Sixth Edition

Managing Change

Bernard Burnes

PEARSON

Harlow, England • London • New York • Boston • San Francisco • Toronto • Sydney
Auckland • Singapore • Hong Kong • Tokyo • Seoul • Taipei • New Delhi
Cape Town • São Paulo • Mexico City • Madrid • Amsterdam • Munich • Paris • Milan

son Education Limited
burgh Gate
ow CM20 2JE
ed Kingdom
Tel: +44 (0)1279 623623
Web: www.pearson.com/uk

First published under the Pitman imprint 1992 (print)
Second edition published under the Pitman imprint 1996 (print)
Third edition published 2000 (print)
Fourth edition published 2004 (print)
Fifth edition published 2009 (print)
Sixth edition published 2014 (print and electronic)

The Financial Times. With a worldwide network of highly respected journalists, *The
Financial Times* provides global business news, insightful opinion and expert analysis
of business, finance and politics. With over 500 journalists reporting from 50 countries
worldwide, our in-depth coverage of international news is objectively reported
and analysed from an independent, global perspective. To find out more, visit
www.ft.com/pearsonoffer.

ISBN: 978-0-273-77896-7 (print)
      978-0-273-77899-8 (PDF)
      978-0-273-77897-4 (eText)

British Library Cataloguing-in-Publication Data
A catalogue record for the print edition is available from the British Library

Library of Congress Cataloging-in-Publication Data
Burnes, Bernard, 1953-
   Managing change / Bernard Burnes. -- Sixth edition.
    pages cm
   ISBN 978-0-273-77896-7
1. Organizational change--Management.   I. Title.
   HD58.8.B882 2014
   658.4'06--dc23

                                            2013047259

10 9 8 7 6 5 4 3 2 1
18 17 16 15 14

Print edition typeset in 9.5/12pt Charter ITC Std by 35
Print edition printed and bound by Ashford Colour Press Ltd, Gosport

NOTE THAT ANY PAGE CROSS REFERENCES REFER TO THE PRINT EDITION

Mar

To Sue, Duncan and Stuart

Contents

Part 2 Strategy development: theory, practice and choice

Part 3 Change management: past, present and future

Introduction

There is nothing so practical as a good theory.   Kurt Lewin

All models are wrong, some models are useful.   George Box

The McKinsey & Company (2008: 1) global survey of organisational transformation concluded that 'organizations need to change constantly'. This is yet further evidence, if needed, that for society at large, and organisations in particular, the magnitude, speed, impact and especially unpredictability of change are greater than ever before. Certainly, since the first edition of this book was published in 1992, new products, processes and services have appeared at an ever-increasing rate. In 1992, the VCR still ruled supreme, the DVD recorder was merely an interesting concept, and the iPod, never mind the iPhone, was not even a twinkle in Steve Jobs' eye. Also, since 1992, whether for good or ill, local markets have become global markets, protected or semi-protected markets and industries have been opened up to fierce competition, and public bureaucracies and monopolies have either been transferred to the private sector or have themselves adopted much more market-orientated practices (Burnes, 2009a; Rodrik, 2012).

When Hammer and Champy (1993: 23) declared that 'change has become both pervasive and persistent. It *is* normality', many people thought this was something of an exaggeration. Most people would now see this as a statement of the blindingly obvious. Certainly, the period since the publication of the first edition of this book has seen organisations having to cope with massive swings in their fortunes. The period began with a global recession and was followed in the mid-1990s by a takeover and merger boom of unprecedented proportions (Burton *et al*, 1996; *The Economist*, 1998). Warner (1997: 3) commented:

> To find a similar period of economic change and merger frenzy, you might need to go back all the way to the 1890s ... Out of it were born such companies as Standard Oil and American Tobacco, the very prototypes of the vertically integrated modern corporation.

The period leading up to the new millennium saw the dotcom boom. This was rapidly followed by the dotcom collapse in which companies previously valued in billions of dollars suddenly became worthless – *see* the Marconi case study in Chapter 6 (Bryce, 2002; Cassidy, 2002; Cellan-Jones, 2003; Kaplan, 2002; Sirower, 2003). This period also saw the bankruptcy of Enron and the exposure of fraud on a massive scale by its leaders – yet another reminder of the fragility and unpredictability of organisational life. It was the spectacular collapse of companies such as Enron, which had grown rapidly and collapsed equally rapidly, that led the American investment guru Warren Buffett to make his now famous remark: 'It's only when the tide goes out that you see who has been swimming with their trunks off.'

Nevertheless, after the first two years of the new millennium, the world economy began to recover. Then came the 2008 credit crunch, which began with the sub-prime scandal in the US and quickly spread across the world (Clark, 2008; Doran, 2008; Hutton, 2008a). Not only did this lead to the worst economic crisis since the Great Depression of the 1930s, but it also appeared to have rolled back decades of economic orthodoxy. In particular, the mantra that free market competition was good and that publicly provided services were bad appeared to have been overthrown with some force. Arch-exponents of the free market, the banks, queued up for government handouts on a truly massive scale, and many of them also had to be nationalised – a fate which only a little while ago many of them would have considered as representing the worst excesses of state interference in the running of the free market (Hutton, 2008b). Since then, though, the financial sector seems to have reverted to type; it is fighting regulations designed to prevent a repeat of the 2008 credit crunch while at the same time awarding ever-bigger bonuses (Alloway, 2013; Guthrie, 2013).

Therefore, even in the relatively short period since the publication of the first edition of this book, organisations have had to cope with very different types of challenges. These range from globalisation, rapid growth, mergers and acquisitions, and the emergence of new technologies and new competitors, to falling markets, depressed economies, de-mergers and consolidations, and the collapse of some customers, suppliers, competitors and even the financial institutions which lend them money. It is the experience of organisations struggling to cope with events such as these, year in and year out, that underlies the quotation from McKinsey at the beginning of this Introduction: 'Organizations need to change constantly.' Yet McKinsey & Company (2008) also found that only a third of organisations managed change successfully.

This brings us to the purpose of this book – *Managing Change*. Though organisational change would not be considered particularly important if products and markets were stable and organisational change was rare, it would be considered even less of an issue if it were easily managed and success could be guaranteed. Alas, it is not just McKinsey which has found substantial evidence that managing change successfully is extremely difficult. Over the years, there has been a continuous stream of examples of change projects that have gone wrong, some disastrously so (*see* Brindle, 1998a; Burnes and Weekes, 1989; Bywater, 1997; Chatterjee, 2007; Chua and Lam, 2005; Cummings and Worley, 1997; Howarth, 1988; Kanter *et al*, 1992; Kelly, 1982a, 1982b; Kotter, 1996; Ojiako and Maguire, 2008; Stace and Dunphy, 1994; Stickland, 1998). Indeed, two of the most respected commentators in the field of organisational change, Beer and Nohria (2000), claim that nearly two-thirds of all change efforts fail, while one of the world's leading management consultancies, Bain & Co., claims the general failure rate is around 70 per cent (Senturia *et al*, 2008).

Though these seem implausibly high rates of failure, studies of particular types of change initiatives appear to reach similar conclusions. For example:

Culture change: A study of major European, Asian and North American companies by Bain & Co. found that the failure rate for culture change initiatives was a shocking 90 per cent (Rogers *et al*, 2006).

Computerisation: The micro-electronics revolution of the 1980s, which saw the rapid expansion of computers and computer-based processes into most areas of organisational life, was the subject of a great many studies. These found that the failure rate of new technology change projects was anywhere between 40 per cent and 70 per cent (AT Kearney, 1989; Bessant and Haywood, 1985; McKracken, 1986; New, 1989; Smith and Tranfield, 1987; Voss, 1985). Nor do the problems in this area appear to be teething troubles limited to the 1980s (Goulielmos, 2003). In 1998, for example, the UK government had to admit that its £170 million programme to replace the computer system that holds the National Insurance records of everyone in the country was in such a mess that the system had collapsed, throwing its social security system into turmoil (Brindle, 1998a, 1999). Similarly, in 2007, one of the main reasons given for BA's Terminal 5 fiasco was the failure of its computerised baggage-handling system (Done and Willman, 2008). In 2012, the US Air Force announced that it had scrapped an Expeditionary Combat Support System (ECSS), which it had begun developing in 2004 and had cost $1 billion (Charette, 2012).

Total Quality Management (TQM): The move by Western organisations to adopt TQM began in the US in the mid-1970s (Dale and Cooper, 1992). In the US, one of the founders of the TQM movement, Philip Crosby (1979), claimed that more than 90 per cent of TQM initiatives failed. Studies of TQM in European countries found a failure rate of 70 per cent or more (AT Kearney, 1992; Cao et al, 2000; Cruise O'Brien and Voss, 1992; Dale, 1999; Economist Intelligence Unit, 1992; Nwabueze, 2001; Patwardhan and Patwardhan, 2008; Whyte and Witcher, 1992; Witcher, 1993; Zairi et al, 1994).

Business Process Re-engineering: This was hailed as 'the biggest business innovation of the 1990s' (Mill, 1994: 26). However, successful BPR initiatives seem rare (Cao et al, 2001; Tarokh et al, 2008). Bryant (1998) cites a reported failure rate for BPR initiatives of 80 per cent, Breslin and McGann (1998) put the failure rate at 60 per cent, while Bywater (1997) puts the figure at 70 per cent. Even the founding father of BPR, Michael Hammer, acknowledges that in up to 70 per cent of cases it leaves organisations worse off rather than better off (Hammer and Champy, 1993).

We should, of course, be wary of extrapolating from a few studies and assuming that they cover all organisations and all situations. Certainly, there is evidence that some of the studies and assertions regarding the rate of change failure may be less than robust (Burnes, 2011a; Hughes, 2011). Even so, the available evidence, both hard and anecdotal, does seem to suggest that many organisations do struggle when seeking to implement change. The striking factor about the four types of change discussed above is that there is a plethora of information, advice and assistance that organisations can and do call upon in planning and executing change, and yet they still fail. This is perhaps why managers consistently identify the difficulty of managing change as one of the key obstacles to the increased competitiveness of their organisations (Dunphy et al, 2003; Hanson, 1993; IBM, 2008; Industrial Society, 1997; Senturia et al, 2008; Worrall and Cooper, 1997).

To many, this must seem paradoxical. On the one hand, there is now more advice on how to manage change than ever before. On the other hand, the failure rate of change initiatives is astronomical. The two quotations from Lewin and Box at the beginning of this Introduction hold the key to this paradox. What almost everyone would like is a clear and practical change theory that explains what changes organisations need to make and how they should make them. Unfortunately, what is available is a wide range of confusing and contradictory theories, approaches and recipes. Many of these are well thought out and grounded in both theory and practice; others, unfortunately, seem disconnected from either theory or reality. Also, though change theory requires an interdisciplinary perspective, each of the major approaches tends to view organisations from the disciplinary angle of their originators – whether it be psychology, sociology, economics, engineering or whatever – which can result in an incomplete and unbalanced picture. So, regardless of what their proponents may claim, we do not possess at present an approach to change that is theoretically holistic, universally applicable, and which can be practically applied. Nevertheless, we do know that, to paraphrase George Box, while all change theories are partial, some theories are useful. This means that for those wishing to understand or implement change, the prime task is not to seek out an all-embracing theory but to understand the strengths and weaknesses of each approach and the situations in which each can best be applied.

There can be few who now doubt the importance to an organisation of the ability to identify where it needs to be in the future, and how to accomplish the changes necessary to get there – although there is a great deal of dispute about how difficult or possible this is. Some might assume that managers do not need to understand organisation theory, strategy theory, change theory or any other theory in order to manage and change their organisations, but this would be to underestimate the extent to which managers and others in organisations are influenced, assisted or potentially misled by theory. Increasingly, managers are exhorted to adopt the teachings of the latest management guru. As Part 1 will demonstrate, and as Mintzberg and Quinn (1991: xii) observe:

> One can, however, suffer not just from an absence of theories, but also from being dominated by them without realizing it. To paraphrase the words of John Maynard Keynes, most 'practical men' are the slaves of some defunct theorist. Whether we realize it or not, our behavior is guided by the systems of ideas that we have internalized over the years. Much can be learned by bringing these out into the open, examining them more carefully, and comparing them with alternative ways to view the world – including ones based on systematic study, that is, research.

These 'systems of ideas', or organisation theories as they are more commonly called, are crucial to change management in two respects. First, they provide models of how organisations should be structured and managed. Second, they provide guidelines for judging and prescribing the behaviour and effectiveness of individuals and groups in an organisation.

To understand why and how to change organisations, it is first necessary to understand their structures, management and behaviour. As Mintzberg and Quinn indicate, in many organisations there is no clear understanding of these theories. It follows that choices with regard to the appropriateness of particular structures and practices, the way they are chosen and implemented, are founded on limited knowledge and perhaps false assumptions. Change cannot hope to be fully successful under these circumstances. On the contrary, a full understanding of these theories is necessary if informed choices are to be made when instigating and implementing change. For this reason, theories will be examined critically in relation to each other, and also in comparison with how organisations actually operate, as opposed to how theorists suppose them to. The aim is not to provide a 'hands-on' practical guide to organisational change – though readers should find this book useful in that respect as well. Rather the aim is to provide an understanding of the theories and approaches to change on offer, to indicate their usefulness and drawbacks, and to enable the reader to choose for themselves which 'models are useful' and when.

The central purpose of this book, then, is to aid this search for understanding both by describing and discussing the key approaches to organisational change, and by setting these within the broader framework of the development, operation and behaviour of organisations and those who populate them. The intention is to allow those who study and carry out organisational change to make their own judgements about the benefits, applicability and usefulness of the approaches on offer.

The key themes underpinning the book are as follows:

● There is a need to understand the wider theoretical and historical context within which organisations operate and the pressures and options they face for change.

- Organisational change cannot be separated from organisational strategy, and vice versa.
- Organisations are not rational entities *per se*, though those who manage them strive to present their deliberations and decisions as being based on logic and rationality.
- There is a strong tendency to present the various approaches to change as being limited in number and mutually exclusive. However, in practice, the range of approaches is wide, and they can be and often are used either sequentially or in combination.
- The appropriateness of each of the available approaches is dependent upon the type of change being considered and the constraints under which the organisation operates, although these constraints and objectives can themselves be changed to make them more amenable to an organisation's preferred approach to change or style of management.
- Organisations and managers can and do exercise a wide degree of choice in what they change, when they change and how they change.

The book is organised into four parts.

Part 1: The rise and fall of the rational organisation provides a comprehensive review of organisation theory and behaviour. It shows that organisation theory is primarily concerned with control, especially in terms of shaping and controlling human behaviour in organisations. It shows that organisation theories are also, implicitly or explicitly, theories of change. Chapter 1 deals with the development of organisations from the Industrial Revolution through to the early years of the twentieth century, when the first fully fledged organisation theory, the Classical approach, appeared. This is followed in Chapter 2 with reviews of the next two organisation theories to appear: the Human Relations approach and Contingency Theory. Chapter 3 examines and compares the three main and most influential contemporary approaches to structuring and managing organisations: the Culture–Excellence and organisational learning approaches, primarily developed in the West, and the Japanese approach. Chapter 4 sets the review of organisational theories in a wider context by reviewing the postmodern, realist and complexity perspectives on organisations. Chapter 5 examines the importance and implications of culture, power and politics. Chapter 5, and Part 1, conclude that, by accident or design, organisation theories attempt to remove choice from organisations by specifying what they need to do in order to be successful. However, the review of culture, power and politics, together with evidence from the earlier chapters, shows that managers do have a wider scope for shaping decisions than much of the organisation literature suggests. This theme of managerial choice is continued in Part 2.

Part 2: Strategy development: theory, practice and choice comprises two chapters, examining the literature on strategic management. Chapters 6 and 7 examine the dominant approaches to strategy, and the main tools and techniques available to organisations for its development and implementation. In particular, these two chapters draw attention to the differences between the Prescriptive and Analytical schools of strategy, and they highlight the importance of the relationship between organisational strategy, organisational change and managerial choice.

Part 3: Change management: past, present and future comprises four chapters. Chapter 8 covers fundamental issues related to organisational change, including why organisations wish to change, the issue of resistance to change and the role of change agents. Chapters 9 and 10 review the two dominant approaches to organisational change: the Planned/Organization Development approach and the Emergent approach. These chapters show that both approaches have their strengths and weaknesses, and that neither separately nor in combination do these approaches cover all change situations. Chapter 11 goes beyond the Planned and Emergent approaches to develop a *framework for change* that relates the various change situations organisations face to the range of approaches to managing change on offer. Chapter 11 concludes Part 2 by arguing that, though organisations face significant constraints on their freedom of choice, these constraints can be influenced and changed in order to allow organisations to choose the particular approach to strategy and change that best suits them.

Part 4: Managing choice comprises the concluding three chapters of the book. Chapters 12 and 13 combine the insights and perspectives from Parts 1, 2 and 3 to create a Choice Management–Change Management model of organisational change. This model, which comprises three interlinked processes – choice, trajectory and change – provides an understanding of how managers and organisations can and do exercise choice and manage change. Given the importance attached to the role of managers in developing strategy and managing change, Chapter 14 reviews what managers do and how they do it. In particular, the role of leadership and management development is examined and related to approaches to change management. The chapter and the book conclude that, as managers have considerable choice over what to change and how to change it, a considerable responsibility lies on their shoulders. How organisations change and develop has enormous consequences, not just for their employees and owners but for society at large. In order to minimise social fragmentation and exclusion, and the destruction of the natural environment, managers need to act in the broader interests of all their stakeholders – employees, shareholders, themselves and the wider community.

The sixth edition

Since the publication of the fifth edition of this book, I have received many helpful comments and suggestions for improving and developing this book, both from my students and colleagues at the University of Manchester and from readers and users elsewhere. I am very grateful for these and have tried to utilise them in preparing this sixth edition.

I have updated all the chapters to reflect developments in the field since the fifth edition. I have taken the opportunity to clarify and re-organise material to make it more accessible to readers. In addition, I have made quite substantial changes to a number of the chapters, including creating two new chapters. The main changes from the fifth edition are as follows:

- All the chapters have new mini case studies at the beginning. There are also four new, longer case studies, which appear at the end of Chapters 5, 12, 13 and 14.

- The first part of Chapter 1 has been revised to incorporate more material on the pre-history of organisations. It shows that for much of human history, those who controlled organisations tended to prefer stability over change.

- A new section has been added to Chapter 2 to highlight the importance of the work of Mary Parker Follett. It also helps to emphasise the importance of the role of women in the development of modern organisations and organisation theories.

- In Chapter 5, the section on culture has been revised. The section on national cultures has, in particular, been expanded to include the GLOBE (Global Leadership and

Organizational Effectiveness) study, which was established to examine how different cultures viewed leadership.

- A new Chapter 8 has been inserted. This brings together and expands material which was previously divided among a number of chapters and dealt with only briefly. In particular, this new chapter includes a section on readiness for and resistance to change, and a discussion of small-scale/slow versus large-scale/fast change.

- Chapter 9 has been substantially revised to provide more information on the history and purpose of Organization Development (OD).

- Chapter 10 has been significantly revised to update the current status of Emergent change and to show that it is being challenged by complexity-based Emergence and a renaissance of OD.

- Chapter 11 in the fifth edition, which covered the Choice Management–Change Management model, has been divided into two chapters, now Chapters 12 and 13. The new Chapter 13, which is solely devoted to an expanded discussion of the Change process, draws especial attention to the importance of behavioural change.

Acknowledgements

Author's acknowledgements

The sixth edition of this book, like the previous five, has been written during the 28 happy and productive years I have spent at the University of Manchester, but by the time this book is published, I will have moved to Stirling University Management School. Therefore, I would like to express my sincere and abiding gratitude to my colleagues and students at the University of Manchester whose generous encouragement and assistance have made this edition and the previous five editions possible. I would particularly like to thank Paul Whittle who, among other things, is responsible for many of the (better) diagrams and figures in this book. In addition, Pearson Education deserve many thanks for their encouragement and patience.

Above all, I am irredeemably indebted to my wife, Sue. Her painstaking reading and editing of draft after draft of this book have improved it beyond recognition. It is not too much to say that she deserves as much credit as I do for what is good about this book.

Nevertheless, despite all the help and assistance I have received, any faults or shortcomings in the final product are mine and mine alone.

Publisher's acknowledgements

We are grateful to the following for permission to reproduce copyright material:

Figures

Figure 5.1 from *Organization Development and Change*, 6th ed., South-Western (Cummings, T.G. and Worley, C.G. 1997) Cengage Learning Inc; Figures 6.3 and 12.5 adapted from Patterns in strategy formation, *Management Science* 24(9), p. 13 (Mintzberg, H. 1978), Reprinted by permission, Copyright (1978), The Institute for Operations Research and the Management Sciences (INFORMS), 5521 Research Park Drive, Suite 200, Catonsville, MD 21228 USA; Figure 7.4 adapted from *The Strategy Concept and Process: A Pragmatic Approach*, 2nd ed., Prentice Hall: New Jersey, USA (Hax, A.C. and Majluf, NS 1996) p. 302 (Figure 17.15), Adapted by permission of Pearson Education Inc., Upper Saddle River, NJ; Figure 10.1 from *Beyond the Boundaries: Leading and Re-Creating the Successful Enterprise* 2nd ed., McGraw-Hill: Sydney, Australia (Stace, D. and Dunphy, D. 2001) p. 107, Copyright 2001, Stace, D and Dunphy, D; Figure 12.6 adapted from *Organisational Behaviour and Analysis* 2nd ed., FT/Prentice Hall: Harlow (Rollinson, D. 2002) p. 254, © Pearson Education Limited 1998.

Tables

Table 10.1 from *Managing Change in Organizations* 4th ed., FT/Prentice Hall: Harlow (Carnall, C.A. 2003) p. 133, © Pearson Education Limited 2003; Table 12.5 from *Organisational Behaviour and Analysis* 2nd ed., Financial Times Prentice Hall: Harlow (Rollinson, D. 2002),

xix

© Pearson Education Limited 1998; Table 14.1 adapted from *The Art and Science of Leadership* 2nd ed., Prentice Hall: Upper Saddle River, NJ, USA. (Nahavandi, A. 2000), Adapted by permission of Pearson Education Inc., Upper Saddle River, NJ.

Text

Case Study 1.1 from Bosses are reining in staff because they can, *The Financial Times*, 27/02/2013, p. 9 (Gapper, J.), © The Financial Times Limited (2013). All Rights Reserved; Case Study 2.1 from Employers: Companies strive to avoid uniformity, *The Financial Times*, 11/04/2013, p. 4 (Devi, S.), © The Financial Times Limited (2013). All Rights Reserved; Case Study 3.1 from Analysis – Corporate culture – Lofty aspirations, *The Financial Times*, 16/07/2012, p. 13 (Hill, A.), © The Financial Times Limited (2012). All Rights Reserved; Case Study on page 218 from Ikea: Against the grain, *The Financial Times*, 13/11/2012, p. 11 (Milne, R.), © The Financial Times Limited (2012). All Rights Reserved; Case Study 5.1 from Hewlett-Packard: Down in the valley, *The Financial Times*, 24/11/2012, p. 6 (Nuttall, C. and Waters, R.); Box 5.8 from Understanding organisational culture and the implications for corporate marketing, *European Journal of Marketing*, p. 357 (Wilson, A.M. 2001), Emerald Group Publishing Limited, (c) Emerald Publishing Ltd, All rights reserved; Case Study 6.1 from Interview: 'Company leaders need battlefield values', *The Financial Times*, 10/04/2013, p. 2 (Boersma, M.), © The Financial Times Limited (2013). All Rights Reserved; Case Study 6.2 from The master strategist: Michael Porter, *The Financial Times*, 15/08/2003, p. 11 (Witzel, M.), © The Financial Times Limited (2003). All Rights Reserved; Case Study 6.3 from The great iconoclast: Henry Mintzberg, *The Financial Times*, 05/08/2003, p. 11 (Witzel, M.), © The Financial Times Limited (2003). All Rights Reserved; Case Study 6.4 from The brashness and bravado in big deals, *The Financial Times*, 17/10/2012, p. 11 (Kay, J.), © The Financial Times Limited (2012). All Rights Reserved; Case Study 7.1 from *Management Tools 2001: An Executive's Guide*, Bain & Company: Boston, MA (Rigby, D. and Bilodeau, B. 2011) pp. 10–11, Used with permission from Bain & Company, Inc. http://www.bain.com/publications/articles/management-tools-trends-2011.aspx; Case Study 7.2 from Row between Virgin and Sky is reignited, *The Financial Times*, 19/05/2007, p. 14 (Edgecliffe-Johnson, A.), © The Financial Times Limited (2007). All Rights Reserved; Case Study 7.3 from Stewardship of a sprawling empire, *The Financial Times*, 18/11/2005, p. 13 (Bickerton, I. and Marsh, P.), © *The Financial Times Limited* (2005). All Rights Reserved; Case Study 7.4 from Apple invites consumers to take a bite of its core philosophy, *The Financial Times*, 16/06/2013, p. 18 (Bradshaw, T.), © *The Financial Times Limited* (2013). All Rights Reserved; Case Study 7.5 from Germany: the engine of success, *The Financial Times*, 09/05/2011, p. 6 (Schaefer, D.), © The Financial Times Limited (2010). All Rights Reserved; Case Study 7.6 from Thin times for lean car production, *The Financial Times*, 09/05/2008, p. 16 (Reed, J. and Soble, J), © *The Financial Times Limited* (2008). All Rights Reserved; Case Study 7.7 adapted from When some of the parts don't add up: Conglomerates that thrive are ruthless in their scrutiny of when to shed beloved but worn-out assets, *The Financial Times*, 07/08/2008, p. 10 (Baer, J. and Guerrera, F), © The Financial Times Limited (2008). All Rights Reserved; Case Study 8.1 from Case study: Minimal change can be best, *The Financial Times*, 30/04/2012, p. 12 (Mueller, U. and Etzold, V.); Case Study 9.1 adapted from Firms grow smarter on strategy, *The Financial Times*, 29/11/2012, p. 4 (Sengupta, R.), © The Financial Times Limited (2012). All Rights Reserved; Box 9.2 from It's just a phase we're going through: A review and synthesis of OD phase analysis. *Group and Organization Management*, 10(4), pp. 383–412 (Bullock, R.J. and Batten, D. 1985), copyright © 1985 by SAGE Publications. Reprinted by permission of SAGE Publications; Box 9.4 from Wanted: OD More Alive Than Dead! *Journal of Applied Behavioral Science*, 40 (4), pp. 374–91 (Greiner, L.E. and Cummings, T.G. 2004), copyright © 2004 by SAGE Publications. Reprinted by permission of SAGE Publications; Case Study 10.1 from IBM (2012) Leading Through Connections: Insights from the Global Chief Executive Officer Study, pp. 6–8., Reprint Courtesy of International Business Machines Corporation, © 2012 International Business Machines Corporation; Case Study 11.1 from SUPPORT SERVICES – G4S chief remains as heads roll, *The Financial Times*, 29/09/2012, p. 18 (Plimmer, G., Warrell, H. and Wembridge, M.), © *The Financial Times Limited* (2012). All Rights Reserved; Case Study on page 447 from Lex in depth: Samsung, *The Financial Times*, 09/08/2012, p. 5 (Hughes, J. and Kirk, S.), © *The Financial Times Limited* (2012). All Rights Reserved; Case Study 12.1 from John Kay – Why the Walkman did not give rise to the Sony iPod, *The Financial Times*, 05/09/2012, p. 9 (Kay, J.), © *The Financial Times Limited* (2012). All Rights Reserved; Case Study 12.2 from Microsoft's direct connection to the customer, *The Financial Times*, 31/12/2001, p. 7 (Harvey, F.), © The Financial Times Limited (2001). All Rights Reserved.; Case Study 13.1 from How an outsider institutes change, *The Financial Times*, 19/02/2013, p. 12 (Pfeffer, J.); Case Study 13.3 adapted from *Changing Behaviour at Work*, Routledge: Abingdon (Makin, P. and Cox, C. 2004), Copyright (© 2004) Routledge, Reproduced by permission of Taylor & Francis Books UK; Case Study on page 534 from Nokia: From 'burning platform' to a slimmer management model, *The Financial Times*, 25/02/2013, p. 12 (Hill, A.), © The Financial Times Limited (2013). All Rights Reserved; Case Study 14.1 from Time to stand up to the crisis junkies, *The Financial Times*, 06/09/2011, p. 14 (Broughton, P.D.).

In some instances we have been unable to trace the owners of copyright material, and we would appreciate any information that would enable us to do so.

The rise and fall of the rational organisation

From trial and error to the science of management

The rise of organisation theory

Learning objectives

After studying this chapter, you should be able to:

- understand the main features of the Classical approach;
- discuss the differences and similarities between the work of Taylor, Fayol and Weber;
- list the main advantages and disadvantages of the Classical approach to structuring organisations, designing jobs and controlling behaviour;
- describe the key features of the Classical approach to organisational change;
- understand why the Classical approach developed as it did in the US, France and Germany;
- understand the development of work organisation from the Industrial Revolution until the beginning of the twentieth century;
- appreciate the reasons for the antagonistic relations between labour and employers in the nineteenth century;
- discuss the different roles played by technology and people in the development of the factory system.

Managers are reining in staff – because they can

Marissa Mayer, Yahoo's new chief executive, has caused consternation by insisting that employees who have worked from home must in future come to the office. Her critics have pointed out that home workers are as productive, if not more so, as those in cubicles. They are, however, missing the point. Ms Mayer is mostly doing this as a rough and ready way to reform Yahoo's notoriously dysfunctional and disorganised culture. She is also doing it because she can.

The lesson to draw from Ms Mayer's whip-cracking – in Silicon Valley, of all places – is that this is an age of harder work. From intense teamwork at the top to monitoring and surveillance at the bottom, managers are squeezing more from employees than they previously would have dared. Even Santa Clara County, where Yahoo's headquarters is located, has a 7.5 per cent unemployment rate, and Yahoo is among the old Valley companies shedding layers of employees so it can regain its edge. The US and Europe still suffer from high unemployment long after the 2008 financial crisis. That has undermined employees' bargaining power, enabling managers to impose greater demands on their shrinking workforces. "For several years, managers have been able to ask workers to do two jobs without any of them quitting," says Peter Cappelli, a management professor at the Wharton School of the University of Pennsylvania.

Managers also have more technology than in the past to measure what each employee contributes, from billing software at law firms to tracking technology in warehouses. The incentive, particularly when any worker who leaves can easily be replaced, is to push this to its limits. On the face of it, Silicon Valley is at the benign end of the scale – it is devising software to measure others rather than being measured itself. Valley companies were pioneers of teamworking and employee autonomy compared with tough methods elsewhere. "There are military type organisations in which the person at the top issues an order and it is passed down the line until the person at the bottom does as he or she is told without question or reason. This is precisely the type of organisation we at HP did not want," wrote David Packard, the co-founder of Hewlett-Packard, about his company in the 1950s. Indeed, companies such as Google sound like holiday camps by comparison. Free buses from San Francisco with WiFi! Free food! Free haircuts! Wacky furniture!

Saunas! Bring your dog to work! But these perks are there to entice employees to spend as much time alongside each other as possible. "There is something magical about sharing meals. There is something magical about spending the time together, about noodling on ideas," Patrick Pichette, Google's chief financial officer, told a conference in Australia last week. Ms Mayer, a Google alumna, presumably wants to achieve the same effect at Yahoo.

Engineers at start-ups, and at the most successful of the big companies such as Google and Apple, have plenty of autonomy, and are paid and rewarded highly. They also work very hard. These companies use an extreme version of the motivational technique called Theory Y by management theorist Douglas McGregor in 1960. The opposite approach, Theory X, assumes that workers need to be tightly managed and supervised because they are inherently slackers. Theory X goes back to the "scientific management" notions of Frederick Taylor, a mechanical engineer who, in 1911, advocated breaking down the work of unskilled labourers and assembly line workers into small tasks and then telling them exactly what to do, while watching them closely. Theory Y has been in the ascendant for several decades, partly because it has worked out well at companies such as Google, and partly because of the rise in white-collar work. But a combination of new technology and a shift in the balance of managerial power is bringing back Taylorism.

A recent *Financial Times* article on an Amazon UK warehouse gave an insight into what is happening in the logistics industry. The "pickers" who collect items from the warehouse shelves carry handheld computers that tell them exactly where to go and check how fast they do it. Technology is enabling the kind of surveillance of which Taylor could only have dreamed. Managers used to be able to check with technology when a worker clocked in or out. Now, those who run call centres and logistics depots know the worker's every move in real time. "If you have a plentiful supply of labour and don't need to worry about quality, the temptation is to nail your workers for every minute of the day," says Kirstie Ball, reader in surveillance and organisation at the Open University.

Even professionals are not immune to surveillance. Law firms use software to calculate the time that lawyers spend on individual cases in order to bill clients by the hour, or even in ten-minute blocks. The computers that hum on most people's desks can easily spy on their users.

Ms Mayer is not attempting to implement command and control at Yahoo. But her edict has one thing in common with Amazon's approach: it is calculated to intensify effort. Commuting to the office to work in a group ensures that everyone knows what you are doing. Peer pressure can be as powerful a management tool as surveillance. That need not be sinister. I would prefer to work hard at a successful company than idle at a demoralised, lethargic one. But a combination of high unemployment and technology hands managers a lot of power. Some will abuse it.

Introduction

In the UK and the rest of the developed world, and increasingly in the developing world, it is almost impossible to imagine life without the plethora of organisations that comprises and makes possible our everyday life. Yet organisations in their modern form – indeed, in almost any form – were virtually unknown before the beginning of the Industrial Revolution in the late eighteenth century. In the intervening period, as Morgan (1986) remarked, we have developed into an 'organizational society'. Not only have organisations, in their many shapes, sizes and manifestations, come to reach into every facet of our lives, they have also acquired an equally diverse range of theories, nostrums and semi-sacrosanct beliefs about how they should be structured, managed and changed. Yet, as Mini Case Study 1.1 shows, there is still no agreement on the most basic and fundamental of organisational questions: what is the best way to manage and motivate employees?

This chapter sets out to explore and discuss the origins of organisations, from the Industrial Revolution to the early years of the twentieth century, when the Classical approach to running organisations emerged. This approach was the first detailed and comprehensive recipe or theory for running organisations, and was founded on the work of Frederick Taylor in the US, Henri Fayol in France and Max Weber in Germany. As Mini Case Study 1.1 shows, though it was developed more than 100 years ago, Taylor's scientific management, which many see as being outdated and just plain wrong, is still hugely influential in determining how people are managed and work is structured. This chapter will review the development of the Classical approach and show why, despite the advent of many competing approaches, it exerts such a strong influence on managers.

The key themes of this chapter are as follows:

- The Industrial Revolution marked a significant shift in how change was perceived. Beforehand, those who controlled organisations, whether those organisations were countries, religions or medieval craft guilds, tended to resist change, considering it a threat to their power. After the Industrial Revolution, though change was strongly resisted by workers, the emerging class of entrepreneurs and industrialists came to see it as the prime mechanism for gaining wealth and power.

- Although industrialisation was primarily characterised by the move from a subsistence economy to a money-market economy, its main enabling mechanism was the creation of the factory system, and its main characteristic was the battle between managers and workers over control of the work process.

● The development of organisation theory was synonymous with the need by managers to legitimate and enhance their authority to control workers' behaviour and initiate changes to production methods. Thus the Classical approach to running organisations stresses the need to remove decision-making powers from workers and vest planning and control of the work process in the hands of managers and specialists.

● As a result, two of the overarching and complementary characteristics of this period were the conflict between workers and managers, and the search for a systematic, scientific and above all efficient approach to running and changing organisations.

The chapter begins by looking at the pre-history of modern organisations. It shows that the opportunities for vast wealth which arose from the rapid expansion of national and international commerce in the seventeenth and eighteenth centuries could not be met by existing forms of production technologies and work organisation. Thus it was that entrepreneurial opportunities created the conditions for the Industrial Revolution in Britain, from which emerged the factory system, the precursor of all modern organisations, and whose two key features were its *ad hoc*, trial-and-error nature and the antagonistic relationship between owners and employees, or – to use the terminology of the times – masters and servants.

The chapter describes how British industrial practices, methods and technologies were 'exported' to other European countries and the US, with similar results in terms of employer–employee relations. As the nineteenth century progressed, and organisations grew in number and size, trial and error increasingly gave way to more considered and consistent approaches to work organisation. This development was especially pronounced in the US and mainland Europe, as industrial leadership moved away from Britain towards these areas.

What emerged, separately, were three different but complementary attempts by Frederick Taylor in the US, Henri Fayol in France and Max Weber in Germany to replace the *ad hoc*, rule-of-thumb approach to organisations with a universally applicable blueprint or theory for how they should be managed. These three approaches, each focusing on different organisational aspects, coalesced into what later became known as the Classical school of organisation theory. This approach to organisations is characterised by:

● the horizontal and hierarchical division of labour
● the minimisation of human skills and discretion
● the attempt to construe organisations as rational–scientific entities.

One of the key objectives of the Classical school was to ensure that managers were the only group with the legitimate right to plan and implement change. It was argued that management was the only group with the skills and authority to analyse the work situation scientifically and rationally, and to devise the most appropriate and efficient methods of operation in order to meet the organisation's goals.

The chapter concludes by arguing that the Classical approach, while being a significant advance on what went before, was badly flawed. In particular, its view of human nature and motivation was not only inaccurate but also counterproductive in that it alienated workers from the organisations that employed them and created resentment. However, the precepts of the Classical school were not aimed solely at constraining workers' ability to make or block change; in addition, by laying down hard-and-fast rules of what was and was not best practice, they constrained management's freedom of action, thus alienating many managers as well as workers.

The pre-history of modern organisations

Before moving on to examine the changes to organisational life brought about by the Industrial Revolution, it is important to recognise that our current preoccupation with change is relatively new, as is the study of change itself. It was only with the advent of the Industrial Revolution that organisations began to focus on change rather than stability. Only in the last 70 years has organisational change emerged as a subject for systematic academic study, and indeed, it is really only since the 1980s that it has become a main-stream subject on undergraduate and postgraduate courses in management and business.

To understand why this is so, we have to recognise that while organisational change is as old as organisations, it has not always been the case that those who lead organisations have welcomed change or seen it as the norm. For most of recorded human history, leaders appear to have favoured stability and tradition rather than change and newness. In a review of managerial practices in the 2,500 years before the Christian era, Rindova and Starbuck (1997) showed how Chinese leaders fostered stable social structures and established a bureaucratic state apparatus geared to the purpose of maintaining the status quo rather than challenging it. Though Weber (1948) saw bureaucracy as a modern approach to achieving order, predictability and control, the Chinese example shows that this is not the case. Nor is it an isolated example. We can see this preference for stability across the ancient world. In Egypt, Greece and Rome, the structure, laws and practice of the state, and social norms such as ancestor worship and respect for age, promoted tradition and stability over newness and change (Antonaccio, 1994; Beyer, 1959; Jones, 1984). As Robbins (1987) noted, this preference for bureaucratic-type organisations can be found in *The Bible*. When Moses, having led his people out of Egypt, began to find the strain of leadership too much, his father-in-law offered the following advice:

> Thou shalt provide out of all the people able men . . . and place such over them, to be rulers of thousands, and rulers of hundreds, rulers of fifties, and rulers of tens: and let them judge the people at all seasons: and it shall be, that every great matter they shall bring unto thee, but every small matter they shall judge: so shall it be easier for thyself, and they shall bear the burden with thee.
> (Exodus 18, 21–23, The Bible, 1962)

Of course, it could be argued that these examples are not typical organisations but nation states or, in the case of Moses and the Israelites, a proto-state. This, though, would miss the point that until the emergence of craft guilds in Europe around the fourteenth century, the only organisations of any significance were feudal states/principalities and, from the fourth century onwards, the 'one, holy catholic church' whose structure tended to mirror that of the states in which it operated (Gonzalez, 1999; Keen, 1991).

In the Christian world, people were subject to two sets of laws: Divine Law, protected and promoted by the Catholic Church, and Human Law, enforced by civil government (Foster, 1977). However, the belief was that civil rulers were appointed by God and subject only to God's laws (which later grew into the Divine Right of Kings). Therefore, Human Law was seen as subservient to Divine Law. This was enshrined in the doctrine of Natural Law, which states that there are certain enduring rules of behaviour to which humans are subject, primarily obedience to the laws of God as prescribed by the church. Anything or anyone who challenged these laws and the pre-eminence of the church, or the Divine Right of Kings, was deemed to be heretical and had to be suppressed, often, as the Inquisition demonstrated, in an extremely violent manner (Green, 2008). It follows that the preference for stability in the church, the state and their institutions was regarded not merely as an attitude of mind but as the natural order of things as laid down by God.

Even when the duopoly of church and state started to be challenged by the advent of powerful and rich craft guilds, this did not noticeably challenge the preference for stability over change. A guild was a monopoly which regulated entry into a trade or craft in a city and sought to control price and supply, quality and methods of production (Gadd and Wallis, 2006). Technological or organisational innovations were seen as threats by guilds as these could undermine their control over their craft. Consequently, for guilds, the pursuit of stability was an economic necessity rather than a religious imperative, but was no less powerful for that. This of course did not mean that changes did not take place in church, state or guild; they clearly did and were often momentous in nature (Davis, 1997; Epstein and Prak, 2010). However, the point is that stability rather than change was seen as the norm. The leaders of organisations, whether they be popes, kings or guild masters, saw it as their duty to maintain the status quo, in terms of religious doctrine, existing social relations or methods of production.

The rise of commerce and the birth of the factory

It was only with the commencement of the Industrial Revolution in the eighteenth century, buttressed by the rise of sectarian Protestantism and the new thinking of the Enlightenment, that change began to be seen as preferential to stability (Hampson, 1990; Hobsbawm, 1979). The emergence of the factory system led to the creation of a new entrepreneurial-industrial class who saw stability and tradition as obstacles to their pursuit of wealth and power. They saw organisational, technological and scientific progress as the key to increased wealth. However, for their workers, the reverse appeared to be the case. They saw change as a threat to their skills and livelihood, and tradition and stability as things to be valued and protected (Burnes, 2009a). Therefore, even at the beginning of what Morgan (1986) refers to as the 'organizational society', the fault lines between employers and employees were evident. Change posed a challenge for both. For employers the challenge was how to accomplish it; for employees the challenge was how to prevent it.

Therefore, the Industrial Revolution was the pivotal event that shaped the world into the form we now see around us. Previously, most societies were based on small-scale, self-sufficient agricultural production, with the vast majority of the population, some 80–90 per cent, living in the countryside. By the end of the nineteenth century, after the Industrial Revolution had run its course, the reverse became the case, in the leading industrialised countries at least, with most people living in urban centres and depending on industrial and commercial activities for their livelihood (Landes, 1969).

Britain was the pioneer industrial country; it was the model that other European nations and the US sought to emulate in their attempts to transform traditional agrarian economies into urban societies based on science and technology (Kemp, 1979). The key development of the Industrial Revolution towards this process of societal transformation was the creation of the factory system. It was this that gave the impetus to and created the model for all that was to follow. As Weber (1928: 302) pointed out, the factory's distinguishing characteristic was:

> in general . . . not the implements of work applied but the concentration of ownership of workplace, means of work, source of power and raw materials in one and the same hand, that of the entrepreneur.

Or, to put it another way, it was the way the entrepreneur 'organised' the elements of production that distinguished it from what went before.

This tells us what changed, but it does not explain why or how in a few score years organisations came to dominate our lives. To answer this, it is necessary to appreciate the great surge of economic activity – especially the international trade in textile products – that arose in the seventeenth and eighteenth centuries. This trade gave an enormous impetus to textile production in Britain, which in turn had a knock-on effect in all other spheres of economic activity (Mathias, 1969).

Before and during the early part of the Industrial Revolution, textile production was carried out as an agricultural by-occupation based on family units. However, as demand increased in the eighteenth century, some 'men and women [became] specialist spinners or weavers, thinking first of wool, treating work on the land as, at most, a by-occupation' (Ashton, 1948: 23). Allied to this, a new mechanism sprang up to link producer and consumer: the 'putting-out' system, whereby a large merchant would 'put out' work to a number of independent domestic producers. The advantage to the merchant was threefold:

- It was cheap – there were few overheads.
- It was flexible – production could be easily expanded or contracted.
- It avoided the difficulties involved in directly employing a workforce.

However, as demand continued to increase in the late eighteenth century, this system became more complex and more costly, and eventually it became too cumbersome (Mathias and Davis, 1989). The chain of intermediaries linking producer to consumer became increasingly difficult for the large merchant to control. There were many problems with the putting-out mechanism: dishonesty (on both sides) was rife; deliveries were late; and quality was often poor. Laws attempting to control producers could do nothing to rectify the fundamental weaknesses in the system. The incompatibility between the large and complex organisation of distribution and the multitude of tiny domestic workshop units, unsupervised and unsupervisable, was bound to create tensions and drive merchants to seek new ways of production – ways whereby they could establish their own managerial control over the production process (Pollard, 1965).

There was also an incompatibility between different cultures. For the merchant, the expansion of markets was a chance to maximise profits in order to live in the grand style. For the rural domestic producer, involved in long hours of back-breaking work, it created the conditions for increased leisure. As Marglin (1976: 35) commented:

> Wages rose and workers insisted on taking out a portion of their gains in the form of greater leisure. However sensible this may have been from their own point of view, it is no way for an enterprising capitalist to get ahead.

Therefore, it was the merchant who began the change towards the factory system – not because the merchant had an innate desire to run factories or exercise direct control over labour, but because they needed to do so in order to reap ever greater profits by being able to take full advantage of expanding market opportunities.

Nevertheless, there was no headlong rush to create a new economic order overnight. The earliest factories, if that is not too grand a word for them, were small, unpowered weaving or spinning sheds that used existing technology and methods. A few very large factories – such as Wedgwood's Etruria Works in Stoke-on-Trent – were established, but these were the exceptions. Indeed, in 1780, the investment in fixed equipment and stock in the textile industry, which was the leading edge of the Industrial Revolution, was only £10 per worker, and the average factory employed no more than 10 or 12 people. By 1830, when the textile industry had grown to employ 100,000 people and the average factory size was 137, the investment in fixed equipment and stock had increased to only £15 per worker, and 50 per cent of the workforce was still home-based (Hobsbawm, 1968; Pollard, 1965, 1981; Tillett, 1970). Given this situation, it is hardly surprising that capital investment was quickly recovered and that it was running expenses, mainly wages and raw materials, that formed the bulk of manufacturing costs. This is why controlling labour and reducing labour costs were such priorities for the early factory owners. It also explains the prevailing antagonistic attitude of employers towards labour in the nineteenth century.

The relationship between employers and employees

British employers based their attitude towards employees on two basic propositions:

1. Labour is unreliable, lazy and will work only when tightly controlled and closely supervised.

2. The main controllable business cost is labour. Therefore the key to increased profits is to make it cheaper, and/or increase its productivity, by getting employees to work harder, or for longer hours, for the same, or less, money.

In this respect, as contemporary writers such as Charles Babbage (1835) and Andrew Ure (1835) observed, workers' skill was seen as at best an inconvenience and at worst a threat, because it could be scarce, costly and allowed workers a strong bargaining position.

As might be expected, employers' hostility was reciprocated by labour. Workers exhibited a strong dislike for the factory system, and a reluctance to become part of it. As Pollard (1965) noted, this was for three main reasons:

1. It involved a wholesale change of culture and environment and the destruction of small, tightly knit communities in which they lived. Hard though the life of cottage industry was, it had given workers a measure of independence and some control over what they did, when they did it and how.

2. The discipline of the factory was harsh and unremitting, with men, women and even small children all expected to work long hours, often seven days a week, in appalling conditions.

3. Given the lack of alternative organisational forms on which to establish factory life, employers often modelled them on workhouses or prisons. Indeed, to square the circle, some workhouses and prisons turned themselves into factories and their inmates into little more than slaves. Thus factories acquired the same stigma as that attached to prisons and workhouses.

Therefore, the antagonism that existed between owners and workers was based on a genuine clash of interests – one which has echoed through the industrial world ever since.

If this picture of the factory system in the nineteenth century seems bleak to us, it is nevertheless accurate, as is shown in the work of its proponents such as Charles Babbage and Andrew Ure, social reformers such as Seebohm Rowntree, political activists such as Friedrich Engels and contemporary novelists such as Charles Dickens. Nor was this aspect of industrialisation restricted to Britain. Studies of other European countries and the US have shown similar tensions, sometimes even more violent, between the old and the new methods of working, and between employers and employees (Bruland, 1989; Chapman and Chassagne, 1981; Mantoux, 1964; Pelling, 1960).

In defence of the factory owners, who must take responsibility for what emerged, it should be said that their own experience was limited and there were no textbooks to guide them. That they should 'copy' the models that existed reflected both the common view of labour among the owning classes and a lack of alternative organisational forms on which to base the emergent factory system. As other nations industrialised, notably Germany, France and the US, they too adopted similar organisational forms and espoused similar attitudes towards labour. Partly this was because they were seeking to emulate Britain's success by copying her approach. It was also because these societies, like Great Britain, were riven by hierarchical and horizontal divisions that were inevitably reproduced in the workplace.

Industrialisation and the organisation of work

The system of organising work that came to characterise industrial life in Britain, most of continental Europe and the US by the end of the nineteenth century was based on the hierarchical and horizontal division of labour. Though this represented a significant change from the past in terms of how work had previously been organised, it was not out of step with the social stratification of European society or with feudal traditions of obedience. The articulation and propagation of the principle of the division of labour owed much to the work of Adam Smith. In his book *The Wealth of Nations*, published in 1776, Smith used the now famous example of pin-making to illustrate what he saw as the advantages of the division of labour. He pointed out that a pin could be made entirely by one person doing everything, or by a number of people, each specialising in one aspect of its production. For three reasons, he believed the latter was more efficient:

1. A worker who constantly performs one simple task will quickly acquire greater dexterity than one who performs a variety of tasks.
2. It avoids the loss of time necessitated by one person moving from one task to another.
3. The concentration of attention on one special task leads to the invention of machines that aid the productivity of labour and allow one person to do the work previously performed by many.

Smith's ideas were given flesh and form in Britain by pioneering factory owners such as Josiah Wedgwood, and Matthew Boulton and James Watt. At his Etruria pottery works, Wedgwood developed a production system that split the work process into separate departments, each with its own specialist supervisor. Work was organised almost on a flowline basis, with the skill involved in each operation reduced to a minimum in order, in

11

Wedgwood's own words, 'to make machines of men as cannot err' (quoted in Tillett, 1970: 37). Matthew Boulton and James Watt developed a similar approach at their Soho Works in Birmingham in the 1770s. They also kept detailed production records, a practice virtually unknown at the time (Roll, 1930). Wedgwood, Boulton, Watt and a few others were the architects of the factory system. By their organisation of work on and off the shopfloor, they created models that later managers would copy and adapt to their own needs and circumstances.

This approach to the organisation and control of work spread outwards from Britain. As Bruland (1989: 165) observed:

> There was a fairly direct international diffusion of these changes from Britain, the originating economy: British workers, in most parts of Europe, played a significant role in spreading the new work systems, in training local workers, and in the adaptation of the work force to the new rhythms of work.

As the nineteenth century progressed, this approach to work organisation became more developed and systematised. Charles Babbage (1835) developed a method of applying the division of labour principle to the detailed analysis of any job. He emphasised the need for and advantage of dividing tasks between and within mental and manual labour. He envisaged three 'classes' employed in the work process:

- The entrepreneur and his technical specialists who would design machines and plan the form of work organisation.

- Operative engineers and managers who would be responsible for executing such plans and designs, based on only partial knowledge of the processes involved.

- The mass of employees, needing only a low level of skill, who would undertake the actual work.

Thus, in Babbage's (1835: vii) view:

> The master manufacturer, by dividing the work to be executed into different processes, each requiring different degrees of skill or force, can purchase exactly the precise quality of both which is necessary for each process.

Though coming from separate traditions, Smith's work was also in tune with the Prussian bureaucratic school, and undoubtedly the efficient organisation of German industry in the late nineteenth century owes much to a combination of the two approaches.

The pioneers of these developments in work organisation, whether in Britain, Germany or other European countries, tended to be strict disciplinarians who used their personal authority to impose the new working arrangements on a usually reluctant workforce (Chapman and Chassagne, 1981). Therefore, change tended to be managed by imposition and force rather than negotiation and agreement. Nor is it surprising that it should be so. In the main these were countries which had been, in the recent past, feudal economies dominated by warrior elites. In Germany, this was still the case. Even where, as in France, there had been a decisive break with the past, this seems merely to have reinforced rather than removed patterns of social rigidity and authoritarianism.

In such situations, resistance to or questioning of change was unlikely to be met by understanding or tolerance. Predictably, there was strong resistance, both active and passive, to the introduction of new working patterns and methods (Kriedte *et al*, 1981). Though this resistance could and did take the form of physical violence against factories and equipment, a more frequent manifestation was high labour turnover. One of the largest

Manchester cotton-spinning firms, McConnell and Kennedy, had an average turnover in the early nineteenth century of 100 per cent per year, a high but not uncommon rate (Fitton and Wadsworth, 1958; Pollard, 1965). A similar situation existed in other European countries. As Lee (1978: 460) noted, in Germany employers:

> were generally satisfied if they achieved partial success in creating a stable core of skilled workers . . . Turnover was the most persistent labour problem confronting employers.

This situation clearly gave those workers whose skills were most in demand a significant bargaining position, which allowed them to increase their wages and determine the pace of work. However, it also acted as a spur to employers to seek methods of reducing their reliance on skilled labour (Bruland, 1989). One of the main ways that entrepreneurs responded was through technological developments aimed at replacing or reducing employers' reliance on skilled labour.

A contemporary observer of the nineteenth-century industrial scene, Andrew Ure (1836: viii–ix), drew special attention to the role that technology could play in this process:

> By developing machines . . . which require only unskilled instead of skilled labour, the cost of labour can be reduced [and] the bargaining position of the worker reduced.

It becomes clear why workers not only opposed the advent of the factory system but also, even when it became established, continued to oppose strongly changes in work practices and the introduction of new equipment. Even in the present day, where change tends to be preceded by consultation and its beneficial effects are stressed, there is still a tendency for those concerned to feel apprehensive of, if not downright resistant towards, change (Dent and Goldberg, 1999; Oreg, 2003). Therefore, in a harsher and more authoritarian age, where organisational and technological change was seen as a weapon in the battle for control of the workplace, it is not surprising that change management should be achieved by imposition and coercion, and occasion the response that it did.

Despite the increasing opposition of 'organised' labour, the work practices associated with the factory system gradually permeated every aspect of industrial and commercial life, albeit only on a piecemeal basis. In Europe as a whole, for the most part, those who created and controlled the large business organisations that were becoming the norm still had to rely on their own experience and judgement, but with growing frustration over their inability to control and organise these bodies fully and effectively. Even by the end of the nineteenth century, there was no unified or accepted approach that managers could apply to organisations in their entirety, though in Germany, which had overtaken Britain as the leading European industrial nation, the application of the Prussian bureaucratic model allied to the approach to industrial organisation of Adam Smith was proving influential (Borchardt, 1973; Kemp, 1979). Yet the developing factory system could not shake off the legacy of its origins or ignore the continuing battle between labour and management over control, rewards and skill. Therefore, there was also a realisation among some that, while change was inevitable, they lacked an effective and, as far as their employees were concerned, acceptable way of managing it. Consequently, there was a growing awareness of the need to develop an approach to organising work that was more systematic and less harsh and arbitrary than what had gone before. Although this was already, to an extent, taking place in Germany with the rise of bureaucracy, the US was the country where the most conscious and consistent search was being pursued for a comprehensive theory of how to structure and run organisations.

In the US, for a number of reasons, the need for a workable, overall approach to organisational design and control, which legitimised the authority of managers to initiate change, was perhaps more acute than anywhere else. The US had industrialised far more rapidly and on a larger scale than any other nation. Only in the 1860s, after the Civil War, did it begin to industrialise in earnest, but by 1914 it had become the premier industrial nation, with the highest per capita income in the world. In the period 1860 to 1914, employment in manufacturing rose from 1.3 million to 6.6 million, and the population as a whole rose from 31 million to 91 million (Habakkuk and Postan, 1965). The US at this time was still heavily influenced by Europe, and initially at least adopted similar approaches and methods in organising and running industry. However, the size of the typical American organisation quickly grew much larger than those in Europe. While the average British and French business was still the small, family-owned firm, in the US it was the monopoly, which dominated an entire industry, or the conglomerate, which had substantial holdings in several industries. As an example, in 1900 Dale Carnegie sold his steel company for the enormous sum of $419 million to a group of financiers. They merged it with other steel concerns to create a monopoly steel producer employing 200,000 workers and valued at $1.3 billion. This was at a time when the British steel industry, which had led the world, comprised 100 blast furnaces owned by 95 separate companies.

As might be imagined, the numbers of Americans employed in factories and offices grew rapidly – almost tripling between 1880 and 1910 (Levine, 1967; Zinn, 1980). The rocketing increase in demand for labour could not be met by the existing population alone and was fuelled by successive waves of immigration. While solving one problem – the shortage of labour – this created others. The culture shock of industrial work, a foreign language, and problems of housing and social integration created enormous pressures in American society. Alongside this was the arbitrary and ruthless discipline of the factory system, where workers were treated as so much industrial cannon fodder. It was a time of rapid social, technological and organisational change: a time when entrepreneurs did not so much expect to manage change as to impose it, and those who could not or would not accept this situation were treated harshly. Consequently, most industries found themselves sitting on a pressure cooker which could, and frequently did, explode in unexpected and violent ways. If management–labour relations were poor in most European countries, they were far worse in the US (Pelling, 1960).

The American approach to industrial development owed little to government aid or encouragement, and much to individual entrepreneurship. For this reason American entrepreneurs had much more in common with the free market approach to industrial expansion of their British counterparts than with the state-sponsored traditions of Germany or France. Therefore, the German approach to industrial organisation, bureaucracy, which might seem appropriate given the size of American companies, was not attractive. In any case, it tended to operate best in situations where growth and demand were stable or predictable, which in Germany the government tried to facilitate. However, US growth patterns were volatile and unpredictable.

Consequently, there was great pressure to find organisational arrangements that would allow employers to control and organise their employees in a manner that reduced conflict, was cost-effective, and was applicable to the American environment and philosophy. It was also becoming recognised that it was not sufficient just to develop a more systematic approach to the organisation of work; there was also a need to develop an approach to managing change that would persuade workers to accept rather than reject or resist the introduction of new methods, techniques and technologies. Therefore, with the spirit of endeavour, determination and confidence that seemed so much a part of the American character at this time, managers and engineers set out to remedy this situation. Though similar developments were taking place in Europe, they lacked the intensity, commitment and scale of events in the US. This is no doubt why one of the earliest and most enduring approaches to organisation theory emerged in the US, and why the US has continued to dominate the development of organisation theory.

Organisation theory: the Classical approach

So, at the end of the nineteenth century, many managers saw a clear need to replace the rule-of-thumb approach to organisational design and management with a more consistent and organisation-wide approach which could effectively control workers' behaviour (Sheldrake, 1996; Taylor, 1911a; Tillett, 1970). This was not because of an academic interest in the functioning of organisations, though this was present, but in order to improve their performance, enhance their competitiveness and – an increasing concern at the time – sustain and legitimate managerial authority. This was certainly the case in the US, where explosive growth and a workforce suffering from culture shock had created dangerous social pressures that questioned the legitimacy of managerial power, and even of the capitalist system itself. This was also true in Europe: although Europe industrialised earlier, it was not only having to come to grips with the increase in size and complexity of business life, it was also facing considerable, and unexpected, competitive pressure from the US.

Even so, these difficulties could not quench the innate optimism of the age. It was a time, much more than now, when people dealt in certainties and universal truths. There was a feeling of confidence that any goal, whether it be taming nature or discerning the best way to run a business, could be achieved by the twin powers of scientific study and practical experience. All over the industrialised world, groups of managers and technical specialists were forming their own learned societies to exchange experiences, to discuss common problems, and to seek out in a scientific and rational fashion the solution to all organisational ills: to discover 'the one best way'.

Out of these endeavours emerged what was later termed the Classical approach to organisational design and management. As the name suggests, it was an approach that drew heavily on what had gone before, taking from writers such as Adam Smith and practitioners such as Josiah Wedgwood, and leavening their ideas with contemporary experience, views and experiments. This approach, reflecting the age in which it emerged, portrays organisations as machines, and those in them as mere parts which respond to the correct stimulus and whose actions are based on scientific principles. The emphasis was on developing universal principles of organisation which would ensure the efficiency, stability and predictability of internal functions. Once these principles were established and in operation, organisations were seen as closed and changeless entities unaffected by the outside world. Though this approach originated in the early part of the twentieth century, it still influences managerial practices and assumptions today, but its credibility among academics has long since waned (Kelly, 1982a, 1982b; Rose, 1988; Scott, 1987).

The Classical approach, or the Scientific–Rational approach as it is sometimes called, while not homogeneous, is characterised by three common propositions:

- **Organisations are rational entities** – they are groups of individuals who, through their organisation into highly formalised, differentiated and efficient structures, pursue relatively specific goals and display output-maximising behaviour.

- **The design of organisations is a science** – through experience, observation and experiment, it has been established that there is one best universal organisational form for all types of jobs and organisations, which shapes human behaviour to the needs of organisational efficiency. Organisations are conceived of as machines which, once set in motion, will inexorably and efficiently pursue and achieve their pre-selected goals.

- **People are economic beings** – they are solely motivated by money. This instrumental orientation means that they will try to achieve the maximum reward for the minimum work, and will use whatever bargaining power their skills or knowledge allow to this end. Therefore, through the hierarchical and horizontal division of labour and functions, jobs must be designed and structured in such a way as to minimise an individual's skill and discretion, and maximise management control.

In essence, the Classical approach seeks to regulate the behaviour of workers through the removal of their control over the work process, the increased division of labour, work standardisation, close supervision and financial incentives and in so doing make real Josiah Wedgwood's ambition 'to make machines of men as cannot err' (quoted in Tillett, 1970: 37).

The key figures in the development of the Classical approach were Frederick Taylor (1856–1915) and two of his main promoters, the pioneers of motion study, Frank and Lillian Gilbreth (1868–1924 and 1878–1972 respectively) in the US, Henri Fayol (1841–1925) in France and Max Weber (1864–1920) in Germany. All were writing in the first two decades of the twentieth century, though Weber's work was not generally available in English until the 1940s. Below is an outline of their work.

Frederick Taylor's Scientific Management

Frederick Winslow Taylor, considered the 'father of Scientific Management', was an engineer who later became one of the first management consultants. He was born into a prosperous Quaker–Puritan family in Germantown, Pennsylvania. Although he passed the entrance exam for Harvard Law School, instead of becoming a lawyer as his family wished, in 1874 he took a manual job in an engineering company and became a skilled pattern maker and machinist. In 1878, he joined the Midvale Steel Company as a labourer, but eventually rose to become its chief engineer. Having had enough of working for other people, in 1893 he set up his own consultancy (Sheldrake, 1996). Taylor was an accomplished and talented engineer, and became a leading authority on metal cutting and a successful inventor. However, he is most famous (or infamous) for developing an approach to controlling workers' behaviour, based on detailed specification of tasks, monetary motivation and close supervision, which restricted their ability to deviate from managerial requirements.

Taylor was a highly controversial figure during his lifetime and remains so some 100 years after his death. This was partly because his theory of management was a direct challenge to both workers and managers. However, a large part of the hostility he generated during his lifetime was due to his character. Rose (1988: 23) stated: 'Taylor was a notorious neurotic – many would not hesitate to write crank; and there is even a case for upgrading the diagnosis to maniac.' He was certainly a zealot when it came to promoting his ideas and would brook no challenge to them, whether from workers or management. Not surprisingly, though he attracted devoted followers, he also engendered fierce dislike.

Through his experience as a shopfloor worker, manager and consultant, Taylor made a major contribution to the development of managerial theory and practice in the twentieth century (Locke, 1982; Rose, 1988). Yet his original attempts to improve productivity (or, as he put it, to stamp out 'soldiering') were less than successful. Not only was his use of sacking, blacklisting and victimisation counterproductive, but the bitterness that this provoked haunted him for the rest of his life. It was his failure to achieve change by, as Rose (1988: 37) termed it, 'managerial thuggery' that led him to seek an alternative method of change management that the workers, and management, would accept because they could see that it was rational and fair. Thereafter, his prime preoccupation became the pursuit and promotion of a scientific approach to management.

Drawing on his work at the Midvale Steel Company and the Bethlehem Steel Company, Taylor constructed a general ideology of efficiency. It was only in 1911, when a group of his supporters met to discuss how better to promote his work, that the term 'Scientific Management' was first used to describe his approach to work organisation (Sheldrake, 1996). Though initially sceptical, Taylor embraced the term and there can be little doubt that the publication, in the same year, of his *Principles of Scientific Management* laid the foundation stone for the development of organisation and management theory. Taylor's primary focus was on the design and analysis of individual tasks; this process inevitably led to changes in the overall structure of organisations. Such was the impact of his work that it created a blueprint for, and legitimated, the activities of managers and their support staff. In so doing, he helped to create the plethora of functions and departments that characterises many modern organisations.

Before Taylor, the average manager tended to operate in an idiosyncratic and arbitrary manner, with little or no specialist support. Taylor saw this as being at the root of much industrial unrest and workers' mistrust of management. Though criticised for his anti-labour postures, Taylor was also highly critical of management behaviour, which may account for this group's initial lack of enthusiasm for his ideas (Scott, 1987). After Taylor, managers were left with a 'scientific' blueprint for controlling workers' behaviour through his 'one best way' approach to job design and his 'fair day's work for a fair day's pay' approach to motivation.

These last two phrases sum up Taylor's basic beliefs:

- It is possible and desirable to establish, through methodical study and the application of scientific principles, the one best way of carrying out any job. Once established, the way must be implemented totally and made to operate consistently.

- Human beings are predisposed to seek the maximum reward for the minimum effort, which Taylor referred to as 'soldiering'. To overcome this, managers must lay down in detail what each worker should do, step by step; ensure through close supervision that the instructions are adhered to; and, to give positive motivation, link pay to performance.

Taylor incorporated those beliefs into his precepts for Scientific Management, comprising three core elements:

- The systematic collection of knowledge about the work process by managers.

- The removal or reduction of workers' discretion and control over what they do.

- The laying down of standard procedures and times for carrying out each job.

The starting point is the gathering of knowledge:

> The managers assume . . . the burden of gathering together all the traditional knowledge which in the past has been possessed by the workman and then of classifying, tabulating and reducing this knowledge to rules, laws and formulae.
> (Taylor, 1911a: 15)

This lays the groundwork for the second stage: increased management control of workers' behaviour. As long as workers possess a monopoly on knowledge about the work process, increased control is impossible. But once the knowledge is also possessed by managers, it becomes possible not only to establish what workers actually do with their time but also, by 'reducing this knowledge to rules, laws and formulae', to decrease the knowledge that workers need to carry out a given task. It also, importantly, paves the way for the division of labour.

The last stage is that 'all possible brain work should be removed from the shop and centred in the planning . . . department' (Taylor, 1911b: 98–9). The divorce of conception from execution removes control from the worker, who no longer has discretion as to how tasks are carried out.

> Perhaps the most prominent single element in modern scientific management is the task idea. The work of every workman is fully planned out by management . . . and each man receives in most cases complete written instructions, describing in detail the task which he is to accomplish, as well as the means to be used in doing the work. . . . This task specifies not only what is to be done but how it is to be done and the exact time allowed for doing it.
> (Taylor, 1911a: 39)

Allied to this last element was Taylor's approach to worker selection and motivation. Taylor carried out many experiments to identify and reward workers. He believed that organisations should employ only 'first class men' and they would get the best results only if they were paid by results. As he commented on his time as a consultant at the Bethlehem Steel Company (Taylor, 1911a: 18–21):

> The Bethlehem Steel Company had five blast furnaces, the product of which had been handled by a pig-iron gang for many years. This gang, at this time, consisted of about 75 men. . . . Our first step was the scientific selection of the . . . proper workman to begin with. We therefore carefully watched and studied these 75 men for three or four days . . . A careful study was then made of each of these men. We looked up their history as far back as practicable and thorough inquiries were made as to the character, habits, and ambitions of each of them. Finally, we selected [Schmidt] . . . as the most likely man to start with. . . . Schmidt started to work, and all day long, and at regular intervals, was told by the man who stood over him with a watch, 'Now pick up a pig and walk. Now sit down and rest. Now walk – now rest,' etc. He worked when he was told to work, and rested when he was told to rest . . . And throughout this time he averaged a little more than $1.85 per day, whereas before he had never received over $1.15 per day . . . One man after another was picked out and trained to handle pig iron . . . receiving 60 per cent more wages than other workmen around them.

The 'task idea' allied to Taylor's approach to selecting and rewarding workers completes the process of managers gaining control over workers' behaviour. The workers become 'human machines', told what to do, when to do it and how long to take. But, more than this, it allows new types of work organisation to be developed, and new work processes and equipment introduced. Thus workers move from having a monopoly of knowledge and control over their work to a position where the knowledge they have of the work process is minimal, and their control vastly reduced. The result is not only a reduction in the skills required and the wages paid but also the creation of jobs that are so narrow and tightly specified that the period needed to train someone to do them is greatly reduced. This removes the last bargaining counter of labour: scarcity of skill.

According to Taylor, this transforms not only workers' behaviour but also managers' behaviour:

> The man at the head of the business under scientific management is governed by rules and laws . . . just as the workman is, and the standards which have been developed are equitable.
> (Taylor, 1911b: 189)

Taylor stated that the 'scientific' basis and equal applicability of his methods meant they were neutral between labour and management; therefore they legitimated managerial action to analyse and change work methods, because managers are merely applying science to determine the best method of work. He claimed that his approach benefited both the worker and the company. The worker was enabled and encouraged to work to his maximum performance and be rewarded with a high rate of pay, while the company benefited from a high rate of output:

> It is absolutely necessary, then, when workmen are daily given a task which calls for a high rate of speed on their part, that they should also be insured the necessary high rate of pay whenever they are successful. This involves not only fixing for each man his daily task, but also paying him a large bonus, or premium, each time that he succeeds in doing his task in the given time. . . . The remarkable and almost uniformly good results from the correct application of the task and the bonus must be seen to be appreciated.   (Taylor, 1911a: 63)

Though seen as something of an anti-trade unionist, which he probably was, as the above implies, he was also strongly critical of management. He believed that many of the problems organisations faced in implementing change were due to the arbitrary and inconsistent approach of managers. In fact, though trade unions were suspicious of Scientific Management in general, and Taylor in particular, managers seemed even more antagonistic. Indeed, after his death, Taylor's acolytes spent much time in the 1920s wooing the American unions with a considerable degree of success; they never achieved the same success with management (Rose, 1988). The main reason for this was that, though managers were anxious to find an approach that would curtail labour resistance to change and improve productivity, they were not prepared to subject themselves to a similar degree of discipline.

As Taylor's biographer, Copley (1923: 146), stated in relation to managerial resistance to Scientific Management at the Bethlehem Steel Company:

> Let us consider what Taylor was contending for. It was essentially this: that the government of the Bethlehem Steel Company cease to be capricious, arbitrary and despotic; that every man in the establishment, high and low, submit himself to law [i.e. that managers should obey the principles of Scientific Management].

Taylor believed passionately in the need to reform managerial behaviour: to base it on competence and fairness rather than the power to hire and fire. However, it is one thing to introduce changes which allow greater controls over one's subordinates' behaviour in order to get them to change their ways and accept new rules and methods; it is another thing entirely for management to introduce similar changes to practices and procedures in order to change their behaviour. No wonder that Taylor met managerial as well as worker resistance.

Yet, even though managers resisted the full implementation of Taylorism, the new and rapidly expanding breed of industrial engineers, charged with developing and implementing new methods, techniques and technologies, found in the work of Taylor and his contemporaries a blueprint for transforming the workplace and increasing their control and status. One consequence of this, brought about by the use of job cards and other forms of work recording and analysis systems, was a massive increase in the amount of paperwork that needed to be processed. Managers complained about the growth of 'industrial bureaucracy', but the benefits it brought by enabling average times and costs, etc. to be calculated easily outweighed the increase in clerical costs.

Nowhere was this demonstrated more dramatically than at Henry Ford's Highland Park plant, the home of the world's first mass-produced motor car, the Model T Ford. From 1909–10, when 18,664 Model Ts were sold, sales and production doubled year-on-year. Every increase in production required a commensurate increase in the plant's workforce. In 1911/12, the plant produced 78,440 Model Ts with 6,867 employees. The next year production doubled and the number of employees doubled. Not surprisingly, Ford was desperate for ways of increasing employee productivity. The solution he adopted was to redesign the assembly operation around Scientific Management principles and then couple this with the introduction of the moving assembly line. This allowed Ford once again to double production, but this time the workforce actually decreased (Lacey, 1986). So the 1910s saw the birth of the twin, and very much related, neologisms that both dominated and revolutionised industrial life for much of the twentieth century – Taylorism and Fordism.

Throughout the 1920s, the adoption of Scientific Management grew in the US, though rarely in the full form laid down by Taylor. It was also introduced on a very limited basis into Europe, but met with much scepticism from managers and hostility from workers (Rose, 1988). Only in Russia did there seem to be any great enthusiasm for it. Indeed, Lenin saw Scientific Management combined with common ownership as the prime basis for Russian industrialisation: 'We must organize in Russia the study and teaching of the Taylor system and systematically try it out and adapt it to our own ends' (Lenin, 1918: 25). Taylor's work also attracted some interest in Japan. However, it was not until after the Second World War, through the auspices of the Marshall Plan for rebuilding Europe's war-torn economies, that Scientific Management was promoted and adopted on any significant scale outside the US. Ironically, the contribution of American trade unions, through their role in the Marshall Plan, was crucial in promoting Scientific Management in European enterprises (Carew, 1987).

Taylor claimed that his system was innovative and unique, which indeed it was in terms of the way he synthesised and systematised a host of previously disparate practices and presented them as scientific and neutral (Aitken, 1960; Rose, 1988). Yet in reality it can be seen that Taylor drew on many of the management practices and negative attitudes towards labour that were prevalent during the nineteenth century. He was also heavily indebted to many contemporaries and associates who helped develop the work study techniques necessary to implement Scientific Management, especially Henry Gantt and Carl Barth, who worked closely with him (Kempner, 1970; Sheldrake, 1996). Perhaps his greatest debt was to Frank and Lillian Gilbreth. As well as being the pioneers of motion study, they were the driving force in establishing the Society for the Promotion of Scientific Management, which was later renamed the Taylor Society, and did much to promote Taylor's work both before and after his death in 1915 (Rose, 1988; Sheldrake, 1996).

The Gilbreths and motion study

Much of modern work study (a central element of the Classical approach) owes its origins to the methods and techniques of motion study developed in the first quarter of the twentieth century by Frank and Lillian Gilbreth (*see* Gilbreth and Gilbreth, 1914). Their work on motion study was initiated by Frank Gilbreth, who was a contemporary of Taylor's. In many respects their careers were similar. Taylor, turning his back on Harvard Law School, began his career on the shopfloor and later rose to eminence as a manager and management consultant. Frank Gilbreth, after passing the entrance exam for but declining to enter the Massachusetts Institute of Technology, rose from being a bricklayer to running his own construction and consultancy companies. He was also, along with his wife, a leading campaigner for Scientific Management.

Although the development and promotion of motion study were begun by her husband, there is no doubt that Lillian Moller Gilbreth was an equal partner. Despite contemporary prejudices against women and education, she obtained Bachelor's and Master's degrees in English. She was denied a doctorate in psychology by the University of California only because family commitments prevented her, after her thesis had been approved, from spending the post-thesis year on campus that the regulations required (Sheldrake, 1996; Thickett, 1970).

In justifying their work, Frank Gilbreth stated in his 1909 book on bricklaying that motion study:

> will cut down production costs and increase the efficiency and wages of the workman . . . To be preeminently successful: (a) a mechanic must know his trade; (b) he must be quick motioned; and (c) he must use the fewest possible motions to accomplish the desired results.
>
> (Quoted in Sheldrake, 1996: 28)

The Gilbreths developed a number of procedures for breaking work down into its constituent components. Flow process charts were used which split human motion into five basic elements: operations, transportation, inspection, storage and delay. Arising out of this, they developed a method of minutely analysing tasks which broke handwork into 17 basic elements. Examples of these are as follows:

> *Grasp* Begins when hand or body member touches an object. Consists of gaining control of an object.
>
> *Release* Begins when hand or body member begins to relax control of object. Consists of letting go of an object.
>
> *Plan* Begins when hand or body members are idle or making random movements while worker decides on course of action. Consists of determining a course of action. Ends when course of action is determined.

The purpose of this microanalysis was not only to establish what was done but also to discover whether a better method of performing the task in question could be developed. In this respect, they did much original work in establishing the distinction between necessary and unnecessary movements. The latter were to be eliminated immediately and the former further analysed in more detail to see if they could be improved, combined or replaced by special equipment.

If this sounds remarkably similar to Adam Smith's observations on pin-making, mentioned earlier, this is no accident. The Classical approach is descended from Smith through the nineteenth-century pioneers of work organisation. Though remarkable in the level of minute detail to which they reduced the motions individuals make when undertaking manual tasks, the Gilbreths were only, as they saw it, taking Smith's maxims to their logical conclusion. If in the process they give the impression of dealing more with machines than people, that too is no accident. Like others who propounded the Classical approach, they viewed organisations and workers very much as machines. The term 'workers' behaviour' can sometimes seem quite nebulous, but the Gilbreths showed that under Scientific Management it is a concrete concept whereby workers were told when to move, how to move and how long to take in making the movement. Also, if this seems like something from another age, it is not. The work study methods developed by the Gilbreths and their successors are still widely used today, not just in manufacturing industries but in all areas of life from hospitals to computer programming, and especially in the design and supervision of work in modern call centres, which was based on similar principles and techniques to those developed by the Gilbreths and the other Taylorites (Grant, 1983; Holman, 2002).

The Gilbreths were also concerned that, having established the best way to carry out a task, this should not be undermined by selecting the wrong person to carry it out or by creating the wrong environment. Therefore, they set about analysing employee selection and establishing environmental criteria with the same determination they had applied to analysing work performance. However, in neither case could they achieve the same micro-analysis that characterised their work study technique; what finally emerged were effectively opinions based on their own 'experience', rather than being the product of experiment and observation.

The Gilbreths, like Taylor, were devoted to one objective: to discover the best method of doing any job. The difference was that whereas Taylor was concerned with reducing the time taken to perform a task, the Gilbreths were more concerned with reducing the motions taken to accomplish the task. Though this differing emphasis did lead to some friction with Taylor (Nadworthy, 1957), they were, nonetheless, among his main promoters and saw their efforts as complementary to, and aimed at enhancing, Scientific Management. The fact that work study is now often labelled 'time and motion' study perhaps reflects this. Like Taylor, they saw themselves as creating a neutral system that benefited both labour and management. They felt that any increase in boredom or monotony brought about by their methods would be compensated for by workers' opportunities to earn more money.

While the Gilbreths and Taylor devoted their efforts to controlling workers' behaviour in order to improve the productivity of individual workers, there were others who took a wider but complementary perspective.

Henri Fayol and the principles of organisation

Though French, Henri Fayol was born in Istanbul. He was educated at the *lycée* in Lyon and the National School of Mines in St Etienne. Fayol was promoting his ideas in France at the same time as Taylor was propounding his views on Scientific Management in the US. He began his working life as a mining engineer in 1860 and, in 1888, was appointed managing director of an ailing mining company, which he quickly turned into a much-admired and financially strong enterprise. He retired as managing director in 1918, though he stayed on the board until his death in 1925. In his 'retirement' he founded the Centre d'Etudes Administratives, whose role was to propagate Fayol's ideas through management education. He chaired weekly meetings of prominent industrialists, writers, government officials, philosophers and members of the military. This direct contact with opinion-formers and decision-makers is undoubtedly one of the main reasons why the Centre had such a profound influence on the practice and theory of management in both the public and private sectors in France.

Fayol's approach to managing organisations and shaping workers' behaviour is described in his book *General and Industrial Management*, which was published in France in 1916 but did not appear in English until 1949 (Lamond, 2004). Fayol did not draw his views on managing organisations solely from his own experience as a manager. His education at one of the *grandes écoles*, and his subsequent career as an executive of a large mining company, placed him among the elite of senior administrators in business, government and the armed forces. Therefore, though he spent his working life in the coal mining industry, his practical knowledge of business was informed by and fits within the intellectual and administrative traditions of French society.

His working life, in the late nineteenth and early twentieth centuries, coincided with a period of rapid industrialisation in France. It was a time when industrial unrest was rife, with frequent strikes by railway workers, miners and civil servants. As was the case in the US, in this period of rapid growth and change there was an unwritten consensus that French business and government needed a theory of management, no matter how basic (Cuthbert, 1970). Unlike Taylor and the Gilbreths, however, Fayol's focus was on efficiency at the organisational level rather than the task level: top-down rather than bottom-up (Fayol, 1949). Though this clearly reflects Fayol's own practical experience, it also indicates the combined influence of the French intellectual tradition, with its preference for addressing philosophies rather than practicalities, and the administrative tradition, which sought to identify and lay down general rules and restrictions applicable to all situations.

Given his background, it is not surprising that Fayol was more concerned with general rather than departmental or supervisory management, and with overall organisational control as opposed to the details of tasks. This does not, however, place him in opposition to Taylor. Rather, the combination of Taylor's work at the task level and Fayol's at the organisational level makes their views complementary rather than contradictory. In addition, both emphasised strongly the need for professionally educated managers who would 'follow the rule' rather than acting in an arbitrary or *ad hoc* fashion.

As the following shows, Fayol (like all the Classical school) was concerned with developing a universal approach to management that was applicable to any organisation:

> There is no one doctrine of administration for business and another for affairs of state; administrative doctrine is universal. Principles and general rules which hold good for business hold good for the state too, and the reverse applies. (Quoted in Cuthbert, 1970: 111)

Fayol established 14 'universal' principles of organisation (*see* Ideas and perspectives 1.1). According to Fayol (1949), it is the prime responsibility of management to enact these principles. In order to achieve this, he prescribed the main duties of management as follows:

- **Forecasting and planning** – examining the future, deciding what needs to be done and developing a plan of action.
- **Organising** – bringing together the resources, human and material, and developing the structure to carry out the activities of the organisation.
- **Commanding** – ensuring that all employees perform their jobs well and in the best interests of the organisation.
- **Coordinating** – verifying that the activities of the organisation work harmoniously to achieve its goals.
- **Controlling** – guaranteeing that all actions are correctly carried out in accordance with established rules and expressed commands.

23

IDEAS AND PERSPECTIVES 1.1

Henri Fayol's principles of organisation

1. **Division of work**. The object is to produce more and better work from the same effort, through the advantages of specialisation.

2. **Authority and responsibility**. Wherever authority is exercised, responsibility arises. The application of sanctions is needed to encourage useful actions and to discourage their opposite.

3. **Discipline**. This is essential for the efficient operation of the organisation. Discipline is in essence the outward mark of respect for agreements between the organisation and its members.

4. **Unity of command**. In any action, any employee should receive orders from one superior only; dual command is a perpetual source of conflicts.

5. **Unity of direction**. In order to coordinate and focus effort, there should be one leader and one plan for any group of activities with the same objective.

6. **Subordination of individual or group interests**. The interest of the organisation should take precedence over individual or group interests.

7. **Remuneration of personnel**. Methods of payment should be fair, encourage keenness by rewarding well-directed effort, but not lead to over-payment.

8. **Centralisation**. The degree of centralisation is a question of proportion and will vary in particular organisations.

9. **Scalar chain**. This is the chain of superiors from the ultimate authority to the lowest ranks. Respect for line authority must be reconciled with activities that require urgent action, and with the need to provide for some measure of initiative at all levels of authority.

10. **Order**. This includes material order and social order. The object of material order is avoidance of loss. There should be an appointed place for each thing, and each thing should be in its appointed place. Social order requires good organisation and good selection.

11. **Equity**. There needs to be fairness in dealing with employees throughout all levels of the scalar chain.

12. **Stability of tenure of personnel**. Generally, prosperous organisations have a stable managerial team.

13. **Initiative**. This represents a source of strength for the organisation and should be encouraged and developed.

14. **Esprit de corps**. This should be fostered, as harmony and unity among members of the organisation are a great strength in the organisation.

Source: Mullins (1989: 202–3).

Fayol was a gifted and highly successful businessman who attributed his success to the application of his principles rather than personal ability. Certainly, he was one of the pioneers of management theory, and many of his principles are still taught and practised today (Lamond, 2004). Indeed, Wren (1994: 193) commented that Fayol's work 'represents the most useful way of conceptualising the manager's job'. However, part of the success of his work lay in the fact that he was writing for a receptive audience, and at a time when management practice and ideas were becoming international currency. Just as Taylor's system arose at the time when a need for a management theory had grown among the business community in the US, so Fayol's was aimed at a similar demand in France, where the business community was developing rapidly but in an unplanned way.

Unlike Taylor, though, he attempted neither to denigrate trade unions openly nor to castigate managers. Nor did he share with Taylor a belief that the interests of managers and workers were necessarily the same or ultimately reconcilable. He did, however, believe that much industrial unrest could be eliminated by fairer, more consistent and firmer management, particularly where this reduced the need for trade unions or their ability to organise. He also believed in the need to educate and train managers. His views were not seen as a direct attack on existing managers; rather, they were in harmony with the approach taken by managers in the larger private enterprises and those operating in government and the armed services. This is not surprising because, by and large, they and Fayol were educated in the *grandes écoles* and shared a common intellectual approach. In addition, Fayol did not generally try to impose his ideas directly on individual organisations. Instead, he preferred to influence managers indirectly through a process of education. In the light of the reaction to Taylor's attitude in the US, many would consider this a wise move.

Though there were attempts in France to promote '*Fayolisme*' in opposition to Taylorism, Fayol rejected this, preferring to see the two approaches as complementary (Sheldrake, 1996). As Urwick (1949: 9–10) commented in the Introduction to the English version of Fayol's *General and Industrial Management*:

> The work of Taylor and Fayol was, of course, essentially complementary. They both realized that the problem of personnel and its management at all levels is the key to industrial success. Both applied scientific method to this problem. That Taylor worked primarily at the operative level, from the bottom of the industrial hierarchy upwards, while Fayol concentrated on the managing director and worked downwards, was merely a reflection of their very different careers.

The US and France were not the only countries where developments in management practice and thought were being studied and documented. In Germany, at this time, Max Weber was charting the growth and merits of bureaucracy.

Max Weber on bureaucracy

Weber was born in 1864 into a well-to-do Prussian family. He pursued an academic career, obtaining a doctorate in 1889. In 1894, he was appointed Professor of Political Economy at the University of Freiburg, and in 1896 he accepted the Chair in Economics at Heidelberg. Unfortunately, in 1897, he suffered a mental breakdown, which plagued him for many years. He resigned from his university post and spent much of his time travelling in Europe and the US. He also moved the focus of his academic studies from economics to sociology.

Weber was an ardent German nationalist, and at the age of 50 he volunteered for military service in the First World War. Until his honourable discharge in 1915, he was responsible for establishing and running nine military hospitals. Despite this, he was a fierce and open critic of the Kaiser, whom he accused of being a dilettante hiding behind the divine right of kings. He believed that Germany's problems at home and abroad could be solved only if the monarchy were replaced with a constitutional democracy. After the war, he became a member of the commission that drew up the constitution for the Weimar Republic, and once again took up university teaching, this time in Munich. Unfortunately, when he died in 1920, most of his work was unpublished and his papers were in a state of chaos. It was not until the 1930s that his work began to be organised and published, and it was the 1940s before his work on bureaucracy was published in English (Sheldrake, 1996; Weber, 1948).

There is a considerable affinity between Weber's work on bureaucracy and Fayol's work on the principles of management. Both were concerned with the overall structuring of organisations, and the principles which guide senior managers in this task. Though a contemporary of Fayol and Taylor, it is unlikely that they were aware of Weber's work on bureaucracy, though he may have been aware of their work.

However, unlike Taylor and Fayol, Weber was never a practising manager. His observations on administrative structures and organisational effectiveness arose from his study of the development of Western civilisation. From this, Weber concluded that the rise of civilisation was a story of power and domination. He noted (Weber, 1948) that each social epoch was characterised by a different form of political rule, and that for a ruling elite to sustain its power and dominance, it was essential for them both to gain legitimacy and to develop an administrative apparatus to enforce and support their authority.

Weber (1947: 328) identified what he called 'three pure types of legitimate authority':

1. **Rational–legal** – resting on a belief in the 'legality' of patterns of normative rule, and the right of those elevated to authority under such rules to issue commands.

2. **Traditional** – resting on an established belief in the sanctity of immemorial traditions and the legitimacy of those exercising authority under them.

3. **Charismatic** – resting on devotion to the specific and exceptional sanctity, heroism or exemplary character of an individual person, and of the normative patterns or order revealed or ordained by them.

For Weber, legitimacy is central to almost all systems of authority. He argued that there are five concepts on which rational–legal authority is based. According to Albrow (1970: 43), these are as follows:

1. That a legal code can be established which can claim obedience from members of the organisation.

2. That the law is a system of abstract rules which are applied in particular cases, and that administration looks after the interests of the organisation within the limits of the law.

3. That the man exercising authority also obeys this impersonal law.

4. That only *qua* [in the capacity of] member does the member obey the law.

5. That obedience is due not to the person who holds authority but to the impersonal order that has granted him his position.

Weber argued that, in the context of the rational–legal authority structures which prevailed in Western societies in the early twentieth century, the bureaucratic approach to controlling human behaviour was the most appropriate and efficient. Under bureaucracy, laws, rules, procedures and predefined routines are dominant and not subject to the vagaries and preferences of individuals. They give form to a clearly defined system of administration – whether it be public administration, such as a government department dealing with pensions and social security payments, or private administration, such as an insurance company – where the execution of routine, pre-programmed procedures is all-important. Weber considered this approach to be both appropriate, because it was the ideal tool for a centralised administration where the legitimacy of those in power was underpinned by the rule of law, and efficient, because the bureaucratic approach mechanises the process of administration in the same way that machines automate the production process in factories.

Weber frequently asserted that the development of bureaucracy eliminates human fallibility:

> Its [bureaucracy's] specific nature, which is welcomed by capitalism, develops the more perfectly the more bureaucracy is 'dehumanised', the more completely it succeeds in eliminating from official business, love, hatred, and all purely personal, irrational and emotional elements which escape calculation.   (Weber, 1948: 215–16)

Bureaucracy is characterised by the division of labour, a clear hierarchical authority structure, formal and unbiased selection procedures, employment decisions based on merit, career tracks for employees, detailed rules and regulations, impersonal relationships, and a distinct separation of members' organisational and personal lives. It must be borne in mind, however, that Weber's bureaucratic model (or 'ideal' organisation), though inspired by developments in Germany at the time, was a hypothetical rather than a factual description of how most organisations were structured. It was his view of the characteristics that organisations should exhibit in modern societies based on rationality and law. How Weber saw these organisational characteristics supporting and reproducing rational–legal authority is best seen by contrasting them with the traditional administrative forms based on patronage (*see* Ideas and perspectives 1.2) (Weber, 1947, 1948).

For Weber, therefore, bureaucracy provided a rational–legal form of organisation which distinguished itself from, and eradicated the faults and unfairness of, previous administrative forms by its mechanical adherence to set rules, procedures and patterns of authority. In essence, Weber was seeking to control not just workers' behaviour but also managers' behaviour. Bureaucracy removed the system of patronage and eliminated human variability, replacing it by the rule of law. In Weber's view, the principles of bureaucracy, especially the legitimation of authority and the subordination of all in the organisation to the same rules and procedures, were universally applicable to all organisations, big or small, public or private, industrial or commercial.

It can be seen that Weber's belief in the standardisation of rules and procedures, and obedience by all to them, is the counterpart of the standardisation of production techniques advocated by Taylor and akin to the principles of administrative management prescribed by Fayol. Also, just as the work of Taylor and Fayol can be understood as representing a combination of their backgrounds and the state of the societies in which they lived, the same is true of Weber. The Prussian bureaucratic tradition dominated both the public and, to a large extent, the private sectors in Germany. It was seen by the ruling elite as the ideal method for ensuring that the objectives of the state and the objectives of individual enterprises were adhered to. It also fitted in with the Prussian militaristic tradition of unquestioning obedience to superiors, which was prevalent in both public and private organisations. It must be remembered, of course, that the state and private enterprises in Germany were not primarily obsessed with profitability or individual aggrandisement. The key objective was to build Germany as the premier military and industrial power in Europe. Competition at the level of the individual or the individual enterprise was a concept that carried much less force in Germany, and even France, than in the US or Britain. German industry and government were more concerned with ensuring that all sections of the country pulled in

IDEAS AND PERSPECTIVES 1.2

Rational–legal authority versus traditional authority

Characteristics of rational–legal authority	Characteristics of traditional authority
Areas of jurisdiction are clearly specified: the regular activities required of personnel are allocated in a fixed way as official duties. The organisation of offices follows the principle of hierarchy: each lower office is controlled and supervised by a higher one. However, the scope of authority of superiors over subordinates is circumscribed, and lower offices enjoy a right of appeal.	The allocation of labour is not defined, but depends on assignments made by the leader, which can be changed at any time. Authority relations are diffuse, being based on personal loyalty, and are not ordered into clear hierarchies.
An intentionally established system of abstract rules governs official decisions and actions. These rules are relatively stable and exhaustive, and can be learned. Decisions are recorded in permanent files.	General rules of administration either do not exist or are vaguely stated, ill-defined, and subject to change at the whim of the leader. No attempt is made to keep permanent records of transactions.
The 'means of production or administration' (e.g. tools and equipment or rights and privileges) belong to the office, not the office-holder, and may not be appropriated. Personal property is clearly separated from official property, and working space from living quarters.	There is no separation of a ruler's personal household business from the larger 'public' business under their direction.
Officials are personally free, selected on the basis of technical qualifications, appointed to office (not elected) and recompensed by salary.	Officials are often selected from among those who are personally dependent on the leader, e.g. slaves, serfs and relatives. Selection is governed by arbitrary criteria, and remuneration often takes the form of benefices – rights granted to individuals that, for instance, allow them access to the ruler's stores, or give them grants of land from which they can appropriate the fees or taxes. Benefices, like fiefs in feudalistic systems, may become hereditary and sometimes are bought and sold.
Employment by the organisation constitutes a career for officials. An official is a full-time employee and looks forward to a lifelong career in the agency. After a trial period, he or she gains tenure of position and is protected against arbitrary dismissal.	Officials serve at the pleasure of the leader, and so lack clear expectations about the future and security of tenure.

the same direction. Where competition threatened this, it was eliminated by the state, either by direct intervention, such as nationalisation of the railways, or by indirect intervention, through the formation of cartels and monopolies. In carrying out this grand plan for German development, bureaucracy was found to be the ideal tool.

In Germany, the advent of the First World War highlighted the incompatibility between industrial bureaucracies based on the rule of law and a government run on autocratic lines for militaristic ends. Weber argued that the rule of law applied not only to the operation of organisations but also, and more importantly, to the running of society. If society was not based on the rule of law, if democratically elected governments did not hold power, then the authority of those who ruled must be called into question. This was the basis of Weber's attacks on the Kaiser and the military during the First World War. He believed that, in the modern age, rational–legal authority, based on democratically elected governments and laws governing property rights, was the best and most effective way for society and organisations to be governed. For Weber, the rise of bureaucracy and the rise of liberal democracy went hand in hand.

It is evident that bureaucracy did not need a Taylor or a Fayol to develop or promote it; it already existed, was accepted by management, and was prospering, in Germany and other advanced countries, especially in the public sector. What Weber did was to give it intellectual respectability by arguing that it was particularly suited to the needs of (what he saw as) the rational, secular and increasingly democratic societies that were becoming the norm in the Western world.

The appeal of bureaucracy, to governments and large organisations at least, can be seen in the way that bureaucracy is an ever-present and pervasive feature of modern life. However, it would be misleading to give the impression that its development in Germany, or elsewhere, was uncontentious. In Germany, in the early years of the twentieth century, it tended to be the purpose and consequences of bureaucracy rather than its principles that were attacked. At an overall political level, the growth of radical parties of the left reflected growing concerns over Germany's military aims and the state's concomitant close links with business, and in particular its perceived preference for aiding capital rather than labour. At the level of the individual enterprise, the growth of militant trade unions, often linked to the parties of the left, reflected the growing frustration of workers who resented the autocratic approach of management and its resistance to collective bargaining.

Conclusions

It is not an inevitable fact of life that modern societies are characterised by organisations, of all shapes and sizes; this is the product of a particular combination of circumstances. The rise of capitalism in Britain and other European countries in the seventeenth and eighteenth centuries created new opportunities and new problems that could not be accommodated under the old order. The result was a move away from self-sufficient, autonomous, individual units to collective units of production controlled by an entrepreneur. It was entrepreneurs who, in pursuit of ever greater profits, created the factory system in Britain, which became the basis of modern organisational life. The central features of the factory system were autocratic management, the division of labour and a battle for control of the work process between management and labour.

Though starting at different times and moving at their own pace, most European countries, followed by the US, adopted and adapted the British approach to industrial organisation. However, as the nineteenth century progressed, the nature of industrialisation began to vary from country to country, reflecting the unique circumstances and needs of the host society. In Germany, the objectives of the state determined that large-scale public and private bureaucracies became the norm. In France, the state also played a role in shaping industrialisation, but in this case it was to perpetuate small-scale, inefficient business and agricultural operations. In both countries, individual pursuit of profit maximisation was less important than in either Britain or the US.

In the transition from a subsistence economy to a money economy, one clear image stands out above all else: the antagonism between employers and employees. The factory did not emerge because it was a more efficient means of production *per se*; it emerged because it offered entrepreneurs a more effective means of controlling workers' behaviour. This meant that the factory was also a battleground, with employers seeking to impose new conditions and technologies, and workers – when they could – attempting to resist change.

As the nineteenth century progressed, managers became increasingly aware of the shortcomings of their *ad hoc* and inconsistent responses to new challenges and opportunities, and the counterproductive nature of resistance to change. The need for a more coherent approach to structuring and running organisations was required: one that legitimated managerial authority, especially to initiate change. This crystallised into the Classical approach.

Though writing in different countries and from different perspectives, the proponents of what later came to be known as the Classical school all adopted a similar perspective towards what they saw as one of the main issues for modern societies: how to create organisations that efficiently and effectively pursue their objectives. Taylor, supported by the work of the Gilbreths and others, concentrated very much on the operational level, arguing for his 'scientific' method of analysing, designing and managing jobs. However, his insistence on the consistent and unbiased application of scientific principles, and the emphasis he placed on all members of an organisation obeying rules and procedures, were as much a challenge to managerial beliefs and behaviour as they were to the beliefs and behaviour of shopfloor workers. Fayol, in contrast, was concerned less with operational issues and more with the overall administration and control of organisations. Therefore, to an extent, his could be called a top-down approach, while Taylor was working from the bottom up. Weber sought to put organisations in a wider historical and societal context, bringing together both the detailed tasks to be carried out in organisations and the general principles governing them.

Though Taylor's approach required a radical change in managerial behaviour and a significant increase in organisational bureaucracy, the objective of his system was to change manual workers' behaviour by redesigning their jobs and thus increasing their efficiency and productivity. Everything else was, as Taylor would have put it, the outcome of pursuing this objective to its logical conclusion. The need to provide managers with rules and systems for running the entire enterprise, and not just that part of it dealing with manual labour, was a means of achieving his objective rather than a prime aim. This is where the work of Fayol and Weber has proved so crucial: together with Taylor's work, it comprises a system for running an entire business in a coherent, standardised and consistent fashion.

Therefore, taken together, their views are, broadly, complementary, and reflect an approach to organisations and people based upon a number of basic assumptions (*see* Ideas and perspectives 1.3).

Seen in the context of the early twentieth century, when there appeared to be a substantial questioning of – and challenge to – managerial authority by workers, the Classical approach had many merits, not least in its attempt to replace arbitrary and capricious management with rules and procedures that apply equally to everyone in the organisation. With

---

IDEAS AND PERSPECTIVES 1.3

The Classical approach – basic assumptions

- There is a 'one best way' for all organisations to be structured and operate.
- This approach is founded on the rule of law and legitimate managerial authority and is designed to ensure that employees' behaviour is geared solely to the efficient pursuit of the organisation's goals.
- Organisations are rational entities: groups of individuals who consistently and effectively pursue rational, quantifiable goals, which should be specified as tightly as possible.
- People are motivated to work solely by financial reward.
- Human fallibility and emotions, at all levels in the organisation, should be eliminated because they threaten the consistent application of the rule of law and the efficient pursuit of goals.
- For this reason, the most appropriate form of job design is achieved through the use of the hierarchical and horizontal division of labour to create narrowly focused jobs encased in tight, standardised procedures and rules, which remove discretion, dictate what job-holders do and how they do it, and allow their work to be closely monitored and controlled by their direct superiors.

---

hindsight, the attempt by Taylor, Fayol and Weber each in their own way to formulate a system of reciprocal obligations between managers and workers appears to be less a decisive break with the past and more an attempt to recast feudalism in a more scientific–rational framework. Certainly, in the late nineteenth century, French, German and American managers of European descent did share a recent and common feudal heritage which might make them well disposed towards a system that replaced management–worker conflict with a code of joint obligation. Indeed, in Germany, the rise of bureaucracy that Weber described was itself a direct product of the Prussian feudal tradition. However, though many managers undoubtedly did long for and believe in an – albeit mythical – age when workers readily did as they were told, this ignored the fact that most American immigrants left Europe to escape just such a system, while French workers took pride in the belief that their Revolution had ended feudal despotism. Only in Germany was it possible to say that the feudal tradition remained strong, though not unopposed.

Therefore, it is important to see the work of the Classical school in terms of what went before. Weber explicitly drew on history to support his views; the historical debts of Taylor and Fayol, though not openly acknowledged in their work, are clearly there. From Smith, through Wedgwood, Boulton and Watt, Babbage and Ure can be traced key elements of the Classical approach: the division of labour, the distrust of human variability, the need for written rules, procedures and records, and the need for rational and consistent management and objectives. Parallel to these are key themes that run through other aspects of nineteenth-century life: the search for the rational, scientific, universal principles that govern the natural world, the belief in the Protestant work ethic, the emergence of Social Darwinism, the greater democratisation of societies, and the gradual reduction of laws favouring one class or group over another.

All these strands coalesced – not always neatly – in the Classical approach, creating (in retrospect) the first real and consistent attempt at a theory, a set of guidelines, for constructing, managing and changing organisations. However, given that it grew out of and was designed to meet particular circumstances, so its appropriateness began to be questioned and criticised as these circumstances changed.

Taylor and his adherents have been criticised both for their lack of scientific rigour and for their one-dimensional view of human motivation (Burnes, 1989; Kelly, 1982a, 1982b). Indeed, as Rose (1988) argued, Taylor portrayed human beings as 'greedy robots': indifferent to fatigue, boredom, loneliness and pain, driven solely by monetary incentive. For Taylor, material incentives are the only effective incentives to work. For this reason, he opposed everything else in the workplace that, in his opinion, undermined managers' attempts to introduce individual incentive systems, whether it be friendships, group loyalty, trade unions, or whatever. Taylor has also been attacked for over-emphasising the merits of the division of labour. The critics' argument is that the creation of jobs which have little intrinsic satisfaction leads to poor morale, low motivation and alienation. Indeed, such are the forces aligned against Scientific Management that it is difficult to find a facet of it that has not been attacked (Argyris, 1964; Littler, 1978; Locke, 1982).

Fayol has been attacked on three fronts: first, that his principles are mere truisms; second, that they are based on questionable premises; and third, that the principles occur in pairs or clusters of contradictory statements (Massie, 1965; Mintzberg, 1973, 1975; Simon, 1947). In addition, Fayol, like Taylor, can be construed as being against trade unions. Certainly, he believed in the pre-eminence of management and its right to make changes how and when it wanted, so long as these were based on his general principles. He also believed, unlike Taylor, that management and labour were fundamentally in conflict. Therefore, his recommendations were partly aimed at eliminating the conditions in which trade unions can flourish, in the interests of his overall aim of establishing the legitimacy of managers to manage.

Weber's arguments for bureaucracy have also received criticism. For instance, Udy (1959) questioned Weber's assertion that bureaucracies are necessarily rational, while Parsons (1947) suggested that Weber puts forward contradictory arguments for the basis of authority within bureaucracies. Robbins (1987) pointed out that bureaucracy is most frequently attacked for encouraging goal displacement:

- Rules become ends in themselves rather than means to the ends they were designed to achieve.

- Specialisation and differentiation create sub-units with different goals which then become primary to the sub-unit members. Not only does this lead to conflict between sub-units, but the accomplishment of sub-unit goals becomes more important than achieving the organisation's overall goals.

- Rules and regulations become interpreted as setting minimum standards of performance rather than identifying unacceptable behaviour. Staff can become apathetic and merely perform the bare minimum of work.

- The unthinking and rigid application of standardised rules and procedures can lead to their being applied in inappropriate situations, with dysfunctional consequences.

Robbins (1987) also pointed out that bureaucracy can alienate both employees and customers or clients. For the former, being treated as mere cogs in a machine leads to a sense of powerlessness and irrelevance. For the latter, being presented with a rigid and face-less organisation, which appears to serve its own ends rather than those of its customers or clients, can be frustrating and, when the provision of welfare services is involved, even heartbreaking. Mullins (1993) also pointed out that bureaucracy is often associated with secrecy and attempts to prevent legitimate public access to vital information on the performance of government and large organisations. Weber's work on bureaucracy has also received criticism because of his lack of attention to informal and social processes, in particular the way that individuals and groups can and do struggle to promote their own interests and goals above those of others in the organisation (Crozier, 1964).

It should also be noted that, though broadly complementary, the approaches of Taylor, Fayol and Weber were developed separately and with different objectives in mind. There are, consequently, tensions and inconsistencies between them. Fayol stresses the importance of *esprit de corps* and individual initiative. Taylor and Weber would find the former irrelevant and the latter dangerous. Likewise, the unchanging rigidity of bureaucracy, as portrayed by Weber, leaves little scope for the continuous search for improvement in methods and productivity advocated by Taylor and Fayol. Taylor's advocacy of functional supervision, which in effect meant a worker being responsible to different supervisors for different aspects of his or her job (some four or five supervisors in total), would have been viewed as a threat to discipline and good order by both Weber and Fayol, who were fierce advocates of unity of command – each worker should receive orders from one superior only.

One of the main criticisms of the Classical approach as a whole is that its view of people is negative. Bennis (1959: 263) called the Classical perspective one of 'organisations without people' because it is founded on the belief that people can be reduced to the level of cogs in a machine. It can also be argued that, in any case, it is impossible to remove the element of human variability from the running of organisations and that attempts to do so are counterproductive. Rather than making people work more efficiently in pursuit of organisational goals, it alienates them from their work and makes them resentful of it (Argyris, 1964; Mayo, 1933). In addition, Stickland (1998) points out that the Classical approach's view of change is limited. Change is the responsibility of management, and workers should not be involved because they have nothing to contribute, given that all valid knowledge should lie with the organisation's managers and technical experts.

> Hence, change was largely an internal planned affair, driven by a unitary world view and focused on the rational, mechanical nature of work at the operational level.
>
> (Stickland, 1998: 31)

Argyris (1964) claims that the rational, de-humanising and excluding focus of the Classical approach was its Achilles heel because it restricts the psychological growth of individuals and causes feelings of failure, frustration and conflict. Instead, he maintained that the organisational environment should provide a significant degree of individual responsibility and self-control; commitment to the goals of the organisation; productiveness and work; and an opportunity for individuals to apply their full abilities. These developed as central issues for the proponents of the Human Relations approach, which emerged in the 1930s as a reaction to the 'de-humanised' Classical approach. This, together with Contingency Theory – the third approach to organisations to emerge in the twentieth century – will be discussed in the next chapter.

TEST YOUR LEARNING

Short discussion topics

The purpose of these is to enable students to check and reflect on the topics. The discussions should last for no more than 5–10 minutes. Depending on the length of the lecture, there could be one, two or three such discussions in a session.

The following are five suggested topics which address issues raised in this chapter:

1. What are the key tenets of Scientific Management?

2. According to Fayol, what are the prime functions of a manager?

3. What was Weber's main justification for advocating bureaucracy?

4. What are the main arguments for the Classical approach?

5. What are the main arguments against the Classical approach?

Class debates

The purpose of class debates is to enable students to explore a topic in depth by setting up a 'for and against' debate. The class can be split into two and one half asked to research the 'for' case and the other the 'against' case. Individuals can then be chosen at random to introduce their side of the debate. Alternatively, two individuals for each side can be told in advance that they will be introducing the debate. The length of such debates depends on the time available, the size of the class and their enthusiasm for the topic. However, less than 30 minutes is probably too short and more than 60 minutes probably too long.

The following are three suggested topics which address issues raised in this chapter:

1. The Classical approach provides an effective way to manage organisational change.

2. Bureaucracy is still the best way to manage large organisations.

3. Scientific Management is the most effective basis on which to organise work in call centres.

Essay questions

1. To what extent and why can it be said that the Industrial Revolution made change rather than stability an organisational priority?

2. Evaluate the similarities, differences and complementarities of the work of Taylor, Fayol and Weber.

3. Discuss the following statement: The Classical approach works only if employees can be reduced to the level of 'greedy robots'.

Suggested further reading

Pollard, S (1965) *The Genesis of Modern Management*. Pelican: Harmondsworth.

Though published nearly 50 years ago, Sydney Pollard's book still provides one of the best descriptions of the development of management and the reaction of labour in the eighteenth and nineteenth centuries.

Rose, M (1988) *Industrial Behaviour*. Penguin: Harmondsworth.
Michael Rose's book provides a well-researched and thorough account of the rise and development of Scientific Management.

Sheldrake, J (1996) *Management Theory: From Taylorism to Japanization*. International Thompson Business Press: London.
John Sheldrake gives an excellent summary of the lives and contributions of Taylor, Fayol and Weber.

Taylor, FW (1911) *The Principles of Scientific Management*. Dover (1998 edition): New York.
This is perhaps the most cited, if least read, of all management books. However, as it numbers only 76 pages and is couched in quite accessible language, it is well worth reading.

Wilson, JF (1995) *British Business History, 1720–1994*. Manchester University Press: Manchester.
Despite its title, this book neither confines itself to British history nor examines business in a narrow sense. Among other things, John Wilson's book provides an excellent review of the development of management in Britain, Germany, Japan and the US from the early days of the Industrial Revolution.

CASE STUDY 1

Nissan's approach to supplier development

Background

Nissan's Sunderland assembly plant is the most productive in Europe and produces almost one in every four cars built in the UK. However, when it opted for a UK base in 1984, the company faced a major challenge in bringing its European suppliers up to the same standard as those in Japan. Nissan recognised that European – especially UK – component suppliers fell far short of Japanese standards of quality, reliability and cost. Measuring suppliers' capabilities on a scale of 0 to 100, Nissan rated Japanese suppliers at 100, suppliers in mainland Europe at 80 and UK suppliers at 65–70. Nissan was required by the European Union to produce cars which contained, by value, 80 per cent local content. Therefore, it needed to improve the capabilities of its European suppliers if it was to maintain the quality and cost standards achieved by its plants in Japan.

To this end, Nissan decided in 1987 to form a Supplier Development Team (SDT) based at its Sunderland plant. The aim of the SDT is to help suppliers to develop their business to the stage where they can meet Nissan's present and future performance requirements. A similar function had been in operation for some 30 years in Japan, and this was considered to be a suitable model for its UK operation. Indeed, the big three Japanese car companies, Toyota, Honda and Nissan, all carry out extensive supplier development programmes (Sako, 2004).

Initially, two engineers were sent to Japan for a nine-week training course. This training included extensive practice in undertaking improvement activities within Nissan's Japanese suppliers. On their return, based on the techniques learned in Japan, the engineers developed a 'ten-day improvement activity' for use with UK suppliers. Their aim was to establish an approach which, while achieving immediate productivity and quality improvements, would convince UK suppliers to adopt the Japanese approach to manufacturing. Consequently, though Nissan was concerned that the outcome of any improvement activity should be positive, its ultimate objective was for suppliers to recognise the value and benefits of adopting the Japanese approach, and to continue with it once the SDT had left.

The SDT approach was officially launched in the UK in November 1988 and involved a group of 12 medium-sized suppliers. Since these small beginnings, the size of the SDT has grown and it has become an established and important part of Nissan's operations. It has worked with the majority of Nissan's suppliers, and has established a reputation among them for its expertise and commitment. Though it originally concentrated on shopfloor improvement projects, which still form the core of its work, it has also provided a broader range of assistance, such as cost-reduction initiatives, joint product development, supervisory training and strategic planning programmes. In essence, it offers a consultancy service to Nissan's suppliers which is, normally, free of charge.

The SDT in action

The SDT approach is to work cooperatively with suppliers to help them identify areas for improvement, and then to assist them to develop and monitor improvement plans. In particular, the SDT will train supplier personnel in quality and production improvement methods, and support supplier initiatives to improve production and reduce defects. The idea of free consultancy by an organisation such as Nissan sounds attractive, but suppliers can also perceive such an offer as either domineering or patronising. Nissan's relations with its suppliers are very positive; however, given the history of antagonism between customers and suppliers in the UK car industry, it tends to tread warily and prepare the ground carefully before offering assistance.

Initial approach: Before undertaking the first improvement activity with a supplier, the SDT makes a presentation to the senior managers of the company concerned. This is because it regards senior management commitment and understanding as an essential precondition for success. Unless this commitment is gained, the SDT cannot and does not proceed further. Though the SDT approach is now well established and valued by suppliers, in the early days some suppliers were sceptical and resistant to such an approach. Nevertheless, most suppliers respond favourably to the initial presentation.

The SDT's standard presentation begins by describing what continuous improvement (Kaizen) is and the benefits it brings. The SDT then outlines a typical improvement activity, including the various tools and techniques used. The team stress that most improvement activities can be carried out at little or no cost, provided that the employees working in the area concerned are involved in planning and making the necessary changes.

If, after the presentation, senior managers are willing to proceed, the SDT briefs other staff and undertakes a factory assessment.

The factory assessment: The length of time devoted to a factory assessment varies, but typically it takes a day. Assessments are not compulsory, but most suppliers welcome an independent review of their operations, especially by a world-class company such as Nissan. The factory assessment does not form part of Nissan's formal supplier-assessment procedure and, therefore, is less threatening than might otherwise be the case.

Factories are assessed under ten headings:

- Company Policy.
- Quality Performance and Procedures.
- Delivery Control Methods and Performance.
- Productivity.
- Equipment Maintenance Procedures.
- Stock Control.
- Production Process Development.
- Housekeeping (how tidy and orderly the factory is).
- Health and Safety.
- Employee Morale.

Each heading is scored out of five and the scores are recorded on a factory assessment summary sheet. The assessment is then discussed with and explained to the supplier's management. From the assessment, the supplier and the SDT can begin to identify areas of concern and possible targets for improvement. The SDT then proceeds to suggest how it might be of assistance and, if this offer is accepted, agrees an improvement project with the supplier.

Improvement activities: Though the ten-day improvement activity offered by the SDT is based on the tools, techniques and experience of Nissan in Japan, it has been tailored to meet the specific needs of its European suppliers (who are mainly based in the UK). Improvement activities usually include some or all of the following:

- Reducing assembly time and improving methods.
- Reducing overhead costs – including reducing inventory and improving equipment availability.
- Reducing work-in-process.
- Preventing defects.
- Improving productivity by reducing through-put times and introducing just-in-time scheduling.

As stated earlier, most improvement activities are usually achieved at little or no cost to the supplier;

however, the supplier does need to commit time and personnel to the activity. The improvement process revolves around a multi-functional team composed of the supplier's own staff, who are assisted by the SDT. The supplier's team includes operators and supervisors from the production area concerned as well as maintenance, process engineering, quality and sometimes administrative staff. The team is led by someone from the supplier. The SDT stress that the most important members of the team are the shopfloor employees working on the process which is to be improved. Not only does this prevent change simply being imposed on those who will be directly affected by it, with all the scope for resentment and mistrust that this can cause, but it also ensures that the valuable knowledge of the shopfloor employees is utilised. Perhaps more importantly, it provides them with the skills and motivation to continue to improve the process even after the SDT have ceased to be involved. An independent study (Lloyd *et al*, 1994) found that this approach led to greater commitment to the activity, and improved morale in the areas concerned. It also found that improvement activities helped to break down functional barriers, and assisted the development of greater cooperation and team spirit.

Once the process or activity which is to be improved has been agreed, targets for the improvement are then established (e.g. reductions in lead time, improvements in quality). The supplier prepares the ground for the activity by briefing staff and making any necessary resources available, such as a dedicated meeting room. If the improvement activity is likely to cause a disruption to production, a stock of components may be built up before the activity commences to compensate for this.

Day One of the ten-day improvement activity is devoted to providing training for the supplier's team. If it is the first time the supplier has been involved in such an activity, the SDT will take the lead in this. However, if the supplier has experience of SDT improvement activities, then a member of its staff is expected to take the lead. The SDT sees its prime purpose as ensuring that everyone understands the concept of Kaizen, the procedures for the ten-day activity are clear, and the team becomes familiar with the tools and techniques necessary for its task. In this latter respect, the most frequently used tools and techniques are flow charts, work flow diagrams, pareto charts, cause and effect (fish bone) diagrams, brainstorming and critical path analysis. Where necessary, these are reinforced and supplemented as the ten-day improvement activity develops.

On **Day Two** of the improvement activity, the team splits into smaller groups to analyse and discuss the process to be improved. The groups use a combination of hard data, such as scrap rates, equipment downtime and stock levels, and more subjective opinions, such as comments about layout, ease of use and the provision of information, to identify causes of waste and possible counter-measures. The SDT encourages the use of stopwatches and even video cameras to assist the supplier's team to analyse the process in question, though these can sometimes be viewed with suspicion by operators.

Once the individual groups have completed their deliberations, they reconvene as a team. The team usually makes a flow diagram of the entire process so that everyone can appreciate what is involved and agree the changes which will bring the best benefits. The data that has been collected by the groups is analysed by the entire team. To make this easier, it is ordered and analysed under a number of standard headings:

1. **Quality:** Are quality problems due to material, process, design or training deficiencies?

2. **Technology:** Is the equipment appropriate, well maintained and used correctly?

3. **Ease of operation:** Can work be made easier through ergonomic improvements such as eliminating the need to bend, or through modifications to the equipment?

4. **Layout:** Does the layout of the process result in time delays or excessive work-in-process?

For each of the above categories, the team proceeds to identify Concerns, Causes and Counter-measures. Most suppliers' teams find this a demanding approach. In the space of two days, not only do they have to learn new tools and techniques but they also have to deploy these in a rigorous and constructive fashion. Nevertheless, by the end of the second day, teams have normally identified what the problems are, what is causing them and the measures necessary to correct them. Sometimes, the outcome is a recognition that existing equipment is inadequate for its task, but it is more usually the case that the team comes up with a list of low-cost/no-cost changes which they can implement themselves. In some cases, other members of the supplier's staff may be called in to discuss the feasibility of some of the ideas generated. However, in the main, the suppliers' teams are usually capable of making their own judgements.

Days Three to Eight of the improvement activity are spent implementing the agreed improvements.

Case study 1 (*continued*)

Though the SDT does come back on Day Six to observe progress and can be contacted for assistance at any time, the responsibility for this phase of the programme lies firmly with the supplier's personnel. The changes they make may be small and simple, or may involve the re-arrangement of complete areas of a factory. Where feasible, the team makes the changes in conjunction with personnel in the area concerned. The changed process is then tested, re-analysed and, if necessary, fine-tuned. To minimise disruption, any major changes in layout tend to take place during the weekend which falls in the middle of the improvement activity.

For **Days Nine and Ten** of the improvement activity, the SDT returns to help the team review what they have learned and achieved, and to ensure that all changes are fully documented. They also discuss outstanding issues and concerns, and potential improvement projects. The final task is to prepare and deliver a presentation to the company's senior managers describing the changes achieved and the benefits gained. Not only does this give staff the opportunity to show senior managers what they have achieved (and receive well-earned praise), it also helps those unused to public speaking to develop their skills in this area.

Summary

The SDT has come to be considered as a valuable resource by Nissan's suppliers, and there is always a queue for its services. From the suppliers' perspective, this is understandable. Improvement activities usually meet or exceed their targets. Productivity increases of 20–40 per cent are quite common, as are similar improvements in quality and reductions in work-in-process. From Nissan's point of view, it is not the individual improvement projects *per se* which are important but the ability of suppliers to carry on making improvements once the SDT presence is removed. For many, this is the case, and individual improvement

projects act as a catalyst to the development of continuous improvement both on and off the shopfloor. Nevertheless, this does not always occur, and some suppliers do appear to find difficulty sustaining and spreading the SDT philosophy, which may affect their longer-term position as a Nissan supplier. After all, Nissan is not a charity. It helps its suppliers to improve their competitiveness in order to improve its own competitiveness. Therefore, it would be misleading to believe that Nissan was in any way 'soft' on suppliers. It promotes cooperative working with suppliers (and encourages suppliers to work cooperatively with their own staff) because it believes it makes sound business sense. Nissan is prepared to enter into long-term partnerships with its suppliers but the suppliers must reciprocate by continuously improving their performance – not an easy task. As Sir Ian Gibson, Nissan's former managing director, stated: 'Co-operative supply relationships are not an easy option, as many imagine, but considerably harder to implement than traditional buyer–seller relationships' (quoted in Burnes and Whittle, 1995: 10).

Questions

1. Compare the Gilbreths' approach to performance improvement with that of Nissan. What factors should an organisation take into account when deciding which approach to use?

2. Given Frederick Taylor's insistence on the 'removal or reduction of workers' discretion and control over what they do', what are the benefits and disadvantages of Nissan training shopfloor workers to have such a key role in improvement programmes?

3. If Frederick Taylor's perception of human beings is as 'greedy robots', what is Nissan's? What are the implications of this for how staff should be managed?

Developments in organisation theory

From certainty to contingency

Learning objectives

After studying this chapter, you should be able to:

- understand the reasons for the emergence of the Human Relations approach;
- identify the key features and key proponents of the Human Relations approach;
- list the advantages and disadvantages of the Human Relations approach;
- describe the differences between the Human Relations approach and the Classical approach to organisational design;
- discuss the reasons for the emergence and popularity of Contingency Theory;
- identify the key features and key proponents of Contingency Theory;
- state the advantages and disadvantages of Contingency Theory;
- appreciate how Contingency Theory seeks to incorporate both the Classical and Human Relations approaches;
- recognise the implications for organisational change of the Human Relations approach and Contingency Theory.

MINI CASE STUDY 2.1

Companies strive to avoid uniformity

Organisations seek simultaneously to adopt best HR practices while projecting a unique brand. Sharmila Devi reports Human Resources professionals could learn a lot from marketing in how to get and keep the loyalty of talented individuals, says David Richardson, managing director of People in Business, an employer brand consultancy. 'Marketeers understand the consumer, how to attract and retain their loyalty, and we in HR need to do the same in the world of work,' he says. 'It is a lot more complex than the consumer relationship and we don't measure it or quantify it as well but HR should take the opportunity to think as marketeers.'

Such a move would enable companies to differentiate themselves amid increasingly common best practices that run the risk of making global entities appear uniform as they seek to attract talent. Mr Richardson says a careful blend of science and art is needed. The science part is making sure a company has the right elements, such as processes, pay, career development and management. A review could easily spot gaps. The art involves thinking about people, not processes, he says. 'Best practice doesn't always bring out what people feel. For example, a lot of companies talk about innovation and have it in their messaging but do they know what it looks like and how to bring it to life?'

GE, the US manufacturer, focuses on 'lean manufacturing', so its people look for opportunities to do things differently at all times, he says. Disney takes a cultural approach, in which people think constantly about how to deliver their 'magic'. Meanwhile, Channel 4, the TV company, is more about 'making trouble', so its brand of innovation centres on creating debate. 'Everyone has their own approach to bringing innovation to life,' says Mr Richardson.

Cherise Mendoza, Microsoft's human resources leader for West, East and Central Africa and the Indian Ocean islands, says some harmonisation of best practices was necessary for any big company operating on the global market but this needed to be coupled with differentiation to provide competitive edge. 'One of the benefits of being a global company is that so many of our policies, such as talent management and succession planning, are set on a global basis – but we can localise them in specific regions,' she says. 'In Africa, flexible working has been tested and it's one of the most important factors to our employees so we give them the tools and resources to work from home.' Other important differentiating factors involve offering a career for the long term and giving opportunities to see the world and experience different markets in one of Microsoft's many global divisions, she says. Meanwhile, feedback, particularly through an annual poll of Microsoft's 95,000 employees, is taken seriously.

Japan Tobacco International, which has about 25,000 employees in more than 120 countries, also says it listens to employees and is heartened by the results. It found in an employee engagement survey conducted last year that 88 per cent would recommend the company to a friend while 94 per cent were willing to make extra effort to help the company succeed. 'The survey proved to us that what's very important is that we listen to our employees and that makes a big difference with other companies,' says Ilona Alonso, JTI's HR vice-president for western Europe. An average of 80 per cent of JTI's leaders are appointed internally and since 2004, the number of international assignments has quadrupled. Ms Alonso says: 'One of our strengths is very robust succession planning.'

'People are seen as important as brands because brands are created by people,' says Mark Phillips, JTI HR vice-president for central Europe. Infosys, the IT outsourcing company based in Bangalore, says it aims to set its legacy for the next 100 years through the Infosys Leadership Institute, which focuses on developing more than 800 leaders. 'We are unique, to the best of our knowledge, in focusing on senior leadership through science and our work with academics as we seek to rebrand the company around leadership and around the world, not just India, with a move into consulting and entrepreneurship,' says Matt Barney, vice-president and director of the institute. 'We treat our senior leaders like gold medallists and our 330-acre campus is the Taj Mahal of education. We offer psychometrics and a customised portfolio of knowledge based on the latest science on thought leadership. We treat our leaders like a private banker would treat high net worth individuals,' he says.

It also tries to be eclectic and fun. A game, 'Grandmasters of Influence', seeks to develop the principles of client relevance and ethical influence, says Chitra Sarmma, the institute's senior manager for leadership and organisation development: 'There are foibles and fun and we've found that the science and practical have blended well together and help leaders to achieve in the real world.'

Mr Richardson says the institute is one of several initiatives he has seen in the developing world that aims to foster local talent and leadership. In more mature markets, as companies cut budgets for training and development, they risk missing an external focus to the company: 'If people aren't being sent off to Harvard or wherever, they miss out on making strategic alliances across businesses and industries,' he says.

Source: Employers: Companies strive to avoid uniformity, *The Financial Times*, 11/04/2013, p. 4 (Devi S.),

Introduction

The emergence of the Classical approach to managing and changing organisations was one of the most significant events in the history of organisation theory and practice. From the 1920s until the 1960s, in the public sector, and in large private-sector concerns, bureaucracy was unquestionably seen as the 'one best way'. The other key element of the Classical approach, Scientific Management, had a more mixed reception. In the US, the death of the irascible Taylor did much to overcome the early opposition to Scientific Management, especially among trade union leaders. It was enthusiastically taken up by capitalists in Japan and communists in Russia, though it met with stiff resistance in other European countries. In the 1930s, Scientific Management and a streamlined version, the Bedeaux system, were rejected by both unions and management in a large number of European countries, though after the Second World War, Scientific Management was heavily promoted as part of the Marshall Plan for the rebuilding of Europe (Carew, 1987; Rose, 1988). Even today, as Mini Case Study 1.1 showed in the previous chapter, Scientific Management exerts a strong influence over how jobs are designed and people are managed.

Despite its growing dominance, from the 1930s the Classical approach began to encounter both intellectual and practical opposition. The core of the Classical approach's argument was that processes are more important than people; get the processes right, construct the machine in the right way, and then people can be reduced to the status of unthinking and obedient cogs which can be slotted in or replaced as the needs of the machine dictate. In the 1930s a new creed began to emerge, one that is epitomised in Mini Case Study 2.1. In a world where everyone can adopt the same best practices, where everyone has the ability to build the same machine, it is 'people, not processes' which make the difference, which create unique products and services, and establish dominant brands. From the 1930s onwards, new ideas about the nature of organisations and the role of people and how they should be managed began to emerge which strike at the very heart of the Classical approach:

1. Organisations are not machines but cooperative systems. To operate effectively and efficiently, they require the active cooperation of workers and not just their passive obedience.

2. People are motivated by a range of rewards, including social esteem, not just monetary ones.

3. Motivating factors change over time; what motivates a person one day may be ineffectual the next.

What makes many of these arguments all the more damaging to the Classical approach is that they came from practising managers, such as Chester Barnard who was President of the New Jersey Bell Telephone Company, rather than 'unworldly' academics.

Therefore, although the Classical school could claim much success, especially in the US, there was also a rising tide of evidence against it. This could have led to the development and strengthening of the Classical approach, and clearly this did happen to an extent (*see* the work of Ralph Davis, 1928, on rational planning). However, as this chapter will show, what emerged were two new approaches to managing and changing organisations: the Human Relations approach, which originated in the 1930s and in which Chester Barnard was a key figure, and the Contingency approach, which was developed in the 1960s.

The first half of this chapter describes the Human Relations approach. This approach was a reaction against the mechanistic view of organisations and the pessimistic view of human nature put forward in the Classical approach. It attempted to reintroduce the human element into organisational life, and claim for itself the title of the 'one best way'. In particular, it contended that people have emotional as well as economic needs, that organisations are cooperative systems that comprise informal structures and norms as well as formal ones, and that workers have to be involved in change if it is to be successful. This left managers with something of a dilemma as to which 'one best way' to adopt – the Classical or the Human Relations approach.

As the second half of this chapter will show, it was in response to this dilemma that Contingency Theory developed in the 1960s. Contingency Theory began by questioning and rejecting the idea that there is a 'one best way' for *all* organisations. Instead, it argued for a 'one best way' for *each* organisation. It did not, therefore, reject the Classical approach and the Human Relations approach; instead it maintained that the structures and practices of an organisation are dependent (i.e. contingent) on the circumstances it faces. Similarly, the approach to organisational change is also dependent on circumstance. In some situations change can be achieved successfully by Tayloristic imposition, while in other cases the greater involvement advocated by the Human Relations school will be required. The main circumstances or contingencies which need to be taken into account are environmental uncertainty and dependence, technology and organisation size. After discussing the merits and drawbacks of the Human Relations approach and Contingency Theory, the chapter concludes that neither appears to be the solution to all known organisational ills that their proponents claim. In particular, it is argued that both fail to reflect and explain the complexities of day-to-day organisational life.

The Human Relations approach

Even while the Classical approach was still struggling to establish itself, the seeds of a new approach to organisational design and change were already being sown. The origins of what later became known as the Human Relations approach can be traced to studies on work fatigue carried out in Britain during the First World War and work in the US, at the same time, on employee selection, which gave new insights into employee motivation (Burnes, 1989). This work was developed and extended in the 1920s by Mayo (1933) in the US and Myers (1934) in Britain, providing new perspectives on organisational life. These studies gave substance to a growing suspicion that the Classical view of organisations as being peopled by human robots motivated by money was badly flawed. Indeed, in 1915, the United States Congress took a stand against the use of Taylor's techniques in their establishments – although Scientific Management was becoming more accepted in private industry and was beginning to cross national boundaries, not always successfully (Rose, 1988). Similarly, though the growth of bureaucracy was gathering pace, so too was people's antagonism towards faceless, machine-like organisations where employees and customers alike lost their individuality and became numbers.

In addition, as Davis and Canter (1956) argued, it is necessary to recognise that jobs and work organisation are social inventions put together to suit the specific needs of the time and to reflect its culture, ideology and the governing concept or ethos. Therefore, to understand the emergence of the Human Relations movement, it is necessary to be aware of the changes taking place in Western society prior to and just after the Second World War.

In the 1930s, in many countries, there was the emergence of a more collectivist ethos than had previously been the case. In the US, this was brought about by the reaction to the Depression of the 1920s and 1930s. The election of FD Roosevelt and the advent of his 'New Deal' introduced a new element of collective provision and concern into a previously highly individualistic nation. It also heralded the advent of 'Big Government' in the US. In Europe, this collectivist ethos led to greater social concern; collective provision was led by the Scandinavian countries, and reflected the election of social democratic governments and a general mood of cooperation rather than conflict in industry in these countries. Similar developments became the cornerstone of the rebuilding of Western Germany after the end of the Second World War. The legacy of the collective effort needed to win the war was also evident in the UK with the construction of the Welfare State.

It was in the US in the 1930s and 1940s that substantial evidence first emerged in print which challenged the Classical view of organisations and allowed the Human Relations approach to stand alongside, if not quite supersede, it. The basic assumptions of the Human Relations approach, as shown in Ideas and perspectives 2.1, were almost diametrically opposed to those of the Classical approach and its view of organisations as predictable, well-oiled machines in which people were relegated to the role of obedient cogs.

In most respects, the Human Relations approach represents a distinct break from the ideas of the Classical school. However, in two important ways, similarities exist. The first is their shared belief in organisations as closed, changeless entities. Once organisations have structured themselves in accordance with the correct precepts, then, regardless of external or even internal developments, no further changes are necessary or desirable. This leads on to the second similarity: proponents of both believed they had discovered the 'one best way' to run organisations; regardless of the type, nature or size of organisation, their precepts were the correct ones.

IDEAS AND PERSPECTIVES 2.1

The Human Relations approach – basic assumptions

- **People are emotional rather than economic–rational beings.** Human needs are far more diverse and complex than the one-dimensional image that Taylor and his fellow travellers conceded. People's emotional and social needs can have more influence on their behaviour at work than financial incentives.

- **Organisations are cooperative, social systems rather than mechanical ones.** People seek to meet their emotional needs through the formation of informal but influential workplace social groups.

- **Organisations are composed of informal structures, rules and norms as well as formal practices and procedures.** These informal rules, patterns of behaviour and communication, norms and friendships are created by people to meet their emotional needs. Because of this, they can have more influence on individual behaviour and performance, and ultimately on overall organisational performance, than the formal structure and control mechanisms laid down by management.

With that in mind, we can now begin to examine in detail the move from the Classical school to the Human Relations approach, beginning with the work of Mary Parker Follett, who is seen as a pivotal figure in this process.

Mary Parker Follett – from Scientific Management to Human Relations

Mary Parker Follett (1868–1933) was born into a Quaker family in Quincy, near Boston, Massachusetts. She was educated at the 'Harvard Annex', later Radcliffe College, which had been established to allow women to be taught by Harvard staff, in order to sidestep Harvard's policy of not admitting women undergraduates. Follett studied a mixed degree comprising philosophy, law, history and political science. While undertaking her course she also spent time at the Sorbonne in Paris and Newnham College, Cambridge. Subsequently, she made frequent visits to England, settling there permanently in 1928 (Graham, 1987; Witzel, 2003a).

For much of her life, Follett was best known in the US as a political thinker and social pioneer. The publication in 1896 of her college research dissertation, *The Speaker of the House of Representatives*, drew her to the attention of the political classes, especially Theodore Roosevelt. She continued to contribute to political thought in America, especially with the publication of *The New State* in 1918 in which she offered her own views on how democracies should be run. This was particularly contentious work because, in a society which valued individuality and free enterprise, Follett argued that both were inseparable from and should take account of the needs of the wider society. Her argument was not just that groups are more important than individuals, but that individuals can only fully develop their potential through their participation in group life (Wren, 1994). In addition, in her call for the need to view individual actions from the viewpoint of their impact on wider society, Follett was in effect articulating stakeholder theory many decades before the phrase was actually coined (Schilling, 2000).

In her views of the relationship between the individual and wider society, Follett was greatly influenced by Gestalt psychology, which stresses that human behaviour is a product of the interaction of the individual with their environment (*see* Chapter 9 for a further elaboration of the Gestalt concept) (Wren, 1994).

However, important though her contribution to political theory was, Follett's main pre-occupation comprised a range of social improvement initiatives designed to better the education and employment prospects of working-class and immigrant families. These included the development of national schemes to provide evening classes and vocational guidance (Sheldrake, 1996).

It was from the combination of her political philosophy, especially in terms of participative democracy, and practical experience of establishing and running organisations that Follett developed her views on management, which had a powerful impact on management thinking in the 1920s and 1930s. These came to the notice of a wider audience through a series of lectures she gave to the Bureau of Personnel Administration in New York. These lectures attracted the attention of Seebohm Rowntree, the social reformer and Chairman of Rowntree and Co., who invited Follett to lecture in England. At the same time, she met and influenced the work of Lyndall Urwick, one of the leading management consultants in the UK and an adherent of the work of Frederick Taylor. Indeed, not only was Follett warmly received in the UK, but her ideas found more support there than in the US (Witzel, 2003a).

The core tenets of Follett's approach to managing organisations were as follows:

- The need to create a system where workers accepted managers' authority and where managers acted in an impartial fashion, basing their actions on the needs of the situation rather than on their self-interests. In this she was very much in line with Frederick Taylor and the rest of the Classical school (Sheldrake, 1996).

- However, she stressed the group above the individual and the need for individuals to achieve a sense of identity and psychic growth through meaningful work. She argued that pride in their work and a sense of self-worth were important motivators and provided workers with an almost spiritual dimension to their working life (Phipps, 2011; Wren, 1994).

- Unlike Taylor, she believed that conflict could play a positive role in encouraging participation and creating a common purpose, which could reconcile individual self-interest with the needs of the wider organisation (Phipps, 2011).

- She saw the command and control system advocated by Taylor and Co. as being inefficient. She argued that in a democratic society, the most important form of control in organisations was self-control, which arises from the pursuit of a common purpose. In effect, the common purpose provides an 'invisible leader' and, consequently, the role of the manager is not to tell people what to do but to coordinate and integrate their activities in pursuit of the common purpose (Witzel, 2003a).

- She also rejected the notion of 'experts' who did the thinking and planning for the rest of the organisation. Instead, she sought to promote a form of 'organisational learning' through individual and group self-development and participation (Witzel, 2003a).

Follett's work is often considered to have created a bridge between Taylor's Scientific Management and the social psychology that began to challenge Taylor's work in the 1920s and 1930s (Rosenfeld and Smith, 1966; Wren, 1994). However, if one looks at the above, Follett's work seems to be less of a bridge and more of a slip road leading from the one-lane, machine-like approach to people and organisations of the Classical approach to the broader, more humane highway of the Human Relations school. Despite her role in the emergence of the Human Relations approach, no one doubts that it began in earnest with the famous Hawthorne Experiments.

Elton Mayo and the Hawthorne Experiments

Elton Mayo (1880–1949) was born in Adelaide, Australia in 1880. He had a somewhat chequered career. He failed three times to qualify as a medical doctor, and eventually became a lecturer in logic, psychology and ethics at the University of Queensland in 1911. There he developed a strong interest in the political problems of industrial society, and a lifelong commitment to achieving social and industrial harmony. However, he was never happy at Queensland and, in 1922, he emigrated to America. There, Mayo was fortunate in that his ideas on resolving industrial conflict attracted the attention of the Laura Spelman Rockefeller Memorial Foundation, which funded his entire career at Harvard Business School. In effect, this meant that Mayo could pursue his own research without let or hindrance from university authorities. This was a major factor in the single-mindedness and success with which he undertook his work.

Elton Mayo is considered by many as the founder and leading light of the Human Relations movement. On his retirement as Professor of Industrial Research at Harvard

Business School in 1947, Mayo was one of the most celebrated social scientists of the age. In praise of his achievements, the business magazine *Fortune* wrote of him:

> Scientist and practical clinician, Mayo speaks with a rare authority that has commanded attention in factories as well as universities. His erudition extends through psychology, sociology, physiology, medicine and economics, and his experience comes from a lifelong first-hand study of industry.   (Quoted in Smith, 1998: 222)

Much of his fame rested on the Hawthorne Experiments carried out at Western Electric's Hawthorne Works in Chicago in the 1920s and 1930s. However, within ten years of his departure from Harvard, his reputation was in tatters: his expertise as a researcher was seriously questioned, his work was criticised for being too 'managerialist' and, perhaps most importantly, his contribution to the Hawthorne Experiments was considered as no more than a public relations exercise for Western Electric (Rose, 1988; Sheldrake, 1996; Smith, 1998).

The Hawthorne Experiments, as Gillespie (1991: 1) commented:

> are still among the most frequently cited and most controversial experiments in the social sciences . . . They are acclaimed as a landmark study in both sociology and psychology . . . Surveys in the key developments in organization and management theory consistently note the seminal contribution of the experiments to their field.

Yet for most of the 90 years since the Hawthorne Experiments were initiated, it has been difficult to identify Mayo's exact role (Smith, 1987). That the name of Elton Mayo is inextricably linked with the Hawthorne Experiments is undeniable. That Mayo publicised and was given credit for masterminding them is also undeniable. Until recently, though, key questions have remained unanswered: did Mayo design and implement the experiments himself? What was the role of his colleagues at Harvard? How frequently did he visit the Hawthorne Works? Now, with the availability of family records and other archive material, Smith (1998) claims to have answered Mayo's detractors and to have re-established him as both the key figure in the Hawthorne Experiments and the dominant figure in the Human Relations movement. Nevertheless, given the vehemence of Mayo's critics (Rose, 1988; Sheldrake, 1996; Wren and Bedeian, 2009), one suspects that the debate over the 'Mayo mystique' is not yet over.

Despite the difficulty in separating out the myth from the man, we should not let that undermine the significance of the Hawthorne work or what we know of Mayo and his colleagues' contribution, even if we cannot clearly identify who did what. The Hawthorne programme was originally devised by Western Electric's own industrial engineers in 1924. Western Electric was the manufacturing division of the American Telephone and Telegraph Company. The Hawthorne Works, which at the time employed some 30,000 people, was considered a prime example of the application of the mass production techniques and work organisation methods advocated by Frederick Taylor and Henry Ford. However, this was tempered by the company's personnel and welfare policies, which provided pension, sickness and disability benefits, a share purchase plan, medical treatment, extensive recreational facilities and a system of worker representation. This example of 'welfare capitalism' had the twin aims of reducing worker dissatisfaction and resisting trade union influence (Sheldrake, 1996).

The first phase of the Hawthorne Experiments, which lasted on and off until 1927, was the Hawthorne Illumination Tests (HIT), which were designed to examine the effects of various levels of lighting on workers' productivity. The engineers established control and experimental groups: the latter were subject to different levels of illumination as they carried out their work while the lighting of the control group was left unchanged. At the outset this looked like a standard Scientific Management experiment in the mould of Taylor and the Gilbreths. What the engineers were expecting was a set of unambiguous results that would allow them to establish the 'one best' level of illumination. This did not happen and, instead, data began to emerge that challenged the very basis of Scientific Management.

The engineers had expected the performance of the experimental group to vary, with increases and decreases in illumination, and for an optimum level to be established, but as the illumination was varied, so output continued to increase. Indeed, output decreased in the experimental group only when the lighting became so dim that it was difficult to see. More puzzling still, output in the control group, where no changes were made, also increased.

In 1927 the company began the second phase of the Hawthorne Experiments. Building on the HIT work, the company wanted to establish the effects on productivity of increased rest periods, a shorter working day, a reduced working week, free refreshments, changes to payment systems, better and friendlier communication, and a relaxation in the customary discipline usually imposed by firstline supervisors. The first group to be involved were six women in the Relay Assembly Test Room (RATR). As Gillespie (1991: 59) noted:

> [Their] privileged status and a modicum of control over work days brought about a strong identification with the test room among the workers . . . With the introduction of refreshments during the morning rest period, the women's status soared higher still.

By 1929, productivity in the RATR group had increased by some 30 per cent. In the interim, the company also initiated a further series of experiments in which, from 1928 onwards, Elton Mayo and his colleagues were closely involved. In the years that followed, successive groups of workers were subjected to changes in hours, payment systems, rest periods, etc. The subsequent changes in output, and the reasons put forward for these, undermined many of the assumptions regarding organisations and human behaviour previously perceived as sacrosanct (Mayo, 1933; Roethlisberger and Dickson, 1938).

The experiments were monitored continuously. From this work, Mayo and his colleagues concluded that it was not the changes in working conditions that affected output but the fact that those workers involved had been singled out for special attention. This acted to increase their morale and make them want to perform better. It was the very fact that they were being studied which produced the increased performance; this later became known as the 'Hawthorne Effect'. This accounted for the improved performance by the original HIT control group, even with no changes to the lighting in their area: they also felt 'special' because they were being studied. These findings led Mayo and his group to move the focus of their work away from the reaction of individual workers to changes in their working conditions. Instead, they began to investigate the role and behaviour of the 'informal' groups that workers themselves established, and the norms and attitudes of these groups.

As a result of this work, Mayo and his colleagues put forward two major propositions that came to form the core of the Human Relations approach. The first related to the importance of informal groups within the formal structure of organisations. The Western Electric studies demonstrated the need to see the work process as a collective, cooperative activity as opposed to an individual, isolated one. The studies showed in particular the important effect that the informal, primary work group has on performance. These groups tend to develop their own norms, values and attitudes that enable them to exert strong social, peer group pressure on individuals within the group to conform to group norms, whether this be in relation to the pace of work or attitudes towards other groups and supervisors. Taylor, years before, had also noted the pressure that groups of workers could exert over their members to make them conform; however, he believed that this was abnormal behaviour which could be remedied by tight managerial control. What the Western Electric studies demonstrated was that far from being abnormal, such behaviour was perfectly normal.

The second proposition put forward by Mayo and his colleagues was that humans have a deep need for recognition, security and belonging. Rather than being purely economic beings, it was argued that the Hawthorne Experiments demonstrated that workers' performance and attitudes could be influenced more by their need for recognition and security, and also by the feeling of belonging engendered by informal groups. This latter point in particular reflected, in Mayo's view, a deep-seated desire by humans as social beings for intimacy, consistency and predictability. Where these social certainties were lacking, workers would deliberately seek to manufacture them by creating their own informal work groups. Therefore, rather than seeking to eradicate or undermine the workings of these informal groups, as Taylor had advocated, the Western Electric studies showed that management needed to gain the collaboration and cooperation of such groups if they were to get the best performance from workers.

The contribution of the Western Electric studies has been strongly disputed, with some calling them brilliant and original, while others have seen them as seriously flawed and offering no new insights (Muldoon, 2012). Nevertheless, it is generally agreed that they had a dramatic effect on management and organisation theory (Mullins, 1989; Rose, 1988). The studies ushered in an era where the Economic Man of the Classical approach was supplanted by Social Man. It was no longer possible for managers to ignore the effects of organisational structures and job design on work groups, employee attitudes and management–worker relations. The crucial issue became one of social relationships – Human Relations – in the workplace. In future, the focus of good management practice would shift to the importance of leadership and communication in order to win over employees. As the 1930s and 1940s progressed, other work began to emerge which both substantiated and broadened those findings.

Chester Barnard and cooperative systems

Chester Barnard (1886–1961) was born in Malden, Massachusetts. On leaving school, he became a piano tuner, but later attended Harvard University where he studied economics. On leaving university, he went to work for the American Telephone and Telegraph Company, in whose subsidiary, Western Electric, the Hawthorne studies were carried out. He was initially employed as a statistician, but quickly rose to hold a number of senior executive positions including, by the age of 41, President of the New Jersey Bell Telephone Company. He also established his credentials as a prolific writer and lecturer with strong links to a number of universities, including Harvard. On retiring in 1948, he became President of the Rockefeller Foundation.

Barnard is best known for his book *The Functions of the Executive* (1938), which has a comparable place in the Human Relations literature to that of Fayol's work in the literature of the Classical school. In this work, Barnard put forward the idea of organisations as cooperative systems. In so doing, this gave him a double claim to fame: not only did he draw attention to the cooperative nature of organisational life, he was also one of the first to treat organisations as systems rather than machines. He was in frequent touch with Mayo and his colleagues at Harvard, and closely followed their work at Western Electric. Therefore, although *The Functions of the Executive* was a personal and idiosyncratic work, reflecting Barnard's distinct views and opinions, it was far from being bereft of academic substance. Indeed, his book was the first systematic attempt in English (Weber's work on bureaucracy was still not translated into English at this time) to outline a theory of organisations as a whole. In this respect, Barnard can claim both to have made a substantial contribution to the Human Relations approach and to have laid the groundwork for subsequent writers such as Selznick and Simon (Robbins, 1987; Scott, 1987).

Barnard had close links with Harvard Business School and, along with Elton Mayo, Talcott Parsons (who first translated Weber's work into English) and Joseph Schumpeter, was a member of the Harvard Pareto Circle. This group was established to discuss and promote the work of the Italian sociologist Vilfredo Pareto, whose writing placed great emphasis on social systems and social equilibrium (Sheldrake, 1996).

The influence of Pareto's social systems view can be seen in Barnard's depiction of organisations as cooperative systems. An organisation is a cooperative system, he argued, because without the willingness of its members to make contributions to its goals and to pursue them, it cannot operate effectively. Like others who espoused the Human Relations approach, he believed cooperation could not be achieved solely by monetary incentives. Instead, he advocated a mixture of monetary and non-monetary inducements. Similarly, cooperation by itself would not be effective unless an organisation also possessed a common purpose: clear and realistic goals and objectives that the organisation's members could understand, relate to and pursue. Establishing this common purpose, in Barnard's opinion, had to be the responsibility of those at the top of the organisation, but achieving it required the cooperation of those at the bottom, and all levels in between. This leads to another of Barnard's assertions: the flow of authority is not from the top down but from the bottom up. He defined authority not as a property of management but as a response by subordinates to superiors. If subordinates did not respond willingly and appropriately, then no authority existed. In this example, as in many others, he both reflected the influence of and supported the findings of the Western Electric studies, which drew attention to the ability of workers through social groupings to facilitate or frustrate the will of management.

In order to avoid a negative response from workers, Barnard advocated systematic and purposeful communication. He saw communication, through both formal and informal structures, as being the key function of the executive. Indeed, he portrayed the organisation as a purposeful, coordinated system of communications linking all participants in a manner that not only encouraged the pursuit of the organisation's common purpose but also legitimated the premises on which it was based. However, he argued that this does not happen automatically or accidentally; it is the product of effective leadership. This is why Barnard stressed the key role of the executive in leading the organisation by facilitating communication and motivating subordinates to high levels of performance; such developments could only come from the top. He also saw the executive as having a role in shaping and reinforcing the organisation's value systems or, as modern writers would put it, its culture.

Given the weight placed by Barnard on the setting and pursuit of clear objectives, and the stress he places on the need for hierarchical organisations and formal lines of authority, there is a degree of overlap with the work of the Classical school. However, what significantly distinguishes him from them is his insistence that organisations are cooperative social systems and his emphasis on the non-rational, informal, interpersonal and indeed moral basis of organisational life. His view of effective leadership also distinguishes him from the Classical school. Rather than seeing leadership as dependent on position, Barnard argued that successful leadership arises from the interplay between the individual leader, the followers and the context.

Above all, Barnard rejected the idea of material incentives being the only incentives to make people work purposefully. Indeed, he saw them as being 'weak incentives' that needed to be supported by other psychological and sociological motivators if organisations were to be successful in achieving their common purpose. In thus challenging the effectiveness of material incentives, he was to receive substantial support a few years later from a more academic source.

Abraham Maslow's hierarchy of needs

Abraham Maslow (1908–1970) was born in Brooklyn, New York. He trained as a psychologist at the University of Wisconsin and, apart from a brief period working in the family business, spent his working life in academia. Maslow was one of the first to differentiate between and classify different types of human need. For Taylor and his adherents, there was only one form of need: material or monetary need. Mayo *et al* and Barnard took a different view; they drew a distinction between material and non-material needs, but made no distinction within these two categories.

Maslow (1943) identified five distinct forms of human need which he placed in a hierarchical order. As Figure 2.1 shows, the five levels in Maslow's hierarchy of needs, in ascending order, are:

- **Physiological needs** – hunger, thirst, sleep, etc. Only when these basic needs have been satisfied do other needs begin to emerge.

- **Safety needs** – the desire for security and protection against danger.

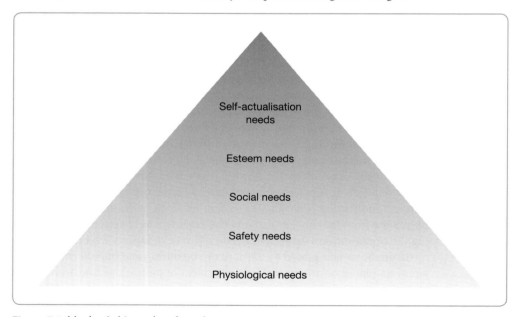

Figure 2.1 Maslow's hierarchy of needs

- **Social needs** – the need to belong, to gain love and affection; to be in the company of others, especially friends.
- **Esteem needs** – these reflect a person's desire to be respected – esteemed – for their achievements.
- **Self-actualisation needs** – this is the need to achieve one's full potential. According to Maslow, this will vary from person to person and indeed may differ over time, as a person reaches a level of potential previously considered unattainable and so goes on to strive for new heights. For these reasons, self-actualisation is a continuously evolving process throughout a person's lifetime.

Maslow argued that, beginning at the lowest level, a person had to satisfy substantially the needs at one level before they could move up the hierarchy and concentrate on 'higher-order' needs. Maslow (1943: 383) recognised that there were weaknesses in his theory of needs: 'Since, in our society, basically-satisfied people are the exception, we do not know much about self-actualisation, either experimentally or clinically.' He accepted that the strength of the hierarchy might differ with individual circumstances – some people's aspirations may be so deadened by their experiences that they would be satisfied by having enough to eat. He also saw that cultural differences between societies could have an impact on the extent and order of needs. Nevertheless, he did believe that his theory was generally applicable and that where people's higher aspirations were thwarted or unmet, the result was likely to be frustration and de-motivation.

Though not designed specifically for organisational analysis, but rather in the context of life in general, it can be seen why Maslow's work was so readily accepted by proponents of the Human Relations approach. For them, it explained why in some situations Tayloristic incentives were effective, while in other situations, such as the Hawthorne Experiments, other factors proved more important.

Applying Maslow's hierarchy of needs to human behaviour in organisations, it can be seen that people will first of all be motivated by the desire to satisfy physiological needs through monetary rewards. Once those have been substantially satisfied, however, workers will seek to satisfy – be motivated by – their safety needs, such as job security and welfare benefits. In a similar fashion, once safety needs are substantially met, these will fade into the background and social needs will come to the fore; people will want to be accepted as part of a group, to share common intents and aspirations with the group, to experience the bonds of friendship and loyalty. Clearly, these social needs played an important role in the Hawthorne Experiments, as did esteem needs. After social and esteem needs are substantially met, finally self-actualisation needs come to the fore. However, as mentioned above, the need for self-actualisation never wanes but tends to act as a continuing spur to further achievements.

Clearly, Maslow's work cannot be transferred fully into the organisational setting, given that the constraints on freedom of action imposed by most jobs do not allow individuals to approach, let alone attain, self-actualisation (Rose, 1988). Even very basic physiological needs are beyond the reach of many millions of people in the world. Nevertheless, in pointing to the negative effects of thwarting an individual's aspirations, and in distinguishing between types of intrinsic (non-material) and extrinsic (material) motivators, and arguing that, at any one time, it is the unmet needs which act as positive motivators, Maslow has had an enormous impact on job design and research (*see* Child, 1984; Smith *et al*, 1982). The influence of Maslow's theory of needs can be seen in the work of other exponents of Human Relations, especially Douglas McGregor.

Douglas McGregor and Theory X–Theory Y

Douglas McGregor (1906–1964) was born in Detroit. He received his doctorate in psychology from Harvard, and spent much of his working life at the Massachusetts Institute of Technology where, from 1954 until his death in 1964, he was the first Sloan Fellows Professor. McGregor is one of the most widely cited Human Relations writers. McGregor was a close associate of Kurt Lewin and can be considered one of the pioneers of organization development (OD) (*see* Chapter 9) and, therefore, he was as interested in changing organisations as he was in understanding them (Burnes and Cooke, 2012b). He developed his views from his personal experience and observations as an academic, consultant and university administrator rather than from empirical research.

His book *The Human Side of Enterprise* (1960) played a central role in the ascendancy of the Human Relations movement in the 1960s. In the book, McGregor argued that decisions taken by top managers on the best way to manage people were based on their assumptions about human nature. McGregor maintained that there are basically two commonly held views of human nature: a negative view – Theory X – and a positive view – Theory Y (*see* Ideas and perspectives 2.2). He believed that managers' behaviour towards their subordinates was based upon one or other of these views, both of which consist of a certain grouping of assumptions about human behaviour.

McGregor saw Theory X, which he believed dominated the literature and practice of management, as a very negative view of human nature, whereas he saw Theory Y as a much more positive view. Theory X and Theory Y are not statements about what people are actually like but rather the general assumptions that managers, and the rest of us, hold about what people are like. The fact that such views may not have a base in reality is irrelevant if managers act as though they are true. Managers who adhere to Theory X will use a combination of stick and carrot methods to control their subordinates, and will construct

---

IDEAS AND PERSPECTIVES 2.2

McGregor's Theory X and Theory Y

Theory X assumptions	Theory Y assumptions
The average person dislikes work and will avoid it wherever possible.	Most people can view work as being as natural as rest or play.
Employees must be coerced, controlled or threatened with punishment if they are to perform as required.	Workers are capable of exercising self-direction and self-control.
Most people try to avoid responsibility and will seek formal direction whenever possible.	The average person will accept and even seek responsibility if they are committed to the objectives being pursued.
Workers place security above other factors relating to employment and will display little ambition.	Ingenuity, imagination, creativity and the ability to make good decisions are widely dispersed throughout the population and are not peculiar to managers.

organisations that restrict the individual's ability to exercise skill, discretion and control over their work. Those managers who adhere to Theory Y will adopt a more open and flexible style of management. They will create jobs that encourage workers to contribute towards organisational goals and allow them to exercise skill and responsibility, and where the emphasis will be on non-material incentives.

Obviously, Theory X is akin to the Classical view of human nature and organisational design, whereas Theory Y falls more in the Human Relations tradition. Though McGregor favoured Theory Y, he recognised that it could not be fully validated. Instead, he saw Theory Y as a challenge to the orthodoxy of Theory X and, as he put it (McGregor, 1960: 53), as an 'invitation to innovate'. He argued that there was nothing inevitable about which approach to adopt. The choice lies with managers. Those who adhere to Theory X will create a situation where workers are only able and willing to pursue material needs (as Maslow observed); such workers will be neither prepared nor in a position to contribute to the wider aims and objectives of the organisation that employs them. Managers who follow Theory Y precepts are likely to receive an entirely different response from their employees; workers will identify more clearly with the general interests of the organisation, and be more able and more willing to contribute to their achievement.

Though stressing the element of choice, McGregor, along with other Human Relations adherents, believed that changes in the nature of modern societies meant that organisations were moving, and should move, more in the direction of Theory Y.

Warren Bennis and the death of bureaucracy

By the 1950s and 1960s, the Human Relations approach and the values it espoused were in the ascendancy. One clear sign of this was the widely held view in the 1960s that bureaucracy was dying and being replaced by more flexible, people-centred organisations that allowed and encouraged personal growth and development. One of the main exponents of this view is Warren Bennis.

Bennis (1925–) was born in Westwood, New Jersey. He trained as an industrial psychologist and held a number of senior academic appointments, including Professor of Management at the University of Southern California. He is now best known for his work on leadership, and has acted as an adviser to four US presidents. In terms of the Human Relations movement, Bennis (1966) is credited with coining the phrase and making the case for 'the death of bureaucracy'. Bennis argued that every age develops an organisational form appropriate to its time. Bureaucracy was, in his view, appropriate for the first two-thirds of the twentieth century but not beyond that. He believed that bureaucracy emerged because its order, precision and impersonal nature acted as the correct antidote for the personal subjugation, cruelty, nepotism and capriciousness that passed for management during the Industrial Revolution.

Bureaucracy, he stated, emerged as a creative and wholesome response to the needs and values of the Victorian age. Up to this point, there is little to distinguish Bennis from Weber; however, he then went on to argue that the Victorian age and its needs were dead and that new conditions were emerging to which bureaucracy was no longer suited (*see* Ideas and perspectives 2.3).

For Bennis and others such as Daniel Bell (1973), Alvin Toffler (1970) and EF Schumacher (1973), bureaucracy was rightly dying and being replaced by more diverse, flexible structures which could cope with the needs of the modern world.

IDEAS AND PERSPECTIVES 2.3

The case against bureaucracy

- **Rapid and unexpected change** – bureaucracy's strength lies in its ability to manage efficiently the routine and predictable; however, its pre-programmed rules and inflexibility make it unsuitable for the rapidly changing modern world.

- **Growth in size** – as organisations become larger, then bureaucratic structures become more complex and unwieldy, and less efficient.

- **Increasing diversity** – rapid growth, quick change and an increase in specialisation create the need for people with diverse and highly specialised skills. These specialists cannot easily or effectively be fitted within the standardised, pyramid structure of bureaucratic organisations.

- **Change in managerial behaviour** – the increasing adoption of the Human Relations approach by managers challenges the simplistic view of human nature put forward by the Classical school, which underpins bureaucracy. If coercion and threats administered in a depersonalised, mechanistic fashion are counterproductive as a way of controlling people in organisations, then the case for bureaucracy is severely diminished.

Job Design: operationalising Human Relations

Though intellectually strong, the Human Relations school remained operationally weak up to the 1950s and 1960s because, unlike the Scientific Management element of the Classical school, it lacked a clear set of operational definitions and guidelines that allowed organisations to understand and implement it. This lack of a practical alternative to Taylorism was further highlighted by the emergence of the OD approach to change with which, through the work of Douglas McGregor, it had strong affinities. Thus the Human Relations school had a sound critique of existing organisation practices and a method for changing these, but no practical alternative model to change them for. However, the advent of the Job Design movement in both the US and Europe rectified this to an extent, at least as far as the design of jobs was concerned.

In the last 60 years, Job Design, or work humanisation as it has also been called, has become a powerful technique for rolling back the worst excesses of the Classical school, especially in the area of manual work, where Scientific Management and its clones have had such an impact. It was in the US in the 1950s that Davis and Canter (1955), influenced by the work of the Human Relations school, questioned the Tayloristic basis of job design and work organisation. They suggested that it would be possible to design jobs that satisfied not only human needs but organisational ones as well. They argued that increased job satisfaction and increased organisational performance went hand in hand. Since then many other writers, especially in Europe, have contributed to the development of Job Design theory (Davis *et al*, 1955; Guest, 1957; Hackman and Oldham, 1980; Likert, 1961; Trist *et al*, 1963; Warr, 1987).

Job Design is a direct attack on the precepts of the Classical approach. Whereas Taylorist tradition seeks to fit people to rigidly defined and controlled jobs, Job Design theorists argue that jobs can and should be fitted to human needs. The basic tenets of Job Design are relatively straightforward and follow on from the work of the proponents of the Human

Relations approach, especially Maslow. It is argued that in pursuit of efficiency maximisation, the Classical approach to jobs, with its emphasis on fragmenting jobs and reducing workers' autonomy and discretion, is counterproductive to both individual fulfilment and organisational performance. This is because boring, monotonous and meaningless jobs lead to decreased employee satisfaction and motivation, increased turnover and absenteeism, and difficulties in managing employees' industrial unrest (Arnold *et al*, 1998; Hackman and Lawler, 1971; Humphrey *et al*, 2007).

The solution to these problems follows from the analysis. If Tayloristic trends in job design are counterproductive, then they should be reversed and 'variety, task completeness and, above all, autonomy' should be built into jobs (Wall *et al*, 1984: 15). Such a move would promote workers' mental health and job satisfaction, bringing in turn increased motivation and performance. Just as Taylor believed his approach would benefit both workers and management, so too do the proponents of Job Design. The difference is that the benefit to the worker is personal fulfilment rather than increased wages, though in both systems the benefit to management is increased productivity (Friedman, 1961; Hackman and Lawler, 1971; Hackman and Oldham, 1980; Herzberg *et al*, 1959; Kelly, 1982a, 1982b). Indeed, a meta-analysis of 259 studies of job design covering some 220,000 participants found that 34 per cent of the variance in performance and more than 55 per cent of the variance in job satisfaction was a function of job design characteristics (Humphrey *et al*, 2007). Or, to put it another way, good job design substantially increases not only workers' job satisfaction but also their productivity.

In practice, as Ideas and perspectives 2.4 shows, there are three main variants of Job Design.

IDEAS AND PERSPECTIVES 2.4

The three main variants of Job Design

- **Job enlargement**, which concentrates on increasing work variety by combining previously fragmented tasks, or by rotating people between different types of work (Guest, 1957).

- **Job enrichment**, which concentrates on increasing workers' control over what they do by rearranging work so that some of the responsibilities previously borne by supervisors and support staff are given to individuals or, more often, semi-autonomous work groups (Herzberg, 1968).

- **Socio-technical Systems theory**, which is a variant on Job Design involving a shift of focus from the individual job to the organisation as a whole. Socio-technical Systems theory sees organisations as being composed of interdependent social and technical systems. The theory argues that there is little point in reorganising the social system in isolation from the technology being used, and that the level of performance achieved is dependent on the degree of fit between the two. This view sees technology as acting as a limitation on the scope for redesigning individual jobs (Davis, 1979; Dunphy and Griffiths, 1998; Trist *et al*, 1963). It follows, therefore, that Job Design must go hand in hand with technological change if it is to be successful.

Job Design emerged and attracted so much attention in the 1950s and 1960s for three main reasons:

1. The first flows from the work of Maslow (1943). As workers have become better educated and more affluent, their higher-order needs such as self-actualisation have come to
the fore. This means that in order to obtain the best performance from workers, jobs have
to be designed to meet their psychological as well as their financial needs (Kelly, 1982b).

2. As markets have become more global, more competitive and more volatile, organisations
need to be more responsive to the needs of their customers. This requires workers to be
more flexible, possess a greater range of skills, and be able to work as part of a team
rather than on an individual basis (Aglietta, 1979; Streeck, 1987).

3. Low unemployment in the 1950s, 1960s and 1970s led to high rates of labour turnover,
absenteeism and endemic industrial unrest in industries and organisations with poor job
design (Pruijt, 1997). This was certainly a major reason for Volvo's adoption of Job
Design in the 1970s (Blackler and Brown, 1978).

Since the 1950s, the US and most European countries have initiated some form of officially sponsored 'Work Humanisation' programme. Not surprisingly, Norway and Sweden,
with their traditions of industrial cooperation and democracy, and what was West Germany,
with its post-war commitment to industrial consensus and worker rights, led the way
in terms of financial and legal backing. Norway initiated the process with its Industrial
Democracy Project (1962–1975). Sweden has probably been the most consistent, however,
establishing the Work Environment Fund in 1972, with a budget of SEK 500 million per
year, and creating the New Factories Programme at the same time. In 1976 it enacted the
Co-determination Act, which ensures that trade unions have a right to be consulted on all
major changes in working conditions. In 1977, the Swedish government created the Centre
for Working Life (later the Institute for Work Life Research) to initiate and promote work
humanisation. In the 1980s, it initiated the Swedish Development Programme (1982–
1987), the Leadership, Organisation and Co-determination Programme (1985–1990), and
the People, Data, Working Life Programme (1987–1992). Germany has seen a similarly
consistent approach with the Humanisation of Working Life Programme (1974–1989)
and, from 1990, the Work and Technology Programme, which was given a budget of DM
100 million per year to subsidise the adoption of Job Design practices (Pruijt, 1997).

Some of the Job Design initiatives in these countries were inspired by Norwegian
researchers such as Einar Thorsrud, who propagated the concept of semi-autonomous work
groups. Others derived from the work on the socio-technical systems approach carried out
by the Tavistock Institute in London (Auer and Riegler, 1990). In the UK, however, despite
the presence of the Tavistock Institute and the establishment of the government's Work
Research Unit in 1974, official backing has been noticeably lukewarm. Indeed, even the
modest expenditure devoted to the Work Research Unit was cut back considerably in the
1980s, and the Unit was eventually disbanded in the 1990s. Successive UK governments
now seem to share the American view that 'Quality of Working Life' programmes are the
purview of individual organisations rather than something to be promoted by government.

To a great degree, the popularity of Job Design seems to have fluctuated with employment levels. In the full-employment era of the 1950s and 1960s, governments and employers
in the West seemed relatively receptive to it. With the recessions of the 1970s and 1980s,
however, interest fell away in most countries (Humphrey *et al*, 2007). The exceptions were
Germany and particularly Sweden, both countries where unemployment remained relatively low in the 1970s and 1980s. Despite this, there can be little doubt that Job Design
precepts have permeated Western society on a significant scale, and provide the main

operational alternative to the Classical approach. As Pruijt (1997) noted, however, Tayloristic work practices have proved far more persistent than the proponents of Job Design had expected.

The Human Relations approach: summary and criticisms

Though many tend to associate the Human Relations movement exclusively with the work of Mayo, the above shows that it is a much more diverse school of thought. Indeed, some have argued that to call it a school owes more to academic convenience than to reality (Rose, 1988). Nevertheless, there are continuing and overlapping themes in the work of the writers cited above which strongly bond them together. The first, and most obvious, is their almost total rejection of the Classical movement's mechanistic–rational approach towards people and organisation structures. As Dunphy and Griffiths (1998: 21) noted:

> In particular, they attacked the notion of employees as interchangeable parts, stressing that individual employees had different motivations; that the specialisation of labour and deskilling had created widespread alienation and demotivation; and that excessive supervision had crushed employee initiative.

The second and more fundamental feature is that while approaching the issues involved from different perspectives and emphasising separate aspects, the proponents of Human Relations create an organisational model that possesses both coherence and plausibility.

The Human Relations model stresses three core elements:

- leadership and communication;
- intrinsic job motivation (as well as extrinsic rewards);
- organisation structures and practices which facilitate flexibility and involvement.

These elements are underpinned by two central propositions:

- **Organisations are complex social systems**, with both formal and informal social structures, and are not mechanical contrivances. Therefore, they cannot effectively be controlled by close supervision, rigid rules and purely economic incentives.
- **Human beings have emotional as well as economic needs.** Organisation and job structures need to be designed in such a way as to enable workers to meet both their material and non-material needs. Only in this way will workers perform efficiently and effectively in the best interests of the organisation.

It is not difficult to see why the Human Relations approach proved popular. In a period when many people were becoming increasingly worried about the growth of impersonal bureaucracies, it provided an attractive alternative. It is an approach that stresses that human beings are not mere cogs in a machine but have emotional needs: humans want to 'belong', achieve recognition, and develop and fulfil their potential. As mentioned earlier, the Depression of the 1930s and the Second World War and its aftermath created, in the US and Europe, a greater sense of collectivism and community than had hitherto been the case – another reason why the Human Relations doctrine found such a ready audience. Also, implicitly, it offers an approach to change management that has a surprisingly modern ring to it. The stress on organisations having clear objectives, effective communication systems and proactive leadership, coupled with the need to obtain the willing cooperation of employees, are central to many modern approaches to change management. This is not so surprising given the overlap in terms of personnel and ideas with the OD movement, which has provided the dominant approach to change for much of the last 60 years (Burnes and Cooke, 2012b).

Despite its attractiveness and plausibility, a substantial and often vitriolic body of opinion came to be ranged against the Human Relations approach in the 1950s and 1960s (Muldoon, 2012; Rose, 1988). Economists rejected the argument that non-material incentives have a potentially stronger motivating influence than material incentives. The emphasis placed by the proponents of Human Relations on people's need for 'togetherness' and 'belonging' was seen by some as a denial of individualism. Others thought that it belittled workers and portrayed them as irrational beings who, given the chance, would cling to management as a baby clings to its mother. It was also attacked from both a management and a trade union viewpoint. Some of the former felt that its supposedly powerful manipulative techniques were either useless or inoperable, while representatives of the latter saw Human Relations as a vehicle for manipulating labour, and undermining – or attempting to eliminate – trade unions. Sociologists criticised it for attempting a sociological analysis of organisations without taking into account the larger society within which each organisation exists (Kerr and Fisher, 1957; Landsberger, 1958; Rose, 1988; Whyte, 1960).

Many of the criticisms were clearly directed at the work of Mayo and his colleagues, including inconsistencies between them. Landsberger (1958), for example, was one of the first to point out the difference between Mayo's (1933) interpretations of the Hawthorne Experiments and those of his colleagues, Roethlisberger and Dickson (1938), though Smith (1998) disputes this and many of the other criticisms of Mayo. However, by no means were all the criticisms levelled at Mayo and his colleagues. Maslow's work, a key theoretical cornerstone of the Human Relations approach, was found to lack empirical substance when researchers attempted to validate it (Sheldrake, 1996). For example, some of Maslow's hierarchical needs do not appear to exist for some people, and monetary rewards seems to fit into more than one level of his hierarchy (Makin and Cox, 2004). Certainly later theories of motivation seem to adopt a different approach (Arnold et al, 2005; Hall and Nougaim, 1968; Hitt et al, 2009; Lawler and Suttle, 1972; Wahba and Bridwell, 1976). Similarly, Bennis's views were attacked. The Aston Studies in the 1960s (Pugh et al, 1969a, 1969b) showed that bureaucracy was growing rather than declining. Also, Miewald (1970) argued that Bennis did not understand the nature of bureaucracy; in his view, far from being rigid, it could and did adapt to changing and dynamic environments. Kelly (1982b) also attacked the proposition that increased job satisfaction leads to increased performance.

There is one further criticism of the Human Relations approach, one that it shares with the Classical approach: it claims for itself the title of the 'one best way'. Yet the question was posed: how can any approach claim that there is only one method of structuring and managing organisations, and that it holds good for all organisations and for all time? Indeed, the seed of this criticism can be found in Bennis's (1966) work, where he argued that organisations in the last third of the twentieth century would experience rapid and unexpected change, continue to increase in size – with the problems of complexity which this brings, and become more diverse and specialised. Clearly, while not explicitly advocating it, Bennis was making the case for an approach to organisations that recognised not only that they face different situations but also that these are not stable over time. Similarly, Trist et al's (1963) argument regarding the need to fit social systems to technical ones can also be seen as making a case for a situationalist approach to job design. Indeed, the most telling argument against the 'one best way' approach is that presented by Davis and Canter (1955), mentioned earlier. If jobs and work organisation are social inventions designed to meet the needs of societies and organisations at particular points in time, then there can never be a one best way for all organisations and for all times. What is needed, instead, is an approach that links approaches to work design to the particular context to which they are best suited. In the 1960s and 1970s, such an approach emerged.

The Contingency Theory approach

Contingency Theory emerged in the 1960s out of a number of now classic studies of organisation structure and management (*see* Burns and Stalker, 1961; Lawrence and Lorsch, 1967; Pugh *et al*, 1969a, 1969b; Thompson, 1967; Woodward, 1965). Since the 1970s, it has proved – as a theory at least – to be more influential than either the Classical or Human Relations approaches. In essence, Contingency Theory is a rejection of the 'one best way' approach previously sought by managers and propounded by academics. In its place is substituted the view that the structure and operation of an organisation, including the way jobs are designed and control over labour exercised, is dependent (i.e. 'contingent') on the situational variables it faces – the main ones being environment, technology and size (Burnes, 1989). It follows from this that no two organisations will face exactly the same contingencies; therefore, as their situations are different, so too should their structures and operations be different. Consequently the 'one best way' for *all* organisations is replaced by the 'one best way' for *each* organisation.

One of the earliest writers to lay the groundwork for Contingency theorists was Herbert Simon. Writing in the 1940s (Simon, 1947), he criticised existing approaches as providing managers with nothing more than proverbs or lists of 'good practice' based on scant ideas, many of which contradicted each other. He argued that organisation theory needed to go beyond superficial and over-simplified precepts, and instead study the conditions under which competing principles could be applied.

Nevertheless, it was not until the 1960s that a considered approach emerged, which broke with the Classical and Human Relations movements' attempts to establish a universal approach suitable to all organisations. The former had concentrated on the formal structure and technical requirements of organisations, and had attempted to establish sets of general principles. The latter, the Human Relations movement, focused on the informal aspects of organisations and the psychological and social needs of their employees. As with the Classical approach, this produced lists of good practice and desired objectives, but it lacked precise guidance on how these should be applied.

Contingency theorists adopted a different perspective, which created a clear distinction between them and proponents of the Classical approach and Human Relations school. Contingency theorists based their approach on systems theory, adopting the premise that organisations are open systems whose internal operation and effectiveness are dependent upon the particular situational variables they face at any one time, and that these vary from organisation to organisation (*see* Ideas and perspectives 2.5). As Scott observed (1987: 23):

> The previous definitions tend [implicitly] to view the organisation as a closed system, separate from its environment and comprising a set of stable and easily identified participants. However, organisations are not closed systems, sealed off from their environments but are open to and dependent on flows of personnel and resources from outside.

IDEAS AND PERSPECTIVES 2.5

What is a system?

Simply put, a system is an organised collection of elements or parts, interconnected with relationships and contained within some identifiable boundary. In addition:

- A system has an identity which sets it apart from its environment and is capable of preserving that identity within a given range of environmental scenarios.
- Systems exist within a hierarchy of other systems. They contain subsystems and exist within some wider system. All are interconnected with the subsystems being less complex than the containing system.

(Stickland, 1998: 14)

Put at its simplest, a system is a collection of interrelated parts which form some whole. Typical systems are the solar system and, the human body, communication networks and social systems. Systems may be 'closed' or 'open'. Closed systems are those, which, for all practical purposes, are completely self-supporting, and thus do not interact with their environment. An example would be an astronaut's life-support pack. Open systems are those which do interact with their environment, on which they rely for obtaining essential inputs and for the discharge of their system outputs. Social systems (e.g. organisations) are always open systems . . . A key feature of open systems is their interdependence on the environment, which may be relatively stable or relatively uncertain at a particular point in time. (Cole, 2001: 5)

Systems theory has been around for over 100 years. It began to emerge in the natural and physical sciences around the beginning of the twentieth century (Wren, 1994). One of the pioneers of systems theory, or general systems theory to give it its correct title, was the eminent biologist Ludwig von Bertalanffy (1972). He argued that the fundamental characteristic of a living organism is its organisation and that one cannot understand the organism unless one understands its total organisation – its biological system. Merely looking at individual parts or processes cannot provide a complete explanation of the whole. He was concerned with the dynamic nature of systems, arguing that the interconnectedness of the elements which make up a system means that changes to one part affect other parts and in turn the whole system. As a biologist, von Bertalanffy (1972: 412) was especially interested in the concept of 'open systems', 'that is systems exchanging matter with the environment as every "living" system does'. He argued that his open systems theory was applicable to all sciences and also to organisations.

From the perspective of open systems theory, changes in one part of an organisation's system, whether internal or external, will cause changes to other parts of the system. Though one can see the open systems concepts in Follett's espousal of Gestalt psychology and also in Barnard's (1938) reference to the influence of outside stakeholders, its application to organisation only really emerged in the 1960s with the advent of Contingency Theory. As Robbins (1987) noted, there is wide agreement that the systems approach offers important insights into the working of an organisation. It views the organisation both as a whole and as part of a larger environment. The idea is that any part of an organisation's activities affects all other parts. Organisations, rather than being closed (as previous theories implicitly assumed), are viewed as open systems operating within a wider environment and having multiple channels of interaction (Mullins, 1993). Therefore, organisations are not in complete control of their own fate; they can be, and often are, affected by the environment in which they operate, and this can and does vary from organisation to organisation.

This view is consistent with evidence that not all organisations – or even all successful ones – have the same structure, and that even within organisations, different structural forms can be observed (Mintzberg, 1979). Though many situational variables, such as the age of the organisation and its history, have been put forward as influential in determining structure, it is generally agreed that the three most important contingencies are environment, technology and size (*see* Ideas and perspectives 2.6).

IDEAS AND PERSPECTIVES 2.6

The three main contingencies

- **Environmental uncertainty and dependence.** It is argued that the management of any organisation is undertaken in circumstances of uncertainty and dependence, both of which change over time. Uncertainty arises because of our inability ever to understand and control events fully, especially the actions of others, whether outside or inside an organisation. Because of this, forecasting is an inexact and hazardous enterprise. Similarly, the dependence of management upon the goodwill and support of others, whether they be internal or external groupings, makes an organisation vulnerable, and may in some circumstances even threaten its very existence. Levels of uncertainty and dependence will vary, but can never be totally eliminated and must therefore be taken into account – treated as a contingency – when designing organisational structures and procedures (Burns and Stalker, 1961; Child, 1984; Lawrence and Lorsch, 1967; Pugh, 1984; Robbins, 1987; Thompson, 1967).

- **Technology.** The argument for technology being a key variable follows similar lines to that of environment. Organisations creating and providing different products and services use different technologies. Indeed, even those producing similar products may use differing techniques. Given that these technologies can vary from the large and expensive, such as a car assembly line, to the relatively small and cheap, such as a personal computer, the form of organisation necessary to ensure their efficient operation will also vary. If so, there is a need to treat technology as a contingent variable when structuring organisations. There are distinct variants of the case for technology, however, which reflect the different definitions of technology that theorists and researchers have employed. The two best-developed approaches are found in Woodward's (1965, 1970) studies of 'operations technology' and Perrow's (1967, 1970) analysis of 'materials technology'. The former refer to the equipping and sequencing of activities in an organisation's work flow, while the latter refer to the characteristics of the physical and informational materials used. Woodward's work tends to relate more to manufacturing organisations, whereas Perrow's is more generally applicable (Hickson *et al*, 1969; Thompson, 1967; Zwerman, 1970).

- **Size.** Some would argue that this is not just *a* key variable but *the* key variable. The case for size being a significant variable when designing organisations has a long antecedence within organisation theory, being first cited by Weber in the early part of the twentieth century when making the case for bureaucracy (Weber, 1947). The basic case is quite straightforward. It is argued that the structure and practices necessary for the efficient and effective operations of small organisations are not suitable for larger ones. For small organisations, centralised and personalised forms of control are claimed to be appropriate, but as organisations grow, more decentralised and impersonal structures and practices become more relevant (Blau, 1970; Mullins, 1989; Pugh *et al*, 1969a, 1969b; Scott, 1987).

The main figures in developing and establishing Contingency Theory were academics in Britain and the US, among whom the pioneers were Burns and Stalker.

Tom Burns and George Macpherson Stalker: the importance of environment

The first major study to establish a relationship between organisations' environment and their structure was carried out by Burns and Stalker (1961) in Britain. They examined 20 firms in a variety of industries in order to assess how their structures responded to the environment in which they operated. Their findings were to have a major impact on organisation theory, and provide concrete evidence for rejecting a universal, 'one best way' approach to organisational structure and practice. They identified five different types of environment, based upon the level of uncertainty that was present, ranging from 'stable' to 'least predictable'. They also identified two basic or ideal forms of structure: 'Mechanistic' and 'Organic'. Their data showed that Mechanistic structures were more effective in stable environments, while Organic ones were better suited to less stable, less predictable environments (*see* Figure 2.2).

Burns and Stalker neither reject nor accept what went before. Instead, they argued that both the Classical approach and the Human Relations approach can be appropriate, but that this depends on the nature of the environment in which the organisation is operating. As Ideas and perspectives 2.7 shows, Mechanistic structures are akin to the Classical approach, while Organic structures resemble the Human Relations approach. In this respect, they not only built on the past rather than rejecting it, they also restored some responsibility to managers. Instead of being called on to adopt blindly the orthodoxy with regard to structure, managers would in future have to assess their organisation and its needs, and then adopt the structure and practices suitable to its situation (Child, 1984; Mullins, 1989; Scott, 1987).

IDEAS AND PERSPECTIVES 2.7

Burns and Stalker's ideal forms of structure

Characteristics of Mechanistic structures	Characteristics of Organic structures
• The specialisation of tasks.	• Job and task flexibility.
• Closely defined duties, responsibilities and technical methods.	• Adjustment and continual redefinition of tasks.
• A clear hierarchical structure with insistence on loyalty to the organisation and accountability to superiors.	• A network structure of control, authority and communication.
• Instructions and information flow (mainly) from the top to the bottom in a hierarchical manner.	• Lateral consultation based on information and advice rather than instructions and decisions.
• Obedience to the organisation and its rules.	• Commitment to the work group and its tasks.
• Importance and prestige determined by position in hierarchy.	• Importance and prestige determined by an individual's contribution to the tasks of their work group rather than their position in the hierarchy.

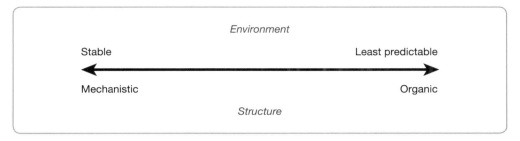

Figure 2.2 The environment–structure continuum

Paul Lawrence and Jay Lorsch: the case for environment continued

Burns and Stalker's findings on the relationship between organisational environment and structure were examined and developed by a number of researchers in Europe and the US. One of the most significant pieces of work was that carried out by Lawrence and Lorsch (1967) in the US. Their work went beyond that of Burns and Stalker, in that they were interested in not only the relationship between environment and a company's overall structure but also how individual departments within companies responded to, and organised themselves to cope with, aspects of the external environment that were of particular significance to them. They undertook a study of six firms in the plastics industry, followed by a further study of two firms in the container industry and two in the consumer foods industry. The structure of each of the firms was analysed in terms of its degree of 'differentiation' and 'integration':

- **Differentiation** refers to the degree to which managers and staff in their own functional departments see themselves as separate and have distinct practices, procedures and structures from others in the organisation.

- **Integration** refers to the level and form of collaboration that is necessary between departments in order to achieve their individual objectives within the environment in which the firm operates.

Therefore, differentiation is the degree to which departments are distinct from each other, while integration refers to the degree to which they have common structures, procedures, practices and objectives at the operational level. Generally, the greater the interdependence among departments, the more integration is needed to coordinate their efforts in the best interests of the organisation as a whole. This may not always be easy to achieve, however. In a rapidly changing environment, the conditions faced by individual departments may differ greatly and a high degree of differentiation may be necessary. In such a situation, the need for integration is also likely to be great, but the diversity and volatility of the environment are likely to push individual departments in the opposite direction (Cummings and Huse, 1989).

In their study of the plastics industry, Lawrence and Lorsch (1967) found clear differentiation between key departments such as research, production and sales. Research departments were more concerned with long-term issues and were under pressure to produce new ideas and innovations. These departments, in Burns and Stalker's terminology, tended to adopt an Organic form of structure. Production departments meanwhile were, for obvious reasons, concerned with short-term performance targets relating to output, costs, quality and delivery. Such departments tended to operate in a fairly stable environment and had Mechanistic structures. Sales departments tended to fall in between research and production in terms of environment and structure. They operated in a moderately stable environment and were concerned more with getting production to meet deliveries than with long-term issues.

While highlighting the degree of differentiation between key departments, the study also found that the degree of integration was critical to a firm's overall performance. Indeed, the two most successful firms in their sample were not only among the most highly differentiated, they also had the highest degree of integration. These findings were confirmed by their studies of the container and consumer foods industries, which showed that differentiation and integration in successful companies varies with the demands of the environment in which they operate. The more diverse and dynamic the environment, the more the successful organisation will be differentiated and highly integrated. In a more stable environment, the pressure for differentiation is less, but the need for integration remains. Therefore, Lawrence and Lorsch found that the most effective organisations had an appropriate fit between the design and coordination of departments and the amount of environmental uncertainty they faced. The most successful firms, however, were the ones that, while operating in an environment that required a high level of differentiation, also managed to achieve a high level of integration.

Clearly, in a situation where departments have dissimilar structures, practices and procedures, achieving integration is not easy or conflict-free. Indeed, in such situations, organisational politics can be rife. Lawrence and Lorsch found that the effective firms avoided such a situation by openly confronting conflict, and by working problems through in the context of the overall needs of the organisation. In addition, in firms that dealt successfully with conflict, the success of those responsible for achieving integration was based mainly on their knowledge and competence rather than their formal position. This was because their colleagues in the different departments respected and responded to their perceived understanding of the issues involved. It follows that to achieve high levels of integration and differentiation, an organisation cannot rely solely on the formal managerial hierarchy. This must be supplemented with liaison positions, task forces and teams, and other integrating mechanisms.

As with Burns and Stalker, Lawrence and Lorsch did not reject the Classical and Human Relations approaches *per se* but instead saw them as alternative options, depending on the environment in which an organisation operates. In looking at the internal operations of organisations in this way, Lawrence and Lorsch raised the issue of dependence as well as uncertainty. This was a subject that James Thompson tackled in greater depth.

James Thompson: environmental uncertainty and dependence

Thompson's (1967) influential work took the environmental perspective forward in three important ways. The first was to argue that although organisations are not rational entities, they strive to be so because it is in the interests of those who design and manage the organisation that its work be carried out as effectively and efficiently as possible. In order to achieve this, organisations attempt to insulate their productive core from the uncertainty of the environment. However, it is not possible to seal off all, or perhaps even any, parts of an organisation, given that it must be open to and interact with its environment if it is to secure resources and sell its products. This leads on to Thompson's second major contribution: different levels of an organisation may exhibit, and need, different structures and operate on a more rational or less rational basis. Thompson's third contribution was to recognise that organisational effectiveness was contingent not only on the level of external environmental uncertainty but also on the degree of internal dependence present. This echoes Lawrence and Lorsch's argument for integration and differentiation. However, Thompson made this point much more explicitly and related it to different structural forms. He formulated a three-type classification in relation to internal dependence (*see* Ideas and perspectives 2.8).

Thompson went on to argue that the type of interdependence could be related to the degree of complexity present: simple organisations rely on pooled interdependence; more complex organisations demonstrate both pooled and sequential interdependence; and in the most complex organisations, all three forms of interdependence may be present. Thompson envisaged that each form of interdependence would require distinct methods for coordinating activities. Pooled interdependence would be characterised by standardisation through the use of rules and procedures. Sequential interdependence would require the use of detailed plans and written agreements, while reciprocal interdependence would achieve coordination by means of personal contact and informal agreements between members of those parts of the organisation involved.

Therefore, in a nutshell, Thompson's main arguments are as follows:

- Different sections of an organisation will be characterised by varying levels of complexity, rationality and formalisation, depending on the extent to which managers can shield them from the level of uncertainty present in the environment.

- The higher both the overall level of uncertainty and that faced by each area of an organisation, the greater will be the dependence of one area on another.

- As this interdependence increases, coordination through standardised procedures and planning mechanisms will become less effective and the need for more personal contact and informal interaction will grow.

- The more that coordination is achieved through mutual reciprocity in this manner, the less rational will be the operation of the organisation.

Thompson's work is of seminal importance in the development of organisation theory, not only because of the case he made for linking external uncertainty to internal dependence

IDEAS AND PERSPECTIVES 2.8

Thompson's classification of internal dependence

- **Pooled interdependence** – where each part of an organisation operates in a relatively autonomous manner, but by fulfilling their individual purposes they enable the organisation as a whole to function effectively.

- **Sequential interdependence** – where the outputs from one part of an organisation constitute the inputs for other parts of the system.

- **Reciprocal interdependence** – where overall effectiveness requires direct interaction between an organisation's separate parts.

but also, as a number of writers have observed (*see* Robbins, 1987; Scott, 1987), because of the attention he drew to the fact that technology can influence organisation structures as well as environmental factors. Thompson's contribution in this respect lay in creating a classification scheme for technology, and arguing that technology determines the selection of the specific structural arrangements for reducing the effect of uncertainty on the various functions of an organisation. The issue of technology and structure had been raised earlier in a major study by Joan Woodward published in 1965.

Joan Woodward: the case for technology

In the 1960s, Joan Woodward carried out a major study of 100 UK manufacturing firms in south-east Essex, in order to establish the validity of the claims made by advocates of the Classical approach that the adoption of a bureaucratic–mechanistic structure was essential for organisational success (Woodward, 1965, 1970). After much work, Woodward concluded that no such correlation existed. What she found, however, was that the more successful companies adopted an organisational form that varied according to their main production technology. By technology, Woodward meant not only the machinery being used but also the way it was organised, operated and integrated into a distinct production process. From her sample, she identified three distinct types of production technology, ranging from least to most complex (*see* Figure 2.3).

Woodward defined these three types of production technology as follows:

- **Small batch (or unit) production** – where customers' requirements were for one-off or small-volume specialist products.
- **Large batch (or mass) production** – where standardised products were made in large numbers to meet a forecast demand.
- **Process production** – where production was in a continuous flow, such as an oil refinery.

When the firms were grouped in this manner, a pattern emerged that showed that though they apparently differed considerably in terms of their organisational structure, many of the variations for the more successful firms could be explained by reference to the technology employed. Among firms engaged in small batch production, the most appropriate structure appeared to be one with relatively few hierarchical levels and wide middle management spans of control (i.e. an Organic-type structure). Woodward noted that technology became more complex as firms moved from small batch to large batch and finally process production. In turn, structures became taller and more narrowly based, with smaller middle

Figure 2.3 Woodward's technology–structure continuum

management and larger chief executive spans of control (i.e. a Mechanistic-type structure). Within each category of technology, the best-performing companies were those closest to the median in the type of structure adopted. Therefore, Woodward's work clearly established a link between technology, structure and success which ran counter to the notion that there was a 'one best way' for all organisations.

Though qualified by later studies (*see* Child, 1984; Handy, 1986; Smith *et al*, 1982), Woodward's research remains a milestone in the development of Contingency Theory. In particular, she demonstrated the need to take into account technological variables in designing organisations, especially in relation to spans of control. Nevertheless, a major drawback of her work was the difficulty of applying it to non-manufacturing companies. This was remedied by the work of Charles Perrow.

Charles Perrow: the case for technology continued

In the US, Charles Perrow (1967, 1970) extended Joan Woodward's work on technology and organisation structure by drawing attention to two major dimensions of technology:

- the extent to which the work being carried out is variable or predictable;
- the extent to which the technology can be analysed and categorised.

The first dimension, *variability*, refers to the incidence of exceptional or unpredictable occurrences, and the extent to which these problems are familiar and can be easily dealt with, or are unique and difficult to solve. For example, an oil refinery should experience few non-routine occurrences, while an advertising agency will encounter many unpredictable and exceptional occurrences. The second major dimension, *analysis and categorisation*, refers to the extent to which the individual task functions can be broken down and tightly specified, and also whether problems can be solved by recourse to recognised, routine procedures or if non-routine procedures have to be invoked. Bringing together these two major dimensions of technology, Perrow constructed a technology continuum ranging from routine to non-routine (*see* Figure 2.4). With the latter, there are a large number of exceptional occurrences requiring difficult and varied problem-solving techniques to overcome them. Routine technology, meanwhile, throws up few problems, which can be dealt with by recourse to standard, simple techniques.

Perrow argued that by classifying organisations according to their technology and predictability (routine to non-routine) of work tasks, it is then possible to identify the most effective form of structure in any given situation or for any activity. Perrow's

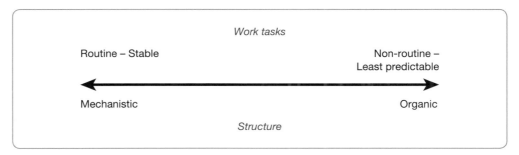

Figure 2.4 Perrow's technology–structure continuum

routine–non-routine continuum can be equated with Burns and Stalker's Mechanistic and Organic dimensions for organisation structures. In routine situations, where few problems arise and those that do are easily dealt with, a Mechanistic structure is more effective because of the stable and predictable nature of the situation. In a dynamic and unpredictable situation, however, a more flexible, Organic form of structure will be more effective in dealing with the non-routine and difficult problems that occur. By formulating his work in this manner (i.e. by combining technology and predictability) it became possible to apply it to non-manufacturing situations. Therefore, Perrow's work both reinforced and extended Woodward's case for recognising technology as a key situational variable to be taken into account when designing organisations. Nevertheless, while Perrow was developing his ideas, a further group of researchers was making the case for yet another 'key' contingency – size.

The Aston Group: the case for size

Though there are many proponents of the case for organisational size being a key contingency (*see* Child, 1984; Robbins, 1987), perhaps the earliest and most ardent was a group of British researchers based at the University of Aston in Birmingham (who became known as the Aston Group). In the 1960s, they carried out a series of studies to examine and identify the relationship between different forms of organisational structures and their determinants (*see* Pugh *et al*, 1969a, 1969b). The Aston Group began in the early 1960s by examining a sample of 87 companies and, as the work developed, further samples were added to their eventually impressive database. In analysing their results, the Aston Group found that size was the most powerful predictor of specialisation, use of procedures and reliance on paperwork. In effect, what they found was that the larger the organisation, the more likely it was to adopt (and need) a mechanistic (bureaucratic) structure. The reverse was also found: the smaller the organisation, the more likely it was to adopt (and need) an organic (flexible) structure (*see* Figure 2.5).

This was clearly a major finding. Not only did it support (at least in terms of larger organisations) Weber's earlier work on bureaucracy, it also struck a blow against those, such as Bennis, who saw bureaucracy as dysfunctional and dying. The work of the Aston Group, along with that of others such as Blau and Schoenherr (1971), who also argued that size is the most important condition affecting the structure of organisations, gave bureaucracy if not a new lease of life then, at least, a new lease of respectability. Bureaucracy, according to the Aston results, was both efficient and effective, at least for larger organisations, and given the tendency for the average size of private-sector companies and public bodies to increase throughout the twentieth century, its applicability would grow.

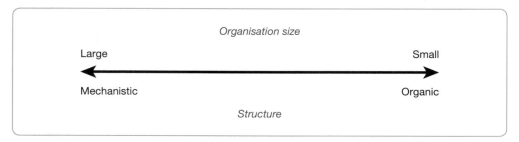

Figure 2.5 The size–structure continuum

There are two explanations for the relationship between size and bureaucracy, both of which have similar implications for organisational efficiency and effectiveness:

1. Increased size offers greater opportunities for specialisation – the Adam Smith argument, in effect. This will manifest itself in terms of greater structural differentiation and a high degree of uniformity among sub-units. In the first instance, this will make managerial coordination more difficult, especially with the emergence of functional autonomy. To counter this, senior managers will move to impose a system of impersonal controls through the use of formal procedures, standardised reporting and control systems, the written recording of information, etc.

2. The difficulty of directing ever larger numbers of staff makes it highly inefficient to continue to use a personalised, centralised style of management. Instead a more decentralised system, using impersonal control mechanisms, has to be adopted. The introduction of such a system inevitably leads to the expansion of the administrative core (the bureaucracy) in organisations (Child, 1984).

As with all the Contingency theorists, those who argued for size as the key situational variable were not attempting to reinvent the 'one best way' approach for *all* organisations. Rather, they were rejecting it in favour of an approach that saw organisational performance as dependent upon the appropriateness of the organisation's structure for its size. Therefore, like all the Contingency theorists, the Aston school adopted an approach which stressed that there is a 'one best way' for *each* organisation.

Contingency Theory: summary and criticisms

The Contingency approach can be considered to be a far more cohesive school of thought than either the Classical or the Human Relations approach. It has three unifying themes:

● Organisations are open systems.

● Structure, and therefore performance, is dependent upon the particular circumstances, situational variables, faced by each organisation.

● There is no 'one best way' for *all* organisations but there is a 'one best way' for *each* organisation.

The attractions of Contingency Theory are obvious. First, it was in tune with the times in which it emerged – the 1960s and 1970s. This was a period of rapid economic and technological change, with a tendency towards much larger organisations and a significant increase in domestic and international competition. In this situation, Contingency Theory offered not only a plausible explanation as to why these events were causing problems for organisations but also a way to resolve them (Burnes, 1989). Second, on the surface at least, it was simpler to understand and apply than the Human Relations approach. As Figure 2.6 shows, proponents of Contingency Theory maintain that if organisations adopt a structure which aligns with their environment, technology and size, the result will be good performance. However, if they do not, the result will be poor performance.

Finally, like the Classical approach, Contingency Theory seeks to apply rationality to organisation design. In order to achieve good performance, organisations are told that they need to analyse their situation rationally and adopt the organisation structure which is most appropriate for the contingencies they face, i.e. as Figure 2.6 shows, they have to align their structure with their size, technology and environment.

Environment Technology Size / Structure	Stable Process Large	Dynamic Unit Small
Mechanistic	Good performance	Poor performance
Organic	Poor performance	Good performance

Figure 2.6 Matching structure to contingencies

In terms of implementing an appropriate organisation structure and of maintaining its appropriateness in the face of changing circumstances, the approach to change management offered by Contingency theorists was similar to that of the Classical school. In a rational fashion, managers should collect and analyse data on the situational variables the organisation faces and match these to the appropriate structural option. The theory then implies that for employees, faced with a plan for change based on such a 'scientific' approach, the only rational course of action is to accept the validity of the situation and cooperate with managers to achieve the required structural changes. However, it is at this point – the attempt to apply Contingency Theory rationally and mechanically – that problems and drawbacks emerge which give rise to a number of major criticisms of this approach, the main ones being as follows:

● Difficulty arises in relating structure to performance. A number of writers have pointed out that there is no agreed definition of 'good performance', and it therefore becomes difficult to show that linking structure to situational variables brings the benefits claimed (Hendry, 1979, 1980; Mansfield, 1984; Terry, 1976). Congruence theorists take a slightly different perspective on the relationship between contingencies and performance (Milliman *et al*, 1991). They argue that it is the general alignment or 'fit' between an organisation and its environment which is important, and that this relates to the broader concept of organisational effectiveness rather than performance (Hayes, 2002). However, even this ignores the fact that there is a wide range of factors which can influence performance or effectiveness, not least of which is luck. Davis and Star (1993) show that in the early 1990s seven of the twelve most profitable firms in the world were pharmaceutical companies, and that three of these produced anti-ulcer drugs. They conclude that the profitability of the pharmaceutical sector was attributable less to the nature of these organisations than to the over-generosity of health systems in funding such treatments – clearly a case of an industry that was in the right place at the right time.

● Despite the length of time that Contingency Theory has been in circulation, there is still no agreed or unchallenged definition of the three key situational variables – environment, technology and size. The literature gives a wide and conflicting range of definitions of these, making it difficult not only to establish a link between them and structure but also to apply the theory (Dastmalchian, 1984; Mullins, 1989; Pugh and Hickson, 1976; Robbins, 1987; Warner, 1984; Wood, 1979).

- While, as argued above, a relationship has been established between size and structure, it has proved difficult to show that this relationship has an appreciable impact on performance. Some researchers have suggested that the link between size and structure relates to preferred systems of control, which may have more to do with the political and cultural nature of organisations than any attempt to improve performance (Allaire and Firsirotu, 1984; Child, 1984; Mansfield, 1984; Pugh and Hickson, 1976; Salaman, 1979).

- In examining the link between structure and contingencies, researchers use the organisation's formal organisational structure for comparison purposes. Yet, as the Hawthorne Experiments showed, the actual operation of an organisation may depend more on the informal structures created by workers than the formal ones laid down by management. This was a point made by Woodward (1965) in her study of technology and structure. She noted that organisation charts failed to show important relationships that, taken together, can have a significant impact on performance (Argyris, 1973; Burawoy, 1979; Selznick, 1948).

- Structure and associated practices and policies may be strongly influenced by external forces (Mullins, 1993). In the UK, privatised utilities are subject to regulation and face restrictions that have a significant influence on how they are structured and operate. Similarly, in the UK, financial service organisations are required to establish 'Chinese walls' between different parts of their business to avoid market-sensitive information being passed from one area to another.

- Rather than managers being the virtual prisoners of organisational contingencies when making decisions regarding structure, the reverse may be the case. Managers may have a significant degree of choice and influence over not only structure but also the situational variables. Whether this is called 'strategic choice' (Child, 1972), 'organisational choice' (Trist *et al*, 1963) or 'design space' (Bessant, 1983), the meaning is the same: those senior managers responsible for such decisions can exercise a high degree of freedom in selecting and influencing the technology to be used, the environment in which they operate and even the size of the organisation. Indeed, one of the architects of the technology–structure hypothesis, Charles Perrow, later claimed that technology is chosen and designed to maintain and reinforce existing structures and power relations within organisations rather than the reverse (Perrow, 1983). Other writers made the case for size and environment being manipulated in similar ways (Abell, 1975; Clegg, 1984; Hendry, 1979; Leifer and Huber, 1977; Lorsch, 1970).

- The postmodernists (*see* Chapter 4) also make a case for managerial choice. They argue that an organisation's environment is socially constructed and managers have the ability to 'construct' an environment which serves their needs (Hatch, 1997). As Grint (2005: 1467) comments:

  > Decision-makers are much more active in the constitution of the context than conventional contingency theories allow, and that a persuasive rendition of the context . . . legitimizes a particular form of action that often relates to the decision-maker's preferred mode of engagement, rather than to what 'the situation' apparently demands.

- It is assumed that organisations pursue clear-cut, well-thought-out, stable and compatible objectives that can be fitted into a Contingency perspective. Researchers and practising managers argue that this is not the case, however – in fact, even two of the proponents of Contingency Theory, Lawrence and Lorsch (1967), highlighted the presence and danger of conflicting objectives. In reality, objectives are often unclear, and organisations may pursue a number of conflicting goals at the same time. Clearly, the objectives of an organisation will impact on its situation and its structure. If these objectives are arbitrary, conflicting or open to managerial whim, it becomes difficult to apply a Contingency approach (Abodaher, 1986; Edwardes, 1983; Hamel and Prahalad, 1989; Mintzberg, 1987; Sloan, 1986).

● The last criticism is that Contingency Theory is too mechanistic and deterministic, and ignores the complexity of organisational life. As argued by the Human Relations school, organisations are by no means the rational entities many would like to believe (a point also made by Thompson (1967) in his support of Contingency Theory). There is a need to see organisations as social systems, with all the cultural and political issues that this raises. In this view, structure is the product of power struggles between individuals and groups within the organisation, each arguing and fighting for their own perspective and position (Allaire and Firsirotu, 1984; Buchanan, 1984; Hickson and Butler, 1982; Morgan, 1986; Pfeffer, 1981; Robbins, 1987; Salaman, 1979).

Therefore, despite its attractiveness, Contingency Theory, like the Classical and Human Relations approaches, fails to provide a convincing explanation for the way in which organisations do and should operate.

Conclusions

For organisations, if not for academics, the key purpose of any organisation theory or approach is to help them analyse and rectify the weaknesses and problems of their current situation, and to assist them in bringing about the changes necessary to achieve their future objectives. Over the past 100 or so years, the design and management of organisations have moved from an *ad hoc* process based on – at best – guesswork to one that is highly complex and informed by a host of practical and theoretical considerations. To the uninitiated, it might appear that this has made running organisations an easier and more certain process. Yet a close examination of most organisations will reveal that this is far from being the case. Not only are organisations, in general, larger and more complex than in the past, but also the practical and theoretical reference points on which managers can draw are diverse and give conflicting and confusing signals.

Not surprisingly in such a situation, many managers look for simple, foolproof solutions: often ones that, as Douglas McGregor noted, appeal to their own basic orientation – whether that be Theory X or Theory Y. This is one of the reasons why the Classical approach, with its deep roots in the Industrial Revolution and its straightforward mechanical approach to organisations and their members, has proved so enduring – despite strong evidence of its lack of suitability in many situations. This search for simple, often quick-fix solutions to the problems of organisational life has been manifested in many ways in the last three decades, not least the emergence of a series of 'panaceas' such as new technology, human resources management, Total Quality Management, culture change, etc. This is not to deny the benefits these can bring but, taken on their own, at best they encourage a fragmented approach, and at worst they create an atmosphere of resignation within organisations as one 'fad' is succeeded by yet another, and none is given the time necessary to prove itself (Collins,

2000). Clearly, in such situations, without an overall, long-term plan, the result of these various 'solutions' is to make the situation worse rather than better (Burnes, 1991; Burnes and Weekes, 1989).

Organisations clearly need to reject a short-term piecemeal approach and instead see themselves in their totality and adopt a consistent and long-term approach. But which approach should they choose? We have seen in this and the previous chapter that well-thought-out and well-supported cases exist for a number of different approaches, but each has its drawbacks and critics. It may well be that each is capable of assisting organisations to analyse and understand the strengths and weaknesses of their present situation. Whether they can provide more effective organisational arrangements for the future is more debatable, however. Similarly, it is not obvious how organisations should actually achieve the process of transformation.

The Human Relations movement offers pertinent advice with regard to having clear objectives, good communication and leadership, but is less forthcoming on how change objectives should be set, and the concomitant changes planned and implemented. Contingency Theory, though, does give a procedure for setting objectives. It stresses the need to identify and analyse the situational variables an organisation faces in order to choose the most appropriate structure. However, it is also silent on the issues of planning and implementation, other than to imply that rational workers will accept rational propositions for change. In addition, even if organisations do manage to implement the recommendations of the Human Relations or Contingency advocates, it is not clear what degree of benefit they would derive from this, given the criticisms of these approaches.

In short, neither of the approaches discussed in this chapter appears to be the solution to all known organisational ills that their proponents seem to claim. They fail to reflect and explain the complexities of day-to-day organisational life that we all experience. In particular, the issue of organisational culture (Allaire and Firsirotu, 1984) barely gets a mention, yet, over the last three decades, its importance as both a promoter of and a barrier to organisational competitiveness has become apparent. Nor do they appear to take account of national differences and preferences, or for that matter pay regard to many of the wider societal factors that now impact on our lives, such as the need to show greater social responsibility, whether it be in the area of 'green' issues or equal opportunities. Yet it is clear that enormous changes are taking place in the world, and that others will be necessary if some of the worst predictions for the future are to be avoided. In the face of these changes and challenges facing organisations, the Classical approach, the Human Relations school and Contingency Theory have all fallen out of favour. The next chapter describes the three newer perspectives on organisational life that have become increasingly influential in the last 30 years.

TEST YOUR LEARNING

Short discussion topics

The purpose of these is to enable students to check and reflect on the topics. The discussions should last for no more than 5–10 minutes. Depending on the length of the lecture, there could be one, two or three such discussions in a session. The following are five suggested topics which address issues raised in this chapter:

1. What were the main findings of the Hawthorne Experiments?

2. What are the main differences between Theory X and Theory Y?

3. Define the term 'contingency' as used by Burns and Stalker.

4. What are the respective attributes of Mechanistic and Organic structures?

5. According to the Aston Group, size is the key contingency. State their case for this assertion.

Class debates

The purpose of class debates is to enable students to explore a topic in depth by setting up a 'for and against' debate. The class can be split into two and one half asked to research the 'for' case and the other the 'against' case. Individuals can then be chosen at random to introduce their side of the debate. Alternatively, two individuals for each side can be told in advance that they will be introducing the debate. The length of such debates depends on the time available, the size of the class and their enthusiasm for the topic. However, less than 30 minutes is probably too short and more than 60 minutes probably too long. The following are three suggested topics which address issues raised in this chapter:

1. Contingency Theory offers a better way of managing change than either the Classical or Human Relations approaches.

2. The presence of multiple contingencies in most organisations makes Contingency Theory unworkable in practice.

3. Warren Bennis's argument for the 'death of bureaucracy' has not stood the test of time.

Essay questions

1. Maslow's hierarchy of needs is a nice idea but its lack of empirical support means that it has been replaced by newer theories of motivation.

2. Evaluate the following statement: The main contribution of Contingency Theory is to see the Classical and Human Relations approaches as alternatives and not competitors.

Suggested further reading

Hendry, C (1979) Contingency Theory in practice, I. *Personnel Review*, 8(4), 39–44.
Hendry, C (1980) Contingency Theory in practice, II. *Personnel Review*, 9(1), 5–11.
Wood, S (1979) A reappraisal of the contingency approach to organization. *Journal of Management Studies*, 16, 334–54.
  Taken together, these three articles provide an excellent review of Contingency Theory.

Rose, M (1988) *Industrial Behaviour*. Penguin: Harmondsworth.
  Michael Rose gives an invaluable account of the development of the Human Relations movement and provides an interesting review of the work of Joan Woodward and the Aston Group.

Sheldrake, J (1996) *Management Theory: From Taylorism to Japanization*. International Thompson Business Press: London.
  John Sheldrake also provides an excellent review of the lives and work of the key figures in the Human Relations movement.

CASE STUDY 2

Jobs International (India) Ltd[1]

Background

Jobs International (India) Ltd is based in New Delhi and is a subsidiary of Jobs International (UK) Ltd. It is a family-owned company whose managing director and major shareholder is David Jacobs. He established the company in India in 1998 to provide advice to Indian nationals wanting to work in the UK and for UK companies wanting to recruit staff from India. It is now one of the largest job consultancies in India and represents over 100 major UK public and private sector employers. Its Indian head office is in New Delhi and there is a network of nine regional offices spread throughout India.

JI (UK) is based in London and its workload is quite light compared with the Indian operation. When JI was set up, Mr Jacobs spent most of his time in India developing the business there. Once JI (India) was firmly established, he moved back to run the London office.

In 2005, Mr Jacobs became concerned that JI's fortunes were based too much on the success of the Indian operation and began to look for opportunities to expand the London office. He came to the following conclusions:

1. The expansion of the EU into Eastern Europe and concomitant changes to UK immigration rules could lead to a reduced demand for Indian nationals by UK organisations.

2. There was a growing demand by UK organisations, including JI's main customers, for Eastern European workers and a reciprocal demand by them for UK jobs.

3. Though the UK market for Indian nationals might decline, the same did not appear to be the case in Australia and North America.

After much discussion with his parents, who were the other shareholders, Mr Jacobs decided upon a two-pronged expansion programme:

- JI would open offices in Eastern Europe, the first one being in Poland. These would operate on a similar basis to the Indian operation. Over the next

three years, the London office would concentrate most of its time on building this business.

- The activities of JI (India) would be expanded and refocused on North America and Australia. This would involve recruiting an Australian and a North American to lead the two new activities in India. However, both would be responsible to the Indian managing director, who would still have overall control.

Mr Jacobs had little doubt that he could make the Eastern European operation a success. However, he was more concerned with the changes to the Indian operation. He had established the business in India and had worked there full-time for the first three years of its existence. He then appointed his deputy, an English man who had spent most of his adult life in India, as managing director. This had worked well until 2004 when the managing director of JI (India) announced he was going to retire and move his family back to the UK. There was no obvious successor and eventually Mr Jacobs appointed his cousin, an English woman, to take over. She had no direct experience of India and had not worked for JI before but she had worked as a recruitment consultant with a number of major international companies and she was a very experienced manager. The fact that she was also a family member meant that she was unlikely to use the job to learn about JI and then set up a rival business in India, which was always one of Mr Jacobs' fears.

However, after 12 months, Mr Jacobs began to have doubts about the appointment. She often complained about the staff in the Indian offices, especially New Delhi, and he had heard that they were less than impressed with her. Therefore, before proceeding with the expansion of the Indian operation, he decided to carry out a change readiness audit.

The change readiness audit

Mr Jacobs contacted a consultant he knew in India who was experienced at carrying out such audits. The consultant was English but had worked in India for 30 years. Mr Jacobs was aware that he had to be sensitive in dealing with his cousin, the managing director of JI (India). He knew that if he upset her, she would contact her parents, who would contact his parents and

[1] This case study is based on research conducted by Ambika Nagar. I am very grateful for her permission to draw on her work.

things could become quite fraught. As he said to a colleague, 'I'm now finding out the downside of employing family.' Therefore, Mr Jacobs told his cousin that the audit was to help her sort out the problems she had encountered and prepare the way for the expansion of business. The consultant told the same story.

The consultant spent a month examining the Indian operation. He visited the nine regional offices but spent most of his time in New Delhi. The main findings from his audit were as follows.

Organisation and operation: Overall, the Indian operation is very profitable, though how profitable only the Indian managing director, her finance director and Mr Jacobs know. The managers of the individual offices do not know whether they make or lose money, though the new managing director has told all of them that they are less profitable than each other as an incentive to get them to change their ways and take more individual responsibility. This does not seem to have worked.

The consultant considered the organisational structure to be more traditional and hierarchical than many similar companies in India. This tended to be more in terms of attitudes rather than actual grade levels. Staff tend to wait to be told what to do and not to act on their own initiative. The consultant also thought there was lack of professionalism in how staff carried out their jobs and that the company seemed to work as separate units rather than an integrated whole. These issues were in many ways a hangover from when Mr Jacobs ran the Indian operation. He had appointed all the staff and had a paternal attachment to them. This was reflected in his style of management, which was both informal and highly centralised – he did not like to delegate. However, the operation was then much smaller. His successor tended to operate in the same way. He was also, as the consultant said, 'an old India hand and he knew how to get the best out of his staff'. Mr Jacobs' cousin, the new managing director, had a very different style. She had worked in large organisations where professionalism, teamwork and individual initiative were the order of the day. She told the staff that this was how she wanted to run JI (India). To this end, she tried to flatten the hierarchy and instil a more professional attitude among staff, but this had generated a great deal of resentment.

The consultant felt that slotting two new divisions, one for Australia and one for North America, into the existing structure might make matters worse. He also felt that neither an Australian nor a North American would be prepared to be left in the dark as to financial performance.

Staff: The new managing director stated that she wanted to be open and honest and involve all staff in the business, especially middle managers. However, attempts at 'straight talking' by the managing director appeared to be counterproductive as this was construed as negative feedback rather than open dialogue. The consultant pointed out that 'straight talking' did not sit well with the Indian culture, which tended to be more circumspect in terms of making or receiving criticism.

The staff were nervous about moves into new markets and the introduction of two new senior members of staff, neither of whom would be Indians. They had felt very comfortable in promoting the UK brand, but the proposed changes seemed to have a paralysing effect on staff. The consultant stated that 'staff are taking even less initiative than in the past and have stopped taking responsibility as they feel that they will be used as scapegoats if things go wrong'.

The staff blame the managing director for their low morale and lack of initiative. They claim that the two previous managing directors were more proactive and took a close interest in the well-being of the staff. As one employee stated, 'Mr Jacobs had his finger on the pulse of the organisation, the new managing director has no idea where the pulse is. We understand that each leader has different leadership styles, and it is not fair to compare, but the earlier levels of professionalism, commitment and service are not followed any more.' Another middle manager stated, 'We no longer feel it's our company. We're just used as target practice.'

Leadership: The managing director believes that she has been given the remit to shake JI (India) 'out of its complacent and unprofessional ways'. She is openly critical about her immediate predecessor, who she feels let staff 'get away with murder'. For example, previously, farewell gifts were presented to staff who left after being with the company for five years. She discontinued this because 'we should not reward people for leaving'. Also, staff in financial hardship could ask for an advance on their salary. This was discontinued because she felt that, 'if staff can't manage their own money, how can we trust them with the company's?'. Employees interpret such changes as showing a lack of respect. In addition, they point out that the managing director takes time off in office hours to go swimming and to the movies.

A key initiative taken by the managing director was to create a team spirit among the New Delhi and regional managers. Previously, they had tended to go their own way, with the New Delhi staff feeling superior to the regional managers whom they see as subordinates rather than colleagues. She spoke to them individually and as a group, telling them they were being unprofessional and should work as a team. The result was that both groups felt they were being bullied and shown a lack of respect.

She initiated communication sessions with staff where she would discuss the company's and individual departments' performance and areas for improvement. However, staff were hostile to discussing such matters in an open forum, and the managing director tended to be the only person who spoke. She also expressed the need for a management development programme for the company to 'bring in modern ideas and develop new talent'. Once again, staff and managers tended to see this as criticism of their performance rather than as an opportunity to develop themselves or the organisation.

Despite her somewhat rough ride since taking over, the managing director stated that she did not foresee any problems with re-orientating the existing staff towards the new business opportunities in Australia and North America. Indeed, she welcomed the idea of appointing an Australian and a North American to the company because it would give her the opportunity to bring in allies who would support her. The consultant took a much more pessimistic view of the introduction of new business and new people.

The consultant's view

The consultant's view is that there are serious problems with JI (India) which make it unlikely that the introduction of the Australian and North American business will be successful. He believes that the problems stem from three sources:

1. The company has grown quickly since it was established, but staff still see it as a small business and expect the managing director to operate as an 'owner–manager' responsible for its day-to-day operation.

2. Staff are nervous of the changes the managing director has been trying to introduce and of the proposed expansion of the business. There is also some resentment, especially among the managers, that a non-Indian and a woman was appointed as managing director. A number of the managers had hoped that they would be offered the job.

3. The managing director has been used to working in big organisations and believes that JI (India) should adopt the same standards of professionalism and teamwork she is used to. Her view is that she has made a big effort to create a team spirit but is not receiving the support and response she deserves. She is aware that some staff are resentful that she has not been prepared to adapt to Indian culture. However, she points out that it is a UK-owned company placing prospective employees with UK companies and, therefore, Indian staff need to adapt to UK ways of doing business. As to her taking time off in working hours, she points out that she is always the last to leave and often works weekends. Therefore, if she takes few hours off during the day, it is no one's business but her own.

Questions

1. If the consultant had adopted a contingency perspective, would this have changed or reinforced his view of what was wrong with JI (India)?

2. Evaluate the following statement: The main problem with the new managing director's approach was that she could not decide whether to adopt a Theory X or Theory Y approach to managing her staff.

3. To what extent is Contingency Theory irrelevant in situations such as JI (India) where the main issue is a clash of cultures?

In search of new paradigms

Learning objectives

After studying this chapter, you should be able to:

- understand the reasons for the emergence of new organisational paradigms in the 1980s and 1990s;
- describe the principal features of the Culture–Excellence approach;
- list the core advantages and disadvantages of the Culture–Excellence approach;
- describe the central elements of the Japanese approach to management;
- understand the key advantages and disadvantages of the Japanese approach;
- discuss the main features of organisational learning;
- appreciate the chief advantages and disadvantages of organisational learning;
- compare the similarities and differences between Culture–Excellence, organisational learning and Japanese management;
- appreciate the implications for organisational change of these three paradigms.

MINI CASE STUDY 3.1

Culture – the great cure-all?

Lofty aspirations

On July 4 [2012], Bob Diamond, Barclays' former chief executive, spent just under three hours answering questions from a House of Commons committee about the UK bank's role in the industry-wide rigging of benchmark interest rates. Committee members and Mr Diamond himself kept coming back to one lofty concept, directly referred to 50 times during the hearing: culture. There is a lot of it about. Culture was the "secret sauce" at Goldman Sachs, of which there is now "virtually no trace", according to Greg Smith, a disgruntled former employee of the US investment bank. The "ingrained conventions of Japanese culture" were behind the crisis at the tsunami-hit Fukushima nuclear plant, says the man chairing the probe into the disaster. British pharmaceutical group GlaxoSmithKline has made "a culture of putting patients first" a priority, having clamped down on aggressive selling and marketing of blockbuster drugs that this month resulted in a $3 billion settlement with the US government. Five years after the global financial and economic crisis began, political and regulatory reforms have either not yet taken effect or failed to allay public fury and frustration about corporate excess.

In the financial services sector, dissonance between banks' traditional image as prudent and conservative, and successive revelations of misselling and misbehaviour – particularly in investment banking operations, such as those at Barclays – has fuelled the anger. It has also shifted the political rhetoric from a focus on legal and regulatory solutions to a wider debate about the need to change a corporate culture focused on short-term profits and bonuses. As Texas Democratic Representative Ruben Hinojosa told Jamie Dimon, JPMorgan Chase chief executive, at a June congressional hearing into a trading fiasco that has cost the US bank $5.8 billion this year: "There needs to be an evaluation of not only prudent regulations but also the broken culture of Wall Street." Increasingly, bad culture seems to be the obvious culprit at organisations and industries in crisis, and good culture the potential saviour.

Letters released this week show that in 2010 Hector Sants, then chief executive of Barclays' regulator, the Financial Services Authority, was concerned, in assessing Mr Diamond's suitability to become chief executive, that he should "set the right culture" for the bank. His letter echoes speeches made around the same time in which Mr Sants expressed his personal view that the watchdog could intervene to modify an unacceptable culture. "I think we do have the means of intervention," he told a conference in June 2010. "For example, influencing the composition of management; influencing incentives for good behaviour; influencing the training and competence regime; and deterring poor behaviour."

It was McKinsey consultants Tom Peters and Robert Waterman who popularised culture as a management tool with their 1982 analysis of the best US companies, *In Search of Excellence*. "Without exception, the dominance and coherence of culture proved to be an essential quality of the excellent companies [we identified]," they wrote. Moreover, "the stronger the culture and the more it was directed toward the marketplace, the less need was there for policy manuals, organisation charts, or detailed procedure and rules".

It is no coincidence that today's obsession with culture coincides with concerns about whether multinationals have become too big to manage, just as the earlier vogue bloomed as companies became more complex and global. In an echo of the Peters and Waterman findings, Bob Diamond, former Barclays chief executive, said in a speech last year: "For me the evidence of culture is how people behave when no one is watching." But even the original studies pointed out that a strong culture could be dangerous if it led to "group think", or mutually reinforcing bad behaviour.

One of the drivers behind the 1980s analysis was the realisation in the US that successful Japanese groups boasted strong shared values. Yet in recent months, the Olympus scandal – in which directors helped chairmen of the Japanese photographic company keep accounting tricks secret for years – has been blamed on the same close-knit local culture. This month, the chairman of the commission looking into the Fukushima disaster laid the blame for the 2011 nuclear plant failure on Japan's "reflexive obedience; our reluctance to question authority; our devotion to 'sticking with programme'; our groupism; and our insularity". Paradoxically, a good corporate culture only lasts if its adherents are also allowed, even encouraged, to challenge it.

Introduction

Organisations have come a long way from the days of Frederick Taylor, who saw them as machines and employees as mere cogs in them, or Henry Ford, who believed that his customers should unquestioningly accept the products his 'machine' turned out; once famously declaring: 'A customer can have a car of any color he wants, so long as it is black' (Witzel, 2003a: 113). Nowadays, the customer is seen as king or queen and woe betide the organisation that fails to cater for their ever-changing and fickle tastes (Denegri-Knott *et al*, 2006).

Similarly, and not unrelatedly, the view that organisations are machines has been replaced by the notion that they are social systems with their own distinct and unique cultures. Crucially, the notion of machine efficiency has been replaced by cultural effectiveness. As Mini Case Study 3.1 shows, 'good' cultures allegedly lead to success and 'bad' cultures to failure.

There has been a sea change in how organisations are seen and managed. Out has gone the preoccupation with structure of the Classical school and Contingency Theory; similarly, out has gone the narrow focus on people and jobs of the Human Relations school. In their place is an emphasis on organisations as social systems, mini societies, with their own unique cultures. Indeed, such has been the change in attitudes towards running organisations in the past three decades that many now speak of organisations as having gone through a paradigm shift. If this is so, what do we mean by a paradigm shift and what brought it about?

Although he did not invent the word, it was the American philosopher of science Thomas Kuhn (1962) who, in his book *The Structure of Scientific Revolutions*, gave a new importance to the notion of 'paradigms'. He defined a paradigm as a universally recognised scientific achievement that over a period of time provides model problems and solutions to a community of practitioners. Kuhn was interested in how new ideas and frameworks for carrying out scientific work (i.e. paradigms) supplant old ones in the physical sciences. However, from the late 1960s onwards, a growing body of social scientists adopted the Kuhnian approach to their own disciplines with great enthusiasm. In the intervening period, new, varying, competing and controversial definitions of the term have been put forward (Burrell, 1997). As far as its applicability to organisations is concerned, a paradigm can be defined as a way of looking at and interpreting the world: a framework of basic assumptions, theories and models that are commonly and strongly accepted and shared within a particular field of activity at a particular point in time (Collins, 1998; Mink, 1992; Reed, 1992). However, as situations change and people's perceptions change, existing paradigms lose their relevance and new ones emerge. Handy (1986: 389) noted:

> When Copernicus suggested that the earth was not at the centre of the universe he was, though he knew it not, a paradigm revolutionary. But it was the minds of men that changed, not the motions of the planets, and the way in which they now viewed that same universe had a profound effect on their beliefs, values and behaviour.

In the previous two chapters we have discussed the paradigms that, in the West at least, have emerged and become common currency in the field of management and organisation theory. Though these paradigms have their adherents as well as critics, increasingly managers have experienced real difficulties in achieving competitive success when applying them in today's turbulent, complex and diverse business world. In consequence, especially over the last three decades, both academics and practitioners have been searching for new recipes for organisational success.

It was in the US that the search for new paradigms first became apparent. It was the rise of Japanese industrial and economic might that forced American businesses to question what they did and how they did it, as Morgan (1986: 111) relates:

> During the 1960s the confidence and impact of American management and industry seemed supreme. Gradually, but with increasing force, through the 1970s the performance of Japanese automobile, electronic, and other manufacturing industries began to change all this. Japan began to take command of international markets.

The productivity gap between Japanese and American companies was starkly high-lighted in a *Harvard Business Review* article by Johnson and Ouchi (1974). The authors claimed that Japanese workers, assembling the same product using the same technology, were 15 per cent more productive than their American counterparts.

> For an American audience this was a shocking statement, confirming the worst fears of a decline in the USA's competitive edge over the rest of the world. Since the Second World War American manufacturers had grown accustomed to out-producing and out-performing every foreign competitor. The era of the Cold War had led Americans to believe that the only danger to their general security sprang from communism and specifically the Soviet Union. The notion that their comprehensively vanquished enemies and strategic clients, the Japanese, might be poised to overhaul them technically and even economically was unpalatable, even unbelievable.
>
> (Sheldrake, 1996: 185)

It was not only the US that took fright; in the 1970s and 1980s, all over the Western world, businesses and governments too woke up to the Japanese challenge. Even West Germany, which prided itself on producing well-engineered and high-quality products such as BMW and Mercedes cars, found that the Japanese were producing cars such as the Lexus that were not only half the price but also better engineered and of far superior quality (Williams *et al*, 1991).

Nor was it just the Japanese challenge that frightened the West. The 1970s also saw the return of unemployment and inflation, both assumed to have been eliminated, and the occurrence of the two 'oil shocks', which highlighted most Western nations' precarious reliance on imported energy. Therefore, old certainties were being challenged and new orthodoxies began to arise. Rather like Copernicus, Japan made the West see the world, and its place in it, from a new perspective. In effect, in the last 30 years or so, the world has turned on its axis. The days of the mass production of standardised products appear to be over; the key words now are variety, flexibility and customisation.

In the 1980s, Perez (1983) and Freeman (1988) described the characteristics of this emerging techno-economic rationale (*see* Ideas and perspectives 3.1). It has been given a variety of names. In the 1970s, Daniel Bell (1973) heralded *The Coming of Post-Industrial Society*. In the 1980s, other writers spoke of the 'post-Fordist' or 'post-Taylorist' era (Whitaker, 1992). Increasingly, in the 1990s, the term 'postmodernism' was used to describe the changes taking place in the world in general and organisations in particular (Hassard, 1993). These

---

IDEAS AND PERSPECTIVES 3.1

The new techno-economic rationale

- A shift towards information-intensive rather than energy- or materials-intensive products.

- A change from dedicated mass production systems towards more flexible systems that can accommodate a wider range of products, smaller batches and more frequent design changes – 'economies of scale' are being replaced by 'economies of scope'.

- A move towards the greater integration of processes and systems within companies and between suppliers and customers, which permits a more rapid response to market and customer requirements.

Source: Perez (1983) and Freeman (1988).

terms, particularly the debate around postmodernism and its alternatives, will be discussed in Chapter 4. For now, however, what we need to recognise is that it is not necessarily that the nature of organisations themselves has changed fundamentally, though significant changes in size, technology and complexity have certainly taken place. It is rather that, like those who listened to Copernicus, we are seeing their role in the established order from a different perspective and beginning to see new possibilities and new challenges.

It is the emergence of these new possibilities and challenges that has motivated Western organisations to undertake a fundamental reassessment of their objectives and operations, rather than a mere change in fashion or managerial whim – though this is obviously present as well (Collins, 2000; Huczynski, 1993; Kennedy, 1994). In effect, what we can see from the beginning of the 1980s is the emergence of a paradigm shift, or, to be more accurate, the search for new, more appropriate paradigms. It seemed as if the changes taking place in the business environment were so enormous and rapid that existing paradigms, whatever their past merits, were breaking down and new ones emerging.

In this chapter, we examine the three proto-paradigms that have come to dominate Western managerial thinking and writing since the 1980s: the Culture–Excellence approach, the Japanese Management approach and the Organisational Learning approach. What links all these three is the notion of culture. As Mini Case Study 3.1 shows, we now live in an era where culture is seen as the great cure-all. Whatever the problem, culture is the answer, even (or especially) if the problem is 'bad' culture. However, as this chapter will show, these three proto-paradigms are distinct approaches to running organisations with different origins and differing implications for management. Culture–Excellence arose as an attempt to counter Japanese competitiveness by drawing on and re-shaping the American and British traditions of individualism and free market liberalism. It emerged in the early 1980s, and its principal exponents (Tom Peters and Robert Waterman, 1982; Rosabeth Moss Kanter, 1989; and Charles Handy, 1989) have attempted both to predict and to promote the ways in which successful (excellent) companies will and should operate in the future.

Though the Japanese management paradigm is a very different animal, which has been developed in Japan over the last 60 years, its success is seen as stemming from the unique culture of Japanese firms. Because of the success of the Japanese economy and Japanese companies in the 1960s, 1970s and 1980s, the Japanese approach attracted much interest in the West – a classic case of 'if you can't beat them, join them'. This was especially the case in the UK, where Japanese inward investment (by household names such as Honda, Nissan and Toyota) generated a great deal of debate regarding the impact and merits of 'Japanisation' and whether or not the culture of Japanese firms could be replicated in Western settings (Ackroyd et al, 1988; Dale and Cooper, 1992; Hannam, 1993; Turnbull, 1986; Whitehill, 1991). This was also the case in the US, where Japan and Japanese methods were seen, in turn, as either a threat or a lifeline to American industrial pre-eminence (Kanter et al, 1992; Pascale and Athos, 1982; Peters, 1993; Schonberger, 1982).

The third approach, organisational learning, came to the fore in the early 1990s. Leading management thinkers, in particular Chris Argyris (1992), have been interested in organisational learning for over 40 years. However, it is only in the last 20 years or so that the concept has become popularised as an engine for organisational competitiveness through the work of Senge (1990) in the US and Pedler, Boydell and Burgoyne (1989) in the UK. One of the key benefits claimed for organisational learning is that it is a universal approach which draws on and is consistent with both Western and Japanese organisational traditions (Hedlund and Nonaka, 1993; Probst and Buchel, 1997). However, like the other two approaches, the success of the learning approach is predicated on organisations possessing or developing an effective learning culture.

Of course, the emergence of these paradigms has been played out in an era when globalisation has advanced apace (see Chapter 14). With the increase in globalisation has come the notion that the integration of the world economy and ready availability of core technologies will have a 'convergence' effect whereby national differences, especially in terms of institutional structures and practices, will disappear (Dowrick and DeLong, 2003). However, this convergence does not seem to be taking place with organisational theories and practices. Though the Culture–Excellence and Japanese approaches have some similarities, for example the resemblance between the Japanese passion for quality and the Culture–Excellence school's fervent advocacy of the pursuit of excellence, the two also have significant differences, as will become clear. While the Japanese approach has clearly influenced the Culture–Excellence thinkers, the influence of the latter in Japan has been small: the two may be competing approaches in the West, but certainly not in Japan. Though they are dynamic and developing paradigms, and have some common elements, the fact that they have both been around for quite a long time now makes it unlikely that a merger between the two is going to happen. The organisational learning approach, though it draws on both Western and Japanese organisational traditions, is not an attempt to fuse or merge the Culture–Excellence and Japanese approaches, nor does it seem as if it is likely to replace either of them. Instead, it represents an alternative attempt to provide Western countries, particularly the US, with an approach to managing organisations that will allow them in the twenty-first century to enjoy the sort of dominance they enjoyed for much of the twentieth century.

It will be argued in the conclusion to this chapter that, although these three proto-paradigms offer new possibilities, they also raise familiar controversies, not least regarding the role and treatment of people. Therefore, as the following discussion of the three approaches will show, while attempting to become new paradigms, they still have to answer old questions.

The Culture–Excellence approach

The core of the Culture–Excellence approach is summed up in the following quote from a report by the management consultants Bain & Company:

> Culture is at the heart of competitive advantage, particularly when it comes to sustaining high performance. Bain & Company research found that nearly 70 percent of business leaders agree: Culture provides the greatest source of competitive advantage. In fact, more than 80 percent believe an organization that lacks a high-performance culture is doomed to mediocrity.
>
> (Rogers *et al*, 2006: 1)

Though predominantly a North American perspective, the Culture–Excellence approach has also found strong adherents in Europe. Therefore, the examination of this approach will draw on the work of key writers from both sides of the Atlantic, namely Tom Peters and Robert Waterman, Rosabeth Moss Kanter and Charles Handy. These writers are all practising and internationally recognised management consultants; Handy and Kanter are also distinguished academics. Consequently, though their work is attempting to predict and promote the way firms will or should operate in the future, it is firmly based on what they believe the best companies are doing now or planning to do in the future.

The work of these four people formed the spearhead of the movement that simultaneously charted and created the new organisational forms that have appeared over the last 30 years. Their work – though both complementary and distinct – is of profound influence in shaping our understanding of what the future holds in the field of management. This work will now be examined in detail, starting with the American perspectives of Peters and Waterman, and Kanter, and concluding with Handy's British perspective.

Tom Peters and Robert Waterman's search for excellence

> If Drucker was the first guru, it was Tom Peters who elevated gurudom to high art. . . . Mr Peters remains one of the handful of A-list gurus able to command $50,000-plus a day to address a senior management retreat or sales conference. His highly charged stage performance still draws crowds.
> (London, 2005: 11)

Tom Peters has been, arguably, the most influential management consultant of the last 30 years. His books sell in millions, his seminars fill auditoriums, and his newspaper column was syndicated across the world (Collins, 2008). He catapulted to international fame when he co-authored, along with Robert Waterman, *In Search of Excellence: Lessons from America's Best-Run Companies* (Peters and Waterman, 1982). Not only is this the best-selling business book of all time, it has also been called the greatest business book of all time (Collins, 2008). It is difficult to overestimate the impact this book has had. At a time when Western economies were on the rocks and Japanese companies appeared to be sweeping all before them, *In Search of Excellence* seemed to offer a way, perhaps the only way, for Western companies to regain their competitiveness (Crainer, 1995).

The origins of the book lie in a major study of the determinants of organisational excellence, which Peters and Waterman carried out when working for the management consultants McKinsey and Company. They used the now-famous McKinsey 7 S Framework (*see* Ideas and perspectives 3.2), which they had developed jointly with Richard Pascale and Anthony Athos, to study 62 of America's most successful companies.

IDEAS AND PERSPECTIVES 3.2

The 7 S Framework

Strategy: plan or course of action for the allocation of scarce resources in order to achieve specified goals.

Structure: the main features of the organisation chart and how the various parts of an organisation are linked.

Systems: the organisation's formalised procedures and processes.

Staff: the composition of the workforce, i.e. engineers, managers, etc.

Style: the behaviour of key managers and also the cultural style of the organisation.

Shared values: the guiding concepts and meanings that infuse the organisation's members.

Skills: the distinctive capabilities possessed by individuals, groups and the organisation as whole.

Source: Peters and Waterman (1982).

Peters and Waterman concluded that it was the four 'soft' Ss (staff, style, shared values and skills) that held the key to business success. In stressing the 'soft' Ss, they challenged the rational theories of management described in previous chapters. They argue that the rational approach is flawed because it leads to the following:

- **Wrong-headed analysis** – situation or information analysis that is considered too complex and unwieldy to be useful. This is analysis that strives to be precise about the inherently unknowable.
- **Paralysis through analysis** – the application of the rational model to such an extent that action stops and planning runs riot.
- **Irrational rationality** – where rational management techniques identify the 'right' answer irrespective of its applicability to the situation in question.

In the light of these criticisms, Peters and Waterman argue that the analytical tools that characterise the rational approach should be used only as an aid to, rather than a substitute for, human judgement. They believe that it is the freedom given to managers and employees to challenge the orthodox and to experiment with different solutions which distinguishes the excellent companies from the also-rans. In place of the rational approach, Peters and Waterman argue that there are eight key attributes that organisations need to demonstrate if they are to achieve excellence:

1. A bias for action.
2. Closeness to the customer.
3. Autonomy and entrepreneurship.
4. Productivity through people.
5. Hands-on, value-driven.
6. Stick to the knitting.
7. Simple form, lean staff.
8. Simultaneous loose–tight properties.

These are discussed in detail below.

1 A bias for action

One of the main identifiable attributes of excellent companies is their bias for action. Even though they may be analytical in approach, they also favour methods that encourage rapid and appropriate response. One of the methods devised for achieving quick action is what Peters and Waterman term 'chunking'. Chunking is an approach whereby a problem that arises in the organisation is first made manageable (i.e. broken into 'chunks') and then tackled by a small group of staff brought together specifically for that purpose. The main reason for the use of such groups, variously called project teams, task forces or quality circles, is to facilitate organisational fluidity and to encourage action. Key characteristics of these groups are as follows:

- They usually comprise no more than ten members.
- They are voluntarily constituted.
- The life of the group is usually between three and six months.
- The reporting level and seniority of the membership is appropriate to the importance of the problem to be dealt with.

- The documentation of the group's proceedings is scant and very informal.
- These groups take on a limited set of objectives, which are usually determined, monitored, evaluated and reviewed by themselves.

Chunking is merely one example of the bias for action that exists in excellent companies and reflects their willingness to innovate and experiment. These companies' philosophy for action is simple: 'Do it, fix it, try it.' Therefore, excellent companies are characterised by small, *ad hoc* teams applied to solving designated problems which have first been reduced to manageable proportions. Achieving smallness is the key, even though the subject or task may be large. Smallness induces manageability and a sense of understanding, and allows a feeling of ownership.

2 Close to the customer

Excellent companies really do get close to the customer, while others merely talk about it. The customer dictates product, quantity, quality and service. The best organisations are alleged to go to extreme lengths to achieve quality, service and reliability. There is no part of the business that is closed to customers. In fact, many of the excellent companies claim to get their best ideas for new products from listening intently and regularly to their customers. The excellent companies are more 'driven by their direct orientation to the customers rather than by technology or by a desire to be the low-cost producer. They seem to focus more on the revenue-generation side of their services' (Peters and Waterman, 1982: 197).

3 Autonomy and entrepreneurship

Perhaps the most important element of excellent companies is their 'ability to be big and yet to act small at the same time. A concomitant essential apparently is that they encourage the entrepreneurial spirit among their people, because they push autonomy markedly far down the line' (Peters and Waterman, 1982: 201). Product champions are allowed to come forward, grow and flourish. Such a champion is not a blue-sky dreamer, or an intellectual giant. The champion might even be an ideal thief. But above all, the champion is the pragmatist, the one who latches on to someone else's idea, and doggedly brings something concrete and tangible out of it.

In fostering such attitudes, the excellent companies have what they label 'championing systems' which comprise three key elements (*see* Ideas and perspectives 3.3). The essence of the championing system is to foster, promote and sustain the budding entrepreneur. It is claimed that the three elements of the championing system are essential to its operation and credibility.

IDEAS AND PERSPECTIVES 3.3

The three elements of the championing system

- **The product champion** – a zealot or fanatic who believes in a product.
- **A successful executing champion** – one who has been through the process of championing a product before.
- **The godfather** – typically, an ageing leader who provides the role model for champions.

Source: Peters and Waterman (1982).

Another key part of this system is that, in some companies, product champions tend to be allocated their own 'suboptimal divisions'. These are similar to small, independent businesses and comprise independent new venture teams, run by champions with the full and total support of senior management. The suboptimal division is independent in that it is responsible for its own accounting, personnel activities, quality assurance and support for its product in the field. To encourage entrepreneurship further, teams, groups and divisions are highly encouraged by the companies' reward structures to compete among themselves for new projects.

Autonomy and entrepreneurship are also encouraged by the type of no-holds-barred communications procedures adopted by excellent companies. These exhibit the following characteristics:

- **Communication systems are informal** – even though there are lots of meetings going on at any one time, most meetings are informal and comprise staff from different disciplines gathering to talk about and solve problems.

- **Communication intensity is extraordinary** – given the freedom, the encouragement and the support (financial, moral and physical) in the organisations, it is no wonder that the level of communication between and among workers is not only informal and spontaneous but also intense. This is borne out by the common occurrence of meetings without agendas and minutes. Also, when presentations are made in these meetings, questioning of the proposal is unabashed and discussion is free and open. Those present are expected to be fully involved in such meetings and there are no 'sacred cows' that cannot be questioned.

- **Communication is given physical support** – blackboards, flip-charts and small tables that foster informal small group discussions are everywhere. The aim is to encourage people to talk about the organisation: what needs changing; what is going on; and how to improve things around the place. There are also people, variously described as dreamers, heretics, gadflies, mavericks or geniuses, whose sole purpose is to spur the system to innovate. Their job is to institutionalise innovation by initiating and encouraging experimentation. They can also call on staff in other divisions of the organisation to assist them in this process, as well as having financial resources at their disposal.

This intense communication system also acts as a remarkably tight control system, in that people are always checking on each other to see how each is faring. This arises out of a genuine desire to keep abreast of developments in the organisation rather than any untoward motive. One result of this is that teams are more prudent in their financial expenditure on projects. Another is that the sea of inquisitors act as 'idea generators', thereby ensuring that teams are not dependent entirely on their own devices to innovate and solve problems. This usually also ensures that all options are considered before a final decision is made. The concomitant result of this fostering of creativity is that senior management is more tolerant of failure, knowing full well that champions have to make many tries, and consequently suffer some failures, in the process of creating successful innovations.

4 Productivity through people

A cherished principle of the excellent companies is that they treat their workers with respect and dignity; they refer to them as partners. This is because people, rather than systems or machines, are seen as the primary source of quality and productivity gains. Therefore, there is 'tough-minded respect for the individual and the willingness to train him, to set reasonable and clear expectations for him, and to grant him practical autonomy to step out and contribute directly to his job' (Peters and Waterman, 1982: 239). There is a closeness and family feeling in such companies; indeed many of the 'partners' see the organisation as an extended family. The slogans of such companies tend to reflect this view of people: 'respect the individual', 'make people winners', 'let them stand out', 'treat people as adults'.

5 Hands-on, value-driven

Excellent companies are value-driven; they are clear about what they stand for and take the process of value-shaping seriously. There is an implicit belief that everyone in the organisation, from the top to the bottom, should be driven by the values of the organisation; hence the great effort, time and money spent to inspire people by and inculcate them with these values:

> These values are almost always stated in qualitative, rather than quantitative, terms. When financial objectives are mentioned, they are almost always ambitious but never precise. Furthermore, financial and strategic objectives are never stated alone. They are always discussed in the context of the other things the company expects to do well. The idea that profit is a natural by-product of doing something well, and not an end in itself, is almost always universal. (Peters and Waterman, 1982: 284)

Implanting these values is a primary responsibility of the individual members of the management team. They set the tone by leading from the front. Coherence and homogeneity must, however, first be created among senior management by regular meetings (both formal and informal). The outcome of this is that management speaks with one voice. They are passionate in preaching the organisation's values. They unleash excitement, not in their offices, but mainly on the shopfloor where the workers are. Inculcating these values, however, is a laborious process and persistence is vital in achieving the desired goal.

6 Stick to the knitting

Acquisition or internal diversification for its own sake is not one of the characteristics of excellent companies. They must stick to the knitting – do what they know best. But when they do acquire, they do it in an experimental fashion, by first 'dipping a toe in the water'. If the water does not feel good, they get out fast. Acquisitions are always in fields related to their core activities and they never acquire any business that they do not know how to run. As a general rule, they 'move out mainly through internally generated diversification, one manageable step at a time' (Peters and Waterman, 1982: 279).

7 Simple form, lean staff

A guiding principle in excellent companies is to keep things simple and small. Structurally, the most common form is the 'product division'. This form, which is rarely changed, provides the essential touchstone that everybody understands and from which the complexities of day-to-day life can be approached. Since the use of teams, groups and task forces for specific projects is a common stock-in-trade of these companies, most changes in structure are made at the edges, such as by allocating one or two people to an *ad hoc* team. By adopting this approach, the basic structure is left in place, while all other things revolve and change around it. This gives these organisations great flexibility but still enables them to keep their structures simple, divisionalised and autonomous.

Such simple structures require only a small, lean staff at the corporate and middle management levels. This results in fewer administrators and more doers: 'It is not uncommon to find a corporate staff of fewer than 100 people running a multi-billion dollar enterprise'

(Peters and Waterman, 1982: 15). Therefore, in excellent companies, flat structures, with few layers, and slimmed-down bureaucracies – which together allow flexibility and rapid communication – are the order of the day.

8 Simultaneous loose–tight properties

This is the 'firm and free' principle. On the one hand, it allows the excellent companies to control everything tightly, while on the other hand allowing and indeed encouraging individual innovation, autonomy and entrepreneurship. These properties are jointly achieved through the organisation's culture – its shared values and beliefs. By sharing the same values, self-control and self-respect result in each person becoming their own, and everyone else's, supervisor. The individual members of the organisation know they have the freedom, and are encouraged, to experiment and innovate. They also know that their actions will be scrutinised and judged, however, with the utmost attention paid to the impact they have on product quality, targets and, above all, the customer. The focus is on building and expanding the frontiers of the business. The ultimate goal is to be the best company, and in the final analysis, this is the benchmark against which the discipline and flexibility of the individual will be measured.

In summary, Peters and Waterman maintain that the main attributes of excellent companies are flat, anti-hierarchical structures; innovation and entrepreneurship; small corporate and middle management staffs; reward systems based on contribution rather than position or length of service; brain power rather than muscle power; and strong, flexible cultures.

Peters and Waterman's vision of the organisation of the future, based on their study of leading American companies, has proved extremely influential, not only in the business world but in academia as well. This is not to say (as will be shown later) that they are without their critics; however, there is little doubt that they laid the groundwork, especially in highlighting the important role played by culture, for other leading thinkers whose work draws on and gels with theirs.

Their vision of the future has not stood still. Peters formed his own consultancy, The Tom Peters Group, and has used this as a vehicle for developing and implementing the Culture–Excellence approach. Though not fundamentally changing his view of the need for excellent organisations, in *Thriving on Chaos* (Peters, 1989) he argued that none existed in the US. In *Liberation Management* (Peters, 1993), he placed more emphasis on the need to break organisations into smaller, more independent, more flexible units. Only by doing this, he argued, would managers be 'liberated', and thus able to achieve their – and their organisation's – full potential. In this book, Peters maintains that the age of the large corporations such as IBM and General Motors is over. He sees such companies as outmoded and uncompetitive dinosaurs, which are doomed to extinction unless they change rapidly and irreversibly. Peters argues that only rapid structural change can create the conditions for entrepreneurial cultures to emerge that both liberate managers and empower workers. Indeed, this book is nothing short of an out-and-out attack on the very existence of corporate America.

The Circle of Innovation: You Can't Shrink Your Way to Greatness (Peters, 1997a) is perhaps his most iconoclastic book. Even the format of the book is different from what has gone before. Indeed, its use of a multitude of different images, font types and font sizes and, in some cases, almost surreal page layouts, makes it more like a pop video than a traditional book. The message could not be clearer: just as this book is innovative in its format, so organisations must be innovative if they are to survive. His attack on present and past organisational practices, stability and any sense of permanence is keener and more vitriolic than ever. Professionalism, rules, balance, propriety, logic and consensus are all outmoded concepts, he argues. Peters (1997a: 76) quotes Dee Hock, founder of the Visa Network, who said: 'The problem is never how to get new, innovative thoughts into your mind, but how to get the old ones out.'

For Peters, organisational forgetting is far more important than organisational learning. Future success, he argues, is not related to what an organisation has done in the past, nor what is bringing it success now, but how innovative it will be in identifying new products, services and markets. He makes a strong, almost messianic, plea for organisations to centre themselves on innovation. Peters argues that innovation demands obsession, tension, being provocative, and having no market peers looking over your shoulder. As firms achieve parity in terms of quality and costs, he believes that only a constant commitment to being different, to continuous innovation, will allow companies to differentiate themselves from their competitors.

Just as quality was seen as everyone's job in the 1980s, so Peters maintains that innovation must also become everyone's job now. In terms of structure, organisations must adopt a network or even a virtual structure, where small groups and even individuals have the freedom to self-manage themselves, to make connections and break connections as they see fit. Indeed, the subtitle of this book could well be 'Anarchy rules!'.

Whereas in *In Search of Excellence*, he and Robert Waterman put forward their eight attributes of excellence, this book is structured around his 15 points on The Circle of Innovation (*see* Ideas and perspectives 3.4).

Trying to follow Peters' train of thought through his various books is like trying to catch mist – just when you think you have got it, it slips through your hands. Indeed, Peters (1997a: xv) takes pride in his inconsistency: '"They" call me inconsistent. I consider that a badge of honor.' As Peters often remarks: 'If you're not confused, you're not paying attention'

IDEAS AND PERSPECTIVES 3.4

The Circle of Innovation

- Distance is dead.
- Destruction is cool.
- You can't live without an eraser.
- We are all Michelangelos.
- Welcome to the white-collar revolution.
- All values come from the professional services.
- The intermediary is doomed.
- The system is the solution.
- Create waves of lust.
- Tommy Hilfiger knows.
- Become a connoisseur of talent.
- It's a woman's world.
- Little things are the only things.
- Love all, serve all.
- We're here to live life out loud.

Source: Peters (1997a).

(London, 2005). Originally he saw the pursuit of 'excellence' as the only way to save corporate America from annihilation by its Japanese competitors (and thus maintain the US as the premier industrial nation). Then, in *Liberation Management*, Peters (1993) argued that corporate America needed to be destroyed in order for America to survive. The message from *The Circle of Innovation* is that, with the business world in a permanent state of chaos, the only way for any organisation to survive is by constantly reinventing itself through a ceaseless process of innovation and change.

Nevertheless, though he offers some new tools and techniques, and the tone of his work has become more strident and zealot-like over the years, in essence he is still promoting the concepts first developed in *In Search of Excellence*. He argues (Peters, 2006) that the eight key attributes of excellence which formed the core of the book have proved their staying power and become the way that winning businesses organise themselves and motivate their people. He continues to maintain that the market is not simply the final arbiter of success, but the only arbiter. Meeting the ever-increasing appetite for instant gratification is the only way to survive. Innovation, i.e. autonomy and entrepreneurship, is now the prime attribute of excellence and the only guarantee of success. For Peters, large, bureaucratic organisations based on command and control systems are the enemy of excellence. Peters' (1997a: 493) view of how organisations should be run is, perhaps, best summed up by a quotation he cites from the racing driver Mario Andretti: 'If things seem under control, you're just not going fast enough.'

Yet for all Peters' continued stridency in presenting his recipe for corporate resurgence, his later books also seem to contain a greater sense of frustration. More than 30 years after *In Search of Excellence*, Peters' message has still not been acted upon by the vast majority of the business world and, as Collins (2008: 331) noted: 'Peters' relationship with the corporate world is strained, and, increasingly, unproductive.'

Rosabeth Moss Kanter's post-entrepreneurial model

Kanter is a professor at the Harvard Business School. Her early work concerned Utopian communities, such as the Shakers, but she then went on to study business organisations. O'Hara (2008: 1) commented that:

> At 65, Kanter boasts an impressive CV. She has 22 honorary doctorates, was editor of the Harvard Business Review in the early 1990s, was named one of the '50 most influential business thinkers in the world', and has spent decades studying corporate governance and advising governments and business.

Kanter first came to prominence with her (1977) book, *Men and Women of the Corporation*. This was an intensive examination of corporate America, which she saw as bureaucratic, unimaginative and uninspiring. In her next book, *The Change Masters* (Kanter, 1983), she offered her personal recipe for overcoming what she saw as the malaise and lack of competitiveness of the US. The book painted corporate America as being in transition; it recognised that the corporatism of the past no longer worked, but was not sure where the future lay. Kanter (1983) argued that it lay in American and not Japanese ideas, and particularly in unleashing individual dynamism through empowerment and greater employee involvement.

Though her earlier books were clearly in tune with Peters and Waterman's work, it is Kanter's (1989) *When Giants Learn to Dance: Mastering the challenges of strategy, management, and careers in the 1990s* that most complements and develops their work by attempting to define what organisations need to be like in the future if they are to be successful. Kanter called for a revolution in business management to create what she termed post-entrepreneurial organisations. She used this term:

> because it takes entrepreneurship a step further, applying entrepreneurial principles to the traditional corporation, creating a marriage between entrepreneurial creativity and corporate discipline, cooperation, and teamwork. (Kanter, 1989: 9–10)

Kanter maintained:

> If the new game of business is indeed like Alice-in-Wonderland croquet, then winning it requires faster action, more creative maneuvering, more flexibility, and closer partnerships with employees and customers than was typical in the traditional corporate bureaucracy. It requires more agile, limber management that pursues opportunity without being bogged down by cumbersome structures or weighty procedures that impede action. Corporate giants, in short, must learn how to dance. (Kanter, 1989: 20)

She argues that today's corporate elephants need to learn to dance as nimbly and speedily as mice if they are to survive in our increasingly competitive and rapidly changing world. Companies must constantly be alert and on their guard, and keep abreast of their competitors' intentions. By evaluating the response of modern organisations to the demands placed upon them, Kanter produced her post-entrepreneurial model of how the organisation of the future should operate. She sees post-entrepreneurial organisations as pursuing three main strategies:

1. Restructuring to find synergies.

2. Opening boundaries to form strategic alliances.

3. Creating new ventures from within – encouraging innovation and entrepreneurship.

These are detailed below.

1 Restructuring to find synergies

Synergy occurs where the whole adds up to more than the sum of its constituent parts. In an age where resources are scarce, one of the priorities of organisations is to make every part of the business add value to the whole. The essence of this approach is to identify and concentrate on the core business areas and to remove all obstacles and impediments to their efficient and effective operation. Therefore, all non-core activities are eliminated, and authority is devolved to the appropriate levels of the business: those in the front line. In practice this means selling off a company's non-core activities and ensuring that what remains, especially at the corporate and middle-management levels, is lean and efficient. Nevertheless, it is not sufficient merely to have a strategy of reducing the size of the organisational bureaucracy. Companies must also ensure that the essential tasks that these people previously carried out are still undertaken. This can be accomplished in a number of ways, such as the use of computers to carry out monitoring and information-gathering, devolving greater responsibility and power down to individual business units, and contracting out services and tasks previously carried out in-house.

The result is to create flatter, more responsive and less complex organisations that have a greater degree of focus than in the past. Kanter argues that such radical changes need to be well planned, however, and executed with care and in a way that ensures that employee motivation is increased, not eliminated.

2 Opening boundaries to form strategic alliances

With the slimming-down of the organisation and the contracting-out of some of its functions, there arises the need to pool resources with other organisations, to band together to exploit opportunities and to share ideas and information. These alliances take three forms: service alliances, opportunistic alliances and stakeholder alliances. The first, a service alliance, is where two or more organisations form a cross-company consortium to undertake a special project with a limited lifespan. Such alliances are usually considered when the resources of the various partners are insufficient to allow them to undertake the project by themselves. For this reason, and not surprisingly, many such alliances involve research and development (R&D) projects. The collaboration between Ford and General Motors on research into the development of new materials for making cars is an example of this. This approach allows organisations to mobilise resources, often on a large scale, while limiting their exposure and protecting their independence. It is the limited purpose of the consortium that makes it possible even for competitors to join together for their mutual benefit.

The second form, an opportunistic alliance, comprises a joint venture whose aim is to take advantage of a particular opportunity that has arisen: 'the two principal advantages behind this kind of alliance are competence-enhancing ones: technology transfer or market access or both' (Kanter, 1989: 126). An example of such an alliance was the link-up between the Rover Group and Honda Motors; the former gained access to Japanese know-how, while the latter gained greater access to the European market. However, as Kanter (1989: 126) pointed out, such alliances are not always equally beneficial: 'Once one of the partners has gained experience with the competence of the other, the alliance is vulnerable to dissolution – the opportunity can now be pursued without the partner.'

The third form, a stakeholder alliance, unlike the previous two, is seen as a continuing, almost permanent partnership between an organisation and its key stakeholders, generally considered to be its employees, customers and suppliers. There is a growing awareness among employees, trade unions and management of the need to see each other as partners in the same enterprise rather than rivals. A similar case is made for treating customers and suppliers as partners too. The main reason for the organisation to exist is to serve its customers; therefore, there is a need to keep close to them, not only to be aware of their present concerns and future needs but also to gain ideas regarding potential joint product development. In the same way, the organisation relies on its suppliers, who will in any case want to get closer to them as their customers. Stakeholder alliances have gained a growing band of adherents in Britain in recent years, especially, though not exclusively, among Japanese companies such as Nissan Motors (Partnership Sourcing Ltd, 1991a; Wickens, 1987). As Kanter points out, major innovations in technology and organisational systems require longer-term investments. Companies can only enter into such investments if they are secure in the knowledge that their key stakeholders are themselves committed to the same aims and approach.

The result of these alliances is that structures and positions within organisations will change, sometimes quite dramatically. This is especially the case among senior and line managers, but even previously protected groups – such as R&D specialists – will also see their roles and responsibilities change. They will have to work more closely not only with colleagues internally but also with external groupings.

3 Creating new ventures from within – encouraging innovation and entrepreneurship

Traditional organisations face a difficult balancing act between gaining the full benefits from existing mainstream business, and, at the same time, creating new activities that will become the mainstream business of the future. Kanter argues that there is a feeling in many traditional companies that opportunities are being missed owing to their inability to give staff the flexibility to pursue new ideas and develop new products. The job of creating new products or ventures used to be the sole domain of the strategic planners or the R&D departments. However, in the post-entrepreneurial organisation, this will no longer be the case: innovation will move from these specialised domains to the centre stage.

As the case studies in this book show, some organisations are deliberately forming new, independent units or entirely restructuring themselves to nurture innovation and entrepreneurship. New cultures are being created which encourage and aid innovation, and old barriers and restrictions are being eradicated. As a result of such changes, the innovative potential of employees is being tapped, and a proliferation of new ideas, products and ways of working are emerging.

The consequences of the post-entrepreneurial model

There is no doubt that the post-entrepreneurial model carries profound implications for both organisations and their employees. However, Kanter, unlike Peters and Waterman, does not see these new developments as being an unalloyed blessing, especially in the case of employees. In particular, she draws attention to three areas where the changes will have a major impact on employees: reward systems, career paths and job security, and lifestyle.

Reward systems

Employers and employees will increasingly come to look for new and more appropriate ways of rewarding and being rewarded. Indeed, with the advent of performance-related pay, in both the private and public sectors, there is already a gradual change from determining pay on the basis of a person's position and seniority to basing it on their contribution to the organisation. These changes are being driven by four main concerns: cost, equity, productivity and entrepreneurial pressure (*see* Ideas and perspectives 3.5).

These concerns are being approached through the application of three different, though not necessarily mutually exclusive, payment methods:

● The first is profit-sharing, whereby the pay of the employee is pegged to the company's performance. This means that salaries are not fixed but instead are related, by the use of a predetermined formula, to the profit of the organisation over a given period of time, usually the previous financial year.

IDEAS AND PERSPECTIVES 3.5

Drivers for changes to reward systems

Cost – the concern is that the present system is too expensive for companies that must conserve resources to be competitive.

Equity – organisations are concerned to ensure that employees are fairly rewarded for their efforts.

Productivity – organisations want to adopt reward systems that motivate high performance from employees.

Entrepreneurial pressure – companies are aware that the present system does not always adequately reward entrepreneurs for their efforts.

Source: Kanter (1989).

- The second method is the use of individual performance bonuses, which are paid on top of basic salary and are related to a predetermined performance target. This method has the advantage of enabling individuals to establish a direct correlation between their personal effort and the bonus payment they receive. Though this method is not new, the sums involved are – sometimes as much as twice basic salary.

- The last is the venture returns method, which represents perhaps the most radical break with the past. This is a scheme whereby entrepreneurs and inventors within an organisation are given the opportunity to earn returns based on the performance, in the marketplace, of the particular products or services for which they are responsible. Through this mechanism, the entrepreneur or inventor remains within the corporate fold but is paid on a similar basis to the owner of a small, independent business. The advantage is that they get the personal satisfaction and reward of running their 'own' business, while the larger organisation benefits from having highly motivated and innovative people in charge of part of its operations.

The picture created by new reward systems is not, of course, totally rosy. Where there are winners, there may also be losers; not everyone will have the opportunity or drive to be an entrepreneur, or will be in a position that lends itself to some form of bonus system. Also, many people who currently benefit from reward systems based on seniority and position may find they lose out. Older workers, established in organisations and well down their chosen career path, could be particularly adversely affected by such changes. In addition, such payment systems may be divisive and create conflict. Kanter stresses the need for teamwork, yet a situation where some members of the team are receiving high bonuses is bound to create tensions which undermine cooperation and collaboration. It may be that profit-sharing schemes, which encompass everyone in the organisation, overcome this threat to teamworking, but if everyone receives the same share of the profits irrespective of their individual contribution, the motivating effect is likely to be diminished. The result of these various approaches to pay could be minimal in terms of motivation, or could even be demotivating and indeed drive out the most experienced people in the organisation.

Careers and job security

As organisations have become slimmer and more tasks are contracted out, organisation structures are becoming flatter as entire layers of hierarchy are dispensed with. The resultant effect threatens the demise of traditional forms of career path. Kanter argues that the idea of staying with one organisation and climbing the corporate career ladder is being replaced by hopping from job to job, not necessarily in the same organisation. Therefore, instead of people relying on organisations to give shape to their career, in future the onus will be on individuals to map out and pursue their own chosen route.

This change is also affecting skill development in organisations. It will no longer be sufficient just to be skilled in a particular job or specialism, because these will certainly change over time or even entirely disappear. Increasingly, individuals are finding that the concept of job security is being replaced by 'employability security' – the ability to adapt and enhance one's skills so as to be able to perform well in different types of jobs and organisations. Careers, therefore, are being shaped by professional and entrepreneurial principles, the ability to develop and market one's skills and ideas, rather than by the sequence of jobs provided by one company. People will join organisations or accept particular jobs not, as in the past, because of job security or career progression, but in order to develop their skills, add to their knowledge and enhance their future employability.

Kanter argues:

> What people are increasingly working to acquire is the capital of their own individual reputation instead of the organisational capital that comes from learning one system well and meeting its idiosyncratic requirements. For many managers, it might be more important, for example, to acquire or demonstrate a talent that a future employer or financial investor might value than to get to know the right people several layers above in the corporation where they currently work.
> (Kanter, 1989: 324)

Having painted this picture, it must also be acknowledged that there are contradictions and dilemmas that need to be resolved. What is being created are organisations and cultures that facilitate innovation and entrepreneurship, and change and flexibility. These will be organisations where employability and loyalty are transient concepts and what matters, almost exclusively, is the individual's present performance rather than their past or potential future contribution. The two main dilemmas from the organisational perspective are, therefore, how to reconcile the above with their stated objective of treating employees as long-term partners, and how to motivate employees to work in the organisation's interest rather than their own interest. This is an especially pointed dilemma in the case of the champions and entrepreneurs on whom it is argued the future of organisations depends. This is because it is this group of highly marketable individuals who are most likely to see their careers in terms of many different jobs and organisations.

Workers' lifestyle

There are now many organisations where people have been given greater freedom to innovate and experiment, where there are strong financial rewards for increased performance levels and where people are given greater control over their area of the business. There is little doubt that in such situations people are expected, and indeed wish, to work longer hours and centre what social life they have around their work. Indeed, there is now much evidence that in most developed countries, people are working longer hours than they did in the 1980s and 1990s (Kodz *et al*, 2003; Taylor, 2007). To encourage this, many companies now provide key employees with 'concierge' services that do their shopping, find them plumbers, sort out their new car and even find them a new house and arrange the move. The purpose of this is, of course, to allow staff to focus more effectively on their job. Nevertheless, where there are benefits to the organisation, there may also be disbenefits to the individual:

> The workplace as a centre for social life and the workmate as a candidate for marriage mate is, on one level, a convenience for overloaded people who have absorbing work that leaves little time to pursue a personal life outside. It is also an inevitable consequence of the new workforce demographics. But on another level, the idea is profoundly disturbing. What about the large number of people whose personal lives are not contained within the corridors of the corporation? What about the people with family commitments outside the workplace? (Kanter, 1989: 285)

We already know the adverse cost that such work patterns can have on people's physical and mental health and on their family life. Indeed, there is now a growing tendency among senior managers of both sexes to give up work or move to less well-paid but less demanding jobs (downshifting) in order to spend more time with their families (Carvel, 2002; Etzioni, 2004; Frith, 2003). One particularly high-profile example of this in the UK was the decision in 2008 by the then Minister of Transport, Ruth Kelly, to resign as an MP in order to spend more time with her children as they grow up. However, as a survey by Hamilton (2003: vii) revealed, downshifting is not just for the rich and powerful:

The results show that 25 per cent of British adults aged 30–59 have downshifted over the last ten years. This is remarkably high and much higher than previous estimates. The proportion rises to 30 per cent if those stopping work to look after a baby or set up their own businesses are included.

The downshifting phenomenon may be the reason why Kanter believes unmarried or divorced executives are thought to be preferred to their married counterparts by some companies because it is assumed they can focus more on their job and that they are less likely to downshift given their lack of home life. Indeed, one of the UK's most high-profile businessmen, Sir Alan Sugar, recently said that he was reluctant to hire women because they might take time off to have children (Ashley, 2008). However, the consequence of this approach for organisations that have a long-hours, high-pressure culture is that they may find themselves fishing for talent in a smaller and smaller pool. However, those who seek to promote a work–life balance for their staff may find it much easier to recruit and retain the best people. The consequence, therefore, of crossing the line between motivation and exploitation may prove detrimental for both staff and the organisations which employ them.

Kanter shares Peters and Waterman's view that traditional, bureaucratic organisations stifle creativity and innovation (*see* Ideas and perspectives 3.6) and enthusiastically agrees with their call for radical organisational change. Furthermore, on the issues of innovation

---

IDEAS AND PERSPECTIVES 3.6

Rules for stifling innovation

1. Regard any new idea from below with suspicion – because it's new, and because it's from below.
2. Insist that people who need your approval to act first go through several other layers of management to get their signatures.
3. Ask departments or individuals to challenge and criticise each other's proposals. (That saves you the job of deciding; you just pick the survivor.)
4. Express your criticisms freely, and withhold your praise. (That keeps people on their toes.) Let them know they can be fired at any time.
5. Treat identification of problems as signs of failure, to discourage people from letting you know when something in their area isn't working.
6. Control everything carefully. Make sure people count anything that can be counted, frequently.
7. Make decisions to reorganise or change policies in secret, and spring them on people unexpectedly. (That also keeps people on their toes.)
8. Make sure that requests for information are fully justified, and make sure that it is not given out to managers freely. (You don't want data to fall into the wrong hands.)
9. Assign to lower-level managers, in the name of delegation and participation, responsibility for figuring out how to cut back, lay off, move people around, or otherwise implement threatening decisions you have made. And get them to do it quickly.
10. And above all, never forget that you, the higher-ups, already know everything important about this business.

Source: Kanter (1983: 100–1).

and entrepreneurship, culture and flexibility, and structure and jobs, they share much common ground. To an extent we might expect this, given that they are all writing from an American perspective, and basing their views on the experience and plans of leading US companies. Where she differs from them is that Kanter is aware that such developments have a downside as well as an upside. In particular, she draws attention to the contradiction that lies at the heart of the post-entrepreneurial model: are people – their skills, motivation and loyalty – central to the success of the organisation of the future, or are they just another commodity to be obtained and dispensed with as circumstances and their performance require?

In *The Challenge of Organizational Change*, Kanter and her co-authors (Kanter *et al*, 1992) turn their attention to the issue of managing change, and propose 'ten commandments for executing change' (*see* Ideas and perspectives 3.7).

Looking at approaches to change, Kanter *et al* (1992) distinguished between 'Bold Strokes' and 'Long Marches' (*see* Ideas and perspectives 3.8). The former relate to major strategic decisions or economic initiatives. These, they argue, can have a clear and rapid

---

IDEAS AND PERSPECTIVES 3.7

Ten commandments for executing change

1. Analyse the organisation and its need for change.
2. Create a shared vision and a common direction.
3. Separate from the past.
4. Create a sense of urgency.
5. Support a strong leader role.
6. Line up political sponsorship.
7. Craft an implementation plan.
8. Develop enabling structures.
9. Communicate, involve people, and be honest.
10. Reinforce and institutionalise change.

Source: Kanter et al (1992: 383).

IDEAS AND PERSPECTIVES 3.8

Bold Strokes and Long Marches

	Bold Strokes	Long Marches
Objective	Major strategic or economic change	Behavioural/cultural change
Timescale	Rapid, short-term change	Slow, long-term change
Involvement	Senior managers	The whole organisation

Source: Kanter et al (1992).

impact on an organisation, but they rarely lead to any long-term change in habits or culture. The Long March approach favours relatively small-scale and operationally focused initiatives that are slow to implement and whose full benefits are achieved in the long term rather than the short term. The Long March approach can impact on culture over time. Bold Strokes are initiatives taken by a few senior managers, sometimes only one; they do not rely on the support of the rest of the organisation for their success. The Long March approach, however, does. Without the involvement and commitment of the majority of the workforce, such initiatives cannot succeed.

Kanter *et al* argue that Bold Strokes and Long Marches can be complementary, rather than alternatives. For example, a major restructuring can lead to short-term economic benefits, but if the organisation is to prosper in the long term it may need to transform its culture through a Long March. However, in practice, companies appear to favour one or the other.

Kanter's works, unlike those of Peters, go far beyond the confines of the individual business enterprise to look at the workings of society as a whole. She co-authored a book, *Creating the Future*, with Michael Dukakis, the former Governor of Massachusetts (Dukakis and Kanter, 1988) and worked on his failed campaign for the US Presidency. The influence of Dukakis and successive Democrat administrations in Massachusetts can be seen in Kanter's *World Class: Thriving Locally in the Global Economy* (Kanter, 1997). Here she argues that if local communities and regions are to achieve economic security, they must see themselves as competing bodies in a mercilessly competitive global economy. Kanter paints a picture of the global economy as one where free enterprise reigns supreme and where goods, and many services, can be supplied from anywhere in the world. She points out that in the 1980s and 1990s, both blue- and white-collar American jobs were exported to whichever part of the world offered the lowest labour costs. Though supporting this example of the working of the free enterprise system as being ultimately to everyone's benefit, Kanter argues that if local communities and regions are to survive and prosper in such a fierce climate, they must learn how to defend themselves. In particular, she argues for an interventionist local state which forms alliances with local private enterprises and manipulates the local economy. By creating a business-friendly taxation system and by the selective use of public expenditure for education and infrastructure projects, it can aim to attract and retain employers, especially large corporations.

In *Innovation: Breakthrough Thinking at 3M, DuPont, GE, Pfizer, and Rubbermaid* (Kanter *et al*, 1997), Kanter returned to the internal world of the organisation and the tried and tested ground of the Culture–Excellence approach. The core arguments of the book are neatly summed up on the dust jacket, which states that inside you will discover:

- why it is impossible to approach innovation from a business school mentality;
- why investigations of any cost or size will fail if tied too tightly to current marketplace needs;
- why managers must learn to operate more intuitively;
- why cross-functional teams are more productive than any other organisational configuration;
- how fostering a competitive internal environment results in a healthy, creative tension and hungry, entrepreneurial employees.

These points are fleshed out by drawing upon the practices of the companies in the book's title and the editors' own, anecdotal, experiences. In a book whose Foreword is written by

Tom Peters, it is not perhaps surprising that many of the arguments mirror those of Peters' own book on innovation (Peters, 1997a). Indeed, the key thrust of the book is succinctly summed up in a phrase from Tom Peters' (1997b) Foreword: 'Tomorrow's victories will go to the masters of innovation! Period!' It speaks volumes for the credibility which the Culture–Excellence approach has achieved in the business world that, after nearly two decades, its two leading American proponents are still in agreement about what it takes to achieve success.

Over the last decade, Kanter has continued to develop these views (*see* Kanter, 2006). However, she has also given increased attention to issues of social and corporate responsibility, especially the relationship between what she refers to as 'principled' business practices, robust democracy and a healthy civil society (O'Hara, 2008). This is perhaps why she now argues that successful, leading, innovative organisations are not just profitable but also progressive, socially responsible human communities (Kanter, 2010). In a *Harvard Business Review* article (Kanter, 2008a), she examines the practices of leading global companies, such as IBM, Procter and Gamble and Cisco, to show how they are meeting business and societal challenges such as maintaining economic growth while achieving environmental sustainability. As Ideas and perspectives 3.9 shows, she argues that these organisations are achieving this by resolving long-standing contradictions, such as between innovation and standardisation, and business value and societal value. As always with Kanter, the key to resolving these contradictions is the marriage of culture and excellence.

IDEAS AND PERSPECTIVES 3.9

Having it both ways

When do you know a paradigm is shifting? When long-standing contradictions begin to resolve. In the giants my research team and I studied, I was struck by the number of areas in which they achieved a balance between seemingly opposing goals.

- They both globalize and localize, deriving benefits from the intersections.
- They both standardize and innovate, endeavoring to prevent consistency from becoming stifling conformity.
- They foster a common universal culture but also respect for individual differences, seeking inclusion and diversity.
- They maintain control by letting go of it, trusting people educated in the shared values to do the right thing.
- They have a strong identity but also a strong reliance on partners, whom they collaborate with but do not control.
- They produce both business value and societal value.
- They bring together the 'soft' areas (people, culture, and community responsibility) and the 'hard' areas (technology and product innovation).
- They do not abandon values in a crisis; in fact, as leaders put them to the test, crises serve to strengthen commitment to values.

Source: Kanter (2008a: 48).

In the next (and last) section on Culture–Excellence, we will examine the emergence of new organisational forms from the perspective of a British theorist: Charles Handy.

Charles Handy's emerging future organisations

Charles Handy is one of Britain's leading management thinkers. Indeed, in a 1997 European league table of global management gurus, he was placed third; all the others in the top ten were American (Rogers, 1997). Handy was educated at Oxford University and the Sloan School of Management at the Massachusetts Institute of Technology. He has been an oil executive, an economist and a professor at the London Business School. He has also acted as a consultant to a wide range of organisations in business, government, the voluntary sector, education and health.

Handy's book, *Understanding Organizations*, which was first published in 1976, has become a standard text on management courses. However, the book that brought him to public prominence and where he first began to articulate his views about the future direction of organisations was *The Future of Work* (Handy, 1984). Like Kanter and Peters, his work was inspired by the rise of Japan and the apparent decline of the West. In particular, he was concerned with the high level of unemployment in the UK at that time. Handy argued that if organisations were to survive and meaningful jobs were to be created for all those who wished to work, then both organisations and individuals would have to change the way they perceived jobs and careers. It was in his book *The Age of Unreason* (1989) that Handy fully articulated his views on the requirements for organisational success. He argued that profound changes were taking place in organisational life:

> The world of work is changing because the organisations of work are changing their ways. At the same time, however, the organisations are having to adapt to a changing world of work. It's a chicken and egg situation. One thing, at least, is clear: organisations in both private and public sectors face a tougher world – one in which they are judged more harshly than before on their effectiveness and in which there are fewer protective hedges behind which to shelter.
>
> (Handy, 1989: 70)

He asserted that British companies were fast moving away from the labour-intensive organisations of yesteryear. In future, new knowledge-based structures, run by a few smart people at their core who will control a host of equally smart computerised machines, will be the order of the day. Already, he noted, leading British organisations were increasingly becoming entities that received their added value from the knowledge and the creativity they put in, rather than from the application of muscle power. He contended that fewer, better-motivated people, helped by clever machines, could create much more added value than large groups of unthinking, demotivated ones ever could.

Like Peters and Kanter, Handy believes that the emerging future organisations will be smaller, more flexible and less hierarchical. Similarly, he also believes that the new organisations will need to treat people as assets to be developed and motivated, rather than just so much industrial cannon fodder. However, he does not assume that the future will be without diversity in relation to the organisational forms that emerge. Unlike Peters and Waterman, and to a lesser extent Kanter, he recognises that companies will continue to face differing circumstances and will need to respond in different manners. Therefore, instead of trying to re-establish a new 'one best way' for all organisations, with all the contradictions that arise from such attempts, Handy identifies three generic types of organisation that he argues will dominate in the future (*see* Ideas and perspectives 3.10).

IDEAS AND PERSPECTIVES 3.10

Handy's generic organisations

Organisation type	Core principles
1. Shamrock	Three distinct groups of staff – Core, Contractual Fringe and a Flexible Labour Force.
2. Federal	A collection or network of individual organisations allied together to achieve a common purpose.
3. Triple I	Information, Intelligence and Ideas = Added Value.

Source: Handy (1989).

---

1 The Shamrock organisation

This form of organisation, like the plant of the same name with three interlocking leaves, is composed of three distinct groups of workers who are treated differently and have different expectations: a small group of specialist 'core' workers, a contractual fringe and a flexible labour force.

The *core workers* are the first leaf, and the main distinguishing feature of the Shamrock form of organisation. These are a group of specialists, professional workers who form the brain, the hub or what we might call the 'nerve centre' of the organisation. These are people who are seen as being essential to the organisation. It is these few intelligent and articulate personnel in whose hands and heads reside the secrets of the organisation. They are both specialists and generalists, in that they run the organisation and control the smart machines and computers that have replaced, to a large extent, much of the labour force. This 'all puts pressure on the core, a pressure which could be summed up by the new equation of half the people, paid twice as much, working three times as effectively' (Handy, 1989: 118–19).

For their well-rewarded jobs, they are expected to be extremely loyal to the organisation, and to live and breathe their work. It is their responsibility to drive the organisation forward to ever greater success; to be flexible enough to meet the constantly changing challenge of competitors and the equally changing and sophisticated needs of customers. Core workers operate as colleagues and partners in the organisation, as opposed to superiors and sub-ordinates. In a very real sense, it is their company, and as such they expect to be recognised and rewarded for their roles and achievements, rather than the position they occupy on the organisation's ladder. It follows that they are managed differently – by consent: asked and not told what to do.

The *contractual fringe* is the second leaf of the Shamrock. A central feature of Shamrock organisations is their smallness in relation to their productive capacity. This is achieved by two methods: first, as mentioned above, by the use of machines to replace people; and secondly, by the contracting-out to individuals and other organisations of services and tasks previously done in-house. This leads to the creation of a contractual fringe, who may or may not work exclusively for the company in question. They are contracted to carry out certain tasks, for which they are paid a fee based on results, rather than a wage based on time taken. The arguments put forward in favour of such arrangements are numerous, but tend to boil down to three main ones:

- **It is cheaper** – companies only pay for what they get.

- **It makes management easier** – why keep the people on the payroll with all the attendant human management problems if it is not necessary?

- **Workload balancing** – when business is slack, it is the contractor who bears the impact of the reduced workload.

The *flexible labour force* is the third and fastest-growing leaf of the Shamrock and comprises a pool of part-time workers available for use by organisations. These are people with relevant skills who are not in need of, or who cannot obtain, full-time employment, but who are prepared to work on a part-time basis.

Increasingly, among this group of flexible workers are women who left their skilled jobs to raise families, but who are willing to return to work on a part-time basis, while still maintaining their child-rearing commitments. Included in this also is the growing army of young or retired executives, who prefer to hop from one job to another, doing bits and pieces of work on a part-time basis. These workers are sometimes referred to as temps (temporaries) or casuals. The growth of this group can be measured by the proliferation of employment agencies, catering solely for these groups, which have been established in the UK since the early 1980s. However, the flexible workforce never:

> have the commitment or ambition of the core. Decent pay and decent conditions are what they want, . . . They have jobs not careers and cannot be expected to rejoice in the organisation's triumphs any more than they can expect to share in the proceeds, nor will they put themselves out for the love of it; more work, in their culture, deserves and demands more money.
>
> (Handy, 1989: 80–1)

The picture, therefore, of the Shamrock organisation is one where structure and employment practices allow it to be big in terms of output, while being small in terms of the number of direct employees. For the latter reason, it is lean with few hierarchical layers and even less bureaucracy. It achieves this by the application of smart machines and a combination of part-time staff and subcontractors, whose work can be turned on and off as circumstances dictate. However, in a departure from past practice, the people involved may be highly skilled and competent. This also has the advantage of requiring much less office and factory accommodation than more traditionally organised companies. Other than the core staff, the rest are all scattered in different organisations or their own homes, often linked through sophisticated communication systems.

Such organisations, with their flexibility and skills, are well-suited to the provision of high-performance products and services to demanding and rapidly changing markets. The beauty of it all, as Handy argues, is that they do not have to employ all of the people all of the time or even in the same place to get the work done. According to Handy, small is not only beautiful but also increasingly preferable.

2 The Federal organisation

This is the second type of generic organisation that Handy sees as becoming dominant in the future. He defines this type of organisation as a collection or network of individual organisations allied together under a common flag with some shaped identity. Federations arise for two reasons. The first is that, as Shamrock organisations grow bigger, the core workers begin to find the volume of information available to them to make decisions increasingly difficult to handle. Secondly, they constitute a response to the constantly changing and competitive environment of the business world. Modern organisations need not only to achieve the flexibility that comes from smallness but also to be able to command the resources and power of big corporations.

As Handy (1989: 110) puts it:

> It [Federalism] allows individuals to work in organisation villages with the advantages of big city facilities. Organisational cities no longer work unless they are broken down into villages. In their big city mode they cannot cope with the variety needed in their products, their processes, and their people. On the other hand, the villages on their own have not the resources nor the imagination to grow. Some villages, of course, will be content to survive, happy in their niche, but global markets need global products and large confederations to make them or do them.

Federalism, therefore, implies the granting of autonomy to Shamrocks. Autonomy requires that Shamrocks are headed by their own separate chief executives, supported by a team of core workers, who take full responsibility for running the company. In such situations the Shamrocks become separate, but related, entities, under the umbrella of the Federal Centre. With the devolving of power to the Shamrocks, which still remain in the Federal portfolio, the Federal Centre is left to pursue the business of providing a common platform for the integration of the activities of the Shamrocks. The Federal Centre has the role of generating and collating ideas from the different Shamrocks and making them into concrete, achievable strategic objectives. Therefore, the Federal Centre is concerned mainly with the future; with looking forward, generating ideas, and creating scenarios and options of what the future will look like. All this is done with the ultimate aim of moving the organisation forwards and keeping it ahead not only of its rivals but also of its time.

Another feature of the Federal organisation is what Handy refers to as the 'inverted do'nut'.

> The do'nut is an American doughnut. It is round with a hole in the middle rather than the jam in its British equivalent . . . This, however, is an inverted American do'nut, in that it has the hole in the middle filled in and the space on the outside; . . . The point of the analogy begins to emerge if you think of your job, or any job. There will be a part of the job which will be clearly defined, and which, if you do not do, you will be seen to have failed. That is the heart, the core, the centre of the do'nut . . . [but] . . . In any job of any significance the person holding the job is expected not only to do all that is required but in some way to improve on that . . . to move into the empty space of the do'nut and begin to fill it up.
>
> (Handy, 1989: 102)

Through this approach, the Federal organisation seeks to maximise the innovative and creative potential of staff members. It does this by specifying the core job, the target and the quality standard expected of a given product or service. Outside of this specified domain, within the do'nut's empty space, however, staff members are given enough room and latitude to challenge and question existing ideas, to experiment and to come up with new methods of doing things, and new products or services. The aim is to encourage enquiry and experimentation that lead to higher standards. It follows from this that the essence of leadership under a Federal system is to provide a shared vision for the organisation; one which allows room for those whose lives will be affected by it – either directly or indirectly – to modify it, ponder over it, expand it, accept it and then make it a reality. Leadership in such situations is about providing opportunities for staff to grow and test their potential to the limit.

3 The Triple I organisation

This is the third of Handy's new organisational forms, although in fact it comprises a set of principles rather than a structural model. From the above, it is clear that both Shamrock and Federal organisation types introduce new dimensions into the world of work. Traditional perspectives are being transformed, and the established criteria for judging organisational effectiveness are being re-evaluated. Issues such as the definition of a productive contribution to work, reward systems, managerial skills and many more are being examined in the light of new management ideas. Indeed, according to Handy, we appear to be on the verge of a revolution in management thought and practice.

An examination of the attributes of the core workers in both Shamrock and Federal organisations gives an indication of what will constitute the new formula for success and effectiveness in tomorrow's companies. The core workers, as seen by Handy, use their *Intelligence* to analyse the available *Information* to generate *Ideas* for new products and services. Thus we find that Handy's first two organisational forms contain the seeds to produce his third form, the Triple I – organisations based on Intelligence, Information and Ideas. Since the three Is constitute the prime intellectual capital of the new organisations, clearly the Triple I principle applies most importantly to the core group of workers who are in a position to possess these attributes.

In future, it is argued, the equation for organisational success will be:

Triple I = AV
Intelligence, Information and Ideas = Added Value

A Triple I organisation will be 'obsessed with the pursuit of truth, or, in business language, of quality' (Handy, 1989: 113). This will not depend solely on human ability but will be a combination of smart people and smart machines. Therefore, organisations of the future will increasingly have to:

- invest in smart machines to remain competitive and effective;
- recruit skilled and smart people to control the machines;
- ensure that this group of skilled people is rewarded equitably.

For the Triple I organisation to emerge and remain successful, it must keep the skills, knowledge and abilities of its staff up to date. This means that it must become a learning organisation; one that provides a conducive environment for the development of its intellectual capital. Time and effort must be consciously and officially devoted to learning and study, at all levels of the organisation. The core, especially, must spend more time than their equivalents in more traditional companies on thinking and study: meeting with other external professionals and experts, going on study tours and listening more to 'partners' within the organisation, all with the objective of improving the organisation's human capital. The new organisations will be dynamic, interactive societies where information is open to all, freely given and freely received. In the Triple I organisation, everyone will be expected to think and learn as well as to do. Nevertheless, it is the core worker from whom most will be demanded. Such people will be increasingly:

> expected to have not only the expertise appropriate to his or her particular role, but will also be required to know and understand business, to have the technical skills of analysis and the human skills and the conceptual skills and to keep them up to date. (Handy, 1989: 124)

This is one of the key features that make the Triple I organisation unique; it is a hotbed of intellectual discourse, where the prevailing culture is one of consent rather than instruction. Staff are unsupervised in the traditional sense, and instead are trusted to do what is right and given room to experiment with new ideas and concepts. Finally, the flexibility of such organisations, and the unpredictability of the environments in which they operate, mean that careers will become more variegated and less permanent.

As can be seen, therefore, Handy's view of the future shape of organisations does not appear dissimilar to that of Kanter, and Peters and Waterman. However, he does depart from their views in at least two crucial respects. First, he explicitly acknowledges that not all organisations will adopt the same form or move at the same pace. His three generic forms indicate that organisations will have to exercise choice and judgement in order to match their particular circumstances to the most suitable form. Also, it is clear that he views this as an evolutionary as well as a revolutionary process: companies cannot immediately become a Triple I type of organisation; they have to develop into one over time. Second, he explicitly states what is only hinted at by the other writers, namely that in the new organisations where everyone is to be treated as an equal 'partner', some will be more equal than others, i.e. the core workers will be treated and rewarded in a more preferential manner than the contractual fringe or the flexible labour force.

Handy does not give specific guidance as to how existing organisations can adapt themselves to take on these new forms, although he does indicate that a lack of empowerment and self-belief among individuals in organisations presents a major obstacle to change. However, in an earlier work (Handy, 1986), he does state very clearly that fundamental change is a long-term process and that people tend to react emotionally rather than rationally to change.

After the publication of *The Age of Unreason*, Handy appeared to grow increasingly concerned with the unanticipated consequences of his prescriptions for the world of work. This is made clear in the first paragraph of his 1994 book, *The Empty Raincoat*:

> Four years ago, my earlier book, The Age of Unreason, was published. In that book I presented a view of the way work was being reshaped and the effects which the reshaping might have on all our lives. It was, on the whole, an optimistic view. Since then, the world of work has changed very much along the lines which were described in the book. This should be comforting to an author, but I have not found it so. Too many people and institutions have been unsettled by the changes. Capitalism has not proved as flexible as it was supposed to be. Governments have not been all-wise or far-seeing. Life is a struggle for many and a puzzle for most.
>
> What is happening in our mature societies is much more fundamental, confusing and distressing than I had expected.   (Handy, 1994: 1)

In *The Empty Raincoat*, Handy returns to and restates many of the themes of his earlier work, but with two differences. First, he explicitly acknowledges that the types of careers that these new organisational forms will create will have a severely adverse effect on the home life of employees, especially senior managers. They will be called on to be company men and women above all else, including their families.

Second, there is an almost evangelical feel to the book. This is especially noticeable in the later section of the book, where Handy argues that the modern world has taken meaning out of people's lives and that, while the pursuit of profit may motivate senior managers:

> Not many in the lower realms of the organisation can get excited by the thought of enriching shareholders. 'Excellence' and 'quality' are the right sort of words, but they have been tarnished by repetition in too many organisations.   (Handy, 1994: 265)

This more pessimistic view of the future is still there in his 1997 book, *The Hungry Spirit* (Handy, 1997: 3):

> Many of us are, I believe, confused by the world we have created for ourselves in the West . . . the new fashion for turning everything into a business, even our own lives, doesn't seem to be the answer. A hospital, and my life, is more than just a business. What good can it possibly do to pile up riches which you cannot conceivably use, and what is the point of the efficiency needed to create those riches if one third of the world's workers are now unemployed or under-employed as the ILO calculates? And where will it end, this passion for growth? . . . I am angered by the waste of so many people's lives, dragged down by poverty in the midst of riches. I am concerned by the absence of a more transcendent view of life and the purposes of life, and by the prevalence of the economic myth which colours all we do. Money is the means for life and not the point of it.

In the book, Handy argues that, in the West, people's spiritual needs have been sacrificed to the pursuit of their material needs; and he examines the options, and where the responsibility lies, for putting balance back into people's lives. In particular he is concerned with the distribution of wealth, the role that education can play in giving everyone a good start in life, and how we can look after ourselves while having a care for others as well. He even touches on, perhaps, the biggest question of all: 'What, ultimately, is the real purpose of life?' (Handy, 1997: 5). In addressing these issues he ranges widely, looking at markets, organisations and the role of business, government and religion. He believes the answer lies in the pursuit of 'Proper Selfishness'. This is a redefinition of individualism; he sees individuals as moving away from the pursuit of narrow self-interest, and instead realising that it is in their best interests to pursue a fairer society for all. Though he identifies a role for government and business in creating Proper Selfishness, he believes it is individuals themselves who bear the main responsibility for its achievement. In particular, he draws attention to the role of individual entrepreneurs in changing the world:

> Entrepreneurs, whether social or commercial, often discover aspects of themselves in the pursuit of something beyond themselves. Such people are not content to let the status quo be the way forward. They itch to make a difference . . . Almost accidentally, corporations have become the nursery for frustrated entrepreneurs. They should turn this to a positive account and do it more deliberately, in the hope that they can retain some of the best for themselves, including women, while seeding the community with the others. The workplace has always been the real school for life. Perhaps it just needs to change its curriculum a little to tune in with the new age of personal initiative.
>
> (Handy, 1997: 262)

In recent years, Handy has seen himself less as a management guru and more as a social philosopher (Handy, 2007a, 2007b). He is concerned that blind greed still drives many people and that the pursuit of riches has created a mercenary society which lacks a moral or spiritual compass. Handy calls for a new sense of purpose for individuals, organisations and society. He wants to see a strong ethical approach to business and society, and a re-creation of the concept that people exist to help and serve each other as well as themselves. These are sentiments that many of us would probably share but, unfortunately, he fails to show how the unleashing of individual entrepreneurship and the creation of the new organisational forms he advocates will aid this search for meaning. Instead, he asks us to put our faith in the goodness of people and to be optimistic about the future. A recurrent theme in Handy's work, however, has been the many paradoxes thrown up by contemporary society, especially the presence of dire poverty amidst extreme wealth, and the potential of technology for creating meaningful work compared with the increasing tendency for the quality of life to decline. Therefore, it seems strange that the one paradox that Handy appears to ignore is that the forms of organisations that he advocates may well be creating the poor jobs and poverty he deprecates.

Culture–Excellence: summary and criticisms

In its third biennial Global CEO Study, IBM (2008: 54) stated that 'The Enterprise of the Future constantly searches for new ways to compete'. In particular, IBM noted that such an enterprise:

- thinks like an outsider;
- draws breakthrough ideas from other industries;
- empowers entrepreneurs;
- experiments creatively in the market, not just the lab;
- manages today's business while experimenting with tomorrow's model.

Such phrases could have been written by Tom Peters or any of the proponents of Culture–Excellence. The IBM Study shows that Culture–Excellence has had a major impact on the thinking and practice of businesses globally, and not just in the UK and the US. It is not surprising, therefore, that Peters is, arguably, the leading business guru of his generation, and that Kanter and Handy have likewise achieved the pre-eminence in business circles that they had previously only occupied in academia. A look in the business section of any bookshop will show that there are many more authors who have jumped on the bandwagon. Barely a day seems to go by without the publication of yet another blockbuster proclaiming that it has discovered the recipe for success. Some of these achieve a degree of prominence in business circles, though many seem to disappear without trace. Nevertheless, the fact that publishers keep publishing them, and that in different ways and shapes they repeat and project the Culture–Excellence message, emphasises the thirst of managers for the message.

Nor is it just a case that managers buy them to leave them on the shelf. In 1997, a survey by the Industrial Society showed that in the UK alone 94 per cent of respondent organisations either had recently been through or were going through a culture change programme (Industrial Society, 1997). The IBM (2008) Global CEO Study also stressed the importance of a common corporate culture. Indeed, a recent article by Fleming (2012: 18), while being strongly critical of the concept, acknowledged that 'corporate culturalism' is still a 'dominant force in managerial practice and ideology'. Therefore, over the last 30 years, on both sides of the Atlantic, managers have been attempting to reshape their companies along the Culture–Excellence lines.

The reason for its emergence, and for its continuing popularity, was that in a world where old certainties had disappeared, where new and more dangerous competitors seemed to appear every day, it rejected the communal and corporatist approach of the Japanese, and offered instead a recipe for success that was in tune with the free market liberalism, with its stress on individualism, that has dominated much of the West for the last three decades. Nor was it merely a rehash of what had gone before. The Culture–Excellence approach to organisations is significantly different from previous approaches; although we might note that the new forms, especially Handy's Shamrock type, bear an interesting resemblance to the first budding of organisational life during the Industrial Revolution. The entrepreneurial style of management, the stress on a privileged core of skilled workers, and the contracting-out of whole areas of organisational activities are all hallmarks of the early industrial organisations. However, the big differences between then and now relate to the level of sophistication and complexity of the new organisations that are emerging, the degree of integration of both internal functions and external relationships, the grade of intelligence and skill required of all staff, whether they be core or periphery – and, of course, the conditions of employment. For Watson (1986: 66), who coined the term 'Culture–Excellence school' to describe proponents of this approach, there is one further and crucial difference:

> [In these new organisations] what brings the activities of the organisational members to focus upon those purposes which lead to effective performance is the existence of a strong and clearly articulated culture.
> (Watson, 1986: 66)

It is this which makes it clear that the Culture–Excellence approach that has been developing since the early 1980s is remarkably different from most of the theory and practice that has grown up in the last 100 years.

Peters, Kanter and Handy argue that organisations are in a new age, where familiar themes are taking on different meanings and are being expressed in a new language. Contrasting the old with the new, they argue that what is important in the new is not muscle power, but brain power: the ability to make intelligent use of information to create ideas that add value and sustain competitiveness. The new organisation is flatter in structure, though it might be more accurate to say that structure is decreasing in importance and that its role as a directing and controlling mechanism is being taken over by cultures that stress the need for, and facilitate, flexibility and adaptation (though in passing we should note that Peters (1993) also sees the dismembering of hierarchical structures as an important step in creating these new cultures). The Culture–Excellence approach wishes to sound the death knell of hierarchical organisations and the concept of promotion through the ranks. Careers and skills are taking on new meanings, as are established ideas of reward.

In future, it is argued, careers are likely to depend on the individual and his or her ability to remain employable. In turn, the skills needed for 'employability' will tend to be generic and broad-based rather than organisation or function/specialism-specific. Likewise, career paths and promotion will no longer be shaped by the particular employing organisation and its structures and criteria, but will be driven more by individuals creating their own opportunities by taking on new roles and responsibilities, either in one organisation or, more likely, by moving from company to company. As for pay, it seems that this will take the form not so much of a wage related to the particular post occupied, but more that of a fee paid for actual performance.

On human relations, the message being transmitted is that the new forms of organisations will treat their employees in a more responsible and humane fashion than has been the norm, though this may only apply to 'core' staff. Employees will be seen and treated as 'partners', capable of making a substantial contribution to the growth of the organisation. This approach, it is argued, will manifest itself in a tough-minded respect for the individual, who will receive training, be set reasonable and clear objectives, and be given the autonomy to make his or her own contribution to the work of the organisation. The new organisations will seek to develop open, flexible and pragmatic cultures, which help to maintain a learning environment that promotes creativity and entrepreneurship among all employees.

Another feature of the new organisational forms, it is claimed, will be their ability to grant autonomy and encourage flexibility and initiative while at the same time keeping tight control of their operations. Like so much else, this is to be achieved through culture rather than structure, and values rather than rules. Everything is to be monitored closely, not by the watchful eye of superiors, but by the creation of a homogeneous environment in which all take an equal responsibility for, and legitimate interest in, the work of their colleagues.

In terms of its approach to change, Culture–Excellence does not offer a clear message. Handy (1986), seems to adopt a gradualist approach to change – big changes over long periods. Both Kanter and Peters, meanwhile, see past approaches as too slow, too incremental and outmoded, but do not agree about how future change should be managed. Peters sees the need for change to be fast, furious and continuous, while Kanter argues for rapid and discontinuous change followed by a period of more incremental changes. Therefore, how the organisational forms and arrangements recommended by the Culture–Excellence school will be implemented and kept fit for purpose is unclear.

Even so, the new organisation forms that have emerged offer much that is admirable, especially the replacement of rigid and faceless bureaucracy with more flexible structures and more empowered workers. Equally clearly, their adherents and promoters raise more questions than they answer. To an extent this was inevitable when dealing with something that was emerging rather than an existing and concrete reality. However, as this concept has now been around for over 30 years, it would be remiss to ignore or gloss over the questions and dilemmas that seem apparent. Many writers have drawn attention to the shortcomings of the Culture–Excellence approach. Carroll (1983) and Lawler (1985) were both scathing about the methodological shortcomings of the research on which Peters and Waterman's (1982) book was based. Indeed, Peters himself appears to have admitted that he and Waterman 'faked' some of the data in order to obtain their results (Kellaway, 2001). This would seem to give additional support to Wilson's (1992) claim that the book lacks any apparent empirical or theoretical foundations. Additionally, extensive research in leading European companies by Stadler (2007) challenges some of the central tenets of the Culture–Excellence movement, especially the notion that organisations need to change radically and continually if they are to survive. Stadler and his colleagues studied 40 European companies which had survived for more than 100 years and which were listed in the *Fortune* Global 500 in 2003. What Stadler (2007: 2) found was that:

- throughout their history, the great companies in our sample have all emphasised exploiting existing assets and capabilities over exploring for new ones;

- good companies tend to stick to their knitting, but the great companies know when to diversify;

- great companies very seldom make radical changes.

From an even more critical perspective, Willmott (1993) and Fleming (2012) see the entire concept of Culture–Excellence as a form of Orwellian tyranny which is designed to instil unquestioning obedience.

Though some of these criticisms may seem exaggerated, it is certainly arguable that the Culture–Excellence approach does have serious weaknesses, especially in three areas that are crucial to the operation of organisations:

1. **People**. There are serious concerns and contradictions regarding the role and behaviour of people in the new organisations. On the one hand, they are proclaimed as the chief asset of the new organisations. On the other hand, there are clearly different grades of employee, from core to periphery, and these different grades will be treated and rewarded in a markedly dissimilar manner; furthermore, none of the different grades can expect any real job security. The new organisations will only value employees as long as they and their areas perform to the highest of standards. Not only does this pit individual against individual but also one part of the organisation against another. While healthy competition may enhance organisational competitiveness, from what we know of motivation theory (Arnold *et al*, 1998) it is not clear that the Culture–Excellence approach is particularly healthy. The Culture–Excellence approach also encourages teamwork, yet the pursuit of individual advancement and reward often leads to conflict rather than cooperation (Schein, 1988).

2. **Politics**. Though Western companies traditionally either deny the existence of internal struggles or argue that such behaviour is perverse, it is clear that the struggle for resources, power and survival is as great within organisations as it is between them (Buchanan and Badham, 1999; Pfeffer, 1981; Robbins, 1986). As stated above, the recommendations of the Culture–Excellence school would seem to exacerbate political behaviour by and between individuals and groups, yet in the main they ignore this drawback to their approach, even though it is potentially damaging to both organisational and individual performance.

3. **Culture**. The proponents of Culture–Excellence are advocating a 'one best way' (one best culture) approach for all organisations, irrespective of their size, environment and other circumstances. Also, as Wilson (1992) pointed out, Culture–Excellence assumes a simple causal relationship between culture and performance. For the proponents of the Culture–Excellence school, culture is the great cure-all – the creation of a culture of excellence is seen as answering all questions and solving all problems. This assumes that the creation of new cultures will itself be unproblematic. However, as Chapter 5 will show, culture and politics appear to be the Achilles heel of approaches to managing organisations.

It would also be remiss to ignore the differences between the main proponents of Culture–Excellence. Peters is a free market liberal in the classic American mould. He believes that individual and organisational competition untrammelled by government is what makes societies strong. Kanter agrees with most of this, but believes that local communities, working with big business, have a positive role to play in attracting and keeping well-paid jobs for their communities. She has also become increasingly concerned with issues of social justice and environmental sustainability, but believes that these are best tackled by enlightened big business. Handy is also committed to the free market, but has become increasingly concerned with the outcome of his prescriptions. He appears to be turning his back on pure individualism, arguing instead for a less rapacious, more caring capitalism, driven by what he terms 'Proper Selfishness' and more concerned with the collective good than individual wealth creation. Though Peters and Kanter may continue to hold to the Culture–Excellence line, it is difficult to see that the direction which Handy is now taking is consistent with it.

There is one final concern that is wider than the Culture–Excellence approach *per se* or its impact on organisations, but which is reflected in the differences between Peters, Kanter and Handy. The move towards creating segmented workforces of the type described by Handy (1989), and the emphasis on the temporary nature of employment championed by Peters and Waterman (1982) and Kanter (1989), are part of a continuing trend in the West, driven by neo-liberal economic and social policies, towards worsening job security and conditions of service, in order to create a vast pool of under-employed, especially part-time, labour that can be turned on or off as the situation dictates (Watson, 1994). For example, in 2003, Germany introduced the concept of the 'mini-job':

> German 'mini-jobs' are just what it says on the tin: precarious employment for up to €400 (£315) per month . . . 'Mini-jobbers' thus forgo core benefits of regular employment, such as building up pension claims. Beyond a basic threshold, income from 'mini-jobs' also entails the reduction of unemployment benefit for recipients. . . . According to the most recent figures of the German Employment Agency, 7.3 million Germans, or one in every five employees, held 'mini-jobs' in September 2010 – an increase of 1.6 million since 2003.
>
> (Blankenburg, 2012)

The UK version of this appears to be the 'zero-hours contract', which has been around for a number of years, but is now being applied to professional jobs, including ones in the NHS.

> The aim of zero hours contracts, which are sometimes known as casual contracts, is not to contract with, and pay, individuals to work a set number of hours per week, but to use and to pay individuals only as and when required. . . . [They] are inextricably linked with low-paid jobs, a lack of employment rights and only being paid for the work you actually do. . . . They are normally restricted to low-skilled jobs, such as catering, cleaning and security. . . . If a fast-food restaurant is having a quiet Sunday afternoon, why pay the individuals for not working? It is a waste of money. They can be sent home or to a rest room. This might leave the employer a bit short-staffed, but if someone has to wait four minutes longer for a burger and fries, no-one gets hurt. The issue is whether you can apply the same line of thinking and working practice to more highly-skilled jobs, where it actually could be a matter of life or death, as opposed to a longer wait for lunch. (von Hagen, 2012)

The move to insecure, temporary and part-time employment is not new, but rose rapidly in the 1980s and 1990s (Hutton, 1995; Saul, 1997). The provision of temporary, contract labour is now a global business which, in 2005, was worth some $240 billion and was dominated by a group of ten multinational corporations (EWERC, 2007). It is also reflected in the growing gap between the income of the highest- and lowest-paid workers in the UK, which is now wider than at any time in the last 40 years (Brindle, 1998b; Dorling *et al*, 2007; Elliott, 2008; Green, 2008; White, 1999). Nor is this bleak picture restricted to the UK: the gap between rich and poor in the US is now wider than at any time since 1928 (Johnston, 2007). Globally, the poorest 40 per cent of the world's population receives 5 per cent of global income and the richest 20 per cent get three-quarters of global income (United Nations Development Programme, 2007). Given this, Guest's (1992) assessment of *In Search of Excellence*, 'Right enough to be dangerously wrong', may well find favour with many people.

Despite these concerns and criticisms, Culture–Excellence has become the most influential approach to running organisations in the US and Europe, as is apparent from the many articles on its merits and case studies of its use that appear regularly in management journals. Meanwhile, since the 1950s, the Japanese have been developing an alternative approach to structuring and managing organisations that is not only markedly different from the Culture–Excellence one but also has a proven track record of success.

The Japanese approach to management

The last 60 years have seen the rebirth of Japan. Reduced almost to ashes at the end of the Second World War, by the 1980s Japan had built an industrial empire second to none (Francks, 1992). Even now, despite the bursting of the asset-price bubble in 1989 and two decades of very low growth, it is still the fourth largest economy in the world (CIA, 2012; *The Economist*, 2008). As Morgan (1986: 111) stated:

> With virtually no natural resources, no energy, and over 110 million people crowded in four small mountainous islands, Japan succeeded in achieving the highest growth rate, lowest level of unemployment and, at least in some of the larger and more successful organizations, one of the best-paid and healthiest working populations in the world.

Though writers suggested many reasons for Japan's success, ranging from culture to economic institutions, time and again, its approach to managing organisations was cited as the key factor (Hunter, 1989; Laage-Hellman, 1997; Sako and Sato, 1997; Schonberger, 1982; Smith and Misumi, 1989; Whitehill, 1991).

Before proceeding to examine what is meant by the Japanese approach to management, it is useful briefly to trace Japan's development as an industrial nation. Up to the middle of the nineteenth century, Japan was an intensely nationalistic society which practised a deliberate policy of isolating itself from the outside world. Therefore, for most of its inhabitants, Japan was the world. It was a feudal country that laid strong emphasis on obligation and deference, and where obedience to authority in general, and to the Emperor in particular, was unquestioned (Sheridan, 1993).

For all its deliberate isolation, Japan was a sophisticated and well-educated country with a high degree of literacy. Education was based on a set of Confucian principles which stressed unquestioning obedience to the family; total loyalty to one's superiors; and reverence for education and self-development. The abiding influence of these can still be seen in Japanese society today, and underpins the strength of Japanese organisations (Smith and Misumi, 1989). However, from the mid-nineteenth century, Japan began to experience internal tensions. The feudal aristocracy experienced escalating financial difficulties while the merchant class, considered social inferiors, began to prosper. At the same time, it became clear that the growing military might of other countries posed a potential threat to Japan. In response to these developments, Japan adopted a twin-track policy of economic and military growth, not dissimilar to that being developed in Germany at this time (Hunter, 1989).

Missions were dispatched abroad to study and bring technologies and practices back to Japan. On one such visit in 1911, Yukinori Hoshino, a director of the Kojima Bank, became acquainted with the work of Frederick Taylor and obtained permission to translate his work into Japanese. Following this, Taylor's Scientific Management principles, and allied approaches to work study and production management, were rapidly and enthusiastically adopted by the Japanese (McMillan, 1985). Indeed, such was the impact of Taylor's work that, according to Wren (1994: 205), it 'led to a management revolution, replacing the entrepreneur-dominated age'. By the 1920s, Japan had moved from being an agrarian economy to one dominated by industry. As in many Western countries, industrialisation was accompanied by considerable industrial conflict, sometimes violent (Urabe, 1986). However, in contrast to most Western countries, this was not accompanied by a growing democratisation of society. Instead, democratic tendencies were quashed by a growing coalition between industry and the military that promoted intense nationalism and led, almost inexorably, to Japan's involvement in the Second World War. After Japan's defeat, its shattered society was occupied by the US, which stripped the Emperor of his traditional powers and established a Western-style democracy (Sheridan, 1993; Whitehill, 1991).

Given the state of the Japanese economy after the Second World War, the success of its reconstruction is nothing short of miraculous. The Korean War in the 1950s proved a stroke of good fortune for Japan, in that the US used Japan as an important staging post for troops and supplies. This injected billions of American dollars into Japan's economy. However, perhaps much more important was America's contribution to management education in Japan. In the immediate post-war years, Japanese companies acquired a reputation for bitter industrial disputes, shoddy workmanship and poor quality. The main responsibility for tackling these problems lay with US engineers working for the Civilian Communications Section of the Occupation Administration (Sheldrake, 1996). Four men in particular have been credited with turning this situation around and creating the basis of Japan's fearsome reputation for the productivity of its workforce and quality of its products: Charles Protzman, Homer Sarasohn, Joseph Juran and W Edward Deming. Interestingly, the last three of these had all worked at Western Electric's Hawthorne Works and were, therefore, familiar, though not necessarily always in agreement, with the Human Relations approach. All of them were far removed from the narrow concept of the engineer. They took a wide view of how enterprises should be run and in particular of the need for managers to show leadership and gain the commitment of their workforces. Their approach, which covered business policy and organisation as well as production methods and techniques, was enthusiastically received, adopted and disseminated by the senior managers who attended their courses and lectures. As Horsley and Buckley (1990: 51) noted, Deming, especially, met with enormous success:

> W E Deming became a legend in Japan. He gave hundreds of lectures . . . to eager managers on the vital importance of statistical quality control . . . Among his pupils were many who were to become captains of Japanese industry in the 1960s and 1970s, heading firms like Nissan, Sharp and the Nippon Electric Company (NEC). The annual Deming Prize for good management was highly coveted in the 1950s, and is still being awarded today.

Yet, despite the economic and technical assistance of the US, there is little doubt that the main credit for the country's success can be attributed to the hard work, commitment and intelligence of Japanese managers and workers. Under the umbrella of a supportive economic and political framework, Japanese enterprises overcame their severe industrial relations and quality problems of the 1950s and created the distinctive and hugely successful Japanese approach to developing and managing their businesses that allowed them to take the world by storm in the 1970s and 1980s (Fruin, 1992; Pascale and Athos, 1982; Sako and Sato, 1997; Sheldrake, 1996; Smith and Misumi, 1989).

What is the Japanese approach to management?

As one might expect, it is difficult to find an all-embracing definition of the Japanese approach to management that satisfies all commentators or can be found in all Japanese companies. In particular, there are distinct differences between larger and smaller enterprises in Japan, and in the treatment of full-time and part-time, and male and female employees in all enterprises (Cole, 1979; Laage-Hellman, 1997; Sako and Sato, 1997). Such are these differences that some argue there is either no such thing as a distinctive Japanese approach to management or that, if it does exist, no one has been able to capture it accurately (Dale, 1986; Keys and Miller, 1984; Sullivan, 1983). Nevertheless, the vast majority of observers do seem to agree that it exists and can, broadly, be defined (Abegglen and Stalk, 1984; Ackroyd *et al*, 1988; Hatvany and Pucik, 1981; Holden and Burgess, 1994; Pascale and Athos, 1982; Smith and Misumi, 1989).

Perhaps the most influential work, and still the best-selling book, on Japanese management was William Ouchi's (1981) *Theory Z: How American Business Can Meet the Japanese Challenge*. Drawing on the theoretical insights of Douglas McGregor and Chris Argyris, Ouchi argues that Japanese success stemmed from:

- the involvement and commitment of the entire workforce;
- a set of internally consistent norms, practices and behaviours based on trust and strong personal ties between the individual and the organisation, particularly their immediate work group;
- practices such as lifetime employment, slow evaluation and promotion and collective decision-making;
- the belief that workers want to build cooperative and close working relationships.

Many other writers have also tried to capture the essence of Japanese management. McKenna (1988) believes that the key elements are:

- lifetime employment;
- the seniority principle with regard to pay and promotion;
- enterprise unionism (which will be explained later).

Pang and Oliver (1988) agree with McKenna but also draw attention to:

- training and education;
- company-based welfare schemes;
- quality circles;
- manufacturing methods such as Just-in-Time production.

Keys and Miller (1984) claim that the hallmarks of Japanese management are:

- long-term planning;
- lifetime employment;
- collective responsibility.

Laage-Hellman (1997) emphasises the presence of:

- a consensus-seeking decision-making process;
- incremental planning through the development of a long-term vision;
- the use of short-term action plans;
- passive owners who do not usually interfere with managers;
- strategies that give priority to long-term growth and survival;
- the effective use of external resources through partnerships with suppliers and customers.

Other commentators have come up with similar lists. One of the most quoted of these is by Pascale and Athos (1982) who used the McKinsey 7 S Framework (*see* Ideas and perspectives 3.2), which they had developed jointly with Tom Peters and Robert Waterman, to analyse Japanese management. Like Peters and Waterman's Culture–Excellence approach, Pascale and Athos stressed the four 'soft' Ss (staff, style, shared values and skills). This was not to dismiss the 'hard' Ss (strategy, structure and systems), but to emphasise that the real difference between Japanese companies and their Western counterparts was that the latter tended to concentrate on the 'hard' Ss and ignore the 'soft' Ss. Pascale and Athos argued that, in contrast, Japanese companies had developed the ability to combine and blend the 'soft' and 'hard' Ss to their competitive benefit. Their work differed from other studies of Japanese management at the time by examining the management style of Japanese companies operating in the US. In a similar vein, Peter Wickens, who was Personnel Director of Nissan Motor Manufacturing (UK) Ltd for more than ten years, also commented on the transfer of Japanese management to the West. In his 1987 book, *The Road to Nissan*, written when he was still at Nissan, he argued that the Japanese approach can be characterised by three factors:

● teamwork;

● quality consciousness;

● flexibility.

Interestingly, after he left Nissan, Wickens (1995) commented that Ouchi and others tended to miss, or underplay, one very important element of Japanese companies:

● a very strong control culture, especially in relation to shopfloor workers.

As Figure 3.1 shows, the factors identified by the above writers can be separated into two categories: those relating to personnel issues and those relating to business practices.

Personnel issues

The dedication, commitment and ability of Japanese workers are seen as a major factor in the success of Japanese companies. Though much credit for this has been given to the culture of Japanese society, especially its Confucian tradition of obedience and loyalty, similar levels of motivation have been reproduced in Japanese companies operating in the West

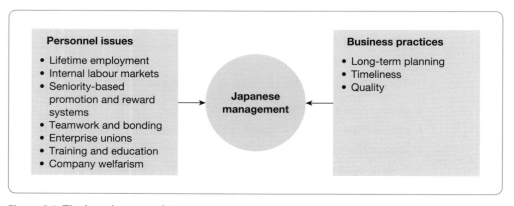

Figure 3.1 The key elements of Japanese management

(Wickens, 1987), which would imply that other factors are also at work. Chief among these is the crucial role played by the personnel policies prevalent in many Japanese enterprises, especially the larger ones. The core of the Japanese approach to personnel comprises a combination of practices and policies designed to align their behaviour with, and bind employees to, the organisation, and promote their long-term development and commitment. The principal practices and policies concerned are listed below.

1. **Lifetime employment**. Many employees are recruited straight from school or university, and expect, and are expected, to spend the rest of their working lives with the same organisation. This 'guarantee', based as it is on an age-old sense of mutual obligation and belonging, creates an intense sense of loyalty to and dependence on the organisation. Indeed, Holden and Burgess (1994) observed that while a Japanese worker might survive the loss of his family, the collapse of his employing organisation would be unbearable. Therefore, lifetime employment is a central feature of the Japanese approach and supports so much else, including a willingness to change and the maintenance of a stable organisational culture. However, the fact that organisations prefer to recruit school or university leavers also makes it difficult for individuals to move between companies once they have accepted an appointment. It follows that if someone is fired, their chances of securing other employment are negligible.

2. **Internal labour markets**. Most positions are filled from inside the company. This is a corollary to lifetime employment which demonstrates to the employee that satisfactory performance will bring promotion, and it eliminates the potential for tension which can be brought about by the recruitment of outsiders.

3. **Seniority-based promotion and reward systems**. Employees are ranked and rewarded primarily, but not exclusively, on their length of service, and independent of the precise nature of the job they perform.

4. **Teamwork and bonding**. Although Japanese employees are made to feel part of the organisation and see it as some sort of extended family, they are first and foremost a member of a particular work group or team. The group is not just a collection of individuals; it is constructed and developed in such a way that it comprises a single entity which takes collective responsibility for its performance. Japanese companies use a variety of techniques, both at work and in a social setting, for bonding team members to each other and to the organisation.

5. **Enterprise (single-company) unions**. Unlike practice in the West, Japanese companies tend to allow only one union to represent the interests of the workforce. In addition, Japanese unions tend to be single-company or enterprise unions. From a Western point of view, they are not so much trade unions as company associations. This is illustrated by the practice of senior managers, at some stage in their careers, being expected to serve as union officials.

6. **Training and education**. Extensive and continuous training and education form an integral part of Japanese personnel policies. This emphasis on the continuous development of employees, to enable them to carry out their work better and to prepare them for promotion, represents a significant investment by Japanese companies in their human capital. Much of the training is done on the job and is always geared to the twin aims of improving organisational performance and individual development. Though encouraged by the company, employees are expected to take responsibility for their own self-development.

7. **Company welfarism**. Many Japanese companies provide a wide range of welfare benefits for their employees. These can cover medical treatment, education for children and even housing. Some of the larger companies are almost mini-welfare states in themselves.

Many other practices and policies could be added to the list, but these appear to be at the core. They are designed to instil the following in employees:

- loyalty and gratitude to the company and a commitment to its objectives;
- a sense of security;
- a strong commitment to hard work and performance improvement;
- an atmosphere of cooperation rather than conflict;
- a belief in self-development and improvement.

These are the cornerstones of Japanese company life; their presence is the reason why Japanese national culture is often cited as being at the heart of Japan's ability to compete in a world market. These operate within organisation structures which, to Western eyes at least, appear complex, highly formalised and very hierarchical (Whitehill, 1991). However, these personnel issues cannot be seen in isolation from the working practices that Japanese companies use or the objectives they pursue. It is the combination of the two that makes Japanese companies so effective (Wood, 1991). Without overall direction and the appropriate work systems, even the best skilled and motivated workers are ineffective. This is why Japanese business practices and work systems should receive as much attention as personnel issues.

Business practices

The Japanese ability to satisfy customers, and thereby capture markets, by developing and producing products to a higher specification and at a lower cost than their competitors, is staggering considering the state of their industry in the 1940s and 1950s. Indeed, even as recently as the 1960s, 'Made in Japan' was synonymous with poor quality. What has changed, or rather what has come to fruition, has been the methods they apply to all aspects of business, but especially to manufacturing (Hannam, 1993). The fact that some of these methods have, quite naturally, Japanese names (such as *Hoshin Kanri* – policy deployment; *Genba Kanri* – workshop management; *Kaizen* – continuous improvement; *Kanban* – a paperless form of scheduling) tends, for the Western audience, to cloak and mystify the core principles and systems being used, and also to disguise the extent to which these have been adopted from the West. Leaving aside the jargon and terminology, Japanese business practices and work systems can be characterised by four interrelated elements: long-term planning, timeliness, quality and change management.

1. **Long-term planning.** This will be discussed further in Chapters 6 and 7, but for now let us say that the timescale on which Japanese enterprises operate is far longer than that of many of their Western competitors, and their focus on building a strong market position similarly contrasts with the short-term profit maximisation objectives prevalent in the US and UK in particular (Hamel and Prahalad, 1989). Needless to say, this is an enormous advantage when considering investment decisions, whether this be for products, processes or people (Smith and Misumi, 1989).

IDEAS AND PERSPECTIVES 3.11

The *ringi* system

This is a procedure whereby proposals for new policies, procedures or expenditure are circulated throughout the firm for comment. The proposal is circulated in written form and is then sent to all who might be affected if it were to be implemented, in ascending order of seniority. The proposal is modified in line with comments, and only when all agree is it implemented. This joint approach to decision-making is also operated through production councils and quality circles, and covers the planning and scheduling of production, work allocation, changes to production methods, problem-solving, etc. (Inagami, 1988).

This system of involving large numbers of people in decision-making is the reason why the Japanese are notorious for the slowness with which they make decisions, and famous for their ability to get it right first time (Hannam, 1993; Smith and Misumi, 1989).

---

2. **The *ringi* system.** In any investigation of the Japanese approach to long-term planning, timeliness and quality, it is necessary to recognise the role played by employees in decision-making. Most discussions of Japanese management emphasise the occurrence of upward influence, particularly through the *ringi* system (*see* Ideas and perspectives 3.11).

As well as aiding decision-making, the *ringi* system has another equally important benefit:

The ringi is as much a process for exploring and reaffirming values as it is for setting a direction . . . In the American view objectives should be hard and fast and clearly stated for all to see. In the Japanese view they emerge from a more fundamental process of exploring and understanding the values through which a firm is or should be operating. A knowledge of these values, the limits that are to guide actions, defines a set of possible actions. An action chosen from this set may not be the very best, but it will satisfy parameters deemed crucial for success.

(Morgan, 1986: 93)

3. **Timeliness.** The Japanese are seen as having a crucial competitive edge in their ability to develop products and bring them to market faster than their competitors. Part of the explanation for this relates to teamwork. While many Western companies are still designing and developing products on a sequential basis (whereby one part of the design is completed before another is begun), the Japanese work in teams to undertake these tasks simultaneously. This form of teamwork extends to working jointly with customers and suppliers as well (Laage-Hellman, 1997). Not only does this cut the overall time required, it also leads to fewer errors and misunderstandings because all the relevant parties are involved (Womack *et al*, 1990). Another major contribution to the timeliness of the Japanese is a series of practices designed to cut manufacturing lead times. The main one is Just-in-Time production. Under Just-in-Time, parts are supplied and used only as and when required. This method reduces stock and work-in-progress and thus reduces cost. However, to achieve this (as proponents of lean/agile manufacturing have stressed), everything must be 'right first time', otherwise such a system would quickly grind to a halt for lack of usable parts (Kidd and Karwowski, 1994; Lamming, 1993). Consequently, it is necessary to drive waste and inefficiency out of the system, and the key mechanism for achieving this is the Japanese commitment to quality (Dale and Cooper, 1992).

4. **Quality.** The Japanese commitment to quality is now legendary. Their approach owes much to the inspiration of three Americans: MacArthur, Deming and Juran (Wilkinson, 1991). General MacArthur, who (on behalf of the US) virtually ruled Japan in the early post-war years, encouraged Japanese industry to improve production quality as part of the rebuilding of their shattered industrial base. Deming (1982) showed the Japanese that statistical process control (SPC), and other such techniques, are powerful methods of controlling quality. Juran (1988) showed the Japanese that quality was determined by all departments in an organisation, and thus set them on the road to developing Total Quality Management. Though imported, the Japanese developed the original concepts considerably. In particular, they introduced the concept of continuous improvement – *Kaizen*. Despite the widespread acceptance of the need for improved quality in the West, the Japanese appear to be the only nation so far capable of diffusing successfully the ideas and practices throughout their industry (Dale and Cooper, 1992; Hannam, 1993; Schonberger, 1982; Womack *et al*, 1990).

5. **Change management**. Another key factor in the Japanese approach is the ability to manage change speedily and effectively. This arises from three elements of the Japanese approach:

- First, 'strategic intent' (*see* Chapter 5) – the creation and pursuit of a vision of their desired future which embraces all staff in the organisation (Hamel and Prahalad, 1989). This provides a basis for judging what changes need to take place why.

- Second, *ringi*-type decision-making. This ensures that changes are fully thought-out and planned before they are implemented.

- Lastly, *Kaizen*-type approaches to change, which ensure that those affected are involved in implementing change and have the skills and commitment to undertake it successfully.

It is the combination of these three elements which, in contrast to most Western companies, allows Japanese companies to get it 'right first time'. Japanese companies tend to spend 90 per cent of the change process on planning and only 10 per cent on implementation. Exhaustive planning allows them to identify and sort out potential problems in advance, thus ensuring that implementation is speedy and successful. In the West, the tendency is to plan rapidly and cursorily, with the result that the implementation process is a long drawn-out affair as 'unforeseen' problems keep cropping up. Unlike Japanese companies, the end result is often failure or a sub-optimal outcome.

One factor only mentioned briefly so far is the importance – or not – of culture to the Japanese approach to management. Certainly, early studies laid great stress on the relationship between Japanese culture and business success (Abegglen, 1958). The argument emerged that it was the nature of Japanese society and its impact on individuals and companies that gave Japan its competitive edge. For this reason, it was argued, the West would never be able to replicate Japanese practices and competitiveness successfully. In fact, one reason why Pascale and Athos (1982) chose to study Japanese companies operating in America was that Pascale doubted whether American companies could learn much from the Japanese in Japan because their cultures were so different (Crainer, 1995). Obviously, as Hofstede (1980, 1990) demonstrates, national cultures do impinge on organisational practices, but whether this means that such practices cannot successfully be adopted in other societies is another question. A number of studies have undermined the argument for considering the Japanese approach to management to be dependent on Japanese culture. It has been shown that many of the distinctive practices of Japanese companies are relatively new and not embedded in Japanese history, that the role of culture is less influential than other factors, and that the Japanese approach can be successfully replicated outside Japan (Ackroyd *et al*, 1988; Buckley and Mirza, 1985; Cole, 1979; Marsh and Mannari, 1976; Pascale and Athos, 1982; Smith and Misumi, 1989; Urabe, 1986; Wickens, 1987).

The future of the Japanese approach

In discussing the distinctive Japanese approach to management, we must not forget the strong reciprocal links between government and business, especially the importance of Japanese industrial policy in stimulating and guiding the country's economic progress. This is seen most clearly in the close links between business and the Ministry of International Trade and Industry (MITI). As part of its remit to establish Japan as a leading industrial nation, MITI played a crucial role in the 1950s and 1960s in establishing national programmes in key industries to encourage joint action, to develop the country's science and technological base, among companies and public research institutions. The ultimate goal of these programmes has been to create a strong, competitive and world-class industrial base for Japan. These collaborative programmes have not been at the expense of competition between companies; rather they have helped to improve the competitiveness of all the companies both in relation to each other and, importantly, in relation to international rivals (Laage-Hellman, 1997).

After successfully coping with the second oil crisis of 1979 and the effects of a rapidly – appreciating currency in the mid-1980s, Japan enjoyed a good economic growth until the late 1980s. Despite the competitiveness of Japanese firms and the active support of the Japanese government, the asset-price bubble burst in 1989. Since then the economy has been in protracted recession, with only occasional signs of recovery (McCormick, 2007; Statistics Bureau, 2003). Nevertheless, successive banking and political scandals have undermined the stability of the political and financial system on which Japan's industrial might was built (Barrie, 1999; Shirai, 1997). This has led to some political and business reforms, and attempts to introduce Western-style deregulation in order to foster competition and cut costs, though, as Keizer (2009) notes, there has been a lot more talk about change than actual change.

Many explanations have been put forward for the decline of the Japanese economy. One of the most persuasive is that while Japan developed a world-class manufacturing base, this was undermined by a failure to develop the rest of its economy to similar standards (Pilling, 2003). In particular, the service sector, especially retailing, is only half as productive as its US counterparts. Similarly, the Japanese public sector is seen as being far less efficient than its Western equivalents. The banking sector also did the Japanese economy no favours by making vast loans to property companies to purchase over-priced land and buildings, which became worth only a fraction of what they paid for them when the asset bubble burst in 1989. The fact that these problems generally lay outside manufacturing helps to explain why, despite all its economic problems, even in the worst years of the 1990s, Japan's leading industrial companies generally continued to outperform those of its competitors in the West (Pilling, 2003; Shirai, 1997). It follows that Japan's economic problems over the last two decades do not appear to invalidate the Japanese approach to management as developed in, and applied to, the manufacturing sector. Even so, low growth, domestic recession, increasing international competition, technological developments that have led to changes in industrial and job structures, and an ageing population have all created pressures to change the Japanese approach to management (Harukiyo and Hook, 1998; Sako and Sato, 1997; Thomas, 2003).

In the larger Japanese companies, these pressures have led to structural changes designed to flatten the hierarchy and create greater flexibility (Koji, 1998). In the motor industry, in particular, there has also been a weakening of the previously strong supply chain links, with second and third-tier suppliers being exposed to greater levels of competition (Masayoshi, 1998). Looking at the Japanese approach to production systems, here too there have been changes; but these do not seem to have radically changed the main characteristic of the Japanese approach, which has been one of blending mass production with flexibility (Masayuki, 1998).

Perhaps the area where the pressures for change have been the greatest is in personnel practices, especially those relating to lifetime employment, seniority-based promotion and reward systems, and the treatment of female workers (Sako and Sato, 1997). As far as lifetime employment is concerned, there is some evidence that the economic, industrial and technological changes of the 1980s and 1990s have had an effect on this (Barrie, 1999). For white-collar workers, especially the older and higher-paid ones, there is evidence that continuous employment within one enterprise is giving way to continuous employment within a group of enterprises (Inagami, 1995; Sako, 1997). In the past, if a worker's job was eliminated, they would be given another one in the same workplace. Increasingly, the tendency is now to transfer redundant workers to another job within the same group or affiliated group of companies but not necessarily the same workplace. In some cases, this can be hundreds of miles away, and can also involve a reduction in pay (Watts, 1998). Yet for blue-collar male workers, where the distinctions between East and West were always the most marked, job security seems to have improved, if anything. This is because of the falling birth rate, which has also led to an increase in the retirement age from 55 to 60, and again in 2012 to 65 (Seike, 1997; Warnock, 2012). There has also been an increase in insecure, temporary and part-time employment, though this tends to be more in evidence in the service sector. Where part-time or contract labour is used in the manufacturing sector, it does not seem to have resulted in the same level of job insecurity as in the service sector (Keizer, 2009; Kezuka, 2001; Wakisata, 1997). Another significant change which has taken place is the increased use of performance-related pay, although this does not seem to have had a major impact on pay levels or job security (Keizer, 2009).

Overall, it appears that stability of employment does not seem to be diminishing, and in some cases may even be increasing. In terms of lifetime employment for male workers, though there have been some changes to the system, it appears that most Japanese corporations have maintained this (McCormick, 2007). Certainly, most Japanese managers, as well as workers, do seem to believe it is desirable and feasible to maintain it, especially as it is seen as essential to manager–worker cooperation (Ohmi, 1997; Sako, 1997; Sugeno and Suwa, 1997). As the finance director of a large Japanese corporation commented:

> To secure our employees living life in good shape is one of the corporation's duties . . . We cannot believe in cutting employees to sustain profitability. It is a kind of failed management philosophy.
> (Quoted in Barrie, 1999: 13)

In the area of the seniority principle, there does seem to be a greater willingness to make changes. There is growing pressure from both employers and unions to consider an increased role for other criteria, such as ability, alongside seniority when determining pay and promotion (Sugeno and Suwa, 1997). In a 1995 survey, two-thirds of responding managers saw the introduction of ability-based reward and promotion systems as a priority in order to create greater flexibility, although very few managers seemed prepared to abandon the seniority principle totally (Kawakita, 1997; Sako, 1997). A more recent study has confirmed that the seniority principle still applies quite widely in Japan but that meritocracy is on the increase (Fukushige and Spicer, 2007). What seems to be taking place is fine-tuning of the traditional Japanese reward system rather than its dismantling (Keizer, 2009).

However, significant changes do seem to be taking place with regard to female workers (Fukushige and Spicer, 2007). As in the West, there has been a significant increase in the proportion of women in the workforce in Japan in the last 40 years. In 1960, there were 18.1 million working women (40.8 per cent of the adult female population); by 1992, this had grown to 26.2 million (75.4 per cent of the adult female population) (Wakisata, 1997). This growth was accompanied by legal changes to promote equal opportunities and practical assistance with child care arrangements. Like men, women have also benefited from greater security of employment. The average length of service of women workers increased from 4.5 years in 1970 to 7.4 years in 1992; the respective figures for men are 8.8 and 12.5 years. In addition, there seems to be a gradual reduction in the very significant gap between male and female rates of pay: in 1970, women earned on average some 50 per cent of male wage levels; by 1992, this had increased to around 60 per cent. For female university graduates in their 20s, the figure was over 90 per cent (Wakisata, 1997).

So, a combination of legal, economic and demographic drivers does seem to have led to a significant rise in gender equality in Japanese workplaces, (Fukushige and Spicer, 2007). All the same, this was from a very low base, and in 2009 the United Nations ranked Japan 57th out of 109 countries in terms of political and economic participation for women, with female legislators, senior officials, and managers totalling only 9 per cent of its workforce (Kitayama, 2010).

Clearly, there have been and remain significant pressures on the Japanese economy, which have led to changes in how companies are structured and run, especially their HR practices, and in their relations with customers and suppliers (McCormick, 2007; Thomas, 2003). However, these do not seem designed to undermine or alter significantly the core of the Japanese approach to management (Harukiyo and Hook, 1998). The strong ties that bind workers and Japanese enterprises together and which lie at the heart of the Japanese approach to management have not weakened (Sako and Sato, 1997). As Shirai (1997: xv) commented: 'It appears from all the indicators that the foundations of stable labour–management relations in Japan remain unshaken and intact.' More than a decade later, research by Keizer (2009: 1532) supported this view:

> There is an important continuity behind these changes, a continuity created by the rules of the internal labour [market] and in particular the practice of lifetime employment. Without a convincing alternative, the support for lifetime employment remains strong and determines the legitimacy and direction of adjustments. This has constrained the opportunities for change and, by introducing performance-related pay, firms have changed the rules of the internal labour market rather than question its existence. Moreover, the support has not just constrained but also enabled change as the duality that lifetime employment creates in the labour market has been instrumental to the rise in non-regular employment. As a consequence, the flexibility in employment practices has been surprisingly large and firms have been relatively successful in their adaptations.

So although there has been much talk of Japan becoming more like the US in its business practices and personnel policies, recent research suggests that there are still distinct differences between the two countries and that a distinct Japanese model still exists (McCormick, 2007). Overall, there seems little evidence for the case that globalisation is bringing about the convergence of national cultures and business practices (Leung *et al*, 2005). This does not mean that the Japanese approach to management is not changing – it is – but it is still recognisably a Japanese approach to management and not a Western one (Fukushige and Spicer, 2007).

The Japanese approach: summary and criticisms

It can be seen that there are distinctive practices and policies which have a coherence and can be described as 'the Japanese approach to management'. But it is not simply the merits of the individual practices that have given the Japanese their competitive edge. Rather, it is that they are devised and adopted in such a way that they are integrated and mutually supportive of each other; in particular, Japanese companies have a unique way of combining hard and soft practices (Laage-Hellman, 1997; Ouchi, 1981; Pascale and Athos, 1982; Sako and Sato, 1997). This is not to say that this approach is universal in Japan or that all elements are present in those companies that do practise it. Nonetheless, there is sufficient evidence available to justify a claim that it has been the dominant approach in Japan since at least the 1960s and remains so today (Keizer, 2009; McCormick, 2007; Smith, 2008).

This does not imply that it will not change. Indeed, given that most of these practices have been evolving over the last 50 years, it would be surprising if they did not continue to evolve (McCormick, 2007; Smith, 2008; Smith and Misumi, 1989; Thomas, 2003; Whitehill, 1991). Already, as described above, there is strong evidence to show that changes are taking place. Even in large companies, such as Toyota and Honda, policies of lifetime employment and the reluctance to recruit staff mid-career are being modified, owing to the need to recruit skills that are in short supply, and because of economic and social pressures. These include especially the pressures for equal opportunities for men and women, the implications of an ageing population, and the need to recruit foreigners (Dawkins, 1993, 1994; Keizer, 2009; Thomas, 1993; Wakisata, 1997).

The Japanese approach has delivered impressive economic results, but there are those who would question the social cost involved. Japanese workers are expected, some would say coerced, to work much longer hours than their Western counterparts, and in addition are expected to participate in many work-related social events (Clark, 1979; Smith, 2008). There is also considerable evidence to show that Japanese workers are less satisfied with their lot than their Western counterparts, especially in relation to working hours and pay (Kamata, 1982; Lincoln and Kalleberg, 1985; Luthans *et al*, 1985; Naoi and Schooler, 1985; Odaka, 1975).

In many respects this is not surprising. From a Western standpoint at least, Japanese companies appear to operate very oppressive and authoritarian regimes that, through the combination of personnel practices and work systems discussed above, together with peer group pressure, leave workers little option but to conform and perform to very high standards (Kamata, 1982; Smith, 2008; Smith and Misumi, 1989). This accounts, in part at least, for the common observation that the Japanese are a nation of workaholics. There are other serious criticisms of the Japanese approach:

- Most companies operate a two-tier labour market, whereby a significant minority of the workforce have good conditions and lifetime employment, at the expense of less well-paid and less secure jobs for the majority, especially women – although there is now some evidence that this is changing, especially for women (Wakisata, 1997).

- Even those with lifetime employment are little more than slaves to the corporation because they cannot move to other jobs (Morgan, 1986; Smith, 2008).

- The merits of teamwork are only gained thanks to the unremitting peer group pressure on individuals continually to improve their performance (Kamata, 1982).

- The lack of independent trade unions leaves workers defenceless in the face of managerial pressure to work ever harder (Kazunori, 1998; Yutaka, 1998). Indeed, chronic overwork has now reached such levels in Japan that cases of death by overwork are common, and the Japanese have now coined an expression for this phenomenon: *karoshi* (Smith, 2008).

Whatever the merits or demerits of the Japanese approach, there is little doubt that it has had an enormous impact on organisational performance; consequently, many attempts have been made to introduce 'Japanisation' into Western companies (Ackroyd *et al*, 1988; Hannam, 1993; McCormick, 2007; Pang and Oliver, 1988; Pascale and Athos, 1982; Schonberger, 1982; Thomas, 2003; Turnbull, 1986). Despite some reservations about how well the system might travel, Japanese companies have shown that they can transfer their approach to the West. Nissan's Sunderland car assembly plant in the UK was judged by the Economist Intelligence Unit to be the most productive in Europe for the second year running in 1998, while in the same year its Smyrna, Tennessee plant was cited as the most productive in North America by the Harbour Report.

On the other hand, transferring the Japanese approach to indigenous Western companies appears to have been more problematic. Even the UK car components industry, which, owing to the presence of Nissan, Honda and Toyota, has received more support and encouragement than probably any industry outside Japan, seems to have failed to adopt the Japanese approach successfully (Hines, 1994; Lamming, 1994). This may be a major reason why many companies in the West, while not rejecting the lessons of Japanese management *per se*, are now turning to other approaches to increase their competitiveness, especially organisational learning.

Organisational learning

Though Culture–Excellence and the Japanese approach continue to exert a powerful influence over Western companies, in the 1990s a third approach to organisational success came forward to challenge them: organisational learning. Despite its new-found popularity in the 1990s, organisational learning was not a new concept. The highly respected American academic Chris Argyris has been writing about organisational learning for over 40 years (Argyris, 1992). Yet, there can be no doubt that interest in the concept of organisational learning, or the learning organisation as it is sometimes called, grew considerably in the 1990s. Crossan and Guatto (1996) noted that there were as many academic papers published on the topic in 1993 as in the whole of the 1980s. Many of these articles are dotted with emotive statements such as 'the rate at which individuals and organizations learn may become the only sustainable competitive advantage' (Stata, 1989: 4). Though statements like this have the power to attract the attention of business leaders, there are really two factors which appear to have moved organisational learning from being a subject for serious academic study to a hot boardroom topic: the pace of change, and the rise of corporate Japan.

There is considerable support for the view that the pace of change is accelerating as never before, and that organisations have to chart their way through an increasingly complex environment. Organisations are having to cope with the pressures of globalisation, climate change, changes in technology, the rise of e-commerce, situations where customers and suppliers can be both competitors and allies, and a change in emphasis from quantity to quality and from products to services. To cope with this growing complexity, organisations are recognising the need to acquire and utilise increasing amounts of knowledge if they are to make the changes necessary to remain competitive (Chawla and Renesch, 1995). As Pautzke (1989) stated:

> Careful cultivation of the capacity to learn in the broadest sense, i.e. the capacity both to acquire knowledge and to develop practical abilities, seems to offer a realistic way of tackling the pressing problems of our time.　　　　　(Quoted in Probst and Buchel, 1997: 5)

The second, and perhaps main, factor that generated such interest in organisational learning was the rise of corporate Japan. In attempting to explain and/or combat Japanese penetration of Western markets, many commentators argued that one of the main strengths of Japanese companies is the speed with which they gather information on markets and competitors, and disseminate and act upon this information internally (Nonaka, 1988; Pascale and Athos, 1982). Moreover, Japanese companies' ability to learn, adapt and develop also extended to their commitment to continuous improvement, in processes as well as products, both internally and jointly with customers and suppliers (Laage-Hellman, 1997; Sako and Sato, 1997). The result, as described earlier in this chapter, is their fearsome reputation for producing the right product, in the right time and at the right price.

Underpinning this is an ability to translate a commitment to individual learning into organisational learning (Hedlund and Nonaka, 1993; Nonaka, 1988; Ouchi, 1981; Whitehill, 1991). This idea, that the promotion of collective learning is crucial to organisational success, has not only led to the upsurge in interest in organisational learning but it also provides a bridge between Western and Eastern approaches to managing organisations. For these reasons, Probst and Buchel (1997: 1) claim that 'Organizational learning offers an alternative paradigm by which systems can change, thus permitting us to redefine the economy and society'.

What is organisational learning?

The term 'organisational learning' is often used interchangeably with the term 'learning organisation'. The difference, according to Tsang (1997: 74–5), is that:

> organizational learning is a concept used to describe certain types of activity that take place in an organization while the learning organization refers to a particular type of organization in and of itself. Nevertheless, there is a simple relationship between the two – a learning organization is one which is good at organizational learning.

In effect, the difference appears to be between 'becoming' and 'being'. Organisational learning describes attempts by organisations to become learning organisations by promoting learning in a conscious, systematic and synergistic fashion that involves everyone in the organisation. A learning organisation is the highest state of organisational learning, in which an organisation has achieved the ability to transform itself continuously through the development and involvement of all its members (Argyris and Schön, 1978; Burgoyne *et al*, 1994; Chawla and Renesch, 1995; West, 1994).

A further, and perhaps more significant, distinction between the two terms relates to those who use them. Argyris (1999: 1) asserts:

> We divide the literature that pays attention to organizational learning into two main categories: the practice-oriented, prescriptive literature of 'the learning organization,' promulgated mainly by consultants and practitioners, and the predominately skeptical scholarly literature of 'organizational learning', produced by academics.

In fact the term 'learning organisation' is used much less now than in the 1980s and 1990s. This appears to be because very few organisations, if any, appear to have achieved learning organisation status (Easterby-Smith, 1997; Probst and Buchel, 1997; Tsang, 1997). For this reason, organisational learning now appears to be the term of choice for both the sceptical and prescriptive camps.

Having said that, one of the problems in coming to grips with organisational learning is that its advocates appear to offer a multitude of definitions or models of what it is. Ideas and perspectives 3.12 gives a sample of the definitions that have been advanced, but it is probably no exaggeration to say that there are nearly as many definitions of organisational learning as there are writers on the topic (Tsang, 1997).

Easterby-Smith (1997) attempts to explain this confusion of definitions by identifying the different disciplinary backgrounds of those writing on organisational learning. He argues that most writers come from one of six disciplines: psychology, management science, sociology,

IDEAS AND PERSPECTIVES 3.12

What is organisational learning?

Organizational learning can be described as a process of individual and shared thought and action in an organizational context, involving cognitive, social, behavioural and technical elements.
(Rashman *et al*, 2009: 470)

Organizational learning is the process by which the organization's knowledge and value base changes, leading to improved problem-solving ability and capacity for action.
(Probst and Buchel, 1997: 15)

A learning organization is an organization skilled at creating, acquiring and transferring knowledge, and at modifying behavior to reflect new knowledge and insights.
(Garvin, 1993: 80)

Organizational learning means the process of improving actions through better knowledge and understanding.
(Fiol and Lyles, 1985: 803)

An entity learns if, through its processing of information, the range of its potential behaviors is changed.
(Huber, 1991: 89)

Organizational learning occurs through shared insight, knowledge and mental models and builds on past knowledge and experience, that is, on memory.
(Stata, 1989: 64)

organisation theory, production management and cultural anthropology. Wang and Ahmed (2003) note that it is not just the different disciplinary backgrounds of the proponents of organisational learning that leads to confusion. They identify five different focuses on the concept, and believe that researchers tend to centre their attention on only one of these. The five focuses are: 'focus on the collectivity of individual learning; focus on the process or system; focus on culture or metaphor; focus on knowledge management; and focus on continuous improvement' (Wang and Ahmed, 2003: 9).

Like Argyris (1999), Easterby-Smith (1997) draws attention to the difference between the long-established contributors to the field, the academic sceptics, who have been attempting to analyse, describe and understand learning processes within organisations, without necessarily wishing to change them (e.g. Argyris, 1992; Bateson, 1972), and the relatively newer entrants, the practitioners and consultants, who are attempting to prescribe what an organisation should do to maximise learning (e.g. Pedler et al, 1989; Senge, 1990). This is a point also made by Tsang (1997), who notes that, up to the 1980s, it was the analytical writers who dominated the field, but in the 1990s, with the upsurge in interest in organisational learning, it was the prescriptive writers who came to the fore.

Though the variety of disciplinary backgrounds and perspectives of those writing about organisational learning helps to explain the plethora of definitions, it does not help to resolve them. For this reason, as Probst and Buchel (1997) state, there is as yet no comprehensive theory of organisational learning. Nevertheless, there is one area where there is growing clarity and agreement: 'In today's environments . . . learning is directed increasingly at transformational change' (Cummings and Worley, 2001: 520). It is the potential of organisational learning to enable organisations to reinvent themselves in order to compete in the changing and increasingly uncertain and competitive environment that is making it such an attractive proposition for many managers.

Although many writers have contributed to the concept of organisational learning, those who have done most to popularise the concept in the UK are Pedler, Boydell and Burgoyne (1989). Perhaps the most influential writer of the 1990s was Peter Senge in the US, whose book *The Fifth Discipline* (1990) caught the imagination of corporate America. Its success motivated a whole host of consultants and academics to follow suit and produce books and articles extolling the virtues of the learning organisation, and the steps necessary to become one (Tsang, 1997). Part of the success of his book lies in the fact that it combines the individualism of the Culture–Excellence approach with the knowledge-generating ability of the Japanese approach. Senge contends that there are five interrelated disciplines that organisations need to foster among individuals and groups in order to promote learning and success (*see* Ideas and perspectives 3.13).

In contrast to Senge, who stresses the attributes an organisation needs to possess in order to learn, others stress the learning styles of individuals and organisations. Perhaps the most influential in this area are Argyris and Schön (1978) who, building on the work of Bateson (1972), proposed a three-level evolutionary model of learning (*see* Ideas and perspectives 3.14).

Burgoyne (1995) suggests that the importance of learning at Level III, Argyris and Schön's (1978) triple-loop learning, lies as much in its ability to allow an organisation to create and transform its environments as it does in allowing it to transform itself. He also considers that this is reflected in the ability of the organisation to stabilise the context in which it operates and/or its relationship with it. It is at this level that the concept of the learning organisation can fully emerge.

IDEAS AND PERSPECTIVES 3.13

Senge's five disciplines

1. **Personal mastery** – individual growth and learning.

2. **Mental models** – deeply ingrained assumptions that affect the way individuals think about people, situations and organisations.

3. **Shared visions** – the development of a common view of the organisation's future.

4. **Team learning** – the shift from individual learning to collective learning.

5. **Systems thinking** – the 'Fifth Discipline' that links the others together and which, he argues, is missing in most organisations:

> The art of systems thinking lies in being able to recognize increasingly (dynamically) complex and subtle structures . . . amid the wealth of details, pressures and cross-currents that attend all real management settings. In fact, the essence of mastering systems thinking as a management discipline lies in seeing patterns where others see only events and forces to react to.

Source: Senge (1990: 73).

IDEAS AND PERSPECTIVES 3.14

Three levels of learning

- **Level I – single-loop learning**. This is adaptive learning, which involves detecting and rectifying errors or exceptions within the scope of the organisation's existing practices, policies and norms of behaviour in order to ensure its objectives are met. Typical examples of this would be the monitoring of quality standards or adherence to sales targets in order to detect and correct variance. However, this would not feed back into the questioning of, or amendment to, the organisation's original objectives.

- **Level II – double-loop learning**. This goes beyond correcting variance in standards and targets and, instead, involves challenging the appropriateness of the organisation's basic norms, values, policies and operating procedures that create these standards and targets in the first place. This is reconstructive learning, which involves reconstructing basic aspects of an organisation's operations. Typically, this might involve questioning whether some functions should be outsourced rather than continuing to be performed in-house or whether the organisation should adopt a flatter, more open structure to remain aligned with its environment. Out of such changes, new practices, policies and norms of behaviour are generated.

- **Level III – triple-loop learning**. This involves questioning the rationale for the organisation and, in the light of this, radically transforming it. A typical example of this might be a traditional manufacturing organisation attempting to reinvent itself as a service company with all the implications for culture, structure and practices that such a move would require.

Source: Argyris and Schön (1978).

Cummings and Worley (2001: 522–4) identify a three-phase process designed to help an organisation move from adaptive, Level I, learning to transformative, Level III, learning, but they warn that:

> Although the phases are described linearly below, in practice they form a recurrent cycle of overlapping learning activities.

1. Discover theories in use and their consequences. This first step involves uncovering members' mental models or theories in use and the consequences that follow from behaving and organising according to them.

2. Invent and produce more effective theories in use. Based on what is discovered in the first phase of this change process, members invent and produce theories in use that lead to more effective actions and that are more closely aligned with [Level II and Level III] learning.

3. Continually monitor and improve the learning process. This final phase involves . . . learning how to learn. Here learning is directed at the learning process itself and at how well [Level II and Level III] learning characteristics are reflected in it. This includes assessing OL strategies and the organisational structures and processes that contribute to them.

Cummings and Worley (Ideas and perspectives 3.15) also identify five organisational characteristics that promote organisational learning.

As can be seen, Cummings and Worley identify both the phases that organisations need to go through to move from adaptive to transformational learning, and the characteristics which promote organisational learning. Probst and Buchel (1997: 16), on the other hand, take a very different view, claiming that 'Organizational learning is unique to an institution'. That is to say that each organisation can and should find its own way to become a learning organisation. They suggest that there are at least four different generic approaches (*see* Ideas and perspectives 3.16).

Despite the diversity and contradictions evident among those promoting the concept of organisational learning, one thing is clear: they all see the main purpose of learning as facilitating organisational change. Like the Culture–Excellence and the Japanese approaches,

---

IDEAS AND PERSPECTIVES 3.15

Promoters of organisational learning

- **Structure** – this needs to be flat and teamwork-based in order to promote networking both internally and externally.

- **Information systems** – these need to be geared toward the rapid acquisition, processing and sharing of information.

- **Human resource practices** – these need to include appraisal and reward systems which promote the acquisition and sharing of new skills and knowledge.

- **Organisational culture** – this needs to be based on values and norms which promote openness, creativity and experimentation in order to support successful learning.

- **Leadership** – managers throughout the organisation must lead, promote and be involved in organisational learning.

Source: Cummings and Worley (2001).

IDEAS AND PERSPECTIVES 3.16

Approaches to organisational learning

- **Learning by developing a strategy** – shaping the organisation's future through a participative and practical learning exercise.

- **Learning by developing a structure** – developing structural forms, such as matrix and network structures, that promote learning.

- **Learning by developing a culture** – the creation of shared values, norms and attitudes that promote collective success over individual attainment.

- **Learning by developing human resources** – developing staff through participative and group-orientated learning.

Source: Probst and Buchel (1997).

---

its popularity owes much to its posited beneficial link to organisational performance; but unlike them, it is the only organisation theory whose main purpose is to enable organisations to cope with and promote change. As Probst and Buchel (1997: xi) comment:

> Learning is attracting increasing attention both in academic circles and business practice. One of the main reasons for this is the increasing pressure of change on companies . . . The rate of change accelerates steadily, and companies must find their bearings in an increasingly complex environment. The ability to learn is thus of paramount importance. Companies which do not successfully implement organizational changes, and which fail to cultivate their potential to develop, may soon find themselves among the losers.

It is clear that there are considerable arguments in favour of the learning approach, yet there are also arguments against it.

Organisational learning: summary and criticisms

Though there has been considerable interest in the concept of organisational learning, this does not seem to have created the clarity one might have wished for. As Antonacopoulou and Chiva (2007) comment:

> The OL debate appears to have reached a point of stalemate where little progress seems to be noticeable in terms of some of the prominent questions that still remain unresolved. Although there seems to be some agreement that emotion, power and politics are part of the OL process and support learning in the presence of diversity there is still lack of agreement about how OL takes place and the mechanisms or processes involved, what factors facilitate its development, or what aspects to look for when we investigate OL.

In a similarly critical fashion, Shipton (2006) suggests that research on the topic is diverse, fragmented and with little overlap between the various disciplinary perspectives on organisational learning. This is perhaps why, according to Huczynski and Buchanan (2001), for every positive statement about organisational learning, one can also find a negative one (*see* Ideas and perspectives 3.17).

Consequently, it is difficult to summarise a concept that has been defined in so many different ways, from so many different perspectives and about which there is so much dispute.

IDEAS AND PERSPECTIVES 3.17

Organisational learning

Positives	Negatives
A rich, multi-dimensional concept affecting many aspects of organisational behaviour	A complex and diffuse set of practices, difficult to implement systematically
An innovative approach to learning, to knowledge management and to investing in intellectual capital	An attempt to use dated concepts from change management and learning theory, repackaged as a management consulting project
A new set of challenging concepts focusing attention on the acquisition and development of individual and corporate knowledge	A new vocabulary for encouraging employee compliance with management directives in the guise of 'self-development'
An innovative approach to organisation, management and employee development	An innovative approach for strengthening management control
Innovative use of technology to manage organisational knowledge through databases and the Internet or intranets	A technology-dependent approach that ignores how people actually develop and use knowledge in organisations

Source: Huczynski and Buchanan (2001: 135).

However, there are perhaps five aspects of organisational learning that most writers would agree upon:

- An organisation's survival depends on its ability to learn at the same pace as or faster than changes in its environment.

- Learning must become a collective and not just an individual process.

- There must be a fundamental shift towards systems (or triple-loop) thinking by an organisation's members.

- By adopting organisational learning, an organisation not only acquires the ability to adapt quickly and appropriately to changing circumstances but it can also transform itself if necessary.

- As well as the ability to transform itself, an organisation can adapt to, influence and even transform its environment.

In summary, while one can see the attraction of organisational learning, one can also distinguish six major criticisms which have been levelled against it:

1. As is apparent from the above review, there is no agreed definition of organisational learning (Burnes *et al*, 2003; Easterby-Smith, 1997; Probst and Buchel, 1997; Rashman *et al*, 2009; Tsang, 1997; Wang and Ahmed, 2003). Even Tom Peters (1993: 385), who might be expected to be attracted to the concept, stated that: 'Most talk about "learning organisations" is maddeningly abstract or vague – and perpetually falls short on the specifics.'

2. Despite the volume of publications on the subject, there is a scarcity of rigorous, longitudinal empirical studies in the area, and what there are tend to focus on private sector organisations (Rashman *et al*, 2009). As Tsang (1997) pointed out, one of the main

reasons for this is that many of those writing on organisational learning are practitioners and consultants seeking to prescribe and sell rather than describe or analyse. He claims that, as well as promoting the concept, they are also trying to promote themselves and the organisations they work for. A similar point was also made by Easterby-Smith (1997: 1107):

> Much of the existing research into learning organizations is based on case studies of organizations that are said to be successful, and these sometimes seem to rely more on public relations than on any rigorous and grounded studies.

If this is the situation, then much of the research on organisational learning, and the recommendations and conclusions that flow from it, have to be treated with a degree of scepticism.

3. As Thompson (1995) pointed out, 'The term organizational learning is actually a misnomer. In fact an organization itself doesn't learn – people learn.' It follows that, in most organisations, the achievement of a high level of organisational learning will necessitate a fundamental shift in how individuals learn. This is not just a case of collecting and sharing information in new ways but, crucially, of thinking in new ways (Argyris and Schön, 1978). This requires individuals to undergo difficult and sometimes painful changes involving unlearning old ways of thinking and the redrawing of their cognitive maps – the way they perceive and make sense of the world around them. Many writers have commented on the serious obstacles to achieving such changes (Argyris, 1990; Hedberg, 1981; Probst and Buchel, 1997; Wang and Ahmed, 2003). Above and beyond these difficulties lies a further issue. In engineering such changes in an individual's thought processes, it is not just their perception of the organisation that is being changed, but their perception of the world outside work and how they relate to it and to others around them. What are being tampered with are deep-rooted personality traits and constructs that are fundamental to an individual's psychological make-up. In such cases, one has to question not only the extent to which such attempts can ever be successful but also whether it is even ethically justifiable to try.

4. Probst and Buchel (1997) maintain that organisational learning requires the generation of diversity of opinion and, at the same time, the creation of consensus. They argue that these contradictory tasks can be reconciled and achieved through the development of a collective view of reality. Their view assumes that it is in everyone's interest to participate in organisational learning and the ensuing changes. Although some writers, especially Argyris (1990) and Easterby-Smith et al (2000) recognise that there are major barriers to organisational learning, the assumption is that these can be overcome. However, according to Alvesson and Spicer (2012), many managers oppose organisational learning because they see it as a threat to stability and order. Also, as Chapter 1 demonstrated, much of our organisational experience since the Industrial Revolution has shown that managers view knowledge and control as almost synonymous. To this end, managers have systematically attempted to reduce workers' knowledge and increase their own (Rose, 1988). As will be discussed further in Chapter 5, organisations are riven by political battles, and the possession and selective use of knowledge is a potent weapon in such situations (Pfeffer, 1981). Even if we ignore politics, many traditional managers are unlikely to welcome the creation of organisations which encourage openness, and allow subordinates to seek out their own knowledge and question the expertise and authority of their superiors. As Garratt (1999: 205) puts it:

A few, often senior, people can see the concept as highly challenging and unnerving. They are concerned that existing organisational power balances may be upset by too much 'transparency'.

Given what we know about resistance to change, given what we know about power and politics in organisations, it is surprising that so little attention has been paid to these issues by those investigating and promoting organisational learning (Blackler and McDonald, 2000; Coopey and Burgoyne, 2000).

5. Though Japanese companies are often held up as exemplars of organisational learning, most theory and practical advice in this area has been developed in the West, especially the US. The proponents of organisational learning claim that the recipes they have developed are applicable to all organisations and cultures; but many writers have drawn attention to the problem of transferring theories and practices developed in one culture to another (Deresky, 2000; Fagenson-Eland et al, 2004; Hedlund and Nonaka, 1993; Hofstede, 1993; Rosenzweig, 1994; Thomas, 2003; Trompenaars, 1993). For example, openness and the encouragement of public debate and criticism are seen as an essential part of organisational learning (Chawla and Renesch, 1995). Although US managers might not find this too difficult to accept, it is doubtful whether, for example, Japanese or Chinese managers, with their tradition of preserving face, would find it so easy (Deresky, 2000). Face involves both maintaining one's own dignity and decorum and, at the same time, not undermining or attacking the dignity and decorum of others. Therefore, Japanese and Chinese managers, and managers from other non-Western countries, might find it very difficult openly to challenge and criticise the behaviour and ideas of others or for others to do this to them (Ho, 1976; Jones et al, 2000; Tsang, 1997). Similarly, as was noted in the previous chapter, proponents of Contingency Theory argued against universal approaches to organisational effectiveness and in favour of a context-based approach (Burns and Stalker, 1961; Child, 1984; Woodward, 1965). In particular, they maintain that theories and practices developed with one sort of organisation or situation in mind may be much less effective in a different set of circumstances (Burnes, 1991).

6. Burnes et al (2003) point out that the case for the general adoption of organisational learning is based on the assumption that all organisations operate in a fast-moving and unpredictable environment. In such a situation, the ability to learn and adapt must be possessed by all members of the organisation and not just a few at the top. Burnes et al argue that this may be the case for companies in the IT sector, but other sectors may experience a much lower level of environmental disturbance. Also, they maintain, even in fast-moving sectors such as IT, there are companies, such as Microsoft, whose dominant position allows them a degree of predictability and stability (Coupland, 1995; Wallace and Erickson, 1992). In addition, Burnes et al pose the question: if an organisation can develop the ability to transform its environment, what is to stop it creating an environment where organisational learning is unnecessary? After all, given the many obstacles and barriers to developing and maintaining organisational learning, this would appear an attractive proposition.

Given the intense debate over the nature and utility of organisational learning, we can perhaps agree with Probst and Buchel (1997: xi) that:

We should be wary of dismissing it [organisational learning] as the latest fad, since the topic of learning is attracting increasing attention both in academic circles and in business practice.

At the same time, we can perhaps also agree with Mintzberg *et al*'s (1998b: 228) double-edged compliment that:

> [organisational learning] is all the rage right now, and mostly for good reasons. But it is no panacea for anything. People have to learn, but they also have to get on with doing the regular work efficiently. (Horses wear blinders for good reasons.) There can be a time to learn and a time to exploit previous learning . . . So learning is wonderful, but there can be too much of a wonderful thing!

Conclusions

This chapter has examined the three main approaches to managing and structuring organisations that have dominated Western thinking and practice over the last three decades. The proponents of all three approaches claim that theirs is a new paradigm that contrasts sharply and favourably with the organisational theories discussed in Chapters 1 and 2. This does not mean there are not some similarities with what has gone before. For example, all of them adopt the open systems approach of the contingency theorists, though only organisational learning makes it an explicit and central part of its approach. Also, the Japanese use the industrial engineering concepts developed by Taylor and his contemporaries to study and design jobs. However, the context in which they are deployed (the lack of payment by results, the use of teamwork and worker involvement, and above all else, guaranteed jobs) is markedly different. In a similar way, the Culture– Excellence approach can be seen to bear some similarities with the Human Relations movement, especially in its emphasis on leadership and communication. On the other hand, the emphasis on culture, individual achievement and all-round excellence makes it a distinct approach. The same can be said of organisational learning, which builds on, but develops in a wider context, past practices for encouraging individual and group learning.

There are also points of contact between the three approaches, not least that in some way they all offer recipes for 'excellence' and they all stress the importance of culture (Dahlgaard-Park and Dahlgaard, 2007; de Waal, 2013). In addition, organisational learning consciously draws on the methods used by the Japanese to gather and use information speedily, and like with Culture–Excellence, it highlights the importance of individuals in promoting innovation. However, it also clashes with the other two approaches. Advocates of organisational learning stress that it can enable companies to shape and create their environment, while supporters of Culture–Excellence stress that organisations have no choice but to adapt to their environment. Organisational learning is at odds with the Japanese approach to change. The Japanese favour directed continuous incremental change, whereas the organisational learning approach encourages continuous but often undirected adaptation and also transformational change.

There are also points of contact between the Japanese approach and the Culture–Excellence approach (the emphasis on excellence, the importance of culture); but, again, there are marked differences. Lifetime employment and loyalty to the organisation contrast strongly with the stress on the transient nature of jobs proposed by the proponents of Culture–Excellence (Hughes, 1995; Rafferty, 1995). Likewise, payment by seniority and payment by performance are significant points of departure (though there is an increasing, but still small-scale, use of performance pay in Japan). It is noticeable as well that neither the Culture–Excellence nor the organisational learning approach really concerns itself with the sort of hard, manufacturing and quality practices so important in Japan.

Finally, the Culture–Excellence school seems obsessed with downsizing and arguing for smallness. The Japanese, meanwhile, are committed to growth. As Ferguson (1988: 57) remarked, in the 1970s and 1980s the US was outperformed not by small, nimble organisations but by 'high industrial complexes embedded in stable, strategically coordinated alliances often supported by protectionist governments'.

On balance, though there are similarities, these three approaches conflict with, rather than complement, each other. This was shown by Dahlgaard-Park (2007) and Dahlgaard-Park and Dahlgaard (2007) who, after reviewing the literature on excellence, concluded that there was no agreement about how to define it or the factors that lead to sustained continuing excellence. The Japanese approach, with its combination of tried-and-tested hard and soft techniques, provides a coherent and comprehensive approach to organisations which stresses both innovation and stability. The Culture–Excellence approach tends to emphasise soft techniques, innovation, dynamism and unpredictability, and, particularly, draws attention to the role of culture. Organisational learning, as an attempt to provide a coherent paradigm for organisational competitiveness, is the newest and least concrete of the three. At one level it has affinities with the other two approaches, but its emphasis on learning as the principal source of competitiveness also distinguishes it from them. This does not mean that if Western organisations become more adept at adopting Total Quality Management and other such techniques, and if Japanese companies broaden their use of external labour markets and adopt more flexible structures, the three may not coalesce, especially given the common emphasis on learning. But, after three decades of running in parallel, they seem happier remaining as competitors rather than collaborators.

Needless to say, none of the three approaches is without its drawbacks or criticisms. In particular, there are five concerns that should be highlighted, relating to 'one best way', people, politics, culture and change management.

One best way

The first three chapters of this book have been concerned with approaches to managing and structuring organisations. The one clear message that has emerged so far is to beware of any theory or proposition which claims that it is the 'one best way' for all situations and all organisations. Yet all three of the approaches we have discussed in this chapter appear to advocate just that.

People

The Culture–Excellence and Japanese approaches also leave much to be desired with regard to people. Both approaches rely on a workforce split into a privileged core and a relatively unprivileged periphery. Under both approaches there is a strong emphasis on commitment to the organisation taking precedence over all else, even family life. Therefore, long hours and short holidays are the norm under both systems. The Japanese approach appears to offer more job security, at least for the privileged core. However, the price of this is that competition for jobs in the better organisations begins, quite literally, at birth. Though some weakening of the system is taking place, to get a job with the best companies, applicants generally have to have been to the best universities; to enter those, they have to have been at the best schools; and to enter the best schools, they have to have been at the best nurseries (Bratton, 1992; Fruin, 1992). The lack of clarity of the organisational learning concept makes it difficult to be certain what its implications are for people. It does project an intensity of work and commitment that aligns it with the Culture–Excellence approach. In addition, its emphasis on restructuring individuals' cognitive processes in order to overcome their resistance to learning is, potentially at least, very worrying. Therefore, taking all three approaches together, one cannot escape the conclusion that the social cost of achieving excellence, in either West or East, is high.

Politics

The issue of organisational power and politics has received extensive attention over the last 30 years (Buchanan and Badham, 1999; Chang *et al*, 2009; Ferris and Treadway, 2012; Huczynski and Buchanan, 2001; Kotter, 1982; Minett, 1992; Pfeffer, 1992; Willcocks, 1994; Yammarino and Dansereau, 2002) and will be explored in Chapter 5. Given that organisations are social entities and not machines, power struggles, political infighting and conflict are inevitable. They may not always be prominent, but tend to come to the fore in situations where resources are scarce or organisations are in transition (Baillien *et al*, 2011; Chang *et al*, 2009; Morgan, 1986). It is perhaps here that Peters and Waterman, with their notion of total openness and trust to the extent of employees effectively allowing others to monitor their work, could most easily be accused of being out of touch with reality. There is a tendency in the West to treat politics and conflict as illegitimate; but, as Pascale (1993) and Thompkins (1990) pointed out, conflict is part and parcel of the creative process, and political skills may be a key competence for managers if they are to be successful leaders and persuaders. To ignore the presence of conflict or underestimate its tenacity is usually a recipe for disaster (Kanter *et al*, 1992; McLennan, 1989; Pfeffer, 1992; Robbins, 1986).

Yet, in the Japanese, organisational learning and Culture–Excellence approaches, little is said on the subject of organisational politics and conflict. As far as the Culture– Excellence and organisational learning perspectives are concerned, there appears to be an assumption that employees working in smaller business units, having greater autonomy and more satisfying jobs, will work with each other, pursuing a common purpose. As Chapter 5 will show, this is perhaps an unrealistic expectation. It may well be that in Japanese organisations, with their consensual and open approach to decision-making, strong commitment to organisational goals, high peer group pressure and, for some at least, lifetime employment, conflict is either minimised or channelled into creative directions (Keizer, 2009; Smith, 1984); though Allen (1994), Ishizuna (1990), Kamata (1982) and Sakai (1992) illustrate that this is not always the case. However, in the West, with companies reshaping their businesses, where job security is being eroded, where an individual's current performance outweighs all other considerations, and where only the fittest and fleetest of foot can expect to survive, it is foolish to deny or underestimate the importance of power and politics or to believe that culture can act as a cure-all.

Culture

This brings us to the next concern generated by these three approaches. Proponents of all three approaches treat culture in a rather simplistic fashion. For the Culture–Excellence school, all problems are resolved through the creation of strong, flexible, pragmatic cultures which promote the values of trust, cooperation and teamwork. A similar point can also be made with regard to the creation of a learning culture. In neither approach is there any real discussion or acknowledgment of the difficulties in defining or changing culture, despite much evidence to the contrary (Allaire and Firsirotu, 1984; Alvesson and Sveningsson, 2008; Hatch, 1993; Schein, 1985; Wilson, 1992). Nor do those who seek to promote the Japanese approach treat the subject of culture any more thoroughly. Either it is portrayed as an immutable feature of Japanese companies which prevents the West from adopting the Japanese approach or, more frequently these days, the Japanese approach is seen as somehow independent of culture (Furuya *et al*, 2009; Sheldrake, 1996; Smith and Misumi, 1989). Very few writers acknowledge that Japanese companies, like their Western counterparts, can find themselves with apparently inappropriate cultures that they wish to change (Ishizuna, 1990). All three approaches clearly leave themselves open to the accusation that they gloss over the difficulty of changing culture. The role of organisational culture will be examined in Chapter 5.

Change management

There is one last issue that should be broached: the management of change. Organisation theories are also theories of change. Most organisation theories claim to show organisations how to identify where they are and where they should be. They also, either explicitly or implicitly, address the issue of change management.

For the Classical school, change management is relatively easy: it tells organisations what they should be and, because managers and workers are rational beings, they should accept any concomitant changes because it's the logical thing to do! A similar approach is adopted by the Contingency theorists. The Human Relations movement, on the other hand, sees change as more problematic. Organisations are social systems, change is not a rational process, emotions come into play as well. Therefore, persuasion and leadership play a key role in changing organisations.

The Culture–Excellence approach has little to say explicitly about how change should be achieved, despite acknowledging the radical transformation it is advocating. Peters (1993) advocated a 'Big Bang' approach to change: 'change radically and do it quickly' seems to be his advice. Handy (1986), meanwhile, seems to adopt a more gradualist approach to change – big changes over long periods. Kanter *et al* (1992) advocate a combination of both; they suggest that major changes, especially in behaviour, can only be achieved over time. Yet they believe that dramatic gestures are also necessary to improve performance in the short term. As a result, their approach to change is a combination of 'Bold Strokes' and 'Long Marches'. Taken as a whole, the message from the Culture–Excellence school is somewhat mixed and the process and details are lacking, notwithstanding Kanter *et al*'s (1992) book on change.

The Japanese approach, however, is more specific. Japanese companies create a vision of the future (strategic intent) and move towards it in incremental steps (*Kaizen*) with decisions on what to change, when to change and how to change decided through the slow, participative *ringi* approach. The Japanese are extremely able at planning and executing change, which has given them a reputation as a nation that makes ambitious long-term plans which are slowly, relentlessly and successfully achieved. However, whether this approach could work in many Western countries, where managers appear to be wedded to quick decision-making and planning, is debatable, especially given that the financial institutions that invest in Western firms appear to favour companies whose senior managers appear decisive and who quickly respond quickly to changing circumstances.

Though organisational learning is explicitly directed at enabling organisations to change, its proponents are vague and inconsistent in specifying how one leads to the other, and particularly how the ultimate goal, of becoming a learning organisation, can be achieved (Probst and Buchel, 1997). Nor is it clear how the plethora of change initiatives generated by learning will lead to effective, coordinated and complementary overall change (Easterby-Smith, 1997; Tsang, 1997).

In summary, though the organisational learning, Japanese and Culture–Excellence approaches have their strong points, they also have their drawbacks, at least as far as Western companies are concerned. For this reason, none has achieved the same intellectual dominance enjoyed by past paradigms, though the Culture–Excellence approach has come to exert a powerful influence on managerial attitudes and behaviour over the past three decades. However, this lack of a dominant paradigm is not necessarily a problem *per se*. Instead, what it may reflect is managerial choice. Rather than slavishly following the precepts of Tom Peters or other gurus and advocates, managers are trying to make sense of their situation and identify what will work for their organisation and their stakeholders. Some managers at least do appear to recognise that the future is not immutable and that they are not powerless: they do have some freedom of choice and action, and the possibility does exist to influence the future shape of work by promoting the good and avoiding the bad. This is a point which will be explored further in subsequent chapter.

The remaining parts of this book will further consider managerial choice and the degree to which organisations are free to shape their own future. Before moving on to this, however, the final two chapters in Part 1 will round off the review of organisation theory by examining, in Chapter 4, the case for and alternatives to the postmodern perspective on organisations and, in Chapter 5, the role of culture, power and politics in constraining and enabling organisational choice.

TEST YOUR LEARNING

Short discussion topics

The purpose of these is to enable students to check and reflect on the topics. The discussions should last for no more than 5–10 minutes. Depending on the length of the lecture, there could be one, two or three such discussions in a session. The following are five suggested topics which address issues raised in this chapter:

1. What is a paradigm?

2. Why did *In Search of Excellence* become an instant best-seller when it was first published?

3. What did Kanter mean when she said that 'corporate elephants need to learn to dance'?

4. What are the main personnel and business issues that distinguish Japanese management from Western management?

5. What is organisational learning?

Class debates

The purpose of class debates is to enable students to explore a topic in depth by setting up a 'for and against' debate. The class can be split into two and one half asked to research the 'for' case and the other 'against' case. Individuals can then be chosen at random to introduce their side of the debate. Alternatively, two individuals for each side can be told in advance that they will be introducing the debate. The length of such debates depends on the time available, the size of the class and their enthusiasm for the topic. However, less than 30 minutes is probably too short and more than 60 minutes probably too long. The following are three suggested topics which address issues raised in this chapter:

1. In terms of organisational success, culture is the only thing that matters: everything else flows from it.

2. If organisations learn faster than their competitors, success is assured.

3. Given the choice between working for an American company practising Culture-Excellence and a Japanese company practising Japanese management, I would always choose the Japanese company.

Essay questions

1. To what extent and why do you agree with the following statement: *In Search of Excellence* has proved so popular among managers because it only requires them to parrot a few meaningless phrases rather than needing to work hard or change their behaviour.

2. Describe and evaluate the effectiveness of each of the following as approaches to organisational change: (a) Culture–Excellence, (b) Japanese management and (c) organisational learning.

Suggested further reading

Peters, TJ and Waterman, RH (1982) *In Search of Excellence: Lessons from America's best-run companies*. Harper & Row: London.
> In order to capture the essence of Culture–Excellence, there is no better book to read than the one that began it all.

Probst, G and Buchel, B (1997) *Organizational Learning*. Prentice Hall: London.
> For a brief, comprehensive and comprehensible look at organisational learning, this is excellent.

Sako, M and Sato, H (eds) (1997) *Japanese Labour and Management in Transition*. Routledge: London.
> A comprehensive review of Japanese management.

Sheldrake, J (1996) *Management Theory: From Taylorism to Japanization*. International Thompson Business Press: London.
> John Sheldrake provides a brief but useful review of the work of Charles Handy and also of the rise of Japanese management.

Wilson, DC (1992) *A Strategy of Change*. Routledge: London.
> David Wilson's book provides a pithy and critical analysis of the shortcomings of the Culture–Excellence approach.

CASE STUDY 3

The transformation of XYZ Construction: Phase 1 – culture change

Background: XYZ Construction employs 500 staff and is part of a Europe-based multinational enterprise. Its main business is the provision of specialist services to major construction projects. As is typical for the construction industry, XYZ operates in a highly competitive and at times hostile and aggressive environment. Disputes between contractors and subcontractors can become bitter and frequently end in litigation, though there have been a number of attempts over the last decade to create better relationships. Just as relationships between organisations tended to be hostile, so relationships within organisations were also less than friendly.

Up to 1996, XYZ had been run by an autocratic managing director who was feared by his colleagues and who treated the company as his own personal fiefdom. His style of management was not liked and many felt that it was counterproductive but, as one manager commented, 'You didn't challenge him, you didn't put your head above the parapet, or he'd make life hell for you.' When he retired, the parent company took the view that XYZ was underperforming and that much of this was due to poor management and a lack of cooperation within the company. His replacement was appointed with the remit to improve the performance of the company and develop its managerial competency. This he did to great effect. Over a four-year period, he transformed the operation, culture and structure of the organisation.

Focusing on people and performance: The new managing director was appointed in 1996. He had trained as an engineer at XYZ but had then left and worked for a number of other companies in the construction industry. Construction is a close-knit industry, however, and he still knew XYZ and its staff quite well. He came with a reputation as an enlightened manager who could deliver performance improvements. The construction industry was notorious for the antagonistic relations between the main contractors and subcontractors such as XYZ, who specialise in one aspect of the construction process. The managing director recognised, however, that the industry was attempting to change, and conflict was being replaced by 'partnership' initiatives – contractors and subcontractors working in a more cooperative and team-based manner (Burnes and Coram, 1999).

The managing director also recognised that external partnerships needed internal partnerships and teamworking if they were to be successful. In turn this would require a new style of participative management in XYZ. Therefore, the managing director set out not just to upgrade XYZ's management but to undertake a root-and-branch overhaul of the company's operations and culture.

As a signal of his way of working, as a first step in creating better relationships among managers, he broadened out the senior management team to include key staff who were not directors. In what had been a very hierarchical and status-conscious company, this was a significant change. The managing director knew that the staff in the company, particularly at a senior level, were experienced and competent people. He believed it was in the company's interest to retain staff rather than replace them. However, he also believed that they would need to change their attitudes and behaviours and upgrade their managerial skills if the company was to achieve the changes he believed were necessary.

His strategy for transforming the company rested on carrying out two crucial activities in parallel: to introduce new practices and techniques into the company in order to provide a better service to customers (and thus improve the company's overall performance), and to change attitudes and behaviours within the company, especially those of managers. He did not see these as being separate activities or programmes: he saw them as being linked. New practices, such as customer care and customer partnering, were not mere technical exercises. They required behavioural changes and new managerial skills. Therefore, the managing director wanted to create a change programme whereby any change designed to improve the organisation's performance, whether it be new skills, new techniques or whatever, also had to promote and reinforce behavioural and culture change. The converse was also the case: any effort designed to change culture or behaviour also had to have the objective of improving the organisation's performance.

Between 1996 and 2000, the company undertook a series of organisational, management and staff development initiatives designed collectively to transform the organisation's performance and culture. The main initiatives are as follows:

Case study 3 (continued)

Date	Event
June 1996	New managing director appointed
August 1996	*Kaizen* Phase 1
October 1996	Customer care programme launched
March 1997	Investors in People launched
April 1997	*Kaizen* Phase 2
September 1997	Customer care programme extended to construction sites
January 1998	Construction supervisors' new role launched
June 1998	New senior management team formed
November 1998	*Kaizen* Phase 3
March 1999	Site-based trainers appointed
June 1999	XYZ culture redefined
July 1999	Leadership and behaviours review

The managing director's first initiative was to introduce a small-scale *Kaizen* programme. *Kaizen* is a Japanese technique for achieving small-scale improvements through teamwork (Witzel, 2002). The managing director saw his *Kaizen* initiative as delivering four benefits: it would show the organisation that improvements could be achieved on a quick low-cost/no-cost basis; it would promote teamworking; it would give managers confidence to delegate to and empower their staff; and it would allow both staff and managers to acquire new skills. In a traditional company such as XYZ, it was not easy to introduce new ideas and new ways of working, especially where managers might perceive them as a threat. But the managing director made it clear he was committed to this initiative and that it had to work. Over the next few years the *Kaizen* approach was rolled out throughout the organisation.

The next initiative, in October 1996, was a customer care programme. This was designed to engender a positive view of customers by promoting joint teamworking. In an industry where antagonism between customers and suppliers (contractor and subcontractors) was the order of the day, where settling disputes through the courts was almost a standard practice, it was never going to be easy to promote customer care. The managing director knew, however, that the future

of the company depended on working with customers to understand what they wanted and to give it to them. Once again, this initiative was a combination of organisational change and management development; but, much more than the *Kaizen* initiative, it was also central to changing the culture of the organisation. It began with a few key customers and a few key managers, but such was its perceived success that a year later it was extended to the actual construction sites.

Other initiatives were introduced over the next few years, including Investors in People, and a redesigning of the construction supervisors' role to ensure that the post-holders possessed the skills, competencies and behaviours necessary to work closely with customers and staff under the new regime. Once again this was designed to achieve a combination of aims, including changes to working practices, the upgrading of managerial competency on the construction sites, and the promotion and development of a more team-based culture in the organisation.

By the end of 1999, the managing director felt the company had made sufficient changes to its behaviour and practices to believe its culture was very different from when he took over in 1996. However, he felt that the new culture needed to be formalised and consolidated. Therefore, he initiated a company-wide review of each manager's leadership abilities and behaviours in order to ensure they were compatible with and promoted the new culture. However, he was aware that the basic structure of the company was unchanged and that he would need to address this issue in the near future (*see* Case Study 9 at the end of Chapter 9).

Questions

1. Evaluate and comment upon the extent to which XYZ can be said to have adopted the Culture–Excellence approach to running its business.

2. The transformation of XYZ appears to have taken place with very little resistance or opposition from staff and managers. Discuss why this should be so.

3. To what extent and why do you agree with the following statement: The new managing director has not changed the culture of XYZ but has merely introduced a new management style.

Critical perspectives on organisation theory

Postmodernism, realism and complexity

Learning objectives

After studying this chapter, you should be able to:

- discuss the contribution of postmodernism to organisational theory;
- list the strengths and shortcomings of postmodernism with regard to the design and management of organisations;
- understand the main tenets of the realist perspective;
- discuss the strengths and weaknesses of the realist perspective for organisations;
- describe the influence of complexity theories on our understanding of organisations;
- state the main advantages and disadvantages of the complexity approach to organisations;
- appreciate the limitations of rational approaches to organisations;
- comprehend how postmodernism, realism and complexity widen the scope for organisational choice.

MINI CASE STUDY 4.1

If you don't like who you are, just reinvent yourself . . .

Charlie Ergen made waves from Wall Street to Tokyo yesterday when the reclusive billionaire who lives in Colorado injected himself into the dealmaking that is reshaping the US telecommunications industry, writes David Gelles.

Offering $25.5 billion for Sprint Nextel in a bid that trumps an agreed deal from SoftBank is classic Mr Ergen – brash, unpredictable and deeply ambitious. . . . Mr Ergen is attempting to **reinvent** his business once more (Gelles, 2013: 19).

Mini case study 4.1 (*continued*)

Barclays' chief executive sought to put a torrid year of scandals and management upheaval behind him yesterday, as he unveiled a far-reaching ambition to **reinvent** a bank that has become a byword for aggressive financial engineering. Antony Jenkins laid out a vision of a bank "doing well financially and behaving well" (Jenkins *et al*, 2013: 1).

Too many shops, too few shoppers and not enough ecommerce: the formula does not make for a durable retail business and last year's lacklustre Christmas shopping season in the US was the latest reminder. . . . The point has resonance for JC Penney, the listed department store reporting today, whose plan to **reinvent** itself by scrapping yo-yoing discounts has led to a very public collapse in sales (Jopson, 2013: 16).

Time Warner named Jeff Zucker as president of CNN Worldwide, tapping a veteran television news executive to **reinvent** the international cable news enterprise. Mr Zucker takes the reins at CNN amid turmoil over the role for the once-pioneering 24-hour cable news network in today's changing news environment (Steel, 2012: 18).

Gas-guzzlers are out of fashion as the industry tries to **reinvent** itself, . . . Since it restarted work in August last year after an 18-month shutdown, [General Motors' Lake Orion assembly plant] has focused mainly on building the Chevrolet Sonic, the smallest mass-production passenger car being built in the US. Lake Orion's revival as a centre for small car production is testament to the eagerness of US carmakers to **reinvent** themselves (Wright, 2012: 25).

Introduction

It is now commonly believed that our world is changing significantly and that we are entering a new era (Cooper and Jackson, 1997; Deresky, 2000; Giddens, 2002; Handy, 1997; Hardaker and Graham, 2001; Hatch and Cunliffe, 2006; IBM, 2008; Kanter, 2006; Peters, 2006; Thomas, 2003). Whether we refer to this development as 'the Information Age', 'the Age of the Internet', 'the Age of Innovation', 'the Age of Unreason', 'Post Industrial Society', 'the Postmodern Age' or 'Globalisation', the message is the same: what worked in the past will not work in the future, and organisations, like society at large, will have to change in unprecedented and unanticipated ways if they are to survive.

One of the recurring themes of this new age, as Mini Case Study 4.1 shows, is that if organisations do not like their present reality they can construct a more favourable reality by 'reinventing' themselves. However, in the wake of the 2008 financial crisis, for more and more companies this reinvention appears to be more a case of searching for some twenty-first century form of realism than the grand visions of rapid growth, pliable consumers and easy money which dominated the preceding 20 years or so (Kay, 2008; Stiglitz, 2010). Certainly, if one looks at the examples in Mini Case Study 4.1, it might be possible to argue that Charlie Ergen and CNN are seeking to shape reality to their needs: in the other examples, the reverse seems to be the case. General Motors has had to accept that in a world of dwindling oil reserves and rising oil prices, the era of the gas guzzler is over; JC Penney is having to bend to the needs of the market rather than vice versa; and Barclays has had to accept that it cannot act as if laws, ethical standards and consumer interests do not apply to its world.

As was the case with past economic crises, such as the dotcom collapse in 2000, reality has a habit of catching up with the grandiose visions that organisations construct. In the process, many companies, such as Lehman Brothers and HBOS, go out of business or are taken over, and others, such as Barclays, General Motors and JC Penney, go through a painful process of realigning themselves with reality. As a *Financial Times* (20 March, 2007:

15) headline put it: *Dreams are no basis for a sound corporate strategy*. Of course, there are many who argue that their grand visions were realistic and that the post-2008 world crunch reality will prove too pedestrian and lacking in ambition. In a sense, this sums up the problem many organisations now face: in a world of competing realities, whose reality should they believe? This chapter will examine three critical perspectives on organisation theory with a view to understanding how they view 'reality' and the implications of their differing views for organisations.

The previous three chapters have described the development of organisations and organisation theory from the Industrial Revolution through to the present day, in order to show the various approaches to and options for designing and running organisations so as to meet the challenges they face. What has emerged is a somewhat confusing picture of theories which claim, each in their own way, to be the answer to all organisational ills, yet which are all open to potentially damning criticisms. All the theories we have examined claim to give practical and coherent advice to managers on how to structure and run their organisations. Yet, as Ideas and perspectives 4.1 shows, it is in their limited applicability to the range and

IDEAS AND PERSPECTIVES 4.1

Criticisms of organisation theories

- The tendency to assume a unitary frame of reference, in which the interests of workers and managers, blue-collar and white-collar staff, and people of different genders, ethnicity and religions either coincide or can be easily reconciled, is a clear shortcoming in all these theories.

- The belief of the Classical school and the Human Relations movement that contextual factors – the external environment, size, technology, etc. – are either irrelevant or easily accommodated is another obvious flaw.

- The assumption by both the Contingency theorists and the proponents of Culture–Excellence that managers are powerless to change the situational variables they face, and have no choice but to accept the prevailing recipe for success, is not borne out in reality.

- There is a growing scepticism regarding the ability of rational, objective science to provide an explanation for the many fundamental changes taking place in organisations and the wider society.

- One of the most serious drawbacks is that only the Culture–Excellence school, and to a lesser extent the organisational learning and Japanese approaches, give any importance to the role of organisational culture – and even then it is treated in a simplistic fashion.

- None of the theories gives serious consideration to the role of power and politics in influencing decision-making in organisations. Not only does this go against a great deal of research that has been produced over the last 20 years but it also runs counter to most people's own experience of organisational life.

- Lastly, these theories explicitly or implicitly reject the notion of choice. Their basic argument is that organisations need to follow 'their' recipe for success or they will fail. Yet, if we look at the panoply of organisations, we can see a vast variety of approaches to their design and management. Some, for periods of time at least, may seem more successful than others, but most organisations appear capable of surviving whether they adopt the current recipe in full, in part or totally reject it.

complexity of situations found in everyday organisational life that these theories are most open to criticism.

This, and the following chapter, which is devoted to an examination of culture, power and politics, will address the issues raised in Ideas and perspectives 4.1, especially the final three points. This chapter examines three important and critical perspectives on organisations: postmodernism, realism and complexity (*see* Ideas and perspectives 4.2, 4.3 and 4.4).

IDEAS AND PERSPECTIVES 4.2

Postmodernism

This is a loosely defined philosophical movement which, though originally based in the arts, has become increasingly influential in the social sciences over the last 25 years. It is a way of looking at the world that rejects rationality and objectivity. Instead, it concentrates on the ways in which human beings attempt to shape reality and invent their world. Therefore, for postmodernists, reality is socially constructed and for this reason, there is not one reality but multiple realities.

IDEAS AND PERSPECTIVES 4.3

Realism

Like postmodernism, realism is a philosophical doctrine that was first applied to the arts but has in the last two decades been taken up by organisation theorists. Also like postmodernists, realists believe that reality is socially constructed. But, unlike the postmodernists, realists reject the notion of multiple realities. The essence of realism is that there is only one reality and it exists even if we have not yet discovered it. They see both the natural and social worlds as consisting of complex structures which exist even if we are not aware of them or how they influence our behaviour. For realists, events and patterns of events are generated or caused by mechanisms and powers that exist independently of the events they generate. Therefore, realists do not deny the ability of human beings to shape their world, but they see this ability as being limited by an ensemble of real and concrete structures, practices and conventions in society.

IDEAS AND PERSPECTIVES 4.4

Complexity

Contrary to postmodernism and realism, complexity arose from the natural sciences before being taken up by social scientists. Complexity theories are concerned with how order is created in dynamic non-linear systems. In particular, those applying this approach to organisations maintain that successful organisations need to operate at the 'edge of chaos' and can only maintain this position by the presence of appropriate order-generating rules.

The chapter concludes by arguing that, while these three approaches differ significantly, what they have in common is that they open up the prospect that organisations have choices in what they do and how they do it. Rather than being the prisoners of organisation theories or contingencies, managers (potentially) have considerable, though by no means unconstrained, freedom of choice over the structure, policies and practices of their organisations, and even over the environment in which they operate. This then leads on, in Chapter 5, to an examination of the role of culture, power and politics in the identification, shaping and pursuit of choices.

The postmodern perspective

From modernism to postmodernism?

As described in Chapter 3, a sea change has taken place over the last 30 years in terms of how we view organisations. The Culture–Excellence model, the Japanese approach and organisational learning all have links with the past but they also represent a break with what has gone before. Running alongside these developments and to a large extent giving them a theoretical respectability, albeit mainly an unacknowledged one, is the view that we have moved from the modern to the postmodern world (Boje, 2006).

For Alvesson and Deetz (1996: 191–2), it was the changing nature of work and competition in the 1980s that forced organisation theorists to question existing and entrenched assumptions about the world:

> The increased size of organizations, rapid implementation of communication/information technologies, globalization, changing nature of work, reduction of the working class, less salient class conflicts, professionalization of the workforce, stagnant economies, widespread ecological problems and turbulent markets are all part of the contemporary context demanding a research response.

Initially, in the 1980s, much of the debate about the changing nature of the modern world revolved around the posited move from 'Fordist' to 'post-Fordist' or 'neo-Fordist' forms of work organisation. This debate, over the move from mass production to flexible specialisation, initially centred on the work of Piore and Sabel (1984). Their argument was that the age of Taylorism and Fordism, the age of mass production, was dead. Mass production was concerned with the production of standardised goods for stable mass markets using a form of work organisation that was characterised by the intense division of labour, the separation of conception from execution and the substitution of unskilled for skilled labour (Tomaney, 1990). Piore and Sabel argue that the market conditions that allowed Fordism to thrive have passed. The emergence of segmented and highly volatile markets, brought about by changes in consumer tastes and technological innovation, require organisations to be highly flexible in order to succeed in these post-Fordist conditions (Laudon and Starbuck, 1997).

According to Piore and Sabel (1984), only decentralised, worker-run firms have the flexibility, skills and commitment to cope with sudden shifts in consumer demands, volatile input prices and rapid changes in technology. They drew on the operation of loose alliances of small firms in Italy to substantiate their case. Though an attractive proposition to some, there does not appear to have been any great movement to create the decentralised worker cooperatives envisaged by Piore and Sabel, as Williams *et al* (1987) show. Instead, other writers began to argue in favour of the emergence of neo-Taylorist or neo-Fordist organisational forms (Smith, 1994; Whitaker, 1992). Rather than the age of industrial bureaucracy coming to an end, these writers argued that it was going through a two-pronged programme of change. On the one hand, computerised automation was linking together machines and processes and thus eliminating labour. On the other hand, where this was not possible, managers were shifting production to low-wage regions of the world (Froebel *et al*, 1980).

As Smith (1994) observes, the problem with this perspective is that though it fits, for example, General Motors, it does not fit Toyota, which has proved by far the more successful car company in the world. Sayer (1989) complains that the post-Fordist literature is confused, riddled with speculation and selective in its use of evidence. Piore and Sabel (1984) in particular have come in for much criticism, especially in relation to what some see as their over-optimistic view of the developing nature of work. Amin and Robins (1990: 202) commented: 'What we are seeing in the present period are organisational developments that are in significant ways an extension of Fordist structures. What is at work is not corporate fragmentation, but, in fact, more effective corporate integration.' Therefore, though Piore and Sabel's supporters can point to examples of flexible specialisation and post- and neo-Fordism, the explanations they gave for these and the implications they drew from them have attracted much criticism (Whitaker, 1992). Indeed, given the breadth and magnitude of the new organisational developments and forms discussed in Chapter 3, terms such as flexible specialisation, post-Fordism and neo-Fordism seem to have only a limited ability to explain the many changes taking place in organisational life. Nevertheless, what this debate did was to create a receptivity among a wider audience for the work of the postmodernists, who provided a more substantial and complex explanation for the changes taking place in the world around us.

Depending on whom one reads, postmodernism is either a relatively new concept or it has been around at least since the 1930s, if not longer (Appignanesi and Garratt, 1995; Featherstone, 1988a). Certainly, the term became fashionable among young writers, artists and critics in New York in the 1960s. In the 1970s and 1980s, the term became more widely used in architecture, music and the visual and performing arts (Hassard, 1993). Its adoption by organisation theorists stems from the work of the poststructuralist movement in French philosophy, which emerged in the 1960s. In the 1970s and 1980s, it became most closely associated with the work of Jean Baudrillard (1983), Jacques Derrida (1978), Michel Foucault (1977) and Jean-François Lyotard (1984). The interest in meaning and interpretation by symbolic-interpretive organisation theorists, drawing on linguistic, semiotic and literary theory, also served to increase interest in postmodernism (Hatch, 1997).

Researchers in organisation and management studies came relatively late to postmodernism. It was only in the late 1980s, with, for example, the work of Smircich and Calás (1987) and Cooper and Burrell (1988), that postmodernism started to impact on organisation theory. The interest in postmodernism by many social scientists and organisation theorists stemmed from their growing belief that existing, modernist theories, such as the Contingency approach, could no longer account for the changes taking place in the world of work and society in general. In particular, there was an increasing scepticism concerning the ability of rational, objective science to provide absolute and unitary knowledge of the world. In its place, postmodernists argue for a relativist position that emphasises multiple realities, fragmentation and subjectivity (Linstead, 1993).

Postmodernism, as the term implies, is something that carries on from, succeeds or takes its frame of reference from modernism. Therefore, it is necessary to understand how the proponents of postmodernism define modernism in order to appreciate their arguments. Modernism is a term used to describe the values, rationale and institutions that have dominated Western societies since the Age of Enlightenment in the eighteenth century. This was the period in which European thought, led by France and Great Britain, is considered to have made a decisive break with the superstition, ignorance and tradition of the Middle Ages. In its place emerged a strong belief in progress, economic and scientific rationality, a search for the fundamental rules and laws that govern both the natural world and human nature, and a commitment to a secular, rationalist and progressive individualism (Gergen, 1992; Hassard, 1993). As Hobsbawm (1979: 34) notes: 'Liberty, equality and (it followed) the fraternity of all men were its slogans.' Linstead (1993: 99) comments that the Enlightenment:

> produced a commitment to the unfolding of progress through history, the incremental growth of knowledge through science and the resulting inevitable subordination of nature to culture and the control of man.

Also, as Gergen (1992: 211) states, modernist 'presumptions remain vital throughout contemporary culture, and have left an indelible mark on theories of organization from early in the [twentieth] century to the present'. Modernists, therefore, assume that the world, both social and natural, and its structuring principles, are accessible through the correct (scientific) methods of observation and analysis. In relation to organisational life, the term modernism is used to describe the form of organisation that has dominated both the public and private sectors over the past 100 years (Biberman and Whitty, 1997). In the previous chapters, we have termed this the Classical or bureaucratic model, though others use terms such as Taylorist, Fordist or the machine-era paradigm (Fox, 1994; Smith, 1994; Tomaney, 1990). It is an organisational form which, its proponents argue, is based on rationality, logic and the pursuit of scientific rules and principles. Such organisations are characterised by mechanistic and hierarchical structures based on the extreme division of labour, and control systems that suppress people's emotions and minimise their scope for independent action.

It is clear from Ideas and perspectives 4.5 that postmodernism offers a very different view of the world from that of the modernists. Postmodernism opposes or denies the validity of

IDEAS AND PERSPECTIVES 4.5

Some features of postmodernism

Fragmentation: the breaking up of established structures into fragments.

De-differentiation: the blurring or dissolution of established boundaries.

Hyper-reality: confusion and mixing of the real with artificial/virtual realities.

Chronology: interest in the past and its imitation alongside/instead of the future.

Pastiche: the playful mixing of styles of decoration, dress, expression, etc.

Anti-foundationalism: rejection of all basics, absolutes, fundamentals, universals, etc.

Pluralism: all of the above happening simultaneously!

Source: Thomas (2003: 214).

the Enlightenment's emphasis on reason, logic and rationality as the foundation of scientific method and the basis for the establishment of truth. Postmodernism challenges the claim of science to establish authoritative or absolute knowledge. Instead, it argues that scientific knowledge is a social construction by the scientific community, and that new scientific paradigms are brought about by changes in the community of scientists rather than scientific discoveries *per se* (Hassard, 1990).

Therefore, for postmodernists, knowledge is relative, not absolute. According to Watson (1997: 383), postmodernism is:

> A way of looking at the world which rejects attempts to build systematic explanations of history and human activity and which, instead, concentrates on the ways in which human beings 'invent' their worlds, especially through language and cultural innovations.

One of the crucial distinctions between modernists and postmodernists is how they view the nature of language:

> For the modernist, language was simply a tool for the logical representation of the real . . . Within the postmodernist view, language . . . gains its meaning and significance through its placement within social interchange. Words fail to make sense (they remain nonsense) until there is at least one other person to give assent to their meaningfulness.
>
> (Gergen, 1992: 213–14)

So if language is a social construct, one cannot take the statements, rules and practices of particular groups and organisations at face value. Instead, taking their cue from Derrida (1978), postmodernists often begin their analysis of a situation or event by 'deconstructing' the language used. Deconstruction is an approach that seeks to reveal and overturn the assumptions underlying an argument, proposition or theory. Overturning assumptions opens up space for previously unconsidered alternatives. In the postmodernist approach, alternatives are left open to multiple interpretations, and the acceptance of multiple, fragmented realities is seen to displace the idea of one unitary transcendent reality (Hatch, 1997). Like many others, postmodernists recognise that the various stakeholders in an organisation each have different perceptions of what the organisation should do and whose views and interests should be paramount. Where they differ, however, is that they do not believe that there is a correct view or that one view has a right to be paramount. Instead, postmodern management and organisation theory, beginning with a process of deconstruction, 'seeks to reconstruct organizations by restoring a sense of harmony and balance in our species, our institutions, and our theories' (Gephart *et al*, 1996: 364).

This leads on to another prevailing theme within postmodernism: self-reflexivity – a critical suspicion of one's own suppositions. If reality and language are social constructs, then, so the postmodernist argument goes, to avoid the modernist error of believing they have discovered a fundamental truth or reality, postmodernists must constantly question and be suspicious of their own assumptions, statements and actions (Lawson, 1985).

Moving on to the links between postmodernism and organisation theory, the concept of self-reflexivity has similarities to Argyris and Schön's (1978) notion of double- and triple-loop learning, which promotes the questioning and challenging of existing organisational assumptions (*see* Chapter 3). Other aspects of Argyris' work also show postmodernist leanings, particularly his questioning of the inner contradictions of research methods (Argyris, 1980). We can also see postmodernist tendencies in Morgan's (1986) *Images of Organizations*, in which he treats existing organisation theories as metaphors.

In the heartland of organisation theory, Linstead (1993) argues that under postmodernism, hierarchies of merit, legitimacy and authority give way to networks, partnerships and organisational structures of a shifting, fluid and social nature. These are driven by external forces, such as markets or competition, and are *ad hoc*, short-term, fragmentary and localised. According to Daft (1998), necessity will force postmodern organisations to develop more flexible and decentralised organisation structures with fuzzy boundaries both internally and externally. In such organisations, he believes, leaders will become facilitators who will communicate through informal, oral and symbolic channels; control will be exercised through self-regulation; planning and decision-making will be inclusive; and egalitarian principles will hold sway. In a similar vein, Boje (2006: 27) argues:

> Postmodern theory holds out the possibility for a liberatory, non-predatory version of capitalism, if you will, a liberatory-grand narrative. This postmodern grand narrative professes democratic governance, transparency in monitoring corporate ethics, and a revision to the surplus value equation of maximizing exploitation that favors worker rights, community sovereignty over corporations, and eco-sustainability.

Consequently, as Clegg (1990) maintains, there are clear distinctions between modernist and postmodernist organisational forms (*see* Table 4.1).

For Clegg, and an increasing number of organisation theorists, postmodernism has arrived, it is having a major impact on the nature and functioning of organisations, and it will continue to do so (Addis and Podesta, 2005). Clegg acknowledges that postmodern forms of organisation are somewhat ill-defined. He argues that they are associated with developments such as flexible specialisation and post-Fordism, and that examples of postmodern organisations can be found in Japan, Sweden, East Asia and Italy. He also points out that while they can be associated with progressive developments, such as the extension of industrial democracy in Sweden, they can also be linked to more repressive and elitist developments, such as the segmented labour force policies adopted by Handy's Shamrock organisation (*see* Chapter 3). In the Shamrock organisation, there are three classes of employees – *core workers*, the *contractual fringe* and the *flexible labour force*. Each of these three segments of the organisation's workforce has very different conditions of employment and is treated and valued very differently.

There are two areas of organisational life to which the postmodernists have paid particular attention: culture and power. The postmodern approach to organisational culture rejects both the integrationist perspective, which sees culture as being shared by all members of an organisation, and the differentiation perspective, which sees organisational unity as being broken by coherent and stable sub-cultures. Instead, it takes a fragmentation perspective, believing that organisational cultures are inconsistent, ambiguous, multiplicitous and in a

Table 4.1 Comparison of modernist and postmodernist organisational forms

	Modernist organisations	Postmodernist organisations
Structure	Rigid bureaucracies	Flexible networks
Consumption	Mass markets	Niche markets
Technology	Technological determinism	Technological choice
Jobs	Differentiated, demarcated and deskilled	Highly de-differentiated, de-demarcated and multi-skilled
Employment relations	Centralised and standardised	Complex and fragmentary

constant state of flux (Martin, 1992; Meyerson and Martin, 1987). Hatch (1997: 231) observes of the postmodern perspective on culture that:

> In this view, alliances or coalitions can never stabilize into subcultures and certainly not into unified cultures because discourse and its focal issues are always changing – hence the image of fragmentation.

Therefore, for postmodernists, organisational culture is important, and indeed is clearly linked to their interest in symbols and language. However, postmodernists are sceptical of attempts to manipulate and change culture, as Hatch (1997: 235) points out:

> When you attempt to change organizational culture, while it is true that something will change, generally the changes are unpredictable and sometimes undesirable (e.g., increases in employee cynicism towards cultural change programs).

Where power is concerned, postmodernists take a very different view from most other writers on organisations. They are less concerned with the power that individuals or groups possess, acquire or deploy. Rather they believe that power resides in the combination of linguistic distinctions, ways of reasoning and material practices which make up the body of taken-for-granted knowledge that exists in society and organisations (Alvesson and Deetz, 1996). Perhaps the most influential postmodernist writer on power has been the French philosopher, Michel Foucault (1983). Foucault argues for a strong link between knowledge and power. He believes that knowledge, when it becomes socially legitimised and institutionalised, exerts control over what we think and do. However, there is a power struggle between different bodies of knowledge, each fighting for legitimacy and supremacy. For Foucault, though these bodies of knowledge are seeking to represent reality, at the same time they socially create it. He argues that power moulds everyone, both those who use it and those who are used by it. He maintains that power and knowledge depend on each other, so that an extension of a group's power is dependent upon and accompanied by an extension of its knowledge, and vice versa (Appignanesi and Garratt, 1995). Gergen (1992: 221) takes a similar perspective, claiming:

> Power is inherently a matter of social interdependence, and it is achieved through the social coordination of actions around specified definitions.

The postmodernist perspective on power has important implications for how a particular view of reality comes to the fore and is maintained in an organisation. Rather than being the product of an objective and rational process, it is the product of power and politics in an organisation. In some organisations, there does not appear to be a settled and generally agreed view of reality; rather what we see are competing interpretations put forward by competing groups and individuals. In other organisations, a definite view does appear to be held and does appear to be maintained. This is achieved when a coalition of groups and forces is able to wield power and use political processes to achieve a dominant position over others in the organisation. When this occurs, it is their view of reality which takes shape and comes to be accepted. Therefore, not only is power deployed to legitimate their view of the world but, in turn, its legitimacy bolsters their power.

The implications for organisations

What we can see from this review of postmodernism is the influence that both modernism and postmodernism have had on organisational theory and practice in the twentieth century.

Clearly, the Classical approach, and especially Weber's contribution, with its emphasis on rationality and scientific knowledge, definitely lies within the tradition of modernism. Indeed, the same can be said of the Human Relations literature, with its use of scientific methods to identify the 'one best way', and certainly the literature on Contingency Theory would appear to fall squarely into the modernist camp. On the other hand, the Culture–Excellence approach seems more comfortable with the rhetoric of postmodernism. Not only does it share a similar view of the current state of the world, i.e. that it is chaotic and unpredictable, but it also shares some of the language. For example, Charles Handy (1989) entitled one of his books *The Age of Unreason*, while Rosabeth Moss Kanter (1989) writes of 'post-entrepreneurial' organisations. Though Tom Peters does not necessarily use the language of the postmodernists, the essence of his message, and certainly the pastiche style of his books, sits comfortably with postmodernism (e.g. Peters, 1997a). The same can be said of organisational learning, with its emphasis on knowledge acquisition, rapid change and, most importantly, the ability of organisations to create their own realities (Hatch, 1997). The Japanese approach, with its inclusion of hard and soft elements, on the other hand, seems to reconcile elements of modernism and postmodernism. Indeed, it may be that one of the main criticisms of modernism and postmodernism is that both come from a Western, especially European, intellectual and cultural tradition and, consequently, may not be coherent with other, particularly Eastern and Islamic, intellectual and cultural traditions (Appignanesi and Garratt, 1995).

Even so, at least in the West, postmodernism does appear to be having a powerful and pervasive impact on both theory and practice in organisations. But, perhaps the main reason why it is having such an impact is that there are many forms of postmodernism which have a multiplicity of meanings and have been utilised in a wide variety of ways (Alvesson and Deetz, 1996). In particular, postmodernism seems to have fragmented into something of a smorgasbord from which both left and right, capitalists and anti-capitalists, can choose those morsels which take their fancy. As one of the key writers in the field of postmodernism and organisations noted:

> What is the postmodern approach to organizations? There is no one approach. Postmodern approaches fragmented into naïve postmodern (calling late modern postindustrialism or complex/adaptive organizations postmodern); more radical approaches (Baudrillard and Lyotard's era-breaks with modernity and some of Foucault); more critical theory approaches (Jameson, Debord, and Best and Kellner, etc. combine critical theory with postmodern theory). Then there are approaches I would call post-postmodern: hybridity (Latour's thesis that we have never been modern, instead there is hybridity of discourses, mostly modern with some post-modern); dark side of postmodern (global reterritorialization, postmodern warfare, and Biotech Century).   (Boje, 2006: 22)

In summary, despite the somewhat impenetrable and contradictory nature of the literature, the core of postmodernism concerns the nature of reason and reality. For postmodernists, reason and logic have proved illusory, and reality is a social construct. In organisational terms, an organisation, or rather those individuals and groups that dominate it, create their own reality – their own view or views of the world. Whether they see themselves as successful or not, whether they view the world as chaotic, whether they believe they can shape their own future, is to a large part determined not by any objective data or what is happening in their environment as such, but by their own ability to shape their own reality. The extent to which they can impose their view of reality on others both inside and outside will, to a large degree, determine whether they and the organisation are seen as successful or not.

Seen in this light, postmodernism has three important implications for the organisation theories and practices discussed in the previous three chapters:

1. **Culture**. As we saw in Chapter 3, the Culture–Excellence school has been highly influential in bringing the issue of organisational culture to the forefront of management thought and practice over the last two decades. In essence, what they argue is that, in order to achieve excellence, managers need to create a strong, unified and appropriate culture for their organisation. A core component of this approach is to manipulate and use language and symbols to create a new organisational reality. Though acknowledging the importance of culture, and sharing a concern with symbols and language, postmodernists view the results of attempts to manipulate and change culture as generally unpredictable and sometimes undesirable. This is because the outcomes depend upon the multiplicity of meanings and interpretations that others in the organisation put on such attempts, which are inherently unmanageable (Hatch, 1997).

2. **Reality**. How does a particular view of reality come to the fore and how is it maintained in an organisation? The answer for postmodernists concerns the role of power and politics. In some organisations, there does not appear to be a settled and generally agreed view of reality; rather what we see are differing interpretations put forward by competing groups and individuals. In other organisations, a definite view does appear to be held and does appear to be maintained. This is achieved when a coalition of groups and forces is able to wield power and use political processes to achieve a dominant position over others in the organisation. When this occurs, it is their view of reality that takes shape and comes to be accepted.

3. **Choice**. As we saw in the three previous chapters, most organisational theorists and practitioners in the twentieth century tended to believe that there was a 'one best way' to run organisations. The postmodernist perspective, however, has raised significant questions about whether these 'one best ways' represent some form of objective knowledge, or whether they are socially constructed realities which pertain to particular times, countries, industries and organisations. If organisational reality is socially constructed, then, in theory at least, it is open to organisations to construct whatever reality they wish. From this perspective, organisations have a wide degree of choice about what they do, how they do it and where they do it.

The influence of postmodernism on organisational thinking and practice cannot be denied (Boje, 2006). Nevertheless, despite its attractions, there are some serious reservations about its validity and usefulness.

Postmodernism – some reservations

Perhaps the main drawback of postmodernism is the difficulty in defining the concept (Boje, 2006). In the social sciences, the term has acquired a wide and often conflicting set of definitions, including a social mood, a historical period filled with major social and organisational changes, and a set of philosophical approaches to organisational and other studies (Alvesson and Deetz, 1996; Featherstone, 1988b; Hassard and Parker, 1993). Hatch (1997: 43) believes postmodernism has been defined in so many different ways that:

> It is impossible to choose a core theory, or a typical set of ideas, to exemplify postmodernism – the incredible variety of ideas labelled postmodern defies summarization, and the postmodern value for diversity contradicts the very idea of unifying these different understandings into a single, all-encompassing explanation.

According to Appignanesi and Garratt (1995: 4):

> The confusion is advertised by the 'post' prefix to 'modern'. Postmodernism identifies itself by something it isn't. It isn't modern anymore. But in what sense exactly is it post . . .
>
> - as a result of modernism?
> - the aftermath of modernism?
> - the afterbirth of modernism?
> - the development of modernism?
> - the denial of modernism?
> - the rejection of modernism?
>
> Postmodern has been used in a mix-and-match of all these meanings.

The confusion and variety of postmodernism can be seen in Ideas and perspectives 4.6, which shows a list of terms which postmodernists use instead of *modern* and *postmodern*.

However, there is little consistency in how these terms are used or defined. Not only are postmodernity and postmodernism used to describe different phenomena but there is no agreement or even consistency as to what the individual terms mean either (Boje, 2006; Featherstone, 1988a). Indeed, Burrell (1988: 222) remarked of one of the key influences on the postmodernist debate, Michel Foucault, that:

> it is important to note that Foucault's iconoclasm takes him into positions which are not readily defensible and his refusal to retain one position for longer than the period between his last book and the next is certainly problematic.

As well as the difficulty in defining postmodernism, there are also powerful voices that defend modernism and attack postmodernism as a form of intellectual nihilism or neo-conservatism (Aronowitz, 1989; Callinicos, 1989). Hassard (1993: 119) states that:

> The most influential critic of postmodernism, however, is Jürgen Habermas . . . [He] argues that theories of postmodernism represent critiques of modernity which have their ideological roots in irrationalist and counter-Enlightenment perspectives . . . Habermas suggests that as many French writers [especially Derrida, Foucault and Lyotard] take their lead from the counter-Enlightenment statements of Nietzsche and Heidegger, this can be interpreted as a disturbing link with fascist thinking . . . Habermas wishes to defend robustly 'a principle of modernism', which he suggests is an unfinished project that holds great, unfulfilled emancipatory potential.

IDEAS AND PERSPECTIVES 4.6

Terms used by postmodernists

modern	postmodern
modernity	postmodernity
modernité	postmodernité
modernisation	postmodernisation
modernism	postmodernism

Source: Featherstone (1988a: 197).

IDEAS AND PERSPECTIVES 4.7

Critics of postmodernism

1. Those who claim there has never been a fully modernist era and claim there cannot, consequently, be a 'post' modernist one.

2. Those who maintain that the current developments in society are merely an extension of what has gone before rather than any significant break with the past.

3. Those who accept that the world is entering a new age, but believe globalisation (see Chapter 12) and not postmodernism is its defining characteristic.

Source: Lyon (2000).

For Lyon (2000), the main critics of postmodernism fall into three camps (*see* Ideas and perspectives 4.7).

No matter how one groups the criticisms of postmodernism, it cannot be denied that a number of serious reservations have been expressed regarding the validity of the concept. These include its lack of consistency and clarity, that its proponents misread the current state of the world, that it may be correct but it is not important, and its posited alignment on the far right of the political spectrum. Its proponents accept that the postmodernist message is not always clear and consistent but, in the main, they would reject most of the other criticisms, especially that it is an ideology of the right. On the other hand, there can be little doubt that the postmodernist message has provided some justification and encouragement for the neo-liberal policies, such as privatisation and deregulation, adopted by most Western governments in the last 30 years. Regardless of the merits or not of postmodernism, there are two other non-modernist perspectives on organisations which are also having a significant impact on organisation theory: realism and complexity.

The realist perspective

What is realism?

As discussed above, there appear to be two dominant philosophical perspectives on the social world: the modernist, or positivist, perspective which believes in objective reality, logic and reason, and the postmodernist perspective, which sees multiple and competing realities which are socially constructed. In the field of organisations, over the past 20 to 30 years, it is the postmodernist perspective which has come to the fore. However, Ackroyd and Fleetwood (2000a) believe that there is an alternative to both. They point out that there is much substantive research on organisations that is based on neither modernism (positivism) nor postmodernism. This work is built on a long-established seam of social science which strongly maintains that, in order to understand and explain events, it is necessary to take into account both social structures, such as organisations, routines, rules and power, and the meaning that individuals and groups apply to these. Underpinning this work are well-developed philosophical doctrines that are neither modernist nor postmodernist. One

> ## IDEAS AND PERSPECTIVES 4.8
>
> ### Realism
>
> To be a realist is, minimally, to assert that many entities exist independently of us and our investigations of them. Clearly, then, most people are realists in this basic sense: we differ in what entities we are realists about. The realist social scientist, however, is likely to claim that social entities (such as markets, class relations, gender relations, social rules, social customs or discourse and so on) exist independently of our investigations of them.
>
> *Source*: Ackroyd and Fleetwood (2000a: 6).

of the most important of these is realism, which offers support for a non-modernist and non-postmodernist approach to organisations and management.

The essence of realism, as Easton (2000: 207) notes, 'is that there is a reality "out there" waiting to be discovered'.

Since the 1970s, realism has been applied to the social sciences by a number of writers (Bhaskar, 1979, 1986; Collier, 1994; Dobson, 2001; Harré, 1972; Outhwaite, 1987; Sayer, 2000). Though few have explicitly applied it to management, it is said to underpin much work in the field of institutional and regulation theory, and there is now a growing interest in its application to the wider issues of management and organisations (Ackroyd and Fleetwood, 2000b). Like postmodernism, the term realism has influenced many areas such as the arts, literature, philosophy and the social sciences. The term tends to be used differently in each of these areas, but, the core belief of realists is that many entities, such as class relations and markets, exist independently of us and our investigation of them (*see* Ideas and perspectives 4.8). This does not mean that such entities cannot be discovered, but it does mean that discovering them will not be easy. As Easton (2000: 207) succinctly puts it: 'We see through a glass darkly but there is something there to see.'

Realism, organisations and change

In applying realism to organisations, there is an increasing tendency to prefix the term with the word *critical* (Fleetwood and Ackroyd, 2004). This follows on from Bhaskar's use of the term critical realism in his work on science and social science (Collier, 1994). Those using this form of words in relation to organisations appear to do so in order to signal that they approach the study of organisations from a critical rather than dogmatic or naïve standpoint (Dobson, 2001). They are signalling that their attitude is one of self-reflection and that they are aware of the hidden presuppositions which abound in social systems. However, the use of the 'critical' prefix is not always consistent. For example, Ackroyd and Fleetwood (2000b), in their edited book on realism and organisations, do not use the prefix, while in their later edited book on the same topic (Fleetwood and Ackroyd, 2004) they do. While bearing this in mind, we will continue to use the term without its prefix.

Tsoukas (2000) states that realist philosophers see both the natural and social worlds as consisting of complex structures that exist independently of our knowledge of them. For realists, events and patterns of events are generated (are caused to be brought about) by causal mechanisms and causal powers that operate independently of the events they generate. Realists seek to identify the generative structures, i.e. the causal mechanisms that bring about events, and to identify their capabilities, i.e. their causal powers (Harré and Madden, 1975; Harré and Secord, 1972). Though these causal mechanisms possess certain capabilities, causal powers, the actual outcome of their operation will be dependent, i.e. contingent, on circumstances. For example, the Japanese approach to management has the potential to engender teamworking and organisational commitment, but whether it will or not depends on a whole host of situational variables, such as the nature of the society in which the organisation operates and the expectations of the employees concerned (Delbridge, 2004). Organisations also contain competing and contradictory organising principles, such as class, gender and ethnicity, and they are composed of different groups with their own distinct priorities and agendas that can undermine the dominant causal mechanisms (Reed, 2000). Yet, despite the potential of these competing forces and groups to create disorder, in many cases the interaction between them occurs in such a way that it produces organisational integration, a degree of continuity and stability, and sufficient change to maintain the organisation's viability (Ackroyd, 2000).

In terms of organisations and management, a central issue is the extent to which organisations and their practices are produced by human beings but still exist externally to them and shape their behaviour. Realists are very clear on this point. They maintain that while the social world, including organisations, is a product of human action, it is not necessarily a product of human design but exists independently of human beings (Connelly, 2000; Easton, 2000). Realists also argue that social phenomena can exist without those involved having any knowledge of them. For example, markets only exist in and through human activity, yet there is no necessity that those people involved should be conscious of the part they play in sustaining them. Ackroyd (2011: 233) states:

> For realists, change is endemic to social relationships and to groups: it is the nature of these things. The reasons for this are several, but the basic reason is that groups and organizations are routinely produced and reproduced by the everyday actions of individuals. Analytically considered, organizations are sets of processes put in motion by the mutually regarding actions of members, and so change is present in groups and organizations if only because the behaviour of participants varies over time.

Therefore, realists acknowledge the socially constructed nature of the world but, unlike postmodernists, do not see the world as being merely a social construction (Ackroyd and Fleetwood, 2000b; Fleetwood and Ackroyd, 2004). This can be seen in terms of the structure and operation of organisations. Realists contend that a structure is a set of simultaneously enabling and constraining rules and resources which shapes the interactions of those who work in or have to deal with the organisation. That is to say, a structure can be considered as a causal mechanism which has the potential and capability to act in certain ways, i.e. it has causal powers (Giddens, 1984; Manicas, 1980; Tsoukas, 2000). Consequently, as Tsoukas (1992) observes, just because a person may have friendly relations with a bank manager does not by itself mean that the person will be able to obtain a loan – the key issues are the lending rules of the bank and the creditworthiness of the borrower. Organisations may give groups and individuals certain powers but they also prescribe how and when these powers are to be deployed (Whittington, 1989). This does not imply that those concerned know how the rules are generated, the obvious and less obvious ways in which compliance is ensured, or their role in maintaining and developing these rules.

To continue the banking example, the bank manager knows the lending rules but not necessarily why they are as they are. Also, though he or she is aware of the penalties for non-compliance, they are less likely to be aware of the subtle pressures exerted by cultural norms to behave in certain ways. Yet the lending decision is not a mechanical process. The manager does have the ability to exert judgement and a degree of discretion in what they do. Likewise, the potential borrower can present their case in a more or a less convincing fashion.

This is why the causal powers possessed by a causal mechanism are seen as capabilities and not determinants. While causal powers limit what can be done, and while they have the potential to bring about (cause) certain actions, whether they do occur or not is dependent on a range of other factors as well, not least human action or inaction. As a result, when studying management and organisations, realists stress the need to give due weight to both people and structure, and the complex interplay between them. They claim that human action is shaped by the simultaneous constraining and enabling nature of an organisation's structure, which tends to favour certain types of outcome, but that any actual outcome is contingent on the prevailing circumstances (Tsoukas, 1989; Whittington, 1994). In addition, not only do these constraining and enabling forces lie outside the control of those concerned but those concerned are often unaware of them (Kumar, 1995).

Realists seek to understand and explain events by focusing on the mechanisms, structures, powers and relations that bring them about. In seeking an explanation in this way, realists begin by postulating the existence of a possible mechanism and proceed by collecting evidence for or against its existence and evidence of possible alternative mechanisms (Outhwaite, 1987; Reed, 2000). In revealing the mechanisms which bring about events, realists also seek to engender debates about alternative ways of structuring the social world and alternative forms of relationships, be they concerned with class, gender or power.

The use of realism in the field of management and organisations is most closely associated with the work of Bhaskar. His argument (Bhaskar, 1989: 36) is that nothing happens out of nothing:

> People do not create society. For it always pre-exists them and is a necessary condition for their activity. Rather society must be regarded as an ensemble of structures, practices and conventions which individuals reproduce and/or transform, but which would not exist unless they did so. Society does not exist independently of human activity . . . But it is not the product of it.

Bhaskar (1986) makes a distinction between human action and social structure. He claims that common propositions which are applied to people assume such a distinction: 'He cashed a cheque' assumes a banking system; 'He pleaded guilty' assumes a legal system (Bhaskar, 1979; Connelly, 2000). The two are mutually influential and interdependent but can be analysed separately, and are fundamentally different in that social structures pre-exist and are sustained and changed through human action, but human action is constrained and enabled by social structures. Realists do not deny that there are multiple perspectives or competing claims about the nature of the social world. They also share with postmodernists a recognition of the role of culture, power and politics in shaping organisational choices. However, they reject the possibility that there are multiple realities. Therefore, unlike the postmodernists, they claim that truth exists and what exists can be found, though the finding may be very difficult (Easton, 2000). As Stacey (2003: 7) comments:

Realists do not see any inherent limitation on human ability to comprehend reality in its entirety. For them, it is only a matter of time before research progressively uncovers more and more of reality.

Realism - some reservations

Realism is a riposte to both modernism and postmodernism. It attacks the former for placing too much reliance on science, rationality and logic, while criticising the latter for rejecting reality in favour of multiple and competing realities. Though it would be unfair to characterise realism as being a halfway house between modernism and postmodernism, it does tend to open itself up to criticism from both camps (Klein, 2004). The modernists object to the social construction side of the realists' reality, while the postmodernists object to the realists' claim that there is only one reality and it can be discovered. Furthermore, realism is not as well-developed or supported as postmodernism (Ackroyd, 2011).

It is also the case that the battle as to which perspective on the world will carry most weight with organisation theorists is not just between postmodernists and realists; over the last 20 years or so, a third perspective, complexity, has entered the fray, which, unlike realism and postmodernism, owes its origins not to philosophy but to the natural sciences.

The complexity perspective

What is complexity?

Over the last two decades or so, an increasing number of academics and practitioners have come to view organisations through the lens of complexity theories, and this is having a profound impact on views of how organisations should be structured and changed (Arndt and Bigelow, 2000; Bechtold, 1997; Black, 2000; Burnes, 2005; Fitzgerald, 2002a; Lewis, 1994; MacIntosh and MacLean, 2001; Morgan, 1997; Stacey, 2003; Tetenbaum, 1998; Wheatley, 1992b). Complexity serves as an umbrella term for a number of theories, ideas and research programmes that are derived from many different disciplines in the natural sciences (Rescher, 1996; Stacey, 2003; Styhre, 2002). To emphasise the diversity of viewpoints among complexity researchers, we will follow Black's (2000) lead and use the term complexity theories rather than theory.

Complexity theories are concerned with the emergence of order in dynamic non-linear systems operating at the edge of chaos, such as weather systems, which are constantly changing and where the laws of cause and effect appear not to apply (Beeson and Davis, 2000; Haigh, 2002; Wheatley, 1992b). Order in such systems manifests itself in a largely unpredictable fashion, in which patterns of behaviour emerge in irregular but similar forms through a process of self-organisation, governed by a small number of simple order-generating rules (Black, 2000; MacIntosh and MacLean, 2001; Tetenbaum, 1998). Many writers have argued that organisations are also complex systems that, to survive, need to operate at the edge of chaos and have to respond continuously to changes in their environments through just such a process of spontaneous self-organising change (Hayles, 2000; Lewis, 1994; Macbeth, 2002; MacIntosh and MacLean, 1999, 2001; Stacey, 2003; Stickland, 1998).

Complexity theories stem from attempts by meteorologists, biologists, chemists, physicists and other natural scientists to build mathematical models of systems in nature (Gleick, 1988; Lorenz, 1993; Styhre, 2002). In the process, a number of different but related theories have emerged, the key ones being chaos theory (Bechtold, 1997; Haigh, 2002; Lorenz, 1979, 1993), dissipative structures theory (Prigogine and Stengers, 1984; Prigogine, 1997), and the theory of complex adaptive systems (Goodwin, 1994; Stacey *et al*, 2002). The main difference between these three theories, according to Stacey (2003), is that chaos and dissipative structures theories seek to construct mathematical models of systems at the macro level (i.e. whole systems and populations), while complex adaptive systems theory attempts to model the same phenomena at the micro level by using an agent-based approach. Instead of formulating rules for the whole population, it seeks to formulate rules of interaction for the individual entities making up a system or population. However, all three see natural systems as both non-linear and self-organising. There are three central concepts that lie at the heart of complexity theories – the nature of chaos and order; the 'edge of chaos'; and order-generating rules.

Chaos and order

Chaos is often portrayed as pure randomness, but from the complexity viewpoint, it can be seen as a different form of order (Arndt and Bigelow, 2000; Fitzgerald, 2002b; Frederick, 1998). Fitzgerald (2002a) states that chaos and order are twin attributes of dynamic, non-linear (complex) systems, and, within chaos, a hidden order may be concealed beneath what looks completely random. For complexity theorists, chaos describes a complex, unpredictable and orderly disorder in which patterns of behaviour unfold in irregular but similar forms; snowflakes are all different but all have six sides (Tetenbaum, 1998). Stacey (2003) identifies three types of order–disorder:

- **Stable equilibrium** – such systems can become so stable that they ossify and die.
- **Explosive instability** – such systems can become too unstable and, as with cancer, get out of control and destroy themselves (Frederick, 1998).
- **Bounded instability** – these are complex systems which, torn between stability and instability, have the ability to transform themselves in order to survive.

Edge of chaos

Under conditions of 'bounded instability', systems are constantly poised on the brink between order and chaos. Elsewhere, Stacey (Stacey *et al*, 2002) refers to this as a 'far-from-equilibrium' state, while Hock (1999) uses the term 'chaordic'. However, the term most commonly used to describe this condition is 'the edge of chaos':

> Complex systems have large numbers of independent yet interacting actors. Rather than ever reaching a stable equilibrium, the most adaptive of these complex systems (e.g., intertidal zones) keep changing continuously by remaining at the poetically termed 'edge of chaos' that exists between order and disorder. By staying in this intermediate zone, these systems never quite settle into a stable equilibrium but never quite fall apart. Rather, these systems, which stay constantly poised between order and disorder, exhibit the most prolific, complex and continuous change.
> (Brown and Eisenhardt, 1997: 29)

161

It is argued that creativity and growth are at their optimal when a complex system operates at the edge of chaos (Frederick, 1998; Jenner, 1998; Kauffman, 1993; Lewis, 1994). It is the presence, or not, of appropriate order-generating rules, which permit self-organisation to take place, that allows some systems to remain at the edge of chaos, while others fall over the edge.

Order-generating rules

In complex systems, the emergence of order is seen as being based on the operation of simple order-generating rules which permit limited chaos while providing relative order (Frederick, 1998; Lewis, 1994; MacIntosh and MacLean, 2001; Reynolds, 1987; Stacey *et al*, 2002; Wheatley, 1992b). As Gell-Mann (1994: 100) puts it:

> In an astonishing variety of contexts, apparently complex structures or behaviors emerge from systems characterized by very simple rules. These systems are said to be self-organized and their properties are said to be emergent. The grandest example is the universe itself, the full complexity of which emerges from simple rules plus chance.

Therefore, the concept of order-generating rules explains how complex, non-linear, self-organising systems manage to maintain themselves at the edge of chaos even under changing environmental conditions. Complex systems have a further trick up their sleeve. Under certain conditions they can even generate new, more appropriate, order-generating rules when the old ones can no longer cope with the changes in the system's environment (Bechtold, 1997; MacIntosh and MacLean, 1999; Wheatley, 1992b).

The implications for organisations

A growing number of academics and practitioners maintain that organisations are complex, non-linear systems, the behaviour of whose members is characterised by spontaneous self-organisation, underpinned by a set of simple order-generating rules (Arndt and Bigelow, 2000; Bechtold, 1997; Black, 2000; Fitzgerald, 2002a; Lewis, 1994; MacIntosh and MacLean, 2001; Morgan, 1997; Stacey, 2003; Tetenbaum, 1998; Wheatley, 1992b).

Frederick (1998) argues that companies that relentlessly pursue a path of continuous innovation succeed because they operate at the edge of chaos, and, indeed, because they inject so much novelty and change into their normal operations, they constantly risk falling over the edge. Brown and Eisenhardt (1997) draw a similar conclusion from their research into innovation in the computer industry. They maintain that continuous innovation is necessary for survival and that this is brought about by a process that resembles self-organisation in nature.

Perhaps the most well-known example of a self-organising organisation is Visa. Hock (1999) reported that Visa had grown by 10,000 per cent since 1970, comprised 20,000 financial institutions, operated in 200 countries and had over half a billion customers. Yet, as Tetenbaum (1998: 26) points out:

> You don't know where it's located, how it's operated, or who owns it. That's because Visa is decentralized, non-hierarchical, evolving, self-organizing and selfregulating. . . . it is a chaordic system conceived as an organization solely on the basis of purpose and principle. Its structure evolved from them.

If organisations are complex systems, management and change take on a new dimension. Beeson and Davis (2000) make the point that while it might be fruitful to see organisations as non-linear systems, to do so will require a fundamental shift in the role of management. Like many others (e.g. Boje, 2000; Stacey *et al*, 2002; Sullivan, 1999; Tetenbaum, 1998; Wheatley, 1992b), they point out that self-organising principles explicitly reject cause-and-effect, top-down, command-and-control styles of management. Brodbeck (2002) suggests that the belief by managers that order and control are essential to achieve their objectives needs to be redressed. Morgan (1997) maintains that complexity will require managers to rethink the nature of hierarchy and control, learn the art of managing and changing contexts, promote self-organising processes, and learn how to use small changes to create large effects. For Tetenbaum (1998), the move to self-organisation will require managers to destabilise their organisations and develop the skill of managing order and disorder at the same time. Managers will need to encourage experimentation and divergent views, even allow rule-breaking, and recognise that 'people need the freedom to own their own power, think innovatively, and operate in new patterns' (Bechtold, 1997: 198). For Jenner (1998: 402), the key to achieving this is a flexible, decentralised structure.

Brown and Eisenhardt (1997: 29) refer to such flexible structures as 'semistructures', which they maintain 'are sufficiently rigid so that change can be organized, but not so rigid that it cannot occur'. They claim that organisations can only survive in highly competitive environments by continuously innovating and improvising, which, they argue, relies on intensive, real-time communication within a structure of a few, very specific, rules. Beeson and Davis (2000) echo this point and argue that, in such situations, change becomes an everyday event undertaken by all in the organisation. Brown and Eisenhardt (1997: 28) also claim that in the firms they studied:

> The rate and scale of innovation . . . was such that the term 'incremental' seemed, in retrospect, stretched. Yet it was not radical innovation [but] . . . a third kind of process that is neither incremental nor radical and that does not fit the punctuated equilibrium model.

Similarly, Brodbeck (2002) draws attention to studies that cast doubt on the effectiveness of large-scale change programmes (*see* Clarke, 1999; Harung *et al*, 1999). For Styhre (2002), the problem is that such programmes assume that it is possible to predict the outcomes of change and attempt to plan, control and manage it in a rational, top-down, linear fashion.

These writers are depicting organisations operating at the edge of chaos and, therefore, needing to respond continuously to changes in their environments through a process of spontaneous self-organising change in order to survive. As is the case in the natural world, this process is driven by order-generating rules that themselves can be subject to transformation in certain situations (Lewis, 1994; MacIntosh and MacLean, 1999, 2001; Stacey, 2003). When this takes place in nature, it is an automatic process; in organisations, this is rarely likely to be the case. As Stacey (2003) argues, people are not unthinking molecules; they can and do exercise free will, they can and do pursue their own objectives, they can and do utilise power and political manoeuvring to achieve their own ends, and they can and do interpret events in widely differing ways. Therefore, self-organisation may not occur even when appropriate order-generating rules are present, nor, if such rules cease to be appropriate, can it be assumed that they will automatically be transformed. Instead both will depend on the nature of the organisation (Griffin, 2002).

MacIntosh and MacLean (2001) provide evidence of the existence and importance of order-generating rules, based on a case study of a long-established manufacturing company that had been in decline for over 30 years. This decline appeared to be caused by a combination of inappropriate order-generating rules (such as 'don't innovate unless it leads to cost reduction') and a rigid structure that stifled innovation. Once this was recognised, the company evolved more appropriate order-generating rules (such as 'better, faster, cheaper') and implemented a new structure that gave greater freedom for self-organisation to its constituent parts.

In order for organisations to promote change through self-organisation, a number of writers have argued that organisations need to operate on democratic principles, i.e. their members will have to have the freedom to self-organise. For example, Bechtold (1997) argues that organisations seeking to adopt a complexity approach need a balanced distribution of power, strong customer focus, a strategy of continuous learning and an orientation towards community service. A further strand in this argument is provided by Kiel (1994), who argues that because small actions can have large and unpredictable consequences, individual human activity assumes great importance. Jenner (1998) claims that for self-organisation to work, authority must be delegated to those who have access to the broadest channels of information that relate to the issue concerned. Nevertheless, Stacey (2003: 278) sounds a note of caution:

> This seems to assume that self-organisation is some new form of behaviour rather than a different way of understanding how people have always behaved. The question is whether such self-organising behaviour produces patterns that block or enable change.

In considering complexity theories and organisational change, one of the key questions is to ask: 'What's new?' (Frederick, 1998). If we look at what appears to be being said about management, structure, behaviour and change, much of it seems very familiar. Writers from Peters and Waterman (1982) onwards have been arguing that managers need to abandon top-down, command-and-control styles, that organisational structures need to be flatter and more flexible, and that greater employee involvement is essential for success (Handy, 1989; Kanter, 1989, 1997; Kanter *et al*, 1997; Kotter, 1996; Peters, 1989, 1993, 1997a). However, as the implications listed in Ideas and perspectives 4.9 show, there are three areas where those seeking to apply complexity theories to organisations appear to depart from, or significantly extend, the received wisdom of the previous 20 years.

IDEAS AND PERSPECTIVES 4.9

Applying complexity theories to organisations

Implication 1 There will be a need for much greater democracy and power equalisation in all aspects of organisational life, instead of just narrow employee participation in change (Bechtold, 1997; Jenner, 1998; Kiel, 1994).

Implication 2 Small-scale incremental change and large-scale radical-transformational change will need to be rejected in favour of 'a third kind' which lies between these two, and which is continuous and based on self-organisation at the team or group level (Brodbeck, 2002; Brown and Eisenhardt, 1997).

Implication 3 In achieving effective change, order-generating rules have the potential to overcome the limitations of rational, linear, top-down, strategy-driven approaches to change (MacIntosh and MacLean, 1999, 2001; Stacey, 2003; Styhre, 2002).

The basis for *Implication 1* is that unless employees have the freedom to act as they see fit, self-organisation will be blocked and organisations will not be able to achieve continuous and beneficial innovation. The rationale for *Implication 2* is that neither small-scale incremental change nor radical-transformational change work: instead, innovative activity can be successfully generated only through the 'third kind' of change, such as new product and process development brought about by self-organising teams. *Implication 3* is based on the argument that because organisations are complex systems, which are radically unpredictable and where even small changes can have massive and unanticipated effects, top-down change cannot deliver the continuous innovation that organisations need in order to survive and prosper. Instead, it is argued that organisations can only achieve continuous innovation if they position themselves at the edge of chaos. This position can be achieved and maintained only through self-organisation, which in turn depends on the possession of appropriate order-generating rules. However, should these rules cease to be appropriate for the organisation's environment, the process of self-organisation allows new, more appropriate, rules to be generated. Therefore, in a chicken-and-egg fashion, order-generating rules create the conditions for self-organisation, and self-organisation creates the conditions that enable order-generating rules to be transformed (Bechtold, 1997; Hoogerwerf and Poorthuis, 2002; Tetenbaum, 1998).

Complexity – some reservations

Like postmodernism and realism, complexity has much to commend it. It offers an explanation of the apparent complexity and chaos of modern life and, potentially at least, a way of managing this complexity and chaos. Also, for managers, it is an approach based on 'hard' science and not 'airy-fairy' philosophy. Nevertheless, writers have raised four main reservations about the application of complexity theories to organisations (Burnes, 2005):

1. The complexity approach requires a significant shift towards greater organisational democracy and power equalisation. This appears to go far beyond the more limited, and often failed, attempts to redistribute power through empowerment, flatter organisational structures and quality improvement programmes which have been called for over the last 20 years (Eccles, 1993; Foegen, 1999; Lawler *et al*, 1998; Lee, 1999; Pfeffer, 1996; Stohl and Cheney, 2001; Wetlaufer, 1999; Whyte and Witcher, 1992; Witcher, 1993; Zairi *et al*, 1994). Therefore, convincing organisations that they are complex systems is likely to prove far easier than for organisations to achieve the profound internal realignments necessary to implement this concept (Beeson and Davis, 2000; Stacey, 2003).

2. In applying complexity theories to organisations, it is important to bear in mind that, even in the natural sciences, there are variants of these and disputes about their definition and implications (Black, 2000; Stacey, 2003; Stacey *et al*, 2002). As Arndt and Bigelow (2000: 36) observe, they have 'caused consternation as well as delight'. Therefore, one needs to be extremely careful not to treat complexity theories as though they are established, unitary, unquestioned and uncontroversial (Houchin and MacLean, 2005; Stickland, 1998).

3. There appears to be a lack of clarity or explicitness regarding how writers are applying complexity theories to organisations (Arndt and Bigelow, 2000; Brodbeck, 2002; Burnes, 2005; Hayles, 2000; Morgan, 1997; Stacey, 2003; Stacey *et al*, 2002). For example, some

see them as a metaphorical device which provides a means of gaining new insights into organisations, while others see them as a way of mathematically modelling how and why organisations operate as they do (Stickland, 1998). If the former, then it could be argued that the complexity perspective is just another of the multiple realities so beloved of the postmodernists. If the latter, then its proponents will have to show how mathematical modelling techniques can be applied to complex and dynamic human processes in organisations, though there is no indication that anyone has yet attempted to do so (Stacey, 2003).

4. There are also those who, while supporting a complexity perspective on organisations, argue that complexity cannot stand alone as a means of understanding and changing organisations. Perhaps the prime example of this can be found in the work of Boje, who seeks to align the science of complexity with the philosophy of postmodernism through the use of narrative and storytelling (Boje and Wakefield, 2011; Luhman and Boje, 2001). He, and others, refers to this coming together of philosophy and science as *emergence* (not to be confused with emergent change or emergent strategy). Emergence will be discussed further in Chapter 9, but for now it is enough to note that even some strong supporters of complexity do not see it as a stand-alone approach to organisations and change.

Although complexity theories may be bringing about a fundamental re-evaluation of how we view the natural world, Burnes (2005) takes the view that there is as yet insufficient evidence to support the claim that they also have the potential to bring about the same sort of fundamental re-evaluation of the nature, purpose and operation of organisations.

Conclusions

In Chapters 1–3, we reviewed the main theories and approaches to structuring and running organisations. These three chapters showed that, over the past 100 years, organisation theory had moved a long way from the mechanical certainties of the Classical school as exemplified by the work of Frederick Taylor. We no longer perceive organisations as simple machines, nor of people as cogs, or 'greedy robots', in those machines. We now recognise the convoluted nature of organisations and their environments, and the even more convoluted nature of human beings. Contemporary approaches to running organisations have attempted to move away from the mechanical certainties of Frederick Taylor *et al* by developing theories that focus on, or incorporate, the human–social dimension of organisational life. Consequently, for the Culture–Excellence school, the key issue has been organisational culture; for the Japanese, the key issue has been to blend together the 'hard' and 'soft' elements of organisational life; whereas for the learning school, the main topic has been to understand how humans learn, and how this can be translated from individual learning to collective, organisational learning. Though there are some common elements between all three approaches, there are also major differences. This has not prevented proponents of all three from seeking to promote their approach as the 'one best way'.

What this chapter has shown is the need to set and understand approaches to running and designing organisations into a wider theoretical frame. None of the three perspectives on organisations reviewed in this chapter was developed specifically with organisations in mind; indeed, their originators might have been somewhat surprised to see this development. Two of them, postmodernism and realism, are based on well-developed philosophical doctrines, and the other, complexity, comes from a great deal of research carried out in a wide variety of disciplines in the natural sciences. All three are inspired by the desire to understand the world around us in its widest context, whether this be art, history, science or why it always seems to rain in Manchester. All three have significant implications for structuring and managing organisations.

- Postmodernism, with its denial of an absolute reality and promotion of competing, and socially constructed, multiple realities, offers enormous scope for the emergence of alternative strategies and choices, but it also stresses the importance of culture, power and politics in how the strategies are selected and legitimised, and how choices are made.

- The realists reject the concept of multiple realities in favour of just one. They do not deny the socially constructed nature of their reality, though they claim that it is no less real for all that. Nor do they deny that this social construction offers organisations a great deal more scope for choice and manoeuvre than conventional approaches appear to acknowledge. The difference between these two perspectives is that while the postmodernists believe that anything is possible, the realists see organisations' room for manoeuvre and choice as limited by intricate structures in both the natural and social worlds which exist even if we are not aware of them.

- The complexity perspective sees organisations as complex, self-organising systems that, in order to maximise their innovative capacities, need to operate at the edge of chaos (bounded instability). In order to remain in this position, rather than falling off the edge, they need to develop and maintain appropriate order-generating rules. In order to do so, organisations are required to become far more democratic than they are now and allow 'people the freedom to own their own power, think innovatively, and operate in new patterns' (Bechtold, 1997: 198). In effect, choice moves from the few to the many. Though it does appear to be the case that organisations can survive for long periods of time without appropriate rules, complexity theorists maintain that this will reduce the organisation's innovative capacity and threaten its long-term survival.

As can be seen, all of these three critical perspectives have important but different implications for organisational life, and each has fundamental differences from the other two. Nevertheless, there is one very important implication which all three perspectives share; this is that organisations do have a wide range of options and choices open to them as to how they are structured and operate. This is the case even if one concedes that some postmodernist realities are more dominant than others, that 'real' social entities, such as markets, class relations, gender relations, social rules, etc., limit choice, or that eventually organisations need to adopt or develop appropriate order-generating rules. If choice is far wider than most organisation theories acknowledge, this poses questions as to how to identify options, and who will make the decisions as to which ones to choose.

In Chapter 3, we drew attention to the importance of culture in shaping organisations and the actions of those in them. Chapter 3 also drew attention to the lack of interest paid to power and politics in running organisations and making decisions. In this chapter, especially in considering postmodernism, we have also drawn attention to the role of culture, power and politics in shaping decisions in organisations. The next chapter will return to these issues and show how they impact on the choices made by those who run organisations.

TEST YOUR LEARNING

Short discussion topics

The purpose of these is to enable students to check and reflect on the topics. The discussions should last for no more than 5–10 minutes. Depending on the length of the lecture, there could be one, two or three such discussions in a session. The following are five suggested topics which address issues raised in this chapter:

1. What is flexible specialisation?

2. Define postmodernism.

3. What is realism?

4. What do complexity theorists mean by the 'edge of chaos'?

5. What are the implications for organisational change of (a) postmodernism and (b) realism?

Class debates

The purpose of class debates is to enable students to explore a topic in depth by setting up a 'for and against' debate. The class can be split into two, and one half asked to research the 'for' case and the other 'against' case. Individuals can then be chosen at random to introduce their side of the debate. Alternatively, two individuals for each side can be told in advance that they will be introducing the debate. The length of such debates depends on the time available, the size of the class and their enthusiasm for the topic. However, less than 30 minutes is probably too short and more than 60 minutes probably too long. The following are three suggested topics which address issues raised in this chapter:

1. Postmodernism is an ill-defined concept which rejects logic and rationality, denies that managers can plan their organisation's future, and seeks to replace hard facts with unsupported opinions.

2. Realism's support for social constructionism and the use by its supporters of terms such as 'causal mechanism' and 'causal powers' make it no more use to managers than postmodernism.

3. Complexity may be an essential science for predicting the weather, but it has absolutely no practical value for organisations.

Essay questions

1. Discuss the following statement: In practice, the multiple realities of postmodernism mean nothing more than 'different people have different opinions'.

2. To what extent and why does the concept of 'simple order-generating rules' offer organisations a novel and effective way of managing radical change?

Suggested further reading

Ackroyd, S and Fleetwood, S (eds) (2000) *Realist Perspectives on Management and Organisations*. Routledge: London.
   This edited collection of essays provide an excellent introduction to realism and how it can be applied to organisations.

Black, JA (2000) Fermenting change: exploring complexity and chaos. *Journal of Organizational Change Management* (Special Edition), 13(6).

Fitzgerald, LA (2002) Chaos: applications in organizational change. *Journal of Organizational Change Management* (Special Edition), 15(4).

These two special editions of the *Journal of Organizational Change Management* offer a thought-provoking and informative overview of complexity theories.

Stacey, RD (2003) *Strategic Management and Organisational Dynamics: The challenge of complexity*. Financial Times Prentice Hall: Harlow.

Taken together, these two books provide a good overview of the postmodernist slant on organisations.

Hatch, MJ (1997) *Organization Theory: Modern, symbolic and postmodern perspectives*. Oxford University Press: Oxford.

CASE STUDY 4

File sharing and the music industry[1]

Background

Though the creation of music is as old as mankind itself, in its commodity form, as a saleable product, it is a relatively recent phenomenon. The market for music began with the sale of sheet music in the nineteenth century. In the twentieth century, with the emergence of and demand for recorded music in the form of vinyl records, cassettes, CDs, etc., the market expanded enormously to become a global industry. However, though the physical product might have changed, the distribution channels and the division of labour within the industry remained relatively stable: artists created music, record labels promoted and distributed it and the fans consumed it. As this case study will show, however, the advent of the internet and file-sharing technologies caused a seismic shift in the way music was distributed, and facilitated music piracy on a massive scale.

The credit or blame, depending on whether you are a music industry executive or a music fan, will go to Shawn Fanning. Fanning is the classic American computer geek who dropped out of college because he wanted to spend his time developing a computer

program which would make it easier to find and swap music via the internet. He called the program, and the company he launched, Napster, after his school nickname. Napster quickly became one of the legends of the internet. As Alderman (2001a: 4) commented:

The program launched in June 1999 and took off with unprecedented speed. For many, using Napster was an epiphany. One would fire it up, type in a song and instantly be connected with possibly thousands of other users who had what you wanted. Sure, you could get the studio version of Led Zeppelin's Whole Lotta Love. But if you were on at the right time, you could also get live versions of the song recorded in LA in 1977, San Francisco in 1975 or Tokyo in 1972. You might also get the new Radiohead or Eminem album weeks before their official release dates. Millions did. Using Napster was easier than going to a record store, and easier than ordering records online, and it allowed the discovery of music in ways that had not existed before. Record stores, for instance, didn't give you the opportunity to identify the cool people and investigate what else they were listening to. If there was another Napster user whose songs you liked, you could check what other music they had on their hard drive and send them instant messages. As a bonus, the whole Napster experience (excluding the computer and net costs) was free. The industry's response was incredulity and, initially, inaction.

---

[1] This case study is based on work carried out with Gary Graham of the Manchester School of Management and Glenn Hardaker of Huddersfield University Business School. A fuller version of this case can be found in Graham *et al* (2002).

The Napster software was very simple to use. You installed it, you placed your favourite music files in a folder on your hard disk and then connected to the internet. Immediately, you could share every other Napster user's music files and they could share yours. At its height in 2000, more than 80 million users per month were treating themselves to free music. Not surprisingly, the industry was not inactive for long. While Napster might seem a good idea to its millions of users, to the big record labels it meant piracy on a scale that could eventually lead to their bankruptcy.

The music industry and the internet

Music-making is economically as well as technically a complex process. Like books, films, television and other art forms, music is rarely just a product. Not only is it difficult to identify, develop and manage successful artists, the artistic value (and therefore the commercial value) of music depends upon consumers' aesthetic preferences, which are neither stable nor predictable. Just because an artist has sold millions of records in the past does not mean they will in the future. The reverse is also the case. Before getting a record contract, even the biggest-selling artists, such as the Beatles, had usually been turned down by a number of record companies who failed to spot their sales potential.

For organisations involved in any form of distribution, the internet offered the opportunity to replace 'bricks' with 'clicks' and thus improve their competitiveness (profitability) by removing stages in the distribution process. This issue was particularly acute for the music industry in that the on-line delivery of music transformed the way music was distributed and could lead to the elimination of its physical manifestations such as CDs, record shops, etc.

Prior to the advent of the internet, the supply chain for music comprised three main activities: the creation of music; the marketing of music; and the distribution of music. The big record labels dominated the music industry, rather than the artists who actually created the music. This was because it was the record labels that controlled access to, and in some cases actually owned, the major distribution and marketing channels. According to Parikh (1999), it was the dominant position of the labels that prevented artists from independently distributing their own material, and it was this dominant position that explained why the labels collected approximately 85–90 per cent of the profit from music sales.

Parikh (1999) also argues that the structure worked against the interests of consumers. This is because the number of intermediaries and elements between the artist and the consumer made it relatively inefficient. While each stage in the chain added costs, it is not clear to what extent they provided any added value for the consumer. It was this potential to remove cost, without necessarily removing value to the final consumer, that made the supply chain for music ripe for transformation by the internet.

As Amazon showed initially with books, the internet offered the potential to remove some layers and elements in the distribution channel for music. As with books, the need physically to produce and distribute music, in the form of CDs and cassettes, used to limit the extent to which intermediaries could be eliminated and costs reduced. However, the advent of digital technology in the 1980s, which enabled music to be recorded and stored digitally in the form of CDs and minidiscs, also allowed it to be transmitted digitally via the internet. This development took layers out of the supply chain for music, and thus threatened the livelihood of those involved in manufacturing and distributing physical products such as CDs. But, as such, it did not threaten or challenge the dominance of the record labels, which still retained control over production and distribution. By itself, so long as consumers downloaded and paid for copyrighted musical content through legitimate online trading organisations, this would not be a problem for the record companies. Indeed, the internet offered enormous scope for the music industry to bring music to a wider public, afford niche artists access to their audiences, and distribute old, new and unusual music at affordable prices.

What threatened the dominance of the labels, however, was the advent of file-sharing technologies such as Fanning's Napster. These developments enabled consumers to bypass the record labels by swapping music files directly between themselves without any money flowing to the record labels. Music piracy was not new; however, what really scared the music industry was the sheer scale and ease of the piracy allowed by the internet. In theory, and increasingly in practice, it is possible to download (i.e. pirate) any piece of music without paying for the privilege of doing so.

Summary

On the one hand, the internet offered an enormous potential to reduce the complexity and the cost of music production and distribution by eliminating the need for CD manufacturers, music shops, transportation, etc. Certainly, the popularity of online music stores such as Apple's iTunes showed that this was increasingly the preferred way for customers to purchase music. On the other hand, it was estimated that 19 out of 20 downloads at the turn of the millennium were from illegal sites. Therefore, the internet facilitated piracy on a scale previously unknown, which had a significant and adverse impact on the income of the record labels. Consequently, the music industry was faced with a major strategic dilemma. How could it maximise the use of the internet to generate revenue while minimising the use of the internet for piracy?

Update[2]

During the last decade, since the original work on which this case study is based, there have been some significant changes in the music industry, but the illegal downloading of music is still a major concern for the industry (Bradshaw, 2012). A report by the Institute for Policy Innovation (Siwek, 2007) estimated that it cost the American music industry some $12.5 billion per annum in lost output. In the UK, the cost is said to be around £219 million per year, with some 1.2 billion tracks being illegally downloaded in 2010, making three out of every four downloads illegal (Robinson, 2010). This is despite the fact that music is now cheaper and easier to download legally than ever before. There are now two main models for purchasing music legally through the internet: either through a subscription-based service such as Spotify, or a 'pay and download' service – essentially an internet shop – such as Apple's iTunes. Spotify works like a virtual jukebox, hosting content from which subscribers choose and listen on demand; with a 'pay and download' service, users buy a digital product which is then their property. The fact that Apple was one of the first companies to provide music in this way and has remained a major player for a decade in such a turbulent and rapidly changing environment is a tribute to their ability to predict customer trends accurately and to adapt accordingly.

The situation for the big record labels has also changed dramatically. Squeezed between lost revenue from piracy and the bargaining power of legal download sites such as iTunes, the big labels have struggled to make profits. This is one of the main reasons why the 'big six'

of the late 1990s (Warner Music Group, EMI, Sony Music, BMG, Universal Music Group and Polygram) have now become the 'big three' (Universal Music Group, Sony Music Entertainment and Warner Music Group). In an attempt to compensate, they now place greater emphasis on touring by well-known artists. Touring now generates a greater proportion of major artists' income than it did a decade ago. At the highest level, a 'stadium' tour can be a great money earner, although at the lower end of the touring market, the lack of record label support can mean some acts struggle to finance tours which are solely dependent on ticket sales.

Even here, though, the record labels face competition from artists' managers themselves, who can cut out the record label intermediaries and simply market artists' music directly. One means of self-promotion for both well-known and less well-known artists is simply to give music away for free. Unthinkable 20 years ago, this is now standard practice. For example, Daft Punk's recent album was available for free for a week before its official release to buy. So, some 15 years after the launch of Napster, the major record labels are still effectively struggling to establish a distinct role for themselves in the digital age.

Questions

1. Imagine that you are a consultant with Postmodern Perspectives, a management consultancy which offers its clients a postmodern approach to strategy. You have been asked by a major record label to provide it with advice on how to maximise income and minimise piracy from the internet. What advice would you offer, why, and what would be specifically postmodern about it?

2. Imagine that you are a consultant with Realist Consultants, a management consultancy which offers its clients a realist approach to strategy. You have been asked by a major record label to provide it with advice on how to maximise income and minimise piracy from the internet. What advice would you offer, why, and what would be specifically realist about it?

3. Imagine that you are a consultant with Complexity Management, a management consultancy which offers its clients a complexity-based approach to strategy. You have been asked by a major record label to provide it with advice on how to maximise income and minimise piracy from the internet. What advice would you offer, why, and what would be specifically complexity-based about it?

---

[2] I am grateful to Chris White and Chris Howett of the University of Sheffield Students' Union for the following update.

Culture, power, politics and choice

Learning objectives

After studying this chapter, you should be able to:

- understand the main tenets of organisational culture;
- discuss the strengths and weaknesses of the cultural approach to organisations;
- describe the role of power and politics in organisations;
- state the main advantages and disadvantages of the power–politics perspective on organisations;
- understand the scope, methods and limitations for the exercise of choice in terms of organisational design and change.

MINI CASE STUDY 5.1

Managerial Behaviour

Down in the valley

The story of Hewlett-Packard, an outwardly staid technology company, has come to resemble the plotline of an improbable corporate soap opera. It has included, during the past decade, the firings of three chief executives, one after a probe into claims of sexual harassment; a salacious boardroom spying scandal that resulted in the resignation of its then chairwoman; and a spate of highly controversial multibillion-dollar deals, including one that sparked a public feud between management and heirs of the company's founders. Now, to top it off, come claims of massive accounting distortion at

Autonomy, the British software company that was the object of the latest of those deals. By the end of this week at least one criminal investigation had been launched into the affair, by the FBI. This trail of destruction has done more than shred management reputations and clean out boardrooms. There has also been a significant financial toll. The latest $8.8bn charge this week, largely caused by the Autonomy mess , has lifted the total write-offs at HP during the past year, taken against a decade of acquisitions, to $19.7bn. And that does not even count a seemingly endless round of restructuring charges that have topped $100m in every one of the past 13 years, reaching $11bn in all.

The numbers are a stark reminder of what has befallen a company that played a central part in the postwar rise of Silicon Valley. HP has become ensnared in an endless cycle of deals, reorganisations and job cuts, as successive managers have tried, and failed, to jolt its moribund business back to life. Meg Whitman, the former eBay boss and Republican candidate for governor of California, took the helm last year with a promise to break this pattern. Yet, contemplating the Autonomy scandal, she ruefully admitted this week: "When we have an event like this, you have to work harder. It doesn't make it any easier." No wonder Mike Lynch, the former Autonomy boss , has been having a field-day in the media, defending himself against charges of accounting impropriety by turning the fire back on to HP. "There is a part of the HP management that would like to blame other people for failures," he told the Financial Times. "They ought to look to themselves."

Deserved or not, Mr Lynch's barb will have hit a nerve with long-suffering shareholders. As HP's reputation as the company that cannot shoot straight has grown to almost legendary proportions, its stock price has collapsed. Though third to Samsung and Apple in the ranks of global technology companies judged by sales, HP's stock market value has slumped to $23.5bn, from more than $100bn in early 2010. "Every time there's a disaster, the management says it's the last person who was responsible – but it's the shareholders who keep holding the bag, over and over," said Charles Elson, a professor of corporate governance at the University of Delaware. "At some point, the music has to stop."

Ms Whitman, already fighting long odds in her effort to turn HP round, now finds herself with another crisis on her hands. It doesn't help that she was among the directors who unanimously backed CEO Leo Apotheker last year when he proposed the Autonomy acquisition. The exorbitant price, about 80 per cent more than Wall Street had thought the company was worth before HP showed up, was a big part of the reason that Mr Apotheker was later shown the door. Ms Whitman now tries to distance herself and other directors from the decision, putting the blame squarely on the former CEO. "We decided to vote for what we thought was the right thing to do," she says. "We thought it was a high price. You do rely on the CEO that you hired."

Absolving HP's directors of responsibility for this latest debacle may not be so easy. In their eagerness to pull off a deal that seemed to promise a partial answer to HP's business challenges, they failed to dig as deeply as they should into possible problems at Autonomy, according to critics. That is despite warnings from some analysts about suspect accounting. "It was a desperation move and I think things were maybe overlooked," said Mark Williams, an academic at Boston University's School of Management. Advisers, including the company's accountants and investment bankers, also slipped, says David Yoffie, a professor at Harvard Business School, although he adds that some of the blame rests with HP's management and board, "for not asking enough questions or spotting signs of trouble".

Ms Whitman can at least point to a thorough board overhaul, undertaken just before the Autonomy deal, that was designed to put paid to HP's reputation of bad governance once and for all. And she claims a more direct personal management style that has led to the latest directors being better informed than their predecessors. "I tell my board everything," she says. "That's quite a different board management style than, I think, my predecessors." "HP probably had more governance problems than any large company in America but Meg cleaned house in 2011," says Mr Yoffie. "It is hard to ascribe deeper systemic governance problems when the board and the CEO are new."

Whether justified or not, meanwhile, the accounting scandal has contributed to a public perception of HP as a dysfunctional company let down by inadequate leadership. As Ms Whitman herself conceded, "there have been questions going back to the beginning of the [last] decade" about failures in the HP boardroom. Those will linger. Ms Whitman must now prevent the Autonomy debacle from derailing her efforts at a turnaround. Wall Street has voted with its feet: the stock market wiped 10 per cent off HP's bargain-basement stock price on the news of the Autonomy debacle. This week's news "adds further weight to the overall view that they are not really competent enough to turn this company around," says Richard Windsor, a former analyst.

The catalogue of HP's problems makes daunting reading. One of the arguments for conglomerates has always been that they offer investors greater stability: if one part of the business is losing money, others will be doing better and help even out the performance. HP, however, is a conglomerate in which all the cylinders have stopped firing at once. Its giant PC division, struggling with a secular downturn as customers turn to tablets, was further

Mini case study 5.1 (*continued*)

dented last year by Mr Apotheker's public musing over whether to sell the business. Its IT services operation has struggled ever since the $13.9bn acquisition four years ago of EDS, leading to an $8bn writedown of its own in August. And in the servers and hardware it sells to corporate IT departments, HP has long suffered from a creeping commoditisation that has hurt profit margins. Even the one division whose profits had long bailed out the rest of the company, based on ink-jet printers, is facing decline. With customers printing fewer photographs on their home PCs as they turn to the cloud, sales of ink cartridges – the cash cow that funded HP for more than a decade – are under pressure. As Ms Whitman says: "This is an enormous company with an extraordinary list of challenges". Her remedy: stop the dealmaking, which has left HP deeply in debt, and get back to doing the basic research and development needed to give the company back a technology edge lost during a long period of under-investment by previous management.

Having cleared the decks with a series of write-offs, including at Autonomy, she now faces two possible futures. In one, says Frank Gillett, an analyst at Forrester Research, HP will "soldier on, there's

nothing that will force an immediate change in their structure – but there's no quick fix to their problems either". Ms Whitman has asked shareholders for five years to complete a turnround, an almost unimaginably long time given the short horizon of most investors. Like other analysts, Mr Gillett also says that HP has promising new technologies it is nurturing – including from smaller acquisitions – and the main challenge will be to overcome the perceptions of failure that dog the company, made all the worse by the Autonomy news. Alternatively, however, the weight of the past could prove too much and Ms Whitman may be forced to sell assets or even break up the company. "People just have no confidence that management has made the right strategic decisions to turn this company around and invest for growth – it's trading on the assumption that HP will fail," says Richard Windsor, a Nomura analyst and author of the Radio Free Mobile blog. The HP chief completely rules out the break-up option. "There isn't a Plan B," she insists. "I'm confident we can turn this company around." But in the wake of the latest bombshell from a company now notorious for having America's most dysfunctional boards, such assurances risk sounding increasingly hollow.

 Source: Adapted from Chris Nuttall and Richard Waters, *Financial Times*, 24 November 2012, p. 6. © *The Financial Times Limited* (2012). All Rights Reserved.

Introduction

In reading Mini Case Study 5.1, and in considering the many studies of managerial behaviour in organisations (Dawson, 2003; Kakabadse *et al*, 2007; Pettigrew, 1985; Pfeffer, 1992), one might be forgiven for believing that managers are free to pursue their own dysfunctional agendas regardless of the damage it does to the organisations which employ them. Indeed, such behaviour recently led one commentator to declare that 'The lunatics have taken over the boardroom' (Johnson, 2012: 14). However, this view stands in stark contrast to the evidence seen in the first three chapters of this book, which described the main and most influential approaches to running organisations that have emerged in the last 100 years. If these 'recipes for effectiveness' can be said to have one common feature, it is that each of them claims to have discovered the 'one best way' to run organisations (Rose, 1988; Witzel, 2007). As such, the result of these innovations ought to be the reduction or elimination of managerial choice and discretion. After all, if there is a sure-fire way of running organisations, the main job of senior managers, overseen by their key stakeholders, is to implement it and see that no one, especially themselves, deviates from it. Indeed, if there is a sure-fire recipe for success, then we should also see the elimination, or at the very least the downgrading, of senior managerial posts and powers because almost anyone should be capable of implementing the recipe. Given the cult of the transformational leader (*see* Chapter 14) and the concomitant increase in executive salaries on both sides of the Atlantic in the last 20 years – including the last few years – when both economies have been in trouble, this is clearly not the case (AFL-CIO, 2003; DeCarlo, 2008; Finch and Treanor, 2003; Gilbert *et al*, 2012; Green, 2008; Ruse, 2012; Treanor and Neville, 2012). Similarly, if such sure-fire recipes exist, why is there such a wide disparity in organisational success, and why do so few, if any, companies manage to achieve long-term prosperity? In the 80 years from 1917 to 1997, only two of America's 100 largest companies, GE and Kodak, outperformed the market, and one of these, Kodak, has recently filed for bankruptcy (Foster and Kaplan, 2003; Reuters, 2012).

Witzel (2007: 14) commented that a recipe for effectiveness 'can be a source of competitive advantage, if you know how to exploit it', and, one might add, *if* you want to exploit it. The reason why these recipes have not led to the removal of managerial authority and choice is that, as Mini Case Study 5.1 shows, many managers are given free rein to follow their instincts, regardless of the consequences for their organisations. In essence, recipes for effectiveness cannot be implemented unless managers choose to implement them. Consequently, the choices that managers make regarding which recipes to adopt and how to implement them are at least as important as the recipes themselves. As an example, Sheldrake (1996) notes that the Japanese approach to quality was developed by Americans, but American companies have signally failed to gain the same level of competitive advantage from it as their Japanese rivals.

The importance of managerial choice was noted in the conclusion to the previous chapter when discussing postmodernism, realism and complexity. It was argued that rather than being the prisoners of circumstances, rather than rational beings unquestioningly following rational recipes, managers may have a surprisingly wide degree of choice and discretion. Even if one rejects the 'boundless' view of choice advocated by the postmodernists in favour of the 'bounded' view of the realists and complexity theorists, managers are still far from the 'executive robots' implied by those who promote 'one best way' approaches to running organisations. However, if the recipes for success are not straitjackets, if managers are not rational beings, if they do have scope for choice, on what do they base their choices? In this chapter, we will examine the argument that the answer lies in the areas of culture, power and politics.

The chapter begins with a review of organisational culture. It is shown that many organisations lack a cohesive culture that bonds them together in a common purpose. Even where strong cultures exist, they may not always be appropriate, contrary to the arguments of the Culture–Excellence school, cultures may also be undermined owing to the absence of clear or uncontested organisational goals. The review of culture concludes:

- Although organisational culture may have important implications for organisational performance, there is little agreement about the nature of culture, whether it can be changed or the benefits to be gained from attempting to do so.

- Instead of culture being seen as an all-important and malleable determinant of performance, organisational life in many cases is dominated by political power battles which may be more influential than culture in shaping key decisions.

Consequently, the review of culture leads on to an examination of the nature and role of power and politics in organisations. Many writers maintain that organisations are essentially political entities. In exploring the arguments for this view, the chapter shows that:

● The decisions, actions and major developments of organisations are influenced and determined by shifting coalitions of individuals attempting to protect or enhance their own interests.

The behaviour of managers in attempting to protect their own interests raises the issue of the degree to which they can exert choice over what they do and how they do it. The issue of choice is examined in the final section of this chapter. The examination draws not only on the review of culture, power and politics from this chapter but also on the conclusions of the previous chapter. In summing up the implications for managerial choice of the two chapters, it is argued that:

● Rather than being the prisoners of organisational theories or contingencies, managers (potentially) have considerable, though by no means unconstrained, freedom of choice over the structure, policies and practices of their organisations, and even over the environment in which they operate.

● In exercising choice, managers are influenced by organisational theories and constraints, but they are also influenced by their concern to ensure that the outcome of decisions favours, or at least does not damage, their personal interests.

The conclusion to this chapter – and indeed of Part 1 of the book – is that, whether illegitimate or useful, political behaviour is an ever-present part of organisational life, and that such behaviour is particularly prevalent when major change initiatives are being considered or implemented.

The cultural perspective

What is organisational culture?

Recalling the discussion in Chapter 3 of the Culture–Excellence school and, to a lesser extent, organisational learning and Japanese management, many writers point out that managers and employees do not perform their duties in a value-free vacuum. Their work and the way it is done are governed, directed and tempered by an organisation's culture – the particular set of values, beliefs, customs and systems that is unique to that organisation. As Chatman and Cha (2003: 23) observe:

> The irony of leadership through culture is that the less formal direction you give employees about how to execute strategy, the more ownership they take over their actions and the better they perform.

Peters and Waterman's (1982) view that organisational culture is the prime determinant of organisational performance has been highly influential, and received much support from business leaders, consultants and academics (Flamholtz, 2001; Kotter and Heskett, 1992; Rigby and Bilodeau, 2011; Rogers *et al*, 2006). Others stress different, but no less important, aspects of culture. Keuning (1998: 46), for example, argues that the two most important functions of culture are 'to provide relatively fixed patterns for handling and solving problems . . . [and to] . . . reduce uncertainty for members of the organization when confronted with new situations'. Nevertheless, as Wilson (1992) noted, so influential has Peters and Waterman's view become that culture has come to be seen as the great 'cure-all' for the majority of organisational ills.

The fascination of business with organisational culture began in the 1980s with the work of writers such as Allen and Kraft (1982), Deal and Kennedy (1982, 1983), and above all Peters and Waterman (1982). Yet academics had drawn attention to its importance much earlier. As Allaire and Firsirotu (1984) and Albrow (1997) point out, there was already a substantial academic literature on organisational culture well before the work of Peters and Waterman (*see* Eldridge and Crombie, 1974; Turner, 1971). Blake and Mouton (1969), for example, were arguing that there was a link between culture and excellence in the late 1960s. For all this, organisational culture remains a highly contentious topic whose implications are far-reaching.

The 1980s and 1990s were a period when both academics and practitioners became obsessed with culture (Fleming, 2012). Turner (1986) traced this 'culture craze' to the decline of standards in manufacturing quality in the US, and the challenge to its economic supremacy by Japan. He comments that the concept of culture holds out a new way of understanding organisations, and has been offered by many writers as an explanation for the spectacular success of Japanese companies in the 1970s and 1980s. Bowles (1989), among others, observes that there is an absence of a cohesive culture in advanced economies in the West, and that the potential for creating systems of beliefs and myths within organisations provides the opportunity for promoting both social and organisational cohesion. As van den Berg and Wilderom (2004: 571) note, this notion of culture being 'the glue that holds the organisation together' has proved highly influential. The case for culture was probably best summed up by Deal and Kennedy (1982, 1983), who argued that culture, rather than structure, strategy or politics, is the prime mover in organisations.

Silverman (1970) contends that organisations are societies in miniature and can therefore be expected to show evidence of their own cultural characteristics. But culture does not spring up automatically and fully formed from the whims of management. Allaire and Firsirotu (1984) consider it to be the product of a number of different influences: the ambient society's values and characteristics, the organisation's history and past leadership, and factors such as industry and technology. Other writers have constructed similar lists but, as Brown (1995) comments, there does seem to be some dispute over which factors shape organisational culture and which are an integral part of it. Drennan (1992), for example, lists company expectations as a factor that shapes culture, but these might just as easily be seen as a reflection of an organisation's values which, according to Burnes and Jackson (2011), are a key component of an organisation's culture. The difficulty in distinguishing between the factors that shape culture and those that comprise culture is a reflection, as Cummings and Huse (1989: 421) point out, of the 'confusion about what the term culture really means when applied to organizations'. Brown (1995: 6–7) estimated that there are literally hundreds of definitions of culture: – examples of these are shown in Ideas and perspectives 5.1.

While there is a similarity between the definitions shown in Ideas and perspectives 5.1, there are also some distinct differences. Is culture something an organisation is or something it possesses? Does it mainly apply to senior managers or does it embrace everyone in the organisation? Is it a weak or a powerful force? Perhaps the most widely accepted definition is that offered by Eldridge and Crombie (1974: 78), who state that culture refers:

> ## IDEAS AND PERSPECTIVES 5.1
>
> ### Definitions of culture
>
> The culture of the factory is its customary and traditional way of thinking and doing things, which is shared to a greater or lesser degree by all its members and which new members must learn, and at least partially accept, in order to be accepted into service in the firm.
>
> (Jacques, 1952: 251)
>
> Culture describes patterns of behavior that form a durable template by which ideas and images can be transferred from one generation to another, or from one group to another.
>
> (Haggett, 1975: 238)
>
> Culture . . . is a pattern of beliefs and expectations shared by the organization's members. These beliefs and expectations produce norms and powerfully shape the behavior of individuals and groups in the organization. (Schwartz and Davis, 1981: 33)
>
> A quality of perceived organizational specialness – that it possesses some unusual quality that distinguishes it from others in the field. (Gold, 1982: 571– 2)
>
> By culture I mean the shared beliefs top managers in a company have about how they should manage themselves and other employees, and how they should conduct business(es).
>
> (Lorsch, 1986: 95)
>
> Culture represents an interdependent set of values and ways of behaving that are common in a community and that tend to perpetuate themselves, sometimes over long periods of time. (Kotter and Hesketh, 1992: 141)
>
> Culture is 'how things are done around here'. (Drennan, 1992: 3)

to the unique configuration of norms, values, beliefs, ways of behaving and so on, that characterise the manner in which groups and individuals combine to get things done.

Certainly, after more than three decades of research on the topic, Schein's (2010: 18) definition looks remarkably similar:

> The culture of a group can now be defined as a pattern of shared basic assumptions learned by a group as it solved its problems of external adaptation and internal integration, which has worked well enough to be considered valid and therefore, to be taught to new members as the correct way to perceive, think, and feel in relation to these problems.

Therefore, what we can say of culture is that it:

- defines how those in the organisation should behave in a given set of circumstances;
- affects all, from the most senior manager to the humblest cleaner;
- ensures that the actions of a member of an organisation are judged by themselves and others in relation to expected norms of behaviour;
- legitimises certain forms of action and proscribes other forms.

This last view is supported by Turner (1971), who observes that cultural systems contain elements of 'ought' which prescribe forms of behaviour or allow behaviour to be judged acceptable or not. Other writers have suggested a wide variety of different aspects of culture as being important in shaping behaviour. For example, Martin *et al* (1983) point to the role

---

IDEAS AND PERSPECTIVES 5.2

Fundamental questions of behaviour in organisations

1. Can employees break the rules?

2. Is the big boss human?

3. Can the little person rise to the top?

4. Will I get fired?

5. Will the organisation help me if I have to move?

6. How will the boss react to mistakes?

7. How will the organisation deal with obstacles?

Source: Martin *et al* (1983).

---

of organisational stories in shaping the actions and expectations of employees. They iden-tify seven basic types of story prevalent in organisations which provide answers to seven fundamental questions of behaviour (*see* Ideas and perspectives 5.2).

Alongside stories, much attention has been paid to the role of ceremonies, rites and rituals in reinforcing behaviour. Trice and Beyer (1984) found that these include the following:

● **Rites of passage** – designed to facilitate and signal a change in status and role through events such as training and induction programmes.

● **Rites of questioning** – to allow the status quo to be challenged, for example through the use of outside consultants.

● **Rites of renewal** – to enable the status quo to be updated and renewed through participative initiatives including strategy development, vision-building and job redesign programmes.

Another common theme in the literature is the role of 'heroes'. Peters and Waterman (1982) stress the importance of corporate heroes in shaping the fortunes of their 'excellent' compan-ies. Deal and Kennedy (1982, 1983) likewise see the corporate hero as the great motivator, the person everyone looks up to, admires and relies on. Indeed, there is a tendency, not just in the US, to attribute much of business success to the actions and personality of individuals, such as Pierre du Pont, Henry Heinz, Henry Ford, Steve Jobs, Kiichiro Toyoda, Konosuke Matsushita, Edward Cadbury and Sir John Harvey-Jones. Current corporate heroes include Richard Branson at Virgin, Paul Polman at Unilever, Ratan Tata at Tata Group and, perhaps the biggest of them all, Warren Buffett at Berkshire Hathaway. Of course, heroes can also become villains. Tony Hayward was seen as a very effective CEO of BP until his handling of the Deepwater Horizon disaster saw him labelled as 'the most hated – and clueless – man in America' (Kennedy, 2010). Similarly, James Murdoch's tenure at BskyB was much lauded until the advent of the News of the World phone-hacking scandal.

Perhaps the biggest fall from grace of the last decade was that of Jeffrey Skilling, who in 2006 was sentenced to 24 years in jail for his role in Enron's financial collapse. *Fortune* magazine named Enron as 'America's Most Innovative Company' for six years in a row until 2001, when it was revealed that its spectacular growth was an illusion created by fraud on a truly massive scale. Skilling quickly moved from being the CEO that everyone should copy to the villain whose behaviour should be avoided at all costs.

Leadership is just one aspect of culture. Brown (1995) offers a long list of 38 key elements of culture that have been identified by writers in the field, which include organisational climate, metaphors, attitudes, history and basic assumptions. Identifying these separate elements of culture helps us to flesh out and better understand how organisational culture manifests itself and impacts on individual and group behaviour. However, as Brown also shows, producing lists of elements or focusing on the role of particular elements tends to present a confusing and partial picture of culture. It becomes difficult to determine which are the more and which are the less important elements and, in terms of changing culture, which elements can be easily altered and which are more immutable.

To overcome this lack of clarity, there have been a number of attempts to identify and categorise culture's constituent elements. Hofstede (1990) develops a four-layered hierarchical model of culture which ranges from *values* at the deepest level through *rituals*, *heroes* and, at the surface level, *symbols*. In a similar way, Schein (1985) suggests a three-level model, with *basic assumptions* being at the deepest level, *beliefs*, *values* and *attitudes* at the intermediate level, and *artifacts* at the surface level. Based on an analysis of the different definitions of culture, Cummings and Worley (2001) produce a composite model of culture, comprising four major elements existing at different levels of awareness (*see* Figure 5.1).

Cummings and Worley (2001: 502–3) define these four major layers of culture as follows:

1. *Artifacts*. Artifacts are the highest level of cultural manifestation. These are the visible symbols of deeper levels of culture, such as norms, values, and basic assumptions. They include observable behaviors of members, as well as the structures, systems, procedures, rules, and physical aspects of the organization.

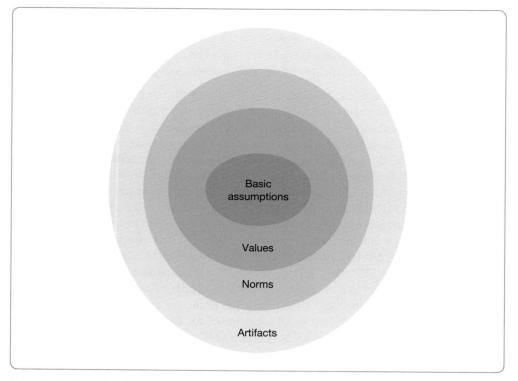

Figure 5.1 The major elements of culture

2. *Norms*. Just below the surface of cultural awareness are norms guiding how members should behave in particular situations. These represent unwritten rules of behavior. [. . .]

3. *Values*. The next-deeper level of awareness includes values about what ought to be in organizations. Values tell members what is important in the organization and deserves their attention. [. . .]

4. *Basic assumptions*. At the deepest level of cultural awareness are taken-for-granted assumptions about how organizational problems should be solved. These basic assumptions tell members how to perceive, think, and feel about things. They are nonconfrontable and nondebatable assumptions about relating to the environment and human nature, human activity, and human relationships. [. . .]

While the various hierarchical models of culture elements are useful, we should always remember that, as Brown (1995: 8–9) observes, 'actual organisational cultures are not as neat and tidy as the models seem to imply'. Indeed, Fang (2005–2006) questions the usefulness of what he calls the 'onion' view of culture, i.e. that culture comprises a number of layers which can be peeled back in order to reveal the true essence of an organisation. Instead, Fang (2005–2006: 82) views culture as an 'ocean':

It is useful to conceive of culture as having a life of its own. Seen longitudinally or historically, every culture has a dynamic life full of energies, sentiments, dramas, and contradictions. In its entire life span, every culture encompasses an ocean of infinite potential value orientations . . . At a given point, many cultural values have been endorsed, promoted, and legitimized, while other 'value cousins' are dampened, suppressed, and destroyed.

Where there are cultures, there are also usually sub-cultures, and where there is agreement about cultures there can also be disagreements and counter-cultures (de Chernatony and Cottam, 2008). In particular, there can also be significant differences between espoused culture and culture-in-practice (Yaniv and Farkas, 2005), all of which can adversely affect an organisation's performance.

This lack of neatness and tidiness has not prevented numerous attempts to define organisational culture, or attempts to categorise the various types of culture. Deal and Kennedy (1982) identify four basic types of culture, as do Quinn and McGrath (1985) – but the two categorisations are very different (*see* Ideas and perspectives 5.3 and Ideas and perspectives 5.4).

IDEAS AND PERSPECTIVES 5.3

Deal and Kennedy's four types of culture

1. The *Tough Guy, Macho culture*, characterised by individualism and risk-taking, e.g. a police force.
2. The *Work-Hard/Play-Hard culture*, characterised by low risks and quick feedback on performance, e.g. McDonald's.
3. The *Bet-Your-Company culture*, characterised by high risks and very long feedback time, e.g. aircraft companies.
4. The *Process culture*, characterised by low risks and slow feedback, e.g. insurance companies.

Source: Deal and Kennedy (1982).

IDEAS AND PERSPECTIVES 5.4

Quinn and McGrath's four types of culture

1. The *Market*, characterised by rational decision-making and goal-orientated employees, e.g. GEC under Arnold Weinstock (*see* the Marconi case study in Chapter 6).
2. The *Adhocracy*, characterised by risk-orientated and charismatic leaders and value-driven organisations, e.g. Apple and Microsoft in their early days.
3. The *Clan*, characterised by participation, consensus and concern for others, e.g. voluntary organisations such as Médecins Sans Frontières.
4. The *Hierarchy*, characterised by hierarchical, rule-based authority that values stability and risk avoidance, e.g. government bureaucracies.

Source: Quinn and McGrath (1985).

These two examples show the difficulty researchers encounter when trying to describe and categorise something as nebulous as culture. This difficulty can also be seen with Handy's (1979) attempt to categorise culture. Developed from Harrison's (1972) work on 'organization ideologies', Handy's is perhaps the best-known typology of culture and the one which has been around the longest. Handy (1986: 188) observes: 'There seem to be four main types of culture . . . *power*, *role*, *task* and *person*.' As shown in Ideas and perspectives 5.5, he relates each of these to a particular form of organisational structure.

IDEAS AND PERSPECTIVES 5.5

Handy's four types of culture

A **power culture** is frequently found in small entrepreneurial organisations such as some property, trading and finance companies. Such a culture is associated with a web structure with one or more powerful figures at the centre, wielding control.

A **role culture** is appropriate to bureaucracies and organisations with mechanistic, rigid structures and narrow jobs. Such cultures stress the importance of procedures and rules, hierarchical position and authority, security and predictability. In essence, role cultures create situations in which those in the organisation stick rigidly to their job description (role), and any unforeseen events are referred to the next layer up in the hierarchy.

A **task culture** is job- or project-orientated; the onus is on getting the job in hand (the task) done rather than prescribing how it should be done. Such types of culture are appropriate to organically structured organisations where flexibility and teamworking are encouraged. Task cultures create situations in which speed of reaction, integration and creativity are more important than adherence to particular rules or procedures, and where position and authority are less important than the individual contribution to the task in hand.

A **person culture** is, according to Handy, rare. The individual and their wishes are the central focus of this form of culture. It is associated with a minimalistic structure, the purpose of which is to assist those individuals who choose to work together. Therefore, a person culture can be characterised as a cluster or galaxy of individual stars.

Source: Handy (1986).

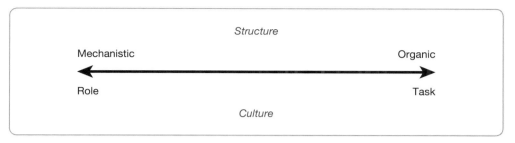

Figure 5.2 A structure–culture continuum

Handy (1986) believes that role cultures (with their accompanying mechanistic structures) and task cultures (with their accompanying organic structures) tend to predominate in Western organisations. Relating these two types of culture to Burns and Stalker's (1961) structural continuum, with mechanistic structures at one end and organic at the other, we can see that Handy is in effect seeking to construct a parallel and related cultural continuum, with role cultures at the mechanistic end and task cultures at the organic end (*see* Figure 5.2).

This categorisation certainly accommodates the five Western approaches to organisation theory discussed in the previous chapters. However, it is difficult to accommodate Japanese organisations within this framework, as their cultures contain elements of each extreme. As described in Chapter 3, Japanese companies have tightly structured jobs, especially at the lower levels; they are hierarchical and deferential, while at the same time achieving high levels of motivation, initiative and creativity in problem-solving. They tend to be heavily group/team-orientated, with such teams having a great deal of autonomy.

This difficulty of where to place Japan highlights one of the main criticisms of the various attempts to categorise culture, which is that they appear to give insufficient weight to the influence of national cultures on the types of organisational culture that predominate in particular countries. Increasingly over the last decade, and to an extent before, strong reservations have been expressed about the ethnocentric nature of organisational theory. The main reservation concerns the generalisability and applicability of management theories developed in the West, predominately the US, to the very different cultures and societies of Asia, the Middle East and Africa (Deresky, 2000; Fagenson-Eland *et al*, 2004; Fang, 2005–2006; Ho, 1976; Rosenzweig, 1994; Sullivan and Nonaka, 1986; Thomas, 2003; Trompenaars, 1993). Lowe *et al* (2007: 246), looking at the various approaches to culture, believe that the problem is:

> They all unconsciously adhere to the structuralist inheritance of western philosophy and the rationalist consequences of Enlightenment thinking. They are all, therefore, western culture-bound accounts of culture, and . . . ignore possible alternative models of culture from other perspectives. They describe culture using a western rationalist world-view.

Such criticisms have not and should not prevent Western researchers from attempting to study the differences between national cultures. In this respect, one of the most comprehensive, widely cited and influential studies was carried out by Hofstede (1980, 1990, 2001, 2011) and Hofstede and Bond (1988). Hofstede suggests that national cultures can be clustered along the lines of their similarities across a range of cultural variables, as follows:

- **Power Distance** – the degree to which people in a country accept a hierarchical or unequal distribution of power (i.e. the degree of centralisation, autocratic leadership and number of levels in the hierarchy).

- **Individualism versus Collectivism** – the degree to which people in a country prefer to work as individuals rather than working in groups, and prefer take care of themselves rather than looking to any collective provision.

- **Masculinity versus Femininity** – the degree to which people in a country emphasise so-called masculine traits, such as heroism, assertiveness and material reward for success, rather than modesty, cooperation, consensus and compassion.

- **Uncertainty Avoidance** – the degree to which people in a country feel uncomfortable with uncertainty and ambiguity, and prefer structured rather than unstructured situations.

- **Long-term versus Short-term orientation** – the degree to which people in a country prefer to save and invest for the future rather than spend now.

Based on these cultural variables, Hofstede (1980 and 1990) classifies industrialised countries into four broad clusters (shown in Ideas and perspectives 5.6).

Hofstede's work has come in for its fair share of criticism in the way it portrays different national cultures and the fact that it is based on only one multi-national company, IBM (*see* Fang, 2005–2006; Lowe *et al*, 2007; McSweeney, 2002). For example, though Wilson (1992: 90) observes that 'the similarity of the factors in [Hofstede's] national culture study to Handy's (1986) four organizational forms is striking', there are also striking dissimilarities. While one can see that Scandinavia can be classed as exhibiting task culture characteristics, and the group containing (the former) West Germany can be seen as exhibiting role culture characteristics, the other two groupings (Great Britain *et al* and Japan *et al*) are more difficult to place. Rather than placing Great Britain and the US in one category, according to where they are positioned on Hofstede's dimensions, it might be more accurate to follow Handy's lead and say that both task and role cultures are prevalent. This still leaves us with where to place Japan *et al*. From the point of view of Hofstede's dimensions, Japan appears to exhibit characteristics of Handy's role culture but, as pointed out above, this is only part of the story of Japanese organisational life.

IDEAS AND PERSPECTIVES 5.6

Hofstede's national clusters

1. Scandinavia (primarily Denmark, Sweden and Norway): these cultures are based upon values of collectivism, consensus and decentralisation.

2. West Germany (prior to unification), Switzerland and Austria: these are grouped together largely as valuing efficiency – the well-oiled machine – and seeking to reduce uncertainty.

3. Great Britain, Canada, the US, New Zealand, Australia and the Netherlands: these lie somewhere between 1 and 2 but cluster on the value they place on strong individuals and achievers in society.

4. Japan, France, Belgium, Spain and Italy: these are clustered on bureaucratic tendencies – the pyramid structure – favouring a large power distance.

Consequently, Hofstede's work should be seen as initiating a conversation rather than providing the last word on the subject. Certainly, it seems to have inspired others to examine cultural differences between countries. One of the most influential is Trompenaars' (1993) ten-year study of management in 28 countries covering 47 national cultures. This identifies seven dimensions of culture: universalism v particularism; individualism v communitarianism; specific v diffuse; neutral v affective; achievement v ascription; attitude to time, i.e. sequential v synchronistic; and internal v external. Though some of these resemble Hofstede's dimensions, others do not. Based on this work, Trompenaars, along with his collaborator Hampden-Turner, founded a thriving consultancy, which advises major companies how to 'deal with cross-cultural challenges and dilemmas, whether they relate to national or corporate cultures, within your own organization or among stakeholders' (Trompenaars Hampden-Turner, 2012).

Perhaps the most extensive and in-depth attempt to unravel the vagaries of national culture has been the GLOBE (Global Leadership and Organizational Effectiveness) study, which was established to examine how different cultures viewed leadership. The study was conceived by Robert J House in 1991 and now comprises 17,000 leaders in more than 950 organisations in 62 countries and involves over 200 academic coordinators (Chhokar *et al*, 2007; Javidian and Dastmalchian, 2009). The twin aims of the study were to categorise national and organisational cultures and to establish the extent to which leadership attributes and behaviours are influenced by cultures. The GLOBE study identified 22 key leadership attributes, including trustworthiness, foresight, dynamism and decisiveness, which were universally viewed as positive, and a further eight which were universally viewed as negative, including ruthlessness, non-cooperation, irritability and being a loner (House *et al*, 1999). In addition, they found 12 attributes, including ambition, caution, compassion and individualism, that were culturally dependent, i.e. in some countries these were seen as positive leadership attributes, and in others negative attributes.

The research found that the national cultures it examined could be grouped into ten distinct clusters (*see* Ideas and perspectives 5.7). Gupta *et al* (2002: 14–15) maintain:

> The results indicate that societal clusters effects account for more than two-thirds of the inter-society differences in values as well as practices of uncertainty avoidance, future orientation and institutional collectivism. In other words, the clusters captured shared societal attributes of the kind of goals pursued (individual or collective), the frame of the goals (short-term or futuristic), and the structure of the goals (rule-based or uncertainty avoidance). . . . This suggests that the societal cluster is an appropriate and relevant unit of analysis, and that the GLOBE cluster classifications are reliable indicators of world-wide cultural attributes.

What Ideas and perspectives 5.7 shows is that an organisation with a Germanic culture would be likely to find it relatively easy to do business with an organisation with an Anglo culture, but rather more difficult to do business with an organisation with a Latin America one. Similar issues might occur within organisations. A mixed-sex team drawn from Latin Europe cultures and Sub-Sahara cultures would be more likely to work together effectively than a team comprised mainly of people from Arab-Middle East Cultures. The issue of national cultures will be revisited in Chapter 14 when we examine the impact of national cultures on the management and leadership of organisations. For now, it is necessary to recognise that though national cultures do play a significant role in shaping organisational behaviour, each individual organisation will still have its own distinct culture. While the culture of each organisation within a particular country will be influenced by its societal

IDEAS AND PERSPECTIVES 5.7

The GLOBE 10 societal clusters

Anglo cultures: England, Australia, South Africa (white sample), Canada, New Zealand, Ireland, US
Key characteristics:
Performance Orientation – High
Assertiveness – Medium
Future Orientation – Medium
Humane Orientation – Medium
Institutional Collectivism – Medium
In-Group Collectivism – Low
Gender Equalisation – Medium
Power Distance – Medium
Uncertainty Avoidance – Medium

Latin America cultures: Costa Rica, Venezuela, Ecuador, Mexico, El Salvador, Columbia, Guatemala, Bolivia, Brazil, Argentina
Key characteristics:
Performance Orientation – Low
Assertiveness – Medium
Future Orientation – Low
Humane Orientation – Medium
Institutional Collectivism – Low
In-Group Collectivism – High
Gender Equalisation – Medium
Power Distance – Medium
Uncertainty Avoidance – Low

Latin Europe cultures: Israel, Italy, Portugal, Spain, France, Switzerland (French speaking)
Key characteristics:
Performance Orientation – Medium
Assertiveness – Medium
Future Orientation – Medium
Humane Orientation – Low
Institutional Collectivism – Low
In-Group Collectivism – Medium
Gender Equalisation – Medium
Power Distance – Medium
Uncertainty Avoidance – Medium

Sub-Sahara Africa cultures: Namibia, Zambia, Zimbabwe, South Africa (black sample), Nigeria
Key characteristics:
Performance Orientation – Medium
Assertiveness – Medium
Future Orientation – Medium
Humane Orientation – High
Institutional Collectivism – Medium
In-Group Collectivism – Medium
Gender Equalisation – Medium
Power Distance – Medium
Uncertainty Avoidance – Medium

Nordic Europe cultures: Finland, Sweden, Denmark
Key characteristics:
Performance Orientation – Medium
Assertiveness – Low
Future Orientation – High
Humane Orientation – Medium
Institutional Collectivism – High
In-Group Collectivism – Low
Gender Equalisation – High
Power Distance – Low
Uncertainty Avoidance – High

Arab-Middle East cultures: Qatar, Morocco, Turkey, Egypt, Kuwait
Key characteristics:
Performance Orientation – Medium
Assertiveness – Medium
Future Orientation – Low
Humane Orientation – Medium
Institutional Collectivism – Medium
In-Group Collectivism – High
Gender Equalisation – Low
Power Distance – Medium
Uncertainty Avoidance – Low

Germanic Europe cultures: Austria, Switzerland (German speaking), The Netherlands, Germany (former East), Germany (former West)
Key characteristics:
Performance Orientation – High
Assertiveness – High
Future Orientation – High
Humane Orientation – Low
Institutional Collectivism – Low
In-Group Collectivism – Low
Gender Equalisation – Medium
Power Distance – Medium
Uncertainty Avoidance – High

Southern Asia cultures: India, Indonesia, Philippines, Malaysia, Thailand, Iran
Key characteristics:
Performance Orientation – Medium
Assertiveness – Medium
Future Orientation – Medium
Humane Orientation – High
Institutional Collectivism – Medium
In-Group Collectivism – High
Gender Equalisation – Medium
Power Distance – Medium
Uncertainty Avoidance – Medium

Ideas and perspectives 5.7 (*continued*)

Eastern Europe cultures: Hungary, Russia, Kazakhstan, Albania, Poland, Greece, Slovenia, Georgia
Key characteristics:
Performance Orientation – Low
Assertiveness – High
Future Orientation – Low
Humane Orientation – Medium
Institutional Collectivism – Medium
In-Group Collectivism – High
Gender Equalisation – High
Power Distance – Medium
Uncertainty Avoidance – Low

Confucian Asia cultures: Taiwan, Singapore, Hong Kong, South Korea, China, Japan
Key characteristics:
Performance Orientation – High
Assertiveness – Medium
Future Orientation – Medium
Humane Orientation – Medium
Institutional Collectivism – High
In-Group Collectivism – High
Gender Equalisation – Medium
Power Distance – Medium
Uncertainty Avoidance – Medium

Source: Compiled from Gupta *et al*, 2002: 13 and Javidan *et al*, 2006.

---

culture, it will also be influenced by a range of other factors, such as its history, past leadership, industry and technology (Allaire and Firsirotu, 1984). Therefore, important as it is to classify national cultures, it is just as important, if not more so, to classify types of organisational culture.

In this respect, Handy's categorisation of types of culture is very useful, in that it takes us beyond vague generalisations and gives us a picture of differing cultures. It must still be recognised that Handy's classification is merely one among many. A number of researchers have attempted to rationalise the plethora of types of culture by attempting to group the various classifications. Wilson (2001) attempts to make sense of the literature on culture by identifying the perspective of those writing about it. As Ideas and perspectives 5.8 shows, he identifies three main perspectives on culture: integration, differentiation and fragmentation. Taking a very different angle, the Organizational Culture Inventory (OCI) (Jones *et al*, 2006) attempts to group types of culture by their impact on the behaviour of individuals and groups in an organisation (*see* Ideas and perspectives 5.9).

What this review of culture types and classifications highlights is both the difficulty of defining cultures clearly and the profound implications of the cultural approach to organisations. These implications fall under four main headings.

- First, Deal and Kennedy (1982) argue that behaviour, instead of reacting directly to intrinsic and extrinsic motivators, is shaped by shared values, beliefs and assumptions about the way an organisation should operate, how rewards should be distributed, the conduct of meetings, and even how people should dress.

- Second, if organisations do have their own identities, personalities or cultures, are there particular types of cultural attributes that are peculiar to top-performing organisations? As discussed in Chapter 3, the Culture–Excellence school reply to this question with a resounding *yes*!

- Third, the received wisdom is that culture guides the actions of an organisation's members without the need for detailed instructions or long meetings to discuss how to approach particular issues or problems. It also reduces the level of ambiguity and

IDEAS AND PERSPECTIVES 5.8

Wilson's culture perspectives

The integration perspective: This portrays a strong or desirable culture as one where there is organisation-wide consensus and consistency (e.g. Deal and Kennedy, 1983; Peters and Waterman, 1982; Schein, 1985). Espoused values are consistent with formal practices, which are consistent with informal beliefs, norms and attitudes. Cultural members share the same values, promoting a shared sense of loyalty and commitment. Where inconsistencies, conflict or sub-cultural differentiation occur, this is portrayed as being a weak or negative culture.

The differentiation perspective: This emphasises that rather than consensus being organisation-wide, it occurs only within the boundaries of a sub-culture. At the organisational level, differentiated sub-cultures may co-exist in harmony, conflict or indifference to each other. Van Maanen (1991), in his study of Disneyland, found groups of employees who considered themselves as being distinct. These sub-cultures related to different jobs, different levels of organisational status, gender and class. Claims of harmony from management masked a range of inconsistencies and group antagonisms. What is unique about a given organisation's culture, then, is the particular mix of sub-cultural differences within an organisation's boundaries.

The fragmentation perspective: This approach views ambiguity as the norm, with consensus and dissension co-existing in a constantly fluctuating pattern influenced by events and specific areas of decision-making. As stated by Frost *et al* (1991), consensus fails to coalesce on an organisation-wide or sub-cultural basis, except in transient, issue-specific ways. Rather than the clear unity of the integration perspective, or the clear conflicts of the differentiation viewpoint, fragmentation focuses on that which is unclear.

Source: Wilson (2001: 357).

IDEAS AND PERSPECTIVES 5.9

Organizational Culture Inventory classifications

Constructive cultures. Cultures in which members are encouraged to interact with others and approach tasks in ways that will help them to meet their higher-order satisfaction needs (includes Achievement, Self-Actualisation, Humanistic-Encouraging and Affiliative cultures).

Passive/Defensive cultures. Cultures in which members believe they must interact with people in defensive ways that will not threaten their own security (includes Approval, Conventional, Dependent and Avoidance cultures).

Aggressive/Defensive cultures. Cultures in which members are expected to approach tasks in forceful ways to protect their status and security (includes Oppositional, Power, Competitive and Perfectionist cultures).

Source: Jones *et al* (2006: 18).

misunderstanding between functions and departments (*see* Brown, 1998). In effect, it provides a common context and a common purpose for those in the organisation. However, this is the case only when an organisation possesses a strong culture, and where the members of the organisation have internalised it to the extent that they no longer question the legitimacy or appropriateness of the organisation's values and beliefs.

● Fourth, one of the most important implications is that it is possible to change or manage a culture (Barratt, 1990; O'Reilly, 1989).

This last implication is particularly contentious, with many writers supporting the view that organisations can deliberately change their culture but with others arguing strongly against it.

Changing organisational culture?

That cultures do change is not in question. No organisation's culture is static: left to itself, it tends to evolve in a slow and unplanned fashion as a result of changes in leadership, the turnover of group members, developments in the organisation's environment and general changes in society (Fang, 2005–2006; Kotter and Heskett, 1992). However, many writers claim that organisations can deliberately choose to change their culture (Brown, 1998; Burke, 2010; Cummings and Worley, 2001; Dobson, 1988; Industrial Society, 1997). In order to examine this claim, three questions will be addressed:

1. Why should an organisation wish to change its culture?

2. Is culture, or significant elements of it, amenable to deliberate change?

3. Are there established approaches available for changing culture?

We will begin by examining the first of these questions.

1 Why should an organisation wish to change its culture?

Given the discussion of culture in the previous section, one might assume that organisations would be wary of attempting to change it, but this does not appear to be the case. Despite the fact that culture is locked into the beliefs, values and norms of each individual in the organisation, and despite the difficulty of changing these, the majority of organisations appear to have attempted or wished to change their culture over the last 30 years (Boddy, 2002; Brown, 1998; Burnes, 1991; Kavanagh and Ashkanasy, 2006; Keuning, 1998; Rogers *et al*, 2006; Schein, 1985). This motivation for culture change stems from the argument put forward by the proponents of Culture–Excellence that success stems from culture, and that a successful culture is one based on values and assumptions appropriate to the unpredictable and fast-moving environment in which they believe modern organisations operate. That this view is still prevalent was illustrated by a 2009 global survey of international executives carried out by Bain & Co.: 80 per cent of respondents stated that culture was as important as strategy for business success (Rigby and Bilodeau, 2009).

In looking at culture change, we also need to take account of the argument that to operate effectively and efficiently, an organisation's culture needs to be aligned with its structure (Allaire and Firsirotu, 1984; Handy, 1986). Therefore, in changing its culture, an organisation may also need to change its structure, or vice versa. Looking at Figure 5.2, we can see that organisations with mechanistic structures are said to operate effectively and efficiently

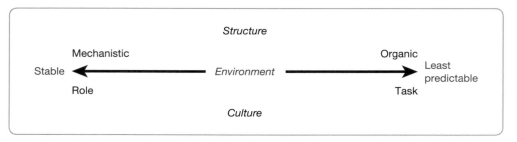

Figure 5.3 A structure–culture–environment continuum

if they have role cultures (Handy, 1986). If we refer back to the work of Burns and Stalker (1961) discussed in Chapter 2, we can merge Figure 2.2 with Figure 5.2 to show how different structures relate to different environments and, by extension, how different cultures relate to different environments (*see* Figure 5.3). As can be seen, mechanistic structures and role cultures are suitable for stable environments and organic structures and task cultures are suitable for least predictable (highly dynamic) environments.

Given that an organisation's environment can change rapidly, situations will arise where an organisation's culture and structure may be out of step with its environment, e.g. it may have a mechanistic structure and a role culture but find itself operating in a least predictable environment. In response to this, an organisation can change its mechanistic structure deliberately and relatively quickly to an organic one which would be more suitable to its new environment. However, it should not assume that its culture will adjust to the new circumstances in a natural (unplanned) manner: it is likely to find that this is a slow and unpredictable process. Consequently, a company that moves quickly to replace a mechanistic structure with a more organic structure, to cope with increasing uncertainty in its environment, might find that the change does not improve its effectiveness and efficiency because it still has a role culture which not only is incompatible with its changed environment but also clashes with its new organic structure (*see* Figure 5.4).

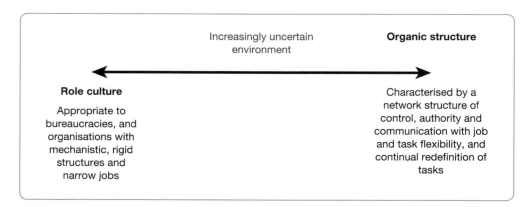

Figure 5.4 A structure–culture mismatch

As Handy (1986: 188) comments, this mismatch between culture and other key organisation variables is not uncommon or unimportant:

> Experience suggests that a strong culture makes a strong organisation, but does it matter what sort of culture is involved? Yes, it does. Not all cultures suit all purposes or people. Cultures are founded and built over the years by the dominant groups in an organisation. What suits them and the organisation at one stage is not necessarily appropriate for ever – strong though that culture may be.

Flynn (1993) describes how, with the introduction of a more market-orientated philosophy, such situations arose across organisations in the public sector in the UK. Jack Welch faced the same situation at GE in the 1980s. He had delayered, downsized and got rid of under-performing units. In the process he had reduced the workforce by 70,000 employees and earned the nickname 'Neutron Jack'. Yet, as he stated to a group of GE employees, he came to recognise that 'a company can boost productivity by restructuring, removing bureaucracy, and downsizing, but it cannot sustain high productivity without cultural change' (quoted in Ghoshal and Bartlett, 2000: 201).

Many similar cases can be found elsewhere in the private sector (*see* Boddy, 2002; Brown, 1995; Cummings and Worley, 2001; Dobson, 1988; Industrial Society, 1997). In such situations, rather than facilitating the efficient operation of the organisation, its culture may obstruct it. This is why, if one looks at the content of leading business journals, such as *The Harvard Business Review*, over the last three decades, one will find a plethora of examples of organisations that have attempted to change their culture in order to pursue competitive advantage (e.g. Jemison and Sitkin, 1986; Kanter, 2008a; Katzenbach *et al*, 2012; Prokesch, 1997).

Therefore, the answer to the question *Why should an organisation wish to change its culture?* is because its existing culture is no longer fit for purpose and is having a detrimental effect on its competitive performance. This now leads on to the second question.

2 Is culture, or significant elements of it, amenable to deliberate change?

The literature on culture is extensive and confusing, with many writers arguing the case for culture being something that can be deliberately and successfully changed, but with a substantial number of writers taking either an openly hostile view or a much more cautious one. Ogbonna and Harris (2002) label these three groups of writers the optimists, the pessimists and the realists.

The optimists claim that 'values, beliefs and attitudes are learnt, can be managed and changed and are potentially manipulable by management' (Barratt, 1990: 23). O'Reilly (1989) maintains that it is possible to change or manage a culture by choosing the attitudes and behaviours that are required, identifying the norms or expectations that promote or impede them, and then taking action to create the desired effect. Therefore, there is a body of opinion that sees culture as something that can be managed and changed (Cummings and Worley, 2001; Deal and Kennedy, 1983; Industrial Society, 1997; Jones *et al*, 2006; Peters and Waterman, 1982; Raz, 2009).

The pessimists question the notion that management has the capacity to control or change culture (Filby and Willmott, 1988). They point out that this ignores the way in which an individual's values and beliefs are conditioned by experience outside the workplace – through exposure to the media, through social activities, as well as through previous occupational activities. Hatch (1997: 235) warns against attempts to change organisational culture:

> Do not think of trying to manage culture. Other people's meanings and interpretations are highly unmanageable. Think instead of trying to culturally manage your organization, that is, manage your organization with cultural awareness of the multiplicity of meanings that will be made of you and your efforts.

A further concern expressed by a number of writers relates to the ethical issues raised by attempts to change culture (Van Maanen and Kunda, 1989; Willmott, 1995). This concern is succinctly articulated by Watson (1997: 278) who concludes:

> Employers and managers engaging in these ways with issues of employees' self-identities and the values through which they judge the rights and wrongs of their daily lives must be a matter of serious concern. To attempt to mould cultures – given that culture in its broad sense provides the roots of human morality, social identity and existential security – is indeed to enter 'deep and dangerous waters'.

The realists seem to take a position somewhere in between those who see culture as something that is amenable to managerial choice and those who see it as immutable. These writers appear to agree that culture as a whole cannot be changed, but argue that certain key elements, such as norms of behaviour, can be influenced by management through changes to recruitment, socialisation and reward processes (Chatman and Cha, 2003; Schein, 1985). This viewpoint is summed up by Meek (1988: 469–70), who argues:

> Culture as a whole cannot be manipulated, turned on or off, although it needs to be recognised that some [organisations] are in a better position than others to intentionally influence aspects of it.

As the labels they ascribe to the three groups might imply, Ogbonna and Harris (2002) tend to believe that the realists have the best of the argument; culture as a whole cannot be changed but it is possible intentionally and successfully to change key aspects of culture. In essence, the realists' argument appears to be that those wishing to change culture should concentrate on changing the behaviour of staff by manipulating the two upper layers of culture as depicted in Figure 5.1, i.e. artifacts and norms. Fang (2005–2006) notes that, according to Festinger's (1957) theory of cognitive dissonance (*see* Chapter 10), if one can change behaviour, this can then lead to a change in values, the third layer in the culture 'onion' depicted in Figure 5.1. Burnes and James (1995: 17) sound a cautionary note with regard to cognitive dissonance and behaviour change:

> It has been argued that, where individuals are required to change their behaviour in such a fashion that it clashes with their attitudes and gives rise to dissonance, an attitude change will only occur if the people concerned believe, rightly or wrongly, that they have a choice as to whether to adopt the new behaviour or not. If, on the other hand, they feel that they are being compelled against their will to change their behaviour, this can lead to high levels of dissonance and perhaps open defiance.

This view is also supported by many of the writers on power and politics (*see* the following section of this chapter) who see the use of remunerative and coercive power as counterproductive, because those on the receiving end of such power tend to view it negatively and resent it (Rollinson, 2002).

Therefore, the answer to the question *Is culture, or significant elements of it, amenable to deliberate change?* is yes, but . . . There is considerable evidence that the surface elements of culture can be changed, i.e. artifacts, such as rules and procedures, and norms of behaviour, such as the degree of openness and cooperation employees are expected to show to col-leagues, customers and suppliers. There is also some evidence that changes to behaviour can lead to changes in values (the third layer in the culture 'onion') but only if those con-cerned feel that they have choice and are adopting the new behaviours of their own free will. If this is not the case, attempts to change culture may result in resistance rather than cooperation. The actual practice of culture change can be understood more easily by mov-ing on to examine the third question.

3 Are there established approaches available for changing culture?

Over the last 30 years, many organisations have attempted to change their culture in order to improve or regain their competitiveness. In the 1980s, a survey of the UK's 1,000 largest public and private sector organisations revealed that more than 250 of them had been involved in culture change programmes (Dobson, 1988). The pace of culture change initiatives increased enormously in the 1990s. A survey covering more than 4,000 UK organisations found that 90 per cent of them were either going through or had recently gone through a culture change programme (Industrial Society, 1997). This was not just a Western phenomenon. Raz (2009) reports that many South Korean companies also embarked on culture change programmes in the 1990s.

Nor does there seem to be any slackening of the pace of culture change. In 2006, the management consultants Bain & Co. undertook a survey of 365 companies in Europe, Asia and North America which found that 76 per cent believed that their cultures could be changed and 65 per cent believed that they needed to change their cultures (Rogers *et al*, 2006).

While many organisations perceive the need for culture change, a major shock to the system is often required before they actually embark on such a change. It was only following the Enron crash, with the subsequent severe criticisms of its auditors, that the Big Four accounting companies in the US began to change their cultures to become more risk-averse (Michaels, 2004). Similarly, it was only with the onset of the 'credit crunch' in 2008, brought about by reckless sub-prime loans (Hutton, 2008a), that the rest of the financial services sector followed suit. Banks and other financial bodies make their money by lending money. In the boom times of the 1990s and 2000s, they overwhelmingly adopted a lend, lend, lend culture. However, the credit crunch triggered a stampede from a risk-inclined to a risk-averse culture (Aiyar, 2011; Balakrishnan and Collinson, 2007; Elliott, 2007).

Nevertheless, a willingness or compelling reason to change is not enough. As the Bain & Co. survey showed, some 90 per cent of culture change initiatives fail, which draws attention to the importance of the process of culture change (Rogers *et al*, 2006). In suggest-ing how organisations can change their cultures, some writers take a prescriptive view, e.g. Peters and Waterman (1982) with their eight steps to excellence (discussed in Chapter 3). Similarly, Dobson offers a four-step approach to culture change, which involves actions designed to shape the beliefs, values and attitudes of employees (*see* Ideas and perspectives 5.10). These simple, step-by-step guides to culture change were very popular in the 1980s and 1990s. For example, an article in *Management Today* took just four pages to show how organisations could quickly, and with apparent ease, identify and change their cultures (Egan, 1994).

A more considered approach is that offered by Cummings and Worley (2001). Drawing on the work of a wide range of researchers, they constructed an approach to culture change

---

IDEAS AND PERSPECTIVES 5.10

Dobson's guide to changing culture

Step 1 Change recruitment, selection and redundancy policies to alter the composition of the workforce so that promotion and employment prospects are dependent on those concerned possessing or displaying the beliefs and values the organisation wishes to promote.

Step 2 Reorganise the workforce to ensure that those employees and managers displaying the required traits occupy positions of influence.

Step 3 Effectively communicate the new values. This is done using a variety of methods such as one-to-one interviews, briefing groups, quality circles, house journals, etc. The example of senior managers exhibiting the new beliefs and values is seen as particularly important.

Step 4 Change systems, procedures and personnel policies, especially those concerned with rewards and appraisal.

Source: Adapted from Dobson (1988).

---

comprising six 'practical' steps (*see* Ideas and perspectives 5.11). Though wider in scope than Dobson's approach, the actual mechanics are quite similar.

In looking at what companies actually do, the Industrial Society (1997) survey mentioned above found that they tended to use similar methods to those advocated by Dobson, and Cummings and Worley, i.e. strategic planning, training, organisation redesign to promote teamwork, and changes to appraisal systems. At one level this is comforting because it shows a strong academic–practitioner link in the culture field. At another level it is quite worrying because, on the evidence of the 90 per cent failure rate of culture change initiatives, both groups seem to have got it badly wrong (Rogers *et al*, 2006). The problem appears to be that, as many researchers have observed, generic approaches to culture change ignore the complexity of organisational life and instead offer simplistic recommendations which are far too general to be of use to individual organisations with their specific circumstances and needs (Brown, 1995; Buchanan *et al*, 1999; Gajendran *et al*, 2012; Gordon, 1985; Harris and Ogbonna, 2002; Hassard and Sharifi, 1989; Hatch and Cunliffe, 2006; Nord, 1985; Seel, 2000; Uttal, 1983).

Regardless of whether the approaches to culture change are more or less prescriptive, regardless of whether they are simplistic or sophisticated, they all appear to be attempting to manipulate or change the two upper elements of culture shown in Figure 5.1 – artifacts and norms of behaviour – rather than attempting to change basic assumptions or even values. This can be seen clearly from Ideas and perspectives 5.10 and 5.11.

If we examine the concrete actions that these approaches propose, they are designed to promote new, more desired forms of behaviour by:

- changing organisational structures, systems and policies, i.e. arifacts;
- altering the composition of the workforce by recruiting or promoting staff who exhibit the desired behaviours or getting rid of staff who do not, i.e. norms of behaviour.

IDEAS AND PERSPECTIVES 5.11

Cummings and Worley's six steps to culture change

1. **Formulate a clear strategic vision**. Effective cultural change should start from a clear vision of the firm's new strategy and of the shared values and behaviour needed to make it work. This vision provides the purpose and direction for cultural change.

2. **Display top-management commitment**. Cultural change must be managed from the top of the organisation. Senior managers and administrators need to be strongly committed to the new values and the need to create constant pressure for change.

3. **Model culture change at the highest level**. Senior executives must communicate the new culture through their own actions. Their behaviours need to symbolise the kind of values and behaviours being sought.

4. **Modify the organisation to support organisational changes**. Cultural change must be accompanied by supporting modifications in organisational structure, human resource systems, information and control systems, and management style. These organisational features can help to orientate people's behaviours to the new culture.

5. **Select and socialise newcomers and terminate deviants**. One of the most effective methods for changing culture is to change organisational membership. People can be selected in terms of their fit with the new culture, and provided with an induction clearly indicating desired attitudes and behaviour. Existing staff who cannot adapt to the new ways may have their employment terminated, for example, through early retirement schemes. This is especially important in key leadership positions, where people's actions can significantly promote or hinder new values and behaviours.

6. **Develop ethical and legal sensitivity**. Most cultural change programmes attempt to promote values that emphasise employee integrity, control, equitable treatment and job security. However, if one of the key steps in pursuing culture change is to replace existing staff with new recruits, not only can this send out the wrong message to newcomers and the remaining staff but, depending how staff are selected for replacement, it could also contravene employment laws. Therefore, organisations need to be especially aware of these potential ethical and legal pitfalls.

Source: Adapted from Cummings and Worley (2001: 509–11).

There are two final and very important issues that need to be recognised when looking at approaches to culture change. The first is that it is a brutal process. There is a tendency to think that because culture is seen as encompassing the 'soft' side of the organisation, culture change is in some way about winning hearts and minds through the persuasive power of transformational leadership: people are not forced to change – they want to change (Burns, 1978). Ideas and perspectives 5.10 and 5.11 show that the reality is very different. The key actions involve restructuring the organisation and its workforce. As Dobson states, the first step is to:

> Change recruitment, selection and redundancy policies to alter the composition of the workforce so that promotion and employment prospects are dependent on those concerned possessing or displaying the beliefs and values the organisation wishes to promote.

Cummings and Worley are even more explicit when they speak of the need to *terminate deviants*. Culture change is mainly focused on getting rid of those who oppose or cannot fit in with the new culture, putting supporters in key positions and ensuring that reward systems reward those who support the new culture. Careers are destroyed, people either sacked or sidelined, and power and rewards are redistributed to supporters of the new order. This is not participative change but directive and coercive change: there is nothing soft or cuddly about it. Take, for example, this starkly illustrative statement by Stuart Rose, describing his actions in transforming Marks and Spencer's culture:

> [Each of] The stores were run differently, as if by their own management teams, and the different divisions were five or six robber barons, all competing under the umbrella of one retailer. Anyone coming in from the outside was strangled at birth. But I had already worked at M&S and I knew which levers to pull. I got the company by the balls and squeezed very hard until one or two people took notice. I butchered the Board.
>
> (In conversation with Grant, 2006: 24)

The second issue relates to the extent that changes to artifacts and norms will lead to changes in values and thus to an overall change in an organisation's culture. As mentioned above when discussing question 2, according to the theory of cognitive dissonance, behaviour change can lead to a change in values, but only if free will is involved, i.e. only if those affected feel that they have a choice.

In examining the various approaches to culture change, what is striking is the directive and coercive nature of the process. It may well be that newcomers to the organisation feel they have a choice in whether to join the organisation and sign up to the new behaviours. It may also be that those who see themselves as benefiting from the culture change may feel that they have chosen to adopt the new ways. Yet the majority of an organisation's members are likely to feel that they had no choice, which in turn may lead to a degree of resentment and even resistance (*see* Chapter 8 for a further discussion on the relationship between choice and resistance). This may be why a large proportion of culture change efforts are seen to fail (Brown, 1995; Jones *et al*, 2006; Rogers *et al*, 2006).

So the answer to the question *Are there established approaches available for changing culture?* is yes, but . . . The 'but' being that these approaches tend to focus on changing behaviour and not culture *per se*. These approaches may lead to changes in values, but only if those involved feel they have a choice. However, the approaches to culture change tend also to be directive and coercive and therefore do not promote choice for many of those involved. The difficulty of accomplishing culture change has led many writers to express reservations about attempting to change culture.

Changing organisational culture: some reservations

Though there are a large number of writers who believe that culture can be changed, others take a more cautious view of the results of such attempts. A major study of cultural transformation in 530 organisations by Gilmore *et al* (1997) found that organisations experienced both positive and negative outcomes, with senior managers reporting that quality and productivity improved and employees reporting that morale decreased and workload increased. Even more worrying for proponents of culture change were the results of the 2006 survey by Bain & Co., which found that fewer than 10 per cent of organisations were successful in changing their cultures (Rogers *et al*, 2006).

Such findings underlie Brown's (1998) warning that organisations must be sure that the problems they wish to address through cultural change are actually caused by the existing culture. He maintains that there is a tendency to assume that culture is the root cause of organisational problems, when in fact they might arise from inappropriate organisational structure. By pursuing culture change instead of the real cause of their problems, organisations doom themselves to failure. Brown also points out that senior managers may use the issue of culture to redirect blame for poor performance away from themselves and onto the rest of the organisation. In addition, he warns against taking an overly simplistic view of culture by believing that organisations have a single unitary culture, or by assuming that all employees can be made to share a single purpose or vision. This was also a point made by Hatch (1997) on behalf of the postmodernists.

One of the most influential writers on the subject of culture, Schein (1985), takes a similarly cautious view. He warns that before any attempt is made to change an organisation's culture, it is necessary to understand the nature of its existing culture and how this is sustained. According to Schein, this can be achieved by analysing the values that govern behaviour, and uncovering the underlying and often unconscious assumptions that determine how those in the organisation think, feel and react. Difficult though he acknowledges this to be, he argues that it can be achieved by:

- analysing the process of recruitment and induction for new employees;
- analysing responses to critical incidents in the organisation's history, as these are often translated into unwritten, but nevertheless strong, rules of behaviour;
- analysing the beliefs, values and assumptions of those who are seen as the guardians and promoters of the organisation's culture;
- discussing the findings from the above with staff in the organisation, and paying special attention to anomalies or puzzling features which have been observed.

Schein's approach, therefore, is to treat the development of culture as an adaptive and tangible learning process. His approach emphasises the way in which an organisation communicates its culture to new recruits. It illustrates how assumptions are translated into values and how values influence behaviour. Schein seeks to understand the mechanisms used to propagate culture, and how new values and behaviours are learned. Once these mechanisms are revealed, he argues, they can then form the basis of a strategy to change the organisation's culture.

Hassard and Sharifi (1989) propose a similar approach to that advocated by Schein. In particular, they stress two crucial aspects of culture change:

> Before a major [cultural] change campaign is commenced, senior managers must understand the implications of the new system for their own behaviour: and senior management must be involved in all the main stages preceding change. In change programmes, special attention must be given to the company's 'opinion leaders.' (Hassard and Sharifi, 1989: 11)

Schwartz and Davis (1981), meanwhile, adopt a different stance with regard to culture. They suggest that, when an organisation is considering any form of change, it should compare the strategic significance (the importance to the organisation's future) of the change with the cultural resistance that attempts to make the particular change will encounter. They term this the 'cultural risk' approach. They offer a step-by-step method for identifying the degree of cultural risk involved in any particular change project. From this, they argue, it is then possible for an organisation to decide with a degree of certainty whether to ignore the culture, manage round it, attempt to change the culture to fit the strategy, or change the strategy to fit the culture. Although Schwartz and Davis' method relies heavily on managerial judgement, they maintain that it constitutes a methodical approach to identifying, at an early stage, the potential impact of strategic change on an organisation's culture, and vice versa.

It should, of course, be pointed out that though Schein's approach and Schwartz and Davis' approach are different, this does not mean they are in conflict or are not compatible. Indeed, both could be considered as different aspects of the same task: deciding whether culture needs to be changed and, if it does, in what way.

No one should dispute the difficulty of changing an organisation's culture. The work of Schein (1985), Schwartz and Davis (1981), Cummings and Worley (2001) and Dobson (1988) provides organisations with the guidelines and methods for evaluating the need for and undertaking cultural change. Schein's work shows how an organisation's existing culture, and the way it is reinforced, can be revealed. Schwartz and Davis' work shows how the need for cultural change can be evaluated and the necessary changes identified. Finally, the work of Cummings and Worley (2001) and Dobson (1988) shows how cultural change can be implemented.

Taking a different tack, Schein (1984, 1985) also claims that there is a negative side to creating (or attempting to create) a strong and cohesive organisational culture. He argues that shared values, particularly where they have been seen to be consistently successful in the past, make organisations resistant to certain types of change or strategic options, regardless of their merit.

In addition, Schein is critical of the idea that culture change can be achieved by a top-down, management-led approach (Luthans, 1989). Instead, he appears to advocate a contingency or context-specific view of culture (Schein, 1989). From the point of view of an organisation's life-cycle, he suggests that an organisation may need a strong culture in its formative years to hold it together while it grows. However, it may reach a stage where it is increasingly differentiated geographically, by function and by division. At this stage, managing culture becomes more a question of knitting together the warring factions and sub-cultures. In such a case, a strong culture may outlive its usefulness.

It must also be noted that, as is the case in society at large, although there may be a strong or dominant culture in an organisation, there will also be sub-cultures, as Ideas and perspectives 5.8 indicates (Hofstede, 1998; Jermier *et al*, 1991; Salaman, 1979). These may be peculiar to the organisation or may cut across organisations. Examples of the latter are occupational groups such as accountants and lawyers who have their own professional cultures which extend beyond the organisations who employ them (Trice, 1993). Davis (1985) examined the culture of white- and blue-collar lower-level employees. He found that not only do these groups have their own distinctive cultures but these can often be in conflict with the dominant (managerial) culture of their organisation. Therefore, sub-cultures exist in a complex and potentially conflicting relationship with the dominant culture. If that dominant culture is seen by some groups to have lost its appropriateness (and thus legitimacy), then potential conflicts can become actual conflicts. The reverse can also be the case: cultural values and methods of operation which one group adopts may be seen as being out of step with 'the way we've always done things'. This in turn can lead to an undermining of the authority of managers and specialists – endangering the efficient operation of the organisation (Morieux and Sutherland, 1988).

Uttal (1983) is another who expresses caution with regard to the difficulties and advisability of culture change. In particular, he observes that even where it is successful, the process can take anywhere from 6 to 15 years. Meyer and Zucker (1989) went further, arguing that while managing cultural change may result in short-term economic benefits, in the longer term it may result in stagnation and demise. Another difficulty in achieving culture change, according to Brown (1995: 153), is:

> Most employees in an organisation have a high emotional stake in the current culture. People who have been steeped in the traditions and values of the organisation and whose philosophy of life may well be caught up in the organisation's cultural assumptions will experience considerable uncertainty, anxiety and pain in the process of change . . . Even if there are personal gains to be made from altering the habits of a lifetime these are likely to be seen as potential or theoretical only, as against the certainty of the losses.

Therefore, any attempt to change an organisation's culture is inevitably going to meet with some resistance. Sometimes this will be open and organised; often it will be covert and instinctive, with people trying to hold on to old ways and protect the old order. Unlike many other forms of change, the main resistance may well come from middle and, especially, senior managers who see their status, power and personal beliefs challenged. This is a point made by Cummings and Worley (2001), who observed that culture change programmes often result in or require the removal of managers from key leadership positions.

A further reservation expressed by a number of writers relates to the ethical issues raised by attempts to change culture. Van Maanen and Kunda (1989) argued that behind the interest in culture is an attempt by managers to control what employees feel as well as what they say or do. Their argument is that culture is a mechanism for disciplining emotion. Seen in this light, attempts to change culture can be conceived of as Taylorism of the mind. Frederick Taylor sought to control behaviour by laying down and enforcing strict rules about how work should be carried out. Van Maanen and Kunda in effect argue that culture change programmes attempt to achieve the same end through a form of mind control. Willmott (1995) expresses similar concerns. He believes that the overriding aim of culture change is to win the 'hearts and minds' of employees by achieving control over the 'employee's soul'. As quoted earlier, Watson (1997: 278) considers this 'a matter of serious concern'.

Changing organisational culture: conflicts and choices

Like so much else to do with organisations, there is no agreement among those who study culture as to its nature, purpose or malleability. Certainly, few writers doubt its importance, but beyond that there is much disagreement. The result, to quote Brown (1995: 5), is that we are presented with 'an embarrassment of definitional riches'. The Culture–Excellence proponents argue that there is only one form of culture that matters in today's environment – strong and flexible – and that organisations should adopt it quickly or face the consequences. The proponents of the Japanese approach to management and the organisational learning camp adopt a similar, though less strident, view.

Schein (1984, 1985, 1989) agrees that culture is important and that in certain cases a strong culture is desirable. However, in other situations, shared values and strong cultures may have a negative effect by stifling diversity and preventing alternative strategies arising. He also doubts that managers acting in isolation from the rest of an organisation have the ability by themselves to change the existing culture or impose a new one. Hofstede (1998) also drew attention to the presence and role of sub-cultures, and their potential for creating conflict. Meek (1988) takes the view that culture as a whole is not amenable to conscious managerial change, but that elements of culture might be open to deliberate change. The postmodernists take a firmer line against deliberate culture change. Though they consider organisational culture to be important, they are sceptical of attempts to manipulate and change culture, believing that the outcomes of such attempts are unpredictable and can alienate rather than motivate employees – remember Hatch's (1997: 235) warning not even to 'think of trying to manage culture'.

As cited earlier, Ogbonna and Harris (2002) believe that the writers on culture can be divided into three groups: the optimists, the pessimists and the realists. They argue that the realists probably have the better of the argument, i.e. that culture as a whole cannot be changed but that certain elements, such as artifacts and norms, can be changed. However, the lack of consensus among writers has to be acknowledged. Bearing this in mind, there are three main conclusions we can draw from the above review of the culture literature:

- First, in the absence of unambiguous guidelines on organisational culture, managers must make their own choices based on their own circumstances and perceived options as to whether or not to attempt to change all or part of their organisation's culture.

- Second, directive and coercive approaches to culture change may be successful in changing the behaviour and values of some existing members of an organisation, and they may allow the recruitment of staff more amenable to the new ways of working. However, such approaches may also alienate a considerable number of staff who feel they are being forced to change. In such cases, covert and overt resistance to change may arise with the organisation dividing into warring camps rather than a unified body.

- Lastly, in the absence of strong or appropriate cultures that bind their members together in a common purpose and legitimate and guide decision-making, managers may find it difficult either to agree among themselves or to gain agreement from others in the organisation. As Robbins (1987) argued, in such a situation, there is a tendency for conflict and power battles to take place.

Therefore, in understanding how organisations operate and the strengths and weaknesses of the theories we have been discussing in the previous chapters, it is necessary to examine the power–politics perspective on organisations.

The power–politics perspective

Political behaviour in organisations

The cultural perspective on organisational life reinforces the argument developed in previous chapters that organisations are not rational entities where everyone subscribes to, and helps to achieve, the organisation's overarching goals, as Mini Case Study 5.1 shows. The power–politics perspective puts forward a similar view, arguing that organisations often act irrationally, that their goals and objectives emerge through a process of negotiation and influence, that they are composed of competing and shifting coalitions of groups and individuals, and that critical decisions have less to do with the best interests of the organisation and more to do with the best interests of those making the decisions (Alvesson and Spicer, 2012; Brown, 1995; Buchanan and Badham, 1999; Change et al, 2009; Mintzberg et al, 1998a; Robbins, 1986, 1987). This perspective began to emerge strongly in the late 1970s and early 1980s, and is especially associated with research by Pettigrew (1973, 1980) and Pfeffer (1978, 1981). Before then, as Gandz and Murray (1980) discovered when they reviewed the literature on organisational politics, there was very little general interest in the topic, and very few publications on it.

Of the early work in the field, Lindblom's (1959) work on the 'science of muddling through' and Cyert and March's (1963) book, *A Behavioral Theory of the Firm*, can be said to have laid the basis for the later explosion of interest in power and politics in organisations. Writing from the viewpoint of public sector organisations, Lindblom argued that political constraints on policy make a rationalist approach to decision-making impossible. Cyert and March extensively developed Lindblom's work, showing that private sector firms were no less political entities than public sector organisations. The intention behind their work was to provide a better understanding of decision-making by supplementing existing theories, which tended to focus on market factors, with an examination of the internal operation of the firm. Cyert and March characterised firms as competing and shifting coalitions of multiple and conflicting interests, whose demands and objectives are constantly, but imperfectly, reconciled and where rationality is bounded by uncertainty over what goals to pursue and how to pursue them. Under such circumstances, managers 'satisfice': rather than searching for the best solution, they select one that is satisfactory and sufficient (Simon, 1947).

Cyert and March's work on the political dimension of decision-making and the nature of organisational life now forms part of the received wisdom on organisational behaviour (Mallory, 1997). This is not to refute or marginalise the role of organisational culture. As Handy (1993) observes, the extent to which agreement exists about the tasks an organisation undertakes, how it undertakes them, and the extent to which members of the organisation are committed to achieving them, will be affected by the strength and the perceived legitimacy or suitability of the organisation's culture. Willcocks (1994: 31) takes the view that diverse interests are part of organisational culture. They include, he argues, 'for example, the goals, values and expectations of the organizational participants and have been described as cognitive maps or personal agendas'. The importance of the power–politics perspective is that it shows that, even where a strong culture may be present, the cohesiveness, willingness and stability of an organisation's members is unlikely to be uniform either across an organisation or over time. Rather the extent of cooperation and commitment they exhibit will vary with the degree to which they perceive the goals they are pursuing as broadly consistent with their own interests (Mullins, 1993; Rollinson, 2002). Therefore, as Pfeffer (1978: 11–12) comments:

> It is difficult to think of situations in which goals are so congruent, or the facts so clear-cut that judgment and compromise are not involved. What is rational from one point of view is irrational from another. Organizations are political systems, coalitions of interests, and rationality is defined only with respect to unitary and consistent ordering of preferences.

It might be comforting to believe that individuals and groups within organisations are supportive of each other, that they work in a harmonious and cooperative fashion. Such a non-political perspective portrays employees as always behaving in a manner consistent with the interests of the organisation. In contrast, as Robbins (1986: 283) remarks:

> A political view can explain much of, what may seem to be, irrational behaviour in organizations. It can help to explain, for instance, why employees withhold information, restrict output, attempt to 'build empires'.

Handy (1986) also observes the tendency for individuals and groups to pursue courses of action that promote their interests, regardless of the organisation's formal goals and objectives. He notes that where individuals perceive that the actual or proposed goals of the organisation or the tasks they are asked to perform are out of step with their own interests, they will seek where possible to bring the two into line. In some cases, individuals and groups may be persuaded to change their perceptions; in others, they may seek to change or influence the goals or tasks. It is this phenomenon of individuals and groups, throughout an organisation, pursuing differing interests, and battling with each other to shape decisions in their favour, that has led many commentators to characterise organisations as political systems (Buchanan and Badham, 1999; Dawson, 2003; Mintzberg *et al*, 1998a; Morgan, 1986; Pettigrew, 1985, 1987; Pfeffer, 1981, 1992). Bradshaw-Camball and Murray (1991: 380), in describing the conditions necessary for political behaviour to occur, demonstrate why so many commentators see it as an intrinsic part of organisational life:

> Virtually all [writers] agree that for politics to occur, certain conditions must exist. There must be two or more parties (individuals, groups or large entities), some form of interdependence between the parties, and a perception on the part of at least one of the parties that divergent interests exist between them such that there is, or may potentially arise, conflict between the parties. Once these conditions exist, the subsequent actions of the parties involved will be deemed 'political'.

This echoes Zaleznik's (1970) view that where there are scarce resources (which is the case in most organisations), the psychology of scarcity and comparison take over. In such situations, possession of resources becomes the focus for comparisons, the basis for self-esteem and, ultimately, the source of power. Such situations will see the emergence not only of dominant coalitions but also, Zaleznik argues, of unconscious collusion based on defensive reaction. Therefore, while some individuals will perceive their actions as 'political' or self-interested, others may act in the same manner, but believe they are pursuing the best interests of the organisation.

Drory and Romm (1988) argue that those in managerial positions are less likely than those in non-managerial positions to define (or recognise) their actions as political. This may be explained by the findings from a survey of 428 managers carried out by Gandz and Murray (1980). They found that managers are more involved in political behaviour, and therefore tend to see it as a typical part of organisational life. If this is the case, it could be argued that the more individuals and groups are involved in political behaviour, the more it becomes the norm, and they become blind to its political nature and see it merely as standard practice. Those less involved in such behaviour, on the other hand, recognise its political nature because it stands out from their normal practices. It is also the case that those lower down the organisation, while affected by resource allocation decisions, are less likely, on a regular basis, to be in a position to influence such decisions. For managers, however, arguing for additional resources or allocating existing resources is the currency of everyday life. This is reflected in Gandz and Murray's survey, where 89 per cent of respondents thought that successful executives had to be good politicians. Despite this, over 50 per cent of respondents also thought that organisations would be happier places if they were free of politics, and a similar number thought that political behaviour was detrimental to efficiency. As Kanter (1979) and Pfeffer (1992) note, this ambivalent attitude, i.e. believing that political behaviour is necessary but deploring its use, is rife in organisations.

As mentioned in Chapter 4, postmodernists take a very different view of power and politics to that of most other writers on organisations. They are not greatly concerned with the way individuals and groups acquire and hold on to power as such. Instead, they focus on the relationship between power and knowledge, and on the way that power is used to promote particular views of reality and to legitimate particular forms of knowledge in organisations.

Power and politics: towards a definition

It is relatively easy to provide simple definitions of power and politics:

Power – the possession of position and/or resources.

Politics – the deployment of influence and leverage.

However, it is more difficult to distinguish between the two, as Drory and Romm (1988) explain. They argue that the two concepts are often used interchangeably and that the difference between the two has never been fully settled. Indeed, a brief examination of each shows the difficulty, and perhaps danger, in separating them. First, however, it is also necessary to understand the difference between power and authority.

Robbins (1987: 186) drew an important distinction between them:

Authority: 'The right to act, or command others to act, toward the attainment of organizational goals. Its unique characteristic, we said, was that this right had legitimacy based on the authority figure's position in the organization. Authority goes with the job.'

Power: 'When we use the term power we mean an individual's capacity to influence decisions . . . . the ability to influence based on an individual's legitimate position can affect decisions, but one does not require authority to have such influence.'

In support of his view, Robbins quotes the example of high-ranking executives' secretaries, who may have a great deal of power, by virtue of their ability to influence the flow of information and people to their bosses, but have very little actual authority. Pfeffer (1992) extends this view by pointing out that power can stem from three sources:

- formal authority to act;
- control over information;
- control over resources.

He believes this latter source of power is particularly important. According to Pfeffer (1992: 83), we must recognise the truth of the 'New Golden Rule: the person with the gold makes the rules'.

Moving from power to politics, Robbins (1987: 194) defines organisational politics as:

[the] efforts of organizational members to mobilize support for or against policies, rules, goals, or other decisions in which the outcome will have some effect on them. Politics, therefore, is essentially the exercise of power.

Robbins' argument, then, is that:

- power is the capacity to influence decisions;
- politics is the actual process of exerting this influence.

This view, that politics is merely the enactment of power, is held by many writers. Gibson *et al* (1988: 44), for example, states that organisational politics comprises:

those activities used at all levels to acquire, develop or use power and other resources to obtain individual choices when there is uncertainty or disagreement about choices.

This view is also central to Pfeffer's (1981: 7) widely accepted definition, that organisational politics:

> involves those activities taken within organizations to acquire, develop and use power and other resources to obtain one's preferred outcome in a situation where there is uncertainty or descensus about choices.

In his major work *Power in Organizations*, Pfeffer (1981) took the view that decisions in organisations are the result of political games among players with different perceptions and interests. This was a theme developed by Mintzberg (1983) in his comprehensive review of power and politics in organisations. He lists 13 political games that are common in organisations, the key ones being:

- games to resist authority;
- games to counter resistance;
- games to build power bases;
- games to defeat rivals;
- games to change the organisation.

Like all games, political ones have particular tactics associated with them. Ideas and perspectives 5.12 lists the seven most common ploys used by managers when seeking to influence superiors, equals and subordinates.

IDEAS AND PERSPECTIVES 5.12

Political ploys

- **Reason** – facts and information are used selectively to mount seemingly logical or rational arguments.
- **Friendliness** – the use of flattery, creation of goodwill, etc. prior to making a request.
- **Coalition** – joining forces with others so as to increase one's own influence.
- **Bargaining** – exchanging benefits and favours in order to achieve a particular outcome.
- **Assertiveness** – being forceful in making requests and demanding compliance.
- **Higher authority** – gaining the support of superiors for a particular course of action.
- **Sanctions** – using the promise of rewards or the threat of punishment to force compliance.

Source: From Kipnis *et al* (1980, 1984), Schilit and Locke (1982).

Robbins (1986) observes that the most popular tactic or ploy is the selective use of reason, regardless of whether the influence was directed upwards or downwards. Although cloaked in reason, arguments and data are deployed in such a way that the outcome favoured by those using the tactic is presented in a more favourable light than the alternatives. So although reason may be deployed, it is not done so in an unbiased way; it is used as a screen to disguise the real objective of the exercise. In deciding which tactic to use, Kipnis *et al* (1984) identify four contingency variables that affect the manager's choice:

- the manager's relative power;
- the manager's objectives in seeking to influence others;
- the manager's expectations of the target person's/group's willingness to comply;
- the organisation's culture.

Having gained a clearer picture of power and politics, we can now move on to examine one of the central issues that arises from this: the distinction between the legitimate and illegitimate use of power and politics.

Power, politics and legitimacy

Thompkins (1990) firmly believes that the use of politics is a direct contravention of or challenge to the legitimate rules of an organisation, but many see organisational politics as existing in a grey area between prescribed and illegal behaviour (Drory and Romm, 1988). Porter *et al* (1983) differentiate between three types of organisational behaviours: prescribed, discretionary and illegal. They believe that political behaviour falls within the discretionary rather than the illegal category. The most common view is that the use of politics in organisations can best be described as non-sanctioned or informal or discretionary behaviour, rather than behaviour that is clearly prohibited or illegal (Farrell and Petersen, 1983; Mayes and Allen, 1977). This definition of politics helps to distinguish between the formal and legitimate use of officially sanctioned power by authorised personnel, and power that is exercised either in an illegitimate manner by authorised personnel or used by non-authorised personnel for their own ends.

Most organisations and many writers see political behaviour as dysfunctional (Drory and Romm, 1988). Batten and Swab (1965), Pettigrew (1973) and Porter (1976) believe that political behaviour goes against and undermines formal organisational goals and interests. Thompkins (1990), on the other hand, argues that political manoeuvring in organisations results from a failure by senior managers to set and implement coherent and consistent goals and policies in the first place. This results in uncertainties, which in turn lead to conflict between groups and individuals. In such a situation, Thompkins (1990: 24) argues:

> Management is then left without top level guidance to run company operations. They will, then, by their own nature of survival, over a period of time, make decisions that will perpetuate their own safety and security. This is the beginning of political power, where legitimate discipline begins to decline and illegitimate discipline begins to strangle the organisation. In short, the tail begins to wag the dog. 'Politics' in this form is created by the neglect of top executive management.

Pfeffer (1981) takes a different view of organisational politics. Rather than political behaviour arising from a lack of clear-cut goals and policies, he suggests that the construction of organisational goals is itself a political process. This does not always mean that political behaviour is detrimental to organisational effectiveness. Mintzberg (1983) maintains that, when used in moderation, political games can have a healthy effect by keeping the organisation on its toes. Mayes and Allen (1977) take a similar view. Pascale (1993) goes further, putting forward the view that conflict and contention are necessary to save an organisation from complacency and decline. The argument that the use of politics and power are central to the effective running of organisations is most strongly put by Pfeffer (1992: 337–8) in his book *Managing with Power*, where he argues:

> ## IDEAS AND PERSPECTIVES 5.13
>
> ### The use of power and politics
>
> **1.** Decide what your goals are, what you are trying to accomplish.
>
> **2.** Diagnose patterns of dependence and interdependence; what individuals are influential and important in your achieving your goal?
>
> **3.** What are their points of view likely to be? How will they feel about what you are trying to do?
>
> **4.** What are their power bases? Which of them is more influential in the decision?
>
> **5.** What are your bases of power and influence? What bases of influence can you develop to gain more control over the situation?
>
> **6.** Which of the various strategies and tactics for exercising power seem most appropriate and are likely to be effective, given the situation you confront?
>
> **7.** Based on the above, choose a course of action to get something done.
>
> *Source:* From Pfeffer (1992: 29).

Computers don't get built, cities don't get rebuilt, and diseases don't get fought unless advocates for change learn how to develop and use power effectively. . . . In corporations, public agencies, universities, and government, the problem is how to get things done, how to move forward, how to solve the many problems facing organizations of all sizes and all types. Developing and exercising power requires both will and skill. It is the will which often seems to be missing.

For Pfeffer, will and skill are exercised through the pursuit of a focused and consistent personal agenda which is implemented through a seven-step programme (*see* Ideas and perspectives 5.13). Certainly, there does seem to be strong body of opinion that political skills are an essential part of the successful manager's toolkit (Bacharach, 2005; Drory and Vigoda-Gadot, 2010). However, Mintzberg (1983) sounds a note of warning. He argues that if too many people pursue their own personal agenda, or if the use of power and politics becomes too aggressive and pervasive, it can turn the whole organisation into a political cauldron and divert it from its main task.

To an extent, the degree to which the balance between positive and negative benefits is tipped one way or the other in an organisation is dependent on the type of power deployed and how it is used. Etzioni (1975) identifies three distinct types of power used in organisations:

- **Coercive power** – the threat of negative consequences (including physical sanctions or force) should compliance not be forthcoming.

- **Remunerative power** – the promise of material rewards as inducements to cooperate.

- **Normative power** – the allocation and manipulation of symbolic rewards, such as status symbols, as inducements to obey.

Robbins (1986) develops this further by identifying not only types of power but also the sources of power. To Etzioni's three types of power, he adds a fourth:

- **Knowledge power** – the control of information.

> We can say that when an individual in a group or organization controls unique information, and when that information is needed to make a decision, the individual has knowledge-based power.
> (Robbins, 1986: 273)

Robbins suggests that these four types of power stem from four separate sources:

- a person's position in the organisation;
- personal characteristics;
- expertise;
- the opportunity to influence or control the flow of information.

All four types of power can be and are deployed in organisations. The degree to which they will be effective is likely to depend upon the source from which they spring. Coercive power is usually the prerogative of those in senior positions, while even quite junior members of an organisation may, in particular circumstances, control or possess information that enables them to exert knowledge power. The interesting point to note is that the use of knowledge power – the selective and biased use of information (often deployed under the guise of reason) – is shown to be effective in gaining willing compliance and cooperation from those at whom it is directed. According to Huczynski and Buchanan (2001), however, the favourite influencing strategies are:

- for influencing up (managers) – the use of reason;
- for influencing across (co-workers) – the use of friendliness;
- for influencing down (subordinates) – the use of reason.

This appears to fit in well with the view of many observers that the use of remunerative and coercive power, i.e. the opposite of reason and friendliness, is often counter productive because those on the receiving end of such power tend to view it negatively and resent it (Bachman *et al*, 1968; Ivancevich, 1970; Robbins, 1986; Student, 1968).

This is perhaps why the most detrimental outcomes from the deployment of power arise when people feel they are being coerced into a particular course of action that goes against their beliefs or self-interest (Rollinson, 2002). Therefore, irrespective of the source or type of power, it is perhaps the willingness to use it in situations where there will be clear winners and losers, and where the covert activities of warring coalitions turn into open warfare, that leads to the more dysfunctional and damaging consequences. Such battles, where groups and individuals fight to influence key decisions and in so doing bolster their own position, especially where the stakes are high, can end with senior figures either leaving or being forced out of the organisation.

Liverpool Football Club is a case in point. The club was bought jointly by US entrepreneurs Tom Hicks and George Gillett in March 2007. However, after the takeover, the two men appeared to become bitter enemies and argued repeatedly and publicly over the running and ownership of the club (Hunter, 2008). The end result was that the club was sold against the wishes of both owners and at a price far lower than either Hicks' or Gillett's valuation (Gabbatt, 2010). Thus, this was a power battle where both sides seemed to have lost.

In the mainstream business world, there are many such examples. Take the case of BMW when it was considering selling Rover. The battle over the future of Rover's Longbridge plant in the UK led to both Bernd Pischetsrieder, BMW's chairman, and his long-time boardroom rival, Wolfgang Reitzle, BMW's marketing director, being forced to resign (Gow, 1999a; Gow and Traynor, 1999).

A similar situation occurred with Pehr Gyllenhammar, the man who ran Volvo for more than two decades. His 1993 attempt to merge Volvo with Renault, the French state-controlled car company, was opposed by a coalition of shareholders and managers, who felt that it was not so much a merger of equals as a takeover by Renault. Both shareholders and managers felt that in such a situation their interests would be damaged, and a very public power struggle ensued, with both sides claiming to act in Volvo's best interests (Done, 1994).

Both these cases could be classed as battles between individuals fighting to maintain their own power. However, the reality was that in both cases major issues concerning the future viability of these organisations were at stake. The irony in Volvo's case was that six years after rejecting a merger with Renault because it was seen as disadvantageous to the company's interests, the company sold its car division to Ford Motors, whose work practices were seen as the antithesis of all that Volvo held dear.

The battle for control of the advertising agency Saatchi & Saatchi, which resulted in the founders leaving, also shows how a power struggle can leave an organisation damaged (Barrie, 1995; Donovan, 1995). Another very public example of a power clash was the on–off merger of SmithKline Beecham and Glaxo. In 1998, the two companies announced that they planned to merge and form the largest pharmaceutical company in the world, worth an estimated $165 billion. However, the merger was quickly called off owing to a rumoured clash between SmithKline's chief executive, Jan Leschly, and Glaxo's chairman, Sir Richard Sykes, over who would run the merged company (although given that it later emerged that Mr Leschly's pay, perks and shares package was worth over £90 million, one can understand why he would be reluctant to step down (Buckingham and Finch, 1999)). It was only when Leschly and Sykes both announced their retirements that the merger proceeded.

In some cases, such clashes can become endemic and linger on even after the initial cause has long gone. Lonrho is a case in point. After the successful battle to oust Tiny Rowland from the company he founded and for so long dominated, Lonrho was split up and sold off. Yet the political battles for control still rumbled on even among its demerged parts (Laird, 1998).

Clearly, as the above examples show, the deployment of coercive power can be very damaging; however, other forms of power can also have adverse effects, though perhaps in a more insidious fashion. The use of remunerative power by senior managers in the UK and US is a good example. Over the last two decades, executive salaries in both countries have run far ahead of inflation, the pay of salaried staff and company profits (Business Notebook, 2003; DeCarlo, 2008; Dunphy and Griffiths, 1998; Green, 2008; Ruse, 2012; Treanor and Neville, 2012). This has caused much controversy, especially in the privatised, but once public, utilities such as gas, electricity and water. In these organisations, executives, the so-called 'fat cats', appeared to use their power to give themselves extremely generous remuneration packages; at the same time, they cut jobs and wages for many staff elsewhere in their organisations (Smithers, 1995). For a time, this practice was condoned by both shareholders and governments because the UK economy and UK companies were doing well and those controlling them could argue that they were being rewarded for success. However, the criticisms of fat-cat salaries became more strident and widespread after the economy started to falter. Government, shareholders and trade unions began to sing with one critical voice that those leading companies were being rewarded for failure. Given that among the

---

IDEAS AND PERSPECTIVES 5.14

Nardelli's style helps to seal his fate

Four months ago, a defiant Bob Nardelli said he had no intention of resigning as chairman and chief executive of Home Depot. "I love this company," he told the Financial Times. "I've been in business 35 years and I've never been in a company with more growth potential. As long as I have my health and support from the board I will continue." It now seems likely that, even as Mr Nardelli spoke those words, the support of the board was already wavering. Home Depot's directors accepted his resignation, by mutual agreement, at a board meeting on Tuesday following a traumatic year for the home improvement retailer.

Mr Nardelli's departure marks a second low point for the combative executive who arrived at Home Depot from General Electric six years ago after losing out in the race to succeed Jack Welch, his mentor, as chairman of GE. His fate may have been sealed as early as last May, when he infuriated many investors by refusing to answer questions at its annual meeting about his hefty compensation package and the company's sagging share price. Mr Nardelli was already a target for shareholder activists, having received more than $120m in compensation, excluding stock options, during his first five years as chief executive, while the share price slumped. But the anger was intensified by his belligerent attitude towards rebel shareholders and activist investors who were preparing a fresh campaign against him ahead of this year's annual meeting.

Source: Adapted from Ward, A (2007): Nardelli's style helps to seal his fate. *The Financial Times*, January 4, p. 22.

UK's top 100 companies, the pay of directors rose 84 per cent in the three years to 2003 but the stock market value of these companies fell by 50 per cent, the outcry is understandable (Finch and Treanor, 2003). This disgruntlement became even more strident when it was realised that some companies were giving big payoffs to executives who appeared to have failed in their jobs, such as Gerald Corbett, who walked away from Railtrack with a payoff of £3.7 million (Treanor and Finch, 2003).

The issue is not so much whether the way executives distribute rewards in their organisations is fair or not, but the corrosive effect such a blatant use of power has on employee morale, shareholder support and customer loyalty. One of the best (or worst) examples of this is the case of Bob Nardelli's reign at Home Depot (*see* Ideas and perspectives 5.14).

These very public manifestations of power battles in organisations represent merely the tip of the iceberg. They illustrate the tendency for such battles to be fought under the banner of 'the best interests of the organisation'. Political in-fighting, the seeking of allies, the influencing of decisions, and the protection or promotion of one's own or one's group's interests are nearly always justified by recourse to the best interests of the organisation, just as the parties involved in any armed struggle always seem to justify it on the grounds that justice is on their side. It is not that the participants necessarily believe their own propaganda, though often they do; it is that, without it, they would find it very difficult to justify, to themselves and their allies, the use of blatantly illegitimate tactics such as challenging, undermining or explicitly ignoring their organisation's official goals and policies.

Consequently, in opposing or promoting a particular decision or development, those indulging in even a low level of political behaviour rarely openly declare their own personal

---

IDEAS AND PERSPECTIVES 5.15

Power tactics

- **Image-building** – action that enhances a person's standing, such as backing the 'right' causes.
- **Selective information** – withhold unfavourable information from superiors.
- **Scapegoating** – blame someone else.
- **Formal alliances** – form or join a coalition of the strong.
- **Networking** – make friends with those in power.
- **Compromise** – be prepared to give in on unimportant issues in order to win on the important ones.
- **Rule manipulation** – interpret rules selectively to favour friends and thwart opponents.
- **Other tactics** – if all else fails, use dirty tricks such as coercion, undermining the expertise of others, playing one group off against another, and get others to 'fire the bullet'.

Source: Buchanan and Badham (1999: 27–9).

---

interest in the outcome. As Pfeffer (1981) maintains, a major characteristic accompanying political behaviour is the attempt to conceal its true motive. This can be seen from Buchanan and Badham's (1999: 27–9) list of power tactics, shown in Ideas and perspectives 5.15. Concealing motives is essential because, as Allen *et al* (1979), Drory and Romm (1988) and Frost and Hayes (1979) observe, those involved believe that such tactics would be judged unacceptable or illegitimate by others in the organisation, and as such resisted. Accordingly, a false but acceptable motive is presented instead.

The picture of power and politics that emerges from Ideas and perspectives 5.15 tends to be a negative one, portraying individuals and groups as using power and politics purely to pursue their own selfish interests. Others take a more positive view. Morgan (1986) offers a model of interests, conflicts and power, accepting that diversity of interests can create conflict. In such circumstances, power and influence are, he suggests, the major means of resolving conflict. Buchanan and Boddy (1992) argue that the use of power and politics is a necessary component in the toolkit of those responsible for managing change in organisations. Seen in this light, political behaviour can have a positive effect on improving the working of organisations by enabling them to manage change more effectively. Pfeffer (1992), in a similar vein, maintains that the use of power is an important social process that is often required to get things done in interdependent systems. In fact, he maintains that a failure to deploy power and politics is harmful:

> By pretending that power and influence don't exist, or at least shouldn't exist, we contribute to what I and others (such as John Gardner) see as the major problem facing many corporations today, particularly in the United States – the almost trained or produced incapacity of anyone except the highest-level managers to take action and get things accomplished.
>
> (Pfeffer, 1992: 10)

Perhaps Gardner (1990: 57) sums up the issues involved in the power–politics debate most succinctly when, in relation to those who possess and deploy power, he states:

The significant questions are: What means do they use to gain it? How do they exercise it? To what ends do they exercise it?

We can see from the above why writers have found it difficult to separate power from politics. While it is possible to examine the potential for power without also examining how power might be exercised, for students of organisational life this is rather a sterile endeavour. For the purpose of understanding what makes organisations tick, how decisions are arrived at, why resources are allocated in a particular way and why certain changes are initiated and others not, we have to comprehend both the possession and exercise of power, whether it be by official or political means.

Though Robbins rightly draws a distinction between formal authority and the possession/deployment of power, we should not fall into the trap of assuming that there is not a close relationship between the two. An examination of the ability to exert influence (power) over key decisions and the possession of position (authority) shows that these tend to lie within dominant coalitions rather than being spread evenly across organisations (*see* Buchanan and Badham, 1999; Pfeffer, 1978, 1981, 1992; Robbins, 1987). The dominant coalition is the one that has the power to affect structure. The reason why this is so important is that the choice of structure will automatically favour some groups and disadvantage others. This is why, as shown earlier in this chapter, restructuring organisations is one of the first steps taken by those seeking to create a new culture – they need to destroy the power base of those who benefit from the old order and are likely to resist the new order. A person or group's position in the structure will determine such factors as their influence on planning, their choice of technology, the criteria by which they will be evaluated, allocation of rewards, control of information, proximity to senior managers, and their ability to exercise influence on a whole range of decisions (Morgan, 1986; Perrow, 1983; Pfeffer, 1981, 1992; Robbins, 1987).

Though the postmodernists would not disagree with this analysis *per se*, as mentioned earlier their view of power in organisations is a much broader one. For them, power is the mechanism by which groups in organisations create and reinforce their view of reality. In turn, postmodernists maintain, it is this shaping and construction of reality that, in the main, allows dominant groups in organisations to impose their will on others rather than the use of sanctions and other control mechanisms (Reed and Hughes, 1992).

Strangely enough, the one topic that is rarely raised when discussing power and politics in organisations is ethics. The last 20 years or so have seen increasing pressure on organisations to act ethically, through initiatives such as Corporate Social Responsibility (Korner, 2005; Matten and Moon, 2004; United Nations, 2010), but this does not embrace the ethical dimension of power and politics in organisations. According to Tseng *et al* (2010: 587) ethics is 'the study and philosophy of human conduct with an emphasis on the determination of right and wrong'. Though some writers debate whether power and politics are good or bad for an organisation's performance, there seems to be little consideration of whether the use of power and politics is right or wrong in terms of the effects it has on those individuals and groups on the receiving end of such behaviour. Indeed, as Buchanan and Badham state in Ideas and perspectives 5.15:

> If all else fails, use dirty tricks such as coercion, undermining the expertise of others, playing one group off against another, and get others to 'fire the bullet'.

We will return to the topic of ethics in Chapters 8–11, when we discuss approaches to organisational change, and Chapter 14 when we discuss leadership.

Managing and changing organisations: bringing back choice

In the previous chapter, we examined the postmodernist, realist and complexity perspectives on organisations. The postmodernists argue that reason and logic have had their day, and that organisations are social organisms in which individuals and groups construct their own views of reality based on their own perceptions of the world and their place in it. Realists, while accepting the social construction hypothesis, argue that reality does exist and that it imposes limits, though sometimes very broad ones, on what individuals and organisations can do. The proponents of complexity, for their part, see organisations as complex, self-organising systems where, in order to maintain appropriate order-generating rules, choice and decision-making must move from the few to the many. What Chapter 4 showed, with its review of these three perspectives, was that organisations have a great deal more choice and freedom in what they can do and how they can do it than the organisation theories discussed in Chapters 1–3 allowed.

In this chapter we have sought to develop this argument further by looking at how choices are made in organisations and on what basis. The chapter began by examining the literature on organisational culture, which revealed that, despite its popularity as a promoter of organisational excellence, culture is difficult to define, change and manipulate. Strong cultures may have a positive effect on organisations, in that they can bond disparate groups together in a common purpose; and weak cultures may have a negative impact, in that individuals and groups can pursue separate and conflicting objectives. In some situations, however, especially where there is major environmental disruption, the reverse may also be true, with strong cultures being a straitjacket on innovation and weak ones allowing new ideas and new leaders to come to the fore. In such situations, where the organisation's dominant coalition is split, or is so ossified it cannot entertain change, power and politics come to the fore.

As the examination of the literature on power and politics showed, in cases where a clash of interests and a clash of perspectives is present, where the status quo is being challenged, major decisions about the future direction, structure and operation of an organisation are likely to be dominated by issues of power and politics (Buchanan and Badham, 1999).

Murray (1989: 285), reporting on a major study of the introduction and use of information technology, comments:

> The use of new technology is subject to processes of organizational decision-making and implementation characterized by often conflicting managerial objectives, rationalities and strategies developed through the mobilization of organizational power.

Therefore, as far as Buchanan and Badham (1999), Dawson (1994), Morgan (1986), Pfeffer (1992), Robbins (1987) and many others are concerned, the process of organisational change is inherently a political one.

Though the postmodern, realist, complexity, cultural and power–politics perspectives on organisational life are very different, there are also strong overlaps. In particular, the management of meaning and the creation of legitimacy through the construction and manipulation of symbols is an area of common ground. This can be seen in Pettigrew's (1985) study of organisational change in ICI. He maintains that the process of change is shaped by the interests and commitments of individuals and groups, the forces of bureaucratic momentum, significant changes in the environment, and the manipulation of the structural context around decisions. In particular, Pettigrew (1987: 659) argues:

The acts and processes associated with politics as the management of meaning represent conceptually the overlap between a concern with the political and cultural analyses of organizations. A central concept linking political and cultural analyses essential to the understanding of continuity and change is legitimacy. The management of meaning refers to a process of symbol construction and value use designed to create legitimacy for one's ideas, actions and demands, and to delegitimate the demands of one's opponents . . . [Therefore] structures, cultures and strategies are not just being treated here as neutral, functional constructs connectable to some system need such as efficiency or adaptability; those constructs are viewed as capable of serving to protect the interests of the dominant groups. . . . The content of strategic change is thus ultimately a product of a legitimation process shaped by political/cultural considerations, though often expressed in rational/analytical terms.

This view that the choice and use of structure, and other key decisions, is the outcome of a political process rather than the application of rational analysis and decision-making has significant implications for organisation theory. While it does not necessarily invalidate the appropriateness or otherwise of particular approaches, it does mean that managerial aspirations and interests are seen as more important than might otherwise be the case. It also means that, rather than being the prisoners of organisation theory (as some might suppose or hope), managers do have significant scope for the exercise of choice with regard to structure and other organisational characteristics.

In his review of the influence of power and politics in organisations, Robbins (1987) notes that no more than 50–60 per cent of variability in structure can be explained by strategy, size, technology and environment. He then goes on to argue that a substantial portion of the residual variance can be explained by those in positions of power choosing a structure that will, as far as possible, maintain and enhance their control. He points out that proponents of other determinants of structure, such as size, technology, etc., assume that organisations are rational entities: 'However, for rationality to prevail an organisation must have either a single goal or agreement over the multiple goals. Neither case exists in most organisations' (Robbins, 1987: 200). Consequently, he argues that structural decisions are not rational. Such decisions arise from a power struggle between special-interest groups or coalitions, each arguing for a structural arrangement that best suits them. Robbins (1987: 200) believes that while strategy, size, technology and environment define the minimum level of effectiveness and set the parameters within which self-serving decision choices will be made, 'both technology and environment are chosen. Thus, those in power will select technologies and environments that will facilitate their maintenance of control'.

As both the realists and complexity advocates argue, however, the extent to which those in power can please themselves has limits. Markets do exist, economies can fall as well as rise and, as the dotcom collapse in 2000 and the credit crunch in 2008 showed, new technologies do not always deliver on their promise, and market bubbles can and do burst. The power–politics perspective, therefore, does not totally undermine the case against the rational view of management but it might explain the dismal long-term performance of America's largest companies mentioned earlier in this chapter (Foster and Kaplan, 2003). After all, if executives are busy pursuing their own (usually) short-term interests, they can hardly be pursuing the long-term interests of their organisations.

There is also other strong and significant evidence that challenges the view of management as rational and neutral implementers of decisions determined by objective data. In particular, the detailed case studies of organisational decision-making and change at ICI and Cadbury Ltd carried out, respectively, by Pettigrew (1985, 1987) and Child and Smith

(1987) lend a great deal of weight to the view that management in general, and the management of change in particular, is inherently a political process. Murray (1989) made the telling point that, given the insecurity of many managers' positions, particularly during periods of major upheaval and change, it is not surprising that managers and other groups attempt to influence decisions in order to protect, enhance or shore up their position in the organisation.

Nevertheless, one needs to be wary of ascribing the purpose of all organisational decisions and actions to self-interest. Politics plays a part but, to view Robbin's (1987) finding from another perspective, so too do strategy, size, technology and environment. As the realists would argue, these can act as a constraint on the freedom of action of groups and individuals, as can the need to be seen to act in the organisation's best interests, in line with agreed goals and in a rational manner. So although the political perspective has become very influential in the last 30 years, it does not explain all actions and all decisions in organisations. We need to see power and politics as an important influence on organisations, but not the only influence. Indeed, we need to remember the original objective of Cyert and March's (1963) work on organisational politics. They sought to show that external factors were not the only factors that affected decision-making in organisations. This is not, of course, the same as saying that external factors do not matter. As Child and Smith (1987) show with their firm-in-sector perspective (*see* Chapter 6), the external environment does matter. In a whole host of concrete and symbolic ways, it constrains and impinges on organisational decision-making and behaviour. It may well be, as Robbins (1987) comments, that strategy, size, technology and environment only define the minimum level of effectiveness and set the parameters within which decisions are taken, but this is still a very important constraint on managers. It is also an important rejoinder to those management theorists who have become, according to Hendry (1996: 621), 'overfocused on the political aspects of the change [decision-making] process'.

In summary, therefore, power and politics are among the most important factors influencing decision-making in organisations. Indeed, by linking the arguments of Robbins, Pettigrew and Murray regarding managerial choice of structure to the discussion on culture, two very interesting points arise:

- First, it is argued by Allaire and Firsirotu (1984), and others, that culture and structure need to be mutually supportive if an organisation is to operate efficiently and effectively. If, as the power–politics perspective argues, structure is in part at least the outcome of self-interested choice by the dominant coalition, the degree of congruence between the two may be due more to accident than design.

- Second, it was also argued earlier that organisational culture is the product of long-term social learning in which dominant coalitions play a key role. This clearly opens up scope for choices over both structure and culture. However, the development of culture and approaches to changing it are long-term processes. Dominant coalitions, on the other hand, change their composition and priorities over time, sometimes over quite short periods of time.

Consequently, although it can be argued that the possibility exists for managers to choose both the structure and culture that best suit their own self-interests, this is only likely to result in a balanced and effective structure–culture nexus if the dominant coalition holds sway and is consistent in its aims over long periods of time.

As many observers note, while these conditions may exist in some Western companies (e.g. News International under Rupert Murdoch, General Electric under Jack Welch, Virgin under Richard Branson), these are the exception. In any case, as the departure of Arnold Weinstock from GEC showed (*see* the Marconi case study in Chapter 6), such situations often rely on dominant individuals to hold coalitions together; when they go, the dominant coalition falls apart and a new one emerges with a radically different vision for the organisation (Brummer and Cowe, 1998; Brummer, 1999). Sometimes the departure of such individuals can even bring an organisation perilously close to collapse, as was the case with GEC when Weinstock stepped down, Apple Computers when Steve Jobs was fired in 1985, and with Tiny Rowland's forced departure from Lonrho in 1995 (Laird, 1998; Morgan, 1986). Even Japanese corporations, with their reputation for dominant coalitions maintaining their unity of purpose through successive changes of personnel, are not immune to this problem (Fruin, 1992; Pascale and Athos, 1982; Whitehill, 1991). For example, Nissan's appointment of a new chief executive in 1985 was followed by an attempt to change its culture in order to overcome what were seen as major mistakes by the previous incumbent (Ishizuna, 1990). This and other changes failed and, in the end, Nissan was, in effect, taken over by the state-owned French car-maker Renault.

However, in some companies, so forceful and coercive is the personality of a dominant individual or group that their will cannot be questioned, and fundamental problems are only discovered once they depart (Bowers, 1996). Certainly, this seems to have been the case with the Japanese firm Olympus. It was only when an outsider, the British-born Michael Woodward, was appointed as CEO of Olympus in 2011 that it became clear that fraudulent activities totalling £1 billion had taken place under the previous management (Neate, 2011).

To sum up, what we can see is that managers have a degree, arguably a wide degree, of choice or influence over major organisational variables such as structure, technology, environment and perhaps even culture, or at least some elements of it. Despite the arguments of the postmodernists, however, their freedom of action is constrained by a whole host of factors such as market conditions, technological development, organisational goals, policies and performance, their own and other people's self-interests, and the need to portray their actions as being rational and in the best interests of their organisation. In addition, in a reciprocal way, some of the factors over which they have a degree of choice, such as structure and culture, can limit managers' freedom of manoeuvre. These constraints will vary from organisation to organisation at any one time and, within and between organisations, over time but will never be fully absent. Strong though these constraints may be, however, choice will also never be totally absent.

Conclusions

In reviewing the main approaches to and perspectives on organisation theory, Part 1 of this book has shown that, by succeeding stages, these have moved from the mechanical-rational outlook of the Classical school to the, arguably, culture-based perspectives of the Culture–Excellence, Japanese and Organisation Learning approaches, passing through the social perspective of the Human Relations school and the rational perspective of the Contingency theorists. They all argue for a 'one best way' approach (though the Contingency theorists believed in this for 'each' rather than 'all' organisations). Because of this approach they all, in effect, seek to remove choice from managers: their mantra is 'do as we tell you, or else!'. Indeed, it was one of the main claims of the Classical school that it removed discretion not only from workers but also from managers. As Frederick Taylor (1911b: 189) stated:

> The man at the head of the business under scientific management is governed by rules and laws . . . just as the workman is, and the standards which have been developed are equitable.

The role of managers, from these perspectives, is to apply rationally the dictates of the particular theory promoted. To do otherwise would be sub-optimal and irrational.

By building on the discussions of postmodernism, realism and complexity in Chapter 4, this chapter has sought to move managerial choice back to centre stage. By exploring organisational culture, it was shown that the degree to which culture influences behaviour is dependent upon the presence of clear and consistent organisational goals. If these are not present, which appears to be the case in many organisations, conflict and disagreement emerge regardless of the nature of the culture. Similarly, if the environment changes to the extent that existing ways of working are no longer appropriate, once again, conflict and disagreement may emerge. In such situations, it is the political perspective on organisational life that offers the better opportunity for understanding how and why decisions are taken, particular courses of action are embarked upon, and why some changes to the management and structure of the organisation are pursued and others discarded.

The examination of organisational politics and power added further weight to the criticisms of the approaches to organisation theory considered in previous chapters, particularly concerning the scope for rational decision-making and choice. To an extent, the key issue was raised when discussing Contingency Theory, namely the question as to whether managers are the prisoners of the situational variables they face, or whether they can influence or change these. Certainly, some critics of Contingency Theory argue that managers can, partly at least, influence or choose the contingencies they face. This casts doubts not only on the deterministic nature of Contingency Theory but also on all organisational theories, because – either openly or implicitly – they are all founded on the notion that organisations face certain immutable conditions that they cannot influence and to which they must therefore adapt.

This does not necessarily mean that the various theories and their attendant structures and practices we have discussed so far in this book are invalid, unhelpful or inapplicable. It does mean that it may be possible, within limits, for organisations, or rather those who control organisations, to decide upon the structure and behaviours they want to promote, and then shape the conditions and contingencies to suit these, rather than vice versa. Indeed, as far as the public sector in the UK is concerned, this appears to be exactly what governments have done. From 1979 to 1997, successive Conservative governments took the view that they wanted managers in the public sector to be cost-focused and entrepreneurial, and shaped the conditions in which the public sector operates (i.e. its environment) in order to promote those attributes (Ferlie *et al*, 1996; Flynn, 1993). Following its election in 1997, the 'New Labour' government similarly manipulated the public sector environment to encourage a more market-orientated approach to service delivery (Salauroo and Burnes, 1998; Vidler and Clarke, 2005). The election of a Conservative-Liberal Democrat coalition in 2010 has once again led to a change of role and behaviour for the public sector. Under the banner of deficit reduction, the public sector is ceasing its service delivery role and instead is becoming a regulator and commissioner of outsourced services provided by the private sector (PwC, 2011).

If organisations are *not* the prisoners of situational variables, as most organisation theories maintain, if those who manage them do have a degree of leeway in what they do, one then has to ask what factors do influence the actions of decision-makers. The review of the power–politics literature showed organisations as shifting coalitions of groups and individuals seeking to promote policies and decisions that enhanced or maintained their position in the organisation. From the literature, a persuasive argument is mounted for seeing politics and power – usually promoted under the cloak of rationality, reasonableness and the organisation's best interests – as a central, though not exclusive, determinant of the way organisations operate.

In particular, though political behaviour appears to be an ever-present feature of organisational life, politics comes to the fore when major issues of structural change or resource allocation are concerned. Such decisions have crucial importance for achieving and maintaining power or position, or even – when the chips are down – for keeping one's job when all around are losing theirs.

Therefore, it is surprising that much of organisation theory, which after all is primarily concerned with major decisions concerning structure and resource allocation, seems to dismiss or gloss over power and politics. What is clear from this chapter is that managers, despite the constraints they face, have a far wider scope for shaping decisions than most organisation theories acknowledge, and that the scope for choice and the deployment of political influence is likely to be most pronounced when change, particularly major change, is on the managerial agenda.

Having examined the merits and drawbacks of the main organisation theories, and in particular having raised the issue of the way in which major decisions are reached and implemented, we can now turn our attention in the following chapters to an in-depth examination of how organisations decide upon and carry out change.

TEST YOUR LEARNING

Short discussion topics

The purpose of these is to enable students to check their learning and reflect on the topics covered in this chapter. The discussions should last for no more than 5–10 minutes. Depending on the length of the lecture, there could be one, two or three such discussions in a session. The following are five suggested topics which address issues raised in this chapter:

1. What are Cummings and Worley's four elements of culture?

2. Briefly describe Handy's four types of culture.

3. Give three benefits of Robbins' addition of knowledge power to Etzioni's three types of power.

4. Define organisational politics.

5. For each of the following, briefly state their implications for organisational change: (a) organisational culture and (b) power and politics.

Class debates

The purpose of class debates is to enable students to explore a topic in depth by setting up a 'for and against' debate. The class can be split into two and one half asked to research the 'for' case and the other 'against' case. Individuals can then be chosen at random to introduce their side of the debate. Alternatively, two individuals for each side can be told in advance that they will be introducing the debate. The length of such debates depends on the time available, the size of the class and their enthusiasm for the topic. However, less than 30 minutes is probably too short and more than 60 minutes probably too long. The following are three suggested topics which address issues raised in this chapter:

1. 90 per cent of the evidence for current organisational theories comes from studies of American organisations. Given what we now know about the differences between national cultures, this means that most organisational theories are wrong.

2. Only an idiot would try to change their organisation's culture.

3. The use of power and politics in organisations is always unethical.

Essay questions

1. To what extent and why do you agree with the following statement: No matter what their nationality, it is the responsibility of employees to adapt to the culture of the organisation which employs them.

2. 'Computers don't get built, cities don't get rebuilt, and diseases don't get fought unless advocates for change learn how to develop and use power effectively' (Pfeffer, 1992: 337). Critically evaluate Pfeffer's view on power in organisations.

Suggested further reading

Brown, A (1998) *Organisational Culture* (2nd edition). FT/Pitman: London.
Andrew Brown's book gives a useful introduction to the uses and abuses of organisational culture.

Chhokar, JS, Brodbeck, FC and House, RJ (eds) (2007) *Culture and Leadership Across the World: The GLOBE book of in-depth studies of 25 societies*. Lawrence Erlbaum Associates: Mahwah, NJ.
The GLOBE work shows how organisational cultures differ from country to country.

Pfeffer, J (1992) *Managing with Power: Politics and influence in organizations*. Harvard Business School Press: Boston, MA.
This is a useful guide to the power–politics perspective on organisations.

Ikea – against the grain

It is 7am in Almhult and 240 of Ikea's staff have gathered to celebrate the opening of a cavernous new store. Ingvar Kamprad, now 86, has come back to the town of 9,000 people where he founded Ikea six decades ago. One of his co-workers, as Ikea calls all its staff, stands by a colleague's pram with a baby inside and says: "We are so proud to think something so big has come out of this little town." A few hours later, it seems as if the whole population of the town in southern Sweden has packed the store's windswept car park to see a grand opening performed Ikea-style. No champagne or ribbon cutting here. Instead, the mayor, the store manager and an Ikea designer ceremonially saw a log into pieces. The designer thrills the crowd by referring to the town as the "Mecca of furniture".

Mr Kamprad founded the company in 1943 just to the north of Almhult, a community surrounded by dense forests and little else. Fifteen years later he opened the first shop in the town in what would become a global empire of flat-pack furniture. Local pride is palpable. In Almhult's Ikea hotel, there is reading material on the bedside table: the New Testament and the Ikea catalogue. Mikael Ohlsson, Ikea's chief executive, puts it simply: "[Almhult] is in a way the heart and soul of Ikea. It is here it started."

Ikea is one of the most extraordinary success stories in post war European business. Famed for its Scandinavian chic-but-cheap tables, bookcases and beds, its self-assembly wares inspire admiration and frustration in equal measure. Now the privately held group is looking to cement its status as the world's biggest furniture retailer by increasing the number of stores by 50 per cent by the end of the decade and almost doubling its sales and customer numbers. But the expansion raises questions over whether the unique corporate culture forged in Almhult is fully steeled for such rapid growth from China to the Dominican Republic.

Steen Kanter, a senior executive at Ikea from 1971 to 1994, says: "I'm concerned about Ikea's culture. I think the foundation of Ikea is its culture and I hope it doesn't go by the wayside." Mr Kanter says he was in an Ikea store in Boston this month. "I don't feel the same spirit when I go into Ikea. There is a danger that Ikea just turns into another big impersonal company," he says. Christopher Bartlett, an emeritus professor at Harvard Business School who has written several case studies over three decades on Ikea, has similar concerns: "In any

company that is as large and diverse as Ikea it does become a challenge [to maintain the culture]."

The way in which Mr Kamprad built up the company has entered folklore. As a schoolboy he used a milk float to deliver goods to farmers. Becoming more sophisticated, he offered pens and watches by mail order before opening first a showroom and then a store for furniture in Almhult. Culture soon became important and stories – some apocryphal, some not – abounded of Mr Kamprad's penny-pinching nature. Perhaps such tales offer some explanation of the company's reputation for cutting prices, which fall by an average of 2 per cent a year. Critics have derided the Almhult culture, with Johan Stenebo, a former personal assistant to Mr Kamprad, portraying the company as a cult-like dictatorship with the province of Smaland seemingly filling in for North Korea.

Most of its Chief Executives, including Peter Agnefjall, who will take over next year, have worked as Mr Kamprad's personal assistant and they seem to echo one another over the decades. Mr Agnefjall himself says that Almhult is "in many ways the heart of Ikea". Mr Kamprad has struck an almost evangelical tone at times, calling a 1976 manifesto "The Testament of a Furniture Dealer". With a mixture of homely advice – "only while sleeping one makes no mistakes" – and almost Soviet-style slogans – "Most things remain to be done. A glorious future!" – it still forms part of the induction of every new worker. But the culture goes much deeper. Mr Ohlsson says: "We always recruit through values. We spend an enormous effort in strengthening the values: togetherness, down to earth and hard working." An article in the *MIT Sloan Management Review* corroborates this, noting how Ikea's standard jobs questionnaire plays down skills, academic credentials or experience to focus on values and beliefs. Mr Ohlsson contends that such a strong culture allows senior executives to have deep trust in country and store managers. "We can have a very decentralised organisation with the culture as a foundation. We can have a very flat and unbureaucratic organisation," he says.

Tina Petersson-Lind, the head of Ikea's range which is designed for the world from Almhult, says products are split into three categories: the vast majority are global, some have local differences such as a darker wood in one market than another, while a few are designed specifically for a set country.

Case study 5 (*continued*)

Tailor-made products are very much the exception because Ikea takes little notice of the modern management tenet of "think global, act local" by imposing similar store design and product offering whether in Bangkok or Baltimore. That allows Ikea to save on costs on volume and logistics. But it has caused problems in some parts of the world, says Mr Kanter, who ran part of the Swedish group's operations in the US in the 1980s and 1990s. He recalls how Ikea's launch ran quickly into trouble in the US because the mattresses were too hard, drinking glasses too small and kitchens not big enough for the Thanksgiving turkey. Still, as Mr Kanter says: "Ikea is relatively good at admitting when they screw up." The US business was turned round by changing the products to suit local tastes. Even for that seemingly obvious step, Mr Kanter says he had to guarantee he could generate enough work for an entire factory with the new, larger kitchen units before he received approval to change it. The recent mistakes have had more serious implications.

In Russia, Ikea fired two senior executives in 2010 for tolerating bribery, while this year a man with apparent connections to another top manager was jailed for corruption. The case attracted particular attention because Ikea had adopted a tough stance against corruption. But as Prof Bartlett notes: "There is often a tension between the corporate culture and a national culture." Another case came to light when it emerged that women had been airbrushed out of certain pictures in the Saudi catalogue over several years. Amid global media interest, the Swedish group admitted that this was partly due to its production guidelines and promised a change. Perhaps most serious was the case in France where Ikea sacked the country head, finance director, risk manager and head of human resources following allegations the company had gained illegal access to police files and used private detectives to pry into the home lives of employees and dissatisfied customers. Ikea responded with workshops on its code of conduct over the summer with its 9,000 French staff encouraged to discuss what happened, and by appointing an ethical committee.

Mr Ohlsson says the problems are isolated, not a sign of the culture buckling as the company expands. "The culture has been an anchor for a long, long time. It is really the inner strength of Ikea. In our co-worker survey, spirit and culture are voted as one of the real assets of Ikea. We are very much against prestige and hierarchies. [But] with 140,000–150,000 co-workers there can always be an exception," he says. One worry is about the pace at which Ikea plans to grow. It wants to open 20 to 25 stores a year until the end of the decade, rising to 500 in 2020 from 338 today. It opened just seven last year.

But Prof Bartlett says that, for all his concerns, Ikea has been one of the most successful companies at preserving its culture as it grows. Returning to visit Ikea in 2006, a decade after a previous case study, he saw little difference: "The culture had been remarkably robust and well maintained and it is very well embedded. It tends to be transferred mouth to ear." Almhult plays a critical role in that process with managers from around the world arriving to exchange ideas and hear the latest thinking from Smaland. Mr Agnefjall says the expansion makes the focus on culture all the more important. "Every company needs something that glues it together. For some companies it is an organisational chart. For other companies such as Ikea it's our culture. If we share the same values and the same vision we can put more trust in people working in the organisation," says the future Chief Executive.

Questions

Using the evidence in the Ikea case study, and other publicly available material, address the following questions:

1. To what extent does Ikea need to adapt its company culture and managerial practices to the national cultures of the countries it operates?

2. Using Cummings and Worley's four elements of culture (Figure 5.1), critically evaluate the nature and coherence of Ikea's culture.

3. Compare Ikea against the types of culture suggested by Deal and Kennedy (1982) and Quinn and McGrath (1985) (see Ideas and perspectives 5.3 and 5.4). What are the implications of your answer for Ikea's planned global expansion?

PART 2

Strategy development:
theory, practice and choice

Chapter 6

Approaches to strategy

Managerial choice and constraints

Learning objectives

After studying this chapter, you should be able to:

- discuss the origins, development and popularity of organisation strategy;
- describe the main features of the Prescriptive stream of strategy;
- list the strengths and weaknesses of the Prescriptive stream;
- discuss the key elements of the Analytical stream of strategy;
- state the major advantages and shortcomings of the Analytical stream;
- understand the key differences between the Prescriptive and the Analytical streams of strategy;
- describe the constraints faced by organisations and whether these can be manipulated or overcome;
- appreciate the relationship between strategy and change.

MINI CASE STUDY 6.1

Company leaders need battlefield values

In Damian McKinney's experience, former military personnel work mainly in management consultancy, financial services, charity, recruitment or security. Mr McKinney's passion for business transformation led him to the first of those. But he did not leave his battlefield mindset behind: the chief executive and founder of McKinney Rogers, a global management consultancy, sees today's workplace as a battleground and believes executives have much to learn from military leaders. He has recorded lessons from his 18 years as a Royal Marines commando, serving on operations around the world, in a book *The Commando Way: Extraordinary Business Execution*. He says in the book: "The word 'strategy' is a military term that is at the centre of any business's thinking; it comes battle-hardened into the business vocabulary. The potential lessons for the business world have been apparent since

Mini case study 6.1 (*continued*)

General von Clausewitz wrote the book *On War* nearly 200 years ago. Though the military learned, business is only just starting to do so."

Mr McKinney founded McKinney Rogers in Devon in 1999. It advises leadership teams around the world and its clients have included large businesses such as Wal-Mart, Diageo, ITV, JP Morgan and Pfizer. With offices in New York, Tokyo, Nairobi, Barbados, London, Hong Kong and elsewhere, the company uses "Mission Leadership" philosophy – a holistic approach that begins with understanding the organisation's vision – to advise on business performance. The values of the military remain deeply ingrained: Mr McKinney says those robust values made him a Royal Marine and he recalls how shocked he was to learn the business world does not take company values as seriously. "It's admirable to reiterate the importance of your company values, as Barclays has done recently, but every business should remember that values need to be absolutely true to the DNA of a company and be internalised by everyone," he says.

"Some people have had lucky careers based on ambiguity. You can't rely on luck, you need clarity and future-looking intelligence." He suggests the military is much better at gathering competitive intelligence, which involves thinking ahead and putting themselves in the position of their opposition or competitors in order to plan what to do. "The thinking commando might have limited resources to deploy, but he can use them well because he has thought 'Where is the competitor's focus? What new products will he have? What's the pricing policy?'

"My favourite historical figure must be Stonewall Jackson, a Confederate general during the American Civil War. He believed in the power of reconnaissance in planning for the future strategic battle. The business world does not understand it. It makes do with business intelligence – slicing and dicing of the data – rather than competitor intelligence which forecasts what might happen." Perhaps the biggest difference Mr McKinney has seen between business and the military is the business world's focus on rank, status and following orders. "Ironically, companies are much more focused on what I call 'command and control' than their military counterparts. This is even more pronounced during uncertain times like the current recession," he explains. "The 'Do as I Say' model is old and designed for an ordered, predictable world. In the current, uncertain world this model leads to a lack of pace, accountability and agility to deal with fast-changing events. It paralyses the front line, leading to internal friction that hampers performance and the corporate machine freezes because different parts of the organisation don't work together."

Mr McKinney's own mentors include his mother, who had to leave Kenya with her family and went on to forge a career in the civil service, and his grandfather who was a citizen soldier, volunteering at 16 and again at 40 to serve his country in two world wars, before returning to commercial life after each. He is still driven by his grandfather's advice, which he thinks equally applies to business: "Be prepared to be more frightened than you have ever been but show no fear. Don't let your men lie down too long on the battlefield, you must maintain momentum and remember your duty is to bring all your men back alive. These words would have served Lehman Brothers well."

Introduction

In Part 1 of this book, we discussed the options open to organisations in terms of their structures, cultures, behaviours and practices. By examining the development of organisational theory in the 200 years since the Industrial Revolution, we saw that, in the beginning, management was almost exclusively concerned with strict labour discipline and long working hours. The methods used to pursue these were *ad hoc*, erratic, short-term and usually harsh and unfair. As the period progressed, more structured and consistent approaches came to the fore. Up to the 1960s, the Classical and Human Relations approaches dominated organisational thinking. With the advent of these two approaches, the emphasis moved more to the effectiveness and efficiency of the entire organisation, rather than focusing purely on discipline and hours of work.

Both these approaches tended to dwell on internal arrangements and to assume that organisation structures and practices were in some way insulated from the outside world. The development of Contingency Theory in the 1960s, with its underlying Open Systems perspective, changed all this. The nature of the environment (both internal and external) in which organisations operate emerged as a central factor in how they should structure themselves. This theme has been continued with the development of new paradigms in the last 30 years, and the importance of situational variables, especially environmental turbulence, which organisations face, is seen by many as an unchallengeable fact (Kanter, 2006; Peters, 2006).

As argued in Part 1, the degree to which organisations are the prisoners of these situational variables (as opposed to being able to exercise influence and choice) is certainly open to debate. Similarly, as shown in Chapters 4 and 5, the credibility of the rational approach to decision-making has been considerably undermined in the last three decades. The increasing appreciation of the complexity of organisational life has been paralleled by a growing recognition that organisations cannot cope successfully with the modern world and all its changing aspects purely on an *ad hoc* and piecemeal basis. Whether decision-makers operate on the basis of rationality or are influenced by personal considerations or organisational cultures, the received wisdom is that for organisations to succeed there must be a consistency and coherence to the decisions taken – which is another way of saying that they must have a strategy (Johnson *et al*, 2011). Unfortunately, it is easier to say that an organisation needs a strategy than it is to say what that strategy should be or how it should be derived. There are a great number of approaches to strategy and an even greater number of strategic planning tools. Some of the approaches to strategy have an instinctive appeal to managers, such as Damian McKinney's military metaphor which sees the marketplace as a battle ground, competition as war and business leaders as heroic generals leading their troops into battle (*see* Mini Case Study 6.1). Appealing though this may be to some leaders, it can also be dangerous and ignores that there are other metaphors which stress cooperation rather than annihilation, and win–win instead of win–lose (Clegg *et al*, 2011; De Wit and Meyer, 2010). Even the two most influential writers on strategy over the past 30 years, Michael Porter and Henry Mintzberg, have radically different views of what strategy is, and how it can be developed and implemented, as the discussion of their work in this chapter will show.

In this chapter, we shall examine the development and shortcomings of the main approaches to strategy that have been put forward in the last 60 years. It will be shown that, since the end of the Second World War, organisations have begun to take a strategic perspective on their activities. They have increasingly sought to take a long-term overview in order to plan for and cope with the vagaries of the future. In many respects, the development of strategic management has tended to mirror the development of organisational theory. In the 1940s and 1950s, the strategy literature considered only one aspect of an organisation's activities – the external environment. It tended to seek rational, mathematical approaches to planning. With the passing of time, more intuitive and less rational approaches to strategic management have been developed which claim to incorporate the totality of organisational life.

The chapter concludes by arguing that, rather than managers being the prisoners of mathematical models and rational approaches to strategy development, they have considerable freedom of action and a wide range of options to choose from. They are still not totally free agents; their freedom of action is seen as being constrained or shaped by the unique set of organisational, environmental and societal factors faced by their particular organisation. Fortunately, these constraints are not immutable. As argued in Part 1, it is possible for managers to manipulate the situational variables they face with regard to structure. Similarly, managers can exert some influence over strategic constraints and, potentially at least, can select the approach to strategy that best suits them.

Understanding strategy: origins, definitions and approaches

The origins of strategy

It is commonly believed that our concept of strategy has been passed down to us from the ancient Greeks. Bracker (1980: 219) claims that the word strategy comes from the Greek *stratego*, meaning 'to plan the destruction of one's enemies through the effective use of resources'. Even today, this 'strategy as war' concept is still highly influential, as evidenced by the continuing popularity among business leaders of Karl von Clausewitz's nineteenth-century book '*On War*' (Witzel, 2012). However, von Claueswitz and others developed the concept purely in relation to the successful pursuit of victory in war. The concept remained a military one until the nineteenth century, when it began to be applied to the business world, though most writers believe the actual process by which this took place is untraceable (Bracker, 1980; Chandler, 1962). Chandler (1962) puts forward the view that the emergence of strategy in civilian organisational life resulted from an awareness of the opportunities and needs – created by changing population, income and technology – to employ existing or expanding resources more profitably.

Hoskin (1990) largely agrees with Chandler's view of the development of modern business strategy since the Industrial Revolution. However, he takes issue with both Chandler and Bracker on two crucial points. First, he argues that the modern concept of organisational strategy bears little resemblance to military strategy, at least as it existed up to the First World War. Secondly, he challenges the view that the origins of business strategy are untraceable. When investigating the emergence of modern strategy, he did find a link with the military world, though it was not quite the link that Bracker and Chandler proposed. Like Chandler, Hoskin argues that one of the most significant developments in business management in the nineteenth century occurred in the running of the US railways. Unlike Chandler, however, Hoskin gives the credit for initiating business strategy to one of the Pennsylvania Railroad's executives, Herman Haupt. He states that Haupt:

> changes the rules of business discourse: the image in which he reconstructs business, on the Pennsylvania Railroad, is that of the proactive, future-oriented organization, which is managed by the numbers . . . How does he do so? By importing the practices of writing, examination and grading . . . On the Pennsylvania Railroad we find for the first time the full interactive play of grammatocentrism [writing and recording] and calculability [mathematical analysis of the recorded data].
> (Hoskin, 1990: 20)

This approach created the bedrock on which strategic management grew in the US, especially after the Second World War. It also ensured that strategic management became a quantitatively orientated discipline, whose focus was on the use of numerical analysis to forecast market trends in order to plan for the future. Hoskin also points out that Haupt was a graduate of the US military academy at West Point, which pioneered the techniques of 'writing, examination and grading' in the military world. From there its graduates, particularly Haupt, took them out into the business world – hence the link between military and civilian management techniques.

Thus it is possible to see why strategic management developed in the way it did – as a quantitative, mathematical approach. We can also see that there are links between the military and business worlds, but that they are not as some have claimed. Management strategy has not developed from the approach to military campaigns of the ancient Greeks; instead it has adopted and made its own the techniques of record-keeping and analysis that were developed at West Point in order to measure the performance, and suitability for military life, of the US army's future officer class.

The contribution of the American armed forces to the quantitative approach to strategy did not end with West Point or in the nineteenth century. In 1945, with the end of the Second World War, the US experienced an extraordinary trading boom. McKiernan (1992) comments that this forced many American companies to rethink their business planning systems. In order to justify and implement the capacity expansion necessary to cope with the boom, companies began to abandon short-term, one-year, budgeting cycles in favour of more long-range planning techniques. The development of this strategic approach to planning and investment was given a significant impetus when some of the people involved in the USAAF's wartime strategic planning activities returned to civilian life. Most notable among them was Robert McNamara, who became Chairman of the Ford Motor Company, Secretary of State under John F Kennedy and President of the World Bank (Moore, 1992). Their main vehicle for influencing business was the Harvard Business School's approach to business policy teaching, which steadily moved the focus of management away from a preoccupation with internal organisational issues (as proposed by the Classical and Human Relations schools) towards an external orientation. This was best exemplified by the development of two important concepts: marketing, with its emphasis on analysing demand and tailoring products to meet it; and systems theory, with its emphasis not only on the interconnectedness of different parts of an organisation but also the links between internal and external forces.

In the intervening years, first in the US and later across the Western world, these techniques and approaches have become more widely disseminated and used (Bracker, 1980). Much credit for this must go to three key figures, Kenneth R Andrews, Alfred D Chandler and H Igor Ansoff, for their work in developing and fleshing out the concept of strategic management, and especially for demonstrating the importance of the product–market mix. Nevertheless, in highlighting the importance of the outside world, and thus breaking managers' Classical school-inspired fixation with internal structures and practices, they can be criticised for not making the link between the two. So managers moved from believing that internal arrangements alone would bring success to believing that an external, market focus was the key.

The rise and fall of long-range planning

In order to cope with the new and rapidly changing technological, economic and organisational developments that followed the end of the Second World War, American organisations, which were at the forefront of these developments, began to adopt long-range planning techniques. This necessitated first defining the organisation's objectives, then establishing plans in order to achieve those objectives, and finally, allocating resources, through capital budgeting, in line with the plans. A key aim of this process was to reduce the gap that often occurred between the level of demand that a firm expected, and planned for, and the level of demand that actually occurred (Fox, 1975). Therefore, long-range planning was a mechanism for plotting trends and planning the actions required to achieve the identified growth targets, all of which were heavily biased towards financial targets and budgetary controls. However, this process proved incapable of accurately forecasting future demand, and the problem of the gap between the level of expected demand and actual demand remained.

Long-range planning failed for a variety of internal and external reasons (McKiernan, 1992). Internally, many planning systems involved little more than an extrapolation of past sales trends. Little attention was paid to wider external economic, technological or social changes, or even changes in the behaviour of competitor firms. Thompson (2008: 15) cites Queen Victoria's funeral as a classic example of this type of planning:

> The route of her funeral procession was laid down as exactly the same route as for her uncle, the previous monarch. The dress rehearsal was by all accounts either hilarious or a farce, depending on your sense of humour. The planners had not taken into account the fact that London had changed considerably in the 60-odd years of Victoria's reign. Some streets were no longer accessible. Many were not even there any more!

Externally, in the 1960s, the relatively comfortable conditions of high market growth gave way to lower levels of growth, which led to increased competition as companies tried to increase, or at least maintain, their market share to compensate for lower growth. One outcome of this was that strategic planners had to adapt to a world where growth was not steady; it could slow down, increase or be interrupted in an unpredictable and violent manner. Also, unforeseen opportunities and threats could and did emerge. Furthermore, it became evident that closing the gap between the plan and what actually occurred was not necessarily the most critical aspect of strategy formulation. Indeed, since the early 1970s, volatile markets, over-capacity and resource constraints have taken over as dominant management considerations (Koch, 1995).

Long-range planning techniques could not cope with such environmental turbulence which, to say the least, limits forecasting accuracy. In addition, the nature of American business had begun to change. Slower growth and increased competition led to a situation where large single-business firms, which in the past might have dominated a single industry, were being replaced by multinational conglomerates operating in a wide range of increasingly competitive industries and markets. Therefore, rather than managing a single, unified enterprise, corporate managers found themselves managing a diverse portfolio of businesses. Richard Branson's Virgin empire is a good example of this sort of development:

> Virgin is a leading international investment group and one of the world's most recognised and respected brands. Conceived in 1970 by Sir Richard Branson, the Virgin Group has gone on to grow successful businesses in sectors ranging from mobile telephony, travel, financial services, leisure, music, holidays and health & wellness. Across its companies, Virgin employs approximately 50,000 people, in 34 countries and global branded revenues in 2011 were around £13 billion ($21 billion).   (Virgin.com, 2013)

In response to the emergence of conglomerates and the failure of long-range planning, in the late 1960s, the concept of strategic management began to emerge. Unlike long-range planning, strategic management focuses on the environmental assumptions that underlie market trends and incorporates the possibility that changes in trends can and do take place, and is not based on the assumption that adequate growth can be assured (Elliot and Lawrence, 1985; Mintzberg and Quinn, 1991). Consequently, strategic management focuses more closely on winning market share from competitors, rather than assuming that organisations can rely solely on the expansion of markets for their own growth (De Wit and Meyer, 2010). As Johnson and Scholes (2002: 15–16) comment:

> Strategic management is concerned with complexity arising out of ambiguous and non-routine situations with organisation-wide rather than operations-specific implications. . . . Nor is strategic management concerned only with taking decisions about major issues facing the organisation. It is also concerned with ensuring that the strategy is put into effect. It can be thought of as having three elements within it . . . understanding the strategic position of an organisation, strategic choices for the future and turning strategy into action.

Strategic management sought to take a broader and more sophisticated view of an organisation's environment than long-range planning. Initially at least, it was closely associated with a number of portfolio planning techniques which also emerged in the late 1960s (Hax and Majluf, 1996; McKiernan, 1992). The most famous of these is the Boston Consulting Group's Growth Share Matrix (*see* Figure 7.2 in Chapter 7). As Chapter 7 will show, this and other portfolio planning techniques were developed to assist managers in running large, diversified enterprises operating in complex environments. Much of this work was sponsored and used by big American corporations, such as General Electric, in order to identify the market position and potential of their strategic business units (SBUs) and to decide on whether to develop, sell or close them down. This 'positioning' approach to strategic management, the latest variant of which is Porter's (1980, 1985) 'competitive forces model' (*see* Figure 7.1 in Chapter 7), dominated the practice of strategic management from the 1960s onwards, and to a large extent still does (Galagan, 1997; Johnson *et al*, 2011; Rigby and Gillies, 2000). It has also led many companies to adopt a harsh, and to an extent unthinking, approach to business success, epitomised by the words of Jack Welch when he was CEO of GE: 'We will run only businesses that are number one or two in their markets' (quoted in Kay, 1993: 339). Therefore, if businesses are not, or do not have the potential to become, leaders in their field, they are sold off or closed down (Koch, 1995).

As Stacey (2010), and many others, point out, this approach to strategic management portrays strategy as a rational process whereby managers gather hard, quantitative data on their companies, and from this information come to rational decisions regarding their future. However, from the late 1970s onwards, the rational perspective on strategy has come under increasing attack, not least by the leading management thinker of his generation, Henry Mintzberg (1976, 1978, 1983, 1987, 1994, 1998, 2001, 2007). The main criticisms of the rational approach to strategy are threefold:

● that hard data are no more reliable, and in some cases less so, than qualitative data;

● that organisations and managers are not rational entities and do not apply a rational approach to decision-making; and

● that an organisation's strategy is as likely to emerge from unplanned actions and their unintended consequences over a period of time as it is from any deliberate process of planning and implementation (Hatch, 1997; Mintzberg *et al*, 2009; Pettigrew *et al*, 1992; Stacey, 2010; Whittington, 1993).

Defining strategy

As the above shows, like many other concepts in the field of management, there are many approaches to strategy but none are universally accepted (Stacey, 2003). Indeed, as Khalifa (2008: 894) comments:

> The plethora of strategy concepts, theories, frameworks, and claims of superiority dazzles many who may not be able to see the forest from the trees. Managers and practitioners are overwhelmed by the flood of advice coming from different directions and each dismisses the other as out of date, short sighted, incomplete, inadequate, or even misleading.

Even one of the pioneers of business strategy, Igor Ansoff (1987), warned that strategy is an elusive and somewhat abstract concept. This must be expected when dealing with an area that is constantly developing. Nor should this inhibit the search for a definition, or definitions, because in doing so we can see how the debate on strategy is developing and where the main areas of dispute lie.

Rather than leading to clarity, the eclipse of long-range planning merely heralded the arrival of a range of different and often confusing perspectives on strategy (Kay *et al*, 2003). As early as the 1960s, two schools of thought vied with each other: the Planning school and the Design school (Mintzberg *et al*, 2009). The Planning school was based on formal procedures, formal training, formal analysis and a large dose of quantification. Its underlying assumption was that a strategy could be put together and work in the same way as a machine. It led to the creation of strategic planning departments in large organisations, reporting directly to the chief executive; that person's role – though notionally to be the architect of strategy – was to approve the planners' plan.

The chief proponent of the Planning school was Igor Ansoff. Ansoff was a Russian–American engineer, mathematician, military strategist and operations researcher whose *Corporate Strategy* was published in 1965 to great acclaim (Koch, 1995; Martinet, 2010). In this book he assumes that the purpose of a firm is profit maximisation, and he portrays strategic management as being primarily concerned with the external, rather than internal, concerns of the firm, especially the matching of products to markets (the product–market mix). As Figure 6.1 shows, Ansoff sought to show that organisations needed to tailor their strategies to the mix of markets they were operating in or wished to operate in, and the

Figure 6.1 Product–market mix

products they produced or intended to produce. So for example, looking at Quadrant 1, he argues that where an organisation was selling existing products into existing markets, it needed a market penetration strategy aimed at enabling them to take a greater share of the market. However, looking at Quadrant 4, where the company wished to sell new products into new markets, it would need a diversification strategy. Ansoff's book provided managers with a plethora of checklists and charts to enable them to derive objectives, assess synergy between different parts of an organisation, appraise its competence profile and decide how, where and in which way to expand. But, as a number of writers remark, the book, and indeed the precepts of the Planning school as a whole, have not aged well (Koch, 1995; Mintzberg *et al*, 2009).

The Design school, though sharing some features with the Planning school, adopted a less formal and machine-like approach. It proposed a model of strategy that emphasises the need to achieve a fit between the internal capabilities of an organisation and the external possibilities it faces. The foundations of the Design school lay in the work of Alfred Chandler, one of the most eminent and influential American economic historians of his generation. His main contribution to the Design school is encapsulated in his 1962 book, *Strategy and Structure*, which was based on a major study of US corporations between 1850 and 1920. In the book, Chandler defined strategy as the determination of the basic long-term goals and objectives of an enterprise, and the adoption of courses of action and the allocation of resources necessary for carrying out these goals. The book also suggested three important precepts for running organisations which challenged the conventional wisdom of the time:

- First, that an organisation's structure should flow from its strategy rather than being determined by some universal 'one best way'.

- Second, that the 'visible hand of management' was more important than Adam Smith's 'invisible hand of the market' in meeting customer need.

- Lastly, that large organisations need to decentralise and divisionalise in order to remain competitive.

Though Chandler's work proved very influential in shaping the strategy debate, the real impetus for the Design school came from the work of the General Management group at Harvard Business School, especially the work of Kenneth R Andrews (Mintzberg *et al*, 1998a). The model of strategy developed by Andrews and his colleagues places primary emphasis on the appraisal of an organisation's external and internal situations. To facilitate this, Andrews developed the now-famous SWOT technique (*see* Figure 6.2 and also Chapter 11).

The purpose of a SWOT analysis is to enable an organisation to assess its internal Strengths and Weaknesses in the light of the Opportunities and Threats posed by the environment in which it operates (Andrews, 1980). Based on this assessment, organisations then generate and evaluate a number of strategies in order to choose the best one (Johnson *et al*, 2011; Rumelt, 1997).

Like the Planning school, the Design school has attracted its fair share of criticism (*see* Mintzberg *et al*, 2009). In particular, Chandler's view that structure should follow strategy has been heavily criticised. Tom Peters (1993: 148), for example, remarked that:

> I understand Chandler's reasoning, but I think he got it exactly wrong. For it is the structure of the organization that determines, over time, the choices that it makes about the markets

Internal factors	Strengths	Weaknesses
External factors	Opportunities	Threats

Figure 6.2 SWOT analysis

it attacks [i.e. its strategy]. Give me a vertically integrated, hierarchically steep organization and perhaps, even today, I can do a few things well. But one thing is certain: I can't shift course very rapidly! A McKinsey or EDS or CNN chooses to do what it does – i.e. continually reinvent itself, with apparent ease – because of its 'structural' shape much more than its chosen strategy.

Regardless of the criticisms levelled at it, the Design school can be seen as an advance on the Planning school. Whereas Ansoff and the Planning school regard strategy as almost exclusively concerned with the relationships between the firm and its environment, Chandler, Andrews and the Design school take a broader view. Its approach takes account of internal as well as external factors. In particular, the Design school sees issues such as organisational structures, production processes and technology as being essentially strategic. The key point proponents of the Design school make is that the external and internal cannot be separated, as the Open Systems theorists would be the first to point out (*see* Scott, 1987, and Chapters 2 and 8). The external affects the internal, and vice versa. Therefore, strategic management must encompass the totality of the organisational domain and must not be restricted to one aspect, such as determining the product–market mix (Andrews, 1980; De Wit and Meyer, 2010).

This brings us a little nearer to a definition but still leaves us with a hazy concept. Henry Mintzberg claims that it is necessary to recognise explicitly that there are multiple definitions of strategy and that we need to use these to manoeuvre through this difficult field. According to Mintzberg *et al* (1998b), there are five main and interrelated definitions of strategy: *plan, ploy, pattern, position* and *perspective* (*see* Ideas and perspectives 6.1).

In a manner that has a postmodernist feel to it, Mintzberg *et al* (1998b) do not argue that one definition should be preferred to the others. In some senses they can be considered as alternatives or complementary approaches to strategy. Also, they are useful in adding important elements to the discussion of strategy. They draw our attention to the distinction between conscious and unconscious strategy, and between emergent and planned strategy. They also highlight the role of the organisation's collective mind in developing and implementing strategy.

In a similar way to Mintzberg *et al*, Johnson (1987) also distinguishes between different views of the strategic management process. As Ideas and perspectives 6.2 shows, he argues that there are three basic views that reflect more general distinctions in the social sciences. One way of considering these various definitions or views of strategy, following on from

IDEAS AND PERSPECTIVES 6.1

Mintzberg's five definitions of strategy

- **Strategy as a plan**. According to this view, strategy is some form of consciously intended course of action which is created ahead of events. This can be either a general strategy or a specific one. If specific, it may also constitute a ploy.

- **Strategy as a ploy**. This is where strategy is a manoeuvre to outwit an opponent. An example of this is when a firm threatens to lower its prices substantially to deter new entrants into its market. It is the threat to lower prices that is the consciously intended course of action, and not any actual plan to do so.

- **Strategy as a pattern**. This is where we observe, after the event, that an organisation has acted in a consistent manner over time, i.e. whether consciously or not, the organisation exhibits a consistent pattern of behaviour. We can say from this that an organisation has pursued a particular strategy. This may not be the strategy it intended to pursue, but it is the one that has emerged from the action of the organisation. Therefore, though the organisation's realised strategy could be the product of a conscious and deliberate plan, this is often not the case.

- **Strategy as a position**. From this perspective, strategy is about positioning the organisation in order to achieve or maintain a sustainable competitive advantage. Mintzberg *et al* argue that most organisations try to avoid head-on competition. What they seek to achieve is a position where their competitors cannot or will not challenge them. In this sense, strategy is also seen as a game: groups of players circling each other, each trying to gain the high ground.

- **Strategy as perspective**. This definition sees strategy as a somewhat abstract concept that exists primarily in people's minds. For members of an organisation, the actual details of its strategy, as such, are irrelevant. What is important is that everyone in the organisation shares a common view of its purpose and direction which, whether people are aware of it or not, informs and guides decision-making and actions. Consequently, without the need for detailed plans, the organisation, through a shared understanding, pursues a consistent strategy or purpose.

Source: Mintzberg *et al* (1998b).

IDEAS AND PERSPECTIVES 6.2

Johnson's three basic views of strategy

- **The rationalistic view** – which sees strategy as the outcome of a series of preplanned actions designed to achieve the stated goals of an organisation in an optimal fashion.

- **The adaptive or incremental view** – which sees strategy evolving through an accumulation of relatively small changes over time.

- **The interpretative view** – which sees strategy as the product of individual and collective attempts to make sense of, i.e. interpret, past events.

Source: Johnson (1987).

IDEAS AND PERSPECTIVES 6.3

Morgan's organisational metaphors

- Organisations as machines
- Organisations as organisms
- Organisations as brains
- Organisations as cultures
- Organisations as political systems
- Organisations as psychic prisons
- Organisations as flux and transformations
- Organisations as instruments of domination

Source: Morgan (1986).

Morgan (1986), is as metaphors. Morgan (1986) identifies eight influential metaphors that are applied to organisations (*see* Ideas and perspectives 6.3).

Morgan (1986: 12–13) comments:

> Our theories and explanations of organizational life are based on metaphors that lead us to see and understand organizations in distinctive yet partial ways. . . . By using different metaphors to understand the complex and paradoxical character of organizational life, we are able to manage and design organizations in ways that we may not have thought possible before.

Like Morgan's use of metaphors, the postmodernist viewpoint, discussed in Chapter 4, would see the varying definitions of strategy as competing realities which managers attempt to impose on their organisations. Realists would acknowledge that these are different perspectives that do influence organisational strategy, but would also argue that there is a 'real world out there' which has to be addressed if strategies are to be successfully realised. Complexity theorists would take a similar view, acknowledging that different perspectives do exist and are influential, but claiming that the social world, like the natural world, is governed by order-generating rules which organisations ignore at their peril. Therefore, while most would see Mintzberg *et al*'s and Johnson's definitions of strategy as metaphors or alternative perspectives, some would also argue that they represent competing realities, while others would argue that there is only one reality (though this can and does change with circumstances and time).

The explicit recognition that there are multiple definitions of strategy can help us to make sense of the confusion of terms which litter the literature and which different writers use in different ways (Johnson *et al*, 2011). Many writers seem to treat corporate planning, long-range planning, strategic planning and formal planning as synonymous. However, not all would agree. Naylor (1979), for example, defines strategic planning as long-range planning with a time horizon of 3–5 years. Litschert and Nicholson (1974) take the opposite view: they state that strategic and long-term planning are not synonymous, arguing that strategic planning is a process which involves making a sequence of interrelated decisions aimed at achieving a desirable future environment for an organisation. Andrews (1998: 51), similarly, defines strategy as a:

pattern of decisions in a company that determines and reveals its objectives, purposes, or goals, produces the principal policies and plans for achieving those goals, and defines the range of business the company is to pursue, the kind of economic and human organisation it is, or intends to be, and the nature of the economic and non-economic contribution it intends to make to its shareholders, employees, customers and communities.

What is clear from the above is that, knowingly or not, writers are using different definitions of strategy and thus interpreting particular terms or phrases in the light of their own implicit or explicit definitions, which have changed radically over the years. For example, in the third edition of their best-selling textbook on strategy, Johnson and Scholes (1993) describe strategy as:

- concerning the full scope of an organisation's activities;

- the process of matching the organisation's activities to its environment;

- the process of matching its activities to its resource capability;

- having major resource implications;

- affecting operational decisions;

- being affected by the values and beliefs of those who have power in an organisation;

- affecting the long-term direction of an organisation.

In the ninth edition of their book, Johnson *et al* (2011: 21) argue that strategy needs to be viewed through four lenses, as follows:

- **Strategy as design**. This takes the view that strategy development can be 'designed' in the abstract, as an architect might design a building using pens, rulers and paper. The architect designs and then hands over the plans for the builders actually to build. . . . Taking a design lens to a strategic problem means being systematic, analytical and logical.

- **Strategy as experience**. The experience lens recognises that the future strategy of an organisation is often heavily influenced by its experience and that of its managers. . . . The experience lens suggests that the personal experience and interests of key decision-makers needs to be understood. It sets low expectations of radical change.

- **Strategy as variety**. Neither of the above lenses is likely to uncover radical new ideas in strategy. Design approaches risk being too rigid and top-down; experience builds too much on the past. . . . Somebody with a variety lens would look for future strategies at the bottom and periphery of organisations. They should be ready for surprises.

- **Strategy as discourse**. Managers spend most of their time talking, persuading and negotiating. They are always using language, or what here is called 'discourse'. The discourse lens points to how command of strategy discourse becomes a resource for managers by which to shape 'objective' strategic analyses to their personal views and gain influence, power and legitimacy. . . . The discourse lens tries to look under the surface of strategy to uncover the personal interests and politicking in organisations. Taking a discourse lens thus encourages a somewhat sceptical view.

Approaches to strategy: the Prescriptive versus the Analytical stream

In defining strategy, especially bearing in mind the various definitions of strategy suggested by Mintzberg *et al* (2009) and Johnson *et al* (2011), there are two further issues to be considered:

1. Is strategy a process or the outcome of a process?

2. Is strategy an economic–rational phenomenon or is it an organisational–social phenomenon?

Taking these two questions together, it can be seen that there are two parallel, competing and, to an extent, interacting streams of ideas. The first, the Prescriptive stream, sees strategy as a controlled, intentional, prescriptive process, based on a rational model of decision-making, which produces complete deliberate strategies (Ansoff, 1965; Argenti, 1974; Steiner, 1969). The second, the Analytical stream, which is more interested in understanding how organisations actually formulate strategy rather than prescribing how they should formulate it, argues that it is the outcome of the complex social and political processes involved in organisational decision-making (Hamel and Prahalad, 1989; Miles and Snow, 1978; Mintzberg *et al*, 2009; Pettigrew, 1980; Quinn, 1980a).

The Prescriptive stream grew out of the long-range planning initiatives of the 1940s and 1950s, and is aimed primarily at the practitioners of strategy. Through the work of the Planning and Design schools, this stream dominated the practice of strategy in the 1960s and 1970s. They not only saw strategy as an economic–rational process but also considered its options and usefulness as primarily restricted to issues relating to market share and profit maximisation (Ansoff, 1965; Porter, 1980). However, with growing disillusionment among academics and practitioners over the ability of this approach to deliver competitiveness, a new variant of this approach came to the fore in the 1980s: the Positioning school.

The Positioning school is most closely identified with Michael Porter (1980, 1985), who is regarded by many as the world's leading consultant on strategy, as well as being a professor at the Harvard Business School (*see* Mini Case Study 6.2).

Porter's (1980) *competitive forces framework* reinvigorated the Prescriptive approach and allowed it to maintain its dominance on the practice of strategy through to the present day (Johnson *et al*, 2011; Teece *et al*, 1997; Witzel, 2012). The main difference between the Positioning school and the earlier Planning and Design schools is that:

> Both the planning and design schools put no limits on the strategies that were possible in any given situation. The positioning school, in contrast, argued that only a few key strategies – as positions in the economic market place – are desirable in any given industry: ones that can be defended against existing and future competitors. Ease of defense means that firms which occupy these positions enjoy higher profits . . . By thereby dispensing with one key premise of the design school – that strategies have to be unique, tailor-made for each organization – the positioning school was able to create and hone a set of analytical tools dedicated to matching the right strategy to the conditions at hand . . .   (Mintzberg *et al*, 1998a: 83)

The work of Porter and the Positioning school will be discussed in more detail in Chapter 7. However, for now, the key points to note are that the three schools that comprise the Prescriptive stream have dominated the practice of strategy within organisations since the 1960s. The reason for this is threefold:

- First, the proponents set out deliberately to address the needs of industry and commerce by providing them with a blueprint for strategy formulation and implementation.

- Second, they interacted closely with a number of leading consultants, notably the Boston Consultancy Group, and business schools, notably Harvard, to promote their work and tailor it to the needs of organisations. By reinforcing and promoting each other, this triple alliance of researchers, consultants and educators created an iron orthodoxy that organisations, especially large ones, felt they ignored at their peril.

MINI CASE STUDY 6.2

The master strategist: Michael Porter

Michael Porter became famous in the 1990s as a consultant on competitiveness to business and governments. In the 1980s, however, he wrote several popular and respected books on business strategy, introducing basic tools of strategic thinking such as the 'five forces' model and the value chain.

It is for this work on strategy that he is likely to be remembered, and his ideas have had a wide impact. In 1999, *Fortune* called him the single most important strategist working today, and possibly of all time.

Prof. Porter was born in Ann Arbor, Michigan, in 1947. He studied at Princeton and Harvard and joined the faculty at Harvard in 1973. He has also become a highly respected consultant, working with companies such as DuPont and Shell, and the US, Canadian, New Zealand and Swedish governments.

Prof. Porter views strategy from the standpoint of economics, and his ideas on how strategy should be implemented are based on an understanding of competition and other economic forces. Strategy is not devised in isolation; a company's options will always be limited by what is going on around it.

His famous 'five forces' model shows the constraining impact that competition and environment have on strategy.

The five forces identified by Prof. Porter are: the threat of new entrants and the appearance of new competitors; the degree of rivalry among existing competitors in the market; the bargaining power of buyers; the bargaining power of suppliers; and the threat of substitute products or services that could shrink the market.

The strength of each of these forces varies from industry to industry, but taken together they determine long-term profitability. They help to shape the prices companies can charge, the costs they must pay for resources and the level of investment that will be needed to compete.

From the external environment, he turns to the company itself. Companies make products and deliver them to consumers, but they can also add value to the basic product in a variety of ways and through different functions.

Value can be added directly, for example by giving a product new technology features, or indirectly, through measures that allow the company to become more efficient. Prof. Porter argues that every product follows a critical path through the company, from its inception to its delivery as a finished article. At every stage along this path there are opportunities to add value. This path he calls the 'value chain'.

The value chain is crucial, he says, because it demonstrates that the company is more than just the sum of its parts and activities: all activities are connected, and what is done at one stage affects work at other stages.

The company needs to examine its value chain and decide where it can add value most effectively to meet competitive pressures in the industry.

These concepts can be applied to entire sectors and national economies as well as individual companies, and Prof. Porter went on to develop his theories of national competitiveness in great detail.

- Lastly, because all three groups in this triple alliance were in effect engaged in a business activity, selling strategy as a product, they were able to invest in promoting and developing their product in a way that others were not. As the following examination of the Analytical stream of strategy will show, though, this did not mean that other important perspectives on strategy were not developed or did not achieve acceptance by a wide audience. It did, however, mean that these alternative perspectives have never had the same impact on practice within organisations as those promoted by the Prescriptive stream.

The Analytical stream, which began to appear in the 1970s and represents a more sceptical and more academically orientated face of strategic management, views strategy not as a process but as an outcome of a process. Its proponents' emphasis is not on the construction of detailed plans, which in any case they believe to be a misdirected approach, but on the organisational and social aspects of strategy formation. Their argument is that the capabilities of an organisation, in terms of its structure, systems, technology and management style, restrict the range of strategic options the organisation can pursue. Consequently, in a very real sense, it is the day-to-day stream of decisions regarding the development of its capabilities that determines an organisation's strategic direction, rather than the reverse (Mintzberg, 1994; Mintzberg *et al*, 2009).

The key figure in the Analytical stream is Henry Mintzberg, who is widely considered as the leading management scholar of his day (*see* Mini Case Study 6.3).

Mintzberg's (1978) concept of emergent strategy is seen as transforming the understanding of strategy development (Mirabeau and Maguire, 2013). With the concept of emergent strategy, Mintzberg explains why an organisation's intended strategy, the objectives it sets

MINI CASE STUDY 6.3

The great iconoclast: Henry Mintzberg

Henry Mintzberg had been called 'the great management iconoclast' for his willingness to attack previously sacred concepts in business and management. But his commonsense approach to management problems has won him a broad following, particularly among students and working managers. He is best known for his work on business strategy, where he exposed the gap between academic concepts of strategy and reality.

Born in Montreal in 1939, Mintzberg studied engineering and worked for Canadian National Railways before obtaining a doctorate from the Massachusetts Institute of Technology in 1968. He joined the faculty of management at McGill University, Canada, where he has remained. Mintzberg was interested in defining what managers really do and how they carry out their tasks. He discovered a vast body of what he termed 'managerial folklore': research studies that considered managers rational beings who made decisions based on careful analysis of all available information.

Experience told Mintzberg that managerial work was not like that. Not only was it less structured and ordered than assumed but its true nature was also hard to define. His observations of managers in action confirmed this. He found that decisions were made quickly, often on the move, usually based more on intuition and experience than on considered analysis. Action was more important than reflection. Half the daily management tasks he observed took less than 10 minutes each and only 10 per cent took more than an hour.

The portrait of the manager and his task that emerges from Mintzberg's work is a sympathetic one. Managers are constantly 'firefighting', dealing with problems under pressure. Rather than the best possible solution, they seek the best solution that can be implemented given the resources available. And, says Mintzberg, because each organisation has its own culture and needs, managers' responses to problems will vary. There may be no one 'right' way to manage a business.

These affect strategy. Academic conceptions of strategy regarded it as the province of top management, who consider and make strategic decisions with detachment. Again, Mintzberg disagrees. In the real world, strategy-making is ad hoc and instinctive, not structured and planned. The concept of 'strategic planning' becomes an oxymoron.

Mintzberg sees this approach to strategy as a virtue. 'Emergent strategy', as he calls it, is strategy that evolves according to need, constantly adjusted and adapted. He also speaks of 'crafting strategy', a process by which managers develop strategy according to the needs of their organisation and environment. Here, strategy creation and implementation are interdependent. He compares the art of strategy making to pottery and managers to potters sitting at a wheel moulding the clay and letting the shape of the object evolve in their hands.

Successful management is about knowing the business – in all its aspects and not just in specialist areas – and an ability to manage through discontinuity.

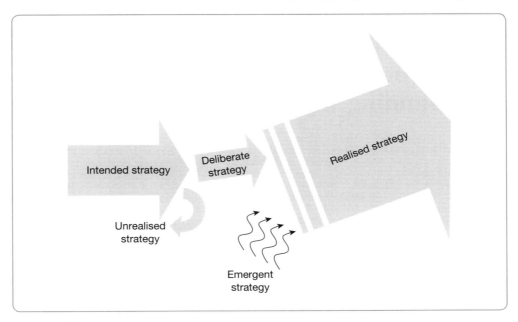

Figure 6.3 Emergent strategy

Source: Adapted from Patterns in strategy formation, *Management Science* 24(9), p. 13 (Mintzberg H. 1978), Reprinted by permission, Copyright (1978), The Institute for Operations Research and the Management Sciences (INFORMS), 5521 Research Park Drive, Suite 200, Catonsville, MD 21228 USA.

out to achieve, is rarely the same as its realised strategy, the objectives it actually achieves. As Figure 6.3 shows, Mintzberg maintains that organisations start out with an intended strategy but, due to unrealistic expectations or changing circumstances, many of the elements of this fall by the wayside. This is because organisations have to respond to unexpected events on a day-to-day basis and, based on the decisions taken, the strategy develops and changes with some elements being dropped and others emerging to take their place (Mintzberg 1994, 2007). In many cases, managers may not even realise the impact of such day-to-day decisions on strategy, but, as such decisions are taken in response to changing events, the intended strategy changes, with the emergent elements of strategy combining with the remaining deliberate elements of the intended strategy to form the organisation's realised strategy.

Perhaps the starkest example of this in recent years was the 2008 financial crisis. At the beginning of 2007, the intended strategies of most financial service organisations revolved around sales growth and increased profit. By the end of 2007, with the advent of the credit crunch, the realised strategies focused on coping with falling growth and decreased profit – in some cases, the key strategy issue was survival (Doran, 2008). The decisions taken by each financial service organisation in responding to the credit crunch were influenced by their circumstances and capabilities, which allowed some to survive relatively unscathed while others went out of business or had to be rescued by competitors or governments. Nor was this just one very big exception to the rule. Almost every day, the financial pages of the newspapers carry examples of major organisations making large, damaging and unexpected changes to their strategies. A prime example recently was the on-off merger of BAE Systems and EADS, which was literally announced one week and humiliatingly called off the next (*see* Mini Case Study 6.4).

MINI CASE STUDY 6.4

Sift through the brashness and bravado surrounding any big deals

In 2006, BAE Systems, formerly known as British Aerospace, sold its stake in Airbus for a disappointing price. Airbus, a civil aviation consortium established by several European governments, is now Boeing's only competitor in the market for large commercial jets. BAE told the world it had decided to leave this market, with a view to focusing on its core defence business. In 2012, the company proposed a merger with EADS, owner of Airbus, emphasising the complementarity of defence with civil aviation.

There may be advantages to a company from concentrating its activities, and there may also be advantages in diversifying into related businesses. It is possible the balance of these advantages has shifted between 2006 and 2012, though it is difficult to see why. Several other advantages were claimed for the merger. But the claim that diversification promotes earnings stability seems to confuse the role of a company director with that of a portfolio manager.

Some corporate executives perceive their role in this way, trading a collection of businesses as a fund manager might trade a portfolio of stocks. But history suggests few of them are good at it – recall ICI or GEC, for example. And the transaction costs involved in dealing in businesses are higher than those for stocks. Another confusion of perspective is found in the claim – made for most acquisitions – that the merged business will create a stronger competitor. Usually, stronger is just another word for bigger. The normal meaning of "stronger competitor", however, is a business with better products and keener prices, a goal generally accomplished through operational improvements rather than transformational deals.

I once thought that however thin the public arguments for large corporate transactions, there was probably some serious analysis going on behind the scenes. Just as I once thought that whatever nonsense politicians might talk on public platforms, more substantive discussion took place when they retired to their offices. But closer acquaintance with business and politics dispelled both illusions. What you see and hear is more or less what there is.

When I was sometimes employed to explain the economic rationale for a corporate transaction, I discovered that it was rarely useful to ask the principals why they were doing it. Usually you just heard those familiar clichés. Sometimes you got closer to the truth, sniffed the testosterone, glimpsed the inflated egos. And, of course, observed the fees earned by the cheerleaders.

The merger of BAE and EADS fell apart in Europe's field of broken dreams – the Berlin office of Chancellor Angela Merkel. The traditional stance of the British government has been that it did not care where corporate control rested. The French, German and US governments, however, do care and their requirements were irreconcilable. And perhaps people in London are learning to care too. The other threat to the deal came from the English market town of Henley, where BAE's largest shareholder, Neil Woodford of Invesco Perpetual, is based. Mr Woodford epitomises the style of fund management favoured in the review of equity markets and long-term decision making I completed this summer – concentrated portfolios and material and committed shareholdings. Mr Woodford criticised the deal, having presumably failed to obtain in private the explanation of its rationale that he then sought in public. There needs to be more such interrogation, to help distinguish sound bites from sound strategy.

In contrast to the botched strategies of many Western companies, such as BAE Systems and EADS, Japanese companies have received many plaudits over the years for their ability to establish and successfully pursue long-term strategic goals, especially their commitment to strategic intent (Hirota *et al*, 2010). Pascale and Athos (1982) and Hamel and Prahalad (1989) argue that Japanese business success is not based on detailed and well-thought-out strategies *per se*, but on strategic intent – the commitment of Japanese managers to create and pursue a vision of their desired future. The vision is then used to bind an organisation together and give it a common purpose to which all can contribute. There is strong evidence that this type of strategic consensus has a positive effect on organisational performance (Kellermanns *et al*, 2011). A key part of this strategic consensus purpose is the identification and development of the core competences and capabilities necessary for the achievement of the organisation's vision.

This theme has been taken up by other Western writers on strategy (Bartkus *et al*, 2006; Bartkus and Glassman, 2008; De Wit and Meyer, 2010; Kotter and Heskett, 1992). Kay (1993) uses the term 'distinctive capabilities' rather than 'core competences', but is clearly describing the same thing. He argues that a firm's distinctive capabilities fall under four headings: reputation, architecture (i.e. internal and external structures and linkages), innovation and strategic assets. Kay asserts that an organisation's competitiveness is dependent not upon any strategic plan as such, but upon the uniqueness and strength of its capabilities. It is these that allow an organisation to take advantage of opportunities and avoid threats, whether foreseeable or not. In a similar way, Stalk *et al* (1992) use the term 'core capability' in referring to an organisation's practices and business routines; and Grant (1991a) proposes a framework for analysing a firm's competitive advantage in terms of its resources and capabilities.

To an extent, the case made by Kay, Stalk *et al* and Grant is complementary to Mintzberg's (1987) concept of emergent strategy. Based on the many Western companies he has studied, Mintzberg argues that successful companies do not start out with detailed strategic plans. Instead, their strategies emerge over time from the pattern of decisions they take on key aspects of their activities. Mintzberg *et al* (1998a: 189–90) draw a distinction between planned or deliberate strategies and emergent ones:

> Deliberate strategy focuses on control – making sure that managerial intentions are realized in action – while emergent strategy emphasizes learning – coming to understand through the taking of actions what those intentions should be in the first place. . . . The concept of emergent strategy . . . opens the door to strategic learning, because it acknowledges the organization's capacity to experiment. A single action can be taken, feedback can be received, and the process can continue until the organization converges on the pattern that becomes its strategy.

Clearly, there are similarities between the Japanese intent and/or competence approach to strategy, Mintzberg's view of strategy and Kay and co.'s distinctive capabilities. However, the Japanese consciously work out their shared vision and consciously pursue it (Hirota *et al*, 2010), while the emergent approach, at least in its pure form, lacks the concept of 'vision' and doubts the presence of conscious intent. Even so, Mintzberg (1994: 25) does recognise that in practice some organisations pursue:

> Umbrella strategies: the broad outlines are deliberate while the details are allowed to emerge within them. Thus emergent strategies are not bad and deliberate ones good; effective strategies mix these characteristics in ways that reflect the conditions at hand, notably the ability to predict as well as the need to react to unexpected events.

Kay (1993) takes a similar view. While doubting the efficacy of corporate vision *per se*, he does stress that the development of capabilities is, or at least can be, a conscious and planned process.

As mentioned in Chapter 4, complexity theories have had an increasing influence on organisation theorists over the last decade. However, their influence on the strategy literature has been limited by the fact that complexity theorists do not appear to share a common view of complexity and organisational strategy. For Stacey (2003: 319–20):

> Strategy comes to be understood as the evolving patterns of an organisation's identity. . . .
> Strategy as the identity of an organisation is continuously constructed and enacted in the
> interaction of organisational practice.

For MacIntosh and MacLean (2001), strategy also has an emergent dimension to it but,
for them, a key feature of strategy is to identify and maintain the appropriateness of the
organisation's order-generating rules. It is the presence of appropriate order-generating
rules that allows a consistent, and beneficial, pattern of action to emerge which forms
the organisation's strategy. Bechtold (1997) and Brown and Eisenhardt (1997) stress that
the purpose of order-generating rules is to keep an organisation operating at the edge of
chaos. For them, the purpose of strategy is to create an organisation where self-organisation
can take place. It is the ability to self-organise that they see as being crucial to maintaining
and/or developing appropriate order-generating rules and thus bringing about beneficial
change.

Like complexity theories, population ecology is borrowed from the physical sciences. It is
a Darwinist-type approach that focuses on how organisations adapt and evolve in order to
survive within the general population of organisations to which they belong (Carroll, 1988;
Morgan, 1990). Watson (1997: 273) comments that:

> One way of considering the relationship of organisations to other organisations in the
> environment is to regard them as involved in a process of natural selection: a fight for survival
> within the ecological system of which they are part. . . . They go through both planned
> and unplanned 'variations' in their form, and, largely through processes of competition, the
> environment 'selects' the form which best suits the organisation. Organisations then 'retain'
> the form which best suits their particular 'niche' or 'domain'.

Population ecologists do not, therefore, challenge the importance of the fit or correspondence between an organisation and its environment, but they do question the extent to
which achieving this is a conscious and planned process. In particular, as Pettigrew *et al*
(1992: 25) maintain: 'Ecologists are unimpressed by the possibility that managers can turn
their organizations round, and instead stress organizational inertia.' This argument echoes
Hannan and Freeman's (1977: 957) assertion that:

> for wide classes of organizations there are very strong inertial pressures on structure arising
> from both internal arrangements (for example, internal politics) and from the environment
> (for example, public legitimation of organizational activity). To claim otherwise is to ignore the
> most obvious feature of organizational life.

Population ecologists argue that an organisation's survival, the extent to which it
achieves a fit with its environment, depends on a combination of the organisation's own
(planned and unplanned) actions, the activities of other organisations in its field and a
strong element of luck (i.e. being in the right place, with the right combination of characteristics and at the right time).

The stress on luck or serendipity in business life is also present in the work of writers such
as Hamel (1996), Williamson (1991), Yukl (2013) and Weick (1979). Weick, in particular,
views the world as an essentially ambiguous place in which it is unrealistic, and indeed
impossible, to make detailed plans. This is clearly a strong challenge to those who emphasise
the need for, and ability of, organisations to pursue environmental match or correspondence.
However, Child's (1972) concept of equifinality takes this challenge even further.
Equifinality, according to Sorge (1997: 13):

quite simply means that different sorts of internal arrangements are perfectly compatible with identical contextual or environmental states. The principle goes against the idea of a quasi-ideal 'match' which is inherent in the principle of correspondence. Whereas correspondence [i.e. Contingency] theory suggests that rigid and bureaucratic structures are not a good match for volatile and shifting product markets, equifinality theorists claim that it may very well turn out to be a good match but only if the level and diversity of the workforce is large and organization culture produces motivated and flexible actors.

Mintzberg *et al* (1998a) note in relation to equifinality that managers need to recognise that achieving a successful outcome is more important than imposing the method of achieving it.

Pettigrew (1985, 1987) and Child and Smith (1987), through their respective studies of ICI and Cadbury, also offer important insights and perspectives on approaches to strategic management and environmental fit. Pettigrew argues that there is a need for a change theory that sees organisations and how they operate in their entirety, one that recognises the importance and influence of the wider environment and appreciates the dynamic and political nature of strategy development and change. He is critical of theories which assume that organisations are rational entities pursuing agreed goals that reflect their best interests. Instead, he contends that organisations have to be understood in the context of the constraints and possibilities offered by the environment in which they operate and in relation to the self-interests of the individuals and groups that compose them.

So Pettigrew sees organisations primarily as political systems in which groups and individuals, under the guise of rationality, seek to mobilise support for, and legitimate the pursuit of, strategies and actions that promote or sustain their personal or sectional interests. Particular groups or individuals may achieve a position of dominance, but that dominance is always subject to prevailing intra-organisational and environmental conditions. Consequently, Pettigrew rejects the view that strategy is a rational process of deliberate calculation and analysis. Instead he believes that organisational strategy – though often cloaked in rational and analytical terms – is in reality the outcome of a combination of internal political struggles, between groups and individuals seeking to influence policy in their favour, and external environmental pressures and constraints (this argument was examined in more detail in Chapter 5).

Child and Smith's (1987) firm-in-sector perspective has some similarities with Pettigrew's work; however, they take a more realist perspective, arguing for a stronger determining link between the individual firm and the sector in which it operates, and a lesser role for organisational politics. As shown in Ideas and perspectives 6.4, they suggest three areas of firm–sector linkage that shape and constrain the strategies organisations pursue.

Child and Smith's (1987) view draws on economic theories of the firm and suggests that the sector, particularly when strongly competitive, determines the path, the trajectory, a firm must take for its future success. Though not denying a role for organisational politics, they claim that, unless the strategic decisions a firm takes are consistent with the conditions prevailing in its sector, success may be jeopardised. So although falling in the Analytical stream, Child and Smith appear to exhibit a greater faith in a rational and linear progression from market sector analysis to strategy formulation and implementation than Pettigrew and many other writers.

The Analytical stream also has a number of other variants, most notably those that see the role and personality of leaders as being the key determinants of successful strategy (Bennis and Nanus, 1985). Leadership will be touched on later in this chapter, and covered

---

IDEAS AND PERSPECTIVES 6.4

Child and Smith's firm-in-sector perspective

1. **The 'objective conditions' for success**. In essence, this is an argument for 'sector or environmental determinism'. Though each firm within a sector may pursue a different strategy, these will all tend to focus on or be determined by similar success factors such as customer satisfaction, quality, profitability, etc. Therefore, 'a firm's viability depends upon the extent to which its behaviour is appropriate to those environmental conditions'.

2. **The prevailing managerial consensus**. '[A]t least within well-established sectors, the senior managers of constituent firms hold very similar constructs of the sector's operational dynamics which effectively furnish the rules of the game for the sector.' It follows that 'the sector is the bearer of external exemplars against which a firm's current strategy and structure, and the ideology underlying these, can be compared'.

3. **The collaborative networks operating in the sector**. Firms do not exist in isolation from the rest of the sector but are joined together in patterns of cooperation and affiliation with other firms in the sector. Consequently, 'a sector does not only consist of product competitors; it is also a *network* of potential and actual collaborators'. Such collaborations may be with customers, suppliers, outside experts or even competitors.

Source: Child and Smith (1987: 566–9).

---

more extensively in Chapter 14; mentioning it here serves to emphasise the somewhat disparate nature of the Analytical stream of strategy. Proponents of this stream are united by a number of factors, such as their attempt to understand rather than prescribe strategy, their orientation, mainly, to an academic rather than a business audience, and their view of organisations as complex social entities operating within dangerous, dynamic and unpredictable environments. Meanwhile, the proponents of the elements which make up the Analytical stream are divided by their emphasis on different aspects of strategy, such as politics, the industry sector, the general environment, organisational and national cultures, leadership, etc. They are also divided by their explicit or implicit adherence to postmodernist, realist or complexity perspectives.

So, although it is true to say that proponents of the Japanese-inspired strategic intent and/or competence argument came to the fore in the 1990s, it is also true to say that they are challenged by the proponents of the other elements in this stream who still exert a powerful influence on the debate over strategy (De Wit and Meyer, 2010; Hirota *et al*, 2010). It follows that their differences with each other are as important as their differences with proponents of the Prescriptive stream of strategy.

Understanding strategy: choices and constraints

While the above identifies key themes in the debate over organisational strategy, it still presents a somewhat confusing picture. Clearly there is a distinction between those who adhere to the Prescriptive stream of strategy, which arose from the long-range planning approach of the 1940s and 1950s, and the Analytical stream as represented by, among others, the strategic intent and/or competences approach of the 1980s and 1990s. What is not clear, however, is the degree to which a common understanding and perspective exists among those collected under the Analytical umbrella. Certainly, a number of writers have tried to argue that a common perspective does exist. Brown and Jopling (1994) believes that the main distinction lies between the writers of the 1950s and 1960s who, they argue, saw strategy as basically concerned with fitting the organisation to its environment, and the writers of the 1980s and 1990s who, they argue, saw strategy as focusing on internal issues, mainly to do with the development of core competences. They base their case on a Contingency perspective. The earlier approach, they argue, was suitable to organisations operating in relatively stable and predictable environments, who had a limited product range, and where competition was restricted. With the advent of greater competition and more unstable environments, this approach was no longer viable, and firms had to look internally at how they could organise themselves to cope with the new situation.

To an extent, this is an attractive analysis. However, though it is true that the earlier writers on strategy – such as Ansoff and company – did concentrate on product–market mix issues, it is also true that they later came to appreciate the link between the outside and the inside (Moore, 1992). Also, while Mintzberg and others have concentrated on internal capabilities, the Japanese approach has been to see the internal and external as two sides of the same coin, which is why they emphasise the importance of the strategic outward-looking vision driving the development of internal capabilities (De Wit and Meyer, 2010; Hirota *et al*, 2010).

All the same, such a simple distinction, based on one dimension of organisational life, cannot resolve the complex differences between and within the Prescriptive and Analytical streams. Mintzberg *et al* (2009) note that the strategy field is now more eclectic and more populous, in terms of different approaches, than ever before. In such a situation, attempts to fit writers into two camps, whether they be early and late, external and internal, are bound to fail. The multiple-definition view of strategy argued by Mintzberg *et al* (2009), and particularly their proposition that the various definitions of strategy are both competing and complementary, offers another perspective. Strategy can be considered as either a process or an outcome. It can also be considered as either a rational approach or a political and/or social phenomenon. The various approaches to strategy do not reflect some underlying truth; rather they are different approaches that organisations can choose (consciously or not) to adopt, depending on their circumstances, objectives and management (Johnson *et al*, 2011).

So maybe instead of looking for a theory or approach to strategy that unifies and encompasses all the others, we should turn the argument on its head and ask, as we did with organisational theory, whether there needs to be a 'one best way' for strategy?

In approaching this question, it is valuable to return to Child's (1972) concept of equifinality. As stated earlier, Sorge (1997: 13) writes that equifinality 'quite simply means that different sorts of internal arrangements are perfectly compatible with identical contextual or environmental states'. To paraphrase this definition, and to stretch the concept a little further than Child might have intended, it could be argued that different approaches to strategy formulation may be perfectly compatible with positive outcomes. This may especially be the case if one takes account of the growing opinion, as expressed in this and the previous chapters, that though organisations are constrained by their circumstances, they do possess the ability to manipulate and influence these circumstances to their own advantage. If this is the case, then, as Mintzberg *et al* (1998a: 365) maintain, 'the question is not whether there exists strategic choice, but how much'. To approach this question, we need to attempt to classify the various approaches to strategy in order to establish the degree to which they incorporate or exclude choice.

Though the above review of approaches to strategy cannot claim to be all-embracing, it does cover the key protagonists in the area. While it separates the main approaches into two streams, however, it does not provide a classification or taxonomy of the various approaches. Whittington (1993) attempted to make sense of the many definitions and categories of strategy by identifying four generic approaches to strategy: the Classical, Evolutionary, Processual and Systemic (*see* Ideas and perspectives 6.5).

Whittington's categorisation of generic approaches to strategy is extremely useful in making sense of the plethora of approaches on offer. As one would expect, it is not perfect; some writers, such as Mintzberg, could fall under more than one heading, while others, like Child and Smith, are difficult to locate. Nevertheless, the Classical approach, with its modernist leanings, would clearly incorporate the work of the Planning, Design and Positioning school and the early Western writers on strategy. The Evolutionary approach has links with both the work of the complexity theorists and population ecologists; Mintzberg's (1994) work on emergent strategy might also fall under this heading. The Processual approach could also cover Mintzberg's work, certainly includes Pettigrew's (1985, 1987) work on organisational politics and sits reasonably comfortably with the post-modernists. The Systemic perspective, which has a realist tinge to it, clearly owes much to the Japanese approach to strategy as described by Hamel and Prahalad (1989).

Whittington (1993) also categorises these four approaches to strategy in terms of how they view outcomes and processes. He argues that the Classical and Evolutionary approaches see profit maximisation as the natural outcome of strategy. The Systemic and Processual approaches, meanwhile, believe other outcomes are both possible and acceptable, such as stability, environmental responsibility or maintenance of an organisation's dominant coalition. With regard to processes, the groupings change. Here the Classical and Systemic approaches both agree that strategy can be a deliberate process; but the Evolutionists and Processualists, though, see strategy as emerging from processes governed by chance and confusion.

Whittington's four categories of strategy can be summarised as follows:

- Classicists see strategy as a rational process of long-term planning aimed at maximising profit.

- Evolutionists also believe that the purpose of strategy is profit maximisation, but regard the future as too volatile and unpredictable to allow effective planning. Instead, they advise organisations to focus on maximising chances of survival today.

- The Processualists are equally sceptical of long-range planning, and see strategy as an emergent process of learning and adaptation.

- The Systemic perspective argues that the nature and aims of strategy are dependent upon the particular social context in which the organisation operates.

To an extent, the four approaches to strategy have some similarity to the Western approaches to organisation theory discussed in Part 1. The Classical, Evolutionary and Processual approaches are clearly 'one best way' or 'only possible way' approaches, whereas the Systemic approach offers a Contingency perspective on strategy. They also share some

IDEAS AND PERSPECTIVES 6.5

Whittington's generic approaches to strategy

- **The Classical approach**. This is the oldest and most influential approach to strategy. It portrays strategy as a rational process, based on analysis and quantification, and aimed at achieving the maximum level of profit for an organisation. It argues that, through rigorous analysis and planning, senior managers can predict future market trends and shape the organisation to take advantage of these.

- **The Evolutionary approach**. As the name implies, this uses the analogy of biological evolution to describe strategy development. It believes that organisations are at the mercy of the unpredictable and hostile vagaries of the market. Those organisations that survive and prosper do so not because of their ability to plan and predict, which is impossible, but because they have been lucky enough to hit on a winning formula. From this perspective, successful strategies cannot be planned, but emerge from the decisions managers take to align and realign their organisations to the changing environmental conditions.

- **The Processual approach**. This perspective concentrates on the nature of organisational and market processes. It views organisations and their members as shifting coalitions of individuals and groups with different interests, imperfect knowledge and short attention spans. Markets are similarly capricious and imperfect but, because of this, do not require organisations to achieve a perfect fit with their environment in order to prosper and survive. Strategy under these conditions is portrayed as a pragmatic process of trial and error, aimed at achieving a compromise between the needs of the market and the objectives of the warring factions within the organisation.

- **The Systemic approach**. This approach sees strategy as linked to dominant features of the local social system within which it takes place. The core argument of this perspective is that strategy can be a deliberate process, and planning and predictability are possible, but only if the conditions within the host society are favourable. Therefore, to an extent, this is a contingency approach to strategy which can accommodate situations where firms do not seek to maximise profit or bow to market pressures. If the conditions within the host society are supportive, markets can be manipulated, financial considerations can become a secondary issue, and stability and predictability can be achieved. Also, under such conditions, the objectives managers seek to pursue may be related more to their social background, degree of patriotism or even professional pride, than to profit maximisation. Therefore, from the Systemic perspective, the strategy an organisation adopts and the interests managers pursue reflect the nature of the particular social system within which it operates.

Source: Whittington (1993).

common ground with organisation theory on the issue of rationality. The Classical and Systemic approaches argue that strategy is or can be rational and intentional in its development and objectives. The Processualists believe that it is rational in neither aspect; the Evolutionists take a similar view of process, but appear to adopt a rational perspective on outcomes, in that profit maximisation is seen as the only outcome that guarantees survival. In their view of the scope for managerial choice and judgement, three of these four

Figure 6.4 Constraints on managerial choice

approaches to strategy do appear to be more flexible than much of organisation theory, which tends to see little scope for managers to exercise choice. Clearly, the Classical strategy theorists leave little scope for either: their instruction seems to be to follow the textbook in terms of outcomes and processes, or else! However, both the Evolutionists and the Processualists emphasise the need for managers to be fleet of foot and percipient in making key decisions responding to opportunities or threats; although the Evolutionists (rather like Napoleon in his view of generals) appear to believe that, at the end of the day, a lucky manager may be more desirable than an able one. For advocates of the Systemic approach, choice and judgement are important, but tend to be constrained by the limits and objectives of the society in which they are located.

It would appear, therefore, that managerial choice, preference and judgement, for all but the Classicists, do have a role to play in determining not just an organisation's strategy, but also the particular approach to strategy it adopts. In our examination of the strategy literature, however, it is clear that choice is constrained and can be exercised only within limits (from some perspectives, very narrow limits indeed). As Figure 6.4 shows, these limits or constraints, which are suggested by or inferred from the literature, can be classified under four headings.

National objectives, practices and cultures

The case for country-specific constraints very much follows the argument of the Systemic perspective on strategy. This view sees the operation of organisations as strongly influenced by the social system in which they operate. In some cases, such as in Japan and Germany, patriotism, national pride and a collectivist ethos have created a business environment that supports the pursuit of long-term national objectives. This is reflected in the behaviour of individual firms and financial institutions that favour stable growth over the medium to long term, rather than short-term profit maximisation. In Britain and the US, on the other hand, the climate is far more supportive of individual endeavour and short-term profit maximisation rather than the national interest *per se*.

The difference between these two approaches is neatly summed up in the old saying that 'What's good for General Motors is good for America'. The Japanese would, of course, transpose this to read 'What is good for Japan is good for Toyota'. This view also draws support from Hofstede's (1980, 1990) work on national cultures discussed in Chapter 5. The implication, therefore, is that organisations ignore national norms at their peril: the pursuit of short-term profit maximisation in Japan and Germany is likely to be as difficult, and perhaps as counterproductive, as the pursuit of a long-term strategy of growing market share, which ignores short-term profitability, would be in the UK or the US. Nevertheless, these constraints are open to manipulation and avoidance. The move by many British companies – Dyson, GKN, etc. – to manufacture outside the UK and/or to form international alliances is an example of this, as is the Japanese trend to establish manufacturing plants in the US and Europe in order to avoid high production costs on the one hand and import quotas on the other. Another example is the lobbying of governments and national and international bodies for changes in laws and regulations that particular organisations or industries see as operating against their interests.

Industry and sector practices and norms

This section follows from Child and Smith's (1987) firm-in-sector perspective. As discussed earlier, they believe that the objective conditions operating in a sector, managers' understanding of the dynamics of the sector, and the nature and degree of inter-firm collaboration all combine to determine the path a firm must take for its future success. This is especially the case where the sector is highly competitive. In effect, Child and Smith's argument is that firms must stick to the rules of engagement in their sector or perish. They do concede that, where competition is less intense, then managers have a greater degree of freedom with regard to the selection of strategy. Indeed, the low level of competition may explain how Japanese companies were able to change the rules of engagement to their advantage in many industries in the 1960s and 1970s (Hamel and Prahalad, 1989), although it is also the case that Japanese companies pay less attention to sectoral constraints than to reshaping the rules of the game to create competitive conditions more favourable to themselves (Turner, 1990). Another method of overcoming sectoral constraints and conditions is by diversifying into new products and different sectors (Allaire and Firsirotu, 1989).

Business environment

For nearly all the approaches to strategy that we have discussed, their proponents assume, explicitly or implicitly, that they are operating in a particular type of environment. The Classical approach to strategy is clearly predicated on the existence of a relatively stable and predictable environment. If this exists, then predicting the future and planning accordingly is a much less hazardous exercise than would otherwise be the case. The Systemic view also seems to assume a degree of environmental stability. As the history of Japan and Germany shows, however, stability needs to be actively promoted by government–industry co-operation rather than relying on the invisible, and often volatile, hand of the market. For Processualists, and even more so for Evolutionists, the environment is a hostile, unpredictable and uncertain place. Planning is almost impossible, and success comes either from continuously adapting to changes in the environment, or from being in the right place at the right time.

For three of these perspectives, the environment is a given, even if they disagree about exactly what is given. However, for those advocating a Systemic approach, the environment is not a given: it can be changed. As this chapter and Part 1 have shown, there are strong supporters of this view (Hatch and Cunliffe, 2006; Morgan, 1997; Stacey, 2003). Shapiro (1989) utilises the tools of game theory to show how firms influence the behaviour and actions of their competitors, and in so doing change the environment in which they operate. In a similar way, Teece *et al* (1997) argue that investments in production capacity, R&D and advertising can all be used to alter an organisation's environment favourably. Weick (1979) takes a different perspective. He argues that the world is so complex and ambiguous that an organisation cannot possibly 'know' its environment. Instead, organisations have to 'enact' their environment; that is to say, they have to develop and act upon their own interpretation of their environment. This is very similar to the learning organisation and postmodernist perspectives, as discussed in Chapters 3 and 4, that organisations have the ability to 'invent' their own reality.

The implication from these different perspectives is that though many companies may have to adjust their strategic approach to environmental conditions, some companies may be able to do the opposite. The UK National Health Service is a good example of this. Burnes and Salauroo (1995) relate that the NHS operated prior to 1990 as a typical government bureaucracy. The government allocated resources and gave policy direction, while the NHS centrally planned how resources would be allocated and policies operationalised (i.e. the Classical approach to strategy). This meant that there was considerable stability and pre-dictability in its environment. However, the government of the day wanted the NHS to operate in a more cost-conscious and entrepreneurial mode. To facilitate and encourage this, it changed the way funds were provided and distributed. Rather than funds being given as of right to service providers (e.g. hospitals), they were reallocated to service purchasers (e.g. local doctors) who could decide what to buy and from whom. This cre-ation of a market for the provision of medical services destabilised the environment and made planning and prediction very hazardous exercises (thus making an Evolutionary or Processual approach to strategy more relevant). However, with a change of government in 1997, the pendulum began to swing back. While wishing to retain some of the perceived benefits of a market system, the new government announced that it would modify the purchaser–provider system to create greater stability (Salauroo and Burnes, 1998). Since then, of course, successive governments have again swung the pendulum back towards market forces, something which has not always been wholeheartedly welcomed by staff in the NHS (Roberts, 2008).

Normally, attempts at manipulating the environment aim to reduce uncertainty, or at least cope with it rather than increase it. Allaire and Firsirotu (1989) identified three ways of coping with uncertainty:

- The first of these is through predicting and planning (the Classical approach).
- The second is to restructure for flexibility (the Contingency approach).
- The third, in contrast, is to manipulate or control the environment.

In terms of the latter, Allaire and Firsirotu (1989) cite the examples of Boeing and IBM, which created and subsequently dominated their environments. Another major approach they identify is the use of cooperative strategies – collusion, market-sharing and other methods of reducing competition. An example of this in the UK was the agreement in the early 1990s by the main companies in the milk industry to 'carve up the country so they stop competing with each other' for doorstep sales (Cowe, 1995: 40). Perhaps one of the most famous (or notorious) recent examples is Microsoft's attempt to dominate the market for internet products by providing its web browser 'free' to everyone who bought its Windows operating system (Windrum, 2004).

So, there is certainly sufficient evidence to show that it is possible to change, control or manipulate the environment in which an organisation operates, and thus either necessitate or make possible a particular approach to strategy.

Organisation characteristics

Obviously, there are many organisation characteristics that act to constrain or facilitate managerial choice. There appear to be four that have particular importance: structure, culture, politics and managerial style. Apart from the last, these have been reviewed extensively in Chapters 3 and 4 and can be discussed relatively briefly. An organisation's structure and culture have clear implications for managerial choice in the area of strategy. Organisations with organic structures and task cultures are likely to be resistant to or incapable of operating a Classical form of strategy. Similarly, organisations with mechanistic structures and role cultures are likely to have a somewhat hostile attitude towards Processual or Evolutionary approaches to strategy. Moving on to the issue of organisational politics: where decisions are heavily influenced by individual and/or group self-interest, as opposed to organisational objectives, it is unlikely that a Classical or Systemic approach to strategy would be successful. Yet a Processual or Evolutionary approach would have clear applicability.

There remains the subject of managerial or leadership style. There has been considerable interest in applying Burns's (1978) pioneering work on political leadership to leadership in organisations (Barker, 2001; Bass, 1995; Beatty and Lee, 1992; Burnes and James, 1995; Gibbons, 1992; Price, 2003; Storey, 2004; Yukl, 2006). Burns identifies two basic organisational states:

- **Convergent** – a stable state.
- **Divergent** – where predictability and stability are absent.

For each of these states, he argues, there is an appropriate managerial style.

- Convergent states require managers with a *transactional style* – ones who are good at optimising the performance of the organisation within the confines of existing policy.
- Divergent states require managers with a *transformational style* – ones who challenge the status quo and create new visions.

It follows from this that transactional managers will prefer approaches to strategy that stress continuity and predictability (i.e. the Classical or, in some circumstances, Systemic approach), while transformational managers will be more comfortable with a Processual or Evolutionary type of approach. Managerial style will be further discussed in Chapters 12 and 14.

As was the case with the other three forms of constraint, organisational characteristics can be amended. The debate on structure and culture has been well covered already, but the level of political behaviour is also open to change. As Pfeffer (1981, 1992) showed, though political behaviour is never absent from organisations, there are situations where it is likely to be more prevalent. In particular, political behaviour is likely to be most evident where major structural changes are taking place that affect the power distribution in organisations. By recognising that this is the case, by taking steps to reduce ambiguity and by trying to increase the transparency and openness of the decision-making process, the ability of individuals to pursue their own interests can be reduced. This is demonstrated by the

Japanese *ringi* system, which promotes extensive and open debate over decisions in order to ensure that they fit in with the company's objectives rather than those of sectional interests. As far as changing managerial styles is concerned, although there is evidence that these are shaped and changed by the organisations in which managers work, there is also considerable evidence that senior managers tend to change organisations to fit their style (Morgan, 1997; Yukl, 2013).

Choices and constraints: summary

It should be borne in mind that the particular mix of these four forms of constraint will vary from organisation to organisation, even where these operate in the same country and industry. Also, it needs to be recognised that these constraints are as likely to conflict with each other as they are to complement each other: for example, car companies operating in the UK may find that the culture of the UK's financial institutions favours short-term profit maximisation, while the car industry appears to require long-term investment in building market share. This may be one reason why the UK motor industry is now mostly foreign-owned. In addition, it should be noted that while managers are not obliged to take account of the constraints they face, they may well pay a price for this in terms of the performance of their organisation. Successful firms are likely to be ones whose managers are aware of, and can balance, the various constraints they face. This obviously raises the issue of managerial ability and competence, an issue we shall explore in some depth in Chapter 14.

Therefore, the key point to recognise from the above review is that the type of strategic approach adopted is a matter of managerial choice, but that choice is constrained by a variety of organisational, environmental, sectoral and national factors, as are the outcomes which flow from it. As was argued in Part 1, organisations and managers may be able to influence or change the constraints they face. By recognising that there are real constraints on managerial choice, as shown in Figure 6.4, one is acknowledging that both the realist and complexity perspectives on organisations have much to offer. At the same time, by recognising that some constraints can be consciously manipulated or influenced and changed, one is also acknowledging that the postmodernists' arguments should not be lightly dismissed.

Even so, both the case for managerial choice and the argument for manipulating constraints need to be taken with a pinch of salt. The fact of the matter is that in the West, as noted by many writers, the Classical approach to strategy, latterly through the work of the Positioning school, still dominates the practice of strategy (De Wit and Meyer, 2010; Johnson *et al*, 2011; Mintzberg *et al*, 2009). Also, as was noted in Chapter 5, there is a tendency for decision-makers to 'satisfice'. That is to say, rather than undertaking an extensive examination of the issues involved and searching for all the possible solutions, decision-makers tend to accept the first satisfactory solution to a problem (Butler, 1997). This equates to Argyris and Schön's (1978) concept of single-loop learning (*see* Chapter 3). It is also similar to Cohen *et al*'s (1972) comment that decisions are often not taken but happen. They suggest that decisions occur when four independent streams meet: problems, solutions, participants and choice opportunities – the so-called Garbage Can model of decision-making (*see* Figure 6.5).

Cohen *et al* argue that when a problem becomes severe it demands attention. Solutions, on the other hand, are answers looking for a problem. Participants are the people in the organisation possessing problems and/or solutions, while choice opportunities are occasions

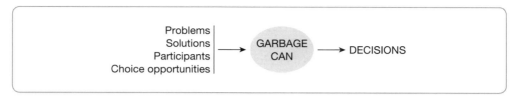

Figure 6.5 The Garbage Can model of decision-making

when organisations are required to make a decision. When these four elements come together, decisions occur. Seen in this way, decision-making is not conscious, rational or systematic; on the contrary, decisions are haphazard, accidental and unplanned. From a slightly different perspective, Nelson and Winter (1982) argue that in many cases decision-making is an unconscious and automatic process, based on a repertoire that individuals develop over time of responses to particular situations. This is similar to Ashforth and Fried's (1988) observation that there is a tendency in some organisations for behaviour to become almost mindless – employees and managers, as a result of organisational social-isation and experience, respond automatically to events in a programmed way. Consequently, though the potential for choice exists, the reality is that many managers appear not to exercise it, preferring instead to stick to tried-and-tested, routine, orthodox, textbook approaches – regardless of their suitability.

Yet it is important to note that, in the academic world, the weight of the argument appears to have shifted from seeing strategy as a rational, mathematical process, to seeing it as the outcome of the ability of an organisation's management to utilise its strengths and competences in the competitive pursuit of success. In contrast, there are some writers who believe that in the business world managers still prefer to opt for rational decision-making approaches to strategy based on value-maximising financial techniques and quantitative analysis of market positions (Grandori, 2013; Grant, 1991b; Levinthal, 2011; Rigby and Bilodeau, 2011; Teece *et al*, 1997). Kay (1993: 357) maintains:

> To observe [as the proponents of the Analytical stream of strategy do] that organizations are complex, that change is inevitably incremental, and that strategy is inevitably adaptive, however true, helps very little in deciding what to do. Managers wish to be told of a process which they can at least partially control and, whatever its weaknesses, that is what rationalist [Prescriptive] strategy appears to offer.

Whatever the validity or otherwise of this view, the main strategies favoured by organisations – as the following chapter will show – are still, though no longer exclusively, market- and quantitatively orientated, and certainly give greater credence to rational decision-making than to more qualitative approaches (De Wit and Meyer, 2010; Johnson *et al*, 2011; Rigby and Bilodeau, 2011).

Conclusions

Strategic planning or management has moved in and out of fashion over the years and is once again firmly back in fashion (De Wit and Meyer, 2010; Galagan, 1997; Hill and Jones, 2006; Johnson *et al*, 2011; Joyce and Woods, 2001; Kay, 1993; Rigby and Gillies, 2000). It has developed (and fragmented) considerably since it began to be widely used in America in the 1950s and 1960s (Brews, 2003; Hambrick and Frederickson, 2001). No longer is strategy purely about the external world; no longer is it solely seen as a rational, quantitative process. Neither is it any longer seen as a process that is geared towards predicting the future, but instead it seeks to shape or create the future (Joyce and Woods, 2001). Indeed, writers and practitioners from different backgrounds and countries, such as Hamel and Prahalad (1994), Mintzberg *et al* (2009), Ohmae (1986) and Stacey (2010), argue that it is not a process at all, but the outcome of a process: an outcome that is shaped not by mathematical models but by human creativity.

The move towards this more emergent perspective on strategy has been brought about by the mounting criticisms against the Classical or Prescriptive approach to strategy. The main criticisms are that it is mechanistic, inflexible, and reliant on quantitative tools and techniques of dubious validity. The result is that organisations that attempt to construct strategies using the Classical approach fall foul of what Peters and Waterman (1982) described as 'Paralysis Through Analysis' and 'Irrational Rationality'. In effect, organisations contort themselves in a vain attempt to make the real world fit the constraints and limitations of their mathematical models, rather than vice versa.

The alternative view is that organisations should move away from exclusive reliance on mathematical models (Stacey, 2010). Instead, human creativity should be brought into play. Senior managers should create a vision of the organisation's future – establish its strategic intent. This should then be pursued relentlessly by the organisation. In the process of doing so, the strategy emerges from the decisions that are taken with regard to resource allocation, organisation structure and the other key areas of operation (Mintzberg, 1994). From different perspectives, a number of writers have come to the same conclusion (Mintzberg *et al*, 2009; Mirabeau and Maguire, 2013; Weike, 2000). For successful companies, strategy does not appear to be a preconceived and detailed set of steps for achieving a coherent package of concrete goals within a given timescale. Neither does it seem to be a rational process that is amenable to mathematical modelling. Rather, it is the outcome of a process of decision-making and resource allocation that is embarked upon in pursuit of a vision (though even here there is disagreement about how conscious this process is). Such an approach is inherently irrational, inherently unplannable – it cannot be modelled or quantified, though it can and must be pursued with rigour and determination. Needless to say, just as the rational approach to strategy sat easily with a modernist perspective, so the more intuitive, less rational approach sits better with the postmodernist view of the world.

The problem is that, though we can identify two major perspectives on strategy, within and between them there are a great number of variants which, as Khalifa (2008) notes, serve to confuse managers rather than help them. In the face of this confusion, the tendency is for managers to limit their strategic domain and to focus on the use of one particular strategic tool (such as the Boston Consulting Group's Growth Share Matrix) regardless of the drawbacks and limited applicability of such tools (Coyne and Subramaniam, 1996; Hambrick and Frederickson, 2001; Mintzberg and Lampel, 1999; Rigby and Bilodeau, 2011).

In this chapter, we have suggested a third approach to strategy, one which sides with neither the quantitative nor the qualitative schools of thought but which instead seeks to promote (rather than reduce) managerial choice. It has been argued in this chapter that the approach to strategy that organisations adopt is or can be the outcome of managerial choice and preference. However, choice in this respect, as in most others, is constrained. The key constraints identified were societal, sectoral, environmental and organisational. While on the face of it this appears to impose severe limitations on the degree of freedom managers have with regard to the choice of strategy, it was also argued that managers can influence or manipulate the constraints they face in order to create their own preferred organisational reality. Therefore, though being very much in the realist and complexity camps, it does not totally reject the postmodernist view either.

This follows on from Part 1, where it was claimed that managers are not the passive creatures portrayed by much of organisation theory. Instead of having to adapt their organisations to the circumstances in which they find themselves, they can attempt to amend or even reinvent the circumstances. So managers in organisations faced by a dynamic and unpredictable environment could seek to change markets and/or products, influence the behaviour of competitors, or change customers' perceptions, in order to reduce uncertainty and increase predictability. By so doing, an organisation could still function efficiently at the more mechanistic end of the mechanistic–organic spectrum, if that was the type of structure preferred by its managers.

This argument would seem equally applicable to the constraints managers face when choosing an approach to strategy. Some managers might prefer an Evolutionary or Processual approach to strategy, either because it suits their own temperament or because they believe that a hostile and turbulent environment suits them better than their competitors (the move by Rupert Murdoch's newspapers in the UK in the 1990s to start a price-cutting war was an example of this). On the other hand, constraints might be manipulated or changed for ideological reasons, such as the attempt by most Western governments to privatise or introduce market forces into the public sector (Burnes, 2009a). The point is that the possibility does exist for managers to choose not only their approach to strategy but also, to an extent at least, the constraints they face.

To choose an approach to strategy is one thing; to apply it is an entirely different matter. As Mintzberg *et al* (1998a, 1998b) observe, whether one takes the view that strategy drives change or that it emerges from the changes an organisation makes, the two are inseparable. Therefore, just as this chapter has reviewed the main arguments with regard to strategy, so the remaining chapters in Part 2 will review the strengths and weaknesses of the main approaches to applying strategy and implementing change.

TEST YOUR LEARNING

The purpose of these is to enable students to check their learning and reflect on the topics covered in this chapter. The discussions should last for no more than 5–10 minutes. Depending on the length of the lecture, there could be one, two or three such discussions in a session. The following are five suggested topics which address issues raised in this chapter:

1. What is long-range planning?

2. What is the Prescriptive school of strategy?

3. What is the Analytical school of strategy?

4. What are the main constraints on organisational choice?

5. Describe the relationship between organisational strategy and organisational change.

Class debates

The purpose of class debates is to enable students to explore a topic in depth by setting up a 'for and against' debate. The class can be split into two and one half asked to research the 'for' case and the other 'against' case. Individuals can then be chosen at random to introduce their side of the debate. Alternatively, two individuals for each side can be told in advance that they will be introducing the debate. The length of such debates depends on the time available, the size of the class and their enthusiasm for the topic. However, less than 30 minutes is probably too short and more than 60 minutes probably too long. The following are three suggested topics which address issues raised in this chapter:

1. Emergent strategy is just a description of poor management.

2. In terms of the merits of the Prescriptive and the Analytical approaches to strategy, it is better to have an approach that gives you some ideas of what to do than one that just tells you what you did.

3. In terms of strategic planning, the problem is not that managers have too little choice but that they are faced with too many choices.

Essay questions

1. Critically evaluate the Emergent approach to strategy and discuss how it could be applied in practice.

2. To what extent and why do you agree with the following statement: Managers should always seek to act in rational manner when developing and implementing strategy.

Suggested further reading

Johnson, G, Whittington, R and Scholes, K (2011) *Exploring Corporate Strategy* (9th edition). Financial Times Prentice Hall: Harlow.

This is the best-selling European textbook on strategy and rightly so.

Mintzberg, H, Ahlstrand, B and Lampel, J (2009) *Strategy Safari* (2nd edition). Pearson: Harlow.

Almost anything with Henry Mintzberg's name on it is worth reading and this book is no exception. It provides a succinct and pertinent review of the main perspectives on strategy.

Whittington, R (2001) *What Is Strategy and Does It Matter?* (2nd edition). Thomson Learning: London.

In this short and eminently readable book, Richard Whittington challenges much of the orthodox thinking on strategy.

CASE STUDY 6

The rise and fall of Marconi[1]

Background

There can be few in the business world who are not aware of the spectacular crash of Marconi, which, in the space of two years, went from a share value of £12.50 to under 2p, a stock market valuation of £35 billion to just a few million pounds, and a profit of £750 million to a loss of some £5.6 billion, one of the biggest in UK corporate history.

Marconi grew out of GEC, the giant industrial conglomerate built by Arnold Weinstock. In a period when the UK's industrial competitiveness, and its base, declined, GEC was one of the UK's leading and most successful industrial enterprises. Weinstock, who died in 2002 at the age of 77, created GEC and was the UK's leading industrialist for over 30 years.

Weinstock had a knack for running businesses profitably where others had failed. This was down to his famously intimidating management style, which produced profits and, in the early years at least, gained him much praise from financial markets. For their time, his methods were revolutionary, at least in the UK. He was legendary for tight control of cash and focus on financial measures. He moved cash out of the separate GEC businesses and held it in the centre. He drove and monitored each business on its financial performance. Budgets became key growth mechanisms that put managers under enormous pressure to deliver on their forecasts. By ruthlessly cutting out overheads, introducing tight financial controls and forcing managers to think intelligently about their businesses, GEC grew in size and increased shareholder value.

Throughout his period in charge, GEC profits grew. Indeed, in 1990–2, when the UK economy was undergoing one of its worst recessions, GEC broke the £1 billion profit barrier. Despite this, however, in the 1990s, GEC and particularly Weinstock became increasingly unpopular with investors in the City of London. Two of the City of London's main ways of making money are to lend it or to charge for their services in mergers and takeovers. GEC's stockpile of cash meant it did not need to borrow money, and Weinstock's insistence that he would not buy companies that were

either overpriced or did not fit into GEC's portfolio appeared to enrage the City money men. There was also a common view in the City that GEC had missed the high-tech boat and that it was stuck in the 'old economy' when the smart money was moving into the 'new economy' (Heller, 2002).

Having passed the age of 70, Weinstock was finally pressured into resigning as GEC's managing director in 1996 and became its president emeritus. Under pressure, he recruited George Simpson as a replacement, but regarded this as an interim measure until his son Simon was ready to take over. Simon Weinstock's sudden death in late 1996 changed these plans and George Simpson became undisputed head of GEC. Simpson had run and sold both Rover and Lucas, was much admired in the City of London, and was considered to have the entrepreneurial qualities needed to reinvigorate GEC.

Whatever criticisms there were of Weinstock in his later years, his legacy was huge. Not only had he built an enormously successful industrial conglomerate in a period when British industry was in decline but also, as Brummer (2002: 1) comments:

> The fact that Britain is still a leading player in the global power industry, and has a world-class research-based defence industry, can largely be attributed to his precocious skills.

The rise of Marconi

Simpson bought into the popular view that GEC needed to get out of the old economy, characterised by its involvement in defence and heavy engineering, and into the new, high-tech world of telecoms and the internet. He believed it also needed to stop being a UK/European company and become a global player. As he later said:

> What else were we going to do? The old GEC had had it and everyone told us that focus was what was needed. Telecoms was the obvious industry to expand into.   (Quoted in M Harrison, 2002: 24)

He began to bring in his own people, notably John Mayo as finance director. Mayo had been an investment banker before moving to Zeneca as Finance Director, from where he was recruited by Simpson. It

---

[1] I am very grateful for the comments and suggestions made by Brian Wolf, a former director of GEC-Marconi.

was Simpson and Mayo who charted GEC's push into the new dotcom economy through a whirlwind series of sales and acquisitions. The crucial period was 1999 to 2001. In 1999, GEC divested itself of its defence business to BAe. This halved the size of GEC and sold off its most consistently profitable elements. To mark this momentous step, GEC was renamed Marconi to signal its intention to become a leading telecoms company, and began a process of acquiring new businesses in the then growing international market for high-capacity telecoms networks. Simpson and Mayo believed, like many more, that the future lay with dotcom companies, and they wanted a big share of it. Not only did they spend the proceeds from selling businesses they did not want and the money that Weinstock bequeathed them but they borrowed over £4 billion as well. In the three years up to the middle of 2001, they sold off almost all of Marconi's non-telecoms business, i.e. the vast majority of the old GEC, and purchased over 20 telecoms businesses, for prices ranging from a few hundred million to a few billion pounds. Mayo stated that:

> The common theme between our [new] core businesses is the ability to securely capture, manage and communicate enormous amounts of data. The 'data wave' is turning into a tidal wave and we have positioned ourselves to ride the wave.
>
> (Quoted in Gow, 1999c: 25)

At another time, the speed of Marconi's transformation into a rapidly growing telecoms equipment provider might have been a cause for concern. But this was taking place at the height of the dotcom bubble. It seemed that everyone wanted to have a slice of the telecoms/internet cake and was not too concerned how much they paid. Rather than worrying the financial markets, Marconi's splurge of buying, selling and borrowing seemed to please them enormously. The share price soared to £12.50 and Marconi was the darling of the financial markets.

The fall of Marconi

Marconi's popularity with the stock market was to prove short-lived. By late 2000, while Simpson and Mayo were still issuing optimistic forecasts of what was to come, other telecoms companies such as Nortel, Alcatel, Nokia and Ericsson began issuing sales and profit warnings as the telecoms recession, and the dotcom collapse, began to bite. Almost to the last,

Marconi denied there were any problems, but in July 2001 it asked for its shares to be suspended ahead of a profits warning, a highly unusual move for a FTSE 100 company.

Though Marconi's profits warning was clearly going to damage the company's standing, the lateness and severity of the warning led to a disastrous fall in the share price, a rapid exit from the Board of senior staff and the virtual destruction of the company. Indeed, such was the concern for the way the Board handled the profits warning that the UK's financial watchdog, the Financial Services Authority (FSA), conducted a lengthy investigation into it, and issued its report in April 2003. The FSA pointed out that the company had a legal obligation to keep the market informed of price-sensitive information in a timely manner, and that in this instance it had not, and had therefore broken the FSA's rules. Treanor and Wray (2003) reconstructed the events leading up to and just after the profits warning:

> Marconi says the first six months of 2001 are unlikely to show an improvement on the previous year's figures.
>
> **12 June** Trading figures show a 10 per cent decline for April and May. No public statement is made.
>
> **21 June** Accounts for April and May show a loss of £180 million, £156 million more than the previous year. No public statement is made.
>
> **26 June** The financial forecast for the six months to September 2001 show a loss of £47 million, as opposed to the £320 million profits that analysts had predicted. The forecast also shows that profits for the year to March 2002 will be £491 million as against the predicted £807 million. The Board disputes these figures and asks for them to be recalculated. No public statement is made.
>
> **28 June** A Board meeting is called for 4 July.
>
> **30 June** The revised financial forecasts are even worse than those presented to the Board on June 26. Full-year profits are projected to be only £272 million, and half-year losses have risen to £121 million. No public statement is made.

4 July	At 7.40 am, Marconi asks for its shares to be suspended pending a meeting of the Board at 4 pm. At 6.41 pm, the Board issues a statement saying that profits are likely to halve, with sales down 15 per cent.
5 July	When the markets open, Marconi's shares fall by nearly 50 per cent. John Mayo tells investors that business will recover in 2002 when the telecom networks 'will be running so hot they'll fall over' and that there will be no change in Marconi's management. Marconi's share price continues to collapse. At 9.40 pm John Mayo resigns.

Two months later, George Simpson also resigned. Both men received substantial payoffs. As a Leader in the *Financial Times* (2003: 20) stated, 'we can only speculate whether more could have been saved had directors been quicker to acknowledge that their headlong rush into telecoms oblivion was flawed'. Regardless of this, the events of June and July meant that, for Marconi, the dotcom bubble had burst with a vengeance. From then on, it was downhill all the way. In May 2002, Marconi announced one of the biggest yearly losses in UK corporate history: some £5.6 billion. Its share price plunged to below 2p, making the company in effect bankrupt and its shares worthless. It then began a long process of trying to stay alive by negotiating with its creditors. In May 2003, Marconi finally agreed a debt restructuring deal with its creditors. In return for writing off over 90 per cent of the approximately £4.5 billion they were owed, Marconi's creditors received 99.5 per cent of the company's equity. The refinanced company would be valued at just over £600 million. The previous shareholders would own just 0.5 per cent, thus reducing the value of their holding to £3 million from £35 billion at its peak, always assuming that anyone would want to buy the shares.

Summary

Simpson and Mayo argued that they were taking GEC through a much-overdue reinvention. However, there is a world of difference between reinventing a company around its core business and spending billions to construct a new one from scratch. What Simpson and Mayo did was to sell off most of what was GEC and to use the money from the sale, and much more besides, to create a new telecoms company that could rival established companies such as Alcatel, Siemens and Lucent. Unfortunately for them, their vision of creating a leading telecoms company came at a time when the dotcom bubble was about to burst. Even taking this into account, they made three classic business mistakes.

First, they bought at the top of the market. In the space of three years they bought some two dozen companies for billions of pounds that very quickly became almost worthless as their markets collapsed. The US company Fore Industries is a prime example of this. Marconi bought the company for £2.8 billion in 1999. In 2002, a financial analyst commented: 'The business has very little value. If Marconi tried to dispose of it, there may even be costs associated with it' (quoted in Hirst, 2002: 1). Marconi was brought low by the combination of massive over-capacity in the industry, a world-wide economic slowdown and the enormous financial drain on telecom operators of paying for third-generation mobile phone licences. This led Marconi's customers, especially its biggest customer, BT, to cut their purchasing of telecoms equipment quickly and savagely. In effect, Marconi's market collapsed.

Second, Simpson and Mayo knew little of the businesses they were buying or the industry they were moving into. Simpson had made his reputation on running, and selling, Rover and Lucas, both firmly established in the 'old economy'. Mayo was an investment banker turned finance director. They were both deal-makers who had never worked in the telecoms industry. As Weinstock commented, 'They knew nothing about the business they were in, and nothing about the businesses they were buying' (quoted in Aris, 2002: 8).

Lastly, they lost financial control of the business. GEC under Weinstock was legendary for its tight financial controls. The corner-stone of these controls was Weinstock's Eight Business Ratios which formed the framework of the monthly reports that had to be submitted to Weinstock by the managing director of each of the GEC businesses. These financial controls were discarded under the new regime with an almost fanatical belief that they constituted old-fashioned thinking. The result was that, as the events of June and July 2001 show, the Marconi Board seemed unaware until the very last minute that the company was in deep financial trouble.

It is difficult to exaggerate the disaster that happened at Marconi. Whatever the criticisms of the old GEC, when Weinstock handed over power in 1996, it was a strong and profitable company. The parts that were

Case study 6 (*continued*)

sold off by Simpson and Mayo still appeared profitable. On the other hand, by 2002, the new Marconi was bankrupt and worthless. When he stepped down, Weinstock was the biggest private investor in GEC, with some 45 million shares valued at over £400 million. At the time of his death in 2002, these were practically worthless. Simpson and Mayo, who were both forced out, received handsome payoffs, and appeared not to accept that they bore any personal responsibility for the Marconi debacle, preferring to cite bad luck, poor timing and other people for the collapse of Marconi (M Harrison, 2002; Hirst, 2002). Hardly surprising, therefore, that Weinstock commented: 'I'd like to string them up from a high tree and let them swing there for a long time' (quoted in Aris, 2002: 8).

Questions

1. Analyse the Marconi case study from both the rational and emergent perspectives on strategy. What does Marconi tell us about these two perspectives?

2. Imagine you are Michael Porter. What advice would you have offered to George Simpson when he took over GEC-Marconi in 1996? How would his advice have changed the fate of Marconi when the dotcom bubble burst in 2000?

3. Imagine you are Henry Mintzberg. What advice would you have offered to George Simpson when he took over GEC-Marconi in 1996? How would his advice have changed the fate of Marconi when the dotcom bubble burst in 2000?

Applying strategy

Models, levels and tools

MINI CASE STUDY 7.1

Strategic management tools

Bain's global 2011 Management Tools & Trends survey

Since launching our first survey of Management Tools & Trends in 1993, we have tracked executives' attitudes and behaviors through a wide range of economic cycles. We watched as managers pulled away from the recession of 1990–91, maneuvered through the speed bumps of 1996, slowed for the painful 2001 recession and slammed into the Great Recession of 2007–09. Familiar patterns are emerging: profound fear that the world has deteriorated forever is followed by increasing optimism that economic challenges strengthened companies' positions and the future will now be brighter.

In 2009, executives expressed deep concerns about the long-term effects of the downturn. Seven out of

10 worried about their ability to meet earnings targets, and growing numbers turned to cost-cutting tools such as downsizing and outsourcing to cope with slowing sales. Today, executives overwhelmingly cite revenue growth as their organizations' most important priority over the next three years – three times more often than any other priority, and six times more often than cost containment. (p. 1)

To determine if [something] is a passing fad or a valued tool to help spur growth, companies often start by testing the waters – beginning with a limited investment. If they're satisfied with the results, then they up the ante. But this approach carries two risks. First, while it's understandable that companies do not want to make major investments before they fully understand how a tool will work, we have found that using tools on a limited basis consistently leads to lower satisfaction, so caution may inadvertently result in failure. The second risk we have found: companies start using a tool because their competitors are using it, or because it's the hot topic in the business press, but if they do not fully understand how and why to use it, the experience ends up in failure. Think of business process reengineering, where we witnessed an inverse relationship between usage and satisfaction rates when it was the hot tool of the 1990s. We witnessed reengineering drop from the tool with the fifth highest satisfaction rate in 1993 all the way to 21st in the late 1990s. It was only after usage rates declined that satisfaction began to improve again. Any time we see high usage but low satisfaction, there is cause for concern. (p. 5)

We ask executives to rate their satisfaction with the tools they use. Strategic planning is the tool with the highest satisfaction rating. Other tools with above-average satisfaction scores include mission and vision statements, total quality management, customer segmentation and strategic alliances. There were clear satisfaction losers. Downsizing, outsourcing and shared services centers – all of which are used to reduce head count – are three of the five tools with below-average satisfaction scores. The other two tools with low satisfaction ratings are knowledge management and social media programs. (p. 7 & 8)

Breaking out tool use by region highlights distinct differences among the top 10 tools.

- In addition to being the heaviest users of social media programs, North American executives use downsizing more frequently than their counterparts elsewhere in the world.
- European firms lead in the use of change management programs.
- Asian companies are top users of knowledge management, a tool companies use to strengthen their organizations by taking full advantage of intellectual assets.
- Latin American firms use more tools than any other region. Their willingness to embrace a wide range of tools reflects their efforts to identify growth opportunities and increase revenues in a vigorous economy. They're the lightest users of downsizing, rapid prototyping and CRM. (p. 10 & 11)

Source: Rigby and Bilodeau (2011).

Bain's global 2007 Management Tools & Trends survey

On the basis of our research to date, we offer four suggestions for the use of tools:

1. Get the facts. Every tool has its own strengths and weaknesses. To succeed, you must understand the effects (and side effects) of each tool, then combine the right tools in the right ways at the right times. Use the research. Talk to other tool users. Don't naïvely accept hyperbole and simplistic solutions.

2. Champion enduring strategies, not fleeting fads. Managers who promote fads undermine employees' confidence that they can create the change that is needed. Executives are better served by championing realistic strategic directions – and viewing the specific tools they use to get there as subordinate to the strategy.

3. Choose the best tools for the job. Managers need a rational system for selecting, implementing and integrating the tools that are appropriate for their companies. A tool will improve results only to the extent that it helps discover unmet customer needs, helps build distinctive capabilities and helps exploit the vulnerabilities of competitors – or a combination of all three.

4. Adapt tools to your business system (not vice versa). No tool comes with prepackaged instructions and a guarantee. Every tool must be adapted to a company's particular circumstance.

Source: Rigby and Bilodeau (2007: 7).

Introduction

This chapter begins where the previous one ended. Chapter 6 reviewed the main perspectives on strategy. In seeking to understand and define strategy formulation, it identified two streams of thought: the Prescriptive and the Analytical. As the name implies, the Prescriptive stream comprises approaches that seek to 'prescribe' how organisations should undertake strategy but, in so doing, tends to ignore or downplay the irrational and highly convoluted nature of organisational life. The Analytical stream, rather than telling organisations how they should build strategy, seeks to analyse – to understand and describe – the complexity and range of forces that affect how organisations actually do build strategy. This divergence is reflected in their respective views of strategy.

The Prescriptive stream, which was the first on the scene and is very much practitioner-orientated, sees strategy formulation as an economic–rational process based on mathematical models. The Analytical stream, which began to appear in the 1970s, represents the more reflexive and more academically orientated face of strategy. It views strategy not as a process, but as an outcome of a process. Its proponents' emphasis is not on the construction of detailed plans, which in any case they believe to be an unworkable approach, but on the organisational, social and political aspects of strategy formulation. The two streams represent markedly different perspectives on strategy formulation, and while the Analytical stream has tended to win the academic arguments over the last 20 years, the Prescriptive one has had considerably more impact and influence on the practice of strategy.

That said, as the surveys of Management Tools & Trends by Bain & Company (Mini Case Study 7.1) show, while quantitative tools, such as strategic planning, are as popular as ever, more qualitative ones, especially mission and vision statements, are now being used alongside them. It is also the case that nine out of ten respondents also rated culture as important as strategy for business success (Rigby and Bilodeau, 2007 and 2011). This shows that while the arguments of the Analytical stream may not have displaced those of the Prescriptive stream, they are being listened to and are having an effect on the choice of tools organisations use to develop their strategies.

The aim of this chapter is to examine how organisations apply strategic planning concepts and theories and the tools they use to do so. It begins by examining the three most popular types or models of strategy that organisations adopt: the Competitive Forces model; the Resource-Based View; and the Strategic Conflict model. The chapter then moves on to look at the three levels of strategic decision-making in organisations: corporate, business and functional. This is followed by a review of the main strategic planning tools.

The chapter ends by arguing that one of the principal reasons for the dominance of prescriptive approaches to strategy has been the alliance between leading consultancies and business schools in America to develop, market and update these. In so doing, the Prescriptive school has established itself as the orthodox, safe and practical approach to strategy formulation. However, with the take-up of more analytically based types of strategy, this is beginning to change. As Chapter 6 maintained, the model or type of strategy an organisation should adopt, and the associated planning tools that accompany it, are dependent upon the constraints the organisation faces. Alternatively, organisations can choose to seek to influence or mould the constraints they face in order to make them more amenable to the type or model of strategy they wish to pursue. So the approach to strategy an organisation adopts may have less to do with the merits of the different models on offer and more to do with the type of organisation it is and the orientation of its managers.

Types of strategy

As the previous chapter explained, there is a wide, and often confusing, variety of approaches to strategy development that organisations can adopt. It follows that the same comment can be made with regard to the types of strategy that organisations do actually adopt in order to achieve competitive advantage over their rivals (De Wit and Meyer, 2010; Johnson *et al*, 2011). However, in practice, there are only three basic types or models of strategy that organisations do adopt: the Competitive Forces model, the Resource-Based View and the Strategic Conflict model, with the first two being the most popular (Campbell *et al*, 2012; Lockett *et al*, 2009; McNeilly, 2012; Mintzberg *et al*, 2009; Teece *et al*, 1997).

The Competitive Forces model

This stems from the Positioning school and, since its inception in the 1980s, has become the dominant approach to strategy (Johnson *et al*, 2011). Its purpose is to relate a company's strategy to the products it makes and the markets is sells them in. The central tenet of this approach is the need to align the organisation with its environment, the key aspect of which is the industry or industries in which it competes. Proponents of this view believe that industry structure strongly influences the competitive rules of the game as well as the range of strategies open to the organisation. This model is most closely associated with the work of Michael Porter (1980, 1985) and his 'five forces' framework (*see* Figure 7.1).

According to Porter, it is these five industry-level competitive forces, the bargaining power of buyers and sellers, the threat of potential substitute products and new entrants,

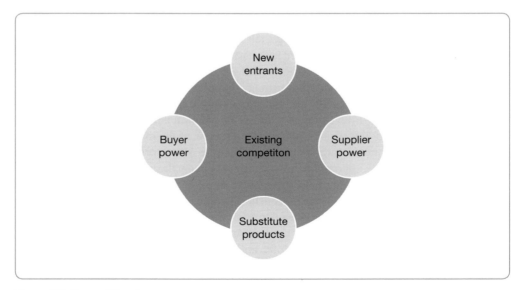

Figure 7.1 Competitive forces
Source: Based on Porter (1980).

and rivalry among existing competitors, that determine the inherent profit potential of an industry. Consequently, he argues, these are the main factors which an organisation needs to take into account when developing its strategy. For Porter (1985: 47), strategy is concerned with 'positioning a business to maximize the value of the capabilities that distinguish it from its competitors'. Porter (1980) maintains that there are only three basic generic strategies a firm can adopt in order to outperform competitors: *cost leadership, product differentiation* and *specialisation by focus* (these are discussed in more detail below). Porter believes that a firm's ability to increase its profits is dependent on its ability to influence the competitive forces in the industry or to change its market position in relation to competitors and suppliers. This approach obviously has links to Contingency Theory (*see* Chapter 2), given that it is based on a systematic empirical search for relationships between external conditions and internal strategies. In addition, because of its focus on the importance of sector and industry factors, it has an affinity with Child and Smith's (1987) firm-in-sector perspective discussed in Chapter 6.

There is little doubt that the Positioning school in general, and Porter's work in particular, has had a huge influence on the practice of strategy within organisations (Campbell *et al*, 2012; Hussey and Jenster, 1999; Johnson *et al*, 2011). As one would expect, it has also attracted considerable criticism (Huggins and Izushi, 2011). One of the most serious is that the choice of forces in the model appears to be arbitrary and without justification; nor is there any indication as to how to assess the relative power of the forces or how they interact (O'Shaughnessy, 1984; Speed, 1996). In terms of more specific charges, Miller (1992) criticises the model as too narrow and inflexible, and thus likely to leave organisations vulnerable if social, technological or economic developments lead, as can happen, to rapid changes in the marketplace. Ghemawat (2008) argues that rather than organisations focusing on a single variable, such as cost or differentiation, they need to be able to be competitive on a range of variables. Mintzberg *et al* (2009) believe that the Positioning school's assumption of rationality ignores the political nature of organisations; that it is biased towards big business, where market power is greatest, and therefore has little to say to small and medium-sized enterprises; and that its dependence on analysis and calculation impedes both learning and creativity. For Fleisher and Bensoussan (2003), the key weaknesses of Porter's approach are its lack of explicit recognition of the importance of socio-political factors, its lack of a longitudinal focus and that it underestimates the importance of core competences.

A further and telling criticism is that the big competitive battles of the last 40 years, especially between Japanese and American firms, tend not to have been won by those who have identified and defended their market position, such as General Motors and Xerox, but by those, such as Toyota and Cannon, who have used their unique resources to change the rules of the game itself (Acedo *et al*, 2006; Armstrong and Shimizu, 2007; Furrer *et al*, 2008; Lockett *et al*, 2009; Hamel and Prahalad, 1989, 1994; Newbert, 2007; Peteraf, 1993). For these reasons, the last decade has seen a growing interest in both the Resource-Based and Strategic Conflict models of strategy.

The Resource-Based View

Lockett *et al* (2009: 9) claim that 'Over the last 20 years, the Resource-Based View (RBV) has reached a pre-eminent position among theories in the field of strategy, but debate continues as to its precise nature'. The focus of the Resource-Based View of competitive advantage is on the relationship between an organisation's resources and its performance (Furrer *et al*, 2008; Newbert, 2007; Peteraf, 1993). The Resource-Based View argues that a firm's ability to achieve above-average profitability, by having lower costs or better products, depends on achieving a strategic position based on the deployment of superior or unique resources, rather than from tactical manoeuvring or product market positioning (Acedo *et al*, 2006; Fahy, 2000). Such resources include tangible assets, such as plant and equipment; intangible assets, such as patents and brands; and capabilities, such as the skills, knowledge and aptitudes of individuals and groups, (Amit and Schoemaker, 1993; Hall, 1993; Lockett *et al*, 2009; Wernerfelt, 1995). Resources such as these are not free-standing assets that a firm can obtain or dispose of easily or quickly, but are deeply embedded in an organisation's processes and as such are very difficult for others to replicate (Ordanini and Rubera, 2008; Peteraf, 1993).

The Resource-Based View grew from the work of economists who, in seeking to identify the factors which gave rise to imperfect competition and super-normal profits, drew attention to differences between firms in terms of technical know-how, patents, trademarks, brand awareness and managerial ability (Chamberlin, 1933; Learned *et al*, 1965; Penrose, 1959; Wernerfelt, 1984). Consequently, proponents of the Resource-Based View see firms as being heterogeneous in respect of their resources, i.e. no two firms possess exactly the same combination of these. In relation to strategic management, this view really came to the fore in the 1980s and 1990s initially through the work of Wernerfelt (1984), who asserted that an organisation's competitiveness stemmed from the possession and ability to exploit resources, but it attracted attention mainly as an explanation for the rise of corporate Japan.

It was out of research into the competitiveness of Japanese firms that Prahalad and Hamel (1990) produced their seminal article 'The core competence of the corporation'. In it, they argue that real competitive advantage comes from the ability to build, at lower cost and more speedily than competitors, those core competences that spawn unanticipated products. They also argue that senior managers should spend a significant proportion of their time developing a corporation-wide architecture for establishing objectives for competence-building. The influential study of the car industry by Womack *et al* (1990), *The Machine that Changed the World*, came to a similar view of Japanese competitiveness. Support for this perspective has also come from a number of studies of Western firms. Cool and Schendel (1988) show that there are systematic and significant performance differences among firms in the same industry sectors. Rumelt (1991) shows that intra-industry profit differentials are greater than inter-industry differentials. Kay's (1993) work on strategy also comes to the conclusion that an organisation's success comes from developing distinctive capabilities.

Hax and Majluf (1996: 10) state:

> The essence of the resource-based model . . . [is] that competitive advantage is created when resources and capabilities that are owned exclusively by the firm are applied to developing unique competencies. Moreover, the resulting advantage can be sustained due to the lack of substitution and imitation capabilities by the firm's competitors.

The influence of the Resource-Based View has grown considerably over the last two decades (Fahy, 2000; Ordanini and Rubera, 2008). It is now the received wisdom that organisations should, in Peters and Waterman's (1982) phrase, 'stick to the knitting' and discard activities that are not part of their core business and which do not build on their core competences (Hax and Majluf, 1996; Newbert, 2007; Peteraf, 1993). Studies of the effectiveness of the Resource-Based View provide evidence which strongly challenges the view of Porter and earlier writers on strategy that competitive advantage arises mainly from environmental factors (Data Systems International, 2007). Instead, the Resource-Based View maintains that the possession of valuable, rare, inimitable and non-substitutable resources may result in sustained superior performance (Acedo *et al*, 2006; Armstrong and Shimizu, 2007; Furrer *et al*, 2008; Lockett *et al*, 2009; Newbert, 2007).

Even so, there are criticisms which have been raised against this view of strategy, including the lack of empirical support, that it has no managerial implications, complex and ambiguous definitions of resources, and that it is merely a rehash of the SWOT analysis (Fleisher and Bensoussan, 2003; Kraaijenbrink *et al*, 2010). A further criticism is that the concept of what constitutes a valuable resource is based on a tautology. As Priem and Butler (2001) note, the main method for identifying a valuable resource is that it already has value. In addition, because resources cannot easily or quickly be acquired or developed, in the short run firms are stuck with the ones they possess. Consequently, depending on the circumstances, and how they change, these firm-specific assets can be either a boon or a curse. Perhaps the main criticism of this approach comes from population ecologists who argue that, because these competences take so long to develop and environments change so quickly, any beneficial match between an organisation's competences and its environment is likely to be accidental or fortuitous rather than the result of deliberate or foresightful actions by managers (Barney, 2002; Hannan and Freeman, 1988; Lockett *et al*, 2009). This is perhaps why there has also been a growing interest in the Strategic Conflict model, which draws attention to the dynamic nature of organisational strategy.

The Strategic Conflict model

This model harks back to the military metaphor, and portrays competition as war between rival firms. In particular, there is a tendency to draw on the work of military strategists such as von Clausewitz (von Clausewitz *et al*, 2001) and Sun Tzu (Michaelson, 2001) and attempt to apply their military aphorisms to modern business organisations (Mintzberg *et al*, 2009). Sayings such as, 'No battle plan ever survived the first encounter with the enemy' are used to illustrate not just the dynamic nature of strategy but also the need to respond to competitors who do not always behave as anticipated. In its current manifestation, it came to prominence with the publication of Carl Shapiro's (1989) article 'The theory of business strategy'. Central to this approach is the view that a firm can achieve increased profits by influencing the actions and behaviour of its rivals and thus, in effect, manipulate the market environment. This can be done in a number of ways, such as by investment in capacity (Dixit, 1980), R&D (Gilbert and Newbery, 1982) and advertising (Schmalensee, 1983). However, such moves will have little impact if they can be easily undone; to be effective, they require irreversible commitment.

Furthermore, it is argued, these various manoeuvres are crucially dependent on what one firm thinks another firm will do in a particular situation. Therefore, the model incorporates the role of strategic signalling as an important mechanism for influencing or intimidating rivals. This includes such practices as predatory pricing (Kreps and Wilson, 1982) and limit pricing (Milgrom and Roberts, 1982). In addition, the model has come to embrace issues relating to the role of commitment and reputation (Ghemawat, 1991) and the simultaneous use of competition and cooperation (Brandenburger and Nalebuff, 1996).

So from the Strategic Conflict perspective, an organisation's ability to increase its profits is dependent on its ability to outwit, out-bluff and out-manoeuvre its rivals. This approach also draws on game theory to understand the nature of competitive interaction between rival firms. Game theory has allowed established intuitive arguments concerning various types of business tactics and strategy (e.g. predatory pricing) to be explained and formalised. In terms of the Prescriptive and Analytical streams of strategy, although Porter (1980) acknowledges the benefits of strategic manoeuvring, it does not fit in with his or the rest of the Positioning school's work. Instead, its emphasis on quick-wittedness, gut instinct and the more emotional elements of decision-making means it sits better with the Analytical stream.

Given that conflict-based strategies do not take account of the wide range of external and internal factors which also contributes to an organisation's competitiveness, its usefulness may well be limited. As Teece *et al* (1997) note, strategic conflict is likely to be more appropriate in situations where there is an even balance between rivals in an industry (e.g. Coca-Cola and Pepsi) rather than in situations where one organisation has a substantial competitive advantage over its rivals (e.g. Microsoft). In these latter situations, it is perhaps the Resource-Based View of strategy that is of most interest.

These three types or models of strategy are all currently fashionable, though Porter's Completive Forces model and the Resource-Based View tend to be more dominant. They are, however, very different in their emphasis and timescales:

- The Strategic Conflict model is outward-facing and very much about out-manoeuvring the opposition. It tends to have a short-term focus, although a number of its tactics do have longer-term implications.

- The Competitive Forces model is also outward-facing but is concerned with identifying and occupying a defensible market position, and thereby achieving higher profits than others in the industry. This tends to have a medium-term focus.

- The Resource-Based View is the only one which has an internal focus; it also has a much longer-term focus than either of the other two. Its proponents believe that organisations need to build strategic competences that, almost through a process of serendipity, will allow it to meet future and unanticipated market needs.

There are, of course, as Mintzberg *et al* (2009) and others have shown, many more strategies than these three. The popularity of these three tends to emphasise the point made by a number of writers that many managers tend to have a preferred approach to strategy which they stick to regardless (or perhaps because) of the fact that it tends to narrow their perspective and limit their options (Khalifa, 2008; Hambrick and Frederickson, 2001; Mintzberg and Lampel, 1999). Nevertheless, just because managers have preferred approaches to strategy, and just because the proponents of particular strategies put theirs forward as the 'one best way', that does not prevent organisations from drawing on a combination of strategies which can be deployed as the circumstances warrant.

In 2007, a very bitter and public row broke out between the satellite broadcaster BSkyB and the cable company Virgin Media (*see* Mini Case Study 7.2). The flashpoint for the battle between the two companies was BSkyB's steep increase in the price it charged Virgin Media to carry its channels. However, underlying this was Virgin Media's manoeuvring to challenge BSkyB's dominance on the UK satellite market, and the latter's attempt to maintain its position. Therefore, on the surface, this appears to be a prime example of the Strategic

MINI CASE STUDY 7.2

Row between Virgin and Sky is reignited

Virgin Media and British Sky Broadcasting traded more accusations as an exchange of letters between the two rivals' chief executives prompted claims on both sides of bad faith and negotiation through the media. The long-running argument about the price Virgin Media pays to carry channels such as Sky One and Sky News flared again yesterday, after the satellite group released letters claiming that its cable rival had rejected a compromise offer.

Sky shows such as Lost and 24 have not been aired on Virgin Media's rebranded service since February 28 after the cable group refused to meet BSkyB's demand for an increase in its carriage fees. The two sides have since disputed each other's claims on the prices demanded and offered.

Yesterday, BSkyB released a letter sent on May 10 by James Murdoch, its chief executive, to Steve Burch, his opposite number at Virgin Media. Mr Murdoch offered to split what he claimed was a £10 million difference between the offers made by the two companies in February. Virgin Media disputed

the figures as it released Mr Burch's response, faxed to BSkyB on May 17. Mr Burch said he was 'fully prepared to negotiate' but claimed the new proposal would simply reduce 'an excessive and anti-competitive price' by 15 per cent. The fax also highlighted a shift in the cable group's negotiating position, arguing that any new offer should reflect 'the damage inflicted on Virgin Media' by the loss of the channels. 'Most of the damage has been to the Virgin Media customers who continue to pay for something they no longer get,' BSkyB said.

Mr Burch had given 'no indication of the terms he would be prepared to accept', added Jeremy Darroch, BSkyB finance director.

In a second letter, sent yesterday, Mr Murdoch claimed BSkyB had 'no choice' but to publish the correspondence, citing 'consumer interest' in the issue and highlighting Virgin Media's own use of the media in the dispute. Virgin Media accused its rival of 'a crude attempt to exert undue pressure by putting negotiations under the public spotlight'.

Source: Row between Virgin and Sky is reignited, *The Financial Times*, 19/05/2007, p. 14 (Edgecliffe-Johnson A.),
© The Financial Times Limited (2007). All Rights Reserved.

Conflict model in action. Both organisations are seeking to gain an advantage over the other through, in this case, some very public tactics. It also has to be remembered that BSkyB is part of Rupert Murdoch's News International empire and that Virgin Media is part of Richard Branson's Virgin empire, and that both men have form as corporate warriors. In Murdoch's case, a good example is his long-running battles with his UK newspaper rivals. In Branson's case, the prime example is the long-running battle between his Virgin Atlantic and British Airways.

Therefore, both Murdoch and Branson appear to give support to the case for the Strategic Conflict model. However, it also needs to be acknowledged that both men have built their empires on strong brands – in Branson's case, it is Virgin; in Murdoch's case, it is newspapers such as the *Times* and *Sun* and broadcasters such as BSkyB. The possession and development of strong brands is a key element of the Resource-Based View of strategy. Beyond that, of course, both men have sought to achieve strong positions in their market by, in Murdoch's case, being the lowest-cost producer, or in Branson's case the use of product/service differentiation or specialisation by focus. Consequently, they can be seen to offer support for the Competitive Forces model. This illustrates clearly that successful organisations such as Virgin and News International rarely limit themselves to one approach to strategy. They tend to be pragmatists – using the approach which offers the best chance of success in their particular circumstance. Sometimes this will be to battle it out with their rivals, sometimes it will be to achieve a particular market position by differentiation, focus or low cost, but in pursuing these strategies they are unlikely to forget the need to develop unique resources which their rivals cannot copy.

The key points to remember are that all types of strategies have weaknesses as well as strengths, and that while they are applicable to some situations, there will be many others where their applicability will be limited. Therefore, as Coyne and Subramaniam (1996) maintain, and Murdoch and Branson have demonstrated, managers need to be familiar with the available range of strategic approaches and tools, and use the ones best suited to their circumstances. Sometimes they might engage in strategic conflict; sometimes they might concentrate on their market position and at other times on resource-building. Consequently, rather than being viewed as mutually exclusive, the three approaches to strategy discussed in this section might be seen as complementary.

Levels of strategy

It is easier to see how the three types of strategy above are applied in practice by examining the three levels of strategic decision-making in organisations: corporate, business and functional/operational (Johnson *et al*, 2011 (*see* Ideas and perspectives 7.1)).

Each of these three levels has its own distinct strategic concerns and each can draw on a different battery of strategic tools, techniques and approaches to aid them, but it is important to remember that they are interrelated. Traditionally, it has been assumed that the corporate level sets the direction for each of its constituent businesses and, in turn, these set the direction for their various functions. Though this is true for some organisations, it is now recognised that these three levels interact in an iterative and dynamic fashion (Johnson *et al*, 2011; Lynch, 2006). Just as business-level and functional-level strategy can be seen as being imposed or driven by corporate-level decisions, so corporate-level strategy can be seen as emerging from, or being shaped by, functional-level and business-level decisions and actions (Mintzberg, 1994). It follows that although there are strategies at the corporate level that have their counterparts at the business and the functional levels, it would be wrong to assume that this is always a product of a top-down rather than a bottom-up process.

IDEAS AND PERSPECTIVES 7.1

Levels of strategic decision-making

- **The corporate level**. Strategy at this level concerns the direction, composition and coordination of the various businesses and activities that comprise a large and diversified organisation, such as Rupert Murdoch's News International or Richard Branson's Virgin empire.

- **The business level**. Strategy at this level relates to the operation and direction of each of the individual businesses within a group of companies, such as Nissan's car assembly plant at Sunderland.

- **The functional/operational level**. Strategy at this level concerns individual business functions and processes such as finance, marketing, manufacturing, technology and human resources.

IDEAS AND PERSPECTIVES 7.2

Strategic questions

Corporate strategy is concerned with questions such as:

- What is the mission of the organisation?
- What are its unique attributes?
- How should the business portfolio be managed?
- Which existing businesses should be disposed of and which new ones acquired?
- What priority and role should be given to each of the businesses in the current portfolio?

The central strategic concerns at the individual business level are:

- How should the firm position itself to compete in distinct, identifiable and strategically relevant markets?
- Which types of products should it offer to which groups of customers?
- How should the firm structure and manage the internal aspects of the business in support of its chosen competitive approach?

Functional-level strategy concerns itself with the following issues:

- How can the strategies formulated at the corporate and business levels be translated into concrete operational terms in such a way that the individual organisational functions and processes (marketing, R&D, manufacturing, personnel, finance, etc.) can pursue and achieve them?
- How should the individual functions and processes of the business organise themselves in order not only to achieve their own aims but also to ensure that they integrate with the rest of the business to create synergy?

When running a diversified enterprise whose activities cut across a number of different areas of business, there is a tendency for senior managers to focus on corporate-level strategy, what Fleisher and Bensoussan (2003) refer to as the corporate 'game plan', and ignore or consider less strategic the concerns of the individual businesses and the functions within them. However, as Ideas and perspectives 7.2 shows, each level of an organisation has its own strategic concerns.

Given the different concerns of these three levels, it becomes easier to appreciate the need to integrate the strategies and structures at all three levels. Otherwise, for example, the corporate level may pursue a strategy of diversification while the individual businesses are busy concentrating their efforts on fewer products and markets. It is also easy to appreciate why in practice it is so difficult for large diversified organisations to identify and pursue a consistent strategy through all areas of their activities (Joyce and Woods, 2001; Lynch, 2006). As argued in the last chapter, strategy formulation and implementation is not a mechanical process that begins at the corporate level and moves in a linear and logical fashion through to the functional level. Strategy formulation is inherently iterative, and aims to optimise the operation of the organisation in its entirety rather than maximising the product of any one particular part. These issues, and the main differences in scope and focus of the individual levels, can clearly be seen by a brief examination of the types of strategy that are pursued at the corporate, business and functional levels.

Corporate-level strategy

Large corporations by their nature tend to comprise a wide range of businesses operating increasingly on a global basis and offering a diverse range of products and services. The purpose of corporate strategy is to decide on the composition of such organisations and their overall direction. As Mini Case Study 7.3 shows, even well-established and well-resourced companies such as Philips find this a very difficult job.

Broadly speaking, there are six basic forms of strategy that organisations pursue at the corporate level.

Stability strategy

Also known as maintenance strategy, as its name implies, strategies under this heading are designed to keep organisations quiet and stable. They are most frequently found in successful organisations, operating in medium-attractiveness industries, which are faced with unpredictable circumstances outside the range of their normal business experience.

MINI CASE STUDY 7.3

Stewardship of a sprawling empire

If Philips did not exist, it is unlikely anyone would invent it. The great survivor of European industry has weathered innumerable crises and restructurings in the past quarter of a century, and its battered history shows up in the diverse range of operations that comes under its stewardship. In spite of this, the Dutch electronics business that makes products from coffee machines to medical scanners has entered a calmer period, which is in no small part down to Gerard Kleisterlee, its chief executive since 2001. Yet the challenges he still faces underline the difficulty of bringing order to a sprawling collection of businesses with a long and illustrious past.

Under Mr Kleisterlee, the 114-year-old company has closed down underperforming factories and some surplus operations. Operating profit trebled last year to €1.6 billion (£1.08 billion) on sales of €30.3 billion and, with steady progress during 2005, Mr Kleisterlee says the company is on course to hit its target of operating margins of 7 to 10 per cent by 2007. But Mr Kleisterlee still has to convince onlookers that he can knit together Philips' operations into a rational business capable of steady performance across all its divisions. One possible strategy is to sell off two of the company's five business groups – semi-conductors and consumer electronics – even though these represent a considerable part of its heritage. That would leave Philips with three main divisions – medical equipment; lighting; and small electric appliances, such as shavers – in each of which the company appears capable of generating reasonable profits over the next decade. While Mr Kleisterlee gives few hints that he may want to do this in the near future, many see such a strategy as being high on his list of options.

'You must credit Mr Kleisterlee with making Philips a smoother running company', says Janardan Menon, an analyst at Dresdner Kleinwort Wasserstein. 'But Philips still comprises a bunch of parts that seem to have little link with each other. Mr Kleisterlee has got to show he has a vision for what to do with them.'

The chief executive of a large US capital goods company, who has followed Philips' progress for more than 20 years, is somewhat more unkind. 'They have had their ass kicked so many times I have lost count. But in spite of all the restructurings, they are still stuck with high-volume, low-margin businesses that they would be better off out of.'

 Source: Stewardship of a sprawling empire, *The Financial Times*, 18/11/2005, p. 13 (Bickerton I. and Marsh P.), © *The Financial Times Limited* (2005). All Rights Reserved.

Because of their markets and products, such organisations believe they have no need to make sudden changes and have the time and position to allow events to unfold before making any response (Meier *et al*, 2010; Wheelen and Hunger, 1989).

Miles and Snow's (1978) 'Defenders' would fall into this category (see Ideas and perspectives 7.3). A typical example would be an established mortgage lender whose business would both necessitate and allow it to take a longer-term perspective.

Growth strategy

This is possibly the most common form of all corporate strategies, and involves either concentrating on dominating one industry (e.g. Intel) or growing by diversification across a number of industries (e.g. Virgin). As a number of writers have suggested (*see* Argenti, 1974; Byars, 1984; Cunill, 2009), its basic attraction is twofold. First, it is claimed that there is a strong and proportional correlation between increased turnover and increased profit. Second, the performance of senior managers tends to be measured in terms of the annual increase in turnover and profit.

However, there are those who point out that increases in turnover are not necessarily matched by increases in profits and that, given the need to invest to achieve growth in turnover, growth may actually weaken a company's financial health (Byars, 1984; Drucker, 1974; Soirinsuo and Mäkinen, 2011).

Portfolio extension

This is another variant of the growth strategy, but is achieved through mergers, joint ventures or acquisitions, rather than through internally generated organic growth (Byars, 1984; Faulkner *et al*, 2012; Little, 1984; Leontiades, 1986. The first two of these, mergers and joint ventures, allow growth or development to take place, without the organisations involved having to invest the level of resources that would be necessary if they were operating in isolation. The third variant, acquisition, is usually resource-intensive but brings immediate gains in the form of an established and, hopefully, profitable business.

Retrenchment strategy

This strategy is usually embarked upon only when an organisation is in trouble or, because of adverse market conditions, sees trouble ahead. It usually involves a process of downsizing, i.e. cutting back on numbers employed and activities undertaken, or even selling off the entire enterprise. The general aim is to cut back in order to match expenditure to projected income, and refocus the organisation so as to be able once again to attain prosperity in the future (Bowman and Asch, 1985; Schoenberg *et al*, 2013; Thompson and Strickland, 1983). In the wake of the 2008 credit crunch, most financial service companies appear to have pursued a retrenchment strategy.

Harvesting strategy

This involves reducing investment in a business or area of activity in order to reduce costs, improve cash flow and capitalise on whatever residual competences or areas of advantage still remain. This approach can be implemented at different rates depending on the urgency of the situation. Slow harvesting means to reduce financial support at such a slow rate that it almost appears to be a maintenance strategy; at the other extreme, fast harvesting can result in budgets being cut at such a rate that it seems almost indistinguishable from liquidation (Harrigan, 1980; Johnson *et al*, 2011; Kotler, 1978; Porter, 1980).

Combination strategy

The above strategies are not mutually exclusive, and can be linked together in whatever combination seems appropriate given the circumstances of the organisation in question. Combination strategies are clearly more appropriate, or at least more necessary, in large multi-divisional organisations where the circumstances faced by the different activities are likely to vary. In such situations, organisations may experience a constant flurry of change, where some parts are being run down and/or disposed of while new units are being acquired and other areas of the business rapidly expanded (Glueck, 1978; Leitner and Güldenberg, 2010; Pearson, 1977).

The above list is not exhaustive, nor can it be, given that each organisation is free to develop its own strategic variant in relation to its own circumstances. As argued in Chapter 6, it is the circumstances of the particular organisation in question that should dictate the type of strategy adopted by its managers, rather than any attempt to copy what has been successful elsewhere. Though Porter's Competitive Forces model can be applicable to all these forms of strategy, the Strategic Conflict and Resource-Based View appear to be more applicable to situations where growth is being pursued or where companies have a strong market position. Yet it needs to be remembered that it is the precepts and assumptions of Porter and the Positioning school which still dominate the practice of strategy. A further point to note is that all except the first, stability strategy, imply fundamental restructuring of the internal operations of the organisation. In such situations, there are likely to be winners and losers, and managers may be more concerned with preserving their jobs and power than choosing the best strategy for the organisation (Mintzberg, 2009).

The importance of an appropriate and effective corporate strategy has been demonstrated by many businesses (Johnson *et al*, 2011). Nevertheless, in the 1980s and 1990s, in both America and Europe, there was a backlash against corporate strategy, or rather against the large corporate centres responsible for developing corporate strategy and which wielded so much power in the 1970s and 1980s (Kanter *et al*, 1992; Peters and Waterman, 1992). The case against them is summed up by Koch (1995: 78), who maintains that:

> Anything other than a minimal [corporate] Centre can only be justified if the Centre adds more value than it costs and subtracts from the business. . . . Yet it should be clear that . . . independent of their cost, most corporate Centres destroy more value than they add.

This negative view of corporate strategy has, perhaps, been most vociferously championed by Peters and Waterman (1982), but has also received strong support from academic researchers (Goold *et al*, 1994). The result of this is that there has been an increasing recognition that strategists at the corporate level need to allow space within their corporate strategies for business units to develop their strategies (Johnson *et al*, 2011).

Business-level strategy

While corporate-level strategies are mainly concerned with managing diversified enterprises whose activities span a number of different areas, business-level strategies relate to the different ways that an individual business unit can compete in its chosen market(s). This does not mean that the strategies are necessarily determined by the individual businesses; they may be set at the corporate level. For example, Marks and Spencer comprises a range of different businesses – clothing, food, furniture, financial services, etc. The strategies for each of these businesses are set at corporate level and not the level of the individual business, though the responsibility for enacting the strategy lies at the business level.

Therefore, it must be remembered that business-level strategies are chosen and deployed within the framework of an overall corporate strategy and not in isolation from it, though the degree of freedom allowed to individual business units in this respect will vary from organisation to organisation (Johnson *et al*, 2011). To this end, the strategic concerns of managers at the business level tend to be, according to Hax and Majluf (1996: 46):

> the mission of the business, the attractiveness of the industry in which the business belongs, and the competitive position of the business unit within the industry. These are the inputs that determine the strategic agenda of a business and lead to the formulation and implementation of its strategy.

As was the case at the corporate level, the strategies available at the business level are many and varied. Rather than attempt to describe them all, we shall examine the main variants by addressing Porter's (1980, 1985) work in this area.

As mentioned earlier, Porter (1985: 11) argues that there are only two basic types of competitive advantage a firm can possess: low cost or differentiation. He adds to these the 'scope' of the business (i.e. the range of its markets) to create 'three generic strategies for achieving above average performance': cost leadership, product differentiation and specialisation by focus. As Figure 7.2 shows, the first two of these are strategies for achieving competitive advantage across an entire industry while the third, specialisation by focus, relates to achieving competitive advantage in a particular segment of an industry only.

Cost leadership

The aim of this strategy is to achieve overall lower costs than one's competitors, without reducing comparable product quality. To do this requires a high volume of sales in order to allow organisations to structure themselves in such a way that they can achieve economies of scale. In the UK, the epitome of this strategy is the supermarket Tesco, which takes £1 in every £7 spent on the high street (*Observer*, 2008). With a market share twice that of its nearest rival, its sales volumes allow it to strike better deals with suppliers and offer customers lower prices while still maintaining better margins than its rivals. To achieve such a competitive advantage, as Porter (1980: 15) states, requires:

> [the] aggressive construction of efficient scale facilities, vigorous pursuit of cost reductions from experience, tight cost and overhead control, avoidance of marginal customer accounts, and cost minimization in areas like R&D, services, sales force and so on.

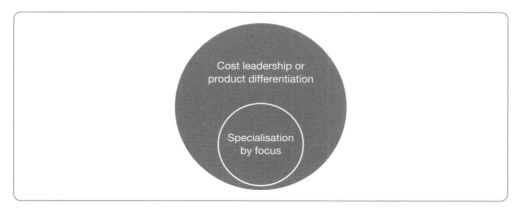

Figure 7.2 Generic strategies

Product differentiation

This strategy attempts to achieve industry-wide recognition of different and superior products and services compared to those of other suppliers. This recognition can be accomplished through the design of special brand images, technology features, customer service or higher quality, all of which have implications for the structure and operation of companies. Achieving differentiation is likely to result in insulation against competitive rivalry due to securing customer loyalty. The resultant competitive advantage also leads to increased returns, sometimes through making customers less sensitive to high product price. Perhaps the pre-eminent example of product differentiation is Apple Computers, which has always had the most loyal, not to say fanatical, customers. There are hundreds, if not thousands, of computers on the market but there has only ever been one Mac – nobody else does anything like it. There are many, many MP3 players, but the iPod is the player of choice for the discerning, fashion-conscious consumer. Similarly, there are many smart phones, but only one iPhone. Apple differentiates itself by its products, but, as Mini Case Study 7.4 demonstrates,

MINI CASE STUDY 7.4

Apple invites consumers to take a bite of its core philosophy

Tim Cook last week attempted to settle the argument about whether Apple can still innovate, unveiling not only new products but a new manifesto for how he will lead the iPhone maker.

At its annual Worldwide Developer Conference in San Francisco, Mr Cook, Apple's chief executive, showcased new Macs, a new internet radio service and a radical redesign of iOS, the software that powers the iPhone and iPad. But at the beginning and end of the two-hour presentation, Apple showed two short films that Mr Cook said explained "the values we live by". "We spend a lot of time on a few great things," one ad's voiceover says, over slow-motion images of schoolchildren using iPads, young lovers shooting selfies with iPhones and grandparents watching a MacBook slideshow. "Designing something requires focus," says the other video, a minimal, black-and-white animation that opened the event. "There are a thousand no's for every yes." Each ends with a slogan that the ads liken to an artist's signature: "Designed by Apple in California".

The ads mark a break with the past but also an attempt to tap into Apple's history. The values they convey – such as focusing on a few products rather than churning out many ill-thought-out devices and attention to detail – are little changed from Steve Jobs' founding principles. But Apple's advertising has traditionally tried to demonstrate them through its products – to create what executives describe as "lust" for its latest gadgetry – rather than talking about them explicitly. "This was an inspirational message that things have changed a bit at Apple," says Regis McKenna, a communications adviser to Jobs. "They certainly have a different voice but they were trying to show that they are no less focused and no less creative . . . It was to put a marker down that Apple is alive and well and that it is going to continue to innovate."

The last time Apple attempted to convey such a message about itself, rather than its products, was 1997's "Think Different" campaign. Jobs commissioned those ads, which showed black-and-white images of icons such as Thomas Edison, Bob Dylan and Albert Einstein, to rally the Apple faithful when he returned to lead the company as it teetered on the brink of bankruptcy. "At the time, Steve was trying to recruit people, and they hadn't seen any [new] products and he was trying to tell the troops: we're different," says Mr McKenna. Apple is no longer the underdog of 1997, it is attempting to cement itself as the tastemaker at the heart of the mainstream. Ensuring that Apple's mainstream brand is as appealing to its customers today as the "crazy ones" and "rebels" celebrated by Jobs' marketing is just as important a part of Mr Cook's role as creating innovative new products.

it also differentiates itself by what Tim Cook, Apple's CEO, refers to as 'the values we live by'. It is these values which make Apple different from its competitors, and it is these values which make Apple's products different from the products of its competitors.

Specialisation by focus

In this case the strategy is concerned with selecting (focusing upon) only certain markets, products or geographical areas in which to compete. As Mini Case Study 7.5 shows, not only can capturing a niche market aid an individual business ride out a recession and thrive in the good times but it can also become the 'engine of success' for an entire economy. The strength of the German economy is its *Mittelstand*, and the competitive advantage of these 'small, medium-sized and often family owned companies' is their ability to capture and hold niche markets.

Porter argues that by focusing in this way, it becomes feasible for a firm to dominate its chosen area(s). The method of achieving domination could either be through cost advantage or product differentiation. According to Porter (1980: 15), however, such niche markets must have certain characteristics which separate them out from the market in general:

> The target segment must either have buyers with unusual needs or else the production and delivery system that best serves the target must differ from that of the other industry segments.

MINI CASE STUDY 7.5

The engine of success

When the financial crisis hit in 2008, the main owner of SMS, the German engineering group, embarked on a rather counter-intuitive strategy. Instead of slashing the company's workforce or cutting development and capital expenditure, Heinrich Weiss, its chairman, decided to increase spending on training, research and machinery. Despite not receiving any orders of meaningful size for months, he doubled SMS's investment budget for 2009 to €70m ($104m). "After the party, it is time for spring-cleaning," Mr Weiss says. "And the most important thing during times of crisis is to look after your workforce." The strategy paid off, not only for SMS but for other German industrial companies. In the past year, the volume of German goods sold abroad rose 18.5 per cent to €951.8 billion – a rapid bounce-back from the 19.3 per cent drop the year before.

A mixture of financial prudence, enterprising spirit and a strategy to retain a highly skilled workforce has been at the heart of the country's success. But are there any lessons for the UK, which is itself seeking to expand its export base? One important reason why export-driven companies in sectors such as machinery, cars and chemical goods have emerged from the crisis stronger in Germany is that many specialise in highly advanced niche markets.

Germany is home to a host of small, medium-sized and often family owned companies – the so-called Mittelstand – that are dedicated to the production of often-sophisticated and expensive products. These include the likes of Ebm-Papst, the world's leading producer by sales of energy-saving industrial fans used in products ranging from refrigerators to car air-conditioning. What appear to be commodities that could easily be copied by mass-market manufacturers in the emerging markets are in fact highly engineered components. About 500 engineers and technicians are responsible for Ebm-Papst's range of almost 15,000 fans, ventilators and electric engines. The group's specialisation and research focus are emblematic of Mittelstand strategies. "A large part of Germany's products are simply indispensable. Companies can postpone such investments but they cannot skip them altogether," says Hermann Simon, founder and chairman of Simon-Kucher & Partners, a strategy consultancy.

 Source: Germany: the engine of success, *The Financial Times*, 09/05/2011, p. 6 (Schaefer D.),
© *The Financial Times Limited* (2011). All Rights Reserved.

If the niche market grows, or is incorporated, into a larger market, then market dominance is unlikely to be retained. In such circumstances, the previously dominant organisation will find itself having to compete for market share with others. In effect, the rules of the game will have changed and a different strategy is required – either attempting to gain cost leadership across the entire market, or adopting a product differentiation policy that neutralises other competitors' cost advantage.

Porter's assertion concerning these three strategies is that they are distinct and cannot be mixed. That is to say, it is not possible to pursue successfully a cost leadership strategy and a product differentiation strategy at the same time, because each requires different organisational arrangements to be successful. Also, if a firm does not achieve cost leadership, product differentiation or specialisation in its products, services or market, it is bound to produce low profitability and have below-average performance. Porter (1980: 41) refers to these sorts of firms as 'stuck in the middle' because they lack:

> the market share, capital investment, and resolve to play the low cost game, the industry-wide differentiation necessary to obviate the need for a low cost position, or the focus to create differentiation or low cost in a more limited sphere.

Influential though Porter's work is, there are many who disagree with him on this point (Mintzberg et al, 2009). Hlavacka et al (2001), in a study of public and private hospitals in the Slovak Republic, found that those which pursued a 'stuck in the middle' strategy had the best performance. An earlier study by Dess and Davis (1984) also questioned Porter's view. They found evidence to show that businesses with both a low cost and a high differentiation position can be very successful.

Miller (1992) challenges Porter's assertion that firms should pursue only one strategy. He points out that such strategic specialisation can lead to inflexibility and narrow an organisation's vision. In addition, Gilbert and Strebel (1992) point to the success of 'outpacing' strategies. This is where firms enter a market as low-cost producers and then, once established, differentiate to capture a larger slice of the market. This was the approach, i.e. moving from one successful form of strategy to another, used by Japanese companies to capture Western markets in the 1970s and 1980s (Johnson et al, 2011). In so doing, Japanese firms used a Strategic Conflict approach, but this was underpinned by their commitment to building and developing their core competences. A further criticism of Porter's work is that it is not as applicable to emerging economies, where the market is less important in determining competitive advantage than non-market institutional relationships (Guillen, 2000; Peng et al, 2005).

Therefore, though Porter's work has tended to dominate the practice of strategic management in Western firms, both the Resource-Based View and Strategic Conflict models have shown their worth, as mentioned above. Regardless of which business-level approach to strategy organisations have followed, prompted by the success of Japanese companies, there is now recognition of the importance of functional/operational-level strategies (Hax and Majluf, 1996; Johnson et al, 2011; Schonberger, 1982; Slack et al, 1998).

Functional/Operational-level strategies

Organisations can construct good corporate strategies and good business strategies, but in order to achieve their objectives, they need good functional strategies as well. For example, Dyer's (1996) study of the reason why Toyota outperformed its American and Japanese

Thin times for lean car production

Presenting its annual earnings in Tokyo yesterday, the world's most profitable carmaker [Toyota] also briefed investors on some new wrinkles in its much-studied manufacturing process. Alongside its financial results and market-share statistics, Toyota outlined measures it was taking to reduce the thickness of resins it uses in its cars by more than 30 per cent, and to cut its use of sheet steel by 20 per cent. The carmaker suffered a 25 per cent rise in the price of rolled steel charged by Japanese producers last month, and said that 'soaring raw material costs', alongside the stronger yen and other factors, presented a major challenge to its global operations.

'The business environment is extremely tough,' said Katsuaki Watanabe, the company's president. Toyota said it was looking to reduce materials costs starting at the development phase, for example by reducing the number of costly electronic control units it designs into its vehicles. The company is regarded as an industry leader in lean production, and its competitors will have been listening closely as they too struggle with rising prices for virtually all the raw materials that go into their cars.

rivals found that the key to its success was a better supply chain strategy. Similarly, as Mini Case Study 7.6 shows, in responding to rises in world commodity prices, coupled with stagnant or falling demand, Toyota did not change its corporate or business strategy but instead changed its product design strategy to take cost out of its vehicles (which was also likely to lead to changes to its supply chain and manufacturing strategies). This emphasises the crucial role that functional strategies play in achieving and maintaining competitive advantage.

The main functional-level strategies concern marketing, finance, R&D, technology, human resources, manufacturing/operations and supply chain. Of the three levels of strategic decision-making, the functional level has probably been the most neglected by Western organisations. This is for three reasons:

● First, the concentration at both the corporate and business levels on the external world, i.e. the market, led to a lack of interest in the internal operation of organisations. The assumption was that the internal world was malleable, and could and should adjust to the priorities set by corporate and business strategists (Schonberger, 1982).

● Second, key elements of functional-level strategy, especially concerning finance, marketing, R&D and technology, were in effect determined and constrained by corporate strategists. Indeed, in many organisations, even the human resource strategy was determined at the corporate level.

● Finally, even though the 1980s saw a renewed interest in functional-level strategy, this tended to be one-sided, stressing soft, personnel-type issues.

As discussed in Chapter 3, in seeking to understand and emulate Japanese success, Western researchers created the 7 S Framework: strategy, structure, systems, staff, style, shared values and skills (Peters and Waterman, 1982; Pascale and Athos, 1982). Though acknowledging that the Japanese were strong in and integrated all the seven Ss, the tendency in the West was to stress the so-called soft Ss: staff, style, shared values and skills. This not only continued to neglect areas such as manufacturing/operations and supply chain but also, in so doing, failed to produce the sort of integrated corporate, business- and functional-level strategies that were seen as lying at the core of Japanese competitiveness.

Once again, this highlights the difficulty that Western strategy practitioners, consultants and theorists have with creating an approach to strategy that goes beyond focusing on particular aspects to take an all-encompassing view (Mintzberg *et al*, 1998a).

In examining the corporate, business and functional levels, it can be seen that there are only a limited number of forms of strategy that organisations tend to adopt and which flow from the Competitive Forces, Strategic Conflict and Resource-Based View models of strategy discussed earlier. The appropriateness of any of these for a particular organisation is, as maintained in Chapter 6, related to the nature of the societal, sector, environmental and organisational constraints it faces. These include the stage of product–market evolution, the competitive position the firm has, the competitive position it seeks, the business strategies being used by rival firms, the internal resources and distinctive competences at a firm's disposal, the prevailing market threats and opportunities, the type and vigour of competition, customer needs, and the conditions that financial institutions place on capital availability, to mention only the more obvious ones (Hax and Majluf, 1996; Hill and Jones, 2006; Johnson *et al*, 2011; Koch, 1995; Thompson and Strickland, 1983). In addition, it must be acknowledged that generic strategies will always give rise to a host of variants and, therefore, at any one time, the choice of the most suitable strategy will be a highly complex task. Indeed, this is what one would expect. If choosing and implementing strategy was easy, then all firms would be successful. But, given that success is usually measured in relative terms, by definition not everyone can be successful; therefore, strategy formulation will and must remain fraught with danger and difficulty.

A major point to note, though, is that almost without exception, whatever form of strategy is adopted, it will require the organisation to achieve a fit between its external environment and internal structures, culture and practices. Contrary to the views of earlier writers on strategy (such as Ansoff, 1965), if organisations are driven by their external environment, internal arrangements may, and usually do, need to change, often radically, in order to achieve the desired marketplace objectives. This once again emphasises the importance of functional-level strategy and shows why it should not be treated as a lesser issue. It should also be borne in mind, as argued in previous chapters, that the possibility does exist for organisations to shape their external environment to fit in with their internal arrangements. The fact that many do not do so may say more about the type of organisation they are than the constraints they face.

Types of organisation

Miles and Snow (1978) developed an important variant of the argument on types of strategy. Rather than attempting to classify the types or levels of strategy that organisations can adopt, they classify the organisations themselves as strategic types, based on the rate at which an organisation changes its products or markets. Miles and Snow identify four strategic types (*see* Ideas and perspectives 7.3).

Miles and Snow's classification has proved been an extremely influential for understanding both organisations and strategy (Hambrick, 2003). Though it has received empirical support from some researchers (e.g. Shortell and Zajac, 1990), others have questioned its applicability across industries (e.g. Hambrick, 1983, 2003). Notwithstanding this, as Waldersee and Sheather (1996) point out, there are some similarities between Miles and Snow's work and Porter's work. They argue that successful firms pursue one of two basic types of strategy – innovative or stability.

IDEAS AND PERSPECTIVES 7.3

Miles and Snow's classification of strategic types

- **Defenders**. These seek internal stability and efficiency by producing only a limited set of products, directed at a narrow but relatively stable segment of the overall market, which they defend aggressively. Such organisations are characterised by tight control, extensive division of labour and a high degree of formalisation and centralisation.

- **Prospectors**. These are almost the opposite of defenders. They aim for internal flexibility in order to develop and exploit new products and markets. To operate effectively in a dynamic environment they have a loose structure, low division of labour and formalisation, and a high degree of decentralisation.

- **Analysers**. These types of organisation seek to capitalise on the best of both the preceding types. They aim to minimise risk and maximise profit. They move into new markets only after viability has been proved by prospectors. Their internal arrangements are characterised by moderately centralised control; with tight control over current activities but looser controls over new undertakings.

- **Reactors**. This is a residual strategy. These types of organisation exhibit inconsistent and unstable patterns caused by pursuing one of the other three strategies erratically. In general, reactors respond inappropriately, perform poorly, and lack the confidence to commit themselves fully to a specific strategy for the future.

Source: Miles and Snow (1978).

Organisations pursuing innovative strategies, which embrace both Porter's product differentiators and Miles and Snow's prospectors, seek to achieve success through reducing price competition by offering products and services that are considered unique in terms of their design, brand image and features. Organisations pursuing stability strategies, which embrace Porter's cost leaders and Miles and Snow's defenders, seek to achieve success by locating and maintaining secured niches in stable product areas where they can produce higher-quality or lower-price products than their competitors.

Covin (1991) agrees with the proposition that successful organisations pursue one of two forms of strategy, though he labels them 'entrepreneurial' and 'conservative'. The former falls within Waldersee and Sheather's innovative category, while the latter falls within their stability category. Covin argues that the strategy an organisation adopts reflects its basic nature (i.e. its culture). Therefore, for Covin, the selection and pursuit of strategy is driven by managerial style and organisational culture. However, Waldersee and Sheather dispute this. Their work sought to examine the relationship between strategy and managerial style, and whether one drove the other. Their conclusion, which was tentative, was that different types of strategy may predispose managers to act in different ways (i.e. managerial style follows strategy type) rather than managers' styles predisposing them to a particular type of strategy. Yet, recalling Chapter 6's discussion of strategy and the constraints on managerial choice, it could be argued that these writers are taking too narrow and deterministic a view. It might well be that, depending on the constraints faced by managers and their perceptions of these, in some situations strategy does require managers to adopt a particular style of working, while in other situations managerial style does influence the nature of the strategy adopted. This discussion of the relationship between managerial style and organisational context will be returned to in the concluding chapter of this book.

Before moving on to examine the strategic tools that organisations have at their disposal, it is important to remember, as discussed in Chapter 6, that the concept of strategy (whether at the functional, business or corporate level) is contentious. There are many influential writers, especially Henry Mintzberg (2007, *et al*, 2009, who do not believe in strategy as a conscious and planned process. This does not invalidate corporate, business or functional/operations strategies *per se*, but it does mean that they occupy a problematic and contested terrain.

Strategic planning tools

This section briefly reviews the main tools that organisations use to select and construct their strategies. By and large, these tools tend to have either a quantitative or a qualitative bias. In the past, and to a major extent even now, it was the quantitative tools (mathematical models) that tended to dominate. This is largely a reflection of the types of strategy organisations adopt, and a (not unrelated) preference for quantification, especially in the financial arena, in the US, where many of the leading strategic tools and approaches to strategy originated (Grant, 1991b; Hax and Majluf, 1996; Moore, 1992). It should be noted, though, that other leading industrial nations, especially Japan and Germany, place less reliance on financial measures such as return ROI (return on investment) and other quantitative measures in determining strategy (Carr *et al*, 1991; Dearlove, 2011; Whittington, 1993; Williams *et al*, 1991).

Beginning in the 1990s, even in the US and the UK where financial considerations appear paramount, there has been a movement away from a sole reliance on quantitative techniques, and a growing interest in softer, qualitative tools such as scenario- or vision-building (Fleisher and Bensoussan, 2003; Joyce and Woods, 2001; Rigby, 2001; Rigby and Bilodeau, 2011). In part, this interest in more qualitative techniques is a result of the perceived failure, especially in the face of Chinese and Japanese competition, of more quantitative approaches favoured by proponents of the Positioning school to deliver a genuine and sustainable competitive advantage (Mintzberg *et al*, 2009). This interest in qualitative techniques has also received a boost from the growing interest in the Strategic Conflict and Resource-Based View approaches to strategy. In addition, it forms part of, and has been given impetus by, the move away from quantification and towards the use of more qualitative techniques in organisation theory in general.

As one would expect, there are an enormous range and number of tools and techniques available to the strategist. However, perhaps the ones that have attracted most attention are, in chronological order:

1. The PIMS (Profit Impact on Marketing Strategy) model;
2. The Growth-Share Matrix;
3. The Scenario- or Vision-Building approach.

The first two focus on corporate and business-level strategies and are biased towards large organisations that have an established and significant presence in the markets they serve. The third, though, has no such restrictions or biases and can be applied to a wide range of situations.

PIMS

The PIMS (Profit Impact on Marketing Strategy) programme was developed at General Electric in the 1960s and was derived from work by Sidney Schoeffler (Schoeffler, 1980). It was further developed with the Management Science Institute at Harvard University and, in 1975, the Strategic Planning Institute (SPI) was launched as an independent body to house the programme (www.pimsonline.com). Since then, PIMS has grown to become one of the largest privately owned databases in the world, comprising over 3000 major corporations and individual business units. PIMS operates as a form of club. It collects financial, strategic, competitive, and background data on each of its members. Each business is profiled in terms of 500 variables, including income, balance sheet data, quality and price relative to competitors, new products, market share, distribution channels, and competitive tactics (www.pimsonline.com). This information is fed into the PIMS database and is then used to provide individual members with answers to questions such as:

- What profit rate is 'normal' for a given business?
- What strategic changes are likely to improve performance?
- What are the likely effects on profitability, cash flow, etc., of adopting a particular strategy?

The rationale underlying the PIMS model is that certain characteristics of a business and its markets determine profitability (McNamee, 1985; Moore, 1992; Shankar and Carpenter, 2012). Consequently, understanding these characteristics and acting upon them will aid a company to become more profitable. The model is based upon the belief that there are three major factors which determine a business unit's performance: its strategy, its competitive position, and the market or industry characteristics of the field in which it competes (Moore, 1992; Moore, 2004). Underpinning the model are two key assumption (Buzzell, 2004; Buzzell and Gale, 1987; Farris and Moore, 2004; Schoeffler, 1980). The first is that all business situations are basically alike and obey the same laws of the marketplace. The second is that the future will resemble the past, i.e. if certain linkages between strategy and performance resulted in profitability in the past, they will do so again in the future.

There has been much discussion as to the success of PIMS; certainly, some of its users, as well as academic observers, regard it as an invaluable tool, while others see it as having only a limited use (Abell, 1977; Anderson and Paine, 1978; Andrews, 1980; Buzzell, 2004; Ford, 1981; Farris and Moore, 2004; Koch, 1995; McKiernan, 1992; Mitroff and Mason, 1981; Naylor, 1981). The main criticisms levelled against PIMS are as follows:

- It is flawed because it uses historic data, without consideration for future changes. The argument is that, as organisations operate in a dynamic environment, to use the past to predict the future can be a dangerous exercise. Indeed, PIMS seems to be useful only in a stable environment, where companies stick to doing what they know best. It is even questioned whether PIMS can be regarded as a tool for policy in a strategic sense, since it can be argued that the 'variables' it so relies on, such as market share, are performance variables, not strategic ones.
- It is highly analytical, but very limited in solving problems. In addition, because PIMS has to use a very large database for its analysis, it is argued that this creates a major problem for managers in terms of absorbing all the data generated. In turn, since the statistical errors in its output are rarely openly discussed, there is a tendency for managers not to question its findings because 'the computer is always right'.

- Its most famous, and contentious, assertion, that profitability is closely linked to market share, and that an improvement in market share can be associated with a proportionate increase in return on investment, is of dubious validity. As Smith (1985) maintains, it could equally be argued that both are due to common factors, such as low costs and good management. It is also said to be responsible for inculcating in managers and consultants a belief that low-market-share businesses are bad and must either increase their market share or withdraw from the industry in question, regardless of profitability.

- Most of the factors that govern the forecasts of the model are beyond the control of individual companies. Therefore, since PIMS relies heavily on these data, whatever conclusions it reaches about the fate of a company are final. It is neither comforting nor particularly useful to be told that you cannot do anything to turn a negative forecast around, because the factors responsible are out of your hands.

- It assumes that a rather large set of quantitative variables, primarily of a financial nature, is sufficient to capture the state of a business and from this determine a realistic strategy. Also, as Mintzberg *et al* (1998a: 99) comment, 'finding a correlation between variables . . . is one thing; assuming a causation, and turning that into an imperative, is quite another'.

- It is based on the premise that business problems are orderly or well-structured. PIMS thus assumes that the determination or classification of the level of the organisation or business unit, the customer group, the competition, the market and the product line to which the analysis applies are all either well-known or well-specified. It is, therefore, not equipped to handle imprecise, let alone conflicting, definitions of business problems.

In summary, the main criticisms of PIMS are that it is too mechanistic, overly complex, based on unreliable data, and cannot cope adequately with dynamic and unpredictable environments. Yet, despite the criticisms levelled against it, many researchers still believe that PIMS is a useful tool (Buzzell, 2004; Chang, 1997; Farris and Moor, 2004; Thompson, 1996). The PIMS method has also been praised for the insight it has given into the true nature of the relationships between strategic variables such as profit and market share. Obviously, managers deal with these variables and their relationships on a daily basis, but attempts at conceptualising these relationships had been lacking until the advent of the PIMS research programme (Anderson and Paine, 1978; Ford, 1981; Mitroff and Mason, 1981).

This is not, however, to minimise the shortcomings of the PIMS model. It is biased towards, and contains data almost exclusively provided by, large and well-established corporations that already occupy significant positions in their markets. Therefore, as Mintzberg *et al* (1998a: 99) observe, its emphasis is on 'being there' or 'staying there' rather than 'getting there'. It follows that its prescriptions may have little relevance for new, small or innovative businesses seeking to enter new markets.

The Growth-Share Matrix

This was the brainchild of the Boston Consulting Group (BCG) in the US and is arguably the most famous strategic tool ever developed (Johnson *et al*, 2011; Koch, 1995; Nippa *et al*, 2011; Srivastava and Prakash, 2011). BCG was formed in 1963 by Bruce Henderson, and it is generally considered to be the pioneer of business strategy analysis. The Growth-Share Matrix, or 'Boston Box' as it is colloquially referred to, arose from two concepts developed by BCG: the experience curve and the sustainable growth formula (McKiernan, 1992).

The experience curve, which Henderson claims to have discovered in the 1960s, suggests that 'as the cumulative production of a product doubles, the cost of producing it seems to decrease by a constant percentage (usually 10 to 30 per cent)' (Mintzberg *et al*, 1998a: 97). From this, BCG concluded that if costs fall in relation to production volume (i.e. experience), then cost must also be a function of market share. Therefore, the company with the largest market share should also have the greatest competitive advantage and, it follows, the highest profit margin.

The sustainable growth formula, which was developed by BCG in the early 1970s, is based on the relationship between growth, investment and returns. It maintains that companies with the highest rate of returns on investments can, theoretically, grow the fastest (McKiernan, 1992).

It was bringing together these two concepts (that the company with the highest returns can grow the fastest and that the company with the highest market share should have the highest profit margin) that created the basis for the Growth-Share Matrix. The matrix is based on the assumption that all except the smallest and simplest organisations are composed of more than one business. The collection of businesses within an organisation is termed its business portfolio. Using pictorial analogies (*see* Figure 7.3), it posits that businesses in an organisation's portfolio can be classified into stars, cash-cows, dogs and problem children (Smith, 1985).

- **Stars** are business units, industries or products with high growth and high market share. Because of this, stars are assumed to use and generate large amounts of cash. It is argued that as they, generally, represent the best profit and investment opportunities, then the best strategy for stars, usually, is to make the necessary investments to maintain or improve their competitive position.

- **Cash-cows** are defined as former stars whose rate of market growth is in decline. They were once market leaders, during the early days when the market was growing rapidly, and have maintained that position as the growth tapered off. They are regarded as businesses

Figure 7.3 BCG Growth-Share Matrix

with low growth but high market share. Because they are entrenched in the market, they have lower costs and make higher profits than their competitors. These businesses are cash-rich; therefore the appropriate strategy for such businesses is to 'milk' them in order to develop the rest of the organisation's portfolio.

- **Dogs** are businesses that have low market share and which operate in markets with low growth potential. Low market share normally implies poor profit, and because the market growth is low, investment to increase market share is frequently prohibitive. Also, in such situations, the cash required to maintain a competitive position often exceeds the cash generated. Thus, dogs often become cash traps. It follows from this that, generally, the best strategy is for dogs to be sold off.

- **Problem children** or **question marks**, as they are sometimes labelled, are regarded as having a high growth rate and low market share. They have high cash requirements to keep them on course, but their profitability is low because of their low market share. They are so named because, most of the time, the appropriate strategy to adopt is not clear. With their high growth rate, it might be possible to turn them into stars, by further investment. However, because of the uncertainty that surrounds this type of business, the best strategy might be to sell them off altogether.

The originators of the Growth-Share Matrix see it as a dynamic tool for assessing and planning market and business developments. For example, the matrix predicts that as growth in their industries slows down, the original stars will move into the position of cash-cows, as long as they keep maintaining their high market share; otherwise they will become dogs. It also claims to predict how cash-cows and dogs will develop as their markets change. Therefore, the Growth-Share Matrix can be used to forecast the development of a business portfolio over a period of time. There are two basic assumptions underlying the matrix:

1. That those industries, products or businesses that have a high growth rate can be differentiated from those that have a low growth rate.

2. That those that have a high competitive position or market share can be differentiated from those that have a low competitive position or market share.

Based on these assumptions, the matrix classifies business units or activities according to the growth rate of the industry of which they are part and by their market share (Koch, 1995; McKiernan, 1992; Moore, 1992).

The matrix was widely and rapidly adopted by American corporations in the 1970s. This was for two reasons: first, the matrix's simplicity and ease of construction; and second, because most large corporations were busy splitting their organisation into strategic business units focusing on particular industries and products. The corporate centres were looking for a simple means of categorising and directing the activities of these units, and the matrix was seen by them as an ideal tool for this purpose. McKiernan (1992), however, argues that its advantages go far beyond merely its simplicity and ease of construction. He maintains that it aids strategic planning, balancing cash flow between businesses, investment decisions and competitive benchmarking.

Understandably, as many commentators note, over the years, the Growth-Share Matrix has attracted its fair share of criticisms as well as praise (Koch, 1995; McKiernan, 1992; Nippa *et al*, 2011; Mintzberg *et al*, 2009). One of the obvious objections to the matrix is the labels it employs for the classification of businesses. Andrews (1980) described these labels as a 'vulgar and destructive vocabulary', while others see such labels as too simplistic (Nippa *et al*, 2011). There are, however, other more substantial criticisms concerning the assumptions underlying, and the operation of, the 'Boston Box' (Johnson *et al*, 2011; Nippa *et al*, 2011). The main one is that the uniqueness of an organisation and its problems may not be adequately captured by this or any other tight classification scheme (Hax and Majluf, 1996). This is reflected in the views of Mitroff and Mason (1981), who argue that the critical assumptions underlying the matrix are tautologous and simplistic, e.g. that the classification scheme applies to all businesses, because all businesses can be classified as one of the four basic types, or that the classification scheme is relevant to all businesses, meaning that all businesses should be able to be classified as one of the four types.

Researchers have also drawn attention to the difficulty in defining and measuring the major variables, such as growth, market share and profitability, on which the matrix relies (Hax and Majluf, 1982; Hax and Nicholson, 1983; Johnson *et al*, 2011). Hax and Nicholson (1983) also question whether market share really is the major factor determining profitability, and whether industry growth is really the only variable that fully explains growth opportunities. These reservations are echoed by Smith (1985). A further concern is that the matrix assumes that a good portfolio analysis should identify the competitive strengths and the industry attractiveness of each business unit. Alternatives to the Growth-Share Matrix, however, reject this assertion. Instead they start by assuming that these two dimensions cannot be revealed by a single measurement, but require a wider set of critical factors for reliable positioning of the business units (Hax and Majluf, 1982; Hofer and Schendel, 1978). Another reservation, expressed by Fawn and Cox (1985), is the difficulty of defining what constitutes a single business. One of the most telling criticisms is that many of the companies that have used the matrix found, to their alarm, that all their component businesses were classed as dogs even though these businesses were actually profitable!

Perhaps the key and most common criticism relates to the way the matrix, and other similar tools, have been used. As Hax and Majluf (1996: 313) observe:

> Matrices tend to trivialize strategic thinking by converting it into simplistic and mechanistic exercises, whose final message is dubious at best. Also the matrix methodology has tended to take strategic analysis and, subsequently, strategic thinking away from managers and into the realms of planning departments.

In the face of such criticisms, a number of alternatives were developed to BCG's original portfolio matrix. Hax and Majluf (1996) identified the following as the most popular:

● The Industry Attractiveness–Business Strength Matrix developed by General Electric in association with management consultants McKinsey (Hax and Nicholson, 1983). (A similar system called the Directional Policy Matrix (DPM) was developed by Shell Chemicals in the UK (Hussey, 1978).)

● The Life-Cycle Matrix developed by the consultants Arthur D Little. As well as identifying the appropriate strategy for each business in a portfolio, this also provides detailed guidance on action programmes to implement the strategies.

● The Alternative BCG Matrix developed by the Boston Consulting Group to update the original matrix.

● The Profitability Matrix developed by the consultants Marakon Associates. This seeks to identify the profitability, growth and cash-generating capabilities of each business in a portfolio.

Table 7.1 Main external and internal factors of matrices

Matrices	External factors	Internal factors
Original BCG Matrix	Market growth	Relative market share
Industry Attractiveness–Business Strength Matrix	Overall industry attractiveness: • Critical structural factors • Five-forces model	Sources of competitive advantage: • Critical success factors • Value chain
Life-Cycle Matrix	Industry maturity	Overall measurement of business position
Alternative BCG Matrix	Ways to compete (opportunities for differentiation)	Size (sustainability) of competitive advantage
Profitability Matrix	Market growth potential Cost of capital	Profitability Cash generation

Source: Adapted from *The Strategy Concept and Process: A Pragmatic Approach*, 2nd ed., Prentice Hall: New Jersey, USA (Hax AC and Majluf NS 1996) p. 302 (Figure 17.15), Adapted by permission of Pearson Education Inc., Upper Saddle River, NJ.

Table 7.1 shows the main external and internal factors which each of these matrices seeks to identify. It also needs to be noted that many other organisations have developed or employed similar schemes to meet their organisational needs (Johnson *et al*, 2011; Koch, 1995; McKiernan, 1992; Patel and Younger, 1978). It remains true that portfolio models all seem to attract similar criticisms to those levelled at the Growth-Share Matrix (Fleisher and Bensoussan, 2003; Mintzberg *et al*, 2009; Turner, 1990).

Regardless of the merits of these criticisms, even its proponents would not dispute that, like PIMS, the Growth-Share Matrix is primarily suited to well-structured planning problems in which the basic definition of a business unit, product or competition is not an issue (Bowman and Asch, 1985). Unfortunately, because of the uncertain and rapidly changing nature of business today, such situations are becoming less and less common. This, to an extent, may account for the increase in the popularity of the next approach.

The scenario- or vision-building approach

As a way of overcoming some of the criticisms of the above quantitative approaches, scenario-building techniques emerged in the 1970s. The use of scenarios is based on the assumption that, in a rapidly changing and uncertain world, if you cannot predict the future, then by considering a range of possible futures, an organisation's strategic horizons can be broadened, managers can be opened up to new ideas and, perhaps, the right future can even be identified (O'Connell *et al*, 2011; Ringland, 1998). Scenarios allow organisations to exercise strategic choice in terms of whether to try shaping the future, adapting to the future or keeping their options open by investing in a range of products, technologies and markets (Courtney *et al*, 1997). Johnson *et al* (2011: 51–2) observe that:

> When a business environment has high levels of uncertainty arising from either complexity or rapid change (or both), it is impossible to develop a single view of how environmental influences might affect an organisation's strategies – indeed it would be dangerous to do so. Scenario analyses are carried out to allow for different possibilities and help prevent managers from closing their minds about alternatives. Thus scenarios offer plausible alternative views of how the business environment might develop in future, based on key drivers of change about which there is a high level of uncertainty. . . . The point is not to predict, but to encourage managers to be alert to a range of possible futures.

The rationale for the scenario approach is that it allows an organisation to carry out an intensive examination of its own unique and complex circumstances and needs, rather than attempting to fit itself to standard strategic planning tools such as PIMS and the Growth-Share Matrix (Johnson *et al*, 2011; Linneman and Klein, 1979; O'Connor *et al*, 2011).

Kahn and Weiner (1978) defined a scenario as a hypothetical sequence of events constructed for the purpose of focusing attention on causal processes and decision points. For them, the purpose of scenarios is to display, in as dramatic and persuasive a fashion as possible, a number of possibilities for the future. To Norse (1979), scenarios are a means of improving our understanding of the long-term global, regional or national consequences of existing or potential trends or policies and their interaction. Essentially, therefore, building scenarios can be regarded as making different pictures of an uncertain future (business or otherwise) through the construction of case studies, either quantitatively or qualitatively (McNulty, 1977). The quantitative variant of scenario-building, sometimes called the hard method, uses mathematics, models and computers to make pictures of the future, through the production of a vast array of numbers and figures. The main approach, however, is the qualitative, or soft, method, which is essentially intuitive and descriptive; it is based on the resources of the human mind and derived from the methods of psychology and sociology (Joyce and Woods, 2001; Ringland, 1998).

The two main scenario-building approaches that have become well established are the *Delphi method* and the *Cross Impact method*. In addition, in recent years, a third approach has become increasingly influential: *vision-building*. Though this bears some relation to other scenario-building techniques, it comes from a different tradition. The scenario approach and especially vision-building have some similarities with the postmodernist view that organisations exist in and represent multiple realities which compete with each other for supremacy (Joyce and Woods, 2001). From the postmodernist perspective, organisations have the ability to create their own reality and, therefore, both scenario- and vision-building can be viewed as processes that assist organisations, or the dominant group within an organisation, to select or construct the reality that most suits their needs. However, scenario- and vision-building are also compatible with the realist and complexity approaches described in Chapter 4. For realists, scenarios could provide a way of separating real constraints from the plethora of different perspectives that surround them; whereas for adherents of complexity, they can be used to locate the 'edge of chaos' and the order-generating rules necessary to maintain an organisation in this position.

One of the main functions of scenario-type approaches is that they enable organisations to question the very foundations of their existence, to examine the usefulness of their values and norms. Instead of asking how they can improve what they are doing, they begin to ask: Why are we doing this at all? What alternatives are there? This questioning of basic assumptions is something that is alien to the quantitative tools discussed above, especially given that most managers do not understand the assumptions built into such models in the first place. Indeed, quantitative models appear to remove the necessity for managers to think by providing them with 'answers' rather than information on which to base their own decisions (Hax and Majluf, 1996; Johnson *et al*, 2011). The three main qualitative approaches are designed specifically to make managers think radically about their organisation, its purpose and its future.

The Delphi method

This uses a panel of experts, who are interrogated about a number of future issues within their area of expertise (Mitchell, 1991). In the classic application, the interrogation is conducted under conditions where each respondent is unknown to the others, in order to avoid effects of authority and the development of a consensual bandwagon. After the initial round of interrogations, the results are reported to the panel and another round of interrogations is conducted. Several rounds may be carried out in this manner (Hasson *et al*, 2000).

Results produced from these interrogations may be amenable to statistical treatment with a view to yielding numbers, dates and ranges from them. At the end of the process, depending on whether a quantitative or qualitative approach is taken, either a detailed numerical forecast of the future is obtained, or a more descriptive and richer picture. In both cases, the central tendencies of majority opinion and the range of minority disagreements will also be included (McNulty, 1977; Zentner, 1982).

The Cross Impact method

This is a variation to the Delphi method. It uses essentially the same interrogation method as the Delphi, i.e. a panel of experts; the difference, however, lies in what they are asked to do. The Delphi requires the experts to identify a number of future issues that they think will affect the organisation or business within their area of expertise. The Cross Impact method, meanwhile, asks its panel of experts to assign subjective probabilities and time priorities to a list of potential future events and developments supplied by the organisation. The emphasis is on identifying reinforcing or inhibiting events and trends, to uncover relationships and to indicate the importance of specific events. The accruing data from this exercise are used to create yield curves of the probabilities for each event as a function of time (Bañuls and Turoff, 2011; Lanford, 1972).

Vision-building

As regular surveys by Bain & Co. have shown, over the last decade or so, vision-building has established itself as one of the key management tools (Rigby, 2001; Rigby and Bilodeau, 2007). While it certainly bears a resemblance to the other scenario-building techniques, it is influenced more by Japanese management practices than by those in the West (Baum *et al*, 1998; Collins and Porras, 1991; Hamel and Prahalad, 1989; O'Connell *et al*, 201). Despite being one of the most popular management tools, it is perhaps also one of the least understood and idiosyncratic (Cummings and Worley, 2009; Stacey, 1992). This is perhaps because it is a much less structured approach than the other two scenario-building techniques, and relies more on a company's own management. According to research by Collins and Porras (1997), compelling visions have two components:

- a core ideology which describes the organisation's core values and purpose; and
- a strong and bold vision of the organisation's future which identifies specific goals and changes.

The major elements of vision-building are as follows:

- the conception by a company's senior management team of an 'ideal' future state for their organisation;
- the identification of the organisation's mission, its rationale for existence;
- a clear statement of desired outcomes and the desired conditions and competences needed to achieve these.

Vision-building is an iterative process that is designed to move from the general (the vision) to the specific (desired outcomes and conditions), and back again. By going round the loop in this manner, according to Cummings and Huse (2009), an ambitious yet attainable future can be constructed and pursued. This owes much to the Japanese, who pioneered the concept of strategic intent on which vision-building is based. The work of Hamel and Prahalad (1989) is of particular importance in this respect. They argued that the strategic approach of Japanese companies is markedly different from that of their Western counterparts. Rather than attempting to lay down a detailed plan in advance, Japanese companies operate within a long-term framework of strategic intent. They create a vision of their desired future – their 'intent' – which they then pursue in a relentless but flexible manner. Hamel and Prahalad quote examples of leading Japanese companies who, in the 1960s, when they were insignificant in world terms, set out to dominate their markets:

- Honda's strategic intent was to be the 'Second Ford'.

- Komatsu's was to 'Encircle Caterpillar'.

- Canon's was to 'Beat Xerox'.

These companies then mobilised their resources towards achieving their individual strategic intent. In this, the prime resource they deployed was the commitment, ingenuity and flexibility of their workforces.

Like all approaches to strategic planning, these scenario-/vision-building approaches have many criticisms (Cummings and Worley, 2001; Conger and Ready, 2004; Fleisher and Bensoussan, 2003; Joyce and Woods, 2001; Keshavan and Rakesh, 1979; Porter, 1985; Wack, 1985; Whittington, 1993), the main ones being:

- They are prone to subjectivity and bias. The fact that any five management specialists can interpret the same situation in totally different ways is an oft-quoted example of this type of criticism.

- They can encourage retrospection. People's ideas of the future are informed by their knowledge and experience of the past. Since experience is not always the best teacher, scenarios and visions may be based on false assumptions.

- Participants can be strongly influenced in their preference of scenario by their own sectional and personal interests.

- The process cannot be carried out by novices and can, therefore, be time-consuming and expensive in terms of senior management time and outside experts.

- There is much debate about how many scenarios to construct and how they should be used.

- The more radical the vision or scenario, the more difficult it will be to get managers and others to commit to it.

- Visions often require strong visionary leaders, which are in short supply.

Despite these criticisms, the use of scenarios and visions now forms an important part of the managerial toolbox (Collins and Porras, 1997; Cummings and Worley, 2005; Hamel, 2007; Leemhuis, 1990; Rigby and Bilodeau, 2011).

In describing and discussing the main strategic planning tools, it is sometimes difficult to get a sense of how important businesses consider them to be. However, as Mini Case Study 7.7 shows, for those who run companies such as General Electric, buying and selling businesses, reviewing and renewing their portfolios, trying to assess future trends and when to move into and out of markets, lie at the core of what they do. It is not a once-a-year event

MINI CASE STUDY 7.7

Shaping and reshaping businesses

When some of the parts don't add up; conglomerates that thrive are ruthless in their scrutiny of when to shed beloved but worn-out assets

As Chris Zook, head of the global strategy practice at Bain, the management consultancy, says: 'Conglomerates tend to have around a third of their divisions in businesses they have no long-term logical reason to be in.'

Every month, the slide presentations arrive in Pam Daley's e-mail inbox. They come from each of General Electric's business leaders, offering updated lists of their leading candidates for acquisitions and partnerships. Initiated in 2001 by Jeffrey Immelt, chief executive, the process requires division heads to submit five of each, says Ms Daley, GE's senior vice-president of corporate business development. 'None of these guys can count to five,' Ms Daley says. 'You get lists of 20 from some, which is exactly what you want if the opportunities are there.'

At GE, the process of adding to its portfolio of businesses is as stringent as the one that determines what is subtracted. The similarities reflect the fact that any company, even one with pockets as deep as GE, has only so much capital to invest. The business heads then travel to GE's Fairfield, Connecticut, headquarters for a meeting with the company's senior executives to discuss changes to their so-called pipeline list and, when necessary, seek Mr Immelt's blessing to enter negotiations or make a bid. Very few items escape Mr Immelt's radar, Ms Daley notes; managers need their boss's approval to pursue any deal worth more than $3m.

Then, after the business heads have made their pitches and left the room, Mr Immelt, Ms Daley and other corporate officers stay behind to discuss the other pipeline – those businesses GE thinks might be better off owned by another company. In his seven years at the helm, Mr Immelt has jettisoned more than $50 billion in businesses. Gone are insurance, plastics and industrial supply, among others. 'This is a 130-year-old company, and it does evolve,' Ms Daley says.

but a continuous process of shaping and reshaping their organisations. They are not unaware of the weaknesses of strategic planning tools but they are reliant on them to aid decision-making. This is why organisations such as General Electric invest in the development and refinement of such tools. It is also why, despite the continuing popularity of quantitative tools and quantitative strategies, there has been a growth in more qualitative tools and techniques to match the increasing popularity of less prescriptive and more qualitative models of strategy (Rigby and Bilodeau, 2011).

Conclusions

Just as the aim of Chapter 6 was to examine the main approaches to understanding strategy, the aim of this chapter has been to examine the main approaches to applying strategy. The chapter began by describing the three main models of strategy which organisations have tended to utilise over the last 25 years: the Competitive Forces model, the Resource-Based View and the Strategic Conflict model. This was followed by an examination of the different organisational levels at which strategy is applied and the main forms of strategic planning tools on offer.

What the examination of these areas has shown is that, in the West at least, it is the approaches, tools and techniques of the Prescriptive stream of strategy that organisations have tended to favour. The continuing prominence of the Positioning school, through the work of Michael Porter, clearly demonstrates the enduring influence of the Prescriptive stream. This of course should not be surprising. After all, the livelihood of those who make up the Prescriptive stream, whether they be consultants, consultancies, business schools or individual academics, is dependent to a large extent upon creating a market for its strategic planning products. It is also probably the case that when leading consultancies, business schools and large corporations are all arguing for a particular approach, there is enormous pressure on managers elsewhere to follow. To paraphrase the old slogan that 'no one ever got fired for buying IBM', one could also say, 'no one ever got fired for calling in the Boston Consultancy Group or Michael Porter'.

Even so, the Resource-Based View and the Strategic Conflict model have been growing in importance in the last two decades, as this chapter has shown. Both tend to be located in and draw support from the Analytical stream of strategy. The Strategic Conflict model has its roots in the perspective of strategy as a battle between warring organisations; but its renewed prominence, as discussed, has arisen both from practical concerns about the applicability of the Competitive Forces model, and from new theoretical insights from areas such as game theory. The Resource-Based View, meanwhile, owes much to researchers like Prahalad and Hamel (1990), who have sought to understand and explain the Japanese approach to strategy. In both cases it can be seen that strategy is conceived of as an emergent rather than a planned process. Therefore, though the Prescriptive stream of strategy is still extremely influential in determining how managers develop and implement strategies, the influence of the Analytical stream is also growing.

To return, however, to the argument developed in Chapter 6, it would be wrong to fall into the trap of seeing the Analytical stream as being the 'right' way to apply strategy and the Prescriptive as the 'wrong' way, or vice versa. Instead, it may be that approaches from both the Prescriptive and Analytical streams have much to offer organisations, depending on their circumstances or constraints. For organisations with a dominant position in a relatively stable market, an approach from the Prescriptive stream, such as the Competitive Forces model, may be suitable. Likewise for organisations seeking to enter new markets or grow their business over a long time-frame, an approach from the Analytical stream, such as the Resource-Based View, has much to commend it. Similarly, in evenly balanced competitive situations, the Strategic Conflict model may be more appropriate. This is not to propose a Contingency model of strategy; rather, as was argued in Chapter 6, what is being suggested is that organisations have a choice. They can seek to influence or mould the constraints they face in order to make them more amenable to the type or model of strategy they wish to pursue. As indicated earlier in this chapter when looking at the work of Miles and Snow (1978), the approach to strategy an organisation adopts may have less to do with the merits of the different models on offer and more to do with the type of organisation it is and the orientation of its managers.

Choosing the type or model of strategy to pursue is one thing; implementing it is an entirely different matter. This is especially so if one recognises that the Prescriptive and Analytical streams of strategy have distinctly different, indeed almost opposite, perspectives on implementation. For the former, implementation flows from the organisation's strategic plan. For the latter, the strategy emerges from and is given shape by the actions and decisions organisations make on a day-to-day basis to change and adapt themselves to their circumstances. But no matter which model of strategy one subscribes to, it is only when organisations implement changes that strategies come alive. This highlights the crucial importance of organisational change. Consequently, just as this chapter and the previous one have reviewed the main arguments with regard to strategy, so the next four chapters will review the strengths, weaknesses and implications of the main approaches to change management.

TEST YOUR LEARNING

Short discussion topics

The purpose of these is to enable students to check their learning and reflect on the topics covered in this chapter. The discussions should last for no more than 5–10 minutes. Depending on the length of the lecture, there could be one, two or three such discussions in a session. The following are five suggested topics which address issues raised in this chapter:

1. What is the Competitive Forces model of strategy?

2. Define the Strategic Conflict model of strategy.

3. Briefly discuss the case for the Resource-Based View of strategy.

4. Describe Miles and Snow's four strategic types of organisations.

5. What are the strengths and weaknesses of the BCG Growth-Share Matrix?

Class debates

The purpose of class debates is to enable students to explore a topic in depth by setting up a 'for and against' debate. The class can be split into two and one half asked to research the 'for' case and the other 'against' case. Individuals can then be chosen at random to introduce their side of the debate. Alternatively, two individuals for each side can be told in advance that they will be introducing the debate. The length of such debates depends on the time available, the size of the class and their enthusiasm for the topic. However, less than 30 minutes is probably too short and more than 60 minutes probably too long. The following are three suggested topics which address issues raised in this chapter:

1. The Resource-Based View is good for identifying whether an organisation has unique resources, but no good at creating them.

2. Developing visions is easy; deciding which vision to pursue, and how to pursue it, is the hard bit.

3. The problem with the Competitive Forces model is that it can only ever apply to a few companies in an industry.

Essay questions

1. Use Miles and Snow's classification of strategic types to analyse one of the case studies which appear at the end of each chapter in this book or a case of your own choosing. Discuss how useful their classification is in judging the appropriateness of strategic leadership in an organisation.

2. Critically evaluate the following statement: Rupert Murdoch's preference for the Strategic Conflict approach to strategy was a key factor in the *News of the World's* aggressive use of phone-hacking.

Suggested further reading

There are a vast number of books on strategy but, unfortunately, no one book covers all the main tools and techniques. However, the following three books, while leaning towards the Prescriptive approach, do cover the main strategic planning methods, techniques and processes.

Bensoussan, BE and Fleisher, CS (2013) *Analysis without Paralysis: 12 tools to make better strategic decisions* (2nd edition). Pearson: Upper Saddle River, NJ.

Grant, RM (2010) *Contemporary Strategy Analysis* (7th edition). John Wiley: Hoboken, NJ.

Johnson, G, Whittington, R and Scholes, K (2011) *Exploring Corporate Strategy* (9th edition). Financial Times Prentice Hall: Harlow.

CASE STUDY 7

Process Control Inc.

Background

Process Control Inc. (PCI) is the European manufacturing arm of an American conglomerate. Its present operation came into being in 1979, through a merger with a subsidiary of a British-owned electronics company. PCI specialises in the assembly of printed circuit boards (PCBs) and process control equipment. It produces over 95 per cent of the conglomerate's total PCB needs, and has a staff of 395.

In recent years, with a rapid expansion of PCB assembly, the company began to experience major operational problems relating to quality and delivery. This in turn caused increasing difficulties for the parent company in the US, which found its own deliveries and quality suffering as a consequence. Despite efforts by PCI, its performance worsened rather than improved and a large proportion of its target completion dates could not be met. Similarly, its quality problems worsened.

As a consequence, the parent company sacked the plant's British CEO and replaced him with an American who was to be seconded to PCI for a one- to two-year period. This came as a shock not only to the CEO but also to the entire workforce. There was widespread feeling, at all levels in the company, that he had been treated shabbily, especially given that he had been with the company, in its various forms, for 25 years. This shock was compounded by the character of the new CEO. He was a colourful and flamboyant person who wore a Mickey Mouse watch, dressed

as Father Christmas and the Easter Bunny at the appropriate time of the year, and was given to public soul-searching.

In his first three months, the chief executive flattened the management hierarchy. The previous CEO had only three managers reporting directly to him, with a further tier of eight managers reporting to them. The new CEO combined these two layers and created a new 11-person management team responsible to him. This levelling-up created some resentment among the original three team members, which was compounded when two of them were told to switch jobs with their former subordinates. Indeed, at one point there was talk that these managers might resign.

Developing a strategy

After six months, when these changes had failed to improve the company's performance, the CEO organised a weekend-long, off-site management seminar. This was led by an outside facilitator and was, the CEO said, about soul-searching and team-building. At the end of this, he felt that the weekend was a turning-point in the organisation's fortunes. Not only did they emerge as a more coherent and committed team but they also came up with the bones of a Strategic Plan which they saw as the solution necessary to pull the organisation out of its predicament. According to the CEO, who introduced the concept and continued to be its main champion, the initial reaction of the management team to the idea of developing a manufacturing strategy was: 'Yes, we need to do planning but Jesus!, we are in a deep mess, we don't have time to do it.' The CEO said that, 'in the end, I had to force the idea of strategic planning on the organisation'. The vision produced by the management team was:

> To empower the organisation to be a world-class manufacturing unit and thereby achieve customer delight.

Throughout the summer, the management team and various sub-groups met to develop and approve the elements of the manufacturing strategy. However, while some maintained their original enthusiasm, others became more sceptical. Some managers felt the process was being rushed, and that as a consequence the time available for thinking through and discussing the proposals was limited. The sub-groups did not have the time to meet and the chairman of each group wrote the plans with little input from others. Notwithstanding this, by September, the complete strategy was agreed by the management team, along with the priorities and timetables for the next 12 months.

The CEO then organised a meeting of all supervisory and middle management staff to brief them on the strategy and to attempt to involve them. This was not particularly successful. The main reason for this was the sheer volume of information presented. Therefore, a second meeting was organised. The problem, however, with both meetings was that because the organisation was under pressure for quick results to turn its fortunes around, much of the time was spent on the action required to achieve the plan, rather than taking enough time to explain the rationale underlying the plan and what the outcomes would mean for the workforce. It was left to the members of the management team to explain these to their own subordinates. However, some of the managers themselves were unclear or in need of convincing of the merits of the proposed changes. Consequently, rather than giving reassurance, these briefings had the opposite effect – especially when staff compared what different managers were saying. Also, the trade union, usually very supportive of the company, complained about 'the looming prospects of redundancy'. There was also a fear among the supervisors and middle managers about their future in the plant, because the plans involved structural changes which would result in the removal of some of their posts.

The management team's response was to introduce a series of weekend and lunch-break meetings aimed at educating the workforce. These were able to calm some of the fears but, overall, they could not fully come to grips with people's worries, because most of the meetings (especially the plant-wide monthly lunch-break meetings) were too large, and so personal concerns and sensitive questions were not even asked, let alone discussed in the open.

Nevertheless, by December elements of the strategy were being implemented. However, there was still much to do both in implementing what had been decided and in clarifying what the new organisational structure should look like. Indeed, the question of structure emerged as the main issue of uncertainty and contention in the management team. Though the CEO said he was clear about the new structure, the rest of his team were not. Despite this, the CEO pushed ahead with a plan to create 'mini' factories within a new matrix-type structure. This clearly demonstrated the growing gap between the CEO and his team – even those who supported him. The gap was particularly obvious among those managers who controlled support functions such as quality, purchasing and production control, because they felt their specialism would be dismembered and career prospects threatened.

All change

In the week before Christmas, all this was thrown into confusion when the CEO announced he was leaving. He had been offered, and had accepted, the chance to take over a more important plant in the company's portfolio in the US. It was not clear who would take over – though there had been an undercurrent of fighting for succession in the management team all along, especially between the production manager and the materials manager. It was announced that there would be a delay before a new, permanent, CEO could be appointed and that an interim, part-time CEO would take over. However, he could make only intermittent visits to PCI and the management team were mainly left to their own devices. Most of the management team were content to await the appointment of the permanent CEO rather than continuing with the more controversial elements of the strategy. However, the production manager, who had been won over by the previous CEO's ideas, and who saw himself as a potential successor, began to push the strategy very strongly. This was quickly put down by the rest of the team through non-cooperation. Most managers reverted to their former state of dealing with the day-to-day running of the plant, and the strategy, which was of top priority a few weeks previously, now came to play a secondary role.

After 12 months without an on-site or full-time CEO, it was announced that the materials manager would be the new CEO. This news was welcomed by most people, though the production manager was extremely upset at being passed over. The new CEO surprised most of his colleagues by declaring that he wanted to resuscitate the strategy. This was partly as an olive branch to the production manager and partly because he recognised that the company was still underperforming in major areas. The CEO decided to present the strategic plan to his superiors in the US in order to get their backing and improve its chances of being accepted in PCI. However, the outcome was not what he expected. His superiors liked the plan but were doubtful of PCI's ability to implement it. Instead, they gave the CEO three months to evaluate the following options and make a recommendation of which one to adopt:

1. Close the plant entirely and contract out all the work to the Far East.

2. Subcontract out the manufacture of PCBs to the Far East and leave a much-reduced PCI responsible for

some managerial functions and the assembly of certain larger systems.

3. Convince his superiors that PCI could overcome its difficulties.

The CEO was left in no doubt that his superiors were sceptical about the third option or that his own future with the company would depend not only on which option he recommended but also on whether it was successful in achieving the company's targets. However, they did concede that they had no hard evidence that firms in the Far East were equipped to do a better job than PCI.

Questions

1. Analyse the case study from the perspectives of the Prescriptive and Analytical streams of strategy. Which perspective, if any, offers the best insight into PCI's failure to implement its strategy?

2. Imagine that you are consultant for Prescriptive Strategy Inc. What advice would you offer the CEO in terms of how he should evaluate and decide upon the three options?

3. Imagine that you are consultant for Analytical Strategy Inc. What advice would you offer the CEO in terms of how he should evaluate and decide upon the three options?

PART 3

Change management: past, present and future

Change management: fundamental questions for organisations

Learning objectives

After studying this chapter, you should be able to:

- define organisational effectiveness and how this relates to organisational change;
- appreciate the difference between individual, group and system change;
- understand the nature of resistance to change and how it relates to commitment and readiness for change;
- be aware of the change agent's role and skills;
- discuss the frequency and magnitude of change in modern organisations.

MINI CASE STUDY 8.1

Minimal change can be best option: Why Berlin snack bar resisted change

The story. Konnopke's Imbiss is probably Berlin's most famous snack bar. Set up in 1930 in Prenzlauer Berg, a then working-class district, it has become legendary for its currywurst, a Berlin speciality of fried sausage served with ketchup, chilli sauce and curry powder. By 2010, it had been run in the same location for 34 years by Waltraud Ziervogel – who took over from her father, Max Konnopke, who started the business and ran it until 1976. The snack bar had two branches – the original at the Eberswalder Strasse subway station and another in the suburban district of Pankow.

The challenge. Until the Berlin Wall came down in 1989, customers at Konnopke's Imbiss were mostly workers who called in during the morning or at lunchtime, or families. But by the turn of the century that had changed, as Prenzlauer Berg had become a hip neighbourhood of young, affluent freelancers, tourists and partygoers. Then, in 2010, Ms Ziervogel learnt that the snack bar would have to close for a year because of nearby construction work on a subway station.

Strategic considerations. The proposed disruption offered an opportunity for some fundamental rethinking about the positioning and marketing of Konnopke's Imbiss, not to mention the business model. Should it move to a spot with even more tourists and potential customers? Should it have a healthier menu? Other questions included whether to raise prices, extend the opening hours (the snack bar often had to turn away customers when it closed at 8pm) and even whether it should sell merchandise or start franchise operations. Received wisdom on strategy and marketing would have recommended changes on many if not all of the classic "four Ps": product, price, place and promotion. The new, affluent locals and the tourists could easily afford higher prices, while later opening hours and a more comfortable location would be in line with their expectations on service quality. The same would be true of more healthy options on the menu. At 74, Ms Ziervogel also had to consider potential succession planning and her children, Mario and Dagmar, who, respectively, worked at the original and the suburban location.

What happened. During the construction work, the snack bar operated from a small stand just 100m away. Despite being offered a substantial sum of money by city authorities to move away permanently, and potentially attract even more customers at one of the tourist hotspots, Ms Ziervogel declined. She decided to rebuild her stand in exactly the same place with almost the same 1960s' look and feel, save for a refurbished, bigger seating area and a slightly

different outward appearance. The menu remained unchanged, as did the opening hours and the prices. Ms Ziervogel resisted all temptations to modernise her business. After the reopening, the queues patiently waiting for a currywurst every day were as long as ever.

Key lessons. In sticking to the same modus operandi, Ms Ziervogel understood three important issues. First, many customers – especially tourists, who make up 90 per cent of its customers – care about "authenticity". By not radically changing, Konnopke's positioned itself as Berlin's most authentic snack bar. Second, as owner and manager, Ms Ziervogel had clear opinions about how to run her business, what to focus on and how to lead people. Too much change simply would not have fitted her or the culture of her business. Third, successful businesses need to carefully balance and align different elements such as strategy, formal organisation, critical tasks, people and culture. Substantial changes in any of the "four Ps" would have required the rearranging of these elements in order to maintain their equilibrium. For instance, increasing the price from EUR3.20 to something nearer the EUR17 charged by some five-star hotels would have required different processes, people and organisational culture.

Introduction

This chapter follows on from the discussion of strategy in the two previous chapters. Chapters 6 and 7 were essentially concerned with approaches to determining and charting an organisation's strategic direction. Underpinning both chapters was the division between the Prescriptive stream of strategy, whose members seek to tell organisations how they should formulate strategy, and the Analytical stream of strategy, whose members seek to understand what organisations actually do to formulate strategy. The former tend to see strategy as a formal, rational and pre-planned process. The latter tend to see strategy as a more messy, less rational, emergent process. Therefore, for the Prescriptive stream, organisational change flows from, and is concerned with implementing, an organisation's predetermined strategy. For the Analytical stream, organisational change is not an outcome of strategy but the process by which it is created and given form. For both streams, change management is vital, whether it be for strategy implementation or development. Indeed, the ability to manage change effectively is seen by leading organisations as one of their most important forms of competitive advantage (Rigby and Bilodeau, 2011).

Consequently, this and the next three chapters will focus on understanding change and categorising the main approaches to planning and implementing the changes required to achieve, or shape, strategic objectives. The received wisdom in much of the business world is that change has to be fast, large-scale and transformational if organisations are to survive (Peters, 2006). However, as the story of Konnopke's Imbiss (Mini Case Study 8.1) shows, this does not always have to be the case; sometimes incremental change which does not disturb the essence of a successful business is what is required. As Etzold and Mueller (2012: 12) state, 'successful businesses need to carefully balance and align different elements such as strategy, formal organisation, critical tasks, people and culture'. In order to create the conditions for successful change, organisations have to address five fundamental sets of questions:

1. Why do we want to change?

2. Should we focus on individual, group or system change?

3. Will there be resistance and, if so, where from? How can we gain employee commitment? Are we ready for change?

4. Who will manage the change process? Do they have the appropriate skills?

5. What are the frequency and magnitude of the changes required in order for us to survive?

Why do organisations change?

In the Introduction to this book, we discussed the failure rate of change initiatives. We can dispute whether or not the failure rate is 70 per cent, we can dispute whether or not some types of change are more difficult to undertake than others, and we can also dispute whether or not some organisations are more able than others to achieve successful change. However, what seems beyond dispute is that managing change is one of the most problematic tasks organisations undertake. If this is so, why is it that change initiatives seem to be increasing both in frequency and magnitude (IBM, 2008)?

In the previous chapters, we examined the development of the main approaches to running organisations which have emerged since the Industrial Revolution. In essence, these have been developed to deal with the problems organisations perceive they face in surviving in an increasingly hostile world. For private sector organisations, these problems tend to come under the heading of 'competitiveness', in the public sector they are often given the sobriquet of 'value for money', whereas in the third sector, they can be covered by a wide variety of terms, most of which can come under the heading of the 'care, health and well-being of society'. However, there is one term which embraces all these different reasons for change – 'organisational effectiveness'. Whether we are dealing with a bank seeking greater profitability, the UK Department of Energy which seeks to ensure that the country has secure, clean, green and affordable energy supplies, or a hospice wanting to provide better care for sick children, they are all looking to become more effective in what they do.

Nevertheless, as Rollinson (2002: 468) states:

'Effectiveness' is one of the most frequently used (and misused) words in discussing organisations. There is no universally accepted theory of organisational effectiveness. Neither is there a universally accepted definition and set of criteria that allows the effectiveness of an organisation to be measured.

Pick up any book on management, organisational behaviour or indeed anything to do with organisations, and sooner or later the term 'organisational effectiveness' will be used. It tends to be deployed as a form of measure against which to compare the appropriateness of whatever is being discussed, whether this concerns people, systems or strategy. This is not surprising; if one is seeking to promote, denigrate or just evaluate a particular approach, it is much more convincing to say that it does or does not improve organisational effectiveness rather than merely to say that one does or does not like it.

The surprising thing is not that the term 'organisational effectiveness' is used so often but that so few writers seek to explain what they mean by it. Some people appear to consider that the term is so readily understandable that there is no need to define it, while others take the opposite view – that it is so difficult to explain that they will not even try. However, as Ideas and perspectives 8.1 shows, there are those who have attempted to grasp the essence of the term.

Though there are some commonalities in the definitions given in Ideas and perspectives 8.1, there are also many differences. For example, Barnard's 'common purpose' is not the same as Drucker's 'economic characteristics'. Nor is Mullins' 'doing the right thing' the same as Schein's 'capacity to survive'. In reviewing the topic, Robbins (1987) notes that in the 1950s, organisational effectiveness tended to be defined as the degree to which an organisation achieved its goals. However, this definition raised more questions than it answered: for example, whose goals? Organisations have multiple stakeholders – shareholders, managers, employees, customers, suppliers and even society at large. They all have goals for and

IDEAS AND PERSPECTIVES 8.1

Organisational effectiveness

The test of effectiveness is the accomplishment of a common purpose or purposes.
(Barnard, 1932: 60)

Effectiveness focuses on opportunities to produce revenue, create markets, and to change the economic characteristics of existing products and markets. (Drucker, 1977: 32)

[Effectiveness is] . . . the degree to which an organisation attains its short- and long-term goals, the selection of which reflects strategic constituencies, the self-interest of the evaluator and the life stage of the organisation. (Robbins, 1987: 51)

A system's effectiveness can be defined as its capacity to survive, adapt, maintain itself, and grow, regardless of the particular functions it fulfils. (Schein, 1988)

Effectiveness is achieved when the organisation pursues appropriate goals.
(Lewis et al, 1998)

Effectiveness can be considered in terms of profitability, in terms of the pursuit of organisational goals (at whatever cost), or in terms of quality of life for those involved.
(Huczynski and Buchanan, 2001: 561)

Effectiveness is concerned with impact – does the service achieve its intended purpose?
(Doherty and Horne, 2002: 340)

Effectiveness is concerned with 'doing the right things'. (Mullins, 2002: 233)

expectations of the organisation (Jones, 2001). This is why those studying organisational effectiveness now prefer to take a multi-goal–multi-stakeholder perspective (Rollinson, 2002). However, this does not eliminate the 'whose goals?' question. Though some goals and some stakeholders are compatible, others are not (Cameron, 2005). For example, when a government announces plans to build a new road, some, such as road haulage groups, will support the decision and some, such as people who live near the proposed new road, will oppose it.

Even if we focus on the goals of just one group, say senior managers, we often find a wide range of opinions over what an organisation's goals are or should be (Pfeffer, 1992). Some managers will stress that the goal should be increased profitability, but argue about whether this is short-term or long-term; others will argue for market share or market growth; many will stress share price and dividend payments; and some will advocate measures of effectiveness which promote their own goals or self-interest (Pfeffer, 1992).

There have been many studies of organisational effectiveness, but the fact that criteria as diverse as product quality, absenteeism, profit, stability, motivation and communication were used to define effectiveness shows how difficult the concept is to define (Robbins, 1987). The problem appears to be that many researchers focus on whether the goals being pursued are appropriate and the degree to which they are achieved (Rollinson, 2002). They do not ask how organisations structure and organise themselves to achieve their goals. Yet if one looks at studies of other types of effectiveness, such as managerial effectiveness, they focus not on what is achieved but how it is achieved (Yukl, 2002). Take perhaps the most popular book on managerial effectiveness, Stephen Covey's (1989) *The Seven Habits of Highly Effective People*. Covey does not emphasise goals as such but the skills and competences managers need to develop in order to achieve their own and their organisation's goals. Similarly, the *Longman Dictionary of Contemporary English* (1978: 350) defines effectiveness as:

the ability or power to have a desired effect.

Like Covey's work, this definition of effectiveness focuses on the process by which an outcome is achieved. Handy (1993), in looking at organisational effectiveness, is one of the few writers who has sought to identify the factors or variables which affect the achievement of goals, including leadership, reward systems and organisational structure. He points to the need to see these variables and factors not as isolated features of organisational life but as parts of organisational theories, i.e. consistent and coherent approaches to structuring and running organisations. Burnes (1998a) and Sowa *et al* (2004) support Handy's view, arguing that organisational effectiveness stems from the approach that organisations adopt towards how they are structured and run. This can be seen in Mini Case Study 8.1, where the effectiveness of Konnopke's Imbiss in meeting its customers' needs and so remaining successful came from its unique alignment of 'processes, people and organisational culture', and not from the goals it set for itself. Therefore, the achievement of an organisation's goals is dependent on the appropriateness of the way it is structured and run. This means that, as Cameron (2005: 293) observes, 'organizational effectiveness lies at the center of all theories of organization'. From this perspective, the five chapters in Part 1 of this book can be seen as dealing with the main theories and perspectives on organisational effectiveness, while the two chapters in Part 2 have dealt with how organisations choose their approach to effectiveness. Consequently, the four chapters in this part of the book will deal with the way that changes to effectiveness processes are implemented. However, a word of caution: this does not mean that the process of developing, selecting and implementing measures to improve effectiveness is a straightforward and linear one. As stated in the last section, strategy and change interact in a dynamic and non-linear fashion. It is as true to say that change drives strategy as it is to say that strategy drives change. Indeed, a more realistic view would be that the relationship between recipes for organisational effectiveness, strategy and change is messy, iterative, unclear and ambiguous. Even the change management field itself is far from straightforward, as the remainder of this chapter will show.

Individuals, groups and open systems

Change management is not a distinct discipline with rigid and clearly defined boundaries. Rather, the theory and practice of change management draw on a number of social science disciplines and traditions. For example, theories of management education and learning, which help us to understand the behaviour of those who manage change, cannot be fully discussed without reference to theories of child and adult psychology. Neither can these be discussed without touching on theories of knowledge (epistemology), which is itself a veritable philosophical minefield. Having said that, it has long been recognised that organisational change tends to focus on the achievement of one of three types of outcome – individual change, group change and system change (Katz and Kahn, 1978). Each of these has its advocates as to which is most important. For example, Maslow (1943) and the early Human Relations school focused very much on the importance of individual motivation and behaviour. Lewin (1947a, 1947b) and Schein (1988), while recognising the importance of individual behaviour to overall organisational performance, argued that modifying group behaviour was the best way to improve performance. Senge (1990), though, took a systems approach to improvement. He saw the interconnectedness of organisational life as being the most important factor and, therefore, change has to start from this perspective. It is not that supporters of these three forms of change ignore the other two, but rather that they see their form as being the lynchpin that holds the others together. This can be seen from examining the three schools of thought that form the central planks on which change management theory is built:

- the Individual Perspective school;
- the Group Dynamics school;
- the Open Systems school.

The Individual Perspective school

The supporters of this school are split into two camps: the Behaviourists and the Gestalt-Field psychologists, notably Kurt Lewin. The former view behaviour as resulting from an individual's direct interaction with their environment. They maintain that human beings are simply the sum of their parts, and that the individual parts can be identified and the causes of behaviour related to individual external stimuli (Deutsch, 1968). Gestalt-Field psychologists, meanwhile, challenge this view, arguing that an individual's behaviour is derived from the totality of coexisting and interdependent forces that impinge on them and make up the field or life space in which the behaviour takes place (Lewin, 1942). They believe that individuals function as whole, total organisms and are capable of understanding the forces which make up their life space and changing them so as to amend their behaviour (Burnes and Cooke, 2012a; French and Bell, 1990).

In Behaviourist theory, all behaviour is learned; the individual is the passive recipient of external and objective data. Among the earliest to work in the field of conditioning of behaviour was Pavlov (1927). In an experiment that has passed into folklore, he discovered that a dog could be 'taught' to salivate at the ringing of a bell, by conditioning the dog to associate the sound of the bell with food. Arising from this, one of the basic principles of the Behaviourists is that human actions are conditioned by their expected consequences. Behaviour that is rewarded tends to be repeated, and behaviour that is ignored tends not to be. Therefore, in order to change behaviour, it is necessary to change the conditions that cause it (Skinner, 1974).

In practice, behaviour modification involves the manipulation of reinforcing stimuli so as to reward desired activity. The aim is to reward all instances of the wanted behaviour, but to ignore all instances of the unwanted behaviour (because even negative recognition can act as a reinforcer). This is based on the principle of extinction: a behaviour will stop eventually if it is not rewarded (Lovell, 1980). Not surprisingly, given the period when it emerged, the Behaviourist approach mirrors in many respects that of the Classical school, portraying humans as cogs in a machine, who respond solely to external stimuli.

For Gestalt-Field theorists, change is a process of gaining or amending insights, outlooks, expectations or thought patterns. In explaining an individual's behaviour, this group takes into account not only a person's actions and the responses these elicit but also the interpretation the individual places on these. As French and Bell (1984: 140) explain:

> Gestalt therapy is based on the belief that persons function as whole, total organisms. And each person possesses positive and negative characteristics that must be 'owned up to' and permitted expression. People get into trouble when they get fragmented, when they do not accept their total selves . . . Basically, one must come to terms with oneself, . . . must stop blocking off awareness, authenticity, and the like by dysfunctional behaviours.

Therefore, from the Gestalt-Field perspective, behaviour is not just a product of external stimuli; rather, it arises from how the individual uses reason to interpret these stimuli. Consequently, the Gestalt-Field proponents seek to help individual members of an organisation change their understanding of themselves and the situation in question, which in turn, they believe, will lead to changes in behaviour (Smith *et al*, 1982). The Behaviourists, meanwhile, seek to achieve organisational change solely by modifying the external stimuli acting upon the individual.

Both groups in the Individual Perspective school have proved influential in the management of change; indeed, some writers even advocate using them in tandem. This is certainly the case with advocates of the Culture–Excellence school, who recommend the use of both strong individual incentives (external stimuli) and discussion, involvement and debate (internal reflection) in order to bring about organisational change (*see* Chapter 3). The importance of the Gestalt-Field approach will be further discussed when looking at the work of Kurt Lewin in Chapter 9.

This combining of extrinsic and intrinsic motivators owes much to the work of the Human Relations movement, which (especially through the work of Maslow, 1943) stresses the need for both forms of stimuli in order to influence human behaviour. Though acknowledging the role of the individual, however, the Human Relations movement also draws attention to the importance of social groups in organisations, as does the Group Dynamics school.

The Group Dynamics school

As a component of change theory, this school has the longest history (Schein, 1969) and, as will be shown in Chapter 9, it originated with the work of Kurt Lewin. Its emphasis is on bringing about organisational change through teams or work groups, rather than individuals (Bernstein, 1968). The rationale behind this, according to Lewin (1947a, 1947b), is that because people in organisations work in groups, individual behaviour must be seen, modified or changed in the light of groups' prevailing practices and norms.

Lewin (1947a, 1947b) postulated that group behaviour is an intricate set of symbolic interactions and forces that not only affects group structures but also modifies individual behaviour. Therefore, he argued that individual behaviour is a function of the group environment or field, as he termed it. This field produces forces and tensions, emanating from group pressures on each of its members. An individual's behaviour at any given time, according to Lewin, is an interplay between the intensity and valence (whether the force is positive or negative) of the forces impinging on the person. Because of this, he asserted that a group is never in a 'steady state of equilibrium' but is in a continuous process of mutual adaptation which he termed 'quasi-stationary equilibrium'.

To bring about change, therefore, it is useless to concentrate on changing the behaviour of individuals, according to the Group Dynamics school. The individual in isolation is constrained by group pressures to conform. The focus of change must be at the group level and should concentrate on influencing and changing the group's norms, roles and values (Cummings and Worley, 2005; French and Bell, 1999; Smith *et al*, 1982).

Norms are rules or standards that define what people should do, think or feel in a given situation. For the Group Dynamics school, what is important in analysing group norms is the difference between implicit and explicit norms. Explicit norms are formal, written rules which are known by, and applicable to, all. Implicit norms are informal and unwritten, and individuals may not even be consciously aware of them. Nevertheless, implicit norms have been identified as playing a vital role in dictating the actions of group members.

Roles are patterns of behaviour to which individuals and groups are expected to conform. In organisational terms, roles are formally defined by job descriptions and performance targets, though in practice they are also strongly influenced by norms and values as well. Even in their work life, individuals rarely have only one role. For example, a production manager may also be secretary of the company's social club, a clerical officer may also be a shop steward, and a supervisor may also be the company's safety representative. A similar situation exists for groups. A group's main role may be to perform a particular activity or service, but it might also be expected to pursue continuous development, maintain and develop its skills, and act as a repository of expert knowledge for others in the organisation. Clearly, where members of a group and the group itself are required to conform to a number of different roles, the scope for role conflict or role ambiguity is ever-present. Unless roles are both clearly defined and compatible, the result can be sub-optimal for the individual (in terms of stress) and for the group (in terms of lack of cohesion and poor performance).

Values are ideas and beliefs that individuals and groups hold about what is right and wrong. Values refer not so much to what people do or think or feel in a given situation;

instead they relate to the broader principles that lie behind these. Values are a more problematic concept than either norms or roles. Norms and roles can, with diligence, be more or less accurately determined. Values, however, are more difficult to determine because group members are not always consciously aware of, or can easily articulate, the values that influence their behaviour. Therefore, questioning people and observing their actions is unlikely to produce a true picture of group values. Nevertheless, the concept itself is seen as very important in determining, and changing, patterns of behaviour.

The Group Dynamics school has proved to be influential in developing both the theory and practice of change management. This can be seen by the very fact that it is now usual for organisations to view themselves as comprising groups and teams, rather than merely collections of individuals (Mullins, 1989).

As French and Bell (1984: 127–9) pointed out, the importance given to teams is reflected in the fact that:

> the most important single group of interventions in OD [Organization Development] are team-building activities, the goals of which are the improved and increased effectiveness of various teams within the organization. . . . The . . . team-building meeting has the goal of improving the team's effectiveness through better management of task demands, relationship demands, and group processes. . . . [The team] analyzes its way of doing things, and attempts to develop strategies to improve its operation.

In so doing, norms, roles and values are examined, challenged and, where necessary, changed.

Nevertheless, despite the emphasis that many place on groups within organisations, others argue that the correct approach is one that deals with an organisation as a whole.

The Open Systems school

Having examined approaches to change that emphasise the importance of groups and individuals, we now come to the systems approach, which seeks to view and understand the organisation in its entirety. This approach, as mentioned in Chapter 2, sees organisations as composed of a number of interconnected sub-systems. However, the Open Systems school does not see organisations just as systems in isolation; instead it views them as 'open' systems. It sees them as open in two respects. First, they are open to, and interact with, their external environment. Second, they are open internally: the various sub-systems interact with each other. Therefore, internal changes in one area affect other areas, and in turn have an impact on the external environment, and vice versa (Buckley, 1968; Cole, 2001). It follows that any change to one part of the organisation system can have an impact on other parts of the system, both internal and external, and, in turn, on its overall performance (Mullins, 2002; Scott, 1987). The Open Systems school's approach to change is based on a method of describing and evaluating these sub-systems, in order to determine how they need to be changed so as to improve the overall functioning of the organisation. The objective of the Open Systems approach is to structure the functions of a business in such a manner that, through clearly defined lines of coordination and interdependence, the overall business objectives are collectively pursued. The emphasis is on achieving overall synergy, rather than on optimising the performance of any one individual part *per se* (Cummings and Huse, 2001; Mullins, 1989). As Fernandez and Rainey (2006: 173) state: 'Managerial leaders must develop an integrative, comprehensive approach to change that achieves subsystem congruence.'

Miller (1967) argues that there are four principal organisational sub-systems:

- **The organisational goals and values sub-system.** This comprises the organisation's stated objectives and the values it wishes to promote in order to attain them. To operate effectively, the organisation has to ensure that its goals and values are compatible not only with each other but also with its external and internal environments.

- **The technical sub-system.** This is the specific combination of knowledge, techniques and technologies which an organisation requires in order to function. Once again, the concern here is with the compatibility and appropriateness of these in relation to an organisation's particular circumstances.

- **The psychosocial sub-system.** This is also variously referred to as organisational climate and organisational culture. In essence, it is the fabric of role relationships, values and norms that binds people together and makes them citizens of a particular miniature society (the organisation). It is influenced by an organisation's environment, history and employees, as well as its tasks, technology and structures. If the psychosocial sub-system is weak, fragmented or inappropriate, then instead of binding the organisation together, it may have the opposite effect.

- **The managerial sub-system.** This spans the entire organisation. It is responsible for relating an organisation to its environment, setting goals, determining values, developing comprehensive strategic and operational plans, designing structure and establishing control processes. It is this sub-system that has the responsibility for consciously directing an organisation and ensuring that it attains its objectives. If the managerial sub-system fails, so does the rest of an organisation.

Over the years, different researchers have placed the boundaries of these sub-systems in different places and proffered their own labels (Cummings, 2005). However, there is general agreement that the main sub-systems are the ones that cover leadership, people, structure and technology (Huczynski and Buchanan, 2001; Mullins, 2002). However, regardless of the definition and labelling of sub-systems, the Open Systems approach is concerned with understanding organisations in their entirety; it attempts to take a holistic rather than a particularistic perspective. This is reflected in the fact that it sees change from an organisational rather than an individual, group or sub-system perspective (Burke, 1980; Senge, 1990; Stickland, 1998).

Though the Open Systems perspective has attracted much praise, attention has also been drawn to its alleged shortcomings (Bryant, 2002; Stickland, 1998). Butler (1985: 345), for example, while hailing it as a major step forward in understanding organisational change, points out: 'Social systems are extremely dynamic and complex entities that often defy descriptions and analysis. Therefore, one can easily get lost in attempting to sort out all the cause-and-effect relationships.' Beach (1980: 138), in a similar vein, argues that Open Systems theory:

> does not comprise a consistent, articulated, coherent theory. Much of it constitutes a high level of abstraction. To be really useful to the professional practice of management, its spokesmen and leaders must move to a more concrete and operationally useful range.

Despite these criticisms, the level of support for this approach, from eminent theorists such as Burns and Stalker (1961), Joan Woodward (1965) and Lawrence and Lorsch (1967), is formidable. This is why, as explained in Chapter 2, it has proved so influential.

In looking at the three schools that form the central planks of change management theory, four major points stand out:

- First, with the exception of the Behaviourists, these schools of thought stand, generally, in sharp contrast to the mechanistic approach of the Classical school towards organisations and people. Furthermore, in their approach to individuals, groups and organisations as a whole, they form a link to the emerging organisational paradigms that were discussed in Chapter 3. Indeed, it might be possible to go further and say that these three schools provide many of the core concepts of the new paradigms, especially in respect of teamwork and organisational learning. If this is so, the claim (by, among others, Kanter, 1989; Senge, 1990) that these new forms of organisation constitute a radical break with the past should be reconsidered.

- Second, the three theoretical perspectives focus on different types of change – individual, group and system. In most cases, each of these forms of change will focus on distinct outcomes and, in all probability, will need to be managed differently. It follows that any approach to managing change can be classified by whether or not it is applicable to all or only some of the types of change covered by these perspectives.

- Third, though each school can be seen as an independent and distinct approach to change, they are not necessarily in conflict or competition. Indeed, it could well be argued that they are complementary approaches. The key task, which will be examined in more detail in the next three chapters, is to identify the circumstances in which each is appropriate: does the problem or the objective of change lie at the level of the organisation, group or individual? Can any of these levels be tackled in isolation from the others? This can be illustrated using the Konnopke's Imbiss case at the beginning of this chapter. It was faced with change owing to its temporary closure and possible relocation. However, it recognised that its success/effectiveness came from its unique blend of 'processes, people and organisational culture', i.e. its entire system and not just parts of it. Therefore, its priority in dealing with the enforced change was to maintain the integrity of its system, but it also recognised that this was composed of 'processes, people and organisational culture' and that any change in these had to be consistent with and support the overall system.

- Last, the Open Systems perspective has a valid point in claiming that change at one level or in one area should take into account the effect it will have elsewhere in the organisation, and vice versa. However, whether the perspective adopted is organisation-wide or limited to groups and individuals, in the final analysis, what is it that is being changed? The answer, surely, is the behaviour of individuals and groups, because organisations are, as the proponents of these three perspectives on change admit, social systems. To change anything requires the cooperation and consent, or at least acquiescence, of the groups and individuals that make up an organisation, for it is only through their behaviour that the structures, technologies, systems and procedures of an organisation move from being abstract concepts to concrete realities. This may be why Schein (1988: 12) observed 'that all organizational problems are fundamentally problems involving human interactions and processes'. However, from a systems perspective, the receptivity or not of individuals and groups to change results not so much from their innate response to change but more from the nature of the organisation and its sub-systems. This can be seen by looking at resistance and commitment to change.

Resistance, commitment and readiness

The prevailing view in the organisational change literature appears to be that employee resistance to change is innate, pervasive, irrational and dysfunctional (Dent and Goldberg, 1999; Ford *et al*, 2008). Indeed, many see resistance as the main reason for the failure of so many change efforts (Maurer, 1996; Waddell and Sohal, 1998). Peiperi (2005: 348) defines such resistance as:

> active or passive responses on the part of a person or group that militate against a particular change, a program of changes, or change in general.

Consequently, it is argued that for change to be successful, change agents have to anticipate and overcome employee resistance (Kreitner, 1992; Palmer, 2004). Even if we put aside evidence that managers may be more resistant to change than employees (O'Toole, 1995; Smith, 1982; Spreitzer and Quinn, 1996), there are still two serious problems with this view, namely that it assumes: (a) that resistance is always wrong and (b) that resistance arises from within the individual (Ford *et al*, 2008). Taking point (a) first, as Ford *et al* (2008) note, this view assumes that those who initiate and manage change are neutral parties who are acting in the best interests of the organisation and its stakeholders. However, as noted in the earlier discussion of effectiveness, organisations have many stakeholders and it is unwise to assume that they all share the same interests. Nor should one assume that the managers who initiate change are necessarily pursuing the organisation's best interests rather than their own (Burnes and By, 2012; Pfeffer, 1992; Storey, 2004).

Stickland (1998) identifies a number of different forms of resistance, including situations where resistance plays a constructive role in the change process. This is because resistance can signal that the proposed change may be ill thought out, not radical enough or just plain wrong. In this latter respect, consider two recent major organisational scandals in the UK. The first was the phone-hacking scandal which led to the closure of the *News of the World*, the most profitable of News International's UK newspaper portfolio. The Leveson Inquiry (2012) found that some journalists did, rightly, try to resist the pressure to conduct illegal and unethical practices. Similarly, the Mid Staffordshire NHS Foundation Trust Public Inquiry (2013) found that some staff tried to resist the changes to care practices which may have caused the deaths of hundreds of patients. In both cases, staff were right to resist the changes to existing practices. As Maurer (1996: 57) maintains: 'Resistance keeps people in organizations from attaching themselves to every boneheaded idea that comes down the pike.' Weisbord (1987) takes an even more positive view of resistance, arguing that it is a 'valuable passion' that can become a constructive force for organisational renewal.

Moving on to point (b), that resistance arises from within the individual, it is noticeable that Stickland (1998) does not see his various forms of resistance as arising from employees but from conflicting or incompatible objectives within the organisation, i.e. he sees resistance as a product of the system and not of the individuals who make up the system. While this may run counter to many writers' and managers' assumptions, there is strong support for this view. After a series of scandals over payment protection insurance (PPI), the rigging of LIBOR and other financial irregularities, Barclays Bank commissioned Anthony Salz to conduct an independent review of its values, principles and standards of operation. The Salz Review (2013) found that, when faced with the incompatibility between following the company's ethics policy and selling PPI, it was the latter which won out, as the following extracts from the Review show:

> We enquired about the role played by sales incentives. We were told that there were schemes designed to encourage staff to sell PPI. One example we noted was that in 2009 a sales person would earn two and a half times more commission for selling a loan with PPI compared to a loan without PPI. (p. 57)

> Some interviewees observed, and our analysis of relevant minutes confirms, that the Barclays Board did not give as much attention to the culture, values and business practices developing in the Group as, with the benefit of hindsight, these matters are now recognised to deserve. (p. 113)

The idea that resistance arises from within the system and not the individual is not new. Kurt Lewin, who pioneered the study of organisational change, made the same point (Burnes, 2004c). As noted above, Lewin saw the behaviour of individuals and groups as deriving from the totality of coexisting and interdependent forces in their field or life space. If an individual or group appears to resist change, this arises from the balance of forces in their field, i.e. the nature and state of the organisation. This was demonstrated by two of Lewin's colleagues, Coch and French (1948), in what was probably the first, and one of the most widely cited, academic articles to address resistance to change. Their research showed that resistance did not arise from personality factors but from the balance of forces which impinged on the individuals concerned. In order to overcome resistance, Coch and French modified the driving and restraining forces which influenced how they responded to change. In their case, they changed the management system of the organisation from one where change was imposed to one where participation became the order of the day.

Dent and Goldberg (1999) showed how, since the 1950s, the concept of resistance has moved from being seen as an organisational shortcoming which requires system changes to overcome it, to one which arises from individual and group self-interest and/or their psychological make-up. The core argument is that resistance is part of human nature; we are innately programmed to resist change and defend the status quo (Coghlan, 1993a; Diamond, 1986; Maurer, 1996; Oreg, 2003; Piderit, 2000). Consequently, a key role of change agents is to overcome resistance by showing us the error of our ways (Palmer, 2004). In addition, Heath and Heath (2011) argue that resistance is the product of entrenched behaviour patterns. Though the notion that human beings are programmed to resist change appears to have become the received wisdom (Dent and Goldberg, 1999; Oreg *et al*, 2011), there have been a number of studies by leading academics which support the systems view of resistance. For example, Senge (1990) sees resistance as arising from incompatible goals within the system, and Beer *et al* (1993) advocate changing the organisational context in order to overcome such obstacles to change. Kotter (1995) also sees resistance as being generated by obstacles in the total system. This continuing interest in the systems approach to resistance reflects not just the influence of Lewin but also the rise of newer perspectives on organisational life that view organisations as complex social systems (Burnes, 2004b, 2005).

Therefore, we appear to be faced with something of a dilemma. On the one hand, there is strong evidence that resistance occurs due not to the psychological propensities of individuals but to the nature of the organisation where resistance occurs, i.e. forces within the system. On the other hand, there is equally strong evidence that resistance does arise from an individual's psychological make-up (Buchanan and Boddy, 1992). However, the individual and systemic views of resistance need not be seen as contradictory. If one takes the view that organisations are social systems, it is not contradictory to see resistance as arising from the interplay between the characteristics of the individual and the characteristics of the organisation (Dent and Goldberg, 1999; Ford and Ford, 2010; Pardo del Val and Martínez Fuentes, 2003; Schein, 1996). An examination of four theories which are fundamental to the resistance debate provides substantial evidence for this view.

Theory 1 – Dispositional resistance

This is the most recent of the theories which seek to explain resistance to change. The concept of dispositional resistance to change was developed by Oreg (2003) and focuses on the individual as the main source of resistance rather than wider organisational factors. Oreg's research showed that individuals varied in the degree to which they were psychologically 'disposed' to accept or resist change. Consequently, individuals 'who are [highly] dispositionally resistant to change are less likely to voluntarily initiate changes and more likely to form negative attitudes toward the changes they encounter' (Oreg *et al*, 2008: 936). He constructed a resistance to change (RTC) scale to measure 'an individual's tendency to resist or avoid making changes' (Oreg, 2003: 680). The RTC is designed to measure the personality factors that Oreg identified as influencing resistance to change. These are routine-seeking, emotional reaction to imposed change, cognitive rigidity, and short-term focus (Oreg, 2003). Oreg and his collaborators confirmed the validity of the RTC scale in different situations and nations (Oreg, 2006; Oreg *et al*, 2008). Oreg *et al* (2009) have also shown that dispositional resistance can influence an individual's choice of occupation.

Therefore, Oreg's work rejects the notion that all human beings are programmed to oppose change, but it does show that individuals with a high dispositional resistance will be predisposed to resist change. However, Oreg also found that an individual's reaction to change can be moderated by their relationship to the change agent; that is to say, those individuals with a positive view of the change agent would be less likely to resist change regardless of their level of dispositional resistance (Oreg and Sverdlik, 2011). This indicates that context, the nature of the system, also plays a part in determining whether or not an individual will resist change. Research by Michel *et al* (2013) also supports the notion that dispositional resistance is moderated by contextual factors, such as the role of the change agent and the way in which they manage the change process. If this is the case, then what factors in the system are likely to moderate an individual's dispositional resistance? In order to answer this question, we will examine three further theories which are pertinent to understanding resistance to change: the depth of intervention, cognitive dissonance and the psychological contract.

Theory 2 – The depth of intervention

Schmuck and Miles (1971) sought to address resistance to change by examining the way change agents managed change, with a particular focus on the issue of employee involvement. They concluded that the level of involvement required in any change project is related to the psychological impact of the change on the people concerned. Huse (1980) explored this relationship further. Incorporating earlier work by Harrison (1970), Huse categorised change interventions along a continuum based on the psychological 'depth' or impact of the intervention on the individuals concerned, ranging from the 'shallow level' to the 'deepest level'. The greater the depth of the intervention, Huse argues, the more it impacts on the psychological make-up and personality of the individual, and the greater the need for the full involvement of individuals if they are to accept the changes.

The argument, therefore, is that it is necessary to link levels of involvement to the types of change proposed. The key is that the greater the effect on the individual in terms of psychological constructs and values, the deeper the level of involvement required if successful behaviour change is to be achieved. This appears to explain why in some cases, involvement can be dispensed with or minimised, i.e. in cases where the psychological impact is shallow, while in others it is vital. It does not, though, explain why major and rapid attitudinal changes can be achieved without a great deal of employee involvement.

In terms of the debate between those who see resistance as arising from an individual's psychological make-up and those who see it as being more system- or context-based, the Depth of Intervention theory offers two interesting insights. First, it supports the view that resistance can be moderated by the way that it is managed, i.e. by the level of involvement. Indeed, a recent extensive review of the change literature found:

> As a rule, change recipients who experienced high levels of participation tended to report higher readiness and acceptance of change, appraised change as less stressful and exhibited overall support for the change. (Oreg *et al*, 2011).

Second, resistance appears to be moderated by the nature of the change intervention itself, i.e. the degree to which it challenges an individual's psychological make-up. This is corroborated by Burnes and Jackson's (2011) work on the relationship between values and organisational change. This will be explored further by examining the theory of Cognitive Dissonance.

Theory 3 – Cognitive dissonance

In seeking to understand why and how involvement affects receptivity to change, Burnes and James (1995) draw on the theory of cognitive dissonance. This theory states that people try to be consistent in both their attitudes and behaviour. When they sense an inconsistency either between two or more attitudes or between their attitudes and behaviour, people experience dissonance; that is, they feel frustrated and uncomfortable with the situation, sometimes extremely so (Jones, 1990). Therefore, individuals will seek a stable state where there is minimum dissonance. This latter point is important. It is unlikely that dissonance can ever be totally avoided, but where the elements creating the dissonance are relatively unimportant, the pressure to correct them will be low. Where the issues involved are perceived by the individual to be significant, however, the presence of such dissonance will motivate the person concerned to try to reduce the dissonance and achieve consonance, by changing either their attitudes or behaviour to bring them into line (Robbins, 1986; Smith *et al*, 1982). This may involve a process of cognitive restructuring, which is unlikely to be free from difficulties for the individual concerned (Mahoney, 1974). However, as Festinger (1957), one of the originators of the concept, pointed out, in addition to trying to reduce the dissonance, people will actively avoid situations and information that would be likely to increase the dissonance. Since the emergence of the theory of cognitive dissonance in the 1950s, it has been developed and refined (*see* Cooper and Fazio, 1984; Fazio *et al*, 1977; Jones, 1990).

Applying principles of cognitive dissonance to organisational change, it can be seen that, on the one hand, if an organisation embarks on a change project that is decisively out of step with the attitudes of those concerned and/or its own values, assumptions and practices, it will meet with resistance unless those concerned change their attitudes. On the other hand, where the level of dissonance occasioned by proposed changes is low, attitudinal adjustments will be minor and potential resistance negligible, as Burnes and Jackson (2011) found when they explored the issues of values and change. Where the proposed change and the way it was managed broadly aligned with the values of the change recipients, it was accepted, and where it did not, it met with resistance. Therefore, the level and type of involvement should be geared to the level of dissonance that any proposed changes may provoke.

Up to this point, cognitive dissonance supports the work of Schmuck and Miles (1971) and Huse (1980). However, if we apply the theory to situations where old certainties have lost their legitimacy and the very survival of the organisation is at stake, a different picture emerges. The crisis (or potential crisis) raises the level of dissonance in the organisation, as it becomes apparent that existing practices are no longer viable and change is required. Old certainties lose their legitimacy, and those involved become more prepared to accept and promote radical solutions that may have been rejected previously. Not only does this make individuals and groups more receptive to radical change, but, in addition, change can be one of the main ways of reducing dissonance. In such situations, fundamental attitudinal change can be achieved relatively quickly and without a great deal of employee involvement, because management and employees recognise the need for (and indeed want) major change and see the creation and implementation of a new vision as their only hope for the company's survival. Therefore, in such instances, the dissonance is occasioned not by the change but by the condition of the organisation leading up to the change. Ordinarily, however, in many other situations, the absence of a sense of deep crisis prevents existing certainties being successfully challenged. Once again, this shows that context plays an important role in whether individuals resist or accept change, regardless of their personal level of dispositional resistance.

Theory 4 – The psychological contract

A similar and complementary explanation for employees' acceptance or resistance to change is offered by the notion of the psychological contract. Though this concept has been around since the 1950s (*see*, for example, Argyris, 1960), it was only in the 1980s and 1990s that it became widely used by organisation theorists (Arnold *et al*, 1998). As Schein (1988: 22–3) explains:

> The notion of a psychological contract implies that there is an unwritten set of expectations operating at all times between every member of an organization and the various managers and others in that organization. . . . The psychological contract implies further that each role player, that is, employee, also has expectations about such things as salary or pay rate, working hours, benefits and privileges . . . and so on. Many of these expectations are implicit and involve the person's sense of dignity and worth. . . . Some of the strongest feelings leading to labor unrest, strikes, and employee turnover have to do with violations of these aspects of the psychological contract, even though the public negotiations are often over the more explicit issues of pay, working hours, job security, and so on.

We can certainly see why, for example, the employees of a public sector organisation with a public sector ethos might feel as though their psychological contract had been violated if they were suddenly told they were to be transferred to the private sector – particularly as such a change might represent a considerable threat to their job security. However, in other instances, similarly radical change might not produce a significantly adverse reaction from staff. The reason offered for this by proponents of the psychological contract would be that in these cases staff recognised the need and justification for the changes and therefore the legitimacy of the need to change their psychological contracts. Consequently, though the notion of the psychological contract might appear to support the argument that resistance arises from the individual's psychological make-up, it is in effect about the context in which the individual is situated. If the organisation, either wittingly or unwittingly, changes or violates one part of the psychological contract without renegotiating the entire contract, in effect it puts individuals in a situation where the organisation is making conflicting demands on them. However, if the individuals can see why the contract needs to be changed and if this leads to a new psychological contract which aligns the demands on them, they are likely not to resist the changes. The psychological contract also has a strong affinity with the concept of organisational-procedural justice, which refers to the perceived fairness of policies and procedures used as the basis for decision-making (Cohen and Keren, 2008; Colquitt *et al*, 2001; Cropanzano *et al*, 2001). It has been shown that where employees perceive either the process or outcome of change to be unfair, they may resist it (Komodromos, 2013; Novelli *et al*, 1995; Wooten and White, 1999). Once again, this resistance arises not from the individual *per se* but from situations where organisations create a conflict between their espoused values of rationality and fairness and actual practices which employees see as unfair and irrational.

In exploring the issue of resistance to change, we have drawn on four complementary ideas: dispositional resistance, depth of intervention, cognitive dissonance and the psychological contract. This has given rise to three important findings:

1. Resistance to change is not uniform among human beings. Instead, it varies according to a person's level of dispositional resistance. Those with a low level of dispositional resistance will be predisposed to accept change and those with a high level will be predisposed to reject it.

2. An individual's level of dispositional resistance does not necessarily predict their actual level of resistance to any particular change initiative. Instead, it will be moderated by the context and the nature of the change. For example, if a change challenges deep-seated beliefs and values, even individuals with a low level of dispositional resistance are likely to challenge it. However, where the change is consistent with values and beliefs, even individuals with a high level of dispositional resistance would be likely to accept it. The Konnopke's Imbiss example is a case in point. There was little resistance to the proposed changes because they were consistent with and intended to maintain the organisation's values and beliefs. However, had Konnopke's Imbiss proposed significant changes to its 'formal organisation, critical tasks, people and culture', these would probably have met with considerable resistance. This would not be because of the individuals' psychological make-up *per se* but because they would be torn between the organisation's existing values and its new way of working. As such, the resistance would have arisen from conflicting objectives in the system rather than through any fault in the individuals concerned. Of course, had Konnopke's Imbiss been in a crisis, which it was not, radical change could have been viewed as favourable.

3. A further factor that is likely to affect the level of resistance is the way the change is managed, both in terms of the management style of the change agent and the degree of involvement of those affected (Buchanan and Boddy, 1992). It is generally assumed that employee involvement allied to a participative style of leadership are essential for

successful change (Oreg *et al*, 2011). However, this general rule of involvement has to take account of the context of the change situation and the type of change being proposed. In many cases it will be necessary to convince staff, through a process of constructive engagement, of the need to challenge their existing beliefs, behaviours and expectations and to renegotiate their unwritten 'contracts' with the organisation. However, in some instances, the legitimacy of existing beliefs, behaviours and expectations may already have been undermined because the organisation is experiencing a crisis (the restructuring of many financial institutions owing to the 'credit crunch' may be a good example). In such situations, it might be that cultural and behavioural change can be quickly achieved without the need for elaborate involvement techniques. This is because those concerned can see that the old attitudes and ways of behaving are no longer appropriate and unless major or radical changes are made, their jobs or even the entire organisation may cease to exist.

Of course, the reverse may also be the case. Organisations seeking to bring about small changes to structures or tasks might find they meet greater resistance than they expected because they underestimate the psychological importance employees attach to these existing arrangements. Therefore, approaches to change, including the level of employee involvement, have to be tailored to the change context rather than being applied in an unthinking fashion. However, in order to undertake this 'tailoring', managers and change agents have to understand the nature of the existing situation and its readiness for change. Armenakis *et al* (1993: 681) define readiness as:

> [an individual's] beliefs, attitudes, and intentions regarding the extent to which changes are needed and the organization's capacity to successfully undertake those changes.

They argue that the reason so many change initiatives meet resistance is because organisations have not evaluated their readiness for change and/or taken the steps necessary to create a readiness for change. In particular, they draw attention to the role of contextual factors in creating readiness. Such factors include effective leadership, a good relationship between managers and employees, organisational commitment, a positive communication climate, a coherent change strategy that is aligned with the organisation's cultural values and communicated to and debated with those involved, the organisation having the resources necessary to implement the change, a high level of employee participation in change, and the availability of change agents with the necessary change skills (Fitzgerald *et al*, 2007; Jones *et al*, 2005; McMillan and Connor, 2005; Oreg *et al*, 2011; Rafferty *et al*, 2013; Weiner *et al*, 2008). This latter point, the importance of the change agent's role, is highlighted by many writers who see them as playing a crucial role not just in managing the change initiative but also in assessing an organisation's readiness for change (Amiot *et al*, 2006; Dent and Goldberg, 1999; Ford and Ford, 2010; Ford *et al*, 2008). Consequently, in the next section, we will examine the role of the change agent.

The change agent

Whether one is dealing with change at the individual, group or organisational level, whether one perceives change as incremental or continuous, and whatever perspective one is viewing it from, change has to be managed: someone has to take responsibility for ensuring that change takes place. Whether this person is a team leader, facilitator, coach or even a dictator, there is usually one individual who bears the responsibility of being the change agent. Such people are referred to by a variety of titles – change consultant, change practitioner, project manager, etc. For simplicity's sake, we shall use the title 'change agent'.

The concept of the change agent originated with Kurt Lewin and has been extensively developed by the Organization Development (OD) movement (see Chapter 9). Over the last two or three decades, as different perceptions of change have emerged, so different perceptions of the role of the change agent can also be identified. Caldwell (2003) notes that we have seen eulogies to the 'heroic' change leader capable of transforming organisations, calls for line managers and functional specialists to become change agents, and the increased popularity of internal and external management consultants as 'catalysts' for change. However, rather than clarifying the role and competencies of the change agent, these developments appear to have made the picture more confused.

One of the strengths of the Lewin–OD approach to change is that it provides a blueprint for the behaviour and attributes of change agents who, in turn, are buttressed and supported by a host of tools and techniques for analysing organisations and managing change (Cummings and Worley, 2005). The Lewin–OD approach sees the change agent as playing a mainly neutral-facilitating role and working with a transparent and ethical agenda to help those involved to identify the options and make their own choices (French and Bell, 1995). Indeed, the twin issues of trust and choice have been shown over the years to be crucial to establishing a positive environment in which change can take place (Carpenter, 2013; Oreg *et al*, 2011; Vakola, 2013).

An essential task of the change agent is to establish the level of readiness for change. Vakola (2013) argues that an organisation's readiness needs to be assessed at the macro, meso and micro levels. It includes factors such as a well-supported strategic plan, an environment of trust, favourable group norms, and training programmes and appraisal procedures which promote flexibility among staff. This is why OD-influenced change agents begin establishing the organisation's readiness for change by mapping out the field in which the change takes place, i.e. they examine the readiness for change not just of those who are the target of the change but of the entire system (Burnes and Cooke, 2012a). They seek to identify factors at the individual, group and organisational levels which will either hinder or promote change, such as sensitivity to pressures for change, dissatisfaction with the status quo, the degree of trust and shared beliefs between employees and managers, and the availability of resources to support change, including knowledge, skills and the availability of substantial management time (Cummings and Worley, 2001; Holt and Vardaman, 2013).

Newer perspectives on the role of the change agent see change as an open-ended, complex, continuous and political process, and a normal part of everyday life in organisations. Consequently, it must be seen as an increasingly important part of every manager's role rather than a specialist activity driven by an expert (Clarke, 1994). The drawback with this perspective is that it can deflect attention from or even ignores the specialist skills necessary to manage the different types of change, whether this is being done by a manager or by a change specialist. It is also the case that, despite the advice offered to change agents by the OD movement, there has been relatively little empirical research on the nature and effectiveness of their role (Hartley *et al*, 1997). Buchanan and Boddy (1992: 27) provide one of the few studies which sought to analyse the skills needed to be a successful change agent. In particular, they draw attention to the change agent's need to:

support the 'public performance' of rationally considered and logically phased and visibly participative change with 'backstage activity' in the recruitment and maintenance of support and in seeking and blocking resistance. . . . 'Backstaging' is concerned with the exercise of 'power skills', with 'intervening in political and cultural systems', with influencing and negotiating and selling, and with 'managing meaning'.

Buchanan and Boddy suggest a model of the expertise of the change agent which identifies the skills and competences necessary to achieve successful change. Their model begins by listing the diagnostic skills required to identify, in effect, the organisation's readiness for change and plan the change initiative accordingly. These diagnostic skills include the ability to categorise the nature of the organisation on a spectrum of rigid to organic, and to determine whether and where it is moving along this scale and how this will impact on the nature of the change initiative. They also include an understanding of critical events in the organisation's past and how these will affect expectations of and attitudes to change. Buchanan and Boddy's model then goes on to list 15 competences under 5 clusters: goals, roles, communication, negotiation and managing up. The first element deals with 'sensitivity' to the context within which change is taking place. Once again, Buchanan and Boddy are emphasising that the change process begins with the change agent identifying the organisation's readiness for change. What emerges from their work is a picture of the change agent as a highly skilled and well-trained political operator who has not only an in-depth knowledge of change processes and tools but also the personal qualities and experience to use them both in the open and, especially, behind the scenes.

Weick and Quinn (1999) contrast the role of the Buchanan and Boddy-type change agent with that of the OD-type change agent. They see the OD change agent as acting as the prime mover – the person who makes the change happen. They point out that though traditionally focused on small-group change, OD change agents have become increasingly involved in large-scale change projects, such as culture change, where they:

> abandon several traditional organizational development (OD) assumptions. Large-scale interventions rely less on action theory and discrepancy theory and more on systems theory; less on closely held, internal data generation and more on gathering data from the environment and sharing it widely; . . . less on individual unit learning and more on learning about the whole organization; . . . less incremental and more fundamental in terms of the depth of change.
>
> (Weick and Quinn, 1999: 374)

Consequently, new types of OD interventions require new skills. In particular, Weick and Quinn (1999: 374) argue that the quality of the change agent's argument becomes less important than the language they use: 'Language interventions are becoming a crucial means for agents to create change.' Indeed, whether change agents are operating from an OD perspective or not, they argue that the appropriate use of language by change agents is crucial when dealing with larger-scale, open-ended, continuing and complex change. Weick and Quinn (1999: 381) maintain that in such situations, the change agent ceases to be a neutral supporter of those involved and instead becomes a 'prime mover' whose role 'becomes one of managing language, dialogue, and identity . . . and . . . the most powerful change interventions occur at the level of everyday conversations'. Drawing on the work of Ford and Ford (1995), Weick and Quinn (1999: 381) assert that under these conditions, agents bring about change through a combination of five forms of language or speech acts: 'assertives or claims, directives or requests, commissives or promises, expressives that convey affective states, and declarations that announce a new operational reality.' Like

Pettigrew (2000), Weick and Quinn do not see the change agent as a neutral facilitator but as an active manager of the change process with their own agenda, which they seek to promote or impose by managing and shaping the perceptions of those concerned. However, in so doing, they fail to acknowledge the potential damage this does to the change agent's ability to build trust with and create genuine choices for change recipients.

Buchanan and Boddy (1992: 123) also draw attention to the 'prime mover' role of change agents, especially in terms of their creative ability to undertake the 'social construction of the process of change':

> Expertise does not simply involve the mechanical deployment of diagnostic tools, competences and stereotyped solutions, but involves also the innovative and opportunistic exploitation of other dimensions of the organizational context.

Mirvis (1988) is another who focuses on the crucial role played by change agents' innovative and creative skills in achieving successful change.

In an article entitled 'Grace, magic and miracles', Lichtenstein (1997) investigated this side of the change agent's role further by examining the work of three leading change practitioners: Peter Senge, William Torbert and Ellen Wingard. In the article, the three consultants each described their approach to change and the theories which underpin it. They also described how, in applying their approaches, it was insufficient just to follow the steps laid down. Success required the consultants to overcome major obstacles and, in so doing, to adopt novel and experimental methods. Senge, Torbert and Wingard use terms such as 'grace', 'magic' and 'miracles' to describe the moment of breakthrough, the point where serious obstacles were overcome and genuine progress made. In fact, what they describe is the ability of the change agent to recognise the need to depart from the 'script' and to experiment with the unknown in order to make progress. Just as Buchanan and Boddy (1992) identified the need for change agents to be able to present and utilise the rational face of change, while being adept at the less rational 'backstage' skills, so Lichtenstein (1997: 407) concludes that:

> there is a logical framework that produces rational actions in the first stages of an intervention effort. However, at a critical threshold it is non-linear logic and spontaneous felt action – grace, magic and miracles – that actually supports organizational (and personal) transformation.

Drawing on the work of cultural anthropologists, Schuyt and Schuijt (1998) also use the analogy of the change agent as a magician. They point out that magicians, witch doctors and medicine men in non-Western cultures use symbols and rituals to smooth the various transitions in life cycles: birth, puberty, marriage and death. In the same way, Schuyt and Schuijt (1998: 399) ask, are not consultants and change agents 'also, in a certain sense, magicians who guide and structure important transitions through the use of rituals and symbols?' These rituals and symbols have a number of key functions: to establish the change agent's credentials, to prepare the participants mentally for change, to guide them through the transition, and to reinforce the 'participants' feeling that they are taking part in a controlled and well-managed process of change . . . but ultimately the crux is to reduce the client's uncertainty' (Schuyt and Schuijt, 1998: 405).

The argument of many commentators is that, in the modern world, the multi-faceted and multi-level nature of change means that it cannot be left to a few experts or a few managers, but that change is everyone's job (Clarke, 1993; Gilley *et al*, 2001; Markus and Benjamin,

IDEAS AND PERSPECTIVES 8.2

Caldwell's models of change agent

- Leadership models where change agents are senior managers responsible for identifying and delivering strategic/tranformational change.

- Management models where change agents are seen as middle-level managers/functional specialists who have responsibility for delivering or supporting specific elements of strategic change programmes or projects.

- Consultancy models where change agents are external or internal consultants who can be called on to operate at any level.

- Team models where change agents are seen as teams that operate at various levels in an organisation and which are composed of the requisite managers, employees and consultants necessary to accomplish the particular change project set them.

Source: Caldwell (2003).

1997). In contrast, what the work of Buchanan and Boddy, Lichtenstein, Schuyt and Schuijt and, indeed, the OD movement would seem to argue is that the more complex the change process, the more difficult it is to achieve, and the greater the need to utilise the skills and experience of a specialist change agent. The conclusion they draw from this is that there is a 'one best' type of change agent who possesses a generic set of high-level competences that can be employed in any situation.

While recognising the need for specialist change agents, Caldwell (2003) takes issue with Buchanan and Boddy *et al*. He argues for a contingency model of change agency which recognises that different change situations require different types of change agent. From an extensive literature review, Caldwell identifies four models of change agent (*see* Ideas and perspectives 8.2). These four different models highlight the difficulty, not to say the impossibility, of attempting to construct a generic change agent who can operate in any situation.

The type of change agent identified by Buchanan and Boddy may fit into some of these models, but not all of them. Similarly, the OD-type of change agent may fit into some of these models, but not all of them. What Caldwell has done is to direct academics and practitioners away from both the 'it's everyone's responsibility' and the 'one best way' schools and towards identifying the behaviours and competences necessary for each type of change situation. This, of course, highlights the need to identify the different types of change situation. Crucial to this, as the next section will show, is to understand the frequency and magnitude of change in modern organisations.

The frequency and magnitude of organisational change

As has often been mentioned in this book, the view which many leading commentators take is that organisations are changing at a faster pace and in a more fundamental way than ever before (Greiner and Cummings, 2004; IBM, 2008; Kanter, 2008a; Kotter and Rathgeber, 2006; Peters, 2006). These commentators judge the present level of organisational change to be unprecedented, although – as Part 1 of this book showed – the history of the past 200 years could well be characterised as successive periods of unprecedented change. Obviously, an understanding of whether organisational change is to be a continuing feature or a one-off event, whether it is on a small or large scale, and whether change is fast or slow, plays a key role in judging the appropriateness of particular approaches to managing change. It is, therefore, important to go beyond the tabloid-like headlines thrown up by popular management writers such as Tom Peters (1997a):

Destruction Is Cool! (p. 35)

WOW! is the answer. (p. 309)

We need to examine the main models of organisational change that are currently being promoted and also recognise that there are strong disagreements about the nature and pace of change that organisations experience. In this respect, there are three current models that are prominent in the literature.

The incremental model of change

Advocates of this view see change as being a process whereby individual parts of an organisation deal incrementally and separately with one problem and one goal at a time (*see* Figure 8.1). By managers responding to pressures in their local internal and external environments in this way, over time their organisations become transformed, hopefully for the better. Miller and Friesen (1984: 222) explain that:

> The incrementalist perspective on change has been around a relatively, long time. It stems from the work of Lindblom (1959) and Cyert and March (1963), and was further developed by Hedberg *et al* (1976) and especially Quinn (1980b and 1982). Quinn argues that strategic change is best viewed as 'muddling through with purpose,' using a continuous, evolving and consensus building approach.

Pettigrew *et al* (1992: 14) add that: 'The received wisdom therefore is that change will take place through successive, limited and negotiated shifts.' Though Quinn (1980b, 1982)

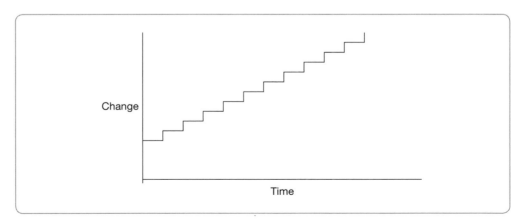

Figure 8.1 Incremental change

and others have marshalled considerable support for the incrementalist perspective from Western sources, the pre-eminent exemplars of incremental change have been Japanese companies (Hamel and Prahalad, 1989). As described in Chapter 3, Japanese companies have an enviable track record of achieving fierce competitiveness through pursuing incremental change year in, year out. Dunphy and Stace (1992) also advocated this approach for Western companies, arguing for a form of managed incrementalism that avoids both the stagnation engendered by fine-tuning and the brutality associated with rapid corporate transformations. However, Mintzberg (1978) argued that though organisations do go through long periods of incremental change, these are often interspersed with brief periods of rapid and revolutionary change. Indeed, given the turbulence of the last 30 years, some writers have argued that it is now the periods of stability which are brief and the revolutionary change periods which are long, at least in Western firms (Pettigrew *et al*, 2001; Weick and Quinn, 1999). Not surprisingly, this has led to an increased interest in how organisations move between periods of stability and instability.

The punctuated equilibrium model of organisational transformation

As shown in Figure 8.2, this somewhat inelegantly titled approach to change:

> depicts organizations as evolving through relatively long periods of stability (equilibrium periods) in their basic patterns of activity that are punctuated by relatively short bursts of fundamental change (revolutionary periods). Revolutionary periods substantively disrupt established activity patterns and install the basis for new equilibrium periods.
>
> (Romanelli and Tushman, 1994: 1141)

The punctuated equilibrium model is associated with the work of Miller and Friesen (1984), Tushman and Romanelli (1985) and Gersick (1991). The inspiration for this model arises from two sources: first, from the challenge to Charles Darwin's gradualist model of evolution in the natural sciences – Steven Jay Gould (1989), in particular, mounted a case for a punctuated equilibrium model of evolution – and second, from the assertion that while most organisations do appear to fit the incrementalist model of change for a period of time, there does come a point when they go through a period of rapid and fundamental change (Gersick, 1991). Orlikowski (1996: 64) notes:

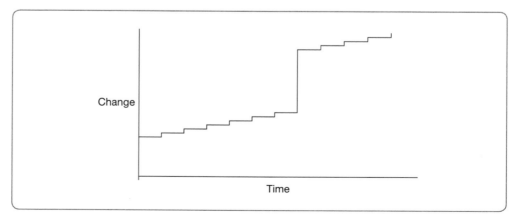

Figure 8.2 Punctuated equilibrium

Punctuated discontinuities are typically triggered by modifications in environmental or internal conditions, for example, new technology, process redesign, or industry deregulation.

Though this view began to take hold in the 1980s, it is by no means new. In the 1970s, Greiner (1972a) observed that as organisations grow, they go through long periods of evolutionary change and short, sharp bursts of revolutionary change. Indeed, Lewin made a similar observation in the 1940s (Lewin, 1947a; Kippenberger, 1998a). However, as even Romanelli and Tushman (1994: 1142) admit: 'Despite the growing prominence and pervasiveness of punctuated equilibrium theory, little research has explored the empirical validity of the model's basic arguments.' Also, research which has looked at the theory suggests that punctuated change can 'destroy competence and appropriateness and so lead to eventual collapse' (Sastry, 1997: 266). In addition, just as the incremental model is criticised for assuming that organisations operate in or go through periods of stability, so too is the punctuated model. The assumption of both is that stability is the natural or preferred state for organisations (Orlikowski, 1996). However, there are some who believe that continuous change is or should be the norm, and this has led them to reject both the incremental and punctuated models of change (Brown and Eisenhardt, 1997).

The continuous transformation model of change

The argument put forward by proponents of this model is that, in order to survive, organisations must develop the ability to change themselves continuously in a fundamental manner (*see* Figure 8.3). From this perspective, Weick and Quinn (1999: 366) argue:

> Change is a pattern of endless modifications in work processes and social practice. It is driven by organizational instability and alert reactions to daily contingencies. Numerous small accommodations accumulate and amplify.

This is particularly the case in fast-moving sectors such as retail where, as Greenwald (1996: 54) notes: 'If you look at the best retailers out there, they are constantly reinventing themselves.' Brown and Eisenhardt (1997: 1) maintain:

> For firms such as Intel, Wal-Mart, 3M, Hewlett-Packard and Gillette, the ability to change rapidly and continuously, especially by developing new products, is not only a core competence,

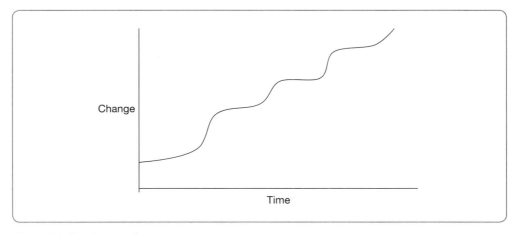

Figure 8.3 Continuous change

it is also at the heart of their cultures. For these firms, change is not the rare, episodic phenom-enon described by the punctuated equilibrium model but, rather, it is endemic to the way these organizations compete. Moreover, in high-velocity industries with short product cycles and rapidly-shifting competitive landscapes, the ability to engage in rapid and relentless continuous change is a crucial capability for survival.

The underpinning rationale for the continuous transformation model is that the environ-ment in which organisations operate is changing, and will continue to change, rapidly, radically and unpredictably. Only by continuous change and adaptation will organisations be able to keep aligned with their environment and thus survive. Though this view has many adherents, there are two groups that are its main promoters. The first is the Culture–Excellence school. This group, especially Tom Peters (1997a, 1997b) and Rosabeth Moss Kanter *et al* (1997), has been arguing for a continuous transformation model of change since the early 1980s. However, as noted in Chapter 3, they provide little solid empirical evidence to support their view. Indeed, research has shown that the success of leading European companies which have remained in business for more than 100 years can be partly attributed to their con-servatism about change; they seldom make radical changes (Stadler, 2007).

The second group are those who seek to apply complexity theories to organisations (Wheatley, 1992b). As described in Chapter 4, complexity theories are concerned with the emergence of order in dynamic non-linear systems operating at the edge of chaos: in other words, systems that are constantly changing and where the laws of cause and effect appear not to apply (Beeson and Davis, 2000; Haigh, 2002; Wheatley, 1992b). Order in such systems manifests itself in a largely unpredictable fashion, in which patterns of behaviour emerge in irregular but similar forms through a process of self-organisation, which is governed by a small number of simple order-generating rules (Black, 2000; MacIntosh and MacLean, 2001; Tetenbaum, 1998). Many writers have argued that organisations are also complex systems which, to survive, need to operate at the edge of chaos and have to respond continuously to changes in their environments through just such a process of spontaneous self-organising change (Hayles, 2000; Lewis, 1994; Macbeth, 2002; MacIntosh and MacLean, 1999, 2001; Stacey, 2003; Stickland, 1998). In applying this perspective to the computer industry, Brown and Eisenhardt (1997: 28) found:

> The rate and scale of innovation . . . was such that the term 'incremental' seemed, in retro-spect, stretched. Yet it was not radical innovation such as DNA cloning, either. . . . Similarly, managers described 'constantly reinventing' themselves. This too seemed more than incre-mental (i.e., unlike replacing top managers here and there) but also not the massive, rare, and risky change of the organizational and strategy literatures. And so we realized that we were probably looking at a third kind of process that is neither incremental nor radical and that does not fit the punctuated equilibrium model.

The problems with this perspective are that (a) it is not clear that one can readily apply theories from the physical sciences to the social sciences, as demonstrated by the fact that even proponents of its use in the social sciences are equivocal on this point; and (b) there have been few empirical studies which provide strong evidence to support the complexity view (Burnes, 2005; Stickland, 1998).

In examining these three perspectives on change, we can see arguments for the incre-mental model, arguments for the punctuated model and arguments for the continuous change model. We can also see arguments against all three. Does this mean that all three are wrong? Certainly, to the extent that they can claim to be universal theories which cover all organisations and situations, they all appear to be wrong. However, they also appear to offer a good explanation for the behaviour of some organisations and for some situations. For example, Konnopke's Imbiss was established in 1930 but appears to have changed little over the intervening 80 or so years, and the changes which have taken place certainly seem to fit the incremental model rather than any other. There is also good evidence that many leading and successful European companies tend to fit this model (Stadler, 2007). We can also find empirical evidence of this sort for the punctuated equilibrium model, the prime example being the banking industry. The 2008 financial crisis precipitated the banking industry into a short period of crisis and massive change (Stiglitz, 2010). However, after this, it settled down basically to business as usual, thus providing a good illustration of punctuated equilibrium (Blumenthal, 2012; Lashinsky, 2012). Similarly, evidence exists for the continuous change model, especially in high-technology companies operating in fast-moving markets, or those where a convergence of the digital, social and mobile spheres is necessary to meet customer expectations (Deeds and Hill, 1996; IBM, 2012). Apple is one of the prime examples of a company that has produced break-through products time after time, and which bears no resemblance to the company Steve Jobs returned to in 1997 (Blumenthal, 2012; Lashinsky, 2012).

Therefore, what we appear to have is not three universal theories but three situational or contingency theories which apply to different organisations in different situations at different times. The implications of this for managing change are that first, organisations have to identify their situation and second, they then have to make choices as to how to respond to it. Though many organisations react to events or seek to fit themselves to their situation, it is clear that some organisations and leaders seek to shape their situation to fit how they want to operate, whether that be in an incremental, punctuated or continuous change mould (Blumenthal, 2012; Etzold and Mueller, 2012; Lashinsky, 2012; Stadler, 2007).

Conclusions

In this chapter, we have sought to address five key sets of questions which organisations need to address before embarking on change:

1. **Why do we want to change?** In addressing this question, it was shown that, in the face of internal and external opportunities and threats, organisations change in order to become more effective at achieving their goals, and that effectiveness is derived from factors such as processes, people and organisational culture.

2. **Should we focus on individual, group or system change?** Organisations are social and technical systems which require individuals and groups to work together effectively if the system is to achieve its goals. When problems, opportunities and challenges arise, the key task for those responsible for maintaining the system is to decide whether the focus of the response lies at the level of the organisation, group or individual. Though these levels cannot be seen in isolation from each other, depending on the situation, the main focus of the response will be at the individual, group or system level.

3. **Will there be resistance and, if so, where from? How can we gain employee commitment? Are we ready for change?** These are three interrelated questions and, in some ways, can be best answered last first. If an organisation is ready for change, employees

will already be prepared to change, commitment will come readily and resistance – if any – will be minimal. Alternatively, if it is not ready for change, gaining commitment may be difficult and resistance can be expected. Resistance will not result from employees' innate aversion to change *per se* but from the nature of the change and the way the organisation manages it, which will give rise to incompatible forces within the system.

4. **Who will manage the change process? Do they have the appropriate skills?** The answer to the first question rather depends on the type of change. Just as some illnesses are best dealt with by general practitioners and some by specialists, so it tends to be the same with change initiatives. Incremental changes which are wholly within one area might best be dealt with by the manager/supervisor in that area. Meanwhile, initiatives which span more than one area and are of a more complex nature might require a specialist change agent. In both cases, though, it depends on the skills of the person leading the change process. Some managers may be experienced at managing change, while some change agents may be limited in the range of change situations they can manage.

5. **What are the frequency and magnitude of the changes required in order for us to survive?** For some organisations, incremental and infrequent adjustments to their activities will be sufficient for them to remain in business. For others, anything but frequent and large-scale change will result in their being overtaken by competitors and put out of business. However, this is not just a case of organisations scanning their environment, recognising the forces for change and acting accordingly. As argued in Chapter 6, organisations can exercise choice in terms of markets, products and other key pressures. As with Konnopke's Imbiss, these choices can minimise the need for change or, as with Steve Jobs and Apple, they can initiate a process of continuing and radical change. Organisations and those who manage them are not always at the mercy of market forces: sometimes they are the ones who create and control those forces.

It follows from the above that an organisation will need to choose an approach to change which is most appropriate in the light of the answers it gives to the above questions. For example, an organisation seeking to bring about transformational change is likely to require a different approach to change than one seeking incremental change. Similarly, an organisation which is unused to and unready for change is likely to require a different approach to one which is ready and where change is the norm. In the next three chapters, we will examine the main approaches to change and identify the situations in which they can most appropriately be used.

TEST YOUR LEARNING

Short discussion topics

The purpose of these is to enable students to check and reflect on the topics. The discussions should last for no more than 5–10 minutes. Depending on the length of the lecture, there could be one, two or three such discussions in a session. The following are five suggested topics which address issues raised in this chapter:

1. Should we judge effectiveness by process or outcome?

2. Give examples of individual, group and system changes.

3. Should change agents use political skills to get their job done?

4. List three factors which would tell you that an organisation was not ready for change.

5. The Konnopke's Imbiss example is an anomaly. The age of incremental change is dead.

Class debates

The purpose of class debates is to enable students to explore a topic in depth by setting up a 'for and against' debate. The class can be split into two and one half asked to research the 'for' case and the other the 'against' case. Individuals can then be chosen at random to introduce their side of the debate. Alternatively, two individuals for each side can be told in advance that they will be introducing the debate. The length of such debates depends on the time available, the size of the class and their enthusiasm for the topic. However, less than 30 minutes is probably too short and more than 60 minutes probably too long. The following are three suggested topics which address issues raised in this chapter:

1. The focus of change should always be on individual behaviour.

2. Resistance is always about the system and never about the individual.

3. Change is everyone's responsibility.

Essay questions

1. Critically discuss the difference between the individual approach to resistance and the systems approach. What are their implications for assessing readiness for change?

2. To what extent and why do you agree with following statement: 'The expertise of the change agent cannot, therefore, be expressed and understood independently of an understanding of the process of change and the context in which it is undertaken.' (Buchanan and Boddy, 1992: 87)

Suggested further reading

The following articles provide further information on and insights into the topics discussed in this chapter.

Brown, SL and Eisenhardt, KM (1997) The art of continuous change: linking complexity theory and time-paced evolution in relentlessly shifting organizations. *Administrative Science Quarterly*, 4(1), March, 1–34.

Caldwell, R (2003) Models of change agency: a fourfold classification. *British Journal of Management*, 14(2), 131–42.

Dent, EB and Goldberg, SG (1999) Challenging resistance to change. *Journal of Applied Behavioral Science*, 35(1), 25–41.

Schein, EH (2002) Models and tools for stability and change in human systems. *Reflections*, 4(2), 34–46.

Sowa, JE, Selden, SC and Sandfort, JR (2004) No longer unmeasurable? A multidimensional integrated model of nonprofit organizational effectiveness. *Nonprofit and Voluntary Sector Quarterly*, 33(4), 711–28.

GK Printers Limited

Background

GK Printers Limited is a small, family-run printing business. It was established just after the Second World War by the present managing director's father. The company was originally a jobbing printers, which is to say they would print anything. 'No job too large or too small' might well have been their motto, although in fact the mainstay of their business was producing stationery, business cards and publicity brochures for local companies. Unlike many other small printers, the company had updated its equipment and processes which enabled it to grow its business while similar companies struggled. Nevertheless, its customers, old and new, were becoming increasingly demanding with regard to price and delivery. In addition, there were signs that its competitors were beginning to win back some of the work they had lost to GK.

Eventually, it became clear that GK was beginning to lose a significant amount of business. This was partly due to increased competition, but mainly it was because its customers, in seeking to cut their own costs, were reducing the size and frequency of their orders (though when orders were placed, they were often required far faster than previously). This presented a double threat to GK. First, the fall in overall volumes was having an adverse effect on turnover and profit. Second, the reduction in size of individual print runs was having an adverse effect on costs because, though the actual volume was smaller, the design, order processing and set-up costs remained constant. In effect, as volumes decreased, the cost of each printed item increased. In addition, there were worrying signs that some customers were using word-processing packages and colour printers to produce their own publicity material instead of going to a printer.

At a time when its customers were pressurising it to cut costs, GK was faced with the dilemma of whether to increase its prices to offset rising costs (and risk customers going elsewhere or developing their own facilities), or to maintain or reduce prices and see its profits plunge. The knee-jerk reaction of many in the company was, 'If customers want smaller runs, the price goes up.' However, the managing director and the other managers in GK came reluctantly to accept that, while the logic was impeccable, the result could be disastrous.

After much seemingly futile discussion, it was the marketing and design manager who eventually came up with a suggestion that, though laughed at initially, later turned out to be the key to GK's survival. He pointed out that to maintain its existing volume of business, and perhaps even increase it, GK needed to improve on its already good level of service. In particular, it needed to cut costs in order to cut prices and improve the efficiency of its internal operations to cut delivery times. The initial reaction to these suggestions was, perhaps predictably, negative. After all, if volumes decrease, unit costs must increase because set-up costs are constant; also, an increase in the number of smaller print runs actually extends turnaround times for a similar reason – more set-ups are required. So the marketing and design manager was attempting to turn the conventional wisdom regarding printing on its head. In addition, he was a relative newcomer to the company and, in some people's eyes, he was believed to lack in-depth knowledge of the printing industry. Finally, GK had already made significant strides in improving efficiency and cutting costs, and there was some doubt as to the scope for any real improvements in these areas.

A false start

Despite the initial adverse comments, the managing director began to wonder whether it might be possible to reduce set-up times and costs. If it could, he reasoned, the company would be able to attract more business, prevent customers seeking in-house solutions, and undermine its competitors. In the past, the managing director had brought in outside consultants to help improve the company. However, in this instance he asked the marketing and design manager to put forward some suggestions for reducing costs and set-up times. This was for two reasons. First, he wanted to give him a chance to prove himself to the rest of the team. Second, the managing director wanted to demonstrate that they had the managerial talent to dispense with outside assistance.

The marketing and design manager quickly responded and within a fortnight presented his proposals to the managing director and other senior staff. He began by identifying what he saw as the main problem the company faced:

1. Though there had been a slight decline in the number of individual orders, the actual reduction in the volume of business was much greater because customers were ordering shorter print runs.

2. The result of this was that, while office staff, marketing, design, administration, etc. were as busy as ever, the print shop was short of work, and it was not unusual to see printers sitting reading the paper with nothing else to do.

3. However, though the printers were underworked, this did not provide much scope for reducing delivery times because most of GK's lead time was accounted for by non-printing activities – especially design, which could take anything up to two weeks.

Having laid out what he saw as the problem, the marketing and design manager went on to offer a solution. He argued that the key to solving the company's problems lay in speeding up design time. He pointed out that there was always a backlog of design work ranging from one to two weeks. Given that everything, even repeat orders, went through design, total lead time could be anything from three to five weeks. While this was considerably better than in the past, it was no longer acceptable as customers were cutting stock to a minimum. Many customers were asking to have their printing back within seven days, sometimes even sooner where promotional material was concerned. The solution, therefore, he argued, was to have more design staff. If one extra designer was employed the marketing and design manager believed that design lead time could be reduced to two or three days.

The managing director and other managers, especially the printing manager, who had been arguing unsuccessfully for new equipment for some time, were taken aback by this proposal. The analysis, they believed, was correct but the solution, they felt, was an outrageous piece of opportunism. The case for more design staff had been raised and rejected in the recent past. The marketing and design manager's colleagues felt that he was blatantly using the company's current problems to empire-build. Not surprisingly, he

vigorously denied this. Nevertheless, the meeting ended acrimoniously and no decision was taken.

The managing director was particularly infuriated, as he had genuinely been expecting an acceptable solution to emerge from the meeting. Instead, the friendly working atmosphere he valued, and which he felt he did much to promote, had been shattered. Nor did he see an easy way to bring his managers back together to seek a cooperative solution. He was also annoyed because he realised that he had made a mistake in asking only one person to put forward their view. Not only would a team have avoided favouring one area rather than another, it would not even occur to anyone to make the accusation. Having made the mistake, however, he was not sure how to remedy it. If a team was set up to examine the options that did not include the marketing and design manager, he would rightly see it as a snub and probably attack any solution that was put forward. If he was included, it was likely that he would continue to push his proposal and the other managers would react badly. His inclination was to impose a solution and tell everyone to get on and implement it. Unfortunately, he did not have a solution to impose.

Questions

1. What were GK's reasons for wanting to change? How would the changes improve their effectiveness?

2. Was GK's focus on individual, group or system change?

3. Was GK ready for change?

4. Why was there resistance and what caused it?

5. How did GK go about gaining commitment for the change?

6. Who was the change agent? Did they have the appropriate skills?

7. Is GK a company which is characterised by incremental, punctuated or continuous change? What was the magnitude of the changes required in this instance?

Planned change and Organization Development (OD)

Learning objectives

After studying this chapter, you should be able to:

- discuss the contribution of Kurt Lewin to managing change;
- state the core elements of Lewin's Planned approach to change;
- show how Planned change provided the core of OD;
- be aware of the history and nature of OD;
- understand the key differences between Lewin's view of Planned change and that promoted by OD;
- appreciate the benefits of Planned change and OD;
- list the main criticisms and defences of Planned change and OD.

MINI CASE STUDY 9.1

Firms grow smarter on strategy

Nearly all the leaders of the firms in the 2012 FT Law 25 had the same observation this year: the market is flat so the only way to grow is to win business from competitors or to create new markets. Most of the top US law firms have similar strategies – to prove to clients that they are unique. This onus on differentiation may be one reason why they have been keener than ever to show the *Financial Times* their innovations. A flat, paralysed market has taken innovation from something that is nice to have, to being a "must-have". The competition in the *FT* report reflects the struggle for market differentiation.

In terms of changing the value proposition of lawyers, the trends have been subtle but more interesting. Brad Malt, chairman of Ropes & Gray, says: "Buggy whip manufacturers went out of business as they did not adapt to the car. We are faced with a buggy whip moment. Firms can pretend that old market dynamics exist – but they don't." For the firms who agree with this, changing the behaviours of their lawyers to align more with clients' demands is imperative.

Paul Hastings has put behaviour change at the centre of its Superior Performance and Coaching programme, designed to place the competencies most valued by clients at the core of its associate career development. The firm analysed the behaviours of role model lawyers in the firm before building a proprietary framework around them. Although this is not new in the corporate world, the systematic and comprehensive way that the firm has sought to replicate desired lawyer behaviour is unusual for the legal profession.

Crowell & Moring realised that to get the whole firm to use professional project management techniques required behaviour change. "We started with the notion that we, not an outside consultant, had to change behaviour before an online tool would be effective," says the firm. After putting more than 400 lawyers through the training, the firm's project management approach is now becoming a differentiator for it in winning pitches.

The nature of the financial crisis has also driven unexpected opportunity. While the image of the bankers is tarnished, the legal profession retains its reputation for integrity and independence. Several law firm leaders felt that clients were increasingly looking to their lawyers instead of the bankers for more all-encompassing business advice. Chris White, chairman of Cadwalader, Wickersham & Taft, says: "There is a void as to who the CEO can turn to. They are relying more on the lawyers and not so much on the bankers. This gives the profession an opportunity to innovate."

Another firm that has done significantly better in the rankings is Weil, Gotshal & Manges – up 16 places – which has appointed younger partners to head the litigation and corporate departments. Executive partner Barry Wolf says: "Our lawyers are adapting to the moving cheese. We preach the wow factor – the idea that you have to continually impress clients."

Introduction

In the last chapter, we examined five fundamental questions which organisations need to address in order to create the conditions for successful change. The next step, in this and the following two chapters, is to focus on understanding and categorising the main approaches to planning and implementing change. As has been shown in previous chapters, there is now a wide recognition that change is not a technical or quantitative exercise, but that successful change is dependent on what Douglas McGregor (1960) referred to, in the title of his famous book, as *The Human Side of Enterprise* (*see* Chapter 2). This recognition is highlighted in the *Financial Times'* review of the top 25 US law firms (*see* Mini Case Study 9.1).

Behind the grand terminology of strategy, uniqueness, differentiation, and innovation, these companies see the key to survival and success as 'changing the behaviours of their lawyers to align more with clients'. This is hardly surprising: as Schein (1988: 12) stated, 'all organizational problems are fundamentally problems involving human interactions and processes'. Therefore, when organisations embark on a change programme, regardless of the terminology or the type of change involved, if the change is to be successful, individuals and groups will have to change their behaviour.

This chapter explores the work of Kurt Lewin and his development of Planned change, which focuses on changing the behaviour of individuals and groups in organisations. It shows how Lewin's work paved the way for and provides the core of organization development (OD). Planned change focuses on the 'human side' of the organisation. The chapter begins by reviewing Lewin's work, especially his creation of Planned change. It then goes on to examine the relationship between Planned change and OD. The chapter shows that Lewin's approach to change, under the umbrella of OD, dominated both the theory and practice of change management from the 1940s until the 1980s, when it began to face increasing levels of criticism, from both those questioning its suitability for organisations operating in dynamic and unpredictable environments, and those who believed that OD had lost its sense of direction and purpose.

The chapter concludes by arguing that, though some of the criticism may be unjustified, the Planned approach does appear to be more suited to incremental–behavioural change than larger-scale and more radical restructuring initiatives.

The Planned approach: from Lewin to Organization Development (OD)

Kurt Lewin and Planned change

Planned change is a term first coined by Kurt Lewin to distinguish change that was consciously embarked upon by an organisation, as opposed to unintended changes such as those that might come about by accident, by impulse, by misunderstanding or that might be forced on an unwilling organisation (Marrow, 1969). Therefore, 'Planned', in this case, does not mean that someone sits down in advance and writes a detailed plan stating what will take place, and when and how it will be achieved. Rather, it means that the organisation pro-actively identifies an area where it believes change is required and undertakes a process to evaluate and, if necessary, bring about change.

Though the significance of his work for contemporary organisations was strongly questioned in the 1980s and 1990s, few social scientists can have received the level of praise and admiration that has been heaped upon Kurt Lewin (Ash, 1992; Bargal *et al*, 1992; Burnes and Cooke, 2012a, 2012b; Dent and Goldberg, 1999; Dickens and Watkins, 1999; Tobach, 1994). As Edgar Schein (1988: 239) enthusiastically commented:

> There is little question that the intellectual father of contemporary theories of applied behavioral science, action research and planned change is Kurt Lewin. His seminal work on leadership style and the experiments on planned change which took place in World War II in an effort to change consumer behavior launched a whole generation of research in group dynamics and the implementation of change programs.

For most of his life, Lewin's main preoccupation was the resolution of social conflict and, in particular, the problems of minority or disadvantaged groups. Underpinning this preoccupation was a strong belief that only the permeation of democratic values into all facets of society could prevent the worst extremes of social conflict. As his wife wrote in the Preface to a volume of his collected work published after his death:

> Kurt Lewin was so constantly and predominantly preoccupied with the task of advancing the conceptual representation of the social-psychological world, and at the same time he was so filled with the urgent desire to use his theoretical insight for the building of a better world, that it is difficult to decide which of these two sources of motivation flowed with greater energy or vigour.
> (GW Lewin, 1948b)

To a large extent, his interests and beliefs stemmed from his background as a German Jew. Lewin was born in 1890 and, for a Jew growing up in Germany at that time, officially approved anti-Semitism was a fact of life. Few Jews could expect to achieve a responsible post in the civil service or universities. Despite this, Lewin was awarded a doctorate at the University of Berlin in 1916 and went on to teach there. Though he was never awarded tenured status, Lewin achieved a growing international reputation in the 1920s as a leader in his field (Lewin, 1992). However, with the rise of the Nazi Party, Lewin recognised that the position of Jews in Germany was increasingly threatened. The election of Hitler as Chancellor in 1933 was the final straw for him; he resigned from the University and moved to America (Marrow, 1969).

In America, Lewin found a job first as a 'refugee scholar' at Cornell University and then, from 1935 to 1945, at the University of Iowa. Here he was to embark on an ambitious programme of research, which covered topics such as child–parent relations, conflict in marriage, styles of leadership, worker motivation and performance, conflict in industry, group problem-solving, communication and attitude change, racism, anti-Semitism, anti-racism, discrimination and prejudice, integration–segregation, peace, war and poverty (Bargal *et al*, 1992; Cartwright, 1952; Lewin, 1948a). As Cooke (1999) notes, given the prevalence of racism and anti-Semitism in America at the time, much of this work, especially his increasingly public advocacy in support of disadvantaged groups, put Lewin on the political left.

During the years of the Second World War, Lewin did much work for the American war effort. This included studies of the morale of front-line troops and psychological warfare, and his famous study aimed at persuading American housewives to buy cheaper cuts of meat (Lewin, 1943a; Marrow, 1969). He was also much in demand as a speaker on minority and inter-group relations (Smith, 2001). These activities chimed with one of his central preoccupations, which was how Germany's authoritarian and racist culture could be replaced with one imbued with democratic values. He saw democracy, and the spread of democratic values throughout society, as the central bastion against authoritarianism and despotism. That he viewed the establishment of democracy as a major task, and avoided simplistic and structural recipes, can be gleaned from the following extracts from his article on 'The special case of Germany' (Lewin, 1943b: 55):

> Nazi culture . . . is deeply rooted, particularly in the youth on whom the future depends. It is a culture which is centred around power as the supreme value and which denounces justice and equality . . . (p. 43)

> To be stable, a cultural change has to penetrate all aspects of a nation's life. The change must, in short, be a change in the 'cultural atmosphere', not merely a change of a single item. (p. 46)

> Change in culture requires the change of leadership forms in every walk of life. At the start, particularly important is leadership in those social areas which are fundamental from the point of view of power.

With the end of the War, Lewin established the Research Center for Group Dynamics at the Massachusetts Institute of Technology. The aim of the Center was to investigate all aspects of group behaviour, especially how it could be changed. At the same time, he was also chief architect of the Commission on Community Interrelations (CCI). Founded and funded by the American Jewish Congress, its aim was the eradication of discrimination against all minority groups. As Lewin wrote at the time:

> We Jews will have to fight for ourselves and we will do so strongly and with good conscience. We also know that the fight of the Jews is part of the fight of all minorities for democratic equality of rights and opportunities. (Quoted in Marrow, 1969: 175)

In pursuing this objective, Lewin believed that his work on Group Dynamics and Action Research would provide the key tools for the CCI. Lewin's work paralleled similar developments at the Tavistock Institute in the UK and he played a key role in the founding of its journal, *Human Relations* (Jaques, 1998; Marrow, 1969).

Perhaps the most crucial event in promoting his work, however, occurred in 1946, when the Connecticut State Inter-Racial Commission asked Lewin to help train leaders and conduct research on the most effective means of combating racial and religious prejudice in communities. This led to the development of the famous (or infamous) T-groups (sensitivity training), which have been described as one of the most important, and contentious, social inventions of the twentieth century (Back, 1972; Campbell and Dunnette, 1968; Highhouse, 2002). It also led to the foundation of the National Training Laboratories (NTL), which championed T-groups and created the basis for the emergence of OD as a powerful change movement. However, Lewin's huge workload took its toll on his health, and on 11 February 1947 he died of a heart attack just at the point when his work on change was beginning to gain momentum and recognition (Burnes and Cooke, 2012b; Lewin, 1992).

The key projects and events which contributed to the development of Planned change and laid the foundations of OD can be seen in Ideas and perspectives 9.1. What this table shows is not just the range of studies in which Lewin was involved but also the importance

IDEAS AND PERSPECTIVES 9.1

Lewin – key projects and events 1939–47

Date	Study/Event	Location	Focus	Concepts	Citation
1938–9	Autocracy–Democracy	Iowa	The effects of different leadership styles on children's behaviour	Participation and group decision-making	Lewin et al (1939)
1939	Employee Turnover	Harwood	Employee retention	Changing supervisory behaviour	Marrow (1969)
1940/1	Group Decision-Making	Harwood	Democratic participation and productivity	Participation and group decision-making	Marrow (1969)
1941	Training in Democratic Leadership	Iowa	Improving leadership behaviours and techniques	Sensitivity training	Bavelas and Lewin (1942)
1942	Food Habits	Iowa	Changing the food-buying habits of housewives	Participation and group decision-making	Lewin (1943a)
1942	Self-Management	Harwood	Increasing workers' control over the pace of work	Group decision-making	Marrow (1969)
1944/5	Leadership Training	Harwood	Improving the interpersonal skills and effectiveness of supervisors	Role play	French (1945)
1944/5	Commission on Community Interrelations (CCI)	New York	The problems and conflicts of group and community life	Action Research	Marrow (1969)
1945	Research Center for Group Dynamics	MIT	Understanding and changing group behaviour	Action Research	Marrow (1969)
1946	Changing Stereotypes	Harwood	Changing attitudes to older workers	Information gathering, discussion and reflection	Marrow (1957 & 1972)
1946	Connecticut State Inter-Racial Commission	New Britain, Connecticut	Leadership training	Sensitivity training/ role play	Marrow (1969)
1947	National Training Laboratory	Bethel, Maine	Leadership training	T-groups (sensitivity training/role play)	Marrow (1967 & 1969)
1947	Overcoming Resistance to Change	Harwood	The impact of different approaches to change on productivity	Participative change/ force field analysis	Coch and French (1948)

Source: Adapted from Burnes (2007).

of his work with the Harwood Manufacturing Corporation. As Dent (2002) commented on the work conducted at Harwood:

> Although this comprehensive effort is much less well-known than the Hawthorne studies, the research which came out of it has perhaps had a greater impact on group decision-making processes, self-management, leadership development, meeting management, stereotyping and resistance to change, among others.

Burnes (2007) also shows that the Harwood studies constitute a milestone in the study of organisational change. Harwood (in Marion, Virginia) became the arena where Lewin developed, tested and proved Planned change, and as such laid the foundations of OD. In particular, they allowed Lewin to move his work from the laboratory to the workplace. Lewin's Autocracy–Democracy study had shown the effectiveness of participative-democratic management in managing and changing group behaviour under experimental conditions (Lewin *et al*, 1939). The Harwood studies showed its effectiveness in real-life industrial situations and laid the foundations for the rapid rise of participative management in the 1950s and 1960s (Cartwright, 1951; Cartwright and Zander, 1953; Likert, 1967; Marrow, 1969; Mosely, 1987; Seashore and Bowers, 1970). What the Harwood studies showed, as did the parallel studies in social change (*see* Ideas and perspective 9.1), was that participative decision-making, where groups were allowed to make their own democratic choices, was a far more effective way of managing and sustaining change than the unilateral imposition of change by management (Burnes, 2007; Burnes and Cooke, 2012a, 2012b). Substantial subsequent research has confirmed that participation and choice are central to effective and sustained change, thus underlining the importance of Lewin's Planned approach to change (Carpenter, 2013; Diamond, 1992; McMillan and Connor, 2005; Oreg *et al*, 2011; Tversky and Kahneman, 1981).

Planned change

Lewin was a humanitarian who believed that only by resolving social conflict, whether it be religious, racial, marital or industrial, could the human condition be improved. He believed that the key to resolving social conflict was to facilitate learning and so enable individuals to understand and restructure their perceptions of the world around them. In this he was much influenced by the Gestalt psychologists he had worked with in Berlin (Burnes and Cooke, 2012a; Smith, 2001). A central theme of much of his work is the view that 'the group to which an individual belongs is the ground for his perceptions, his feelings and his actions' (Allport, 1948: vii). Also, despite the fact that his work covered many subjects and fields, as Gold (1999: 295) states: 'It is quite clear that Lewin thought of his professional activities as a piece, seamless and integrated.' Therefore, though Planned change has four individual elements – Field Theory, Group Dynamics, Action Research and the Three-Step model – and though they are often treated as separate themes of his work, Lewin saw them as a unified whole with each element supporting and reinforcing the others, and all of them necessary to understand and bring about Planned change, whether it be at the level of the individual, group, organisation or even society (Bargal and Bar, 1992; Kippenberger, 1998a, 1998b; Smith, 2001). Allport (1948: ix) states:

> All of his concepts, whatever root-metaphor they employ, comprise a single well integrated system.

This can be seen by examining these four elements of his work in turn.

Field Theory

In developing Field Theory, Lewin was greatly influenced by Gestalt psychology, which emerged in Germany in the early part of the twentieth century (Köhler, 1967). For psychologists, a Gestalt is a perceptual pattern or configuration which is the construct of the individual mind. Lewin referred to the Gestalt by a number of names, the most common being 'life space' or 'field'. Lewin's Field Theory argues that behaviour is derived from the totality of coexisting and interdependent forces which impinge on a person or group and which make up the life space or field in which the behaviour takes place (Burnes and Cooke, 2012a; Lewin, 1942). The field is a coherent whole which has specific properties that can neither be derived from the individual elements nor be considered merely as the sum of them (Kadar and Shaw, 2000).

As Figure 9.1 shows, Lewin conceived of behavioural change as movement from one part of the field to another. Within the field of forces shown in Figure 9.1, **P** is the individual or group, **O** represents their current situation or behaviour, and **G** is the goal that they wish to achieve or the change that they wish to make. Lewin argued that in order to move from **O** to **G**, it is necessary to remove or 'unfreeze' the restraining forces in the sectors of the field which prevent movement, such as personal defences or group norms (Weick and Quinn, 1999).

In order to achieve this, it is first necessary to identify what these restraining forces are. Field Theory provides a method of mapping the totality and complexity of the field in which the behaviour takes place and, consequently, provides a means of identifying the forces which govern group behaviour (Back, 1992). Lewin maintained that to understand any situation it was necessary that: 'One should view the present situation – the *status quo* – as being maintained by certain conditions or forces' (Lewin, 1943a: 172).

As Figure 9.2 shows, the status quo is maintained because forces within a life space or field driving change are in balance with the forces restraining change. Lewin (1947b) postulated that group behaviour is an intricate set of symbolic interactions and forces that not only affects group structures but also modify individual behaviour. Therefore, individual behaviour is a function of the group environment or field, as he termed it. Consequently, any changes in behaviour stem from changes, be they small or large, in the forces within the field, i.e. either an increase in the driving forces or a decrease in the restraining forces (Lewin, 1947a). Lewin defined a field as 'a totality of coexisting facts which are conceived of as mutually interdependent' (Lewin, 1946: 240). Lewin believed that a field was in a continuous state of adaptation and that 'Change and constancy are relative concepts; group life is never without change, merely differences in the amount and type of change exist' (Lewin, 1947a: 199). This is why Lewin used the term 'quasi-stationary equilibrium' to

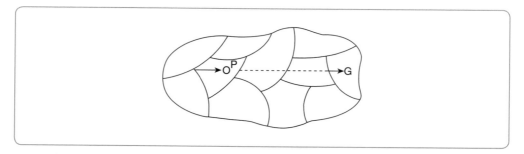

Figure 9.1 Field with person and goal

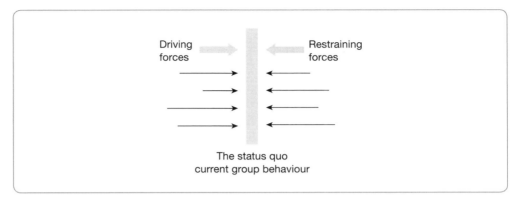

Figure 9.2 Force Field Analysis

indicate that, while there might be a rhythm and pattern to the behaviour and processes of a group, these tended to fluctuate constantly owing to changes in the forces or circumstances that impinge on the group.

Lewin's view was that if one could identify, plot and establish the potency of these forces, then it would be possible not only to understand why individuals, groups and organisations behave as they do but also what forces would need to be diminished or strengthened in order to bring about change. A key belief of Lewin's was that, in general, change could be effective only if people embarked on it of their own free will and could make informed choices about whether and what to change (Burnes, 2004c; Marrow, 1969). Over the years, researchers have found considerable support for Lewin's view that the freedom of individuals and groups to accept or reject change is central to its effectiveness (Carpenter, 2013). Indeed, research has shown that where individuals have a choice over decisions that affect them, they are likely to be more than four or five times more committed to the decision than if the choice has been imposed on them (Bar-Hillel and Neter, 1996).

Because of the need to involve people in decision-making and change, and their need to consider their choices fully, Lewin saw behavioural change as a slow process; however, he did recognise that under certain circumstances, such as a personal, organisational or societal crisis, the various forces in the field can shift quickly and radically. In such situations, established routines and behaviours break down and the status quo is no longer viable; new patterns of activity can rapidly emerge and a new equilibrium (or quasi-stationary equilibrium) is formed (Lewin, 1947a; Kippenberger, 1998a).

With Lewin's death, the interest in Field Theory waned (Back, 1992; Gold, 1992; Hendry, 1996), but in the past two decades it has once again begun to attract interest, especially in terms of understanding and overcoming resistance to change (Argyris, 1990; Hirschhorn, 1988). However, the form which has emerged, Force Field Analysis, tends to focus only on identifying driving and restraining forces, as in Figure 9.2, rather than constructing the entire life space or field of a group or an individual. According to Hendry (1996), even critics of Lewin's work have drawn on Field Theory to develop their own models of change (*see* Pettigrew *et al*, 1989, 1992). Indeed, parallels have even been drawn between Lewin's work on Field Theory and the work of complexity theorists (Back, 1992; Kippenberger, 1998). Nevertheless, Field Theory is now probably the least understood element of Lewin's work, yet, because of its potential to map the forces impinging on an individual, group or organisation, it underpinned the other elements of his work (Burnes and Cooke, 2012a).

Group Dynamics

> The word 'dynamics' . . . comes from a Greek word meaning force. . . . 'group dynamics' refers to the forces operating in groups. . . . it is a study of these forces: what gives rise to them, what conditions modify them, what consequences they have, etc. (Cartwright, 1951: 382)

Lewin was the first psychologist to write about 'group dynamics' and the importance of the group in shaping the behaviour of its members (Allport, 1948; Bargal *et al*, 1992). Indeed, Lewin's (1939: 165) definition of a 'group' is still generally accepted: 'it is not the similarity or dissimilarity of individuals that constitutes a group, but interdependence of fate.' As Kippenberger (1998a) notes, Lewin was addressing two questions:

- What is it about the nature and characteristics of a particular group that causes it to respond (behave) as it does to the forces which impinge on it?
- How can these forces be changed in order to elicit a more desirable form of behaviour?

It was to address these questions that Lewin began to develop the concept of Group Dynamics. Group Dynamics stresses that group behaviour, rather than that of individuals, should be the main focus of change (Bernstein, 1968; Dent and Goldberg, 1999). Lewin (1947b) maintained that it is fruitless to concentrate on changing the behaviour of individuals because the individual in isolation is constrained by group pressures to conform. Consequently, the focus of change must be at the group level and should concentrate on factors such as group norms, roles, interactions and socialisation processes to create 'disequilibrium' and change (Schein, 1988).

Lewin's pioneering work on Group Dynamics not only laid the foundations for our understanding of groups (Dent and Goldberg, 1999; Cooke, 1999; French and Bell, 1984; Marrow, 1969; Schein, 1988) but has also been linked to complexity theories by researchers examining self-organising theory and non-linear systems (Tschacher and Brunner, 1995). Since Lewin's day, much has been written about the nature of groups. Perhaps the best-known works are Belbin's categorisation of team roles and Tuckman's model of the stages of team development. Belbin's (1996) work on team roles has been highly influential in the construction and development of groups. Belbin maintains that individuals in groups fall into one of nine team roles – Plant, Resource Investigator, Coordinator, Shaper, Monitor Evaluator, Teamworker, Implementer, Completer Finisher and Specialist. Tuckman (1965) identified four stages which a team must go through in order to grow and develop its effectiveness – Forming, Storming, Norming and Performing. He later added a fifth stage – Adjourning – to acknowledge that if the original objectives and tasks of a group have been achieved or may no longer be required, the group may need to disband (Tuckman and Jensen, 1977).

Lewin was perhaps the first to recognise the need to study and understand the internal dynamics of a group – the different roles people play and how groups need to change over time. However, for him, this understanding was not sufficient by itself to bring about change. Lewin also recognised the need to provide a process whereby group members could be engaged in and committed to changing their behaviour. This led Lewin to develop Action Research and the Three-Step model of change.

Action Research

This term was coined by Lewin (1946) in an article entitled 'Action Research and Minority Problems'. Lewin stated in the article (p. 201):

In the last year and a half I have had occasion to have contact with a great variety of organizations, institutions, and individuals who came for help in the field of group relations.

However, though these people exhibited:

a great amount of good-will, of readiness to face the problem squarely and really do something about it. . . . These eager people feel themselves to be in a fog. They feel in a fog on three counts: 1. What is the present situation? 2. What are the dangers? 3. And most importantly of all, what shall we do?   (Lewin, 1946: 201)

Lewin conceived of Action Research as a two-pronged process which would allow groups to address the three questions above:

- First, it emphasises that change requires action, and is directed at achieving this.
- Second, it recognises that successful action is based on analysing the situation correctly, identifying all the possible alternative solutions and choosing the one most appropriate to the situation at hand (Bennett, 1983).

To be successful, though, there has also to be a 'felt-need'. Felt-need is an individual's inner realisation that change is necessary. If felt-need is low in the group or organisation, introducing change becomes problematic. However, felt-need only arises where individuals and groups feel they have a choice in whether to change or not, thus once again emphasising the importance of choice to the change process (Carpenter, 2013; Diamond, 1992; Tversky and Kahneman, 1981). The theoretical foundations of Action Research lie in Gestalt psychology, which stresses that change can be successfully achieved only by helping individuals to reflect on and gain new insights into the totality of their situation. Lewin (1946: 206) stated that Action Research 'proceeds in a spiral of steps each of which is composed of a circle of planning, action, and fact-finding about the results of the action'. As Figure 9.3 shows, it is an iterative process whereby research leads to action, and action leads to evaluation and further research. As Schein (1996: 35) comments, it was Lewin's view that 'one cannot understand an organization without trying to change it'. Indeed,

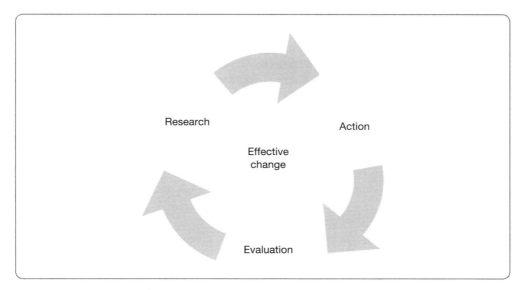

Figure 9.3 Action Research

Lewin's view was very much that the understanding and learning that this process produces for the individuals and groups concerned, which then promotes changed behaviour, is more important than any resulting change as such (Lewin, 1946).

To this end, Action Research draws on Lewin's work on Field Theory to identify the forces that bear on the group to which the individual belongs. It also draws on Group Dynamics to understand why group members behave in the way they do when subjected to these forces. Lewin stressed that the routines and patterns of behaviour in a group are more than just the outcome of opposing forces. They have a value in themselves and have a positive role to play in enforcing group norms (Lewin, 1947a). Action Research stresses that for change to be effective, it must take place at the group level, and must be a participative and collaborative process which involves all of those concerned (Allport, 1948; Bargal *et al*, 1992; Darwin *et al*, 2002; Dickens and Watkins, 1999; French and Bell, 1984; Lewin, 1947b; McNiff, 2000).

Lewin's first Action Research project was to investigate and reduce violence between Catholic and Jewish teenage gangs. This was quickly followed by a project to integrate black and white sales staff in New York department stores (Marrow, 1969). However, Action Research was also adopted by the Tavistock Institute in Britain, and used to improve managerial competence and efficiency in the newly nationalised coal industry. Since then it has acquired strong adherents throughout the world (Dickens and Watkins, 1999; Eden and Huxham, 1996; Elden and Chisholm, 1993). However, Lewin (1947a: 228) was concerned:

> A change towards a higher level of group performance is frequently short lived; after a 'shot in the arm', group life soon returns to the previous level. This indicates that it does not suffice to define the objective of a planned change in group performance as the reaching of a different level. Permanency at the new level, or permanency for a desired period, should be included in the objective.

It was for this reason that he developed his Three-Step model of change.

Three-Step model

This is often cited as Lewin's key contribution to organisational change. It needs to be recognised, however, that when he developed his Three-Step model, Lewin was not thinking only of organisational issues. Nor did he intend it to be seen separately from the other three elements which make up his Planned approach to change (i.e. Field Theory, Group Dynamics and Action Research). Rather Lewin saw the four concepts as forming an integrated approach to analysing, understanding and bringing about change at the group, organisational and societal levels. A successful change project, Lewin (1947a) argued, involved three steps (*see* Figure 9.4).

Step 1: Unfreezing. Lewin believed that the stability of human behaviour was based on a quasi-stationary equilibrium supported by a complex field of driving and restraining forces (*see* Figure 9.2). This can be characterised as inertia – the inability of organisations, groups

Figure 9.4 Lewin's Three-Step model of change

or individuals to change as fast as the environment in which they operate (Pfeffer, 1997). D Miller (1993, 1994) argues that the more successful an organisation or group has been, the greater the inertia. This is because success tends to make organisations focus on those factors which are seen as having brought success and to discard those which are seen as peripheral. Successful organisations also tend to ignore signals which might indicate the need for change. The result is that they sacrifice adaptability and increase inertia. This is why Lewin argued that the equilibrium (the forces of inertia) needs to be destabilised (unfrozen) before old behaviour can be discarded (unlearnt) and new behaviour successfully adopted.

In order to identify what forces needed to be changed or modified, Lewin drew on Field Theory and Group Dynamics. As with other aspects of Lewin's work, choice plays an important role because 'unlearning', letting go of the emotional attachment to current beliefs and arrangements, can take place only if those involved decide of their own volition that these are no longer appropriate or sustainable. Given the type of issues that Lewin was addressing, he did not believe that change would be easy, or that the same methods could be applied in all situations:

> The 'unfreezing' of the present level may involve quite different problems in different cases. Allport . . . has described the 'catharsis' which seems necessary before prejudice can be removed. To break open the shell of complacency and self-righteousness it is sometimes necessary to bring about an emotional stir up. (Lewin, 1947a: 229)

Enlarging on Lewin's ideas, Schein (1996: 28) comments that the key to unfreezing:

> was to see that human change, whether at the individual or group level, was a profound psychological dynamic process that involved painful unlearning without loss of ego identity and difficult relearning as one cognitively attempted to restructure one's thoughts, perceptions, feelings, and attitudes.

Schein (1996) identifies three processes necessary to achieve unfreezing: disconfirmation of the validity of the status quo, the induction of guilt or survival anxiety, and creating psychological safety. He argued that 'unless sufficient psychological safety is created, the disconfirming information will be denied or in other ways defended against, no survival anxiety will be felt, and consequently, no change will take place' (Schein, 1996: 30). In other words, those concerned have to feel safe from loss and humiliation before they can accept the new information and reject old behaviours.

Step 2: Moving. As Schein (1996: 32) notes, unfreezing is not an end in itself; it 'creates motivation to learn but does not necessarily control or predict the direction of learning'. This echoes Lewin's view that any attempt to predict or identify a specific outcome from Planned change is very difficult because of the complexity of the forces concerned. Instead, one should seek to take into account all the forces at work and identify and evaluate, on a trial and error basis, all the available options (Lewin, 1947a). This is, of course, the learning approach promoted by Action Research. It is this iterative approach of research, action and more research that enables groups and individuals to move from a less acceptable to a more acceptable set of behaviours. However, as noted above, Lewin (1947a) recognised that, without reinforcement, change could be short-lived.

Step 3: Refreezing. This is the final step in the Three-Step model. Refreezing seeks to stabilise the group at a new quasi-stationary equilibrium in order to ensure that the new behaviours are relatively safe from regression. The main point about refreezing is that new behaviour must be, to some degree, congruent with the rest of the behaviour, personality and environment of the learner or it will simply lead to a new round of disconfirmation (Schein, 1996). This is why Lewin saw successful change as a group activity, because unless group norms and routines are also transformed, changes to individual behaviour will not be sustained. In organisational terms, refreezing often requires changes to organisational culture, norms, policies and practices (Cummings and Huse, 1989).

Like other aspects of Lewin's work, his Three-Step model of change started to become unfashionable in the 1980s (Dawson, 1994; Hatch, 1997; Kanter *et al*, 1992). Nevertheless, such is its continuing influence that, as Hendry (1996: 624) commented:

> Scratch any account of creating and managing change and the idea that change is a three-stage process which necessarily begins with a process of unfreezing will not be far below the surface.

Hendry's view is supported by the work of Elrod and Tippett (2002), who reviewed a wide range of change models. They found that most approaches to organisational change were strikingly similar to Lewin's Three-Step model. When they extended their research to other forms of human and organisational change, Elrod and Tippett (2002: 273) also found that:

> Models of the change process, as perceived by diverse and seemingly unrelated disciplines [such as bereavement theory, personal transition theory, creative processes, cultural revolutions and scientific revolutions] . . . follow Lewin's . . . three-phase model of change.

Others support this view (Levy and Merry, 1986; Zell, 2003). Carnall (2003) draws on these various models of change to construct a Coping Cycle (*see* Figure 9.5) which shows how people react and adjust when faced with change.

The Coping Cycle comprises five stages:

Stage 1 – Denial: When faced with the need to make or accept significant changes, the first reaction by many people or groups is to deny there is a need for change.

Stage 2 – Defence: Once people realise that change is taking place and they cannot stop it, they may feel rejected and depressed. This can turn into defensive behaviour whereby people will defend their past practices and behaviours and deny that the new ways are suitable to them and their job.

Stage 3 – Discarding: If people realise that the change will take place whether they like it or not, and that it does affect them and that they need to adjust to the new situation,

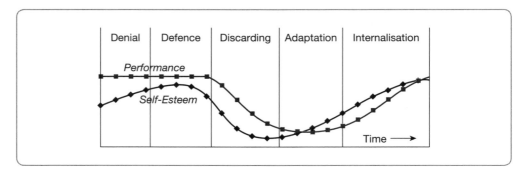

Figure 9.5 The Coping Cycle

they begin the process of discarding past behaviour – recognising that what was suitable in the past is no longer suitable for the current situation.

Stage 4 – Adaptation: No proposed change is ever likely to be 100 per cent suitable at the outset. Therefore, for change to be successful, not only must those affected by it adapt to the new ways but the new ways must also be adapted to fit in with the existing people and circumstances.

Stage 5 – Internalisation: The is the stage of the Coping Cycle where change becomes fully operational, and new ways of working and behaving have been developed. People reach the point where, psychologically, they see the changes not as *new* but as *normal* – the way things should be.

There are four points to note about the Coping Cycle:

- First, individuals will often react differently when faced with the same situation, even though they may be members of the same group. Some will move from Denial to Internalisation very quickly, while others may stick at the Denial or Defence stages and never accept the legitimacy of the changes.

- Second, as Figure 9.5 shows, people's self-esteem and performance can fluctuate wildly as they move through the Coping Cycle. To use a somewhat hackneyed phrase, people can experience an emotional rollercoaster.

- Third, the point between Stage 3, Discarding, and Stage 4, Adaptation, where people are beginning to accept the need for change and embarking on a process of mutual accommodation, is the point where their self-esteem and performance are likely to be at their lowest. It is at this point, when success is almost within reach, that those driving and sponsoring change and those experiencing it may begin to feel that they have chosen the wrong course of action and should abandon it. It is important, therefore, at the outset of any change process to recognise the truth of the old adage: *Things will get worse before they get better!*

- Lastly, following Elrod and Tippet's (2002) argument, if we superimpose Lewin's Three-Step model of change onto the Coping Cycle (*see* Figure 9.6), the remarkable applicability and appropriateness of Lewin's approach to change stands out. Step 1 of Lewin's Model – Unfreezing – aligns with Stages 1 to 3 of Carnall's Coping Cycle and provides the insights and tools necessary to address the issues of Denial, Defence and Discarding.

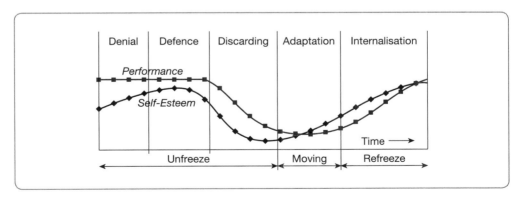

Figure 9.6 Three-Step model and the Coping Cycle

Step 2 – Moving – aligns with Stage 4 and once again provides the means of dealing with the issues and obstacles that arise from Adaptation. Finally, Step 3 of Lewin's model, Refreezing, aligns with Stage 5 of the Coping Cycle and provides an approach to and the mechanisms for achieving Internalisation.

As can be seen, therefore, though Lewin's Planned approach to change was developed some 70 years ago, it still appears to have much to recommend it as an approach to changing the behaviour of individuals and groups. Certainly, the importance he placed on participation, choice and free will have stood the test of time (Carpenter, 2013; Diamond, 1992; McMillan and Connor, 2005; Tversky and Kahneman, 1981; Oreg *et al*, 2011). Also, Lewin's commitment to combining rigorous theory and practical relevance has a very contemporary feel to it. There has been much debate in recent years concerning the need to achieve both rigour and relevance in organisational theory and practice (Bartunek, 2007; Polzer *et al*, 2009). However, it was Lewin (1943/4: 169), who first made the case for this in his famous dictum: 'There is nothing so practical as a good theory', which presaged the current debate by five decades (Gulati, 2007). For Lewin, rigour and relevance are not opposing forces or objectives, but two sides of the same coin. For Lewin, practice which was not underpinned by good theory was poor practice, which was limited in applicability and bound to fail. Similarly, theory which did not have practical relevance was poor theory.

Lewin and change: a summary

Lewin was primarily interested in resolving social conflict through behavioural change, whether this was within organisations or in the wider society. He identified two requirements for success:

1. To analyse and understand how social groupings were formed, motivated and maintained. To do this, he developed both Field Theory and Group Dynamics.

2. To change the behaviour of social groups. The primary methods he developed for achieving this were Action Research and the Three-Step model of change.

Underpinning Lewin's work, as mentioned earlier, was a strong moral and ethical belief in the importance of democratic institutions, values and practices throughout society, including the workplace. Lewin believed that only by strengthening democratic participation in all aspects of life and being able to resolve social conflicts could the scourge of despotism, authoritarianism and racism be effectively countered. Since his death, Lewin's wider social agenda has been mainly pursued under the umbrella of Action Research. For example, Bargal and Bar (1992) described how, over a number of years, they used Lewin's approach to address the conflict between Arab-Palestinian and Jewish youths in Israel through the development of inter-group workshops. The workshops were developed around six principles based on Lewin's work:

(a) a recursive process of data collection to determine goals, action to implement goals and assessment of the action; (b) feedback of research results to trainers; (c) cooperation between researchers and practitioners; (d) research based on the laws of the group's social life, on three stages of change – 'unfreezing,' 'moving,' and 'refreezing' – and on the principles of group decision making; (e) consideration of the values, goals and power structures of change agents and clients; and (f) use of research to create knowledge and/or solve problems.

(Bargal and Bar, 1992: 146)

In terms of the application of his concepts to the organisational sphere, Lewin and his associates had a long and fruitful relationship with the Harwood Manufacturing Corporation, where his approach to change was developed, applied and refined (Burnes, 2007; Marrow, 1969). Coch and French (1948: 512) observed that, at Harwood: 'From the point of view of factory management, there were two purposes to the research: (1) Why do people resist change so strongly? and (2) What can be done to overcome this resistance?' Therefore, in both his wider social agenda and his narrower organisational agenda, Lewin sought to address similar issues and apply similar concepts. Since his death, it is the organisational side of his work that has been given greater prominence by his followers and successors, mainly through the creation of the Organization Development (OD) movement, which will be discussed shortly (Cummings and Worley, 1997; French and Bell, 1999). However, many supporters of Planned change, while attempting to remain true to Lewin's participatory philosophy, and being greatly influenced by his work on Group Dynamics, tend to equate Planned change with Lewin's Three-Step model, rather than treating it as an integrated package that also requires the use of Field Theory, Group Dynamics and Action Research. As a stand-alone approach to change, the Three-Step model is rather underdeveloped, which is why there have been a number of attempts to develop it further.

Phases of Planned change

As Armenakis and Bedeian (1999) have shown, there have been many attempts to elaborate Lewin's Three-Step model. In so doing, writers have expanded the number of steps or phases. For example, Lippitt *et al* (1958) developed a seven-phase model of Planned change, while Cummings and Huse (1989), not to be outdone, produced an eight-phase model and Galpin (1996) proposed a model comprising nine wedges that form a wheel. As Cummings and Huse (1989: 51) point out, however, 'the concept of planned change implies that an organization exists in different states at different times and that planned movement can occur from one state to another'. Therefore, in order to understand Planned change, it is not sufficient merely to understand the processes that bring about change; there must also be an appreciation of the states that an organisation must pass through in order to move from an unsatisfactory present state to a more desired future state.

Perhaps the most comprehensive attempt to elaborate upon Lewin's work was by Bullock and Batten (1985), who developed an integrated, four-phase model of Planned change based on a review and synthesis of over 30 models of Planned change (*see* Ideas and perspectives 9.2). Their model describes Planned change in terms of two major dimensions: change phases, which are distinct states an organisation moves through as it undertakes Planned change; and change processes, which are the methods used to move an organisation from one state to another.

According to Cummings and Huse (1989), this model has broad applicability to most change situations. It clearly incorporates key aspects of many other change models and, especially, it overcomes any confusion between the processes (methods) of change and the phases of change – the sequential states that organisations must go through to achieve successful change.

The focus of Bullock and Batten's model, like Lewin's, is change at the individual and group level. As will be shown below, this very much chimed with the early years of OD, but began to be seen as too narrow a focus from the 1970s onwards (French and Bell, 1995: 3–4).

IDEAS AND PERSPECTIVES 9.2

Bullock and Batten's four-phase model of planned change

1. **Exploration phase**. In this state an organisation has to explore and decide whether it wants to make specific changes in its operations and, if so, commit resources to planning the changes. The change processes involved in this phase are becoming aware of the need for change; searching for outside assistance (a consultant/facilitator) to assist with planning and implementing the changes; and establishing a contract with the consultant which defines each party's responsibilities.

2. **Planning phase**. Once the consultant and the organisation have established a contract, then the next state, which involves understanding the organisation's problem or concern, begins. The change processes involved in this are collecting information in order to establish a correct diagnosis of the problem; establishing change goals and designing the appropriate actions to achieve these goals; and persuading key decision-makers to approve and support the proposed changes.

3. **Action phase**. In this state, an organisation implements the changes derived from the planning. The change processes involved are designed to move an organisation from its current state to a desired future state, and include establishing appropriate arrangements to manage the change process and gaining support for the actions to be taken; and evaluating the implementation activities and feeding back the results so that any necessary adjustments or refinements can be made.

4. **Integration phase**. This state commences once the changes have been successfully implemented. It is concerned with consolidating and stabilising the changes so that they become part of an organisation's normal, everyday operation and do not require special arrangements or encouragement to maintain them. The change processes involved are reinforcing new behaviours through feedback and reward systems and gradually decreasing reliance on the consultant; diffusing the successful aspects of the change process throughout the organisation; and training managers and employees to monitor the changes constantly and to seek to improve upon them.

Source: Bullock and Batten (1985).

The origins of OD

The term 'organization development' and the movement itself began to emerge in the 1950s in the US. Lewin's work, especially the various projects and events listed in Ideas and perspective 9.1, provided the practical and philosophical foundations of OD. Of particular significance was the 1946 New Britain leadership-training workshop, which gave birth to the T-group methodology and the National Training Laboratories (NTL). It was the NTL's promotion of T-groups which created the conditions for OD to flourish (Burnes and Cooke, 2012b). Nevertheless, its central pillar is Lewin's Planned approach to change (Burnes, 2004c, 2007).

According to French and Bell (1995: 1–2):

> Organization development is a unique organizational improvement strategy that emerged in the late 1950s and early 1960s. . . . [It] has evolved into an integrated framework of theories and practices capable of solving or helping to solve most of the important problems confronting

the human side of organizations. Organization development is about people and organizations and people in organizations and how they function. OD is also about planned change, that is getting individuals, teams and organizations to function better. Planned change involves common sense, hard work applied diligently over time, a systematic, goal-oriented approach, and valid knowledge about organizational dynamics and how to change them. Valid knowledge derives from the behavioral sciences such as psychology, social psychology, sociology, anthropology, systems theory, and the practice of management.

Cummings and Worley (2005) relate that OD evolved from five main developments:

- The growth of the National Training Laboratory (NTL).
- Action Research/Survey Feedback.
- Participative Management.
- Quality of Working Life.
- Strategic Change.

Cummings and Worley state that the first three developments derived from work by Kurt Lewin on Planned change in the 1940s, while the last two did not emerge until the 1960s and 1970s. However, Lewin did not just provide OD with a range of tools, techniques and approaches; he also imbued it with a set of radical values. As Mirvis (2006: 77) commented: 'OD was birthed with utopian aspirations. Democracy and freedom were central to Lewin's work.' Consequently, underpinning OD is a set of values, assumptions and ethics that emphasises its humanistic orientation as well as its commitment to organisational effectiveness. Indeed, Wirtenberg *et al* (2004: 469) claim that one of OD's major strengths is the 'values OD brings to practice'. These values have been articulated by many writers over the years (Conner, 1977; French and Bell, 1999; Gellerman *et al*, 1990; Warwick and Thompson, 1980). One of the earliest attempts was by French and Bell (1973), who identified a number of underlying assumptions and values which lie at the core of OD (*see* Ideas and perspectives 9.3).

In a survey of OD practitioners, Hurley *et al* (1992) found these values were clearly reflected in the five main approaches they used in their work:

1. Empowering employees to act.
2. Creating openness in communications.
3. Facilitating ownership of the change process and its outcomes.
4. The promotion of a culture of collaboration.
5. The promotion of continuous learning.

IDEAS AND PERSPECTIVES 9.3

French and Bell's core assumptions and values of OD

- The needs and aspirations of human beings provide the prime reasons for the existence of organisations within society.
- OD places a high value on trust and mutual learning.
- Change agents are committed to improving organisational effectiveness.
- OD is most effective in situations where organisations are committed to cooperative, participative change, and pursue win–win outcomes.

Source: French and Bell (1973).

Within the OD field, there are a number of major theorists and practitioners who have contributed their own models and techniques to its advancement (e.g. Argyris, 1962; Beckhard, 1969; Blake and Mouton, 1976; French and Bell, 1973). OD also shares some concepts with, and sits easily alongside, the Human Relations movement. This can be seen in the fact that McGregor's Theory Y (*see* Chapter 2) takes a similar view of human nature to that of OD. This is not surprising, given that McGregor was a close friend and supporter of Kurt Lewin and, as well as being a key figure in the Human Relations movement, also played a significant role in the early stages of OD (see McGregor, 1967). Thus there are strong links between the Human Relations approach to organisational effectiveness and the Planned/ OD approach to organisational change. However, despite this, there is general agreement that the OD movement grew out of, and became the standard bearer for, Kurt Lewin's pioneering work on behavioural science in general, and his development of Planned change in particular (Burnes, 2007; Burnes and Cooke, 2012b; Cummings and Worley, 1997).

From small beginnings in 1950s, OD grew dramatically in 1960s America, led by the theorists and idealists of the NTL and fuelled by the popularity of the T-group approach. T-groups promoted personal growth, emotional expression, and challenged the efficacy of organisational bureaucracy, seeking to replace it with democratic participation, all of which chimed with the hippy, anti-authoritarian spirit of the age as epitomised by the civil rights and peace movements (Highhouse, 2002; Isserman and Kazin, 2007; Thrift, 2005). Led by the popularity of T-groups, OD began to expand across the globe (Fagenson-Eland *et al*, 2004) and take on the characteristics of a profession with its own professional associations, such as the NTL, the OD Network, the OD Institute, and the International Organization Development Association. These bodies began to offer accreditation, training in OD tools and techniques, and promote their own ethical codes of practice (Cummings and Worley, 1997). Yet by the end of the 1960s, OD found itself under attack, enthusiasm for T-groups began to decline and new, organisation-wide approaches to change began to emerge in the 1970s and 1980s.

The changing nature of OD

The original focus of OD, as described earlier, was on work groups within an organisational setting rather than organisations in their entirety, and it was primarily concerned with the human processes and systems within organisations. However, even in the 1960s, there were those who saw the need for a more organisation-wide approach to change. Greiner (1967: 119), for example, observed:

> Whereas only a few years ago the target of organization change was limited to a small work group or a single department, especially at lower levels, the focus is now converging on the organization as a whole, reaching out to include many divisions and levels at once, and even the top managers themselves.

OD practitioners, whether employed in academic institutions, consultancy practices or private and public organisations, exist to provide consultancy services. Like any profession or trade, unless what they provide is relevant to their customers' needs, they will soon go out of business. By the 1970s, the economic, technological, organisational and workforce conditions were vastly different from those in the 1940s, 1950s and even 1960s (Greiner and Cummings, 2004; Johnson and Ouchi, 1974; Sheldrake, 1996). Large numbers of OD practitioners woke to the realisation that companies no longer wanted to experiment with novel OD ideas; they wanted value-for-money products that worked (Freedman, 1999). As a result, serious questions were raised about the relevance of OD for the needs of contemporary organisations, and the influence of the visionary, academic wing of OD, which had been led by the NTL, began to fade, and the influence of its practitioner wing grew. OD began to be driven by entrepreneurial and pragmatic practitioners who saw the need to transform it into a more hard-headed, results-focused, commercial activity which catered for what companies wanted (Burnes, 2009a; Dent, 2002; Freedman, 1999; Greiner and Cummings, 2004; Krell, 1981). Thus, the bridge between academic rigour and practical relevance, which Lewin had done so much to build, began to crumble. This can be seen in Greiner's (1972b) article 'Red flags in organization development', which was seen as a wake-up call for the OD movement (*see* Ideas and perspectives 9.4).

IDEAS AND PERSPECTIVES 9.4

Greiner's red flags

Flag 1: Putting the individual before the organization. The obsession of OD with individual behavior change caused less focus on the formal organization – its strategy, structure, controls, and so on. As a result, OD neglected to address potential sources of environmental support and reinforcement for behavior change.

Flag 2: Informal before formal organization. There was also an overemphasis on interpersonal values (e.g., openness, trust, etc.) in an attempt to change the informal culture of organizations, often at the expense of the design of the formal organization and its values of efficiency, hierarchy, and accountability. Again, an opportunity was missed to produce a wider impact.

Flag 3: Behavior before diagnosis. OD was preoccupied with behavior change along the lines of OD's core values, not on diagnosing whether the existing behavior was compatible with the strategic thrust or culture of the organization. Thus, OD's goal of promoting more open and trusting relationships became the normative model for change; it was taken for granted without questioning its applicability to particular situations.

Flag 4: Process before task. With its emphasis on how one person should relate to others, OD became enamored with the human dynamics of working together, assuming that team building was the preferred alternative. In doing so, it neglected the realities of technology and the substantive problems in front of people. Contingency theory revealed that some jobs were inherently mechanistic and programmable; therefore, they did not require much teamwork and openness for effective performance.

Flag 5: Experts before the manager. OD programs were designed and conducted by expert consultants. NTL had become an elitist organization of trained experts. Their target of change was the manager in organizations. Unfortunately, managers were relatively uninvolved in the planning and conducting of consultant-led OD programs. They were simply supposed to be the recipients of change and conform to the model being advocated by the consultants.

Flag 6: Package before the situation. Potential clients for OD activities usually preferred packaged change programs – formal activities that were structured, tangible, and easy to explain to employees. Many OD consultants also welcomed this approach because structured programs were easier to sell and administer than open-ended and evolving efforts. The unfortunate result was that organizations were frequently shoehorned to fit the OD program's characteristics rather than customizing the program to fit the uniqueness of the client organization.

Source: Greiner and Cummings (2004: 378–9).

From the 1970s onwards, the OD movement experienced a major shift of focus from the group to the organisation setting, and even beyond, in response to the changing organisational demands (Armenakis and Bedeian, 1999; Pasmore and Fagans, 1992; Sashkin and Burke, 1987; Woodman, 1989). Three developments in particular caused it to broaden out its perspective:

- With the rise of the Job Design movement in the 1960s (*see* Chapter 2), and particularly the advent of Socio-Technical Systems theory, OD practitioners came to recognise that they could not solely concentrate on the work of groups and individuals in organisations but that they needed to look at other systems. Gradually, OD has adopted an Open Systems perspective which allows it to look at organisations in their totality and within their environments.

- This organisation-wide perspective caused OD practitioners to broaden out their perspective in two interrelated ways. First, and not surprisingly, they developed an interest in managing organisational culture. Given that, when working with groups, OD consultants have always recognised the importance of group norms and values, it is a natural progression to translate this into an interest in organisational culture in general. Second, they developed an interest in the concept of organisational learning. Once again, as derived from Lewin's work, OD practitioners tend to stress that their interventions are as much about learning as change. Therefore, it is a natural extension to move from group learning to organisational learning. In both cases, these developments have tended to reflect and follow on from a general interest in such issues by organisations and academics rather than necessarily being generated by the OD profession itself.

- The increasing use of organisation-wide approaches to change (e.g. culture change programmes), coupled with increasing turbulence in the environment in which organisations operate, drew attention to the need for OD practitioners to become involved in transforming organisations in their totality rather than focusing only on changes to their constituent parts.

Therefore, in the 1970s and 1980s, OD moved away from its roots in group-based and Planned change and began to take a far more organization- and system-wide perspective on change. This created something of a dilemma for proponents of OD. As Krell (1981) pointed out, much of what can be conceived of as traditional OD (such as Action Research) had become accepted practice in many organisations by the early 1980s. Even some of the newer approaches, such as Job Design and self-managed work teams, had become mainstream practices in many organisations (Beer and Walton, 1987). By and large, these tried-and-tested approaches still tended to focus on the group level rather than on the wider organisation level. However, the more organisation-wide transformational approaches, which were seen as crucial to maintaining OD's relevance for organisations, were less clear, less well-developed and less well-accepted (Cummings and Worley, 1997; French and Bell, 1995).

Although concepts such as Weisbord's (1987) 'getting the whole system in the room' are attractive, the practical obstacles are difficult to overcome. For example, just because all stakeholders are represented does not mean that all stakeholders have an equal voice (Worley *et al*, 2011). In addition, the more that OD became focused on macro issues, the less it could keep in touch with all the individuals affected by its change programmes and offer them genuine choice and involvement, and thus the less able it was to promote its core humanist and democratic values.

In effect, OD seemed to be pulled in two very different directions. On the one hand, it recognised that 'Organizations are being reinvented; work tasks are being reengineered; the rules of the marketplace are being rewritten; the fundamental nature of organizations is changing' (French and Bell, 1995: 3–4). Therefore, OD had to adapt to these new conditions and broaden its focus out beyond individual and group behaviour in order to maintain its relevance. On the other hand, as Wooten and White (1999) argue, the core values of OD – equality, empowerment, consensus-building and horizontal relationships – were particularly relevant to some of the newer perspectives on organisations that were emerging at the time, especially the notion of the postmodern organisation. Under these circumstances, rather than loosening its ties with its traditional values in order to retain its relevance, OD should have been strengthening them in order to create the 'framework for a postmodern OD science and practice' (Wooten and White, 1999: 17). This tension between two seemingly irreconcilable forces led even leading supporters of OD to argue that it had lost its sense of direction and purpose to the extent that it was no longer clear what constituted OD (Bradford and Burke, 2004; Burke, 1997; Greiner and Cummings, 2004; Marshak, 1993; Nicholl, 1998a, 1998b; Worley and Feyerhern, 2003).

In addition to its internal tensions, from the 1970s OD faced criticisms from other and newer perspectives on organisations. The first signs of this challenge to OD appeared in 1970s when academics began to take an interest in the role of power in organisations, especially in terms of organisational change (Pettigrew, 1973, 1980; Pfeffer, 1978, 1981). Pfeffer (1978: 11–12) took the view that:

> It is difficult to think of situations in which goals are so congruent, or the facts so clear-cut that judgment and compromise are not involved. What is rational from one point of view is irrational from another. Organizations are political systems, coalitions of interests, and rationality is defined only with respect to unitary and consistent ordering of preferences.

Based on his major, longitudinal study of strategic change at ICI, Pettigrew (1985: 17) went on to reject OD, arguing that 'planned change and innovation is both an inadequate way of theorising about what actually happens during change processes and an overtly simple guide for action'. He maintained that OD was too rational, linear, incremental and prescriptive, did not pay enough attention to the need to analyse and conceptualise organisational change, and failed to recognise that change processes were shaped by history, culture, context and the balance of power in organisations (Pettigrew, 1985).

These criticisms of OD, and the new approaches to change they spawned, will be examined at length in the next chapter.

Planned change and OD: summary and criticisms

Planned change, as developed by Kurt Lewin, comprised four elements: Field Theory, Group Dynamics, Action Research and the Three-Step model. It is an iterative, cyclical, process involving diagnosis, action and evaluation, and further action and evaluation. It is an approach that recognises that once change has taken place, it must be self-sustaining (i.e. safe from regression). For Lewin, the key to making change self-sustaining was that those concerned needed to be involved in the change process and be able to make genuine choices. The original purpose of Planned change was to resolve social conflict in society, including conflict within organisations. In organisational terms, its original purpose was to focus on improving the effectiveness of the human side of the organisation. Central to

---

IDEAS AND PERSPECTIVES 9.5

OD dilemmas

Over the years, OD practitioners have sought to focus more on organisational transformation initiatives and less on group behaviour change. This has led to two fundamental dilemmas:

Dilemma 1: OD Expertise

- The group behaviour focus is well understood, accepted and supported by tried-and-tested tools and techniques.
- The organisational transformation focus is unclear, less developed and more contentious.

Dilemma 2: OD values

- The group behaviour focus is based on and promotes humanistic and democratic values through participative learning.
- The organisational transformation focus is more autocratic, less participative and less about individual and group learning.

Planned change in organisations is the emphasis placed on the collaborative nature of the change effort: the organisation, both managers and recipients of change, and the consultant jointly diagnose the organisation's problem, and jointly plan and design the specific changes. Underpinning Planned change and indeed the OD movement is a strong humanist and democratic orientation and an emphasis on organisational effectiveness. Marching hand in hand with this humanist and democratic orientation was the development of a host of tried-and-tested tools and techniques for promoting group participation and change.

Nevertheless, as OD practitioners have developed Planned change over the years, and moved their focus from group behaviour change to organisational transformation initiatives, two fundamental dilemmas have arisen (*see* Ideas and perspectives 9.5).

The first dilemma is that while OD practitioners are well equipped to bring about change in group behaviour, they are far less well equipped to achieve the same in terms of organisational transformation. The former is well understood, OD practitioners find it relatively easy to gain the support of those involved, and Planned change, with its host of tried-and-tested tools and techniques, is ideally suited to this kind of initiative. Yet OD practitioners have found it more difficult to apply their skills and expertise to organisational transformational initiatives. The process of diagnosing the need for transformational change at the organisational level and specifying what is required is much less clear than it is at the group level. Also, the tools and techniques for bringing about transformational change are less developed, and the process tends to be more contentious, conflict-ridden and offer less opportunities for those affected to be involved in decision-making.

The second dilemma concerns the values which underpin OD. As OD has moved more to address large-scale organisational transformation issues, though the emphasis on organisational effectiveness has remained, a difference has emerged with regard to the participatory and democratic nature of its approach. Though this is partly due to the numbers of people involved in such changes, it is largely driven by the approach of top management. As French and Bell (1995: 351) observed, from the 1980s onwards, there has been a growing tendency for top managers to focus less on people-orientated values and more on 'the bottom line and/or the price of stock . . . [consequently] some executives have a "slash and burn" mentality'. Clearly, this tendency is not conducive to the promotion of democratic and humanistic values. This 'slash and burn' mentality has impacted on the role of the change agent. Lewin stressed the need to solve problems through social action (dialogue). He believed that successful change could be achieved only through the active participation of the change adopter (the subject) in understanding the problem, selecting a solution and implementing it. Lewin, and the early OD practitioners, saw the change agent as a facilitator, not a director or a doer. More important even than the solution to the problem, Lewin believed that the change agent's real task was to develop those involved, and to create a learning environment that would allow them to gain new insights into themselves and their circumstances. Only through this learning process could people willingly come to see the need for, and choose to, change.

Bullock and Batten's (1985) model, as with other more recent variants of Planned change, gives the change agent a more directive and less developmental role. Their model seems to place a greater emphasis on the change agent as an equal (or even senior) partner rather than as a facilitator; the consultant is as free to direct and do as the others involved. Those involved are more dependent on the change agent, not just for his or her skills of analysis but also for providing solutions and helping to implement them. Therefore, the focus is on what the change agent can do for those involved, rather than on seeking to enable the subjects to change themselves. This tendency for change agents to have a more directive role, and for employees to have a less participatory one, has become even more pronounced as OD practitioners have shifted their focus from individuals and groups to organisations in their entirety.

Lewin's approach to change was greatly influenced by the work of the Gestalt theorists, who believe that successful change requires a process of learning. This allows those involved to gain or change insights, outlooks, expectations and thought patterns. This approach seeks to provide change adopters with an opportunity to 'reason out' their situation and develop their own solutions (Bigge, 1982). The danger with Bullock and Batten's approach, and certainly with organisational transformation initiatives, is that they appear to be moving more in the Behaviourist direction. The emphasis is on the change agent acting as a consultant who provides expertise that the organisation lacks. As such, their role is less to facilitate participative change and more to provide solutions which can be imposed in a rapid fashion. The risk in this situation is that the learner (the change adopter) becomes a passive recipient of external and, supposedly, objective data: one who has to be directed to the 'correct' solution. Reason and choice do not enter into this particular equation; those involved are shown the solution and motivated, through the application of positive reinforcement, to adopt it on a permanent basis (Skinner, 1974). This appears to be especially the case with the newer, organisation-wide and transformational approaches about which even supporters of OD admit there is some confusion (Bradford and Burke, 2004; Greiner and Cummings, 2004; Worley and Feyerhern, 2003).

Therefore, the move away from its original focus and area of expertise, i.e. the human processes involved in the functioning of individuals and groups in organisations, coupled with a more hostile business environment, appear to be eroding the values which Lewin and the early pioneers of OD saw as being central to successful change.

Though many proponents of OD see its broadening out as necessary and appropriate (Armenakis and Bedeian, 1999; Pasmore and Fagans, 1992; Sashkin and Burke, 1987; Woodman, 1989), not everyone shares this view. These developments in OD, as well as newer perspectives on organisations, have led many to question not only particular aspects of the Planned approach to change but also the utility and practicality of the approach as a whole. The main criticisms levelled against the Planned approach to change, according to Burnes and Salauroo (1995), are as follows.

First, as Wooten and White (1999: 8) observe, 'Much of the existing OD technology was developed specifically for, and in response to, top-down, autocratic, rigid, rule-based organizations operating in a somewhat predictable and controlled environment.' Arising from this is the assumption that, as Cummings and Huse (1989: 51) pointed out, 'an organization exists in different states at different times and that planned movement can occur from one state to another'. An increasing number of writers, however, argue that, in the turbulent and chaotic world in which we live, such assumptions are increasingly tenuous and that organisational change is more a continuous and open-ended process than a set of discrete and self-contained events (Arndt and Bigelow, 2000; Bechtold, 1997; Black, 2000; Brown and Eisenhardt, 1997; Garvin, 1993; IBM, 2008; Kanter *et al*, 1997; Peters, 1997a; Stacey, 2003).

Second, and on a similar note, a number of writers have criticised the Planned approach for its emphasis on incremental and isolated change and its difficulty with incorporate radical, transformational change (Dawson, 1994; Dunphy and Stace, 1993; Harris, 1985; Miller and Friesen, 1984; Pettigrew, 1990a, 1990b; Schein, 1985).

Third, the Planned change approach is seen as being based on the assumption that common agreement can be reached, and that all the parties involved in a particular change project have a willingness and interest in doing so (Dawson, 1994; Hatch, 1997; Wilson, 1992). This assumption appears to ignore organisational conflict and politics, or at least assumes that problem issues can be easily identified and resolved. Given what was said of organisational power, politics and vested interests in Chapter 5, such a view is difficult to substantiate. Also, as Stace and Dunphy (1994) showed, there is a wide spectrum of change situations, ranging from fine-tuning to corporate transformation, and an equally wide range of ways of managing these, from collaborative to coercive. Though Planned change may be suitable to some of these situations, it is clearly much less applicable to situations where more directive approaches may be required, such as when a crisis, requiring rapid and major change, does not allow scope for widespread involvement or consultation.

Fourth, it assumes that one type of approach to change is suitable for all organisations, all situations and all times. Dunphy and Stace (1993: 905), however, argue:

> Turbulent times demand different responses in varied circumstances. So managers and consultants need a model of change that is essentially a 'situational' or 'contingency model', one that indicates how to vary change strategies to achieve 'optimum fit' with the changing environment.

In supporting and adding to this list of criticisms, many writers have drawn attention to the increasing frequency and magnitude of change and, while the Planned approach may be applicable to incremental change, it is less relevant to larger-scale and more radical transformational changes that many organisations have undergone or are experiencing (Brown and Eisenhardt, 1997; Hayes, 2002). The same can be said in relation to the three schools of thought which provide the theoretical underpinnings of organisational change that were discussed in the previous chapter – the individual perspective, Group Dynamics and the Open Systems approach. Planned change is certainly applicable to the individual and group contexts, but seems less appropriate for system-wide change.

Leading OD advocates, as might be predicted, dispute these criticisms and point to the way that Planned change has tried to incorporate issues such as power and politics and the need for organisational transformation (Cummings and Worley, 2005; French and Bell, 1999). Also, as Burnes (1998b) argues, there is a need to draw a distinction between Lewin's original analytical approach to Planned change and the more prescriptive and practitioner-orientated variants that have been developed by the OD profession subsequently. In defence of Lewin, Burnes (2004c) points out that Lewin did not ignore the importance of power and politics, nor did he fail to recognise that change could be fast and dramatic. In particular, Burnes argues that while Lewin saw human behaviour, both at the individual and group level, as being relatively stable over time and capable of moving from one stable state to another (*see* the earlier section on Field Theory), he did not see organisations as stable and changeless entities. In this respect, his view was not dissimilar to that of many of his critics. As already mentioned, a number of proponents of complexity theory have made similar observations. This is a point which will be revisited in the next chapter.

Furthermore, it has to be recognised that Lewin never saw Planned change as being applicable to all change situations, and it was certainly never meant to be used in situations where rapid, coercive and/or wholesale change was required. However, from the 1970s onwards, the incremental, small-group view of change favoured by Lewin and his supporters began to be replaced by one which saw change as being more frequent and of greater magnitude.

Conclusions

This chapter has examined the origins and development of the Planned/OD approach to change, which dominated the theory and practice of change management from the 1940s to the 1980s. It was shown that the foundations of Planned change were laid by Kurt Lewin. After his death, it was taken up, and over time significantly modified, by the OD movement in the US and elsewhere. In terms of organisational change, the Planned approach focused upon resolving group conflicts and improving group performance by bringing together managers, employees and a change agent. Through a process of learning, those involved gain new insights into their situation and are thus able to identify and make choices over more effective ways of working together. Advocates of Planned change, especially the early years, believe that group learning and individual development are at least as important as the actual change process itself. This, in part, arises from the humanist and democratic values that underpin Planned change and which derive from Kurt Lewin's background and beliefs.

Under the auspices of OD, however, the influence of these values has lessened. The focus of Planned change has moved from conflict resolution to performance enhancement, as OD has grown into a consultancy industry aimed almost exclusively at resolving problems within client organisations. Therefore, as was the case with the approaches to strategy discussed in Chapters 6 and 7, it is possible to draw a distinction between the two wings of OD. On the one hand, there are those who take a rigorous, analytical approach to change and who seek to hold true to Lewin's original values and concepts, which we have referred to as the academic wing of OD. On the other hand, there are those who take a more prescriptive approach, especially change consultants whose livelihood depends upon the perceived relevance of the products and services they are seeking to sell, which we have referred to as the practitioner wing of OD.

In the 1960s and 1970s, Planned change/OD, with its increasing array of tools, techniques and practitioners, became the dominant approach to managing organisational change. From the 1980s onwards, however, as the next chapter will show, Planned change faced increasing levels of criticism, principally relating to its perceived inability to cope with radical, coercive change situations or ones where power and politics are dominant. In its defence, as described earlier, there are proponents of Planned change and OD who would argue that these criticisms are not valid, that it is a more flexible and holistic approach than its detractors would acknowledge, and that it is capable of incorporating transformational change (Bradford and Burke, 2004; Bushe, 2011; Cooperrider and Srivastva, 1987; French and Bell, 1999; Greiner and Cummings, 2004; McLennan, 1989; Mirvis, 1990; Worley and Feyerhern, 2003). However, they would acknowledge that OD as a whole does have serious issues which need to be addressed. There are also those who believe that many of the criticisms of Lewin's work are misplaced (Burnes, 2004b, 2004c, 2007; Burnes and Cooke, 2012a, 2012b).

Nevertheless, partly as a consequence of these criticisms of the Planned approach, and partly in the context of newer perspectives on change such as the punctuated-equilibrium and continuous transformation models, newer approaches to change have been gaining ground since the 1980s, one of which in particular has come to dominate the literature. Though aspects of it have been given a number of different labels, such as continuous improvement or organisational learning, it is more often referred to as the *Emergent* approach to change. The Emergent approach tends to see change as driven from the bottom up rather than from the top down; it stresses that change is an open-ended and continuous process of adaptation to changing conditions and circumstances; and it also sees the process of change as a process of learning, and not just a method of changing organisational structures and practices (Dawson, 1994; Mabey and Mayon-White, 1993; Wilson, 1992).

The next chapter will examine the principles and merits of the Emergent approach to change. It will also show that in the face of these newer approaches to change, Planned change/OD appears to have rediscovered its sense of purpose.

TEST YOUR LEARNING

Short discussion topics

The purpose of these is to enable students to check their learning and reflect on the topics covered in this chapter. The discussions should last for no more than 5–10 minutes. Depending on the length of the lecture, there could be one, two or three such discussions in a session. The following are five suggested topics which address issues raised in this chapter:

1. How did Lewin define the term 'Planned change'?

2. What are the main criticisms of the Planned approach?

3. How does OD differ from Lewin's Planned change?

4. What are the main criticisms of OD?

5. Discuss the implications of the Planned approach for managerial behaviour.

Class debates

The purpose of class debates is to enable students to explore a topic in depth by setting up a 'for and against' debate. The class can be split into two and one half asked to research the 'for' case and the other 'against' case. Individuals can then be chosen at random to introduce their side of the debate. Alternatively, two individuals for each side can be told in advance that they will be introducing the debate. The length of such debates depends on the time available, the size of the class and their enthusiasm for the topic. However, less than 30 minutes is probably too short and more than 60 minutes probably too long. The following are three suggested topics which address issues raised in this chapter:

1. Lewin's ethical views on change are too idealistic to be practical.

2. OD is applicable to large-scale change initiatives.

3. The biggest weakness of OD/Planned change is its inability to deal with power and politics.

Essay questions

1. To what extent and why do you agree with the following statement: Lewin's work is as relevant today as it was in the 1940s.

2. Critically examine the Coping Cycle's ability to explain why change fails.

Suggested further reading

The following articles and books provide a comprehensive guide to the origins and practices of Planned change and OD.

Burnes, B (2004c) Kurt Lewin and the planned approach to change: a re-appraisal. *Journal of Management Studies*, 41(6), 977–1002.

Burnes, B (2007) Kurt Lewin and the Harwood studies: the foundations of OD. *Journal of Applied Behavioral Science*, 43(2), 213–31.

Burnes, B and Cooke, B (2012) The past, present and future of organization development: taking the long view. *Human Relations*, 65(11), 1395–429.

Cummings, TG and Worley, CG (2005) *Organization Development and Change* (8th edition). South-Western College Publishing: Mason, OH.

French, WL and Bell, CH (1999) *Organization Development* (6th edition). Prentice-Hall: Upper Saddle River, NJ.

Marrow, AJ (1969) *The Practical Theorist: The life and work of Kurt Lewin*. Teachers College Press (1977 edition): New York.

The transformation of XYZ Construction: Phase 2 – change of structure

Background

XYZ Construction employs 500 staff and is part of a Europe-based multinational enterprise. Its main business is the provision of specialist services to major construction projects. As is typical for the construction industry, XYZ operates in a highly competitive and at times hostile and aggressive environment. In 1996 a new managing director was appointed. He spent much of the next three years developing a more participative culture in the organisation (*see* Case Study 3, Chapter 3). In 1999, XYZ decided it was time to change its structure to reflect its new ways of working and its developing culture.

Towards team XYZ

By 1999, the company was a much more cohesive, open and efficient organisation. However, its basic structure remained the same as when the new managing director had taken over. There was Head Office, which dealt with large, national projects, and five regional offices that dealt with smaller, local projects. Each of these offices was organised on a functional basis; they each had separate departments for Finance, Estimation, Design and Engineering. In addition, the Head Office had a Human Resources function which covered the entire company. This structure gave rise to a number of problems: rivalry between the Head Office and the regional offices; and rivalry and lack of communication within the various offices between departments and functions.

A particular problem was the relationship between Estimation and Design in the Head Office. The former was responsible for dealing with customers and setting the price for a job. The cost of a job, however, was based on the design provided by the Design Office. Though based in the same building, there was friction between the two functions, with each seeking to second-guess the other. The large jobs were often very complex, and even within the two functions of Estimation and Design there could be disputes about the best way to carry out a job. However, there was much more dispute between the two functions. Estimation felt that Design sometimes made jobs too complex and costly, and Design felt that Estimation did not understand the technical aspects of what they were suggesting to customers. This caused problems

for Engineering, which was responsible for the actual construction process. The engineers sometimes found themselves starting jobs where there were still disagreements between Estimation and Design over what had been quoted for and what was required. Nevertheless, the general view was that the company was more efficient, better-run and a friendlier place than it had been three years earlier.

In 1999, the managing director and his deputy began to have discussions in the company over restructuring. Their basic aim was to remove functional barriers and create a more teamwork-based, process-focused organisation. However, they did not underestimate how difficult this would be. It would need a complete reorganisation within and between the offices. It would reduce the power of the regional managers and amalgamate the Head Office empires of some directors. The managing director recognised that such changes could and probably would create friction and resistance. Consequently, he also recognised that XYZ lacked the skills to plan and implement such a change. He, therefore, brought in a change consultant to assist with the exercise. After discussions with the consultant, a five-stage change process was agreed comprising the following activities:

1. Change readiness audit.
2. Evaluation and planning workshops.
3. Communication.
4. Implementation and team-building.
5. Evaluation.

Stage 1

The consultant undertook a change readiness audit to identify key issues and concerns which needed to be addressed. This consisted of face-to-face interviews with all senior managers, and interviews and discussions with other staff from all levels of the company. It also involved a SWOT exercise to assess the company's competitive position. Some 70 people, at all levels, were involved in the SWOT. The interviews showed that there was a general recognition of the problems brought about by the existing structure, but little agreement about any new structure, and some concern over potential loss of status and career opportunities if a flatter, less functional structure was adopted, especially if the new structure involved multi-function teams and a reduced number of departments. However, the audit also showed that managers and staff alike had faith in and respect for the managing director. They also felt that the changes that had taken place over the previous three years had been positive. In addition, there was a strong sense of self-belief in the company that whatever the changes required, they could achieve them.

The SWOT exercise showed that there was considerable agreement that the company had a strong technical base but concerns about lack of teamworking and entrepreneurial flair. In particular, staff in the regional offices felt that opportunities for new business were being missed. They also felt that their skills were under-utilised by being devoted to mainly small jobs rather than having an opportunity to participate in the larger contracts. The findings from the change audit were used to structure and begin the second stage of the change process, the evaluation and planning workshops.

Stage 2

There were five one-day workshops spread over a two-month period. The purpose of these workshops was to establish a set of criteria for evaluating alternative structures, identify what alternatives existed, test these against the evaluation criteria, select a preferred structure and develop plans for implementing it. This was seen as an iterative process. Even when the evaluation criteria had been agreed, it was expected that further discussions about alternative structures and planning would lead to some of these being questioned, challenged and amended. Similarly, once a preferred structure had been agreed, it could still be amended if the planning process threw up issues that had not been considered. At the end of each workshop, participants had an agreed set of actions which they had to undertake, a key one being to go out and discuss what had emerged from the workshops with their colleagues in the rest of the company. A newsletter was also issued from each workshop.

The first two workshops were for the senior management team (SMT) only and the remaining three for the SMT plus the next layer of managers down, an additional 15–20 people. The results of the audit were presented to the first workshop, which began the process of developing a set of evaluation criteria and generating alternative structures. At the end of Workshop 1, a consensus seemed to be emerging with regard to a preferred structure. At the end of Workshop 2, it was agreed that the new structure should be built around

the three core activities of the company, which were labelled: Get Work; Do Work; and Get Paid. It was also agreed that while it was important to keep the regional offices, their staff should be merged into the new structure. In effect, what emerged was a process-orientated flat, matrix structure with staff in the regional offices being responsible both to the Regional Manager and the Process Manager in Head Office. For the Head Office staff, in the main, their line manager and process manager would be the same person. As might be expected, this new structure did not emerge without much discussion, debate and in some cases soul-searching. The SMT also recognised that this was probably the most radical of the proposals they had looked at, and the one likely to meet the most resistance both from regional managers, whose power would be much reduced, and functional specialists in Estimation and Design who would have to be merged to create the 'Get Work' group. In addition, it was clear that some directors were not happy to see their own department dismantled and their own position threatened.

Workshop 3 was devoted to presenting the proposed structure to the new participants, testing it and in some cases agreeing to amend it. Workshops 4 and 5 concentrated on the details of implementing the new structure. This covered everything from where people would sit, to whom they would report, new job descriptions, to communication and team-building. This last exercise was seen as vital to ensuring that staff in the reorganised structure worked as teams and cooperated with other teams rather than merely creating another set of functional barriers. It was at this point that it was agreed that the new structure be named 'Team XYZ' to emphasise that the intention was to create a company where everyone felt they were members of one team. There was also much discussion and consultation between the Workshops with staff in the rest of the company.

At the end of Stage 2, almost all managers and supervisors in the company and a great number of the workforce had been involved in the process and by November 1999, the company was ready to communicate the new structure both internally and externally (to their parent company and customers).

Stage 3

The communication stage was both short and intense. Members of the SMT were given the task of visiting all areas of the company and briefing them on the new structure and how it would impact on them. Though there were also newsletters and information on the company's intranet, it was these face-to-face briefings

Case study 9 (*continued*)

with small groups of staff which generated the most debate. They also raised some questions, mainly of a detailed nature, which had not been addressed. In general, however, the new structure received a positive welcome and the implementation stage then began.

Stage 4

The new structure was rolled out over a three-month period. Ideally everything would have changed overnight, but the logistics of moving staff around from one group to another, physically altering office accommodation, and training managers for their new roles took time. Also, the intention was to ensure that all managers and supervisors, including those on sites, went through Team XYZ team-building workshops. Although, as expected, there were some hiccups and some unanticipated problems, by the end of March 2000 the new structure was fully up and running with remarkably little difficulty.

Stage 5

In April, a two-day meeting of all the company's senior and middle managers was held to evaluate the change that had taken place, identify issues that needed to be addressed, and ensure that the momentum was maintained and that staff did not fall back into old ways of working. As part of this process, each manager was asked to identify two steps that they personally would take to develop the new structure further and promote teamworking. These were all written on flip charts and pinned to the walls for everyone to see. At the beginning of the two days, there was something of an air of exhaustion about the managers; they had been through a period of major upheaval and, as one said, 'We need a period of consolidation'. At the end of the two days, they left not only having agreed that the new structure was working remarkably well but also with a whole host of new changes they wanted to make to improve the structure further.

Summary

Though the development and implementation of a new structure at XYZ was not without its difficulties, it was achieved remarkably quickly and with relatively little disruption. There was significant potential for those who might lose out from the changes to try to prevent, or at least slow down, their implementation. All the regional managers and a number of the directors saw their areas of responsibility, and thus power, reduced. Many of the functional specialists found themselves operating in multi-function teams where their promotion prospects depended less on their technical abilities *per se* and more on their ability to work and manage as a team player. There was also the fact that people who did not like each other suddenly found that they were working side by side.

One explanation as to why the potential dangers to the change process did not emerge is clearly a result of the way it was managed. It was an open process that involved a great number of people either directly or indirectly. At some point, all the issues that needed to be considered, even personality issues, were brought out on the table and discussed, sometimes quite often. There was also a tenacity and momentum to the process. It was clear from the start that the managing director wanted to see a new structure and would not be fobbed off with a sub-optimal compromise. It was also clear from the change audit that many other people in the company recognised that its structure needed changing, even if they were nervous about such a change. In essence, the company was ready for such a change, even if some were uncomfortable with the outcome.

Questions

1. Compare and discuss XYZ's approach to change with Lewin's Three-Step model.

2. Undertake a Force Field Analysis (Figure 9.2) of XYZ prior to the change of structure. Identify and discuss which of the forces were changed, why they needed to be changed and how the changes were achieved.

3. Use the Coping Cycle, Figure 9.5, to analyse and discuss why the change of structure appeared to be accepted with such little resistance.

Developments in change management

Emergence challenges Emergent change as OD strikes back

MINI CASE STUDY 10.1

Insights from the IBM Global Chief Executive Officer Study

How are Chief Executive Officers (CEOs) responding to the complexity of increasingly interconnected organisations, markets, societies and governments – what we call the connected economy? To find out, we spoke with more than 1,700 CEOs and senior public sector leaders from around the globe. For some time now, businesses have been refining and optimising their networks of suppliers and partners. They're streamlining supply chains, creating massive back-office efficiencies and perfecting everything from just-in-time inventory to predictive merchandising. But something just as meaningful has been happening in the marketplace – the

➡

sudden convergence of the digital, social and mobile spheres – connecting customers, employees and partners in new ways to organisations and to each other.

These changes put pressure on the front office to digitise and adapt but also create opportunities for the organisation to innovate and lead. Leaders are recognising that our new connected era is fundamentally changing how people engage. This shift is one reason why, for the first time since this CEO Study series began in 2004, technology now tops the list of external forces impacting organisations. Above any other external factor – even the economy – CEOs expect technology to drive the most change in their organisations over the next three to five years.

Our key findings

CEOs are creating more open and collaborative cultures – encouraging employees to connect, learn from each other and thrive in a world of rapid change.

More than 70 per cent of CEOs are seeking a better understanding of individual customer needs and improved responsiveness. Given the need for deep customer insight, outperformers have a distinct advantage. They are far more adept at converting data into insights and insights into action.

The pressure to innovate is not subsiding and organisations are teaming to meet the challenge. More than half of all CEOs are partnering extensively to drive innovation.

Today's CEOs are leading their organisations through an uncharacteristically disruptive era – one that is quite different from those their predecessors have faced. Many CEOs have found themselves in a position of learning while leading.

To steer their organisations effectively, CEOs told us three leadership traits are most critical: inspirational leadership, customer obsession and leadership teaming across the C-suite [all senior managers]. Interestingly, these characteristics closely align with the goals of empowering employees through values, engaging customers as individuals and amplifying innovation with partnerships. This linkage illustrates what CEOs intuitively know: their evolution as leaders directly impacts their organisations' behaviour, culture and ultimately, results.

Source: IBM (2012), *Leading Through Connections: Insights from the Global Chief Executive Officer Study*, pp. 6–8, Reprint Courtesy of International Business Machines Corporation, © 2012 International Business Machines Corporation.

Introduction

Every two years IBM interviews 1,700 CEOs from across the globe. As the latest CEO Study shows (*see* Mini Case Study 10.1), they view their organisations less and less as stable and enduring institutions, and more and more as 'work in progress' subject to continuous and disruptive change. This was reflected in one of the findings from the latest Study:

> CEOs are . . . becoming increasingly accustomed to volatility. They simply expect unpredictability. For them, there is no 'new normal.' As one U.S. government agency leader told us flatly, 'There isn't a single day I come into work when I know what will happen.' Unable to control or even anticipate economic outcomes, these CEOs have shifted their focus elsewhere.
> (IBM, 2012: 12)

Chapter 8 cast doubt on the argument that all organisations face radical and continuous change. The IBM study does not necessarily refute this doubt, but it does show that, whether from day-to-day experience or some form of global CEO group-think, large numbers of senior managers across the world assume that they are operating in a 'disruptive era' where 'unpredictability' is the order of the day and they will act in accordance with that assumption. This is why many believe that the Planned approach to change, reviewed in Chapter 9, is no longer fit for purpose and instead have sought to promote the Emergent approach. The Emergent approach starts from the assumption that change is not a linear process or a one-off isolated event but is a continuous, open-ended, cumulative and unpredictable process of aligning and re-aligning an organisation to its changing environment (Falconer, 2002). Weick (2000: 225) comments as follows on studies of Emergent change:

> The recurring story is one of autonomous initiatives that bubble up internally; continuous emergent change; steady learning from both failure and success; strategy implementation that is replaced by strategy making; the appearance of innovations that are unplanned, unforeseen and unexpected; and small actions that have surprisingly large consequences.

Advocates of Emergent change argue that it is more suitable to the turbulent and continually changing environment in which firms now operate. They reject both the incremental approach of Planned change, which they characterise as individually separate and distinct change-events, and the large-scale, unexpected, discontinuous and reactive approach of those who espouse the punctuated equilibrium model. Instead, they argue that organisations must continually and synergistically adapt their internal practices and behaviour in real time to changing external conditions (Beer and Nohria, 2000). Consequently, 'The art of leadership in the management field would seem to lie in the ability to shape the process [of change] in the long term rather than direct single episodes' (Pettigrew and Whipp, 1991: 143). As Orlikowski (1996: 65–6) maintains:

> In this perspective, organizational transformation is not portrayed as a drama staged by deliberate directors with predefined scripts and choreographed moves, or the inevitable outcome of a technological logic, or a sudden discontinuity that fundamentally invalidates the status quo. Rather, organizational transformation is seen here to be an ongoing improvisation enacted by organizational actors trying to make sense of and act coherently in the world. . . . Each variation of a given form is not an abrupt or discrete event, neither is it, by itself, discontinuous. Rather, through a series of ongoing and situated accommodations, adaptations, and alterations (that draw on previous variations and mediate future ones), sufficient modifications may be enacted over time that fundamental changes are achieved. There is no deliberate orchestration of change here, no technological inevitability, no dramatic discontinuity, just recurrent and reciprocal variations in practice over time. Each shift in practice creates the conditions for further breakdowns, unanticipated outcomes, and innovations, which in their turn are responded to with more variations. And such variations are ongoing; there is no beginning or end point in this change process.

In a similar vein, Caldwell (2006: 77) refers to Emergent change as 'a long-term complex and incremental process of shaping how change unfolds over time'. For Brown and Eisenhardt (1997: 28) change is 'neither incremental nor radical' but 'a third kind of process' that lies somewhere in between. Though they may disagree with Caldwell about the 'size' of change, all three would agree with a view of change as occurring continuously and synergistically with each change initiative being linked to the critical path of the organisation rather than being a separate or rare event. This is why the advocates of Emergent change argue that it needs to be viewed holistically and contextually (Mintzberg and Westley, 1992). Furthermore, and just as importantly, proponents of Emergent change recognise that organisations are power systems and, consequently, change is a political process whereby different groups in an organisation struggle to protect or enhance their own interests (Orlikowski and Yates, 2006).

To understand the nature of Emergent change, this chapter begins by presenting the case against the Planned/OD approach to change and the rise of the Emergent perspective on change. It then goes on to examine the main arguments for, and characteristics of, Emergent change. This will show that, although they do not always agree with each other, the advocates of Emergent change are united by their antagonism towards Planned change and the emphasis they place on organisational structure, culture and learning, and their perspective on managerial behaviour and the role of power and politics in the change process. However, it is also shown that, some 25 years since its inception, it still lacks the tools and techniques necessary to provide a practical alternative to Planned change. Following this, the chapter examines the merits of complexity-based Emergence as an approach to change. It also shows that, despite the rumours of its demise, the Planned/OD approach to change appears to have staged a remarkable recovery in recent years. In conclusion, it is argued that despite the large body of literature devoted to the topic of change management, and the many tools and techniques available to change agents, there is considerable debate and little agreement regarding the most appropriate approach. One thing is clear: neither the Emergent approach nor the Planned approach is suitable for all situations and circumstances.

From Planned to Emergent change

As was shown in Chapter 9, the OD movement has ensured that the Planned approach to change has been, and remains, highly influential, not just in the US but across the world (Fagenson-Eland et al, 2004: Wirtenberg et al, 2007). It is still far and away the best developed, documented and supported approach to change. This is because OD has taken Kurt Lewin's original concept of Planned change and used it as the basis of a thriving consultancy industry with its own standards, accreditation procedures and membership (Burnes and Cooke, 2012b; Cummings and Worley, 1997). In doing so, Lewin's conception of Planned change as applying to small-group, human-centred change has been extended to include organisation-wide change initiatives. This has led to some confusion between Planned (participative) change as promoted by the OD movement and Planned (directive–transformational) change as promoted by some elements of the strategic planning movement (Beer and Nohria, 2000; Mintzberg et al, 1998a, 1998b).

This section, following on from the previous chapter, is concerned with the Planned approach to change as promoted by Lewin and the OD movement and which, from the late 1940s to the early 1980s, was the dominant approach to change, especially in the US. As was discussed in Chapter 9, from the early 1980s onwards, it has faced increasing levels of criticism regarding its appropriateness and efficacy, especially in terms of its ability to cope with continuous change, its emphasis on incremental change, its neglect of organisational conflict and politics, and its advocacy of a 'one best way' approach to change.

It was the rise of Japanese competitiveness and the apparent eclipse of Western industry in the late 1970s that precipitated the questioning of existing approaches to structuring, managing and changing organisations (e.g. Pascale and Athos, 1982; Peters and Waterman, 1982). Weick (2000: 227) states that the main drawbacks of Planned change were seen as a:

> high probability of relapse; uneven diffusion among units; large short-term losses that are difficult to recover; less suitability for opportunity-driven than for threat-driven alterations; unanticipated consequences due to limited foresight; temptations towards hypocrisy (when people talk the talk of revolution but walk the talk of resistance); adoption of best practices that work best elsewhere because of a different context; ignorance among top management regarding key contingencies and capabilities at the front line; and lags in implementation that make the change outdated before it's even finished.

For Wilson (1992), it is the increasingly dynamic and uncertain nature of the business environment that undermines the case for Planned change and underlines the appropriateness of the Emergent approach. He also believes that the Planned approach, by attempting to lay down timetables, objectives and methods in advance, is too heavily reliant on the role of managers, and assumes (rashly) that they can have a full understanding of the consequences of their actions and that their plans will be understood and accepted and can be implemented. Similarly, Buchanan and Storey (1997: 127) maintain that the main criticism of those who advocate Planned change is:

> their attempt to impose an order and a linear sequence to processes that are in reality messy and untidy, and which unfold in an iterative fashion with much backtracking and omission.

The proponents of Culture–Excellence were perhaps the most vociferous and scathing critics of Planned change, arguing that:

> Lewin's model was a simple one, with organizational change involving three stages; unfreezing, changing and refreezing . . . This quaintly linear and static conception – the organization as an ice cube – is so wildly inappropriate that it is difficult to see why it has not only survived but prospered. . . . Suffice it to say here, first, that organizations are never frozen, much less refrozen, but are fluid entities with many 'personalities'. Second, to the extent that there are stages, they overlap and inter-penetrate one another in important ways.
>
> (Kanter *et al*, 1992: 10)

The advocates of Culture–Excellence, described in Chapter 3, argued that Western organisations were bureaucratic, inflexible and stifled innovation. In place of Lewin's 'wildly inappropriate' model of change, the advocates of Culture–Excellence called for organisations to adopt cultures that promote innovation and entrepreneurship and encourage bottom-up, flexible, continuous and cooperative change. However, they also recognised that top-down coercion, and rapid transformation, might be necessary to create the conditions in which this type of approach could flourish.

As mentioned in Chapter 9, at the same time, other new perspectives on organisations, especially concerning the role of power and politics in decision-making, were also coming to the fore (Pettigrew, 1973, 1980; Pfeffer, 1978, 1981). This paved the way for the development of a processual approach to organisational change (*see* next section), which highlights the continuous, unpredictable and political nature of change (Dawson, 1994; Pettigrew, 1985, 1997; Wilson, 1992). Looking at Planned change versus a processual approach, Dawson (1994: 3–4) comments:

> Although this [Lewin's] theory has proved useful in understanding planned change under relatively stable conditions, with the continuing and dynamic nature of change in today's business world, it no longer makes sense to implement a planned process for 'freezing' changed behaviours. Implementing stability and reinforcing behaviour which conforms to a rigid set of procedures for new work arrangements does not meet the growing requirements for employee flexibility and structural adaptation to the unfolding and complex nature of ongoing change processes. . . . The processual framework . . . adopts the view that change is a complex and dynamic process which should not be solidified or treated as a series of linear events. . . . central to the development of a processual approach is the need to incorporate an analysis of the politics of managing change.

For the postmodernists (*see* Alvesson and Deetz, 1996; Foucault, 1983; Gergen, 1992), power is also a central feature of change, but it arises from the socially constructed nature of organisational life:

> In a socially constructed world, responsibility for environmental conditions lies with those who do the constructing. . . . This suggests at least two competing scenarios for organizational change. First, organization change can be a vehicle of domination for those who conspire to enact the world for others . . . An alternative use of social constructionism is to create a democracy of enactment in which the process is made open and available to all . . . such that we create opportunities for freedom and innovation rather than simply for further domination.
>
> (Hatch, 1997: 367–8)

Thus, from the early 1980s, a powerful consensus built up against the Planned approach to change. It is a consensus, however, that criticises Planned change from very different perspectives: ranging from the free market neo-liberalism of Tom Peters to the neo-Marxism of some of the postmodernists. Therefore, they are certainly a much less coherent group than the advocates of Planned change and, rather than being united by a shared belief, they tend to be distinguished by a common disbelief in the efficacy of Planned change. Nevertheless, they do share at least two beliefs: firstly, instead of seeing change as a phenomenon that is linear, pre-planned and has a finite end point, they see change as an 'emerging' and ongoing process of organisational adaptation and transformation. Secondly, they adopt an open systems perspective. That is, they see individual organisations as interdependent parts or sub-systems of a much larger environment, though they disagree about whether the environment is a concrete reality or a socially constructed phenomenon. The environment impacts upon and affects the actions and decisions of organisations, but they also impact on the environment. Proponents of the Emergent approach see change as emerging from the day-to-day actions and decisions of members of an organisation. In this sense, change can emerge from attempts by members of organisations to align the organisation with its environment, or as the result of different groups battling for domination, or even from attempts to construct a new, or challenge an old, social reality.

Having identified what separates it from the Planned approach to change, we can now move on to examine the Emergent approach in more detail.

Emergent change

For proponents of the Emergent approach, change is a continuous, dynamic and contested process that emerges in an unpredictable and unplanned fashion. For Weick (2000: 227), the advantages of Emergent change include:

> sensitivity to local contingencies; suitability for on-line real-time experimentation, learning, and sensemaking; comprehensibility and manageability; likelihood of satisfying needs for autonomy, control, and expression; proneness to swift implementation; resistance to unravelling; ability to exploit existing tacit knowledge; and tightened and shortened feedback loops from results to action.

The rationale for the Emergent approach stems, according to Hayes (2002: 37), from the belief that:

> the key decisions about matching the organisation's resources with opportunities, constraints and demands in the environment evolve over time and are the outcome of cultural and political processes in organisations.

One of the main strands of the Emergent approach is provided by processual analysts, deriving from the work of Andrew Pettigrew (1973, 1979, 1985, 1990a, 1990b, 1997, 2000; Pettigrew *et al*, 2001). As noted in the previous chapter, Pettigrew (1985) based his work on his major study of ICI, which argued that OD was not effective and should be replaced by a processual approach to change. Processualists, as the name implies, conduct process research in organisations. They define a process as 'a sequence of individual and collective events, actions, and activities unfolding over time in context' (Pettigrew, 1997: 338). Therefore, process research in organisations is the study of organisational change over time and in context.

Processualists reject prescriptive, recipe-driven approaches to change and are suspicious of single causes or simple explanations of events. Instead, when studying change, they focus on the interrelatedness of individuals, groups, organisations and society (Dawson, 2003; Pettigrew and Whipp, 1993). In particular, they claim that the process of change is a complex and untidy cocktail of rational decision processes, individual perceptions, political struggles and coalition-building (Huczynski and Buchanan, 2001). Within this complex and untidy cocktail, processualists recognise 'the importance of planning for change' and the presence of 'processes of continuity'; they also recognise, however, that these are constrained and influenced by 'the complex untidy and messy nature of change' (Dawson, 2003: 25). Pettigrew and Whipp (1991: 165) observed:

> Leading change calls for the resolution of not so much great single issues but rather a pattern of interwoven problems.

The elaborateness of the processualist view of change is shown by Pettigrew (1997: 340), who states that processualists pursue their work through five internally consistent guiding principles (*see* Ideas and perspectives 10.1).

For Pettigrew, change is never a one-off or isolated event. For him, it cuts across functions, spans hierarchical divisions, and has no neat starting or finishing point; instead it is a 'complex analytical, political, and cultural process of challenging and changing the core beliefs, structure and strategy of the firm' (Pettigrew, 1987: 650).

IDEAS AND PERSPECTIVES 10.1

Pettigrew's five guiding principles of processual research

The irreducible purpose of a processual analysis remains to account for and explain the what, why and how of the links between context, processes and outcomes. I would like to conclude this statement of theory of method for conducting processual research by reaffirming five internally consistent guiding assumptions. They are:

1. embeddedness, studying processes across a number of levels of analysis;
2. temporal interconnectedness, studying processes in past, present and future time;
3. a role in explanation for context and action;
4. a search for holistic rather than linear explanations of process; and
5. a need to link process analysis to the location and explanation of outcomes.

Source: Pettigrew (1997: 340).

For these reasons, the Emergent perspective rejects both simple taxonomies of change, and approaches such as Total Quality Management and Business Process Re-engineering, which promise success through following a series of laid-down steps and stages (Beer and Nohria, 2000; Collins, 1998). According to Stace and Dunphy (2001: 5):

> The appealing aspect of the promises held out for these change technologies is that they can absolve the manager from the onerous task of critically reviewing the full range of other competing approaches or devising a custom-made program. They cut through complexity. However, the offer is often illusory, for particular change approaches usually apply to particular situations, and simple solutions sometimes ignore the complexity of real life.

In addition, proponents of the Emergent approach argue that even when changes are operational, they will need to be constantly refined and developed in order to maintain their relevance (Dawson, 2003). Genus (1998: 51) uses an 'interpretive' perspective to explain the messy nature of organisational change, arguing that the 'various political, symbolic and structural factors [involved in the change process] condition the perceptions of individuals or groups'. Finstad's (1998) view of organisational change, while being consistent with the perspectives of Dawson and Genus, appears to adopt a realist perspective on change by drawing an important distinction between the concrete elements of change, such as structures and practices, and the more symbolic elements, such as people's basic understandings and assumptions about their organisations. He maintains, though, that it is the symbolic aspects that dominate the change process rather than the more concrete changes. The importance of symbolism and ritual in the change process is also emphasised by Schuyt and Schuijt (1998), who argue that the management of these is not only central to achieving successful change but also plays a crucial role in reducing the uncertainty which change generates.

Therefore, advocates of Emergent change tend to stress the developing and unpredictable nature of change. They view change as a process that unfolds through the interplay of multiple variables within an organisation, especially context, consultation and political behaviour (Dawson, 2003).

Power, politics and change

Dawson (1994: 180–2) states that:

> In managing these transitions practitioners need to be aware of: the importance of power politics within organizations as a determinant of the speed, direction and character of change; the enabling and constraining properties of the type and scale of change being introduced; and the influence of the internal and external context on the pathways and outcomes of change on new work arrangements. . . . [Also] . . . the management of these changes cannot be characterized as being composed of a linear series of phases, nor do the outcomes represent the results of objective rational decision-making on the part of managers. . . . [nor] as a single reaction to adverse contingent circumstances.

Therefore, successful change is less dependent on detailed plans and projections than on reaching an understanding of the intricacy of the issues concerned, including the central role played by power and politics in initiating and managing change, and in identifying the range of available options (Pettigrew, 1997). The political dimension of change is further emphasised by the postmodernists, for whom the struggle for power and domination is the central feature of change in organisations (Hassard, 1993; Hatch, 1997). As Finstad (1998)

IDEAS AND PERSPECTIVES 10.2

Pugh's four principles for understanding change

Principle One: Organizations are organisms. They are not mechanisms which can be taken apart and reassembled differently as required. They can be changed, but the change must be approached carefully with the implications for the various groupings thought out and the participants convinced of the worthwhileness of their point of view.

Principle Two: Organizations are political and occupational systems as well as rational resource allocation ones. Every reaction to a change proposal must be interpreted not only in terms of rational arguments of what is best for the firm . . . The reaction must also be understood in relation to the occupational system . . . and the political system (how will it affect the power, status, prestige of the group?).

Principle Three: All members of an organization operate simultaneously in all three systems – the rational, the occupational and the political ones. Do not make the mistake of becoming cynical and thinking that the occupational and the political aspects are all that matter, and that rational arguments are merely rationalizations to defend a particular position.

Principle Four: Change is most likely to be acceptable and effective in those people or departments who are successful in their tasks but who are experiencing tensions or failure in some particular part of their work . . . They will have the two basic ingredients [for successful change] of confidence in their ability and motivation to change.

Source: Pugh (1993: 109–10).

notes, however, the difference is that, for the processualists, the political nature of change tends to close off options, whereas for the postmodernists, the presence of conflicting interests gives people a range of new possibilities and ideas to choose from.

Despite their difference in emphasis, proponents of the Emergent approach do agree that power and politics play an important role in the process of organisational change. This is a major point of departure between them and proponents of Planned change. In commenting on the failure to incorporate the political nature of change into the traditional and more prescriptive literature on change, Hardy (1996) argues that this 'aversion' to discussing power has restricted our understanding of change and impeded our ability to manage it effectively. Pugh (1993) makes a similar point about the political nature of organisational life in Principle Two of his analysis of organisational change (*see* Ideas and perspectives 10.2). However, he also argues, in Principle Three, that rational and occupational systems need to be considered alongside, and not subordinate to, the political system. This clearly conflicts with the processualists, who see the political system as being paramount.

The role of managers

It is because change is so complex, multifaceted and pervasive that Carnall (2003) suggests that mastering the challenge of change is beyond the abilities specialist change agents, but an essential part of every manager's role. This is because they are ones who best know their organisation, its priorities and staff, and are thus in the best position to bring about change. Carnall (2003: 125–6) proposes four core managerial competences that are essential for the effective management of change:

- **Decision-making**: this includes intuition and vision, the ability to gather and utilise information, understanding the practical and political consequences of decisions, the ability to overcome resistance, the skill to understand and synthesise conflicting views and to be able to empathise with different groups.

- **Coalition-building**: this comprises the skills necessary to gain the support and resources necessary to implement decisions. These include checking the feasibility of ideas, gaining supporters, bargaining with other stakeholders and presenting new ideas and concepts in a way that wins support.

- **Achieving action**: this includes handling opposition, motivating people, providing support and building self-esteem.

- **Maintaining momentum and effort**: this involves team-building, generating ownership, sharing information and problems, providing feedback, trusting people and energising staff.

Stace and Dunphy (2001) take a more contextual view of managerial competences. Their Change Matrix identifies a spectrum of change situations, ranging from fine-tuning to corporate transformation, and a matching spectrum of styles of change management, ranging from cooperative to coercive. The Matrix identifies at least 16 combinations of change situations and styles of management, each of which requires a different set of managerial competences (*see* Figure 10.1).

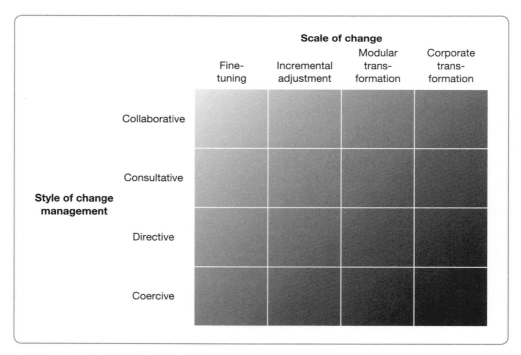

Figure 10.1 The Dunphy–Stace change matrix
Source: Stace and Dunphy (2001: 107).

Contingency

The contingency view of change tallies with that of McCalman and Paton (1992) who suggest that, to be effective in creating sustainable change, managers need an extensive and systemic understanding of their organisation's environment, in order to identify the pressures for change and to ensure that, by mobilising the necessary internal resources, their organisation responds in a timely and appropriate manner. Similarly, Dawson (1994) claims that change must be linked to developments in markets, work organisation, systems of management control and the shifting nature of organisational boundaries and relationships. He emphasises that, in a dynamic business environment, one-dimensional change interventions are likely to generate only short-term results and heighten instability rather than reduce it. This is a point emphasised by many other writers (Beer and Nohria, 2000; Graetz *et al*, 2002; Hartley *et al*, 1997; Senior, 2002).

As can be seen, though not all state it openly, advocates of Emergent change tend to adopt a Contingency perspective (*see* Chapter 2), arguing that approaches to change need to be tailored to the situation of the individual organisation and the type of change it is undertaking (Weick, 2000). This is a point that is central to Pettigrew's contextualist approach to change:

> Context and action are inseparable.
>
> (Pettigrew, 2000: 243)

> Leadership [of change] requires action appropriate to its context.
>
> (Pettigrew and Whipp, 1991: 165)

Therefore, Pettigrew offers a very particularistic view of change whereby each change situation is different and must be approached and managed differently. It follows from this that implicit in the case for Emergent change is the assumption that if organisations operated in more stable and predictable environments, the need for change would be less and it might be possible to conceive of it as a process of moving from one relatively stable state to another. As Dawson (1994: 3) observes:

> Although [Lewin's] theory has proven to be useful in understanding planned change under relatively stable conditions, with the continuing and dynamic nature of change in today's business world, it no longer makes sense to implement a planned process of 'refreezing' changed behaviours.

For advocates of Emergent change, therefore, it is the uncertainty of the environment that makes Planned change inappropriate and Emergent change more pertinent. This is a point emphasised by Stickland (1998: 14), who draws on systems theory to emphasise the way that organisations are separate from but connected to their environment:

> A system has an identity that sets it apart from its environment and is capable of preserving that identity within a given range of environmental scenarios. Systems exist within a hierarchy of other systems. They contain subsystems and exist within some wider system. All are interconnected.

From this systems perspective, Stickland (1998: 76) raises a question that many of those studying organisational change appear not to acknowledge:

> To what extent does the environment drive changes within a system [i.e. an organisation] and to what extent is the system in control of its own change processes?

Finstad (1998: 721) puts this issue in a wider context by arguing that 'the organization is . . . the creator of its environment and the environment is the creator of the organization'.

Though this has a postmodernist sound to it, realists would also recognise that organisations do contribute to the creation or the maintenance of their environment, but they see this as a long-term and largely unconscious process. This reciprocal relationship between an organisation and its environment clearly has profound implications for how organisations conceptualise and manage change. It also serves to emphasise that a key competence for organisations is the ability to scan the external environment in order to identify and assess the impact on them of trends and discontinuities and also to understand how their actions might affect the environment (Graetz *et al*, 2002; McCalman and Paton, 1992; Pettigrew and Whipp, 1993). This involves exploring the full range of external variables, including markets and customers, shareholders, legal requirements, the economy, suppliers, technology and social trends. This activity is made more difficult by the changing and arbitrary nature of organisation boundaries: customers can also be competitors; suppliers may become partners; and employees can be transformed into customers, suppliers or even competitors for scarce resources.

To cope with these complications and uncertainties, Pettigrew and Whipp (1993) maintain that organisations need to become open learning systems, with strategy development and change emerging from the way the company as a whole acquires, interprets and processes information about its environment. Carnall (2003) and Hayes (2002) take a similar view, arguing that an organisation's survival and growth depend on identifying environmental and market changes quickly, and responding opportunistically. This is in line with the discussion on organisational learning covered in Chapter 3. However, as Benjamin and Mabey (1993: 181) point out:

> While the primary stimulus for change remains those forces in the external environment, the primary motivator for how change is accomplished resides with the people within the organization.

Bottom-up, not top-down

Consequently, actual or potential changes in the external environment require organisations to make choices over how and when to respond. Such responses, the supporters of the Emergent approach state, should promote, throughout the organisation, an extensive and deep understanding of strategy, structure, systems, people, style and culture, and how these can function either as sources of inertia that can block change, or alternatively, as levers to encourage an effective change process (Dawson, 2003; Pettigrew, 1997; Wilson, 1992). A concomitant development is the adoption of a 'bottom-up' rather than 'top-down' approach to initiating and implementing change. After all, there is little point in encouraging staff to identify change opportunities unless they are also encouraged to implement them. The case in favour of this move is based on the view that the pace of environmental change is so rapid and complex that it is impossible for a small number of senior managers effectively to identify, plan and implement the necessary organisational responses. The responsibility for organisational change is therefore of necessity becoming more devolved. As described in Chapter 2, this is very much what the advocates of Contingency Theory would expect in such a situation.

The need for a bottom-up approach does not arise solely from external pressures. As Stickland (1998: 93) notes, organisations are continually experiencing 'natural changes', i.e. the unintended consequences of deliberate decisions and actions:

> Within any organisation at a given point in time there are a number of continual shifts and changes playing out at various levels. These are not planned changes with a defined beginning and end, but rather reflect the natural dynamics which take place internally.

Such events may present organisations with unexpected and unlooked-for opportunities, such as new product ideas, but may also present unwelcome threats, such as the departure of key staff. Given that such changes are continually happening at all levels and across all functions, organisations would quickly become paralysed if it was left solely to senior managers to identify and resolve them. Therefore, if they are to be dealt with speedily, these local problems or opportunities have to be dealt with locally. As Senior (2002) comments, this requires organisations to empower their employees to make changes at a local level. This follows from Mintzberg's (1994) assertion that it is from these local and bottom-up actions that the direction of the organisation emerges and is given shape.

In many ways, this is the crux of the Emergent argument – top-down, senior-management-imposed change does not work. What is required is for managers and employees, on a day-to-day basis, to have the authority to be able to shape and reshape their part of the organisation to deal with the threats and opportunities presented by an ever-changing environment. However, as these changes emerge from a host of local responses, if they are to have a synergistic and positive effect on the organisation, as opposed to tearing it apart, such changes must be guided by a common vision of the future and a shared understanding of the organisation's priorities and situation.

Therefore, a bottom-up approach requires a major change in the role of senior managers. Instead of controlling employees, they have to empower people. Instead of directing and controlling change, they have to ensure that the organisation's members are receptive to the change process, and have the necessary skills, motivation and power to take charge of it. There is a distinction here between those who take a narrow view of empowerment, seeing it mainly as devolving some limited managerial responsibility, and those, *à la* Lewin, who see it as an emancipatory process that aims to create genuine organisational democracy, though it must be pointed out that even the former have a poor track record of success (Eccles, 1993; Foegen, 1999; Graetz *et al*, 2002; Huczynski and Buchanan, 2001; Lawler *et al*, 1998; Lee, 1999; Maynard *et al*, 2012; Pfeffer, 1996; Stohl and Cheney, 2001; Wetlaufer, 1999). Nor is this just an issue of managers changing. Wilson (1992) believes that to achieve effective empowerment, senior managers must not only change the way they perceive and interpret the world but achieve a similar transformation among everyone else in the organisation as well. Pettigrew and Whipp (1993: 17–18) contend that the degree to which organisations can achieve such a difficult task, and create a climate receptive to change, is dependent on four conditioning factors:

1. The extent to which there are key actors within the firm who are prepared to champion [environmental] assessment techniques which increase the openness of the organisation [to its environment];

2. The structural and cultural characteristics of the company;

3. The extent to which environmental pressures are recognised and their associated dramas developed; and

4. The degree to which assessment occurs as a multi-function activity which is not pursued as an end in itself but is then linked to the central operation of the business.

As can be seen, the advocates of Emergent change come from a wide variety of backgrounds and each offers their own distinct view on how organisations should and should not manage change. As the following section will show, there are some core similarities which link them.

Key features of the Emergent approach to successful change

Though the proponents of the Emergent approach reject the concept of universally applicable rules for change, the guidance they do provide tends to stress five key features of organisations that either promote or obstruct success (*see* Figure 10.2).

Organisational structure

This is seen as playing a crucial role in determining where power lies, in defining how people relate to each other and in influencing the momentum for change (Carnall, 2003; Dawson, 2003; Hatch, 1997; Huczynski and Buchanan, 2001; Kotter, 1996). Crucially, as Galbraith (2000: 154) notes: 'The theory of organization has always identified some types of [organisational structures] as being more easily changeable than others.' Morgan (1988) claims that there are really only four basic forms of structure which range from the very rigid to the very flexible, as follows: bureaucracy, matrix, project and loosely coupled-organic network. Therefore, an appropriate organisational structure, in both its formal and informal elements, can be an important facilitator of change.

The case for developing more appropriate organisational structures in order to facilitate change very much follows the arguments of the Contingency theorists (discussed in Chapter 2) and the Culture–Excellence school (discussed in Chapter 3), i.e. that dynamic and chaotic

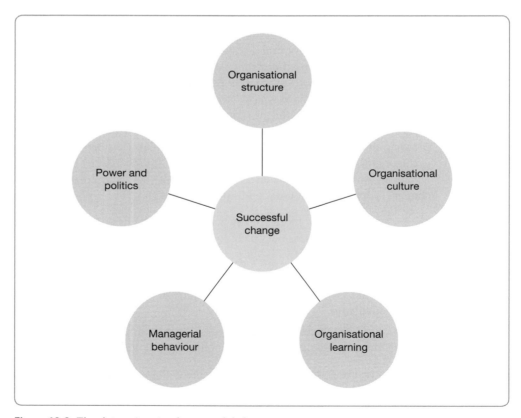

Figure 10.2 The determinants of successful change

environments require organisations to adopt more flexible, less hierarchical structures. Those favouring an Emergent approach to change point out that the 1990s witnessed a general tendency to create flatter organisational structures in order to increase responsiveness by devolving authority and responsibility (Senior, 2002). As Kotter (1996: 169) remarks, the case for such structural changes is that:

> an organization with more delegation, which means a flat hierarchy, is in a far superior position to maneuver than one with a big, change-resistant lump in the middle.

In studying innovating organisations, Brown and Eisenhardt (1997: 29) refer to such flexible structures as 'semistructures', which they claim:

> are sufficiently rigid so that change can be organized, but not so rigid that it cannot occur . . . sustaining this semistructured state is challenging because it is a dissipative equilibrium and so requires constant managerial vigilance to avoid slipping into pure chaos or pure structure.

A similar point is made by Galbraith (2000: 155), who refers to the 'reconfigurable' organisation, which:

> consists of a stable part and a variable part. The stable part consists of 'homes' for specialists in functions, which also host generalists on rotating assignments. . . . The variable part of the structure consists of integrating mechanisms and networks across the functions.

Brown and Eisenhardt (1997) claim that such structures are essential for ensuring organisational survival in highly competitive environments because they facilitate continuous innovation and improvisation and allow intensive, real-time communication within a structure of a few, very specific rules.

A common aspect of these new structures is the move by customer-obsessed leaders to create customer-centred organisations with structures that reflect, and are responsive to, different markets rather than different functions (Galbraith, 2000; Hamel and Prahalad, 1994; IBM, 2012; Stace and Dunphy, 2001). Customer responsiveness places greater emphasis on effective horizontal processes and embodies the concept that, whether one is looking internally or externally, everyone is someone else's customer (Dale, 2003; Jenner, 1998).

One result of attempts to respond rapidly to changing conditions by breaking down internal and external barriers, disseminating knowledge and developing synergy across functions is the emergence of network organisations (Morgan, 1997; Rampersad *et al*, 2010; Wisdom, 2001). Network organisations have been defined in a number of ways and given a number of names – Handy (1989) refers to them as 'federal organisations', Robbins (1997) uses the term 'virtual organisation', after the internet on which many of them either rely or are based, and Senge (2000: 77) writes of 'living human communities'. For Cummings and Worley (2001: 291), the purpose of a network-based structure is that it:

> manages the diverse, complex, and dynamic relationships among multiple organizations or units, each specializing in a particular business function or task.

Birchall and Lyons (1995) stress that networks can be in a constant state of flux as they adjust to the changing needs of their dynamic customer base. They also comment that in some cases, customers are even part of the network. For Snow *et al* (1993), a major benefit of network structures is that the semi-autonomous nature of each part of a network reduces the need for and erodes the power of centrally managed bureaucracies, which, in turn, leads to change and adaptation being driven from the bottom up rather than from the top down. They further argue that the specialisation and flexibility required to cope with globalisation, intense competition and rapid technological change, especially the challenge of the internet, can be achieved only by loosening the central ties and controls that have characterised organisations in the past (Genus, 1998; Hardaker and Graham, 2001; Kanter *et al*, 1997; Kotter, 1996; Wisdom, 2001).

However, is it clear that every organisation will have to adopt such structural changes in order to survive? The premise that this is necessary is based on the assumption that all organisations experience similar levels of environmental turbulence and cannot do anything other than adapt their internal arrangements to these external conditions. As argued in previous chapters, there are three flaws to this argument. First, environmental instability is not uniform; it varies from industry to industry and organisation to organisation. Secondly, even where instability is present, organisations can choose to take action to reduce it rather than merely having to adapt to it. Lastly, as Child's concept of equifinality discussed in Chapter 6 suggests, there are a range of internal arrangements that are compatible with external turbulence, of which flattened hierarchies are only one.

A further point which needs to be recognised is that structures do not stand in isolation from the other elements of an organisation (Mintzberg and Westley, 1992). As Hannan *et al* (2003: 401) comment:

> Organizational analysts commonly distinguish between formal architectural and informal cultural features. Architecture refers to the formal (official) specifications of an organization and its governance. Architectural choices are reflected in the formal structures for assigning work, that is, constructing the units that undertake the subtransactions. The choices also specify the means of coordinating members and units, monitoring them, and allocating resources and rewards. Culture governs how work actually gets completed, how members interact, how decisions are actually made, which units defer to others, and so forth.

Therefore, as argued in Chapter 5, it is not sufficient to have an appropriate structure; it must be matched with an appropriate culture if it is to be effective.

Organisational culture

There can be few people who now doubt the important role culture plays in the life of organisations, especially when it comes to change (Allaire and Firsirotu, 1984; Brown, 1995; De Witte and van Muijen, 1999; Hirschhorn, 2000). Johnson (1993: 64) suggested that the strategic management of change is 'essentially a cultural and cognitive phenomenon' rather than an analytical, rational exercise. Clarke (1994) states that the essence of sustainable change is to understand the culture of the organisation that is to be changed. If proposed changes contradict cultural biases and traditions, it is inevitable that they will be difficult to embed in the organisation. Kotter (1996) takes a similar view, arguing that for change to be successful it must be anchored in the organisation's culture.

Dawson (2003) echoes this theme. He suggests that attempts to realign internal behaviours with external conditions require change strategies that are culturally sensitive. Organisations, he points out, must be aware that the process is lengthy, potentially dangerous, and demands considerable reinforcement if culture change is to be sustained against the inevitable tendency to regress to old behaviours. Pointing to Pirelli's attempt to implement TQM in two of its Australian plants, Dawson (2003: 33) comments that:

Management had a plan and a timeframe for the 'successful' management of change, but they were not prepared for the very different contextual conditions and local operating cultures of the two adjacent plants in South Australia. The cultural socio-political aspects of change turned out to be far more important and influential than had been anticipated, or could be accommodated for, in planning the process of change.

Likewise, Pettigrew (1997) stresses that organisational processes are embedded in an organisation's context, of which culture forms an important part. Pettigrew also points out that, because of this embeddedness, change can be slow. Cummings and Worley (2001) likewise recognise that culture can hinder the speed of change, especially when it is the culture that needs to change. In such cases, they point out, it is necessary to challenge mechanisms that reinforce old or inappropriate behaviour, such as reward, recruitment and promotion structures – all areas where resistance can be expected. In addition, if these reinforcement mechanisms are complemented by managerial behaviour which promotes risk aversion and fear of failure, it is unlikely to create a climate where people are willing to propose or undertake change. Accordingly, as Clarke (1994: 94) suggests, 'Creating a culture for change means that change has to be part of the way we do things around here, it cannot be bolted on as an extra.'

Therefore, for many proponents of the Emergent approach, an essential factor in successful change is for organisations to possess or to be able to develop an appropriate organisational culture. However, Senior (2002) notes that many writers and researchers take a different view. Beer *et al* (1993), for example, suggest that the most effective way to promote change is not by directly attempting to influence organisational behaviour or culture. Instead, they advocate restructuring organisations in order to place people in a new organisational context which imposes new roles, relationships and responsibilities upon them. This, they believe, forces new attitudes and behaviours upon people. This view, as discussed in Chapter 3, is also shared by Tom Peters (1993), who advocates rapid and complete destruction of existing hierarchical organisation structures as a precursor to behavioural change.

In Chapter 5, we discussed the difficulty and relevance of achieving cultural change, by whatever means. This discussion found some support for the Beer *et al* and Peters position. It noted that what many proponents of cultural change appear to advocate are changes to structure, policies and norms rather than attempts to change the deeper elements of culture. It was argued that many writers are highly sceptical about seeing culture as a promoter of change. This view is, perhaps, best summed up by Wilson (1992: 91), who claims:

> To effect change in an organization simply by attempting to change its culture assumes an unwarranted linear connection between something called organizational culture and performance. Not only is this concept of organizational culture multi-faceted, it is also not always clear precisely how culture and change are related, if at all, and, if so, in which direction.

Organisational learning

This was examined in Chapter 3. For advocates of the Emergent approach, learning plays a key role in preparing people for change and enabling them to cope with it (Bechtold, 1997; Rashman *et al*, 2009; Senge, 2000). Put simply, learning means:

> the capacity of members of an organization to detect and correct errors and to seek new insights that would enable them to make choices that better produce outcomes that they seek.
>
> (Martin, 2000: 463)

A willingness to change often stems only from the feeling that there is no other option (Argyris, 1999; Pettigrew *et al*, 1992). Therefore, as Wilson (1992) suggests, change can be precipitated by encouraging dissatisfaction with current systems and procedures or making impending crises real to everyone in the organisation. Kotter (1996) even advocates engineering a crisis in order to build the momentum for change. Whatever the spur for change, however, staff are unlikely to recognise the need for change unless managers create mechanisms which allow them to become familiar with the company's performance, marketplace, customers, competitors, legal requirements, etc. (Fiol and Lyles, 1985; Probst and Buchel, 1997). Pettigrew and Whipp (1993: 18) also contended that 'collective learning' is one of the main preconditions for sustainable change. They argue that 'collective learning' ensures that the full implications of an organisation's view of its environment can then inform subsequent actions over the long term and, in turn, the way in which future shifts in the environment are tackled.

Clarke (1994) and Nadler (1993) suggest that individual and organisational learning stem from effective top-down communication and the promotion of self-development and confidence. In turn, this encourages the commitment to, and shared ownership of, the organisation's vision, actions and decisions that are necessary to respond to the external environment and take advantage of the opportunities it offers. Additionally, as Pugh (1993) points out, in order to generate the need and climate for change, people within organisations need to be involved in the diagnosis of problems and the development of solutions. Carnall (2003) takes this argument further, arguing:

> The effective organization is one which encourages and supports learning from change. This means that an open management style, encouraging initiative and risk, is needed.

Likewise, Clarke (1994: 156) maintains that involving staff in change management decisions has the effect of 'stimulating habits of criticism and open debate', which enables them to challenge existing norms and question established practices.

Clarke goes on to say that although this can create the opportunity for innovation and radical change, challenging the status quo is also akin to challenging managerial judgement and authority. As Benjamin and Mabey (1993) maintain, though the questioning of the status quo is the essence of bottom-up change, it also leads to a form of role reversal whereby, rather than managers pressuring staff to change, the reverse occurs. Therefore, a new, open management style can result in staff putting pressure on managers to address fundamental questions about the purpose and direction of the organisation which previously they might have preferred to avoid. Consequently, as Easterby-Smith *et al* (2000) and Tsang (1997) suggest, organisational learning is neither an easy nor an uncontentious option for organisations. There is also a great diversity of opinion as to what it is and how it can be promoted, which makes organisational learning a more difficult concept to apply than many of its supporters acknowledge (Burnes *et al*, 2003; Wang and Ahmed, 2003).

Managerial behaviour

Chapter 1 showed that the traditional view of managers is that they should direct and control staff, resources and information. It sees managers as being the only ones with the expertise, knowledge and legitimate authority to decide how and when change should take place. The Emergent approach to change, like the Culture–Excellence approach to managing organisations, requires a radical change in the role of managers (Dawson, 2003; Kanter, 2008a; Kotter and Cohen, 2002; Peters, 2006; Weick, 2000). Instead of directing change from the top, managers are expected to operate as facilitators and coaches who, through their ability to span hierarchical, functional and organisational boundaries, can bring together and empower teams and groups to identify the need for, and achieve, change (Bennis, 2000; Carnall, 2003; Mabey and Mayon-White, 1993; Weick, 2000). Crucial to this, according to Kotter (1996), is for managers to develop leadership skills. Drawing on the work of Burns (1978 – *see* Chapter 13), Kotter (1996: 25) argued:

> Management is a set of processes that can keep a complicated system of people and technology running smoothly. The most important aspects of management include planning, budgeting, organizing, staffing, controlling, and problem solving. Leadership is a set of processes that creates organizations in the first place or adapts them to significantly changing circumstances. Leadership defines what the future should look like, aligns people with that vision, and inspires them to make it happen despite the obstacles.

Therefore, in order to be effective, managers must become leaders. They require knowledge of and expertise in strategy formulation, human resource management, marketing and sales, negotiation and conflict resolution, and much more (Beer and Nohria, 2000; Clarke, 1994; Hayes, 2002). But the key to success, the decisive factor in creating a focused agenda for organisational change is, according to many observers, managers' own behaviour (Graetz *et al*, 2002; Kanter, 1989; Kotter, 1999; Pfeffer, 1996). If managers are to gain the commitment of others to change, they must first be prepared to challenge their own assumptions, attitudes and mindsets so that they develop an understanding of the emotional and intellectual processes involved (Buchanan and Boddy, 1992; Burns, 1978; Harrison, R, 2002; Sosik and Megerian, 1999).

For supporters of the Emergent approach, the essence of change is the move from the familiar to the unknown, from the certain to the uncertain (Jones *et al*, 2000). In this situation, it is essential for managers to be able to tolerate risk and cope with paradox and ambiguity (Stacey *et al*, 2002; Weick, 2000). Pugh (1993) takes the view that, in a dynamic environment, open and active communication with those participating in the change process is the key to coping with such uncertainty. This underlines the view expressed by many that top-down, unilaterally imposed change doesn't work and that bottom-up change, based on devolved responsibility and genuine empowerment, is the way forward (Brown and Eisenhardt, 1997; Clarke, 1999; Falconer, 2002; Harung *et al*, 1999; Styhre, 2002). This in turn requires managers to facilitate open, organisation-wide communication via groups, individuals, and formal and informal channels (Hayes, 2002; Kanter *et al*, 1992; Senior, 2002).

An organisation's ability to gather, disseminate, analyse and discuss information is crucial for successful change, from the perspective of the Emergent approach. The reason for this, according to Wilson (1992) is that to effect change successfully, organisations need, consciously and proactively, to move forward incrementally. Large-scale change and more formal and integrated approaches to change (such as Total Quality Management) can quickly lose their sense of purpose and relevance for organisations operating in dynamic and uncertain environments (Hodge and Coronado, 2007). However, if organisations move towards their strategic vision by means of Emergent, continuous, localised and relatively small-scale change efforts, managers must ensure that those concerned, which could potentially be the entire workforce, have access to and are able to act on all the available information. Also, by encouraging a collective pooling of knowledge and information in this way, a better understanding of the pressures and possibilities for change can be achieved, which should enable managers to improve the quality of strategic decisions (Boddy and Buchanan, 1992; Quinn, 1993).

Others take a slightly different view. They reject both small-scale change and large-scale radical-transformational change in favour of 'a third kind' which lies between these two, and which is continuous and based on self-organisation at the team or group level (Brodbeck, 2002; Brown and Eisenhardt, 1997). To a certain extent, part of this difference is about terminology: how big is incremental change? Perhaps the two issues to concentrate on are as follows. First, there is general agreement among proponents of Emergent change that large-scale, top-down change programmes, while sometimes being necessary, rarely succeed (Beer and Nohria, 2000). Secondly, Emergent change, whether incremental or 'a third kind', is not concerned with isolated change events (whether big or small) but sees change as a pattern of interwoven and continuous events which play out over the long term (Pettigrew and Whipp, 1991). This does not mean that there is not a crucial role for managers in identifying issues to be addressed or in developing an organisational vision which can guide Emergent change (Bennis, 2000; Dunphy, 2000). It does mean, however, that successful change is seen as coming from bottom-up initiatives which emerge from local responses to issues, threats or opportunities in the environment (Bennis, 2000; Pettigrew, 2000). It follows that the size of such responses will vary but, because they are local responses, they can never be large-scale.

Whatever the scale of the change, however, the potential for resistance will always be present. As discussed in Chapter 8, resistance to change can arise from a number of sources, including incommensurate objectives and values, and for a number of reasons ranging from different perspectives on what is best for the organisation to sectional or individual self-interest (Dent and Goldberg, 1999; Hayes, 2002; Huczynski and Buchanan, 2001). To cope effectively with resistance, managers will need to acquire and develop a range of skills that enables them to ready organisations for change and deal with resistance if and when it arises (Boddy and Buchanan, 1992; Ford et al, 2008; Kotter, 1996). Promoting openness, reducing uncertainty, encouraging experimentation and seeing the positive side of resistance can be powerful mechanisms for overcoming resistance and promoting change (Ford and Ford, 2010; Mabey and Mayon-White, 1993). In this respect, Coghlan (1993b) and McCalman and Paton (1992) advocated the use of OD tools and techniques (such as transactional analysis, teamwork, group problem-solving, role-playing, etc.), which have long been used in Planned change programmes. However, there is an enormous and potentially confusing array of these; Mayon-White (1993) and Buchanan and Boddy (1992) argue that managers have a crucial role to play in terms of identifying and applying the appropriate ones. The main objective in deploying such tools and techniques is to encourage shared learning through teamwork and cooperation. It is this that provides the framework and support for the development of creative and innovative solutions and encourages a sense of involvement, commitment and ownership of the change process (Carnall, 2003; Kanter et al, 1997; McCalman and Paton, 1992; Peters, 1997a).

Nevertheless, it would be naïve to assume that everyone will want to work, or be able to function effectively, in such situations. The cognitive and behavioural changes necessary for organisational survival may be too large for many people, especially managers (Ghoshal and Bartlett, 2000). An important managerial task will, therefore, be to identify sources of inertia, assess the skill mix within their organisation and, most of all, consider whether their own managerial attitudes and styles are appropriate. It needs also to be recognised that there are different types of change, and that these often require different approaches (Stace

and Dunphy, 2001). Proponents of Emergent change tend to see the world from one perspective but, as will be discussed in Chapter 11, there are other ways of viewing change and
other ways of bringing it about (Beer and Nohria, 2000).

Power and politics

As mentioned earlier in this chapter:

> Change and politics are inexorably linked . . . This means that at the top, middle, and lower
> reaches of the organization, campaigning, lobbying, coalition building, and the sharing of
> information, rewards, and recognition are all fateful for change through all the various
> unpredictable stages and loops of the innovation journey. (Pettigrew, 2000: 250)

The importance of power and politics in organisational life, especially change situations,
was explored in Chapter 5. Though the advocates of Emergent change tend to view power
and politics from differing perspectives, they recognise their importance and that they
have to be managed if change is to be effective. Dawson (1994: 176), for example,
concluded that:

> The central argument is that it is important to try and gain the support of senior management,
> local management, supervisors, trade unions and workplace employees.

According to Weick (2000: 236) gaining support requires 'considerable linguistic skills
to capture and label the flow of events [and] resequence and relabel that sequence'. The
postmodernists also argue that managers manipulate and use language and symbols to
create a new organisational reality (Hatch, 1997). Pettigrew *et al* (1992: 293) take a similar
view, stating that:

> The significance of political language at the front end of change processes needs emphasizing.
> Closures can be labelled as redevelopments. Problems can be re-coded into opportunities
> with . . . broad positive visions being articulated to build early coalitions.

Kanter *et al* (1992: 508) argue that the first step to implementing change is coalition-
building: 'involve those whose involvement really matters . . . Specifically, seek support
from two general groups: (1) power sources and (2) stakeholders.' In a similar vein, Nadler
(1993) advocates the need to shape the political dynamics of change so that power centres
develop that support the change rather than block it. Senior (2002), drawing on the work of
Nadler (1988), proposes four steps that organisations need to take to manage the political
dynamics of change (*see* Ideas and perspectives 10.3).

Important though power and politics are in the change process, Hendry (1996) and Pugh
(1993) remind us that they are not the be-all and end-all of change and that it is important

IDEAS AND PERSPECTIVES 10.3

Managing the political dynamics of change

Step 1 Ensure or develop the support of key power groups.

Step 2 Use leader behaviour to generate support for the proposed change.

Step 3 Use symbols and language to encourage and show support for the change.

Step 4 Build in stability by using power to ensure that some things remain the same.

Source: Senior (2002).

Table 9.1 Political skills and the management of change

Resources	Process	Form
Formal authority	Negotiation	Politics of:
Control of resources	Influencing	Budgets
Control of information	Mobilising support	Careers
Control of agenda	Mobilising bias	Succession
Control of access symbols	Use of emotion	Information
	Ceremony and rituals	Organisational structures
	Professional 'mystery'	Appraisal

Source: (Carnall, 2003: 133).

not to focus on these to the exclusion of other factors. Nevertheless, the focus placed on the political dynamics of change does serve to highlight the need for those who manage change to be aware of and control this dimension of the change process. To this end, Carnall (2003: 133) offers a model of the political skills that can be utilised to manage change, which identifies three basic types of political skill: the ability to utilise resources, such as formal authority and information; the aptitude to understand and manage political processes, such as negotiation and mobilising support; and the capacity to recognise and engage in the various forms of political activity, such as battles over budgets and organisational structures (*see* Table 9.1). Carnall's argument is not that one individual will possess all these skills, but that those managing change will have to gain the support of those who do.

As can be seen, therefore, there are a number of core issues on which the advocates of Emergent change share similar views. Having identified the beliefs which distinguish them as a group, it is equally important to understand what advice they offer for putting their approach into practice.

The five features of organisations discussed above – structure, culture, learning, managerial behaviour, and power and politics – help explain why the advocates of the Emergent approach see change as an enormously complex process. However, in the main, the advocates do not describe how change should be managed in organisations. The next section will address this issue.

Recipes for Emergent change

Pettigrew and Whipp (1993: 6) maintain that there are no universal rules with regard to leading change; rather it involves 'linking action by people at all levels of the business'. However, this has not prevented most of the advocates of Emergent change from suggesting sequences of actions which organisations should follow. Pettigrew and Whipp (1993), for example, propose a model for successfully managing strategic and operational change that involves five interrelated factors (*see* Ideas and perspectives 10.4).

For his part, not to be outdone by Pettigrew and Whipp's five factors, Dawson (1994: 179) puts forward fifteen 'major practical guidelines which can be drawn from a processual analysis of managing organizational transitions'. These guidelines range from the need to maintain an overview of the dynamics and long-term process of change, to the need to take a total organisational approach to managing transitions. On the way, he makes the case for understanding and communicating the context and objectives of change, and ensuring managerial and employee commitment. Wilson (1992: 122) also draws attention to the complex and long-term nature of change, writing that:

IDEAS AND PERSPECTIVES 10.4

Pettigrew and Whipp's five central factors for managing change

- **Environmental assessment** – organisations, at all levels, need to develop the ability to collect and utilise information about their external and internal environments.

- **Leading change** – this requires the creation of a positive climate for change, the identification of future directions and the linking together of action by people at all levels in the organisation.

- **Linking strategic and operational change** – this is a two-way process of ensuring that intentional strategic decisions lead to operational changes and that emergent operational changes influence strategic decisions.

- **Human resources as assets and liabilities** – just as the pool of knowledge, skills and attitudes possessed by an organisation is crucial to its success, it can also be a threat to the organisation's success if the combination is inappropriate or poorly managed.

- **Coherence of purpose** – this concerns the need to ensure that the decisions and actions that flow from the above four factors complement and reinforce each other.

Source: Pettigrew and Whipp (1993).

This book has deliberately taken a particular stance towards the question of organizational change. The argument has largely been against skill-based approaches, ready-made models of good organizational practice (for example, the 'excellence' models) and reliance upon analysing change as primarily the outcome-oriented pursuit of great and charismatic individuals. The arguments have, rather, favoured the potency of organizational structures, of economic determinism, of institutionalization within which the manager must operate. To operate successfully (and in the long term) he or she must understand and learn from the wider context or organization. This is not to say that individual skills are unimportant, only that they cannot be considered in isolation from the wider factors of strategic change.

Unfortunately, the problem with much of the advice for managing change offered by advocates of the Emergent approach, or at least those who come from the more processualist–analytical camp, such as Dawson and Pettigrew, is that it tends to be too general or cursory in nature and thus difficult to apply. It can sometimes also appear almost as an afterthought (Caldwell, 2006). However, those from the more prescriptive camp, as described below, do offer much substantial guidance to managers. Unlike the analytical camp, they are more concerned with telling organisations what they should do than in providing detailed analyses of what they do do. The two leading exponents of change in this respect are Rosabeth Moss Kanter and John P Kotter. Kanter's work has already been discussed extensively in Chapter 3, but to recap briefly, as shown in Ideas and perspectives 10.5, she proposes 'Ten Commandments for Executing Change' (Kanter *et al*, 1992).

Looking at approaches to change, Kanter *et al* (1992) distinguished between 'Bold Strokes' and 'Long Marches'. The former relate to major strategic decisions or economic initiatives, usually of a structural or technological nature. These, they argue, can have a clear and rapid impact on an organisation, but they rarely lead to any long-term change in habits or culture. The Long March approach, on the other hand, favours a host of relatively small-scale and operationally focused initiatives, each of which can be quickly implemented

---

IDEAS AND PERSPECTIVES 10.5

Ten commandments for executing change

1. Analyse the organisation and its need for change.
2. Create a shared vision and a common direction.
3. Separate from the past.
4. Create a sense of urgency.
5. Support a strong leader role.
6. Line up political sponsorship.
7. Craft an implementation plan.
8. Develop enabling structures.
9. Communicate, involve people and be honest.
10. Reinforce and institutionalise change.

Source: Kanter *et al* (1992: 382–3).

---

but whose full benefits are achieved in the long term rather than the short term. However, the Long March approach can, over time, lead to a change of culture. Bold Strokes are initiatives taken by a few senior managers, sometimes only one; they do not rely on the support of the rest of the organisation for their success. In contrast, the Long March approach requires widespread commitment throughout an organisation. Without the involvement and commitment of the majority of the workforce, Kanter *et al* argue, such initiatives cannot succeed. They do maintain that Bold Strokes and Long Marches can be complementary, rather than alternative, approaches to change; though in practice companies appear to favour one or the other. Companies may need both if they are to succeed in transforming themselves. Therefore, though Kanter appears to prefer the Emergent approach of the Long March, she does see situations where Bold Strokes may be a necessary precursor, or adjunct, to the Long March.

Like Kanter, Kotter is a professor at the Harvard Business School and runs his own successful consultancy – Kotter Associates. He is the author of a wide range of books and articles on management and change, including his highly influential 1995 *Harvard Business Review* article, 'Leading change: why transformation efforts fail'. This article immediately jumped to first place among the thousands of reprints sold by the *Review*, which, considering the quality of the articles in its reprint base, is a considerable achievement. Spurred on by the reception of his views on change, Kotter went on to write his 1996 book, *Leading Change*. This elaborates and expands on the ideas in his *Harvard Business Review* article. The book begins by identifying eight key errors that Kotter believes cause transformation efforts to fail (*see* Ideas and perspectives 10.6).

Kotter (1996: 16) maintains that the consequences of these errors are:

- New strategies aren't implemented well.
- Acquisitions don't achieve expected synergies.
- Reengineering takes too long and costs too much.
- Downsizing doesn't get costs under control.
- Quality programmes don't deliver hoped-for results.

> ## IDEAS AND PERSPECTIVES 10.6
>
> ### Why change initiatives fail
>
> **Error 1** Allowing too much complacency.
>
> **Error 2** Failing to create a sufficiently powerful guiding coalition.
>
> **Error 3** Underestimating the power of vision.
>
> **Error 4** Undercommunicating the vision by a factor of 10 (or 100 or even 1000).
>
> **Error 5** Permitting obstacles to block the new vision.
>
> **Error 6** Failing to create short-term wins.
>
> **Error 7** Declaring victory too soon.
>
> **Error 8** Neglecting to anchor changes firmly in the corporate culture.
>
> *Source*: Kotter (1996).

In order to eliminate these errors and their consequences, the book then proceeds to present Kotter's Eight-Stage Process for successful organisational transformation (*see* Ideas and perspectives 10.7).

Kotter (1996: 23) stresses that his eight stages are a process and not a checklist, and that 'Successful change of any magnitude goes through all eight stages . . . skipping even a single step or getting too far ahead without a solid base almost always creates problems.' He also points out that most major change efforts comprise a host of small and medium-sized change projects which, at any one point in time, can be at different points in the process. Kotter (1996: 24–5) cites the example of a telecommunications company where:

> The overall effort, designed to significantly increase the firm's competitive position, took six years. By the third year, the transformation was centered in steps 5, 6 and 7. One relatively

> ## IDEAS AND PERSPECTIVES 10.7
>
> ### Kotter's eight steps to successful change
>
> **Step 1** Establishing a sense of urgency.
>
> **Step 2** Creating a guiding coalition.
>
> **Step 3** Developing a vision and strategy.
>
> **Step 4** Communicating the change vision.
>
> **Step 5** Empowering broad-based action.
>
> **Step 6** Generating short-term wins.
>
> **Step 7** Consolidating gains and producing more change.
>
> **Step 8** Anchoring new approaches in the culture.
>
> *Source*: Kotter (1996).

small reengineering project was nearing the end of stage 8. A restructuring of corporate staff groups was just beginning with most of the effort in steps 1 and 2. A quality program was moving along, but behind schedule, while a few small initiatives hadn't even been launched yet. Early results were visible at six to twelve months, but the biggest payoff didn't come until near the end of the overall effort.

As can be seen, there is a reassuring similarity between Kanter *et al*'s Ten Commandments and Kotter's Eight-Stage Process. Taken together, they provide general guidance for implementing change. However, this does not mean that the Emergent approach is without serious criticism.

Emergent change: summary and criticisms

The proponents of Emergent change are a somewhat broad group who seem to be united more by their scepticism regarding Planned change than by a well-focused and commonly agreed alternative. Indeed, some might argue that any label which spans the prescriptive, consultant-orientated views of Kotter and Kanter and the analytical–processual views of Pettigrew and Dawson is too broad; certainly this is Dawson's (2003) view. Nevertheless, this would ignore two crucial points. First, Planned change is an equally broad church. It ranges from those who see it as applicable only to behavioural change in small groups to those who see it as an approach for transforming entire organisations (Armenakis and Bedeian, 1999; Burnes, 2004c; Burnes and Cooke, 2012b; Greiner and Cummings, 2004; Worley and Feyerhern, 2003). Second, any approach to change which seeks to be applicable beyond the classroom or have validity wider than the management consultancy needs to incorporate both the prescriptive practitioner and the analytical academic. The issue is not how broad the church is but whether what unites them is greater than what divides them. In the former respect, there does seem to be some agreement regarding the main tenets of Emergent change, which are as follows:

- Organisational change is not a linear process or a one-off isolated event but is a continuous, open-ended, cumulative and unpredictable process of experimentation and adaptation aimed at matching an organisation's resources and capabilities to the opportunities, constraints and demands of a dynamic and uncertain environment.

- This is best achieved through an interwoven pattern of (mainly) small- to medium-scale continuous changes which, over time, can lead to a major re-configuration and transformation of an organisation.

- Change is a multi-level, cross-organisation process that unfolds in an iterative and messy fashion over a period of years and comprises a series of interlocking projects.

- Change is not an analytical–rational process. Instead, key change decisions evolve over time and are the outcome of political and cultural processes in organisations.

- The role of managers is not to plan or implement change *per se*, but to shape the long-term process of change by creating or fostering an organisational structure and climate which encourages and sustains experimentation, learning and risk-taking, and to develop a workforce that has the freedom and motivation to take responsibility for identifying the need for change and implementing it.

● Though managers are expected to become facilitators rather than doers, they also have the prime responsibility for developing a collective vision or common purpose that gives direction to their organisation, and within which the appropriateness of any proposed change can be judged.

● The key organisational activities that allow these elements to operate successfully are:

  ● information-gathering – about the external environment and internal objectives and capabilities;

  ● communication – the transmission, analysis and discussion of information;

  ● learning – the ability individually and collectively to develop new skills, identify appropriate responses and draw knowledge from their own and others' past and present actions.

Though not always stated openly, the case for the Emergent approach to change is based on the assumption that the environment in which organisations operate is changing rapidly, radically and unpredictably, and will continue to do so. Just as advocates of Planned change assume that stability, at least in terms of behaviour, is the *natural* or *preferred* state for organisations, so proponents of Emergent change assume the *natural* or *preferred* state for organisations is turbulence and unpredictability (Brown and Eisenhardt, 1997; Orlikowski, 1996). Consequently, if the external world is changing in a rapid, uncertain and continuous way, organisations need to change in a continuous, appropriate and timely manner if they are to remain competitive. It is because they view change as a continuous and open-ended process that proponents of Emergent change see the Planned approach to change as inappropriate. To be successful, changes need to emerge locally and (relatively) incrementally in order to counter environmental threats and take advantage of opportunities.

Presented in this manner, there is an apparent coherence and validity to the Emergent approach. However, it is a fragile coherence and a challengeable validity. As far as coherence is concerned, some proponents of Emergent change, especially Pettigrew (1997) and Dawson (2003), clearly approach it from the processual perspective on organisations. However, it is not clear that Buchanan and Boddy (1992) and Wilson (1992) would fully subscribe to this view. In the case of Carnall (2003), Clarke (1994), Kanter *et al* (1992) and Kotter (1996), it is clear that they do not take a processual perspective. They do not doubt the importance of power and politics in the change process, but for them the issue is one of legitimacy and pragmatism. Managers and change agents have the legitimate right to introduce changes, but to do so they must use political skills in a pragmatic way to build support and overcome or avoid resistance. For the processualists, like the postmodernists, change is about dominant coalitions, and smaller groupings, trying to impose their will on all or part of an organisation in order to maintain or improve their position. Partly, this is explained by the fact that some of these writers (especially Dawson, 2003; Pettigrew, 1997; Wilson, 1992) are attempting to understand and analyse change from a critical perspective, while others (notably Kanter *et al*, 1992; Kotter, 1996) are more concerned with prescribing recipes and checklists for successful change. In addition to these apparent tensions, as Caldwell (2006) notes, there are some open disagreements among advocates of the Emergent approach. For example, Pettigrew's processual stance has been criticised by both the practitioner wing and processual wing for its lack of practicality (Buchanan and Boddy, 1992; Dawson, 2003). Therefore, though the advocates of Emergent change have a number of common bonds, their differing objectives and perspectives do cast doubt on the coherence of their approach.

In terms of the validity or general applicability of the Emergent approach to change, this depends to a large extent on whether or not one subscribes to the twin assumptions that (a) environmental instability and unpredictability is the *natural* or *preferred* state for organisations and that (b) the best way for organisations to cope with this is through a continuous process of small-to-medium-sized changes which emerge from the bottom up and not the top down. As a 2008 IBM report found, and as the consequences from the 2008 financial crisis have demonstrated, there is much evidence that organisations face an increasingly hostile, rapidly changing and unpredictable environment (Elliott, 2013; IBM, 2008). However, as was discussed in Chapter 8, it is debatable whether the environment impacts on all organisations in the same way or whether they should respond with the same approach, a point that Pettigrew and Whipp (1991: 165) acknowledge when they state that: 'Leadership [of change] requires action appropriate to its context.'

If one considers the history of organisations over the past 100 years, there have been many disruptive economic, political and military events which have required rapid, major responses by organisations which could not be coped with or anticipated by the Emergent approach. Indeed, since the year 2000 there have been three major global shocks which have disrupted organisations in a significant fashion and which have required immediate and disruptive responses – the dotcom collapse, 9–11 and the 2008 credit crunch. Therefore, while one might accept that the *preferred* environmental state, at least for advocates of Emergent change, is one that is amenable to being dealt with by Emergent change, it is difficult to accept that this is necessarily the *natural* state of affairs, or at least not for all organisations. For some, Emergent change may be appropriate, for others, the Planned approach may be more appropriate, while in some organisations and in some situations, directive or coercive change may be used.

Obviously, the issues above raise questions over the universal applicability of the Emergent approach; even without reservations regarding its coherence and validity, however, there would still be serious criticisms of this approach. For example, many of its supporters seem to advocate the same approach to organisations as the Culture–Excellence school and are, therefore, open to the same criticisms (*see* Chapter 3). Given this link to Culture–Excellence, not surprisingly, a great deal of emphasis is placed on the need for appropriate organisational cultures. Yet, as the writers on Emergent change seem to sway between advocating the need for culture change (Kanter *et al*, 1992) and advocating the need to work with existing cultures (Pettigrew, 1997), it is not clear what they perceive the role of culture to be. In any case, as was noted in Chapter 5, the whole issue of the role and the manipulability of organisational culture is a veritable minefield. Indeed, as also mentioned in Chapter 5, even Wilson (1992), who supports the Emergent perspective, was sceptical about the case for culture change.

Similar points can be made regarding the 'learning organisation' approach. As Whittington (1993: 130) comments:

> The danger of the purely 'learning' approach to change, therefore, is that . . . managers [and others] may actually recognize the need for change, yet still refuse to 'learn' because they understand perfectly well the implications for their power and status. Resistance to change may not be 'stupid' . . . but based on a very shrewd appreciation of the personal consequences.

A variant of this criticism relates to the impact of success on managerial learning. Miller (1993: 119) observes that, while managers generally start out by attempting to learn all they can about their organisation's environment, over time, as they gain experience, they 'form quite definite opinions of what works and why' and as a consequence tend to limit their search for information and knowledge. So experience, especially where it is based on success, may actually be a barrier to learning, in that it shapes the cognitive structures by which managers, and everyone else, see and interpret the world. Nystrom and Starbuck (1984: 55) observe that:

> What people see, predict, understand, depends on their cognitive structures . . . [which] manifest themselves in perceptual frameworks, expectations, world views, plans, goals . . . myths, rituals, symbols . . . and jargon.

This brings us neatly to the topic of the role of managers. Though this will be discussed extensively in Chapter 13, for now it should be noted that managers are the people who appear to have to make the greatest change in their behaviour. As the above quotations indicate, however, they may neither welcome nor accept such a change, especially where it requires them to challenge and change their own beliefs, and where it runs counter to their experience of 'what works and why'. Also, if the possibility exists (as mentioned above) to manipulate environmental variables and constraints rather than having to change their behaviour, managers may perceive this as a more attractive or viable option.

Though the above reservations regarding the validity of the Emergent approach are fairly significant, there are five further criticisms that are perhaps more serious. The first relates to the difference between that approach and the Planned approach. The Planned approach is attacked because of its reliance on Lewin's Three-Step model of unfreezing, moving and refreezing. It is argued that in a turbulent environment, organisations are in a constant state of change and that, therefore, to speak of unfreezing and refreezing is nonsense (Kanter *et al*, 1992). However, if one examines the process of change advocated by, for example, Dawson (1994), Kotter (1996) and Pettigrew *et al* (1992), though they argue to the contrary, they do speak of change as a 'transition' process with a beginning, middle and end. Indeed, the last of Kanter *et al's* Ten Commandments for Executing Change (*see* Ideas and Perspectives 10.5) is to 'Reinforce and institutionalise change', which sounds very much like the 'refreezing' stage of Lewin's Three-Step model. This is rather ironic given that it appears in the same book in which they strongly criticise Lewin's model claiming that: '. . . *organizations are never frozen, much less refrozen*' (Kanter *et al*, 1992: 10). In addition, Dawson (2011) has advocated the use of action research techniques, one of the core elements of Planned change, to bring about processual change. All this, of course, provides support for Hendry's (1996: 624) comment which was quoted in Chapter 9:

> Scratch any account of creating and managing change and the idea that change is a three-stage process which necessarily begins with a process of unfreezing will not be far below the surface.

There are others who strongly support Hendry's view that the Three-Step model has greater validity and wider usage than its critics acknowledge (Burnes, 2004b, 2004c; Elrod and Tippett, 2002).

The second criticism of the Emergent approach concerns the emphasis placed on the power and politics aspects of change. Advocates this approach have undoubtedly provided a valuable contribution to our understanding of change by highlighting the neglect of these important issues in the past. However, in doing so, as Hendry (1996: 621) argues, 'the management of change has become . . . overfocused on the political aspects of change'. Similarly, Collins (1998: 100), voicing concerns of his own and of other researchers, argues:

> In reacting to the problems and critiques of [the Planned approach], managers and practitioners have swung from a dependence on under-socialized models and explanations of change and instead have become committed to the arguments of, what might be called, over-socialized [political] models of change.

This concurs with those who take a realist perspective on organisations. They argue that while the social world, including organisations, is a product of human action, it is not necessarily a product of conscious human design, but exists independently of human beings and, therefore, an overreliance on a political perspective on organisations can be misleading (Connelly, 2000; Easton, 2000).

The third criticism is that, as Burnes and By (2012: 249) observe:

> Though not explicitly stated, the practice of Emergent change, based as it is on the use of power and manipulation, revealed that its underlying values undermined rather than supported ethical outcomes.

In addition, as Burnes (2009b) argues, its advocates do not always appear to understand or even acknowledge the ethical issues involved in the use of power and politics. It is one thing to acknowledge their importance; it is quite another to advocate, either by omission or commission, their use either in an unethical fashion or to achieve unethical ends.

Fourthly, though the Emergent approach undoubtedly raises key issues, and offers valuable insights and guidance, it does not appear to be as universally applicable as its advocates imply. As Dawson (2003) notes, it is clear that there are many situations where managers find it more appropriate to push change through in a rapid and confrontational manner (*see also* Edwardes, 1983; Franklin, 1997; Grinyer *et al*, 1988; Stace and Dunphy, 2001). In Chapter 8, we identified three different perspectives on change: the individual, group and system perspectives, and three categories of change: incremental, punctuated equilibrium and continuous transformation. The Emergent approach is specifically founded on the assumption that organisations operate in a dynamic environment where they have to transform themselves continuously in order to survive. The focus of Emergent change is continuous, synergistic, interconnected change which, though small- or medium-sized in nature, affects the organisation and its major sub-systems. Consequently, it is by its own definition not applicable to organisations operating in environments which require isolated incremental change at the individual and/or group levels, or punctuated equilibrium change initiatives at the organisation level.

It is also the case that advocates of the Emergent approach seem unclear regarding the degree to which change should be viewed as cooperative and voluntary. On the one hand, great play is made of change being driven from the bottom up by motivated and empowered employees. On the other hand, change is seen as a battle for power, and change agents are expected to have the political skills to manipulate those involved.

The fifth criticism of Emergent change is that it is strong on analysis and weak on practice (Buchanan and Boddy, 1992; Collins, 1998; Morsing, 1997). Certainly, if one looks at the foregoing examination of Emergent change, it does appear to be very global and lacking in the many specific and practical tools and techniques for its application which can be found in most OD textbooks (*see*, for example, Cummings and Worley, 2001 and French and Bell, 1999). This is a point acknowledged by Dawson (2011: 128), one of the major figures in the development of the processual approach, who states that the problem with such research is:

> on the one hand, the inability of this type of study to produce anything of 'practical' value (in the form of systematic predictive capabilities) and. on the other hand, the tendency for studies to produce guidelines that undermine their theoretical foundations through outlining rather banal lists of ingredients on how best to manage change.

In effect, to use the terminology of the rigour-relevance debate (Bartunek, 2007; Polzer *et al*, 2009), the Emergent approach is theoretically rigorous, but lacks practical relevance, and its attempts to address this weakness have tended both to be simplistic and undermine its theoretical strength. This is why some now see Emergent change as having failed in its attempts to supplant Planned change as the dominant approach to organisational change (Burnes, 2011b). In its place, a very different perspective on organisations and change has attracted much attention and interest among those who study and practice change, one which goes under the rubric of Emergence.

Emergence

As discussed in Chapter 4, a wide range of organisational theorists and practitioners have argued that organisations are complex, non-linear systems in which change emerges through a process of spontaneous self-organisation, which is underpinned by a set of simple order-generating rules (Arndt and Bigelow, 2000; Bechtold, 1997; Black, 2000; Fitzgerald, 2002a; MacIntosh and MacLean, 2001; Stacey, 2003). The concept of self-organisation, as well as its implications for organisations, has some similarities with the concept of Emergent change, especially in terms of empowerment and bottom-up change (Burnes, 2005). However, Emergence's origins in the natural sciences and its argument that successful organisations have appropriate underlying order-generating rules make it a very different animal.

Though both Emergence and Emergent change see change as a multi-level, cross-organisation process that unfolds in an iterative and messy fashion over a period of years, they differ significantly on the degree to which it can be intentionally influenced. For proponents of Emergence, the presence of underlying order-generating rules offers a means of intentionally influencing the process and outcome of change by identifying and modifying these rules (MacIntosh and MacLean, 2001). This is something that proponents of Emergent change would seriously challenge. Therefore, in its philosophy and practice, Emergence does offer a significantly different approach to change. Though this approach to organisations still parades under labels such as complexity and chaos, these are increasingly being subsumed under the overarching concept of Emergence.

The term Emergence, to describe one of the defining properties of complex physical and social systems, has been around for some 100 years (Goldstein, 1999). However, as Seel (2006) notes, it is a somewhat difficult concept to define. In essence, Emergence is the process by which patterns of behaviour or global-level structures arise from the interaction of local-level processes and agents interacting according to their own local order-generating rules. Such behaviours and structures do not arise from intention or planning, and cannot even be predicted from the local rules of behaviour (Mihata 1997; Stacey, 1996). One of the reasons why it is such a difficult concept to define is because it has its roots in a number of scientific disciplines, such as meteorology, biology, physics, chemistry and mathematics, and uses a plethora of strange and exotic terms, such as autocatalytic change, fitness landscapes, non-linearity, bifurcation, Feigenbaum constants, Mandelbrot sets, strange attractors and many, many more (Burnes, 2005). Another reason is that, among organisational scholars, the science of complexity has also been combined with postmodernist and other philosophies, which makes it an even more difficult concept to grasp (Boje and Wakefield, 2011; Goldstein, 1999; Luhman and Boje, 2001).

Emergence theorists argue that the best-run companies survive because they operate at the edge of chaos by relentlessly pursuing a path of continuous innovation brought about by a process that resembles self-organisation in nature (Brown and Eisenhardt, 1997; Frederick, 1998; Jenner, 1998). However, Beeson and Davis (2000) make the point that while it might be fruitful to see organisations as non-linear systems, to do so will require a fundamental shift in the role of management. Like many others (e.g. Boje, 2000; Stacey *et al*, 2002; Sullivan, 1999; Tetenbaum, 1998; Wheatley, 1992b), they point out that self-organising principles explicitly reject cause-and-effect, top-down, command-and-control styles of management. Brodbeck (2002) suggests that the belief by managers that order and control are essential to achieve their objectives should be rejected. For Tetenbaum (1998), the move to self-organisation will require managers to destabilise their organisations and develop the skill of managing order and disorder at the same time. Managers will need to encourage experimentation, divergent views, even allow rule-breaking, and recognise that 'people need the freedom to own their own power, think innovatively, and operate in new patterns' (Bechtold, 1997: 198). Beeson and Davis (2000) echo this point and argue that, in such situations, change becomes an everyday event undertaken by all in the organisation.

The implication of this for Bechtold (1997) is that organisations seeking to adopt a Emergence approach will need to have a balanced distribution of power, strong customer focus and a strategy of continuous learning. A further strand in this argument is provided by Kiel (1994), who claims that because small actions can have large and unpredictable consequences, individual human activity assumes great importance. Similarly, Jenner (1998) claims that for self-organisation to work, authority must be delegated to those who have access to the broadest channels of information that relate to the issue or problem concerned.

As can be seen, Emergence claims to offer a rigorous, theoretical approach to understanding change in organisational life. However, in its current state of development, it has much less to offer on the practical side of the rigour-relevance divide – even less than the Emergent approach. Nevertheless, its origins in the natural sciences do allow it to avoid some of the ethical pitfalls awaiting those proponents of Emergent change who advocate unethical approaches to change through the misuse of power and politics (Burnes and By, 2012). Another advantage owing to its origins is that, not having arisen in opposition to Planned change, it is able to draw on Lewinian OD change tools and techniques to manage change under conditions of Emergence. For example, Boje and Rosile (2010) draw on Lewin's field theory, MacIntosh and MacLean (2001) advocate the use of the Three-Step approach to identify and change order-generating rules, and Seel (2006) suggests that newer variants of OD, such as Appreciative Inquiry, can be used to influence the general direction of Emergence in organisations. Also, Goldstein (1999: 52) points out that the concept of Gestalt, which is fundamental to Lewin's formulation of Field Theory, strongly resembles a description of Emergence, in its claim that '. . . perception takes place through recognizing whole patterns' and that 'the whole is greater than the sum of the parts'. However, he goes on to argue that Gestalt is a static concept while Emergence is a dynamic one. Yet this ignores the fact that in formulating Field Theory, Lewin showed that Gestalt could be used as a dynamic approach to understanding and managing change (Burnes and Cooke, 2012a). Finally, it may be noted that there are a number of Lewin/OD supporters among proponents of the complexity approach to change (Back, 1992; Olson and Eoyang, 2001; Tschacher and Brunner, 1995; Worley and Feyerherm, 2003). So one can agree with Holman (2010) that there are interesting and perhaps mutually beneficial similarities between Emergence and OD.

In terms of its influence on the study of organisations, Goldstein (1999) maintains that the self-organising and participative nature of Emergence offers the opportunity to promote the sort of informal structures, leadership and networks that are seen as more suited to the nature of the modern world than what he considers to be the outmoded and rigid command and control systems that have characterised organisational life over the last hundred years. Its influence is also demonstrated by the fact that it has generated a number of dedicated research centres, such as the Complexity and Management Centre at the University of Hertfordshire, consultancy organisations, such as New Paradigm Organisation Consulting, and even its own journal – *Emergence: Complexity & Organization (E:CO)*. Therefore, despite the fact that as a concept it is still difficult to understand, and in many ways vague, there is strong evidence that Emergence may be supplanting Emergent change as the main alternative to Planned change and OD. However, the mutual interest between supporters of Emergence and OD is also offering new insights into and support for the Lewinian stance on organisational change. This is one of the reasons why, along with the failure of the Emergent approach to provide a practical alternative, there has been a resurgence of interest in OD over the last decade or so.

The renaissance of OD

For OD, the 1980s and 1990s were difficult times; the OD community itself became embroiled in a turmoil of soul-searching, debate, and dispute over the nature and future of OD and its Lewinian heritage (Bennis, 2000; Burke, 1997; Farias and Johnson, 2000; Hornstein, 2001; Marshak, 1993; Worley and Feyerherm, 2003). Many commentators were asking if OD had lost its sense of direction or even still existed (Greiner and Cummings, 2004; Wirtenberg *et al*, 2004), and many managers considered it 'an out-of-date fad' (Porras and Bradford, 2004: 401).

Yet, despite the torrent of criticism and self-doubt, the 1990s saw two major developments which led to renewed support for Lewin and OD. First, a new generation of scholars started to take a critical and surprisingly supportive interest in the work of Kurt Lewin. In 1992 the *Journal of Social Issues* (48, 2) published a special issue to mark (belatedly) the centenary of Lewin's birth in 1890. This brought Lewin's work to a new generation and argued that it was still highly relevant to the needs of organisations and society at large, claiming that '. . . psychology as a field has moved much closer to Lewin's worldview than it was during his lifetime' (Bargal *et al*, 1992: 4). Other writers have also made claims for the continuing relevance of Lewin's work (Boje *et al*, 2011; Burnes, 2004b, 2007, 2009b, 2011a, 2011b, 2011c; Burnes and By, 2011; Burnes and Cooke, 2012a, 2012b; Coghlan and Jacobs, 2005). Burnes (2004c), in a reappraisal of planned change, also observed that many of Lewin's critics appear to have misread, or perhaps even not read, his work, which has generated a simplistic and misleading picture of Lewin's contribution to the field. Therefore, while many in the OD community were busy questioning its purpose and values, other scholars, often from outside the community, were rehabilitating Lewin and OD.

The second development, or rather continuing development, was that OD did not stand still. OD practices were increasingly being incorporated into HRM and HRD, creating strong overlaps between the three areas (Grieves and Redman, 1999; Ruona and Gibson, 2004), and the internationalisation of OD continued apace (Cummings and Worley, 2009; French and Bell, 1999; Mirvis, 2006; Piotrowski and Armstrong, 2005; Wirtenberg *et al*, 2004 and 2007). Also, long-standing OD bodies became increasingly international in their membership and outlook, such as the OD Network, the OD Institute, the International Organization Development Association and the NTL Institute; and newer bodies have been created, including the Asia OD Network. Some, though, have questioned whether OD is still growing in its traditional markets (Alban, 2003). However, the issue here may be that while some organisations, especially the big consultancies, have shied away from the term OD, they have not necessarily shied away from its practice (*see*, for example, Human Synergistics International's 'Planned Culture Change' programme which appears to draw on core OD practices (Jones *et al*, 2006)). One can also see this rebadging with some scholar-practitioners who use labels such as 'Long March' (Kanter *et al*, 1992) and 'Theory O' (Beer and Nohria, 2000) for approaches which have a distinctly OD flavour.

In addition, just as different varieties of OD emerged in the US and Europe to reflect differing social and economic conditions, so is the case now in the many other countries in which OD is active (Neumann *et al*, 2009; Paquin *et al*, 2007). Just as importantly, new approaches to OD, often incorporating newer perspectives on the nature of organisational life, such as social constructionism-postmodernism and complexity theories, continue to emerge and be well received (Bushe, 2011; Freedman, 1999; Oswick and Marshak, 2011). It may seem strange that OD, which in the 1980s and 1990s was under attack from social constructionist-postmodernist critics (Hatch, 1997), should itself attempt to incorporate these perspectives (Oswick, 2009). However, a number of leading OD scholars see social constructionism as a way of providing OD with a more coherent theoretical underpinning (Cummings and Worley, 2009; Marshak and Grant, 2008; Worley and Feyerherm, 2003). As Van Nistelrooij and Sminia (2010) maintain, dialogue is one of the primary methods whereby a plurality of perspectives is created, sustained and revealed, and dialogue is central to many OD techniques. A related area in which supporters of OD have shown an interest is that of organisational storytelling (Rhodes, 2011), which has links with both dialogic OD and social constructionism (Bryant and Wolfram Cox, 2011). Storytelling is seen as enabling the exploration of the dialogic nature of organisations in which the organisation is seen as a 'multiplicity of discourses' which reflect different perspectives on reality (Grant *et al*, 1998: 7). Furthermore, storytelling shares much common ground with sensemaking, which has also found favour among proponents of OD (Werkman, 2010). Similarly, one of the most prominent new approaches in OD is Appreciative Inquiry (AI), which is based on dialogic OD and social constructionist theory (Bushe, 2011; Cooperrider and Srivastva, 1987).

Therefore, as can be seen, while the Emergent approach has been losing ground and Emergence has yet to establish itself as a practical approach to change, OD has been experiencing something of a renaissance.

Conclusions

Organisations come in all shapes and sizes, provide a vast variety of products and services, and face an enormous array of challenges. Perhaps the only factor common to all organisations is change. Organisations never stand still, though the speed and magnitude of change does vary from organisation to organisation and over time. It is now generally accepted that the ability to manage change effectively is a crucial component of an organisation's ability to compete successfully. As Chapter 9 demonstrated, for many years, the Planned/OD approach was considered to be the best way of managing change. However, as was shown at the beginning of this chapter, from the early 1980s onwards, the Planned/OD approach has faced a torrent of criticisms as to its suitability in a world of rapid and unpredictable change. In particular, its detractors claim that the notion that organisations operate in stable environments and can move from one fixed state to another is, to quote Kanter *et al* (1992: 10), a 'quaintly linear and static conception . . . [and] . . . wildly inappropriate'.

In the light of these criticisms of the Planned approach, the chapter went on to examine the Emergent approach and its claim of being the best way to manage change. The Emergent approach sees organisational change as an ongoing process of adaptation to an unpredictable and ever-changing environment. For proponents of this view, change is a messy, unpredictable, open-ended and political affair. In such a situation, it is impossible for a few managers at the top of an organisation to identify and implement all the changes necessary to keep the organisation aligned with its environment. Consequently, successful change is a bottom-up, emergent, response to events. However, just as the Planned approach to change can be criticised as limited and flawed, similar criticisms can be made of the Emergent approach. In particular, it may be less a coherent approach to change and more a label for a collection of approaches critical of Planned change. In addition, questions have been raised about key elements of Emergent change such as its perception of culture, organisational learning and the role of managers. The Emergent approach has also been criticised for its over-emphasis on the political dimension of change and its view that all organisations operate in a dynamic and unpredictable environment. However, the most telling criticism is that after being around for over 25 years, it still has not provided a practical approach to managing change, which is why it appears to be falling out of favour. The complexity-based Emergence appears to be taking its place. Though it also suffers from the lack of a practical base, there is evidence that its supporters are addressing this shortcoming in a more effective manner than those of the Emergent approach. In addition, and perhaps surprisingly, the Planned/OD approach of Lewin has experienced something of a renaissance and once again looks to be the dominant approach to change.

Nevertheless, even a resurgent OD cannot claim to cover the full extent of the broad spectrum of change events organisations encounter. In order to address this, the next chapter will examine the change situations faced by organisations, and will construct *a framework for change* that identifies the range of change situations and a matching range of approaches to change.

TEST YOUR LEARNING

Short discussion topics

The purpose of these is to enable students to check and reflect on the topics in this chapter. The discussions should last for no more than 5–10 minutes. Depending on the length of the lecture, there could be one, two or three such discussions in a session. The following are five suggested topics which address issues raised in this chapter:

1. Describe the Processual approach to change.

2. What are the main attributes of the Emergent approach to change?

3. What is Emergence and how can it be applied to organisations?

4. What similarities are there between Kotter *et al's* Ten Commandments for Executing Change and Lewin's Three-Step model of change?

5. Why has OD experienced a resurgence of support?

Class debates

The purpose of class debates is to enable students to explore a topic in depth by setting up a 'for and against' debate. The class can be split into two and one half asked to research the 'for' case and the other 'against' case. Individuals can then be chosen at random to introduce their side of the debate. Alternatively, two individuals for each side can be told in advance that they will be introducing the debate. The length of such debates depends on the time available, the size of the class and their enthusiasm for the topic. However, less than 30 minutes is probably too short and more than 60 minutes probably too long. The following are three suggested topics which address issues raised in this chapter:

1. 'With the continuing and dynamic nature of change in today's business world, it no longer makes sense to implement a planned process of 'refreezing' changed behaviours' (Dawson, 1994: 3).

2. Emergence offers a different way of seeing organisations rather than a different way of changing them.

3. OD and social constructionism are an ideal match.

Essay questions

1. Discuss and evaluate the following statement: Emergent change does not offer a coherent alternative to Planned change but merely provides an umbrella for those who oppose it.

2. In what ways can Emergence be seen as a different way of seeing organisations rather than a different way of changing them?

Suggested further reading

Burnes, B and Cooke, B (2012) The past, present and future of organization development: taking the long view. *Human Relations*, 65(11), 1395–429.
This comprehensive review of OD explains why it has experienced a renaissance in recent years.

Dawson, P (2003) *Organizational Change: A processual approach*. Routledge: London.
Patrick Dawson's book is an excellent guide to the Processual approach to change which raises some important questions about both Planned and Emergent change.

Kotter, JP (1996) *Leading Change*. Harvard Business School Press: Boston, MA.
John Kotter's work represents the more prescriptive and pragmatic wing of Emergent change.

CASE STUDY 10

Midshires College of Midwifery and Nursing

Background

This case study describes the attempt to merge five colleges of midwifery and nursing to form the new Midshires College of Midwifery and Nursing. The existing colleges, between them, serviced hospitals in ten different Health Authorities. The Health Authorities, in consultation with the Regional Health Authority, appointed a Steering Group of senior managers, drawn from the Boards of Governors of the five colleges, to oversee the merger. The Steering Group comprised General Managers from NHS Hospital Trusts within the Health Authorities, Chief Nursing Officers, and representatives from the Regional Health Authority, 24 members in all.

The remit of the Steering Group was fairly straightforward: To oversee the amalgamation of the five colleges.

In the past, such mergers had been relatively straightforward with everyone keeping their jobs and, for managers at least, an increase in pay to reflect the increased size of the new college. However, there were three issues which made this process significantly different and potentially more complicated than past amalgamations.

First, there was uncertainty over the demand for nurse education in the future (both in terms of numbers and function). Therefore, there was a threat to jobs.

Second, a potential conflict of interest existed between the General Managers on the Steering Group on the one hand and the new college on the other. This was owing to the fact that in the past NHS policy had tied hospitals to a particular college of nursing, whether they liked it or not. This policy had changed and, in future, the General Managers would be able to choose which college of nursing would educate their

trainee nurses. They could, if they so wished, put their requirements for training new nurses out to open tender to any college in the country, as one Trust elsewhere in the UK had already done. In addition, and in the short term more probably, they could seek alternative suppliers for post-experience courses (i.e. courses for already trained nurses who needed to upgrade their skills), or even provide these courses themselves in competition with the new college. Indeed, two of the Health Authorities had already established their own organisation for delivering post-experience nurse education in competition with the new college. This is perhaps why some members of the Steering Group suggested that the new college should not have in its remit the provision of post-experience courses (with implications for the jobs of some 30 per cent of existing staff in the five colleges to be amalgamated). Therefore, key players in establishing the college found themselves placed in a somewhat ambiguous position with regard to its purpose and remit.

Lastly, it was expected that qualifications gained at the new college would be validated by a higher education institution and that eventually, as similar colleges were doing, it would actually merge into the university sector.

There seems to have been no formal acknowledgment of these potential problems or that this amalgamation was in any way different from previous ones. It might have been expected that the Steering Group would seek to clarify these key issues before proceeding to resolve the structure and organisation of the new college. After all, how could decisions regarding its structure and functioning be resolved in advance of key decisions on student numbers, course content, areas of operation, and whether or not it would merge with a higher education institution? Nevertheless, the Steering Group avoided consciously tackling these issues prior to commencing the merger process.

Developing the strategy

The Steering Group decided that merging the five colleges could and should be managed as a straightforward and uncomplicated, almost mechanical, process. They established a 24-month timetable for merging the colleges and appointed a Project Leader, on a fixed-term contract of 24 months, to accomplish the task.

The appointee was the principal of one of the colleges being merged. He had no direct experience of merging colleges, but had only two years' service left prior to retirement. This meant that, unlike the other four college principals, he would not be a potential candidate for the principal's post in the new college. Surprisingly, the Project Leader was given no budget or support, not even a secretary. He could, though, call on the resources of the five colleges, providing that the principals agreed.

Within 48 hours of his appointment, the Project Leader contacted the principals of the other colleges, by fax, and announced both the formation of a Project Board and its membership. The membership included the Project Leader and the principals of the five colleges, including the acting principal from his own college. There were also three external members brought in as advisors to the project group. These were a Finance Manager and a Personnel Manager from the Regional Health Authority and the Education Officer from the English National Board for Nursing.

By the time of the Project Board's first meeting, the Project Leader had produced a plan which, among other objectives, proposed the immediate integration of some administrative processes and the centralisation of student recruitment. The core of the plan was the establishment of four sub-projects aimed at integrating the major functions of the five colleges: pre-registration courses for nursing; post-registration courses for nursing; midwifery education; and education support services.

The first meeting of the Project Board discussed its own membership, the Project Leader's project plan, the roles of the Project Board members, communications, the development of new courses, and the accountability of the Project Board to the Steering Group. The Project Leader stated that he had been given clear instructions by the Steering Group, and that the task of the Project

Board was to get on with the job of integrating the five colleges as laid down in his project plan. This first meeting set the pattern for the future; the Project Leader would act as the only conduit between the Steering Group and the Project Board, and questions relating to the pace, purpose and form of the proposed merger were not part of the Board's remit. Within these constraints, scope for questions and initiatives existed, but the Project Leader had the final say on all matters.

Time for a rethink

In month 5 of the merger timetable, a one-day staff conference was organised for everyone employed at the five colleges. The purpose of the day was to brief staff on developments and get feedback from them. It was apparent as the day progressed that, although staff in the colleges were enthusiastic about the change, and indeed appeared to have more enthusiasm and ideas than the Project Board itself, there were key issues which were not being addressed and which were causing increasing concern. The main concern for staff was that no one seemed to have a clue as to how many staff would retain their posts in the new college, or what mix of skills would be required. However, staff were just as concerned, if not more so, by the lack of any clear direction for the new college: What was its mission? What products and services would it provide? How would it be structured? Who would make these decisions, when and on what basis? What seemed to shock and dismay many of the staff was that the Project Leader seemed as uncertain and powerless as they were regarding these issues.

The conference brought home to the Project Leader the lack of progress made towards amalgamation. The sub-groups had met frequently and produced extremely detailed plans; but the ability to turn these plans into actions seemed to elude them, partly because key issues had still not been resolved.

For the Project Leader, the conference had crystallised a number of his concerns regarding both the pace of the amalgamation and the effectiveness of the Project Board system. He also, privately, expressed the view that he had become a 'piggy in the middle' between the Project Board and the Steering Group, having critics in both camps but supporters in neither. In addition, some members of the Project Board were meeting informally but regularly to discuss and promote alternative ideas to those of the Project Leader, though whether he was aware of this was unclear. Similarly, Board members were seeing members of the Steering Group informally as well. So a great deal of behind-the-scenes lobbying and jockeying for position was taking place. This was hardly surprising, given the uncertainty – particularly over jobs – which was present.

Shortly after the staff conference, the Project Leader called a one-day Project Board meeting to discuss progress, and he invited the Chair of the Steering Group to part of the meeting. Though members were told that the meeting was to examine the situation and discuss options, they were in effect presented with a *fait accompli* by the Project Leader. He made a number of major announcements at this meeting which in effect tore up the previous four months' work:

- The Project Board was to be disbanded and replaced by an interim Management Committee for the new college.

- The four existing principals would become part of the Management Committee with specific areas of responsibility.

- The role of the existing principals in the five individual colleges would be replaced by the appointment of heads of sites.

- The sub-projects were to be abandoned; in their place, the Project Leader announced a structure for the new college which would, he stated, be fully operational by month 12 of the merger timetable.

Despite these changes, decisions had still not been taken regarding the number of students the new college would have in the future, whether it would be allowed to offer post-registration courses, or whether it would be moving into higher education. Without this information, it was almost impossible to determine staffing levels and the skill mix for the new college, or judge the appropriateness of the proposed structure. In such a situation, inevitably, staff morale continued to decline, especially among staff on short-term contracts. One example of this was the high number of staff, especially in managerial positions, who were on long-term sick leave with stress-related illnesses.

Time for another rethink

The creation of the Management Committee appeared to have had little positive impact upon the new college.

The new structure still existed only on paper. The reports from the Management Committee were vague, irregular and fragmented. However, in month 9 of the merger timetable, a new Chair of the Steering Group was appointed. The new Chair came in with a sense of urgency to resolve staffing issues because it had been decided by the Regional Health Authority that his Trust would take over formal responsibility for the college by month 18 of the merger timetable. This meant that any redundancies that might arise, and any associated costs, would be borne by his Trust.

Questions

1. Imagine that you are the new Chair of the Steering Committee. You have decided to take direct charge of the merger process yourself without the aid of any outside assistance.

   a. What is your analysis of what has gone wrong so far and who is to blame?

   b. What are the main steps you need to take to merge the colleges successfully?

   c. What obstacles might you expect to encounter and how might you overcome these?

2. Imagine that you are an outside consultant brought in to advise the new Chair of the Steering Committee.

   a. What are the key issues he needs to address and resolve?

   b. What are the main steps he needs to take to merge the colleges successfully?

   c. What obstacles might he expect to encounter and how might he overcome these?

3. Imagine that you are the Project Leader. The new Chair of the Steering Committee has asked you to produce a report on the current state of the merger and plans for successfully completing the merger within the 24-month timetable. The report should include:

   a. An analysis and explanation of the slow progress to date.

   b. The main steps that need to be taken to complete the merger on time.

   c. The main obstacles to achieving the merger and how they can be overcome.

A framework for change

Approaches and choices

Learning objectives

After studying this chapter, you should be able to:

- recognise that, even taken together, the Planned and Emergent approaches do not cover all change situations;
- list the range of change situations that organisations face;
- appreciate the variety of approaches to change;
- understand the situations in which the various approaches to change are most appropriately used;
- describe how organisations can increase their degree of choice when undertaking change.

MINI CASE STUDY 11.1

G4S chief remains as heads roll

The fallout from the Olympics security fiasco claimed two scalps at G4S yesterday and triggered a radical shake-up of senior management – in a move that the company hopes will draw a line under the high-profile contract failure. But Nick Buckles – the chief executive who has been the public face of the Olympics debacle – has defied calls from MPs to resign. Despite his admission that the failure to deliver sufficient staff at games venues had been a "humiliating shambles", Mr Buckles had already won support from investors to continue at the helm

of the global security group, which operates in 125 countries. However, David Taylor-Smith – head of the UK and Ireland division, and widely tipped as a potential successor to Mr Buckles – was axed. Ian Horseman Sewell, managing director of global events, was also sacked. Just weeks before the games, Mr Horseman Sewell had promised he could "deliver two Olympics" at the same time.

A damning review by the audit firm PwC published yesterday concluded that the company's "management framework and practices [on the contract] were ineffective". In its own review of the fiasco, G4S said: "While the CEO has ultimate responsibility for the company's performance, the review did not identify significant shortcomings in his performance or serious failings attributable to him in connection with the Olympic contract."

The contract problems were revealed when G4S admitted, only a fortnight before the games began, that it could not provide a promised 10,400 guards. The company has agreed to reimburse the military after the army was called in to make up the shortfall. An expected £10 million profit on the £284 million contract has turned into a £50 million loss. Keith Vaz, Labour MP and chairman of the Commons Home Affairs Committee, called for the government to withhold £57 million still owed to G4S on the contract. "This is the right step forward but it doesn't end the problem," he said. "There's still a lot of unfinished business as far as G4S's relationship with the taxpayer is concerned."

In a move to reassure the government over its ability to handle future contracts, G4S has appointed Richard Morris – currently head of care and justice services – as UK chief executive. Kim Challis, who runs welfare-to-work programmes and other projects in the UK, has become responsible for all government business. The company is already searching for two additional non-executives and a full-time chief operating officer, who will be recruited from outside the organisation. G4S has pointed to a five-year deal to provide electronic tagging for offenders in Scotland as evidence that it would continue to be one of the public sector's favourite suppliers. The £13 million-a-year deal was announced last Friday.

John Connolly, chairman of G4S since June, said he was confident that the security company would not be categorised as an underperforming supplier by the government. "Clearly, our credentials prevailed there [in Scotland]. We anticipate that because of our record and success, we would not feature in such a blacklist," he said. But Kevin Lapwood at Seymour Pierce, the broker, said: "The government will be under pressure not to appoint G4S on sensitive outsourcing contracts such as prisons for some time yet."

Government deals account for more than half of G4S's £1.8 billion UK revenue. The group, which employs 625,000 staff worldwide, is expected to achieve total revenues of £8 billion this year.

 Source: SUPPORT SERVICES – G4S chief remains as heads roll, *The Financial Times*, 29/09/2012, p. 18 (Plimmer G., Warrell H. and Wembridge M.), © *The Financial Times Limited* (2012). All Rights Reserved.

Introduction

Since the Industrial Revolution, the conventional wisdom has been that the private sector is the leader in terms of efficiency and customer responsiveness and the public sector is the laggard (van der Mandele and van Witteloostuijn, 2013). This view is based on the belief that only free-market competition will drive organisations and individuals to innovate, change and deliver value-for-money products and services on time and within budget. Consequently, if the public sector is to improve, it needs to learn from the private sector; certainly, this was the view in the 1980s and 1990s, when not just ideas and techniques were imported from the private sector but many managers as well. However, as far as the organisation and delivery of the London Olympic Games is concerned, one of the biggest public construction and sporting projects ever undertaken in the UK, this was clearly not the case. As Mini Case Study 11.1 shows, the Games were a triumph for public management and a 'humiliating shambles' for the private sector in the form of G4S. This came as something of a shock to those members of the UK government who came into office believing that all things private were good and all things public were bad. Philip Hammond, Minister of Defence, commented:

I came into the [Ministry of Defence – MoD] with a prejudice that we have to look at the way the private sector does things to know how we should do things in government," Mr Hammond told the Independent newspaper. "But the story of G4S and the military rescue is quite informative." He added: "I'm learning that the application of the lean commercial model does have relevance in areas of the MoD but, equally, you can't look at a warship and say, 'How can I bring a lean management model to this?' – because it's doing different things with different levels of resilience that are not generally required in the private sector.

(Warrell, 2012: 2)

Actually, this should not have come as such a surprise to Mr Hammond, as successive governments in the UK and elsewhere have put considerable pressure on their respective public sectors to deliver more cost-effective and more customer-responsive services (Buchanan *et al*, 2006; Burnes, 2009a; By and Macleod, 2009; Stern, 2011). The notion that the private sector is always the leader and the other sectors always the followers when it comes to developing, managing and changing organisations is something of a misconception. All the same, though the public sector may have something to teach the private sector when it comes to delivering value-for-money services and products, the real lesson is that while different sectors and different organisations can learn from each other, they can also face widely differing challenges, and what is appropriate for one organisation or sector is not necessarily appropriate for another. Consequently, a 'one-size-fits-all' approach is unlikely to work, whether based on private- or public-sector experiences. This is particularly the case when considering organisational change. As Stickland (1998: 14) remarks:

The problem with studying change is that it parades across many subject domains under numerous guises, such as transformation, development, metamorphosis, transmutation, evolution, regeneration, innovation, revolution and transition to name but a few.

The last two chapters have reviewed the Planned and Emergent approaches to change, examining their strengths and weaknesses and the situations they are designed to address. Though the Planned approach seemed to have been eclipsed by the Emergent approach, in recent years it has been experiencing a renaissance; while the Emergent approach is itself being challenged by the relatively new concept of Emergence. Nevertheless, the Planned and Emergent approaches still dominate the change literature, despite the fact that – even taken together – they do not cover the broad spectrum of change events that organisations encounter, as the rise of Emergence, for example, shows. Pettigrew (2000: 245–6) observes:

There is a long tradition in the social sciences and in management and organization theory of using bipolar modes of thinking: dichotomies, paradoxes, contradictions and dualities. . . . The duality of planned versus emergent change has served us well as an attention director but may well now be ready for retirement.

Though both Planned and Emergent change have made important contributions to our understanding of change, their dominance of the change literature has led to a neglect of other approaches. In order to address this neglect, this chapter will seek to identify the range of change situations organisations face and match these to a wider group of approaches. This will enable a framework to be constructed which will allow different change situations to be matched to appropriate approaches to managing change. It will then be argued that, by manipulating key variables in this framework, it is possible for organisations to have genuine choices in what to change, how to change and when to change.

Varieties of change

Chapter 8 explained that types of change can be categorised as to whether their primary focus applies to individuals, groups, or systems and sub-systems. As far as models or theories of change are concerned, once again as noted in Chapter 8, the three main ones are the Incremental model, the Punctuated Equilibrium model and the Continuous Transformation model. Figure 11.1 brings these together to create a change matrix that appears to cover most situations, as the examples illustrate.

However, there are other types, models and forms of change that expand on, cut across or are not included in this matrix. Senior (2002), drawing on the work of Grundy (1993), identifies three categories of change:

- **smooth incremental**, covering slow, systematic, evolutionary change;
- **bumpy incremental**, pertaining to periods where the smooth flow of change accelerates;
- **discontinuous change**, which is similar to the punctuated equilibrium model.

As discussed in Chapter 10, Kanter *et al* (1992), in addressing the issue of transformational change, argued that it can be achieved either by:

- a **Bold Stroke** approach – rapid overall change; or
- a **Long March** approach – incremental change leading to transformation over an extended period of time.

In a similar vein, Beer and Nohria (2000) identify two basic archetypes or theories of change:

- **Theory E**: This is similar to Kanter *et al*'s Bold Stroke. The main objective of this approach is to maximise shareholder value. It is applied in situations where an organisation's performance has diminished to such an extent that its main shareholders demand major and rapid change to improve the organisation's financial performance. Typically

	Incremental	Punctuated	Continuous
Individuals	IT training	Promotion Dismissal	Career development
Groups	Kaizen	Forming, Storming, Norming, Performing and Adjourning	Changes in composition and tasks
Systems	Fine-tuning	BPR, Organisation restructuring	Culture

Figure 11.1 Varieties of change

this is a 'hard' approach based on downsizing, divestment of non-core or low-performing businesses, and the heavy use of financial incentives.

● **Theory O**: This is similar to Kanter *et al*'s Long March. Theory O is also aimed at improving an organisation's performance, but this is more a 'soft' approach based on a slow incremental development of the organisation's culture and its human capabilities, and promoting organisational learning.

Beer and Nohria (2000) believe that these are both valid models of change but that both have their flaws. Theory E can achieve short-term financial gains but at the cost of denuding an organisation of the human capabilities and organisational culture necessary for long-term survival. Theory O, while focusing on people and culture, falls into the trap of not restructuring to concentrate on core activities, thus failing to deliver shareholder value. To achieve the gains of both these approaches, while avoiding the pitfalls, Beer and Nohria advocate using these in tandem by focusing on the rapid restructuring elements of Theory E but following this with the slow human capability development offered by Theory O.

Cummings and Worley (2001: 30) identify a 'continuum ranging from incremental changes that involve fine-tuning the organization to quantum changes that entail fundamentally altering how it operates'. Stace and Dunphy (2001), in a similar but more detailed way, identify a four-stage change continuum that comprises the following: fine-tuning, incremental adjustment, modular transformation and corporate transformation (*see* Figure 10.1 in Chapter 10). Looking at the last of these, Stace and Dunphy argue that corporate transformations can take four forms: developmental transitions, task-focused transitions, charismatic transformations and turnarounds. For Peters (1989), rapid, disruptive and continuous change is the only appropriate form of change there is. With echoes of Peters, Quinn (1996) differentiates between incremental change, which he sees as leading to slow death, and deep, radical change leading to irreversible transformation. Pettigrew *et al* (1992) distinguish between types of change by their scale and importance. Their change continuum spans:

● operational change – small-scale, relatively unimportant;
● strategic change – major and important structural changes.

Buchanan and Boddy's (1992) classification is almost the same as Pettigrew *et al*'s, but they use two dimensions:

● Incremental change to radical change.
● Changes that are of central importance to the organisation to those that are peripheral to its purpose.

Kotter (1996) ignores the notion of a continuum of change as such and, instead, argues that organisations need to be continuously transforming themselves through a series of large and small interlinked change projects spanning different levels and functions and having different timescales.

One could of course extend this review further by including other writers (e.g. Carnall, 2003; Dawson, 2003; Stickland, 1998; Wilson, 1992); however, the end product would be the same: change can be viewed as running along a continuum from incremental to transformational. Incremental or fine-tuning forms of change are geared more to changing the activities, performance, behaviour and/or attitudes of individuals and groups, whereas transformational change is geared towards the processes, structures and culture of the entire organisation. Obviously, there are differences in how these writers construe these concepts. Some writers see fine-tuning or incremental change as being relatively isolated and/or relatively unimportant (i.e. Stace and Dunphy, 2001; Pettigrew *et al*, 1992), while others see it as being part of an overall plan to transform an organisation (e.g. Kanter *et al*, 1992; Senior, 2002). In contrast, all seem to view transformational change as being strategic and important; though there are those who see it as being a relatively slow process (Kotter, 1996), those who see it as being a relatively rapid one (Peters, 1989), and those who argue that it can take both forms (Kanter *et al*, 1992; Stace and Dunphy, 2001).

Regardless of these differences, the overall view as shown by Figure 11.2 is that change can be seen as running along a continuum from small-scale incremental change to large-scale transformational change. This of course is no surprise; intuitively, one would expect change to range from small-scale to large-scale and from operational to strategic. The important consideration is perhaps not the type of change but how it should be conceived and managed. Implicit in the arguments of the Emergent approach is the view that Planned change stands at the left-hand end of this spectrum and Emergent change at the right-hand end, and that what separates them is the nature of the environment (*see* Figure 11.3).

Chapter 9 argued that Lewin saw Planned change as being effective for changing the behaviour of individuals and groups, which does tend to be relatively stable over time. On the other hand, the proponents of Emergent change, discussed in Chapter 10, see it as better suited to more turbulent, organisation-wide environments. Therefore, as argued in Chapters 9 and 10, neither approach can be considered to be effective for all situations and types of change. For example, the Planned approach tends to stress collaborative and consultative change. However, Stace and Dunphy's (2001) four approaches to managing change effectively are based on the degree to which employees are involved in planning and executing change (see Figure 10.1 in Chapter 10). They take the collaborative and consultative approaches of Planned change and add directive and coercive change, which they consider to be widely used. They argue that consultative and directive approaches are the most popular forms of change, but that more coercive approaches tend to be seen as effective for situations where rapid organisational transformations are required. Kotter (1996)

Figure 11.2 Change continuum

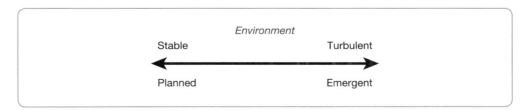

Figure 11.3 Approaches to change

takes a different view, considering these approaches not as alternatives, but as complementary. Kotter believes that the overall direction of change is decided in a directive-coercive manner by senior managers, and its implementation is played out in a collaborative-consultative manner by empowered managers and employees at all levels.

Burnes and Jackson (2011) relate the effectiveness of change approaches to organisational culture. They argue that organisations with participative cultures will find collaborative and consultative approaches more effective, while those with command-and-control cultures will find directive and coercive approaches more effective. Boddy and Buchanan (1992) believe that the choice of approach will vary depending on whether the change is viewed as central or peripheral to the organisation's purpose. Davenport's (1993) perspective on change seems to incorporate both the cultural and importance dimensions. He identifies five principal factors that influence how a project will be managed: the scale of change, the level of uncertainty about the outcome, the breadth of change across the organisation, the magnitude of change in terms of attitudes and behaviour, and the timescale for implementation. Storey (1992), taking a slightly different tack, begins by identifying two key dimensions:

- The degree of collaboration between the parties concerned: varying from change that is unilaterally constructed by management, to change brought about by some form of joint agreement with those involved.
- The form that change takes, ranging from change that is introduced as a complete package, to change comprising a sequence of individual initiatives.

From these two dimensions, Storey constructs a fourfold typology of change:

1. **Top-down systemic change** aimed at transforming the organisation.
2. **Piecemeal initiatives** devised and implemented by departments or sections in an unconnected fashion.
3. **Bargaining for change** where a series of targets are jointly agreed between managers and workers, but are pursued in a piecemeal fashion.
4. **Systemic jointism** where managers and workers agree a total package of changes designed to achieve organisational transformation.

As was the case with the earlier review of the varieties of change, in order to make sense of this review of the nature of change and how it should be managed, we need to find a way of categorising and tabulating the various viewpoints. However, this is far from being a straightforward exercise. Stace and Dunphy's (2001) fourfold categorisation of approaches to change, ranging from cooperative to coercive, is useful in that it appears to cover most of the managerial approaches on offer.

However, it is the circumstances in which each of these might best be used that are perhaps of most concern. Boddy and Buchanan's categorisation of central–peripheral is interesting but, in most instances, this appears to boil down to an issue of project size. Almost by definition, all major projects can be considered as central by virtue of their size and, for a similar reason, most smaller projects are, relatively speaking, peripheral. Davenport's five factors are perhaps more useful in helping us to categorise change, especially those concerning uncertainty, behaviour and attitudes, and timescale. As we have noted frequently in this book, uncertainty tends to be present when the environment is changing in a rapid and unpredictable fashion. This requires organisations to respond quickly; advocates of the Emergent approach believe this is best done by small- to medium-scale local or cross-functional or process changes. The ability to do this, however, is dependent on having appropriate structures, attitudes and cultures in place. If this is not the case, then change will be delayed or not quick enough and, as Stace and Dunphy (2001) showed, will be likely to require rapid transformational change undertaken in a directive or coercive fashion. Yet both Kanter *et al* (1992) and Beer and Nohria (2000), as well as the review of culture in Chapter 5, argue that changes in attitudes and culture cannot be achieved in a rapid and coercive manner. That type of approach tends to be effective in changing structures and processes, but achieving attitudinal and/or cultural change is a much slower process.

A framework for change

If we summarise the above views, we can create yet another change continuum (*see* Figure 11.4). At one end is slow change, where the focus is on behavioural and cultural change. At the other end of the continuum is rapid change, where the focus is on major changes in structures and processes.

If we merge Figure 11.4 (putting it along the horizontal axis) with Figures 11.2 and 11.3 (putting them along the vertical axis), what we get, as Figure 11.5 shows, are four quadrants, each of which has a distinct focus in terms of change.

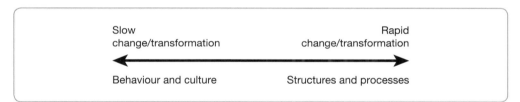

Figure 11.4 Speed and focus of change

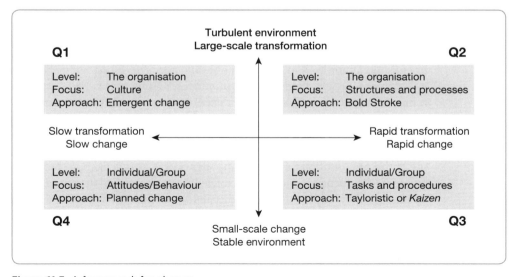

Figure 11.5 A framework for change

The top half of Figure 11.5, Quadrants 1 and 2, represents situations where organisations need to make large-scale, organisation-wide changes to either their culture or structure. These changes may be required because the organisation's structure/culture, though appropriate in the past, is inappropriate for the turbulent environment in which it finds itself operating. The bottom half of the figure, Quadrants 3 and 4, represents situations where organisations need to make relatively small-scale, localised adjustments to the attitudes and behaviours or tasks and procedures of individuals and groups. Such changes must be sustained and, therefore, it is crucial to ensure that the post-change environment is stable.

The left-hand side of the figure, Quadrants 1 and 4, represents situations where the main focus of change is the human side of the organisation, i.e. cultural and attitudinal and/or behavioural change. As argued above, these sorts of changes are likely to be best achieved through a relatively slow, participative approach, rather than a rapid and directive or coercive one. The right-hand side of Figure 11.5, Quadrants 2 and 3, represents situations where the primary focus is on achieving changes to the technical side of the organisation, i.e. structures, processes, tasks and procedures. These types of changes tend to be less participative in nature and relatively rapid in their execution.

Let's take each of the quadrants in turn. Quadrant 1 identifies situations where the culture of an organisation operating in a turbulent environment is no longer appropriate. For such relatively large-scale initiatives, where the main focus is culture change at the level of the entire organisation or large parts of it, the Emergent approach (e.g. Kanter *et al*'s Long March), which emphasises both the collaborative and political dimensions of change, may be appropriate. A growing number of researchers also maintain that Emergence, discussed in Chapter 10, with its emphasis on participative self-organisation, may be appropriate. Both have their supporters because, as described in Chapter 5, successful culture change is less likely to be the product of a top-down, deliberate process and more likely to 'emerge' from a host of initiatives that arise in response to changes in the environment. This does not necessarily exclude some elements of deliberation and guidance from senior managers. Although the organisation may be operating in a turbulent environment and, therefore, individual elements of the cultural change may be rapid, the overall cultural transformation is likely to be a slow process.

Quadrant 2 relates to situations where the focus is on achieving major changes in structures and processes at the level of the entire organisation (e.g. Kanter *et al*'s Bold Stroke). Situations where such changes are required arise for a variety of reasons. It may be that an organisation finds itself in serious trouble and needs to respond quickly to realign itself with its environment (e.g. financial institutions responding to the credit crunch). Alternatively, it may be that an organisation is not experiencing a crisis, but that it perceives that it will face one unless it restructures itself to achieve a better fit with its environment. In such cases, it may not be possible or advisable to change the structure slowly or on a piecemeal basis and, therefore, a major and rapid reorganisation is necessary. Because it involves the entire organisation or major components of it, this is likely to be driven by the centre and to be the focus of a political struggle, given that major structural changes are usually accompanied by major shifts in the distribution of power. Therefore, the new structure will be imposed from the top in a directive or even coercive way, depending on the balance between winners and losers.

Quadrant 3 presents a different picture. This represents situations where change is aimed at the individual and group level rather than at the level of the entire organisation. The aim is to improve the performance of the areas involved through changes to the technical side of the organisation. Such changes tend to be relatively small-scale and piecemeal and with few (if any) implications for behaviour and attitudes. A key objective is to ensure the predictability and stability of the performance of the areas involved but at a higher level. How these changes are managed will depend on the culture of the organisation. In a traditional, bureaucratic organisation, a Tayloristic approach may be adopted, i.e. specialist managers and engineers will identify the 'best way of working' and impose it. In a more participative culture, such as a Japanese company, a more collaborative approach may be appropriate, such as a *Kaizen* initiative that brings together a team comprising workers and specialists. But either is possible and both can be achieved in a relatively speedy fashion.

Finally, Quadrant 4 covers relatively small-scale initiatives whose main objective is performance improvement through attitudinal and behavioural change at the individual and group level. As was the case in Quadrant 3, a key objective is to ensure the predictability and stability of the performance of the people involved but at a higher level. In such situations, Planned change, with its emphasis on collaboration and participation, is likely to be the more appropriate approach. However, because of the focus on behavioural and attitudinal change, the process may be relatively slow.

Of course, it could be argued that, at the organisational level, it is difficult to identify situations that involve solely cultural changes or solely structural changes. A similar comment could be made with regard to attitudinal and/or behavioural change and changes to tasks and procedures at the individual or group level. Such comments are valid to an extent, but the real issue is to identify the main focus of the change. Chapter 3 examined the work of the Culture–Excellence approach. Here it was shown that writers like Tom Peters and Rosabeth Moss Kanter argued for structural change in order to promote the values and behaviours necessary for organisations to survive in an increasingly complex world. Therefore, though significant structural changes are recommended, these are part of the process of culture change and not an end in themselves. Kotter, as noted in the previous chapter, advocates the need for organisations to restructure themselves on a continuous basis in order to meet the challenges of the future. At different times and in different areas, he believes that this can involve all of the types of change shown in Figure 11.1. There are also many cases, according to Kotter, where an organisation already has an appropriate culture and where changes to its overall structure, and piecemeal changes to its component parts, are seen as working with and reinforcing the existing organisational culture rather than leading to its replacement.

Therefore, the question of whether changes can be labelled as mainly structure-orientated or mainly people-orientated is partly a matter of sequencing: what does the organisation need to do first? It is also partly concerned with the extent to which environmental turbulence has a uniform effect across an organisation. As shown in Chapter 2, in the 1960s, James Thompson (1967) identified that different sections of an organisation, by accident or design, could experience different levels of uncertainty. On this basis, it would be perfectly feasible for some parts of an organisation to be experiencing relatively low levels of uncertainty and concentrating on small-scale, piecemeal changes while at the same time the overall organisation was going through a process of rapid transformation.

Where does this leave us? Drawing on the work of Davenport (1993), we need to distinguish between initiatives that focus on fundamental attitudinal change and those aimed at fundamental structural change. It was argued in Chapter 5 and by Allaire and Firsirotu (1984) that there is a strong relationship between organisational structures and organisational cultures, and so changes in one may require corresponding changes in the other. It was also argued earlier, however, that it is much easier and quicker to change structures than to change cultures. Consequently, we need to take into account the timescale for change. Culture change, to be effective, is likely to be slow and involves incremental changes to the human side of the organisation; also, because of its nature, it is likely to be participative and collaborative. Rapid change is likely to be effective or necessary only where the main changes are to structure, or where the organisation is in such trouble that delay is not an option (e.g. the many and rapid bank mergers and takeovers which followed the 2008 credit crunch). In the case of structural change, this may involve some consultation but is likely to have a large element of direction from the centre. In the latter case, where the organisation is in trouble because of the urgency of the situation, change is likely to be directive and, probably, coercive.

There is one further point that needs to be noted, and that relates to how these various approaches can be used in combination. In a manner reminiscent of Mintzberg's (1994) definition of 'umbrella' strategies, Pettigrew *et al* (1992: 297) write of instances where change is both 'intentional and emergent'. Storey (1992) identifies the need for change projects whose outlines are decided at corporate level with little or no consultation, but whose implementation comprises an interrelated series of change initiatives, some or all of which could be the product of local cooperation and consultation. Kotter (1996) takes a similar perspective. He sees strategic change as comprising a series of large and small projects aimed at achieving the same overall objectives but which are begun at different times, which can be managed differently and which vary in nature. Buchanan and Storey (1997) also hint at this when criticising Planned change for attempting to impose order and a linear sequence to processes that are untidy, messy, multi-level and multi-function, and that develop in an iterative and backtracking manner. This is also identified by Kanter *et al* (1992) when speaking of Long Marches and Bold Strokes. They argue that Bold Strokes often have to be followed by a whole series of smaller-scale changes over a more extended timescale in order to embed the changes brought about by the Bold Stroke. Beer and Nohria (2000) are even more explicit in arguing for the use of Theory E and Theory O in tandem. Similarly, Burnes (2004a) also shows that major change projects that involve both structural and cultural change can successfully utilise both Planned and Emergent approaches. Consequently, when considering major change projects, one should not see them as being managed solely in a cooperative fashion or solely in a coercive fashion. Instead, they may have elements of both but at different levels, at different times and managed by different people. They may also, indeed probably will, unfold in an unexpected way which will require rethinking and backtracking from time to time.

A framework for employee involvement

Figure 11.5 can also be seen as a framework for employee involvement, given that the types of change in each quadrant appear to require different degrees of involvement if they are to be achieved successfully. Certainly, the received wisdom in the literature on organisational change is that employee involvement is crucial to successful change, especially in situations that require changes to attitudes and values (Burnes and Cooke, 2012b; Oreg *et al*, 2011). There is considerable support for the view that cultural and behavioural change (Quadrants 1 and 4) require greater levels of employee involvement than those that focus on restructuring tasks or even entire organisations (Quadrants 2 and 3). The implication of this is that rapid organisational transformations can only be successful if they focus on structural as opposed to cultural change. As Chapters 9 and 10 showed, this conclusion can certainly find plenty of support in the literature on both Planned and Emergent change. It is also supported by Kanter *et al* (1992), who believe that an organisation's structure can be changed relatively quickly through a 'Bold Stroke' but that cultural change can be achieved only by a 'Long March' requiring extensive participation over time. Beer and Nohria (2000) make a similar point with their Theory E and Theory O approach to change, and the XYZ case study provides an illustration of this (see Chapters 3 and 9). However, the case study of Oticon at the end of this chapter shows that this is not always the case. Sometimes, cultural change can be relatively swift and employee involvement relatively low. To understand why this should be so, it is necessary to revisit the discussion of resistance to change in Chapter 8.

In that discussion, it was stressed that the degree of resistance, which is clearly related to the need for employee involvement and speed of change, arises from two factors: the type of change and the context within which the change takes place. In terms of the type of change, the depth of intervention theory stressed that the level of involvement required in any change project is dependent on the impact of the change on the people concerned. The greater the depth of the intervention, the more it impacts on the psychological make-up and personality of the individual, and the greater the need for the full involvement of individuals if they are to accept the change. Cultural and behavioural change would normally be expected to a greater psychological impact than changes to structure or tasks. However, the other three theories examined in the discussion of resistance tend to modify this view by drawing attention to contextual factors.

If we consider the theory of dispositional resistance, for example, this maintains that individuals' reactions to change vary. In organisations where employees have very low levels of dispositional resistance, the level of involvement required to achieve cultural or behavioural change would be much lower than in an organisation where dispositional resistance was higher, even though the type of change might be the same. There is a similar argument when we consider cognitive dissonance and the psychological contract. In both cases, the level of involvement required would be moderated by the degree to which the type of change aligned with or challenged existing values, practices and expectations.

Consequently, it is necessary to treat the issue of employee involvement with some caution. In general, we can say that cultural and behavioural changes, i.e. the left-hand side of Figure 11.5, are likely to require greater levels of employee involvement than the more structural changes of the right-hand side of Figure 11.5. However, if we draw on the four complementary theories of dispositional resistance, depth of intervention, cognitive dissonance and the psychological contract, we see that this general rule of involvement has to take account of the context of the change situation and not just the type of change being proposed. In many cases it will be necessary to convince staff, through a process of constructive engagement, of the need to challenge their existing beliefs, behaviours and expectations and to renegotiate their unwritten 'contracts' with the organisation. However, in some instances, the legitimacy of existing beliefs, behaviours and expectations may already have been undermined because the organisation is experiencing a crisis (*see*, for example, the case of Oticon, discussed at the end of this chapter). In such situations, it might be that cultural and behavioural change can be achieved relatively quickly, without the need for extensive involvement procedures, because those concerned can see that the old attitudes and ways of behaving are no longer appropriate and, unless major or radical changes are made, their jobs or even the entire organisation may cease to exist. Of course, the reverse may also be the case. Organisations seeking to bring about small changes to structures or tasks might find they meet greater resistance than they expected because they under-estimate the psychological and symbolic importance employees attach to these existing arrangements. Therefore, approaches to change, including the level of employee involve-ment, have to be tailored to the change context rather than being applied in an unthinking fashion. The next section explores the possibility of influencing the change context to make it more amenable to particular approaches to change.

A framework for choice

As can be seen from Figure 11.5, what appears to be on offer is a menu approach to change whereby organisations, or more accurately those who manage them, can choose the approach which fits their circumstances. This conception of a multiplicity of approaches is in line with the call by Dunphy and Stace (1993: 905) for 'a model of change that is essentially a "situational" or "contingency model", one that indicates how to vary strategies to achieve "optimum fit" with the changing environment'. If we were to stop at this point, it might be considered that we had indeed made significant progress in our understanding of change; yet there would still be one essential question outstanding: what about choice? We have identified situations where these various approaches seem appropriate or not, but does that mean they cannot be used in other situations and does that mean that the context cannot be changed? Supposing organisations whose management prefers a cooperative approach find themselves seriously out of alignment with their environment: is their only option rapid and coercive structural change? Or, alternatively, where managers prefer a more directive, less participative style, are they compelled to adopt a more participative style and culture?

These questions revolve around two issues. The first issue concerns the extent to which an organisation can influence the forces driving it to change. If we accept that the speed and nature of the changes that organisations are required to make are dependent upon the nature of the environment in which they are operating, then choice will relate to the extent that organisations can influence, manipulate or recreate their environment to suit their preferred way of working. This is a subject that has been examined a number of times so far, especially in Chapters 5 and 6, and will be touched on again in Chapters 12 and 13. The conclusion reached was that organisations could influence their environment, either to stabilise or to destabilise it. If this is the case, then the important question is not just how organisations can do this, but whether, finding themselves in trouble, they have the time to influence their environment.

This leads on to the second issue: to what extent and for how long can an organisation operate with structures, practices and cultures that are out of line with its environment? The answer to this question draws on Child's (1972) concept of equifinality. Discussed in Chapter 6, equifinality 'quite simply means that different sorts of internal arrangements are perfectly compatible with identical contextual or environmental states' (Sorge, 1997: 13). This does not imply that any structure is suitable for any environment. What it does suggest, though, is that total alignment between structure and environment is not always necessary. The duration for which this non-alignment is sustainable will clearly vary with the degree of non-alignment and the circumstances of the organisation in question; at the very least, however, it does offer organisations the potential to stave off realignment for some time during which they can influence or change their circumstances. Indeed, this is exactly what Nissan did when they first established their Sunderland plant in the 1980s. Its partnership-based supply chain structures and practices were out of alignment with the UK's antagonistic customer–supplier relationships. Nevertheless, instead of changing its own structures and practices, it worked to change the practices of its suppliers to align them with its preferred way of working. Given the possibility that organisations can change their environment, it follows that Figure 11.5 depicts not only a framework for change but also a framework for choice.

In summary, therefore, what we can see, as Pettigrew (2000) suggested, and as the previous chapter showed, is that the debate between Planned change and Emergent change is too narrow. It is too narrow in the sense that there are other approaches to change that organisations have available to them; in particular, it tends to ignore the more coercive and directive approaches to change that, in many organisations, may be more prevalent than cooperative ones. It is also too narrow in the sense that it assumes that the impetus for change can come from only one direction, i.e. it is driven by the environment. Organisations do have the opportunity to make choices about what to change, how to change and when to change. This does not mean that all organisations will exercise such choices or that those which do will be successful. Nor, as Chapter 6 argued, does it mean that choice is not severely constrained. What it does mean is that those who do not recognise that choice exists may be putting themselves in a worse competitive position than those who do.

Conclusions

The previous two chapters focused primarily, though not exclusively, on the Planned and Emergent approaches to change, which have dominated the theory and, to a large extent, the practice of organisational change over the past 60 years. Chapter 9 was devoted to the Planned approach to change. It was argued that, though still appropriate for changing the behaviour of groups in organisations, attempts by OD practitioners to apply it to organisation-wide change initiatives have led to confusion and a loss of direction. In the increasingly dynamic and unpredictable business environment of the 1980s, writers began to question the appropriateness of a top-down approach that saw the process of change primarily in terms of a 'beginning, middle and end' framework. In place of the Planned approach, as was shown in Chapter 10, the Emergent approach began to gain support. With its emphasis on bottom-up and open-ended change, it appeared to offer a more appropriate method of accomplishing the stream of adaptations organisations believed they needed to make in order to bring themselves back into line with their environment. However, Chapter 10 also showed that Emergent change has many shortcomings, not least its failure to develop the tools, techniques and practitioner base which would have allowed it to provide a practical alternative to Planned change. This is why, as Chapter 10 concluded, Emergent change has found itself under threat from both the complexity-based Emergence and a resurgent Lewinian OD.

Nevertheless, this should not blind us to the fact that Planned change and Emergent change appear to have some important similarities, especially the emphasis they place on change as a learning process. They also share a common, and major, difficulty, which is that while both the extended form of Planned change represented by OD and Emergent change claim to be universally applicable, they were developed with particular change situations, organisation types and environments in mind. Originally, the Planned approach was developed to focus on behaviour change in small groups. It is based on the assumption that group behaviour is relatively stable and predictable. It also assumes that managers can identify where change is required and that change is about moving from one stable mode of behaviour to another more appropriate, but no less stable, mode of behaviour, and that the steps or phases in between are relatively well-understood and achievable. Later OD elaborations have sought to apply this approach to entire organisations. The Planned approach is also based on the assumption that organisations, managers and employees are open and frank, they welcome involvement, and are willing to change, or that these attributes can be achieved with the application of the appropriate tools and techniques.

The Emergent approach assumes that organisations are open and fluid systems that operate in unpredictable and uncertain conditions over which they have little control. It further assumes that change is a continuous process of adaptation and transformation which, because of its speed and frequency, managers can neither fully identify nor effectively control centrally. Therefore, from the Emergent perspective, identifying and managing change has to be the responsibility of everyone in the organisation. This view portrays managers, who are assumed to be highly competent and adaptable, as capable of changing themselves from outmoded controllers and coordinators to new-style facilitators and partners; and employees are assumed to be willing to take responsibility for identifying deficiencies and implementing change. Above all, and perhaps somewhat contradictorily, change is seen as being a political process whereby different groups and individuals strive to protect or enhance their power and position. It is on this last point – the overriding importance of power and politics in the change process – that postmodernists are most in agreement with the Emergent approach and realists most in disagreement.

Chapter 9 demonstrated that the Planned approach has had a considerable impact on organisation practice since its inception in the 1940s. However, despite its undoubted merits, it does appear limited in terms of the situations in which it can successfully be applied. In particular, the Planned approach has been criticised for its lack of suitability to situations requiring large-scale change and/or those where political and power considerations are prevalent. Nonetheless, Chapter 10 demonstrated that the Emergent approach also has drawbacks in terms of its applicability to large-scale and abrupt change programmes, preferring a continuous programme of small- to medium-sized changes, and the lack of practical guidance, tools and techniques which allow it to be implemented. In addition, criticisms have been raised over its heavy emphasis on the political dimension of change and its contradictory tendency, both implicitly and explicitly, to characterise change as a slow and cooperative process. Consequently, even taken together, the Planned and Emergent approaches do not cover all change situations. In particular, neither approach seems suitable for situations where the primary focus is rapid and radical structural change.

Instead of portraying the argument regarding the most appropriate approach to change as a contest between the merits of the Planned and Emergent approaches, the framework for change (Figure 11.5) provides an overview of the range of change situations organisations face, the approaches available to them and the types of situations in which they can best be applied.

Though this Contingency-type approach to change appears to have some merit, it is subject to the same sort of criticisms levelled at Contingency Theory in Chapter 2. However, this chapter has also argued that, if we adopt the perspective developed in previous chapters and see the environment and other organisational constraints as potentially subject to manipulation or managerial choice, many of these criticisms can be answered and new possibilities opened up. It has to be recognised that there is dispute between the realists and postmodernists as to what can be manipulated and the degree of choice which exists. However, this is a matter of degree; both acknowledge the existence of choice. Therefore, some organisations will find that the organisational adjustments required to accommodate their position on the environmental continuum coincide with the dominant view in the organisation of how it should operate. In that case, whether the approach to change adopted is Planned or Emergent, directive or cooperative, it will fit in with both how the organisation wishes to operate and the needs of the environment. Some organisations will, obviously, find that the dominant view internally of how they should operate is out of step with what is required to align or realign them with their environment. Such organisations face a number of choices ranging from whether to attempt to change their structure, culture or style of management to accommodate the environment, or whether to attempt to manipulate the environment and other constraints so as to align them more closely with the dominant view within the organisation of how it should operate. Still further, there will be other organisations that face severe problems either because they failed to respond quickly enough or in an appropriate manner to changes in their environment, or because the environment moved too rapidly for an incremental approach to respond adequately. Nevertheless, by showing that a more conducive environment can be brought about, the framework also provides those who wish to promote more cooperative approaches to change with the means to argue their case in situations where previously more directive and coercive measures appeared to be the only option.

The concept of a framework for change that allows approaches to change to be matched to environmental conditions and organisational constraints is clearly attractive. The fact that it incorporates the potential for managers, and others, to exercise some choice or influence over their environment and other constraints allows the model to move beyond the limitations of mechanistic and rational perspectives on organisations, and into the heartland of organisational reality. In addition, though not by accident, it is in harmony with the approach to strategy developed in Chapters 6 and 7.

Nevertheless, though such a model of change has its attractions, its usefulness depends on how well it accommodates the reality of organisational life. This will be addressed in the remaining chapters of the book.

TEST YOUR LEARNING

Short discussion topics

The purpose of these is to enable students to check their learning and reflect on the topics covered in this chapter. The discussions should last for no more than 5–10 minutes. Depending on the length of the lecture, there could be one, two or three such discussions in a session. The following are five suggested topics which address issues raised in this chapter:

1. In Storey's (1992) fourfold topology of change, what are the differences between 'top-down systemic change' and 'systemic jointism'?

2. In what way is the framework for change shown in Figure 11.5 also a framework for employee involvement?

3. Give specific examples of the types of changes that would fit into each of the quadrants of the framework for change shown in Figure 11.5.

4. How might an organisation change or manipulate the contingencies or constraints it faces?

5. What factors should managers take into account when choosing an approach to change?

Class debates

The purpose of class debates is to enable students to explore a topic in depth by setting up a 'for and against' debate. The class can be split into two and one half asked to research the 'for' case and the other 'against' case. Individuals can then be chosen at random to introduce their side of the debate. Alternatively, two individuals for each side can be told in advance that they will be introducing the debate. The length of such debates depends on the time available, the size of the class and their enthusiasm for the topic. However, less than 30 minutes is probably too short and more than 60 minutes probably too long. The following are three suggested topics which address issues raised in this chapter:

1. 'The duality of planned versus emergent change has served us well as an attention director but may well now be ready for retirement.' (Pettigrew, 2000: 245–6)

2. At the organisation level, change can either be structure-orientated or culture-orientated but it cannot be both at the same time.

3. Bottom-up (employee-led) change is always more effective than top-down (management-driven) change.

Essay questions

1. How can the leadership of an organisation manipulate or recreate its environment to suit its preferred way of working? Illustrate your answer with recent real-life examples.

2. Use the framework for change, Figure 11.5, to analyse change in one of the case studies which appear at the end of each chapter in this book or for a case of your own choosing. In particular, identify the type of change or changes involved, the selection and suitability of the approach to change and the degree to which the approach was aligned with the management style of the organisation.

Suggested further reading

Beer, M and Nohria, N (eds) (2000) *Breaking the Code of Change*. Harvard Business School Press: Boston, MA.

This edited collection contains contributions by many of the leading thinkers on organisational change. It covers the main approaches to change, including the Planned and Emergent.

Oticon – the disorganised organisation

Background

Oticon, a Danish company founded in 1904, was the first hearing instrument company in the world. In the 1970s, it was the world's number one manufacturer of 'behind-the-ear' hearing aids. However, as the market for 'in-the-ear' products grew in the 1970s and 1980s, its fortunes plummeted and it lost money and market share. However, its fortunes began to change with the appointment of Lars Kolind as president of the company in 1988. In order to revitalise the company, Kolind resolved to 'think the unthinkable':

> Maybe we could design a new way of running a business that could be significantly more creative, faster, and more cost-effective than the big players, and maybe that could compensate for our lack of technological excellence, our lack of capital, and our general lack of resources.

The vision was to create a knowledge-based organisation. Kolind realised that the industry was totally technology-focused, but he thought this was short-sighted. He believed Oticon was not in the hearing-aid business *per se*; they were in the business of 'making people smile' – restoring the enjoyment of life that hearing impairment can destroy. To this end, the company adopted a new mission statement:

> To help people with hearing difficulties to live life as they wish, with the hearing they have.

Kolind had the vision for Oticon's role in meeting customers' needs, but he still had to find a way of implementing it. He believed the key lay in the mix of expertise necessary to provide each customer with an effective hearing aid: micro-mechanics, microchip design, audiology, psychology, marketing, manufacturing, logistics, and all-round service capability. If Oticon were to move away from merely making hearing aids and instead provide a total package of support for people with hearing difficulties, it would have to develop a whole new concept in hearing-aid service. In short, they would have to move from being a technology-based manufacturing company to a knowledge-based service business. They had to build a learning organisation where experts put aside their expertise and work as a team to 'make people smile'.

For Kolind, a knowledge-based or learning organisation:

> should not work like a machine, it should work like a brain. Brains do not know hierarchies – no boxes – no job descriptions; there is a very chaotic set of thousands of relationships tangled in with each other based on certain knowledge centres, with an interaction which may seem chaotic. It is the reflection of the brain into the organisation that creates companies that are able to manage that knowledge process.

Kolind began by redefining his role as CEO. Instead of seeing himself as the captain that steers the ship, he saw himself as the naval architect who designs it. He believed that it was more important to design the organisation to act in a clever and responsible way than to control every action. On this basis, he drafted plans for the company's future which he first presented in April 1990. He wanted to create 'the spaghetti organisation' – a chaotic tangle of relationships and interactions that would force the abandonment of preconceived ideas and barriers to innovation and competitiveness.

The strategy

Having identified the vision for the organisation, the next step was to set about fleshing out and implementing his strategy for change. Beginning with the Head Office, which comprised the finance, management, marketing and product development functions, he decided to abandon the concept of a formal organisation; instead he wanted to create a 'disorganised organisation'. Formal structures, job descriptions and policies were seen as creating barriers to cooperation, innovation and teamwork rather than facilitating it. Kolind's new disorganised organisation would be founded on four principles:

- Departments and job titles would disappear and all activities would become projects initiated and pursued informally by groupings of interested people.

- Jobs would be redesigned into fluid and unique combinations of functions to suit each employee's needs and capabilities.

- All vestiges of the formal office would be eradicated and replaced by open space filled with workstations that anyone could use.
- Informal, face-to-face dialogue would replace memos as the acceptable mode of communication.

Therefore, Oticon got rid of departments, departmental heads and other managerial and supervisory positions. Job descriptions and titles and anything else that created a barrier between one member of staff and another were also eliminated. The company wanted to get rid of everything associated with traditional organisations, including budgets. The intent was to see what happened when staff were 'liberated' to do what they thought best. Kolind wanted everyone in the organisation, from secretaries to technical experts, to work much more closely together to make things happen more creatively, faster and more cost-effectively.

Implementing the strategy
Oticon now operates on a project basis. Anyone can start a project, provided they have the permission of one of five senior managers. Some projects are also initiated by management. Whomsoever the idea comes from, the main criterion for acceptance is that a project is customer-focused. Anyone can join a project, provided they have the agreement of the project leader. The basic idea, going back to the concept that Oticon treats everyone as an adult, is that it is the individual's responsibility to fill their day usefully. If people do not have anything to do, it is their job to find something useful to do – either by starting a project or by joining one.

Kolind's view of Oticon would send shivers down the spine of most traditional CEOs: 'Hearing aids are not the core of what this company is about. It's about something more fundamental. It's about the way people perceive work. We give people the freedom to do what they want.' This is perhaps why, as well as the 100 or so 'authorised' projects, as Kolind comments, 'We have a lot of skunk work going on that's not in any official priority.' There is a saying in Oticon that 'It's easier to be forgiven than to get permission.' Basically, this means, 'If in doubt do it. If it works, fine. If it doesn't, we forgive you.'

The physical embodiment of this new 'structureless' structure is the workplace. Gone are individual offices, gone are corridors – all the walls were taken out and everyone works in the same open-plan office. Staff gather where they wish to work. Instead of individual offices, everyone has a little filing cabinet on wheels. Staff come in each morning, pick up their mobile office and trundle it to where they are working that day. Oticon is also a genuinely 'paperless office'. All incoming mail is scanned into the computer and then shredded. The reason for this is simple: Oticon wants staff to move around from project group to project group as work requires. It does not want this process hindered by staff having to transport masses of paper as happens in most offices – the solution is to get rid of the paper.

This requires everyone to have access to and to be able to use a computer. However, the emphasis at Oticon is on face-to-face, informal communication (although, for example, e-mail is used but not extensively). This is why the office is littered with stand-up coffee bars to encourage small, informal (but short) meetings. Three or four people will meet to discuss an issue or exchange ideas and information and then return to where they are working that day and follow up ideas and suggestions. These are usually fed straight into the computer and are available to everybody else. There is also an expectation not only that all information is open to staff in this manner but that staff actually want to know the information. Therefore, rather than putting up barriers or operating on a need-to-know basis, Oticon tries to be transparent about all aspects of its business, whether it be new products, staff salaries or finance in general. The view is that the more a person knows, the more valuable they are to the company.

Staff did not take to this radically new way of working overnight. This is perhaps not surprising. Staff were not originally recruited for their teamworking and project management skills, and some found it hard to come to terms with these new arrangements. Nor did they welcome the loss of routine and clear authority relationships or find the resultant uncertainty easy to adjust to. This was especially the case with managers for whom the loss of their power base, information monopoly and status symbols was difficult to accept.

In addition, under the new arrangement, managers were reclassified as project leaders and had to compete for the best staff, rather than having their own dedicated subordinates. Some groups of staff also found it difficult to find a role in the project team environment; for some time, receptionists, for instance, still answered the telephone.

The biggest boost to the new arrangements came when staff could see they actually worked better than the old ones. One immediate benefit was that Oticon 'found' that it had already developed the industry's first automatic, self-adjusting hearing aid in the 1980s. However, owing to technical problems (the solution to which was given a very low priority), lack of communication between the R&D and sales staff, and a lack of imagination, nobody seemed to have realised that they had developed a potentially world-beating product. In the transformed Oticon, this new type of hearing aid quickly resurfaced, the technical problems were rapidly ironed out, and the MultiFocus hearing aid, as it became known, was launched in late 1991. In the next two years, three more powerful variants of the MultiFocus were developed and its size reduced by half.

Where next?

The changes to – or rather the transformation of – Oticon started at 8 am on 8 August 1991. At the beginning, all was chaos. It took months before everyone understood their new roles, and for the organisation to cast off its old ways and begin to operate in the manner Kolind had envisaged. By 1994, however, the results were impressive:

- 15 new products had been launched (twice as many as the company had previously).

- New product lead time had been halved.

- The company's sales were growing at 20 per cent per year, after a period of 10 years without real growth and at a time when the market had begun shrinking by 5 per cent per year.

- Oticon's market share increased from 8 per cent to 12 per cent in the two years following the changes.

Nor did the progress stop there. In 1995, Oticon launched the world's first digital hearing aid, the DigiFocus. This is, in effect, a four-gram computer that fits in the ear but has the processing power of a desk-top machine. Not only was this a technological breakthrough for which Oticon has won a number of major innovation awards but it also allowed Oticon to regain its position as one of the world's top three hearing aid producers. Also, by 1995 turnover had increased by 100 per cent on 1990 and profits had increased tenfold.

For some, this would have been a time to sit back and feel satisfied. Yet Kolind was becoming increasingly dissatisfied. The launch of the DigiFocus had dominated 1995 and the long-standing project teams created to develop and launch the product had taken on an air of permanency. He believed the company was in danger of slipping back into a traditional departmental organisational form.

Questions

1. Imagine that you are Lars Kolind. The changes you have made have been far more successful than you could have imagined. The company is profitable, producing innovative products and the workforce is pleased with the new arrangements.

    a. What are the advantages and disadvantages of allowing the company to regain a more formalised structure?

    b. What are the advantages and disadvantages of once again 'disorganising' the company?

    c. Which course of action do you intend to take and why?

2. Imagine that you were formerly a senior manager with Oticon and are now one of its most successful project leaders. Lars Kolind has shared his concerns with you and asked you to produce a report on the options for future organisation of the company from your perspective. In particular, he wishes you to address the following questions:

    a. What are the advantages and disadvantages of allowing the company to regain a more formalised structure?

    b. What are the advantages and disadvantages of once again 'disorganising' the company?

    c. Which course of action would you recommend and why?

3. Imagine that you are an outside consultant brought in to advise Lars Kolind. He wishes you to address the following questions:

    a. What are the advantages and disadvantages of allowing the company to regain a more formalised structure?

    b. What are the advantages and disadvantages of once again 'disorganising' the company?

    c. Which course of action would you recommend and why?

PART 4

Managing choice

Organisational change and managerial choice

Part 1: The choice process and the trajectory process

Learning objectives

After studying this chapter, you should be able to:

- understand the rationale underlying the Choice Management–Change Management model;
- discuss the three organisational processes which make up the Choice–Change model;
- describe the choice process;
- describe the trajectory process;
- identify the range of choices that organisations have when considering change;
- appreciate how organisations can influence their circumstances to align them with their preferred way of working.

MINI CASE STUDY 12.1

Why the Walkman did not give rise to the Sony iPod

A decade ago Apple launched the iPod with the slogan "1,000 songs in your pocket". The claim encapsulated seamless integration of content and delivery. The launch of the iPod mattered not just for what it did, but for what it implied for the future.

The age of the personal computer was ending, giving way to an era in which a single handheld device would be the gateway to every service that could be delivered electronically. So why didn't Sony do it?

Mini case study 12.1 (*continued*)

The company created the Walkman, the analogue predecessor to the iPod. For a generation, Sony was the world's most successful consumer electronics company. It developed a vision of integration of devices and content long before Apple dreamt of going into the music business. The route Sony followed was acquisition. In 1987, Sony bought CBS records. Two years later the company purchased Columbia Pictures. Sony had seen the future. And it worked, but not for them. Apple went on to dominate the new markets, transforming itself from a computer company into both a leading consumer electronics company and a major retailer. Sony didn't even come close . . .

However, its failure is hardly unique. The acquisition of AOL by Time Warner is now notorious as possibly the worst merger in history, although Royal Bank of Scotland's purchase of the Dutch bank ABN Amro runs it close. As at Sony, Time Warner's vision of the future was correct. But, as at Sony, it didn't work for them. Amazon, a retailer, transformed the distribution of print media: just as Apple, a computer company, has transformed the distribution of audio-visual media. And paradoxically, Sony, which didn't have a book business, proved more effective in e-publishing than in exploiting new distribution systems for audio and video. AT&T saw in the 1980s that the emergence of computing and telecommunications would define the future of both industries. The vision was again well-founded. But the belief that the means of influencing that future was to buy a computer company was a preposterous misconception, and AT&T would play only a secondary role in the dramatic events that followed.

Narratives of industry evolution often represent fairy tales constructed by corporate financiers, or ambitious chief executives. They relentlessly seek rationale, however spurious, for the next deal. Remember the cradle-to-grave financial services business that would arise from the merger of Travelers and Citibank? Or the seamless home-to-destination service that would follow from United Air Lines' purchase of car hire and hotel businesses? But the narratives that were used as justification for the Sony or Time Warner or AT&T transactions were not fantasies. So why did they not come to pass?

The explanation can be found in Clayton Christiansen's analysis of the innovator's dilemma. Established companies in an industry are naturally resistant to disruptive innovation, which threatens their existing capabilities and cannibalises their existing products. A collection of all the businesses which might be transformed by disruptive innovation might at first sight appear to be a means of assembling the capabilities needed to manage change. In practice, it is a means of gathering together everyone who has an incentive to resist change. The executives of music companies, film studios and book publishers did not rush to embrace the opportunities offered by new channels of distribution. They saw these technological developments as threats to well established business models in which they had large personal and corporate investments. And they were right to think this.

So convergence was accomplished by groups such as Apple and Amazon, which had no similar vested interests to oppose change. These companies succeeded precisely because they were outsiders. Economic growth is held back by industries where established interests are so powerful that disruptive innovation can be staved off for ever.

Introduction

In Mini Case Study 12.1, John Kay argues that organisations such as Apple and Amazon have succeeded because their leaders had an ambitious, compelling and achievable vision of the future of their industries. Others, such as AOL and Royal Bank of Scotland, failed because their vision was faulty. However, there is a third group of organisations, such as Sony, whose vision was good but who failed to achieve it. According to Kay, such organisations appear to fail for two basic reasons. The first is that their history of success makes it difficult for them to overturn what they are and change radically. In effect, their forward trajectory is overly influenced by their backward trajectory. The second reason is that their ability to plan and manage change lets them down. They know where they want to be, but they just do not have the ability to get there. Obviously, the ability to identify and realise a sustainable future is crucial to any organisation's survival. It is equally obvious that it is not a simple or easily achieved process. The purpose of this and the next chapter is to examine how organisations can create visions, develop trajectories and implement change successfully.

As previous chapters have shown, while organisational change can be a complex, ambiguous and open-ended phenomenon, it can also be relatively straightforward with understandable and limited objectives. This in itself is not a new or radical finding – anyone who works in or studies organisations will have noted that change comes in a wide variety of shapes and sizes. It was argued in Chapter 11, however, that in order to cope with the wide variety of types of change, there is a need for a corresponding variety of approaches to strategy development and change management.

This point – the need to match types of change with appropriate approaches to managing change – is not as prominent in the literature on organisational change and behaviour as one might expect. As Parts 2 and 3 of the book showed, despite the widespread influence of Contingency Theory, the majority of writers and practitioners are committed to a 'one best way' approach to strategy and change. The call by Dunphy and Stace (1993) for a situational or contextual approach to these issues has been taken up by few others. Though there are writers on strategy, such as Mintzberg *et al* (1998a) and Whittington (1993), who identify the various approaches to strategy, in most cases they tend, eventually, to opt for one as their preferred approach. This is even more pronounced in the change literature, where there is a clear distinction between those who support the Planned approach (such as Cummings and Worley, 2009; and Gallos, 2006) and those who adhere to a more Emergent approach (such as Dawson, 2011; Pettigrew, 1997; and Weick, 2000).

Many of those arguing for their own favoured approach to strategy and change do so, either explicitly or implicitly, on the basis of their perception of the nature of the environment in which organisations operate. Those arguing for a Planned approach to strategy and/or change appear to assume that the environment is relatively stable, predictable and controllable. Those who take a more Emergent approach seem to operate on the assumption that the environment is turbulent, unpredictable and uncontrollable.

Furthermore, most writers seem to assume that the principal role of managers and the ultimate objective of strategy and change is to align or realign an organisation with its environment. In the preceding chapters, a case has been built for rejecting this argument and adopting a different stance. Rather than accepting the view that managers are prisoners of the circumstances in which their organisations operate or find themselves, it was argued that managers can and do exercise a considerable degree of choice. Even so, the scope and nature of the choices managers face and make are constrained by a range of external factors (national characteristics, the business environment and industry norms) and internal organisational characteristics (especially structure, culture, politics and managerial style). This argument goes much further than many by challenging the assumption that managers are in some way the passive agents of forces beyond their control, but it still leaves them as prisoners of circumstances – although the prison in this case is much roomier than many of the writers we have discussed would acknowledge.

The arguments in Chapters 5, 6 and 11 challenged even this definition of managerial choice. It was suggested that many of the constraints on choice are themselves amenable to managerial actions – in effect, organisations can influence or change the constraints under which they operate. This possibility was first suggested when examining Contingency Theory in Chapter 2; it was further developed in subsequent chapters and shown to be more than a possibility. In particular, some managers are even capable of reinventing their organisations or, as the postmodernists would have it, creating a preferable reality for them. As the case studies in previous chapters have illustrated, although some organisations do try to align and realign themselves with their environment, some also attempt to influence and restructure the environment and other constraints in their favour. This is one reason why organisations such as Apple and Dyson spend so much money on protecting their patents and – like McDonald's and Coca-Cola – on promoting their brands. Sometimes, by accident or design, success results in a reconfiguration of the accepted rules by which the industry in which they operate competes: Apple's iPhone is a prime example. In other instances, such as McDonald's brand recognition, success provides protection from rivals and prevents organisations being forced to undertake more radical internal upheavals.

Previous chapters have given detailed examples of organisations that have shaped their environments to fit their needs, and vice versa. For example, Oticon (Chapter 11) deliberately set out to change the basis on which it competed by reinventing itself as a service-based rather than a technology-driven organisation. Lacking the technological strength of its competitors, which was the accepted cornerstone of competition in its industry, it proposed to offer a superior level of service instead. By changing the rules of the game in its industry, Oticon hoped to steal a march on its competitors. At XYZ (Chapters 3 and 9), the new managing director sought to change the internal constraints in the company, in terms of its culture, management style and structure, in order to improve its performance and align it with the changing nature of the construction industry and the desires of its parent company. In essence, the new managing director was attempting to reinvent the company, based on more cooperative internal relationships, in order to create more stable relationships with customers and establish a less uncertain external environment.

So, as the case studies show, organisations can and do influence and change the constraints under which they operate. On the other hand, the case studies give some support to those, such as proponents of the realist perspective discussed in Chapter 4, who maintain that there are some types of constraint that are not amenable to change. This is illustrated by the Marconi example (Chapter 6), where no amount of effort on behalf of its management could alter the situation that they had borrowed too much money to buy overpriced assets at the top of the dotcom boom that, when the demand for telecoms equipment went into freefall, were found to be virtually worthless.

Therefore, we can see that organisations do have considerably more freedom of choice than many commentators on strategy and change would acknowledge, even if there are some constraints that appear beyond the scope of individual organisations to change. The implications of this wider perspective on managerial choice for the nature and focus of change management are significant. Change management need not be seen as a mechanism for achieving a specified and predicted outcome (the Planned approach). Nor need it be conceived of as a continuing process of aligning and realigning the organisation with its environment (the Emergent approach). Instead, as this chapter will explain, by linking managerial choice to the management of change, organisations can open up a much wider spectrum of options. These range from focusing on achieving radical internal change to align an organisation with its external constraints, doing the same in an attempt to restructure such constraints, to influencing or changing external constraints in order to avoid internal upheavals. In such a situation, not only are managers trying to make sense of their situation for themselves and others but they are also seeking to construct a more favourable environment as well.

Building on this insight into managerial choice, the next section in this chapter will present an overview of the Choice Management–Change Management model for understanding and implementing organisational change. This is followed by a detailed description of two of the three processes in the model: the choice process and the trajectory process, with the third component of the model, the change process, being discussed in detail in the next chapter.

The Choice Management–Change Management model

The Choice Management–Change Management model in Figure 12.1 demonstrates that organisational change can be viewed as the product of three interdependent and iterative organisational processes:

- **The choice process** – which is concerned with the nature, scope and focus of organisational decision-making.
- **The trajectory process** – which relates to an organisation's past and future direction and is seen as the outcome of its vision, purpose and future objectives.
- **The change process** – which covers approaches to, mechanisms for achieving, and outcomes of change.

These processes are interdependent and iterative: as Figure 12.2 shows, the change process is an integral part of the trajectory process and this, in turn, is a vital part of the choice process. Also, within each of these processes there are a group of elements, or forces, which interact, clash with and influence each other in subtle and complex ways. For example, after careful consideration of the information available to them (which may be limited or even misleading), the senior managers of an organisation may make choices which shape its strategic priorities. These priorities will shape its 'deliberate' strategy, which will identify and require the organisation to make certain specified changes if the strategy is to be realised. However, as explained in Chapter 6, Mintzberg (1978) argues that day-to-day responses to unexpected events will lead to 'emergent' changes that were not part of the organisation's deliberate strategy, which will reshape the strategy, sometimes very significantly. In turn, this will influence the choices senior managers face.

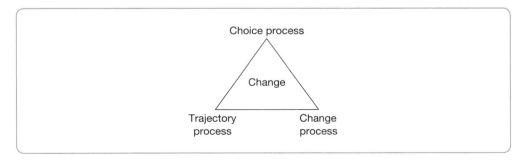

Figure 12.1 The Choice Management–Change Management model

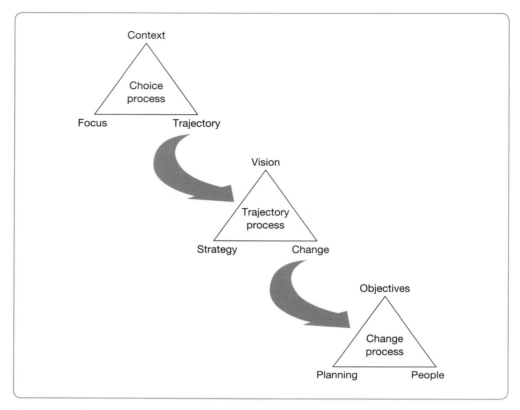

Figure 12.2 Choice and change processes

This is why these three processes are both interdependent and iterative; none of these three processes exists in isolation or independently from the others, and just as choices made by senior managers will affect intended changes, so the actual changes that take place may require senior managers to review and alter their original choices. It is this interaction of elements or forces, especially the clash between the 'deliberate' change it wants to make and the 'emergent' changes it does make, which prevents decision-making and change management from being a totally, or even predominantly, rational–mechanical process, and ensures that they are based on subjective and imperfect judgement.

Chapter 11 presented the *framework for change*, which shows the main forms of change and how they relate to the main approaches to change. What it did not show is how organisations choose between the different forms and approaches to change. Figure 12.3 addresses this issue by relating the Choice Management–Change Management model to the framework for change. This shows that the choices regarding which type of changes to make and which approaches to change to adopt are influenced by all three of the processes shown in the Choice Management–Change Management model.

For example, an organisation operating in a rapidly changing context, where old ways of working are no longer seen as appropriate, is likely to focus on transformational change (Quadrants 1 and 2 of the framework). Whether it chooses to change its culture or its structure, and how these changes might be undertaken, will depend on other aspects of its context, such as its financial position, the pressure from stakeholders to change, its readiness

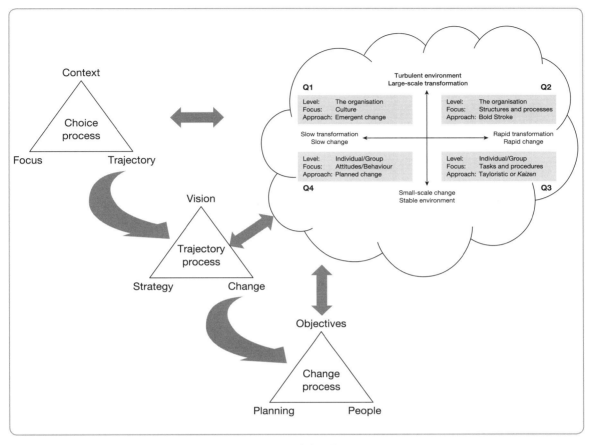

Figure 12.3 The Choice–Change model and the Framework for Change

for change and its preferred managerial style. These choices would also be influenced by the organisation's trajectory, both in terms of the radical nature of its future ambitions and the success of past attempts to make large-scale and radical changes, and its current change capabilities, especially its preferred approach to change.

Furthermore, because the relationship between choice and change is not one-way but reciprocal, the framework for change will also influence the choices an organisation makes. For example, even though it might want to change its culture, an organisation might decide that the timescale, complexity and the way it would have to be managed are beyond its capabilities and instead opt for the smaller scale and relatively quicker changes of Quadrants 3 and 4. Even here, managers might base their choice of whether to opt for Quadrant 3 change or Quadrant 4 change on the degree to which their organisation' underlying values align with their own managerial beliefs and values rather than what the context would ideally require. Consequently, though the organisation's circumstances might indicate that Quadrant 1 or 2 forms of radical change might be needed, the difficulty of achieving these, and thus the relative attractiveness of Quadrant 3 and 4 approaches, might incline them to choose more small-scale forms of change.

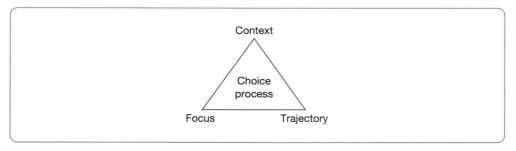

Figure 12.4 The choice process

Having clarified the relationship between the framework for change and the Choice Management–Change Management model, we will now move on to discuss the three processes in the model in more detail. This will not only show their complexity and interdependence but also provide a guide to putting the model into practice. The description of the change process in the next chapter will pay particular attention to the steps necessary to accomplish change successfully.

The choice process

As can be seen from Figure 12.4, the choice process comprises three elements:

● organisational context;
● focus of choice;
● organisational trajectory.

Organisational context

One of the standard prescriptions for successful organisations is that they should know their own strengths and weaknesses, their customers' needs and the nature of the environment in which they operate, in order to understand the options open to them. As the case studies show, however, many organisations appear only to begin collecting this sort of information when they are in trouble.

No one would suggest that assembling information on past, present and anticipated future performance is easy or that understanding the nature of the constraints faced by an organisation is simple. However, there are relatively well-established methods for benchmarking an organisation's performance against a range of internal and external comparators (Camp, 1989). There are also a number of tried-and-tested tools that organisations can use for gathering information on and evaluating the main internal constraints, such as structure, culture, politics and management style, and the main external constraints, such as national characteristics, industry and sector norms, and the business environment. Ideas and perspectives 12.1 and 12.2 show two of the tools most widely used by organisations for this purpose: the SWOT analysis and the PESTEL framework (Johnson *et al*, 2011; Lynch, 2006).

As in Phase 2 of the XYZ case study (Chapter 9), one advantage of adopting such well-understood tools, which are easily explained and do not require expert assistance, is that organisations can use them to promote openness and reduce, though probably not eliminate, political behaviour and conflict. Even so, some organisations will find that owing

IDEAS AND PERSPECTIVES 12.1

SWOT analysis

What is a SWOT analysis?	What does it do?
SWOT stands for: Strengths (internal) Weaknesses (internal) Opportunities (external) Threats (external)	A SWOT analysis enables managers to identify the key internal and external issues they need to take into account in order to understand the context in which the organisation operates. Also, by identifying key issues, it begins to focus managers on the areas where they need to make choices, and helps to identify some of the constraints and risks involved.

IDEAS AND PERSPECTIVES 12.2

PESTEL framework

What is the PESTEL framework?	What does it do?
PESTEL stands for: Political Economic Sociocultural Technological Environmental Legal	The PESTEL framework is a rigorous approach to identifying and understanding the main external environmental factors which affect an organisation. Like the SWOT analysis, it plays a role in focusing organisations on the choices open to them and the constraints and risks involved in these choices.

to the context in which they operate, teamwork, cooperation and openness are very difficult to achieve without first changing those factors which hinder or prevent these. Perhaps the prime consideration in this respect is the prevalent style of management. The issue of management style will be discussed in Chapter 14; however, as Ideas and perspectives 12.3 shows, different styles of management can have significantly different implications for the way managers see, run and change their organisations.

Though others can exert pressure, managers are really the only group who can initiate change, but will rarely (as a group) voluntarily adopt changes which adversely affect them (Pfeffer, 1992). It follows that, faced with a mismatch between their organisation and its environment, rather than pursuing an internal reorganisation that may involve changes in management style and personnel, some managers will ignore the pressures for change while others will seek realignment by influencing the environment.

An organisation's management style will also influence how and by whom information is gathered and discussed. If an accurate picture of an organisation's context is to be constructed, it will require the involvement of a wide range of people. Not only should this provide a robust basis for decision-making, it can also develop a sense of teamwork, cooperation and mutual understanding among those concerned. If only a few managers are involved, it is likely to result in a skewed and biased picture of the organisation. It should

---

IDEAS AND PERSPECTIVES 12.3

Styles of management

Strengths	Weaknesses
Traditionalist management	
● Practical common sense	
● Attentive to facts	● Makes snap decisions
● Systems focus	● Lacks responsibility for change
● Steady worker	● Poor at relationships
● Super-dependable	● Concerned with difficulties
● Realistic about timescales	
Catalyst management	
● Charisma and commitment to staff	● Can be drawn into pleasing others
● Communicates well	● Has difficulties with rules and conventions
● Comfortable with changing environment	● May spend too long on issues
● Comfortable with diversity	● Takes over problems and responsibilities
Visionary management	
● Strong on intellectual vision	● May be insensitive to others
● Creative and progressive	● Devalues others who are not intellectual
● Enjoys problem-solving	● Expects too much of people
● Outspoken	● Restless and easily bored

Source: From Maddock (1999: 40), based on Vinnecombe (1987).

---

also be recognised that no matter how rigorously information is collected, analysed and argued over, there will always be a large element of subjectivity in this process. This is why, as a number of writers have commented, one of the key tasks managers perform is 'sensemaking' (Weick, 1995). As Weick (1995: 13) explains:

> Sensemaking is about the ways people generate what they interpret. Jury deliberations, for example, result in a verdict. Once jurors have that verdict in hand, they look back to construct a plausible account of how they got there.

For managers in organisations, sensemaking is about understanding, interpreting and explaining their organisation's world for themselves and others in such a way that it provides a rationale and justification for past, present and future actions. Sensemaking is also the process by which managers attempt or can attempt to impose their view of reality on others. The Oticon case study (Chapter 11) is a prime example of where a CEO first made sense of the world for himself and then imposed this sense on others in such a way that it allowed the organisation to move successfully forward. Marconi (Chapter 6) is another example where a senior manager attempted to impose his 'sense' on others in order to justify and guide actions. In this case, however, the outcome was far from successful. Grint (2005: 1470–1) suggests:

> The context or situation is actively constructed by the leader, leaders, and/or decision-makers. In effect, leadership involves the social construction of the context that both legitimates a particular form of action and constitutes the world in the process. If that rendering of the context is successful – for there are usually contending and competing renditions – the newly constituted context then limits the alternatives available such that those involved begin to act differently.

Focus of choice

Many organisations can find themselves in a situation where they appear to be constantly reacting to events and indulging in 'fire-fighting' rather than being proactive. Certainly, this seems to be the current position in the music industry, as the case study in Chapter 4 shows. One of the characteristics of successful sensemaking (i.e. context construction) is that, as Grint remarks, it 'limits the alternatives available' and focuses managers' attention on a narrow range of short-, medium- and long-term issues. Some of these will relate to the organisation's performance, while others may be more concerned with building or developing particular competences or technologies. In some instances, the issues may be of passing interest only, while in other instances they may be fundamental to the organisation's survival. Certainly, in most situations, organisations will in one way or another focus on aligning themselves with or even influencing or changing the constraints under which they operate.

How an organisation decides upon which issues to focus, and whether this is done in a collaborative and coordinated way (as was the case at XYZ in Chapters 3 and 9), or in a disjointed and fractious way (as was the case at GK Printers in Chapter 8), is a fundamental factor in any organisation's decision-making process. Certainly, the received wisdom is that a concerted and coordinated approach, which focuses upon a small number of issues at any one time, is more effective than a fragmented one (Kay, 1993; Senge, 1990). It is interesting to note that Weick (1995) appears to consider the Japanese approach to decision-making as an example of sensemaking in action. This may explain why Japanese organisations are particularly good at identifying the key aspects of their strategy on which they need to focus.

The technique many Japanese companies use is called *Hoshin Kanri* (*see* Ideas and perspectives 12.4). *Hoshin Kanri*, or Policy Deployment as it is often termed in the West, was developed in Japan to communicate a company's policy, goals and objectives throughout its hierarchy in a structured and consistent fashion (Lee and Dale, 2003). One of its main benefits is that it focuses attention on key activities for success. It is a process that is undertaken annually to ensure that everyone in the company is conscious of and addressing the same objectives, and that these inform actions and decision-making at all levels in the organisation (Akao, 1991).

Organisational trajectory

An organisation's trajectory or direction is shaped by its past actions and future objectives and strategies. As such it provides a guide or framework within which to judge the acceptability,

IDEAS AND PERSPECTIVES 12.4

Hoshin Kanri

The word *hoshin* can be broken into two parts. The literal translation of *ho* is *direction*. The literal translation of *shin* is *needle*, so the word *hoshin* could translate into *direction needle* or the English equivalent of *compass*. The word *kanri* can also be broken into two parts. The first part, *kan*, translates into control or channeling. The second part, *ri*, translates into reason or logic. Taken altogether, *hoshin kanri* means management and control of the organization's direction needle or focus.

Source: Total Quality Engineering Inc (2003).

relevance or urgency of issues, concerns and proposed actions. The trajectory process encompasses the determination of and interplay between an organisation's vision, strategies and approach to change. This can be seen from Volvo's strong commitment to Job Design, which arose from the interplay of events over more than 20 years (Karlsson, 1996).

The concept of trajectory comprises not only an organisation's 'memory' of past events but also its intent in terms of future ones. For some organisations, such as Nissan (Chapter 1) with its commitment to partnership working, the trajectory will be clear and unambiguous, unless there is some major disturbance which throws into question past practice. In others, like Marconi (Chapter 6), making sense of past events and agreeing proposals for future actions can be the subject of much dispute, uncertainty and bitterness. Certainly, after its crash, one would assume that there was much rewriting of history in the Marconi boardroom, especially with regard to the supposed failure of GEC and the attractiveness of telecoms. Similarly, in the light of the 2008 banking crisis, one might assume that many financial service organisations, and their shareholders, have encountered a great deal of trouble and disagreement in trying to make sense of their past, present and future direction. A recent example was the on, then rapidly off, merger between BAE Systems and EADS (Mini Case Study 6.4 in Chapter 6). In 2006, BAE sold its large shareholding in EADS, saying it wanted to concentrate on defence contracts and that an involvement in civil aviation was not part of its core business. 'In 2012, the company proposed a merger with EADS, owner of Airbus, emphasising the complementarity of defence with civil aviation' (Kay, 2012: 11). The failure of the merger has left BAE Systems with an unclear trajectory and struggling to find a strategy (Lex Column, 2013).

Some organisations will deliberately and consciously attempt to plot their trajectory in minute detail, such as PCI (Chapter 7), while others, such as Oticon (Chapter 11), may adopt a more global and distant set of objectives from which their trajectory emerges. Whatever the approach, as Mintzberg (1994: 25) observes:

> Few, if any, strategies can be purely deliberate, and few can be purely emergent. One suggests no learning, the other, no control. All real-world strategies need to mix these in some way – to attempt to control without stopping the learning.

So an organisation's trajectory can be seen as a blend of, or clash between, the deliberate and emergent elements of its strategy (*see* Figure 12.5). Whether or not this blend or clash produces the intended or expected outcomes for the organisation appears to depend partly on the quality of its sensemaking and partly on the degree of control it can exert, or chooses to exert, over events. Furthermore, as the case studies show, it is also dependent on an organisation's ability to learn from, deal with and take advantage of unexpected events as they emerge. For Oticon and XYZ, the ability to learn and successfully move on was crucial. For Marconi, the inability to do so was disastrous. It is the interplay between the interpretation of past actions and future intent coupled to the ability of organisations to shape developing events to their advantage that makes decision-making so complex.

Each of the three elements of the choice process, context, focus and trajectory, is complex in itself, but they also interact with each other in an intricate and unpredictable way. An organisation's trajectory, whether it is seen as successful or not, can influence both the focus of its decision-making, and the context within which the organisation operates. Likewise, the context provides a framework within which the trajectory is developed. Similarly, the focus of choice will influence which aspect of the organisation's context its trajectory will be directed towards, not only in the short term but also in the medium and long term.

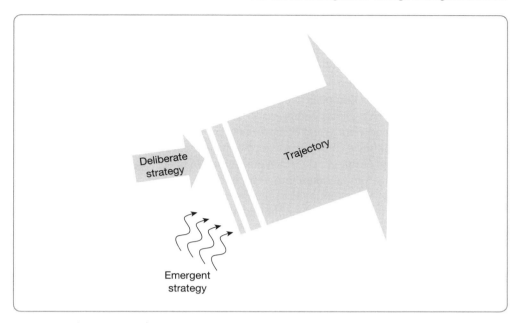

Figure 12.5 Organisational trajectory

Source: Adapted from Patterns in strategy formation, *Management Science* 24(9), p. 13 (Mintzberg H. 1978), Reprinted by permission, Copyright (1978), The Institute for Operations Research and the Management Sciences (INFORMS), 5521 Research Park Drive, Suite 200, Catonsville, MD 21228 USA.

Decision-making is a complex and multifaceted process. One reason for this is the type of decisions that have to be addressed when organisations deal with major questions. Rollinson (2002) maintains that decisions can be classed on a spectrum that runs from 'bounded' to 'unbounded' (*see* Figure 12.6). Bounded decisions are usually small, have relatively easily defined parameters, and tend to be relatively separable from the environment or context in which they arise. A typical example might be the purchase of a tablet computer. In a relatively speedy and accurate manner, a purchaser can determine what they want from a computer, calculate how much they can afford to spend, gather information on competing products and choose the one that best meets their needs for the price they are prepared to pay.

However, unbounded decisions usually concern large and important issues, have difficult-to-define parameters, are ambiguous and are intertwined with other issues and factors

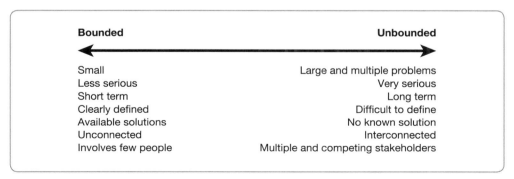

Figure 12.6 Types of decision

Source: Adapted from Rollinson (2002: 254).

in the environment or context in which they arise. An obvious example of an unbounded decision is the question of global warming. Even getting key stakeholders such as governments and large corporations to admit that there is a question to be addressed has been a major problem. More problematic still is getting agreement on what causes it, how to tackle it, what the priorities are, what the timescale for action is and who should pay. Similarly, the complexity of the European Union's economic woes, and its 'glacial decision-making process', arise from the fact that it comprises 27 very different countries each with its own very different economic, political and cultural concerns (Buiter, 2013: 24). Even before policy-makers can start building a consensus over what measures are necessary to tackle the European Union's economic problems, they face the herculean task of identifying and exploring all the factors which need to be taken into account. Though most of the major strategic issues facing an organisation are not on the same scale as global warming or the European Union's finances, they do tend to lie at the unbounded rather than bounded end of the spectrum.

Given the unbounded nature of strategic decisions, it is not surprising, as the models of decision-making described in Ideas and perspectives 12.5 illustrate, that managers are less

IDEAS AND PERSPECTIVES 12.5

Decision-making models

Model	Assumptions
The Rational Choice model of decision-making	<ul><li>Decision-makers have knowledge of all possible alternative solutions.</li><li>They have complete knowledge of the consequences of all these alternatives.</li><li>They have a robust set of criteria for evaluating these alternatives.</li><li>They have unlimited resources, including time, money and abilities.</li><li>They follow a systematic and orderly sequence of decision steps.</li></ul>
The Bounded Rationality model of decision-making	<ul><li>Decision-makers do not have complete knowledge. They rely on hunches and intuition.</li><li>Decision-makers do not have fixed and consistent preferences.</li><li>Decision-makers do not have unlimited resources.</li><li>An optimal solution may not exist or even be necessary.</li><li>Decision-makers do not optimise or seek a solution that maximises the expected benefits.</li><li>They 'satisfice' – seek a solution or decision option which is 'good enough' rather than ideal.</li><li>They do follow a systematic and orderly sequence of steps.</li></ul>
The Garbage Can model of decision-making	<ul><li>Decisions involve four elements: problems, solutions, participants and choice opportunities.</li><li>Some decisions will only be made when all four elements come together.</li><li>Political motives can lead to these elements being manipulated.</li><li>Decision-making is volume-sensitive – managers cannot be everywhere at once or deal with all issues at once.</li><li>As the number of problems increases, decision opportunities decrease.</li><li>Novel problems are likely to attract more attention than mundane ones.</li><li>Decision-makers do not follow an orderly sequence of steps.</li><li>Chance plays a large part in what decisions get made and when.</li></ul>

Source: Adapted from Rollinson (2002).

rational and more haphazard in their approach to decision-making than they themselves would often openly acknowledge. As the case studies in this book show, and as writers have pointed out for many years, there is a tendency for managers to 'muddle through' rather than attempt an exhaustive and exhausting examination of all the available options (Lindblom, 1968). Nor is it surprising that some managers prefer 'fire-fighting' to tackling fundamental issues (Burnes, 1991) – at least the objective is immediate and clear, and a favourable outcome can be achieved (though it is often short-lived).

Appreciating the complexity of decision-making also casts the Japanese *ringi* system (discussed in Chapter 3) in a favourable light. Only by an exhaustive analysis of the issue concerned and the options available is the most appropriate decision likely to be arrived at. Moreover, the *ringi* system is usually carried out within the framework of a strong corporate vision and clear strategies for its pursuit, rendering decisions less 'unbounded', thus making it easier to identify which choices and actions are appropriate. According to Heath and Heath (2013), the basis of good decision-making is to ensure that decisions are framed in such a way that they are wide enough to include information or options that need to be considered, but not so wide that decision-makers become paralysed in the face of an avalanche of information. Japanese companies achieve this delicate balance by creating a strategic frame of reference which allows them to explore only those possibilities and issues which are in harmony with their vision, strategy and intent. In this way, the entire choice process is simplified and made more achievable.

Japanese companies have shown themselves to be masters of developing visions and strategies that not only make them successful but also, and not incidentally, reduce the uncertainty in their environment, alter the basis of competition in their favour, and narrow the focus of decision-making (Hamel and Prahalad, 1989). The result is that though the choice process remains complex, not only does it have a greater degree of consistency between the elements and people involved but it is also more focused in the range of issues and decisions required.

It is clear that while the choice process is uncertain, complex and time-consuming, there are approaches that do reduce these factors and can make the process more transparent and effective. Even so, the degree of transparency and the efficacy of the choice process are heavily influenced by an organisation's ability to turn choices into workable strategies and to turn strategies into successful actions. The success of these, in turn, will influence future choices. In order to understand the choice process further, we shall now examine the trajectory process, followed, in the next chapter, by the change process.

The trajectory process

As shown by Figure 12.7, like the choice process, the trajectory process comprises three elements:

- organisational vision;
- organisational strategy;
- organisational change.

Vision

As described in Chapter 7, a great many organisations now use scenario-building and 'visioning' techniques (Rigby and Bilodeau, 2011). The purpose of these techniques is to

Figure 12.7 The trajectory process

generate different organisational futures, or realities, in order to select the one that seems most favourable or appropriate. The case of Konnopke's Imbiss in Chapter 8 shows that not all organisations have or need visions, and the case of Marconi (Chapter 6) shows that not all visions lead to success. Nevertheless, the concept of organisations driving themselves forward by creating an ambitious vision (or intent or scenario) of where they wish to be in the long term has become 'one of the most popular yet least understood practices in management' (Cummings and Worley, 2001: 159). Its ubiquitousness has also provoked increasing levels of cynicism (Alvesson and Spicer, 2012; Collins, 1998; Watson, 1994). The argument, in brief, for visions is that previous attempts to plan the future have either fallen foul of the difficulty of accurately translating past trends into future projections, or have not been ambitious enough because they have allowed future plans to be constrained by present resources (Collins and Porras, 1997; Hamel and Prahalad, 1989). The process of developing an organisation's vision attempts to overcome this by encouraging senior managers to think freely, without considering present resource constraints, about possible futures for their organisation in the long term. In a recent review of the literature, O'Connell *et al* (2011: 103) concluded:

> Vision impacts organizational performance, group effectiveness and growth in entrepreneurial firms. It can create the spark that lifts organizations beyond the mundane and can build both staff and customer satisfaction.

Vision-building can help organisations to produce very ambitious objectives, such as Honda's declaration in the 1960s (when it was barely more than a motorcycle producer little known outside Japan) that it wanted 'to become the second Ford'. As the Marconi case shows, however, the possession of an ambitious vision is, by itself, no guarantee of success, though the rigour with which a vision is developed may help to overcome or avoid some of the more obvious pitfalls. Though vision statements vary enormously, O'Connell *et al* (2011) found that they tend to have three common attributes: they are goal-orientated; they describe how the organisation intends to conduct its business; and they identify the type of environment that would best enable staff to achieve the vision. These attributes can be seen in Cummings and Huse's (1989) guidelines for constructing a vision (Ideas and perspectives 12.6).

Vision-building is almost always led by senior managers, whose personal values play a key role in shaping the vision. Certainly, this was the case with Oticon (Chapter 11). But they cannot build the vision alone; they have to 'negotiate' with other stakeholders in order to create a shared view of the future (Zaccaro and Banks, 2001). This process can, and in some cases does, eventually encompass everyone in the organisation. This co-creation

IDEAS AND PERSPECTIVES 12.6

Constructing a vision

The four elements of a vision

1. **Mission**. This states the organisation's major strategic purpose or reason for existing. It can indicate such factors as products, markets and core competencies.

2. **Valued outcomes**. Visions about desired futures often include specific performance and human outcomes the organisation would like to achieve. These can include types of behaviour and levels of skill as well as more traditional outcomes such as turnover and profit. These valued outcomes can serve as goals for the change process and standards for assessing progress.

3. **Valued conditions**. This element of creating a vision involves specifying what the organisation should look like to achieve the valued outcomes. These valued conditions help to define a desired future state towards which change activity should move. Valued conditions can include issues relating to structure, culture, openness and managerial style as well as external issues such as relations with customers and suppliers.

4. **Mid-point goals**. Mission and vision statements are by nature quite general and usually need to be fleshed out by identifying more concrete mid-point goals. These represent desirable organisational conditions but lie between the current state and the desired future state. Mid-point goals are clearer and more detailed than desired future states, and thus, they provide more concrete and manageable steps and benchmarks for change.

Source: Cummings and Huse (1989).

perspective sees 'the emergence of vision as a dance among multiple partners with senior leaders playing a key role in the choreography' (O'Connell *et al*, 2011: 106). To sum up, the creation of visions is an iterative and negotiated process whereby options are identified, an initial vision is created, and the gap between this and the present circumstances is identified. Then the organisation considers its strategic options to bridge the gap, and in so doing refines the vision. This refining process serves partly to ensure that the vision is discussed widely within the organisation, and to gain employees' commitment to its objectives, thus using the vision as a motivating and guiding force for the organisation. Over time, by this process of revisiting and refining the vision, loose and intangible ideas become transformed into an achievable vision with concrete medium-term goals that people can relate to and pursue. In terms of achievability, Baum *et al* (1998) identify seven attributes of effective visions: brevity; clarity; abstractness; challenge; future orientation; stability; and desirability or the ability to inspire.

The organisational vision can best be described as a beacon shining from a faraway hillside at night that guides travellers to their destination. Travellers can usually see only a few feet ahead but are prevented from getting lost by the beacon. Occasionally the traveller will have to make a detour, or sometimes even reverse course, but this is done in the certain knowledge that they still know where it is that they are travelling to. The concept of the beacon is a useful analogy, in that it highlights one of the main differences between vision-building and other forms of long-range planning. Normally it is only the leadership of an organisation that has a clear view of where the organisation is going in the long term. The vision, like the beacon, should shine clearly for everyone in the organisation to see, so that they can all know where they are heading for, and use it to judge the appropriateness of their actions.

By constructing a vision in this manner, the organisation not only has a picture of what it wishes to become but also some concrete targets to aim for. At Oticon, its vision of becoming a knowledge-based organisation sprang from the mind of its CEO, Lars Kolind. But, to give it flesh and to be able to construct his 'disorganised organisation' required the involvement of everyone else in the organisation. It was an iterative process of trial and error. Above all, it was a process of experimentation. He and they knew how they wanted to operate, what they wanted to achieve, but the actual details had to be worked out.

The Marconi vision, meanwhile, seemed both to start and end with two senior managers. The extent to which they required the commitment and understanding of others, as opposed to their compliance, appears to be small. Also, unlike Kolind, they seemed unable to adapt their strategy to save their vision. When the downturn in demand for telecoms equipment became evident to other companies, which took action to protect themselves, Marconi did not. Instead, it continued its strategy of selling profitable companies and borrowing money to buy ones which fitted its vision but whose viability diminished with the decline in demand for telecoms equipment. The point is that visions (and components of visions) identify the intent, and mid-point goals are then needed to help identify a way forward. As the vision is implemented, these goals will periodically have to be renewed and revisited in the light of changing circumstances, usually within the context of the vision, as was the case with Oticon. As the Marconi example shows, however, the possibility always exists that changing circumstances, or the process of implementation, can raise serious questions about the viability of the vision itself. It is through the development of strategy that visions are implemented, brought to life and, if necessary, changed.

Strategy

In the context of a vision, strategy can be defined as a coherent or consistent stream of actions which an organisation takes or has taken to move towards its vision (*see* Chapters 6 and 7). This stream of actions can be centrally planned and driven, they can be delegated and distributed throughout the organisation, and they can be either conscious actions in pursuit of the vision, or unconscious or emergent ones resulting from past patterns of decisions or resource allocations, or from current responses to problems and opportunities. In reality, as Figure 12.5 illustrates, an organisation's strategy tends to be a combination of, and be pursued through, a mixture of formal and informal plans and planned and unplanned actions.

Chapter 7 showed that formal strategies usually cover marketing, product development, manufacturing, personnel, purchasing, finance, information technology and quality. The characteristics of conscious strategies are that they generally look 5 years or more ahead, but contain firm and detailed plans for only the next 12 to 18 months (because changing circumstances usually prevent most companies from being firm about their intentions for any longer than this). These strategies are put together in one strategic plan that is, usually, formally reviewed annually, but is frequently reviewed informally and when major and unexpected events occur. Because strategies are not ends in themselves but means to an end (the vision), they should by necessity be both flexible and pragmatic. They should be constructed and pursued only to the extent that they facilitate the pursuit of the vision. Indeed, even when their strategies appear to fail, the more successful organisations seem to have an innate ability to turn failure into success. Pascale (1984) documented the disastrous entry of Honda into the US motorcycle market in 1959. It tried to sell the wrong bikes, to the wrong customers at wrong time of year, yet by 1966 it had 63 per cent of the market. How did it do this? It learned fast, was not afraid to change a losing strategy, and acted fast.

We can see something similar to the Honda experience in Mini Case Study 12.2. In 1995, Microsoft launched MSN in order to become an internet content provider. It quickly saw

MINI CASE STUDY 12.2

The development of MSN

Microsoft's direct connection to the customer

Sometimes it seems that even when Microsoft loses, it wins. . . . Take MSN, the company's internet portal. This unit of Microsoft has lost money ever since it was set up . . . But to Microsoft that does not really matter. The real point of MSN is not to make money at all. Instead, the division serves a peculiar mixture of purposes including research and development, testing the company's software, advertising its services and even product distribution. What is more, these capabilities set Microsoft apart from its rivals.

In the next phase of Microsoft's plans, its .Net vision, in which software becomes a service delivered over the internet – a vision on which Bill Gates admits he has 'bet the company' – the site will become even more vital. MSN is quietly emerging as the centrepiece of the whole .Net strategy. This is a far cry from the original MSN, named for the Microsoft Network. The website was initially set up as a media play in 1995, the early days of the dotcom boom. It produced content including news and sport, horoscopes, and e-commerce offers. For a while it looked as if Microsoft had serious ambitions in media.

That phase did not last long. The career of Geoff Sutton, now Managing Director of MSN in the UK, illustrates the change of heart. Mr Sutton was originally brought into the company in 1997 to run a team of journalists writing news for the portal. In 1998, the news team was scrapped and Mr Sutton found himself working in a software company.

'It quickly became apparent that Microsoft shouldn't try to be a content player,' he says. Judy Gibbons, vice-president of MSN for EMEA [Europe, the Middle East and Africa], agrees: 'Microsoft is a software company, that's what we do, and we shouldn't stray away from our core competences.'

With its foray into content, however, Microsoft had managed to gather up something very useful: an audience. Through MSN, Microsoft found it had a direct line with consumers that it had never experienced before. People visited the site regularly . . . in the process being exposed to Microsoft branding and services. Today, MSN is one of the world's top three internet destinations, along with Yahoo and AOL, receiving some 270m visitors a month, while its Hotmail has 110m users.

Once this kind of connection with customers was in place, all kinds of things became possible. Microsoft could start marketing services to its customers direct. It could even start giving them software direct, over the internet. This interactive and instant relationship with customers even gave Microsoft a testing ground for new software products, as people could be asked to download beta software, software still in the process of development, from the site for comments and suggestions.

The .Net strategy neatly takes advantage of all these aspects of Microsoft's portal. Users will plug into a web of services running across a wide variety of devices, including PCs, handheld computers, phones, television sets, and even games consoles. 'MSN will provide the entry point for consumers to .Net services, as you will be able to go up to the site and sign on and get access to all the pieces you want,' says Ms Gibbons.

Microsoft estimates that the market for such services could run into trillions of dollars by 2010, in what it terms the 'digital decade'. No other internet portal can yet offer anything similar. And no other software company boasts its own internet portal through which to dispense rival versions of these web services. The huge MSN user base forms a ready-made audience to which Microsoft can market its services with ease. The fact that all the visitors attracted to the portal by this range of services can be 'monetised' by charging advertisers to market them is just the icing on the cake. If MSN can reach break-even from these advertising dollars, so much the better, if not, it scarcely matters.

that this was not where its core competences lay, but what it also saw was that MSN gave it a direct link to an enormous customer base. The original strategy of adding content provision to its software activities was abandoned in favour of a much more ambitious strategy of delivering its services over the internet directly to customers. It is also something that contributes directly to Microsoft's vision of remaining the world's dominant software company.

Strategy is not an end in itself; its purpose is to allow an organisation to pursue and achieve its vision, which is the ultimate measure of whether a strategy is working or not. If not, then, following the examples of Honda and Microsoft, successful companies change their strategies. Unfortunately, when companies – like Marconi – continue to pursue a failing strategy, the results can be disastrous. One of the strengths of anchoring a strategy to an overarching vision is that the vision creates a general awareness of how to act or respond to opportunities and threats, or successes and failures. Honda's vision was to establish a dominant presence in the US motorcycle market, not to sell a particular type of bike. Microsoft's intention was to use the internet to reinforce its position as the world's dominant software company, rather than see it as a money-generating venture.

From this perspective, one way of viewing strategy is to see it as a series of links in a chain which stretch from the present to the indeterminate future where the vision lies. Each link in the chain represents particular strategies or groups of decisions that organisations pursue to move themselves forward, in the light of both their eventual target and the prevailing circumstances of the time. The links (strategies) are continually having to be forged and reforged (or to use Mintzberg's (1987) term, 'crafted') over time as events develop and circumstances change. For Microsoft, MSN was a link forged for one purpose which became reforged for another purpose but with the same end in sight: to bolster Microsoft's dominance of the software market. So an organisation's strategy is likely to comprise both deliberate (planned) and emergent (unplanned) elements – the exact balance being determined by the circumstances of the particular organisation in question rather than any intrinsic merit of either the deliberate or emergent approaches to strategy.

One final point: it follows from this that organisations do not need to be able to see all the links in the strategic chain: merely those that will guide them over the next few years. Nor do they need to dictate centrally or identify in detail what should be done and when. Instead, they need to establish both a climate of understanding and a general willingness to pursue certain courses of action, as the opportunity arises or circumstances necessitate. It is only when a course of action is pursued, however, that organisations begin to change and move towards their vision.

Change

Just as an organisation's trajectory is both an important element of the choice process and a process in its own right, the same applies to change. The change process is discussed extensively in the next chapter, but in the context of the trajectory process it is necessary to note that, though visions and strategies can be crucial in shaping the life of organisations, it is only when some facet of the organisation is changed or changes that visions and strategies advance from being mere possibilities to become reality. This is also a two-way street. On the one hand, visions and strategies shape and direct change; they indicate what needs to change and where. They also create the conditions and climate within which change takes place. On the other hand, because visions and strategies become reality only through the actions of the organisation, it is these changes, these actions, which shape visions and strategies.

In summary, we can see that the trajectory process, while playing a key role in shaping choice, is also itself a complex process comprising vision, strategy and change. Though it is difficult to conceive of any organisation that does not possess some elements of all three, the degree to which they are held in common or are consistent with each other or are part of a conscious effort clearly varies. Partly this relates to the circumstances of the organisation. Under conditions of stability and predictability, even without prompting from senior managers, it is much easier for people to make sense of their situation and develop a common view of how their organisation should operate, what its future should be and what changes need to be made. In rapidly changing circumstances, however, where certainties and fixed points of reference are few and far between, a common understanding is unlikely to arise automatically. Even if a common understanding does exist in such situations, it is likely to be outmoded and inappropriate. In such cases, one of the key roles of senior managers is to make sense of the situation for themselves and others by constructing a new vision which can unite the organisation in a common cause. Such a vision should reduce uncertainty, make sense of what is happening, and create a broad understanding of what needs doing, and how. For many organisations, the merit of this approach is not only that it makes change easier but that it also allows staff to judge for themselves what changes need to be made and what approach to adopt. In order to explore this further, we shall next examine the change process itself.

Conclusions

In presenting the Choice Management–Change Management model, this chapter has sought to merge the theory and practice of strategy development and change management as presented in Chapters 6–11. In doing so, it has also drawn on many of the arguments and insights into the behaviour, operation and rationality of organisations presented in Chapters 1–5. The Choice Management–Change Management model comprises three interrelated organisational processes: the choice process, the trajectory process and the change process (*see* Figure 12.2). It was also shown how this model relates to the framework for change presented in Chapter 11 (*see* Figure 12.3).

In examining the choice process, it was argued that choice is an uncertain, complex and time-consuming process, but that there are approaches that do reduce these factors and can make the process more transparent and effective. Even so, the degree of transparency and the efficacy of the choice process are heavily influenced by an organisation's ability to turn choices into workable strategies and to turn strategies into successful actions. This led on to the discussion of the trajectory process which, while playing a key role in shaping choice, is also itself a complex process comprising vision, strategy and change. A key factor in the alignment of these is the last of these factors – change. Though change is driven by an organisation's vision and strategy, change also helps to shape these. Indeed, it is only when change takes place that decisions mean anything, visions cease to be words on paper and strategies start to be enacted. This will be explored in detail in the next chapter, which is devoted to the change process.

Short discussion topics

The purpose of these is to enable students to check and reflect on the topics. The discussions should last for no more than 5–10 minutes. Depending on the length of the lecture, there could be one, two or three such discussions in a session. The following are five suggested topics which address issues raised in this chapter:

1. What are the main elements of the choice process?

2. How does a SWOT analysis differ from a PESTEL analysis?

3. What are the key features of the trajectory process?

4. What are the key factors an organisation needs to take into account when constructing a vision for itself?

5. What is *Hoshin Kanri*?

Class debates

The purpose of class debates is to enable students to explore a topic in depth by setting up a 'for and against' debate. The class can be split into two and one half asked to research the 'for' case and the other 'against' case. Individuals can then be chosen at random to introduce their side of the debate. Alternatively, two individuals for each side can be told in advance that they will be introducing the debate. The length of such debates depends on the time available, the size of the class and their enthusiasm for the topic. However, less than 30 minutes is probably too short and more than 60 minutes probably too long. The following are three suggested topics which address issues raised in this chapter:

1. The only real ability senior managers need is the ability to recognise and make choices.

2. Vision statements are not worth the paper they are written on and should be replaced with clear instructions and objectives from senior managers.

3. Organisations need to concentrate on the future and ignore anything that happened the past.

Essay questions

1. In Mini Case Study 12.1, John Kay argues that even companies who have an achievable vision for their future fail because they are prisoners of their past trajectory. To what extent and why do you agree with Kay's argument?

2. Use the Choice–Change model to assess one of the case studies in this book or another organisation of your choice.

Suggested further reading

Baum, JR, Locke, EA and Kirkpatrick, SA (1998) A longitudinal study of the relation of vision and vision communication to venture growth in entrepreneurial firms. *Journal of Applied Psychology*, 83(1), 43–54.

O'Connell, D, Hickerson, K and Pillutla, A (2011) Organizational visioning: an integrative review. *Group & Organization Management*, 36(1) 103–25.

Wilson, I (1992) Realising the power of strategic vision. *Long Range Planning*, 25(5), 18–28.
These three articles provide a good review of the theory and practice of vision-building.

Rollinson, D (2008) *Organisational Behaviour and Analysis* (4th edition). Financial Times Pearson: Harlow.
Rollinson's book provides a good review of the different approaches to decision-making.

CASE STUDY 12

Samsung: dynamic leadership and a long-term vision?

South Korea's largest company has leapfrogged US and Japanese rivals to become the biggest technology group by sales – but its lack of creativity and low profit margins explain its modest valuation. Reading this on the move? If so, the chances are you are using an Apple or a Samsung Electronics device. By the time you have finished (we give you 10 minutes), the two companies will have sold almost 5,000 smartphones. Everyone knows about Apple. The iPhone has been flying off the shelves since 2007. But it is currently being outsold by Samsung. Of every five smartphones sold by the two companies, three will be a Samsung. Most impressively, South Korea's largest company began to gain traction in this market only in 2010. That was also the year it became the world's biggest technology company by sales, leapfrogging the likes of Hewlett-Packard and Hitachi.

Proving it has arrived, Samsung is now facing the ultimate accolade (and nightmare): battling Apple in a Californian courtroom over claims its success is based on copying Apple's designs. Investors stand to learn whether Samsung is a new breed of deep-pocketed, creatively minded Asian giant genuinely challenging Apple, or merely a more successful version – for now – of the likes of Sony, Sharp or Panasonic, Japan's one-time cutting-edge electronics giants whose decade of decline is only worsening.

If California's technology giants began with student geeks in basements, the Asian equivalent started off with more basic products, if a little more organised. Samsung began making transistor radios in 1969. As late as the mid-1990s it was still so stuck in a mid-market mass-production mindset that Lee Kun-hee, son of the founder, and chairman since 1987, made a bonfire of 150,000 mobile phones and

threatened to do so again unless workers did better. This is a company with dynamic leadership and a long-term vision. But sending $50 million of inventory up in smoke is hardly a sign that Samsung worries much about shareholders. Welcome to Korea's *chaebol*, the linked groups of companies that dominate business life, of which Samsung is the biggest. Companies named Samsung, or linked to it, make up about a quarter of Seoul's Kospi benchmark index.

If there is a high-tech acronym, the likelihood is that Samsung dominates it. In addition to its top spot as a smartphone seller, it is number one in D-Ram (memory chips for PCs) and in LCD (liquid crystal display) TVs, and is joint leader in NAND flash memory (for mobiles and tablets). Samsung has come a long way from middle-of-the-range mobiles, for sure. But this sort of leadership costs serious money to maintain – before even factoring in the ever-shorter product cycles and the need to be consistently developing the next big thing. Samsung labours hard at this. About a quarter of its 220,000 employees work in research and development, and it has been the second-biggest filer of tech patents in the US, behind IBM, for each of the past six years (take note, Apple). In addition to R&D spending, each year Samsung announces a capital expenditure budget so large it appears partly designed to terrify rivals into throwing in the towel. This year it has already spent $12 billion and is only just over halfway through its planned budget. Capex has accounted for about 11 per cent of sales per year for the past five, trailing Intel's spending by only 3 percentage points. Tellingly, Sony – whose capex has been declining over a decade of persistent restructuring – uses just 5 per cent of sales on capex.

Case study 12 (*continued*)

Apple taking on Samsung is not just fascinating because the world's two biggest tech companies are facing off in public, but because the outcome could lead to one of the messiest business divorces. This is because the two, as well as competing, depend heavily on each other. Samsung estimates that it provides about a quarter of all the components inside the iPhone and the iPad, including the much talked-about retina display and the processor and memory chips. Apple is also Samsung's single biggest customer. Neither can walk away from this relationship quickly, however nasty the court battle gets – and this is only the latest of many. For investors, the case may also help answer whether Samsung is simply a clever copier or a genuinely innovative firm. History suggests the former; its name means three stars, which is widely seen as a challenge to Mitsubishi's three diamonds logo. Certainly, Samsung's earliest years were spent in the shadow of Japan's electronic giants, such as Sony, Panasonic and Sharp. The truth is probably somewhere between Samsung being an Apple and a copier. It is an early adopter – but rarely a first-mover – and a fast innovator. Samsung will not change the game like Apple, but it will be the company that rapidly deploys its resources and execution ability to produce the iterative innovations now driving new phone models, such as large, sharper screens and more powerful chips.

But any company wanting to be the biggest, fastest follower requires its management to make consistently brilliant bets on the next big thing. In Samsung's case, this means investors have to trust that the Lee family will make the right calls. Granted, Mr Lee has an impressive record from his quarter-century at the helm. Company lore says he personally made the critical decisions on which particular semiconductors would become indispensable. So far, investors have been rewarded for their trust. Over the past five years, the Samsung stock has returned 125 per cent. While that pales next to Apple's 360 per cent, it is great versus the flat performance of the Kospi or the S&P 500. Mr Lee is now 70, however. His son and heir apparent, Jay Lee, is currently chief operating officer. Can he spot the next big thing as his father has? Who knows?

The group has pledged $21 billion of investment by 2020 in five promising areas: solar cells, rechargeable batteries for hybrid cars, LED technology, biopharmaceuticals and medical equipment. Each involves Samsung Electronics, or a unit it is heavily invested in. That gives another five businesses investors must get to grips with – assuming they work out. Still, having the nerve to try new areas shows that Samsung is not relying on blockbuster smartphones to carry the company forward. The Lees are also clearly signalling there will be no change in the group's essential model. They identify a potentially game-changing industry then produce innovations, rather than taking the risk of trying to change the game itself. That makes Samsung one of the world's best at what it does but not a world leader, like Google or Apple. Investors understand the difference and Samsung is priced accordingly.

Share price performance: Though shareholders are not a priority at Apple, Sony or Samsung Electronics, Apple has delivered extraordinarily high returns on the back of great products while investors are depressed by Sony's four straight years of losses, made worse by the strength of the yen. Samsung is unlikely to stay in the middle of the road forever.

 Source: Lex in depth: Samsung, *The Financial Times*, 09/08/2012, p. 5 (Hughes J. and Kirk S.), © *The Financial Times Limited* (2012). All Rights Reserved.

Questions

Using the evidence in the Samsung case study, and other publicly available material, address the following questions:

1. To what extent and why do you agree with the statement that Samsung has 'dynamic leadership and a long-term vision'?

2. What evidence is there from Samsung's trajectory that it really is 'a new breed of deep-pocketed, creatively minded Asian giant genuinely challenging Apple'?

3. If you had £20 million which you could invest only in either Samsung or Apple, and you could not withdraw the money for 20 years after it had been invested, which of the two companies would you invest in? Explain and justify your selection.

Organisational change and managerial choice

Part 2: The change process

Learning objectives

After studying this chapter, you should be able to:

- understand the change process element of the Choice Management–Change Management model;
- appreciate how the change process relates to the choice and trajectory processes;
- understand the importance of behavioural change in achieving successful organisational change;
- establish objectives and outcomes, plan change and manage the people side of the change process.

MINI CASE STUDY 13.1

How an outsider institutes change

In 1998, Gary Loveman left teaching at Harvard Business School to take up the role of chief operating officer at Harrah's Entertainment (now Caesars Entertainment), the US casino operator. Mr Loveman, who had earlier undertaken some consulting and training for Harrah's, was offered the job by Phil Satre, the chief executive, who did not tell his board or other senior executives about the appointment beforehand.

The challenge. Mr Loveman faced resistance from senior, experienced leaders who thought they should

have the job for which he seemed manifestly unqualified. He had to gain credibility and support while leading Harrah's transition to a more marketing-focused company that achieved better financial results. As Mr Loveman says, "in Las Vegas, you could go to a 40-year-old casino that looked like a riverboat or go a few blocks down the street and play the identical games at the Bellagio, one of the most beautiful properties in the world".

The strategy. In order to overcome internal resistance, Mr Loveman initiated the following: He identified

---

Mini case study 13.1 (*continued*)

critical relationships that just had to work and spent time and effort with those people. One was the chief financial officer, a talented executive who thought he should have had the COO job. Mr Loveman spent time every day in the CFO's office. He sought his advice on decisions, kept him informed about what he was doing and how things were going, and made sure he and other senior executives knew that if Harrah's became more successful financially, their stock options would be worth much more. Any mistakes were admitted to Mr Satre and others straight away. This built trust.

Mr Loveman stayed out of any operational details or areas, such as buildings, where he had no special expertise. Harrah's recruited new people who could help turn it into an analytical marketing organisation. Mr Loveman enthused people with his energy – intellectual and physical – when he visited casino locations and talked to employees at all levels. Mr Satre, a very popular figure in the company, used his social capital to help Mr Loveman gain credibility.

Mr Loveman also signalled that Harrah's had to operate at a higher level of intensity. So executives held planning meetings at night and weekends to show that the company was being run differently. He also made sure he explained what was required when he met people at all levels of the organisation: what each of them could do on their next eight-hour shift to increase the chances that a customer would

come back more often. Harrah's rewarded employees whose units recorded higher levels of customer satisfaction, regardless of financial performance, to signal that customer focus mattered.

Underpinning all this, Harrah's implemented data analytics so it could identify its best customers – it found that 26 per cent of visitors generated 82 per cent of revenues, for instance – and focus on making them feel special: this included making sure they did not wait in queues to check in, and that they were visited by chefs in the dining room.

The outcome. Harrah's financial performance improved, with the stock price rising from about $16 when Mr Loveman initiated his changes to $90 when Harrah's went private in a leveraged buyout in 2007. Mr Loveman became CEO in 2003 and is now regarded as one of the best executives in the gaming industry.

Key lessons. First, pay attention to relationships that matter, and build trust even among people who do not like you. Second, focus on aspects where you can add value, and keep your agenda simple: Mr Loveman sometimes asks people to list the Ten Commandments in order to show that even ten is a lot to remember and that performance comes from focusing on the few areas of a business that are actually key to its success. Last, build an evidence-based decision-making culture, as conventional wisdom about what drives performance is often wrong.

Source: Jeffrey Pfeffer, *Financial Times*, 19 February 2013, p. 12, © The Financial Times Limited (2013). All Rights Reserved.

Introduction

The previous chapter introduced the Choice Management–Change Management model, and discussed the decision process and the trajectory process components of the model. This chapter will complete the examination of the model by examining the change process element. In so doing, particular attention is paid to the behavioural aspects of change because, recalling Chapter 8, 'all organizational problems are fundamentally problems involving human interactions and processes' (Schein, 1988: 12). The chapter concludes by arguing that though organisations may choose to restructure their internal operations and practices in order to align them with the external circumstances they face, they can also choose to change or modify external and internal conditions and constraints in order to avoid extensive internal upheaval and/or to bring the constraints into line with their preferred *modus operandi*. Whatever choices are made, it is the role of managers consciously to explore and identify all the available options, however improbable they seem, rather than assuming that they have no, or only limited, choice in the matter.

The importance of the behavioural side of change can be seen in Mini Case Study 13.1. When Gary Loveman became Chief Operating Officer at Harrah's Entertainment, it would have been very easy for him to follow the tried-and-tested path to improving financial performance: cut costs, make people work harder and sack those who complained. Instead, he recognised that the key to success was to focus on getting the 'human side' of the business right. He treated his senior colleagues as allies and not competitors, recognising that a dysfunctional senior management team leads to a dysfunctional organisation. He also made sure that he met and encouraged staff at all levels. Loveman appreciated that it is difficult for employees to make customers 'feel special' if they do not feel valued themselves. Above all, Loveman recognised that though change needs to be well managed and well organised, at its heart it is about people changing their behaviour. If the appropriate behavioural change is not achieved, then the change will fail.

It may seem like something of an exaggeration to say that the success or failure of any or all change initiatives depend on achieving the required behavioural change, but this does seem to be the case. Consider the nine types of change shown in Figure 11.1 in Chapter 11. These range from changes aimed at individuals, such as IT training, to changes aimed at the entire system, such as organisational restructuring. In terms of the former, an example of this would be an organisation upgrading from Windows 7 to Windows 8 and providing staff with training to use the new operating system. The success of the IT training, and the upgrade itself, would be judged by how many people changed their behaviour to stop using Windows 7 and started using Windows 8. Many people would see this as straightforward technical change; after all, once Windows 7 has been removed from a person's computer and replaced with Windows 8, they have no alternative but to use it. However, this is not the case. It is possible in Windows 8 to change the user interface to be more like Windows 7. If people choose to do this, the full benefits of Windows 8 will not be realised and the organisation would have wasted its money in upgrading its computer system. The lesson from this is that IT training should not be treated merely as a technical exercise of showing people how to use the new system, but as a process of behavioural change that convinces users to adopt the new system.

With IT training, it is clear that its purpose is to persuade the individuals to change their behaviour, and it is clear what this change involves – to stop using Windows 7 and to start using Windows 8. However, can the same perspective be applied to organisational restructuring? Take the case of an organisation that has a bureaucratic structure and wants to move to a loosely coupled organic network. As Morgan (1989: 64) points out, with a bureaucratic structure: 'The organization has tried to codify all important operational principles, and is run in accordance with these principles.' The behaviour expected of staff is to obey the rules and procedures without question or deviation. An organic network, however, according to Morgan (1989: 67):

> changes from month to month as different ideas and products come on line, and as the core organization experiments with different partners. The firm is really a system of firms – an open-ended system of ideas and activities, rather than an entity with a clear structure and definable boundary.

The behaviour expected of staff in such an organisation is to do what is necessary to get the job done, which is likely to be different from day to day and situation to situation.

If an organisation decides to move from a bureaucratic to an organic structure, redrawing its organisation chart is relatively easy, as might be moving staff into new groups and issuing new job descriptions. However, changing staff behaviour from obeying the rules with no discretion to making up the rules up as they go along is a very different issue. As Makin and Cox (2004: 34) put it, we are motivated to behave as we do at work because we receive a combination of rewards and punishments:

1. We receive something nice.
2. Something nasty is taken away.
3. Something nice is taken away.
4. We receive something nasty.

For example, we tend to report for work each day because we receive something *nice* – a salary. We tend not to stay at home all day because we would receive something *nasty* – dismissal from our job.

When organisations attempt to change staff behaviour, though, they do not always identify or seek to modify the *'nice-nasty'* combination of motivators. For example, if an organisation wants to move from individual to team working, it needs to understand the factors which promoted individual rather than group effort. These might be a combination of a bonus scheme which rewarded individual effort and initiative, career development, praise from managers and admiration/envy from colleagues. If, under the teamwork regime, all that changes is that managers praise group effort rather individual effort and other motivators remain unchanged, it should come as no surprise that staff resist team work. However, the source of the resistance does not lie with the individual, but stems from the organisation's formal and informal reward systems. In effect, as was argued in Chapter 8, resistance tends to arise from a lack of alignment between the behaviours/changes the organisation wishes to promote and the combination *'nice-nasty'* signals it sends to staff. Nonetheless, McMillan and Connor (2005: 231) also point out:

> Individuals are motivated to change by a wide variety of factors. Being aware of the potentially negative consequences of behavior is not enough to prevent that behavior being performed and being aware of the potential beneficial consequences of a behavior is not enough to ensure action. . . . Self-empowerment techniques, which include participatory learning . . . are more likely to succeed as they encourage individuals to become personally involved and develop self-regulatory strategies to increase their likelihood of success.

Therefore, in examining the change process, special attention will be paid to approaches and techniques for understanding and changing behaviour.

The change process

Change can be viewed as a one-off event, an exception to the normal running of an organisation and, therefore, something to be dealt with on an issue-by-issue basis as it arises. Yet some organisations see change not as an exception but as the norm, a continuous process that forms part of the organisation's day-to-day activities. As the case studies in this book have shown, where change is seen as the exception, such as in GK (Chapter 8), organisations tend to have difficulty in choosing the most appropriate approach and there also tends to be no structured, or even informal, procedure for capturing the lessons from one change project and making them available for future projects. Each change is seen as a unique

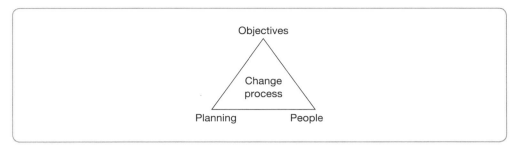

Figure 13.1 The change process

event, and seems to involve an element of reinventing the wheel as the organisation struggles to determine how best to deal with it. However, in organisations where change is seen as a continuous process, such as XYZ (Chapters 3 and 9), they appear to be able not only to treat each project as a learning opportunity but to capture this learning and pass it on. This allows them to select the most appropriate approach for each situation. In such organisations, not only is change seen as an everyday event but the management of it is also seen as a core capability that needs to be developed and in which all staff need to become competent.

As Figure 13.1 shows, the change process itself, like the choice and trajectory processes, comprises three interlinked elements:

● objectives and outcomes;

● planning the change; and

● people.

Objectives and outcomes

It is a widely held view that some 70 per cent of change efforts end in failure (Beer and Nohria, 2000; Burnes, 2011a; Rogers *et al*, 2006; Senturia *et al*, 2008). Many reasons for this have been given, including complacency, poor communication, weak leadership, lack of value alignment, inappropriate culture and political infighting (Burnes and Jackson, 2011; Huczynski and Buchanan, 2001; Hoag *et al*, 2002; Kotter, 1996). In terms of this last point, the detrimental effect of political behaviour was highlighted in Chapter 5. Because change often affects the distribution of power and resources in an organisation, it is, therefore, an inherently political process which can be undermined by sectional interests rather than driven by organisational needs.

Though it is difficult to envisage a situation where political interests are not present, Burnes (1988) suggested an approach to assessing the need for and type of change that attempts to make the process of establishing objectives and outcomes more rigorous and open. Openness and rigour not only make it harder to disguise political considerations, they also allow assumptions regarding the merits (or lack of them) of particular options to be tested. Burnes's approach has four elements – the trigger, the remit, the assessment team and the assessment.

The trigger

In Chapter 8, it was argued that the only legitimate reason why an organisation should embark upon change is to improve its effectiveness. Organisations should only investigate change (other than relatively minor projects that can be easily accommodated) for one of the following reasons:

- The company's vision or strategy highlights the need for change or improved performance.

- Current performance or operation indicates that severe problems or concerns exist, or, because of changing circumstances, are likely to arise in the future.

- Suggestions or opportunities arise (either from the area concerned or elsewhere) that potentially offer significant benefits to the organisation.

If one or more of the above arises, then this should trigger the organisation to assess the case for change, which leads to the next phase.

The remit

This should state clearly the reasons for the assessment, its objectives and timescale, and who should be involved and consulted. The remit should stress the need to focus as much on the behavioural aspects of the change process as the technical and financial considerations involved. In addition, it must make clear that those who will carry out the assessment must look at all options rather than merely considering one or two alternatives. Organisations need to be clear who draws up such remits and who has the final say on the assessment team's recommendations. As shown by Burnes and Weekes (1989), this responsibility is often unclear. In traditional organisations, this responsibility would lie with senior managers. In many of today's organisations, the responsibility for such activities is often devolved. There is usually a requirement to inform senior managers of change, however, and certain types of major change remain the responsibility of senior managers. Also, where change affects more than one area or activity, coordination between areas will be essential. The important point is that there must be clarity and agreement about who has the responsibility and authority to initiate change before an assessment begins.

The assessment team

These are the people who will assess the need for change. In most cases, this should be done by a multi-disciplinary team consisting of representatives from the area or areas affected (both managers and staff), specialist staff (e.g. finance, technical and personnel), and, where appropriate, a change specialist, either an internal facilitator or an external consultant who is a specialist in organisational change. It may also require the involvement of senior managers. Furthermore, just as it is important to have the appropriate blend of skills and authority, it is also important to have the appropriate blend of personalities or what Belbin (1996) refers to as 'team roles' (*see* Ideas and perspective 13.1). Though one might not necessarily expect to see all these roles represented in an assessment team, it is important for the team not to be unbalanced. For example, completer finishers are crucial to ensuring that an assessment team completes its task. However, a team composed of only completer finishers would lack creativity, enthusiasm and coordination, and would be likely to take too narrow and detailed a perspective on its remit. Consequently, in assembling the assessment team, it is important to pay attention to personalities as well as other attributes. To this end, as well as identifying the nine roles, Belbin (1996) also develops the 'self-perception inventory' questionnaire, which is designed to allow individuals to identify their team roles.

> ## IDEAS AND PERSPECTIVES 13.1
>
> ### Belbin's nine team roles
>
> - **Plant** – creative, imaginative, unorthodox. Solves difficult problems, but can be a poor communicator.
> - **Resource investigator** – extrovert, enthusiastic, exploratory. Explores opportunities. Develops contacts but can lose focus.
> - **Coordinator** – mature, confident, a good chairperson. Clarifies goals, promotes decision-making. Can end up delegating everything.
> - **Shaper** – dynamic, challenging. Has drive and courage to overcome obstacles. Too many shapers leads to conflict.
> - **Monitor evaluator** – sober, strategic, discerning. Sees all options. Can become cynical and demotivating.
> - **Teamworker** – cooperative, mild, perceptive, diplomatic. Listens, builds, averts friction. Can lack decisiveness.
> - **Implementer** – disciplined, reliable, conservative. Turns ideas into practical action. Can become locked into a particular trajectory.
> - **Completer Finisher** – painstaking, conscientious, anxious. Searches out errors and omissions, delivers on time. Not good at delegating and can become fixated on minor details.
> - **Specialist** – single-minded, self-starting, dedicated. Provides knowledge and skill in rare supply. Can become disinterested in anything outside their area of expertise.
>
> *Source*: Belbin (1996).

The assessment

The first task of the assessment team is to review and if necessary clarify or amend its remit. Only then can it begin the assessment, which should comprise the following four steps:

1. **Clarification of the problem or opportunity**. This is achieved by gathering information, especially from those involved. In some situations it might be found that the problem or opportunity is redefined, or does not exist, or can be dealt with easily by those most closely concerned. If so, this is reported back and probably no further action needs to be taken. If the clarification reveals that a significant problem or opportunity does exist, then the remaining steps need to be completed. The change readiness audit carried out at XYZ was aimed at clarifying whether the proposed restructuring of the organisation would deliver the benefits senior managers expected (*see* Case Study 9, Chapter 9). The outcome of this was that staff felt that re-organisation would be beneficial, which allowed XYZ to move onto the next stage – appraising alternative solutions.

2. **Investigate alternative solutions**. A wide-ranging examination should take place to establish the range of possible solutions. These should be tested against an agreed list of criteria covering costs and benefits, in order to eliminate those solutions that are clearly inapplicable and to highlight those that appear to offer the greatest benefit. Companies will usually seek to define benefits in monetary terms. It should be recognised, however,

that not all changes, particularly those of a behavioural or strategic nature, like Oticon's restructuring and XYZ's move to teamworking, can be assessed on purely financial criteria. In any case, changes rarely have single benefits. For example, a change in technology that brings financial benefits may also offer opportunities to increase teamworking and to develop the skill and knowledge base of the organisation. Therefore, organisations need to find ways of defining and assessing non-monetary benefits. Also, where there are benefits there are usually disbenefits. Where new skills are gained, old ones are discarded. For example, Nissan's partnership approach to customer–supplier relations has many benefits, but it can also lead to a loss of negotiating and bargaining skills. Similarly, moves to greater teamworking, such as at XYZ, can undermine the authority of line managers and middle managers. If such disbenefits are to result from change, it is better to recognise this in advance and prepare for them rather than finding out later when the damage is done. This then leads on to the next step.

3. **Feedback**. The definition of the problem or opportunity and the range of possible solutions should be discussed with interested or affected parties, particularly those from whom information was collected in the first place. This helps to counter the tendency to fit solutions to problems; it makes it more difficult for people to promote their favoured solution regardless of its suitability; and it helps to prepare people for any changes that do take place. In addition, the response to feedback can provide an important source of information on the advantages and disadvantages of the possible solutions on offer and, thus, it helps to establish the criteria for selecting the preferred solution or solutions. Evidence of the effectiveness of this approach can be seen in Stages 2 and 3 of the XYZ case study at the end of Chapter 9. In the XYZ case, not only did this help managers to test and improve their preferred option, it also helped to prepare staff for the change of structure.

4. **Recommendations and decision**. The team should present their recommendations in a form that clearly defines the problem or opportunity, identifies the range of solutions, establishes the criteria for selection and makes recommendations. These recommendations should include not only the type of change but also the mechanics and timescale for making such changes and the resource implications, as well as performance targets for the new operation. Crucially, they should identify the nature of any behavioural change and the importance of it for success.

This then leaves those responsible for making the final decision in a position to assess, modify, defer or reject the assessment team's recommendations in the light of the vision and strategic objectives of the organisation.

Indeed, some change programmes and projects are so complex that it is possible to judge their worth only in relation to an organisation's long-term intent. For example, in the 1990s, one of the UK's largest biscuit makers established an assessment team to determine whether the company should build a new factory solely dedicated to the production of chocolate biscuits (the biggest growth area for the company). The team recommended that one should be built next door to an existing factory in the north of England. The Board accepted the recommendation for the new factory but decided, because of its long-term ambitions to develop in Europe, to locate the new factory in France. This decision could be justified as being in the long-term interests of the company, but even so, such decisions are more an act of faith than a racing certainty, though managers may choose to present them as closer to the latter in order to garner support. For example, the biscuit company were assuming the strategic advantage of location would outweigh the inevitable operational issues of setting

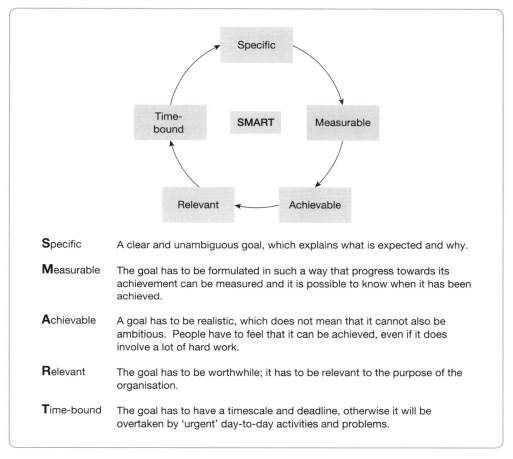

Specific	A clear and unambiguous goal, which explains what is expected and why.
Measurable	The goal has to be formulated in such a way that progress towards its achievement can be measured and it is possible to know when it has been achieved.
Achievable	A goal has to be realistic, which does not mean that it cannot also be ambitious. People have to feel that it can be achieved, even if it does involve a lot of hard work.
Relevant	The goal has to be worthwhile; it has to be relevant to the purpose of the organisation.
Time-bound	The goal has to have a timescale and deadline, otherwise it will be overtaken by 'urgent' day-to-day activities and problems.

Figure 13.2 The SMART framework for goal-setting

up what was, in effect, a new business in a country with a different language, different culture and different employment laws and practices.

Once an organisation has accepted the case for change, it is for senior managers to ensure that the goal or objective of the change is specified as clearly as possible. Goal-setting theory is relatively new, having emerged in the 1960s from the management by objectives movement. There is substantial evidence of the benefits both to organisations and employees of adopting a rigorous and systematic approach to setting their change objectives (Day and Tosey, 2011; Locke and Latham, 2006). One of the most widely used approaches to goal-setting is the SMART framework (*see* Figure 13.2). SMART has become a popular approach for establishing clear and attainable objectives for organisations, groups and individuals (Day and Tosey, 2011). Ideas and perspectives 13.2 shows how SMART can be applied to becoming healthier. From this we can see why some change initiatives might be flawed from the start. If an organisation decided it wanted to change its culture, it would need to specify what new behaviours it wanted from staff. If it did not or could not do this, then it would fail the SMART test and would be likely to fail.

Although a robust goal is the foundation for any change initiative, the change still has to be planned and implemented.

IDEAS AND PERSPECTIVES 13.2

The SMART way to improving your health

Consider a person who decides as their New Year's resolution to become healthier. If they were to apply the SMART framework to this goal, they would find that 'healthier' is not Specific – it is not a clear and unambiguous goal. Therefore, it fails the SMART test; if it is not Specific, it is not Measurable, and if it cannot be measured, how can you tell if you have attained your objective or not? What is required is to reformulate the objective in such a way that it passes the SMART test.

For an increasing number of people, the key health issue is to lose weight. In order to decide how much weight they needed to lose, they might use the Body Mass Index (BMI), which looks at a person's weight in relation to their height. A BMI of less than 18.5 is considered to be underweight, 18.5–24.9 indicates a healthy weight, 25–29.9 is overweight and 30 or more is obese. There are many websites which provide BMI weight calculators (see www.nhs.uk, for example), so finding your BMI is straightforward. Once this has been obtained, the next step is to calculate how much weight needs to be lost to achieve a healthy BMI, which gives the person a weight loss goal. We can now apply the SMART framework test to the goal:

Specific   The goal is to lose a quantifiable amount of weight, therefore, it is specific.

Measurable   All that is required is a pair of scales and for the person to stand on them every day. Therefore, the goal is measurable.

Achievable   Though the goal may be specific and measurable, it may not be attainable. Supposing a person is 20 kilos overweight and decides to set a weight loss target of 1 kilo per month. They may find that this is too little over too long a period of time for them to see any appreciable benefit. The result might be that their motivation ebbs and the weight loss regime fails. Similarly, if they decide they want to lose all the 20 kilos in one month, this may be too ambitious and, once again, the weight loss regime fails. This is why it is important to check the initial goal against all elements of the SMART framework, to ensure that it is not just specific but also achievable. This also shows the iterative nature of the SMART framework.

Relevant   If a person is concerned about their health and feels that losing weight will address that concern, then they will see it as worthwhile. However, if they see it as something that is imposed on them by someone else, say a doctor, or feel pressured by social norms to look thin, they may feel less committed to a weight-loss regime.

Time-bound   As mentioned when looking at attainability, the timescale is important; too short, and it may be impossible to achieve; too long, and it loses any sense of urgency. However, the time factor also covers the issue of when to start. It is probably not a good idea to try to diet while one is on holiday or during Christmas or other festivals.

What this illustrates is that the SMART framework provides a useful way of way of checking the robustness of goals.

Planning the change

Whether the need for change is driven by an organisation's strategy or emerges from its day-to-day activities, once it has been established that it should take place and what form it should take, it is then necessary to plan the change. Just as assessing the need for change and setting goals are iterative processes, so too is planning. It is rarely a straightforward, step-by-step process and those involved will find it necessary occasionally to backtrack and check or change earlier decisions, or even question the original goal. As the Japanese have shown, time spent getting it right at the planning stage saves far more time at the implementation stage (*see* the Nissan case in Chapter 1 and the section on Japan in Chapter 3).

A key factor which impacts on planning is the approach to change adopted. Chapter 11 showed that there are many different approaches to change and that their appropriateness depends on what is to be changed, and the management style and culture of the organisation. For example, an organisation with a bureaucratic culture and a directive management style is unlikely to find it easy to adopt a participative approach to change; an organisation with a collaborative culture and management style may find a directive approach difficult to undertake (*see* the case study on *Organisational change: The role of values* at the end of this chapter). Such issues have, of course, to be balanced against what are seen as the most appropriate ways of managing specific types of change, as was discussed in Chapter 11.

Small-scale and relatively technical or structural changes can usually be planned and executed relatively quickly, and may not require extensive consultation or the involvement of the staff affected. Similarly, changes which are isolated to one part of the organisation and seen as 'inevitable' may also be relatively straightforward. However, unless the need for radical change is already accepted, as it was at Oticon, to adopt a rapid-change, low-involvement approach to larger-scale changes, particularly where people's attitudes and behaviours are the prime object of the change process, can bring with it a high risk of failure. Therefore, as the two XYZ examples show (Chapters 3 and 9), planning and execution, and consequent development, in such cases can be extensive, span hierarchical levels and horizontal processes and include a high degree of involvement. For these reasons, the success of large-scale change will depend, to a significant extent, on the involvement and commitment of all those concerned with and affected by the change.

Consequently, the range of change situations and approaches, and the nature of the organisation embarking upon them, need to be borne in mind when considering the following six interrelated activities that make up the planning and change process.

1 Establishing a change management team

In order to maintain continuity, the team should include some, if not all, of those responsible for the original assessment of the need for change. It will usually also have a greater user input, especially at the implementation stage. For example, in 1997, the UK government asked the Inland Revenue to undertake a review as to whether the Contributions Agency, then a semi-autonomous body, should become part of the Inland Revenue. The man who led the assessment team, and who recommended that the Contributions Agency should become part of the Inland Revenue, was also made responsible for leading the change management team that had to implement his recommendation. Similarly, in the case of Phase 2 of the changes at XYZ, all the original assessment team became members of the change management team, along with a much wider spectrum of middle and line managers. For large change projects, it is usual to establish sub-groups responsible for discrete elements of the change programme. These will generally comprise those most closely affected by the changes, both managers and staff. Their role is to handle the day-to-day implementation issues.

It must be recognised that all the people in the change management team, and its sub-groups, are in effect 'change agents'. In addition, as was the case at XYZ, change specialists should be involved, i.e. people whose primary input is their experience in managing change. The role of change agents – discussed in Chapter 8 – is not just a technical one concerned with establishing plans and ordering their implementation. Change agents need a wide range of skills, not least of which is what Buchanan and Boddy (1992: 27) refer to as the ability to deploy 'backstage activity':

> 'Backstaging' is concerned with the exercise of 'power skills', with 'intervening in political and cultural systems', with influencing and negotiating and selling, and with 'managing meaning'.

Change agents also need the ability to deal with the unanticipated events. 'Expect the unexpected' might well be the motto of most change agents. In discussing the role of change agents in Chapter 8, the article on 'Grace, magic and miracles' by Lichtenstein (1997) was cited. This explains that while a structured approach to change is necessary, it is often, by itself, not sufficient to ensure success. Success, Lichtenstein (1997: 393) argues, also requires change agents to have the ability and experience to recognise and take advantage of 'intuitive, unexpected, and serendipitous' situations. So in choosing members of the change management team, it is necessary to have the right blend of skills for the change being undertaken, including the ability to deal with the unexpected. It should also have the right blend of personalities, as discussed above.

2 Management structures

Because larger change projects, especially organisational transitions, are wide-ranging, have multiple objectives and can involve a high degree of uncertainty, existing control and reporting systems are unlikely to be adequate for managing them. For example, the more that a change project challenges existing power relations and resource allocation procedures, the more it is likely to encounter managerial resistance. In such cases, unless the change management team has a direct line to senior managers or the CEO, and their public support, the change process is likely to become bogged down or even abandoned. For example, one of the main reasons why regional managers did not block the organisational changes at XYZ was because the managing director was closely involved in the change process. He was aware that the regional managers might try to block changes that threatened their interests and standing, and he was prepared to take action if they did so, and he made sure the regional managers knew this. Where senior managers are less directly involved, effective reporting and management structures need to be put in place in advance in order to provide direction, support, resources, and where necessary decisive interventions.

The Midshires case in Chapter 10 shows that serious problems, threatening the entire change project, can arise when a change agent is in effect abandoned by senior managers.

3 Activity planning

Beckhard and Harris (1987: 70–1) refer to this as a process of 'getting from here to there'. They state: 'The activity plan is the road map for the change effort, so it is critical that it is realistic, effective and clear.' Ideas and perspectives 13.3 describes Beckhard and Harris's five key characteristics of an effective activity plan.

Activity planning involves constructing a schedule for the change programme, citing the main activities and events that must occur if the transition is to be successful. In establishing the first two elements of an activity plan, i.e. relevance and specificity, those involved might find it helpful to use the SMART approach, described earlier. It must be recognised, though, that not all the elements of a large change programme can be planned in detail in advance.

> ## IDEAS AND PERSPECTIVES 13.3
>
> ### Beckhard and Harris's approach to activity planning
>
> The five characteristics of an effective activity plan:
>
> - **Relevance** – activities are clearly linked to the change goals and priorities.
> - **Specificity** – activities are clearly identified rather than broadly generalised.
> - **Integration** – the parts are closely connected.
> - **Chronology** – there is a logical sequence of events.
> - **Adaptability** – there are contingency plans for adjusting to unexpected forces.
>
> *Source*: Beckhard and Harris (1987: 72).

Such programmes are by their nature multi-level, multi-stage, can stretch over an extended time-frame, and can involve elements of backtracking and rethinking. Nonetheless, as a change programme proceeds, it becomes possible for successive levels and stages to become clearer and for plans to become more detailed. It follows that, in order to stay on course, activity planning should clearly identify and integrate key change events and stages and ensure they are linked to the organisation's change goals and priorities.

Activity planning should also gain top-management approval, should be cost-effective, and should remain adaptable as feedback is received during the change process. Activity planning therefore comprises the final and intermediate objectives, and ensures that where and when possible these are tied to a specific timetable in order to avoid uncertainty among those who have to carry out the changes.

4 Commitment planning

This involves identifying key people and groups whose commitment is needed, and deciding how to gain their support. Beckhard and Harris (1987: 92) observe:

> In any complex change process, there is a critical mass of individuals or groups whose active commitment is necessary to provide the energy for change to occur.

Designating someone as a key person is concerned less with their nominal position or level of authority in an organisation than with their ability to block or promote particular changes. This may be because they have power to dispense or withhold specific resources or information, or because, as Mini Case Study 13.2 shows, others look to them for guidance or leadership, even though they may have no formal role in this respect. The Midshires case in Chapter 10 is a graphic example of a change agent failing to get, or perhaps even to recognise the need for commitment. The case of XYZ (Chapters 3 and 9), meanwhile, is an example where the company recognised it needed to gain the commitment of key staff in planning and implementing change.

Ideas and perspectives 13.4 shows the main steps in developing a commitment plan. Beckhard and Harris (1987) note that even where the commitment of an individual or group is needed, it is not necessary to gain the same level of commitment from all. They identify three kinds of commitment:

MINI CASE STUDY 13.2

The importance of commitment

Getting rid of the bonus

Northern Engineering is a very efficient and progressive manufacturing company which has successfully introduced many Japanese techniques for improving its business. However, it did operate a shopfloor bonus system based on individual output. It recognised that this was detrimental to quality but felt that the workforce would strongly resist any effort to change it. Eventually though, the company decided it would offer the workforce a very tempting financial package to buy out the bonus. The operations director was the man responsible for selling the idea to the workforce. He did this through a series of presentations, to each of the company's three shifts.

The group he was most concerned about were the night shift. These were the people he seldom met and who had shown the least commitment to change in the past. The operations director described his experience with the night shift:

They work ten to six, four nights a week. I went to brief them at the beginning of their shift. The presentation took about 20 minutes and then

I opened it up for questions. All through my presentation, this big bloke on the front row had been staring at me with a disgruntled look on his face. When I finished he stood up and everybody looked at him in an expectant fashion. When he began talking, I thought, 'I'm sunk'. He said, 'It's the same as usual. You only see the bosses when they want to take something off you.' Others on the shift nodded in agreement at this. He then went on, 'Once they take the bonus off us, we won't get it back. Some might be OK, but others'll lose money. But, this is not a bad company, so I think we should give them a chance.' He sat down, nobody else said anything, and it was agreed, the bonus would go. I was totally flummoxed. The bloke's body language, his tone, his first words, all indicated that he was against it. I was very, very lucky; if he'd gone against the idea, I could see that everybody would have gone with him. What I learned that night was a very valuable lesson. The next time I have to talk to the night shift, I'll get hold of that bloke first and win him over.

IDEAS AND PERSPECTIVES 13.4

Beckhard and Harris's approach to commitment planning

A **commitment plan** is a strategy, described in a series of action steps, devised to secure the support of those [individuals and groups] which are vital to the change effort. The steps in developing a commitment plan are:

1. Identify target individuals or groups whose commitment is necessary.
2. Define the critical mass needed to ensure the effectiveness of the change.
3. Develop a plan for getting the commitment of the critical mass.
4. Develop a monitoring system to assess the progress.

Source: Beckhard and Harris (1987: 93).

Let it happen – i.e. do not obstruct the change.

Help it happen – i.e. participate in the change process.

Make it happen – i.e. drive the change.

For most kinds of change, success depends on winning the commitment of key staff. Without this support, it will be impossible to mobilise the energy necessary to start the change process and keep it moving to a successful conclusion. However, while most managers, with some encouragement, might be able to identify the critical mass, many would lack the skills and motivation to win them over. This is why the participation of experienced change agents, with the necessary 'backstage' expertise, is crucial to the change process.

5 Audits and post-audits

It is important to monitor progress and see to what extent objectives are being met. This allows plans to be modified in the light of experience. It also allows for opportunities to improve on the original objective to be identified or created. The more uncertain and unclear the change process, the greater the need for periodic review. After the change, or when a particular milestone has been passed, an audit or post-audit should be carried out (a) to establish that the objectives have really been met, and (b) to ascertain what lessons can be learned for future projects. In addition, periodic reviews give senior managers the chance to praise, support and encourage those carrying out the change.

One very useful tool in this respect is the Deming Cycle, also known as the PDCA Cycle (*see* Figure 13.3). This was developed by the American quality guru Edward Deming, but was first taken up and is now used extensively by the Japanese (*see* Chapter 3), and is one of the key components of their continuous improvement philosophy (Slack *et al*, 1998). At one level, it is a structured way of checking how much progress has been made and what more needs to be done. However, when linked to the Japanese view that improvement is always possible, no matter how well something appears to be working, it becomes a powerful means of countering complacency and encouraging staff to further development.

Though the auditing process can appear straightforward, it rarely is. Large projects, in particular, are collections of a number of relatively smaller sub-projects and, as Kotter (1996: 25) remarks, 'Because we are talking about multiple steps and multiple projects, the end result is often complex, dynamic, messy, and scary.' These 'multiple projects' start at different times and operate at different levels and in different areas of an organisation. Some of these sub-projects will run concurrently, some consecutively and a few may even be largely free-standing. By their nature, they will also be geared to different sub-objectives, which may need to be monitored and measured in different ways. Seen in this way, it

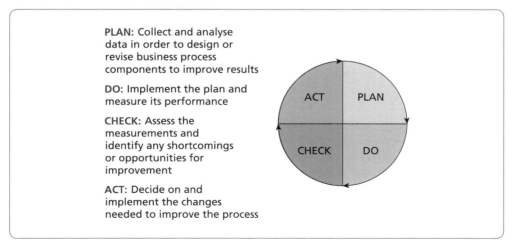

Figure 13.3 The Deming/PDCA Cycle

becomes easier to understand why conducting audits and post-audits, and even day-to-day monitoring of progress, can be exceedingly difficult, but is also exceedingly necessary. If progress is not rigorously monitored, the end result (or lack of) can come as a very nasty shock.

When an audit shows that a project is running late, there is a tendency to throw more resources at it in the hope that it will then be brought back on schedule. Unfortunately, as Fred Brooks found when he led the team that developed the operating system for IBM's 360 range of computers, this can be a misleading idea:

> This was probably the largest non-military software project ever mounted, and it was of vital strategic importance to IBM, which then completely dominated the computer business. It also turned out to be vastly more complex than anyone – including Fred – anticipated, and it rapidly metamorphosed into a kind of death march. The project fell further and further behind schedule. But because IBM was a rich company and OS/360 was so important, it was able to throw more and more resources (ie programmers) at the task. But as it did so, the problems got worse, not better. At which point Fred Brooks had his epiphany: he realised that every time he added a programmer to the team the project fell further behind. . . . Why? Basically because a big software project involves two kinds of work: the actual writing of computer code; and coordinating the work of the dozens – or maybe hundreds – of programmers working on different parts of the overall system. Coordination represents an essential but unproductive overhead: and the more programmers you have, the bigger that overhead becomes. Hence Brooks's law: adding manpower to a late software project makes it later.
>
> (Naughton, 2013).

Many large change projects resemble the IBM experience: they are expensive, vital and complex. When they fall behind schedule, adding more staff merely makes them more complex to manage and slows them down even further. So if a change project is running late, those responsible need to understand why, and what options they have. Sometimes, living with the overrun and perhaps slowing down associated projects may be more effective than trying to bring the project back on schedule. It is also worth bearing in mind that a vital element of good planning is to identify potential problems before they arise, or at least to have contingency plans in place for if they do.

Even when a change programme has been completed, the post-audit should not be treated as the end of the line: a chance for people to rest on their laurels. It can be another opportunity for improvement. The post-audit at XYZ (Chapter 9) was turned into an opportunity for continuing to drive the change process forward, by the simple expedient of asking each manager to identify two initiatives they would personally take to reinforce and enhance the benefits from the company's new organisational structure. This is an example of what Kotter (1996: 21) refers to as 'consolidating gains and producing more change'.

6 Training and development

This is a key part of any change project and takes a number of forms. The obvious one is in relation to new skills and competences that might be necessary. Furthermore, as the case studies in this book show, training and development can have a number of other purposes. They may aim to give staff the skills to undertake the change themselves. It may be the intention to leave them with the ability to pursue continuous improvement, once the change has been substantially achieved, or training and development may be intended to make them aware of the need for change and to win them over. There is also a need to give general awareness training to those in the organisation who might be indirectly affected.

Even where the primary objective is to enhance skills, training can also contribute to other objectives, such as culture change, by structuring it in such a way that training promotes teamworking or inter-departmental cooperation. To ensure that the various types of training are targeted at the right people or groups, a training programme – starting before implementation and continuing after completion – should be established, showing who needs training, the form of the training and when it will take place.

Looking wider than just individual change projects and programmes, as Burnes (2003) argues, there are many benefits to linking an organisation's overall management and staff development programme formally with its various change initiatives. Burnes comments that many of the skills and competences that organisations wish to develop in staff and managers are the same ones necessary for bringing about successful change. Therefore, management and staff development programmes can provide the human resources necessary for managing change, and change projects can provide the real learning opportunities that staff and managers need to develop their skills and competences. The link between management development and change will be returned to in Chapter 14.

There is often a tendency to portray the planning element of change as a technical exercise involved with timetabling and resource allocation. Though planning change is in some ways a 'technical' issue, it is also very much about the people concerned, both those who are managing change and those who are on the receiving end, as the above six activities show. The success of any change effort is always likely to hinge on an organisation's ability to involve and motivate the people concerned and win over those whose support is necessary.

People

Chapter 11 showed that organisational change takes many forms. But, whatever form it takes, its success depends on eliciting the appropriate behavioural response, even if that is just a matter of using Windows 8 instead of Windows 7. Change can be of a predominantly structural or technical nature which requires little of individuals in terms of behavioural or attitudinal change, but if that little is not forthcoming, and users prefer to continue with Windows 7, the change has failed. Increasingly though, as the case studies in this book show, the objective of change is explicitly to modify the attitudes and behaviours of individuals and groups, sometimes radically so. People are being required to reconsider their attitudes towards how work is performed, how they behave towards their colleagues internally, and their attitudes towards their counterparts externally.

In attempting to change the behaviour of their staff, there is a trap that managers often fall into – assuming that it is other people's behaviour that needs to change and that managers' own behaviour can remain the same.

Mini Case Study 13.3 examines how an MSc student working part-time in a bar went about changing the aggressive behaviour of her customers. It reveals that, sometimes, before you can change other people's behaviour, you have to change your own. It was Lewin *et al's* (1939) autocracy-democracy studies which first drew attention to this phenomenon. They found that if a team leader wanted to improve the performance of his/her team, they needed to look at how their own behaviour was influencing and reinforcing others' behaviour. This discovery was reinforced by the New Britain leadership-training workshop (*see* Chapter 9) which also showed that leaders often needed to understand and change their own behaviour before they could change other people's behaviour. Since then, this has been demonstrated in many other studies (Makin and Cox, 2004).

MINI CASE STUDY 13.3

Changing customers' behaviour

Some years ago, a student studying for an MSc in Psychology took a job working behind the bar in a very busy city-centre pub. She had worked in pubs before, but none had been as large and busy as this one, nor had she ever encountered customers who were quite so volubly aggressive. She was one of five people serving behind the bar and, at most times on her shift, she would have 10 or 15 customers clamouring to be served, sometimes even more. With all the shouting and pushing, it was difficult for anyone, including her, to see who should be served next. Both she and the customers found this frustrating, and those who felt they had been passed over, which seemed to be most of the customers, got very aggressive about it. In turn, she found herself responding in an aggressive manner. After two weeks, she was on the verge of quitting the job; she needed the money, but she could not cope with the stress.

In response to a question from one of her lecturers about why she was looking so tired and stressed, she explained the situation to him. He pointed out that what she needed to do was to modify the behaviour of her customers. At the moment, she was responding to their aggressive behaviour; instead she needed to take charge by establishing a 'virtual' queue and letting everyone know where they were in the queue and when they would be served. The lecturer suggested the following procedure:

1. Make eye contact with people when they came to the bar and wave to them to let them know she had seen them.

2. Tell them their place in the queue, e.g. 'you're third in line' or 'there are six people in front of you'.

3. Always serve them in that order.

At first she found this quite an awkward procedure to follow and was not confident it would work, but if it did not, she knew she would have to leave the job. After a few days, though, she found that some people responded favourably to it. As soon as they knew where they were in the queue, they stopped pushing forward and shouting to be served and were happy to wait their turn. After a week she was much more confident and found that most people were happy to queue; the ones who still tried to jump the queue were usually spoken to by other customers rather than her needing to intervene. After ten days, the queue system was working well, her stress levels were down, and she was enjoying the job. As an added, and unexpected, bonus, her tips tripled, whereas previously they had been about the same level as the other staff in the bar.

What this example shows is that through the consistent and fair application of a few simple rules, you can change other people's behaviour, but that in order to do so, sometimes you have to change your own behaviour first.

Source: Adapted from *Changing Behaviour at Work*, Routledge: Abingdon (Makin P. and Cox C. 2004), Copyright (© 2004), Routledge, Reproduced by permission of Taylor & Francis Books UK.

Therefore, whether managers are involved in planning change or executing it, or have to manage the situation once the change has taken place, they need to ask how appropriate their own behaviour is for achieving the desired outcome. This should be borne in mind as we examine three key people-related activities that need to be undertaken in order to manage change successfully: creating a willingness to change, involving people and sustaining the momentum.

Creating a willingness to change

Even where change is purely of a technical or structural form, there has to be willingness among those concerned to change. In an ideal world, organisations would want everyone to buy into a change project. More realistically, as mentioned above, the important issue is to win over what Beckhard and Harris (1987: 92) refer to as the '*critical mass* of individuals or groups whose active commitment is necessary to provide the energy for change to occur'. Some organisations put a great deal of effort into creating a climate where change is accepted as the norm and the critical mass is already present or needs little effort to assemble. The cases of Oticon and the second phase of XYZ's change programme are examples of this. Most organisations, however, are still at the stage where they have to convince staff of the need for change. This is especially the case in those organisations, such as GK (Chapter 8), where each change project is perceived to be a one-off event, almost an exception to the 'normal' flow of organisational life.

For many people, organisational change involves moving from the known to the unknown, with the possibility of loss as well as gain. In such situations, it is often the case that those who fear they will lose out will vociferously oppose any change, while those who believe they will gain from the change will keep quiet for fear of antagonising the losers. This was a point most famously made by Niccolo Machiavelli (1515, Chapter VI, p. 1):

> And it ought to be remembered that there is nothing more difficult to take in hand, more perilous to conduct, or more uncertain in its success, than to take the lead in the introduction of a new order of things. Because the innovator has for enemies all those who have done well under the old conditions, and lukewarm defenders in those who may do well under the new.

So in seeking to create a willingness and a readiness for change, organisations need to be aware that stressing the positive aspects of any proposed change may have much less impact than they might imagine. This point was recognised by Lewin (1947a) when he argued that the *status quo* needs to be destabilised before old behaviour can be discarded (unlearnt) and new behaviour successfully adopted. He referred to this process as 'unfreezing' (*see* Chapter 9). Drawing on his work on Field Theory, Lewin recognised that the *status quo* (which he referred to as the quasi-stationary equilibrium) occurred when the forces driving change and the forces resisting were equal (*see* Figure 13.4). To bring about change, one had to increase the strength of the former and reduce that of the latter. Like Machiavelli, he also recognised that it is often easier to create a readiness for change by making people dissatisfied with their current situation (decreasing the forces resisting change), and thus prepared to consider alternatives, than to try to paint a rosy picture of the future (increasing the driving forces for change). Kotter (1996: 36) echoes this point when he states that: 'Establishing a sense of urgency is crucial to gaining needed cooperation.' To do this, as Kotter (1996: 42) argues, managers need to change their behaviour:

> Increasing urgency demands that you remove sources of complacency or minimize their impact: for instance, eliminating such signs of excess as a big corporate air force; setting higher standards both formally in the planning process and informally in day-to-day interactions; changing internal

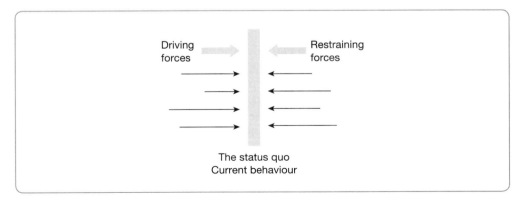

Figure 13.4 Force Field Analysis

measurement systems that focus on the wrong indexes; vastly increasing the amount of external performance feedback everyone gets; rewarding both honest talk in meetings and people who are willing to confront problems; and stopping baseless happy talk from the top.

In order to create a willingness for change, a sense of urgency, a feeling of dissatisfaction with the present, there are four steps an organisation needs to take.

1. Make people aware of the pressures for change. The organisation should inform employees on a continuous basis of its plans for the future, the competitive and/or market pressures it faces, customer requirements and the performance of its key competitors. This should be a participative process where staff have opportunity to question, make comments and make suggestions. Many companies now encourage staff at all levels to spend time meeting and working with customers.

Customers are also increasingly being invited to come and give direct feedback to staff and managers. The aim is to make staff aware of what customers want and do not want and, particularly, to highlight the organisation's shortcomings. This seems to be a development that is common to both private- and public-sector organisations (Crawford *et al*, 2003; Kotter, 1996; Rigby, 2013). Obviously, promoting the vision and explaining the strategic plan are also vital components in this. Through this approach, members of the organisation come to appreciate that change is not only inevitable but is being undertaken to safeguard rather than threaten their future. It is also necessary to use informal as well as formal channels of communication.

In any organisation, department or team, there are individuals who are opinion-formers: people to whom others look for guidance. They may not hold any position of power or authority in the organisation's management structure but, as Mini Case Study 13.2 shows, they do have influence. To get the message across successfully, managers must identify who these people are and seek to ensure that they not only understand the message being transmitted but will also pass a favourable judgement on it.

2. Give regular feedback on the performance of individual processes and areas of activity within the organisation. This allows a company to draw attention to any discrepancy between actual performance and desired present and future performance. The feedback has to be in a form that people can relate to and act on. Telling a team that it is losing money is less useful than giving them feedback on productivity and quality. Feedback also has to be timely. Discussing yesterday's performance is useful in getting staff to identify and address problems; discussing last year's performance is rarely so. Also, giving people the skills and authority to undertake improvement activities, as XYZ did with its *Kaizen* initiatives (Chapter 3), is likely to make people more receptive to feedback because they can do something to improve the situation. In addition, it makes a difference who provides and delivers the feedback. A quarterly or annual meeting led by the CEO may have little impact. However, as mentioned above, direct and timely feedback from customers and product and service users, whether internal or external, is likely to have a much greater impact. Once again, the form of this and the recipient's ability to act upon it is also important.

Feedback can encourage those concerned to begin to think about how their performance can be improved, and prepare them for the need for change. In looking at the case study companies in this book, it is noticeable that there was a greater readiness to change in those organisations where management was open about its objectives and the company's or function's current performance than in those organisations where information was guarded. This can clearly be seen in the Nissan, Oticon and XYZ cases. Conversely, in the Midshires case, suspicion over and opposition to the Project Leader's plans, and political behaviour by members of the Steering Committee and Project Board, led to confusion over and resistance to change. In GK, suspicion over the objectives of the marketing and design manager led to resistance to change. Openness helps people to understand the need for change, which is an essential step on the road to achieving it.

3. Understand people's fears and concerns. In Chapter 9, we discussed the Coping Cycle. This shows that, when undertaking change, individuals go through five psychological states – denial, defence, discarding, adaptation and internalisation. In moving through these states, their performance tends to suffer as they move from something they understand well to trying to adapt to something new, with which they lack competence. Because of this, their self-esteem, their belief in their own abilities, also falls. One of the major mistakes change agents can make when introducing change is to fail to recognise that people react to it emotionally; what can seem a small change from a proposer's point of view may feel like a career-threatening event when viewed by those at the receiving end. Though people's concerns tend to focus on the proposed change, they will also be strongly influenced by the outcome of previous change initiatives. If their past experience of change has been negative, this will tend to increase their normal level of dispositional resistance, but if it has been good, it will tend to reduce it.

In the company in Mini Case Study 13.2 the success of past changes appeared to act to reduce concerns over its move to a new bonus system. Yet, given that the majority of change initiatives appear to fail (Beer and Nohria, 2000), the past experience of change for many people is not a positive one. Consequently, organisations need to recognise that change does create uncertainty and that some individuals and groups may resist, or may not fully cooperate with it, if they fear the consequences or if their views and concerns are ignored. In this respect, resistance can be seen as a signal that there is something wrong with the change process or its objectives rather than with those who are opposing or questioning it. From this perspective, resistance can be viewed as positive: it reminds the organisation that it has not considered all the consequences of its actions or is sending mixed messages, and forces it to review its plans.

It follows that those championing change need to pay special attention to the potential for resistance, both in terms of the adverse consequences it can bring and the underlying problems it may indicate. They also need to pay close attention to the organisation's history of change and the extent to which this reduces or enhances people's fears and concerns. In addition, as mentioned when considering resistance to change in Chapter 8, the way change is managed by the change agent can reduce or increase employees' concerns about and receptiveness to change.

4. Publicise successful change. In order to reduce fears and create a positive attitude towards change, companies should publicise the projects that are seen as models of how to undertake change, and the positive effects change can have for employees. This does not mean that mistakes should be hidden or poor outcomes ignored; these should be examined and explained and lessons should be learned. Staff should be encouraged to expect and set credible and positive outcomes for change programmes. Once again, the experience of the case study companies illustrates this point. Samsung (*see* Chapter 12) has had a long history of successfully developing new products and entering new markets. This has produced a positive attitude towards change by employees and managers alike. Similarly, Nissan's SDT has now been operating in the UK since the 1980s, and has overcome the suspicion by suppliers that they were some sort of spies for Nissan rather than a group intent on helping suppliers to develop their potential.

As the above four steps show, in order to create a willingness for change, an effective two-way flow of information is vital. Even where this is the case, though, organisations should not take for granted the willingness of staff and managers to undertake every change that is proposed. It is noticeable that even after XYZ had spent a number of years creating a willingness for change, it undertook a change readiness audit before embarking on the project to change its organisation structure. Not only did this allow it to estimate the degree of readiness for change but it also formed part of the second people-related activity, involving people in the change project.

Involving people

Chapter 8 reviewed the main theories which explain why people react to change as they do, which were as follows: dispositional resistance, cognitive dissonance, the 'depth' of intervention and the psychological contract. In summary, the argument from these theories is that, though the level of receptivity to change varies from person to person, the more a change challenges a person or group's existing norms of behaviour, beliefs or assumptions, the more resistance it is likely to meet.

It follows from this that the appropriateness of an involvement strategy needs to be judged less by the type of change being considered and more by how people will react to it. Changes that may readily be accepted in some organisations may be strongly resisted in others. Likewise, some major changes may meet with much less reaction than much smaller ones. For example, over the last two decades it has become the norm for staff in public services to give their name on the telephone and wear name badges when meeting members of the public. Previously, staff were not required or even encouraged to do this. When this new policy was first introduced, it was met with a strong emotional reaction by staff, which appeared to be greatly out of proportion to what was being suggested. The reason for this was that many staff felt threatened, exposed to public scrutiny, by having to give their name. It was also the case that the change was imposed on them without consultation and without their being offered a choice in the matter. As was mentioned in Chapters 8 and 9, research has shown that change is likely to prove more effective and commitment will be higher in instances where individuals and groups are offered a choice over whether to accept or reject change (Carpenter, 2013).

In developing an involvement strategy, it is also important to remember Beckhard and Harris's (1987) advice regarding levels of commitment. They argued that the key objective was for organisations to gain the active support of the *critical mass* of people necessary to bring about the change. This is not all, or even necessarily a majority, of those affected. Nor is the same level of support necessary from all of the *critical mass*. Instead it can be split into three groups: those who let it happen, those who help it to happen and those who make it happen. Although it can sometimes be difficult to win over key groups and individuals, it can sometimes be surprisingly easy: as Mini Case Study 13.4 shows, an occasional cup of tea may be all that's necessary to create an ally.

An involvement strategy needs to take account of the size and duration of the proposed change project. Though some change projects can be short-lived and, possibly, easily achieved, many are not. In some cases, achieving a successful change can be a long and complex task. There will be difficult obstacles to overcome, not all of which can be anticipated in advance. To gain and maintain the active involvement of the *critical mass*, and to

MINI CASE STUDY 13.4

Gaining commitment

Tea with the convenor

Mary Davenport is the trade union convenor for a large NHS Hospital Trust in the north of England. This is a full-time post. The hospital site is very big and sprawling and, as she says, 'my office is about as far as you can get from the Trust headquarters'. She believes that this is deliberate. The Trust has tended to see the trade unions as an obstacle to change rather than a partner in the same undertaking. This was reflected in the relationship between Mary and the chief executive of the Trust. She could never get to see him but when he wanted to see her, she was summoned to his office, usually at short notice, whereupon he would either announce a change programme and demand the unions agree to it or complain that the unions were being obstructive in blocking earlier changes he had announced. Not surprisingly, the Trust found it difficult to implement change. Sometimes this was due to poor planning, but often it was due to lack of staff commitment.

One day it was suddenly announced that the chief executive was leaving and that a new chief executive had been appointed. It appeared that his superiors in the NHS and key supporters in the Trust Board had lost patience with the slow pace of change and the chief executive's excuses. The trade unions were as surprised by the sudden change as everyone else, but not optimistic that the new man would be any different. As Mary stated, 'We assumed that he had been given the remit to sort us all out and to do it quickly.' Mary expected that at some point she and her colleagues would be summoned to meet the new chief executive and, as she put it, be 'read the riot act'. However, on the day the new chief executive took up his post, there was a knock on Mary's door and a man she had never seen before walked in and introduced himself as the new chief executive and asked if she 'fancied a cup of tea'. 'We had a long chat over the tea in the canteen where everybody could see me chatting to him. Most of the chat was about our families, he hardly mentioned work. He then said that we ought to do this more often and we now have a cup of tea together in the canteen at least once a month. As well as that, I can see him whenever I like and, as often as not, he'll come to my office.'

After that first meeting, relations between the unions and the management were transformed. Changes which had previously been seen as impossible suddenly became very possible. Now the unions are always consulted and always involved in change. However, the changed relationship stems from that first meeting between Mary and the chief executive. As Mary put it, 'He had the courtesy, on his first day on the job, to come to me and treat me as a valued colleague rather than a despised opponent.'

develop the momentum necessary to ensure that the project is successful, is not a one-off occurrence but an ongoing activity stretching over the lifetime of the change project. There are two main activities that help secure and maintain this level of involvement:

Communication. As well as being key to gaining people's involvement, communication is an essential element of all the above change activities. In terms of involvement, the establishment of a regular and effective communication process can significantly reduce people's levels of uncertainty. In turn, this eliminates one of the major obstacles to people's willingness to get involved in the change process. The purpose of communication is not just to inform staff that change is being considered, but by drawing them into the discussions and debates about the need for and form of the change, and allowing them the freedom to discuss the issues involved openly, to persuade them to convince themselves of the need for change.

The evidence that this is one of the most effective ways of gaining support goes back to the work of Kurt Lewin in the 1940s (Lewin, 1999a). During the Second World War, he was asked by the American government to find an effective way of getting people to change their eating habits. Through a series of now classic experiments, he demonstrated that the most effective method of convincing people to change their behaviour was by providing groups with information for them to evaluate and discuss, and letting the group come to its own decision. Once the decision had been made by the group, it exerted a strong pressure on all the individuals concerned to adhere to the group's decision. Merely telling people they should change had very little effect at all.

Communication should be a regular rather than a one-off exercise. Nor should it be pursued through just one or two channels, such as newsletters or team briefings. As mentioned above when discussing the need to make people aware of the need for change, organisations have a wide range of formal and informal channels for communication. They should consciously use all of these. As a rule of thumb, it should be recognised that, while people are often willing to believe the wildest rumour from unofficial sources, anything from management has to be stated at least six times in six different ways before people start giving it credence. In addition, as Case Study 13 shows at the end of this chapter, communication is most effective when it is tailored to the values of the people concerned. In this instance, Group A had open-democratic values geared to achieving the collective good, which were best served by an informal, participative approach that enabled the discussion and exploration of ideas. Group B, meanwhile, had values based on self-interest, individual ambition and a win-lose philosophy, which were best served by a more formal style of communication that focused on giving answers and identifying best practice rather than encouraging discussion.

In some cases, where all those concerned become directly involved in the change process, as with Nissan's SDT initiatives, communication is less of an issue. However, in most cases, it is impractical to give everyone this level of involvement; therefore, as at XYZ, it is important to communicate proposals from the outset. This involves not only providing information but also listening to the response and taking it seriously. This has a number of benefits. The change management team will very quickly pick up any worries and concerns and can respond to these; they will also be made aware of aspects that need to be taken into consideration which have been overlooked; and assumptions that have been made will be tested and sometimes challenged. In addition, this will assist in identifying issues, individuals and groups who might obstruct change. In terms of the three target groups for commitment, i.e. those who let it happen, those who help it to happen and those who make it happen, communication can secure the commitment of the first but, by itself, is unlikely to secure the commitment of the other two groups. Their commitment will come through (and be tested by) their direct involvement in the change process.

Getting people involved. One of the most vital initiatives an organisation can take with staff is not to treat them as objects of change, or obstacles to it, but to involve them in it and make them responsible for it. There are good examples of this in Oticon, XYZ and Nissan. Particularly where large-scale projects are concerned, not everyone can be involved in all aspects of planning and execution. But, it is important to identify and enrol those whose assistance is necessary and those who are essential to make change happen. This should be the main criterion for selecting who will be involved. Obviously, where it is possible, it is a good idea to ensure that all those most closely affected are involved in some, if not all, aspects.

Similarly, again where possible, responsibility for aspects of the change project should be given to those who will be directly affected by the result. In those cases, where the scale of the project will prevent all those affected being involved, managers will need to select those to involve. Sometimes, volunteers will be asked for. However, remembering the discussion of team composition earlier, it is important to get the right balance between those who are perceived to have 'the right attitude', and those who take a more sceptical view. People prepared to challenge assumptions and ask awkward questions have an essential role to play in ensuring that awkward questions are asked, and answered. If sceptics are won over, they can become powerful advocates for the change. Likewise, it is useful to consider involving key opinion-formers: people to whom their colleagues look for guidance.

As the above shows, communication and involvement are essential to gaining people's understanding of the need for change. Change can be a slow and difficult process, and commitment can diminish unless steps are taken to maintain it. This leads on to the third and final people-related activity: sustaining the momentum.

Sustaining the momentum

Even in the best-run organisations, it sometimes happens that initial enthusiasm and momentum for change wanes and, in the face of the normal day-to-day pressures to meet customer needs, progress becomes slower and can grind to a halt. In any case, as the Coping Cycle illustrates (*see* Chapter 9), in terms of both performance and self-esteem, things do get worse, sometimes considerably so, before they get better. Indeed, in PCI and Midshires, enthusiasm waned very early. In some cases, enthusiasm for change may be lacking at the outset. In such situations, people may not even get through the Denial and Defence stages of the Coping Cycle. Instead, they stick with or quickly return to the methods and types of behaviour with which they are familiar, confident and comfortable. Given that momentum for change does not arise of itself or continue without encouragement, organisations need to consider how to build and sustain it. The points already made above regarding planning and implementation, and especially involvement, are clearly part of this. In addition, organisations should do the following.

Provide resources for change. Kotter (1996: 35) states:

> In an organization with 100 employees, at least two dozen must go far beyond the normal call of duty to produce a significant change. In a firm of 100,000 employees, the same might require 15,000 or more.

For a one-off change project of short duration, it might be acceptable to ask staff to 'go far beyond the normal course of duty'. However, for many organisations, as the case studies in this book demonstrate, change is a way of life; and in many organisations, staff and managers have to work long hours merely to get their normal work done. In situations such as these, and indeed in most situations, it is probably difficult, and certainly unwise, to ask staff to undertake change initiatives without some additional resources, whether these be financial or human. In cases where staff are required to keep up the same level of output during the transition phase, considerable additional resources may be required to achieve this. The 1999 case of the UK's Passport Agency, which failed to provide sufficient extra staff to cope with the introduction of a new computer system, is a case in point. Not only did this result in inexcusable delays in issuing passports but the Passport Agency eventually had to recruit 300 extra staff anyway. In all, the additional cost of the measures necessary to deal with the situation was around £12.6 million (NAO, 1999). It is important, therefore, that the need for any extra resources is identified and extra resources are allocated, whether for the provision of temporary staff, the training of existing staff, senior management time or whatever. As the example of the Passport Office showed, nothing is guaranteed to be more demoralising than having to make changes without adequate resources or support.

Give support to the change agents. As Buchanan and Boddy (1992) note, an enormous responsibility falls upon the change management team. They have not only to plan and oversee the change project but also to motivate others and deal with difficulties, sometimes very personal problems. Just as they have to support others, so too must they receive support themselves, otherwise they may be the ones who become demoralised and lose their ability to motivate others. Midshires is a 'good' example of a case where the change agent was not given support, with serious consequences for himself and the project he was managing.

Sometimes change agents can be encouraged by offering them financial rewards, sometimes by the promise of future advancement, but often the most effective method is through public and private praise of the individuals concerned. In Chapter 2, we drew attention to Chester Barnard's (1938) observation that monetary rewards are often less effective than non-monetary ones, such as praise. This does not mean that monetary rewards should be avoided, but it does mean that too great a reliance on them may be counterproductive.

Develop new competences and skills. This reiterates the point made when discussing 'planning the change' above. Change frequently demands new knowledge, skills and competences. Increasingly, managers have to learn new leadership styles, staff have to learn to work as teams, and all are expected to be innovators and improvers. This requires more than just training and re-training. It may also include on-the-job counselling and coaching. Consequently, organisations need to consider what is required, who requires it and – the difficult part – how to deliver it in a way that encourages rather than threatens or alienates staff. Case Study 13, at the end of this chapter, shows that with good preparation it is possible to deliver training and development which is geared to achieving a positive rather than negative outcome. Similarly, XYZ is a good example of a company that recognised that managerial and staff development go hand in hand with organisational change. This can be an expensive process, in terms of both staff time and cost. This, once again, emphasises the need to provide additional resources for change.

Reinforce desired behaviour. As mentioned earlier, in organisations, people generally do those things that bring rewards or avoid punishments. Consequently, one of the most effective ways of sustaining the momentum for change is to reinforce the kinds of behaviour required to make it successful. Sometimes this may be monetary, such as increased pay or bonuses for particular types of activity or progress. Sometimes it may be symbolic, such as Oticon's tearing down of walls and elimination of personal desks. Sometimes it may be through recognition, whereby senior managers openly or privately single out individuals or groups for special praise. At the same time, it is also important that managers recognise, as discussed above, that if they want their staff to change their behaviour, they may have to change their own behaviour first. Such activities are particularly important during the early stages of change. If managers are seen to take a lead in 'modelling' the new behaviour and/or identifying and praising progress, participants are more likely to develop a positive attitude about the change project. In XYZ, it could be argued that the change in organisational structure was a method of reinforcing the behavioural changes that had already taken place. Alternatively, it could be said that they reinforced the new organisational structure. However one views XYZ, the key point is that the behavioural changes might have been difficult to sustain without the new structure and, certainly, the new structure would have been much less effective without the prior behavioural changes.

In looking at the three interlinked elements that make up the change process – objectives and outcomes, planning the change, and people – we can see why change is so complex and why so many initiatives fail. Though there are technical aspects that must be accomplished, no matter what type of change is involved, it can never be a purely technical exercise. Establishing objectives involves testing assumptions and challenging preconceived ideas. It also involves gathering both fact and opinion, and making judgements about which is the most important. Similarly, planning change often involves an impressive and daunting array of challenges and activities, some of which are amenable to straightforward techniques of analysis and decision, many of which are not. The final element, though, is the most complex: people. People are not just important because they are often the 'object' of change, but also because they are the ones who have to carry it out. In a real sense, they are the glue that holds it together. They can influence the choice of objectives and the way change is planned. In turn, objectives and planning can also affect their willingness to accept or become involved in change.

One final point: even after a change project has been 'completed', the story does not end there. As the Japanese maintain, even when change has resulted in a stable state being achieved, there always remains scope for improvement. Furthermore, as is clear from the case studies, many change projects are open-ended. Change will continue to take place. Therefore, both in planning a project and evaluating its outcomes, it is necessary to identify the open-endedness of it, and the degree to which the final outcome will require a continuous improvement approach or a continuing change approach. The Deming/PDCA Cycle mentioned earlier can be a powerful antidote to complacency and an effective spur for further improvement (*see* Figure 13.3). There is a marked difference between organisations where change is seen as an everyday occurrence, and techniques such as the Deming Cycle are extensively used, and those where it is seen as a one-off event which requires no further attention once the change has been implemented. In the latter, it is very difficult to develop the capabilities and commitment necessary to achieve continuous improvement, whereas in the former, continuous improvement and continuous change, and the capabilities, skills and commitment required of both, go hand in hand.

Conclusions

This and the previous chapter have sought to merge the theory and practice of strategy development and change management as presented in Chapters 6–11. In doing so, it has also drawn on many of the arguments and insights into the behaviour, operation and rationality of organisations presented in Chapters 1–5. Based on these 11 chapters, Chapters 12 and 13 have introduced and elaborated on the Choice Management–Change Management model for understanding and managing organisational change. This comprises three inter-related organisational processes: the choice process, the trajectory process and the change process (*see* Figure 12.1 in the previous chapter). It was argued that not only does this model incorporate and go beyond both the Planned and Emergent approaches to strategy and change but it also demonstrates how managers can attempt to change their organisation's circumstances to fit them to the approach that best suits them and their organisation.

It was asserted that the Choice Management–Change Management model incorporates the full scope of the various approaches to strategy and change, including the Planned and Emergent approaches, and that it also accommodates and explains the use of more directive approaches. However, one of the fundamental differences between this model and many other approaches to strategy and change is that it recognises that managers are active players rather than passive spectators in the development of their own organisations. The model is based on the assumption that not only can managers choose to align their organisation with the external conditions and constraints it faces but they can also do the reverse and align these external conditions and constraints to their preferred way of structuring and running their organisation. Whether they choose to attempt to influence or alter the circumstances their organisation faces or to align it with them will depend on a range of issues, not least their own views about whether they or the organisation is better suited by a stable, planned situation or whether more turbulent, emergent conditions are preferable.

Though the Choice Management–Change Management model appears to offer significant theoretical avenues for understanding how organisations and managers operate, it also offers considerable practical benefits. In Chapter 3, we examined the Culture–Excellence perspective on organisations. The proponents of this view, especially Tom Peters, argue that organisations have no choice but to change radically if they are to survive. The Culture–Excellence theory is based on a particular view of the environment and other constraints organisations face. Assuming that this view is accurate, the Choice Management–Change Management model indicates that organisations need not radically restructure themselves, but could seek to influence the constraints they face to bring them more in line with their existing organisational arrangements. Even if, in the long term, organisations did have to structure themselves along the lines advocated by Peters, Kanter and Handy, they could still seek to influence the conditions under which they operated to achieve this over a longer timescale than might otherwise be assumed. Indeed, as Chapter 3 revealed, this is just the approach the Japanese take. Between the 1950s and the 1980s, Japan's leading organisations transformed themselves. This was achieved by slow and gradual transformation rather than by rapid shock tactics. Japanese companies achieved this gradual transformation by a combination of long-term vision allied to the ability to influence and restructure the constraints under which they operate, especially, as explained by Hamel and Prahalad (1989), their ability to change the rules of competition in their particular industries. In so doing, they provide much support for Kanter *et al*'s (1992) view that a Long March is more effective than a Bold Stroke for building competitive organisations.

Therefore, the Choice Management–Change Management model, in conjunction with the framework for change presented in Chapter 11, potentially at least, resolves the dispute between proponents of Planned and Emergent approaches to strategy development and change. Furthermore, it raises fundamental questions about what managers *can* do and what they *do* do in terms of running and shaping their organisations. In particular, it raises questions about the way that managers can make sense of their situation for themselves and others and, in so doing, construct alternative scenarios or realities for their organisation's future. Many writers, especially from the Culture–Excellence perspective, have made a case for visionary leadership being the key to an organisation's success. Certainly, the transactional, steady-as-she-goes type of manager appears very much out of favour (Grint, 2005; Kotter and Rathgeber, 2006; Peters, 2006). The case for transforming managers, as well as organisations, however, tends to be based on a partial view of what managers need to do and, often, only a shallow understanding of what they actually do. In order to come to grips with the nature of managerial work and the extent to which the Choice Management–Change Management model requires a rethink of how managers operate, the concluding chapter of this book will examine the role of managers, management and leadership, and the differences between them.

TEST YOUR LEARNING

Short discussion topics

The purpose of these is to enable students to check and reflect on the topics. The discussions should last for no more than 5–10 minutes. Depending on the length of the lecture, there could be one, two or three such discussions in a session. The following are five suggested topics which address issues raised in this chapter:

1. What is the choice process?

2. Why might managers have to change their behaviour?

3. What does commitment planning involve?

4. How can desired behaviour be reinforced?

5. Why is choice important?

Class debates

The purpose of class debates is to enable students to explore a topic in depth by setting up a 'for and against' debate. The class can be split into two and one half asked to research the 'for' case and the other the 'against' case. Individuals can then be chosen at random to introduce their side of the debate. Alternatively, two individuals for each side can be told in advance that they will be introducing the debate. The length of such debates depends on the time available, the size of the class and their enthusiasm for the topic. However, less than 30 minutes is probably too short and more than 60 minutes probably too long. The following are three suggested topics which address issues raised in this chapter:

1. Giving people choice undermines the authority of the change agent.

2. In achieving change, rewards and punishments are better than choice and involvement.

3. If managers do not change their behaviour, no one else will.

Essay questions

1. Critically evaluate the three elements of the choice process.

2. Use the choice process to assess one of the case studies of organisational change in this book or change in an organisation of your choice.

Suggested further reading

The following three publications give valuable insights into the planning and execution of change.

Day, T and Tosey, P (2011) Beyond SMART? A new framework for goal setting. *Curriculum Journal*, 22(4), 515–34.

Kotter, JP (1995) Leading change: why transformation efforts fail. *Harvard Business Review*, 73(2), 59–67.

Makin, P and Cox, C (2004) *Changing Behaviour at Work*. Routledge: Abingdon.

CASE STUDY 13

Organisational change: the role of values

Background

One of the most remarkable aspects of organisational change initiatives is their low success rate. It has been argued that a major reason for this is a lack of alignment between the value system of the change intervention and of those of the members of the organisation undergoing the change. This case study describes and presents the findings from two change initiatives in two different organisations that test this argument. As will be shown, the case study supports the view that value system alignment may be an important factor in the success of organisational change initiatives.

Much has been written over the years regarding the need to align organisational and individual values, usually from the culture perspective. The main argument is that effective organisations are ones where goals and values are congruent and shared by the leadership and staff of the organisation. In terms of organisational change, perhaps the first person to draw attention to the relationship between value alignment and successful change was Kurt Lewin in the 1940s (*see* Chapter 9). Since then, a wide range of studies has cited organisation, group and individual values as important factors in the success of change interventions. Consequently, there is much support for the view that successful change is associated with the value alignment of three factors:

- those involved in the change intervention;
- the objective of the intervention;
- the approach to change (i.e. the values underpinning the content of the change and the process by which it is managed).

In order to test the assertion that value alignment is a major factor affecting the success of change interventions, a methodology based on Graves' Emergent Cyclical Levels of Existence Theory (ECLET) was used. ECLET is based on eight core values systems (*see* Ideas and perspectives 13.5). The value systems of the individuals involved in the two change initiatives described in this case study were measured using the Values Test, a commercially available psychometric questionnaire.

The change initiatives

Company A is a national charitable organisation and the change initiative involved an 11-member project team based in the north west of England. The change was primarily designed to improve the effectiveness of staff working with people in difficult circumstances. The change was also designed to help the group work together more effectively as a team by developing self-awareness and mutual understanding.

Company B is a privately owned marketing organisation, also located within the north west of England, and the change involved its 13-member management team. This change initiative was primarily designed to improve the company's business performance by developing the management and leadership abilities of the company's leadership team.

In order to test the value alignment concept, it was necessary to gather three essential pieces of information:

1. **The value system of each group**: This was determined using the Values Test mentioned above. All 11 participants in Company A completed the Values Test instrument. The results showed a strong acceptance of the 'Collective' FS value system and a rejection of the egocentric 'Individual' CP system. Therefore, the group's values align very well with what one would expect from individuals working for a charitable organisation.

   The Values Test instrument was completed by 10 of the 13 members of the management team in Company B. This group have a very a different value system from those in Company A. There is a substantial acceptance of the 'Individual' ER system and a strong rejection of 'Collective' CP system, which is what one might expect from managers working for a profit-focused private-sector company.

2. **The value system of the intervention**: In this case, because the values of each group were already known, the two change initiatives were designed around these values (*see* Ideas and perspectives 13.6 for a detailed description of the values). The design of the two change initiatives is shown in Ideas and perspectives 13.7 and 13.8.

3. **The effectiveness of the intervention**: This was determined from feedback data collected shortly after the intervention. The effectiveness of each intervention was assessed on the basis of each

IDEAS AND PERSPECTIVES 13.5

Summary of Graves' value systems hierarchy

Level
Value System

AN
Individual: Express Self for personal survival, do what you can to look after self, take whatever's offered. Effective where there is no competition but growing people numbers build fear through vulnerability. Security is sought through safety in numbers and leads to emergence of . . .

BO
Collective: Deny Self for family and close relations, safety in numbers, traditional ways and ancestral traditions and rituals. Priority is to maintain the security and sustainability of the local community so that the future is the same as the past. Anger at lack of change in the face of inadequacy leads to emergence of . . .

CP
Individual: Express Self for power and immediate gratification. Coercion, superiority and strength enables satiation of selfish needs and to hell with the rest. Leads to personal expression and adrenalin-fuelled releases of energy, both positive and negative. Leads to feudal systems, exploitation and abuse of others, strives for personal (illegitimate) power and control. Guilt over consequences leads to a desire to conform to agreed behaviours and emergence of . . .

DQ
Collective: Deny Self for order and stability, subordinate oneself to the rules of society based on absolutist principles of the one right way, laws and regulations, obey the appointed (legitimate) power and authority and accept penal consequences for transgression and the authority will provide and protect and reward hard work in the long term. Frustration at lack of personal recognition and satisfaction in the short term lead to emergence of . . .

ER
Individual: Express Self for reward now and the material riches and good life but not at the obvious expense of others. Get away with what you can for personal gain now, find the best way rather than the right way, contingent thinking, flexible approaches, manipulate and engineer outcomes to suit personal needs and wants. Success brings isolation and resentment from the 'have-nots' and feelings of loneliness and exclusion lead to emergence of . . .

FS
Collective: Deny Self for equality, sharing and humanity, wealth distribution, charity and working for humanitarian causes to aid social development and community. All are equal in the eyes of society, no one person is in control, consensus decision-making, inclusion and harmony eventually leads to lower efficiencies. Lack of effective progress leads to emergence of . . .

GT
Individual: Express Self but not at the expense of others. Open-minded systemic thinking that allows for the integration of all previous value systems in natural flows, an acceptance of complex/chaotic systems and paradox, stratified democracy, self-gain but also with preservation of life systems in general, and a recognition that knowledge has the greatest value and only the right knowledge can provide systemic solutions to the problems of existence. Frustration at the lack of social action in the light of new knowledge and understanding leads to emergence of . . .

HU
Collective: Deny Self for the benefit of whole world socio-economic systems and community, deny self for ecological existence and planetary sustainability and the continual search for knowledge and meaning in the universe so that new understanding can be applied to enabling a sustainable planetary future.

Source: Cowan and Todorovic (2005).

Case study 13 (*continued*)

IDEAS AND PERSPECTIVES 13.6

Summary of Graves' value systems

Graves ER system values

1. Express self for reward now
2. Multiplistic opportunities
3. Find the best way, survival of the fittest
4. Change to achieve more is OK
5. Play to authority figures
6. Materialistic control/employee utilisation
7. Rule-challenging
8. Manipulation of others – maximum output at minimum cost
9. Avoid being controlled – manage up the hierarchy
10. Contingency management
11. Deny guilt and punishment
12. Autonomous decision-making
13. Modal operators of possibility
14. Secular scientism

Graves FS system values

1. Deny self now for acceptance by others now
2. Relativistic sociocentrism
3. Find the acceptable way by consensus
4. Change to create equality
5. Shared power/rotating leadership
6. Cooperative control/employee involvement and motivation
7. Rules are for guidance
8. Meet needs of others
9. Equalitarian authority – flatten the hierarchy
10. Cooperative management
11. Avoid punishment and guilt – understand all perspectives
12. Consensual decision-making
13. Searching for acceptability
14. Humanitarianism

group's response to questions about the usefulness and suitability of the content of the intervention and the way it was delivered, and the extent to which participants were willing to change as a result of the intervention.

For Company A: A focus group discussion was conducted by one of the facilitators who delivered the change sessions. In summary, it was found that there was substantial alignment between the values of the intervention and the values of the group. There was also substantial agreement that the intervention was a

success and that much of this can be attributed to the alignment of values.

For Company B: The organisation undertook its own qualitative review of the change initiative. There was substantial agreement that the intervention was a success and that much of this can be attributed to the alignment of values.

Summary

This case study has shown support for the concept that value alignment can play an important role in

---

IDEAS AND PERSPECTIVES 13.7

Company A

1. Programme objectives

To develop improvements in effectiveness as measured by perception of team communications, openness in discussions and greater degrees of trust and sharing, and improved effectiveness in dealing with 'client' cases by having a greater understanding of individual differences and stages of value system development.

More specifically, to develop:

- self-awareness through an appreciation of individual differences;
- awareness of others through an appreciation of multiple perspectives;
- knowledge of a range of psychological models (including value systems) affecting human behaviour;
- ability to apply the above to helping others (external clients) in specific difficult circumstances through case studies;
- ability to apply the above to further internal development of the group working together as a team.

2. Delivery style

The delivery consisted of eight one-day workshops. Each was informal and held at the group's premises in a common-room environment seated on small sofas in a circular arrangement with the workshop deliverers sitting as equal members of the group. There was little presentation material, mostly hand-drawn on a flipchart supported by a few handouts. The underlying motive of the sessions was to help the group to apply the intervention content externally to their clients, often prejudiced individuals and groups in society, and themselves. Contribution of existing expertise from group members was actively encouraged as each group member played an equal role in the learning process. No judgement was made of any different perspectives held by any of the group members and all points of view were respected and considered valid.

3. Content

The programme content consisted of a series of workshops exploring Myers Briggs personality dimensions; aspects and models of personal motivation including Maslow, McClelland and motivation models from Neuro Linguistic Programming (NLP); and latterly Graves' Value Systems and their application to participant self-assessment and personal growth and client case studies. The material was presented as being an optional perspective on the subject and not 'the definitive answer', essentially consistent with a subjectivist relativistic philosophy. Ideas, principles and models were put forward as discussion points and explored through interactive conversation among equals such that each member of the group determined their own perception of the meaning of the materials.

---

whether change interventions are accepted or not by members of an organisation. The case study also shows that the Graves' ECLET-based methodology is a potentially useful tool for determining an organisation's value system and ensuring that the values which underpin all elements of the approach to change – the objectives, content and delivery style – are aligned with it.

IDEAS AND PERSPECTIVES 13.8

Company B

1. Programme objectives

To develop improved business performance through better understanding and effectiveness of communication processes, self-management, self-motivation and personal awareness and leadership styles for running the business, and dealing effectively with employees and getting the most from them.
More specifically:

- building rapport and developing relationships with customers and employees;
- understanding perception and reality and seeing multiple perspectives;
- dealing with awkward conversations;
- directive vs coaching styles of leadership;
- individual differences, self-motivation;
- personal prioritisation and time management;
- styles of leadership;
- empowering and motivating others;
- influencing, delegating and coaching.

2. Delivery style

The delivery consisted of three one-day sessions in which the atmosphere was open and relaxed and conducive to self-disclosure. Delivery style was generally semi-formal set by smart-casual office-wear and delivered off the company's premises in a comfortable hotel training room arranged with horse-shoe table and seating plan. Training material was presented largely using PowerPoint supported by flip-charts for capturing discussion points. Materials were delivered using a range of styles including experiential activities, taught theory, group discussions and reviews. The underlying motive of the training sessions was to improve individual and group performance and, therefore, overall business performance.

3. Intervention content

The content was delivered under a range of philosophical styles from the objectivist 'one right answer' to modernist contingent theories focused on finding the 'best way' and postmodern relativistic material allowing each person to define their own way. The content itself can be seen from the bullet point objectives above and included principles of leadership taken from contingency theory, transformational leadership, situational leadership and principles of coaching, empowering and employee engagement as means of gaining improved employee and, therefore, business performance.

Questions

1. What are the main differences between the value system of Company A and that of Company B? What factors might account for the difference?

2. The Company A and Company B change initiatives were directed at developing individual and team capabilities. How might value alignment be used in other change situations?

3. Other than value systems alignment, what other factors might affect the success of a change initiative?

Source: Burnes, B and Jackson, P (2011) Success and failure in organisational change: an exploration of the role of values. *Journal of Change Management*, 11(2), 133–62.

Chapter 14

Management, leadership and change

Learning objectives

After studying this chapter, you should be able to:

- define globalisation and understand the importance of sustainability, workforce diversity and business ethics;
- list the key duties of managers;
- understand that much of what managers do is reactive and driven by expediency;
- describe the three main perspectives on leadership;
- identify the primary approaches to managerial development and education;
- appreciate the differences between management and leadership and the different skills required for each;
- explain the relationships between management, leadership and organisational change;
- appreciate the need for managers to identify and examine the full range of choices facing them;
- understand the impact of managers' decisions on society as a whole, and their wider and longer-term responsibilities.

MINI CASE STUDY 14.1

Time to stand up to the crisis junkies

Ambitious managers love a crisis. It gives them a chance to shine, to deploy all those talents that may lead to greatness. In the US, Bill Clinton has spoken regretfully that no epic challenges occurred while he was president. Negotiating the North American Free Trade Agreement and implementing limited welfare reform will not get him carved on to Mount Rushmore. It is the same in business. Every chief

➡

executive would like to make elephants dance, the way Lou Gerstner did at IBM, or turn round an industrial dinosaur as Sergio Marchionne has at Fiat. No one wants to leave a legacy of average performance in dull times. But there are true crises and manufactured ones – the real-life "burning platform" that leads to change, and the manager who likes to run amok with his hair on fire so that he feels important or because he cannot get people to do what he wants in a less hysterical way.

There are none better than bankers at exaggerating a sense of crisis. They thrive on deadlines and pressure, on price twitches and deal schedules. Creating a permanent sense of siege and looming disaster unless a contract is signed or a trade executed is part of the culture of their industry. It served them well during the depths of the financial crisis, forcing governments into bail-outs that, on deeper reflection, might have been handled differently. But standing up to crisis junkies and distinguishing between the various phases of a crisis is an essential managerial skill. Ronald Heifetz, a leadership expert at Harvard's Kennedy School of Government, has defined two phases in crisis management: the emergency, when your priority is to stabilise the situation and buy time; and the adaptive phase, when you address the underlying causes of the crisis in order to build the strength to thrive anew.

The current row over banking reform in the UK has pitted on one side the banks, who argue that ring-fencing their retail and investment banking and retail operations will stunt general economic growth. On the other side are the politicians and regulators who believe that three years after the financial crisis, it is high time the banks became less risky institutions. However, another way to understand the dispute is as one between banks which argue that the financial crisis is still in the emergency phase and regulators who believe they should be well on their way to adapting.

The distinct phases require two different forms of management. In the emergency phase, managers are expected to respond with certainty, to draw on their experience in order to calm nerves. In the second phase, however, they must be extremely open to change. They must be able to set aside their experience, the default behaviours that enabled them to stabilise the emergency, and draw on new ideas in order to adapt their organisations. It is rare to find managers who can do both. We see variations on this theme throughout business.

Turnround specialists exist purely to come into troubled organisations and fix them, arriving and leaving with no emotional baggage. Start-up entrepreneurs are often replaced by investors as their businesses reach a steady state of growth. The energy and reflexes required for months of high intensity are ill-suited to years of assiduous grunt work. Yet few managers who have led a company well through a crisis will be happy to stand aside for the adaptive phase. In a 2009 paper, written with Alexander Grashow and Marty Linsky, Prof Heifetz wrote: "Many people survive heart attacks, but most cardiac surgery patients soon resume their old ways: only about 20 per cent give up smoking, change their diet, or get more exercise. In fact, by reducing the sense of urgency, the very success of the initial treatment creates the illusion of a return to normalcy. The medical experts' technical prowess, which solves the immediate problem of survival, inadvertently lets patients off the hook."

The banks experienced their heart attack in 2008. Their objection to reform suggests they still do not want to give up smoking. They did not, as Prof Heifetz puts it, use the crisis "to set the organisational reset button". They and their managers appear more comfortable trying to prolong the emergency than doing the hard work of adaptation. Recent studies of the Deepwater Horizon oil spill and the Fukushima nuclear power plant explosion in Japan suggest that private sector organisations and governments need to do a much better job of detailed crisis planning, establishing clear plans for low-probability, high-impact events. This is another crucial part of the adaptive phase of crisis management, introducing a "war game" scenario planning mentality in the private sector so that it is ready to take on the next great emergency. The banks' pleading suggests that their desire to pursue business as usual is stronger than to take the managerially responsible route and hunker down for a changed world.

Introduction

As Mintzberg *et al* (2002) note with some concern, one of the most enduring and eye-catching notions in all of the management literature is the concept of 'Heroic leaders [who] announce magnificent strategies, do dramatic deals and promise grand results' (p. 71). A concept based on 'a massive set of assumptions: that the chief executive is the enterprise, that he or she alone is responsible for the entire performance, and that this performance can be measured and the chief executive rewarded to do' (p. 70). Yet, as Broughton argues in Mini Case Study 14.1, though there may be instances where heroic leaders are needed to deal with a crisis, to save the day, to turn around failing organisations, there are also other situations where a more reflective, participative and less dramatic form of leadership is required. The nub of Broughton and Mintzberg *et al*'s argument is that organisations change, and as they change, leaders face different challenges which need to be managed in different ways. One size does not fit all, no matter how attractive, larger than life, and heroic that size may be. If managers cannot align their leadership style and skills with the circumstances they face, then those managers are likely to be judged failures, regardless of how effective they might have been previously.

Indeed, the inability to adapt to changing circumstances may be the reason why it is claimed that somewhere between 50 and 75 per cent of managers are not effective in their job (Burke, 2011; Hughes *et al*, 2009). The case of George Simpson and John Mayo at Marconi is good example (*see* Chapter 6). Both were considered to be highly effective leaders, but they failed disastrously at Marconi. One explanation for this is that their leadership style, skills and experience were just not appropriate to the situation in which they found themselves, i.e. there was a lack of fit or alignment between the leaders' abilities and the organisation's situation. Whether this was a case of poor leadership selection or just bad luck can be argued about, but the disastrous outcome is there for everyone to see (Burke, 2011; Yukl, 2013).

The misalignment argument may also explain why some two-thirds of leadership teams are considered ineffective (Kakabadse and Korac-Kakabadse, 1999). The type of people who rise to the top in corporate cultures which, at least until recently, have lauded strong, individualistic and transformational leadership tend not to be team players (Storey, 2004). In addition, these claims that around 70 per cent of leaders and leadership teams are ineffective may help to explain the oft-cited statistic that 70 per cent of change initiatives fail (Burnes, 2011a).

The key task for organisations, therefore, is to understand the vast array of present and future challenges they face and determine how best they should be managed, and select and develop managers with the necessary skills and other attributes to manage them (Burke, 2011). Of course, identifying what these challenges will be and what response will be appropriate will not be easy. Many writers and commentators are good enough to provide us with their views on the future. Sometimes these views have a postmodern rosy glow about them, while often, as the world struggles to shake off the after-effects of the 2008 credit crunch, they present a gloomy, doomsday picture of the future. Two things, though, are clear: it is unlikely that the challenges facing managers in the future will get any easier, and attempts to predict the future, as Ideas and perspectives 14.1 shows, usually fall very short of the mark. Nor, as Ideas and perspectives 14.2 illustrates, is this anything new.

IDEAS AND PERSPECTIVES 14.1

Predicting inflation

Mervyn King is the Governor of the Bank of England. He has an army of highly trained economists and advisors who work for him. He can also draw upon a vast array of public and private sector knowledge both in the UK and abroad. Yet even his economic forecasts can be spectacularly wrong, as the following two quotations show.

August 2008:

> 'Price increases will continue to enter the measure of CPI inflation for 12 months, so inflation is likely to remain markedly above the target until well into next year.'

November 2008:

> 'Although CPI inflation did rise above 5% its expected future path has fallen significantly . . . There is obviously a risk that [deflation] could happen.'

Source: The two quotes are from Elliott and Seager (2008: 1).

IDEAS AND PERSPECTIVES 14.2

Predicting the future

This 'telephone' has too many shortcomings to be seriously considered as a means of communication.   (Western Union internal memo, 1876)

Airplanes are interesting toys, but of no military value.   (Marshal Foch, 1911)

Who the hell wants to hear actors talk?   (HM Warner of Warner Brothers, 1927)

I think there is a world market for maybe five computers.
                                                    (Thomas Watson, Chairman IBM, 1943)

This is no excuse for ignoring the many serious and daunting challenges that organisations and those who manage them, not to mention the world at large, have to face in the coming decades. The globalisation of world trade may open up new markets and create new opportunities, but it also brings with it new competitors and new uncertainties. The same holds true for scientific advances. The beneficial effects of computers are there for all to see, with the range of applications expanding daily, but so too is the problem of cyber crime. Similarly, medical advances such as stem cell treatments for cancer and Alzheimer's may be hugely beneficial, but they also raise significant practical and ethical concerns. Then there is the reality of climate change, the dwindling of natural resources, the growing gap between rich and poor countries, and the threat to the natural world of indiscriminate industrialisation; we are reminded of these almost daily (Becker, 2008; Dunphy *et al*, 2007; Newman, 2008).

Nevertheless, nothing is inevitable until it actually happens, and even then it may be reversed. Individual consumers and pressure groups have some influence, and governments can pass laws, but in an age where organisations dominate our lives, where they appear to be more powerful than ever before, the role and performance of managers will be crucial.

Managers will need to recognise that in the future, as in the past, regardless of the particular issues involved, the environment in which their organisations operate will continue to change. They will also have to recognise that the appropriateness of their decisions will be judged by a wider set of criteria and a wider range of stakeholders than in the past. At the same time, managers will continue to have to find ways of ensuring that their organisation and its environment, and the other constraints under which it operates, are, as far as possible, kept aligned. As pointed out in previous chapters, this does not mean that each and every organisation has to change rapidly and radically, though many will. Instead, managers can seek to influence the constraints under which their organisation operates, and the pace and timing of change, to make them more favourable to their preferred way of working.

The case studies in this book show that change is neither easy nor necessarily always successful – something that most people's everyday experiences will confirm. Regardless of this, organisations do change, either by design or default, and managers do play a crucial role in determining whether the outcome is success or failure. Managers are the ones who have the responsibility for ensuring that options are identified, choices made and actions taken. They are also the ones who have the responsibility for making sense, presenting a coherent picture, of the events and developments that make up an organisation's past, present and potential future. Therefore, in concluding this book, it is only right that we look at how well managers are equipped, or can be equipped, for this task.

The chapter begins by examining the implications of globalisation, especially in terms of sustainability, workforce diversity and business ethics. This highlights the need for managers not just to acquire appropriate skills and competences but also to adopt appropriate behaviours. This leads on to a review of the literature on what managers are supposed to do and what they really do. This shows that, despite what leading thinkers such as Fayol and Weber believed and advocated, most managers are driven by expediency and operate in a responsive mode. The chapter then moves on to discuss the importance and nature of leadership in organisations. In particular, it seeks to identify the characteristics and contexts that make for effective leadership. Arising from this, the leadership role played by managers in the case studies is explored. This is followed by an examination of the education and development of managers, which leads on to a discussion of the relationships between management, leadership and change.

The chapter and the book conclude by arguing that managers have an important responsibility to identify and exercise choice, when faced with situations which require change. Though choice can be determined on a very narrow basis of short-term financial return, increasingly managers will have to take into account wider organisational and societal factors. Especially important in this respect is that managers should be prepared to question trends and advice that seem designed to increase organisational and societal instability and fragmentation. The interests of society in general and their own organisations in particular may be better served by seeking stability rather than promoting instability.

Globalisation and the challenge of change

Arguably, the biggest single challenge facing managers today is globalisation: the creation of a unified world marketplace (Dunphy *et al*, 2007). Allied to globalisation are three other challenges: how to achieve sustainability in a world of dwindling natural resources and increasing environmental pollution, how to manage an increasingly diverse workforce and, at a time when business leaders are considered less trustworthy than ever before, how to manage ethically.

Trade between different parts of the world has been taking place for thousands of years. In the last 20–30 years, the integration of the global economy appears to have gone through a step change, hastened by the fall of communism in Eastern Europe and the opening up of China. Whereas in the 1970s and 1980s it was common to talk about international brands such as Coca-Cola and McDonald's, it is now equally common to speak of global, trans-national corporations that dominate their industries and gobble up the smaller companies. Significantly, this is leading to the seat of economic power moving eastwards. In 2008, there was only one non-Western company on the list, Toyota (Fortune, 2008). In 2012 there were four, and three of those were Chinese (Fortune, 2012).

One obvious manifestation of globalisation is that, in the developed world, we take for granted that our supermarkets will be stocked with our favourite foods from every part of the world all year round. Even so, it is perhaps surprising that Wal-Mart appears in the top ten on Fortune's 2008 and 2012 lists of the world's biggest companies. Nor is globalisa-tion merely an issue for large companies; it is affecting smaller organisations as well, whether through the threat of increased competition and takeover, or the promise of new markets.

Like many hot topics that attract a great deal of attention, it is difficult to find an agreed definition of globalisation. For some, it is primarily an economic phenomenon, concerned with the integration and convergence of economic systems through the growth in interna-tional trade, investment and capital flows (Deresky, 2010; Jones, 1995). Others see it as a much wider phenomenon involving social, cultural and technological exchanges that will 'transform our world into the beginnings of a global civilization, a new civilization of civil-izations, that will blossom through the coming century' (Schwartz and Leyden, 1997: 1). For Giddens (2002), the advent of new communications technologies is leading to the 'death of distance' and making it possible to share knowledge and culture across the globe instantaneously and simultaneously. Some argue that globalisation may also be sounding the death knell of the nation state, as large trading blocks, based on Europe, North America and Asia and overseen by the World Trade Organization, take over (Deresky, 2010). Reich (1998), in an attempt to make sense of these differing perspectives, identifies the four main definitions of globalisation: a historical epoch; a confluence of economic phenomena; the hegemony of American values; and a technological and social revolution.

Despite these different views as to what globalisation is, as Reich (1998) shows, there is some agreement among commentators as to what is driving it: the intensification of inter-national competition, the fall of communism, economic liberalisation, the removal of trade barriers, and the advent of new communication technologies such as the internet. It is these very real developments which make globalisation a key issue for managers rather than a passing fad. Globalisation is also a highly contentious issue which has given rise to a great deal of bitter conflict between those who see it as a force for global good and those who see it as the oppression of poor nations by rich ones (*Economist*, 2002; Hobsbawm, 2008; Klein, 2001; Rodrik, 2012; Stiglitz, 2007). To a great extent, much of the pro-and-anti argument revolves around the size and behaviour of the large, transnational corporations that are coming to dominate the global economy. For example, by 2003, more than half of the 100 largest economies in the world were private corporations (GlobalisationGuide.org, 2003), but as we now know, most of these pay very little tax (Arthur, 2013; Inman, 2013). They are very good at making enormous profits from consumers in rich and poor countries alike, but they give very little back (Arthur, 2013; Stiglitz, 2013). This may not be exactly illegal, but neither is it exactly ethical or in line with many of these companies' public utterances, e.g. Google's 'Don't be evil' slogan (Kaiser, 2013).

For the pro-globalisation camp, this provides the rationale for the creation of global institutions such as the World Trade Organization (WTO), the International Monetary Fund (IMF) and the World Bank that can set the rules for such organisations and police them. For the 'antis', this shows that big business is the dominant force in globalisation, and the WTO, IMF and the World Bank exist to do their bidding (Peet, 2012).

Regardless of whether one sees globalisation as a force for good or ill, organisations have to come to terms with the changing nature of domestic and international trade. They have to live with a situation where the rules that govern their behaviour are set by supra-national bodies such as the EU and WTO. In addition, as mentioned above, they need to come to terms with three other issues whose importance has been intensified by globalisation, namely sustainability, workforce diversity and business ethics.

Sustainability

Globalisation both derives from and is driving economic development across the globe; the greater the level of economic integration across the planet, the greater the level of consumption. As we are reminded every day, however, the result of this rush for ever-greater levels of economic growth and consumption is the dwindling and depredation of natural resources, increasing levels of pollution and rapid climate change. The surge in oil prices in recent years reflects the increased demand for oil brought about by globalisation, especially the growth of the Chinese economy (Strahan, 2008). Nor is it just a case of oil running out. As Lines (2002: 126–7) argues:

> The regenerative and assimilative capacities of the biosphere cannot support even the current levels of consumption, much less the manifold increase required to generalize to higher standards of living worldwide. Still less can the planet afford an ever-growing human population striving to consume more per-capita.

Many thought that President Obama would make climate change and sustainability a keystone of his first term in office. Though they are said to be key part of his second term agenda, even many of his loyal supporters are becoming impatient at the lack of action (Eilperin, 2013). As was demonstrated by the failure of the US to sign up to the Kyoto Protocol on achieving reductions in the emissions of greenhouse gases, governments have tended to put short-term economic benefits ahead of long-term environmental survival. As the then UN Secretary General, Kofi Annan, stated in 2006:

> The world remains locked into short-term thinking, from election cycles in politics to profit-taking in the business world. Sustainable development cries out for a long-term perspective. The world remains captive to the old idea that we face a choice between economic growth and conservation. One of two jobs worldwide – in agriculture, forestry and fisheries – depends on the sustainability of ecosystems.   (Quoted in Dunphy *et al*, 2007: 30)

Even if governments can reach an accord over action on climate change, we also know that organisations, driven by market forces, will have a major influence on how such actions are formulated and will have the major responsibility for their implementation. As Dunphy and Griffiths (1998: 183) argue in their book, *The Sustainable Corporation*:

There is a widespread view that governments must solve environmental problems. However, the major multinationals outstrip many of the world's national economies in terms of wealth and power, and their global coverage allows them to escape the requirements of particular governments seeking to place severe environmental restrictions on them. They can simply move their operations across national borders. The world's multinationals are in fact more powerful than most national governments.

Nevertheless, Dunphy and Griffiths do believe that it is possible for these large organisations to change their ways. They point out that those who run organisations live in the same world as the rest of us, and, to a large extent, experience the consequences of their actions in the same way as everyone else. Consequently, they argue, managers cannot divorce their actions from the wider impact they have on society; nor can they ignore the fact that a sustainable future for their organisations requires a sustainable future for the world. This presents a major challenge for managers, particularly at the senior level. While operating in competitive and hostile markets, they have to marry the desire of their shareholders for increased profit with the need to act in the wider and longer-term interests of society as a whole. They will not achieve this without pressure and support from governments and the force of public opinion. Nor, as Dunphy *et al* (2007) point out, will managers be able to create sustainable organisations unless they have the change management skills to do so. Dunphy *et al* claim that both incremental and transformational approaches can be used to create sustainable organisations, with the appropriateness of either depending on the circumstances of the organisation in question. So the role of managers is not just to lead change but to develop the skills necessary to identify which approach to change is suitable for their organisation.

Furthermore, according Docherty *et al* (2002: 12), sustainability is not just about the relationship of organisations to their environment, or the depletion of natural resources:

> Sustainability . . . encompasses three levels: the individual, the organizational and the societal. Sustainability at one level cannot be built on the exploitation of the others. These levels are intimately related to the organization's key stakeholders: personnel, customers, owners and society. An organization cannot be sustainable by prioritizing the goals and needs of some stakeholders at the expense of others . . . Thus sustainability has a value basis in the due considerations and balancing of different stakeholders' legitimate needs and goals.

Therefore, as Dunphy *et al* (2007) argue, life cannot be sustained on earth unless we create sustainable organisations. However, Docherty *et al* (2002) claim that creating sustainable organisations cannot be achieved unless all stakeholders, including the organisation's own members, are treated in an equitable and ethical manner. This is why the issues of workforce diversity and business ethics are so important.

Workforce diversity

Jones *et al* (2000: 166–7) observe:

> Diversity is dissimilarities – differences – among people due to age, gender, race, ethnicity, religion, sexual orientation, socioeconomic background, and capabilities/disabilities . . . Diversity raises important ethical issues and social responsibility issues as well. It is also a critical issue for organizations, one that if not handled well can surely bring an organization to its knees, especially in our increasingly global environment.

Ever since the Industrial Revolution ushered in the age of the organisation, the workforce has become increasingly diverse, though faster in some industries and countries than others. Globalisation is intensifying workforce diversity in three key ways.

The first and most obvious is that the growth of the transnational corporations means that, increasingly, companies are being owned and managed by people from different countries and cultures. The fact that Ford Motors operates its own plants in most major markets and has a partnership with Mazda in Japan and a partnership with Volkswagen in Brazil is a typical example. There are also many examples of Japanese and South Korean companies, such as Honda and Hyundai, establishing factories in Europe and the US. Indeed, the famous MG sports car is now manufactured in the UK by Shanghai Automotive Industry Corporation, the largest carmaker in China. Companies are also increasingly buying products and services from overseas. The epitome of German manufacturing, Mercedes-Benz, now purchases car components from India, and many big UK companies, such as BT and Aviva, have relocated call centres to India.

The second effect of globalisation concerns the migration and recruitment of workers from other countries. Richer countries have always been a magnet for workers from poorer countries. The emigration from Europe to the US in the nineteenth century is a case in point. It offered the potential for a better life for immigrants and met the severe shortage of workers the US was experiencing. The last 50 years has seen the mass migration of people from South America to the US. In some American cities, Hispanics are now the largest ethnic grouping and by 2050 will make up some 25 per cent of the population of the US (Hitt *et al*, 2009). The transport and communications infrastructures that have made globalisation possible also make it easier to move from one country to another, whether legally or illegally, to seek a better life. Also, with globalisation, the need to move skilled labour from where it is plentiful to where it is scarce, or where it can be better rewarded, is an increasingly important factor of competitiveness. In recent years, for example, the UK government has sought to recruit medical staff from across the world to compensate for staff shortages in the National Health Service.

The third effect of globalisation on diversity has been to increase the participation rate of women and minority groups in the workforce. As economies develop, they require greater amounts of labour. The tendency is first of all to recruit male workers, and often to give preference to particular groups, whether these be based on grounds of race, tribe, religion, age or sexual orientation. As demand for labour grows, other groups are drawn into the workforce. In the twentieth century, for example, the participation of women in the workforce of most developed countries probably accounted for the biggest increase in diversity (Nahavandi, 2012; Valerio, 2009; Yukl, 2013).

It has always been the case that the US tends to exemplify workforce diversity. Hitt *et al* (2009: 41) recommend their readers to consider the following:

Over the past decade, more than one-third of people entering the US workforce have been members of racial or ethnic minority groups. Moreover, the proportion of racial and ethnic minorities in the workforce is expected to increase indefinitely. The situation is similar in some European countries.

This echoed a point made by Cummings and Worley (2001: 429–30) who state:

Contemporary workforce characteristics are radically different from what they were just twenty years ago. Employees represent every ethnic background and color; range from highly educated to illiterate; vary in age from eighteen to eighty; may appear perfectly healthy or may have terminal illness; may be single parents or part of dual-income, divorced, same-sex or traditional families; and may be physically or mentally challenged.

Diversity would not be an issue if we all reacted to the same things in the same ways and treated everybody else as we would wish to be treated ourselves. Erez (2010: 389) offers the following illustration of how people from dissimilar cultures can behave radically differently when faced with the same set of circumstances:

Imagine Americans, Israelis and Japanese participating in an international management training program. They all assemble in one lecture room, each with a personal computer with an Internet connection. The training session begins with an in-basket simulation. Each participant gets a set of problems to solve. The instructor lets them know that they can use any method they want to work out the problems. They can sit in class or go outside. They can use Google to get more information, exchange ideas with each other, or both. The instructor then observes their free styles of gathering information. What he sees is the following: The Americans open up Google in search of relevant information, and continue to work on the problem individually. The Israelis look around and signal to each other to go outside and talk in small groups. They exchange ideas about solving the problems, and then approach the instructor to ask whether they can work as a team and submit a team project rather than individual projects. The Japanese participants are most confused with the lack of a clear task structure. They are not sure whether they can go outside and talk to each other or not. They are also not sure about the seniority differences among the group members. Consequently, each Japanese participant stays in the room and does his job, feeling very hesitant and uncomfortable.

In his entertaining and enlightening book *Blunders in International Business*, Ricks (1999) catalogues the mistakes made by businesses in trying to sell their products or establish businesses in other countries. Ricks (1999: 4) maintains:

Cultural differences are the most significant and troublesome variables encountered by the multinational company. The failure of managers to comprehend fully these disparities has led to most international business blunders.

In Chapter 5, we described the work of Hofstede (1980, 1990) and the GLOBE study (Javidian and Dastmalchian, 2009) in seeking to identify the similarities and differences between national cultures and the implications of these for the management of different groups. From their work and that of other researchers (*see* Trompenaars, 1993, for example) it is clear that approaches which might be effective when managing, say, Japanese workers might be considerably less effective when managing employees from the US (*see* Ideas and perspectives 5.7 in Chapter 5). Jones *et al* (2000: 175) comment:

When American and Japanese managers interact, for example, the Americans often feel frustrated by what they view as indecisiveness in the Japanese, and the Japanese are often frustrated by what they perceive as hasty, shortsighted decision making by the Americans.

Managing diversity is not just about how to manage relationships between people with different national cultures effectively. Managing diversity is also concerned with developing appropriate approaches to managing differences in gender, age, abilities, sexuality, ethnicity, etc. For instance, in the West, it is claimed that male and female workers have different strengths and weaknesses and different preferences in how they prefer to manage and be managed (Maddock, 1999; Thomas, 2003; Valerio, 2009). Alimo-Metcalfe (1995a, 1995b) maintains that women tend to be more motivated by organisational goals than their male counterparts and more amenable to change. Women also appear to have different work–life balance priorities, especially in terms of childcare, as British Airways found to its cost in 2003. An attempt by the airline to impose a new clocking-on arrangement on its check-in staff at Heathrow Airport turned out disastrously when the predominantly female workforce went on unofficial strike. This cost British Airways £40 million in lost revenues and an incalculable amount in bad publicity (Harrison, 2003). The company failed to understand its staff's priorities and concerns, as Phillips (2003: 17) relates:

> Currently, shifts are organised three months at a time and women can arrange childcare around their working hours. What they fear is a system in which a computer will decide on a day-to-day, or hour-to-hour, basis when they should come into work. . . . BA, and the unions too, have been caught on the hop because they failed to understand that, for these relatively low-paid, often part-time, women workers, the welfare of children comes first – above money.

Despite the evidence that women have different preferences and priorities to men, and face different career obstacles, it is not clear how this impacts on their leadership style or effectiveness (Nahavandi, 2012). While at one time, it was thought if women were to progress up the managerial hierarchy, they had to conform to male characteristics, such as decisiveness, competitiveness and playing by the rules, this no longer seems to be the case (Schein and Mueller, 1992; Yukl, 2013). Certainly, characteristics that were previously attributed to women, such as a preference for adopting a participative-democratic leadership style, are now seen as important for all leaders, whether male or female (Valerio, 2009). Workforce diversity is not just about gender, however, or even cultural or ethnic differences, as Cummings and Worley (2001: 429–30) point out:

> Such a definition is too narrow and focuses attention away from the broad range of issues that a diverse workforce poses. Diversity results from people who bring different resources and perspectives to the workplace and who have distinctive needs, preferences, expectations and lifestyles. Organizations must design human resource systems that account for these differences if they are to attract and retain a productive workforce and if they want to turn diversity into a competitive advantage.

That people who are different are treated less well than those who conform to whatever the prevailing stereotype is in organisations and society is well known. Most countries now have laws that seek to prevent or punish discrimination. This of course can provide a powerful incentive for organisations to recognise and manage workforce diversity. In raising the issue of competitive advantage, however, Cummings and Worley draw attention to the positive side of diversity. In a fiercely competitive world where markets are expanding and customers are increasingly rejecting standardised products and services in favour of ones tailored to their needs, workforce diversity can bring substantial benefits. It offers the possibility of more creativity, innovation and flexibility, and it provides a heightened sensitivity to different customer groupings and a wider pool of talent to draw from. This is certainly the view taken by Google (2008):

> Diversity and inclusion are fundamental to Google's way of doing things. We strive to be a local company in every country that we operate and we understand that our users all have different cultures, languages and traditions. It drives the projects we work on, the people we hire and the goals we set ourselves. We go to great lengths to create products that are useful to our user wherever they are and we've found that this commitment to diversity and to our users has been key to our success.

Google aspires to be an organization that reflects the globally diverse audience that our search engine and tools serve. We believe that in addition to hiring the best talent, the diversity of perspectives, ideas, and cultures leads to the creation of better products and services. The diversity of our employees and partners serves as the foundation for us to better serve our diverse customers and stakeholders all over the world.

Only by attracting, retaining and motivating workers effectively, including recognising and promoting the benefits of diversity, can organisations expect to prosper or even survive in an increasingly competitive global economy. This means that organisations have to achieve the difficult but essential task of treating workers differently because of their diversity but treating them all fairly. This is a task that can only be achieved if those in positions of power and authority in organisations are also prepared to manage ethically. However, for some companies, as the next section shows, this appears to go against their normal business practices.

Business ethics

The Oxford Dictionary of English (2006: 595) defines ethics as 'Moral principles that govern a person's behaviour or the conducting of an activity'. Thiroux and Krasemann (2007: 27) state that ethics relate to morality, which:

> deals basically with humans and how they relate to other beings, both human and nonhuman. It deals with how humans treat other beings so as to promote mutual welfare, growth, creativity, and meaning and to strive for what is good over what is bad and what is right over what is wrong.

The business scandals of the last 20 years or so have highlighted the importance of ethics, especially in terms of business leaders (Burnes and By, 2011). It is now generally recognised that a leader's behaviour is influenced by their personal ethics (Northouse, 2013). The choices leaders make, the actions they take, how they treat other people and organisations, all these are informed, either explicitly or implicitly, by ethical considerations. This is why it is now commonplace, as the following quotations show, for most books on organisations and management to make some reference to business ethics:

> Ethical behaviour is behaviour that is morally accepted as good and right, as opposed to bad or wrong, in a particular setting. Business scandals resulting in the collapse of high-profile companies such as Enron and Worldcom highlighted the importance of ethics in managerial behaviour. Today a trend is clear: there are increasing demands that government officials, managers, workers in general and the organizations they represent all act in accordance with high ethical and moral standards.
> (French et al, 2008: 37)

> Three issues are prominent in discussions of proper conduct in developed nations: (1) corruption . . . the chief issues involve bribing foreign public officials in order to win business. . . . (2) exploitation of labor . . . [this] involves the employment of children, the forced use of prison labor, unreasonably low wages and poor working conditions. . . . (3) environmental impact . . . [this] relates to pollution and overuse of scarce resources.
> (Hitt et al, 2009: 95–6)

> Managers today are usually quite sensitive to issues of social responsibility and ethical behavior because of pressure from the public, from interest groups, from legal and government concerns, and from media coverage. It is less clear where to draw the line between socially responsible behavior and the corporation's other concerns, or between the conflicting expectations of ethical behavior among different countries.
> (Deresky, 2000: 56)

There is certainly no shortage of advice about what ethics are or how they should be applied to business. The problem, as the last quotation shows, is that, in an increasingly complex, diverse and competitive world, applying an ethical approach to business is not straightforward. Leaders often have to choose between conflicting sets of values and objectives (Hughes *et al*, 2009). This is why many companies and governments, even those that profess to have ethical policies, have difficulty bridging the gap between rhetoric and reality, especially, it seems, the banks. Though such ethical shortcomings can be viewed as examples of corporate management valuing the interests of one group of stakeholders above those of other groups, that is not the end of the story. The last decade has also shown that in many instances, senior and even junior managers have put their own personal interests above those of everybody else, even to the extent of breaking the law. There can be few people unaware of the Enron scandal, where a number of senior managers conspired to line their own pockets at the expense of everyone else and, in the process, ruined the company and destroyed its accountants, Arthur Andersen (Bryce, 2002). Furthermore, as Partnoy (2003: 1) observes, this was not an isolated incident: 'The 1990s were a decade . . . peppered with financial debacles.' In the US, such practices are especially associated with Wall Street, where financial analysts regularly and aggressively oversold shares, as Tran (2003: 1) relates:

> Analysts hoodwinked investors by hyping up the prospects of internet and other hi-tech companies, while privately dismissing them. Former star internet analyst Henry Blodget once privately described as a 'piece of shit' a stock he was publicly touting, according to previously disclosed emails.

According to Teather (2002), the hyping or 'ramping' of shares was central to the operation of Wall Street's financial institutions and not just limited to a few rogue analysts. In May 2003, in an attempt to draw a line under the crimes of the boom years, leading Wall Street financial institutions agreed to pay fines totalling $1.4 billion (Tran, 2003). Even so, neither the jailing of a few brokers and Enron executives nor the levying of billion-dollar fines appears to have changed the behaviour of the financial institutions. Indeed, the behaviour appears to have worsened in the last decade, as the sub-prime mortgage scandal has shown:

> A pair of Bear Stearns executives were arrested and charged with fraud yesterday over the collapse of two hedge funds. In early morning raids, the FBI arrested Ralph Cioffi and Matthew Tannin at their homes in New Jersey and New York. The pair were handcuffed and escorted, grim faced, into court in front of a battery of television cameras. According to the US government, the duo concocted a web of lies to persuade investors to keep funds in two mortgage-heavy funds that evaporated in value in June last year, losing more than $1.4 billion (£710 million) of clients' money. Among the biggest victims was Barclays Bank, which had pumped in $400 million. Benton Campbell, a federal prosecutor, said: 'They lied in the futile hope that the funds would turn around and that their income and reputations would remain intact.'
> (Clark, 2008)

Nor has such financial misbehaviour ben eradicated by the lessons learnt from the 2008 credit crunch. For example, in May 2012, the American bank JP Morgan admitted that one of its London traders had lost $6 billion in six weeks through 'bets' on the bond market. To put this in context, this figure is larger than the GDP of many small countries (CIA, 2012). The bank's management said that the trader, who was colloquially known as the 'London Whale' for the size of his bets on the bond market, had acted without authority and that it had known nothing about his activities. The US Senate, which investigated the matter, took a different view. They found that:

> JPMorgan Chase 'misled investors' before 'lying to investigators' about its $6 billion trading losses, . . . The 300-page report homes in on disclosures by Jamie Dimon, JPMorgan chief executive, and Doug Braunstein, who resigned as chief financial officer after the affair came to light. Mr Dimon had initially played down the significance of credit derivatives trading activity in the bank's London chief investment officer during an hearings call in April last year, saying it was 'a tempest in a teapot'. However, the Senate report found that he was 'already in possession of information about the . . . complex and sizeable portfolio, its sustained losses for three straight months, the exponential increase in those losses during March and the difficulty of exiting the . . . positions'. . . . The report quotes an examiner at the Office of Comptroller of the Currency, JPMorgan's regulator, saying he felt the bank had 'lied to' and 'deceived' the agency over whether it had mismarked its books to hide the extent of losses.
>
> (Braithwaite and Nasiripour, 2013: 1)

This is not just a case of a few incompetent, greedy or corrupt executives. The sub-prime scandal, which precipitated the 2008 financial collapse, stretched from the top to the bottom of the financial sector and was as blatant as it was illegal (Blanton, 2008).

Of course, as the following examples show, unethical behaviour is not just the preserve of the financial sector:

> The arms company BAe secretly paid Prince Bandar of Saudi Arabia more than £1 billion in connection with Britain's biggest ever weapons contract, it is alleged today. A series of payments from the British firm was allegedly channelled through a US bank in Washington to an account controlled by one of the most colourful members of the Saudi ruling clan, who spent 20 years as their ambassador in the US. It is claimed that payments of £30 million were paid to Prince Bandar every quarter for at least 10 years. It is alleged by insider legal sources that the money was paid to Prince Bandar with the knowledge and authorisation of Ministry of Defence officials under the Blair government and its predecessors. For more than 20 years, ministers have claimed they knew nothing of secret commissions, which were outlawed by Britain in 2002.
>
> (Leigh and Evans, 2007)

> Mobile phone company Samsung has admitted to using tin sourced from Indonesia's controversial Bangka Island, where an investigation last year by the Guardian and environmental charity Friends of the Earth (FoE) found that unregulated tin mining depends on child labour, wrecks the environment and kills an estimated 150 miners every year.
>
> (Hodal, 2013)

In public at least, there are two aspects of business ethics that business leaders agree upon: all businesses should have them, and all businesses have difficulty abiding by them. In making ethical decisions, Peale and Blanchard (2000), authors of *The Power of Ethical Management*, suggest that managers should ask themselves the following three questions:

1. **Is it legal?** Does this decision break any laws or violate any company policies?

2. **Is it balanced?** Is it fair to all the parties concerned?

3. **Is it right?** How do you feel about this decision? Would you like your friends and loved ones to know you've made this decision?

Difficult though they are to implement and maintain, if organisations fail to adopt an ethical approach, the result can be disastrous, as demonstrated by the case of Enron, where managers put their own interests above those of shareholders, staff and the law. Indeed, as the sub-prime scandal shows, even entire industries can become corrupt, threatening the entire world economy.

Globalisation is often couched in terms of the competitive challenge it poses for individual organisations, i.e. how can an organisation, whether in the public, private or voluntary sector, survive and prosper in a borderless world that is increasingly dominated by a few giant, transnational corporations? The discussion above of sustainability, diversity and ethics demonstrates that globalisation also raises crucial questions about the role and impact of organisations in and on a global society. This has led to a growing interest in the concept of the 'Triple Bottom Line' (Fry and Nisiewicz, 2013). This is the idea that companies should adopt three bottom-line objectives – people, planet and profit. Promoters of the concept argue that companies can generate profits while simultaneously improving the lives of their employees and the communities in which they operate.

The Triple Bottom Line goes beyond traditional business concerns such as profit and loss, value for money or market share; it is concerned with fundamental issues of the role of organisations in sustaining life on Earth, respect for human diversity and dignity, and the ethical rules by which we live. These issues are not new, but globalisation has accentuated and brought them to the fore as never before. Governments, international bodies and individual organisations have responded by adopting policies that supposedly promote responsible and ethical behaviour. All big organisations, including the financial institutions involved in the sub-prime scandal, and many smaller companies, have policies on minimising their environmental impact, promoting and managing diversity, and on behaving in an ethical fashion. Yet the gap between ethical rhetoric and the reality of unethical behaviour seems to be getting wider rather than narrower.

The real challenge for organisations is to change managerial behaviour so that business ethics become business practices. Policies, skills and good intentions are clearly not enough. The fundamental point is that managers need to behave differently: they need to put the policies and skills into practice. Therefore, in examining the role and development of managers in the rest of this chapter, one of the key issues to be addressed will be what determines managerial behaviour and how can we change it.

The manager's role

It is generally accepted that serious attempts to define the role of managers began in 1916 with the publication of Henri Fayol's (1949) book *General and Industrial Management* (Hales, 1999; Lamond, 2004). There, Fayol stated that the key functions of managers were: forecasting and planning, organising, commanding, coordinating and controlling (*see* Chapter 1). Since then, there have been a great number of other attempts to define the manager's role (*see* Barnard, 1938; Brewer and Tomlinson, 1964; Carlson, 1951; Constable and McCormick, 1987; Golding and Currie, 2000; Griffin, 2002; Handy *et al*, 1987; Horne and Lupton, 1965; Kotter, 1982, 1990; Mintzberg, 1973; Nahavandi, 2000; Silverman and Jones, 1976; Sjöstrand, 1997; Stewart, 1976; Yukl, 2006). As Hales (1986, 1999) found when he reviewed many of these studies, the information available presents the reader with a confusing and conflicting picture of what managers should do and how they should do it. All the same, Fayol's work still attracts support (Lamond, 2004; Duncan, 1999; Wren,

1994) and many textbooks still take a recognisably Fayolian approach when defining the role of managers. For example, Dakin and Hamilton (1990: 32) maintain that:

> [The manager] plans, organises, directs and controls, on proprietors' or own behalf, an industrial, commercial or other undertaking, establishment or organisation, and coordinates the work of departmental managers or other immediate subordinates.

Others, though, have taken a distinctly different approach. Peter Drucker (1985: 53), often referred to as the 'father of modern management', argues that the essence of the manager's role is:

> [the] task of creating a true whole that is larger than the sum of its parts, a productive entity that turns out more than the sum of the resources put into it.

Drucker also likened the manager to the conductor of a symphony orchestra. As conductor, the manager is the one through whose effort, vision and leadership the various instrumental parts, that are so much noise by themselves, become the living whole of music. In this instance, the manager is also the composer as well as the conductor.

Charles Handy (1986: 365–6), whose work was examined in Chapter 3, likened the manager to a doctor:

> The manager, like the GP, is the first recipient of problems. However he may deal with them, whatever role he may choose to assume, he must first (just like the doctor) decide whether it is a problem and if so, what sort of problem it is, before he proceeds to act. He must, in other words:
>
> Identify the symptoms in any situation;
> Diagnose the disease or cause of the trouble;
> Decide how it might be dealt with – a strategy for health;
> Start the treatment.

Such analogies are useful in that they create a concrete picture of the manager's role, but they can also be misleading. Conducting is an art form; is management an art form? Or, as Handy's analogy implies, is it a science in the same way that medicine is a science? As Part 1 of this book showed, the clash between those who see management as a rational, science-based process, and those who believe it to be more intuitive and less rational, is not new.

Duncan (1975) tries to resolve this conflict by taking a holistic view of the job of the manager. He identifies three distinct levels of management activity:

Philosophical – goal formation.

Scientific – goal accomplishment and evaluation.

Art – implementation of decisions.

At the philosophical level in forming goals, Duncan proposes that the manager is mainly concerned with the effects of the actions and reactions of other individuals and groups within the organisation's wider economic and social context. At this level, managers and their associates formulate clear and precise strategies that will encompass all envisaged effects that can result from the set goals, not only on the various pressure groups within its internal and external environment but also on competitors and regulatory agencies. It is also at this level that the ethics of managerial behaviour, values and priorities of the organisation are formulated and established.

At the scientific level, management develops plans, methods and techniques for achieving set goals, and establishes procedures for monitoring and evaluating progress.

The art level is concerned with the implementation of decisions; this is the level at which tactical and administrative decisions are made to deploy the organisation's resources and attain the optimum degree of operational efficiency. This level is an 'art' because, according to Duncan, there appears to be a particular talent necessary to persuade others that management-generated goals and decisions should be accepted.

While one might not necessarily agree with his definitions, especially in terms of strategy formulation, Duncan's three-level approach is extremely useful in that it suggests that management is both a science and an art. By its very nature, management is forced to deal with both rational, science-based activities, such as the design and operation of manufacturing and administrative systems, and less rational, more intuitive activities, especially those concerning managing and motivating people. The extent to which a manager is involved in any of these activities will depend on the kind of organisation the manager works for, the type of job the manager has, and – crucially – the manager's level in the organisation's hierarchy (Hales, 1986). Position in the hierarchy, formally at least, is likely to exert the greatest influence on the role given to and expected of a manager. The three main hierarchical levels are as follows:

- **Top management** – the policy-making group responsible for the overall direction of the company.

- **Middle management** – responsible for the execution and interpretation of policies throughout the organisation and for the successful operation of assigned divisions or departments.

- **First-level or supervisory management** – directly responsible to the middle management group for ensuring the execution of policies by their subordinates. They are also responsible for the attainment of objectives by the units they control, through practices and procedures approved and issued by top or middle management.

Superficially, at least, these three hierarchical levels of management appear to mirror Duncan's three levels of management activity. On a closer examination, however, it becomes more difficult to match them because each hierarchical level of management can encompass philosophical, scientific and art activities, though not necessarily to the same extent. This can be seen more clearly by examining what it is that managers actually do, as opposed to what academics say they should do.

There have been a number of important studies conducted to determine how managers spend their time (*see*, for example, Brewer and Tomlinson, 1964; Child and Ellis, 1973; Kotter, 1982). Hales (1999) claims that the most widely known and replicated work in this area is by Mintzberg (1973, 1975). In *The Nature of Managerial Work* (Mintzberg, 1973), his aim was to replace the 'folklore' about what managers do with the 'fact' of what they actually do. As he later commented:

> If you ask a manager what he does, he will most likely tell you that he plans, organizes, coordinates and controls. Then watch what he does. Don't be surprised if you can't relate what you see to these four words. . . . The fact is that these four words, which have dominated management vocabulary since the French industrialist Henri Fayol first introduced them in 1916, tell us little about what managers actually do. At the best, they indicate some vague objectives managers have when they work.
> (Mintzberg, 1975: 49)

Synthesising his results (Mintzberg, 1973) and previous research on the role of managers, he concluded as follows:

- Although much managerial work is unprogrammed, all managers do have regular, ordinary duties to perform.

- Rather than being systematic, reflective thinkers and planners, managers simply respond to the pressures or demands of their jobs.

- Managerial activities are characterised by brevity, variety and discontinuity.

Some 30 years after Mintzberg's work, Yukl (2002), in reviewing the literature on management, came to similar conclusions:

- The content of managerial work is varied and fragmented.

- Many activities are reactive.

- Interactions often involve peers and outsiders.

- Many interactions involve oral communications.

- Decision processes are disorderly and political.

- Most planning is informal and adaptive.

Yukl (2002: 22) also found that the pace of managerial work was hectic and unrelenting:

> During the typical workday there is seldom a break in the workload. Managers receive almost continuous requests for information, assistance, direction, and authorization from a large number of people, such as subordinates, peers, superiors, and people outside the organization.

Yukl's work confirms Mintzberg's (1973) finding that managers' jobs are remarkably similar, and that their work can be described in terms of ten very important roles that could be categorised under three headings: interpersonal, informational and decision-making.

Interpersonal roles

One of the most time-consuming and important aspects of most managerial jobs is to work with, direct and represent people. The three key roles in this respect are as follows:

- **Figurehead** – as the formal representative of the organisation.

- **Liaison** – forming connections with other organisations.

- **Leader** – in relation to members of a group within the organisation.

Informational roles

Those in managerial positions have unique opportunities to obtain and disseminate information. The three key roles involved are given below:

- **Monitor** – as monitors, managers seek, receive and store information that can be used to the advantage of the company.

- **Disseminator** – the manager must broadcast this useful information to the organisation.

- **Spokesperson** – on behalf of the organisation, the manager communicates information to other relevant groups and bodies, both internal and external.

Decision-making roles

One of the main parts of any manager's job is to take decisions. In this respect, there are four key roles involved:

- **Entrepreneur** – looking for ways to improve the operation of the organisation or for new product or market opportunities.
- **Disturbance-handler** – managers must handle crises effectively.
- **Resource-allocator** – responsible for constructing budgets and allocating resources.
- **Negotiator** – according to Mintzberg, managers spend a great deal of their time as negotiators, because only they have the necessary information and the authority to carry out this role.

As Yukl (2013) notes, though these roles are common to most managerial jobs, the emphasis and importance of these roles varies between managers depending on a range of factors such as organisation size, level of management, level of managerial independence, and the stage the organisation has reached in its life cycle. Mintzberg (1973) argues that the lack of uniformity within managerial jobs can be accounted for by hierarchical and functional differentiation. He contended that chief executives, for example, focus considerable attention on external roles, such as liaison, spokesperson and figurehead, which link the organisation to its environment. At lower levels, work is more focused, more short term in outlook, and the characteristics of brevity and fragmentation are more pronounced. As a result of this, the external managerial roles are less important, and real-time internal roles (disturbance-handler and negotiator) concerned with daily operating problems and maintaining the workflow become relatively more important. Furthermore, he argues that interpersonal roles are more important to sales managers, that staff managers give more attention to informational roles, and production managers focus on decisional roles. Mintzberg's observations have been supported by a number of other studies (Kotter, 1982; Silverman and Jones, 1976).

Stewart (1976, 1982) draws particular attention to demands, constraints and choices in shaping managerial roles:

- **Demands** – these are the expectations that those in positions of power have for a role holder.
- **Constraints** – these are factors peculiar to the organisation and its environment that limit a manager's freedom of manoeuvre.
- **Choices** – though managers are limited in what they can do by the demands and constraints of their jobs, all managers have a degree of discretion (choice) in what to do and when to do it.

One key area where managers are called on to make choices is when faced with role conflicts (Yukl, 2013). For example, managers are often caught between subordinates' expectations that managers will protect their interests and provide resources, and superiors' expectations that managers will act in the best interests of the organisation and minimise costs. Another example of conflict between roles is where managers are expected to spend considerable time, in their figurehead role, dealing with the external world while at the same time colleagues expect them to be present internally carrying out their leadership role.

Nevertheless, despite the presence of conflicts and choices, Hales (1986: 102), in reviewing the research on the manager's role, concludes that:

> Much of what managers do is, of necessity, an unreflective response to circumstances. The manager is less a slow and methodical decision maker, more a 'doer' who has to react rapidly to problems as they arise, 'think on his feet', take decisions in situ and develop a preference for concrete activities. This shows in the pace of managerial work and the short time span of most activities.

Therefore, in examining the role of managers, there appears to be a discrepancy between what the literature says managers should do (as epitomised by Fayol) and what the managers actually do (as shown by Mintzberg). Lamond (2004: 353) takes a different view:

> It is neither Fayol (1949) nor Mintzberg (1973) who captures 'management', but together they encapsulate in a pair of overlapping Venn diagrams some, but not all, of the concerns and behaviours of those charged with executing managerial functions in organizations, whether they are called 'managers' or not. Those with managerial responsibilities may prefer the sense of rationality and sense of purpose that infuses Fayol's (1949) characterisation, but they act in different ways, reflecting the day-to-day exigencies faced by Mintzberg's (1973) managers.

Lamond's argument is that the difference is not between Fayol's view of management and Mintzberg's view but between managers' preferred style of behaviour and their actual style of behaviour. He maintains that, in seeking to be effective, managers' behaviour is shaped by the day-to-day circumstances they face rather than how they would prefer to behave. Therefore, important as it is to understand the manager's role, it is just as important to understand what constitutes effectiveness.

Despite the vast number of books and articles on management and the role of the managers, most writers seem to shy away from defining either organisational or managerial effectiveness. Part 1 of this book reviewed organisation theory and behaviour. What this revealed is that the promoters of these theories, either implicitly or explicitly, state that effectiveness is defined by the extent to which managers adopt the theorists' 'one best way'. From this perspective, effectiveness is something of a moving target; the 'best way' for Frederick Taylor is not the best way for Douglas McGregor or Tom Peters or Peter Senge.

Nahavandi (2000: 5) makes a similar point when commenting that 'leadership effectiveness depends on the point of view of the person who is evaluating the leader'. The concept of effectiveness was reviewed in Chapter 8. Instead of seeing effectiveness as defined by adherence to a particular approach or theory, or lying solely in the eye of the beholder, it was argued that effectiveness is 'the ability or power to have a desired effect' (Longman Dictionary of Contemporary English, 1978: 350). In terms of managerial effectiveness, this means that an effective manager is one who achieves what is required of them, whether that be to transform an organisation or merely to ensure that services continue to be delivered on time, at the right cost and to the right quality. If this is the definition of managerial effectiveness, the next question is: 'What determines managerial effectiveness?' Are there key attributes, skills or competences that managers need to possess in order to 'have a desired effect'? As the next section will explain, there are three main perspectives on what makes an effective manager.

Management and leadership

Regardless of the difficulty in identifying what managers do or how they should do it, there has been a long-held belief that the major factor which distinguishes successful organisations from their less successful counterparts is the presence of dynamic and effective leadership (Northouse, 2013). However, as Yukl (2013: 23) points out, 'There is a continuing controversy about the difference between leadership and management'. This was most clearly stated by Bennis and Nanus (1985: 21) who maintain that 'managers are people who do things right and leaders are people who do the right thing'. Though it is conceptually appealing to separate people into one of two mutually exclusive types, managers or leaders, there is little empirical evidence for this view (Bass, 1990; Hickman, 1990; Mintzberg, 1973; Rost, 1991; Yukl, 2013).

Indeed, Vroom and Jago (1988) specifically argue that managers can and do possess both managerial and leadership skills, which they swap between depending on the situation. Nahavandi (2012) offers a more nuanced view of the leadership versus management debate by arguing that the distinction between the two is about management and leadership processes. He contends that the process of management is essentially concerned with achieving stability. Yet he sees the leadership process as essentially being concerned with bringing about change (*see* Table 14.1).

Nahavandi (2012: 23) also offers the warning:

> Defining managing and leading as distinct roles, processes, or relationships may obscure more than it reveals if it encourages simplistic theories about effective leadership. Most scholars seem to agree that success as a manager or administrator in modern organizations also involves leading. How to integrate these two processes has emerged as a complex and important issue in organizational literature.

Though the topic of leadership, its definition, promotion and difference from management, has dominated the management literature for over 50 years, it still remains an elusive concept, which has spawned many different and conflicting theories (Northouse, 2013). In the early years of the twentieth century, leadership was seen as the ability to control and dominate subordinates. By the 1930s, this view had formalised itself into the trait approach

Table 14.1 Management v leadership processes

Managers	Leaders
Focus on the present	Focus on the future
Maintain status quo and stability	Create change
Implement policies and procedures	Create a culture based on shared values
Remain aloof to maintain objectivity	Establish an emotional link with followers
Use the power of their position	Use personal power

Source: Adapted from *The Art and Science of Leadership* 2nd ed., Prentice Hall: Upper Saddle River, NJ, USA. (Nahavandi A. 2000), Adapted by permission of Pearson Education Inc., Upper Saddle River, NJ.

to leadership, which related good leadership to the possession of certain physical and psychological characteristics. In the 1950s and 1960s, the literature tended to focus on how the leader developed and achieved shared group goals. The 1970s saw a shift from concern with group behaviour and group goals to organisational behaviour and organisational goals. In particular, there was a greater emphasis on leader–follower relations, with the particular attention on how leaders influenced the behaviour of individuals to achieve organisational goals. From the 1980s, continuing through to the present day, there has been a major shift in the leadership literature with the emergence of, not to say obsession with, the notion of the heroic, charismatic, transformational leader.

More than 50 years ago, Bennis (1959: 259) commented:

> Always it seems that the concept of leadership eludes us or turns up in another form to taunt us again with its slipperiness and complexity. So we have invented a proliferation of terms to deal with it . . . and still the concept is not sufficiently defined.

It would be nice to think that we are now in a position to define what leadership is and what leaders should do. Unfortunately, the reverse appears to be the case. Instead of the ideas and theories which have emerged over the last 100 years combining to provide a composite and coherent theory of leadership, what we have is a fragmented and confusing picture, with each theory or nostrum seeking to outpoint the others (Barker, 2001; Northouse, 2013; Yukl, 2012).

While it may be difficult to define leadership, it is possible to bring some clarity to the concept by recognising that researchers on leadership and management can, in the main, be grouped into one of three categories, as follows:

● Those who primarily focus on the personal characteristics/traits of the leader.

● Those who concentrate on the leader–follower situation, especially the characteristics of the follower.

● Those who take a contextual approach by relating leadership and management styles to the overall organisation context and climate.

The personal characteristics/traits approach to effective leadership

The trait approach to leadership flourished between 1930 and 1950, though it still has its adherents today. It maintains that there are individual characteristics or traits that universally differentiate leaders from non-leaders, and that these characteristics explain why some people are effective in leadership roles and others not (House *et al*, 1997). It is based on the assumption that leaders are to a substantial extent born, not made, and possess natural and unique personal traits not possessed by other people (Yukl, 2013). Many psychological traits have been identified as important for leaders, including authoritarianism, intelligence, need for achievement and need for power, as well as a number of physical characteristics, such as gender, height, physical energy and appearance (House *et al*, 1997). This is sometimes known as the 'great man' approach because its proponents tend to use historical figures such as Napoleon, Churchill, Roosevelt, Gandhi, Henry Ford, etc., to support their arguments. Consequently, regardless of the task or situation, if a person possesses the appropriate traits, it is argued that they will be a good or great leader and if they do not possess the appropriate personal attributes, then they will be unlikely to be a good leader (Hughes *et al*, 2009).

Attractive though the 'great man' approach may seem, the numerous studies of leadership have failed to reveal any consistent pattern of universal traits or characteristics related to effective leadership, and the theory has been effectively dismissed for lack of empirical support (Arnold *et al*, 2005; Gibb, 1969; Grint, 2005; Hughes *et al*, 2009; Stogdill, 1948, 1974; Yukl, 2013). Nevertheless, it does attempt to make a comeback from time to time.

In an effort to breathe new life into this approach, attempts were made to view leadership behaviour rather than traits as the main predictor of effectiveness. Fleishman (1953, 1969) identifies two separate classes of behaviour as important in determining effective leadership:

1. **Consideration** – the quality of the interpersonal relationship between the leader and his or her subordinates, and in particular the degree to which a leader shows trust of subordinates, respect for their ideas and consideration for their feelings.

2. **Initiating structure** – the degree to which leaders define and structure their own and their subordinates' roles towards achieving set goals. It also covers the extent to which a leader directs group activities through planning, communication, information, scheduling, trying out new ideas, and praise and criticism.

Another related dimension of leadership behaviour that received much attention in the 1950s and 1960s was participation – whether the leader leans towards an autocratic or democratic style of management. As noted in Chapters 2, 8 and 9, both the Human Relations school and proponents of Planned change believed that, in the aftermath of the Second World War, participation and democracy would prove to be essential components of organisational effectiveness. It was not a coincidence that those studying leadership and those studying organisational change should develop similar views on participation and democracy. Much of the work on leadership at this time was influenced by the ground-breaking studies into leadership styles by Kurt Lewin, Ronald Lippitt and Ralph White (Marrow, 1969). These studies promoted the idea that a democratic leadership style was the most effective (*see* Chapter 9). According to Gastil (1994), there are three key elements of democratic leadership:

- maximising participation and involvement of group members;
- empowerment;
- facilitating group decision-making.

In the 1950s and 1960s, this emphasis on leadership style and behaviour characteristics gave rise to a number of 'universal theories' of effective leader behaviour – which is to say, researchers began to argue for a 'one best way' approach to leadership (*see*, for example, Argyris, 1964; Likert, 1967; McGregor, 1960). These theories postulated that the same style of leadership is optimal in all situations (Yukl, 1994).

Perhaps the best known and most influential of these 'universal theories' is Blake and Mouton's (1969, 1985) Managerial Grid – later re-named the Leadership Grid (Blake and McCanse, 1991). The Grid has two critical dimensions: *concern for people* – similar to *consideration*; and *concern for production* – similar to *initiating structure*. By examining how these two dimensions interact, in both their strong and weak states, Blake and Mouton identified five different styles of management, which they labelled as follows:

- **Team management**. This arises from a high concern for people and a high concern for production. The objectives are to achieve high levels of both performance and job satisfaction by gaining subordinates' willing commitment to achieving their assigned tasks.

- **Country club management**. This occurs when concern for production is low but concern for people is high. The main concern of this approach is to achieve the harmony and well-being of the group in question by satisfying people's social and relationship needs.

- **Middle-of-the-road management**. This situation comes about where there is moderate concern for production and moderate concern for people. Managers who follow this approach tend to have a 'live and let live' philosophy and tend to avoid difficult or contentious issues.

- **Task management**. This can be defined as a high concern for production but a low concern for people. The objective is to achieve high productivity by planning, organising and directing work in such a way that human considerations are kept to a minimum.

- **Impoverished management**. This ensues from a low concern for both production and people. This form of managerial behaviour centres on exacting the minimum effort from subordinates in order to achieve the required result.

Though Blake and Mouton (1985) identify these five styles of management, for them the most effective is team management, where leaders are both task and people-orientated – the so-called 'high–high' leader (i.e. their aim is to ensure subordinates achieve high levels of performance and high levels of job satisfaction). They also argue that while managers have a dominant or preferred style of leadership, many managers are capable of switching from one style to another or of combining styles if they encounter a situation where their preferred style does not work. In a significant departure from other adherents of the personal characteristics approach, Blake and Mouton also argue that a person's dominant style is influenced not only by their personal values and personal history but by the nature of the organisation in which they are operating, and chance – the types of management situations and styles they have encountered in their career.

Despite the wide number of studies seeking to test and elaborate the Managerial Grid approach, however, the evidence in support of it, or for any of the universal theories, is limited (Evans, 1970; Filley *et al*, 1976; Larson *et al*, 1976; Wagner, 1994; Yukl, 2006).

Overall then, despite the hundreds of studies over many decades, researchers have failed to produce convincing evidence of a relationship between universal leadership traits/behaviours and leadership effectiveness (Bass, 2008; Judge *et al*, 2009; Yukl, 2013). Despite this, trait researchers still maintain that certain traits seem to differentiate leaders from non-leaders. (Northouse, 2013). For example, Kirkpatrick and Locke (1991) identify six traits which they maintain characterise good leaders. These are as follows: drive, motivation, honesty and integrity, self-confidence, cognitive ability, and knowledge of business. Others suggest that the list should also include traits such as emotional intelligence, agreeableness, flexibility and extraversion (Northouse, 2013). Having said that, they also seem to acknowledge that these may be situation-specific traits rather than universal ones. For example, a leader who is flexible may be effective in unstable situations but not so in stable ones (House *et al*, 1997). Similarly, two leaders with different traits may both be successful in the same situation (Yukl, 2013). Nevertheless, even this watered-down, situational version of the 'great man' approach remains to be tested (House *et al*, 1997; Northouse, 2013). What it has done, however, is draw attention to the situational aspects of leadership effectiveness and given rise to a contingency-based perspective on leadership. This can be seen in the leader–follower approach, which examines whether the interaction between the characteristics of subordinates (followers) and the characteristics of leaders can offer an explanation of leadership effectiveness.

The leader–follower situation approach to effective leadership

In the 1950s and 1960s, in response to the inability of researchers to make a convincing case for a 'one best way' approach to leadership, attention began to focus on identifying the situations in which leaders were effective, particularly in terms of how leaders influenced group behaviour (Northouse, 2013). By the 1970s, researchers had begun to examine the relationship not just at the group level but at the level of the individual follower as well. In effect, they began to focus on how a leader's behaviour varies from subordinate to subordinate. This leader–follower approach, or leader–member exchange (LMX) as it is sometimes called, focuses on how the leader and the follower develop an interpersonal relationship over time (North *et al*, 1997), influencing each other and negotiating the subordinate's role in the organisation.

The basic premise of the theory is that a leader develops a different relationship with each subordinate and that this will be based on the behaviour (or expected behaviour) of each party. These relationships take one of two forms: the leader will develop a close and trusting relationship with a small number of people, and a much more distant and formal relationship with the rest (Kerr *et al*, 1974). In the first type of relationship, both parties have high expectations of each other. The leader expects loyalty and commitment and the follower expects preferment and advancement. In the more distant types of relationship, both parties have relatively low expectations. The leader expects the subordinate to comply with rules and perform their allocated duties. In turn, the subordinate expects to receive the rate for the job and be treated fairly (Graen and Cashman, 1975; Yukl, 2013).

In examining leader–follower relations, Kerr *et al* (1974) take the two forms of leadership behaviour identified by Fleishman (1969) – consideration and initiating structure – and apply these to a framework that includes three situational variables or contingencies:

1. **Subordinate considerations** – such as the subordinates' experience and abilities, and their expectations of the leader.

2. **Superior considerations** – in particular, the amount of influence subordinates have over the behaviour of their superiors.

3. **Task considerations** – including factors such as time urgency, amount of physical danger, permissible error rate, presence of external stress, degree of autonomy and scope, importance and meaningfulness of work, and degree of ambiguity.

Kerr *et al* (1974) argued that the effectiveness of the two forms of leadership behaviour (consideration and initiating structure) in promoting high levels of performance from subordinates is moderated by the above three situational variables. For example, if the task to be performed is characterised by time pressure, subordinates will be more amenable to a higher level of initiating structure (i.e. direction by superiors) and there will be a stronger relationship between job satisfaction, performance and initiating structure. Alternatively, when a task is seen as intrinsically very satisfying to a subordinate, a leadership style with high consideration will not significantly increase satisfaction or performance. Support for the central premises of Kerr *et al*'s (1974) model has been limited. Research by Schriesheim and Murphy (1976) produced mixed results. There was evidence that high levels of initiating structure did increase performance in high-pressure situations and reduce it under low levels of pressure. Different levels of pressure, however, did not appear to impact on subordinates' satisfaction with their superiors. Nor, where tasks were viewed as having higher clarity, were either consideration-based or initiating-structure-based styles significantly related to satisfaction.

The most influential contingency theory of leadership has been Fiedler's (1967) Least Preferred Co-worker (LPC) model. Based on a decade of research, Fiedler argues that leaders have relatively stable personal characteristics that, in turn, leave them with a particular set of leadership behaviours which they cannot change. Consequently, there is no point in trying to train or educate managers to adopt different behaviours towards their subordinates. Instead, both they and their subordinates have to learn to live with the leader's behaviour. For Fiedler, the key personal characteristics involved in leadership concern how positively or not the leader views his or her Least Preferred Co-worker. Fiedler developed a questionnaire to determine a leader's LPC measure. The questionnaire is built around a scale of 16 bipolar adjectives (e.g. pleasant–unpleasant, distant–close, efficient–inefficient) that attempts to measure whether a person is 'task'- or 'relationship'-orientated. As Arnold *et al* (2005) note, there is some dispute about exactly what a leader's LPC score means and how it relates to other leadership dimensions such as consideration and structure. In general, leaders with a high LPC are often seen as being people or relationship-orientated, while those with a low LPC are seen as being task-orientated. From his work, Fiedler concludes that the effectiveness of particular leadership traits or behaviours, as measured by a high or low LPC score, are moderated by the situation in which they are deployed, making it important to match the leader to the situation (Fiedler and Chemers, 1984).

Fiedler identifies three key aspects of a work situation, which taken together, he argues, determine the effectiveness or not of particular leadership characteristics. In descending order of importance, these are as follows:

1. **The leader–follower relationship** – friendliness and loyalty from subordinates increases the leader's influence over them.

2. **Task structure** – the greater the degree of standardisation, detailed instructions and objective measures of performance, the more favourable the situation is for the leader.

3. **The leader's formal position and power** – the more discretion and authority the leader has regarding the reward and punishment of subordinates, the more influence he or she will be able to exert.

By attributing a high or low score to each of these three aspects, Fielder constructs eight (i.e. $2 \times 2 \times 2$) types of work situation. He maintains that the most favourable situation is where leader–follower relations are good, the task is well-defined and highly structured, and the leader has a high level of formal authority. In contrast, the least favourable situation is where leader–follower relations are poor, the task structure is ill-defined, and the leader has only a low level of formal authority.

Although (or perhaps because) it is the most influential and widely utilised situational theory of leadership, it is also the most widely criticised. The main criticisms are that it lacks empirical support, that it fails to explain how particular types of leadership behaviour affect subordinates' performance, and that the measures used by Fiedler are arbitrary and lack any explicit rationale (Ashour, 1973; Shiflett, 1973; Vecchio, 1983). Fiedler's model has also been subjected to the same type of criticism as other contingency–situational approaches (*see* Chapter 2). In particular, critics maintain that it ignores a manager's ability to change or influence factors such as task structure to favour their style of leadership. In this respect, a number of writers have pointed out that Fiedler treats structure, an important component of his model, as a given, whereas in many instances, determining and changing organisation and job structures is a major component of a manager's role (O'Brien and Kabanoff, 1981). Overall, empirical support for Fielder's LPC model is limited (Yukl, 2013).

In response to these criticisms, Fiedler (1986, 1995) developed cognitive resource theory (CRT), which is built on his LPC work. This examines how the cognitive resources of leaders and subordinates (primarily intelligence and experience) affect group performance. Fiedler maintains the relationship is moderated by the level of interpersonal stress between the leader and their subordinates, their respective levels of task knowledge, and the degree of participation in decision-making. In low-stress situations, he contends that a leader's effectiveness in terms of influencing subordinate performance is related to the leader's intelligence. In high-stress situations, however, leaders rely more on their experience to promote effectiveness.

In considering leadership style, Fielder claims that participative decision-making is more effective when subordinates have more knowledge of the task than leaders. If the reverse is the case, a less participative, more directive approach tends to be more effective (Yukl, 2013). Unfortunately for Fielder, the evidence for CRT is no more convincing than that for LPC (Arnold *et al*, 2005; Nahavandi, 2012; Vecchio, 1992). Also, as Yukl (2013) notes, contingency approaches to leadership, such as Fielder's, are too general; they do not provide enough guidance to help managers identify how they should behave in specific circumstances. In any case, as the next section shows, there are those who believe that managers, rather than having fixed behaviours as Fielder assumes, can and do change their leadership behaviours to accommodate changing circumstances (Bass, 1995; Burns, 1978; Vroom and Jago, 1988).

The contextual approach to effective leadership

One of the weaknesses of the leadership literature, as was demonstrated above, is that it tends to concentrate on the traits of individual managers and their followers and the relation between the two groups. The assumption, both explicit and implicit, is that effectiveness is an attribute of the individual manager, but moderated by the leader–subordinate situation. Yet, as many writers observes, a manager's effectiveness may be determined as much by the nature of the organisation in which he or she operates as by their personal qualities and the nature of their relationship with subordinates (*see* Arnold *et al*, 2010; Burnes, 1991; Griffin, 2002; Hales, 1986; Nahavandi, 2012; Sjöstrand, 1997; Yukl, 2013).

It is out of and in response to such observations that the contextual approach to leadership developed. This approach is a variant of the leader–follower approach to leadership; however, instead of concentrating on leadership behaviour, it focuses on leadership style, and instead of the narrow leader–follower situation, it focuses on the overall organisation context and climate. Thus this approach maintains that leadership effectiveness is contingent on the alignment between an individual's leadership style and the organisational context in which they are operating. In addition, it is the only one of the three main approaches to leadership that incorporates change as a variable (Hughes *et al*, 2009).

One of the most influential contingency approaches to leadership was developed by Vroom and Yetton (1973) and later extended by Vroom and Jago (1988). In contrast to Fiedler, this approach suggests that leaders can and do change their behaviour from situation to situation. The theory identifies five styles of leader decision-making, ranging from the most autocratic to the most democratic. To complement these, Vroom and Jago (1988) also identify some key features of problem situations that leaders have to take into account, such as the need to resolve conflict or achieve goal congruence. By combining leadership styles with problem situations, Vroom and Jago developed a computer package to help managers to identify how suitable their style is for particular situations. Unfortunately, the package proved to be of limited value as it was very complex to use and dealt with only a limited aspect of leadership (Yukl, 2013). Nevertheless, Vroom and Jago express the hope that knowledge of its general principles may be sufficient for most situations. To this end, as Arnold *et al* (2005) note, Vroom and Jago's model has been used to provide some general 'rules of thumb' for leaders, including advice such as:

- where subordinates' commitment is important, a more participative style of leadership is better;
- where subordinates do not share the organisation's goals, group decision-making should be avoided.

However, advice couched in such broad terms is usually too general to be of much use. Even if they were not so general, these rules of thumb are still subject to being overridden by factors such as time constraints, organisational policies and the ability and preferences of managers and subordinates. This is perhaps why other contextual approaches have also been put forward.

One of the most interesting and influential of these was developed not by a social scientist but by a political scientist, James MacGregor Burns, in his 1978 Pulitzer Prize-winning book, *Leadership*. Burns's book combines biography, history and political theory to produce a major study of the nature of leadership. Primarily, he identifies two basic organisation states or contexts, convergent and divergent; and two matching management–leadership styles, transactional management and transformational leadership (*see* Figure 14.1). Most writers tend to use the terms management and leadership interchangeably. Burns was the first to draw a distinction between what he called transactional management (which focuses on maintaining the status quo) and transformational leadership (which focuses on overthrowing the status quo). Burns was primarily concerned with management and

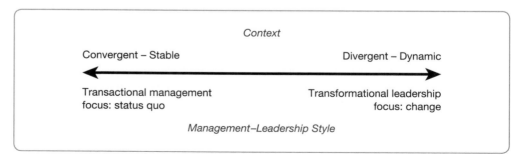

Figure 14.1 Burns's contextual approach to leadership

Table 14.2 Management v leadership

	Transactional management	Transformational leadership
Creating the agenda	Planning and budgeting: developing a detailed plan of how to achieve the results.	Establishing direction: developing a vision that describes a future state along with a strategy for getting there.
People	Organising and staffing: which individual best fits each job and what part of the plan fits each individual.	Aligning people: a major communication challenge in getting people to understand and believe the vision.
Execution	Controlling and problem-solving: monitoring results, identifying deviations from the plan and solving the problems.	Motivating and inspiring: satisfying basic human needs for achievement, belonging, recognition, self-esteem, a sense of control.
Outcomes	Produces a degree of predictability and order.	Produces changes – often to a dramatic degree.

Source: Adapted from Kotter (1990).

leadership in the political context; Bass (1985, 1995) refined Burns' concepts and applied them to organisations.

A *convergent* state occurs when an organisation is operating under stable conditions; where there are established and accepted goals and a predictable external and internal environment. The most appropriate style of management in such a situation, it is contended, is *transactional*. The concept of transactional management stems from the notion that the manager–subordinate relationship is based on a transaction between the two, whereby managers exchange rewards for subordinates' performance. Transactional managers focus on task completion, goal clarification and optimising the performance of the organisation through incremental changes within the confines of existing policy, structures and practices – basically, they seek to work within and maintain the status quo (*see* Table 14.2). Transactional managers motivate followers to perform the tasks expected of them by appealing to their self-interest through the use of incentives and rewards such as pay and promotion.

A *divergent* state occurs when environmental changes challenge the efficiency and appropriateness of an organisation's established goals, structures and ways of working. The Oticon case study in Chapter 11 is an example of an organisation operating in a divergent state. The most appropriate style of leadership in this situation, according to Burns, is *transformational*. Transformational leaders are often portrayed as charismatic or visionary individuals who seek to overturn the status quo and bring about radical change (*see* Table 14.2). Transformational leaders use the force of their personality to motivate followers to identify with the leader's vision and to sacrifice their self-interest in favour of that of the group or organisation. Transformational leaders seek to gain the trust and emotional commitment of their followers by appealing to higher moral and ethical values.

The compatibility between organisational state and leadership style is seen as essential for successful leadership. Where the organisation is required to face new challenges and develop new ways of adapting to these for the sake of survival, then a purely transactional approach would be counterproductive – the phrase 'fiddling while Rome burns' springs to mind. However, transformational leadership is just as likely to be counterproductive during periods where maintenance of the current operational systems would be most appropriate.

Since its publication in 1978, Burns' work has been taken up and cited by a wide range of organisation theorists who subscribe to the view that managers need to, and can, match or adapt their style and approach to the circumstances of the organisation in which they operate (Arnold *et al*, 2005; Bass, 1985, 1995; Beatty and Lee, 1992; Burnes and James, 1995; French and Bell, 1995; Gibbons, 1992; Yukl, 2006). However, the late 1970s and early 1980s, the period when Burns' book was published, were a time of crisis for many Western organisations, when organisations and entire industries and sectors were going through massive changes. Not surprisingly, therefore, there was a tendency for those in the leadership field to focus on transformational leadership, and downplay or even denigrate transactional management (Yukl, 2002). Bass (1985, 1995), while seeking to develop the concept of the transformational leader, nevertheless argues that transformational leadership and transactional management are distinct but not mutually exclusive processes. Transformational leaders may be more effective at motivating their followers but, Bass maintains, effective leaders need to have both transformational and transactional tools in their armouries.

All the same, in situations where radical change is required, as Alimo-Metcalfe and Alban-Metcalfe (2000: 27) found when studying leadership in the UK National Health Service (NHS), 'the transactional competencies of managers, while crucial, are simply not sufficient on their own'. The argument from Bass (1985, 1995) and Alimo-Metcalfe and Alban-Metcalfe (2000) is that someone with purely transactional skills would struggle to deal effectively with the many changes that are an ever-present part of organisational life. Someone with purely transformational skills, meanwhile, would not be able to cope with the day-to-day, routine activities that need to be accomplished even where radical change is taking place. The key issue, therefore, is to identify the optimum balance of transactional–transformational skills in any given circumstances.

Kanter (1989) offers a different perspective on the balance issue by maintaining that good leaders need to incorporate both transactional and transformational characteristics. She argues that archetypal images of managers tend to derive from two basic models: the 'corpocrat' (i.e. the transactional manager) and the 'cowboy' (i.e. the transformational leader). The former is the corporate bureaucrat, the conservative resource-preserver who lives by, and controls the organisation through, established and detailed rules. The latter, the 'cowboy', is a maverick who challenges the established order, who wants to seize every opportunity and question every rule, and who motivates and controls through personal loyalty. Instead of seeking to relate the balance of these two sets of characteristics to their appropriate organisational setting, Kanter (1989: 361) argues that modern organisations require managers who combine the best of both corpocrat and cowboy:

> Without the bold impulses of the take-action entrepreneurs and their constant questioning of the rules, we would miss one of the most potent sources of business revitalization and development. But without the discipline and coordination of conventional management, we could find waste instead of growth, unnecessary risk instead of revitalization. . . . Our new heroic model [of leadership] should be the athlete who can manage the amazing feat of doing more with less, who can juggle the need to both conserve resources and pursue growth opportunities. This new kind of business hero avoids the excesses of both the corpocrat and the cowboy. . . . the business athlete has the strength to balance somewhere in the middle, taking the best of the corpocrat's discipline and the cowboy's entrepreneurial zeal.

As Ideas and perspectives 14.3 shows, Kanter maintains that there are seven skills and sensibilities that this 'new heroic' type of leader needs to possess. Kanter's model avoids the issue of how to determine the optimum balance of transactional and transformational skills

---

IDEAS AND PERSPECTIVES 14.3

Kanter's characteristics of the business hero

Skills and sensibilities of the business athlete:

1. Learn to operate without the might of the hierarchy.
2. Compete in a way that enhances rather than undercuts cooperation.
3. Operate with the highest ethical standards.
4. Have a dose of humility.
5. Develop a process focus.
6. Be multifaceted and ambidextrous.
7. Gain satisfaction from results.

Source: Kanter (1989: 361–4).

---

in a given set of circumstances. Instead, she argues that there is a basic set of transactional and transformational skills or characteristics that all effective leaders need to possess and which can be applied successfully in any situation. In effect, she is attempting to return to the trait approach to leadership, arguing that good leaders are those who possess the requisite set of skills and sensibilities.

Kanter's argument, as mentioned in Chapter 3, is basically that all organisations operate in the same turbulent context, face the same challenges and, consequently, require the same style of leadership. While not necessarily challenging her description of the skills required of transformational leaders, most proponents of the contextual school tend to take the view that there is a wider range of organisational contexts than Kanter acknowledges and, therefore, managers–leaders need to be able to change their approach from transactional to transformational and vice versa as the situation dictates (Hitt *et al*, 2009: 268).

This still leaves the issue of managerial choice – the degree to which managers and leaders have to adapt their approach to the context, as opposed to the degree to which they can influence the context to bring it into line with their preferred way of working. It has been argued in previous chapters that managers do have the ability to adapt the organisational context to make it more amenable to the way they wish to run their organisations. In leadership terms, Grint (2005: 1467) argues that 'decision-makers are much more active in the constitution of the context than conventional contingency theories allow'.

Taking a social-constructionist view (*see* Chapter 4), Grint (2005) argues:

Leadership theories that eschew the dominant and proactive role of the individual leader in favour of more social or structural accounts tend to assume that the context or situation should determine how leaders respond . . . However, I suggest that this is a naïve assumption because it underestimates the extent to which the context or situation is actively constructed by the leader, leaders, and/or decision-makers. In effect, leadership involves the social construction of the context that both legitimates a particular form of action and constitutes the world in the process. (pp. 1470–1)

Hence, CEOs should not be assessed against their ability to 'read' the environment but rather their ability to render that environment suitable for their intended strategies. (pp. 1491–2)

Grint's criticism of the contextual approach to leadership does not invalidate the view that particular situations require a particular set of leadership skills. His argument is that managers have the ability to choose whether to adapt their skills and behaviours to the situation or adapt the situation to their preferred skills and behaviours.

There is one further and very important issue which needs to be considered when looking at the transformational leadership dimension of the contingency approach to leadership, and this relates to ethics. In a highly competitive and rapidly changing world, there has been and still is a strong tendency to see transformational leaders as 'visionary', 'charismatic' and 'heroic' individuals who are far superior to their 'stick-in-the-mud' managerial counterparts (Burnes and By, 2012; Storey, 2004). Because of their almost superhuman powers, they should be allowed free rein to transform their organisations in the way they see fit and expect to be rewarded lavishly for doing so (Gilbert *et al*, 2012; Mintzberg *et al*, 2002). Though there are examples where this freedom of action given to leaders has led to genuine organisational renaissance (e.g. Oticon, Chapter 11), there are also very many other examples where it has been disastrous (e.g. Marconi, Chapter 6). It certainly seems that such unrestricted freedom has contributed to many of the biggest organisational scandals of the last 20 years, and has led to an upsurge in what Einarsen *et al* (2007) refer to as 'destructive' leadership and Gilbert *et al* (2012) call 'toxic behaviors at work' (Burnes and By, 2012; Gopalakrishnan *et al*, 2008; Storey, 2004).

For Burns (1978), at the core of transformational leadership lay an ethical, moral purpose directed at the good of society. For him, it was this moral purpose which ensured that leaders did not abuse the freedom that was granted to them. Unfortunately, as we now know, the ego and greed of many leaders seem to outweigh any ethical considerations, to the detriment of their organisations and the interests of the wider society (Burnes and By, 2012; Leveson Inquiry, 2012; Salz Review, 2013; Soltani, 2013). This has led to a backlash against the concept of the heroic, freewheeling leader, and a renewed interest in models of ethical leadership (Hughes *et al*, 2009; Northouse, 2013).

Yukl (2013: 336–40) describes the three main models of ethical leadership, as follows:

- Servant leadership – is about helping others to accomplish shared objectives by facilitating individual development, empowerment, and collective work that is consistent with the health and long-term welfare of followers.

- Spiritual leadership – describes how leaders can enhance the intrinsic motivation of followers by creating conditions that increase their sense of spiritual meaning at work.

- Authentic leadership – is based on positive psychology and psychological theories of self-regulation. . . . [It] emphasises the importance of consistency in a leader's words, actions, and values.

Mintzberg *et al* (2002: 70) contrast their variant of ethical leadership, which they label 'engaging management', with heroic management (*see* Table 14.3). Their 'engaging' leader does not tower over the organisation like some latter day Colossus who is above mere laws, rules and morality. Instead, the 'engaging' leader is a team player, committed to working with others to achieve the organisation's goals, and is steered by a moral compass.

Though there are a number of variants of ethical leadership, the key message from all of them is that if leaders are to be given the power and responsibility to transform their organisations, they must do so within an ethical framework which allows subordinates and others to check and challenge unethical behaviour. In this respect, Google's 'Don't be evil'

Table 14.3 Heroic management v engaging management

Heroic management	Engaging management
Managers are important people, quite apart from others who develop products and deliver services.	Managers are important to the extent that they help other people be important.
The higher "up" these managers go, the more important they become. At the "top", the chief executive is the corporation.	An organization is an interacting network, not a vertical hierarchy. Effective leaders work throughout; they do not sit on top.
Strategy – clear, deliberate and bold – emanates from the chief who takes the dramatic steps that drive up share price. Everyone else "implements".	Strategies, often initially modest and even obscure, emerge as the people who develop the products and deliver the services solve little problems that merge into new initiatives.
Implementation is the problem, because although the chief embraces change, most others resist it. That is why outsiders – consultants and new managers – must be favored over insiders.	Implementation cannot be separated from formulation. Healthy change requires a respect for the old alongside a recognition of the new.
To manage is to make decisions and allocate resources – including "human" resources. Managing means analyzing, often calculating.	To manage is to bring out the energy that exists naturally within people. Managing thus means inspiring and engaging.
Rewards for increasing the share price go largely to the leader, the risk taker (who pays no penalty for drops in share price).	Rewards for making the company a better place go to everyone, and they are significantly psychic.

Source: Mintzberg *et al* (2002: 70).

slogan, which has empowered subordinates to challenge examples of unethical behaviour, has something to offer (Kaiser, 2013).

In summary, though there are different perspectives on the contextual approach to leadership, taken as a whole, the approach does not seek to invalidate either the trait or leader–follower approaches; rather, it tries to incorporate them within and link them to the wider organisational context. It explicitly recognises that a manager's personal character-istics are an important component of leadership style, and consequently, effectiveness. In addition, it acknowledges the crucial importance not just of the relationship between leaders and followers but also of the overall context within which this takes place (Nahavandi, 2012). In particular, as Gibbons (1992: 5) remarks, 'organizational survival and success are dependent on the ability of leader–follower relations to resolve the prob-lems of internal integration and external adaptation'. Many writers argue, however, that (despite its attractiveness) there is little evidence to support the case for the contextual approach to leadership or to show that is a more suitable approach to running organisations than either the personal characteristics or leader–follower models (Arnold *et al*, 2010; Hinkin and Tracey, 1999; Yukl, 2013).

Leadership research – a note of caution

Just as a review of the role of managers produced a confusing and conflicting picture, so too does an examination of the three approaches to leadership. Nevertheless, the idea of considering context and style together is congruent, partly at least, with the argument developed in the previous parts of this book: namely that there is a need to match the approach to change to the context of the organisation. That argument was developed further to include the possibility that managers could reverse this process and match the organisation's context to their preferred style of working. However, one major caveat needs to be remembered when considering approaches to management: the vast majority of the research and writing on leadership is set in Western, and particularly American, organisations, and addresses their concerns from their cultural perspective (Alimo-Metcalfe and Alban-Metcalfe, 2000; Barker, 2001; House *et al*, 1997). Also, the majority of research studies have tended to focus on male managers and their characteristics (Arnold *et al*, 2010; Maddock, 1999; Thomas, 2003; Valerio, 2009). Therefore, before moving on, we need to return to the issue of diversity raised earlier when discussing globalisation.

To recap, Jones *et al* (2000: 166–7) explain:

Diversity is dissimilarities – differences – among people due to age, gender, race, ethnicity, religion, sexual orientation, socioeconomic background, and capabilities/disabilities.

Diversity is not just about differences within groups of people or between groups of people, it is also about differences between individuals. In terms of differences between people, the posited differences in managerial style between men and women have attracted a great deal of attention (Loden, 1986; Macdonald *et al*, 1999; Maddock, 1999; Mullins, 2002; Thomas, 2003; Valerio, 2009). Davies (1995), for example, found significant differences between masculine and feminine approaches to management. In particular, she found that the masculine approach valued self-esteem, abstract thinking, control and loyalty to superiors. The feminine approach, meanwhile, valued selflessness, contextual thinking, experience and accommodation. It is findings like these that have led writers such as Alimo-Metcalfe (1995a, 1995b) to argue that women prefer to use a more transformational style of leadership while men tend to be more transactionally orientated. While agreeing with Alimo-Metcalfe's findings regarding gender and leadership style, Valerio (2009: 44) points out:

Both men and women [leaders] show a combination of characteristics that include intelligence, sociability, assertiveness, conscientiousness, integrity and the ability to inspire others with their optimistic visions of the future.

Valerio does not argue that women are better managers than men, or vice versa. Her point is that the most successful organisations in America tend to be the ones with a more equal balance of men and women leaders.

It should also be noted that differences in management style are not just gender-related; they can also arise due to age, ethnicity, religion or simple differences in personality (Deresky, 2010; Jones *et al*, 2000).

To complicate the picture, these preferences are not stable between countries and cultures. Much of the work on gender and management has tended to focus on the US and Europe. It is not clear, however, that men and women managers in, for example, Japan and China have the same style preferences as their Western counterparts (Gupta *et al*, 2002; Javidan *et al*, 2006). Indeed, as Trompenaars' (1993) ten-year study of management in 28 countries covering 47 national cultures showed, the differences between countries are as great as the differences within. His work showed that managers as a whole, male and female, in Japan and China tended to possess the characteristics attributed to women managers in the West. For example, they favoured relationships as against rules, they promoted interpersonal trust as against contracts, and they tended to avoid rather than welcome confrontation. This, of course, confirms Hofstede's (1980, 1990) earlier work on cultural differences, which showed that organisational culture, and the values and behaviours of managers, vary from country to country.

Arnold *et al* (1998) maintain there is sufficient evidence to show that leader behaviour is interpreted differently in different cultures. Consequently, managerial behaviour that might be considered supportive in one society may be seen as threatening in another. Therefore, we have to be wary of taking work on managerial styles and behaviour developed in one setting and assuming it applies to all organisations and all societies. This is perhaps why Ricks (1999: 4) comments that 'cultural differences are the most significant and troublesome variables encountered by the multinational company'.

The implications of these findings for management and leadership are significant. First, as was argued earlier in this chapter when discussing diversity, there are no universal rules as to what constitutes an effective manager or leader. An effective manager in one country, company or situation may be less so in others. Second, effectiveness is situation-dependent. In judging what is or is not an effective approach, managers and leaders need to take into account the nature of the organisation and the diversity of its workforce. Lastly, in training and developing managers, there is a need to recognise that while there are some essential generic skills, competences and behaviours, there will also be a need to tailor development programmes to the person and their situation. The issue of management development will be examined next.

Management development

Learning and flexibility

The literature on management and leadership gives support for the notion that different situations require different approaches to change. The literature also show that managers are, sometimes at least, able to change their style of management or leadership, and even exhibit different styles to different parts of their organisations at the same time. This is consistent with the arguments in Chapter 11 that managers can and do adopt both the Planned and Emergent approaches to change management either alternatively or simultaneously as the situation requires. In addition, as Grint (2005) and others maintain, managers can choose to change, or redefine, the context in which their organisations operate to suit their preferred or existing approach to both management and change. As argued in Chapters 10 and 11, changing the situational context can be very important; yet in terms of leadership roles and managerial expectations, one of the main findings from the contextual perspective is the need for managers not only to adapt their style to the particular situation but also to alternate between transactional and transformational approaches as the situation requires (Alimo-Metcalfe and Alban-Metcalfe, 2000; Bass, 1985, 1995).

In part at least, the argument that there are managers who can change their style of leadership runs counter to some of the literature on managerial learning discussed in Chapter 10. D Miller (1993: 119) argues that as they gain experience, managers 'form quite definite opinions of what works and why'. Miller (1994) maintains that this was particularly the case with managers in successful organisations who were highly resistant to changing a 'winning formula'. This view was supported by earlier work from Nystrom and Starbuck

(1984), who maintained that managers interpret the world through their own perceptions and expectations, which are built up over time. Yet, as the Oticon case study illustrated (*see* Chapter 11), some managers do seem capable under certain conditions – especially when faced with a crisis – of restructuring their mental models of how the world is and how they should respond. In Chapter 8, the concepts of dispositional resistance, cognitive dissonance, depth of intervention and the psychological contract were used to explain why it was that people could, in crisis situations, change deeply held attitudes very quickly. This 'crisis mode' only partly helps to explain, however, how some managers, when faced with change situations, appear capable of switching from a transactional approach to a transformational one as the circumstances demand or, indeed, become capable of adopting both at the same time.

The work of Mintzberg (1976) offers some clues as to how managers might accomplish this mental juggling act. In studying brain functions and successful managers, he concludes that effective and proficient managers are 'whole thinkers' – they use both the left and the right hemispheres of their brain. That is, they can combine a rational–analytical approach to management with creativity and lateral thinking. Mintzberg claims that, in general, Western managers tend to think on the left side of their brain – they tend to adopt a rational–analytical approach. Interestingly, this is compatible not only with a transactional approach to management but also with a rational–planned approach to strategy and the directive approach to change.

In contrast, Nonaka (1991) argues that one of the great strengths of Japanese companies is their belief that creating new knowledge depends more on tapping the tacit and often subjective insights and intuitions of all their employees, whether managers or not. He maintains that traditional Western management sees organisations as information processing machines with the only useful knowledge being formal, scientific, quantifiable and rational. He contends that such a perspective limits the creation of new knowledge which, in turn, makes it difficult for organisations to respond to changing and new situations. Nonaka believes that new knowledge always begins with the individual. One of the main foundations of the success of Japanese companies is, he states, managers' ability to gather and combine the insights and intuitions of individual employees and use them for the benefit of the entire organisation. The tendency of Japanese managers to use softer, more creative approaches and to involve staff in decision-making was also noted in Chapters 3, 6 and 7 when discussing approaches to management and strategy.

The success of many Western firms, particularly those concerned with creative processes (such as software development) and the performing arts (such as film-making), show that it is not inevitable that Western managers should operate solely in a rational–analytical mode. Even so, as studies of difference between national cultures have shown, there is a predisposition in Western societies towards more rational–analytical ways of working, whereas in Japan and China managers tend to use more subjective decision-making processes (Gupta *et al*, 2002; Hofstede, 1980, 1990; Javidan *et al*, 2006; Trompenaars, 1993). Also, as D Miller (1993, 1994) points out, a manager's view of the world and what works is shaped by their previous work experience. If this has been in organisations that have operated on traditional Western principles, which are structured in a Classical way and give credence primarily to formal and scientific knowledge, then they undoubtedly will tend to operate on the left side of the brain. This does not mean that such managers cannot develop or access the right side of their brain, but it does mean it is unlikely to come about accidentally or without strong encouragement from the organisations in which they work. To this end, many organisations are seeking to construct management development programmes designed to broaden the outlook and develop the creative, inductive and questioning side of their managers' personalities (Harrison, 2005). Unfortunately, this is unlikely to be achieved through traditional management development programmes, which offer standard packages delivered in classroom situations, because of their low success rate (Burnes, 2003; Lessem, 1998; Mullins, 2002; Mumford *et al*, 2000). If management development programmes are to be effective, in future, as Harrison (2005) contends on behalf of the UK's Chartered Institute of Personnel and Development (CIPD), they will have to be tailored to both the needs of the individual manager and the strategic objectives of their organisation.

In respect of developing managers' creativity, Kirton's (1989) Adaptation–Innovation theory, and subsequent work by Talbot (1993, 1997), provide useful insights. Kirton maintains that not only do people exhibit different degrees of creativity but that they also express their creativity in different ways, along a spectrum which runs from *adaptors* to *innovators*. Those who tend towards the adaptor end of the spectrum prefer to work within the existing system to improve things. Adaptors are efficient, tend to conform to existing norms and like to deal with only a few ideas at a time. Innovators tend to ignore or challenge the system and to come up with radical proposals for change. Figure 14.2 shows how Kirton's ideas relate to transactional management and transformational leadership. As can be seen, it follows from Kirton's work that transactional managers will tend to need lower levels of creativity because they are dealing with changes at the group level, whereas transformational leaders need higher levels of creativity because they are involved in transformational activities at the organisation level.

Figure 14.2 also shows that even within the transformational dimension of leadership, there will be situations which require a more adaptive approach, such as structural rather than cultural change. Similarly, transactional managers may be faced with situations where more innovative than adaptive solutions are required, such as dealing with behavioural issues as opposed to technical ones. Regardless of their levels of creativity, some managers may find it easier than others to switch between innovative and adaptive behaviour. There may also be many managers who can exhibit varying levels of creativity as the situation demands. This may be the reason why some people, as demonstrated by our case studies and the leadership literature, can change their style of leadership or even adopt different styles at the same time.

Figure 14.2 Leadership, management and change

The story does not end there. Talbot (1997) demonstrates that, regardless of the level of creativity a person possesses or where they are located on the adaptor–innovator spectrum, there are proven tools and techniques for increasing their level of creativity and flexibility. By so doing, transactional managers may find it easier to operate in a more transformational and innovative mode, or move between both as circumstances necessitate. Talbot (1993) also points out, though, that such tools and techniques can only overcome barriers to creativity that lie within the individual. Other barriers, he argues, such as the attitudes and behaviours of superiors and colleagues, and the way the organisation operates, can also block individual creativity. Therefore, in management development, as with so many other aspects of organisational life, we cannot consider the individual in isolation from the rest of the organisation.

The management development process

Under different names, management training and education have been around since the Industrial Revolution. In the nineteenth century, training and education tended to be geared towards giving managers specific skills, such as engineering or production control, through either on-the-job training or self-help societies. Though usually thought of as focusing almost exclusively on the training of shop floor workers, Frederick Taylor (1911a: iii–iv) was adamant that leaders needed training as well:

> In the past the prevailing idea has been well expressed in the saying that "Captains of industry are born, not made"; and the theory has been that if one could get the right man, methods could be safely left to him. In future it will be appreciated that our leaders must be trained right as well as born right.

In the twentieth century, more and more, employers took on the job of specifying and providing formal management training, but it still tended to be geared towards giving managers specific skills. Over the last 30 years or so, there has been a significant change in emphasis. Management development programmes are increasingly seeking to change managerial behaviour, especially to promote leadership and creativity, and to align managers' behaviour with the longer-term strategic objectives of their organisations and with society's wider social and ethical considerations (Harrison, 2005). Though management development is big business in all advanced countries, there is no universally agreed definition of what it is. The following quotations give a flavour of the range of definitions on offer:

> ... a conscious and systematic decision-action process to control the development of managerial resources in the organisation for the achievement of organisational goals and strategies.
> (Ashton et al, 1975: 5)

> ... that function which from deep understanding of business goals and organisational requirements, undertakes: (a) to forecast needs, skill mixes and profiles for many positions and levels; (b) to design and recommend the professional, career and personal development programmes necessary to ensure competence; (c) to move from the concept of 'management' to the concept of 'managing'.
> (Beckhard, 1985: 22)

> ... an attempt to improve managerial effectiveness through a planned and deliberate learning process.
> (Mumford, 1987: 29)

> Management development is concerned not only with improving the effectiveness of individual managers but also with an improvement in management performance as a whole and organisational effectiveness.
> (Mullins, 2002: 845)

In an age where organisations are often required to change rapidly and radically, management education and development are taken seriously in most advanced countries and entry into a managerial job often requires formal, university-level qualifications (Arnold *et al*, 2005; Jones *et al*, 2000; Lippitt, 1982; Marsh, 1986; Morgan, 1988; Mullins, 2002; Pearson, 1987; Storey, 1989). The nature of management development varies between countries, however (Keuning, 1998). In Japan, for example, it tends to be a competitive process which begins by recruiting elite cohorts who have usually studied law or engineering at a top university. In Germany, there is a greater emphasis on a formal apprenticeship system which develops managers through a career path that often involves the attainment of higher degrees. France, like Japan, tends to be elitist and managers are expected to have studied for a degree in business or law at one of the *Grandes Ecoles* (R Harrison, 2002).

In the UK, management education tends to be more *ad hoc* and less well regarded, even in large organisations. UK companies also spend a much lower percentage of their turnover promoting education and training than their counterparts in France, Germany, Japan and the US (Constable and McCormick, 1987; R Harrison, 2002; Keuning, 1998). Partly in response to these findings, the 1980s and 1990s saw a growing interest in management development by government and organisations (OECD, 1996; Sissons and Storey, 1988; Storey, 1989, 1990; Worrall and Cooper, 1997, 1998); though these were not particularly successful (Hannagan, 2002; Paton, 2003). This continuing lack of management skills appears to be the main reason why the UK government abandoned most of the management training and development schemes its predecessors launched in the 1980s and 1990s, such as the Management Charter Initiative. In 2002 the government established a new body, the Council for Excellence in Management and Leadership, which itself concluded that most management and business leadership programmes are 'dysfunctional' and that the lack of appropriate leadership skills is detrimental to the UK's economic performance (Paton, 2003). This still appears to be the case, with a recent government report (BIS, 2012) finding that:

- ineffective management is estimated to be costing UK businesses over £19 billion per year in lost working hours;

- 43 per cent of UK managers rate their own line manager as ineffective – and only one in five is qualified;

- nearly three-quarters of organisations in England reported a deficit of management and leadership skills in 2012. This deficit is contributing to our productivity gap with countries such as the US, Germany and Japan;

- incompetence or bad management of company directors causes 56 per cent of corporate failures.

Regardless of the encouragement (or not) of governments, it is individual organisations that initiate such programmes. Given that organisations are different and face different challenges, if management development programmes are to be successful in producing effective managers and improving the performance of organisations, then it is self-evident not only that they will vary from company to company but also that they will need to vary from individual to individual. R Harrison (2002: 348) claims that, despite the differences between organisations, an effective management development process (MDP) has six basic features:

- a clear MDP mission, linked to the organisation's business strategy;
- specific programme objectives that relate to the external challenges that the organisation is facing;
- a focus on major internal organisational issues;
- programmes tailored to organisational and individual needs;
- the systematic assessment of management development needs, aims and outputs;
- a professional business-led approach to MDP.

Harrison's six basic features of an effective MDP represent a clear break with the standard management development programmes of the past that companies required all their managers to pursue, regardless of their individual needs, and which appear to have served them and their managers poorly (Arnold *et al*, 2010; Burnes, 2003; Mangham Working Party, 1987; Sissons, 1989; Storey, 1989; Thornberry, 1987; Yukl, 2002). The two main problems with such standard offerings is that, firstly, they tend to develop managers within an existing behaviour pattern and set of expectations. Therefore, traditional organisations will tend to continue to produce transactional managers, regardless of the presence or absence of formal training and education programmes. The second problem is that they fail to address the needs of individual managers. While they might meet a manager's training requirements in terms of technical skills (such as accountancy or engineering), they rarely address how they could develop the attitudes and behaviours necessary to be an effective manager.

Though formal, classroom-based qualifications such as Management Diplomas and MBAs are still seen as having an important role in most management development programmes, they are now being balanced with more individual and experientially based approaches. These approaches include the use of assessment and assessment centres, coaching and mentoring, self-development and, increasingly, Action Learning. Though experiential learning approaches have been around for a long time, their potential contribution to management development has generally been ignored (Burgoyne and Germaine, 1984; Harrison, 2005; Long, 1986; Mullins, 2002; Newstrom, 1985; Pedler, 1996; Stuart, 1986; Wilkinson and Orth, 1986; Willbur, 1987). It has now become clear, though, as McCall (2010) concludes from a major review of the leadership development literature, that experience is the best teacher and that organisations need to provide challenging job assignments which enable future leaders to learn by doing and through making mistakes. What such assignments should be teaching them, according to Burke (2011: 161), are the five basic demands of the leadership role:

1. Setting and communicating direction – determining purpose, vision, goals, and establishing support for these endeavors.
2. Aligning critical constituencies – making sure that those who need to support these endeavours are 'on board'.
3. Developing an executive temperament – being able to cope with complexity, ambiguity, and the pressures of the leadership role.
4. Setting and living values – clarifying what to believe in and stand for, and making sure that as leader one's words match one's actions.
5. Growth of self and others – practising and supporting in others' lifelong learning, growth, and change.

Changing managerial behaviour

In terms of challenging and changing managerial attitudes and behaviours, the experiential approach as epitomised by Action Learning is particularly interesting. It was developed in the 1940s in the UK by Reg Revans and is based on small groups of managers tackling a set problem or case study. As Pedler (1996: 9) explains:

> Action Learning is a method of problem solving and learning in groups to bring about change for individuals, teams and organisations. It works to build relationships which help any organisation improve existing operations and learn and innovate for the future.

The aim is not only that managers learn how to approach problems together but also that they learn about themselves and challenge the appropriateness of their own attitudes and behaviours. As Revans commented:

> The central idea of this approach . . . is today that of the set, or small group of comrades in adversity, striving to learn with and from each other as they confess failures and expand on victories.
> (Quoted in Crainer, 1996: 195)

Though Revans's ideas were out of fashion for many years, his emphasis on teamworking and the power of groups to solve their own problems, linked with the potential for self-reflection and development, is making it an increasingly popular approach (Mullins, 2002). Contemporary approaches to Action Learning tend to be based on Kolb's cycle of experiential learning (Experience–Understanding–Planning–Action) with sets or groups being guided by a facilitator who acts as a catalyst for ideas (Darwin *et al*, 2002). Also, as its name implies, Action Learning has strong similarities to and can be seen as a derivation of Lewin's Action Research (McLaughlin and Thorpe, 1993). Action Research is one of the four elements of Lewin's Planned approach to change (*see* Chapter 9). Like Action Research, Action Learning places a heavy emphasis on self-reflection, behavioural change and learning. While the latter tends to focus on developing the individual, however, Action Research focuses more on change at the group level. Nevertheless, Revans' statement that 'there is no learning without action and no (sober and deliberate) action without learning' (quoted in Pedler, 1996: 15) could have been written by Lewin.

Burnes (2003) links Action Learning with organisational change. He argues that change projects can double as Action Learning projects, and vice versa. Burnes maintains that there are clearly situations and times when organisational change and management development go hand in hand. These are not situations where it is either necessary or desirable for the objectives of one to become subservient to the other, or to be compromised by the needs of the other. Rather, these are genuinely situations where the need to change an organisation and the need to develop managers are mutually supportive. Unfortunately, as Crainer (1998: 259) comments, though Action Learning is attracting much attention, its complexity makes it a 'daunting prospect'. Given that organisational change projects can, in themselves, be a 'daunting prospect', it is perhaps not surprising that many organisations choose not to link them to management development initiatives. Even so, the benefits, Burnes argues, may be considerable.

As with all general developments, this move away from formal, off-the-job training programmes to more personalised and experiential, on-the-job programmes needs to be viewed critically. Storey (1989), in a major review of the management development literature, argues that drawing a distinction between on-the-job and off-the-job training may miss the main issue. This is the requirement to assess the development and training needs of individual managers accurately and to provide programmes that allow managers to develop a much more critical and intuitive approach to their situation. Argyris (1991) states, however, that one of the main barriers to developing more critical and intuitive approaches is that, within the narrow confines of transactional behaviour, many managers do operate effectively, even though, looking at the wider picture, their organisation may be in trouble. This is akin to Peters and Waterman's (1982) concept of 'irrational rationality' – managers applying the 'right' solution even when the situation means that it is no longer appropriate. Argyris believes that managers need to experience failure or recognise the inappropriateness of their behaviour before they can begin questioning their assumptions and practices, and develop their ability to be critical and creative. Senge (1990) contends that the most important factor in developing such a questioning approach and achieving organisational success is the ability to comprehend in a critical way the overall organisational context. This takes us back to the point made by Talbot (1993, 1997), cited earlier, that it is insufficient to develop managers if the organisation as a whole – people, values and systems – does not also change, or perceive the need for change. The case studies of XYZ and Oticon (Chapters 3, 9 and 11) support this argument. It was the need for transformational change that forced or enabled managers in both companies to break out of their transactional mould and think critically and creatively about solutions to the problems their organisations faced.

So while management development has increasingly come to be seen as a process that must address the needs of individual managers, it must not lose sight of the need to develop management as a whole in organisations. Nowhere is this more apparent than in the areas discussed earlier in this chapter covering sustainability, diversity and ethics. These are areas where organisations have failed significantly in the past, whether it be in terms of environmental depredations, racial and sexual discrimination and stereotyping, or the recent sub-prime mortgage scandal. Organisations often attribute such transgressions to the failure of an individual or small group to follow the organisation's guidelines and policies; but the regular occurrence of illegal and unethical practices in business, especially the sub-prime mortgage scandal, reveals that these are a failure of management in its entirety in organisations, rather than the failure of a few managers.

Though it is necessary for individual managers to address issues of sustainability, diversity and ethics as part of their personal development, by itself this is not sufficient. If organisations and those in them are to behave differently, it is also necessary that the management of an organisation as a whole should address these issues as part of its development. The question, of course, is how this can be done. If organisations are capable of systematically side-stepping the policies and guidelines that they have developed, how can a management development programme make them face up to the issues? One answer might be to utilise Action Learning, where managers 'learn with and from each other as they confess failures'. Yet Action Learning has a number of drawbacks, not least that its focus is on developing individual managers, albeit in a group setting (McGill and Beaty, 1995). It does not appear to be appropriate to situations where behavioural change and reflection need to take place at the group rather than the individual level. Nor does it appear suitable for situations where the issue is the effectiveness of management at the organisational level, rather than the individual level.

There is an approach that was specifically established to enable groups to address the appropriateness of their behaviour, especially in terms of discriminatory activity, and which also has a strong ethical basis. It is, of course, Planned change, as formulated by Kurt Lewin.

Planned change was designed to enable groups, in this case management groups in an organisation, to understand the factors which make them act as they do, and to develop effective ways to change them and then 'freeze' or institutionalise those changes. As described in Chapter 9, Planned change has four elements: Field Theory, Group Dynamics, Action Research and the Three-Step approach to change. Lewin's critics maintain that Lewin's approach is not suitable for large-scale, rapid and coercive change situations, or situations where the focus is on structural rather than behavioural change. However, both Lewin's own work, and that of his successors, has shown that it is a highly effective process for achieving sustained behavioural changes in groups (Burnes and Cooke, 2012b). It has been applied to a wide variety of situations, including the food habits of American housewives, teenage inter-racial gang warfare in American cities, conflict between Palestinians and Israelis, and management behaviour in organisations (Bargal and Bar, 1992; Burnes, 2004c, 2007; Cummings and Worley, 2009; Gold, 1999; Lewin, 1947a; Marrow, 1969). Therefore, as an approach to tackling the failures of management as a group in an organisation, Planned change has a lot to recommend it. This does not undermine the case for other approaches which address the needs of managers as individuals, but does recognise that individual behaviour and effectiveness cannot be separated from group behaviour and effectiveness. Indeed, it may be one of the ironies of management development that, in order to equip managers to meet the challenges of the twenty-first century, it has to look back to the work of Kurt Lewin.

Summary

From the above examination of managerial learning, seven factors can be discerned as important in the ability of managers to operate effectively:

1. The manager's experience, and whether this has reinforced their beliefs or, instead, led them to question their appropriateness.
2. The level of creativity of the manager. Does the manager have a preference for transactional management or transformational leadership, and to what degree can they move between the two?
3. His or her cognitive style: are they adaptors or innovators? Are they 'whole thinkers', or are they more left-hemisphere–rational thinkers or right-hemisphere–creative thinkers?
4. The manager's ability to perceive the whole picture. Can they see the organisation in its context? In particular, do they understand the choices available in terms of changing the organisation itself, its context, and their own approach to leadership, strategy and change?
5. The organisational context: is it amenable, or can it be made amenable, to a more critical, creative and ethical style of leadership?
6. The organisation's management team: does it have a commitment to promoting sustainability, diversity and ethical behaviour, and are the senior managers committed to ensuring that its statement and policies in these areas are implemented through the day-to-day actions of all its members?
7. The organisation's management development process: is it effective? Is it geared to developing individual managers and the management cadre of the organisation as a whole?

Management, leadership and change

The literature on management and leadership goes back many hundreds of years. Indeed, if one takes the view of some writers that *The Art of Warfare* by Sun Tzu, which was written in China around 400 BC, is pertinent to managing today's organisations, then the study of management goes back thousands of years (Michaelson, 2001). As was shown in Chapter 1, however, to all intents and purposes the systematic study of management in Western cultures can be said to have begun with the work of Frederick Taylor at the beginning of the twentieth century. Since then, there have been more books and articles on management than anyone can possibly count. These have thrown up a plethora of theories, studies and terminology which, as Thomas (2003) comments, has probably caused more confusion than clarification. In this chapter, we have tried, as Weick (*see* Chapter 10) might put it, to make sense of the literature on management. This 'sensemaking' began with an examination of the challenges posed to management by globalisation, especially in terms of sustainability, diversity and ethics. This was followed by a review of the literature on the manager's role, which drew attention to the three main theories on leadership, i.e. the personal characteristics approach, the leader–follower approach, and the contextual approach. Finally, we investigated the role played by, or that could be played by, management development in shaping the behaviour of managers and leaders at both the individual and group levels. This attempt to make sense of management and the literature on management has revealed the following:

- The incredible variety and complexity of the role of people who hold the title 'manager'. The title is applied to people in a wide range of hierarchical levels and functional specialisms. These 'managers' are presented with a myriad of responsibilities and challenges, ranging from the mundane, but vital, everyday tasks required to ensure that organisations operate efficiently, to the rarer and far more spectacular need to transform and reinvent organisations.

- The wide range of factors that impinges on managerial effectiveness, including the manager's personality, that of their followers, superiors and peers, and the wider organisational context and objectives in which they operate.

- The ability or potential of managers to increase their level of creativity and change their style of management from transactional to transformational, and back, as situations require.

- The recognition that management development has a key role to play not only in developing individual creativity but also in changing the ethical behaviour of management as a group in organisations.

What conclusions can we draw from this review for the relationship between management, leadership and change in organisations? The first is that there does seem to be some terminological agreement, as shown in Tables 14.1 and 14.2, as to the differences between management and leadership. Management is about the present, it is about maintaining the *status quo*, and it is about objectivity and aloofness. Leadership is about the future, it is about change and it is about values and emotions. But while management and leadership may be different, this does not mean that managers and leaders are or should be different people. This chapter has argued that most management and leadership roles require a mixture of transactional and transformational skills. In an ideal world, managers would be able to adjust the balance of transactional and transformational skills they deploy to match the organisation's requirements at any one time. In our less-than-ideal world, the balance is likely to be static rather than dynamic, and usually determined by the background, experience and personality of the individual manager. At the same time, it would be difficult to think of a manager who never had to deal with organisational change, even on a small scale, and who, therefore, did not need to possess some transformational skills. Similarly, it would be difficult to think of a leader who, regardless of the size of the changes they were responsible for, did not have to possess some of the transactional skills necessary for ensuring that an organisation continued to satisfy its stakeholders. So the balance of management–leadership and transactional–transformational skills an individual needs to possess at any one time is related to the degree of change or stability they encounter.

The second conclusion we can draw, as Figure 14.2 showed, is that management and leadership focus on different types of change. Management tends to focus on small-scale, localised changes, while leadership tends to focus on more radical, organisation-wide changes. The former tend to require only relatively low levels of creativity, while the latter require relatively high levels. Even within these different types of change, there are some forms of change that appear to be more innovative and others more adaptive. Consequently, the ability of managers and leaders to deal effectively with different change situations will be related to the level of creativity they possess and the degree to which their creativity expresses itself in an innovative or adaptive manner.

Having drawn these two conclusions, we are now in a position to relate approaches to management and leadership to approaches to managing change. In Chapter 11, we developed a *framework for change* (*see* Figure 11.5). This related the types of changes organisations experienced, such as cultural or structural change, to the most appropriate approach to change, such as Emergent or Planned. If we merge Figure 11.5 from Chapter 11 with Figure 14.2 from this chapter, we can construct a *framework for management, leadership and change* (*see* Figure 14.3).

The four quadrants in Figure 14.3 show what form of management or leadership is best suited to each form of change and each approach to change management. For example, Quadrant 3 shows that where changes to tasks and procedures are concerned, these can be achieved by either a Tayloristic or a *Kaizen* approach and managed in a transactional manner which requires only a low level of adaptive creativity.

Quadrant 1 presents a much more complex picture. It shows that where an organisation wishes to change its culture, it may be more appropriately achieved by an Emergent approach to change led by someone with a transformational approach to leadership and who exhibits a high degree of innovation. Remembering, however, that Emergent change can encompass a wide range of change initiatives spread over a period of time, which can include Planned change and Bold Strokes, such transformational leaders may also need to possess adaptive and transactional skills, or be able to call on others who possess such skills.

Figure 14.3 also allows us to understand better the obstacles and approaches to dealing effectively with issues of sustainability, diversity and ethics. As was shown in examining globalisation earlier in this chapter, these are issues that organisations are aware of and, at least in large organisations, have policies and procedures to address. Possessing the ability to put these policies and procedures into practice is a different matter. These are issues that, for most organisations, require a major change of culture, especially by management and leadership at all levels. If sustainability, diversity and ethics are treated merely as structural

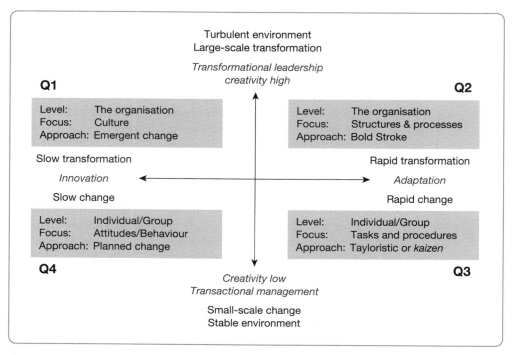

Figure 14.3 A framework for management, leadership and change

or policy issues, as in Quadrant 2, this is unlikely to lead to any permanent or sustained changes in attitudes and behaviour. Similarly, if they are seen as issues that are primarily about individual behaviour and attitudes, as in Quadrant 4, there is unlikely to be an organisation-wide and lasting change to the way that managers and leaders behave. If ethics, diversity and sustainability are treated as issues that need to be embedded in an organisation's culture, however, and if the required changes are managed and led as shown in Quadrant 1, then changes in attitudes and behaviour at the overall level are likely to be achieved and maintained.

Conclusions

In reading some of the literature on strategy and change, one might be forgiven for asking whether managers and what they do matter at all. If strategy is Emergent, often unrelated to conscious decisions, does an important role exist for managers? Or if, as the evolutionary perspective on strategy would have it, luck plays a greater part in success than conscious action, does the quality of the manager matter? However, this chapter has shown that the way an organisation is managed and led can have profound implications not only for the organisation and its members but for society as a whole.

On the negative side, poor management can act to hold back organisations, prevent beneficial change and create a climate of blame and wrong-doing where infighting and discrimination are tolerated or even promoted. On the positive side, good management can identify opportunities for progress, promote ethical behaviour, recognise the opportunities that diversity brings, and create sustainable organisations which achieve harmony with their environment. Good managers and leaders can create the conditions for growth and prosperity. Effective managers are, therefore, for very positive reasons, important to an organisation. At the same time, they do not operate in isolation or have a totally free rein.

The Chief Executives of Oticon (Chapter 11) and Marconi (Chapter 6) both wanted to transform their organisations. They both developed ambitious visions for their organisation's future. The Chief Executive of Oticon sought organisation-wide approval and support for his vision. All Oticon's employees were involved in developing and implementing the strategy to realise the vision. It was a vision that was seen as benefiting all Oticon's employees; and it was a vision which succeeded. The vision for the new Marconi, however, was not seen as benefiting its employees, nor were they involved in developing or implementing it. With hindsight, the vision was badly flawed and it failed disastrously.

There is a strand in the management literature which equates organisational success with strong, clear-sighted and charismatic leadership (Thomas, 2003). Certainly, there are leaders, such as Jack Welch in his time at General Electric, Pehr Gyllenhammar before his departure from Volvo, Richard Branson at Virgin, Bill Gates when at Microsoft or Rupert Murdoch at News International, who through sheer force of personality dominated and transformed organisations. There are also other instances, as this chapter has shown, where 'heroic' leaders have ruined their organisations. The successful charismatic leader appears to be in the minority. Even successful leaders may outstay their welcome, as Arnold Weinstock's example at GEC-Marconi shows (*see* Chapter 6) or the market may change to such an extent that radical surgery is needed in order for an organisation to survive. Nevertheless, as was noted in Chapter 8, one should be wary of the argument that all organisations need to change radically and quickly, or that there are not alternatives to this approach to sustainability.

Most managers, even of very large corporations, have to rely far less on their personality, important though this may be, and far more on their business knowledge, skills, creativity and experience. They are also called upon to perform a wide range of duties and activities. Though the theories and approaches to strategy and change appear to paint managers as either directing change or facilitating it, and the leadership literature tends to dwell on whether they are transactional or transformational managers, the reality is that they are often required to be all of these things and more, depending on the circumstances. Figure 14.3 shows that in bringing about organisational change, there will be occasions when managers and leaders will need to devolve responsibility to subordinates; sometimes, they will need to encourage and support change projects; and, in other instances, they will have to lead the process themselves. Although the approach adopted will depend to a certain extent upon the size and importance of the change project, the timescale involved and the state of the organisation, in the final analysis it will rely on managerial judgement to make the appropriate choice. Changing organisations is a complex process fraught with more opportunities for failure than success. If managers are to accomplish and keep accomplishing this task, as this book has argued, they have to be aware of the choices and approaches available and be willing themselves to change their beliefs and attitudes.

Despite the views of some writers, there can never be any general recipes or formulas for organisational success. The vast variety of organisations, each with its own differing constraints and pressures, makes that impossible. What there is, however, is a large body of theories and associated advice which organisations can draw upon to assist them. As the quotation by George Box at the beginning of this book states: 'All models are wrong, some models are useful.' This book has shown that there is no such thing as an uncontested theory – all have their drawbacks. In particular, most tend to be situation-specific, even if they do not acknowledge this. Managers and organisations need to treat theories with a degree of scepticism; but they also need to realise that if they can identify the main theories for running and changing organisations, and they do understand the context in which they operate, they are in a position to identify choices and make changes.

Sometimes managers may choose or be required by circumstances to change their organisations radically and quickly; sometimes they may choose to influence the context to promote or reduce the need for such changes. In other cases, change may take place more slowly and over a long period, as both organisation and context are shaped and changed. The key factor in all this is to make conscious decisions rather than rely on untested assumptions. This will require those who manage and lead organisations to question and challenge their own and other people's assumptions. It will also require them to gather and be open to a wide variety of information – as Chapter 3 showed, the experience of more and more successful companies is that learning should be an organisation-wide and continuous process, rather than one limited to a few like-minded individuals at one point in time.

Even where choices are identified, managers should not assume that exercising choice is easy or that the results will be beneficial for all concerned, including themselves. For this reason, managers have a responsibility in making and implementing choices to consider the implications in the widest context – not just for themselves, not just for their organisation, but for society as well. In the West, especially the UK and the US, there is a tendency to think mainly in terms of short-term profitability, and ignore the longer-term organisational and social consequences of actions. We can see this in the context of the Classical school, whose concentration on narrow issues of control and efficiency leads to the creation of jobs that are both physically strenuous and mind-numbingly boring. The adverse consequences of organisation theory are not limited to the Classical school, however; in many ways, the policies and approaches advocated by the Culture–Excellence school could be considered even worse. Though both Handy (2007b) and, to a lesser extent, Kanter (1997) are concerned about the impact of fragmented organisations and insecure jobs on society at large and family life in particular, neither appears to believe that these can be avoided.

Yet the consequences of this approach in creating instability and unpredictability in the job market are disastrous. As was noted in Chapter 3, the 1990s saw the UK become more socially divided than at any time since the Second World War, with some 60 per cent of the population either marginalised or living in very insecure circumstances (Hutton, 1995; Saul, 1997; White, 1999). Nor has the situation improved since then: quite the reverse (Clark, 2013; von Hagen, 2012). Increasingly, the rich are choosing to live behind security fences in elite communities (Arnot, 2002). The situation is even worse in the US, where the tendency for the better-off to retreat into walled compounds patrolled by armed guards is widespread and long-established (Dunphy and Griffiths, 1998; Elliott, 1997; Reich, 1997). Even so, recalling the discussion on globalisation, in a borderless world, it will be impossible to escape the consequences of environmental depredation, a lack of business ethics and discriminatory behaviour merely by building walls.

If this seems a somewhat apocalyptic vision, then bear in mind the reality of climate change. Bear in mind the millions of people who lost their savings and pensions in the dot-com boom, and the millions more who lost their jobs and homes in the sub-prime mortgage scandal. Also bear in mind that one of the most fashionable American gurus of the late

1990s, William Bridges, advocates the jobless organisation. He believes that there should no longer be any permanent jobs, not even for managers. Instead, he wants to see the labour force form one enormous pool of labour waiting for temporary employment – the Just-in-Time workforce to complement the Just-in-Time organisation (Bridges, 1996, 1998; Golzen, 1995). In support of his view that jobless organisations are the future, he points out that in the 1990s General Motors ceased to be the largest employer in the US; instead, it was overtaken by the temporary employment agency, Manpower.

Some would argue that these developments are only the inevitable consequence of capitalism (Collins, 1998). However, as Crouch and Streeck (1997) and Whitley (1998) demonstrate, capitalism comes in many forms and guises. The fragmentation and insecurity of the labour market that was a growing characteristic of the US and the UK in the 1980s and 1990s was much less pronounced in some other countries. This was especially the case in those nations that, historically, had seen the objectives of individual organisations as subservient to national interests. In the 1990s for example, despite economic problems associated with reunification, Germany still had an enviable record of attempting to prevent job losses and reduce job insecurity, as did the Scandinavian states and Japan.

This, of course, emphasises that national governments as well as individual organisations have a major contribution to make when considering the wider context and implications of managers' decisions. In the West, led by the US and the UK, the last 20 years have seen an increasing move towards deregulation, privatisation and the introduction of market forces into the operation of the public sector. Whatever the merits of these policies in terms of efficiency, and they are debatable (Ferlie *et al*, 1996; Flynn, 1993; Warrell, 2012), no one can doubt that they acted to increase instability both in public-sector bodies and the economy at large. Whether such changes will eventually lead to a better deal for consumers or not is obviously an issue, but so is the effect on the social fabric. Post-1945, all Western governments used their public sectors both to provide services and as a means of creating employment and maintaining economic and social stability. These latter functions have now been abandoned in many countries, and the resulting insecurity is evident for all to see.

The point of mentioning this is not merely to show concern, but to argue that it need not be the case. The Culture–Excellence concept is only one of many approaches to running organisations. All have their downside, but not all result in job cuts and labour market instability. One alternative is for managers to choose to adopt approaches that reduce instability in their environment, rather than to implement policies that increase the use of short-term contracts and part-time and casual working. If followed widely, this would have two effects. First, the result of many organisations seeking stability would be to reduce the overall level of turbulence in the environment. This is because, as Stickland (1998) maintains, organisations and their environment are not separate entities, but part of the same system. If organisations become more stable, so, too, does the environment. If organisations become more sustainable, so does the planet. Similarly, if, as recommended by Tom Peters, organisations adopt internal chaos to cope with external chaos, this merely acts to increase the overall turbulence in the system; in effect, a vicious spiral of increasing chaos is created which, instead of poising an organisation at the 'edge of chaos', may tear it apart. Furthermore, if organisations focus solely on narrow profitability, environmental and ethical problems will grow. The second consequence of organisations seeking stability is that it increases the stability in society – jobs and communities become more stable and more sustainable.

As Mintzberg *et al* (2002: 74) so succinctly put it:

We can live our lives and manage our enterprises obsessed with getting ever more, with keeping score, with constantly calculating and scheming. Or we can open ourselves to another way, by engaging ourselves to engage others so as to restore our sense of balance.

Therefore, as a final note: organisations face many challenges and choices. Some organisations will find that their room for manoeuvre is very limited. Others may find that there is considerable scope for discretion. It is the role of managers and leaders to ensure that all available options and choices are identified, and that the choices made take account of both the short- and long-term interests of all their stakeholders – whether these be shareholders, employees, the managers themselves or the community at large. The worst managers may not be those who make poor choices; they may be those who fail to recognise that there are choices to be made.

TEST YOUR LEARNING

Short discussion topics

The purpose of these is to enable students to check their learning and reflect on the topics covered in this chapter. The discussions should last for no more than 5–10 minutes. Depending on the length of the lecture, there could be one, two or three such discussions in a session. The following are five suggested topics which address issues raised in this chapter:

1. What is the relationship between sustainability, workforce diversity and ethics?

2. Briefly discuss Mintzberg's (1973, 1975) description of managerial roles.

3. State the key features of the leader–follower approach to leadership.

4. How does Kirton's (1989) Adaptation–Innovation theory help us to understand managerial behaviour?

5. What is the difference between management and leadership?

Class debates

The purpose of class debates is to enable students to explore a topic in depth by setting up a 'for and against' debate. The class can be split into two and one half asked to research the 'for' case and the other 'against' case. Individuals can then be chosen at random to introduce their side of the debate. Alternatively, two individuals for each side can be told in advance that they will be introducing the debate. The length of such debates depends on the time available, the size of the class and their enthusiasm for the topic. However, less than 30 minutes is probably too short and more than 60 minutes probably too long. The following are three suggested topics which address issues raised in this chapter:

1. Ethical organisations cannot survive in a global world.

2. Heroic leadership has been a disaster for most organisations.

3. The best leaders are highly creative.

Essay questions

1. How can the framework for management, leadership and change (Figure 14.3) be used to guide organisational change? Illustrate your answer with reference to one of the case studies in this book or by using an organisation of your choice.

2. Discuss the following statement: Transformational change is driven by the leader's vanity and not market necessity.

Suggested further reading

Deresky, H (2010) *International Management: Managing across borders and culture* (7th edition). Prentice-Hall: Upper Saddle River, NJ.
   This book provides a well-researched and well-written guide to international management. It is especially strong in the areas of culture, diversity and ethics.

Dunphy, D, Griffiths, A and Benn, S (2007) *Organizational Change for Corporate Sustainability* (2nd edition). Routledge: London.
   This is an important book which does not just make the case for creating sustainable organisations but also provides illustrations of and guidance on managing the changes necessary to achieve this.

Yukl, G (2013) *Leadership in Organizations* (8th edition). Pearson: London.
   Gary Yukl's book is an excellent guide to the literature and research on management and leadership.

CASE STUDY 14

Nokia: from 'burning platform' to a slimmer management model

Two years after Chief Executive Stephen Elop warned his company that it faced oblivion, Andrew Hill investigates how it has been restructured and whether it has worked. When Nokia chief executive Stephen Elop booked the Grand Tarabya hotel in Istanbul for the Group's annual leadership meeting at the end of January, he planned a spectacular finale. As the meeting of 200 senior executives drew to a close, musicians introduced themselves into the room, playing Ravel's Bolero, until the whole orchestra was present for the climactic bars. "My message was that the way we would succeed in the end was if each of us played our role, and each instrument came together to build this beautiful symphony," Mr Elop says. The Nokia boss likes a metaphor. It is two years since he stunned the Finnish mobile telecoms company and the sector with a memo – quickly leaked – that warned Nokia was standing on a "burning platform". The company would perish unless it was prepared to jump into the icy water. Days later, on February 11, he announced the leap: a controversial alliance with Microsoft in smartphones to build a "third ecosystem" to rival Apple and Google's Android, and an accelerated pursuit of the "next billion" consumers in emerging markets.

At the time, there were still a few inside Nokia who doubted the situation was that dire. The company was, after all, the biggest handset manufacturer in the world. It was still infected with what one senior executive has called "the arrogance of Nokia". But if some could not yet smell smoke, they quickly felt the flames as Nokia implemented a deep restructuring. Since then, Mr Elop has sought to tackle a trio of internal challenges identified in a two-part Financial Times analysis in April 2011: to become more open, more accountable and more agile. But the company, which launched four new devices on Monday at the Mobile World Congress in Barcelona, has yet to answer adequately the most important question: will consumers buy Nokia's phones in sufficient quantities to guarantee its future?

Mr Elop is often asked whether he has a "Plan B" if the Windows phone plan falters, but there were, and are, few other options short of a break-up of the whole company. The choice of Android as a smartphone platform would have led Nokia into a fragmented, commoditised, overcrowded market. The Microsoft deal "was the only strategy that was really available to them," says Richard Windsor, an independent analyst and founder of the blog Radio Free Mobile. Nokia has adapted its structure and cost base to this reality. The company, which employed 65,000 (excluding the Nokia Siemens Networks joint venture) in early 2011, now has 45,000 staff. It has closed or consolidated 200 out of 500 sites worldwide. Nokia used to launch about 50 new products a year; it now introduces 25. Last year, Nokia sold and leased back its Espoo headquarters, just outside Helsinki. Some analysts interpreted it as a sign of the depth of Nokia's plight, but corporate controller Kristian Pullola says the decision signalled "nothing is sacred when it comes to driving the focus on cash". Nokia went through all cash flow sources to identify the "owner" of every cash-generating item. Nevertheless, between February 2011 and mid-July last year – just after Mr Elop was forced to announce a further 10,000 job losses – the share price fell 83 per cent, and Samsung snatched the mantle of world's biggest handset maker. In January, Nokia cancelled its dividend for the first time in its 148-year history.

Executives say what looked from outside like a deepening crisis reinforced Nokia's determination to reform its overcomplicated management systems.

Mr Elop claims to have increased the "intensity of execution" of the strategy. "Focus" is the word Nokia executives interviewed for this article kept repeating. For instance, Jo Harlow, who leads the smart devices division, has mapped Nokia's management structure against that of its US partner, to improve efficiency. Nokia created the roles of Programme Manager, Head of Quality and Head of Engineering to match similar roles at Microsoft "so that engineers can talk to engineers, quality managers to quality managers, and so on. . . . We have taken a lot of the fluff out of the product programme development cycle so that [product developers] have mature innovations that they can implement in a timely fashion," she says. Examples include "optical image stabilisation" – which produces steady video even when the camera is moving – on the flagship Lumia 920, and the entry-level Lumia 620's "dual shot", two-tone moulded cover. Under the old Nokia system, she suggests, the company would have had to choose between an innovative product, brought to market late, or a punctual product with less innovation. One reason was that decisions that should have been taken locally got stuck at committee level at headquarters. But in the "controlled mania" of producing a first Windows phone by the end of 2011, Ms Harlow says Nokia learnt to "give the teams the authority to run faster". At the same time, she says the company, guilty in the past of overcomplicating new products, has "made hard choices not to do something just because we could", in refining the Windows platform.

Juha Akras, Nokia's head of human resources, says one side-effect of becoming smaller is greater cooperation. To his surprise, internal measures of staff satisfaction have continued to improve, even during the gloomy first half of 2012. But Nokia has also faced setbacks, notably in its attempt to strengthen the second pillar of its strategy: to sell more mobile phones in fast-growing markets such as China and India. The company admits it was slow to bring its most innovative full-touch feature phones into these markets in the first half of 2012, allowing Samsung and HTC to steal market share.

In June, Mr Elop put Juha Putkiranta, in charge of factories, supplies and logistics, and Chris Weber, new Head of Sales and Marketing, into the senior leadership team. Both would now report directly to the Chief Executive. "We really ratcheted up the degree to which the senior leadership and layers below were involved in what was going on," Mr Elop says. A "change task force", put in place in 2011 became a "turnround leadership group" last year as it became clear, Mr Pullola says, that Nokia needed to become "even more disciplined and focused" on cash control. Outsiders still worry that supply chain shortages – such as the Group's inability to get enough Lumia phones into shops in China for the new year holiday – indicate deeper problems. Nokia replies that demand exceeded expectations. Technology companies also have a long history of crimping supply as a marketing ploy, but analyst Mr Windsor says it is clear that "at the very high end, they aren't the customer of choice" for suppliers. Will customers buy it? More worrying is that new Nokia smartphones are not yet the device of choice for customers. "Marketing remains their weakest link in terms of being able to regain that 'wow' factor," says Gartner's Carolina Milanesi.

While Nokia's share of the market for more affordable mobile phones slipped just over four percentage points between 2011 and 2012 to 19.1 per cent, its smartphone share dropped from 17.9 per cent to 5.8 per cent. Better fourth-quarter figures than expected, published last month, did show the first positive underlying profit margin in the core mobile business for a year – as well as an improvement in its net cash position. Following last year's correction of course in full-touch feature phones, these more affordable devices – sold under the sub-brand Asha (meaning "hope") – are selling better, and a revived Nokia Siemens Networks provided unexpectedly strong support to the Group. The sales of Windows phones were in line with expectations. Given the amount Microsoft is spending to market its wider operating system, Ms Harlow believes the customer is just starting to appreciate the advantages of Windows 8 when used on computer, tablet and phone. "The amount of effort going into Windows 8, the amount of advertising – that is going to help," adds Mr Elop, who on Monday announced new affordable Windows models and also said Nokia was winning more corporate business. But Pekka Yla-Anttila, research director at ETLA, a Helsinki economic think-tank, says the "alliance with Microsoft isn't yet flying... No one can say whether it will succeed or not – even six years ago we didn't know anything about iPhones."

In an effort to differentiate Nokia's products, Mr Elop has pushed the company to emphasise how the new phones will improve customers' lives. He suggests to sales staff, for instance, that, rather than detailing the technical attributes of the Lumia phone's cameras, they should say "it takes great pictures at night": "If you go into these stores and look at these devices, it's hard to tell most of them apart. You can look at a piece of paper next to them and see it's got a Snapdragon quad-core blah blah blah... [Instead], we asked 'What are the improved consumer experiences that really make a difference?'"

Pankaj Ghemawat, global strategy professor at IESE Business School, compares Nokia's broader challenge with that which faced Nintendo in the early 2000s when it was trying to get ahead in the video game market. Incremental change was not sufficient to outstrip feuding rivals Microsoft Xbox and Sony PlayStation, so the Japanese company came up with the revolutionary Wii. Nokia "has to build a city and the bridge to get to it at the same time", he says.

Is it enough? Nokia executives seem confident the company has turned a corner. The share price has doubled since last July. The immigration officers at London's Heathrow airport – whom US-born Ms Harlow uses as a barometer of public perception – have started asking her about Nokia's new devices rather than sympathising with her about her employer's problems. Gartner's Ms Milanesi believes Nokia has now finally brought together the elements of a viable software ecosystem and attractive hardware. But nobody else has stood still. Apple and Samsung are still riding high, and the Apple iOS and Android platforms dominate the smartphone market. Even BlackBerry, which looked to be falling faster than Nokia, has bounced back with a well-reviewed new product and operating system, while "white-label" manufacturers chip away at Nokia in emerging markets. Mr Elop made a personal commitment to his senior team in Istanbul that he would "make Nokia sing again". But he still needs to make himself heard above an extraordinary cacophony of other powerful voices.

Key dates in the restructuring of Nokia:

● February 2011 Stephen Elop urges Nokia to leap from "burning platform"; strikes smartphone deal with Microsoft.

Case study 14 (*continued*)

- October 2011 Unveils first Windows phones; launches Asha, a new brand of phones . . . focused on emerging markets.
- June 2012 Reshuffles leadership team and announces 10,000 more job losses; debt downgraded to "junk".

- September 2012 Launches "flagship" Lumia 920 smartphone.
- January 2013 Handset business returns to underlying profitability; dividend cancelled for first time in its 148-year history.

 Source: Nokia: From 'burning platform' to a slimmer management model, *The Financial Times*, 25/02/2013, p. 12 (Hill A.), © *The Financial Times Limited* (2013). All Rights Reserved.

Update: In September 2013, Microsoft bought Nokia.

Questions

Using the evidence in the Nokia case study, and other publicly available material, address the following questions:

1. To what extent do you agree with Richard Windsor's view that: the Microsoft deal 'was the only strategy that was really available to them [Nokia]'.

2. Discuss the following statement:

   Nokia has not transformed itself; it's merely got smaller.

3. Which of the following best describes Mr Elop's leadership style?
   - Heroic
   - Servant
   - Spiritual
   - Engaging

Explain your answer and discuss whether or not you think Mr Elop's leadership style is appropriate for Nokia's situation.

Bibliography

Abegglen, J (1958) *The Japanese Factory*. Free Press: Glencoe, IL.

Abegglen, J and Stalk, G (1984) *Kaisha, the Japanese Corporation*. Basic Books: New York.

Abell, DF (1977) *Using PIMS and Portfolio Analysis in Strategic Market Planning: A comparative analysis*. Intercollegiate Case Clearing House, Harvard Business School: Boston, MA.

Abell, P (1975) Organisations as technically constrained bargaining and influence systems. In P Abell (ed): *Organisations as Bargaining and Influence Systems*. Heinemann: London.

Abodaher, D (1986) *Iacocca*. Star: London.

Acedo, FJ, Barroso, C and Galan, JL (2006) The resource-based theory: dissemination and main trends. *Strategic Management Journal*, 27(7), 621–36.

Ackroyd, S (2000) Connecting organisations and societies: a realist analysis of structures. In S Ackroyd and S Fleetwood (eds): *Realist Perspectives on Management and Organisations*. Routledge: London.

Ackroyd, S (2011) Contemporary realism and organizational change. In D Boje, B Burnes and J Hassard (eds): *The Routledge Companion to Organizational Change*. Routledge: London.

Ackroyd, S and Fleetwood, S (2000a) Realism in contemporary organisation and management studies. In S Ackroyd and S Fleetwood (eds): *Realist Perspectives on Management and Organisations*. Routledge: London.

Ackroyd, S and Fleetwood, S (eds) (2000b) *Realist Perspectives on Management and Organisations*. Routledge: London.

Ackroyd, S, Burrell, G, Hughes, M and Whitaker, A (1988) The Japanisation of British industry. *Industrial Relations Journal*, 19(1), 11–23.

Adams, C, Cavendish, W and Mistry, P (1996) *Adjusting Privatisation: case studies from developing countries*. Heinemann: London.

Addis, M and Podesta, S (2005) Long life to marketing research: a postmodern view. *European Journal of Marketing*, 39(3–4), 386–412.

Aglietta, M (1979) *A Theory of Capitalist Regulation: The US experience*. New Left Books: London.

Aguren, S, Bredbacka, C, Hansson, R, Ihregren, K and Karlsson, KG (1984) *Volvo/Kalmar Revisited: Ten years of experience*. The Development Council: Stockholm, Sweden.

Aitken, H (1960) *Taylorism at the Watertown Arsenal: Scientific Management in Action 1908–1915*. Harvard University Press: Cambridge, MA.

Aiyar, S (2011) *Working Paper No. 42: How did the crisis in international funding markets affect bank lending? Balance sheet evidence from the United Kingdom*. Bank of England: London.

Akao, Y (ed) (1991) *Hoshin Kanri: Policy deployment for successful TQM*. Productivity Press: Cambridge, MA.

Alban, B (2003) The future. In M Wheatley, R Tannenbaum, PY Griffin and K Quade (eds): *Organization Development at Work: Conversations on the values, applications and future of OD*. Pfeiffer: San Francisco, CA.

Albrow, M (1970) *Bureaucracy*. Pall Mall Press: London.

Albrow, M (1997) *Do Organizations Have Feelings*? Routledge: London.

Alderman, J (2001a) *Sonic Boom: Napster, P2P and the battle for the future of music*. Fourth Estate: London.

Alderman, J (2001b) Free for all. *The Guardian*, 4 August, available at www.guardian.co.uk

Alimo-Metcalfe, B (1995a) Female and male constructs of leadership and empowerment. *Women in Management*, 10(2), 3–8.

Alimo-Metcalfe, B (1995b) Leadership and assessment. In S Vinnicombe and NL Colwill (eds): *The Essence of Women in Management*. Prentice-Hall: Englewood Cliffs, NJ.

Alimo-Metcalfe, B and Alban-Metcalfe, R (2000) Heaven can wait. *Health Service Journal*, 12 October, 26–29.

Allaire, Y and Firsirotu, ME (1984) Theories of organizational culture. *Organization Studies*, 5(3), 193–226.

Allaire, Y and Firsirotu, ME (1989) Coping with strategic uncertainty. *Sloan Management Review*, 30(3), 7–16.

Allen, FR and Kraft, C (1982) *The Organizational Unconscious. How to create the corporate culture you want and need*. Prentice-Hall: Englewood Cliffs, NJ.

Allen, M (1994) *Undermining the Japanese Miracle: Work and conflict in a coalmining community*. Cambridge University Press: Cambridge.

Allen, RW, Madison, DL, Porter, LW, Renwick, PA and Mayes, BT (1979) Organizational politics: tactics and characteristics of its actors. *California Management Review*, 22, 77–83.

Alloway, T (2013) Wall St bonuses rise 9% as job cuts mean fewer collect. *Financial Times*, 23 February, 16.

Allport, GW (1948) Foreword. In GW Lewin and GW Allport (eds): *Resolving Social Conflict*. Harper & Row: London.

Alvesson, M and Deetz, S (1996) Critical theory and postmodern approaches to organizational studies. In SR Clegg, C Hardy and WR Nord (eds): *Handbook of Organization Studies*. Sage: London.

Alvesson, M and Spicer, A (2012) A stupidity-based theory of organizations. *Journal of Management Studies*, published online, doi: 10.1111/j.1467–6486.2012.01072.x

Alvesson, M and Sveningsson, S (2008) *Organizational Cultured: Cultural change work in progress*. Routledge: London.

Amin, A and Robins, K (1990) The re-emergence of regional economics? The mythical geography of flexible accumulation. *Environment and Planning D: Society and Space*, 8(1), 7–34.

Amiot, C, Terry, D, Jimmieson, N and Callan, V (2006) A longitudinal investigation of coping processes during a merger: implications for job satisfaction and organizational identification. *Journal of Management*, 32(4), 552–74.

Amit, R and Schoemaker, PJ (1993) Strategic assets and organisational rents. *Journal of Management Studies*, 30, 31–49.

Anderson, C and Paine, F (1978) PIMS: a re-examination. *Academy of Management Review*, 3(3), 602–12.

Andrews, KR (1980) *The Concept of Corporate Strategy*. Irwin: Homewood, IL.

Andrews, KR (1998) The concept of corporate strategy. In H Mintzberg, JB Quinn and S Ghoshal (eds): *The Strategy Process*. Prentice-Hall: London.

Ansoff, HI (1965) *Corporate Strategy*. McGraw-Hill: New York.

Ansoff, HI (1987) *Corporate Strategy* (revised version). McGraw-Hill: New York.

Antonaccio, CM (1994) Contesting the past: hero cult, tomb cult and epic in Early Greece. *American Journal of Archaeology*, 98(3), 398–410.

Antonacopoulou, E and Chiva, R (2007) The social complexity of organizational learning: the dynamics of learning and organizing. *Management Learning*, 38(3), 277–95.

Appignanesi, R and Garratt, C (1995) *Postmodernism for Beginners*. Icon Books: Cambridge.

Argenti, J (1974) *Systematic Corporate Planning*. Nelson: London.

Argyris, C (1960) *Understanding Organizational Behavior*. Dorsey: Homewood, IL.

Argyris, C (1962) *Interpersonal Competence and Organizational Effectiveness*. Irwin: Homewood, IL.

Argyris, C (1964) *Integrating the Individual and the Organization*. Wiley: London.

Argyris, C (1970) *Intervention Theory and Method*. Addison-Wesley: Reading, MA.

Argyris, C (1973) Peter Blau. In G Salaman and K Thompson (eds): *People and Organizations*. Longman: London.

Argyris, C (1977) Double-loop learning in organizations. *Harvard Business Review*, September–October, 115–25.

Argyris, C (1980) *Inner Contradictions of Rigorous Research*. Academic Press: New York.

Argyris, C (1990) *Overcoming Organizational Defenses*: *Facilitating organizational learning*. Allyn & Bacon: Boston, MA.

Argyris, C (1991) Teaching smart people how to learn. *Harvard Business Review*, May–June, 99–109.

Argyris, C (1992) *On Organizational Learning*. Blackwell: Oxford.

Argyris, C (1999) *On Organizational Learning* (2nd edition). Blackwell: Oxford.

Argyris, C and Schön, D (1978) *Organizational Learning: A theory of action perspective*. Addison-Wesley: Reading, MA.

Argyris, C, Putnam, R and McLain-Smith, D (1985) *Action Science: Concepts, methods and skills for research and intervention*. Jossey-Bass: San Francisco, CA.

Aris, S (2002) Weinstock: I wanted to string up Simpson. *The Sunday Times*, 28 July, 8.

Armenakis, AA and Bedeian, AG (1999) Organisational change: a review of theory and research in the 1990s. *Journal of Management*, 25(3), 293–315.

Armenakis, AA, Harri, SG and Mossholder, KW (1993) Creating readiness for organizational change. *Human Relations*, 46(6), 681–703.

Armstrong, CE and Shimizu, K (2007) A review of approaches to empirical research on the resource-based view of the firm. *Journal of Management*, 33(6), 959–86.

Arndt, M and Bigelow, B (2000) Commentary: the potential of chaos theory and complexity theory for health services management. *Health Care Management Review*, 25(1), 35–8.

Arnold, J, Cooper, CL and Robertson, IT (1998) *Work Psychology* (3rd edition). Pitman: London.

Arnold, J, Randall, R, Patterson, F, Silvester, J, Robertson, I, Cooper, C, Burnes, B, Axtell, C and Hartog, DD (2010) *Work Psychology* (5th edition). FT Prentice Hall: Harlow.

Arnold, J, Silvester, J, Patterson, F, Robertson, IT, Cooper, CL and Burnes, B (2005) *Work Psychology* (4th edition). FT Prentice Hall: Harlow.

Arnot, C (2002) Laager toffs. *The Guardian*, 30 January, 2–3.

Aronowitz, S (1989) Postmodernism and politics. In A Ross (ed): *Universal Abandon: The politics of Postmodernism*. Edinburgh University Press: Edinburgh.

Arthur, C (2013) Google Tax Avoidance is 'wrong', insists Ed Miliband. *The Guardian*, 22 May, available at www.guardian.co.uk

Ash, MG (1992) Cultural contexts and scientific change in psychology – Lewin, Kurt in Iowa. *American Psychologist*, 47(2), 198–207.

Ashforth, BE and Fried, Y (1988) The mindlessness of organizational behaviours. *Human Relations*, 41(4), 305–29.

Ashley, J (2008) Equality is tricky, but women are in the workplace to stay. *The Guardian*, 21 July, available at www.guardian.co.uk

Ashour, AS (1973) The contingency model of leadership effectiveness: an evaluation. *Organizational Behavior and Human Performance*, 9, 339–55.

Ashton, D, Easterby-Smith, M and Irvine, C (1975) *Management Development: Theory and practice*. MCB: Bradford.

Ashton, TS (1948) *The Industrial Revolution 1760–1830*. Oxford University Press: Oxford.

AT Kearney (1989) *Computer Integrated Manufacturing: Competitive advantage or technological dead end?* Kearney: London.

AT Kearney (1992) *Total Quality: Time to take off the rose-tinted spectacles*. IFS: Kempston.

AT Kearney Ltd (1994) *Partnership or Powerplay?* AT Kearney: London.

Auer, P and Riegler, C (1990) *Post-Taylorism: The enterprise as a place of learning organizational change – a comprehensive study on work organization changes and its context at Volvo*. The Swedish Work Environment Fund: Stockholm, Sweden.

Ayres, R (1995) Privatisation and distributional equity: the case of Brazil. *International Journal of Social Economics*, 22(12), 36–49.

Babbage, C (1835) *On the Economy of Machinery and Manufacture*. Knight: London.

Bacharach, S (2005) *Get Them on Your Side: Win support, convert skeptics, get results*. Platinum Press: La Crosse, WI.

Bachman, JG, Bowers, DG and Marcus, PM (1968) Bases of supervisory power: a comparative study in five organizational settings. In AS Tannenbaum (ed): *Control in Organizations*. McGraw-Hill: New York.

Back, KW (1972) *Beyond Words: The story of sensitivity training and the encounter movement*. New York: Russell Sage Foundation.

Back, KW (1992) This business of topology. *Journal of Social Issues*, 48(2), 51–66.

Bailllien, E, Neyens, I and De Witte, H (2011) Organizational correlates of workplace bullying in small- and medium-sized enterprises. *International Small Business Journal*, 29(6), 610–25.

Balakrishnan, A and Collinson, P (2007) Merrill Lynch: avoid risk but look for opportunities. *The Guardian*, 16 August, 28.

Bañuls, VA and Turoff, M (2011) Scenario construction via Delphi and cross-impact analysis. *Technological Forecasting and Social Change*, 78(9), 1579–602.

Bar-Hillel, M and Neter, E (1996) Why are people reluctant to exchange lottery tickets? *Journal of Personality and Social Psychology*, 70(1), 17–27.

Bargal, D and Bar, H (1992) A Lewinian approach to intergroup workshops for Arab–Palestinian and Jewish youth. *Journal of Social Issues*, 48(2), 139–54.

Bargal, D, Gold, M and Lewin, M (1992) The heritage of Kurt Lewin – introduction. *Journal of Social Issues*, 48(2), 3–13.

Barker, RA (2001) The nature of leadership. *Human Relations*, 54(4), 469–94.

Barnard, C (1938) *The Functions of the Executive*. Harvard University Press: Cambridge, MA.

Barnard, C and Scott, J (eds) (2002) *The Law of the Single European Market: Unpacking the premises*. Hart Publishing: London.

Barney, JB (2001) Is the resource-based 'view' a useful perspective for strategic management research? Yes. *Academy of Management Review*, 26(1), 41–56.

Barratt, ES (1990) Human resource management: organisational culture. *Management Update*, 2(1), 21–32.

Barrie, C (1995) Saatchi loses accounts to new agency. *The Guardian*, 16 February, 15.

Barrie, C (1999) It's a far cry from safe and secure. *Guardian* – Jobs Section, 2 January, 12–13.

Bartkus, BR and Glassman, M (2008) Do firms practice what they preach? The relationship between mission statements and stakeholder management. *Journal of Business Ethics*, 83(2), 207–16.

Bartkus, B, Glassman, M and McAfee, B (2006) Mission statement quality and financial performance. *European Management Journal*, 24(1), 86–94.

Bartunek, J (2007) Academic–practitioner collaboration need not require joint or relevant research. *Academy of Management Journal*, 50(6), 1323–33.

Bass, BM (1985) *Leadership and Performance beyond Expectations*. Free Press: New York.

Bass, BM (1990) *Handbook of Leadership: A survey of theory and research*. Free Press, New York.

Bass, BM (2008) *Handbook of Leadership: Theory, research, and managerial application* (4th edition). Free Press, New York.

Bass, BM (1995) Transformational leadership redux. *Leadership Quarterly*, 6(4), 463–78.

Bateson, G (1972) *Steps to an Ecology of the Mind*. Ballantine: New York.

Batten, JD and Swab, JL (1965) How to crack down on company politics. *Personnel*, 42, 8–20.

Baudrillard, J (1983) *Simulations*. Semiotexte: New York.

Baum, JR, Locke, EA and Kirkpatrick, SA (1998) A longitudinal study of the relation of vision and vision communication to venture growth in entrepreneurial firms. *Journal of Applied Psychology*, 83(1), 43–54.

Bavelas, A and Lewin, K (1942) Training in democratic leadership. *Journal of Abnormal Psychology*, 37, 115–19.

Beach, SD (1980) *Personnel*. Macmillan: London.

Beatty, CA and Lee, GL (1992) Leadership among middle managers – an exploration in the context of technological change. *Human Relations*, 45(9), 957–89.

Bechtold, BL (1997) Chaos theory as a model for strategy development. *Empowerment in Organizations*, 5(4), 193–201.

Becker, WS (2008) *The 100 Day Action Plan to Save the Planet*. St Martin's Griffin: New York.

Beckhard, R (1969) *Organization Development: Strategies and models*. Addison-Wesley: Reading, MA.

Beckhard, R (1985) Whither management development? *Journal of Management Development*, 4(2), 10–16.

Beckhard, R and Harris, RT (1987) *Organizational Transitions: Managing complex change* (2nd edition). Addison-Wesley: Reading, MA.

Beer, M and Nohria, N (eds) (2000) *Breaking the Code of Change*. Harvard Business School Press: Boston, MA.

Beer, M and Walton, RE (1987) Organizational change and development. *Annual Review of Psychology*, 38, 339–68.

Beer, M, Eisenstadt, RA and Spector, B (1990) *The Critical Path to Corporate Renewal*. Harvard Business School Press: Boston, MA.

Beer, M, Eisenstadt, RA and Spector, B (1993) Why change programmes don't produce change. In C Mabey and B Mayon-White (eds): *Managing Change* (2nd edition). The Open University/ Paul Chapman Publishing: London.

Beesley, ME and Littlechild, SC (1983) Privatisation principles, problems and priorities. *Lloyds Bank Review*, 149, 1–20.

Beeson, I and Davis, C (2000) Emergence and accomplishment in organizational change. *Journal of Organizational Change Management*, 13(2), 178–89.

Belbin, M (1996) *Team Roles at Work*. Butterworth-Heinemann: London.

Bell, D (1973) *The Coming of Post-Industrial Society*. Basic Books: New York.

Bell, RM (1973) *The Behaviour of Labour, Technical Change, and the Competitive Weakness of British Manufacturing*. Technical Change Centre: London.

Benjamin, G and Mabey, C (1993) Facilitating radical change. In C Mabey and B Mayon-White (eds): *Managing Change* (2nd edition). The Open University/Paul Chapman Publishing: London.

Bennett, J and Jayes, S (1995) *Trusting the Team: The best practice guide to partnering in construction*. Reading University, Centre for Strategic Studies in Construction: Reading.

Bennett, R (1983) *Management Research. Management Development Series, 20*. International Labour Office: Geneva.

Bennis, WG (1959) Leadership theory and administrative behaviour. *Administrative Science Quarterly*, 4(3), 259–301.

Bennis, WG (1966) The coming death of bureaucracy. *Think*, November–December, 30–5.

Bennis, WG (2000) Leadership of change. In M Beer and N Nohria (eds): *Breaking the Code of Change*. Harvard Business School Press: Boston, MA.

Bennis, WG and Nanus, B (1985) *Leaders: The strategies for taking charge*. Harper & Row: New York.

Bensoussan, BE and Fleisher, CS (2008) *Analysis without Paralysis: 10 tools to make better strategic decisions*. Financial Times Prentice Hall: Harlow.

Bensoussan, BE and Fleisher, CS (2013) *Analysis without Paralysis: 12 tools to make better strategic decisions* (2nd edition). Pearson: Upper Saddle River, NJ.

Berggren, C (1992) *The Volvo Experience*. Macmillan: London.

Bernstein, L (1968) *Management Development*. Business Books: London.

Bessant, J (1983) Management and manufacturing innovation: the case of information technology. In G Winch (ed): *Information Technology in Manufacturing Processes*. Rossendale: London.

Bessant, J and Haywood, B (1985) *The Introduction of Flexible Manufacturing Systems as an Example of Computer Integrated Manufacture*. Brighton Polytechnic: Brighton.

Beyer, WC (1959) The civil service in the Ancient World. *Public Administration Review*, 19(4), 243–9.

Bhaskar, R (1979) *A Realist Theory of Science* (2nd edition). Harvester: Brighton.

Bhaskar, R (1986) *Scientific Realism and Human Emancipation*. Verso: London.

Bhaskar, R (1989) *Reclaiming Reality*. Verso: London.

Bhote, KR (1989) *Strategic Supply Management*. American Management Association: New York.

Biberman, J and Whitty, M (1997) A postmodern spiritual future for work. *Journal of Organizational Change*, 10(2), 130–8.

Bible, The – Authorized Version (1962), The British & Foreign Bible Society: London.

Bickerton, I and Marsh, P (2005) *Financial Times*, 18 November, 13.

Bigge, LM (1982) *Learning Theories for Teachers*. Gower: Aldershot.

Birchall, D and Lyons, L (1995) *Creating Tomorrow's Organization: Unlocking the benefits of future work*. Pitman: London.

BIS (2012) *Leadership & Management in the UK – The key to sustainable growth*. BIS – Department for Business, Innovation & Skills: London.

Black, JA (2000) Fermenting change: capitalizing on the inherent change found in dynamic non-linear (or complex) systems. *Journal of Organizational Change Management*, 13(6), 520–5.

Blackler, F and Brown, C (1978) *Job Redesign and Management Control: Studies in British Leyland and Volvo*. Saxon House: Farnborough.

Blackler, F and Brown, C (1984) Alternative models to guide the design and introduction of new information technologies into work organisations. *Journal of Occupational Psychology*, 59(4), 287–314.

Blackler, F and McDonald, S (2000) Power, mastery and organisational learning. *Journal of Management Studies*, 37(6), 833–51.

Blake, RR and McCanse, AA (1991) *Leadership Dilemmas – Grid Solutions*. Gulf Publishing: Houston, TX.

Blake, RR and Mouton, JS (1969) *Building a Dynamic Corporation through Grid Organization Development*. Addison-Wesley: Reading, MA.

Blake, RR and Mouton, JS (1976) *Organizational Change by Design*. Scientific Methods: Austin, TX.

Blake, RR and Mouton, JS (1985) *The Managerial Grid III*. Gulf Publishing: Houston, TX.

Blanchard, K (1994) Changing role of executives. *Executive Excellence*, 11(4), 7.

Blankenburg, S (2012) 'Mini-jobs' don't work in Germany, and they won't work in Britain. *The Guardian*, 21 August, available at www.guardian.co.uk

Blanton, K (2008) Broker's clients detail web of dashed dreams. *Boston Globe*, 20 January, 1.

Blau, PM (1970) The formal theory of differentiation in organizations. *American Sociological Review*, 35, 201–18.

Blau, PM and Schoenherr, RA (1971) *The Structure of Organizations*. Basic Books: New York.

Block, P (1981) *Flawless Consulting: A guide to getting your expertise used*. Learning Concepts: Austin, TX.

Blumenthal, K (2012) *Steve Jobs: The man who thought different*. Bloomsbury: London.

Boddy, D (2002) *Management: An introduction*. Financial Times Prentice Hall: Harlow.

Boddy, D and Buchanan, D (1992) *Take the Lead: Interpersonal skills for change agents*. Prentice Hall: London.

Boersma, M (2013) Company leaders need battlefield values. *Financial Times*, 11 April, 2.

Boje, DM (2000) Phenomenal complexity theory and change at Disney: response to Letiche. *Journal of Organizational Change Management,* 13(6), 558–66.

Boje, DM (2006) What happened on the way to postmodern? *Qualitative Research in Organizations and Management: An International Journal*, 1(1), 22–40.

Boje, DM and Rosile GA (2010) Lewin's action research meets Aristotle on the storytelling field: Maybe it's a distinctive niche for CTU. Colorado Springs, CO, Colorado Technical University, 11 July.

Boje, DM and Wakefield, T (2011) Storytelling in systemicity and emergence. In DM Boje, DM, Burnes, B and Hassard, J (eds): *The Routledge Companion to Organizational Change*. Routledge: London.

Borchardt, K (1973) Germany 1700–1914. In C Cipolla (ed): *The Fontan a Economic History of Europe Vol. 4, The Emergence of Industrial Societies – Part 1*. Fontana: London.

Bower, T (1996) *Maxwell: The Final Verdict*. HarperCollins: London.

Bowers, DG, Franklin, JL and Pecorella, P (1975) Matching problems, precursors and interventions in OD: a systematic approach. *Journal of Applied Behavioural Science*, 11, 391–410.

Bowles, M (1989) Myth, meaning and work organisation. *Organization Studies*, 10(3), 405–23.

Bowman, C and Asch, D (1985) *Strategic Map*. Macmillan: London.

Box, GEP and Draper, NR (1987) *Empirical Model-Building and Response Surfaces*. Wiley: New York.

Bracker, J (1980) The historical development of the strategic management concept. *Academy of Management Review*, 5(2), 219–24.

Bradford, DL and Burke, WW (2004) Introduction: Is OD in crisis? *Journal of Applied Behavioral Science*, 40(4), 369–73.

Bradshaw, T (2012) CD sales slide to half their 2004 peak. *Financial Times*, 3 January, 14.

Bradshaw, T (2013) Apple invites consumers to take a bite out of its core philosophy. *Financial Times*, 17 June, 18.

Bradshaw-Camball, P and Murray, VV (1991) Illusions and other games: a trifocal view of organizational politics. *Organization Science*, 2(4), 379–98.

Braithwaite, T and Nasiripour, S (2013) JPMorgan criticised by Senate panel over London whale saga. *Financial Times*, 15 March, 1.

Brandenburger, AM and Nalebuff, BJ (1996) *Co-opetition*. Doubleday: New York.

Bratton, J (1992) *Japanization at Work: Managerial studies for the 1990s*. Macmillan: London.

Breslin, J and McGann, J (1998) *The Business Knowledge Repository: Consolidating and accessing your ways of working*. Quorum Books: Westport, CT.

Brewer, E and Tomlinson, JWC (1964) The manager's working day. *Journal of Industrial Economics*, 12(3), 191–7.

Brews, PJ (2003) Star trek strategy: real strategy at work. *Business Strategy Review*, 14(3), 34–43.

Bridges, W (1996) *Jobshift: How to prosper in a workplace without jobs*. Nicholas Brealey: London.

Bridges, W (1998) *Creating You & Co: Learn to think like the CEO of your own career*. Perseus Books: New York.

Brindle, D (1998a) Benefits payments in chaos: computer collapse wipes out records. *The Guardian*, 10 September, 1.

Brindle, D (1998b) Gap between rich and poor widens again. *The Guardian*, 16 October, 7.

Brindle, D (1999) Pensions computer upgrade hit by 1,900 bugs as deadline looms. *The Guardian*, 26 January, 3.

Brodbeck, PW (2002) Implications for organization design: teams as pockets of excellence. *Team Performance Management: An International Journal*, 8(1/2), 21–38.

Broughton, PD (2011) Time to stand up to the crisis junkies. *Financial Times*, 6 September, 14.

Brown, A (1995) *Organisational Culture*. Pitman: London.

Brown, A (1998) *Organisational Culture* (2nd edition). Financial Times Pitman: London.

Brown, DH and Jopling, D (1994) Some experiences of outsourcing: a systemic analysis of strategic and organisational issues. Paper presented to the British Academy of Management Annual Conference, University of Lancaster, September.

Brown, SL and Eisenhardt, KM (1997) The art of continuous change: linking complexity theory and time-paced evolution in relentlessly shifting organizations. *Administrative Science Quarterly*, 42(1), March, 1–34.

Bruland, K (1989) The transformation of work in European industrialization. In P Mathias and JA Davis (eds): *The First Industrial Revolutions*. Blackwell: Cambridge.

Brummer, A (1999) Weinstock's heirs look for an encore. *The Guardian*, 20 January, 21.

Brummer, A (2002) Lord Weinstock. *The Guardian*, 24 July, available at www.guardian.co.uk

Brummer, A and Cowe, R (1998) *Weinstock*. HarperCollins: London.

Bryant, A (1998) Beyond BPR: confronting the organizational legacy. *Management Decision*, 36(1), 25–30.

Bryant, A (2002) Grounding Systems Research: Re-establishing Grounded Theory. Proceedings of the 35th Hawaii International Conference on System Sciences, 7–19 January.

Bryant, D (1979) The psychology of resistance to change. *Management Services*, March, 9–10.

Bryant, M and Wolfram Cox, J (2011) Narrating organizational change. In D Boje, B Burnes and J Hassard (eds): *The Routledge Companion to Organizational Change*. Routledge: London.

Bryce, R (2002) *Pipe Dreams: Greed, ego, jealousy and the death of Enron*. Public Affairs: London.

Buchanan, DA (1984) The impact of technical implications and managerial aspirations on the organization and control of the labour process. Paper presented to the Second Annual Conference on the Control and Organisation of the Labour Process, UMIST/Aston, 28–30 March.

Buchanan, DA and Badham, R (1999) *Power, Politics and Organizational Change: Winning the turf game*. Sage: London.

Buchanan, DA and Boddy, D (1992) *The Expertise of the Change Agent*. Prentice Hall: London.

Buchanan, DA and Storey, J (1997) Role-taking and role-switching in organizational change: the four pluralities. In I McLoughlin and M Harris (eds): *Innovation, Organizational Change and Technology*. International Thompson: London.

Buchanan, DA, Claydon, T and Doyle, M (1999) Organisation development and change: the legacy of the nineties. *Human Resource Management Journal*, 9(2), 20–37.

Buchanan, DA, Fitzgerald, L and Ketley, D (eds) (2006) *The Sustainability and Spread of Organizational Change: Modernizing healthcare*. Routledge: London.

Buckingham, L and Finch, J (1999) SmithKline bows to revolt over directors' pay. *The Guardian*, 24 April, 22.

Buckley, PJ and Mirza, H (1985) The wit and wisdom of Japanese management. *Management International Review*, 25(3), 16–32.

Buckley, W (1968) *Modern Systems and Research for the Behavioral Scientist*. Aldine Publishing: Chicago, IL.

Buiter, W (2013) The eurozone crisis demands swift debt restructuring. *Financial Times*, 9 May, 24.

Bullock, RJ and Batten, D (1985) It's just a phase we're going through: a review and synthesis of OD phase analysis. *Group and Organization Studies*, 10(December), 383–412.

Burawoy, M (1979) *Manufacturing Consent: Changes in the labor process under monopoly capital*. University of Chicago Press: Chicago, IL.

Burgoyne, J (1995) Feeding minds to grow the business. *People Management*, 1(19), 22–6.

Burgoyne, J and Germaine, C (1984) Self development and career planning: an exercise in mutual benefit. *Personnel Management*, 16(4), April, 21–3.

Burgoyne, J, Pedler, M and Boydell, T (1994) *Towards the Learning Company*. McGraw-Hill: London.

Burke, WW (1980) *Organisation Development*. Little, Brown and Co: Toronto, Canada.

Burke, WW (1997) The new agenda for organization development. *Organizational Dynamics*, Summer, 7–20.

Burke, WW (2011) A perspective on the field of organization development and change: the Zeigarnik effect. *The Journal of Applied Behavioral Science*, 47(2), 143–67.

Burke, W, Michael, RS, Luthems, F, Odiorne, S and Hayden, S (1981) *Techniques of Organisational Change*. McGraw-Hill: London.

Burnes, B (1988) *Strategy for Success: Case studies in advanced manufacturing technologies*. EITB: Watford.

Burnes, B (1989) *New Technology in Context*. Gower: Aldershot.

Burnes, B (1991) Managerial competence and new technology: don't shoot the piano player – he's doing his best. *Behaviour and Information Technology*, 10(2), 91–109.

Burnes, B (1996) No such thing as . . . a 'one best way' to manage organizational change. *Management Decision*, 34(10), 11–18.

Burnes, B (1997) Organisational choice and organisational change. *Management Decision*, 35(10), 753–9.

Burnes, B (1998a) Recipes for organisational effectiveness: mad, bad, or just dangerous to know. *Career Development International*, 3(3), 100–6.

Burnes, B (1998b) The planned approach to change: come back Kurt Lewin – all is forgiven. Paper presented to the Second Maintaining Organizational Effectiveness Conference, Edge Hill University College, Ormskirk, June, 17.

Burnes, B (2003) Managing change and changing managers: from ABC to XYZ. *Journal of Management Development*, 22(7), 627–42.

Burnes, B (2004a) Emergent change and planned change – competitors or allies? The case of XYZ Construction. *International Journal of Operations and Production Management*, 24(9), 886–902.

Burnes, B (2004b) Kurt Lewin and complexity theories: back to the future? *Journal of Change Management*, 4(4), 309–25.

Burnes, B (2004c) Kurt Lewin and the planned approach to change: a re-appraisal. *Journal of Management Studies*, 41(6), 977–1002.

Burnes, B (2005) Complexity theories and organisational change. *International Journal of Management Reviews*, 7(2), 73–90.

Burnes, B (2007) Kurt Lewin and the Harwood studies: the foundations of OD. *Journal of Applied Behavioral Science*, 43(2), 213–31.

Burnes, B (2009a) Organisational change in the public sector: The case for planned change. In RT By and C Macleod (eds): *Managing Organisational Change in Public Services: International issues, challenges and cases*. Routledge: London.

Burnes, B (2009b) Reflections: ethics and organisational change – time for a return to Lewinian values. *Journal of Change Management*, 9(4), 359–381.

Burnes, B (2011a) Introduction: why does change fail and what can we do about it? *Journal of Change Management*, 11(4), 445–50.

Burnes, B (2011b) Understanding the emergent approach to change. In DM Boje, B Burnes and J Hassard (eds): *The Routledge Companion to Organizational Change*. Routledge: London.

Burnes, B and By, RT (2012) Leadership and change: the case for greater ethical clarity. *Journal of Business Ethics*, 108(2), 239–52.

Burnes, B and Cooke, B (2012a) Kurt Lewin's field theory: a review and re-evaluation. *International Journal of Management Reviews*, published online 6 September, doi: 10.1111/j.1468–2370.2012.00348.x

Burnes, B and Cooke, B (2012b) The past, present and future of organization development: taking the long view. *Human Relations*, 65(11), 1395–429.

Burnes, B and Coram, R (1999) Barriers to partnership in the public sector: the case of the UK construction industry. *Supply Chain Management*, 4(1), 43–50.

Burnes, B and Dale, B (eds) (1998) *Working in Partnership*. Gower: Aldershot.

Burnes, B and Jackson, P (2011) Success and failure in organisational change: an exploration of the role of values. *Journal of Change Management*, 11(2), 133–62.

Burnes, B and James, H (1995) Culture, cognitive dissonance and the management of change. *International Journal of Operations and Production Management*, 15(8), 14–33.

Burnes, B and New, S (1996) *Strategic Advantage and Supply Chain Collaboration*. AT Kearney: London.

Burnes, B and New, S (1997) Collaboration in customer–supplier relationships: strategy, operations and the function of rhetoric. *International Journal of Purchasing and Materials Management*, 33(4), 10–17.

Burnes, B and Salauroo, M (1995) The impact of the NHS internal market on the merger of colleges of midwifery and nursing: not just a case of putting the cart before the horse. *Journal of Management in Medicine*, 9(2), 14–29.

Burnes, B and Weekes, B (1989) *AMT: A Strategy for Success?* NEDO: London.

Burnes, B and Whittle, P (1995) Supplier development: getting started. *Logistics Focus*, February, 10–14.

Burnes, B, Cooper, C and West, P (2003) Organisational learning: the new management paradigm? *Management Decision*, 41(5), 443–51.

Burnes, B, Katsouros, M and Jones, T (2004) Privatisation and the European Union: the case of the Public Power Corporation of Greece. *International Journal of Public Sector Management*, 18(1).

Burns, JM (1978) *Leadership*. Harper & Row: New York.

Burns, T and Stalker, GM (1961) *The Management of Innovation*. Tavistock: London.

Burrell, G (1988) Modernism, post modernism and organisational analysis 2: the contribution of Michel Foucault. *Organization Studies*, 9(2), 221–35.

Burrell, G (1997) Organization paradigms. In A Sorge and M Warner (eds): *The IEBM Handbook of Organizational Behaviour*. International Thompson Business Press: London.

Burt, T (2002) Divorcees with a difference: Volvo. *Financial Times*, 4 March, 13.

Burton, F, Yamin, M and Young, S (eds) (1996) *Europe in Transition*. Macmillan: London.

Bushe, G (2011) Appreciative inquiry: theory and critique. In D Boje, B Burnes and J Hassard (eds): *The Routledge Companion to Organizational Change.* Routledge: London.

Business Notebook (2003) Old expressions. *The Guardian*, 2 July, 16.

Butler, R (1997) Decision making. In A Sorge and M Warner (eds): *The IEBM Handbook of Organizational Behaviour*. International Thompson Business Press: London.

Butler, VG (1985) *Organisation and Management*. Prentice Hall: London.

Buzzell, RD (2004) The PIMS program of strategy research: a retrospective appraisal. *Journal of Business Research*, 57(5), 478–83.

Buzzell, RD and Gale, BT (1987) *The PIMS Principles – Linking Strategy to Performance*. Free Press: New York.

By, RT and Burnes, B (2012) (eds). *Organizational Change, Leadership and Ethics: Leading organizations towards sustainability*. Routledge: London.

By, RT and Macleod, C (eds) (2009) *Managing Organisational Change in Public Services: International issues, challenges and cases*. Routledge: London.

Byars, LL (1984) *Strategic Management: Planning and implementation*. Harper & Row: London.

Bywater PLC (1997) *Executive Briefings: The executive role in sponsoring change – making it happen*. Bywater Plc: Reading.

Caldwell, R (2001) Champions, adapters, consultants and synergists: the change agents in HRM. *Human Resource Management Journal*, 11(3), 39–52.

Caldwell, R (2003) Models of change agency: a fourfold classification. *British Journal of Management*, 14(2), 131–42.

Caldwell, R (2006) *Agency and Change*. Routledge: London.

Callinicos, A (1989) *Against Postmodernism*. Polity: Cambridge.

Cameron, K (2005) Organizational effectiveness. In N Nicholson, PG Audia and MM Pillutula (eds): *The Blackwell Encyclopedia of Management (2nd edition) – Organizational Behavior*. Blackwell: Oxford.

Camp, RC (1989) *Benchmarking*. ASQC Quality Press: Milwaukee, WI.

Campbell, A and Warner, M (1988) Organization of new forms of manufacturing operations. In M Wild (ed): *International Handbook of Production and Operations Management*. Cassell: London.

Campbell, D, Stonehouse, G and Houston, B (2012) *Business Strategy: An introduction*. Butterworth-Heinemann: Oxford.

Campbell, JP and Dunnette, MD (1968) Effectiveness of T-group experiences in managerial training and development. *Psychological Bulletin*, 70, 73–104.

Cant, M and Jeynes, L (1998) What does outsourcing bring you that innovation cannot? How outsourcing is seen – and currently marketed – as a universal panacea. *Total Quality Management*, 9(2/3), 193–202.

Cao, G, Clarke, S and Lehaney, B (2000) A systemic view of organisational change and TQM. *The TQM Magazine*, 12(3), 186–93.

Cao, G, Clarke, S and Lehaney, B (2001) A critique of BPR from a holistic perspective. *Business Process Management Journal*, 7(4), 332–9.

Carew, A (1987) *Labour under the Marshall Plan: The politics of productivity and the market.* Manchester University Press: Manchester.

Carlson, S (1951) *Executive Behaviour.* Strombergs: Stockholm.

Carnall, CA (1990) *Managing Change in Organizations.* Prentice Hall: London.

Carnall, CA (1995) *Managing Change in Organizations* (2nd edition). Prentice Hall: London.

Carnall, CA (2003) *Managing Change in Organizations* (4th edition). Financial Times Prentice Hall: Harlow.

Carpenter, CJ (2013) A meta-analysis of the effectiveness of the 'but you are free' compliance-gaining technique. *Communication Studies*, 64(1), 6–17.

Carr, C, Tomkins, C and Bayliss, B (1991) Strategic controllership – a case study approach. *Management Accounting Research*, 2(2), 89–107.

Carr, P and Donaldson, L (1993) Managing healthily: how an NHS region is managing change. *Personnel Management*, October, 48–51.

Carroll, DT (1983) A disappointing search for excellence. *Harvard Business Review*, November–December, 78–88.

Carroll, GR (ed) (1988) *Ecological Models of Organizations.* Ballinger: Cambridge, MA.

Cartwright, D (1951) Achieving change in people: some applications of group dynamics theory. *Human Relations*, 6(4), 381–92.

Cartwright, D (ed) (1952) *Field Theory in Social Science.* Social Science Paperbacks: London.

Cartwright, D and Zander, A (1953) *Group Dynamics: Research and theory.* Row, Peterson and Co: White Plains, NY.

Carvel, J (2002) Long working hours harming family life. *The Guardian*, 25 September, 13.

Cassidy, J (2002) *Dot.con: The greatest story ever sold.* Allen Lane: London.

Caulkin, S (2003) The bosses we love to hate. *Observer*, 6 July, available at www.guardian.co.uk

Caves, R (2001) *Creative Industries.* The Free Press: New York.

Cellan–Jones, R (2003) *Dot.bomb: The strange death of dot.com Britain.* Arum: London.

Chamberlin, EH (1933) *The Theory of Monopolistic Competition.* Harvard University Press: Cambridge, MA.

Chandler, AD (1962) *Strategy and Structure: Chapters in the history of the American industrial enterprise.* MIT Press: Cambridge, MA.

Chang, C-H, Rosen, CC and Levy, PE (2009) The relationship between perceptions of organizational politics and employee attitudes, strain, and behavior: a meta-analytic examination. *Academy of Management Journal*, 52(4), 779–801.

Chang, T–L (1997) Cultivating global experience curve advantage on technology and marketing capabilities. *Journal of Marketing Practice: Applied Marketing Science*, 3(4), 230–50.

Chapman, L (1978) *Your Disobedient Servant Published.* Chatto & Windus: London.

Chapman, SD and Chassagne, S (1981) *European Textile Printers in the Eighteenth Century. A study of Peel and Oberkampf.* Heinemann: London.

Charette, RN (2012) U.S. Air Force blows $1 billion on failed ERP project. IEEE Spectrum, 15 November, available at www.spectrum.ieee.org

Chatman, JA and Cha, SE (2003) Leading by leveraging culture. *California Management Review*, 45(4), 20–34.

Chatterjee, S (2007) Why is synergy so difficult in mergers of related businesses? *Strategy and Leadership*, 35(2), 46–52.

Chawla, S and Renesch, J (1995) *Learning Organizations: Developing cultures for tomorrow's workplace*. Productivity Press: Portland, OR.

Chhokar JS, Brodbeck FC and House RJ (eds) (2007) *Culture and Leadership Across the World: The GLOBE book of in-depth studies of 25 societies*. Lawrence Erlbaum Associates: Mahwah, NJ.

Child, J (1972) Organizational structure, environment and performance: the role of strategic choice. *Sociology*, 6(1), 1–22.

Child, J (1984) *Organization*. Harper & Row: Cambridge.

Child, J and Ellis, T (1973) Predictors of variation in managerial roles. *Human Relations*, 26(2), 227–50.

Child, J and Smith, C (1987) The context and process of organisational transformation – Cadbury Limited in its sector. *Journal of Management Studies*, 24(6), 565–93.

Chin, R and Benne, KD (1976) General strategies for effecting changes in human systems. In WG Bennis, KD Benne, R Chin and KE Corey (eds): *The Planning of Change* (3rd edition). Holt, Rinehart and Winston: New York.

Choi, TY, Dooley, KJ and Rungtusanatham, M (2001) Supply networks and complex adaptive systems: control versus emergence. *Journal of Operations Management*, 19(3), 351–66.

Christopher, M (1998) *Logistics and Supply Chain Management* (2nd edition). Pitman: London.

Chua, A and Lam, W (2005) Why KM projects fail: a multi-case analysis. *Journal of Knowledge Management*, 9(3), 6–17.

CIA (2012) *The World Fact Book*, available at www.cia.gov

Clark, A (2008) Feds charge Bear pair with fraud over $1.4bn sub-prime collapse. *The Guardian*, 20 June, available at www.guardian.co.uk

Clark, P (1972) *Action Research and Organisational Change*. Harper & Row: London.

Clark, RC (1979) *The Japanese Company*. New Haven, CT.

Clark, T (2013) In post-Thatcher Britain there is such a thing as a divided society. *The Guardian*, 16 April, available at www.guardian.co.uk

Clarke, L (1994) *The Essence of Change*. Prentice Hall: London.

Clarke, M (1999) Management development: a new role in social change. *Management Decision*, 37(10), 767–77.

Clegg, CW (1984) The derivation of job design. *Journal of Occupational Behaviour*, 5, 131–46.

Clegg, CW and Symon, G (1991) Technology-led change: a case study of the implementation of CADCAM. *Journal of Occupational Psychology*, 64(4), 273–90.

Clegg, S (1990) *Modern Organisation: Organisation studies in the postmodern world*. Sage: London.

Clegg, S, Carter, C, Kornberger, M and Schweitzer, J (2011) *Strategy: Theory and practice*. Sage: London.

Coch, L and French, JRP, Jr (1948) Overcoming resistance to change. *Human Relations*, 1(4), 512–32.

Coghlan, D (1993a) A person-centred approach to dealing with resistance to change. *Leadership & Organization Development Journal*, 14(4), 10–14.

Coghlan, D (1993b) In defence of process consultation. In C Mabey and B Mayon-White (eds): *Managing Change* (2nd edition). The Open University/Paul Chapman Publishing: London.

Cohen, A and Keren, D (2008) Individual values and social exchange variables: examining their relationship to and mutual effect on in-role performance and organizational citizenship behavior. *Group & Organization Management*, 33(4), 425–52.

Cohen, MD, March, JG and Olsen, JP (1972) A garbage can model of organizational choice. *Administrative Science Quarterly*, 17(1), 1–25.

Cole, G (2001) Organisations as systems. In D Barnes (ed): *Understanding Business: Processes*. Routledge: London.

Cole, RE (1979) *Work, Mobility and Participation: A comparative study of Japanese and American industry*. University of California Press: Los Angeles, CA.

Collier, A (1994) *Critical Realism*. Verso: London.

Collins, D (1998) *Organizational Change*. Routledge: London.

Collins, D (2000) *Management Fads and Buzzwords*. Routledge: London.

Collins, D (2008) Has Tom Peters lost the plot? A timely review of a celebrated management guru. *Journal of Organizational Change Management*, 21(3), 315–34.

Collins, JC and Porras, JI (1991) Organizational vision and visionary organizations. *California Management Review*, Fall, 30–52.

Collins, JC and Porras, JI (1997) *Built to Last: Successful habits of visionary companies*. HarperBusiness: New York.

Colquitt, JA, Conlon, DE, Wesson, MJ, Porter, COLH and Ng, KY (2001) Justice at the millennium: a meta-analytic review of 25 years of organizational justice research. *Journal of Applied Psychology*, 86, 425–45.

Conger, JA and Ready, DA (2004) Rethinking leadership competencies. *Leader to Leader*, 32, 41–47.

Connelly, J (2000) A realistic theory of health sector management: the case for critical realism. *Journal of Management in Medicine*, 14(5/6), 262–71.

Conner, PE (1977) A critical enquiry into some assumptions and values characterizing OD. *Academy of Management Review*, 2(1), 635–44.

Constable, J and McCormick, R (1987) *The Making of British Managers*. British Institute of Management/Confederation of British Industry: London.

Cook, T (1998) New Labour, new NHS . . . new internal market? *Management Accounting*, 76(3), March, 24–6.

Cooke, B (1999) Writing the left out of management theory: the historiography of the management of change. *Organization*, 6(1), 81–105.

Cool, K and Schendel, D (1988) Performance differences among strategic group members. *Strategic Management Journal*, 9(3), 207–23.

Coombs, R and Hull, R (1994) The best or the worst of both worlds: BPR, cost reduction, and the strategic management of IT. Paper presented to the OASIG Seminar on Organisation Change through IT and BPR: Beyond the Hype, London, September.

Cooper, CL and Jackson, SE (eds) (1997) *Creating Tomorrow's Organizations*. Wiley: Chichester.

Cooper, J and Fazio, RH (1984) A new look at dissonance theory. In L Berkowitz (ed): *Advances in Experimental Social Psychology*, Vol. 17, 229–67. Academic Press: New York.

Cooper, R and Burrell, G (1988) Modernism, postmodernism and organizational analysis: an introduction. *Organization Studies*, 9(1), 91–112.

Cooper, Z (2008) Faiths to faith. *The Guardian*, 7 June, available at www.guardian.co.uk

Cooperrider, D and Srivastva, S (1987) Appreciative inquiry in organizational life. In R Woodman and W Pasmore (eds): *Organization Change and Development*. JAI: Greenwich, CT.

Coopey, J and Burgoyne, J (2000) Politics and organisational learning. *Journal of Management Studies*, 37(6), 869–85.

Copley, FB (1923) *Frederick Winslow Taylor: Father of Scientific Management*, Vol. 2. Harper & Row: New York.

Coram, R and Burnes, B (2001) Managing organizational change in the public sector: lessons from the privatisation of the Property Services Agency. *International Journal of Public Sector Management*, 14(2), 205–20.

Coram, WR (1997) The privatisation of the Property Services Agency, Vols 1 and 2. Unpublished PhD Thesis. UMIST: Manchester.

Coulson-Thomas, C and Coe, T (1991) *The Flat Organization*. British Institute of Management: London.

Coupland, D (1995) *Microserfs*. Regan Books: New York.

Courtney, H, Kirkland, J and Viguerie, P (1997) Strategy under uncertainty. *Harvard Business Review*, 75(6), 67–79.

Covey, S (1989) *The Seven Habits of Highly Effective People*. Simon & Schuster: New York.

Covin, JG (1991) Entrepreneurial versus conservative firms: a comparison of strategies and performance. *Journal of Management Studies*, 28(5), 439–62.

Cowan, CC and Todorovic, N (eds) (2005) *The Never Ending Quest: Clare W Graves explores human nature*. ECLET Publishing: Santa Barbara, CA.

Cowe, R (1995) Compete carefully. *The Guardian*, 25 March, 40.

Coyne, KP and Subramaniam, S (1996) Bringing discipline to strategy. *McKinsey Quarterly*, 4, 14–25.

Crainer, S (ed) (1995) *The Financial Times Handbook of Management*. Pitman: London.

Crainer, S (1996) *Key Management Ideas*. Financial Times Pitman: London.

Crawford, M, Rutter, D and Thelwall, S (2003) *User Involvement in Change Management: A review of the literature*. Department of Psychological Medicine, Imperial College: London.

Cressey, P (1996) Enriching production: perspectives on Volvo's Uddevalla plant as an alternative to lean production. *Industrial Relations Journal*, 27(1), 77–80.

Cringely, RX (1992) *Accidental Empires: How the boys of Silicon Valley make their millions, battle foreign competition, and still can't get a date*. Addison-Wesley: Reading, MA.

Cropanzano, R, Byrne, ZS, Bobocel, DR and Rupp, DE (2001) Moral virtues, fairness heuristics, social entities, and other denizens of organizational justice. *Journal of Vocational Behavior*, 58(2), 164–209.

Crosby, PB (1979) *Quality Is Free*. McGraw-Hill: New York.

Crossan, MM and Guatto, T (1996) Organizational learning research profile. *Journal of Organizational Change Management*, 9(1), 107–12.

Crouch, C and Streeck, W (eds) (1997) *Political Economy of Modern Capitalism*. Sage: London.

Crozier, M (1964) *The Bureaucratic Phenomenon*. Tavistock: London.

Cruise O'Brien, R and Voss, C (1992) *In Search of Quality*. Working Paper, London Business School: London.

Cummings, TG (2005) Systems theory. In N Nicholson, PG Audia and MM Pillutula (eds): *The Blackwell Encyclopedia of Management (2nd edition) – Organizational Behavior*. Blackwell: Oxford.

Cummings, TG and Huse, EF (1989) *Organization Development and Change* (4th edition). West: St Paul, MN.

Cummings, TG and Worley, CG (1997) *Organization Development and Change* (6th edition). South-Western College Publishing: Cincinnati, OH.

Cummings, TG and Worley, CG (2001) *Organization Development and Change* (7th edition). South-Western College Publishing: Mason, OH.

Cummings, TG and Worley, CG (2005) *Organization Development and Change* (8th edition). South-Western College Publishing: Mason, OH.

Cummings, TG and Worley, CG (2009) *Organization Development and Change* (9th edition. South-Western College Publishing: Mason, OH.

Cunill, OM (2009) *The Growth Strategies of Hotel Chains*. Routledge: Abingdon.

Cuthbert, N (1970) Readings from Henri Fayol, general and industrial management. In A Tillett, T Kempner and G Willis (eds): *Management Thinkers*. Pelican: Harmondsworth.

Cyert, RM and March, JG (1963) *A Behavioral Theory of the Firm*. Prentice Hall: Englewood Cliffs, NJ.

Daft, RL (1998) *Organizational Theory and Design* (6th edition). Southwestern: Cincinnati, OH.

Dahlgaard-Park, SM (2007) Guest editorial: our dreams of excellence – learning from the past and architecturing the future. *Journal of Management History*, 13(4), 306.

Dahlgaard-Park, SM and Dahlgaard, JJ (2007) Excellence – 25 years evolution. *Journal of Management History*, 13(4), 371–93.

Dakin, SR and Hamilton, RT (1990) How 'general' are your general managers? *Management Decision*, 28(2), 32–7.

Dale, BG (ed) (1999) *Managing Quality* (3rd edition). Blackwell: Oxford.

Dale, BG (ed) (2003) *Managing Quality* (4th edition). Blackwell: Oxford.

Dale, BG and Cooper, CL (1992) *TQM and Human Resources: An executive guide*. Blackwell: Oxford.

Dale, PN (1986) *The Myth of Japanese Uniqueness*. Croom Helm: London.

Darwin, J, Johnson, P and McAuley, J (2002) *Developing Strategies for Change*. Financial Times Prentice Hall: Harlow.

Dastmalchian, A (1984) Environmental dependencies and company structure in Britain. *Organization Studies*, 5(3), 222–41.

Data Systems International (2007) *The Resource-Based View of Strategy: Application to the agricultural industry*. DSI/Asia and Pacific: Kansas, MO.

Davenport, TH (1993) *Process Innovation: Re-engineering work through IT*. Harvard Business School Press: Boston, MA.

Davies, C (1995) *Gender and the Professional Predicament in Nursing*. Routledge: London.

Davis, E and Star, J (1993) The world's best performing companies. *Business Strategy Review*, 4(2), 1–16.

Davis, LE (1979) Job design: historical overview. In LE Davis and JC Taylor (eds): *Design of Work*. Goodyear: Santa Monica, CA.

Davis, LE and Canter, RR (1956) Job design research. *Journal of Industrial Engineering*, 7(6), 275–82.

Davis, LE, Canter, RR and Hoffman, J (1955) Current job design criteria. *Journal of Industrial Engineering*, 6(2), 5–11.

Davis, N (1997) *Europe: A history*. Pimlico: London.

Davis, R (1928) *The Principles of Factory Organization and Management*. Harper & Row: New York.

Davis, TRV (1985) Managing culture at the bottom. In R Kilmann, M Saxton, R Serpa and Associates (eds): *Gaining Control of the Corporate Culture*. Jossey-Bass: San Francisco, CA.

Dawkins, W (1993) Costly burden of tradition. *Financial Times*, 1 December, 10.

Dawkins, W (1994) Loosening of the corporate web. *Financial Times*, 30 November, 15.

Dawson, P (1994) *Organizational Change: A processual approach*. Paul Chapman Publishing: London.

Dawson, P (2003) *Organizational Change: A processual approach*. Routledge: London.

Dawson, P (2011) The contribution of the processual approach to the theory and practice of organizational change. In DM Boje, B Burnes and J Hassard (eds): *The Routledge Companion to Organizational Change*. London: Routledge.

Day, C, Elliott, J, Somekh, B and Winter, R (eds) (2002) *Theory and Practice in Action Research*. Symposium Books: Oxford.

Day, J, Reynolds, P and Lancaster, G (1998) A marketing strategy for public sector organisations compelled to operate in a compulsory competitive tendering environment. *International Journal of Public Sector Management*, 11(7), 583–95.

Day, T and Tosey, P (2011) Beyond SMART? A new framework for goal setting. *Curriculum Journal*, 22(4), 515–34.

de Chernatony, L and Cottam, S (2008) Interactions between organisational cultures and corporate brands. *Journal of Product and Brand Management*, 17(1), 13–24.

de Waal, AA (2013) Evergreens of excellence. *Journal of Management History*, 19(2), 241–78.

De Wit, B and Meyer, R (2010) *Strategy: Process, content, context* (4th edition). Cengage: Andover.

De Witte, K and van Muijen, JJ (1999) Organizational culture: critical questions for researchers and practitioners. *European Journal of Work and Organizational Psychology*, 8(4), 583–95.

Deal, T and Kennedy, A (1982) *Corporate Cultures*. Addison-Wesley: Reading: MA.

Deal, T and Kennedy, A (1983) Culture: a new look through old lenses. *Journal of Applied Behavioural Science*, 19(4), 498–505.

Dearlove, D (2011) The art of Japanese management revisited. *Business Strategy Review*, 22(3), 57–9.

Deeds, DL and Hill, CWL (1996) Strategic alliances and the rate of new product development: an empirical study of entrepreneurial biotechnology firms. *Journal of Business Venturing*, 11(1), 41–55.

Delbridge, R (2004) Working in teams: ethnographic evidence from two 'high performance' workplaces. In S Fleetwood and S Ackroyd (eds): *Critical Realist Applications in Organisation and Management Studies*. Routledge: London.

Deming, WE (1982) *Quality, Productivity and Competitive Position*. MIT Press: Boston, MA.

Denegri-Knott, J, Zwick, D and Schroeder, JE (2006) Mapping consumer power: an integrative framework for marketing and consumer research. *European Journal of Marketing*, 40(9/10), 950–71.

Dent, EB (2002) The messy history of OB&D: how three strands came to be seen as one rope. *Management Decision*, 40(3), 266–80.

Dent, EB and Goldberg, SG (1999) Challenging resistance to change. *Journal of Applied Behavioral Science*, 35(1), 25–41.

Deresky, H (2000) *International Management: Managing across borders and cultures* (3rd edition). Prentice Hall: Upper Saddle River, NY.

Deresky, H (2010) *International Management: Managing across borders and culture* (7th edition). Prentice-Hall: Upper Saddle River, NJ.

Derrida, J (1978) *Writing and Difference*. Routledge and Kegan Paul: London.

Dess, GG and Davis, PS (1984) Porter's (1980) generic strategies as determinants of strategic group membership and original performance. *Academy of Management Journal*, 27(3), 467–88.

Deutsch, M (1968) Field theory in social psychology. In Lindzey, G and Aronson, E (eds): *The Handbook of Social Psychology*, Vol. 1 (2nd edition). Addison-Wesley: Reading, MA.

Devi, S (2013) Companies strive to avoid uniformity. *Financial Times*, 11 April, 4.

Diamond, GA (1992) Field theory and rational choice: a Lewinian approach to modelling motivation. *Journal of Social Issues*, 48(2), 79–94.

Diamond, M (1986) Resistance to change: a psychoanalytic critique of Argyris and Schon's contributions to organization theory and intervention. *Journal of Management Studies*, 23(5), 543–62.

Dickens, L and Watkins, K (1999) Action research: rethinking Lewin. *Management Learning*, 30(2), 127–40.

Dixit, A (1980) The role of investment in entry deterrence. *Economic Journal*, 90(357), 95–106.

Dobson, P (1988) Changing culture. *Employment Gazette*, December, 647–50.

Dobson, PJ (2001) The philosophy of critical realism – an opportunity for information systems research. *Information Systems Frontiers*, 3(2), 199–210.

Docherty, P, Forslin, J, Shani, AB and King, M (2002) Emerging work systems: from intensive to sustainable. In P Docherty, J Forslin, AB Shani and M King (eds): *Creating Sustainable Work Systems: Emerging perspectives and practices*. Routledge: London.

Doherty, TL and Horne, T (2002) *Managing Public Services: Implementing change – a thoughtful approach*. Routledge: London.

Domberger, S (1998) *The Contracting Organization*. Oxford University Press: Oxford.

Done, K (1994) Up to strength once again: Volvo. *Financial Times*, 2 December.

Done, K and Willman, J (2008) BA struggles to escape T5 twilight zone. *Financial Times*, 5 April, 5.

Donkin, R (2002) How to preserve the soul of management: the increasing sophistication of measurement techniques threatens to reduce executives to robots. *Financial Times*, 19 September, 12.

Donovan, P (1995) Saatchis in row over share deal. *The Guardian*, 15 February, 22.

Doran, J (2008) Wall Street's collapse: who is next? *The Observer*, 20 July, available at www.guardian.co.uk

Dorling, D, Rigby, J, Wheeler, B, Ballas, D, Thomas, B, Fahmy, E, Gordon, D and Lupton, R (2007) *Poverty, Wealth and Place in Britain, 1968 to 2005*. Joseph Rowntree Foundation/Polity Press: Bristol.

Dowrick, S and DeLong, JB (2003) Globalization and Convergence. In MD Bordo, AM Taylor and JG Williamson (eds): *Globalization in Historical Perspective*. University of Chicago Press: Chicago, IL.

Drennan, D (1992) *Transforming Company Culture*. McGraw-Hill: London.

Drory, A and Romm, T (1988) Politics in the organization and its perception within the organization. *Organization Studies*, 9(2), 165–79.

Drory, A and Vigoda-Gadot, E (2010) Organizational politics and human resource management: typology and the Israeli experience. *Human Resource Management Review*, 20(3), 194–202.

Drucker, PF (1974) *Management: Tasks, responsibilities, practices*. Harper & Row: London.

Drucker, PF (1977) *People and Performance*. Heinemann: London.

Drucker, PF (1985) *Innovation and Entrepreneurship*. Pan: London.

Dudley, G (1999) British Steel and the government since privatisation: policy 'framing' and the transformation of policy networks. *Public Administration*, 77(1), 51–71.

Dukakis, MS and Kanter, RM (1988) *Creating the Future*. Summit Books: New York.

Duncan, WJ (1975) Organisations as political coalitions: a behavioral view of the goal function process. *Journal of Behavioral Economics*, 5, Summer, 25–44.

Duncan, WJ (1999) *Management: Ideas and action*. Oxford University Press: Oxford.

Dunphy, D (2000) Embracing paradox: top-down versus participative management of organizational change, a commentary on Conger and Bennis. In M Beer and N Nohria (eds): *Breaking the Code of Change*. Harvard Business School Press: Boston, MA.

Dunphy, DD and Griffiths, A (1998) *The Sustainable Corporation: Organisational renewal in Australia*. Allen & Unwin: St Leonards, Australia.

Dunphy, DD and Stace, DA (1988) Transformational and coercive strategies for planned organizational change: beyond the OD model. *Organization Studies*, 9(3), 317–34.

Dunphy, DD and Stace, DA (1992) *Under New Management: Australian organizations in transition*. McGraw-Hill: Roseville, New South Wales.

Dunphy, DD and Stace, DA (1993) The strategic management of corporate change. *Human Relations*, 46(8), 905–18.

Dunphy, D, Griffiths, A and Benn, S (2003) *Organizational Change for Corporate Sustainability*. Routledge: London.

Dunphy, D, Griffiths, A and Benn, S (2007) *Organizational Change for Corporate Sustainability* (2nd edition). Routledge: London.

Dyer, H (1996) Specialized supplier networks as a source of competitive advantage: evidence from the auto industry. *Strategic Management Journal*, 17(4), 271–91.

Easterby-Smith, M (1997) Disciplines of organizational learning: contributions and critiques. *Human Relations*, 50(9), 1085–113.

Easterby-Smith, M, Crossan, M and Nicolini, D (2000) Organizational learning: debates past, present and future. *Journal of Management Studies*, 37(6), 783–96.

Easton, G (2000) Case research as a method for industrial networks: a realist apologia. In S Ackroyd and S Fleetwood (eds): *Realist Perspectives on Management and Organisations*. Routledge: London.

Eccles, T (1993) The deceptive allure of empowerment. *Long Range Planning*, 26(6), 13–21.

Economist, The (1998) All fall down. *The Economist*, 28 February.

Economist, The (2002) *Globalisation: Reasons, effects and challenges*. Economist Books: London.

Economist, The (2008) Grossly distorted picture: If you look at GDP per head, the world is a different – and, by and large, a better – place. 13 March, available at www.economist.com

Economist Intelligence Unit (1992) Making Quality Work – Lessons from Europe's Leading Companies. Economist Intelligence Unit: London.

Eden, C and Huxham, C (1996) Action research for the study of organizations. In SR Clegg, C Hardy and WR Nord (eds): *Handbook of Organization Studies*. Sage: London.

Edgecliffe-Johnson, A (2007) *Financial Times*, 19 May, 14.

Edwardes, M (1983) *Back from the Brink*. Collins: London.

Egan, G (1994) Cultivate your culture. *Management Today*, April, 39–42.

Eilperin, J (2013) On climate change, Obama faces an attack from his left flank. *The Washington Post*, 20 May, available at www.washingtonpost.com

Einarsen, S, Aasland, MS and Skogstad, A (2007) Destructive leadership behaviour: a definition and conceptual model. *The Leadership Quarterly*, 18(3), 207–16.

Elden, M and Chisholm, RF (1993) Emerging varieties of action research: introduction to the special issue. *Human Relations*, 46(20), 121–42.

Eldridge, JET and Crombie, AD (1974) *A Sociology of Organizations*. George Allen and Unwin: London.

Elliot, K and Lawrence, P (1985) *Introducing Management*. Penguin: Harmondsworth.

Elliott, L (2007) Cost of large mortgages hits post-9/11 high as credit squeeze ripples through economy. *The Guardian*, 2 October, 29.

Elliott, L (2008) Up. Up. Up. Child poverty, pensioner poverty, inequality. *The Guardian*, 11 June, available at www.guardian.co.uk

Elliott, L (2013) Eurozone recession sends shares lower. *The Guardian*, 14 February, available at www.guardian.co.uk

Elliott, L and Seager, A (2008) Shape of things to come. *The Guardian*, 13 November, 1.

Elrod II, PD and Tippett, DD (2002) The 'death valley' of change. *Journal of Organizational Change Management*, 15(3), 273–91.

Epstein, SR and Prak, M (2010) *Guilds, Innovation and the European Economy, 1400–1800*. Cambridge University Press: Cambridge.

Erez, M (2010) Culture and job design. *Journal of Organizational Behavior*, 31(2–3), 389–400.

Erridge, A and Nondi, R (1994) Public procurement, competition and partnership. *European Journal of Purchasing and Supply Management*, 1(3), 169–79.

Etzioni, A (1975) *A Comparative Analysis of Complex Organizations*. Free Press: New York.

Etzioni, A (2004) The post affluent society. *Review of Social Economy*, LXII(3), 404–20.

Etzold, V and Mueller, U (2012) Minimal change can be best option: why Berlin snack bar resisted change. *Financial Times*, 1 May, 12.

European Commission (1998) *Work Programme*. The Directorate General for Energy, DG XVII/148–98-EN: Brussels.

Evans, MG (1970) The effects of supervisory behaviour on the path–goal relationship. *Organizational Behavior and Human Performance*, 5, 277–98.

Evans, R, Traynor, I, Harding, L and Carroll, R (2003) Web of state corruption dates back 40 years. *Guardian*, 13 June, available at www.guardian.co.uk

EWERC (2007) The globalization of the temporary staffing industry. *EWERC Research News*, 3 (September), 2.

Ezzamel, M, Green, C, Lilley, S and Willmott, H (1994) *Change Management: Appendix 1 – a review and analysis of recent changes in UK management practices*. The Financial Services Research Centre, UMIST: Manchester.

Fagenson-Eland, E, Ensher, EA and Burke, WW (2004) Organization development and change interventions: a seven-nation comparison. *Journal of Applied Behavioral Science*, 40(4), 432–64.

Fahy, J (2000) The resource-based view of the firm: some stumbling-blocks on the road to understanding sustainable competitive advantage. *Journal of European Industrial Training*, 24(2–4), 94–104.

Falconer, J (2002) Emergence happens! Misguided paradigms regarding organizational change and the role of complexity and patterns in the change landscape. *Emergence*, 4(1/2), 117–30.

Fang, T (2005–2006) From 'onion' to 'ocean': paradox and change in national cultures. *International Studies of Management and Organization*, 35(4), 71–90.

Farias, G and Johnson, H (2000) Organizational development and change management: setting the record straight. *Journal of Applied Behavioral Science*, 36(3), 376–9.

Farrell, D and Petersen, JC (1983) Patterns of political behaviour in organizations. *The Academy of Management Review*, 7, 403–12.

Farris, PW and Moore, MJ (2004) *The Profit Impact of Marketing Strategy Project: Retrospect and prospects*. Cambridge University Press: Cambridge.

Faulkner, D, Teerikangas, S and Joseph, RJ (eds) (2012) *The Handbook of Mergers and Acquisitions*. Oxford University Press: Oxford.

Fawn, J and Cox, B (1985) *Corporate Planning in Practice*. Strategic Planning Society: London.

Fayol, H (1949) *General and Industrial Management* (trans). Pitman: London.

Fazio, RH, Zanna, MP and Cooper, J (1977) Dissonance and self-perception: an integrative view of each theory's proper domain of application. *Journal of Experimental Social Psychology*, 13, 464–79.

Featherstone, M (1988a) In pursuit of postmodernism: an introduction. *Theory, Culture and Society*, 5, 195–215.

Featherstone, M (ed) (1988b) *Postmodernism*. Sage: Newbury Park, CA.

Ferguson, CH (1988) From the people who brought you Voodoo Economics. *Harvard Business Review*, May–June, 55–62.

Ferlie, E, Ashburner, L, Fitzgerald, L and Pettigrew, A (1996) *The New Public Sector in Action*. Oxford University Press: Oxford.

Ferris GR and Treadway, DC (eds) (2012) *Politics in Organizations: Theory and research considerations*. Routledge: New York.

Festinger, L (1957) *The Theory of Cognitive Dissonance*. Stanford University Press: Stanford, CA.

Fiedler, FE (1967) *A Theory of Leadership Effectiveness*. McGraw-Hill: New York.

Fiedler, FE (1986) The contribution of cognitive resources to leadership performance. *Journal of Applied Psychology*, 16(6), 532–48.

Fiedler, FE (1995) Cognitive resources and leadership performance. *Applied Psychology: An International Review*, 44(1), 5–28.

Fiedler, FE and Chemers, MM (1984) *Improving Leadership Effectiveness: The leader match concept* (2nd edition). Wiley: New York.

Filby, I and Willmott, H (1988) Ideologies and contradictions in a public relations department. *Organization Studies*, 9(3), 335–51.

Filley, AC, House, RJ and Kerr, S (1976) *Managerial Process and Organization Behavior*. Scott, Foresman and Company: Glenview, IL.

Financial, The [of Greece] (2000) When would consumers get a better service: if service utilities were government or privately-owned?, 6 October, 14–15.

Financial Times (2003) The madness in Marconi's fall: the FSA report obscures important lessons. 14 April, 20.

Financial Times (2007) Dreams are no basis for a sound corporate strategy. 20 March, 15.

Finch, J and Treanor, J (2003) Shares down 24%. Average earnings up 3%. Boardroom pay up 23%. *The Guardian*, 31 July, 1.

Finstad, N (1998) The rhetoric of organizational change. *Human Relations*, 51(6), 717–40.

Fiol, MC and Lyles, MA (1985) Organizational learning. *Academy of Management Review*, 10(4), 803–13.

Fitton, R and Wadsworth, A (1958) *The Strutts and the Arkwrights 1758–1830*. Manchester University Press: Manchester.

Fitzgerald, LA (2002a) Chaos: the lens that transcends. *Journal of Organizational Change Management*, 15(4), 339–58.

Fitzgerald, LA (2002b) Chaos speak: a glossary of chaordic terms and phrases. *Journal of Organizational Change Management*, 15(4), 412–23.

Fitzgerald, L, Ferlie, E, Addicott, R, Baeza, J, Buchanan, D and McGivern, G (2007) Service improvement in healthcare – understanding change capacity and change context. *Clinician in Management*, 15(2), 61–74.

Flamholtz, E (2001) Corporate culture and the bottom line. *European Management Journal*, 19(3), 268–75.

Fleetwood, S and Ackroyd, S (eds) (2004) *Critical Realist Applications in Organisation and Management Studies*. Routledge: London.

Fleisher, CS and Bensoussan, BE (2003) *Strategic and Competitive Analysis: Methods and techniques for analysing business competition*. Prentice Hall: Upper Saddle River, NJ.

Fleishman, EA (1953) The description of supervisory behaviour. *Personnel Psychology*, 37, 1–6.

Fleishman, EA (1969) *Manual for the Leadership Opinion Questionnaire*. Science Research Associates: Chicago, IL.

Fleming, P (2012) 'Down with Big Brother!': The end of 'corporate culturalism'? *Journal of Management Studies*, published online, doi: 10.1111/j.1467–6486.2012.01056.x

Flynn, J, Dawley, H, Templeman, J and Bernier, L (1995) Suddenly British carmaking is burning rubber. *Business Week*, 3 April, 21.

Flynn, N (1993) *Public Sector Management* (2nd edition). Harvester Wheatsheaf: Hemel Hempstead.

Foegen, JH (1999) Why not empowerment? *Business and Economics Review*, 45(3), April–June, 31.

Ford, JD and Ford, LW (1995) The role of conversations in producing intentional change in organizations. *Academy of Management Review*, 20(3), 541–70.

Ford, JD and Ford, LW (2010) Stop blaming resistance to change and start using it. *Organizational Dynamics*, 39(1), 24–36.

Ford, JD, Ford, LW and D'Amelio, A (2008) Resistance to change: the rest of the story. *Academy of Management Review*, 33(2), 362–77.

Ford, TM (1981) Strategic planning – myth or reality? A chief executive's view. *Long Range Planning*, 14, December, 9–11.

Fortune (1990) Global 500: the world's biggest industrial corporations. *Fortune*, 30 July.

Fortune (2007) 100 Best companies to work for 2007. Available at money.ccn.com/magazines/fortune/bestcompanies/2007

Fortune (2008) Global 500: Our annual ranking of the world's largest corporations. Available at www.cnnmoney.com/magazines/fortune/global500/2008

Fortune (2012) Global 500: Our annual ranking of the world's largest corporations, available at http://money.cnn.com/magazines/fortune/global500/2012/full_list/

Foster, MB (1977) *Masters of Political Thought*. Harrap: London.

Foster, R and Kaplan, S (2003) *Creative Destruction: Why companies that are built to last under-perform the market – and how to successfully transform them*. Doubleday: London.

Foucault, M (1977) *The Archaeology of Knowledge*. Tavistock: London.

Foucault, M (1983) The subject and power. In HL Dreyfus and P Rabinow (eds): *Michel Foucault: Beyond structuralism and hermeneutics* (2nd edition). University of Chicago Press: Chicago, IL.

Fox, JM (1975) Strategic planning: a case study. *Managerial Planning*, 23, May/June, 32–8.

Fox, M (1994) *The Reinvention of Work: A new vision of livelihood for our times*. Harper: San Francisco, CA.

Francks, P (1992) *Japanese Economic Development: Theory and practice*. Routledge: London.

Franklin, B (1997) *Newszak and News Media*. Arnold: London.

Frederick, WC (1998) Creatures, corporations, communities, chaos, complexity: a naturological view of the corporate social role. *Business and Society*, 37(4), 358–76.

Freedman, A (1999) The history of organization development and the NTL Institute: what we have learned, forgotten and rewritten. *The Psychologist–Manager Journal*, 3(2), 125–41.

Freeman, C (1988) The factory of the future: the productivity paradox, Japanese just-in-time and information technology. *ESRC PICT Policy Research Paper 3*. ESRC: Swindon.

French, JRP, Jr (1945) Role playing as a method of training foremen. *Sociometry*, 8, 410–25.

French, JRP, Jr and Raven, BH (1959) The bases of social power. In D Cartwright (ed): *Studies in Social Power*. Institute for Social Research: Ann Harbor, MI.

French, R, Rayner, C, Rees, G and Rumble, S (2008) *Organizational Behaviour*. Wiley: Chichester.

French, WL and Bell, CH (1973) *Organization Development*. Prentice Hall: Englewood Cliffs, NJ.

French, WL and Bell, CH (1984) *Organization Development* (4th edition). Prentice Hall: Englewood Cliffs, NJ.

French, WL and Bell, CH (1995) *Organization Development* (5th edition). Prentice Hall: Englewood Cliffs, NJ.

French, WL and Bell, CH (1999) *Organization Development* (6th edition). Prentice Hall: Upper Saddle River, NJ.

Friedman, G (1961) *The Anatomy of Work*. Heinemann: London.

Frith, M (2003) Brain drain: the men who won't let jobs deprive them of fatherhood. *The Independent*, 14 June, 7.

Froebel, F, Heinrichs, J and Kreye, O (1980) *The New Industrial Division of Labour: Structural unemployment in industrialized countries and industrialization in developing countries*. Cambridge University Press: Cambridge.

Frost, PJ and Hayes, DC (1979) An exploration in two cultures of a model of political behaviour in organizations. In RW Allen and LW Porter (eds): *Organizational Influence Processes*. Scott, Foresman and Co: Glenview, IL.

Frost, PJ, Moore, L, Louis, M, Lundberg, C and Martin, J (eds) (1991) *Reframing Organizational Culture*. Sage: Beverly Hills, CA.

Fruin, WM (1992) *The Japanese Enterprise System*. Oxford University Press: Oxford.

Fry, LW and Nisiewicz, MS (2013) *Maximising the Triple Bottom Line*. Stanford University Press: Stanford, CA.

Fukushige, A and Spicer, DP (2007) Leadership preferences in Japan: an exploratory study. *Leadership and Organization Development Journal*, 28(6), 508–30.

Fullerton, H and Price, C (1991) Culture change in the NHS. *Personnel Management*, March, 50–3.

Fulton, The Lord (1968) *The Civil Service: Report of the Committee Cmnd 3638*. HMSO: London.

Furrer, O, Thomas, H and Goussevskaia, A (2008) The structure and evolution of the strategic management field: a content analysis of 26 years of strategic management research. *International Journal of Management Reviews*, 10(1), 1–23.

Furuya, N, Stevens, MJ, Bird, A, Oddou, G and Mendenhall, M (2009) Managing the learning and transfer of global management competence: antecedents and outcomes of Japanese repatriation effectiveness. *Journal of International Business Studies*, 40(2), 200–15.

Gabbatt, A (2010) Liverpool board agrees sale to owners of Boston Red Sox. *The Guardian*, 6 October, available at www.guardian.co.uk

Gadd, IA and Wallis, P (2006) *Guilds and Associations in Europe, 900–1900*. Centre for Metropolitan History, University of London: London.

Gajendran, T, Brewer, G, Dainty, A and Runeson, G (2012) A conceptual approach to studying the organisational culture of construction projects. *Australasian Journal of Construction Economics and Building*, 12(2), 1–26.

Galagan, PA (1997) Strategic planning is back. *Training and Development*, 51(4), 32–8.

Galbraith, JR (2000) The role of formal structures and processes. In M Beer and N Nohria (eds): *Breaking the Code of Change*. Harvard Business School Press: Boston, MA.

Gallos, JV (Ed) (2006) *Organization Development: A Jossey-Bass reader*. Jossey-Bass: San Francisco, CA.

Galpin, T (1996) *The Human Side of Change: A practical guide to organization redesign*. Jossey-Bass: San Francisco, CA.

Gandz, J and Murray, VV (1980) The experience of workplace politics. *Academy of Management Journal*, 23, 237–51.

Gapper, J (2013) Managers are reining in staff – because they can. *Financial Times*, 28 February, 9.

Gardner, J (1990) *On Leadership*. Free Press: New York.

Garratt, B (1987) *The Learning Organization*. Fontana: London.

Garratt, B (1999) The learning organisation 15 years on: some personal reflections. *The Learning Organization*, 6(5), 202–6.

Garvin, DA (1993) Building a learning organization. *Harvard Business Review*, 71(4), July–August, 78–91.

Gastil, J (1994) A definition and an illustration of democratic leadership. *Human Relations*, 47, 953–75.

Gay, CL and Essinger, J (2000) *Inside Outsourcing*. Nicholas Brealey Publishing: London.

Gell–Mann, M (1994) *The Quark and the Jaguar*. Freeman: New York.

Gellerman, W, Frankel, MS and Ladenson, RF (1990) *Values and Ethics in Organizational and Human Systems Development: Responding to dilemmas in professional life*. Jossey-Bass: San Francisco, CA.

Gelles, D (2013) Brash, unpredictable and deeply ambitious. *Financial Times*, 16 April, 19.

Genus, A (1998) *The Management of Change: Perspective and practice*. International Thompson: London.

Gephart, RP, Thatchenkery, TJ and Boye, DM (1996) Reconstructing organizations for future survival. In DM Boye, RP Gephart and TJ Thatchenkery (eds): *Postmodern Management and Organizational Theory*. Sage: Thousand Oaks, CA.

Gergen, KJ (1992) Organization theory in the postmodern era. In M Reed and M Hughes (eds): *Rethinking Organization: New directions in organization theory and analysis*. Sage: London.

Gersick, CJG (1991) Revolutionary change theories: a multilevel exploration of the punctuated equilibrium paradigm. *Academy of Management Review*, 16(1), 10–36.

Ghemawat, P (1991) *Commitment: The dynamics of strategy*. Free Press: New York.

Ghemawat, P (2008) Reconceptualizing international strategy and organization. *Strategic Organization*, 6(2), 195–206.

Ghoshal, S and Bartlett, CA (2000) Rebuilding behavioral context: a blueprint for corporate renewal. In M Beer and N Nohria (eds): *Breaking the Code of Change*. Harvard Business School Press: Boston, MA.

Gibb, CA (1969) Leadership. In G Lindzey and E Aronson (eds): *Handbook of Social Psychology*, Vol. 4 (2nd edition). Addison-Wesley: Reading, MA.

Gibbons, PT (1992) Impacts of organisational evolution on leadership roles and behaviors. *Human Relations*, 45(1), 1–18.

Gibson, JL, Ivancevich, JM and Donnelly, JH (1988) *Organizations: Behavior–structure–processes*. Business Publications: Plano, TX.

Gibson, O (2003a) Napster: hopes to relaunch before end of year. *The Guardian*, 24 February, available at www.guardian.co.uk

Gibson, O (2003b) Web piracy hits music sales. *The Guardian*, 10 February, available at www.guardian.co.uk

Gibson, O (2003c) EMI to sell music downloads. *The Guardian*, 23 April, available at www.guardian.co.uk

Giddens, A (1984) *The Constitution of Society*. Polity Press: Cambridge.

Giddens, A (2002) *Runaway World: How globalisation is reshaping our lives*. Profile: London.

Gilbert, JA, Carr-Ruffino, N, Ivancevich, JM, Konopaske, R (2012) Toxic versus cooperative behaviors at work: the role of organizational culture and leadership in creating community-centered organizations. *International Journal of Leadership Studies*, 7(1), 29–47.

Gilbert, RJ and Newbery, DMG (1982) Preemptive patenting and the persistence of monopoly. *American Economic Review*, 72, 514–26.

Gilbert, X and Strebel, P (1992) Developing competitive advantage. In H Mintzberg and JB Quinn (eds): *The Strategy Process: Concepts, contexts and cases*. Prentice Hall: London.

Gilbreth, FB and Gilbreth, LM (1914) *Applied Motion Study*. Sturgis and Walton: New York.

Gilchrist, A (2000) The well-connected community: networking to the edge of chaos. *Community Development Journal*, 3(3), 264–75.

Gillespie, R (1991) *Manufacturing Knowledge: A history of the Hawthorne Experiments*. Cambridge University Press: Cambridge.

Gillett, C (1996) *The Sound of the City: The rise of rock & roll* (3rd edition). Souvenir Press: London.

Gilley, JW, Quatro, SA, Hoekstra, E, Whittle, DD and Maycunich, A (2001) *The Manager as a Change Agent*. Perseus: Cambridge, MA.

Gilmore, T, Shea, G and Useem, M (1997) Side effects of corporate cultural transformations. *Journal of Applied Behavioral Science*, 33(2), 174–89.

Gleick, J (1988) *Chaos: The making of a new science*. Heinemann: London.

Globalisationguide.org (2003) Is globalisation shifting power from nation states to undemocratic organisations? Available at www.globalisationguide.org

Glueck, WF (1978) *Business Policy and Strategic Management*. McGraw-Hill: New York.

Gold, KA (1982) Managing for success: a comparison of the private and public sectors. *Public Administration Review*, November–December, 568–75.

Gold, M (1992) Metatheory and field theory in social psychology: relevance or elegance? *Journal of Social Issues*, 48(2), 67–78.

Gold, M (ed) (1999) *The Complete Social Scientist: A Kurt Lewin reader*. American Psychological Association: Washington, DC.

Golding, D and Currie, D (2000) *Thinking about Management: A reflective practice approach*. Routledge: London.

Goldstein, J (1999) Emergence as a construct: history and issues. *Emergence* 1(1), 49–72.

Golzen, G (1995) Jobbing guru. *Human Resources*, 16, January/February, 42–8.

Gonzalez, JL (1999) *The Story of Christianity: The early church to the present day*. Prince Press: Peabody, MA.

Goodwin, B (1994) *How the Leopard Changed Its Spots*. Weidenfeld and Nicolson: London.

Google (2008) Google jobs: Google celebrates diversity. Available at www.google.co.uk/support/jobs

Goold, M, Campbell, A and Alexander, M (1994) *Corporate-Level Strategy: Creating value in the multi-business company*. Wiley: Chichester.

Gopalakrishnan, S, Mangaliso, MP and Butterfield, DA (2008) Managing ethically in times of transformation challenges and opportunities. *Group & Organization Management*, 33(6), 756–9.

Gordon, G (1985) The relationship of corporate culture to industry sector and corporate performance. In R Kilmann, M Saxton, R Serpa and Associates (eds): *Gaining Control of the Corporate Culture*. Jossey-Bass: San Francisco, CA.

Gould, SJ (1989) Punctuated equilibrium in fact and theory. *Journal of Social Biological Structure*, 12, 117–36.

Goulielmos, M (2003) Outlining organisational failure in information systems development. *Disaster Prevention and Management*, 12(4), 319–27.

Gow, D (1999a) Vultures still circling Rover plant as BMW remains silent on investment. *The Guardian*, 6 February, 11–12.

Gow, D (1999b) BMW to put £3bn into Rover car plants. *The Guardian*, 24 June, 25.

Gow, D (1999c) Finance: EC plans global assault: Simpson pledges to double value within five years after Marconi defence sale. *The Guardian*, 6 May, 25.

Gow, D and Traynor, I (1999) BMW split raises fears for Rover plant. *The Guardian*, 2 February, 1.

Grandori, A (Ed) (2013) *Handbook of Economic Organization: Integrating economic and organization theory*. Edward Elgar: Cheltenham.

Graen, GB and Cashman, JF (1975) A role making model of leadership in formal organizations: a developmental approach. In JG Hunt and LL Larson (eds): *Leadership Frontiers*. Kent State University Press: Kent, OH.

Graetz, F, Rimmer, M, Lawrence, A and Smith, A (2002) *Managing Organisational Change*. Wiley: Milton, Queensland.

Graham, G, Burnes, B and Hardaker, G (2002) The peer-to-peer revolution: how the Internet is transforming the supply chain for music. *The International Journal of New Product Development and Innovation Management*, 4(2), June/July, 115–30.

Graham, P (1987) *Dynamic Managing: The Follett way*. British Institute of Management: London.

Grant, A (1983) *Against the Clock*. Pluto: London.

Grant, D. Keenoy, T and Oswick, C (1998) Introduction: organizational discourse: of diversity, dichotomy and multi-disciplinarity. In D Grant, T Keenoy and C Oswick (eds): *Discourse + Organization*. Sage: London.

Grant, L (2006) And the brand played on. *The Guardian Weekend*, 12 August, 18–25.

Grant, RM (1991a) *Contemporary Strategy Analysis*. Blackwell: Oxford.

Grant, RM (1991b) The resource-based theory of competitive advantage: implications for strategy formulation. *California Management Review*, 33(3), 114–22.

Grant, RM (2007) *Contemporary Strategy Analysis* (4th edition). Blackwell: Oxford.

Grant, RM (2010) *Contemporary Strategy Analysis* (7th edition). John Wiley: Hoboken, NJ.

Green, C (2008) Chief executives' pay rises by more than 30 per cent. *The Independent*, 24 May, available at www.independent.co.uk

Green, T (2008) *Inquisition: The reign of fear*. Pan: London.

Greenberg, P and Erios, L (2001) One year ago: MP3.com caves in to legal blow, *Ecommercetimes*, 5 November, 1–3, available at www.ecommercetimes.com

Greenwald, J (1996) Reinventing Sears. *Time*, 23 December, 53–5.

Greiner, LE (1967) Patterns of organization change. *Harvard Business Review*, May–June, 119–30.

Greiner, LE (1972a) Evolution and revolution as organizations grow. *Harvard Business Review*, July–August, 37–46.

Greiner, LE (1972b) Red flags in organization development. *Business Horizons*, June.

Greiner, LE and Cummings, TG (2004) Wanted: OD more alive than dead! *Journal of Applied Behavioral Science*, 40(4), 374–91.

Grey, C (2003) The fetish of change. *Tamara: Journal of Critical Postmodern Organizational Science*, 2(2), 1–19.

Grieves, J and Redman, T (1999) Living in the shadow of OD: HRD and the search for identity. *Human Resource Development International*, 2(2), 81–102.

Griffin, D (2002) *The Emergence of Leadership: Linking self-organisation and ethics*. Routledge: London.

Grint, K (2005) Problems, problems, problems: the social construction of 'leadership'. *Human Relations*, 58(11), 1467–94.

Grinyer, PH, Mayes, DG and McKiernon, P (1988) *Sharpbenders: The secrets of unleashing corporate potential*. Blackwell: Oxford.

Grove, G (1998) The automotive industry – the customer's perspective: a study of Rover group. In B Burnes and B Dale (eds): *Working in Partnership*. Gower: Aldershot.

Grundy, T (1993) *Managing Strategic Change*. Kogan Page: London.

Guest, D (1992) Right enough to be dangerously wrong: an analysis of the *In Search of Excellence* phenomenon. In G Salaman (ed): *Human Resource Strategies*. Sage: London.

Guest, RH (1957) Job enlargement – revolution in Job Design. *Personnel Administration*, 20, 9–16.

Guillen, MF (2000) Business groups in emerging economies: a resource-based view. *Academy of Management Journal,* 43(3), 362–80.

Gulati, R (2007) Tent poles, tribalism, and boundary spanning: The rigor–relevance debate in management research. *Academy of Management Journal*, 50(4), 775–82.

Guthrie, J (2013) Bankers left in no doubt that time for remorse is not yet over. *Financial Times*, 19 June, 2.

Gyllenhammar, PG (1977) *People at Work*. Addison-Wesley: Reading, MA.

Habakkuk, HJ and Postan, M (eds) (1965) *The Cambridge Economic History of Europe*, Vol. VI. Cambridge University Press: Cambridge.

Hackman, JR and Lawler, EE (1971) Employee relations and job characteristics. *Journal of Applied Psychology*, 55, 259–86.

Hackman, JR and Oldham, GR (1980) *Work Redesign*. Addison-Wesley: Reading, MA.

Haggett, P (1975) *Geography: A modern synthesis*. Harper & Row: New York.

Haigh, C (2002) Using chaos theory: the implications for nursing. *Journal of Advanced Nursing*, 37(5), 462–9.

Hales, CP (1986) What do managers do?: a critical review of the evidence. *Journal of Management Studies*, 22(1), 88–115.

Hales, C (1999) Why do managers do what they do: reconciling evidence and theory in accounts of managerial work. *British Journal of Management*, 10, 335–50.

Hall, DT and Nougaim, KE (1968) An examination of Maslow's need hierarchy in an organizational setting. *Organizational Behaviour and Performance*, 3, February, 12–35.

Hall, R (1933) A framework linking intangible resources and capabilities to sustainable competitive advantage. *Strategic Management Journal*, 14, 607–18.

Hambrick, DC (1983) High profit strategies in mature capital goods industries: a contingency approach. *Academy of Management Journal*, 26, 687–707.

Hambrick, DC (2003) On the staying power of defenders, analyzers, and prospectors. *Academy of Management Executive*, 17(4): 115–18.

Hambrick, DC and Frederickson, JW (2001) Are you sure you have a strategy? *The Academy of Management Executive*, 15(4), 48–59.

Hamel, G (1996) Strategy as revolution. *Harvard Business Review*, July–August, 69–82.

Hamel, G (2007) *The Future of Management*. Harvard Business School Press: Boston, MA.

Hamel, G and Prahalad, CK (1989) Strategic intent. *Harvard Business Review*, May–June, 63–76.

Hamel, G and Prahalad, CK (1994) *Competing for the Future*. Harvard Business School Press: Boston, MA.

Hamilton, C (2003) Downshifting in Britain: A sea-change in the pursuit of happiness. Discussion Paper Number 58, November. The Australia Institute: Manuka, ACT, Australia.

Hammer, M and Champy, J (1993) *Re-engineering the Corporation*. Nicolas Brealey: London.

Hammersley, B (2002) Working the web: P2P technology. *The Guardian*, 7 March, available at www.guardian.co.uk

Hampson, N (1990) *The Enlightenment*. Penguin: Harmondsworth.

Handfield, RB and Nichols, EL Jr (1999) *Introduction to Supply Chain Management*. Prentice Hall: Englewood Cliffs, NJ.

Handy, C (1979) *Gods of Management*. Pan: London.

Handy, C (1984) *The Future of Work*. Blackwell: Oxford.

Handy, C (1986) *Understanding Organizations* (3rd edition). Penguin: Harmondsworth.

Handy, C (1989) *The Age of Unreason*. Arrow: London.

Handy, C (1993) *Understanding Organizations* (4th edition). Penguin: Harmondsworth.

Handy, C (1994) *The Empty Raincoat*. Hutchinson: London.

Handy, C (1997) *The Hungry Spirit*. Hutchinson: London.

Handy, C (2007a) *Myself and Other More Important Matters*. Arrow Books: London.

Handy, C (2007b) *The New Philanthropists*. Heinemann: London.

Handy, C, Gow, I, Gordon, C, Randlesome, C and Moloney, M (1987) *The Making of a Manager*. NEDO: London.

Hannagan, T (2002) *Management: Concepts and practices* (3rd edition). Financial Times Pearson: Harlow.

Hannam, R (1993) *Kaizen for Europe*. IFS: Kempston.

Hannan, MT and Freeman, J (1977) The population ecology of organizations. *American Journal of Sociology*, 82, 929–64.

Hannan, MT and Freeman, J (1988) *Organizational Ecology*. Harvard University Press: Cambridge, MA.

Hannan, MT, Pólos, L and Carroll, GR (2003) The fog of change: opacity and asperity in organizations. *Administrative Science Quarterly*, 8(3), 399–432.

Hanson, P (1993) Made in Britain – the true state of manufacturing industry. Paper presented at the Institution of Mechanical Engineers' Conference on Performance Measurement and Benchmarking, Birmingham, June.

Hardaker, G and Graham, G (2001) *Wired Marketing: Energizing business for e-commerce*. Wiley: Chichester.

Hardy, C (1996) Understanding power: bringing about strategic change. *British Journal of Management*, 7(Special Issue), March, S3–16.

Harré, R (1972) *The Philosophies of Science*. Oxford University Press: Oxford.

Harré, R and Madden, EH (1975) *Causal Powers*. Blackwell: Oxford.

Harré, R and Secord, PF (1972) *The Explanation of Social Behaviour*. Blackwell: Oxford.

Harrigan, RK (1980) *Strategy for Declining Businesses*. Lexington Books: Lexington, MA.

Harris, L and Ogbonna, E (2002) The unintended consequences of culture interventions: a study of unexpected outcomes. *British Journal of Management*, 13(1), 31–49.

Harris, PR (1985) *Management in Transition*. Jossey-Bass: San Francisco, CA.

Harrison, M (2002) Lord Simpson speaks out for the first time since leaving Marconi. *The Independent*, 28 November, 24.

Harrison, M (2003) Swipe card strike wipes £40m off BA. *The Independent*, 1 August, 19.

Harrison, R (1970) Choosing the depth of an organisational intervention. *Journal of Applied Behavioural Science*, 6, 181–202.

Harrison, R (1972) Understanding your organization's character. *Harvard Business Review*, 50(3), May/June, 119–28.

Harrison, R (2002) *Learning and Development* (3rd edition). CIPD: London.

Harrison, R (2005) *Learning and Development* (4th edition). CIPD: London.

Hartley, J, Bennington, J and Binns, P (1997) Researching the roles of internal-change agents in the management of organizational change. *British Journal of Management*, 8(1), 61–73.

Harukiyo, H and Hook, GD (eds) (1998) *Japanese Business Management: Restructuring for low growth and globalization*. Routledge: London.

Harung, HS, Heaton, DP and Alexander, CN (1999) Evolution of organizations in the new millennium. *Leadership and Organization Development Journal*, 20(4), 198–207.

Harvey, D and Brown, DR (2001) *An Experiential Approach to Organization Development* (6th edition). Prentice Hall: Upper Saddle River, NJ.

Harvey, F (2001) Microsoft's direct connection to the customer. *Financial Times*, 31 December, 7.

Hassard, J (1990) An alternative to paradigm incommensurability in organization theory. In J Hassard and D Pym (eds): *The Theory and Philosophy of Organizations*. Routledge: London.

Hassard, J (1993) *Sociology and Organization Theory: Positivism, paradigms and postmodernity*. Cambridge University Press: Cambridge.

Hassard, J and Parker, M (eds) (1993) *Postmodernism and Organizations*. Sage: London.

Hassard, J and Sharifi, S (1989) Corporate culture and strategic change. *Journal of General Management*, 15(2), 4–19.

Hasson, F, Keeney, S and McKenna, H (2000) Research guidelines for the Delphi survey Technique. *Journal of Advanced Nursing*, 32(4), 1008–15.

Hatch, MJ (1993) The dynamics of organizational culture. *Academy of Management Review*, 18(4), 657–93.

Hatch, MJ (1997) *Organization Theory: Modern, symbolic and postmodern perspectives*. Oxford University Press: Oxford.

Hatch, MJ and Cunliffe, AL (2006) *Organization Theory: Modern, symbolic and postmodern perspectives* (2nd edition). Oxford University Press: Oxford.

Hatvany, N and Pucik, V (1981) An integrated management system: lessons from the Japanese experience. *Academy of Management Review*, 6, 469–80.

Hax, CA and Majluf, NS (1982) Competitive cost dynamics. *Interfaces*, 12, October, 50–61.

Hax, CA and Majluf, NS (1996) *The Strategy Concept and Process* (2nd edition). Prentice Hall: Upper Saddle River, NJ.

Hax, CA and Nicholson, SM (1983) The use of the growth share matrix in strategic planning. *Interfaces*, 13, February, 46–60.

Hayes, J (2002) *The Theory and Practice of Change Management*. Palgrave: Basingstoke.

Hayles, KN (2000) From chaos to complexity: moving through metaphor to practice. *Complexity and Chaos in Nursing*, 4, available at www.southernct.edu/scsu/chaosnursing/chaos4.htm

Heath, C and Heath, D (2011) Overcoming resistance to change. *School Administrator*, 68(3), 28–32.

Heath, C and Heath, D (2013) *Decisive: How to make better choices in life and work*. Random House: New York.

Hedberg, B (1981) How organizations learn and unlearn. In PC Nystrom and WH Starbuck (eds): *Handbook of Organizational Design*. Oxford University Press: London.

Hedberg, B, Nystrom, P and Starbuck, W (1976) Camping on seesaws: prescriptions for a self-designing organization. *Administrative Science Quarterly*, 17, 371–81.

Hedlund, G and Nonaka, I (1993) Models of knowledge management in the West and Japan. In P Lorange (ed): *Implementing Strategic Processes*. Blackwell: Oxford.

Heller, F (1970) Group feed-back analysis as a change agent. *Human Relations*, 23(4), 319–33.

Heller, R (2002) A legacy turned to tragedy. *The Observer*, 18 August, available at www.observer.co.uk

Hendry, C (1979) Contingency theory in practice, I. *Personnel Review*, 8(4), 39–44.

Hendry, C (1980) Contingency theory in practice, II. *Personnel Review*, 9(1), 5–11.

Hendry, C (1996) Understanding and creating whole organizational change through learning theory. *Human Relations*, 48(5), 621–41.

Herzberg, F (1968) One more time: how do you motivate employees? *Harvard Business Review*, 46, 53–62.

Herzberg, F, Mausner, B and Snyderman, B (1959) *The Motivation to Work*. John Wiley: New York.

Hickman, CF (1990) *Mind of a Manager, Soul of a Leader*. John Wiley: New York.

Hickman, L (2008) Is this the end for Primark? *The Guardian*, 24 June, available from www.guardian.co.uk

Hickson, DJ and Butler, RJ (1982) Power and decision-making in the organisational coalition. Research report presented to the Social Science Research Council, New York.

Hickson, DJ, Pugh, DS and Pheysey, DC (1969) Operations technology and organisation structure: an empirical reappraisal. *Administrative Science Quarterly*, 14, 378–97.

Highhouse, S (2002) A history of the T-group and its early applications in management development. *Group Dynamics: Theory, Research and Practice*, 6(4), 277–90.

Hill, A (2012) Lofty aspirations. *Financial Times*, 16 July, 13.

Hill, A (2013) *Financial Times*, 26 February, 12.

Hill, CWL and Jones, GR (2006) *Strategic Management: An integrated approach* (8th edition). Houghton Mifflin: Boston, MA.

Hines, P (1994) *Creating World Class Suppliers: Unlocking mutual competitive advantage*. Pitman: London.

Hinkin, TR and Tracey, JB (1999) The relevance of charisma for transformational leadership in stable organizations. *Journal of Organizational Change Management*, 12(2), 105–19.

Hirota, S, Kubo, K, Miyajima, H, Hong, P and Park, YW (2010) Corporate mission, corporate policies and business outcomes: evidence from Japan. *Management Decision*, 48(7), 1134–53.

Hirschhorn, L (1988) *The Workplace Within*. MIT Press: Cambridge, MA.

Hirschhorn, L (2000) Changing structure is not enough: the moral meaning of organizational design. In M Beer and N Nohria (eds): *Breaking the Code of Change*. Harvard Business School Press: Boston, MA.

Hirst, C (2002) Marconi's £3bn debt lifeline. *Sunday Independent*, 7 April, 1.

Hitt, MA, Miller, CC and Colella, A (2009) *Organizational Behavior: A strategic approach* (2nd edition). Wiley: Hoboken, NJ.

Hlavacka, S, Bacharova, L, Rusnakova, V and Wagner, R (2001) Performance implications of Porter's generic strategies in Slovak hospitals. *Journal of Management in Hospitals*, 15(1), 44–66.

HMSO (1989) *Working for Patients*, Cmnd 555. HMSO: London.

HMSO (1991) *Competing for Quality*, Cmnd 1730. HMSO: London.

Ho, DYF (1976) On the concept of face. *American Journal of Sociology*, 81(4), 867–84.

Hoag, BG, Ritschard, HV and Cooper, CL (2002) Obstacles to effective organization change: the underlying reasons. *Leadership and Organisation Development Journal*, 23(1), 6–15.

Hobsbawm, EJ (1968) *Industry and Empire*. Pelican: Harmondsworth.

Hobsbawm, EJ (1979) *The Age of Revolution*. Abacus: London.

Hobsbawm, EJ (2008) *Globalisation, Democracy and Terrorism*. Abacus: London.

Hock, D (1999) *Birth of the Chaordic Age*. Berrett-Koehler: San Francisco, CA.

Hodal, K (2013) Samsung admits its phones may contain tin from area mined by children. *The Guardian*, 25 April, available from www.guardian.co.uk

Hodge, B and Coronado, G (2007) Understanding change in organizations in a far-from-equilibrium world. *E:CO*, 9(3), 3–15.

Hofer, CH and Schendel, DE (1978) *Strategy Formulation: Analytical concepts*. West: St Paul, MN.

Hofstede, G (1980) *Culture's Consequences: International differences in work-related values*. Sage: London.

Hofstede, G (1990) The cultural relativity of organizational practices and theories. In DC Wilson and RH Rosenfeld (eds): *Managing Organizations: Text, readings and cases*. McGraw-Hill: London.

Hofstede, G (1993) Cultural constraints in management theories. *Academy of Management Executive*, 7(1), 81–94.

Hofstede, G (1998) Identifying organizational subcultures: an empirical approach. *Journal of Management Studies*, 35(1), 1–12.

Hofstede, G (2001) *Culture's Consequences: Comparing values, behaviors, institutions, and organizations across nations* (2nd edition). Sage: Thousand Oaks, CA.

Hofstede, G (2011) Dimensionalizing cultures: the Hofstede model in context. *Online Readings in Psychology and Culture*, 2(1), available at http://dx.doi.org/10.9707/2307–0919.1014

Holden, N and Burgess, M (1994) *Japanese-Led Companies*. McGraw-Hill: London.

Holman, D (2002) Employee wellbeing in call centres. *Human Resource Management Journal*, 12(4), 35–50.

Holman, P (2010) *Engaging Emergence: Turning upheaval into opportunity*. Barrett-Koehler: San Francisco, CA.

Holt, DT and Vardaman, JM (2013) Towards a comprehensive understanding of readiness for change: the case for an expanded conceptualization. *Journal of Change Management*, 13(1), 9–18.

Hoogerwerf, EC and Poorthuis, A-N (2002) The network multilogue: a chaos approach to organizational design. *Journal of Organizational Change Management*, 15(4), 382–90.

Horne, JH and Lupton, T (1965) The work activities of 'middle managers' – an exploratory study. *Journal of Management Studies*, 2(1), 14–33.

Horsley, W and Buckley, R (1990) *Nippon New Superpower; Japan since 1945*. BBC Books: London.

Horton, S (1996) The civil service. In D Farnham and S Horton (eds): *Managing the New Public Services* (2nd edition). Macmillan: Basingstoke.

Hoskin, K (1990) Using history to understand theory: a re-consideration of the historical genesis of 'strategy'. Paper prepared for the EIASM Workshop on Strategy, Accounting and Control, Venice, Italy.

Houchin, K and MacLean, D (2005) Complexity theory and strategic change: an empirically informed critique. *British Journal of Management*, 16(2), 149–66.

House, JS (1993) John R French, Jr: a Lewinian's Lewinian. *Journal of Social Issues*, 49(4), 221–6.

House, RJ, Hanges, PJ, Ruiz-Quintanilla, SA *et al* (1999) *Cultural Influences on Leadership and Organizations: Project GLOBE. Advance in Global Leadership*, Vol. 1. JAI Press: Stanford, CT.

Howarth, C (1988) Report of the Joint Design of Technology, Organisation and People Growth Conference – Venice, 12–14 October. *Information Services News and Abstracts*, 95 November/December, Work Research Unit: London.

Huber, GP (1991) Organizational learning: the contributing processes and the literatures. *Organization Science*, February, 88–115.

Huczynski, AA (1993) *Management Gurus*. Routledge: London.

Huczynski, A and Buchanan, D (2001) *Organizational Behaviour* (4th edition). Financial Times Prentice Hall: Harlow.

Huggins, R and Izushi, H (eds) (2011) *Competition, Competitive Advantage, and Clusters: The ideas of Michael Porter*. Oxford University Press: Oxford.

Hughes, J and Kirk, S (2012) *Financial Times*, 9 August, 5.

Hughes, M (1995) Halifax and Leeds clear the courts. *The Guardian*, 29 March, 15.

Hughes, M (2011) Do 70 per cent of all organizational change initiatives really fail? *Journal of Change Management*, 11(4), 451–64.

Hughes, RL, Ginnett, RC and Curphy, GJ (2009) *Leadership: Enhancing the lessons of experience* (6th edition). McGraw-Hill: Boston, MA.

Humphrey, SE, Nahrgang, JD and Morgeson, FP (2007) Integrating motivational, social, and contextual work design features: a meta-analytic summary and theoretical extension of the work design literature. *Journal of Applied Psychology*, 92(5), 1332–56.

Hunter, A (2008) Parry's head on block as Americans escalate battle: Liverpool chief executive's rejection of Hicks demand highlights power vacuum in the Anfield boardroom. *The Guardian*, 11 April, available from www.guardian.co.uk

Hunter, JE (1989) *The Emergence of Modern Japan*. Longman: London.

Hurley, RF, Church, AH, Burke, WW and Van Eynde, DF (1992) Tension, change and values in OD. *OD Practitioner*, 29, 1–5.

Huse, EF (1980) *Organization Development and Change*. West: St Paul, MN.

Hussey, DE (1978) Portfolio analysis: practical experience with the Directional Policy Matrix. *Long Range Planning*, 11, August, 2–8.

Hussey, DE and Jenster, P (1999) *Competitive Intelligence: Turning analysis into success*. John Wiley: Chichester.

Hutton, W (1995) *The State We're In*. Cape: London.

Hutton, W (2008a) This reckless greed of the few harms the future of the many. *The Observer*, 27 January, available at www.guardian.co.uk

Hutton, W (2008b) A late call to account. *The Guardian*, 2 December, 30.

IBM (2008) *The Enterprise of the Future: IBM Global CEO Study*. IBM: Somers, NY.

IBM (2012) *Leading Through Connections: Highlights of the Global Chief Executive Officer Study*. IBM Institute for Business Value, available from ibm.com/ceostudy2012

Inagami, T (1988) *Japanese Workplace Industrial Relations*. Japan Institute of Labour: Tokyo.

Inagami, T (1995) *Enterprise Unions in a Mature Society*. Japan Institute of Labour: Tokyo.

Industrial Society (1997) *Culture Change. Managing Best Practice 35*. Industrial Society: London.

Inman, P (2013) OECD prepares new rules to limit corporate tax avoidance. *The Guardian*, 30 May, available at www.guardian.co.uk

Institute of Management (1995) *Finding the Time – A Survey of Managers' Attitudes to Using and Managing Time*. Institute of Management: London.

Ishikawa, K (1985) *What Is Total Quality Control? The Japanese Way*. Prentice Hall: Englewood Cliffs, NJ.

Ishizuna, Y (1990) The transformation of Nissan – the reform of corporate culture. *Long Range Planning*, 23(3), 9–15.

Isserman, M and Kazin, M (2007) *America divided: The Civil War of the 1960s*. 3rd edition. Oxford University Press: Oxford.

Ivancevich, J (1970) An analysis of control, bases of control, and satisfaction in an organizational setting. *Academy of Management Journal*, December, 427–32.

Jaques, E (1952) *The Changing Culture of a Factory*. Dryden Press: New York.

Jaques, E (1998) On leaving the Tavistock Institute. *Human Relations*, 51(3), 251–7.

Javidian, M and Dastmalchian, A (2009) Managerial implications of the GLOBE project: a study of 62 societies. *Asia Pacific Journal of Human Resources*, 47(1), 41–58.

Javidan, M, Dorfman, PW, Du Luque, MS and House, RJ (2006) In the eye of the beholder: cross cultural lessons in leadership from Project GLOBE. *Academy of Management Perspectives*, 20(1), 67–90.

Jemison, DB and Sitkin, SB (1986) Acquisitions: the process can be a problem. *Harvard Business Review*, 64, March, 107–16.

Jenkins, P, Jones, A and Thompson, J (2013) Barclays facelift wins over investors after torrid year. *Financial Times*, 13 February, 1.

Jenner, RA (1998) Dissipative enterprises, chaos, and the principles of lean organizations. *Omega: International Journal of Management Science*, 26(3), 397–407.

Jermier, JM, Slocum, JW, Fry, LW and Gaines, J (1991) Organizational subcultures in a soft bureaucracy: resistance behind the myth and facade of an official culture. *Organization Science*, 2(2), 170–94.

Johnson, G (1987) *Strategic Change and the Management Process*. Blackwell: Oxford.

Johnson, G (1993) Processes of managing strategic change. In C Mabey and B Mayon-White (eds): *Managing Change* (2nd edition). The Open University/Paul Chapman Publishing: London.

Johnson, G and Scholes, K (1993) *Exploring Corporate Strategy*. Prentice Hall: London.

Johnson, G and Scholes, K (eds) (2001) *Exploring Public Sector Strategy*. Financial Times Prentice Hall: Harlow.

Johnson, G and Scholes, K (2002) *Exploring Corporate Strategy* (6th edition). Financial Times Prentice Hall: Harlow.

Johnson, G, Scholes, K and Whittington, R (2006) *Exploring Corporate Strategy* (7th edition). Financial Times Prentice Hall: Harlow.

Johnson, G, Whittington, R and Scholes, K (2011) *Exploring Corporate Strategy* (9th edition). Financial Times Prentice Hall: Harlow.

Johnson, L (2012) The lunatics have taken over the boardroom. *Financial Times*, 7 March, 14.

Johnson, R and Ouchi, W (1974) Made in America (under Japanese management). *Harvard Business Review*, 52(5), 61–9.

Johnston, DC (2007) Income gap is widening, data shows. *The New York Times*, 29 March, available at www.truthout.org

Jones, AHM (1984) *The Greek City from Alexander to Justinian*. Oxford University Press: Oxford.

Jones, EE (1990) *Interpersonal Perception*. Freeman: New York.

Jones, GR (2001) *Organizational Theory* (3rd edition). Prentice Hall: Upper Saddle River, NJ.

Jones, GR, George, JM and Hill, CWL (2000) *Contemporary Management* (2nd edition). McGraw-Hill: Boston, MA.

Jones, H (1989) Private property. *New Civil Engineer*, 29 June, 23.

Jones, RA, Jimmieson, NL and Griffiths, A (2005) The impact of organizational culture and reshaping capabilities on change implementation success: the mediating role of readiness for change. *Journal of Management Studies*, 42(2), 361–86.

Jones, RJB (1995) *Globalization and Interdependence in the International Political Economy: Reality and rhetoric*. Pinter: London.

Jones, Q, Dunphy, D, Fishman, R, Larne, M and Canter, C (2006) *In Great Company: Unlocking the secrets of cultural transformation*. Human Synergistics: Sydney.

Jopson, B (2013) Retailers throw out the rule book in bid to survive. *Financial Times*, 27 February, 16.

Joyce, P and Woods, A (2001) *Strategic Management: A fresh approach to developing skills, knowledge and creativity*. Kogan Page: London.

Judge, TA, Piccolo, RF and Kosalka, T (2009) The bright and dark sides of leadership traits: a review and theoretical extension of the leader trait paradigm. *Leadership Quarterly*, 20(6), 855–75.

Juran, JM (1988) *Quality Control Handbook*. McGraw-Hill: New York.

Kadar, EE and Shaw, RE (2000) Toward an ecological field theory of perceptual control of locomotion. *Ecological Psychology*, 12(2), 141–80.

Kahn, H and Weiner, A (1978) *The Year 2000*. Macmillan: London.

Kaiser, T (2013) Google's Eric Schmidt: "Don't be evil" was stupid. *DailyTech*, 14 May, available at www.dailytech.com

Kakabadse, A, Kakabadse, N and Lee-Davies, L (2007) Three temptations of leaders. *Leadership & Organization Development Journal*, 28(3), 196–208.

Kakabadse, A, Korac-Kakabadse, N and Kouzmin, A (2003) Ethics, values and behaviours: comparison of three case studies examining the paucity of leadership in government. *Public Administration*, 81(3), 477–508.

Kamata, S (1982) *Japan in the Passing Lane*. Pantheon: New York.

Kanter, RM (1977) *Men and Women of the Corporation*. Basic Books: New York.

Kanter, RM (1979) Power failure in management circuits. *Harvard Business Review*, 57(4), 65–75.

Kanter, RM (1983) *The Change Masters*. Simon & Schuster: New York.

Kanter, RM (1989) *When Giants Learn to Dance: Mastering the challenges of strategy, management, and careers in the 1990s*. Unwin: London.

Kanter, RM (1997) *World Class: Thriving locally in the global economy*. Simon & Schuster: New York.

Kanter, RM (2006) Innovation: the classic traps. *Harvard Business Review*, 84(11), November, 72–83.

Kanter, RM (2008a) Transforming giants. *Harvard Business Review*, 86(1), January, 43–52.

Kanter, RM (2008b) *Supercorp: How Vanguard companies create innovation, profits, growth, and social good*. Profile Books: London.

Kanter, RM, Kao, J and Wiersema, F (eds) (1997) *Innovation: Breakthrough thinking at 3M, DuPont, GE, Pfizer, and Rubbermaid*. HarperBusiness: New York.

Kanter, RM, Stein, BA and Jick, TD (1992) *The Challenge of Organizational Change*. Free Press: New York.

Kaplan, PJ (2002) *F'd Companies: Spectacular dot-com flameouts*. Simon & Schuster: New York.

Karlsson, C (1996) Radically new production systems. *International Journal of Operations and Production Management*, 16(11), 8–19.

Karlsson, LE (1973) *Experiences in Employee Participation in Sweden: 1969–1972*. Mimeograph, Cornell University: New York.

Katz, D and Kahn, RL (1978) *The Social Psychology of Organizations*. John Wiley: Hoboken, NJ.

Katzenbach, JR, Steffen, I and Kronley, C (2012) Cultural change that sticks. *Harvard Business Review*, July–August.

Kauffman, SA (1993) *Origins of Order: Self-organisation and selection in evolution*. Oxford University Press: Oxford.

Kavanagh, MH and Ashkanasy, NM (2006) The impact of leadership and change management strategy on organizational culture and individual acceptance of change during a merger. *British Journal of Management*, 17(S1), S81–103.

Kawakita, T (1997) Corporate strategy and human resource management. In M Sako and H Sato (eds): *Japanese Labour and Management in Transition*. Routledge: London.

Kay, J (1993) *Foundations of Corporate Success*. Oxford University Press: Oxford.

Kay, J (2008) How we let down the diligent folk of Halifax. *Financial Times*, 24 September, 13.

Kay, J (2012a) Sift through the brashness and bravado surrounding any big deals. *Financial Times*, 17 October, 11.

Kay, J (2012b) Why the Walkman did not give rise to the Sony iPod. *Financial Times*, 5 September, 9.

Kay, J, McKiernan, P and Faulkner, DO (2003) The history of strategy and some thoughts about the future. In DO Faulkner and A Campbell (eds): *The Handbook of Strategy*. Oxford University Press: Oxford.

Kazunori, O (1998) New trends in enterprise unions and the labour movement. In H Harukiyo and GD Hook (eds): *Japanese Business Management: Restructuring for low growth and globalization*. Routledge: London.

Keen, M (1991) *The Penguin History of Medieval Europe* (Penguin History). Penguin: Harmondsworth.

Keizer, AB (2009) Transformations in- and outside the internal labour market: institutional change and continuity in Japanese employment practices. *The International Journal of Human Resource Management*, 20(7), 1521–35.

Kellaway, L (1998) Manage with mother. *Financial Times*, 2 March, 14.

Kellaway, L (2001) A boast too far: Tom Peters' 'confession' that he faked the data for his most famous management book shows how attitudes have changed in 20 years. *Financial Times*, 3 December, 16.

Kellermanns, FW, Walter, J, Floyd, SW, Lechner, C and Shaw, JC (2011) To agree or not to agree? A meta-analytical review of strategic consensus and organizational performance. *Journal of Business Research*, 64(2), 126–33.

Kelly, JE (1982a) Economic and structural analysis of Job Design. In JE Kelly and CW Clegg (eds): *Autonomy and Control at the Workplace*. Croom Helm: London.

Kelly, JE (1982b) *Scientific Management, Job Redesign and Work Performance*. Academic Press: London.

Kemp, T (1979) *Industrialization in Nineteenth Century Europe*. Longman: London.

Kempner, T (1970) Frederick Taylor and scientific management. In A Tillett, T Kempner and G Wills (eds): *Management Thinkers*. Pelican: Harmondsworth.

Kennedy, C (1994) *Managing with the Gurus*. Century Business Books: London.

Kennedy, H (2010) BP's CEO Tony Hayward: The most hated – and most clueless – man in America. *Daily News*, 3 June, available at www.NYDailyNews.com

Kerr, C and Fisher, L (1957) Plant sociology: the elite and the Aborigines. In M Komarovsky (ed): *Common Frontiers of the Social Sciences*. Greenwood: Westport, CT.

Kerr, S, Schriesheim, CA, Murphy, CJ and Stogdill, RM (1974) Towards a contingency theory of leadership based upon the consideration and initiating structure literature. *Organizational Behavior and Human Performance*, 12, 62–82.

Keshavan, K and Rakesh, KS (1979) Generating future scenarios – their use in strategic planning. *Long Range Planning*, 12, June, 57–61.

Keuning, D (1998) *Management: A contemporary approach*. Pitman: London.

Keys, JB and Miller, TR (1984) The Japanese management theory jungle. *Academy of Management Review*, 9, 342–53.

Kezuka, K (2001) Legal problems concerning part-time work in Japan. In *Japan Institute for Labour Policy and Training: Highlights in Japanese Labour Issues*, Vol. V. JILPT: Tokyo.

Khalifa, AS (2008) The 'strategy frame' and the four Es of strategy drivers. *Management Decision*, 46(6), 894–917.

Kidd, P and Karwowski, W (eds) (1994) *Advances in Agile Manufacture*. IOS Press: Amsterdam.

Kiel, LD (1994) *Managing Chaos and Complexity in Government*. Jossey-Bass: San Francisco, CA.

Kimberley, J and Miles, R (eds) (1980) *The Organizational Life Cycle*. Jossey-Bass: San Francisco, CA.

Kipnis, D, Schmidt, SM and Wilkinson, I (1980) Intraorganizational influence tactics: explorations in getting one's way. *Journal of Applied Psychology*, August, 440–52.

Kipnis, D, Schmidt, SM, Swaffin-Smith, C and Wilkinson, I (1984) Patterns of managerial influence: shotgun managers, tacticians, and bystanders. *Organizational Dynamics*, Winter, 58–67.

Kippenberger, T (1998a) Planned change: Kurt Lewin's legacy. *The Antidote*, 3(4), 10–12.

Kippenberger, T (1998b) Managed learning: elaborating on Lewin's model. *The Antidote*, 3(4), 13.

Kirkpatrick, SA and Locke, EA (1991) Leadership: do traits matter? *The Executive*, 5, 48–60.

Kirton, MJ (1989) *Adaptors and Innovators: Styles of creativity and problem solving*. Routledge: London.

Kitayama, A (2010) Japan lags behind in gender equality. Reuters, 7 March, available at blogs.reuters.com

Klein, HK (2004) Seeking the new and the critical in critical realism: déjà vu? *Information and Organization*, 14(2), 123–44.

Klein, N (2001) *No Logo*. Flamingo: London.

Koch, R (1995) *The Financial Times Guide to Strategy*. Pitman: London.

Kodz, J, Davis, S, Lain, D, Sheppard, E, Rick, J, Strebler, M, Bates, P, Cummings, J, Meager, N, Anxon, D, Gineste, S and Trinczek, R (2003) *Working Long Hours in the UK: Executive summary*. Department of Trade and Industry: London, available at www.dtigor.uk/emar/longhours.htm

Köhler, W (1967) Gestalt psychology. *Psychological Research*, 31(1), XVIII–XXX.

Koji, O (1998) Small headquarters and the reorganisation of management. In H Harukiyo and GD Hook (eds): *Japanese Business Management: Restructuring for low growth and globalization*. Routledge: London.

Komodromos, M (2013) Employees' perceptions of trust, fairness, and management of change using an organisational justice framework: a brief review of the literature. *International Journal of Teaching and Case Studies*, 4(1), 83–94.

Korner, K (2005) Changing governance patterns and CSR. *Corporate Governance*, 5(3), 151–8.

Kotler, P (1978) Harvesting strategies for weak products. *Business Horizons*, 21(4), August, 15–22.

Kotter, JP (1982) *The General Manager*. Free Press: New York.

Kotter, JP (1990) *A Force for Change: How leadership differs from management*. Free Press: New York.

Kotter, JP (1995) Leading change: why transformation efforts fail. *Harvard Business Review*, 73(2), 59–67.

Kotter, JP (1996) *Leading Change*. Harvard Business School Press: Boston, MA.

Kotter, JP (1999) What effective general managers really do. *Harvard Business Review*, 77(2), 145–59.

Kotter, JP and Cohen, DS (2002) *The Heart of Change: Real-life stories of how people change their organizations*. Harvard Business School Press: Boston, MA.

Kotter, JP and Heskett, JL (1992) *Corporate Culture and Performance*. Free Press: New York.

Kotter, J and Rathgeber, K (2006) *Our Iceberg Is Melting*. Macmillan: London.

Kraaijenbrink, J, Spender, JC and Groen, A (2010) The resource-based view: a review and assessment of its critiques. *Journal of Management*, 36(1), 349–72.

Kreitner, R (1992) *Management* (5th edition). Houghton Mifflin: Boston, MA.

Kuhn, TS (1962) *The Structure of Scientific Revolutions*. University of Chicago Press: Chicago, IL.

Krell, TC (1981) The marketing of organization development: past, present and future. *Journal of Applied Behavioral Science*, 10(2), 485–502.

Kreps, DM and Wilson, R (1982) Reputation and imperfect information. *Journal of Economic Theory*, 27, 253–79.

Kriedte, P, Medick, H and Schlumbohm, J (1981) *Industrialization before Industrialization*. Cambridge University Press: Cambridge.

Kumar, K (1995) *From Post–Industrial to Post-Modern: New theories of the contemporary world*. Blackwell: Oxford.

Laage-Hellman, J (1997) *Business Networks in Japan*. Routledge: London.

Lacey, R (1986) *Ford: The men and the machine*. Heinemann: London.

Laird, L (1998) Predators hover over Lonrho's African diamonds. *The Guardian*, 14 November, 28.

Lamming, R (1993) *Beyond Partnership: Strategies for innovation and lean supply*. Prentice Hall: Hemel Hempstead.

Lamming, R (1994) *A Review of the Relationships Between Vehicle Manufacturers and Suppliers*. DTI/SMMT: London.

Lamond, D (2004) A matter of style: reconciling Henri with Henry. *Management Decision*, 42(2), 330–56.

Landes, DS (1969) *The Unbound Prometheus*. Cambridge University Press: Cambridge.

Landsberger, HA (1958) *Hawthorne Revisited: 'Management and the Worker'. Its Critics and developments in human relations in industry*. Cornell University Press: New York.

Lanford, HW (1972) *Technological Forecasting Methodologies: A synthesis*. American Management Association: New York.

Larson, LL, Hunt, JG and Osborne, RN (1976) The great hi-hi leader behavior myth: a lesson from Occam's razor. *Academy of Management Journal*, 19, 628–41.

Lashinsky, A (2012) *Inside Apple: The secrets behind the past and future success of Steve Jobs's iconic brand*. John Murray: London.

Laudon, K and Starbuck, WH (1997) Organization information and knowledge. In A Sorge and M Warner (eds): *The IEBM Handbook of Organizational Behavior*. International Thompson Business Press: London.

Lawler, EE (1985) Challenging traditional research assumptions. In EE Lawler and Associates (eds): *Doing Research That Is Useful for Theory and Practice*. Jossey-Bass: San Francisco, CA.

Lawler, EE and Suttle, JL (1972) A causal correlation of the need hierarchy concept in an organizational setting. *Organization Behaviour and Human Performance*, 7, April, 265–87.

Lawler, EE, Mohrman, SA and Ledford, GE (1998) *Strategies for High Performance Organizations*. Jossey-Bass: San Francisco, CA.

Lawrence, PR (1973) How to deal with resistance to change. In GW Dalton, PR Lawrence and E Grenier (eds): *Organizational Change and Development*. Dorsey: Homewood, IL.

Lawrence, PR and Lorsch, JW (1967) *Organization and Environment*. Harvard Business School: Boston, MA.

Lawson, H (1985) *Reflexivity, the Post Modern Predicament*. Hutchinson: London.

Learned, EP, Christensen, CR, Andrews, KR and Guth, WD (1965) *Business Policy: Texts and cases*. Irwin: Homewood, IL.

Lee, J (1978) Labour in German industrialization. In P Mathias and M Postan (eds): *Cambridge Economic History of Europe*, Vol. VII. Cambridge University Press: Cambridge.

Lee, M (1999) The lie of power: empowerment as impotence. *Human Relations*, 52(2), 225–62.

Lee, RG and Dale, BG (2003) Policy deployment. In BG Dale: *Managing Quality* (4th edition). Blackwell: Oxford.

Leemhuis, JP (1990) Using scenario development strategies at Shell. In B Taylor and J Harrison (eds): *The Manager's Casebook of Business Strategy*. Butterworth-Heinemann: Oxford.

Left, S (2001) Nike. *Guardian Unlimited*, 23 February, available at www.guardian.co.uk

Leifer, R and Huber, GP (1977) Relations amongst perceived environmental uncertainty, organisation structure and boundary-spanning behaviour. *Administrative Science Quarterly*, 22, 235–47.

Leigh, D and Evans, R (2007) BAE accused of secretly paying £1bn to Saudi prince. *The Guardian*, 7 June, available at www.guardian.co.uk

Leitner, K-H and Güldenberg, S (2010) Generic strategies and firm performance in SMEs: a longitudinal study of Austrian SMEs. *Small Business Economics*, 35(2), 169–89.

Lenin, VI (1918) The immediate tasks of the Soviet government. Reprinted in: *On the Development of Heavy Industry and Electrification*. Progress Publishers: Moscow.

Leontiades, M (1986) *Managing the Unmanageable*. Addison-Wesley: Reading, MA.

Leslie, K, Lindsay, V, Mullings, H and Salkeld, N (1999) Why companies have much to learn from charities. *Financial Times*, 9 February, 16.

Lessem, R (1998) *Management Development through Cultural Diversity*. Routledge: London.

Leung, K, Bhagat, RS, Buchan, NR, Erez, M and Gibson, CB (2005) Culture and international business: recent advances and their implications for future research. *Journal of International Business Studies*, 36(4), 357–78.

Leveson, Inquiry, The (2012) *An Inquiry into the Culture, Practices and Ethics of the Press: Report*. The Stationery Office: London.

Levine, AL (1967) *Industrial Retardation in Britain 1880–1914*. Basic Books: New York.

Levinthal, DA (2011) A behavioral approach to strategy – what's the alternative? *Strategic Management Journal*, 32(13), 1517–23.

Levy, A and Merry, U (1986) *Organizational Transformation: Approaches, strategies, theories*. Praeger: New York.

Lewin GW (ed) (1948a) *Resolving Social Conflict*. Harper & Row: London.

Lewin, GW (1948b) Preface. In GW Lewin (ed) (1948): *Resolving Social Conflict*. Harper & Row: London.

Lewin, K (1939) When facing danger. In GW Lewin (ed) (1948): *Resolving Social Conflict*. Harper & Row: London.

Lewin, K (1942) Field Theory and Learning. In D Cartwright (ed) (1952): *Field Theory in Social Science: Selected theoretical papers by Kurt Lewin*. Social Science Paperbacks: London.

Lewin, K (1943a) Psychological ecology. In D Cartwright (ed) (1952): *Field Theory in Social Science*. Social Science Paperbacks: London.

Lewin, K (1943b) The special case of Germany. In GW Lewin (ed) (1948): *Resolving Social Conflict*. Harper & Row: London.

Lewin, K (1943/4) Problems of research in social psychology. In D Cartwright (ed) (1952): *Field Theory in Social Science.* Social Science Paperbacks: London.

Lewin, K (1946) Action research and minority problems. In GW Lewin and GW Allport (eds) (1948): *Resolving Social Conflict*. Harper & Row: London.

Lewin, K (1947a) Frontiers in group dynamics. In D Cartwright (ed) (1952): *Field Theory in Social Science*. Social Science Paperbacks: London.

Lewin, K (1947b) Group decisions and social change. In TM Newcomb and EL Hartley (eds) (1959): *Readings in Social Psychology*. Henry Holt: New York.

Lewin, K (1999a) Group decisions and social change. In M Gold (ed): *The Complete Social Scientist: A Kurt Lewin reader*. American Psychological Association: Washington, DC.

Lewin, K (1999b) The dynamics of group action. In M Gold (ed): *The Complete Social Scientist: A Kurt Lewin reader*. American Psychological Association: Washington, DC.

Lewin, K, Lippitt, R and White, R (1939) Patterns of aggressive behavior in experimentally created 'social climates'. *Journal of Social Psychology*, 10, 271–99.

Lewin, M (1992) The impact of Kurt Lewin's life on the place of social issues in his work. *Journal of Social Issues*, 48(2), 15–29.

Lewis, PS, Goodman, SH and Fandt, PM (1998) *Management Challenges in the 21st Century* (2nd edition). South-Western: St Paul, MN.

Lewis, R (1994) From chaos to complexity: implications for organizations. *Executive Development*, 7(4), 16–17.

Lex Column (2013) BAE Systems. *Financial Times*, 22 February, 12.

Lichtenstein, BM (1997) Grace, magic and miracles: a 'chaotic logic' of organizational transformation. *Journal of Organizational Change Management*, 10(5), 393–411.

Likert, R (1961) *New Patterns of Management*. McGraw-Hill: New York.

Likert, R (1967) *The Human Organization: Its management and values*. McGraw-Hill: New York.

Lincoln, JR and Kalleberg, AL (1985) Work organisation and workforce commitment: a study of plants and employees in the US and Japan. *American Sociological Review*, 50, 738–60.

Lindblom, CE (1959) The science of muddling through. *Public Administration Review*, 19, Spring, 79–88.

Lindblom, CE (1968) *The Policy-Making Process*. Prentice Hall: Englewood Cliffs, NJ.

Lines, WL (2002) *Open Air Essays*. New Holland Publishers: Sydney.

Linneman, RE and Klein, HE (1979) The use of multiple scenarios by US industrial companies. *Long Range Planning*, 12, February, 83–90.

Linstead, S (1993) From postmodern anthropology to deconstructive ethnography. *Human Relations*, 46(1), 97–120.

Lippitt, G (1982) Management development as the key to organisational renewal. *Journal of Management Development*, 1(2).

Lippitt, R and White, R (1960) *Autocracy and Democracy: An experimental inquiry*. Harper & Row: New York.

Lippitt, R, Watson, J and Westley, B (1958) *The Dynamics of Planned Change*. Harcourt, Brace and World: New York.

Litschert, R and Nicholson, E (1974) Corporate long range planning groups – some different approaches. *Long Range Planning*, 7, August, 62–6.

Little, R (1984) Conglomerates are doing better than you think. *Fortune*, 28 May, 60.

Littler, CR (1978) Understanding Taylorism. *British Journal of Sociology*, 29(2), 185–202.

Lloyd, AR, Dale, BG and Burnes, B (1994) A study of Nissan Motor Manufacturing (UK) supplier development team activities. Proceedings of the Institute of Mechanical Engineers, 208, Part D. *Journal of Automobile Engineering*, 63–8.

Locke, EA and Latham, GP (2006) New Directions in Goal-Setting Theory. *Current Directions in Psychological Science*, 15(5), 265–8.

Locke, EW (1982) The ideas of Frederick W Taylor. *Academy of Management Review*, 7(1), 14–24.

Lockett, A, Thompson, S and Morgenstern, U (2009) The development of the resource-based view of the firm: a critical appraisal. *International Journal of Management Reviews*, 11(1), 9–28.

Loden, M (1986) *Feminine Leadership, or How to Succeed in Business without Being One of the Boys*. Time Books: New York.

London, S (2005) There are no false profits in the thriving world of gurudom. *Financial Times*, 19 November, 11, available at www.ft.com

Long, P (1986) *Performance Appraisal Revisited*. IPM (Institute of Personnel Management): London.

Longman (1978) *Longman Dictionary of Contemporary English*. Longman: London.

Lorenz, E (1979) Predictability: Does the flap of a butterfly's wing in Brazil set off a tornado in Texas? Address at the American Association for the Advancement of Science, Washington, DC.

Lorenz, E (1993) *The Essence of Chaos*. UCL Press: London.

Lorsch, JW (1970) Introduction to the structural design of organizations. In GW Dalton, PR Lawrence and JW Lorsch (eds): *Organization Structure and Design*. Irwin-Dorsey: London.

Lorsch, JW (1986) Managing culture: the invisible barrier to strategic change. *California Management Review*, 28(2), 95–109.

Lovell, R (1980) *Adult Learning*. Croom Helm: London.

Lowe, S, Moore, F and Carr, AN (2007) Paradigmapping studies of culture and organization. *International Journal of Cross Cultural Management*, 7(2), 237–51.

Lu, DJ (1987) *Inside Corporate Japan*. Productivity Press: Cambridge, MA.

Luhman, JT and Boje, DM (2001) What is complexity science? A possible answer from narrative research. *Emergence*, 3(1), 158–68.

Luthans, F (1989) Conversation with Edgar H Schein. *Organizational Dynamics*, 17, Spring, 70–5.

Luthans, F, McCaul, HS and Dodd, NG (1985) Organizational commitment: a comparison of American, Japanese and Korean employees. *Academy of Management Journal*, 28(2), 213–19.

Lynch, R (1997) *Corporate Strategy*. Pitman: London.

Lynch, R (2006) *Corporate Strategy* (4th edition). FT Prentice Hall: Harlow.

Lyon, D (2000) Post-modernity. In G Browning, A Halcli and F Webster (eds): *Understanding Contemporary Society*. Sage: London.

Lyotard, J-F (1984) *The Postmodern Condition*. Manchester University Press: Manchester.

Mabey, C and Mayon-White, B (1993) *Managing Change* (2nd edition). The Open University/ Paul Chapman Publishing: London.

Macalister, T (1999) Fury over further 6000 job cuts in utilities. *The Guardian*, 15 December, available at www.guardian.co.uk

Macalister, T (2003) Swiss join oil bribery inquiry. *The Guardian*, 7 May, available at www. guardian.co.uk

Macbeth, DK (2002) Emergent strategy in managing cooperative supply chain change. *International Journal of Operations and Producton Management*, 22(7), 728–40.

Macdonald, M, Sprenger, E and Dubel, I (1999) *Gender and Organizational Change: Bridging the gap between policy and practice*. Royal Tropical Institute: Amsterdam.

Machiavelli, N (1515) *The Prince*. Available at www.constitution.org/mac/prince06.htm

MacIntosh, R and MacLean, D (1999) Conditioned emergence: a dissipative structures approach to transformation. *Strategic Management Journal*, 20(4), 297–316.

MacIntosh, R and MacLean, D (2001) Conditioned emergence: researching change and changing research. *International Journal of Operations and Production Management*, 21(10), 1343–57.

Maddock, S (1999) *Challenging Women*. Sage: London.

Magex (2000a) Liberating the digital economy – creating commercial success in the digital marketplace. Magex.com Whitepaper, 21 February, available at www.magex.com/downloads/ W_Paper_1(1).pdf

Magex (2000b) Online music piracy. Magex.com Whitepaper, 22 June, available at www. magex.com/news/library/list

Maguire, K, Milner, M and Watt, N (2000) The secret deal that left Rover a museum piece. *The Guardian*, 18 March, 4–5.

Mahoney, MJ (1974) *Cognition and Behavior Modification*. Ballinger: Cambridge, MA.

Maitland, A (2001) Managers resort to old tools in a crisis. *Financial Times*, 18 July, 10.

Makin, P and Cox, C (2004) *Changing Behaviour at Work*. Routledge: Abingdon.

Malaska, P, Malmivirta, M, Meristo, T and Hansen, SO (1984) Scenarios in Europe – who uses them and why? *Long Range Planning*, 17, October, 45–9.

Mallory, G (1997) March, James Gardner (1928–) and Cyert, Richard Michael (1921–) In A Sorge and M Warner (eds): *The IEBM Handbook of Organizational Behaviour*. International Thompson Business Press: London.

Mangham Working Party (1987) The Mangham Working Party Report: A Survey of the In-house Activities of Ten Major Companies. British Institute of Management/Confederation of British Industry: London.

Manicas, P (1980) The concept of social structure. *Journal of the Theory of Social Behaviour*, 10(2), 65–82.

Mansfield, R (1984) Formal and informal structures. In M Gruneberg and T Wall (eds): *Social Psychology and Organizational Behaviour*. Wiley: Chichester.

Mantoux, P (1964) *The Industrial Revolution in the Eighteenth Century*. Cape: London.

Marglin, SA (1976) What do bosses do? In A Gorz (ed): *The Division of Labour: The labour process and class struggle in modern capitalism*. Harvester: Brighton.

Markus, LM and Benjamin, RI (1997) The magic bullet theory in it-enabled transformation. *Sloan Management Review*, Winter, 55–68.

Markus, LM, Manville, B and Agres, CE (2000) What makes virtual organisations work? Lessons from the open-source world. *Sloan Management Review*, Fall, 13–26.

Marrow, AJ (1957) *Making Management Human*. McGraw-Hill: New York.

Marrow, AJ (1967) Events leading to the establishment of the National Training Laboratories. *The Journal of Applied Behavioral Science*, 3, 144–50.

Marrow, AJ (1969) *The Practical Theorist: The life and work of Kurt Lewin*. Teachers College Press: New York.

Marrow, AJ (1972) The effects of participation on performance. In AJ Marrow (ed), *The Failure of Success*. Amacom: New York.

Marsh, N (1986) Management development and strategic management change. *Journal of Management Development*, 5(1).

Marsh, RM and Mannari, H (1976) *Modernization and the Japanese Factory*. Princeton University Press: Princeton, NJ.

Marshak, RJ (1993) Lewin meets Confucius: a re-view of the OD model of change. *The Journal of Applied Behavioral Science*, 29(4), 393–415.

Marshak, RJ and Grant, D (2008) Organizational discourse and new organization development practices. *British Journal of Management*, 19(S7), S8–19.

Martin, J (1992) *Cultures in Organizations: Three perspectives*. Oxford University Press: Oxford.

Martin, J, Feldman, MS, Hatch, MJ and Sitkin, SB (1983) The uniqueness paradox in organizational stories. *Administrative Science Quarterly*, 28(3), 438–53.

Martin, R (2000) Breaking the code of change: observations and critique. In M Beer and N Nohria (eds): *Breaking the Code of Change*. Harvard Business School Press: Boston, MA.

Martinet, A-C (2010) Strategic planning, strategic management, strategic foresight: The seminal work of H. Igor Ansoff. *Technological Forecasting and Social Change*, 7(9), 1485–87.

Masayoshi, I (1998) Globalisation's impact on the subcontracting system. In H Harukiyo and GD Hook (eds): *Japanese Business Management: Restructuring for Low Growth and Globalization*. Routledge: London.

Masayuki, M (1998) The end of the 'mass production system' and changes in work practices. In H Harukiyo and GD Hook (eds): *Japanese Business Management: Restructuring for low growth and globalization*. Routledge: London.

Maslow, AH (1943) A theory of human motivation. *Psychology Review*, 50, 370–96.

Massie, JL (1965) Management theory. In JG March (ed): *Handbook of Organizations*. Rand McNally: Chicago, IL.

Mathias, P (1969) *The First Industrial Nation*. Methuen: London.

Mathias, P and Davis, JA (eds) (1989) *The First Industrial Revolutions*. Blackwell: Cambridge.

Matten, D and Moon, J (2004) Corporate social responsibility education in Europe. *Journal of Business Ethics*, 54(4), 323–37.

Matthews, R (2002) Competition, archetypes and creative imagination. *Journal of Organizational Change Management*, 15(5), 461–76.

Maurer, R (1996) Using resistance to build support for change. *The Journal for Quality and Participation*, 19(3), 56–63.

May, B and Singer, M (2001) Unchained melody. *The McKinsey Quarterly*, 1, available at www. Mckinseyquarterly.com

Mayes, BT and Allen, RW (1977) Towards a definition of organizational politics. *Academy of Management Review*, October, 672–8.

Maynard, MT, Gilson, LL and Mathieu, JE (2012) Empowerment – fad or fab? A multilevel review of the past two decades of research. *Journal of Management*, published online 28 March 2012. DOI: 10.1177/0149206312438773.

Mayo, E (1933) *The Human Problems of Industrial Civilization*. Macmillan: New York.

Mayon-White, B (1993) Problem-solving in small groups: team members as agents of change. In C Mabey and B Mayon-White (eds): *Managing Change* (2nd edition). The Open University/ Paul Chapman Publishing: London.

McCall, MW, Jr (2010) Recasting leadership development. *Industrial and Organizational Psychology*, 3(1), 3–19.

McCalman, J and Paton, RA (1992) *Change Management: A guide to effective implementation*. Paul Chapman Publishing: London.

McCormick, K (2007) Sociologists and 'the Japanese model': a passing enthusiasm? *Work, Employment and Society*, 21(4), 751–71.

McDougall, D (2008) Working flat out – the child labour behind your Egyptian cotton sheets. *The Observer*, 8 June, available at www.guardian.co.uk

McGill, I and Beaty, L (1995) *Action Learning*. Kogan Page: London.

McGregor, D (1960) *The Human Side of Enterprise*. McGraw-Hill: New York.

McGregor, D (1967) *The Professional Manager*. McGraw-Hill: New York.

McIvor, G (1995) Retuned Volvo rises from the ashes. *The Guardian*, 24 June, 37.

McKenna, S (1988) 'Japanisation' and recent developments in Britain. *Employee Relations*, 10(4), 6–12.

McKiernan, P (1992) *Strategies for Growth: Maturity, recovery and internationalization*. Routledge: London.

McKinsey & Company (2008) Creating organizational transformations. *The McKinsey Quarterly*, July, 1–7, available at www.mckinseyquarterly.com

McKracken, JK (1986) Exploitation of FMS technology to achieve strategic objectives. Paper to the 5th International Conference on Flexible Manufacturing Systems, Stratford-upon-Avon.

McLaughlin, H and Thorpe, R (1993) Action Learning – a paradigm in emergence. *British Journal of Management*, 4(1), 19–27.

McLennan, R (1989) *Managing Organizational Change*. Prentice Hall: Englewood Cliffs, NJ.

McMillan, B and Connor, M (2005) Motivating personal change. In J Kerr, R Weitkunat and M Moretti (eds): *ABC of Behavior Change*. Elsevier Churchill Livingstone: Edinburgh.

McMillan, J (1985) *The Japanese Industrial System*. De Gruyter: Berlin.

McNamee, BP (1985) *Tools and Techniques of Strategic Management*. Pergamon: Oxford.

McNeilly, MR (2012) *Sun Tzu and the Art of Business*. Oxford University Press: Oxford.

McNiff, J (ed) (2000) *Action Research in Organisations*. Routledge: London.

McNulty, CAR (1977) Scenario development for corporate planning. *Futures*, 9(2), 128–38.

McSweeney, B (2002) Hofstede's model of national cultural differences and their consequences: a triumph of faith – a failure of analysis. *Human Relations*, 55(1), 89–118.

Meek, VL (1988) Organizational culture: origins and weaknesses. *Organization Studies*, 9(4), 453–73.

Meier, KJ, O'Toole, LJ, Jr, Boyne, GA and Andrews, R (2010) Alignment and results testing the interaction effects of strategy, structure, and environment from Miles and Snow. *Administration & Society*, 42(2), 160–92.

Meyer, MW and Zucker, LG (1989) *Permanently Failing Organizations*. Sage: Beverly Hills, CA.

Meyerson, D and Martin, J (1987) Cultural change: an integration of three different views. *Journal of Management Studies*, 24(6), 623–47.

Michaels, A (2004) Survey reveals changing culture at the Big Four. FT.Com, 8 February, available at www.ft.com

Michaelson, GA (2001) *Sun Tzu: The art of war for managers: 50 strategic rules*. Adams Media: Avon, MA.

Michel, A, By, RT and Burnes, B (2013) The limitations of dispositional resistance in relation to organizational change. *Management Decision*, 51(4), 761–80.

Mid-Staffordshire NHS Foundation Trust Public Inquiry, The (2013) *Report of the Mid Staffordshire NHS Foundation Trust Public Inquiry*. The Stationery Office: London.

Miewald, RD (1970) The greatly exaggerated death of bureaucracy. *California Management Review*, Winter, 65–9.

Mihata, K (1997) The persistence of 'Emergence'. In RA Eve, S Horsfall and ME Lee (eds): *Chaos, Complexity & Sociology: Myths, models & theories*. Sage: Thousand Oaks, CA.

Miles, RE and Snow, CC (1978) *Organizational Strategy, Structure and Process*. McGraw-Hill: New York.

Milgrom, P and Roberts, J (1982) Predation, reputation and entry deterrence. *Journal of Economic Theory*, 27(2), 280–313.

Mill, J (1994) No pain, no gain. *Computing*, 3 February, 26–7.

Miller, D (1992) The generic strategy trap. *Journal of Business Strategy*, 13(1), 37–41.

Miller, D (1993) The architecture of simplicity. *Academy of Management Review*, 18(1), 116–38.

Miller, D (1994) What happens after success: the perils of excellence. *Journal of Management Studies*, 31(3), 325–58.

Miller, D and Friesen, PH (1984) *Organizations: A quantum view*. Prentice Hall: Englewood Cliffs, NJ.

Miller, E (1967) *Systems of Organisation*. Tavistock: London.

Miller, E (1993) *From Dependency to Autonomy – Studies in Organization and Change*. Free Association Books: London.

Milliman, J, von Glinow, MA and Nathan, M (1991) Organizational life cycles and strategic international human resource management in multinational companies: implications for congruence theory. *The Academy of Management Review*, 16(2), 318–39.

Milne, R (2012) *Financial Times*, 14 November, 11.

Milner, M (1998) Productivity as seen by hamsters. *The Guardian*, 22 October, 27.

Minett, S (1992) *Power, Politics and Participation in the Firm*. Ashgate: Brookfield, VT.

Mink, OG (1992) Creating new organizational paradigms for change. *International Journal of Quality and Reliability Management*, 9(3), 21–35.

Mintzberg, H (1973) *The Nature of Managerial Work*. Harper & Row: New York.

Mintzberg, H (1975) The manager's job: folklore and fact. *Harvard Business Review*, 53(4), 49–61.

Mintzberg, H (1976) Planning on the left side and managing on the right. *Harvard Business Review*, July/August, 49–58.

Mintzberg, H (1978) Patterns in strategy formation. *Management Science*, 24(9), 934–48.

Mintzberg, H (1979) *The Structure of Organizations*. Prentice Hall: Englewood Cliffs, NJ.

Mintzberg, H (1983) *Power In and Around Organizations*. Prentice Hall: Englewood Cliffs, NJ.

Mintzberg, H (1987) Crafting strategy. *Harvard Business Review*, 19(2), 66–75.

Mintzberg, H (1994) *The Rise and Fall of Strategic Planning*. Prentice Hall: London.

Mintzberg, H (1998) Covert leadership: notes on managing professionals. *Harvard Business Review*, 76(6), 140–7.

Mintzberg, H (2001) Decision-making: it's not what you think. *Sloan Management Review*, 42(3), 89–93.

Mintzberg, H (2007) *Tracking Strategies: Toward a general theory*. Oxford University Press: Oxford.

Mintzberg, H and Lampel, J (1999) Reflecting on the strategy process. *Sloan Management Review*, 40(3), 21–30.

Mintzberg, H and Quinn, JB (1991) *The Strategy Process: Concepts, contexts and cases*. Prentice Hall: London.

Mintzberg, H and Westley, F (1992) Cycles of organizational change. *Strategic Management Journal*, 13, Winter, 39–59.

Mintzberg, H, Ahlstrand, B and Lampel, J (1998a) *Strategy Safari*. Prentice Hall: Hemel Hempstead.

Mintzberg, H, Ahlstrand, B and Lampel, J (2009) *Strategy Safari* (2nd edition). Pearson: Harlow.

Mintzberg, H, Quinn, JB and Ghoshal, S (1998b) *The Strategy Process*. Prentice Hall: London.

Mintzberg, H, Simons, R and Basu, K (2002) Beyond Selfishness. *MIT Sloan Management Review*, 44(1), 67–74.

Mirabeau, L and Maguire, S (2013) From autonomous strategic behavior to emergent strategy. *Strategic Management Journal*, published online: 21 May 2013. DOI: 10.1002/smj.2149

Mirvis, P (1988) Organizational development: an evolutionary perspective. In W Pasmore and R Woodman (eds): *Research in Organizational Change and Development*, Vol. 2. JAI Press: Greenwich, CT.

Mirvis, PH (1990) Organization development: Part 2 – a revolutionary perspective. *Research in Organizational Change and Development*, 4, 1–66.

Mirvis, PH (2006) Revolutions in OD: the new and the new, new things. In JV Gallos (ed): *Organization Development: A Jossey-Bass reader*. Jossey-Bass: San Francisco, CA.

Mitchell, VM (1991) The Delphi technique: an exposition and application. *Technology Analysis & Strategic Management*, 3(4), 333–58.

Mitroff, II and Mason, RO (1981) *Challenging Strategic Planning Assumptions*. Wiley: New York.

Moore, JI (1992) *Writers on Strategy and Strategic Management*. Penguin: Harmondsworth.

Morgan, G (1986) *Images of Organizations*. Sage: Beverly Hills, CA.

Morgan, G (1988) *Riding the Waves of Change*. Jossey-Bass: San Francisco, CA.

Morgan, G (1989) *Creative Organization Theory*. Sage: London.

Morgan, G (1990) *Organisations in Society*. Macmillan: London.

Morgan, G (1997) *Images of Organization* (2nd edition). Sage: London.

Morieux, YUH and Sutherland, E (1988) The interaction between the use of information technology and organization change. *Behaviour and Information Technology*, 7(2), 205–13.

Morris, J and Imrie, R (1992) *Transforming Buyer–Supplier Relationships*. Macmillan: Basingstoke.

Morsing, M (1997) Patrick Dawson: organizational change – a processual approach. *Organization Studies*, 18(3), 523–35.

Mosley, D (1987) System four revisited: some new insights. *Organization Development Journal*, 5(1), 19–24.

Mougayar, W (1998) *Opening Digital Markets: Battle plans and business strategies for internet commerce*. McGraw-Hill: Maidenhead.

Muldoon, J (2012) The Hawthorne legacy: a reassessment of the impact of the Hawthorne studies on management scholarship, 1930–1958. *Journal of Management History*, 18(1), 105–19.

Mullins, L (1989) *Management and Organisational Behaviour*. Pitman: London.

Mullins, LJ (1993) *Management and Organisational Behaviour* (3rd edition). Pitman: London.

Mullins, L (2002) *Management and Organisational Behaviour* (6th edition). Financial Times Pearson: Harlow.

Mumford, A (1987) Myths and reality in developing directors. *Personnel Management*, 19(2), February, 29–33.

Mumford, E (1979) The design of work: new approaches and new needs. In JE Rijnsdorp (ed): *Case Studies in Automation Related to Humanization of Work*. Pergamon: Oxford.

Mumford, MD, Marks, MA, Connelly, MS, Zaccaro, SJ and Reiter-Palmon, R (2000) Development of leadership skills: experience and timing. *Leadership Quarterly*, 11(1), 87–114.

Murray, F (1989) The organizational politics of information technology: studies from the UK financial services industry. *Technology Analysis and Strategic Management*, 1(30), 285–97.

Myers, CS (1934) An Account of the Work Carried out at the National Institute of Industrial Psychology during the Years 1921–34. NIIP: London.

Nadler, DA (1988) Concepts for the management of organizational change. In ML Tushman and WL Moore (eds): *Readings in the Management of Innovation*. Ballinger: New York.

Nadler, DA (1993) Concepts for the management of strategic change. In C Mabey and B Mayon-White (eds): *Managing Change* (2nd edition). The Open University/Paul Chapman Publishing: London.

Nadworthy, M (1957) Frederick Taylor and Frank Gilbreth: competition in scientific management. *Business History Review*, 31(1), 23–34.

Nahavandi, A (2000) *The Art and Science of Leadership* (2nd edition). Prentice Hall: Upper Saddle River, NJ.

Nahavandi, A (2012) *The Art and Science of Leadership* (6th edition). Pearson: Upper Saddle River, NJ.

NAO (1995) Interim Report: PSA services, the sale of PSA projects. Report by the National Audit Office. HMSO: London.

NAO (1996) PSA Services: The transfer of PSA building management to the private sector. Report by the National Audit Office. HMSO: London.

NAO (1999) The United Kingdom Passport Agency. The passport delays of summer of 1999. Report by the National Audit Office. HMSO: London.

Naoi, A and Schooler, C (1985) Occupational conditions and psychological functioning in Japan. *American Journal of Sociology*, 90, 729–52.

Naughton, J (2013) Why big IT projects always go wrong. *The Observer*, 21 April, available at www.guardian.co.uk

Naylor, TH (1979) *Simulation Models in Corporate Measuring*. Draeger: New York.

Naylor, TH (1981) Strategic planning models. *Managerial Planning*, 30, July/August, 3–11.

Neat, R (2011) Michael Woodford: the man who blew whistle on £1bn fraud. *The Guardian*, 23 October, available at www.guardian.co.uk

NEDC (1991a) *The Experience of Nissan Suppliers: Lessons for the United Kingdom engineering industry*. NEDC: London.

NEDC (1991b) *Winning Together: Collaborative sourcing in practice*. NEDC: London.

Nelson, RR and Winter, SG (1982) *An Evolutionary Theory of Economic Change*. Harvard University Press: Cambridge, MA.

Neumann, JE, Lau, CM and Worley, CW (2009) Ready for consideration: international organizational development and change as an emerging field of practice. *Journal of Applied Behavioral Science*, 45(2), 171–85.

New, C (1989) The challenge of transformation. In B Burnes and B Weekes (eds): *AMT: A strategy for success?* NEDO: London.

New, S and Burnes, B (1998) Developing effective customer–supplier relationships: more than one way to skin a cat. *Journal of Quality and Reliability Management*, 15(4), 377–88.

Newbert, SL (2007) Empirical research on the resource–based view of the firm: an assessment and suggestions for future research. *Strategic Management Journal*, 28, 121–46.

Newman, S (ed) (2008) *The Final Energy Crisis*. Pluto Press: London.

Newstrom, J (1985) "Mod" management development: does it deliver what it promises? *Journal of Management Development*, 4(1), 3–11.

Nicoll, D (1998a) Is OD meant to be relevant? *OD Practitioner*, 30(2), 3–6.

Nicoll, D (1998b) Is OD meant to be relevant? Part II. *OD Practitioner*, 30(3), 3–6.

Nichols, NA (1993) From complacency to competitiveness: an interview with Vitro's Ernesto Martens. *Harvard Business Review*, September.

Nippa, M, Pidun, U and Rubner, H (2011) Corporate portfolio management: appraising four decades of academic research. *Academy of Management Perspectives*, November, 50–66.

Nonaka, I (1988) Creating organizational order out of chaos: self-renewal in Japanese firms. *California Management Review*, 30(3), 57–73.

Nonaka, I (1991) The knowledge-creating company. *Harvard Business Review*, 69(6), November/ December), 96–104.

Nord, W (1985) Can organizational culture be managed: a synthesis. In R Kilmann, M Saxton, R Serpa and Associates (eds): *Gaining Control of Corporate Culture*. Jossey-Bass: San Francisco, CA.

Norse, D (1979) Scenario analysis in interfutures. *Futures*, 11(5), 412–22.

Northouse, PG (2013) *Leadership: Theory and practice* (6th edition). Sage: London.

Novelli, L, Kirkman, BL and Shapiro, DL (1995) Effective implementation of organizational change: an organizational justice perspective. In CL Cooper and DM Rousseau (eds): *Trends in Organizational Behavior*, Vol 2. Wiley: Chichester.

Nuttall, C and Waters, R (2012) Down in the valley. *Financial Times*, 24 November 2012.

Nwabueze, U (2001) An industry betrayed: the case of total quality management in manufacturing. *The TQM Magazine*, 13(6), 400–9.

Nystrom, PC and Starbuck, WH (1984) To avoid crises, unlearn. *Organizational Dynamics*, 12(4), 53–65.

O'Brien, GE and Kabanoff, B (1981) The effects of leadership style and group structure upon small group productivity: a test of discrepancy theory of leader effectiveness. *Australian Journal of Psychology*, 33(2), 157–8.

Observer (2008) Tesco in numbers. *The Observer*, 29 June, 25.

O'Connell, D, Hickerson, K and Pillutla, A (2011) Organizational visioning: an integrative review. *Group & Organization Management*, 36(1), 103–25.

Odaka, K (1975) *Towards Industrial Democracy: Management and workers in modern Japan*. Harvard University Press: Cambridge, MA.

OECD (1996) *The OECD Economic Survey: the UK 1996*. OECD: Paris.

Ogbonna, E and Harris, LC (2002) Managing organisational culture: insights from the hospitality industry. *Human Resource Management Journal*, 12(1), 33–53.

O'Hara, M (2008) Prophet for a new age. *The Guardian: Society Guardian*, 12 November, 1.

Ohmae, K (1986) *The Mind of the Strategist*. Penguin: Harmondsworth.

Ohmae, K (1990) Untitled article in Special Report 1202, The Management Briefing, Economist, London.

Ohmi, N (1997) The public sector and privatisation. In M Sako and H Sato (eds): *Japanese Labour and Management in Transition*. Routledge: London.

Ojiako, U and Maguire (2008) Success criteria for systems led transformation: managerial implications for global operations management. *Industrial Management and Data Systems*, 108(7), 887–908.

Olsen, BD (2002) Applied social and community interventions for crisis in times of national and international conflict. *Analyses of Social Issues and Public Policy*, 2(1), 119–29.

Olson EE and Eoyang GH (2001) *Facilitating Organization Change*. Jossey-Bass: San Francisco, CA.

Ordanini, A and Rubera, G (2008) Strategic capabilities and internet resources in procurement: a resource-based view of B-to-B buying process. *International Journal of Operations and Production Management*, 28(1), 27–52.

Oreg, S (2003) Resistance to change: developing an individual differences measure. *Journal of Applied Psychology*, 88(4), 680–93.

Oreg, S (2006) Personality, context, and resistance to organizational change. *European Journal of Work and Organizational Psychology*, 15(10), 73–101.

Oreg, S and Sverdlik, N (2011) Ambivalence toward imposed change: the conflict between dispositional resistance to change and the orientation toward the change agent. *Journal of Applied Psychology*, 96(2), 337–49.

Oreg, S, Vakola, M and Armenakis, A (2011) Change recipients' reactions to organizational change: a 60-year review of quantitative studies. *Journal of Applied Behavioral Science*, 47(4), 461–524.

Oreg, S, Bayazit, M, Vakola, M and 20 others (2008) Dispositional resistance to change: measurement equivalence and the link to personal values across 17 nations. *Journal of Applied Psychology*, 93(4), 935–44.

Oreg, S, Nevo, O, Metzer, H, Leder, N and Castro, D (2009) Dispositional resistance to change and occupational interests and choices. *Journal of Career Assessment*, 17(3), 312–23.

O'Reilly, C (1989) Corporations, culture and commitment. *California Management Review*, 31(4), 9–24.

Orlikowski, WJ (1996) Improvising organizational transformation over time: a situated change perspective. *Information Systems Research*, 7(1), 63–92.

Orlikowski, WJ and Yates, JA (2006) ICT and organizational change: a commentary. *Journal of Applied Behavioral Science*, 42(1), 127–34.

Osborne, D and Gaebler, T (1992) *Reinventing Government: How the entrepreneurial spirit is transforming the public sector*. Addison-Wesley: Reading, MA.

O'Shaughnessy, J (1984) *Competitive Marketing*. Allen & Unwin: Boston, MA.

Oswick, C (2009) Revisioning or re-versioning?: A commentary on diagnostic and dialogic forms of organization development. *Journal of Applied Behavioral Science*, 45(3), 369–74.

Oswick, C and Marshak, RJ (2011) Images of organization development: the role of metaphor in processes of change. In D Boje, B Burnes and J Hassard (eds): *The Routledge Companion to Organizational Change*. Routledge: London.

Oticon (1994) *Oticon's Fundamental Human Values – Vision and Reality*. Oticon: Copenhagen.

O'Toole, J (1995) *Leading Change: Overcoming the ideology of comfort and the tyranny of custom*. Jossey-Bass: San Francisco, CA.

Ouchi, W (1981) *Theory Z: How American business can meet the Japanese challenge*. Addison-Wesley: Reading, MA.

Outhwaite, W (1987) *New Philosophies of Social Science: Realism, hermeneutics and critical theory*. Macmillan: London.

Owen, G (2002) The man who built GEC into an industrial giant. *Financial Times*, 24 July, 23.

Oxford Dictionary of English (2nd edition) (2006) Oxford University Press: Oxford.

Palmer, B (2004) *Making Change Work: Practice tools for overcoming human resistance to change*. ASQ Quality Press: Milwaukee, WI.

Pang, K and Oliver, N (1988) Personnel strategy in eleven Japanese manufacturing companies. *Personnel Review*, 17(3), 16–21.

Paquin, AR, Roch, SG and Sanchez-Ku, ML (2007) An investigation of cross-cultural differences on the impact of productivity interventions: the example of ProMES. *Journal of Applied Behavioral Science*, 43(4), 427–48.

Pardo del Val, M and Martínez Fuentes, C (2003) Resistance to change: a literature review and empirical study. *Management Decision*, 41(2), 148–55.

Parikh, M (1999) The music industry in the digital world: waves of changes. Putting the 'e' in Entertainment: e–music as a case in point, *Industry Round Table*, 17 June. The New York Information Technology Center, available at www.ite.poly.edu

Parker, D (1998) Privatisation in the European Union: an overview. In D Parker (ed): *Privatisation in the European Union: Theory and policy perspectives*. Routledge: London.

Parker, D (2003) Performance, risk and strategy in privatised, regulated industries: the UK's experience. *International Journal of Public Sector Management*, 16(1), 75–100.

Parker, M (2000) *Thatcherism and the Fall of Coal: Politics and economics of UK coal*. Cambridge University Press: Cambridge.

Parsons, T (1947) Introduction. In M Weber (ed): *The Theory of Social and Economic Organization*. Free Press: Glencoe, IL.

Partnership Sourcing Ltd (1991a) *Case Studies in Partnership Sourcing*. Partnership Sourcing Ltd: London.

Partnership Sourcing Ltd (1991b) *Partnership Sourcing*. Partnership Sourcing Ltd: London.

Partnoy, F (2003) When greed is fact and control is fiction. *The Guardian*, 14 February, available at www.guardian.co.uk

Pascale, RT (1984) Perspectives on strategy: the real story behind Honda's success. *California Management Review*, 26(3), 47–72.

Pascale, RT (1993) The benefit of a clash of opinions. *Personnel Management*, October, 38–41.

Pascale, RT and Athos, AG (1982) *The Art of Japanese Management*. Penguin: Harmondsworth.

Pasmore, W and Fagans, M (1992) Participation, individual development, and organizational change: a review and synthesis. *Journal of Management*, 18(2), 375–97.

Patel, P and Younger, M (1978) A frame of reference for strategy development. *Long Range Planning*, 11, April, 6–12.

Paton, N (2003) Leadership skills hold Britain back. *The Guardian: Jobs and Money*, 22 February, 23.

Paton, R, Clark, G, Jones, G, Lewis, J and Quintas, P (eds) (1996) *The New Management Reader*. Routledge/Open University: London.

Patwardhan, A and Patwardhan, D (2008) Business process re-engineering – saviour or just another fad?: One UK health care perspective. *International Journal of Health Care Quality Assurance*, 21(3), 289–96.

Pavlov, IP (1927) *Conditioned Reflexes* (trans). Oxford University Press: London.

Peacock, A (1984) Privatisation in perspective. *Three Banks Review*, December, 3–25.

Peale, NV and Blanchard, K (2000) *The Power of Ethical Management*. Vermilion: London.

Pearson, AE (1987) Muscle-build the organization. *Harvard Business Review*, 65(4), 49–55.

Pearson, B (1977) How to manage turnarounds. *Management Today*, April, 75.

Pedler, M (1996) *Action Learning for Managers*. Lemos & Crane: London.

Pedler, M, Boydell, T and Burgoyne, JG (1989) Towards the learning company. *Management Education and Development*, 20(1), 1–8.

Peet, P (2012) *Unholy Trinity: The IMF, World Bank and WTO* (2nd edition). Zed Books: London.

Peiperi, M (2005) Resistance to change. In N Nicholson, PG Audia and MM Pillutula (eds): *The Blackwell Encyclopedia of Management (2nd Edition) – Organizational Behavior*. Blackwell: Oxford.

Pelling, H (1960) *American Labor*. Chicago University Press: Chicago, IL.

Peng, MW, Lee, SH and Wang, DYL (2005) What determines the scope of the firm over time? A focus on institutional relatedness. *Academy of Management Review*, 30(3), 622–33.

Penrose, E (1959) *The Theory of Growth of the Firm*. Blackwell: Oxford.

Perez, C (1983) Structural change and the assimilation of new technologies in the economic and social systems. *Futures*, 15, 357–75.

Perrow, C (1967) A framework for the comparative analysis of organizations. *American Sociological Review*, 32, 194–208.

Perrow, C (1970) *Organizational Analysis: A sociological view*. Tavistock: London.

Perrow, C (1983) The organizational context of human factors engineering. *Administrative Science Quarterly*, 28, 521–41.

Peteraf, MA (1993) The cornerstones of competitive advantage: a resource-based view. *Strategic Management Journal*, 14(3), 179–91.

Peters, T (1989) *Thriving on Chaos*. Pan: London.

Peters, T (1993) *Liberation Management*. Pan: London.

Peters, T (1995) *The Pursuit of WOW!* Macmillan: London.

Peters, T (1997a) *The Circle of Innovation: You can't shrink your way to greatness*. Alfred A Knopf: New York.

Peters, T (1997b) Foreword. In RM Kanter, J Kao and F Wiersema (eds): *Innovation: Breakthrough thinking at 3M, DuPont, GE, Pfizer, and Rubbermaid*. HarperBusiness: New York.

Peters, T (2006) *Re-imagine! Business Excellence in a Disruptive Age*. Dorling Kindersley: London.

Peters, T and Waterman, RH (1982) *In Search of Excellence: Lessons from America's best-run companies*. Harper & Row: London.

Pettigrew, AM (1973) *The Politics of Decision-Making*. Tavistock: London.

Pettigrew, AM (1979) On studying organizational culture. *Administrative Science Quarterly*, 24(4), 570–81.

Pettigrew, AM (1980) The politics of organisational change. In NB Anderson (ed): *The Human Side of Information Processing*. North-Holland: Amsterdam.

Pettigrew, AM (1985) *The Awakening Giant: Continuity and change at ICI*. Blackwell: Oxford.

Pettigrew, AM (1987) Context and action in the transformation of the firm. *Journal of Management Sciences*, 24(6), 649–70.

Pettigrew, AM (1990a) Longitudinal field research on change: theory and practice. *Organizational Science*, 3(1), 267–92.

Pettigrew, AM (1990b) Studying strategic choice and strategic change. *Organizational Studies*, 11(1), 6–11.

Pettigrew, AM (1997) What is a processual analysis? *Scandinavian Journal of Management*, 13(4), 337–48.

Pettigrew, AM (2000) Linking change processes and outcomes: a commentary on Ghosal, Bartlett and Weick. In M Beer and N Nohria (eds): *Breaking the Code of Change*. Harvard Business School Press: Boston, MA.

Pettigrew, AM and Whipp, R (1991) *Managing Change for Competitive Success*. Blackwell: Oxford.

Pettigrew, AM and Whipp, R (1993) Understanding the environment. In C Mabey and B Mayon-White (eds): *Managing Change* (2nd edition). The Open University/Paul Chapman Publishing: London.

Pettigrew, AM, Ferlie, E and McKee, L (1992) *Shaping Strategic Change*. Sage: London.

Pettigrew, AM, Hendry, C and Sparrow, P (1989) *Training in Britain: Employers' perspectives on human resources*. HMSO: London.

Pettigrew, AM, Woodman, RW and Cameron, KS (2001) Studying organizational change and development: challenges for future research. *Academy of Management Journal*, 44(4), 697–713.

Phipps, STA (2011) Mary, Mary, quite contrary: in a male-dominated field, women contributed by bringing a touch of spirituality to early management theory and practice. *Journal of Management History*, 17(2), 178–92.

Pfeffer, J (1978) *Organizational Design*. AHM Publishing: Arlington Heights, IL.

Pfeffer, J (1981) *Power in Organizations*. Pitman: Cambridge, MA.

Pfeffer, J (1992) *Managing with Power: Politics and influence in organizations*. Harvard Business School Press: Boston, MA.

Pfeffer, J (1996) *Competitive Advantage through People: Unleashing the power of the work force*. Harvard Business School Press: Boston, MA.

Pfeffer, J (1997) *New Directions for Organization Theory*. Oxford University Press: Oxford.

Phillips, A (2003) Childcare before money: as BA has discovered, working mothers will not give up their childcare arrangements without a fight. *The Guardian*, 30 July, 17.

Piderit, SK (2000) Rethinking resistance and recognizing ambivalence: a multidimensional view of attitudes toward an organizational change. *The Academy of Management Review,* 25(4), 783–94.

Pilling, D (2003) How could a corporate sector that dominated the world a decade ago have become so unproductive? *Financial Times*, 21 April, 15.

Piore, M and Sabel, C (1984) *The Second Industrial Divide*. Basic Books: New York.

Piotrowski, C and Armstrong, TR (2005) Major research areas in organization development. *Organization Development Journal*, 23(4), 86–91.

Plimmer, G, Warrell, H and Wembridge, M (2012) G4S chief remains as heads roll. *Financial Times*, 29 September, 18.

Plowden, The Lord (1961) *Control of Public Expenditure*, Cmnd 1432. HMSO: London.

Pollard, S (1965) *The Genesis of Modern Management*. Pelican: Harmondsworth.

Pollard, S (1981) *Peaceful Conquest: The industrialization of Europe, 1760–1970*. Oxford University Press: Oxford.

Polzer, JT, Gulati, R and Khurana, R (2009) Crossing boundaries to increase relevance in organizational research. *Journal of Management Inquiry*, 18, 280–6.

Pontusson, J (1990) The politics of new technology and job redesign: a comparison of Volvo and British Leyland. *Economic and Industrial Democracy*, 11, 311–36.

Porras, JI and Bradford, DL (2004) A historical view of the future of OD: an interview with Jerry Porras. *Journal of Applied Behavioral Science*, 40(4), 392–402.

Porter, LW (1976) Organizations as political animals. Presidential Address, Division of Industrial Organizational Psychology, 84th Annual Meeting of the American Psychological Association, Washington, DC.

Porter, LW, Allen, RW and Angle, HL (1983) The politics of upward influence in organizations. In RW Allen and LW Porter (eds): *Organizational Influence Processes*. Scott, Foresman and Co: Glenview, IL.

Porter, M (1980) *Competitive Strategy*. Free Press: New York.

Porter, M (1985) *Competitive Advantage*. Free Press: New York.

Porter, ME (2001) Strategy and the Internet. *Harvard Business Review*, March, 63–78.

Prahalad, CK and Hamel, G (1990) The core competence of the corporation. *Harvard Business Review*, May/June, 71–91.

Price, TL (2003) The ethics of authentic transformational leadership. *The Leadership Quarterly*, 14(1), 67–81.

Priem, RL and Butler, JE (2001) Is the resource-based view a useful perspective for strategic management research? *Academy of Management Review*, 26(1), 22–40.

Prigogine, I (1997) *The End of Certainty: Time, chaos, and the new laws of nature*. Free Press: New York.

Prigogine, I and Stengers, I (1984) *Order out of Chaos: Man's new dialogue with nature*. Bantam Books: New York.

Probst, G and Buchel, B (1997) *Organizational Learning*. Prentice Hall: London.

Prokesch, SE (1997) Unleashing the power of learning: an interview with British Petroleum's John Browne. *Harvard Business Review*, September.

Pruijt, HD (1997) *Job Design and Technology: Taylorism vs Anti-Taylorism*. Routledge: London.

PSA [Property Services Agency] (1988) *PSA Annual Report 1987–88*. HMSO: London.

PSA [Property Services Agency] (1989) *PSA to be Privatised*. PSA Press Release No. 96, 27 September. DoE: London.

Public Power Corporation (1999) *Human Resource Management*. The PPC Sector of Education: Athens.

Public Power Corporation (2001) *Offering Circular: 35,000,000 shares in the form of shares and global depository receipts*. Hellenic Republic: Athens.

Pugh, DS (ed) (1984) *Organization Theory*. Penguin: Harmondsworth.

Pugh, DS (1993) Understanding and managing organizational change. In C Mabey and B Mayon-White (eds): *Managing Change* (2nd edition). The Open University/Paul Chapman Publishing: London.

Pugh, DS and Hickson, DJ (1976) *Organizational Structure in its Context: The Aston Programme 1*. Saxon House: Farnborough.

Pugh, DS, Hickson, DJ, Hinings, CR and Turner, C (1969a) The context of organization structures. *Administrative Science Quarterly*, 14, 91–114.

Pugh, DS, Hickson, DJ and Hinings, CR (1969b) An empirical taxonomy of structures of work organisation. *Administrative Science Quarterly*, 14, 115–26.

PwC (2011) *Understanding Commissioning Behaviours: Commissioning and competition in the public sector. Report for the Office of Fair Trading*. PricewaterhouseCoopers, London, available from www.pwc.co.uk

Quinn, JB (1980a) Managing strategic change. *Sloan Management Review*, 21(4), 3–20.

Quinn, JB (1980b) *Strategies for Change: Logical incrementalism*. Irwin: Homewood, IL.

Quinn, JB (1982) Managing strategies incrementally. *Omega*, 10(6), 613–27.

Quinn, JB (1993) Managing strategic change. In C Mabey and B Mayon-White (eds): *Managing Change* (2nd edition). The Open University/Paul Chapman Publishing: London.

Quinn, RE (1996) *Deep Change: Discovering the leader within*. Jossey-Bass: San Francisco, CA.

Quinn, RE and McGrath, MR (1985) The transformation of organizational cultures: a competing values perspective. In PJ Frost, LF Moore, MR Louis, CC Lundberg and J Martin (eds): *Organizational Culture*. Sage: Newbury Park, CA.

Rafferty, AE, Nerina, L, Jimmieson, NL and Armenakis, AA (2013) Change readiness: a multi-level review. *Journal of Management*, 39(1), 110–35.

Rafferty, K (1995) Tokyo and Mitsubishi banks to merge to create world's largest bank. *The Guardian*, 25 March, 15.

Rampersad, G, Pascale, P and Troshani, I (2010) Examining network factors: commitment, trust, coordination and harmony. *Journal of Business & Industrial Marketing*, 25(7), 487–500.

Rashman, L, Erin, E and Hartley, J (2009) Organizational learning and knowledge in public service organizations: a systematic review of the literature. *International Journal of Management Reviews*, 11(4), 463–94.

Raven, BH (1965) Social influence and power. In ID Steiner and M Fishbein (eds): *Current Studies in Social Psychology*. Holt, Rinehart, Winston: New York.

Raven, BH (1993) The bases of power – origins and recent developments. *Journal of Social Issues*, 49(4), 227–51.

Raven, BH (1999) Kurt Lewin address: influence, power, religion, and the mechanisms of social control. *Journal of Social Issues*, 55(1), 161–89.

Raz, AE (2009) Transplanting management participative change, organizational development, and the glocalization of corporate culture. *The Journal of Applied Behavioral Science*, 45(2), 280–304.

Reed, J and Soble, J (2008) *Financial Times*, 9 May, 16.

Reed, M (1992) *The Sociology of Organizations*. Harvester Wheatsheaf: Hemel Hempstead.

Reed, M and Hughes, M (eds) (1992) *Rethinking Organization: New directions in organization theory and analysis*. Sage: London.

Reed, MI (2000) In praise of duality and dualism: rethinking agency and structure in organisational analysis. In S Ackroyd and S Fleetwood (eds): *Realist Perspectives on Management and Organisations*. Routledge: London.

Reich, S (1998) *What is Globalization? Four possible answers*. Working Paper No. 261. The Helen Kellogg Institute for International Studies, University of Notre Dame, IN.

Rescher, N (1996) *Complexity: A philosophical overview*. Transaction Publishers: New York.

Reuters (2012) Kodak files for bankruptcy. *The Guardian*, 19 January, available at www.guardian.co.uk

Reynolds, CW (1987) Flocks, herds and schools: a distributed behaviour model. Proceedings of SIGGRAPH '87'. *Computer Graphics*, 21(4), 25–34.

Rhodes, C (2011) The moral of the story: ethics, narrative, and organizational change. In D Boje, B Burnes and J Hassard (eds): *The Routledge Companion to Organizational Change*. Routledge: London.

Ricks, DA (1999) *Blunders in International Business*. Blackwell: Oxford.

Rigby, D (2001) *Management Tools 2001: An executive's guide*. Bain & Company: Boston, MA.

Rigby, D and Bilodeau, B (2007) *Management Tools and Trends 2007*. Bain & Company: Boston, MA.

Rigby, D and Bilodeau, B (2009) *Management Tools and Trends 2009*. Bain & Company: Boston, MA.

Rigby, D and Bilodeau, B (2011) *Management Tools and Trends 2011*. Bain & Company: Boston, MA.

Rigby, D and Gillies, C (2000) Making the most of management tools and techniques: a survey from Bain & Company. *Strategic Change*, 9, 269–74.

Rigby, R (2013) Stay in touch or it can be difficult to reintegrate: Temporary reassignments; The careerist. *Financial Times*, 25 February, 14.

Rindova, VP and Starbuck, WH (1997) Ancient Chinese theories of control. *Journal of Management Inquiry*, 6(2), 144–59.

Ringland, G (1998) *Scenario Planning: Managing for the future*. Wiley: Chichester.

Robbins, SP (1986) *Organizational Behavior: Concepts, Controversies, and Applications*. Prentice Hall: Englewood Cliffs, NJ.

Robbins, SP (1987) *Organization Theory: Structure, design, and applications*. Prentice Hall: Englewood Cliffs, NJ.

Robbins, SP (1997) *Managing Today!* Prentice Hall: Upper Saddle River, NJ.

Roberts, Y (2008) The NHS isn't Ikea. *The Guardian*, 7 July, available at www.guardian.co.uk

Robinson, J (2010) Britons 'downloaded 1.2bn illegal tracks this year'. *The Guardian*, 16 December, available at www.guardian.co.uk

Rodrik, D (2012) *The Globalization Paradox*. Oxford University Press: Oxford.

Roethlisberger, F and Dickson, WJ (1938) *Management and the Worker*. Wiley: New York.

Rogers, P, Meehan, P and Tanner, S (2006) *Building a Winning Culture*. Bain & Company: Boston, MA.

Rogers, R (1997) Handy man. *Training*, November, 19.

Roll, E (1930) An early experiment in industrial organisation: Boulton and Watt, 1775–1805. Reprinted in M Berg (ed) (1979): *Technology and Toil in Nineteenth Century Britain*. CSE Books: London.

Rollinson, D (2002) *Organisational Behaviour and Analysis* (2nd edition). Financial Times Prentice Hall: Harlow.

Rollinson, D (2008) *Organisational Behaviour and Analysis* (4th edition). Financial Pearson: Harlow.

Romanelli, E and Tushman, ML (1994) Organizational transformation as punctuated equilibrium: an empirical test. *Academy of Management Journal*, 37(5), 1141–66.

Rose, M (1988) *Industrial Behaviour*. Penguin: Harmondsworth.

Rosenbrock, H (1982) *Unmanned Engineering*. Report 12 to the FMS Steering Committee. UMIST: Manchester.

Rosenfeld, J and Smith, M (1966) Mary Parker Follett: the transition to modern management thought. *Advanced Management Journal*, 31(4), 33–7.

Rosenzweig, PM (1994) When can management science research be generalized internationally? *Management Science*, 40(1), 28–39.

Rost, JC (1991) *Leadership for the Twenty-First Century*. Greenwood: Westport, CT.

Rost, JC (1993) Leadership development in the new millennium. *The Journal of Leadership Studies*, 1(1), 92–110.

Rothwell, S (1994) Human resources management. *Manager Update*, 5(3), Spring, 22–35.

Rubin, I (1967) Increasing self-acceptance: a means of reducing prejudice. *Journal of Personality and Social Psychology*, 5, 233–8.

Rumelt, RP (1991) How much does industry matter? *Strategic Management Journal*, 12(3), 167–85.

Rumelt, RP (1997) The evaluation of business strategy. In H Mintzberg and JB Quinn, *The Strategy Process* (3rd edition). Prentice Hall: Englewood Cliffs, NJ.

Ruona, WE and Gibson, SK (2004) The making of twenty-first century HR: an analysis of the convergence of HRM, HRD and OD. *Human Resource Management*, 43(1): 49–66.

Rushe, D (2012) American CEOs enjoy 15% pay rise in second year of double-digit hikes. *The Guardian*, 2 May, available at www.guardian.co.uk

Saigol, L (2003) Sex discrimination case could spell the end for City's secretive pay structure. *Financial Times*, 4 April, 8.

Sakai, K (1992) The feudal world of Japanese manufacturing. In RM Kanter, BA Stein and TD Jick: *The Challenge of Organizational Change*. Free Press: New York.

Sako, M (1997) Introduction. In M Sako and H Sato (eds): *Japanese Labour and Management in Transition*. Routledge: London.

Sako, M (2004) Supplier development at Honda, Nissan and Toyota: comparative case studies of organizational capability enhancement. *Industrial and Corporate Change*, 13(2), 281–308.

Sako, M and Sato, H (eds) (1997) *Japanese Labour and Management in Transition*. Routledge: London.

Salaman, G (1979) *Work Organisations*. Longman: London.

Salauroo, M and Burnes, B (1998) The impact of a market system on public sector organisations: a study of organisational change in the NHS. *The International Journal of Public Sector Management*, 11(6), 451–67.

Salz Review (2013) *An Independent Review of Barclays' Business Practices*. Barclays: London.

Sashkin, M and Burke, W (1987) Organization development in the nineteen-eighties. *Journal of Management*, 13, 393–417.

Sastry, MA (1997) Problems and paradoxes in a model of punctuated organizational change. *Administrative Science Quarterly*, 42(2), 237–75.

Sathe, V (1983) Some action implications of corporate culture: a manager's guide to action. *Organizational Dynamics*, Autumn, 4–23.

Saul, JR (1997) *The Unconscious Civilization*. Penguin: London.

Saunders, M (1997) *Strategic Purchasing and Supply Chain Management* (2nd edition). Pitman: London.

Sayer, A (1989) Post-Fordism in question. *International Journal of Urban and Regional Research*, 13(4), 666–95.

Sayer, A (2000) *Realism and Social Science*. Sage: London.

Schaefer, D (2010) *Financial Times*, 10 May, 6.

Schein, EH (1969) *Process Consultation*. Addison-Wesley: Reading, MA.

Schein, EH (1984) Coming to a new awareness of organizational culture. *Sloan Management Review*, 25(2), 3–16.

Schein, EH (1985) *Organizational Culture and Leadership: A dynamic view*. Jossey-Bass: San Francisco, CA.

Schein, EH (1988) *Organizational Psychology* (3rd edition). Prentice Hall: Englewood Cliffs, NJ.

Schein, EH (1989) Organizational culture: what it is and how to change it. In P Evans, T Doz and A Laurent (eds): *Human Resource Management in International Firms*. Macmillan: London.

Schein, EH (1996) Kurt Lewin's change theory in the field and in the classroom: notes towards a model of management learning. *Systems Practice*, 9(1), 27–47.

Schein, EH (2002) Models and tools for stability and change in human systems. *Reflections*, 4(2), 34–46.

Schein, EH (2010) *Organisational Culture and Leadership* (4th edition). Jossey-Bass: San Francisco, CA.

Schein, VE and Mueller, R (1992) Sex role stereotyping and requisite management characteristics: a cross cultural look. *Journal of Organizational Behaviour*, 13(5), 439–47.

Schilit, WK and Locke, EA (1982) A study of upward influence in organizations. *Administrative Science Quarterly*, June, 304–16.

Schilling, MA (2000) Decades ahead of her time: advancing stakeholder theory through the ideas of Mary Parker Follett. *Journal of Management History*, 6(5), 224–42.

Schmalensee, R (1983) Advertising and entry deterrence: an exploratory model. *Journal of Political Economy*, 91(4), 636–53.

Schmuck, R and Miles, M (1971) *Organizational Development in Schools*. National Press: Palo Alto, CA.

Schoeffler, S (1980) *Nine Basic Findings on Business Strategy*. The Strategic Planning Institute: Cambridge, MA.

Schoenberg, R, Collier, N and Bowman, C (2013) Strategies for business turnaround and recovery: a review and synthesis. *European Business Review*, 25(3), 243–62.

Schonberger, RJ (1982) *Japanese Manufacturing Techniques*. Free Press: New York.

Schriesheim, CA and Murphy, CJ (1976) Relationships between leader behavior and subordinate satisfaction and performance: a test of some situational moderators. *Journal of Applied Psychology*, 61, 634–41.

Schumacher, EF (1973) *Small Is Beautiful: A study of economics as if people mattered*. Vintage Books: London.

Schuyt, TNM and Schuijt, JJM (1998) Rituals and rules: about magic in consultancy. *Journal of Organizational Change Management*, 11(5), 399–406.

Schwartz, H and Davis, S (1981) Matching corporate culture and business strategy. *Organizational Dynamics*, 10, 30–48.

Schwartz, P and Leyden, P (1997) The long boom: a history of the future, 1980–2020. *Wired*, July, 1–16, available at www.wired.com

Scott, WR (1987) *Organizations: Rational, natural and open systems*. Prentice Hall: Englewood Cliffs, NJ.

Seashore, SE and Bowers, DG (1970) Durability of organizational change. *American Psychologist*, 25, 227–233.

Seel, R (2000) Culture and complexity: new insights on organisational change. *Organisations & People*, 7(2), May, 2–9.

Seel, R (2006) *Emergence in Organizations*. New Paradigm Organisation Consulting: Chedgrave, Norfolk, available from www.new-paradigm.co.uk

Seike, A (1997) Ageing workers. In M Sako and H Sato (eds): *Japanese Labour and Management in Transition*. Routledge: London.

Selznick, P (1948) Foundations of the theory of organization. *American Sociological Review*, 13, 25–35.

Senge, PM (1990) *The Fifth Discipline: The art and practice of the learning organization*. Century Business: London.

Senge, PM (2000) The puzzles and paradoxes of how living companies create wealth: why single-valued objective functions are not quite enough. In M Beer and N Nohria (eds): *Breaking the Code of Change*. Harvard Business School Press: Boston, MA.

SenGupta, R (2012) Firms grow smarter on strategy. *Financial Times*, 29 November, 4.

Senior, B (1997) *Organisational Change*. Pitman: London.

Senior, B (2002) *Organisational Change* (2nd edition). Financial Times Prentice Hall: Harlow.

Senturia, T, Flees, L and Maceda, M (2008) *Leading Change Management Requires Sticking to the PLOT*. Bain & Company: London.

Shapiro, C (1989) The theory of business strategy. *RAND Journal of Economics*, 20(1), 125–37.

Sheldrake, J (1996) *Management Theory: From Taylorism to Japanization*. International Thompson Business Press: London.

Shelton, CK and Darling, JR (2001) The quantum skills model in management: a new paradigm to enhance effective leadership. *Leadership and Organization Development Journal*, 22(6), 264–73.

Sheridan, K (1993) *Governing the Japanese Economy*. Polity Press: Oxford.

Shiflett, SC (1973) The contingency model of leadership effectiveness: some implications of its statistical and methodological properties. *Behavioral Science*, 18(6), 429–40.

Shipton, H (2006) Cohesion or confusion? Towards a typology for organizational learning research. *International Journal of Management Reviews*, 8(4), 233–252.

Shirai, T (1997) Foreword. In M Sako and H Sato (eds): *Japanese Labour and Management in Transition*. Routledge: London.

Short, JE and Venkatraman, N (1992) Beyond business process redesign: redefining Baxter's business network. *Sloan Management Review*, Fall, 7–21.

Shortell, S and Zajac, E (1990) Perceptual and archival measures of Miles and Snow's strategic types: a comprehensive assessment of reliability and validity. *Academy of Management Journal*, 33, 817–32.

Silverman, D (1970) *The Theory of Organizations*. Heinemann: London.

Silverman, D and Jones, J (1976) *Organizational Work*. Macmillan: London.

Silverman, S (2002) Weill wields his power at Citigroup: revamp represents ongoing structural changes. *Financial Times*, 13 June, 30.

Simon, HA (1947) *Administrative Behavior: A study of decision-making processes in administrative organizations*. Macmillan: New York.

Sirower, M (2003) When mergers can be a scandal. *Financial Times*, 14 August, 17.

Sissons, K (ed) (1989) *Personnel Management in Britain*. Blackwell: Oxford.

Sissons, K and Storey, J (1988) Developing effective managers: a review of the issues and an agenda for research. *Personnel Review*, 17(4), 3–8.

Siwek, SE (2007) *The True Cost of Copyright Industry Piracy to the U.S. Economy*. Institute for Policy Innovation: Lewisville, TX.

Sjöstrand, SV (1997) *The Two Faces of Management: The Janus Factor*. Thomson: London.

Skinner, BF (1974) *About Behaviourism*. Cape: London.

Slack, N, Chambers, S, Harland, C, Harrison, A and Johnson, R (1998) *Operations Management*. Pitman: London.

Sloan, AP (1986) *My Years with General Motors*. Penguin: Harmondsworth.

Smircich, L and Calás, M (1987) Organizational culture: a critical assessment. In F Jabin, L Putnam, K Roberts and L Porter (eds): *Handbook of Organizational Communication*. Sage: Newbury Park, CA.

Smith, A (1776) *The Wealth of Nations*, Vol. 1. Methuen (1950 edition): London.

Smith, A (2008) Working lives: cultural control, collectivism, Karoshi. *Sociology*, 42(1), 179–85.

Smith, JG (1985) *Business Strategy*. Blackwell: Oxford.

Smith, JH (1987) Elton Mayo and the hidden Hawthorne. *Work, Employment and Society*, 1(1), 107–20.

Smith, JH (1998) The enduring legacy of Elton Mayo. *Human Relations*, 51(3), 221–49.

Smith, KK (1982) *Groups in Conflict: Prisons in disguise*. Kendall/Hunt: Dubuque, IA.

Smith, M, Beck, J, Cooper, CL, Cox, C, Ottaway, D and Talbot, R (1982) *Introducing Organizational Behaviour*. Macmillan: London.

Smith, MK (2001) Kurt Lewin: groups, experiential learning and action research. *The Encyclopedia of Informal Education*, 1–15, available at www.infed.org/thinkers/et–lewin.htm

Smith, PB (1984) The effectiveness of Japanese styles of management: a review and critique. *Journal of Occupational Psychology*, 57(2), 121–36.

Smith, PB and Misumi, J (1989) Japanese management – a sun rising in the West. In CL Cooper and I Robertson (eds): *The International Review of Industrial and Organizational Psychology*. Wiley: London.

Smith, S and Tranfield, D (1987) The implementation and exploitation of advanced manufacturing technology – an outline methodology. *Change Management Research Unit, Research Paper No 2*, Sheffield Business School.

Smith, T (1994) Flexible production and capital/wage labour relation in manufacturing. *Capital and Class*, 53, Summer, 39–63.

Smithers, R (1995) Power chiefs pay themselves £72m in share options. *The Guardian*, 13 February, 20.

Snow, C, Miles, R and Coleman, H (1993) Managing 21st century network organizations. In C Mabey and B Mayon-White (eds): *Managing Change* (2nd edition). The Open University/Paul Chapman Publishing: London.

Soirinsuo, J and Mäkinen, P (2011) Growth and economies of scale among timber haulage companies. *Journal of Small Business and Enterprise Development*, 18(1),170–84.

Soltani, B (2013) The anatomy of corporate fraud: a comparative analysis of high profile American and European scandals. *Journal of Business Ethics*, published online 2 March 2013, DOI 10.1007/s10551-013-1660-z

Sorge, A (1997) Organization behaviour. In A Sorge and M Warner (eds): *The IEBM Handbook of Organizational Behaviour*. International Thompson Business Press: London.

Sosik, JJ and Megerian, LE (1999) Understanding leader emotional intelligence and performance: the role of self-other agreement in transformational leadership perceptions. *Group and Organization Management*, 24(3), 367–90.

Sowa, JE, Selden, SC and Sandfort, JR (2004) No longer unmeasurable? A multidimensional integrated model of nonprofit organizational effectiveness. *Nonprofit and Voluntary Sector Quarterly*, 33(4), 711–28.

Speed, RJ (1996) Oh Mr Porter! A re-appraisal of competitive strategy. *Marketing Intelligence and Planning*, 7(5/6), 8–11.

Speller, S (2001) The Best Value initiative. In G Johnson and K Scholes (eds): *Exploring Public Sector Strategy*. Financial Times Prentice Hall: Harlow.

Spiller, K (2003) Realism replaces grand visions. *Financial Times*, 12 March, 2.

Spreitzer, GM and Quinn, RE (1996) Empowering middle managers to be transformational leaders. *Journal of Applied Behavioral Science*, 32(3), 237–61.

Srivastava, R and Prakash, A (2011) Growth-Share Matrix as a tool for portfolio planning: evidence from the Indian telecommunication services industry. *The IUP Journal of Business Strategy*, VIII (2), 22–33.

Stace, DA and Dunphy, DD (1994) *Beyond the Boundaries: Leading and re-creating the successful enterprise*. McGraw-Hill: Sydney.

Stace, D and Dunphy, D (2001) *Beyond the Boundaries: Leading and re-creating the successful enterprise* (2nd edition). McGraw-Hill: Sydney.

Stacey, R (1990) *Dynamic Strategic Management for the 1990s*. Kogan Page: London.

Stacey, R (1992) *Managing Chaos: Dynamic business strategies in an unpredictable world*. Kogan Page: London.

Stacey, R (1993) *Strategic Management and Organisational Dynamics*. Pitman: London.

Stacey, RD (1996) *Complexity and Creativity in Organizations*. Berrett-Koehler: San Francisco, CA.

Stacey, RD (2003) *Strategic Management and Organisational Dynamics: The challenge of complexity*. Financial Times Prentice Hall: Harlow.

Stacey, RD (2010) *Strategic Management and Organisational Dynamics: The challenge of complexity* (6th edition). FT Prentice Hall: Harlow.

Stacey, RD, Griffin, D and Shaw, P (2002) *Complexity and Management: Fad or radical challenge to systems thinking?* Routledge: London.

Stadler, C (2007) The four principles of enduring success. *Harvard Business Review*, July–August, 62–72.

Stalk, G, Evans, P and Shulman, LE (1992) Competing on capabilities – the new rules of corporate strategy. *Harvard Business Review*, March–April, 57–69.

Stata, R (1989) Organization learning – the key to management innovation. *Sloan Management Review*, Spring, 63–74.

Statistics Bureau (2003) *Labour Force Survey – Monthly Results, June 2003*. Ministry of Public Management, Home Affairs, Posts and Telecommunications, available at www.stat.go.jp

Steel, E (2012) Television news veteran Zucker takes reins at CNN. *Financial Times*, 30 November, 18.

Steiner, GA (1969) *Top Management Planning*. Macmillan: London.

Stewart, H (2003) The day investors said enough is enough. *The Guardian*, 20 May, available at www.guardian.co.uk

Stewart, R (1976) *Contrasts in Management*. McGraw-Hill: London.

Stewart, R (1982) *Choices for the Manager: A guide to understanding managerial work*. Prentice-Hall: Englewood Cliffs, NJ.

Stickland, F (1998) *The Dynamics of Change: Insights into organisational transition from the natural world*. Routledge: London.

Stiglitz, J (2007) *Making Globalization Work: The next steps to global justice*. Penguin: Harmondsworth.

Stiglitz, J (2010) *Freefall: Free markets and the sinking of the global economy*. Allen Lane: London.

Stiglitz, J (2013) Globalisation isn't just about profits. *The Guardian*, 27 May, available at www.guardian.co.uk

Stogdill, RM (1948) Personal factors associated with leadership: a survey of the literature. *Journal of Psychology*, 25, 35–71.

Stogdill, RM (1974) *A Handbook of Leadership: A survey of theory and research*. Free Press: New York.

Stohl, C and Cheney, G (2001) Participatory processes/paradoxical practices. *Management Communication Quarterly*, 14(3), 349–407.

Storey, J (1989) Management development: a literature review and implications for future research – Part 1: conceptualisations and practices. *Personnel Review*, 18(6), 3–19.

Storey, J (1990) Management development: a literature review and implications for future research – Part 2: profiles and context. *Personnel Review*, 19(1), 3–11.

Storey, J (1992) *Developments in the Management of Human Resources*. Blackwell: Oxford.

Storey, J (ed) (2004) *Leadership in Organizations: Current issues and key trends*. Routledge: London.

Stournaras, Y (1999) *The Converging Greek Economy: Developments, policies and prospects*. Ministry of National Economy: Athens.

Strahan, D (2008) *The Last Oil Shock: A survival guide to the imminent extinction of Petroleum Man*. John Murray: London.

Streeck, W (1987) The uncertainties of management and the management of uncertainties: employers, labour relations and industrial adjustments in the 1980s. *Work, Employment and Society*, 1(3), 281–308.

Stuart, R (1986) Social learning. *Management Decision*, 24(6), 32–5.

Student, J (1968) Supervisory influence and work-group performance. *Journal of Applied Psychology*, June, 188–94.

Styhre, A (2002) Non-linear change in organizations: organization change management informed by complexity theory. *Leadership and Organization Development Journal*, 23(6), 343–51.

Sugeno, K and Suwa, Y (1997) Labour law issues in a changing labour market: in search of a new support system. In M Sako and H Sato (eds): *Japanese Labour and Management in Transition*. Routledge: London.

Sullivan, J (1983) A critique of Theory Z. *Academy of Management Review*, 8, 132–42.

Sullivan, J and Nonaka, I (1986) The application of organizational learning theory to Japanese and American management. *Journal of International Business Studies*, Fall, 127–47.

Sullivan, TJ (1999) Leading people in a chaotic world. *Journal of Educational Administration*, 37(5), 408–23.

Sviokla, JJ (1998) Virtual value and the birth of virtual markets. In SP Bradley and RL Nolan (eds): *Sense and Respond: Capturing value in the network era*. Harvard Business School Press: Boston, MA.

Taguchi, G (1986) *Introduction to Quality Engineering*. Asian Production Organization: Dearborn, MI.

Talbot, C (2001) UK public services and management (1979–2000): evolution or revolution? *International Journal of Public Sector Management*, 14(4), 281–303.

Talbot, R (1993) Creativity in the organizational context: implications for training. In SG Isaksen, MC Murdock, RL Firestien and DJ Treffinger (eds): *Nurturing and Developing Creativity*. Ablex: Norwood, NJ.

Talbot, R (1997) Taking style on board. *Creativity and Innovation Management*, 6(3), 177–84.

Tarokh, MJ, Sharifi, E and Nazem, E (2008) Survey of BPR experiences in Iran: reasons for success and failure. *Journal of Business and Industrial Marketing*, 23(5), 350–62.

Taylor, A (2007) Work your proper hours, says TUC. *Financial Times*, 23 February, 4, available at www.ft.com

Taylor, FW (1911a) *The Principles of Scientific Management*. Dover (1998 edition): New York.

Taylor, FW (1911b) *Shop Management*. Harper (1947 edition): New York.

Teather, D (2002) Trying to close a can of worms. *The Guardian*, 11 October, available at www.guardian.co.uk

Teather, D (2003) US labels to sue individuals for net music piracy. *The Guardian*, 26 June, 13.

Teece, DJ, Pisano, G and Shuen, A (1997) Dynamic capabilities and strategic management. *Strategic Management Journal*, 18(7), 509–33.

Terry, PT (1976) The contingency theory and the development of organisations. A paper presented for the Study Group for Industrial Sociology of the British Sociological Association, March.

Tetenbaum, TJ (1998) Shifting paradigms: from Newton to chaos. *Organizational Dynamics*, 26(4), 21–32.

Tett, G (1994) Partnerships in business grow. *Financial Times*, 28 June, 12.

Thickett, M (1970) Gilbreth and the measurement of work. In A Tillett, T Kempner and G Willis (eds): *Management Thinkers*. Pelican: Harmondsworth.

Thiroux, JP and Krasemann, KW (2007) *Ethics: Theory and practice* (9th edition). Pearson Prentice Hill: Upper Saddle River, NJ.

Thomas, AB (1993) *Controversies in Management*. Routledge: London.

Thomas, AB (2003) *Controversies in Management: Issues, debates, answers*. Routledge: London.

Thompkins, JM (1990) Politics – the illegitimate discipline. *Management Decision*, 28(4), 23–8.

Thompson, AA Jnr and Strickland, AJ (1983) *Strategy Formulation and Implementation*. Business Publications Inc: Homewood, IL.

Thompson, J (1967) *Organizations in Action*. McGraw-Hill: New York.

Thompson, JW (1995) The renaissance of learning in business. In S Chawla and J Renesch (eds): *Learning Organizations: Developing cultures for tomorrow's workplace*. Productivity Press: Portland, OR.

Thompson, M (1996) Effective purchasing strategy: the untapped source of competitiveness. *Supply Chain Management*, 1(3), 6–8.

Thompson, M (2008) *Introduction to Strategic Management*. MDP (Management Development Partnership): Bangor, Wales.

Thornberry, NE (1987) Training the engineer as project manager. *Training and Development Journal*, 41(10).

Thrift, N (2005) *Knowing Capitalism*. London: Sage.

Tibbs, H and Bailey, K (2008) Empty threat. *The Guardian*, 11 June, available at www.guardian.co.uk

Tighe, C (2002) Less means more in engineering. *Financial Times*, 17 October, 15.

Tillett, A (1970) Industry and management. In A Tillett, T Kempner and G Willis (eds): *Management Thinkers*. Pelican: Harmondsworth.

Tobach, E (1994) Personal is political is personal is political. *Journal of Social Issues*, 50(1), 221–44.

Toffler, A (1970) *Future Shock*. Random House: New York.

Tomaney, J (1990) The reality of workplace flexibility. *Capital and Class*, 40, Spring, 29–60.

Total Quality Engineering Inc. (2003) Hoshin Kanri, available at www.tqe.com/hoshinTR.html

Tran, M (2003) $1.4 bn Wall Street settlement finalised. *The Guardian*, 28 April, available at www.guardian.co.uk

Treanor, J and Finch, J (2003) Directors gains stir revolt by investors. *The Guardian*, 31 July, 4.

Treanor, J and Neville, S (2012) Executive pay among FTSE firms keeps soaring, survey reports. *The Guardian*, 11 June, available at www.guardian.co.uk

Treanor, J and Wray, R (2003) Marconi chiefs defy FSA censure: no apology for shareholders in wake of City watchdog's warning on rules breach. *The Guardian*, 12 April, available at www.guardian.co.uk

Trice, HM (1993) *Occupational Subcultures in the Workplace*. ILR Press: Cornell University, Ithaca, NY.

Trice, HM and Beyer, JM (1984) Studying organizational cultures through rites and ceremonials. *Academy of Management Review*, 9, 653–69.

Trice, HM and Beyer, JM (1990) Using six organizational rites to change culture. In RH Kilmann, MJ Saxton, R Serpa and Associates (eds): *Gaining Control of the Corporate Culture*. Jossey-Bass: San Francisco, CA.

Trist, EL, Higgin, GW, Murray, H and Pollock, AB (1963) *Organisational Choice*. Tavistock: London.

Trompenaars, F (1993) *Riding the Waves of Culture*. Nicholas Brealey: London.

Trompenaars Hampden–Turner (2012) *Our Expertise*, available at www.thtconsulting.com

Tsang, EWK (1997) Organizational learning and the learning organization: a dichotomy between descriptive and prescriptive research. *Human Relations*, 50(1), 73–89.

Tschacher, W and Brunner, EJ (1995) Empirical-studies of group-dynamics from the point-of-view of self-organization theory. *Zeitschrift fur Sozialpsychologie*, 26(2), 78–91.

Tseng, H-C, Duan, C-H, Tung, H-L and Kung, H-J (2010) Modern business ethics research: concepts, theories, and relationships. *Journal of Business Ethics*, 91, 587–97.

Tsoukas, H (1989) The validity of idiographic research explanations. *Academy of Management Review*, 14(4), 551–61.

Tsoukas, H (1992) Postmodernism, reflexive rationalism and organisation studies. *Organisation Studies*, 13(4), 643–9.

Tsoukas, H (2000) What is management? An outline of a metatheory. In S Ackroyd and S Fleetwood (eds): *Realist Perspectives on Management and Organisations*. Routledge: London.

Tuckman, BW (1965) Developmental sequence in small groups. *Psychological Bulletin*, 63, 384–99.

Tuckman, BW and Jensen, MAC (1977) Stages of small group development revisited. *Group and Organizational Studies*, 2, 419–27.

Turnbull, P (1986) The Japanisation of production and industrial relations at Lucas Electrical. *Industrial Relations Journal*, 17(3), 193–206.

Turner, B (1971) *Exploring the Industrial Subculture*. Macmillan: London.

Turner, B (1986) Sociological aspects of organizational symbolism. *Organization Studies*, 7(2), 101–17.

Turner, D (2003) Unemployment falls to two-year low. *Financial Times*, 17 July, 3.

Turner, I (1990) Strategy and organisation. *Manager Update*, 1(3), 1–10.

Tushman, M and Virany, B (1986) Changing characteristics of executive teams in an emerging industry. *Journal of Business Venturing*, 37–49.

Tushman, ML and Romanelli, E (1985) Organizational evolution: a metamorphosis model of convergence and reorientation. In LL Cummings and BM Staw (eds): *Research in Organizational Behavior*, 7, 171–222. JAI Press: Greenwich, CT.

Tversky, A and Kahneman, D (1981) The framing of decisions and the psychology of choice. *Science*, 211(4481), 453–8.

Udy, SH Jnr (1959) 'Bureaucracy' and 'rationality' in Weber's organization theory. *American Sociological Review*, 24, December, 791–5.

United Nations (2010) *United Nations Global Compact*. Available at ww.unglobalcompact.org

United Nations Development Programme (2007) *Human Development Report 2007/2008*. Palgrave Macmillan: Basingstoke.

Urabe, K (1986) Innovation and the Japanese management system. Keynote address, First International Symposium on Management, Japan Society for the Study of Business Administration, Kobe University, 11–49.

Ure, A (1835) *The Philosophy of Manufactures*. Frank Cass (1967 edition): London.

Ure, A (1836) *The Cotton Manufacture of Great Britain*, Vol. 1. Johnson (1970 edition): London.

Urwick, L (1949) Introduction. In H Fayol (ed): *General and Industrial Management* (trans). Pitman: London.

Uttal, B (1983) The corporate culture vultures. *Fortune*, 17 October, 66–72.

Vakola, M (2013) Multilevel readiness for change: a conceptual approach. *Journal of Change Management*, 13(1), 96–109.

Valerio, AM (2009) *Developing Women Leaders*. Wiley-Blackwell: Chichester.

van den Berg, PT and Wilderom, CPM (2004) Defining, measuring, and comparing organisational cultures. *Applied Psychology: An International Review*, 53(4), 570–82.

van der Mandele, HC and van Witteloostuijn, A (2013) *Why Organizations Will Always Ultimately Fail*. Edward Elgar: Cheltenham.

Van der Wiele, A (1998) *Beyond Fads*. Eburon: Delft, The Netherlands.

Van Maanen, J (1991) The smile factory: work at Disneyland. In PJ Frost, L Moore, M Louis, C Lundberg and J Martin (eds): *Reframing Organizational Culture*. Sage: Beverly Hills, CA.

Van Maanen, J and Kunda, G (1989) Real feelings: emotional expression and organisational culture. In B Staw and L Cummings (eds): *Research in Organizational Behaviour*, 11, 43–103.

Van Nistelrooij, A and Sminia, H (2010) Organization development: what's actually happening? *Journal of Change Management*, 10(4), 393–405.

Vecchio, RP (1983) Assessing the validity of Fielder's contingency model of leadership effectiveness: a closer look at Strube and Garcia. *Psychological Bulletin*, 93, 404–8.

Vecchio, RP (1992) Cognitive resource theory: issues for specifying a test for the theory. *Journal of Applied Psychology*, 75, 141–7.

Vickers, J and Yarrow, G (1991) Economic perspectives on privatisation. *Journal of Economic Perspectives*, 5(2), 111–32.

Vidler, E and Clarke, J (2005) Creating citizen-consumers: New Labour and the remaking of public services. *Public Policy and Administration*, 20(2), 19–37.

Vinnecombe, S (1987) What exactly are the differences in male and female working styles? *Women in Management Review*, 3(1).

Virgin.com (2008) *About Virgin*. Available at www.virgin.com

von Bertalanffy, L (1972) The history and status of general systems theory. *The Academy of Management Journal*, 15(4), 407–26.

von Clausewitz, C, von Ghyczy, T, von Oetinger, C and Bassford, C (2001) *Clausewitz on Strategy: Inspiration and insight from a master strategist*. Wiley: Chichester.

von Hagen (2012) Zero hours contracts for NHS staff explained. *BBC News*, 19 September, available at www.bbc.co.uk

Voss, CA (1985) *Success and Failure in Advanced Manufacturing Technology*. Working Paper, Warwick University.

Vroom, VH and Jago, AG (1988) *The New Leadership: Managing participation in organizations*. Prentice Hall: Englewood Cliffs, NJ.

Vroom, VH and Yetton, PW (1973) *Leadership and Decision Making*. Pittsburgh Press: Pittsburgh, PA.

Wack, P (1985) Scenarios: uncharted waters ahead. *Harvard Business Review*, September/October, 73–89.

Waclawski, J (2002) Large-scale organizational change and performance: an empirical examination. *Human Resource Development Quarterly*, 13(3), 289–305.

Waddell, D and Sohal, A (1998) Resistance: a constructive tool for change management. *Management Decision*, 36(8), 543–8.

Wagner, JA (1994) Participation's effects on performance and satisfaction: a reconsideration of research evidence. *Academy of Management Review*, 19, 312–30.

Wahba, MA and Bridwell, LG (1976) Maslow reconsidered: a review of research on the need hierarchy theory. *Organizational Behavior and Human Performance*, 15(2), 212–40.

Wakisata, A (1997) Women at work. In M Sako and H Sato (eds): *Japanese Labour and Management in Transition*. Routledge: London.

Waldersee, R and Sheather, S (1996) The effects of strategy type on strategy implementation actions. *Human Relations*, 49(1), 105–22.

Wall, TD, Burnes, B, Clegg, CW and Kemp, NJ (1984) New technology, old jobs. *Work and People*, 10(2), 15–21.

Wallace, J and Erickson, J (1992) *Hard Drive: Bill Gates and the making of the Microsoft empire*. Wiley: New York.

Waller, DL (1999) *Operations Management: A supply chain approach*. International Thompson: London.

Wang, CL and Ahmed, PK (2003) Organisational learning: a critical review. *The Learning Organization*, 10(1), 8–17.

Ward, A (2007) Nardelli's style helps to seal his fate. *Financial Times*, 4 January, 22.

Warner, M (1984) New technology, work organisation and industrial relations. *Omega*, 12(3), 203–10.

Warner, M (1997) The year of the very big deals. *Fortune*, 24, November, 3.

Warnock, E (2012) Japan bill to raise retirement age passes Lower House. *Wall Street Journal*, 2 August, available at www.wsj.com

Warr, P (ed) (1987) *Psychology at Work*. Penguin: Harmondsworth.

Warrell, H (2012) Hammond concedes G4S debacle was 'informative'. *Financial Times*, 14 August, 2.

Warwick, DP and Thompson, JT (1980) Still crazy after all these years. *Training and Development Journal*, 34(2), 16–22.

Wastell, DG, White, P and Kawalek, P (1994) A methodology for business process redesign: experience and issues. *Journal of Strategic Information Systems*, 3(1), 23–40.

Watson, G (1994) The flexible workforce and patterns of working hours in the UK. *Employment Gazette*, July, 239–47.

Watson, T (1982) Group ideologies and organisational change. *Journal of Management Studies*, 19(3), 259–77.

Watson, TJ (1986) *Management Organisation and Employment Strategy: New directions in theory and practice*. Routledge and Kegan Paul: London.

Watson, TJ (1997) *Sociology, Work and Industry* (3rd edition). Routledge: London.

Watts, J (1998) Japanese 'bullied' out of work. *The Guardian*, 29 August, 13.

Weber, M (1928) *General Economic History*. George Allen & Unwin: London.

Weber, M (1947) *The Theory of Social and Economic Organization* (trans). Free Press: Glencoe, IL.

Weber, M (1948) *From Max Weber: Essays in sociology* (translated, edited and with an introduction by HH Gerth and C Wright Mills). Routledge and Kegan Paul: London.

Weick, KE (1979) *The Social Psychology of Organizing*. Addison-Wesley: Reading, MA.

Weick, KE (1987) Substitute for corporate strategy. In DJ Teece (ed) *The Competitive Challenge: Strategies for industrial innovation and renewal*. Ballinger: Cambridge, MA.

Weick, KE (1995) *Sensemaking in Organizations*. Sage: London.

Weick, KE (2000) Emergent change as a universal in organizations. In M Beer and N Nohria (eds): *Breaking the Code of Change*. Harvard Business School Press: Boston, MA.

Weick, KE and Quinn, RE (1999) Organizational change and development. *Annual Review of Psychology*, 50, 361–86.

Weiner, BJ, Amick, H and Lee, S-Y D (2008) Review: conceptualization and measurement of organizational readiness for change: a review of the literature in health services research and other fields. *Medical Care Research Review*, 65(4), 379–436.

Weisbord, M (1987) *Productive Workplaces: Organizing and managing for dignity, meaning and community*. Jossey-Bass: San Francisco, CA.

Werkman, R (2010) Reinventing organization development: how a sensemaking perspective can enrich OD theories and interventions. *Journal of Change Management*, 10(4), 421–38.

Wernerfelt, B (1984) A resource-based view of the firm. *Strategic Management Journal*, 15(2), 171–80.

Wernerfelt, B (1995) The resource-based view of the firm: ten years after. *Strategic Management Journal*, 16, 171–4.

West, P (1994) The concept of the learning organization. *Journal of European Industrial Training*, 18(1), 15–21.

Wetlaufer, S (1999) Organizing for empowerment: an interview with AES's Roger Sante and Dennis Bakke. *Harvard Business Review*, January–February, 120–1.

Wheatley, MJ (1992a) *The Future of Middle Management*. British Institute of Management: London.

Wheatley, MJ (1992b) *Leadership and the New Science: Learning about organization from an orderly universe*. Berrett-Koehler: San Francisco, CA.

Wheelan, SA, Pepitone, EA and Abt, V (eds) (1990) *Advances in Field Theory*. Sage: Newbury Park: CA.

Wheelen, TL and Hunger, DJ (1989) *Strategic Management and Business Policy*. Addison-Wesley: Reading, MA.

Whitaker, A (1992) The transformation in work: post-Fordism revisited. In M Reed and M Hughes (eds): *Rethinking Organization: New directions in organization theory and analysis*. Sage: London.

White, M (1999) PM's deadline to end child poverty. *The Guardian*, 19 March, 10.

White, S and Mitchell, T (1976) Organization development: a review of research content and research design. *Academy of Management Review*, 1(2), 57–73.

Whitehill, AM (1991) *Japanese Management: Tradition and transition*. Routledge: London.

Whitley, R (1998) *Divergent Capitalisms*. Oxford University Press: London.

Whittington, R (1989) *Corporate Strategies in Recovery and Recession: Social structure and strategic choice*. Unwin Hyman: London.

Whittington, R (1993) *What Is Strategy and Does It Matter?* Routledge: London.

Whittington, R (1994) Sociological pluralism, institutions and managerial agency. In J Hassard and M Parker (eds): *Towards a New Theory of Organisation*. Routledge: London.

Whittington, R (2001) *What Is Strategy and Does It Matter?* (2nd edition). Thomson Learning: London.

Whyte, WH (1960) *The Organization of Man*. Penguin: Harmondsworth.

Whyte, J and Witcher, B (1992) *The Adoption of Total Quality Management in Northern England*. Durham University Business School: Durham.

Wickens, P (1987) *The Road to Nissan*. Macmillan: London.

Wickens, P (1995) *The Ascendant Organization: Combining commitment and control for long term sustainable business success*. Macmillan: London.

Wilkinson, A (1991) *TQM and HRM*. Working Paper, Manchester School of Management, UMIST.

Wilkinson, HE and Orth, DC (1986) Soft skill training in management development. *Training and Development Journal*, 40(3), 34–6.

Wilbur, J (1987) Does mentoring breed success? *Training and Development Journal*, 41(11), 38–41.

Willcocks, SG (1994) Organizational analysis: a health service commentary. *Leadership and Organization Development Journal*, 15(1), 29–32.

Williams, K, Cutler, T and Haslan, C (1987) The end of mass production? *Economy and Society*, 1(3), 404–39.

Williams, K, Haslam, C and Williams, J (1991) Management accounting: the Western problematic against the Japanese application. 9th Annual Conference of the Labour Process, UMIST, Manchester.

Williamson, O (1991) Strategizing, economizing and economic organization. *Strategic Management Journal*, 12, 75–94.

Willmott, H (1993) Strength is ignorance; slavery is freedom: managing culture in modern organizations. *Journal of Management Studies*, 30(40), 515–52.

Willmott, R (2000) Structure, culture and agency: rejecting the current orthodoxy of organisational theory. In S Ackroyd and S Fleetwood (eds): *Realist Perspectives on Management and Organisations*. Routledge: London.

Wilson, AM (2001) Understanding organisational culture and the implications for corporate marketing. *European Journal of Marketing*, 35(3/4), 353–67.

Wilson, DC (1992) *A Strategy of Change*. Routledge: London.

Wilson, I (1992) Realising the power of strategic vision. *Long Range Planning*, 25(5), 18–28.

Wilson, JF (1995) *British Business History, 1720–1994*. Manchester University Press: Manchester.

Windrum, P (2004) Leveraging technological externalities in complex technologies: Microsoft's exploitation of standards in the browser wars. *Research Policy*, 33(3), 385–94.

Wirtenberg, J, Abrams, L and Ott, C. (2004) Assessing the field of organization development. *Journal of Applied Behavioral Science*, 40(4), 465–79.

Wirtenberg, J, Lipsky, D, Abrams, L, Conway, M and Slepian, J (2007) The future of organization development: enabling sustainable business performance through people. *Organization Development Journal*, 25(2), 7–22.

Wisdom, J (ed) (2001) *Digital Futures: Living in a dot-com world*. Earthscan: London.

Witcher, B (1993) *The Adoption of Total Quality Management in Scotland*. Durham University Business School: Durham.

Witzel, M (2002) The sustainable business: continuous search for improvement. *Financial Times*, 19 August, 9.

Witzel, M (2003a) *Fifty Key Figures in Management*. Routledge: London.

Witzel, M (2003b) The master strategist: Michael Porter. *Financial Times*, 15 August, 11.

Witzel, M (2003c) The great iconoclast: Henry Mintzberg. *Financial Times*, 5 August, 11.

Witzel, M (2007) The progressive power of thinking anew. *Financial Times*, 22 November 2007, 14.

Witzel, M (2012) *A History of Management Thought*. Routledge: London.

Wolff, R (2011) Bonuses for bankers, bankruptcy for public services. *The Guardian*, 20 January, available at www.guardian.co.uk

Womack, JP, Jones, DT and Roos, D (1990) *The Machine that Changed the World*. Rawson Associates: New York.

Wood, S (1979) A reappraisal of the contingency approach to organization. *Journal of Management Studies*, 16, 334–54.

Wood, S (1991) Japanisation and/or Toyotaism? *Work, Employment and Society*, 5(4), 567–600.

Woodman, R (1989) Organization change and development: new arenas for inquiry and action. *Journal of Management*, 15, 205–28.

Woodward, J (1965) *Industrial Organization: Theory and practice*. Oxford University Press: London.

Woodward, J (1970) *Industrial Organization: Behaviour and control*. Oxford University Press: London.

Wooten, KC and White, LP (1999) Linking OD's philosophy with justice theory: postmodern implications. *Journal of Organizational Change Management*, 12(1), 7–20.

Worley, CG and Feyerherm, AE (2003) Reflections on the future of organisation development. *Journal of Applied Behavioral Science*, 39(1), 97–115.

Worley, CG, Mohrman, S and Nevitt, JA (2011) Large group interventions: an empirical field study of their composition, process, and outcomes. *The Journal of Applied Behavioral Science*, 47(4), 404–31.

Worrall, L and Cooper, CL (1997) *The Quality of Working Life: The 1997 Survey of Managers' Changing Experiences*. Institute of Management: London.

Worrall, L and Cooper, CL (1998) *The Quality of Working Life: The 1998 Survey of Managers' Changing Experiences*. Institute of Management: London.

Wren, DA (1994) *The Evolution of Management Thought* (4th edition). Wiley: Chichester.

Wren, DA and Bedeian, AG (2009) *The Evolution of Management Thought* (6th edition). Wiley: Chichester.

Wright, R (2012) SUVs take a back seat amid drive towards subcompact transport. *Financial Times*, 3 October, 25.

www.dei.gr The official website of PPC SA.

www.rae.gr The official website of the Greek Regulatory Authority for Energy.

Yammarino, FI and Dansereau, F (2002) *The Many Faces of Multi-Level Issues: Research in multi-level issues*, Vol 1. JAI Press: London.

Yaniv, E and Farkas, F (2005) The impact of person–organization fit on the corporate brand perception of employees and of customers. *Journal of Change Management*, 5(4), 447–61.

Young, H (1990) *The Iron Lady: A biography of Margaret Thatcher*. Farrar Straus and Giroux: London.

Yukl, G (1994) *Leadership in Organizations* (3rd edition). Prentice Hall: Englewood Cliffs, NJ.

Yukl, G (2002) *Leadership in Organizations* (5th edition). Prentice Hall: Upper Saddle River, NJ.

Yukl, G (2006) *Leadership in Organizations* (6th edition). Prentice Hall: London.

Yukl, G (2013) *Leadership in Organizations* (8th edition). Pearson: London.

Yukl, G and Van Fleet, DD (1992) Theory and research on leadership in organizations. In MD Dunnette and LM Hough (eds): *Handbook of Industrial and Organizational Psychology*, Vol. 3 (2nd edition). Consulting Psychologists Press: Palo Alto, CA.

Yutaka, N (1998) Japanese–style industrial relations in historical perspective. In H Harukiyo and GD Hook (eds): *Japanese Business Management: Restructuring for low growth and globalization*. Routledge: London.

Zaccaro, SJ and and Banks, D (2001) Leadership, vision, and organizational effectiveness. In SJ Zaccaro and RJ Klimoski (eds): *The Nature of Organizational Leadership: Understanding the performance imperatives confronting today's leaders*. Jossey-Bass: San Francisco, CA.

Zairi, M, Letza, S and Oakland, J (1994) Does TQM impact on bottom line results? *TQM Magazine*, 6(1), 38–43.

Zaleznik, A (1970) Power and politics in organizational life. *Harvard Business Review*, May–June, 47–60.

Zell, D (2003) Organizational change as a process of death, dying, and rebirth. *Journal of Applied Behavioral Science*, 39(1), 73–96.

Zentner, RD (1982) Scenarios, past, present and future. *Long Range Planning*, 15, June, 12–20.

Zimmerman, BJ (1992) *Chaos and Self-Renewing Organizations: Designing transformation processes for co-evolution*. Faculty of Administrative Studies, York University: Ontario.

Zinn, H (1980) *A People's History of the United States*. Longman: London.

Zwerman, WL (1970) *New Perspectives in Organization Theory*. Greenwood: Westport, CT.

Glossary

Action Learning This approach to management development was devised in the 1940s in the UK by Reg Revans and involves small groups of managers tackling a set problem or case study. The aim is not only that managers learn how to approach problems together but also that they learn about themselves and challenge the appropriateness of their own attitudes and behaviours.

Action Research This is an approach to change which, first, emphasises that change requires action, and is directed at achieving this; and second, recognises that successful action is based on analysing the situation correctly, identifying all the possible alternative solutions and choosing the one most appropriate to the situation at hand. It is one of the four elements of Lewin's Planned approach to change (see *Planned change*).

activity planning This involves constructing a schedule or 'road map' for a change programme, citing the main activities and events that must occur if the change is to be successful.

Adaptation–Innovation theory This maintains not only that people exhibit different degrees of creativity but also that they express their creativity in different ways, along a spectrum which runs from adaptors to innovators. Those who tend towards the adaptor end of the spectrum prefer to work within the existing system to improve things. Innovators tend to ignore or challenge the system and to come up with radical proposals for change.

Analytical stream This phrase is used to describe writers on strategy and change who are more interested in understanding how organisations actually formulate strategy and manage change than prescribing how they should conduct these activities (see *Prescriptive stream*).

artifacts At the highest level of cultural awareness are the artifacts and creations that are visible manifestations of the other levels of culture. These include observable behaviours of members, as well as the structures, systems, procedures, rules and physical aspects of the organisation (see *Organisational culture*).

aston group The work of this group constitutes one of the key building blocks of Contingency Theory. Working in the 1960s, they found that size was the most powerful predictor of specialisation, use of procedures and reliance on paperwork. In effect, what they found was that the larger the organisation, the more likely it was to adopt (and need) a mechanistic (bureaucratic) structure. The reverse was also found: the smaller the organisation, the more likely it was to adopt (and need) an organic (flexible) structure.

Audits and post-audits During and after a change initiative, an audit or a post-audit should be carried out (a) to establish that the objectives have really been met, and (b) to ascertain what lessons can be learned for future projects.

Authority In organisational terms, authority is the right to act, or command others to act, towards the attainment of organisational goals. The right to act is given legitimacy by the authority figure's position in the organisation. Therefore, the level of authority a person possesses is related to their job.

Autonomy This is the ability or requirement of individuals, groups and organisations to act independently and proactively, and without seeking the permission of higher authority, when pursuing organisational goals. Peters and Waterman link it to entrepreneurship and it is seen as an essential attribute of excellent organisations (see *Culture–Excellence approach*).

Backstaging This is concerned with the exercise of power skills during the change process. In particular, it involves influencing the recipients of change to accept it. Buchanan and Boddy (1992) see this as being an essential skill of a change agent.

basic assumptions These are seen as one of the core components of organisational culture. They operate at the deepest level of cultural awareness and are unconscious, taken-for-granted assumptions about how organisational problems should be solved, as well as about the nature of human beings, human activity and human relationships.

Behaviourist psychology This maintains that all human behaviour is learned and that the individual is the passive recipient of external and objective data. One of the basic principles of the Behaviourists is that human actions are conditioned by their expected consequences. Behaviour that is rewarded tends to be repeated, and behaviour that is ignored tends not to be. Therefore, in order to change behaviour, it is necessary to change the conditions that cause it.

benchmarking This is the term given to the process of comparing an organisation's performance, or the performance of part of an organisation, e.g. a product or service, against a range of internal and external comparators.

bias for action This is one of Peters and Waterman's eight key attributes of excellent companies. Even though such companies may have an analytical approach to problems, they are predisposed towards taking rapid and appropriate action rather than getting bogged down in analysis (see *Culture–Excellence approach*).

Bold Strokes These are major strategic or economic initiatives, e.g. restructuring an organisation. They can have a clear and rapid impact on an organisation's performance, but they rarely lead to any long-term change in habits or culture. Bold Strokes are initiatives taken by a few senior managers, sometimes only one; they do not rely on the support of the rest of the organisation for their success (see *Long Marches*; *Culture–Excellence approach*).

Boston Consulting Group See *Growth-Share Matrix*.

bottom-up change This is the opposite of top-down change. Instead of change being driven by a few senior managers from the top, this approach sees change as coming from bottom-up initiatives which emerge from local responses to issues, threats or opportunities in the environment. The size of such responses will vary but, because they are local responses, they can never be large-scale (see *Emergent change*).

BPR See *Business Process Re-engineering*.

bureaucracy This form of organisational structure is characterised by the division of labour, a clear hierarchical authority structure, formal and unbiased selection procedures, employment decisions based on merit, career tracks for employees, detailed rules and regulations, impersonal relationships, and a distinct separation of members' organisational and personal lives. It is one of the core elements of the Classical approach to organisations and corresponds with the mechanistic structure identified by Contingency theorists (see *Contingency Theory*).

business ethics These are moral principles or beliefs about what is right or wrong. These beliefs guide managers and others in organisations in their dealings with other individuals, groups and organisations, and provide a basis for deciding whether behaviour is socially responsible.

Business Process Re-engineering (BPR) This is an approach that aims to achieve a radical rethinking and redesign of organisational processes in order to significantly improve key performance measures, such as quality, cost and delivery.

cash-cows These are companies whose rate of market growth is in decline but which still achieve significant cash surpluses. They became market leaders, during the early days when the market was rapidly growing, and have maintained that position as the growth tapered off. They are regarded as businesses with low growth but high market share (see *Growth-Share Matrix*).

causal mechanisms According to the realist perspective, these are the (usually hidden) processes or pathways through which an outcome is caused to be brought about. An example of a causal mechanism is the process by which a rise in interest rates leads to a fall in house prices. In this case, the causal mechanism linking cause to effect involves decisions by each individual house purchaser about the mortgage repayments they can and cannot afford. It is the aggregate behaviour of these individuals that leads to the overall fall in house prices (see *realism*).

causal powers These are the capabilities or potential for systems and mechanisms to act in a particular way, or to be capable of acting in a particular way (see *realism*).

change agents These are the people responsible for directing, organising and facilitating change in organisations (see *backstaging*).

chaordic This term was coined by Hock (1999) to describe organisations which are poised between order and chaos (see *edge of chaos*; *complexity theories*).

chaos For complexity theorists, chaos describes a complex, unpredictable and orderly disorder in which patterns of behaviour unfold in irregular but similar forms (see *edge of chaos*; *complexity theories*).

chaos theory This is one of the main complexity theories. It seeks to construct mathematical models of systems at the macro level (i.e. whole systems and populations). It portrays natural systems as both non-linear and self-organising.

Classical approach to organisations This approach to organisations is characterised by the horizontal and hierarchical division of labour, the minimisation of human skills and discretion, and the attempt to construe organisations as rational–scientific entities. It comprises the work of Frederick Taylor (see *Scientific Management*), Henri Fayol (see *Principles of Organisation*) and Max Weber (see *Bureaucracy*).

Classical approach to strategy This is the oldest and most influential approach to strategy. It portrays strategy as a rational process, based on analysis and quantification, and aimed at achieving the maximum level of profit for an organisation.

closed systems This is a view of organisations which sees them as being relatively unaffected by events outside their boundaries. It considers organisations to be closed, changeless entities. Once organisations have structured themselves in accordance with the correct precepts, then, regardless of external or even internal developments, no further changes are necessary or desirable (see *Open Systems school*).

coercive power The use of threats, sanctions or force to gain compliance.

cognitive dissonance This theory states that people try to be consistent in both their attitudes and behaviour. When they sense an inconsistency either between two or more attitudes or between their attitudes and behaviour, people experience dissonance; that is, they feel frustrated and uncomfortable with the situation, sometimes extremely so.

Competitive Forces model This is an approach to strategy which stresses the need to align the organisation with its environment, the key aspect of which is the industry or industries in which it competes. Proponents of this view believe that industry structure strongly influences the competitive rules of the game as well as the range of strategies open to the organisation. This model is most closely associated with the work of Michael Porter (1980, 1985).

complexity theories These are concerned with how order is created in dynamic non-linear systems. In particular, those applying this approach to organisations maintain that successful organisations need to operate at the 'edge of chaos' and can only maintain this position by the presence of appropriate order-generating rules.

contextual approach to leadership This is an approach which argues that effective leadership is situation-dependent, i.e. a manager's performance will depend on his or her personal characteristics and the overall context within which they operate (see *transactional management*; *convergent state*; and *transformational leadership*; *divergent state*).

Contingency Theory This maintains that the structures and practices of an organisation, and therefore its performance, are dependent (i.e. contingent) on the circumstances it faces. The main contingencies – situational variables – identified by its proponents are environmental uncertainty and dependence, technology and organisation size (see *environment*).

continuous change This model of change, also referred to as the continuous transformation model, is based on the assertion that the environment in which organisations operate is changing, and will continue to change, rapidly, radically and unpredictably. Consequently, only by continuous transformation will organisations be able to keep aligned with their environment and thus survive.

contracting out See *outsourcing*.

control The ability to impose a desired pattern of activity or behaviour on processes and people (see *authority and power*).

convergent state This occurs when an organisation is operating under stable conditions, where there are established and accepted goals, and a predictable external and internal environment (see *transactional management*).

creativity The ability to produce new, novel or original ideas and solutions.

Cross Impact method This is a scenario-building technique which asks a panel of experts to assign subjective probabilities and time priorities to a list of potential future events and developments supplied by an organisation.

culture See *Organisational culture*.

Culture–Excellence approach Based on the work of Peters and Waterman, Kanter and Handy, this maintains that an organisation's performance (excellence) is determined by the possession of an appropriate, strong and clearly articulated culture. It is culture that ensures that the members of the organisation focus on those activities which lead to effective performance.

Delphi method This is a scenario-building technique which uses a panel of experts, who, independently of each other, are interrogated about a number of future issues within their area of expertise.

Design school The proponents of this approach to strategy emphasise the need to achieve a fit between the internal capabilities of an organisation and the external possibilities it faces. Flowing from this, they place primary emphasis on the appraisal of an organisation's external and internal situations.

dissipative structures These are systems that exist in far-from-equilibrium conditions (i.e. are in a state of constant fluctuation) and which, therefore, use (dissipate) energy. The concept of dissipative structures is one of the core ideas in complexity theories. They are most closely associated with the work of the Nobel Prize-winning physicist, Ilya Prigogine (Prigogine and Stengers, 1984; Prigogine, 1997).

divergent state This situation occurs when environmental changes challenge the efficiency and appropriateness of an organisation's established goals, structures and ways of working (see *contextual approach to leadership*; *transformational leadership*).

diversity See *workforce diversity*.

division of labour The hierarchical and horizontal separation of tasks and responsibilities into their component parts so that individuals are only responsible for a limited set of activities instead of the whole task.

dogs These are businesses that have low market share and which operate in markets with low growth potential (see *Growth-Share Matrix*).

double-loop learning This process involves challenging the appropriateness of an organisation's basic norms, values, policies and operating procedures (see *single-loop learning*; *triple-loop learning*).

edge of chaos This is a state where systems are constantly poised between order and disorder (see *complexity theories*).

Emergence This describes one of the defining properties of complex physical and social systems. In essence, Emergence is the process by which patterns of behaviour or global-level structures arise from the interaction of local-level processes and agents interacting according to their own local order-generating rules.

Emergent change This approach to change is based on the assumption that change is a continuous, open-ended and unpredictable process of aligning and realigning an organisation to its changing environment.

empowerment The delegation of power and responsibility to subordinates.

entrepreneurship The encouragement and pursuit of innovative ideas, products and services (see *Culture–Excellence approach*).

environment Those forces external to an organisation, such as markets, customers, the economy, etc., which influence its decisions and internal operations.

equifinality This concept, coined by Child (1972), states that different sorts of internal arrangements and structures can be perfectly compatible with identical contextual or environmental states. Put simply, this means that there is more than one way for organisations to structure themselves in order to achieve their goals.

esteem needs These reflect a person's desire to be respected – esteemed – for their achievements (see *hierarchy of needs*).

Excellence See *Culture–Excellence approach*.

extrinsic motivators These are material rewards, such as money and promotion, provided by others (see *intrinsic motivators*; *physiological needs*).

felt-need This is an individual's inner realisation that change is necessary. If felt-need is low in a group or organisation, introducing change becomes problematic.

Field Theory This is an approach to understanding group behaviour by trying to map out the totality and complexity of the field in which the behaviour takes place. It is one of the four elements of Lewin's Planned approach to change (see *Planned change*).

firm-in-sector perspective This view of strategy, developed by Child and Smith (1987), maintains that the conditions operating in a sector shape and constrain the strategies which organisations in that sector can pursue.

Fordism This is named after Henry Ford's approach to car assembly. Fordism is seen as the application of Scientific Management to mass production industries through the utilisation of automation, e.g. the moving assembly line.

game theory This approach to strategy can be traced back to the study of war. Game theory has two core assumptions: first, that competitors are rational and will try to win; second, that each competitor is in an interdependent relationship with the other competitors. So all competitors are affected by and will react to what other competitors do.

Generative structures See *causal mechanisms*.

Gestalt-Field psychology This sees an individual's behaviour as the product of their environment and reason. Behaviour arises from the way in which an individual uses reason to interpret external stimuli. Consequently, to change behaviour, individuals must be helped to change their understanding of themselves and the situation in question.

globalisation There is a great deal of dispute as to what this term means. However, at its most basic, it refers to the worldwide integration of markets and cultures, the removal of legal and political barriers to trade, the 'death of distance' as a factor limiting material and cultural exchanges.

Group Dynamics This concept refers to the forces operating in groups. It is concerned with what gives rise to these forces, their consequence and how to modify them. Group Dynamics stresses that group behaviour, rather than that of individuals, should be the main focus of change. It is one of the four elements of Lewin's Planned approach to change (see *Planned change*).

Group Dynamics school As a component of change theory, this school originated with the work of Kurt Lewin and has the longest history. Its emphasis is on bringing about organisational change through teams or work groups, rather than individuals.

Growth-Share Matrix This is a strategic planning tool developed by the Boston Consulting Group. Using pictorial analogies, it posits that businesses in an organisation's portfolio can be classified into stars, cash-cows, dogs and problem children.

Hawthorne Experiments These were carried out at Western Electric's Hawthorne Works in Chicago in the 1920s and 1930s. As a result of this work, two major propositions were put forward: that work is a collective, cooperative activity which is influenced by formal and informal aspects of an organisation; and that humans have a deep need for recognition, security and belonging, rather than being purely economic beings (*see Human Relations approach*).

hierarchy of needs Developed by Maslow (1943), this sees human motivation as based on an ascending order of needs: physiological needs; safety needs; social needs; esteem needs and self-actualisation needs. Only when a lower-order need has been met, does the next level of need begin to motivate an individual.

Hoshin Kanri Also known as policy deployment, this is a Japanese approach to communicating a company's policy, goals and objectives throughout its hierarchy in a structured and consistent fashion in order to ensure that its strategic priorities inform decision-making at all levels in the organisation.

Human Relations approach This was a reaction against the mechanistic view of organisations and the pessimistic view of human nature put forward in the Classical approach to organisations. It reintroduces the human element into organisational life by contending that people have emotional as well as economic needs, and that organisations are cooperative systems which comprise informal structures and norms as well as formal ones (see *Hierarchy of needs*; *Hawthorne Experiments*).

Humanisation of Work See *Job Design.*

incremental model of change Advocates of this view see change as being a process whereby individual parts of an organisation deal incrementally and separately with one problem and one goal at a time.

Individual Perspective school This school of thought is concerned with understanding and promoting behaviour change in individuals. It is split into two camps: the Behaviourists and the Gestalt-Field psychologists.

informal organisations See *Human Relations approach.*

intrinsic motivators These are non-material rewards, such as praise, satisfaction and recognition which are internal to the individual (see *extrinsic motivators; esteem needs; social needs*).

Japanese approach Pascale and Athos (1982) argue that the effectiveness and uniqueness of the Japanese approach to management comes from their ability to combine 'soft' (personnel/industrial relations) elements and 'hard' (business/manufacturing) practices (see *7 S Framework*).

Job Design Also called work humanisation, and arising from the work of the Human Relations approach, proponents of this view argue that the fragmentation of jobs promoted by the Classical approach to organisations creates boring, monotonous, meaningless and demotivating jobs. To reverse this, and to make jobs interesting and intrinsically motivating, they should be designed to provide variety, task completeness and, above all, autonomy.

Kaizen This is a Japanese process of incremental, systematic, gradual, orderly and continuous improvement which utilises a range of techniques, tools and concepts, such as quality circles.

knowledge power This is power based on the control of unique information that is necessary for decision-making.

leadership The process of establishing goals and motivating others to pursue and achieve these goals.

Long Marches The Long March approach to change favours relatively small-scale and operationally focused initiatives, which are slow to implement and whose full benefits are achieved in the long term rather than the short term. The Long March approach can impact on culture over time but it does require the involvement and commitment of most of the organisation (see *Bold Strokes*).

long-range planning This is an approach to strategy based on plotting trends and planning the actions required to achieve the identified growth targets. It is heavily biased towards financial targets and budgetary controls.

management The process of planning, organising and controlling resources and people in order to produce goods or provide services.

management development This is concerned with the training and education of managers so as to equip them with the competences and skills necessary to carry out their duties effectively.

mechanistic structure This forms one end of the structure continuum identified by Contingency theorists, the other end being Organic structure. A mechanistic structure equates to the bureaucratic-type structure advocated by the Classical approach to organisations (see *bureaucracy*).

metaphor This is a linguistic device for describing or seeing one type of experience by suggestion that it is similar to something else, e.g. using the metaphor of a machine to describe a bureaucratic type of organisational structure.

mission statement This states an organisation's major strategic purpose or reason for existing. It can indicate such factors as the organisation's products, markets and core competences. It is part of an organisation's vision.

modernism This is a term used to describe the values, rationale and institutions that have dominated Western societies since the Age of Enlightenment in the eighteenth century. The essence of modernism is a strong belief in progress, economic and scientific rationality, a search for the fundamental rules and laws which govern both the natural world and human nature, and a commitment to a secular, rationalist and progressive individualism (see *postmodernism*; *realism*).

moving This is the second step in Lewin's Three-Step model of change. It involves identifying and evaluating the various types of change on offer, and implementing the chosen one (see *unfreezing*; *refreezing*).

non-linear systems This is a term used by complexity theorists to describe constantly changing systems where the laws of cause and effect appear not to apply. Order in such systems is seen as manifesting itself in a largely unpredictable fashion, in which patterns of behaviour emerge in irregular but similar forms through a process of self-organisation, which is governed by a small number of simple order-generating rules.

normative power This describes the allocation and manipulation of symbolic rewards, such as status symbols, as inducements to obey.

norms These are one of the key components of culture. They represent unwritten rules of behaviour which guide how members of an organisation should behave in particular situations (see *organisational culture*).

OD (Organization Development) This is an approach to change developed in the US. It is based on the work of Kurt Lewin and, originally at least, was concerned with improving the effectiveness of the human side of the organisation through participative change programmes.

'one best way' approach This is a term used to describe any theory or approach which claims to be universally superior to all others on offer, e.g. the Classical approach to organisations.

open-ended change This is a term used especially by proponents of Emergent change to indicate that change is a continuous and unpredictable process which does not have a beginning, middle and end.

Open Systems school Proponents of this view see organisations as systems composed of a number of interconnected sub-systems, where any change to one part of the system will have an impact on other parts of the system, and, in turn, on its overall performance. Organisations are seen as open systems in that they are open to, and interact with, their external environment (see *closed systems*).

order From a complexity perspective, order refers to the patterns of behaviour which emerge in irregular but similar forms in non-linear systems through a process of self-organisation.

order-generating rules In complex systems, the emergence of order is seen as being based on the operation of simple order-generating rules which permit limited chaos while providing relative order (see *complexity theories*).

organic structure This forms one end of the structure continuum identified by Contingency theorists, the other end being mechanistic structure. An organic structure is seen as being flat, informal, flexible and highly adaptable, i.e. the reverse of a bureaucratic structure.

organisational culture This is the name given to the collection of basic assumptions, values, norms and artifacts that are shared by and influence the behaviour of an organisation's members.

organisational learning This term describes the process of collective, as opposed to individual, learning in an organisation. Its aim is to improve the performance of the organisation by involving everyone in collecting, studying, learning from and acting on information.

Organization Development See *OD*.

outsourcing This is the practice of seeking outside organisations to take over activities and services previously carried out within an organisation, e.g. catering, security and IT.

paradigm This is a way of looking at and interpreting the world, a framework of basic assumptions, theories and models that are commonly and strongly accepted and shared within a particular field of activity at a particular point in time.

participation This is the process of involving people in decision-making and change activities within organisations.

person culture The individual and his or her wishes are the central focus of this form of culture. It is associated with a minimalistic structure, the purpose of which is to assist those individuals who choose to work together (see *organisational culture*).

phases of change This is an elaboration of Planned change based on a four-phase model which describes change in terms of two major dimensions: change phases, which are distinct states through which an organisation moves as it undertakes Planned change; and change processes, which are the methods used to move an organisation from one state to another.

physiological needs These relate to hunger, thirst, sleep, etc. (see *hierarchy of needs*).

PIMS (Profit Impact on Marketing Strategy) This is a quantitative strategic planning tool based upon the belief that there are three major factors which determine a business unit's performance: its strategy, its competitive position, and the market/industry characteristics of the field in which it competes.

Planned change This term was coined by Kurt Lewin in the 1940s to distinguish change that was consciously embarked upon and planned by an organisation, as opposed to types of change that might come about by accident or by impulse or that might be forced on an organisation. Lewin's Planned approach to change consists of four interrelated elements: Field Theory, Group Dynamics, Action Research and the Three-Step model of change.

politics This describes the efforts of people in organisations to gain support for or against policies, rules, goals, or other decisions where the outcome will have some effect on them. Politics is seen as the exercise of power.

population ecology This concept is borrowed from the life sciences. It is a Darwinist-type approach that focuses on how organisations adapt and evolve in order to survive within the general population of organisations to which they belong.

Positioning school This approach to strategy is based on the argument that organisations which enjoy higher profits than their competitors do so because they have achieved advantageous and easily defended positions in their markets.

postmodernism This is a loosely defined philosophical movement which, though originally based in the arts, has become increasingly influential in the social sciences over the last 20 years. It is a way of looking at the world that rejects the rationality of modernism and concentrates on the ways in which human beings attempt to shape reality and invent their world (see *Realism*).

power An individual's capacity to influence decisions, to exert their will and achieve outcomes consistent with their goals and priorities.

power culture This is frequently found in small entrepreneurial organisations such as some property, trading and finance companies. It is associated with a web structure with one or more powerful figures at the centre, wielding control (see *organisational culture*).

Prescriptive stream This phrase is used to describe writers on strategy and change who are more interested in developing prescriptions for telling organisations what they should do rather than analysing what they actually do (see *Analytical stream*).

principles of organisation These are a set of rules governing the running of organisations developed by Fayol (1949). He claimed that they were universally applicable to all organisations. The principles of organisation form one of the core elements of the Classical approach to organisations.

privatisation The process of transferring state assets from the public to the private sector.

problem children Also known as question marks, these are units or businesses which have a high growth rate and low market share. They have high cash requirements to keep them on course, but their profitability is low because of their low market share. They are so named because, most of the time, the appropriate strategy to adopt is not clear (see *Growth-Share Matrix*).

processual approach to change This approach sees change as a complex and dynamic process which cannot be solidified or treated as a series of linear events. In particular, it focuses on the need to analyse the politics of managing change.

processual approach to strategy This perspective concentrates on the nature of organisational and market processes. It views organisations and their members as shifting coalitions of individuals and groups with different interests, imperfect knowledge and short attention spans.

Profit Impact on Marketing Strategy See *PIMS*.

psychological contract This concept is based on the assertion that there is an unwritten set of expectations operating at all times between every member of an organisation and the various managers and others in that organisation.

punctuated equilibrium model This view of change sees organisations as evolving through relatively long periods of stability (equilibrium periods) in their basic patterns of activity that are punctuated by relatively short bursts of fundamental change (revolutionary periods).

question marks *See problem children*.

rationality The use of scientific reasoning and logical arguments to arrive at decisions.

realism This philosophical perspective asserts that social entities, such as markets, class relations, gender relations, ethnic groupings, social rules, etc., exist, are real and can be discovered. However, while it rejects the notion of multiple realities, it still acknowledges that social entities arise through a process of social construction. This distinguishes it from both modernism and postmodernism.

refreezing This is the third step in Lewin's Three-Step model of change. It seeks to stabilise new behaviours in order to ensure that they are relatively safe from regression (see *unfreezing*; *moving*).

remunerative power This is the use or promise of material rewards as inducements in order to gain people's cooperation.

resource-based model This approach to strategy sees competitiveness as coming from the effective deployment of superior or unique resources, such as equipment, patents, brands and competences, which allow firms to have lower costs or better products than their competitors.

***Ringi* system** This is a Japanese approach to decision-making which promotes extensive and open debate over decisions, in order to ensure that they fit in with the company's objectives rather than those of sectional interests.

role A set of observable behaviours associated with, and expected of, an identifiable position or job in an organisation.

role culture This type of organisational culture is appropriate to bureaucracies, and organisations with mechanistic, rigid structures and narrow jobs. Such cultures stress the importance of procedures and rules, hierarchical position and authority, security and predictability. In essence, role cultures create situations in which those in the organisation stick rigidly to their role.

safety needs The desire for security and protection against danger (see *hierarchy of needs*).

scenario-building This is an approach to strategy development that allows organisations to construct and test pictures of possible futures and to select the one which is most likely to meet their needs. It is based on the assumption that, if you cannot predict the future, then by considering a range of possible futures, an organisation's strategic horizons can be broadened, and managers can be receptive to new ideas (see *vision-building*).

Scientific Management This is an approach to work organisation developed by Frederick Taylor in the early twentieth century. He claimed that this approach to designing jobs and supervising workers is based on the scientific study of work. It emphasises the division of labour, the removal of workers' discretion and the right of management to make what changes it thinks are necessary for efficient working. It is one of the core elements of the Classical approach to organisations.

Scientific–Rational approach This is an alternative title used to describe the Classical approach to organisations.

self-actualisation needs These constitute the need to achieve one's full potential. According to Maslow (1943), this will vary from person to person, and may differ over time as a person reaches a level of potential previously considered unattainable and so goes on to strive for new heights (see *hierarchy of needs*).

self-organisation This is a term used by complexity theorists to describe how order emerges and is maintained in complex systems (see *order-generating rules*).

semistructures This is a term used by complexity theorists to describe structures which are sufficiently rigid that change can be organised, but not so rigid that it cannot occur.

7 S Framework This is a tool for analysing organisational performance and was developed by Tom Peters, Robert Waterman, Richard Pascale and Anthony Athos when they all worked at McKinsey in the late 1970s. The seven Ss comprise four 'soft' Ss (staff, style, shared values and skills) and three 'hard' Ss (strategy, structure and systems) (see *Japanese approach*).

simple order-generating rules See *order-generating rules.*

single-loop learning This is adaptive learning which involves detecting and rectifying errors or exceptions within the scope of the organisation's existing practices, policies and **norms** of behaviour (see *double-loop learning*; *triple-loop learning*; *organisational learning*).

situational variables See *Contingency Theory.*

size See *Contingency Theory.*

social construction This is an approach concerned with the processes by which people construct, maintain and change social and organisational reality. It is a term used in both postmodernism and realism. For postmodernists, social construction is seen as creating a number of competing 'realities', none of which possesses ultimate truth or reality. Realists, on the other hand, believe in just one socially constructed reality which does exist.

social needs The need to belong, to gain love and affection; to be in the company of others, especially friends (see *hierarchy of needs*).

Socio-Technical Systems theory This is a variant on Job Design which involves a shift of focus from the individual job to the organisation as a whole. It sees organisations as being composed of interdependent social and technical systems.

stars These are business units, industries or products with high growth and high market share. Because of this, stars are assumed to use and generate large amounts of cash. However, they are also likely to be very profitable (see *Growth-Share Matrix*).

Strategic Conflict model This is an approach to strategy which harks back to the military metaphor, and portrays competition as war between rival firms. In particular, this model draws on the work of military strategists, and attempts to apply their military aphorisms to modern business organisations.

strategic intent This is a term which was originally coined to describe the commitment of Japanese managers to create and pursue a vision of their desired future.

strategic management Though often used as a generic term to describe the process by which managers identify and implement their organisation's strategy, it was originally applied only to quantitative, mathematical approaches to strategy.

strategy This is a plan of action stating how an organisation will achieve its long-term objectives.

sustainability This term was originally coined by environmental and ecological campaigners to describe the development of economic, social and industrial practices which would contribute to sustaining the natural environment. It has been extended to include the promotion of organisational practices that contribute to the health of the planet, the survival of humans and other species, the development of a just and humane society, and the creation of work that brings dignity and self-fulfilment (Dunphy *et al*, 2007).

SWOT analysis This is a strategic planning tool which assesses the Strengths, Weaknesses, Opportunities and Threats possessed and faced by an organisation.

Systems Theory See *closed systems and Open Systems school.*

task culture This type of organisational culture is job or project-orientated; the onus is on getting the job in hand (the task) done rather than prescribing how it should be done. Such types of culture are appropriate to organisations with organic structures where flexibility and team-working are encouraged.

Taylorism See *Scientific Management.*

technology See *Contingency Theory.*

Theory X This is a management theory expounded by Douglas McGregor (1960) which states that the average person dislikes work and will avoid it wherever possible, unless coerced to do so (see *Theory Y*).

Theory Y This is a management theory expounded by Douglas McGregor (1960) which states that most people can view work as being as natural as rest or play, they are willing to take responsibility, and are capable of exercising self-direction and self-control (see *Theory X*).

Three-Step model This model of change was developed by Kurt Lewin and sees change as going through three stages: unfreezing, moving and refreezing. It is one of the four elements of Lewin's Planned approach to change (see *Planned change*).

Total Quality Management (TQM) This was developed in Japan and is the systematic application of quality management principles to all aspects of an organisation's activities, including customers and suppliers, and their integration with key business processes.

transactional management This approach stems from the notion that the manager–subordinate relationship is based on a transaction between the two, whereby managers exchange rewards for subordinates' performance. Transactional managers focus on task completion, goal clarification and optimising the performance of the organisation through incremental changes within the confines of existing policy, structures and practices – basically, they seek to work within and maintain the status quo. This approach to management is seen as being appropriate in convergent states (see *contextual approach to leadership; transformational leadership*).

transformational leadership This approach portrays leaders as charismatic or visionary individuals who seek to overturn the status quo and bring about radical change. Such leaders use the force of their personality to motivate followers to identify with the leader's vision and to sacrifice their self-interest in favour of that of the group or organisation. Transformational leadership is seen as being appropriate to divergent states (see *contextual approach to leadership; Transactional management*).

triple-loop learning This involves questioning the rationale for the organisation and, in the light of this, radically transforming it (see *single-loop learning; double-loop learning; organisational learning*).

uncertainty This relates to the degree of doubt, unpredictability and ambiguity that exists in any situation.

unfreezing This is the first step in Lewin's Three-Step model of change. It seeks to destabilise (unfreeze) the complex field of driving and restraining forces which prevent human behaviour from changing (see *moving; refreezing*).

values These are one of the key components of culture. They relate to how things ought to be done in an organisation; they tell members what is important in the organisation (see *organisational culture*).

vision This is a view of an organisation's desired future state. It generally has two components: a description of the organisation's core values and purpose; and a strong and bold picture of the organisation's future which identifies specific goals and actions (see *Vision-building*).

vision-building This is the process of creating a vision. It is an iterative process which involves the conception by a company's senior management team of an 'ideal' future state for their organisation; the identification of the organisation's mission, its rationale for existence; and a clear statement of desired outcomes and the desired conditions and competences needed to achieve these.

workforce diversity This term refers to the dissimilarities – differences – among an organisation's workforce owing to age, gender, race, ethnicity, religion, sexual orientation, nationality, socio-economic background, capabilities/disabilities, etc. It draws attention to the need to take account of these differences when seeking to recruit, retain and motivate staff. In particular, it identifies the need to treat different groups differently if an organisation is to treat all its employees in an ethical and fair manner.

Index

Page numbers in **bold** signify glossary entries